Lecture Notes in Computer Science 11694

More information about this series at http://www.springer.com/series/7410

Alexandra Boldyreva · Daniele Micciancio (Eds.)

Advances in Cryptology – CRYPTO 2019

39th Annual International Cryptology Conference
Santa Barbara, CA, USA, August 18–22, 2019
Proceedings, Part III

 Springer

Editors
Alexandra Boldyreva
Georgia Institute of Technology
Atlanta, GA, USA

Daniele Micciancio
University of California at San Diego
La Jolla, CA, USA

ISSN 0302-9743   ISSN 1611-3349   (electronic)
Lecture Notes in Computer Science
ISBN 978-3-030-26953-1   ISBN 978-3-030-26954-8   (eBook)
https://doi.org/10.1007/978-3-030-26954-8

LNCS Sublibrary: SL4 – Security and Cryptology

This Springer imprint is published by the registered company Springer Nature Switzerland AG
The registered company address is: Gewerbestrasse 11, 6330 Cham, Switzerland

Alexandra Boldyreva · Daniele Micciancio (Eds.)

Advances in Cryptology – CRYPTO 2019

39th Annual International Cryptology Conference
Santa Barbara, CA, USA, August 18–22, 2019
Proceedings, Part III

 Springer

Editors
Alexandra Boldyreva
Georgia Institute of Technology
Atlanta, GA, USA

Daniele Micciancio
University of California at San Diego
La Jolla, CA, USA

ISSN 0302-9743   ISSN 1611-3349   (electronic)
Lecture Notes in Computer Science
ISBN 978-3-030-26953-1   ISBN 978-3-030-26954-8   (eBook)
https://doi.org/10.1007/978-3-030-26954-8

LNCS Sublibrary: SL4 – Security and Cryptology

This Springer imprint is published by the registered company Springer Nature Switzerland AG
The registered company address is: Gewerbestrasse 11, 6330 Cham, Switzerland

Preface

The 39th International Cryptology Conference (Crypto 2019) was held at the University of California, Santa Barbara, California, USA, during August 18–22, 2019. It was sponsored by the International Association for Cryptologic Research (IACR). As in the previous year, a number of workshops took place on the days (August 17 and August 18, 2019) immediately before the conference. This year, the list of affiliated events included a Workshop on Attacks in Cryptography organized by Juraj Somorovsky (Ruhr University Bochum); a Blockchain Workshop organized by Rafael Pass (Cornell Tech) and Elaine Shi (Cornell); a Workshop on Advanced Cryptography Standardization organized by Daniel Benarroch (QEDIT) and Tancrède Lepoint (Google); a workshop on New Roads to Cryptopia organized by Amit Sahai (UCLA); a Privacy Preserving Machine Learning Workshop organized by Gilad Asharov (JP Morgan AI Research), Rafail Ostrovsky (UCLA) and Antigoni Polychroniadou (JP Morgan AI Research); and the Mathcrypt Workshop organized by Kristin Lauter (Microsoft Research), Yongsoo Song (Microsoft Research) and Jung Hee Cheon (Seoul National University).

Crypto continues to grow, year after year, and Crypto 2019 was no exception. The conference set new records for both submissions and publications, with a whopping 378 papers submitted for consideration. It took a Program Committee (PC) of 51 cryptography experts working with 333 external reviewers for over two months to select the 81 papers which were accepted for the conference.

As usual, papers were reviewed in the double-blind fashion, with each paper assigned to three PC members. Initially, papers received independent reviews, without any communication between PC members. After the initial review stage, authors were given the opportunity to comment on all available preliminary reviews. Finally, the PC discussed each submission, taking all reviews and author comments into account, and selecting the list of papers to be included in the conference program. PC members were limited to two submissions, and their submissions were held to higher standards. The two Program Chairs were not allowed to submit papers.

The PC recognized three papers and their authors for standing out amongst the rest. "Cryptanalysis of OCB2: Attacks on Authenticity and Confidentiality", by Akiko Inoue, Tetsu Iwata, Kazuhiko Minematsu and Bertram Poettering was voted Best Paper of the conference. Additionally, the papers "Quantum cryptanalysis in the RAM model: Claw-finding attacks on SIKE" by Samuel Jaques and John M. Schanck, and "Fully Secure Attribute-Based Encryption for t-CNF from LWE" by Rotem Tsabary, were voted Best Papers Authored Exclusively By Young Researchers.

Beside the technical presentations, Crypto 2019 featured a Rump session, and two invited talks by Jonathan Katz from University of Maryland, and Helen Nissenbaum from Cornell Tech.

We would like to express our sincere gratitude to all the reviewers for volunteering their time and knowledge in order to select a great program for 2019. Additionally, we are very appreciative of the following individuals and organizations for helping make Crypto 2019 a success:

- Muthu Venkitasubramaniam (University of Rochester) - Crypto 2019 General Chair
- Carmit Hazay (Bar-Ilan University) - Workshop Chair
- Jonathan Katz (University of Maryland) - Invited Speaker
- Helen Nissenbaum (Cornell Tech) - Invited Speaker
- Shai Halevi - Author of the IACR Web Submission and Review System
- Anna Kramer and her colleagues at Springer
- Whitney Morris and UCSB Conference Services

We would also like to say thank you to our numerous sponsors, the workshop organizers, everyone who submitted papers, the session chairs, and the presenters. Lastly, a big thanks to everyone who attended the conference at UCSB.

August 2019   Alexandra Boldyreva
                                                               Daniele Micciancio

CRYPTO 2019

The 39th International Cryptology Conference

University of California, Santa Barbara, CA, USA
August 18–22, 2019

Sponsored by the *International Association for Cryptologic Research*

General Chair

Muthu Venkitasubramaniam   University of Rochester, USA

Program Chairs

Alexandra Boldyreva   Georgia Institute of Technology, USA
Daniele Micciancio   University of California at San Diego, USA

Program Committee

Manuel Barbosa — INESC TEC, University of Porto, Portugal
Zvika Brakerski — Weizmann Institute of Science, Israel
Mark Bun — Simons Institute, Boston University, USA
Ran Canetti — Tel Aviv University, Israel, and Boston University, USA
Dario Catalano — University of Catania, Italy
Alessandro Chiesa — UC Berkeley, USA
Sherman S. M. Chow — Chinese University of Hong Kong, SAR China
Kai-Min Chung — Academia Sinica, Taiwan
Jean-Sebastien Coron — Luxembourg University, Luxembourg
Jean Paul Degabriele — TU Darmstadt, Germany
Nico Döttling — Cispa Helmholtz Center (i.G.), Germany
Orr Dunkelman — University of Haifa, Israel
Rosario Gennaro — City College, CUNY, USA
Tim Güneysu — Ruhr University Bochum, DFKI, Germany
Felix Günther — UC San Diego, USA
Siyao Guo — NYU Shanghai, China
Sean Hallgren — Pennsylvania State University, USA
Carmit Hazay — Bar-Ilan University, Israel
Susan Hohenberger — Johns Hopkins University, USA
Sorina Ionica — Université de Picardie, France
Bhavana Kanukurthi — Indian Institute of Science, India
Vladimir Kolesnikov — Georgia Institute of Technology, USA

Anja Lehmann	IBM Research Zurich, Switzerland
Vadim Lyubashevsky	IBM Research Zurich, Switzerland
Ilya Mironov	Google
Michael Naehrig	Microsoft Research
Svetla Nikova	KU Leuven, Belgium
Ryo Nishimaki	NTT Secure Platform Labs, Japan
Omer Paneth	MIT, USA
Charalampos Papamanthou	University of Maryland, USA
Chris Peikert	University of Michigan, USA
Giuseppe Persiano	University of Salerno, Italy
Christophe Petit	University of Birmingham, UK
Thomas Peyrin	Nanyang Technological University, Singapore
Benny Pinkas	Bar Ilan University, Israel
Bertram Poettering	Royal Holloway, University of London, UK
Mariana Raykova	Yale University, USA
Silas Richelson	UC Riverside, USA
Adeline Roux-Langlois	University Rennes, CNRS, IRISA, France
Peter Scholl	Aarhus University, Denmark
Dominique Schröder	Friedrich-Alexander-Universität, Germany
Thomas Shrimpton	University of Florida, USA
Damien Stehlé	ENS Lyon, France
Björn Tackmann	IBM Research Zurich, Switzerland
Keisuke Tanaka	Tokyo Institute of Technology, Japan
Eran Tromer	Tel Aviv University, Israel, and Columbia University, USA
Daniele Venturi	Sapienza, University of Rome, Italy
Xiao Wang	MIT, Boston University, USA
Xiaoyun Wang	Tsinghua University, China
Bogdan Warinschi	University of Bristol, UK
Mor Weiss	IDC Herzliya, Israel

Additional Reviewers

Ittai Abraham	Vivek Arte	Paulo S. L. M. Barreto
Shweta Agrawal	Gilad Asharov	James Bartusek
Gorjan Alagic	Tomer Ashur	Carsten Baum
Navid Alamati	Nuttapong Attrapadung	Gabrielle Beck
Younes Talibi Alaoui	Benedikt Auerbach	Amos Beimel
Martin Albrecht	Roberto Avanzi	Sonia Belaid
Joel Alwen	Saikrishna	Fabrice Benhamouda
Prabhanjan Ananth	Badrinarayanan	Pauline Bert
Elena Andreeva	Josep Balasch	Rishabh Bhadauria
Benny Applebaum	Foteini Baldimtsi	Olivier Blazy
Marcel Armour	Marshall Ball	Jeremiah Blocki
Gal Arnon	Achiya Bar-On	Jonathan Bootle

Cecilia Boschini
Katharina Boudgoust
Florian Bourse
Elette Boyle
Jacqueline Brendel
Anne Broadbent
Wouter Castryck
Andrea Cerulli
Yilei Chen
Nai-Hui Chia
Ilaria Chillotti
Arka Rai Choudhuri
Michele Ciampi
Benoit Cogliati
Ran Cohen
Sandro Coretti
Craig Costello
Geoffroy Couteau
Jan Czajkowski
Dana Dachaman-Soled
Wei Dai
Anders Dalskov
Hannah Davis
Akshay Degwekar
Ioannis Demertzis
Patrick Derbez
David Derler
Itai Dinur
Mario Di Raimondo
Benjamin Dowling
Minxin Du
Léo Ducas
Yfke Dulek
Francois Dupressoir
Frédéric Dupuis
Stefan Dziembowski
Gautier Eberhart
Christoph Egger
Maria Eichlseder
Daniel Escudero
Antonio Faonio
Franz Aguirre Farro
Pooya Farshim
Omar Fawzi
Katharina Fech
Ben Fisch

Marc Fischlin
Emmanuel Fouotsa
Danilo Francati
Daniele Friolo
Ariel Gabizon
Tommaso Gagliardoni
Steven Galbraith
Chaya Ganesh
Lydia Garms
Romain Gay
Ran Gelles
Adela Georgescu
David Gerault
Essam Ghadafi
Satrajit Ghosh
Federico Giacon
Aarushi Goel
Junqing Gong
Alonso Gonzalez
Rishab Goyal
Vipul Goyal
Nicola Greco
Daniel Grosse
Zichen Gui
Tim Güneysu
Chethan Kamath Hosdurg
Mohammad Hajiabadi
Lucjan Hanzlik
Patrick Harasser
Carmit Hazay
Julia Hesse
Minki Hhan
Kuan-Yi Ho
Justin Holmgren
Akinori Hosoyamada
Patrick Hough
James Howe
Pavel Hubáček
Shih-Han Hung
Kathrin Hövelmanns
Takanori Isobe
Mitsugu Iwamoto
Malika Izabachène
Joseph Jaeger
Christian Janson
Dirmanto Jap

Stas Jarecki
Zhengzhong Jin
Charanjit Jutla
Guillaume Kaim
Mustafa Kairallah
Yael Kalai
Chethan Kamath
Marc Kaplan
Shuichi Katsumata
Shinagawa Kazumasa
Mojtaba Khalili
Dmitry Khovratovich
Ryo Kikuchi
Sam Kim
Elena Kirshanova
Fuyuki Kitagawa
Susumu Kiyoshima
Karen Klein
Michael Klooss
Kamil Kluczniak
Markulf Kohlweiss
Ilan Komargodski
Venkata Koppula
Evgenios Kornaropoulos
Takeshi Koshiba
Luke Kowalczyk
Stephan Krenn
Mukul Kulkarni
Ranjit Kumaresan
Gijs Van Laer
Russell W. F. Lai
Thalia Laing
Changmin Lee
Eysa Lee
Moon Sung Lee
Tancrède Lepoint
Jyun-Jie Liao
Han-Hsuan Lin
Huijia (Rachel) Lin
Helger Lipmaa
Qipeng Liu
Tianren Liu
Alex Lombardi
Patrick Longa
Julian Loss
Atul Luykx

Julio López
Fermi Ma
Jack P. K. Ma
Bernardo Magri
Mohammad Mahmoody
Christian Majenz
Hemanta Maji
Giulio Malavolta
Mary Maller
Nathan Manohar
Peter Manohar
Daniel Masny
Takahiro Matsuda
Alexander May
Sogol Mazaheri
Jeremias Mechler
Simon-Philipp Merz
Peihan Miao
Romy Minko
Takaaki Mizuki
Amir Moradi
Kirill Morozov
Travis Morrison
Nicky Mouha
Tamer Mour
Pratyay Mukherjee
Jörn Müller-Quade
Kartik Nayak
Gregory Neven
Ka-Lok Ng
Ruth Ng
Ngoc Khanh Nguyen
Ventzislav Nikov
Ariel Nof
Sai Lakshmi Bhavana
    Obbattu
Maciej Obremski
Tobias Oder
Sabine Oechsner
Wakaha Ogata
Miyako Ohkubo
Cristina Onete
Claudio Orlandi
Emmanuela Orsini
Carles Padro
Jiaxin Pan

Lorenz Panny
Dimitris Papadopoulos
Anat Paskin-Cherniavsky
Christopher Patton
Alice Pellet-Mary
Zack Pepin
Jeroen Pijnenburg
Oxana Poburinnaya
Antigoni Polychroniadou
Bart Preneel
Ben Pring
Emmanuel Prouff
Chen Qian
Luowen Qian
Willy Quach
Srinivasan Raghuraman
Adrián Ranea
Divya Ravi
Vincent Rijmen
Peter Rindal
Felix Rohrbach
Razvan Rosie
Dragos Rotaru
Ron Rothblum
Arnab Roy
Paul Rösler
Luisa Siniscalchi
Mohamed Sabt
Rajeev Anand Sahu
Cyprien de Saint Guilhem
Kazuo Sakiyama
Pratik Sarkar
Pascal Sasdrich
Alessandra Scafuro
Falk Schellenberg
Thomas Schneider
Tobias Schneider
Jacob Schuldt
Gregor Seiler
Sruthi Sekar
Karn Seth
Yannick Seurin
Aria Shahverdi
Abhishek Shetty
Sina Shiehian
Javier Silva

Siang Meng Sim
Mark Simkin
Luisa Siniscalchi
Fang Song
Pratik Soni
Katerina Sotiraki
Nicholas Spooner
Caleb Springer
Akshayaram Srinivasan
François-Xavier Standaert
Douglas Stebila
Damien Stehlé
Ron Steinfeld
Noah
    Stephens-Davidowitz
Christoph Striecks
Patrick Struck
Banik Subhadeep
Gelo Noel Tabia
Stefano Tessaro
Sri Aravinda Krishnan
    Thyagarajan
Mehdi Tibouchi
Elmar W. Tischhauser
Yosuke Todo
Junichi Tomida
Patrick Towa
Monika Trimoska
Itay Tsabary
Rotem Tsabary
Sulamithe Tsakou
Ida Tucker
Dominique Unruh
Bogdan Ursu
Vinod Vaikuntanathan
Kerem Varici
Prashant Vasudevan
Muthu
    Venkitasubramaniam
Fernando Virdia
Madars Virza
Ivan Visconti
Satyanarayana Vusirikala
Riad Wahby
Adrian Waller
Alexandre Wallet

Michael Walter
Haoyang Wang
Jiafan Wang
Meiqin Wang
Xiuhua Wang
Yuyu Wang
Gaven Watson
Hoeteck Wee
Weiqiang Wen

Harry W. H. Wong
Tim Wood
Joanne Woodage
Huangting Wu
Keita Xagawa
Shota Yamada
Takashi Yamakawa
Avishay Yanai
Kenji Yasunaga

Kevin Yeo
Eylon Yogev
Yu Yu
Mark Zhandry
Jiapeng Zhang
Yupeng Zhang
Yongjun Zhao
Yu Zheng

Sponsors

Contents – Part III

Trapdoor Functions

Trapdoor Hash Functions and Their Applications

Nico Döttling[1], Sanjam Garg[2], Yuval Ishai[3], Giulio Malavolta[4(✉)],
Tamer Mour[5(✉)], and Rafail Ostrovsky[6]

[1] CISPA Helmholtz Center for Information Security, Saarbrücken, Germany
doettling@cispa.saarland
[2] UC Berkeley, Berkeley, CA, USA
sanjamg@berkeley.edu
[3] Technion, Haifa, Israel
yuvali@cs.technion.ac.il
[4] Carengie Mellon University, Pittsburgh, PA, USA
giulio.malavolta@hotmail.it
[5] Weizmann Institute of Science, Rehovot, Israel
tamer@weizmann.ac.il
[6] UCLA, Los Angeles, CA, USA
rafail@cs.ucla.edu

Abstract. We introduce a new primitive, called *trapdoor hash functions* (TDH), which are hash functions $H : \{0,1\}^n \rightarrow \{0,1\}^\lambda$ with additional trapdoor function-like properties. Specifically, given an index $i \in [n]$, TDHs allow for sampling an encoding key ek (that hides i) along with a corresponding trapdoor. Furthermore, given $H(x)$, a hint value $E(ek, x)$, and the trapdoor corresponding to ek, the ith bit of x can be efficiently recovered. In this setting, one of our main questions is: How small can the hint value $E(ek, x)$ be? We obtain constructions where the hint is only *one bit* long based on DDH, QR, DCR, or LWE.

This primitive opens a floodgate of applications for low-communication secure computation. We mainly focus on two-message protocols between a receiver and a sender, with private inputs x and y, resp., where the receiver should learn $f(x, y)$. We wish to optimize the *(download) rate* of such protocols, namely the asymptotic ratio between the size of the output and the sender's message. Using TDHs, we obtain:
1. The first protocols for (two-message) *rate-1 string OT* based on DDH, QR, or LWE. This has several useful consequences, such as:
   (a) The first constructions of PIR with communication cost polylogarithmic in the database size based on DDH or QR. These protocols are in fact rate-1 when considering block PIR.
   (b) The first constructions of a *semi-compact* homomorphic encryption scheme for branching programs, where the encrypted output grows only with the program *length*, based on DDH or QR.

G. Malavolta—Part of the work done while at Friedrich-Alexander-Universität Erlangen-Nürnberg.

T. Mour—Part of the work done while at Technion.

A. Boldyreva and D. Micciancio (Eds.): CRYPTO 2019, LNCS 11694, pp. 3–32, 2019.
https://doi.org/10.1007/978-3-030-26954-8_1

      (c) The first constructions of lossy trapdoor functions with input to output ratio approaching 1 based on DDH, QR or LWE.

      (d) The first *constant-rate* LWE-based construction of a 2-message "statistically sender-private" OT protocol in the plain model.

  2. The first *rate-1* protocols (under any assumption) for n parallel OTs and matrix-vector products from DDH, QR or LWE.

We further consider the setting where f evaluates a RAM program y with running time $T \ll |x|$ on x. We obtain the first protocols with communication sublinear in the size of x, namely $T \cdot \sqrt{|x|}$ or $T \cdot \sqrt[3]{|x|}$, based on DDH or, resp., pairings (and correlated-input secure hash functions).

1 Introduction

Seminal results from the 1980s [31,55] showed that it is possible for a group of mutually distrustful parties to compute a joint function on their private inputs without revealing anything more than the output of the computation. These foundational results were seen as providing the first theoretical proofs of concept. However, significant theoretical and practical advances over the years provide support for the idea that perhaps secure computation can be as practical and ubiquitous as public-key cryptography.

In the quest to make secure computation efficient, realizing *communication efficient* secure computation protocols has emerged as a central theme of research. Moreover, secure computation protocols with large communication cost can often be prohibitive in practice. Consequently, substantial effort has been put towards realizing communication efficient protocols. Nonetheless, our understanding of communication efficient secure computation protocols remains significantly limited. Specifically, known protocols for circuits with communication independent of the circuit size are only known using fully homomorphic encryption (FHE) [27] and can only be based on variants of LWE. In the two-party case, the communication complexity of such protocols is comparable to the length of the *shorter input* plus the length of the output. For simpler functions that can be represented by log-depth circuits or polynomial-size branching programs, similar protocols were recently constructed from other assumptions such as DDH [9] or a circular-secure flavor of DCR [23]. Here the communication is comparable to the total length of *both inputs* plus the length of the output.

The above state of affairs leaves several types of gaps between secure and insecure communication complexity.[1] First, even when applying the best known FHE schemes, there is a constant-factor gap for functions whose output length is comparable to (or longer than) the length of the shorter input.[2] Second, the communication gap can be even bigger when considering restricted interaction.

---

[1] It seems plausible that these gaps can be closed using indistinguishability obfuscation [25]. However, the focus of this work is on constructions that can be based on more traditional assumptions.

[2] A simple "hybrid FHE" technique [28] can generically convert any FHE scheme into one whose encrypted (long) input is roughly as long as the input. However, no such generic technique is known for compressing the encrypted output.

For instance, when one input is much shorter than the other, FHE cannot be used to get communication-efficient 2-message protocols where the party holding the *long* input sends the first message. Finally, and most importantly for this work, under standard assumptions other than LWE, the gaps between secure and insecure communication are much bigger, especially when considering functions with unbalanced input sizes.

To illustrate the current gaps, consider the fundamental problem of private information retrieval (PIR) [17,44] over m-bit records, where a client wants to privately learn the ith record of a server's database that consists of n records of length m each. Here, a protocol that achieves near-optimal communication from the server to the client (i.e., roughly m bits) is only known under DCR [18,45]. For the case of retrieving m different 1-bit records, the situation is even worse. In the best known protocol, the gap between the server's message length and the output length is a big multiplicative constant [33]. Finally, even for the case $m = 1$, obtaining polylog(n) communication under (subexponential variants of) standard assumptions such as DDH or QR is open.

1.1   Our Setting and Questions of Interest

Setting: Two-Message Secure Computation. We consider two-party protocols in which a receiver and a sender have private inputs x and y, respectively. We consider protocols for evaluating a function $f(x, y)$ using only two messages. First, based on its input x, the receiver sends the first message msg_1 to the sender who, based on its input y, responds with the second message msg_2. Finally, the receiver uses its secret state and msg_2 to compute $f(x, y)$. *Sender's privacy* requires that the receiver learns nothing more about y than $f(x, y)$ and the length of y. Similarly, *receiver's privacy* requires that the sender learns nothing about x other than its length. By default, we only consider security against *semi-honest* parties.[3]

Case I: Large Receiver Output. We are primarily interested in the case where the output of f is long, and define the *download rate* of such a 2-message protocol (or *rate* for short) as the asymptotic ratio between $|f(x, y)|$ and $|\mathsf{msg}_2|$. We will also consider the *overall rate*, defined as the asymptotic ratio between the insecure communication complexity of f and that of the protocol. A fundamental functionality in this regime is oblivious transfer (OT). We start with the special case of *string OT*, implemented via a two-message protocol. Recall that in the string OT functionality the inputs of the sender and receiver are two strings $\mathsf{s}_0, \mathsf{s}_1 \in \{0, 1\}^n$ and a bit $i \in \{0, 1\}$, respectively. For this functionality, the receiver's output should be s_i. Here the download and overall rate are the asymptotic ratios $\frac{n}{|\mathsf{msg}_2|}$ and $\frac{n}{|\mathsf{msg}_1|+|\mathsf{msg}_2|}$, respectively, when the security parameter λ tends to infinity and n is a sufficiently big polynomial in λ (see Definition 3.1

---

[3] Our protocols can be efficiently extended to provide security against malicious parties (under the same assumptions) using sublinear arguments [46]. This increases the number of rounds, but does not affect the asymptotic communication.

for a precise formulation). We also consider *batch OT*; this functionality allows n parallel instances of bit-OT (string OT with 1-bit strings).

Even for the special case of OT, the state-of-the-art with optimal overall rate (or optimal download rate) is quite unsatisfactory.[4] Any 2-message string-OT protocol can be compiled into a similar protocol with rate $1/2$ using *hybrid encryption* as follows: Given a string-OT protocol for messages of size λ, the sender uses the OT protocol to transmit one out of two symmetric keys to the receiver, and uses these keys with a rate-1 symmetric encryption scheme to encrypt the actual messages. The two ciphertexts are sent along with the OT sender message. The receiver recovers one of the two keys and decrypts the corresponding ciphertext. However, going beyond rate $1/2$ seems to hit barriers! Interestingly enough, for information-theoretic OT in the correlated randomness model, rate $1/2$ (as e.g. in Beaver's standard reduction [6]) is optimal [38,54]. In the computational setting, constructions based on additively homomorphic encryption or homomorphic secret sharing hit a similar barrier [10,42,53]. Currently, the only construction of OT known to achieve rate better than $1/2$ is based on the Damgård-Jurik cryptosystem [18], which relies on the DCR assumption. Even here, optimal rate in only achieved by undesirably letting the size of the group used in the scheme grow with the size of the inputs.[5] Moreover, in the more general case of *batch OT*, rate 1 could not even be achieved based on DCR. This brings us to our first motivating question:

> *Can we realize OT with rate$> \frac{1}{2}$ from assumptions other than DCR?*
> *Can we realize such batch OT from any assumption?*

Why care about OT with rate $> \frac{1}{2}$? As mentioned earlier, there is a large body of work on minimizing the communication complexity of secure computation. The special case of OT is not only natural and useful as a standalone application, but it also serves as a stepping stone for other applications. Indeed, high-rate 2-message OT implies: (i) high-rate PIR with polylogarithmic communication complexity in the number of records [40,44]; (ii) a semi-compact homomorphic encryption scheme that supports evaluation of bounded-length branching programs (in particular, finite automata, decision trees and OBDDs) over encrypted data [40], (iii) a high-rate lossy-trapdoor function [51], and (iv) statistically sender-private (SSP) two-message OT with constant rate [4,11]. We will elaborate on these applications below. To sum up, while high-rate OT is a powerful primitive with important consequences, very little is known about how to construct it.

---

[4] The work of Cho et al. [16] on *laconic OT* gives a batch OT protocol where $|\mathsf{msg}_1|$ is independent of $|x|$. This generalizes to arbitrary functions f; however, even in the simple case of batch OT the download rate is sub-constant. The same applies to the more recent work of Quach et al. [52] on laconic function evaluation.

[5] In this work, we consider this question in the more stringent two-message setting. However, we note that no other protocols with rate $> \frac{1}{2}$ are known even when additional rounds of communication are allowed.

Case II: Large Receiver Input. Up to this point, we were mainly concerned with functions $f(x, y)$ that have a long output, where our goal was to make the communication from the sender to the receiver very close to $|f(x, y)|$. Even multi-round protocols of this type were not known prior to our work. A second setting we consider applies to two-round protocols in the case where $|x| \gg |y|$ and the output is short. In this case, an insecure protocol for f can simply have the sender communicate y to the receiver. Since secure computation with only one message is impossible (except in trivial cases), our goal is to obtain a *two-message* secure protocol with similar efficiency features, namely where the total communication complexity is comparable to $|y|$ rather than $|x|$. As a motivating example, consider the case where the receiver has a large n-bit database x, the sender's input y describes a small RAM machine M whose running time is $T \ll n$, and the receiver's output is $M(x)$. For instance, M can select a single entry $y \in [n]$ of x, outputting $M(x) = x_y$. Note that a natural FHE-based protocol where the receiver sends an encryption of x and receives an encryption of $M(x)$ does not meet our efficiency goal of using less than n bits of communication. On the other hand, allowing for a higher round complexity, our goal can be met using any PIR protocol [46].

From here on, we restrict the attention to 2-message protocols with $o(n)$ communication. The recent *laconic function evaluation* primitive [52] provides such a protocol with overall communication of $|y| + \mathsf{poly}(\lambda, T)$, where λ is a security parameter. However, results in this setting are only known under LWE (with subexponential modulus-to-noise ratio). This brings us to our second main question:

> *Are there 2-message protocols computing $M(x)$ with $o(n)$ bits of communication from any assumptions other than LWE?*

1.2   Our Results

In this work, we introduce a new primitive that we call trapdoor hash functions (TDHs).[6] TDHs are hash functions $\mathsf{H} : \{0,1\}^n \to \{0,1\}^\lambda$ with additional trapdoor-function-like properties. Specifically, given an index $i \in [n]$, TDHs allow for sampling an encoding key ek (that hides i) along with a corresponding trapdoor. Furthermore, given $\mathsf{H}(x)$, a hint value $\mathsf{E}(\mathsf{ek}, x)$, and the trapdoor corresponding to ek, the ith bit of x can be efficiently recovered. In this setting, one of our main questions is: how small can the hint value $\mathsf{E}(\mathsf{ek}, x)$ be? We define the rate of TDH as the inverse of the size of the hint.

We obtain constructions of rate-1 TDHs from standard assumptions, namely DDH, QR, DCR, and LWE. The surprising twist in these constructions is the close integration of techniques developed in two very recent and seemingly unrelated lines of investigation: (i) A new type of hash function for constructing

---

[6] The notion of trapdoor hash functions is inspired by the closely related notion of hash encryption [13, 21, 22, 26] and somewhere statistically binding hash functions [36, 43, 49].

identity-based encryption by Döttling and Garg [21] and its extension to constructions of trapdoor functions by Garg, Gay and Hajiabadi [24, 26] and (ii) techniques for homomorphic secret sharing by Boyle, Gilboa and Ishai [9].

Main Result: Rate-1 Two-Message String OT. Our TDHs yield the first construction of string OT with rate-1 from the {DDH, QR, LWE} assumption. Additionally, we get a new construction under DCR, for which, unlike the Damgård-Jurik construction [18], the size of the group used is independent of the size of the inputs. We stress that while our constructions use only two messages; previously, even multi-round constructions with rate $> \frac{1}{2}$ were not known under these assumptions.[7] This allows us to obtain the following new results:

1. *Private Information Retrieval*: We obtain the first constructions of private information retrieval (PIR) from {DDH, QR, LWE} with download rate 1 (for retrieving long records). The total communication complexity grows only logarithmically with the number of records.[8] Previously, such PIR protocols were only known under DCR [45]. This also resolves the longstanding open question of building PIR with polylogarithmic communication (for 1-bit records) from {DDH, QR} [44]. Such protocols were only known under DCR, LWE, and the Phi-hiding assumptions [14, 15, 45, 50]. For example, the best known construction from DDH required $O(2^{\sqrt{\log n}} \cdot \lambda)$ bits of communication, for database size n and security parameter λ [44, 53].

2. *Semi-Compact Homomorphic Encryption for Branching Programs:* We obtain the first encryption schemes based on {DDH, QR} that allow evaluating a branching program on an encrypted input, where the encrypted output grows only with the *length* of the branching program and not with its size. Previously, such schemes were only known under {DCR, LWE} [40].

3. *Lossy Trapdoor Functions:* We obtain the first construction of lossy trapdoor functions [51] with rate 1 from the {DDH, QR, LWE} assumption. Here, rate is defined as the ratio of the input length and output length for the trapdoor function. Very recently, Garg et al. [24] obtained construction from DDH with a small constant rate. However, besides that, no constructions with constant rate were known under these assumptions.

4. *Malicious Statistically Sender Private OT:* We obtain the first LWE-based 2-message OT protocol in the plain model that offers statistical sender privacy against a malicious receiver and has a *constant* rate. This improves over the $1/\log(\lambda)$ rate of a recent LWE-based protocol of Brakerski and Döttling [11]. Similar protocols were previously known under {DDH, DCR} [1, 34, 48].

---

[7] Our protocols achieve asymptotic download rate 1, which is clearly optimal. However, the (additive) difference between the sender's message length and the output length grows with the security parameter λ. In the full version we show that that this gap is necessary even in the more liberal setting of secure computation with preprocessing.

[8] More specifically, as our group-based constructions are black-box in the underlying group, we can count the communication complexity in terms of the number of group elements, which in our case is $\log n \cdot \mathsf{poly}(\lambda)$, where n is the size of the database and λ is the security parameter.

Rate-1 Protocols for Functionalities Generalizing OT. We generalize the techniques for rate-1 OT to yield secure 2-message protocols with *download* rate 1 for other useful functionalities. In these cases, we obtain the first protocols under *any* assumption. We obtain such protocols for the following functionalities.

1. *Batch OT:* Batch OT allows n instances of bit-OT to be performed in parallel. We obtain 2-message batch OT protocol with download rate 1 (but sub-constant upload rate) from QR and LWE. Allowing for inverse polynomial error probability, we obtain a similar protocol under DDH. Protocols with smaller constant download rates (and constant overall rate) were known under a variety of assumptions; see [8, 10, 39] and references therein.
2. *Batch OLE:* An oblivious linear function evaluation (OLE) scheme allows the sender to evaluate an affine function $f(x) = ax + b$ over the receiver's private input x. We obtain the first batch OLE (over either a field of a small characteristic or smooth modulus) with download rate 1 based on QR or LWE. We also get a DDH-based construction if we allow inverse-polynomial error. For the case of fields, smaller constant download rate (and constant overall rate) could be realized under LWE [20, 42] or code-based assumptions [2, 41, 47].
3. *Matrix-Vector Products:* We generalize the above to oblivious matrix-vector product evaluation (OMV), where the sender has a matrix M, the receiver holds a vector v, and the output is Mv. A two-message OMV protocol can be thought as a relaxed form of additively homomorphic encryption. Our techniques can be generalized to construct OMVs over $\mathbb{F}_2$ with optimal download rate, based on QR or LWE. We can also generalize the LWE-based construction to fields modulo small primes or smooth integers. Compared to previous LWE-based constructions (e.g., [42]), we get better (optimal) download rate but worse overall rate.

As mentioned for rate-1 OT, all the aforementioned results were known only under the DCR assumption (and in the case of functionalities generalizing OT, were not known under any standard assumptions), where optimal rate was achieved by letting the size of the group grow with the size of the inputs. Our work improves in this setting. Specifically, assuming only DCR, our work implies all of the above results in groups of size independent of the message length.

As in the context of rate-1 OT, while we consider only two-message protocols, we stress that, prior to our work, none of the above-mentioned results were known even when additional rounds of communication are allowed.

Beyond OT: Two-Message SFE with Sublinear Communication. Armed with our new techniques, we attempt to broaden the class of functionalities for which two-message secure-function evaluation (SFE) can be achieved with sublinear communication. Specifically, we start with the following example setting: Alice would like to share her DNA sequence online so that various medical researchers can use it to provide her with valuable insights about her health. However, Alice wants to keep her "large" genetic information confidential and each researcher wants to keep the specific parts of the genetic code it looks at private. In a bit more detail, Alice wants to publish a hash $h(\mathsf{x})$ of her input x (of length n) online, such that any contractor Bob, with a private machine M with "small running time" (denoted by T) can send Alice a "short" message, enabling her to learn M^{x}, where M has random access to x. In summary, we are interested in a setting that allows Alice to evaluate Bob's private *small machine* on her private *large input* with sublinear communication.

Positive results for the above setting with sublinear communication are only known from lattice assumptions—namely, using laconic function evaluation [52]. In contrast, for the case of DDH-based constructions, such protocols need communication complexity proportional to n. We note that constructions based on laconic OT [16] do not keep the locations accessed by M private and thus, do not suffice for this application.[9]

We obtain the first protocol for non-interactive secure computation on large inputs from DDH with communication proportional to $T \cdot \sqrt{n}$, where T is the running time of the machine and n is the size of the database. Furthermore, using pairings (and appropriate correlated-input secure hash functions [3,7,30,32,37]) we obtain a protocol with communication cost proportional to $T \cdot \sqrt[3]{n}$.

Further, in a scenario where Bob's machine M is repeatedly executed over different large inputs (possibly owned by different Alices), we achieve protocols with communication proportional to T, and *independent* of n, per execution, assuming a non-interactive "offline phase" where Bob publishes an "encoding" of M of length proportional to n or $\sqrt{n}$ (from DDH or pairings, resp.), which can be amortized over all executions.

Our results are obtained by constructing a variant of laconic OT [16], that keeps the locations accessed by M private. We call this primitive *private laconic OT*. The key technical challenge here is to realize this primitive with communication cost sublinear in the size of Alice's large input. By using private laconic OT, rather than laconic OT, in the constructions from in [16], we obtain SFE for RAM programs with sublinear communication which, as opposed to the protocol from [16], also hides the access pattern made by the machine to the input database and therefore achieves a full notion of security.

1.3   Concurrent Work

In a concurrent work, Gentry and Halevi [29] constructed an efficient rate-1 FHE schemes from LWE, which in particular also yield rate-1 OT constructions. When instantiated from LWE with polynomial modulus-to-noise ratio, their construction achieves rate $1 - \epsilon$ for any constant ϵ. In comparison, our OT constructions achieve rate $1 - 1/\lambda$ in this regime and can also be based on DDH or QR.

1.4   Paper Organization

In the following sections, we give a high level overview of the technical contributions of our work. We first introduce trapdoor hash functions, and present

---

[9] For this application, we insist on the two-message setting. Allowing $O(T)$ rounds of interaction, similar protocols can be based on any single-server PIR scheme [46].

the ideas behind our constructions from the different assumptions. We then proceed to discuss the applications of trapdoor hash. More technical details and full formal analysis are provided in the full version.

2   Trapdoor Hash Functions

We start by providing a notational framework for the new primitive, then give an overview of our constructions.

2.1   Defining Trapdoor Hash

A *trapdoor hash scheme (TDH)* defines a family of samplable publicly-parameterized hash functions $H_{hk} : \{0,1\}^n \to \{0,1\}^\eta$, accompanied with the following three algorithms:

– *Key generation:* given the public hash key, Bob generates a pair of an *encoding key* and a *trapdoor* $(ek, td) \leftarrow G(hk, i)$, corresponding to a private index $i \in [n]$.
– *Encoding:* using the encoding key ek, Alice, with a private input $x \in \{0,1\}^n$, can compute a *hint* $e \leftarrow E(ek, x)$, which essentially encodes the bit $x[i]$.
– *Decoding:* Bob, who has the secret trapdoor td, can now decode any encoding e generated for some input x as above, to recover x_i, given only the hash $H_{hk}(x)$. In fact, Bob would be able to generate two encodings $(e_0, e_1) \leftarrow D(td, h)$, where it is guaranteed that $e = e_{x[i]}$.

We actually consider a more general notion of TDH where Bob with a private *predicate* $f : \{0,1\}^n \to \{0,1\}$, chosen from a predefined class of predicates $\mathcal{F}$, generates a key ek, using which Alice encodes the bit $f(x)$, and a corresponding trapdoor, using which Bob decodes. Such a scheme is called trapdoor hash for $\mathcal{F}$, and the above special case is referred to as trapdoor hash for *index predicates*.

Definition 2.1 (Trapdoor Hash Scheme). *Let $\mathcal{F} = \{\mathcal{F}_n\}_{n \in \mathbb{N}}$ be a class of predicates, where each $\mathcal{F}_n$ is a set of predicates defined over $\{0,1\}^n$, and let $\omega := \omega(\lambda) \in \mathbb{N}$ for any $\lambda \in \mathbb{N}$. A rate-$\frac{1}{\omega}$ trapdoor hash scheme (TDH) for $\mathcal{F}$ is a tuple of five PPT algorithms $\mathsf{TDH} = (\mathsf{S}, \mathsf{G}, \mathsf{H}, \mathsf{E}, \mathsf{D})$ with the following properties.*

– ***Syntax :***
  • $hk \leftarrow S(1^\lambda, 1^n)$. *The sampling algorithm takes as input a security parameter λ and an input length n, and outputs a hash key hk.*
  • $(ek, td) \leftarrow G(hk, f)$. *The generating algorithm takes as input a hash key hk and a predicate $f \in \mathcal{F}_n$, and outputs a pair of an encoding key ek and a trapdoor td.*
  • $h \leftarrow H(hk, x; \rho)$. *The hashing algorithm takes as input a hash key hk, a string $x \in \{0,1\}^n$ and randomness $\rho \in \{0,1\}^*$, and deterministically outputs a hash value $h \in \{0,1\}^\eta$.*

- $e \leftarrow E(ek, x; \rho)$. *The encoding algorithm takes as input an encoding key ek, string* $x \in \{0,1\}^n$ *and randomness* $\rho \in \{0,1\}^*$, *and deterministically outputs an encoding* $e \in \{0,1\}^\omega$.
- $(e_0, e_1) \leftarrow D(td, h)$. *The decoding algorithm takes as input a trapdoor td, a hash value* $h \in \{0,1\}^n$, *and outputs a pair of a 0-encoding and a 1-encoding* $(e_0, e_1) \in \{0,1\}^\omega \times \{0,1\}^\omega$.

- **Correctness:** TDH *is* $(1 - \epsilon)$-*correct (or has* ϵ *error probability), for* $\epsilon := \epsilon(\lambda) < 1$, *if the following holds for any* $\lambda, n \in \mathbb{N}$, *any* $x \in \{0,1\}^n$ *and any predicate* $f \in \mathcal{F}_n$.

$$\Pr[e = e_{f(x)}] \geq 1 - \text{negl}(\lambda) \qquad \Pr[e \neq e_{1-f(x)}] \geq 1 - \epsilon - \text{negl}(\lambda)$$

  where $hk := S(1^\lambda, 1^n)$, $(ek, td) := G(hk, f)$, $h := H(hk, x; \rho)$ *and* $e := E(ek, x; \rho)$ *for* $\rho \xleftarrow{\$} \{0,1\}^*$, *and* $(e_0, e_1) := D(td, h)$.
- **Function Privacy:** TDH *is* function-private *if for any polynomial-length* $\{1^{n_\lambda}\}_{\lambda \in \mathbb{N}}$ *and any* $\{f_n\}_{n \in \mathbb{N}}$ *and* $\{f'_n\}_{n \in \mathbb{N}}$ *such that* $f_n, f'_n \in \mathcal{F}_n$ *for all* $n \in \mathbb{N}$, *it holds that*

$$\{(hk_\lambda, ek_\lambda)\}_{\lambda \in \mathbb{N}} \stackrel{c}{\equiv} \{(hk_\lambda, ek'_\lambda)\}_{\lambda \in \mathbb{N}}$$

  where $hk_\lambda \xleftarrow{\$} S(1^\lambda, 1^{n_\lambda})$, $(ek_\lambda, td_\lambda) \xleftarrow{\$} G(hk_\lambda, f_{n_\lambda})$ *and* $(ek'_\lambda, td'_\lambda) \xleftarrow{\$} G(hk_\lambda, f'_{n_\lambda})$.
- **Input Privacy:** TDH *is* input-private *if for any polynomial-length* $\{x_\lambda\}_{\lambda \in \mathbb{N}}$ *and* $\{x'_\lambda\}_{\lambda \in \mathbb{N}}$ *such that* $n_\lambda := |x_\lambda| = |x'_\lambda|$, *it holds that*

$$\{(hk_\lambda, h_\lambda)\}_{\lambda \in \mathbb{N}} \stackrel{c}{\equiv} \{(hk_\lambda, h'_\lambda)\}_{\lambda \in \mathbb{N}}$$

  where $hk_\lambda \xleftarrow{\$} S(1^\lambda, 1^{n_\lambda})$, $h_\lambda = H(hk_\lambda, x_\lambda; \rho)$ *and* $h' = H(hk_\lambda, x'_\lambda; \rho')$ *for* $\rho, \rho' \xleftarrow{\$} \{0,1\}^*$. *We also define statistical input privacy in the natural sense.*
- **Compactness:** *we require that the image length of the hash function,* η, *is independent of* n, *and is bounded by some polynomial in* λ.

For this outline, we think of trapdoor hashing as a protocol where Alice and Bob play the roles of a sender with input x and, respectively, a receiver who wants to learn $x[i]$ (or, generally, $f(x)$). For now, we will mostly focus on receiver privacy, i.e. function privacy, as sender's privacy is much easier to achieve. Our main goal is to construct trapdoor hash with optimal rate of 1, that is a scheme where the hint e consists of a single bit.

2.2 Trapdoor Hash from DDH

We start with our DDH-based construction of trapdoor hash for index predicates. Recall that, roughly speaking, the *Decisional Diffie-Hellman (DDH)* assumption says that an element g^{ab} of a group $\mathbb{G}$ with prime order p, where $g \in \mathbb{G}$ is a generator and $a, b \in \mathbb{Z}_p$ are uniform, is indistinguishable from a uniform group element, given g^a and g^b. We formally state our first result below.

Theorem 2.2. *There exists a rate-1 trapdoor hash scheme for index predicates with error probability* $1/\lambda$, *statistical input privacy, and function privacy based on the DDH assumption.*

The Basic Hash Function. The starting point of is the following group-based hash function mapping $\{0,1\}^n$ to a group $\mathbb{G}$:

$$H(\mathbf{A}, \mathsf{x}) = \prod_{j=1}^{n} g_{j, \mathsf{x}[j]}$$

where $\mathsf{x} \in \{0,1\}^n$ is the input and $\mathbf{A} = (g_{j,b})_{j \in [n], b \in \{0,1\}} \xleftarrow{\$} \mathbb{G}^{2 \times n}$ is chosen uniformly at random and serves as the hash key hk. By choosing n larger than the representation size of a group element in $\mathbb{G}$, this function becomes compressing. Collision resistance of this function can be routinely established from the discrete logarithm assumption in $\mathbb{G}$.

This surprisingly powerful function plays a central role in recent constructions of identity based encryption [21], trapdoor functions [26], deterministic encryption and lossy trapdoor functions [24].

Adding Trapdoors. We show how this function can be made invertible, using techniques of [24]. Clearly, the hash value $\mathsf{h} \leftarrow H(\mathsf{hk}, \mathsf{x})$ is too short to information-theoretically specify x. Thus we will add additional *hints*, which we also call *encodings*, to allow recovery of x. We will first discuss how the receiver can recover a single bit $\mathsf{x}[i]$ of x.

Let $i \in [n]$ be an index of the receiver's choice. The receiver will generate a matrix $\mathbf{B} \in \mathbb{G}^{2 \times n}$, that serves as an encoding key ek, such that the following holds for all $\mathsf{x} \in \{0,1\}^n$: If $H(\mathbf{A}, \mathsf{x}) = \mathsf{h}$, then $H(\mathbf{B}, \mathsf{x}) = \mathsf{h}^s \cdot g^{\mathsf{x}[i]}$ for some $s \in \mathbb{Z}_p$. We can construct such a matrix $\mathbf{B} = (u_{j,b})_{j \in [n], b \in \{0,1\}}$ by choosing $s \xleftarrow{\$} \mathbb{Z}_p$ uniformly at random, and setting

$$u_{j,b} = g_{j,b}^{s}$$

for all $j \neq i$ and

$$u_{i,b} = g_{i,b}^{s} \cdot g^{b}. \tag{2.1}$$

Since s is uniform, we immediately get, via the DDH assumption, that all $g_{j,b}^{s}$ are pseudorandom, and consequently, the matrix $\mathbf{B}$ is pseudorandom as well. Thus, the matrix $\mathbf{B}$ computationally hides the index i.

Given the values $\mathsf{h} = H(\mathbf{A}, \mathsf{x})$ and the hint $\mathsf{e} = H(\mathbf{B}, \mathsf{x})$, as well as a trapdoor consisting of s, the receiver can recover x as follows. As by the above property it holds that $\mathsf{e} = \mathsf{h}^s \cdot g^{\mathsf{x}[i]}$, we can recover $\mathsf{x}[i]$ by testing $\mathsf{e} \stackrel{?}{=} \mathsf{h}^s \cdot g^b$ for both $b \in \{0,1\}$ and setting $\mathsf{x}[i] \leftarrow b$ for the b which satisfies this test. While we can construct a trapdoor hash function in this way, its rate will be far from 1: To encode a single bit $\mathsf{x}[i]$ of x, we need to spend one full group element e. Assuming that a group element has size λ, this will give us a construction of rate $1/\lambda$.

Towards Rate 1. Clearly, sending a group element e to encode a single bit $x[i]$ is wasteful. However, we make the following observation: The term e can only assume two different values, namely h^s and $h^s \cdot g$, depending on whether the bit $x[i]$ is 0 or 1. So what we need is a way for the sender to signal to the receiver that either $e = h^s$ or $e = h^s \cdot g$, without actually sending e. Yet, since the sender does not know i, he generally does not know whether he is encoding 0 or 1, that is, he does not know whether e is of the form h^s or $h^s \cdot g$.

However, assume the sender could somehow determine the *distance to a nearby reference point* of e which is insensitive to small perturbations. This would for instance be the case if the group $\mathbb{G}$ had a subgroup $\mathbb{G}'$, such that we can efficiently test membership in $\mathbb{G}'$ and the quotient $\mathbb{G}/\mathbb{G}'$ is of polynomial size. Since $|\mathbb{G}/\mathbb{G}'|$ is only of polynomial size, we can efficiently compute the *distance* to $\mathbb{G}'$ for every $e \in \mathbb{G}$. That is, the function $\mathsf{Dist}(e)$ which exhaustively searches for the smallest $z \in \mathbb{Z}$ such that $e \cdot g^z \in \mathbb{G}'$ is efficiently computable. Assuming further for simplicity that $|\mathbb{G}/\mathbb{G}'|$ is even, it holds for every $e \in \mathbb{G}$ that

$$\mathsf{Dist}(e \cdot g) \mod 2 = (\mathsf{Dist}(e) + 1) \mod 2.$$

This means that h^s and $h^s \cdot g$ never map to the same bit under the function $\mathsf{Dist}(\cdot)$ mod 2. Via this observation, the sender can signal to the receiver whether e is h^s or $h^s \cdot g$ as follows. Instead of sending e itself to the receiver, he just sends the bit $\hat{e} = \mathsf{Dist}(e) \mod 2 \in \{0,1\}$ to the receiver.

Modifying the recovery procedure of above, the receiver can recover $x[i]$ by testing $\hat{e} \stackrel{?}{=} \mathsf{Dist}(h^s g^b) \mod 2$ for $b \in \{0,1\}$ and setting $x[i] \leftarrow b$ for the b which satisfies this test. This procedure recovers the correct bit $x[i]$ with $\hat{e} = \mathsf{Dist}(h^s \cdot g^{x[i]})$, as the value e computed by the sender must have been either h^s or $h^s \cdot g$, and by the above $\mathsf{Dist}(h^s) \mod 2 \neq \mathsf{Dist}(h^s \cdot g) \mod 2$.

Achieving Rate 1. Alas, since $\mathbb{G}$ is typically a cyclic group of prime order, it has no non-trivial subgroups. But upon closer inspection, the signalling technique above does not really rely on any additional group structure. All we need is that $\mathsf{Dist}(e \cdot g) = \mathsf{Dist}(e) + 1$.

Fortunately, a technique to determine the distance to a reference point was proposed by Boyle, Gilboa and Ishai [9] in the context of homomorphic secret sharing. In a nutshell, instead of computing the distance to a subgroup, we compute the distance to a *moderately dense pseudorandom subset* of $\mathbb{G}$. Such a pseudorandom subset can be succinctly represented via the key of a pseudorandom function by setting S_K to be the set of all points $h \in \mathbb{G}$ for which $\mathsf{PRF}_K(h)$ starts with $k = O(\log(\lambda))$ zeros. By tuning the parameter k appropriately, one can achieve an average separation of the points in S_K by an arbitrary polynomial amount. We can now define $\mathsf{Dist}(e)$ to be the smallest $z \in \mathbb{Z}$ such that $e \cdot g^z \in S_K$, i.e. $\mathsf{PRF}_K(e \cdot g^z)$ starts with k zeros. Note that this function can be computed efficiently for the above choice of k.

However, as the vigilant reader might have observed already, when using this distance function, the above signalling procedure does not have perfect correctness anymore. If h^s and $h^s \cdot g$ decode to different points in S_K, it might be that

$\mathsf{Dist}(\mathsf{h}^s) \bmod 2 = \mathsf{Dist}(\mathsf{h}^s \cdot g) \bmod 2$, in which case the receiver cannot infer whether $\mathsf{x}[i] = 0$ or $\mathsf{x}[i] = 1$ and must declare an erasure.

Fortunately, by choosing k large enough, we can make the probability of such an erasure happening an arbitrarily small polynomial fraction $1/p(\lambda)$, while still ensuring that the decoding procedure runs in polynomial time[10] As it turns out, in many applications, we can deal with this small erasure probability by resorting to standard coding techniques.

Sender Privacy. So far we have not addressed issues concerning the privacy of the sender's inputs. However, in our DDH-based construction this is easy to achieve by providing an additional random input to the hash function H. That is, we define H as

$$\mathsf{H}(\mathbf{A}, \mathsf{x}; r) = g^r \cdot \prod_{j=1}^{n} g_{j, \mathsf{x}[j]},$$

for a uniformly random $r \xleftarrow{\$} \mathbb{Z}_p$. The hash value $\mathsf{h} = \mathsf{H}(\mathbf{A}, \mathsf{x}; r)$ is now uniformly random (over the choice of r) and therefore does not leak information about x. Furthermore, given the trapdoor s and a single bit $\mathsf{x}[j]$ of the input x we can perfectly simulate e by computing $\mathsf{e} \leftarrow \mathsf{h}^s \cdot g^{\mathsf{x}[j]}$. From e we can compute $\hat{\mathsf{e}}$ as before. Thus, the modified construction has perfect sender privacy.

2.3   Trapdoor Hash from QR and LWE

We now briefly discuss instantiations of these techniques based on the Quadratic Residuosity (QR) and Learning With Errors (LWE) assumptions to achieve trapdoor hash for the even more general class of linear predicates. As it turns out, in both these cases we will have structures with exact subgroups. However, in both cases there will also be new challenges which will have to be addressed with slightly different ideas.

Theorem 2.3. *There exists a rate-1 trapdoor hash scheme for linear predicates with negligible error probability, statistical input privacy, and function privacy based on the {QR,LWE} assumption.*

Construction from QR. We will start with the QR-based construction. Instead of relying on the QR assumption directly, we will use the fact that we can construct a group $\mathbb{G}$ in which the subgroup indistinguishability problem is hard under QR [12]. More specifically, the group $\mathbb{G}$ we use has a subgroup $\mathbb{G}'$ such that $|\mathbb{G}/\mathbb{G}'| = 2$. We can represent every $h \in \mathbb{G}$ as $h = (-1)^b \cdot a$, where $b \in \{0, 1\}$

---

[10] We can ensure that both sender and receiver run in strict polynomial time by introducing a suitable polynomial upper bound for the number of trials in the exhaustive search step of $\mathsf{Dist}(\cdot)$. For small erasure probabilities, a near-quadratic improvement in the running time can be obtained via the recent optimal "distributed discrete log" algorithm of Dinur, Keller, and Klein [19].

and $a \in \mathbb{G}'$. For the hash function H, we can use exactly the same construction as above, that is $\mathsf{H}(\mathsf{hk}, \mathsf{x}) = \prod_{j=1}^{n} g_{j, \mathsf{x}[j]}$. The only difference is that we choose the elements in the key $\mathsf{hk} = \mathbf{A}$ from the subgroup $\mathbb{G}'$ instead of $\mathbb{G}$, that is, $\mathbf{A} = (g_{j,b})_{j \in [n], b \in \{0,1\}} \overset{\$}{\leftarrow} \mathbb{G}'^{2 \times m}$. Similar as in the DDH-based construction, for an index $i \in [n]$, the matrix $\mathbf{B}$ generated by G now has the form $\mathbf{B} = (u_{j,b})_{j \in [n], b \in \{0,1\}}$ where

$$u_{j,b} = g_{j,b}^{s}$$

for all $j \neq i$ and

$$u_{i,b} = g_{i,b}^{s} \cdot (-1)^{b}.$$

Here, s is uniformly random in an appropriate domain. The crucial difference is that in $u_{i,b}$, we have replaced the generator g in the DDH-based construction by -1. It follows directly via the subgroup indistinguishabilty assumption that $g_{i,b}^{s} \cdot (-1)^{b}$ is indistinguishable from $g_{i,b}^{s}$. Thus, as before, the index i is hidden.

By a similar analysis as before, it holds that if $\mathsf{h} = \mathsf{H}(\mathbf{A}, \mathsf{x})$, then $\mathsf{e} = \mathsf{H}(\mathbf{B}, \mathsf{x}) = \mathsf{h}^{s} \cdot (-1)^{\mathsf{x}[i]}$. However, there is a crucial difference now: As $\mathsf{e} = \mathsf{h}^{s} \cdot (-1)^{\mathsf{x}[i]}$, the sender can also compute $\mathsf{e} \cdot (-1) = \mathsf{h}^{s} \cdot (-1)^{1-\mathsf{x}[i]}$. That is, one of these two elements is h^{s} and the other one is $\mathsf{h}^{s} \cdot (-1)$. Recall that the receiver can also compute these two elements using the hash value h and the trapdoor s. Thus, the only task left for the sender is to signal to the receiver which one of the two elements the element e he got is. This can be easily done by communicating a single bit: The sender compares e and $\mathsf{e} \cdot (-1)$ under some total order $\succ$, say, by representing both elements as bit strings, and computing the lexicographic order. Now, he sends the bit $\hat{e} = 0$ if $\mathsf{e} \succ \mathsf{e} \cdot (-1)$ and $\hat{e} = 1$ otherwise. The receiver can recover $\mathsf{x}[i]$ as follows: If $\mathsf{h}^{s} \succ \mathsf{h}^{s} \cdot (-1)$ and $\hat{e} = 0$ he sets $\mathsf{x}[i] = 0$, otherwise $\mathsf{x}[i] = 1$.

The main difference of this instantiation compared to our DDH-based construction is that there is no decoding error. We can even leverage this fact to achieve a stronger functionality. So far, we have only discussed how the receiver can recover individual bits $\mathsf{x}[i]$ of the sender's input, namely realize trapdoor hash for *index predicates*. We will now show how this can be upgraded in a way such that the receiver can learn an inner product $\langle \mathsf{y}, \mathsf{x} \rangle \mod 2$, and therefore obtain trapdoor hash for the more general class of *linear predicates*. The vector y is chosen by the receiver and is used to generate the matrix $\mathbf{B}$. Concretely, for a vector $\mathsf{y} \in \{0,1\}^{n}$ the receiver sets

$$u_{j,b} = g_{j,b}^{s} \cdot (-1)^{b \cdot \mathsf{y}[j]}$$

for all $j \in [n]$ and $b \in \{0,1\}$. As before, we can use the subgroup indistinguishability assumption to establish that the matrix $\mathbf{B}$ hides the vector y.

A simple calculation shows that $\mathsf{H}(\mathbf{B}, \mathsf{x}) = \mathsf{h}^{s} \cdot (-1)^{\langle \mathsf{y}, \mathsf{x} \rangle}$. The encoding and decoding procedures are exactly the same as before, with the difference that now the receiver learns the inner product $\langle \mathsf{y}, \mathsf{x} \rangle \mod 2$. While this modification to our construction is nearly straightforward, it has several important applications.

Construction from LWE. We will finally turn to our construction from LWE. On a conceptual level, the construction is very similar to the QR-based construction. We will directly explain the construction for linear predicates, i.e. inner products over $\mathbb{F}_2$. In this instantiation, let $q = 2p$ be an even modulus. The hashing key $\mathsf{hk} = \mathbf{A}$ is a $2 \times n$ matrix of uniformly random column vectors $\mathbf{a}_{j,b} \in \mathbb{Z}_q^k$, that is, each component of this matrix is a vector itself. The hash of an input $\mathsf{x} \in \{0,1\}^n$ is now computed as the sum of the corresponding $\mathbf{a}_{j,b}$, that is

$$H(\mathbf{A}, \mathsf{x}) = \sum_{j=1}^{n} \mathbf{a}_{j,\mathsf{x}[j]}.$$

The encoding key contains a matrix $\mathbf{B} = (u_{j,b})_{j \in [n], b \in \{0,1\}}$, which consists of elements $u_{j,b} \in \mathbb{Z}_q^k$ which are computed by

$$u_{j,b} = \mathbf{s}^\top \mathbf{a}_{j,b} + e_{j,b} + \mathsf{y}[j] \cdot b \cdot (q/2),$$

where $\mathbf{s}$ is chosen uniformly from $\mathbb{Z}_q^k$ and the $e_{j,b}$ are sampled from a short LWE-error distribution such as a discrete gaussian. By the LWE assumption, we immediately get that the values $\mathbf{s}^\top \mathbf{a}_{j,b} + e_{j,b}$ are pseudorandom, and consequently the matrix $\mathbf{B}$ hides the vector y. Assume further that PRF is a pseudorandom function from $\mathbb{Z}_q^k$ to $\mathbb{Z}_q$. For this instantiation, the receiver will also include a uniformly random PRF-key $K \xleftarrow{\$} \{0,1\}^\lambda$ into the encoding key.

As before, the sender computes $\mathsf{h} = H(\mathbf{A}, \mathsf{x})$ and $\mathsf{e} = H(\mathbf{B}, \mathsf{x})$. Notice that it holds that

$$\mathsf{e} = \sum_{j=1}^{n} u_{j,\mathsf{x}[j]} = \mathbf{s}^\top \sum_{j=1}^{n} \mathbf{a}_{j,\mathsf{x}[j]} + \sum_{j=1}^{n} e_{j,\mathsf{x}[j]} + \langle \mathsf{y}, \mathsf{x} \rangle \cdot (q/2) = \mathbf{s}^\top \mathsf{h} + e' + \langle \mathsf{y}, \mathsf{x} \rangle \cdot (q/2),$$

where $e' = \sum_{j=1}^{n} e_{j,\mathsf{x}[j]}$ is a small error.

The challenge in this instantiation is that e is noisy, so the comparison-based technique from the QR-based construction will not work here. Nevertheless, a standard tool to robustly deal with this kind of error in the world of LWE is the rounding technique, introduced by Banerjee, Peikert and Rosen [5]. Define the rounding function $\lfloor \cdot \rceil_2$ by $\lfloor z \rceil_2 = \lceil z \cdot 2/q \rceil \mod 2$. The sender now computes $\hat{\mathsf{e}}$ by

$$\hat{\mathsf{e}} = \lfloor H(\mathbf{B}, \mathsf{x}) + \mathsf{PRF}_K(\mathsf{h}) \rceil_2$$

and sends h along with the bit $\hat{\mathsf{e}}$ to the receiver. The receiver now computes and outputs $(\hat{\mathsf{e}} - \lfloor \mathbf{s}^\top \mathsf{h} + \mathsf{PRF}_K(\mathsf{h}) \rceil_2) \mod 2$.

To establish correctness, we will use the fact that, for a sufficiently large q, the rounding function is insensitive to small perturbations. That is, for a uniformly random $z \xleftarrow{\$} \mathbb{Z}_q$, and a sufficiently *small* noise e, it holds that $\lfloor z + e \rceil_2 = \lfloor z \rceil_2$, except with small probability over the choice of z. Now, since the term $\mathsf{PRF}_K(\mathsf{h})$ is pseudorandom in $\mathbb{Z}_q$, it holds that

$$\hat{\mathsf{e}} = \lfloor H(\mathbf{B}, \mathsf{x}) + \mathsf{PRF}_K(\mathsf{h}) \rceil_2 = \lfloor \mathbf{s}^\top \mathsf{h} + e' + \langle \mathsf{y}, \mathsf{x} \rangle \cdot (q/2) + \mathsf{PRF}_K(\mathsf{h}) \rceil_2$$
$$= \lfloor \mathbf{s}^\top \mathsf{h} + \mathsf{PRF}_K(\mathsf{h}) \rceil_2 + \langle \mathsf{y}, \mathsf{x} \rangle,$$

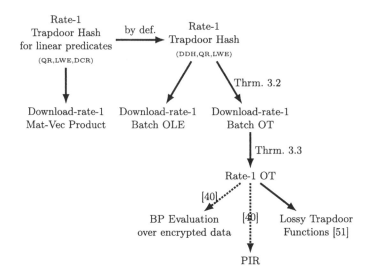

Fig. 1. Overview of the results in this work, Part I: optimal-rate protocols for OT-like sender-receiver functionalities and their applications. Dotted lines correspond to corollaries from prior work.

except with small probability over the choice over K. This is the reason why we include the key K in the receiver's message, that is, to enable the sender to randomize $H(\mathbf{B}, x)$ without increasing the size of the sender message. Correctness of the scheme follows.

The magnitude of the correctness error depends on the modulus-to-noise ratio. If we choose a superpolynomial modulus-to-noise ratio, the correctness error becomes negligible. For a polynomial modulus-to-noise ration the correctness error will be inverse polynomial and we have to compensate with coding techniques.

3   Rate-1 Oblivious Transfer and More

We now present the first family of applications of trapdoor hash (Fig. 1). We show how to use rate-1 trapdoor hash to securely realize basic sender-receiver functionalities through two-message protocols with optimal sender-receiver communication, i.e. optimal *download rate*.

Formally speaking, a two-message protocol for functionality $f : X \times Y \to Z$ is defined through a triple of PPT algorithms $\Pi = (\Pi_1, \Pi_2, \Pi_3)$ where, at first, the receiver computes a message $\mathsf{msg}_1 \leftarrow \Pi_1(1^\lambda, x)$ for security parameter λ and input $x \in X$ and sends it to the sender. The sender with input $y \in Y$ responds by a message $\mathsf{msg}_2 \leftarrow \Pi_2(\mathsf{msg}_1, y)$. Lastly, given the second message msg_2 and possibly a local state st computes the output $f(x, y) = \Pi_3(\mathsf{msg}_2, \mathsf{st})$. We require standard notions of receiver privacy and sender privacy (against a semi-honest receiver). The download rate of a two-message is defined as follows.

Definition 3.1 (Download Rate of a Two-Message Protocol). *Let* $0 \leq \omega \leq 1$. *We say that a two-message protocol Π for functionality $f : X \times Y \to Z$ has download rate ω if there exists a polynomial $B(\lambda)$ such for all polynomial-length input sequences $\{(x_\lambda, y_\lambda)\}_{\lambda \in \mathbb{N}}$ in the domain of f such that $|f(x_\lambda, y_\lambda)| \geq B(\lambda)$ for all λ, we have*

$$\liminf_{\lambda \to \infty} \frac{|f(x_\lambda, y_\lambda)|}{m_\lambda} = \omega$$

where m_λ is the maximal length of the sender-receiver message when Π runs on inputs (x_λ, y_λ) and security parameter λ.

The first fundamental functionality we investigate is *oblivious transfer* (OT), where a receiver with private input bit $i \in \{0, 1\}$ communicates with a sender with secrets s_0, s_1 in order to obtain secret s_i. Rate-1 OT has several important applications, for which we are able to achieve the first constructions under various assumptions, using our trapdoor hash constructions. We also discuss a couple of related primitives: *oblivious linear function evaluation* (OLE), where the sender has a linear function $f(x) = ax + b$ and the goal is to evaluate f on the receiver's private input x, and the more general *matrix-vector product* where the sender has a matrix M, the receiver has a vector v, and the goal is to compute the product $Mv^\top$.

3.1   Rate-1 Oblivious Transfer from Trapdoor Hash

Equipped with our newly developed tool, we show how to construct 2-message OT protocols with rate 1 given any trapdoor hash with the same rate. We consider two flavours of OT where download-rate-1 can be achieved. The first is *batch OT*, where a batch of OT instances with single-bit secrets are invoked in parallel, and the second is *string OT*, which consists of a single OT instance with secrets that are assumed to be sufficiently long. In the latter case, we get optimal *overall* rate (where also receiver-sender communication is taken into account).

Batch OT. Recall that a trapdoor hash scheme for index predicates allows one to recover the ith bit of a string x given the hash value H(hk, x) and a single additional bit e (which we denote ê above). With this tool at hand, we can realize the 1-out-of-2 bit OT functionality by letting the receiver specify the hash key hk and the encoding key ek corresponding to the choice bit $i \in \{0, 1\}$. The sender then sets its input x := $s_0 \| s_1$ to be the concatenation of the two secret bits and computes h = H(hk, x) together with the encoding e. Given such an information, the receiver can recover the chosen secret bit by running the decoding algorithm. The obvious shortcoming of this approach is that it is wasteful in terms of download rate, in the sense that the hash of the string must be included to recover a single bit.

The key observation here is that the hash key hk can be reused across several executions. Therefore the size of the hash h can be amortized across multiple independent bit OT protocols. That is, if the bit OTs are executed in a batch, we can boost the download rate of the construction to approach 1: Given n independent instances of bit OT, the receiver samples a hash key hk as before, this time for inputs of length $2n$ rather than 2, and samples a set of encoding keys $(\mathsf{ek}_1, \ldots, \mathsf{ek}_n)$, where the jth key allows the receiver to learn the input bit at position $(2j + i_j)$, where $i_j \in \{0, 1\}$ is the choice bit of the jth OT instance. It is important that all of the encoding keys are generated with respect to the same hk, since it will allow us to re-use the corresponding hash. The sender defines $\mathsf{x} := \mathsf{s}_{1,0} \| \mathsf{s}_{1,1} \| \ldots, \| \mathsf{s}_{n,0} \| \mathsf{s}_{n,1}$, where $\mathsf{s}_{j,0}, \mathsf{s}_{j,1}$ are the secrets for the jth instance, and computes the hash $\mathsf{h} = \mathsf{H}(\mathsf{hk}, \mathsf{x})$ as before, in addition to the additional hints, i.e. TDH encodings, $(\mathsf{e}_1, \ldots, \mathsf{e}_n)$. The recovery procedure is then run in parallel for each bit OT instance. Note that the sender's message consists of a hash (i.e., a single group element) and n bits. That is, the impact of h in the communication vanishes as n grows, and thus, the download rate of the scheme approaches 1. The above outline gives the following theorem.

Theorem 3.2. *Assume there exists a rate-1 trapdoor hash scheme* TDH, *with error probability* $\epsilon(\lambda)$. *Then, there exists a 2-message batch OT protocol with download rate 1 and independent error probability of* $\epsilon(\lambda)$ *in every (single-bit) OT instance. Further, if* TDH *is statistically input-private, then the obtained batch OT protocol is statistically sender-private.*

String OT. We showed how to obliterate the impact of the hash value h in the second OT message by executing multiple bit OT instances in a batch. The same can be accomplished for a single OT instance, when executed on sufficiently long secret strings (rather than single bits)[11]. The protocol can be derived generically from the batch OT by adapting the encodings of the inputs: The receiver executes the batch OT protocol of above by replicating the same choice bit i over each of the n instances, whereas the sender parses the two strings $(\mathsf{s}_0, \mathsf{s}_1) \in \{0, 1\}^n$ as n pairs of bits and encodes the string x as before. Since the choice bit of the receiver is the same in all positions, the decoding algorithm will recover the string s_i in its entirety.

In the above discussion we omitted a few important aspects of our transformation that need to be addressed in order to obtain a fully-fledged rate-1 OT. More specifically, (i) some instances of trapdoor hash have a correctness error, in the sense that the secret might not be recoverable with a certain probability ϵ. Furthermore, (ii) the upload rate of the construction is inverse polynomial in λ. To resolve the former point we preprocess the sender's inputs with a sufficiently strong error-correcting code. One has to be careful that the encoding function does not affect the download rate of the protocol. Fortunately, our error probability ϵ lies in a regime of parameters that allow us to efficiently instantiate the encoding function. For the latter issue, we show that any string OT with download rate 1 can be generically bootstrapped to a string OT with overall rate 1. Our method is based upon the simple observation that the first message of an OT is always reusable and therefore can be amortized by executing the

---

[11] In fact, string OT can be thought of as a special case of batch OT, where all the choice bits i_j are equal.

same OT over blocks of a sufficiently long string. Thus, overall, our main result in this context is as follows.

Theorem 3.3. *Assume there exists a 2-message batch OT protocol with download rate 1 and independent error probability of $\epsilon(\lambda) = O(1/\lambda)$ in every (single-bit) OT instance. Then, there exists a 2-message string OT protocol with overall rate 1 and negligible error.*

The same techniques can be generalized to 1-out-of-k OT, for any $k \in \mathbb{N}$.

3.2 Applications of Rate-1 OT

We now discuss few interesting applications of rate-1 OT.

Private Information Retrieval. Given a 1-out-of-2 string OT with rate 1, a (block) single-server PIR protocol [44], with optimal download rate and polylogarithmic overall communication, follows as a simple corollary of the main theorem of Ishai and Paskin [40]. We hereby recall the transformation for completeness.

Recall that in (block) PIR, a client queries a server, that holds a database consisting of N blocks, each of length β bits, in order to privately retrieve a block of his choice. Observe that a 1-out-of-2 string OT can be seen as a hash function that compresses the size of its input by a factor of roughly two. The idea is to use such a hash function and let the server compute a Merkle tree over the database $\mathsf{x} \in \{0,1\}^{N \cdot \beta}$. Every node in the tree consists of a block and, for simplicity, we assume that $N = 2^d$ for some $d \in \mathbb{N}$, which is the depth of the tree. Thus, the lowest level in the tree consists of the N database blocks: $\mathsf{x}_0, \ldots, \mathsf{x}_{N-1}$, and every other level $\ell = 1, \ldots, d$ in the tree consists of $N/2^\ell$-many blocks: $\mathsf{h}_{\ell,0}, \ldots, \mathsf{h}_{\ell,N/2^\ell-1}$, that are hashes of the nodes in level ℓ. Notice that every index $i \in \{0, \ldots, N-1\}$ corresponds to a path in the tree, which we denote by $(i_1, \ldots, i_d)$, which represents the path from database block x_i to the root of the tree.

The protocol proceeds as follows: First, the client generates the receiver message $\mathsf{msg}_1^{(\ell)}$ of an OT for strings of appropriate length, for each layer $\ell = 1, \ldots, d$ in the tree, where the choice bit is set to be the index i_ℓ. Then the client sends $(\mathsf{msg}_1^{(1)}, \ldots, \mathsf{msg}_1^{(\ell)})$ to the server, who computes all of the hash values in the Merkle tree, i.e. OT sender messages, and sends the root $\mathsf{msg}_2^{(d)}$ to the client. The client can recover the entry of interest by recursively applying the decoding algorithm of the OT, starting from the top level d.

Evaluating Branching Programs over Encrypted Data. Another result in the work of Ishai and Paskin [40], which can be seen as a generalization of the above, is a compiler that takes any 2-message rate-1 OT[12] into a *semi-compact* homomorphic encryption scheme for branching programs (a superclass of NC^1),

---

[12] In fact they require an OT protocol with a strong notion of sender privacy, which is satisfied by all of our constructions.

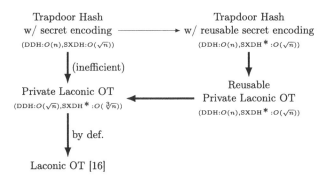

Fig. 2. Overview of the results in this work, Part II: secure function evaluation with sublinear communication. Thin lines correspond to non-generic transformations. (*We also assume correlated-input secure hash over bilinear groups.)

where the size of the evaluated ciphertexts depends only on the length of the branching program but not on its size. This immediately yields a sublinear secure function evaluation protocol where the client's work is independent of the size of the branching program (which is in fact hidden to its eyes).

Lossy Trapdoor Functions. As a yet another application, we show a simple construction of lossy trapdoor functions [35,51] with optimal rate from any 2-message rate-1 OT, and therefore obtain schemes based on DDH, QR, or LWE. Prior to our work, rate optimal schemes were known to exist only under the DCR assumption.

3.3 Rate-Optimal Protocols for Other OT-like Functionalities

It turns out that using trapdoor hash for index predicates, we can already capture a wide variety of predicate classes through a simple transformation. More specifically, if a given predicate class $\mathcal{F}$ is "small", i.e. contains $\mathsf{poly}(n)$ predicates for input size n, then we can obtain TDH for $\mathcal{F}$ on input x by applying TDH for index predicates on input x', where the ith bit in x' is the evaluation of the ith predicate in $\mathcal{F}$ on x.

We use this observation to extend the range of functionalities for which we can construct rate-optimal protocols. For instance, an interesting special case of small predicate classes are functions $f(x) = ax + b$ over $\mathbb{F}_2$, which essentially allow realizing batch oblivious linear function evaluation (OLE) [47] by replacing the TDH for index predicates, in the batch OT construction described above, with TDH for such predicates. Further, one can extend the idea to OLE over other constant size rings (e.g. fields $\mathbb{F}_p$ for constant prime p), by evaluating each output bit separately.

An even more general functionality, that allows evaluating matrix-vector products over $\mathbb{F}_2$ (with the vector and matrix respectively being the receiver's and sender's input), can be realized using the same technique by relying on TDH for linear predicates, which can be instantiated, as mentioned earlier, under the LWE and QR assumptions. The LWE-based TDH scheme can be further extended to allow trapdoor-evaluation of linear functions over small fields, thus yielding *oblivious matrix vector multiplication* (OMV) over such fields. It is worth mentioning that OMV can be also seen as a variant of rate-1 additively homomorphic encryption, where inner products (and in particular matrix multiplication) can be evaluated over encrypted vectors.

Lastly, we note that using OLE and OMV schemes over small fields, we can realize similar functionalities over larger algebraic structures through standard algebraic manipulations. More specifically, we can get OLE and OMV over smooth rings, via the Chinese Remainder Theorem, and over extension fields of small characteristic using basic extension field algebra.

4   Private Laconic Oblivious Transfer

In this section we outline another application of trapdoor hash: *private laconic oblivious transfer* (Fig. 2). As discussed in the introduction, private laconic OT has strong applications in secure computation. In particular, following the outline presented in [16] to utilize laconic OT for non-interactive secure RAM computation with unprotected memory access, we can use private laconic OT to obtain secure RAM computation where the access pattern to the memory is also hidden, and therefore achieve a stronger notion of security.

Recall that in laconic OT (ℓOT) [16], a receiver with an input database $\mathsf{x} \in \{0,1\}^n$ communicates with a sender, with two secrets $\mathsf{s}_0, \mathsf{s}_1 \in \{0,1\}$ and an index $i \in [n]$ as input, in order to learn $\mathsf{s}_{\mathsf{x}[i]}$,while keeping both x and $\mathsf{s}_{1-\mathsf{x}[i]}$ private. In *private* laconic OT ($p\ell$OT), we also require that the index i remains hidden from the receiver.

Our end goal is to realize the $p\ell$OT functionality through a two-message protocol where the overall communication is sublinear in n in order to obtain sublinear SFE protocols (due to [16]).

As a start, however, we aim for *receiver-compact* $p\ell$OT where the upload communication (i.e., the communication from the receiver to the sender) is independent of the receiver's database size n, and set no restrictions on the communication from the sender to the receiver. We then describe such a receiver-compact $p\ell$OT construction with linear sender-receiver communication through our DDH-based trapdoor hash, and then show to get sublinear communication (namely $\sqrt{n}$) using pairings.

Lastly, we show that if we are willing to compromise receiver-compactness, then we can balance our protocols using what we call *reusable private laconic OT* and obtain more efficient SFE protocols with sublinear communication under both DDH and pairings. We start with the basic definition of private laconic OT.

Definition 4.1 (Private Laconic OT). *A private laconic OT scheme is a tuple of four PPT algorithms $p\ell\mathsf{OT} = (\mathsf{Gen}, \mathsf{Hash}, \mathsf{Send}, \mathsf{Receive})$ with the following properties.*

- **Syntax:**
  - pp $\leftarrow$ Gen($1^\lambda, 1^n$). *The generating algorithm takes as input the security parameter* 1^λ, *and the size of the database* n, *and outputs public parameters* pp $\in \{0,1\}^*$.
  - h $\leftarrow$ Hash(pp, x; ρ). *The hashing algorithm takes as input the public parameters* pp, *a database* x $\in \{0,1\}^n$, *and randomness* $\rho \in \{0,1\}^*$, *and deterministically outputs a hash value* h $\in \{0,1\}^\eta$.
  - ct $\leftarrow$ Send(pp, h, i, (s_0, s_1)). *The sending algorithm takes as input the public parameters* pp, *a hash value* h, *an index* $i \in [n]$, *and a pair of secrets* (s_0, s_1) $\in \{0,1\} \times \{0,1\}$, *and outputs a ciphertext* ct $\in \{0,1\}^*$.
  - s $\leftarrow$ Receive(pp, ct, x; ρ). *The receiving algorithm takes as input the public parameters* pp, *a ciphertext* ct, *a database* x $\in \{0,1\}^n$, *and randomness* $\rho \in \{0,1\}^*$, *and deterministically outputs a secret* s $\in \{0,1\}$.
- **Correctness:** $p\ell OT$ *is correct if there exists a negligible function* $\epsilon(\lambda)$ *such that the following holds for all* $\lambda, n \in \mathbb{N}$, *any database* x $\in \{0,1\}^n$, *any index* $i \in [n]$, *and any pair of secrets* $s_0, s_1 \in \{0,1\}$.

$$\Pr\left[s = s_{x[i]} \,\middle|\, \begin{array}{l} pp \leftarrow \text{Gen}(1^\lambda, n) \\ \rho \xleftarrow{\$} \{0,1\}^* \\ h \leftarrow \text{Hash}(pp, x; \rho) \\ ct \leftarrow \text{Send}(pp, h, i, (s_0, s_1)) \\ s \leftarrow \text{Receive}(pp, ct, x; \rho) \end{array} \right] \geq 1 - \epsilon(\lambda).$$

- **Receiver Privacy:** $p\ell OT$ *is statistically, resp., computationally, receiver-private if for any polynomial-length* $\{x_\lambda, x'_\lambda\}_{\lambda \in \mathbb{N}}$ *where* $n_\lambda := |x_\lambda| = |x'_\lambda|$ *for all* $\lambda \in \mathbb{N}$, *the following two distribution ensembles*

$$\{(pp_\lambda, h_\lambda)\}_{\lambda \in \mathbb{N}} \qquad\qquad \{(pp_\lambda, h'_\lambda)\}_{\lambda \in \mathbb{N}}$$

where $pp_\lambda \xleftarrow{\$} \text{Gen}(1^\lambda, 1^{n_\lambda})$ *and* $h_\lambda := \text{Hash}(pp_\lambda, x_\lambda; \rho)$, $h'_\lambda := \text{Hash}(pp_\lambda, x'_\lambda; \rho')$ *for* $\rho, \rho' \xleftarrow{\$} \{0,1\}^*$, *are statistically, resp. computationally, indistinguishable.*
- **Sender Privacy (against a semi-honest receiver):** $p\ell OT$ *is (computationally) sender-private if there exists a PPT algorithm* Sim *such that for any* $s_0, s_1 \in \{0,1\}$, *any polynomial-length* $\{x_\lambda\}_{\lambda \in \mathbb{N}}$ *and any* $\{i_\lambda\}_{\lambda \in \mathbb{N}}$, *where* $n_\lambda := |x_\lambda|$ *and* $i_\lambda \in [n_\lambda]$ *for all* $\lambda \in \mathbb{N}$, *the distribution ensembles* $\{\text{Real}_\lambda\}_{\lambda \in \mathbb{N}}$ *and* $\{\text{Ideal}_\lambda\}_{\lambda \in \mathbb{N}}$, *where*

$$\text{Real}_\lambda = (pp_\lambda, x_\lambda, (ct_\lambda, \rho)) \qquad \text{Ideal}_\lambda = (pp_\lambda, x_\lambda, \text{Sim}(1^\lambda, pp_\lambda, x_\lambda, s_{x_\lambda[i]}))$$

such that $\rho \xleftarrow{\$} \{0,1\}^*$, $pp_\lambda \xleftarrow{\$} \text{Gen}(1^\lambda, 1^{n_\lambda})$ *and* $ct_\lambda \xleftarrow{\$} \text{Send}(pp_\lambda, h_\lambda, i_\lambda,$ $(s_0, s_1))$ *for* $h_\lambda = \text{Hash}(pp_\lambda, x_\lambda; \rho)$, *are computationally indistinguishable.*
- **Receiver Compactness:** $p\ell OT$ *is receiver-compact if the output length of* Hash, η, *is independent in* n, *and is bounded by some polynomial in the security parameter* λ.

4.1 Basic Construction from Trapdoor Hash

Let us first try to realize the relaxed notion of ℓOT using trapdoor hash in a straight-forward way. In order to that, the roles of Alice and Bob from Sect. 2, as a sender and a receiver, must be swapped.

Given a TDH for index predicates, the construction proceeds as follows. The public parameters of the ℓOT scheme simply consist of a hash key hk of the TDH. The receiver (which is now played by Alice) computes a hash value of his database $h = H(hk, x)$, which he sends to the sender (now Bob). Observe that the size of h is independent of the size of x, and thus satisfying our requirement regarding upload communication.

The sender generates a pair (ek, td) of an encoding key and a trapdoor corresponding to the hash key hk and his input index i. Using td and h, he computes two symmetric encryption keys $(e_0, e_1) = D(td, h)$, using which he encrypts his secret inputs s_0 and s_1, respectively, to obtain two ciphertexts. He now sends the key ek as well as the two ciphertexts to the receiver, who will be able to decrypt one of them by recovering $e_{x[i]}$ using the encoding algorithm E of the TDH.

To establish security of this ℓOT construction, we need the following to ensure that (i) the hash h hides x (*receiver privacy*), and (ii) the encoding key ek hides $e_{1-x[i]}$ (*sender privacy*). While receiver privacy is implied directly from the input privacy of the underlying TDH, sender privacy does not generically follow. Thus, we need to augment our definition of TDH with the requirement that, for every i, the value $e_{1-x[i]}$ is uniformly random given hk, ek and x, where $(ek, td) \xleftarrow{\$} G(hk, i)$ and $(e_0, e_1) = D(td, H(hk, x))$. A TDH that satisfies this requirement is said to have *secret encoding*.

Notice that the secret encoding property is in conflict with achieving high rate in a TDH. In particular, in any rate-1 TDH, correctness requires that $e_{1-x[i]} = 1 - e_{x[i]}$ with a high probability.

Fortunately, the basic DDH-based TDH construction without the rate optimization, which is sketched above, fulfills the secret encoding property under DDH. This is not surprising, as so far, this construction is very similar to the original ℓOT construction of [16].

In fact, the above outlined protocol realizes the stronger notion of $p\ell$OT. By relying on the function privacy of the underlying TDH, we immediately get that the sender's input index i is kept hidden from the receiver, and hence, we get the following theorem.

Theorem 4.2. *There exists a receiver-compact $p\ell$OT scheme, with statistical receiver privacy and sender privacy under the DDH assumption, that has communication complexity $O(\mathsf{poly}(\lambda)n)$.*

As hinted earlier, the above construction suffers from an undesired property: download communication is linear in the size of the receiver's database. We propose two solutions. The first relies on the SXDH assumption over bilinear groups and uses pairings in order to reduce the communication to $O(\sqrt{n})$. In the second, we introduce a *reusability* notion of $p\ell$OT, that can be realized under both DDH and SXDH with similar communication. We then show how to transform any reusable $p\ell\mathsf{OT}$ into a (non-reusable) $p\ell\mathsf{OT}$ scheme while reducing the overall communication complexity, to obtain efficient $p\ell\mathsf{OT}$ protocols under DDH, resp. SXDH, with download communication proportional to $\sqrt{n}$ and $\sqrt[3]{n}$, respectively.

4.2   Shrinking the Keys Using Pairings

The bottleneck in the efficiency of the DDH-based $p\ell\mathsf{OT}$ scheme from above lies in the size of the public parameters and sender's message, namely the keys hk and ek of the trapdoor hash, which both grow linearly in n.

Towards achieving sublinear communication, we start with the following observation. The high entropy of the public parameters, i.e. matrix $\mathbf{A}$ in hk, is not essential for security in the DDH-based TDH scheme. Thus, if we could produce such a matrix $\mathbf{A} = (g_{j,b})_{j\in[n],b\in\{0,1\}}$ using a shorter "seed", and then let Alice compute a short "seed" that expands to a matrix $\mathbf{B} = (u_{j,b})_{j\in[n],b\in\{0,1\}}$ which can be used as an encoding key ek, then we are able to reduce the size of hk and ek and, therefore, the communication of the resulted $p\ell\mathsf{OT}$.

Roughly speaking, we choose the seed for $\mathbf{A}$ to be two $2 \times \sqrt{n}$ matrices, $\mathbf{A_1} \in \mathbb{G}^{2\times\sqrt{n}}$ and $\mathbf{A_2} \in \mathbb{H}^{2\times\sqrt{n}}$, for two different groups $\mathbb{G}$ and $\mathbb{H}$. We then use a bilinear map $e : \mathbb{G} \times \mathbb{H} \to \hat{\mathbb{G}}$ to pair elements in $\mathbf{A_1}$ with elements in $\mathbf{A_2}$ and get $2 \times n$ elements in $\hat{\mathbb{G}}$, which we use as the hash key $\mathsf{hk} = \mathbf{A} \in \hat{\mathbb{G}}^{2\times n}$. To generate a seed to the corresponding encoding key $\mathbf{B}$, we begin by defining $\mathbf{B_1} = \mathbf{A_1}^{s_1}$ and $\mathbf{B_2} = \mathbf{A_2}^{s_2}$, which would expand to $\mathbf{B} = \mathbf{A}^{s_1+s_2}$ using the pairing. To achieve functionality, we would want to "puncture" the $(i,1)^{th}$ entry in $\mathbf{B}$ and multiplying it by a random group element (see Eq. 2.1). For this task, we use a bilinear pairing with a special property, that allows us to multiply every element in $\mathbf{B_1}$ and $\mathbf{B_2}$ by carefully sampled random elements from $\mathbb{G}$ and $\mathbb{H}$ (resp.). We do this in a way that when pairing elements from the two matrices to generate $\mathbf{B}$, these random factors cancel each other out, except at the $(i,1)^{th}$ element, which will be randomly distributed. The above idea gives us the following result.

Theorem 4.3. *There exists a receiver-compact $p\ell\mathsf{OT}$ scheme, with statistical receiver privacy and sender privacy under the SXDH assumption, that has communication complexity $O(\mathsf{poly}(\lambda)\sqrt{n})$.*

4.3   Balanced Protocols Through Resuable Private Laconic OT

Having shown how to obtain receiver-compact private laconic OT from DDH and SXDH, we next describe in a high level how to transform such "unbalanced" schemes to $p\ell\mathsf{OT}$ schemes which, despite being non-receiver-compact, have lower overall communication, and in particular, give us sublinear non-interactive secure computation protocols also from DDH.

Theorem 4.4. *There exists a (non-receiver-compact) $p\ell OT$ scheme, with statistical receiver privacy and sender privacy under the $\{DDH, SXDH^{13}\}$ assumption, that has overall communication complexity $\{O(\mathsf{poly}(\lambda)\sqrt{n}), O(\mathsf{poly}(\lambda)\sqrt[3]{n})\}$.*

How to Reuse the Sender's Message. Let us reexamine the $p\ell OT$ scheme from TDH. The sender's message consists of an encoding key ek and encryptions of the two sender's secrets, each under a corresponding TDH encoding. We observe that the encoding key ek, which is actually the larger part of the sender's message, is actually independent of the hash value $\mathsf{h} = \mathsf{H}(\mathsf{hk}, \mathsf{x})$. It can therefore be *reused* for different $p\ell OT$ invocations corresponding to different values of the receiver's database x and the sender's secrets $\mathsf{s}_0, \mathsf{s}_1$ (but that share the same index i).

This brings us to define a notion of *reusable $p\ell OT$*, where we distinguish between two parts of the sender's message: (i) a *reusable* part, of size sublinear in n, that depends only on i and, therefore, can be reused for different inputs $\mathsf{x}, \mathsf{s}_0, \mathsf{s}_1$, and (ii) a *compact* part, of size independent in n, that is generated w.r.t. a specific receiver's database x and sender's secrets s_0 and s_1.

As mentioned above, the $p\ell OT$ construction from TDH already gives reusability, with ek being reusable. However, a subtle issue concerning the sender privacy has to be resolved. Take for instance the $p\ell OT$ construction from the DDH-based TDH. Above, we argued that the encoding $\mathsf{e}_{1-\mathsf{x}[i]}$ is uniformly distributed given hk and ek, in what we called the *secret encoding property*. Notice, however, that this is not sufficient for reusable $p\ell OT$, where many such encodings $\mathsf{e}_{1-\mathsf{x}[i]}$, namely symmetric encryption keys, are generated w.r.t. different values of x. Although each of these encryption keys is individually uniform, they are highly correlated. Encryption under correlated keys is clearly insecure. Thus, we do not get sender privacy when ek is reused.

We handle this issue by defining a related *reusable secret encoding* property for TDH. Both the DDH-based and pairings-based TDH schemes can be extended to have reusable secret encoding using suitable *correlated-input secure hash* [3], which can be fortunately realized under DDH and, resp., appropriate hardness assumptions over bilinear groups.

Reusable $p\ell OT$ can be useful by itself for applications in secure computation, in particular when we allow to amortize the communication cost over many computations of the same functionality on different inputs. Further, as mentioned earlier, reusable $p\ell OT$ turns out to be useful to achieve $p\ell OT$ schemes which, although non-reusable, have smaller download communication.

Exploiting Reusability for More Efficient Schemes. Lastly, we show how to use reusable $p\ell OT$ to achieve more efficient $p\ell OT$ schemes. Our final results are a DDH-based $p\ell OT$ with communication proportional to $\sqrt{n}$, and a pairing-based $p\ell OT$ with communication proportional to $\sqrt[3]{n}$. Although the construction is generic, it is parameterized differently according to the underlying reusable $p\ell OT$. For presentation, we take the DDH-based reusable $p\ell OT$, where the public parameters and sender's message grow linearly in n as a special case.

---

[13] for the SXDH-based construction we further assume the existence of correlated-input secure hash for group-induced correlations over bilinear groups [3,32].

The idea is as follows. We divide the receiver's database x to $\sqrt{n}$ smaller databases, $\mathsf{x}_1, \ldots, \mathsf{x}_{\sqrt{n}}$, each of size $\sqrt{n}$. Consequently, every index $j \in [n]$ is interpreted as $(j_1, j_2) \in [\sqrt{n}]^2$ (particularly, $i = (i_1, i_2)$) where $\mathsf{x}_j := \mathsf{x}_{j_1}[j_2]$. On the sender's side, each of the secrets $\mathsf{s}_0, \mathsf{s}_1$ is additively shared to $\mathsf{s}_{0,1}, \ldots, \mathsf{s}_{0,\sqrt{n}} \in \{0,1\}$ and, respectively, $\mathsf{s}_{1,1}, \ldots, \mathsf{s}_{1,\sqrt{n}} \in \{0,1\}$ s.t. $\sum_j \mathsf{s}_{j,b} = \mathsf{s}_b$ for $\mathsf{b} \in \{0,1\}$. In fact, the sender generates the shares such that $\mathsf{s}_{j,0} = \mathsf{s}_{j,1}$ for any $j \neq i_1$.

The idea is to use the underlying reusable $p\ell\mathsf{OT}$ to send to the receiver, for every $j \in [\sqrt{n}]$, either $\mathsf{s}_{j,0}$ or $\mathsf{s}_{j,1}$, conditioned on $\mathsf{x}_j[i_2]$. For any $j \neq i_1$, both bits are equal, and therefore, the receiver obtains s_j, regardless of the value of $\mathsf{x}_j[i_2]$. The only database bit that matters is $\mathsf{x}[i] := \mathsf{x}_{i_1}[i_2]$, which determines whether the receiver receives $\mathsf{s}_j := \mathsf{s}_{j,0}$, and therefore can compute $\sum_j \mathsf{s}_j = \mathsf{s}_0$, or $\mathsf{s}_j := \mathsf{s}_{j,1}$, which would allow him to compute $\sum_j \mathsf{s}_j = \mathsf{s}_1$.

Acknowledgments. We thank Craig Gentry, Shai Halevi, Srinath Setty, and Vinod Vaikuntanathan for helpful discussions and pointers.

S. Garg supported by DARPA/ARL SAFEWARE Award W911NF15C0210, AFOSR Award FA9550-15-1-0274, AFOSR YIP Award, DARPA and SPAWAR under contract N66001-15-C-4065, a Hellman Award and research grants by the Okawa Foundation, Visa Inc., and Center for Long-Term Cybersecurity (CLTC, UC Berkeley). The views expressed are those of the author and do not reflect the official policy or position of the funding agencies.

Y. Ishai supported by ERC Project NTSC (742754), ISF grant 1709/14, NSF-BSF grant 2015782, and a grant from the Ministry of Science and Technology, Israel and Department of Science and Technology, Government of India.

G. Malavolta supported by a gift from Ripple, a gift from DoS Networks, a grant from Northrop Grumman, a Cylab seed funding award, and a JP Morgan Faculty Fellowship.

T. Mour supported by BSF grant 2012378, and NSF-BSF grant 2015782.

R. Ostrovsky supported by NSF grant 1619348, BSF grant 2015782, DARPA Safe-Ware subcontract to Galois Inc., DARPA SPAWAR contract N66001-15-C-4065, JP Morgan Faculty Research Award, OKAWA Foundation Research Award, IBM Faculty Research Award, Xerox Faculty Research Award, B. John Garrick Foundation Award, Teradata Research Award, and Lockheed-Martin Corporation Research Award. The views expressed are those of the authors and do not reflect position of the Department of Defense or the U.S. Government.

References

1. Aiello, B., Ishai, Y., Reingold, O.: Priced oblivious transfer: how to sell digital goods. In: Pfitzmann, B. (ed.) EUROCRYPT 2001. LNCS, vol. 2045, pp. 119–135. Springer, Heidelberg (2001). https://doi.org/10.1007/3-540-44987-6_8
2. Applebaum, B., Damgård, I., Ishai, Y., Nielsen, M., Zichron, L.: Secure arithmetic computation with constant computational overhead. In: Katz, J., Shacham, H. (eds.) CRYPTO 2017, Part I. LNCS, vol. 10401, pp. 223–254. Springer, Cham (2017). https://doi.org/10.1007/978-3-319-63688-7_8
3. Attrapadung, N., Matsuda, T., Nishimaki, R., Yamada, S., Yamakawa, T.: Constrained PRFs for NC^1 in traditional groups. In: Shacham, H., Boldyreva, A. (eds.) CRYPTO 2018, Part II. LNCS, vol. 10992, pp. 543–574. Springer, Cham (2018). https://doi.org/10.1007/978-3-319-96881-0_19

4. Badrinarayanan, S., Garg, S., Ishai, Y., Sahai, A., Wadia, A.: Two-message witness indistinguishability and secure computation in the plain model from new assumptions. In: Takagi, T., Peyrin, T. (eds.) ASIACRYPT 2017, Part III. LNCS, vol. 10626, pp. 275–303. Springer, Cham (2017). https://doi.org/10.1007/978-3-319-70700-6_10

5. Banerjee, A., Peikert, C., Rosen, A.: Pseudorandom functions and lattices. In: Pointcheval, D., Johansson, T. (eds.) EUROCRYPT 2012. LNCS, vol. 7237, pp. 719–737. Springer, Heidelberg (2012). https://doi.org/10.1007/978-3-642-29011-4_42

6. Beaver, D.: Precomputing oblivious transfer. In: Coppersmith, D. (ed.) CRYPTO 1995. LNCS, vol. 963, pp. 97–109. Springer, Heidelberg (1995). https://doi.org/10.1007/3-540-44750-4_8

7. Bellare, M., Cash, D.: Pseudorandom functions and permutations provably secure against related-key attacks. In: Rabin, T. (ed.) CRYPTO 2010. LNCS, vol. 6223, pp. 666–684. Springer, Heidelberg (2010). https://doi.org/10.1007/978-3-642-14623-7_36

8. Block, A.R., Maji, H.K., Nguyen, H.H.: Secure computation with constant communication overhead using multiplication embeddings. In: Chakraborty, D., Iwata, T. (eds.) INDOCRYPT 2018. LNCS, vol. 11356, pp. 375–398. Springer, Cham (2018). https://doi.org/10.1007/978-3-030-05378-9_20

9. Boyle, E., Gilboa, N., Ishai, Y.: Breaking the circuit size barrier for secure computation under DDH. In: Robshaw, M., Katz, J. (eds.) CRYPTO 2016, Part I. LNCS, vol. 9814, pp. 509–539. Springer, Heidelberg (2016). https://doi.org/10.1007/978-3-662-53018-4_19

10. Boyle, E., Gilboa, N., Ishai, Y.: Group-based secure computation: optimizing rounds, communication, and computation. In: Coron, J.-S., Nielsen, J.B. (eds.) EUROCRYPT 2017, Part II. LNCS, vol. 10211, pp. 163–193. Springer, Cham (2017). https://doi.org/10.1007/978-3-319-56614-6_6

11. Brakerski, Z., Döttling, N.: Two-message statistically sender-private OT from LWE. In: Beimel, A., Dziembowski, S. (eds.) TCC 2018, Part II. LNCS, vol. 11240, pp. 370–390. Springer, Cham (2018). https://doi.org/10.1007/978-3-030-03810-6_14

12. Brakerski, Z., Goldwasser, S.: Circular and leakage resilient public-key encryption under subgroup indistinguishability. In: Rabin, T. (ed.) CRYPTO 2010. LNCS, vol. 6223, pp. 1–20. Springer, Heidelberg (2010). https://doi.org/10.1007/978-3-642-14623-7_1

13. Brakerski, Z., Lombardi, A., Segev, G., Vaikuntanathan, V.: Anonymous IBE, leakage resilience and circular security from new assumptions. In: Nielsen, J.B., Rijmen, V. (eds.) EUROCRYPT 2018, Part I. LNCS, vol. 10820, pp. 535–564. Springer, Cham (2018). https://doi.org/10.1007/978-3-319-78381-9_20

14. Cachin, C., Micali, S., Stadler, M.: Computationally private information retrieval with polylogarithmic communication. In: Stern, J. (ed.) EUROCRYPT 1999. LNCS, vol. 1592, pp. 402–414. Springer, Heidelberg (1999). https://doi.org/10.1007/3-540-48910-X_28

15. Chang, Y.-C.: Single database private information retrieval with logarithmic communication. In: Wang, H., Pieprzyk, J., Varadharajan, V. (eds.) ACISP 2004. LNCS, vol. 3108, pp. 50–61. Springer, Heidelberg (2004). https://doi.org/10.1007/978-3-540-27800-9_5

16. Cho, C., Döttling, N., Garg, S., Gupta, D., Miao, P., Polychroniadou, A.: Laconic oblivious transfer and its applications. In: Katz, J., Shacham, H. (eds.) CRYPTO

2017, Part II. LNCS, vol. 10402, pp. 33–65. Springer, Cham (2017). https://doi. org/10.1007/978-3-319-63715-0_2

17. Chor, B., Goldreich, O., Kushilevitz, E., Sudan, M.: Private information retrieval. In: 36th Annual Symposium on Foundations of Computer Science, Milwaukee, Wisconsin, 23–25 October 1995, pp. 41–50. IEEE Computer Society Press (1995)

18. Damgård, I., Jurik, M.: A generalisation, a simplification and some applications of Paillier's probabilistic public-key system. In: Kim, K. (ed.) PKC 2001. LNCS, vol. 1992, pp. 119–136. Springer, Heidelberg (2001). https://doi.org/10.1007/3-540-44586-2_9

19. Dinur, I., Keller, N., Klein, O.: An optimal distributed discrete log protocol with applications to homomorphic secret sharing. In: Shacham, H., Boldyreva, A. (eds.) CRYPTO 2018, Part III. LNCS, vol. 10993, pp. 213–242. Springer, Cham (2018). https://doi.org/10.1007/978-3-319-96878-0_8

20. Dodis, Y., Halevi, S., Rothblum, R.D., Wichs, D.: Spooky encryption and its applications. In: Robshaw, M., Katz, J. (eds.) CRYPTO 2016, Part III. LNCS, vol. 9816, pp. 93–122. Springer, Heidelberg (2016). https://doi.org/10.1007/978-3-662-53015-3_4

21. Döttling, N., Garg, S.: Identity-based encryption from the Diffie-Hellman assumption. In: Katz, J., Shacham, H. (eds.) CRYPTO 2017, Part I. LNCS, vol. 10401, pp. 537–569. Springer, Cham (2017). https://doi.org/10.1007/978-3-319-63688-7_18

22. Döttling, N., Garg, S., Hajiabadi, M., Masny, D.: New constructions of identity-based and key-dependent message secure encryption schemes. In: Abdalla, M., Dahab, R. (eds.) PKC 2018, Part I. LNCS, vol. 10769, pp. 3–31. Springer, Cham (2018). https://doi.org/10.1007/978-3-319-76578-5_1

23. Fazio, N., Gennaro, R., Jafarikhah, T., Skeith, W.E.: Homomorphic secret sharing from Paillier encryption. In: Okamoto, T., Yu, Y., Au, M.H., Li, Y. (eds.) ProvSec 2017. LNCS, vol. 10592, pp. 381–399. Springer, Cham (2017). https://doi.org/10.1007/978-3-319-68637-0_23

24. Garg, S., Gay, R., Hajiabadi, M.: New techniques for efficient trapdoor functions and applications. Cryptology ePrint Archive, Report 2018/872 (2018). https://eprint.iacr.org/2018/872

25. Garg, S., Gentry, C., Halevi, S., Raykova, M., Sahai, A., Waters, B.: Candidate indistinguishability obfuscation and functional encryption for all circuits. In: 54th Annual Symposium on Foundations of Computer Science, Berkeley, CA, USA, 26–29 October 2013, pp. 40–49. IEEE Computer Society Press (2013)

26. Garg, S., Hajiabadi, M.: Trapdoor functions from the computational Diffie-Hellman assumption. In: Shacham, H., Boldyreva, A. (eds.) CRYPTO 2018, Part II. LNCS, vol. 10992, pp. 362–391. Springer, Cham (2018). https://doi.org/10.1007/978-3-319-96881-0_13

27. Gentry, C.: Fully homomorphic encryption using ideal lattices. In: Mitzenmacher, M. (ed.) 41st Annual ACM Symposium on Theory of Computing, Bethesda, MD, USA, 31 May–2 June 2009, pp. 169–178. ACM Press (2009)

28. Gentry, C., Groth, J., Ishai, Y., Peikert, C., Sahai, A., Smith, A.D.: Using fully homomorphic hybrid encryption to minimize non-interative zero-knowledge proofs. J. Cryptol. **28**(4), 820–843 (2015)

29. Gentry, C., Halevi, S.: Compressible FHE with applications to PIR. Technical report (2019). (Personal communication)

30. Goldenberg, D., Liskov, M.: On related-secret pseudorandomness. In: Micciancio, D. (ed.) TCC 2010. LNCS, vol. 5978, pp. 255–272. Springer, Heidelberg (2010). https://doi.org/10.1007/978-3-642-11799-2_16

31. Goldreich, O., Micali, S., Wigderson, A.: How to play any mental game or a completeness theorem for protocols with honest majority. In: Aho, A. (ed.) 19th Annual ACM Symposium on Theory of Computing, New York City, NY, USA, pp. 218–229, 25–27 May 1987. ACM Press (1987)

32. Goyal, V., O'Neill, A., Rao, V.: Correlated-input secure hash functions. In: Ishai, Y. (ed.) TCC 2011. LNCS, vol. 6597, pp. 182–200. Springer, Heidelberg (2011). https://doi.org/10.1007/978-3-642-19571-6_12

33. Groth, J., Kiayias, A., Lipmaa, H.: Multi-query computationally-private information retrieval with constant communication rate. In: Nguyen, P.Q., Pointcheval, D. (eds.) PKC 2010. LNCS, vol. 6056, pp. 107–123. Springer, Heidelberg (2010). https://doi.org/10.1007/978-3-642-13013-7_7

34. Halevi, S., Kalai, Y.T.: Smooth projective hashing and two-message oblivious transfer. J. Cryptol. **25**(1), 158–193 (2012)

35. Hemenway, B., Ostrovsky, R.: Extended-DDH and lossy trapdoor functions. In: Fischlin, M., Buchmann, J., Manulis, M. (eds.) PKC 2012. LNCS, vol. 7293, pp. 627–643. Springer, Heidelberg (2012). https://doi.org/10.1007/978-3-642-30057-8_37

36. Hubacek, P., Wichs, D.: On the communication complexity of secure function evaluation with long output. Cryptology ePrint Archive, Report 2014/669 (2014). http://eprint.iacr.org/2014/669

37. Ishai, Y., Kilian, J., Nissim, K., Petrank, E.: Extending oblivious transfers efficiently. In: Boneh, D. (ed.) CRYPTO 2003. LNCS, vol. 2729, pp. 145–161. Springer, Heidelberg (2003). https://doi.org/10.1007/978-3-540-45146-4_9

38. Ishai, Y., Kushilevitz, E., Meldgaard, S., Orlandi, C., Paskin-Cherniavsky, A.: On the power of correlated randomness in secure computation. In: Sahai, A. (ed.) TCC 2013. LNCS, vol. 7785, pp. 600–620. Springer, Heidelberg (2013). https://doi.org/10.1007/978-3-642-36594-2_34

39. Ishai, Y., Kushilevitz, E., Ostrovsky, R., Sahai, A.: Cryptography with constant computational overhead. In: STOC 2008, pp. 433–442 (2008)

40. Ishai, Y., Paskin, A.: Evaluating branching programs on encrypted data. In: Vadhan, S.P. (ed.) TCC 2007. LNCS, vol. 4392, pp. 575–594. Springer, Heidelberg (2007). https://doi.org/10.1007/978-3-540-70936-7_31

41. Ishai, Y., Prabhakaran, M., Sahai, A.: Secure arithmetic computation with no honest majority. In: Reingold, O. (ed.) TCC 2009. LNCS, vol. 5444, pp. 294–314. Springer, Heidelberg (2009). https://doi.org/10.1007/978-3-642-00457-5_18

42. Juvekar, C., Vaikuntanathan, V., Chandrakasan, A.: GAZELLE: a low latency framework for secure neural network inference. In: USENIX Security Symposium, pp. 1651–1669 (2018)

43. Koppula, V., Lewko, A.B., Waters, B.: Indistinguishability obfuscation for turing machines with unbounded memory. In: Servedio, R.A., Rubinfeld, R. (eds.) 47th Annual ACM Symposium on Theory of Computing, Portland, OR, USA, 14–17 June 2015, pp. 419–428. ACM Press (2015)

44. Kushilevitz, E., Ostrovsky, R.: Replication is NOT needed: SINGLE database, computationally-private information retrieval. In: 38th Annual Symposium on Foundations of Computer Science, Miami Beach, Florida, 19–22 October 1997, pp. 364–373. IEEE Computer Society Press (1997)

45. Lipmaa, H.: An oblivious transfer protocol with log-squared communication. In: Zhou, J., Lopez, J., Deng, R.H., Bao, F. (eds.) ISC 2005. LNCS, vol. 3650, pp. 314–328. Springer, Heidelberg (2005). https://doi.org/10.1007/11556992_23

46. Naor, M., Nissim, K.: Communication preserving protocols for secure function evaluation. In: 33rd Annual ACM Symposium on Theory of Computing, Crete, Greece, 6–8 July 2001, pp. 590–599. ACM Press (2001)

47. Naor, M., Pinkas, B.: Oblivious transfer and polynomial evaluation. In: 31st Annual ACM Symposium on Theory of Computing, Atlanta, GA, USA, 1–4 May 1999, pp. 245–254. ACM Press (1999)

48. Naor, M., Pinkas, B.: Efficient oblivious transfer protocols. In: SODA 2001, pp. 448–457 (2001)

49. Okamoto, T., Pietrzak, K., Waters, B., Wichs, D.: New realizations of somewhere statistically binding hashing and positional accumulators. In: Iwata, T., Cheon, J.H. (eds.) ASIACRYPT 2015, Part I. LNCS, vol. 9452, pp. 121–145. Springer, Heidelberg (2015). https://doi.org/10.1007/978-3-662-48797-6_6

50. Ostrovsky, R., Skeith, W.E.: A survey of single-database private information retrieval: techniques and applications. In: Okamoto, T., Wang, X. (eds.) PKC 2007. LNCS, vol. 4450, pp. 393–411. Springer, Heidelberg (2007). https://doi.org/10.1007/978-3-540-71677-8_26

51. Peikert, C., Waters, B.: Lossy trapdoor functions and their applications. In: Ladner, R.E., Dwork, C. (eds.) 40th Annual ACM Symposium on Theory of Computing, Victoria, British Columbia, Canada, 17–20 May 2008, pp. 187–196. ACM Press (2008)

52. Quach, W., Wee, H., Wichs, D.: Laconic function evaluation and applications. In: 2018 IEEE 59th Annual Symposium on Foundations of Computer Science (FOCS), pp. 859–870 (2018)

53. Stern, J.P.: A new and efficient all-or-nothing disclosure of secrets protocol. In: Ohta, K., Pei, D. (eds.) ASIACRYPT 1998. LNCS, vol. 1514, pp. 357–371. Springer, Heidelberg (1998). https://doi.org/10.1007/3-540-49649-1_28

54. Winkler, S., Wullschleger, J.: On the efficiency of classical and quantum oblivious transfer reductions. In: Rabin, T. (ed.) CRYPTO 2010. LNCS, vol. 6223, pp. 707–723. Springer, Heidelberg (2010). https://doi.org/10.1007/978-3-642-14623-7_38

55. Yao, A.C.-C.: How to generate and exchange secrets (extended abstract). In: 27th Annual Symposium on Foundations of Computer Science, Toronto, Ontario, Canada, 27–29 October 1986, pp. 162–167. IEEE Computer Society Press (1986)

CCA Security and Trapdoor Functions via Key-Dependent-Message Security

Fuyuki Kitagawa[1]([✉]), Takahiro Matsuda[2], and Keisuke Tanaka[3]

[1] NTT Secure Platform Laboratories, Tokyo, Japan
fuyuki.kitagawa.yh@hco.ntt.co.jp
[2] National Institute of Advanced Industrial Science and Technology (AIST),
Tokyo, Japan
t-matsuda@aist.go.jp
[3] Tokyo Institute of Technology, Tokyo, Japan
keisuke@is.titech.ac.jp

Abstract. We study the relationship among public-key encryption (PKE) satisfying indistinguishability against chosen plaintext attacks (IND-CPA security), that against chosen ciphertext attacks (IND-CCA security), and trapdoor functions (TDF). Specifically, we aim at finding a unified approach and some additional requirement to realize IND-CCA secure PKE and TDF based on IND-CPA secure PKE, and show the following two main results.

As the first main result, we show how to achieve IND-CCA security via a weak form of key-dependent-message (KDM) security. More specifically, we construct an IND-CCA secure PKE scheme based on an IND-CPA secure PKE scheme and a secret-key encryption (SKE) scheme satisfying one-time KDM security with respect to projection functions (projection-KDM security). Projection functions are very simple functions with respect to which KDM security has been widely studied. Since the existence of projection-KDM secure PKE implies that of the above two building blocks, as a corollary of this result, we see that the existence of IND-CCA secure PKE is implied by that of projection-KDM secure PKE.

As the second main result, we extend the above construction of IND-CCA secure PKE into that of TDF by additionally requiring a mild requirement for each building block. Our TDF satisfies adaptive one-wayness. We can instantiate our TDF based on a wide variety of computational assumptions. Especially, we obtain the first TDF (with adaptive one-wayness) based on the sub-exponential hardness of the constant-noise learning-parity-with-noise (LPN) problem.

Keywords: Chosen ciphertext security · Trapdoor functions · Key-dependent-message security

© International Association for Cryptologic Research 2019
A. Boldyreva and D. Micciancio (Eds.): CRYPTO 2019, LNCS 11694, pp. 33–64, 2019.
https://doi.org/10.1007/978-3-030-26954-8_2

1   Introduction

1.1   Background

Public-key encryption (PKE) is one of the most fundamental cryptographic primitives. The most basic security requirement for PKE is indistinguishability against chosen plaintext attacks (IND-CPA security) [23]. However, in many practical applications, PKE schemes should satisfy the stronger notion of indistinguishability against chosen ciphertext attacks (IND-CCA security) [15,35] in order to take active adversaries into consideration [10].

Since IND-CCA security is stronger than IND-CPA security, the existence of IND-CCA secure PKE implies that of IND-CPA secure one. However, the implication of the opposite direction is not known. While a partial negative result was shown by Gertner, Malkin, and Myers [21], the question whether an IND-CCA secure PKE scheme can be constructed from an IND-CPA secure one has still been standing as a major open question in cryptography.

In addition to IND-CCA secure PKE, a family of trapdoor functions (TDF) is also a fundamental primitive whose relationship with IND-CPA secure PKE has been widely studied. It was shown that an IND-CPA secure PKE can be constructed from TDF [6,40]. For the opposite direction, Gertner, Malkin, and Reingold [22] showed a negative result stating that TDF cannot be built from PKE in a black-box way.

In fact, in the random oracle model [7], we can construct both IND-CCA secure PKE and TDF based solely on IND-CPA secure PKE using a simple and unified derandomization technique [6,19]. However, in the standard model, we cannot use such a simple derandomization technique successfully. Especially, in order to construct IND-CCA secure PKE and TDF in the standard model by circumventing the impossibility results [21,22], we need non-black-box techniques or some additional requirements for the building block PKE scheme.

Hajiabadi and Kapron [24] tackled the above question, and as a main result, they built a TDF based on a PKE scheme satisfying circular security [14] and a randomness re-usability property called reproducibility [5]. Since their TDF satisfies one-wayness under correlated products, based on the same assumption, they also obtained a construction of IND-CCA secure PKE by relying on the result by Rosen and Segev [38]. Their TDF construction is elegant and can also be extended to deterministic encryption [4]. However, due to the somewhat strong additional requirement of randomness re-usability, its instantiations are limited to specific number theoretic assumptions.

In this work, we further study the above question. Especially, we aim at finding a unified approach and some additional requirement to realize IND-CCA secure PKE and TDF based on IND-CPA secure PKE.

1.2   Our Results

We show a unified approach to build IND-CCA secure PKE and TDF based on IND-CPA secure PKE by additionally using secret-key encryption (SKE) satisfying a weak form of *key-dependent-message (KDM) security* [9]. Roughly speaking, an encryption scheme is said to be KDM secure if it can securely encrypt a message of the form $f(\mathsf{sk})$, where sk is the secret key and f is a function. The details of our results are as follows.

IND-CCA Security via Key-Dependent-Message Security. As the first main result, we construct an IND-CCA secure PKE scheme based on an IND-CPA secure PKE scheme and an SKE scheme satisfying KDM security. The building block SKE scheme is required to be one-time KDM secure with respect to projection functions (projection-KDM secure). Projection functions are very simple functions such that each output bit depends on at most a single bit of an input. An SKE scheme satisfying one-time projection-KDM security can be built from a wide variety of computational assumptions [3,11–13,16]. We obtain this result based on a construction technique used by Koppula and Waters [30] who showed how to construct IND-CCA secure attribute-based encryption (ABE) from IND-CPA secure one using a pseudorandom generator (PRG) with a special security property called hinting PRG. We extend the techniques of Koppula and Waters in several aspects. See Sect. 2 for the details.

The existence of PKE satisfying projection-KDM security against chosen plaintext attacks implies that of the above two building blocks. Therefore, as a corollary of this result, we see that the existence of IND-CCA secure PKE is implied by that of PKE with projection-KDM security (against CPA!).

Given our result and the result by Koppula and Waters, it is natural to ask what is the relationship between hinting PRG and one-time KDM secure SKE. To clarify this, we show that a one-time projection-KDM secure SKE scheme can be built from a hinting PRG. This means that one-time projection-KDM secure SKE is not a stronger assumption than hinting PRG.

Previously, Matsuda and Hanaoka [33] constructed an IND-CCA secure PKE scheme from a PKE scheme satisfying the sender non-committing property and an SKE scheme satisfying one-time KDM security with respect to circuits of a-priori bounded size. We improve their result in the sense that our construction requires weaker security properties for both of the underlying PKE and SKE schemes compared to theirs.

On Black-Box Usage of Building Blocks. Our construction of an IND-CCA secure PKE scheme is *fully-black-box* [36] and *non-shielding* [21]. A construction of a PKE scheme is said to be shielding if the decryption algorithm of the scheme does *not* call the encryption algorithm of the building block schemes, and otherwise it is called non-shielding. We show that our construction being a non-shielding construction is essential by showing that a fully-black-box and shielding construction of an IND-CCA secure PKE scheme based on our assumptions is *impossible* by extending the impossibility result shown by Gertner et al. [21]. More specifically, we show that there is no fully-black-box and shielding construction of an IND-CCA secure PKE scheme based on a projection-KDM secure PKE scheme that trivially implies both of our building blocks.

Extension to TDF. As the second main result, we extend the above construction of an IND-CCA secure PKE scheme into that of a TDF by additionally requiring a mild requirement for each building block. Our TDF satisfies adaptive one-wayness [27]. Adaptive one-wayness ensures that an adversary cannot invert a function in the family even under the existence of the inversion oracle, and thus it is a much stronger security property compared to ordinary one-wayness.

The additional requirements for the building blocks are as follows.

- First, we require that the underlying IND-CPA secure PKE scheme have the *pseudorandom ciphertext property*. Namely, a ciphertext of the underlying IND-CPA secure PKE scheme needs to be indistinguishable from a uniformly random element sampled from the ciphertext space of the scheme.
- Second, we require that the underlying projection-KDM secure SKE scheme be *randomness-recoverable*. Namely, random coins used to encrypt a message needs to be recovered together with the message in the decryption process.

Both of the above two requirements are mild in the following sense.

For the first requirement, a number of IND-CPA secure PKE schemes based on concrete computational assumptions naturally have this property. In fact, as far as we know, an IND-CPA secure PKE scheme satisfying the pseudorandom ciphertext property can be constructed from any concrete computational assumption implying IND-CPA secure PKE.

For the second requirement, the randomness-recovering property is easy to achieve in the secret-key setting while this property is so hard to achieve in the public-key setting that it immediately yields a TDF. Projection-KDM secure PKE schemes based on projective hash functions [11,12,39] can easily be transformed into SKE variants satisfying the randomness-recovering property. Also, projection-KDM secure SKE schemes based on the learning-parity-with-noise (LPN) and learning-with-errors (LWE) assumptions proposed by Applebaum, Cash, Peikert, and Sahai [3] already satisfy this property. Moreover, even the recent constructions of KDM secure PKE schemes based on the computational Diffie-Hellman (CDH) and factoring assumptions [13,16] can be transformed into one-time projection-KDM secure SKE with the randomness-recovering property.

As noted above, the additional requirements needed to realize a TDF are mild. As a result, we can instantiate our TDF based on a wide variety of computational assumptions. Especially, by combining the previous results [3,42], we obtain the first TDF (with adaptive one-wayness) based on the sub-exponential hardness of the constant-noise LPN problem. Moreover, we also obtain the first TDF satisfying adaptive one-wayness based on the low-noise LPN assumption. Previously to our work, a TDF satisfying ordinary one-wayness based on the low-noise LPN assumption was shown by Kiltz, Masny, and Pietrzak [26].

1.3   Concurrent and Subsequent Works

Very recently, in a concurrent work, Lombardi, Quach, Rothblum, Wichs, and Wu [31] showed how to construct a reusable designated-verifier non-interactive zero-knowledge (DV-NIZK) argument system based on the combination of an IND-CPA secure PKE scheme and a hinting PRG. In one of the steps in their construction, they employed the construction methodology of Koppula and Waters [30], and a hinting PRG is used in the step.

Based on our technique in this paper, Lombardi et al. [32] (in their latest update on May 23, 2019) and Kitagawa and Matsuda [28] independently and concurrently observe that a hinting PRG used in Lombardi et al.'s reusable DV-NIZK argument system can also be replaced with a one-time $\mathcal{P}$-KDM secure SKE in exactly the same way as we do in our work. That is, these works show that a reusable DV-NIZK argument system can be constructed from an IND-CPA secure PKE scheme and a one-time $\mathcal{P}$-KDM secure SKE scheme. This leads to the first reusable DV-NIZK argument system based on the LPN assumption.

Furthermore, Kitagawa and Matsuda [28] show that using the reusable DV-NIZK argument system above and our result on IND-CCA secure PKE, we can transform a KDM-CPA secure PKE scheme into a KDM-CCA secure one without requiring any additional assumption. This leads to the first KDM-CCA secure PKE schemes based on the CDH and LPN assumptions.

1.4 Paper Organization

In Sect. 2, we show an overview of our techniques. In Sect. 3, we review definitions of cryptographic primitives. In Sect. 4, we show our proposed IND-CCA secure KEM. In Sect. 5, we prove the impossibility of fully-black-box shielding constructions. Finally, in Sect. 6, we present our proposed TDF.

Many of the details are omitted due to the space limitation. See the full version [29] for all the details.

2 Technical Overview

We give an overview of our techniques.

2.1 Achieving IND-CCA Security via Randomness-Recovering

One of classical mechanisms for achieving IND-CCA security is adopting a validity checking by re-encryption in the decryption process. In this technique, we make an encryption scheme randomness-recoverable, that is, a randomness used to generate a ciphertext is recovered during the decryption process. Then, when decrypting the ciphertext, we can check that the ciphertext was well-formed by re-encrypting the decrypted message using the recovered randomness.

Such a mechanism can be easily implemented in the random oracle model. Fujisaki and Okamoto [19] showed that by designing the encryption algorithm as $\mathsf{Enc}(\mathsf{pk}, r\|m; \mathsf{H}(r\|m))$, we can construct an IND-CCA secure PKE scheme based on the above strategy, where $\mathsf{Enc}(\mathsf{pk}, \cdot; \cdot)$ is the encryption algorithm of an IND-CPA secure PKE scheme and H is a hash function modeled as a random oracle. On the other hand, in the standard model, realizing a randomness-recoverable encryption scheme is difficult. Almost all existing such schemes are based on a TDF with advanced security properties [27,34,38]. The main theme of this work is how we implement the mechanism in the standard model when starting from an IND-CPA secure PKE scheme.

A naive idea for our goal would be to design the encryption algorithm as $\mathsf{Enc}(\mathsf{pk}, \mathsf{r}\|\mathsf{m}; \mathsf{r})$, where $\mathsf{Enc}(\mathsf{pk}, \cdot; \cdot)$ again denotes the encryption algorithm of an IND-CPA secure PKE scheme. Unfortunately, it seems difficult to prove the security of this construction based on its IND-CPA security, since in order to rely on IND-CPA security, we need to ensure that a message to be encrypted is completely independent of the encryption randomness r.

A natural idea to remove the dependency is to use a variant of the hybrid encryption paradigm. Namely, we design the encryption algorithm as $(\mathsf{Enc}(\mathsf{pk}, \mathsf{s}; \mathsf{r}), \mathsf{E}(\mathsf{s}, \mathsf{r}\|\mathsf{m}))$, where $\mathsf{E}(\mathsf{s}, \cdot)$ is the encryption algorithm of an SKE scheme. At first glance, the dependency is removed, but the construction is in fact at a "dead-lock" and it also seems difficult to prove its security. We can solve the dead-lock by using the *signaling technique*[1] recently introduced by Koppula and Waters [30] who showed how to construct IND-CCA secure ABE from IND-CPA secure one using a PRG with a special security property called hinting PRG.

2.2 Partial Randomness-Recovering Using the Signaling Technique

We now use $2n$ public keys $(\mathsf{pk}_i^v)_{i \in [n], v \in \{0,1\}}$ of the IND-CPA secure PKE scheme to encapsulate a secret key $\mathsf{s} = (\mathsf{s}_1, \ldots, \mathsf{s}_n) \in \{0,1\}^n$ of the SKE scheme, where $[n] := \{1, \ldots, n\}$. Below, let $(\mathsf{sk}_i^v)_{i \in [n], v \in \{0,1\}}$ be secret keys corresponding to $(\mathsf{pk}_i^v)_{i \in [n], v \in \{0,1\}}$. Roughly, we "encode" each bit s_i of s as $(\mathsf{ct}_i^0, \mathsf{ct}_i^1)$, where

$$\mathsf{ct}_i^{\mathsf{s}_i} = \mathsf{Enc}(\mathsf{pk}_i^{\mathsf{s}_i}, 1; \mathsf{r}_i^{\mathsf{s}_i}) \text{ and } \mathsf{ct}_i^{1-\mathsf{s}_i} = \mathsf{Enc}(\mathsf{pk}_i^{1-\mathsf{s}_i}, 0; \mathsf{r}_i^{1-\mathsf{s}_i}).$$

Namely, we encapsulate s by using $2n$ ciphertexts $(\mathsf{ct}_i^0, \mathsf{ct}_i^1)_{i \in [n]}$. During the decapsulation, we decrypt ct_i^0 by using sk_i^0 and set $\mathsf{s}_i := 0$ if the decryption result is 1 and $\mathsf{s}_i := 1$ otherwise.

Of course, if we encrypt all of the random coins $(\mathsf{r}_i^v)_{i \in [n], v \in \{0,1\}}$ used to encapsulate s by the SKE scheme to make the resulting scheme randomness-recoverable, it leads to a dead-lock as before. However, by using the signaling technique used by Koppula and Waters, we can perform the validity check by re-encrypting n out of $2n$ ciphertexts of the IND-CPA secure PKE scheme in the decryption process, and solve the dead-lock as follows.

We say that "an encoding $(\mathsf{ct}_i^0, \mathsf{ct}_i^1)$ signals α" when ct_i^α encrypts 1. By using an (ordinary) PRG and adding a "tag" T_i to each encoding $(\mathsf{ct}_i^0, \mathsf{ct}_i^1)$ as $(\mathsf{ct}_i^0, \mathsf{ct}_i^1, \mathsf{T}_i)$, we can build a mechanism ensuring that it is statistically impossible to generate an encoding $(\mathsf{ct}_i^0, \mathsf{ct}_i^1, \mathsf{T}_i)$ that signals both 0 and 1 at the same time. In order to implement this mechanism, we also add some random strings to the public key that are used to generate tags, but we ignore them for simplicity in

---

[1] Garg, Gay, and Hajiabadi [20] also used a similar technique called *mirroring*.

this overview. In this case, we can perform the validity check of the key encapsulation part $(\mathsf{ct}_i^0, \mathsf{ct}_i^1, \mathsf{T}_i)_{i \in [n]}$ by checking whether $(\mathsf{ct}_i^{\mathsf{s}_i})_{i \in [n]}$ are well-formed encryptions of 1 by re-encryption. This is intuitively because if we confirm that these n ciphertexts are encryptions of 1, we can also be sure that the remaining n ciphertexts $(\mathsf{ct}_i^{1-\mathsf{s}_i})_{i \in [n]}$ are not encrypting 1 due to the added mechanism based on the PRG and tags $(\mathsf{T}_i)_{i \in [n]}$, and thus we can finish the pseudo-validity-check of all $2n$ ciphertexts of the key encapsulation part. Thus, in this construction, in addition to a message to be encrypted, the SKE scheme needs to encrypt only n random coins $(\mathsf{r}_i^{\mathsf{s}_i})_{i \in [n]}$ used to generate $(\mathsf{ct}_i^{\mathsf{s}_i})_{i \in [n]}$.

2.3 Outline of the Proof: Necessity of KDM Secure SKE

We explain how to prove the IND-CCA security of the above construction. A ciphertext of the scheme is of the form

$$\Big((\mathsf{ct}_i^0, \mathsf{ct}_i^1, \mathsf{T}_i)_{i \in [n]}, \ \mathsf{E}(\mathsf{s}, (\mathsf{r}_i^{\mathsf{s}_i})_{i \in [n]} \| \mathsf{m}) \Big).$$

The general picture of the security proof is the same as that for the ordinary hybrid encryption scheme, and thus we first eliminate the information of s from the key encapsulation part $(\mathsf{ct}_i^0, \mathsf{ct}_i^1, \mathsf{T}_i)_{i \in [n]}$ and then complete the entire proof by using the security of SKE.

We first explain how to eliminate the information of s from the key encapsulation part. In the security proof, thanks to the validity check by re-encryption in the decryption process, we can simulate the decryption oracle correctly by using $(\mathsf{sk}_i^{\mathsf{s}_i})_{i \in [n]}$ instead of $(\mathsf{sk}_i^0)_{i \in [n]}$. In this case, we can change the distribution of $(\mathsf{ct}_i^{1-\mathsf{s}_i})_{i \in [n]}$ in the challenge ciphertext by using the IND-CPA security of the PKE scheme since $(\mathsf{r}_i^{1-\mathsf{s}_i})_{i \in [n]}$ used to generate $(\mathsf{ct}_i^{1-\mathsf{s}_i})_{i \in [n]}$ are not encrypted by the SKE scheme and the decryption oracle can be simulated without $(\mathsf{sk}_i^{1-\mathsf{s}_i})_{i \in [n]}$. We can eliminate the information of s from the key encapsulation part $(\mathsf{ct}_i^0, \mathsf{ct}_i^1, \mathsf{T}_i)_{i \in [n]}$ by changing $(\mathsf{ct}_i^{1-\mathsf{s}_i})_{i \in [n]}$ encrypting 0 into ciphertexts encrypting 1. This means that after this change, every encoding $(\mathsf{ct}_i^0, \mathsf{ct}_i^1, \mathsf{T}_i)$ contained in the challenge ciphertext signals 0 and 1 at the same time. While an adversary cannot generate such an encoding that signals 0 and 1 at the same time as noted above, the reduction algorithm can do it by programming random strings contained in the public key that are used to generate tags $(\mathsf{T}_i)_{i \in [n]}$.

Since we eliminate the information of s from the key encapsulation part above, it seems that we can complete the entire security proof by using the security of the SKE scheme. However, in order to do so, we need an SKE scheme that satisfies *KDM security*. This is because the underlying SKE scheme needs to encrypt $(\mathsf{r}_i^{\mathsf{s}_i})_{i \in [n]}$, which is a message depending on the key s. Concretely, $(\mathsf{r}_i^{\mathsf{s}_i})_{i \in [n]}$ can be seen as $f(\mathsf{s})$ for the function f that has $(\mathsf{r}_i^v)_{i \in [n], v \in \{0,1\}}$ hardwired, and given $\mathsf{s} \in \{0,1\}^n$ outputs $(\mathsf{r}_i^{\mathsf{s}_i})_{i \in [n]}$. Such a function is described as a very simple form of functions called projection functions, for which KDM security has been widely studied [2,3,11–13,16]. In our construction, we need an SKE scheme satisfying only *one-time* KDM security with respect to projection functions, since our construction is basically a hybrid encryption scheme. This is the reason KDM secure SKE is needed for our construction of IND-CCA secure PKE.

The Construction by Koppula and Waters [30]. The construction we explained so far is in fact almost the same as the PKE variant of the construction proposed by Koppula and Waters, except that a one-time KDM secure SKE scheme is used instead of a *hinting PRG*. Here, we briefly explain the notion of hinting PRG and how it is used in their construction.

A hinting PRG is a PRG that, given an n-bit string x, outputs an $(n+1) \cdot \ell$-bit string $y_0 \| y_1 \| \cdots \| y_n$, where y_i is an ℓ-bit string for every $i \in [n]$. Then, its security property requires that $Y := y_0 \| (y_{i,0} \| y_{i,1})_{i \in [n]} \in \{0,1\}^{(2n+1) \cdot \ell}$ be indistinguishable from a uniformly random string in $\{0,1\}^{(2n+1) \cdot \ell}$, where $y_{i,x_i} = y_i$ and $y_{i,1-x_i}$ is a uniformly random string in $\{0,1\}^{\ell}$ for every $i \in [n]$. We see that the locations where $y_1, \cdots y_n$ are placed in Y depend on the seed x, and thus Y itself can be seen as a "hint" of the seed x. Therefore, we can say that the security property of a hinting PRG requires that its output be pseudorandom even if such a hint of the seed is revealed.

Koppula and Waters used a hinting PRG HPRG in their construction as follows. When encrypting a message m, their scheme first generates a seed $x = (x_1, \cdots, x_n) \in \{0,1\}^n$ of HPRG and computes $y_0 \| y_1 \| \cdots \| y_n \leftarrow \mathsf{HPRG}(x)$. Then, it generates an encapsulation of x by generating an encoding $(\mathsf{ct}_i^0, \mathsf{ct}_i^1, \mathsf{T}_i)$ of x_i in which y_i is used as the encryption randomness for $\mathsf{ct}_i^{x_i}$ for every $i \in [n]$. Note that $\mathsf{ct}_i^{1-x_i}$ is generated by using truly random coins. Moreover, it generates the data encapsulation part as $\mathsf{m} \oplus y_0$. The resulting ciphertext is of the form

$$\left((\mathsf{ct}_i^0, \mathsf{ct}_i^1, \mathsf{T}_i)_{i \in [n]}, \ \mathsf{m} \oplus y_0 \right).$$

When decrypting the ciphertext, we can first recover x and thus $y_0 \| y_1 \| \cdots \| y_n \leftarrow \mathsf{HPRG}(x)$ from the encapsulation part. Since $(y_1, \cdots, y_n)$ are random coins used to generate $(\mathsf{ct}_i^{x_i})_{i \in [n]}$, we can also perform the pseudo-validity-check of all $2n$ ciphertexts of the key encapsulation part as we explained above. The security proof of their construction also goes through in a similar fashion to the proof of our construction, except that the security property of HPRG is utilized instead of KDM security.

2.4   Extension to TDF

We explain how we extend the above construction of IND-CCA secure PKE based on IND-CPA secure PKE and one-time KDM secure SKE, into a TDF. More concretely, we explain how we make the above construction completely randomness-recoverable.

In the above construction, there are two types of encryption randomness that are not recovered in the decryption process. The first one is $(r_i^{1-s_i})_{i \in [n]}$ for the underlying IND-CPA secure PKE scheme. The other one is the encryption randomness for the underlying SKE scheme. We require an additional requirement for each building block to make it possible to recover these two types of encryption randomness.

First, to deal with $(r_i^{1-s_i})_{i\in[n]}$ for the IND-CPA secure PKE scheme, we require the underlying IND-CPA secure PKE scheme have the *pseudorandom ciphertext property*. Namely, we require that a ciphertext of the underlying IND-CPA secure PKE scheme be indistinguishable from a uniformly random element sampled from the ciphertext space of the scheme. In the above construction, recall that we encode each bit s_i of s as (ct_i^0, ct_i^1, T_i), where $ct_i^{s_i} = \mathsf{Enc}(pk_i^{s_i}, 1; r_i^{s_i})$ and $ct_i^{1-s_i} = \mathsf{Enc}(pk_i^{1-s_i}, 0; r_i^{1-s_i})$. We now modify the way s_i is encoded so that $ct_i^{1-s_i}$ is an element sampled from the ciphertext space uniformly at random. We can still decode s_i correctly with overwhelming probability thanks to the signaling technique even if we add this modification.[2] Then, we see that the issue of recovering $(r_i^{1-s_i})_{i\in[n]}$ is solved by designing the TDF such that $(ct_i^{1-s_i})_{i\in[n]}$ are directly sampled from the ciphertext space as part of an input to the TDF.

Second, to deal with the random coins for the SKE scheme, we simply require that the SKE scheme be *randomness-recoverable*. Namely, we require that random coins used to encrypt a message be recovered with the message in the decryption process. The randomness-recovering property is easy to achieve in the secret-key setting, and it is also the case even if we require the SKE scheme to be KDM secure. In fact, we can easily construct a one-time projection-KDM secure SKE scheme that is randomness-recoverable by modifying existing projection-KDM secure PKE schemes [11–13, 16, 39]. Moreover, the projection-KDM secure SKE schemes based on the LPN and LWE assumptions proposed by Applebaum et al. [3] already satisfy this property.

With the help of these two additional requirements, we can modify our IND-CCA secure PKE scheme into a TDF. Since our TDF is an extension of IND-CCA secure PKE, it naturally satisfies adaptive one-wayness [27].

2.5 Optimizations and Simplifications

Finally, we explain several optimizations and simplifications that are applied in the actual constructions.

The first optimization is on the number of key pairs of the underlying IND-CPA secure PKE scheme. In the above overview, $2n$ key pairs of the underlying IND-CPA secure PKE scheme are used to construct the key encapsulation part $(ct_i^0, ct_i^1, T_i)_{i\in[n]}$. In our actual constructions, we use only two key pairs of the underlying IND-CPA secure PKE scheme. More concretely, in our actual constructions, every encoding (ct_i^0, ct_i^1, T_i) is generated by using the same pair of public keys (pk^0, pk^1). In fact, if we allow a public parameter shared by all users of the resulting schemes, even one of these public keys, pk^1, can be put into the public parameter, and a public key of the resulting IND-CCA secure scheme and an evaluation key of the resulting TDF consist only of a *single* public key pk^0 of the underlying IND-CPA secure scheme. This optimization is possible by devising at which step of the hybrid games we switch the secret keys of the underlying IND-CPA secure PKE scheme used to simulate the decryption oracle.

---

[2] While we cannot achieve perfect correctness by this modification, we can still achieve almost-all-keys correctness [18]. For its formal definition, see Sect. 3.

The second optimization is on how to make each tag T_i contained in each encoding (ct_i^0, ct_i^1, T_i). In the original signaling technique, a one-time signature scheme is additionally used in order to generate tags. We show that we can replace a one-time signature scheme with a target collision resistant hash function. Such a technique was previously used by Matsuda and Hanaoka [33]. Although both of these primitives can be realized using only a one-way function as an assumption [37], this improvement is critical when constructing a TDF since if we attempt to use a one-time signature scheme for constructing a TDF, we would need to recover the random coins used to generate a key pair of the one-time signature scheme during the inversion process. We can avoid this issue by the use of a target collision resistant hash function instead. This modification is made possible due to the use of a deferred analysis technique in the security proof.

Third, we make a simplification by using key encapsulation mechanism (KEM) instead of PKE. In this overview, we have explained how to construct an IND-CCA secure PKE scheme and a TDF based on IND-CPA secure PKE by additionally using KDM secure SKE. In our actual proposals, we construct an IND-CCA secure KEM (and a TDF) based on IND-CPA secure KEM and KDM secure SKE. As explained above, in the original signaling technique, we use an (ordinary) PRG. More precisely, in the original signaling technique, $ct_i^{s_i}$ in each encoding is generated as $ct_i^{s_i} = \mathsf{Enc}(pk_i^{s_i}, 1\|u_i; r_i^{s_i})$, where u_i is a seed of PRG. In our actual construction, in order to hide the use of a PRG from the description and simplify the construction, we use a KEM whose session-key space is sufficiently larger than its randomness space. We can generically transform an IND-CPA secure PKE scheme into a KEM with such a property. We show that the signaling technique can be implemented by using such a KEM.

For the construction of TDF, we also add an optimization that is made possible by the pseudorandom ciphertext property of the underlying IND-CPA secure PKE scheme. By this optimization, an image of a function consists of n ciphertexts of the IND-CPA secure PKE scheme corresponding to $(ct_i^{s_i})_{i \in [n]}$, n tags $(T_i)_{i \in [n]}$, and a ciphertext of the SKE scheme.

We finally remark that all of the above optimizations and simplifications can be brought back to the construction of an IND-CCA secure ABE scheme based on an IND-CPA secure one and a hinting PRG by Koppula and Waters [30].

3 Preliminaries

In this section, we review the basic notation and the definitions of main cryptographic primitives. For the definitions of primitives that are not reviewed here, see the full version of this paper [29].

Basic Notation. $\mathbb{N}$ denotes the set of natural numbers, and for $n \in \mathbb{N}$, we define $[n] := \{1, \ldots, n\}$. For a discrete finite set S, $|S|$ denotes its size, and $x \xleftarrow{r} S$ denotes choosing an element x uniformly at random from S. For strings x and y, $x\|y$ denotes their concatenation. For a (probabilistic) algorithm or a function

A, $y \leftarrow A(x)$ denotes assigning to y the output of A on an input x, and if we need to specify a randomness r used in A, we denote $y \leftarrow A(x; r)$ (in which case the computation of A is understood as deterministic on input x and r). $\mathsf{Sup}(A)$ denotes the support of A. For any values x, y, $(x \stackrel{?}{=} y)$ is defined to be 1 if $x = y$ and 0 otherwise. λ denotes a security parameter. (P)PT stands for *(probabilistic) polynomial time*. A function $f(\lambda)$ is said to be *negligible* if $f(\lambda)$ tends to 0 faster than $\frac{1}{\lambda^c}$ for every constant $c > 0$. We write $f(\lambda) = \mathsf{negl}(\lambda)$ to denote that $f(\lambda)$ is a negligible function. $\mathsf{poly}(\cdot)$ denotes an unspecified positive polynomial.

3.1   Key Encapsulation Mechanism

Here, we review the definitions for a KEM. For the definition of correctness, we formalize "almost-all-keys" correctness, which is naturally adapted from the definition for PKE formalized by Dwork, Naor, and Reingold [18].

A key encapsulation mechanism (KEM) KEM consists of the three PPT algorithms $(\mathsf{KKG}, \mathsf{Encap}, \mathsf{Decap})$. KKG is the key generation algorithm that takes 1^λ as input, and outputs a public/secret key pair $(\mathsf{pk}, \mathsf{sk})$. We assume that the security parameter λ determines the ciphertext space $\mathcal{C}$, the session-key space $\mathcal{K}$, and the randomness space $\mathcal{R}$ of Encap. Encap is the encapsulation algorithm that takes a public key pk as input, and outputs a ciphertext/session-key pair $(\mathsf{ct}, \mathsf{k})$. Decap is the (deterministic) decapsulation algorithm that takes a secret key sk and a ciphertext ct as input, and outputs a session-key k or the invalid symbol $\perp \notin \mathcal{K}$.

Letting $\epsilon : \mathbb{N} \to [0,1]$, we say that a KEM $\mathsf{KEM} = (\mathsf{KKG}, \mathsf{Encap}, \mathsf{Decap})$ is ϵ-*almost-all-keys correct* if we have

$$\mathsf{Err}_{\mathsf{KEM}}(\lambda) := \Pr_{(\mathsf{pk},\mathsf{sk}) \leftarrow \mathsf{KKG}(1^\lambda)} \left[\exists r \in \mathcal{R} \text{ s.t. } \begin{array}{l} \mathsf{Encap}(\mathsf{pk}; r) = (\mathsf{ct}, \mathsf{k}) \\ \wedge\ \mathsf{Decap}(\mathsf{sk}, \mathsf{ct}) \neq \mathsf{k} \end{array} \right] = \epsilon(\lambda).$$

(A public key pk under which incorrect decapsulation could occur is called *erroneous*.) Furthermore, we just say that KEM is *correct* (resp. *almost-all-keys correct*) if $\mathsf{Err}_{\mathsf{KEM}}(\lambda)$ is zero (resp. $\mathsf{negl}(\lambda)$).

Now we review the security definitions for a KEM used in this paper, which are *IND-CCA security*, *IND-CPA security*, and the *pseudorandom ciphertext* property. For convenience, we will define the multi-challenge versions for the latter two notions, which are polynomially equivalent to the single-challenge versions via a standard hybrid argument.

Definition 1 (Security Notions for a KEM). *Let* $\mathsf{KEM} = (\mathsf{KKG}, \mathsf{Encap}, \mathsf{Decap})$ *be a KEM whose ciphertext and session-key spaces are* $\mathcal{C}$ *and* $\mathcal{K}$, *respectively. We say that* KEM *satisfies*

– IND-CCA security *if for all PPT adversaries* $\mathcal{A}$, *we have* $\mathsf{Adv}^{\mathsf{cca}}_{\mathsf{KEM},\mathcal{A}}(\lambda) := 2 \cdot |\Pr[\mathsf{Expt}^{\mathsf{cca}}_{\mathsf{KEM},\mathcal{A}}(\lambda) = 1] - 1/2| = \mathsf{negl}(\lambda)$, *where* $\mathsf{Expt}^{\mathsf{cca}}_{\mathsf{KEM},\mathcal{A}}(\lambda)$ *is defined as in Fig. 1 (left), and in the experiment,* $\mathcal{A}$ *is not allowed to submit* ct^* *to the decapsulation oracle* $\mathsf{Decap}(\mathsf{sk}, \cdot)$.

$\text{Expt}^{\text{cca}}_{\text{KEM},\mathcal{A}}(\lambda):$
  $(\text{pk},\text{sk}) \leftarrow \text{KKG}(1^\lambda)$
  $(\text{ct}^*,\text{k}^*_1) \leftarrow \text{Encap}(\text{pk})$
  $\text{k}^*_0 \leftarrow \mathcal{K}$
  $b \xleftarrow{r} \{0,1\}$
  $b' \leftarrow \mathcal{A}^{\text{Decap}(\text{sk},\cdot)}(\text{pk},\text{ct}^*,\text{k}^*_b)$
  Return $(b' \overset{?}{=} b)$.

$\text{Expt}^{\text{mcpa}}_{\text{KEM},\ell,\mathcal{A}}(\lambda):$
  $(\text{pk},\text{sk}) \leftarrow \text{KKG}(1^\lambda)$
  $\forall i \in [\ell]:$
    $(\text{ct}^*_i,\text{k}^*_{i,1}) \leftarrow \text{Encap}(\text{pk})$
    $\text{k}^*_{i,0} \xleftarrow{r} \mathcal{K}$
  $b \xleftarrow{r} \{0,1\}$
  $b' \leftarrow \mathcal{A}(\text{pk},(\text{ct}^*_i,\text{k}^*_{i,b})_{i\in[\ell]})$
  Return $(b' \overset{?}{=} b)$.

$\text{Expt}^{\text{mprct}}_{\text{KEM},\ell,\mathcal{A}}(\lambda):$
  $(\text{pk},\text{sk}) \leftarrow \text{KKG}(1^\lambda)$
  $\forall i \in [\ell]:$
    $(\text{ct}^*_{i,1},\text{k}^*_{i,1}) \leftarrow \text{Encap}(\text{pk})$
    $(\text{ct}^*_{i,0},\text{k}^*_{i,0}) \xleftarrow{r} \mathcal{C} \times \mathcal{K}$
  $b \xleftarrow{r} \{0,1\}$
  $b' \leftarrow \mathcal{A}(\text{pk},(\text{ct}^*_{i,b},\text{k}^*_{i,b})_{i\in[\ell]})$
  Return $(b' \overset{?}{=} b)$.

Fig. 1. Security experiments for a KEM: IND-CCA experiment (left), (Multi-challenge) IND-CPA experiment (center), and the (multi-challenge) pseudorandom ciphertext property experiment (right).

- IND-CPA security *if for all PPT adversaries $\mathcal{A}$ and all polynomials $\ell = \ell(\lambda)$, we have* $\text{Adv}^{\text{mcpa}}_{\text{KEM},\ell,\mathcal{A}}(\lambda) := 2 \cdot |\Pr[\text{Expt}^{\text{mcpa}}_{\text{KEM},\ell,\mathcal{A}}(\lambda) = 1] - 1/2| = \text{negl}(\lambda)$, *where* $\text{Expt}^{\text{mcpa}}_{\text{KEM},\ell,\mathcal{A}}(\lambda)$ *is defined as in Fig. 1 (center).*
- *the* pseudorandom ciphertext property *if for all PPT adversaries $\mathcal{A}$ and all polynomials $\ell = \ell(\lambda)$, we have* $\text{Adv}^{\text{mprct}}_{\text{KEM},\ell,\mathcal{A}}(\lambda) := 2 \cdot |\Pr[\text{Expt}^{\text{mprct}}_{\text{KEM},\ell,\mathcal{A}}(\lambda) = 1] - 1/2| = \text{negl}(\lambda)$, *where* $\text{Expt}^{\text{mprct}}_{\text{KEM},\ell,\mathcal{A}}(\lambda)$ *is defined as in Fig. 1 (right).*

3.2 Secret-Key Encryption

A secret-key encryption (SKE) scheme SKE consists of the three PPT algorithms $(\text{K},\text{E},\text{D})$. K is the key generation algorithm that takes 1^λ as input, and outputs a secret key sk. We assume that the security parameter λ determines the secret key space $\mathcal{K}$ and the message space $\mathcal{M}$. E is the encryption algorithm that takes a secret key sk and a plaintext m as input, and outputs a ciphertext ct. D is the (deterministic) decryption algorithm that takes a secret key sk and a ciphertext ct as input, and outputs a plaintext m or the invalid symbol $\perp \notin \mathcal{M}$. An SKE scheme $\text{SKE} = (\text{K},\text{E},\text{D})$ is said to be *correct* if for all $\text{sk} \in \mathcal{K}$ and all $\text{m} \in \mathcal{M}$, it holds that $\text{D}(\text{sk},\text{E}(\text{sk},\text{m})) = \text{m}$.

In our proposed constructions of a TDF, we will use an SKE scheme that satisfies the "randomness-recovering decryption" property, which requires that for an honestly generate ciphertext, the randomness used to generate it can be recovered in the decryption process. We formally define the property as follows.

Definition 2 (Randomness-Recovering Decryption). *Let* $\text{SKE} = (\text{K},\text{E},\text{D})$ *be an SKE scheme whose secret key space is $\mathcal{K}$, whose plaintext space is $\mathcal{M}$, and the randomness space of whose encryption algorithm* E *is $\mathcal{R}$. We say that* SKE *satisfies the* randomness-recovering decryption *property, if there exists a deterministic PT algorithm* RD *(called the* randomness-recovering decryption *algorithm) such that for all* $\text{sk} \in \mathcal{K}$, *all* $\text{m} \in \mathcal{M}$, *and all* $\text{r} \in \mathcal{R}$, *we have* $\text{RD}(\text{sk},\text{E}(\text{sk},\text{m};\text{r})) = (\text{m},\text{r})$.

Here, we recall KDM security of an SKE scheme. For simplicity, we only give the definition for the single key setting, which is sufficient for our purpose.

$$\begin{array}{c|c|c}
\begin{array}{l} \mathsf{Expt}^{\mathsf{kdm}}_{\mathsf{SKE},\mathcal{F},\mathcal{A}}(\lambda): \\ \quad \mathsf{sk} \leftarrow \mathsf{K}(1^\lambda) \\ \quad b \xleftarrow{r} \{0,1\} \\ \quad b' \leftarrow \mathcal{A}^{\mathcal{O}_{\mathsf{kdm}}(\cdot,\cdot)}(1^\lambda) \\ \quad \text{Return } (b' \overset{?}{=} b). \end{array} &
\begin{array}{l} \mathcal{O}_{\mathsf{kdm}}((f_0,f_1) \in \mathcal{F}^2): \\ \quad \mathsf{ct} \leftarrow \mathsf{E}(\mathsf{sk}, f_b(\mathsf{sk})) \\ \quad \text{Return } \mathsf{ct}. \end{array} &
\begin{array}{l} \mathsf{Expt}^{\mathsf{aow}}_{\mathsf{TDF},\mathcal{A}}(\lambda): \\ \quad (\mathsf{ek},\mathsf{td}) \leftarrow \mathsf{Setup}(1^\lambda) \\ \quad \mathsf{x}^* \leftarrow \mathsf{Samp}(1^\lambda) \\ \quad \mathsf{y}^* \leftarrow \mathsf{Eval}(\mathsf{ek}, \mathsf{x}^*) \\ \quad \mathsf{x}' \leftarrow \mathcal{A}^{\mathsf{Inv}(\mathsf{td},\cdot)}(\mathsf{ek}, \mathsf{y}^*) \\ \quad \text{Return } (\mathsf{x}' \overset{?}{=} \mathsf{x}). \end{array}
\end{array}$$

Fig. 2. The KDM security experiment for an SKE (left) scheme, the KDM-encryption oracle used in the KDM security experiment (center), and the adaptive one-wayness experiment for a TDF (right).

Definition 3 (KDM Security). *Let* $\mathsf{SKE} = (\mathsf{K}, \mathsf{E}, \mathsf{D})$ *be an SKE scheme with a secret key space* $\mathcal{K}$ *and a plaintext space* $\mathcal{M}$. *For a family of functions* $\mathcal{F}$ *with domain* $\mathcal{K}$ *and range* $\mathcal{M}$ *and an adversary* $\mathcal{A}$, *consider the experiment* $\mathsf{Expt}^{\mathsf{kdm}}_{\mathsf{SKE},\mathcal{F},\mathcal{A}}(\lambda)$ *defined as in Fig. 2 (left), where the KDM-encryption oracle* $\mathcal{O}_{\mathsf{kdm}}$ *is described in Fig. 2 (center).*

We say that SKE *is* $\mathcal{F}$-*KDM secure if for all PPT adversaries* $\mathcal{A}$, *we have* $\mathsf{Adv}^{\mathsf{kdm}}_{\mathsf{SKE},\mathcal{F},\mathcal{A}}(\lambda) := 2 \cdot |\Pr[\mathsf{Expt}^{\mathsf{kdm}}_{\mathsf{SKE},\mathcal{F},\mathcal{A}}(\lambda) = 1] - 1/2| = \mathsf{negl}(\lambda)$.

Furthermore, we say that SKE *is one-time* $\mathcal{F}$-*KDM secure if* $\mathsf{Adv}^{\mathsf{kdm}}_{\mathsf{SKE},\mathcal{F},\mathcal{A}}(\lambda) = \mathsf{negl}(\lambda)$ *for all PPT adversaries* $\mathcal{A}$ *that make a single KDM-encryption query.*

Function Families for KDM Security. We will deal with the following function families for KDM security of an SKE scheme with key space $\mathcal{K}$ and plaintext space $\mathcal{M}$:

- $\mathcal{P}$ *(Projection functions):* A function is said to be a projection function if each of its output bits depends on at most a single bit of its input. We denote by $\mathcal{P}$ the family of projection functions with domain $\mathcal{K}$ and range $\mathcal{M}$.
- $\mathcal{B}_{\mathsf{size}}$ *(Circuits of a-priori bounded size* size): We denote by $\mathcal{B}_{\mathsf{size}}$, where $\mathsf{size} = \mathsf{size}(\lambda)$ is a polynomial, the function family with domain $\mathcal{K}$ and range $\mathcal{M}$ such that each member in $\mathcal{B}_{\mathsf{size}}$ can be described by a circuit of size size.

3.3 Trapdoor Function

Here, we review the definitions for a TDF. As in the KEM case, for correctness, we will define almost-all-keys correctness.

A trapdoor function (TDF) TDF consists of the four PPT algorithms (Setup, $\mathsf{Samp}, \mathsf{Eval}, \mathsf{Inv}$): Setup is the setup algorithm that takes 1^λ as input, and outputs an evaluation key/trapdoor pair $(\mathsf{ek}, \mathsf{td})$. We assume that the security parameter λ determines the domain $\mathcal{X}$. Samp is the domain sampling algorithm that takes 1^λ as input, and outputs a domain element $x \in \mathcal{X}$. Eval is the evaluation algorithm that takes an evaluation key ek and a domain element x as input, and outputs some element y. Inv is the (deterministic) inversion algorithm that takes a trapdoor td and an element y as input, and outputs some element x which could be the invalid symbol $\bot \notin \mathcal{X}$.

Letting $\epsilon : \mathbb{N} \to [0, 1]$, we say that a TDF TDF = (Setup, Samp, Eval, Inv) is ϵ-*almost-all-keys correct* if we have

$$\mathsf{Err}_{\mathsf{TDF}}(\lambda) := \Pr_{(\mathsf{ek},\mathsf{td}) \leftarrow \mathsf{Setup}(1^\lambda)} \left[\exists x \in \mathcal{X} \text{ s.t. } \mathsf{Inv}(\mathsf{td}, \mathsf{Eval}(\mathsf{ek}, x)) \neq x \right] = \epsilon(\lambda).$$

Furthermore, we just say that TDF is *correct* (resp. *almost-all-keys correct*) if $\mathsf{Err}_{\mathsf{TDF}}(\lambda)$ is zero (resp. $\mathsf{negl}(\lambda)$).

Definition 4 (Adaptive One-wayness/(Ordinary) One-wayness). *Let* TDF = (Setup, Samp, Eval, Inv) *be a TDF with domain* $\mathcal{X}$. *We say that* TDF *is* adaptively one-way *if for all PPT adversaries* $\mathcal{A}$, *we have* $\mathsf{Adv}_{\mathsf{TDF},\mathcal{A}}^{\mathsf{aow}}(\lambda) :=$ $\Pr[\mathsf{Expt}_{\mathsf{TDF},\mathcal{A}}^{\mathsf{aow}}(\lambda) = 1] = \mathsf{negl}(\lambda)$, *where* $\mathsf{Expt}_{\mathsf{TDF},\mathcal{A}}^{\mathsf{aow}}(\lambda)$ *is defined as in Fig. 2 (right), and in the experiment,* $\mathcal{A}$ *is not allowed to submit* y^* *to the inversion oracle* $\mathsf{Inv}(\mathsf{td}, \cdot)$.

Furthermore, we say that TDF *is* one-way *if* $\mathsf{Adv}_{\mathsf{TDF},\mathcal{A}}^{\mathsf{aow}}(\lambda) = \mathsf{negl}(\lambda)$ *for all adversaries that never use the inversion oracle* $\mathsf{Inv}(\mathsf{td}, \cdot)$.

4 Chosen Ciphertext Security via KDM Security

In this section, we show our proposed construction of an IND-CCA secure KEM.

Specifically, in Sect. 4.1, we present the formal description of our proposed KEM, state theorems regarding its correctness/security, and discuss its consequences and extensions. Then, in Sects. 4.2 and 4.3, we prove the correctness and IND-CCA security of our proposed construction, respectively.

4.1 Our Construction

Let $\ell = \ell(\lambda)$ be a polynomial, which will denote the session-key length of the constructed KEM. Our construction uses the building blocks KEM, SKE, and Hash with the following properties:

- KEM = (KKG, Encap, Decap) is a KEM such that (1) its session-key space is $\{0, 1\}^{4\lambda}$, (2) the randomness space of Encap is $\{0, 1\}^\lambda$, and (3) the image size of Decap(sk, ·) for any sk output by $\mathsf{KKG}(1^\lambda)$ (other than $\bot$) is at most 2^λ.[3]
- SKE = (K, E, D) is an SKE scheme whose secret key space is $\{0, 1\}^n$ for some polynomial $n = n(\lambda)$ and whose plaintext space is $\{0, 1\}^{n \cdot \lambda + \ell}$, and we denote the randomness space of E by $\mathcal{R}_{\mathsf{SKE}}$.
- Hash = (HKG, H) is a keyed hash function such that the range of H is $\{0, 1\}^\lambda$, which we are going to assume to be target collision resistant.

Using these building blocks, the proposed KEM $\mathsf{KEM}_{\mathsf{cca}} = (\mathsf{KKG}_{\mathsf{cca}}, \mathsf{Encap}_{\mathsf{cca}}, \mathsf{Decap}_{\mathsf{cca}})$ is constructed as in Fig. 3. Its session-key space is $\{0, 1\}^\ell$, and the randomness space $\mathcal{R}$ of $\mathsf{Encap}_{\mathsf{cca}}$ is $\mathcal{R} = \{0, 1\}^n \times (\{0, 1\}^\lambda)^{2n} \times \{0, 1\}^\ell \times \mathcal{R}_{\mathsf{SKE}}$.

For the correctness and security of $\mathsf{KEM}_{\mathsf{cca}}$, the following theorems hold.

---

[3] These three requirements are without loss of generality for an IND-CPA secure KEM: The properties (1) and (3) can be achieved by stretching a session-key of a KEM with session-key space $\{0, 1\}^\lambda$ by using a PRG G : $\{0, 1\}^\lambda \to \{0, 1\}^{4\lambda}$, and the randomness space of Encap can also be freely adjusted by using a PRG.

$$
\begin{array}{l}
\mathsf{KKG}_{\mathsf{cca}}(1^\lambda): \\
\quad \forall v \in \{0,1\}: (\mathsf{pk}^v, \mathsf{sk}^v) \leftarrow \mathsf{KKG}(1^\lambda) \\
\quad A_1, \dots, A_n, B \xleftarrow{r} \{0,1\}^{4\lambda} \\
\quad \mathsf{hk} \leftarrow \mathsf{HKG}(1^\lambda) \\
\quad \mathsf{PK} \leftarrow (\mathsf{pk}^0, \mathsf{pk}^1, (A_i)_{i \in [n]}, B, \mathsf{hk}) \\
\quad \mathsf{SK} \leftarrow (\mathsf{sk}^0, \mathsf{PK}) \\
\quad \text{Return } (\mathsf{PK}, \mathsf{SK}).
\end{array}
$$

$\mathsf{Encap}_{\mathsf{cca}}(\mathsf{PK}):$	$\mathsf{Decap}_{\mathsf{cca}}(\mathsf{SK}, \mathsf{CT}):$
$(\mathsf{pk}^0, \mathsf{pk}^1, (A_i)_{i \in [n]}, B, \mathsf{hk}) \leftarrow \mathsf{PK}$	$(\mathsf{sk}^0, \mathsf{PK}) \leftarrow \mathsf{SK}$
$s = (s_1, \dots, s_n) \leftarrow \mathsf{K}(1^\lambda)$	$(\mathsf{pk}^0, \mathsf{pk}^1, (A_i)_{i \in [n]}, B, \mathsf{hk}) \leftarrow \mathsf{PK}$
$r_1^0, \dots, r_n^0, r_1^1, \dots, r_n^1 \xleftarrow{r} \{0,1\}^\lambda$	$((\mathsf{ct}_i^0, \mathsf{ct}_i^1, T_i)_{i \in [n]}, \mathsf{ct}_{\mathsf{SKE}}) \leftarrow \mathsf{CT}$
$k \xleftarrow{r} \{0,1\}^\ell$	$h \leftarrow \mathsf{H}(\mathsf{hk}, (\mathsf{ct}_i^0, \mathsf{ct}_i^1)_{i \in [n]} \| \mathsf{ct}_{\mathsf{SKE}})$
$\mathsf{ct}_{\mathsf{SKE}} \leftarrow \mathsf{E}(s, (r_i^{s_i})_{i \in [n]} \| k)$	$\forall i \in [n]:$
$\forall (i,v) \in [n] \times \{0,1\}:$	$\quad s_i \leftarrow 1 - (\mathsf{Decap}(\mathsf{sk}^0, \mathsf{ct}_i^0) \overset{?}{=} T_i) \quad (\star)$
$\quad (\mathsf{ct}_i^v, k_i^v) \leftarrow \mathsf{Encap}(\mathsf{pk}^v; r_i^v)$	$\quad = \begin{cases} 0 & \text{if } \mathsf{Decap}(\mathsf{sk}^0, \mathsf{ct}_i^0) = T_i \\ 1 & \text{otherwise} \end{cases}$
$h \leftarrow \mathsf{H}(\mathsf{hk}, (\mathsf{ct}_i^0, \mathsf{ct}_i^1)_{i \in [n]} \| \mathsf{ct}_{\mathsf{SKE}})$	$s \leftarrow (s_1, \dots, s_n) \in \{0,1\}^n$
$\forall i \in [n]:$	$m \leftarrow \mathsf{D}(s, \mathsf{ct}_{\mathsf{SKE}})$
$\quad T_i \leftarrow k_i^{s_i} + s_i \cdot (A_i + B \cdot h) \quad (\dagger)$	Parse m as $((r_i^{s_i})_{i \in [n]}, k) \in (\{0,1\}^\lambda)^n \times \{0,1\}^\ell.$
$\quad = \begin{cases} k_i^0 & \text{if } s_i = 0 \\ k_i^1 + A_i + B \cdot h & \text{if } s_i = 1 \end{cases}$	If $\forall i \in [n]:$
$\mathsf{CT} \leftarrow ((\mathsf{ct}_i^0, \mathsf{ct}_i^1, T_i)_{i \in [n]}, \mathsf{ct}_{\mathsf{SKE}})$	$\quad \mathsf{Encap}(\mathsf{pk}^{s_i}; r_i^{s_i}) = (\mathsf{ct}_i^{s_i}, T_i - s_i \cdot (A_i + B \cdot h))$
Return $(\mathsf{CT}, k).$	$\quad$ then return k else return $\perp.$ $\quad (\dagger)$

Fig. 3. The proposed KEM $\mathsf{KEM}_{\mathsf{cca}}$. $^{(\dagger)}$ $h \in \{0,1\}^\lambda$ is treated as an element of $\{0,1\}^{4\lambda}$ by some canonical injective encoding (say, putting the prefix $0^{3\lambda}$), and the arithmetic is done over $\mathrm{GF}(2^{4\lambda})$ where we identify $\{0,1\}^{4\lambda}$ with $\mathrm{GF}(2^{4\lambda})$. $^{(\star)}$ We call this step the *find step*.

Theorem 1. *Let $\epsilon = \epsilon(\lambda) \in [0,1]$. If* KEM *is ϵ-almost-all-keys correct and* SKE *is correct, then* $\mathsf{KEM}_{\mathsf{cca}}$ *is $(\epsilon + n \cdot 2^{-\lambda})$-almost-all-keys correct.*

Theorem 2. *Assume that* KEM *is almost-all-keys correct and IND-CPA secure,* SKE *is one-time $\mathcal{P}$-KDM secure, and* Hash *is target collision resistant. Then,* $\mathsf{KEM}_{\mathsf{cca}}$ *is IND-CCA secure.*

The proofs of Theorems 1 and 2 are given in Sects. 4.2 and 4.3, respectively.

Implications to Black-Box Constructions/Reductions. It is straightforward to see that our construction uses the underlying primitives in a black-box manner. As will be clear from our security proof, our reduction algorithms also treat the underlying primitives and an adversary in a black-box manner. In fact, our construction/reduction is fully black-box in the sense of [36]. Since there exists a black-box construction of a target collision resistant hash function from a one-way function, which can be trivially constructed from an IND-CPA secure PKE scheme/KEM in a black-box manner, and since an IND-CCA/CPA PKE scheme and KEM imply each other (in a black-box manner), we obtain the following result as a corollary of our theorems.

Corollary 1. *There exists a fully black-box construction of an IND-CCA secure PKE scheme/KEM from an IND-CPA secure PKE scheme/KEM and a one-time $\mathcal{P}$-KDM secure SKE scheme that can encrypt plaintexts of length $\Omega(n \cdot \lambda)$, where $n = n(\lambda)$ is the secret key length of the SKE scheme.*

Furthermore, since a $\mathcal{P}$-KDM secure *PKE* scheme trivially implies both an IND-CPA secure PKE scheme/KEM and a one-time $\mathcal{P}$-KDM secure SKE scheme, we obtain another corollary.

Corollary 2. *There exists a fully black-box construction of an IND-CCA secure PKE scheme/KEM from a $\mathcal{P}$-KDM secure PKE scheme.*

In contrast to Corollary 2, in Sect. 5, we will show that there exists no *shielding* black-box construction [21] of an IND-CCA1 secure PKE scheme from a $\mathcal{P}$-KDM secure PKE scheme.

In [33], Matsuda and Hanaoka showed a construction of an IND-CCA secure PKE scheme/KEM from a PKE scheme satisfying the security notion called the sender non-committing property and a one-time $\mathcal{B}_{\text{size}}$-KDM secure SKE scheme (where size is related to the running time of the sender non-committing encryption scheme). Although their construction uses the underlying primitives as black-boxes, their security reduction (to the $\mathcal{B}_{\text{size}}$-KDM security of the underlying SKE scheme) is non-black-box in the sense that the reduction needs to use the description of one of the algorithms in the sender non-committing encryption scheme as a KDM-encryption query. Compared to the result by Matsuda and Hanaoka, our results are superior in terms of both the strength of the assumptions on the building blocks (IND-CPA security is weaker than the sender non-committing property, and $\mathcal{P}$-KDM security is weaker than $\mathcal{B}_{\text{size}}$-KDM security), and the "black-boxness" of the reductions.

Hinting PRG vs. KDM Secure SKE. As mentioned earlier, the result of Koppula and Waters [30], when specialized to PKE, implies that if there exists an IND-CPA secure PKE scheme and a hinting PRG, one can realize an IND-CCA secure PKE scheme. Given our result in this section and the result of [30], it is natural to ask whether there exists an implication/separation between a (one-time) KDM secure SKE scheme and a hinting PRG. We give a partial affirmative answer to this question. Specifically, we show the following theorem.

Theorem 3. *If there exists a hinting PRG, then for any polynomials $m = m(\lambda)$ and $\text{size} = \text{size}(\lambda) \geq m$, there exists a one-time $\mathcal{B}_{\text{size}}$-KDM secure SKE scheme whose plaintext space is $\{0,1\}^m$. Furthermore, for any polynomial $m = m(\lambda)$, there exists a fully black-box construction of a one-time $\mathcal{P}$-KDM secure SKE scheme with plaintext space $\{0,1\}^m$ from a hinting PRG.*

The formal proof of this theorem is given in the full version of this paper [29]. This result shows that the existence of a KDM-secure SKE scheme is not stronger (as an assumption) than that of a hinting PRG. At this moment, it is not clear if the implication of the opposite direction can be established.

Additional Remarks.

- If we adopt the syntax of a KEM in which there is a public parameter shared by all users, then we can push pk^1, $(A_i)_{i \in [n]}$, B, and hk in PK to a public parameter, so that a key pair of each user consists only of a single key pair (pk^0, sk^0) of the underlying IND-CPA secure KEM.
- Although our proposed construction satisfies only almost-all-keys correctness, a minor variant of our construction can achieve perfect correctness, by using a PKE scheme and a PRG, instead of a KEM, as done in the Koppula-Waters construction [30].

4.2 Proof of Correctness (Proof of Theorem 1)

Let $PK = (pk^0, pk^1, (A_i)_{i \in [n]}, B, hk)$ be a public key. Using pk^0, pk^1, and B in PK, we define the function $f : \{0,1\}^{3\lambda} \to \{0,1\}^{4\lambda}$ by

$$f(r, r', h) : \Big[(ct, k) \leftarrow \mathsf{Encap}(pk^0; r); \ (ct', k') \leftarrow \mathsf{Encap}(pk^1; r'); \ \text{Return } k - k' - B \cdot h \Big].$$

We say that a public key PK is *bad* if (1) pk^0 is erroneous, or (2) some of $(A_i)_{i \in [n]}$ belongs to the image of f. Note that the image size of f is at most $2^{3\lambda}$. Since each A_i is chosen uniformly at random from $\{0,1\}^{4\lambda}$, when $\mathsf{KKG}_{\mathsf{cca}}(1^\lambda)$ is executed, the probability that a bad PK is output is at most $\epsilon + n \cdot \frac{2^{3\lambda}}{2^{4\lambda}} = \epsilon + n \cdot 2^{-\lambda}$.

Now, consider the case that (PK, SK) is output by $\mathsf{KKG}_{\mathsf{cca}}$ and PK is not bad. Let $R = (s = (s_1, \ldots, s_n), (r_i^0, r_i^1)_{i \in [n]}, k, r_{\mathsf{SKE}}) \in \{0,1\}^n \times (\{0,1\}^\lambda)^{2n} \times \{0,1\}^\ell \times \mathcal{R}_{\mathsf{SKE}}$ be a randomness for $\mathsf{Encap}_{\mathsf{cca}}$, and let $(CT = ((ct_i^0, ct_i^1, T_i)_{i \in [n]}, ct_{\mathsf{SKE}}), k) = \mathsf{Encap}_{\mathsf{cca}}(PK; R)$. Moreover, for each $i \in [n]$, let $s_i' := 1 - (\mathsf{Decap}(sk^0, ct_i^0) \overset{?}{=} T_i)$.

Note that if $s_i' = s_i$ holds for all $i \in [n]$, then the decryption result of ct_{SKE} using $s' = (s_1', \ldots, s_n')$ as a secret key is exactly $(r_i^{s_i})_{i \in [n]} \| k$ due to the correctness of SKE. Thus, the validity check done in the last step of $\mathsf{Decap}_{\mathsf{cca}}$ never fails, and $\mathsf{Decap}_{\mathsf{cca}}(SK, CT)$ will output k.

Hence, it remains to show that $s_i' = s_i$ holds for all $i \in [n]$.

- For positions i with $s_i = 0$, we have $(ct_i^0, k_i^0 = T_i) = \mathsf{Encap}(pk^0; r_i^0)$. Thus, the property that pk^0 is not erroneous implies $\mathsf{Decap}(sk^0, ct_i^0) = T_i$, and we have $s_i' = 0$.
- For positions i with $s_i = 1$, we have $(ct_i^0, k_i^0) = \mathsf{Encap}(pk^0; r_i^0)$ and $(ct_i^1, k_i^1 = T_i - A_i - B \cdot h) = \mathsf{Encap}(pk^1; r_i^1)$, where $h = \mathsf{H}(hk, (ct_i^0, ct_i^1)_{i \in [n]} \| ct_{\mathsf{SKE}})$. Since A_i is not in the image of f, we have

$$A_i \neq f(r_i^0, r_i^1, h) = k_i^0 - k_i^1 - B \cdot h = k_i^0 - (T_i - A_i - B \cdot h) - B \cdot h \iff k_i^0 \neq T_i.$$

Furthermore, since pk^0 is not erroneous, we have $\mathsf{Decap}(sk^0, ct_i^0) = k_i^0$. These together imply that we must have $s_i' = 1$.

The above shows that $s_i' = s_i$ holds for all $i \in [n]$.

Putting everything together, except for a probability at most $\epsilon + n \cdot 2^{-\lambda}$ over $(PK, SK) \leftarrow \mathsf{KKG}_{\mathsf{cca}}(1^\lambda)$, there exists no randomness R satisfying $\mathsf{Encap}_{\mathsf{cca}}(PK; R) = (CT, k)$ and $\mathsf{Decap}_{\mathsf{cca}}(SK, CT) \neq k$ simultaneously. $\qquad\qquad \square$ **(Theorem 1)**

4.3 Proof of IND-CCA Security (Proof of Theorem 2)

Let $\epsilon : \mathbb{N} \rightarrow [0,1]$ be such that KEM is ϵ-almost-all-keys correct. Let $\mathcal{A}$ be any PPT adversary that attacks the IND-CCA security of $\mathsf{KEM}_{\mathsf{cca}}$ and makes $q_{\mathsf{dec}} = q_{\mathsf{dec}}(\lambda) > 0$ decapsulation queries. We will show that for this $\mathcal{A}$, there exist PPT adversaries $\mathcal{B}_{\mathsf{tcr}}$, $\{\mathcal{B}_{\mathsf{cpa}}^j\}_{j\in[4]}$, $\mathcal{B}_{\mathsf{cpa}}'$, and $\mathcal{B}_{\mathsf{kdm}}$ (which makes a single KDM-encryption query) satisfying

$$\mathsf{Adv}^{\mathsf{cca}}_{\mathsf{KEM}_{\mathsf{cca}},\mathcal{A}}(\lambda) \leq$$
$$2 \cdot \mathsf{Adv}^{\mathsf{tcr}}_{\mathsf{Hash},\mathcal{B}_{\mathsf{tcr}}}(\lambda) + 2 \cdot \sum_{j\in[4]} \mathsf{Adv}^{\mathsf{mcpa}}_{\mathsf{KEM},n,\mathcal{B}_{\mathsf{cpa}}^j}(\lambda) + 2q_{\mathsf{dec}} \cdot \mathsf{Adv}^{\mathsf{mcpa}}_{\mathsf{KEM},n,\mathcal{B}_{\mathsf{cpa}}'}(\lambda)$$
$$+ 2 \cdot \mathsf{Adv}^{\mathsf{kdm}}_{\mathsf{SKE},\mathcal{P},\mathcal{B}_{\mathsf{kdm}}}(\lambda) + 8\epsilon + n \cdot 2^{-\lambda+3} + n(q_{\mathsf{dec}} + 1) \cdot 2^{-4\lambda+1}. \quad (1)$$

This is negligible by our assumption, and thus will prove the theorem.

Our proof is via a sequence of games argument using the following six games.

Game 1: This is the IND-CCA experiment $\mathsf{Expt}^{\mathsf{cca}}_{\mathsf{KEM}_{\mathsf{cca}},\mathcal{A}}(\lambda)$. However, for making it easier to describe the subsequent games, we change the ordering of the operations for how the key pair $(\mathsf{PK}, \mathsf{SK})$ and the challenge ciphertext/session-key pair $(\mathsf{CT}^*, \mathsf{k}_b^*)$ are generated so that the distribution of $(\mathsf{PK}, \mathsf{SK}, \mathsf{CT}^*, \mathsf{k}_b^*)$ is identical to that in the original IND-CCA experiment.
Specifically, the description of the game is as follows:

- Generate $\mathsf{PK} = (\mathsf{pk}^0, \mathsf{pk}^1, (A_i)_{i\in[n]}, B, \mathsf{hk})$, $\mathsf{SK} = (\mathsf{sk}^0, \mathsf{PK})$, and $\mathsf{CT}^* = ((\mathsf{ct}_i^{*0}, \mathsf{ct}_i^{*1}, T_i^*)_{i\in[n]}, \mathsf{ct}_{\mathsf{SKE}}^*)$ as follows:
    1. Compute $(\mathsf{pk}^v, \mathsf{sk}^v) \leftarrow \mathsf{KKG}(1^\lambda)$ for $v \in \{0, 1\}$, and pick $B \xleftarrow{\mathsf{r}} \{0, 1\}^{4\lambda}$.
    2. Compute $s^* = (s_1^*, \ldots, s_n^*) \leftarrow \mathsf{K}(1^\lambda)$, and pick $r_1^{*0}, \ldots, r_n^{*0}, r_1^{*1}, \ldots, r_n^{*1} \xleftarrow{\mathsf{r}} \{0, 1\}^\lambda$ and $\mathsf{k}_1^* \xleftarrow{\mathsf{r}} \{0, 1\}^\ell$.
    3. Compute $\mathsf{ct}_{\mathsf{SKE}}^* \leftarrow \mathsf{E}(s^*, (r_i^{*(s_i^*)})_{i\in[n]} \| \mathsf{k}_1^*)$.
    4. Compute $(\mathsf{ct}_i^{*v}, \mathsf{k}_i^{*v}) \leftarrow \mathsf{Encap}(\mathsf{pk}^v; r_i^{*v})$ for every $(i, v) \in [n] \times \{0, 1\}$.
    5. Compute $\mathsf{hk} \leftarrow \mathsf{HKG}(1^\lambda)$ and $h^* \leftarrow \mathsf{H}(\mathsf{hk}, (\mathsf{ct}_i^{*0}, \mathsf{ct}_i^{*1})_{i\in[n]} \| \mathsf{ct}_{\mathsf{SKE}}^*)$.
    6. Pick $A_1, \ldots, A_n \xleftarrow{\mathsf{r}} \{0, 1\}^{4\lambda}$.
    7. Compute $T_i^* \leftarrow \mathsf{k}_i^{*(s_i^*)} + s_i^* \cdot (A_i + B \cdot h^*)$ for every $i \in [n]$.
    8. Set $\mathsf{PK} \leftarrow (\mathsf{pk}^0, \mathsf{pk}^1, (A_i)_{i\in[n]}, B, \mathsf{hk})$, $\mathsf{SK} \leftarrow (\mathsf{sk}^0, \mathsf{PK})$, and $\mathsf{CT}^* \leftarrow ((\mathsf{ct}_i^{*0}, \mathsf{ct}_i^{*1}, T_i^*)_{i\in[n]}, \mathsf{ct}_{\mathsf{SKE}}^*)$.
- Then, pick the random session-key $\mathsf{k}_0^* \xleftarrow{\mathsf{r}} \{0, 1\}^\ell$ and the challenge bit $b \xleftarrow{\mathsf{r}} \{0, 1\}$, and run $\mathcal{A}(\mathsf{PK}, \mathsf{CT}^*, \mathsf{k}_b^*)$. From here on, $\mathcal{A}$ may start making decapsulation queries.
- Decapsulation queries $\mathsf{CT} = ((\mathsf{ct}_i^0, \mathsf{ct}_i^1, T_i)_{i\in[n]}, \mathsf{ct}_{\mathsf{SKE}})$ are answered as follows: First, compute $h \leftarrow \mathsf{H}(\mathsf{hk}, (\mathsf{ct}_i^0, \mathsf{ct}_i^1)_{i\in[n]} \| \mathsf{ct}_{\mathsf{SKE}})$. Next, compute $s_i \leftarrow 1 - (\mathsf{Decap}(\mathsf{sk}^0, \mathsf{ct}_i^0) \stackrel{?}{=} T_i)$ for every $i \in [n]$, and set $s \leftarrow (s_1, \ldots, s_n)$. Then, compute $m \leftarrow \mathsf{D}(s, \mathsf{ct}_{\mathsf{SKE}})$ and parse m as $((r_i^{s_i})_{i\in[n]}, k) \in (\{0, 1\}^\lambda)^n \times \{0, 1\}^\ell$. Finally, if $\mathsf{Encap}(\mathsf{pk}^{s_i}; r_i^{s_i}) = (\mathsf{ct}_i^{s_i}, T_i - s_i \cdot (A_i + B \cdot h))$ holds for all $i \in [n]$, then return k to $\mathcal{A}$. Otherwise, return $\perp$ to $\mathcal{A}$.
- At some point, $\mathcal{A}$ terminates with output $b' \in \{0, 1\}$.

For convenience, in the following we will use the following sets:

$$\mathcal{S}_{\text{zero}} := \left\{ j \in [n] \mid \mathsf{s}_j^* = 0 \right\} \quad \text{and} \quad \mathcal{S}_{\text{one}} := \left\{ j \in [n] \mid \mathsf{s}_j^* = 1 \right\} = [n] \setminus \mathcal{S}_{\text{zero}}.$$

Game 2: Same as Game 1, except for an additional rejection rule in the decapsulation oracle. Specifically, in this game, if $\mathcal{A}$'s decapsulation query $\mathsf{CT} = ((\mathsf{ct}_i^0, \mathsf{ct}_i^1, \mathsf{T}_i)_{i \in [n]}, \mathsf{ct}_{\mathsf{SKE}})$ satisfies $\mathsf{h} = \mathsf{H}(\mathsf{hk}, (\mathsf{ct}_i^0, \mathsf{ct}_i^1)_{i \in [n]} \| \mathsf{ct}_{\mathsf{SKE}}) = \mathsf{h}^*$, then the decapsulation oracle immediately returns $\perp$ to $\mathcal{A}$.

Game 3: Same as Game 2, except for how A_i's for the positions $i \in \mathcal{S}_{\text{zero}}$ are generated. Specifically, in this game, A_i for every position $i \in \mathcal{S}_{\text{zero}}$ is generated by

$$\mathsf{A}_i \leftarrow \mathsf{k}_i^{*0} - \mathsf{k}_i^{*1} - \mathsf{B} \cdot \mathsf{h}^*. \tag{2}$$

(At this point, A_i's for the remaining positions $i \in \mathcal{S}_{\text{one}}$ are unchanged.)

Game 4: Same as Game 3, except for the behavior of the decapsulation oracle. Specifically, for answering $\mathcal{A}$'s decapsulation queries $\mathsf{CT} = ((\mathsf{ct}_i^0, \mathsf{ct}_i^1, \mathsf{T}_i)_{i \in [n]}, \mathsf{ct}_{\mathsf{SKE}})$, the oracle in this game first computes $\mathsf{h} = \mathsf{H}(\mathsf{hk}, (\mathsf{ct}_i^0, \mathsf{ct}_i^1)_{i \in [n]} \| \mathsf{ct}_{\mathsf{SKE}})$, and returns $\perp$ to $\mathcal{A}$ if $\mathsf{h} = \mathsf{h}^*$. (This rejection rule is the same as in Game 3.) Otherwise, the oracle uses the "alternative decapsulation algorithm" $\mathsf{AltDecap}$ and the "alternative secret key" SK' defined below for computing the decapsulation result k returned to $\mathcal{A}$.

$\mathsf{AltDecap}$ takes $\mathsf{SK}' := (\mathsf{sk}^1, \mathsf{PK})$ and CT as input, and proceeds identically to $\mathsf{Decap}_{\mathsf{cca}}(\mathsf{SK}, \mathsf{CT})$, except that the "find step" (i.e. the step for computing s_i's) is replaced with the following procedure:

$$\forall i \in [n] : \quad \mathsf{s}_i \leftarrow \left(\mathsf{Decap}(\mathsf{sk}^1, \mathsf{ct}_i^1) \overset{?}{=} \mathsf{T}_i - \mathsf{A}_i - \mathsf{B} \cdot \mathsf{h} \right)$$
$$= \begin{cases} 1 & \text{if } \mathsf{Decap}(\mathsf{sk}^1, \mathsf{ct}_i^1) = \mathsf{T}_i - \mathsf{A}_i - \mathsf{B} \cdot \mathsf{h} \\ 0 & \text{otherwise} \end{cases}.$$

Note that due to this change, the decapsulation oracle answers $\mathcal{A}$'s queries without using sk^0.

Game 5: Same as Game 4, except for how A_i's for the positions $i \in \mathcal{S}_{\text{one}}$ are generated. Specifically, in this game, A_i for $i \in \mathcal{S}_{\text{one}}$ is also generated as in Eq. 2.

Note that due to this change, all of $(\mathsf{A}_i)_{i \in [n]}$ are generated as in Eq. 2. Furthermore, $\mathsf{T}_i^* = \mathsf{k}_i^{*0}$ holds for every $i \in [n]$, no matter whether $\mathsf{s}_i^* = 0$ or $\mathsf{s}_i^* = 1$. Indeed, this is the case for the positions $i \in \mathcal{S}_{\text{zero}}$ by design. For the positions $i \in \mathcal{S}_{\text{one}}$, we have

$$\mathsf{T}_i^* = \mathsf{k}_i^{*1} + \mathsf{A}_i + \mathsf{B} \cdot \mathsf{h}^* = \mathsf{k}_i^{*1} + (\mathsf{k}_i^{*0} - \mathsf{k}_i^{*1} - \mathsf{B} \cdot \mathsf{h}^*) + \mathsf{B} \cdot \mathsf{h}^* = \mathsf{k}_i^{*0}.$$

Hence, in this game, values dependent on s^* appear only in the plaintext of $\mathsf{ct}_{\mathsf{SKE}}^*$ (i.e. $(r_i^{*(\mathsf{s}_i^*)})_{i \in [n]} \| \mathsf{k}_1^*$).

Game 6: Same as Game 5, except that the information of the challenge bit b is erased from the SKE ciphertext $\mathsf{ct}^*_{\mathsf{SKE}}$. Specifically, in this game, $\mathsf{ct}^*_{\mathsf{SKE}}$ in the challenge ciphertext CT^* is generated by $\mathsf{ct}^*_{\mathsf{SKE}} \leftarrow \mathsf{E}(\mathsf{s}^*, 0^{n \cdot \lambda + \ell})$, instead of $\mathsf{ct}^*_{\mathsf{SKE}} \leftarrow \mathsf{E}(\mathsf{s}^*, (r_i^{*(\mathsf{s}_i^*)})_{i \in [n]} \| \mathsf{k}_1^*)$.

For $j \in [6]$, let SUC_j be the event that $\mathcal{A}$ succeeds in guessing the challenge bit (i.e. $b' = b$ occurs) in Game j. By definition, we have $\mathsf{Adv}^{\mathsf{cca}}_{\mathsf{KEM}_{\mathsf{cca}}, \mathcal{A}}(\lambda) = 2 \cdot |\Pr[\mathsf{SUC}_1] - 1/2|$. Thus, the triangle inequality implies

$$\mathsf{Adv}^{\mathsf{cca}}_{\mathsf{KEM}_{\mathsf{cca}}, \mathcal{A}}(\lambda) \leq 2 \cdot \left(\sum_{j \in [5]} |\Pr[\mathsf{SUC}_j] - \Pr[\mathsf{SUC}_{j+1}]| + \left| \Pr[\mathsf{SUC}_6] - \frac{1}{2} \right| \right). \quad (3)$$

In the following, we show how the terms appearing in Eq. 3 are bounded.

Lemma 1. *There exist PPT adversaries $\mathcal{B}_{\mathsf{tcr}}$, $\{\mathcal{B}^j_{\mathsf{cpa}}\}_{j \in [2]}$, and $\mathcal{B}'_{\mathsf{cpa}}$ satisfying*

$$|\Pr[\mathsf{SUC}_1] - \Pr[\mathsf{SUC}_2]| \leq \mathsf{Adv}^{\mathsf{tcr}}_{\mathsf{Hash}, \mathcal{B}_{\mathsf{tcr}}}(\lambda) + \sum_{j \in [2]} \mathsf{Adv}^{\mathsf{mcpa}}_{\mathsf{KEM}, n, \mathcal{B}^j_{\mathsf{cpa}}}(\lambda)$$

$$+ q_{\mathsf{dec}} \cdot \mathsf{Adv}^{\mathsf{mcpa}}_{\mathsf{KEM}, n, \mathcal{B}'_{\mathsf{cpa}}}(\lambda) + 3\epsilon + n \cdot 2^{-\lambda+1} + n(q_{\mathsf{dec}} + 1) \cdot 2^{-4\lambda}. \quad (4)$$

Due to the space limitation, we give the formal proof of Lemma 1 in the full version of this paper [29]. The proof relies on the target collision resistance of the underlying keyed hash function Hash, and uses a deferred analysis (up to Game 4) with (slight variants of) the arguments used in the proofs of Lemmas 2 to 4 stated below.

Lemma 2. *There exists a PPT adversary $\mathcal{B}^3_{\mathsf{cpa}}$ such that $|\Pr[\mathsf{SUC}_2] - \Pr[\mathsf{SUC}_3]| = \mathsf{Adv}^{\mathsf{mcpa}}_{\mathsf{KEM}, n, \mathcal{B}^3_{\mathsf{cpa}}}(\lambda)$.*

In Games 2 and 3, sk^1 is not used. Moreover, r_i^{*1} used to generate ct_i^{*1}, is not encrypted into $\mathsf{ct}^*_{\mathsf{SKE}}$ for $i \in \mathcal{S}_{\mathsf{zero}}$. Thus, from $\mathcal{A}$, we can construct a PPT adversary $\mathcal{B}^3_{\mathsf{cpa}}$ that attacks the IND-CPA security of KEM under the key pk^1 with the advantage stated in the lemma. For the formal proof, see the full version [29].

Lemma 3. *$|\Pr[\mathsf{SUC}_3] - \Pr[\mathsf{SUC}_4]| \leq 2\epsilon + n \cdot 2^{-\lambda+1}$ holds.*

Proof of Lemma 3. Note that Game 3 and Game 4 proceed identically unless $\mathcal{A}$ makes a decapsulation query $\mathsf{CT} = ((\mathsf{ct}_i^0, \mathsf{ct}_i^1, T_i)_{i \in [n]}, \mathsf{ct}_{\mathsf{SKE}})$ such that $\mathsf{h} = \mathsf{H}(\mathsf{hk}, (\mathsf{ct}_i^0, \mathsf{ct}_i^1)_{i \in [n]} \| \mathsf{ct}_{\mathsf{SKE}}) \neq \mathsf{h}^*$ and $\mathsf{Decap}_{\mathsf{cca}}(\mathsf{SK}, \mathsf{CT}) \neq \mathsf{AltDecap}(\mathsf{SK}', \mathsf{CT})$ hold simultaneously. We call such a decapsulation query *bad*. In the following, we will show that if PK is not "bad" in the sense specified below, a bad decapsulation query does not exist in Game 3 and Game 4, and the probability that PK becomes bad is bounded by $2\epsilon + n \cdot 2^{-\lambda+1}$. This will prove the lemma.

Fix the following values in Game 3:

- $(\mathsf{pk}^0, \mathsf{sk}^0), (\mathsf{pk}^1, \mathsf{sk}^1) \in \mathsf{Sup}(\mathsf{KKG}(1^\lambda))$ such that pk^0 and pk^1 are not erroneous, and $\mathsf{hk} \in \mathsf{Sup}(\mathsf{HKG}(1^\lambda))$.

- $s^* = (s_1^*, \ldots, s_n^*) \in \mathsf{Sup}(\mathsf{K}(1^\lambda))$, $r_1^{*0}, \ldots, r_n^{*0}, r_1^{*1}, \ldots, r_n^{*1} \in \{0,1\}^\lambda$, $k_1^* \in \{0,1\}^\ell$, and $r_{\mathsf{SKE}}^* \in \mathcal{R}_{\mathsf{SKE}}$.
- $(\mathsf{ct}_i^{*v}, \mathsf{k}_i^{*v}) = \mathsf{Encap}(\mathsf{pk}^v; r_i^{*v})$ for all $(i, v) \in [n] \times \{0,1\}$.
- $\mathsf{ct}_{\mathsf{SKE}}^* = \mathsf{E}(s^*, (r_i^{*(s_i^*)})_{i \in [n]} \| k_1^*; r_{\mathsf{SKE}}^*)$ and $h^* = \mathsf{H}(\mathsf{hk}, (\mathsf{ct}_i^{*0}, \mathsf{ct}_i^{*1})_{i \in [n]} \| \mathsf{ct}_{\mathsf{SKE}}^*)$.

Let $\mathcal{C}$ be the ciphertext space of KEM. To define the notion of "badness" for a public key, we introduce two types of functions based on the above fixed values.

- For each $i \in \mathcal{S}_{\mathsf{zero}}$ and $v \in \{0,1\}$, we define the function $\hat{g}_{i,v} : \{0,1\}^\lambda \times \mathcal{C} \times (\{0,1\}^\lambda \setminus \{h^*\}) \to \{0,1\}^{4\lambda} \cup \{\bot\}$ by

$$\hat{g}_{i,v}(r, \mathsf{ct}', h) : \left[\begin{array}{l} (\mathsf{ct}, \mathsf{k}) \leftarrow \mathsf{Encap}(\mathsf{pk}^v; r); \quad \mathsf{k}' \leftarrow \mathsf{Decap}(\mathsf{sk}^{1-v}, \mathsf{ct}'); \\ \text{If } \mathsf{k}' = \bot \text{ then return } \bot \text{ else return } \frac{(\mathsf{k}-\mathsf{k}') \cdot (-1)^v - \mathsf{k}_i^{*0} + \mathsf{k}_i^{*1}}{h - h^*} \end{array} \right].$$

We say that a string $B \in \{0,1\}^{4\lambda}$ is *bad* if B belongs to the image of $\hat{g}_{i,v}$ for some $(i, v) \in \mathcal{S}_{\mathsf{zero}} \times \{0,1\}$. Due to the property that the image size of $\mathsf{Decap}(\mathsf{sk}^{1-v}, \cdot)$ is bounded by 2^λ, the image size of $\hat{g}_{i,v}$ (excluding $\bot$) is at most $2^{3\lambda}$ for every $i \in \mathcal{S}_{\mathsf{zero}}$ and $v \in \{0,1\}$. Hence, when choosing $B \xleftarrow{r} \{0,1\}^{4\lambda}$, the probability that B is bad is at most $|\mathcal{S}_{\mathsf{zero}}| \cdot 2 \cdot \frac{2^{3\lambda}}{2^{4\lambda}} = |\mathcal{S}_{\mathsf{zero}}| \cdot 2^{-\lambda+1}$.

- For each $B' \in \{0,1\}^{4\lambda}$ and $v \in \{0,1\}$, we define the function $g_{B',v} : \{0,1\}^\lambda \times \mathcal{C} \times \{0,1\}^\lambda \to \{0,1\}^{4\lambda} \cup \{\bot\}$ by

$$g_{B',v}(r, \mathsf{ct}', h) : \left[\begin{array}{l} (\mathsf{ct}, \mathsf{k}) \leftarrow \mathsf{Encap}(\mathsf{pk}^v; r); \quad \mathsf{k}' \leftarrow \mathsf{Decap}(\mathsf{sk}^{1-v}, \mathsf{ct}'); \\ \text{If } \mathsf{k}' = \bot \text{ then return } \bot \text{ else return } (\mathsf{k}-\mathsf{k}') \cdot (-1)^v - B' \cdot h \end{array} \right].$$

For each $B' \in \{0,1\}^{4\lambda}$, we say that a string $A' \in \{0,1\}^{4\lambda}$ is *bad with respect to* B' if A' belongs to the image of $g_{B',0}$ or that of $g_{B',1}$. Again, due to the property that the image size of $\mathsf{Decap}(\mathsf{sk}^{1-v}, \cdot)$ is bounded by 2^λ, the image size of $g_{B,v}$ (excluding $\bot$) is at most $2^{3\lambda}$ for every $B' \in \{0,1\}^{4\lambda}$ and $v \in \{0,1\}$. Hence, for any fixed $B' \in \{0,1\}^{4\lambda}$, when choosing $A_i \xleftarrow{r} \{0,1\}^{4\lambda}$ for all $i \in \mathcal{S}_{\mathsf{one}}$, the probability that some of $\{A_i\}_{i \in \mathcal{S}_{\mathsf{one}}}$ is bad with respect to B' is at most $|\mathcal{S}_{\mathsf{one}}| \cdot 2 \cdot \frac{2^{3\lambda}}{2^{4\lambda}} = |\mathcal{S}_{\mathsf{one}}| \cdot 2^{-\lambda+1}$.

We say that a public key PK generated in Game 3 is *bad* if (1) either pk^0 or pk^1 is erroneous, or (2) either B is bad or A_i for some $i \in \mathcal{S}_{\mathsf{one}}$ is bad with respect to B. By the union bound, the probability that PK is bad in Game 3 is bounded by $2\epsilon + |\mathcal{S}_{\mathsf{zero}}| \cdot 2^{-\lambda+1} + |\mathcal{S}_{\mathsf{one}}| \cdot 2^{-\lambda+1} = 2\epsilon + n \cdot 2^{-\lambda+1}$.

To complete the proof, below we show that if $\mathsf{PK} = (\mathsf{pk}^0, \mathsf{pk}^1, (A_i)_{i \in [n]}, B, \mathsf{hk})$ is not bad, then for any ciphertext $\mathsf{CT} = ((\mathsf{ct}_i^0, \mathsf{ct}_i^1, T_i)_{i \in [n]}, \mathsf{ct}_{\mathsf{SKE}})$ such that $h = \mathsf{H}(\mathsf{hk}, (\mathsf{ct}_i^0, \mathsf{ct}_i^1)_{i \in [n]} \| \mathsf{ct}_{\mathsf{SKE}}) \neq h^*$, we always have $\mathsf{Decap}_{\mathsf{cca}}(\mathsf{SK}, \mathsf{CT}) = \mathsf{AltDecap}(\mathsf{SK}', \mathsf{CT})$.

Let $\mathsf{CT} = ((\mathsf{ct}_i^0, \mathsf{ct}_i^1, T_i)_{i \in [n]}, \mathsf{ct}_{\mathsf{SKE}})$ be an arbitrary ciphertext satisfying $h = \mathsf{H}(\mathsf{hk}, (\mathsf{ct}_i^0, \mathsf{ct}_i^1)_{i \in [n]} \| \mathsf{ct}_{\mathsf{SKE}}) \neq h^*$. For each $i \in [n]$, define

$$s_i := 1 - \left(\mathsf{Decap}(\mathsf{sk}^0, \mathsf{ct}_i^0) \stackrel{?}{=} T_i \right), \quad \text{and}$$

$$s_i' := \left(\mathsf{Decap}(\mathsf{sk}^1, \mathsf{ct}_i^1) \stackrel{?}{=} T_i - A_i - B \cdot h \right).$$

We consider two cases and show that $\mathsf{Decap}_{\mathsf{cca}}(\mathsf{SK}, \mathsf{CT}) = \mathsf{AltDecap}(\mathsf{SK}', \mathsf{CT})$ holds in either case.

- **Case 1: For all positions $i \in [n]$, there exists a pair $(\mathsf{r}, v) \in \{0,1\}^\lambda \times \{0,1\}$ satisfying $\mathsf{Encap}(\mathsf{pk}^v; \mathsf{r}) = (\mathsf{ct}_i^v, \mathsf{T}_i - v \cdot (\mathsf{A}_i + \mathsf{B} \cdot \mathsf{h}))$.**
  In this case, we show that $\mathsf{s}_i = \mathsf{s}_i'$ holds for all $i \in [n]$. This in turn implies that the output of $\mathsf{Decap}_{\mathsf{cca}}$ and that of $\mathsf{AltDecap}$ agree since these algorithms proceed identically after they respectively compute s.
  Fix $i \in [n]$. The condition of this case directly implies $\mathsf{Decap}(\mathsf{sk}^v, \mathsf{ct}_i^v) = \mathsf{T}_i - v \cdot (\mathsf{A}_i + \mathsf{B} \cdot \mathsf{h})$. This in turn implies that if $v = 0$ then we have $\mathsf{s}_i = 0$, while if $v = 1$ then we have $\mathsf{s}_i' = 1$. In the following, we will show that

$$\mathsf{k}' := \mathsf{Decap}(\mathsf{sk}^{1-v}, \mathsf{ct}_i^{1-v}) \neq \mathsf{T}_i - (1 - v) \cdot (\mathsf{A}_i + \mathsf{B} \cdot \mathsf{h}) \tag{5}$$

  holds, which implies that if $v = 0$ then we have $\mathsf{s}_i' = 0$, while if $v = 1$ then we have $\mathsf{s}_i = 1$. Hence, combined together, we will obtain the desired conclusion $\mathsf{s}_i = \mathsf{s}_i'$ (regardless of the value of v). Also, if $\mathsf{k}' = \bot$, then Eq. 5 is obviously satisfied. Thus, below we consider the case $\mathsf{k}' \neq \bot$.
  The argument for showing Eq. 5 differs depending on whether $i \in \mathcal{S}_{\mathsf{zero}}$ or $i \in \mathcal{S}_{\mathsf{one}}$. If $i \in \mathcal{S}_{\mathsf{zero}}$, then since B is not bad, it is not in the image of $\hat{g}_{i,v}$. Hence, we have

$$\mathsf{B} \neq \hat{g}_{i,v}(\mathsf{r}, \mathsf{ct}_i^{1-v}, \mathsf{h}) = \frac{\left(\mathsf{T}_i - v \cdot (\mathsf{A}_i + \mathsf{B} \cdot \mathsf{h}) - \mathsf{k}'\right) \cdot (-1)^v - \mathsf{k}_i^{*0} + \mathsf{k}_i^{*1}}{\mathsf{h} - \mathsf{h}^*}$$

$$\Longleftrightarrow \quad \mathsf{k}' \neq \mathsf{T}_i - v \cdot (\mathsf{A}_i + \mathsf{B} \cdot \mathsf{h}) - (-1)^v \cdot \left((\mathsf{k}_i^{*0} - \mathsf{k}_i^{*1} - \mathsf{B} \cdot \mathsf{h}^*) + \mathsf{B} \cdot \mathsf{h}\right)$$

$$\overset{(*)}{=} \mathsf{T}_i - \left(v + (-1)^v\right) \cdot (\mathsf{A}_i + \mathsf{B} \cdot \mathsf{h}) \overset{(**)}{=} \mathsf{T}_i - (1 - v) \cdot (\mathsf{A}_i + \mathsf{B} \cdot \mathsf{h}),$$

  where the equality $(*)$ uses $\mathsf{A}_i = \mathsf{k}_i^{*0} - \mathsf{k}_i^{*1} - \mathsf{B} \cdot \mathsf{h}^*$, which is how A_i is generated for the positions $i \in \mathcal{S}_{\mathsf{zero}}$ in Game 3; The equality $(**)$ is due to $v + (-1)^v = 1 - v$ for $v \in \{0,1\}$.
  Similarly, if $i \in \mathcal{S}_{\mathsf{one}}$, then since A_i is not bad with respect to B, it is not in the image of $g_{\mathsf{B},v}$. Hence, we have

$$\mathsf{A}_i \neq g_{\mathsf{B},v}(\mathsf{r}, \mathsf{ct}_i^{1-v}, \mathsf{h}) = \left(\mathsf{T}_i - v \cdot (\mathsf{A}_i + \mathsf{B} \cdot \mathsf{h}) - \mathsf{k}'\right) \cdot (-1)^v - \mathsf{B} \cdot \mathsf{h}$$

$$\Longleftrightarrow \quad \mathsf{k}' \neq \mathsf{T}_i - v \cdot (\mathsf{A}_i + \mathsf{B} \cdot \mathsf{h}) - (-1)^v \cdot (\mathsf{A}_i + \mathsf{B} \cdot \mathsf{h})$$

$$= \mathsf{T}_i - \left(v + (-1)^v\right) \cdot (\mathsf{A}_i + \mathsf{B} \cdot \mathsf{h}) = \mathsf{T}_i - (1 - v) \cdot (\mathsf{A}_i + \mathsf{B} \cdot \mathsf{h}),$$

  where the last equality is again due to $v + (-1)^v = 1 - v$ for $v \in \{0,1\}$.
  We have seen that $\mathsf{Decap}(\mathsf{sk}^{1-v}, \mathsf{ct}_i^{1-v}) \neq \mathsf{T}_i - (1 - v) \cdot (\mathsf{A}_i + \mathsf{B} \cdot \mathsf{h})$ holds regardless of whether $i \in \mathcal{S}_{\mathsf{zero}}$ or $i \in \mathcal{S}_{\mathsf{one}}$, as required. Hence, as mentioned earlier, $\mathsf{s}_i = \mathsf{s}_i'$ holds for all $i \in [n]$, and consequently we have $\mathsf{Decap}_{\mathsf{cca}}(\mathsf{SK}, \mathsf{CT}) = \mathsf{AltDecap}(\mathsf{SK}', \mathsf{CT})$.
- **Case 2: There exists a position $i \in [n]$ for which there exists no pair $(\mathsf{r}, v) \in \{0,1\}^\lambda \times \{0,1\}$ satisfying $\mathsf{Encap}(\mathsf{pk}^v; \mathsf{r}) = (\mathsf{ct}_i^v, \mathsf{T}_i - v \cdot (\mathsf{A}_i + \mathsf{B} \cdot \mathsf{h}))$.**

In this case, both $\mathsf{Decap}_{\mathsf{cca}}$ and $\mathsf{AltDecap}$ return $\perp$. Indeed, the condition of this case implies that there exists a position $i \in [n]$ for which there exists no $\mathsf{r} \in \{0,1\}^\lambda$ satisfying $\mathsf{Encap}(\mathsf{pk}^{\mathsf{s}_i}; \mathsf{r}) = (\mathsf{ct}_i^{\mathsf{s}_i}, \mathsf{T}_i - \mathsf{s}_i \cdot (\mathsf{A}_i + \mathsf{B} \cdot \mathsf{h}))$. Hence, the validity check done in the last step of $\mathsf{Decap}_{\mathsf{cca}}$ cannot be satisfied at the position i, and thus $\mathsf{Decap}_{\mathsf{cca}}$ outputs $\perp$. Exactly the same argument applies to $\mathsf{AltDecap}$, and thus it also outputs $\perp$. Hence, in this case we have $\mathsf{Decap}_{\mathsf{cca}}(\mathsf{SK}, \mathsf{CT}) = \mathsf{AltDecap}(\mathsf{SK}', \mathsf{CT}) = \perp$.

As seen above, if PK is not bad, then for any CT with $\mathsf{h} \neq \mathsf{h}^*$, we have $\mathsf{Decap}_{\mathsf{cca}}(\mathsf{SK}, \mathsf{CT}) = \mathsf{AltDecap}(\mathsf{SK}', \mathsf{CT})$, as desired. $\square$ (**Lemma** 3)

Lemma 4. *There exists a PPT adversary* $\mathcal{B}_{\mathsf{cpa}}^4$ *such that* $|\Pr[\mathsf{SUC}_4] - \Pr[\mathsf{SUC}_5]| = \mathsf{Adv}_{\mathsf{KEM}, n, \mathcal{B}_{\mathsf{cpa}}^4}^{\mathsf{mcpa}}(\lambda)$.

With a similar reason to for Lemma 2 above, from $\mathcal{A}$, we can construct a PPT adversary $\mathcal{B}_{\mathsf{cpa}}^4$ that attacks the IND-CPA security of KEM under the key pk^0 with the advantage stated in the lemma. For the formal proof, see the full version [29].

Lemma 5. *There exists a PPT adversary* $\mathcal{B}_{\mathsf{kdm}}$ *that makes a single KDM-encryption query and satisfies* $|\Pr[\mathsf{SUC}_5] - \Pr[\mathsf{SUC}_6]| = \mathsf{Adv}_{\mathsf{SKE}, \mathcal{P}, \mathcal{B}_{\mathsf{kdm}}}^{\mathsf{kdm}}(\lambda)$.

In Games 5 and 6, s^* is used only when generating $\mathsf{ct}_{\mathsf{SKE}}^*$. Furthermore, we can regard the message $(\mathsf{r}_i^{*(\mathsf{s}_i^*)})_{i \in [n]} \| \mathsf{k}_1^*$ encrypted in $\mathsf{ct}_{\mathsf{SKE}}^*$ as an output of a projection function of s^*. Thus, from $\mathcal{A}$, we can straightforwardly construct a PPT adversary $\mathcal{B}_{\mathsf{kdm}}$ that attacks the one-time $\mathcal{P}$-KDM security of SKE with the advantage stated in the lemma. For the formal proof, see the full version [29].

Lemma 6. $\Pr[\mathsf{SUC}_6] = 1/2$ *holds.*

Proof of Lemma 6. This lemma is true because in Game 6, the information of the challenge bit b is completely erased from $\mathcal{A}$'s view. $\square$ (**Lemma** 6)

   Due to Lemmas 1 to 6 and Eq. 3, we can conclude that there exist PPT adversaries $\mathcal{B}_{\mathsf{tcr}}$, $\{\mathcal{B}_{\mathsf{cpa}}^j\}_{j \in [4]}$, $\mathcal{B}_{\mathsf{cpa}}'$, and $\mathcal{B}_{\mathsf{kdm}}$ (that makes a single KDM-encryption query) satisfying Eq. 1, as desired. $\square$ (**Theorem** 2)

5   Impossibility of Shielding Black-Box Constructions

Gertner et al. [21] showed that there exists no shielding black-box construction of an IND-CCA1 secure PKE scheme from an IND-CPA secure one. Recall that a shielding black-box construction of a PKE scheme $\mathsf{PKE} = (\mathsf{KG}, \mathsf{Enc}, \mathsf{Dec})$ from another PKE scheme $\mathsf{pke} = (\mathsf{kg}, \mathsf{enc}, \mathsf{dec})$ is such that the decryption algorithm Dec in PKE does *not* use the encryption algorithm enc of pke. Put differently, we have $\mathsf{PKE}^{\mathsf{pke}} = (\mathsf{KG}^{\mathsf{kg}, \mathsf{enc}, \mathsf{dec}}, \mathsf{Enc}^{\mathsf{kg}, \mathsf{enc}, \mathsf{dec}}, \mathsf{Dec}^{\mathsf{kg}, \mathsf{dec}})$.

   In this section, we extend Gertner et al.'s result and show the following result.

Theorem 4. *There exists no shielding black-box construction of an IND-CCA1 secure PKE scheme from a $\mathcal{P}$-KDM secure PKE scheme.*

This theorem is proved as a corollary of Theorems 5 and 6 stated below.

We emphasize that this result does not contradict our result in Sect. 4.1 (in particular, Corollary 2), because our construction $\mathsf{KEM}_{\mathsf{cca}}$ is a non-shielding black-box construction in which the decapsulation algorithm $\mathsf{Decap}_{\mathsf{cca}}$ uses the encapsulation algorithm Encap of the underlying IND-CPA secure KEM.

We also note that our result seems incomparable to a similar result by Hajiabadi and Kapron [24], who showed that a PKE scheme satisfying a form of *randomness-dependent-message (RDM) security* is a primitive from which a non-shielding black-box construction of an IND-CCA secure PKE scheme is possible while shielding black-box constructions of an IND-CCA1 secure PKE scheme are impossible. (We note that they used a tailored definition of RDM security that is different from the original definition by Birrell, Chung, Pass, and Telang [8].[4])

Our impossibility of shielding black-box constructions is shown based largely on the framework and technique of [21] and the technique of [24]. Informally, [21] defined a distribution $\mathbf{\Phi}$ of an oracle $\mathbf{O} = (\mathbf{O}_1, \mathbf{O}_2)$ such that $\mathbf{O}_1$ syntactically constitutes a PKE scheme, $\mathbf{O}_2$ is an attacker's "breaking" oracle, and they showed that the following two items hold with high probability over the choice of $\mathbf{O} = (\mathbf{O}_1, \mathbf{O}_2) \leftarrow \mathbf{\Phi}$:

1. $\mathbf{O}_1$ constitutes an IND-CPA secure PKE scheme against any computationally unbounded adversary $\mathcal{A}^{\mathbf{O}_1, \mathbf{O}_2}$ that makes polynomially many queries.
2. The IND-CCA1 security of any candidate shielding black-box construction $\mathsf{PKE}^{\mathbf{O}_1}$ is broken (with more than a constant advantage) by some computationally unbounded adversary $\mathcal{A}'^{\mathbf{O}_1, \mathbf{O}_2}$ with polynomially many queries.

These two items imply (via a standard argument used in black-box separation results) the impossibility of shielding black-box constructions of an IND-CCA1 secure PKE scheme from an IND-CPA secure one.

Since we use exactly the same distribution $\mathbf{\Phi}$ of oracles $\mathbf{O}$ used by Gertner et al., and the second item was already shown by them, for our result, we only need to prove an extension of the first item, namely, $\mathbf{O}_1$ constitutes a $\mathcal{P}$-KDM secure PKE scheme with high probability over the choice of $\mathbf{O} = (\mathbf{O}_1, \mathbf{O}_2) \leftarrow \mathbf{\Phi}$.

In the following, we first recall the definition of the distribution $\mathbf{\Phi}$ of oracles $\mathbf{O}$ used by Gertner et al., then state their result corresponding to the item 2 above. Finally, we state our result corresponding to the item 1 above.

---

[4] Roughly speaking, RDM security used by Hajiabadi and Kapron requires that n ciphertexts encrypting the bit-decomposition of $\mathsf{r} = (\mathsf{r}_1, \ldots, \mathsf{r}_n)$ are indistinguishable from n ciphertexts that all encrypt 0 even if they are all encrypted under the same random coin r itself. In the actual definition, an adversary is given multiple sets of the above n ciphertexts. This setting is somewhat unnatural in the usage of PKE, and a PKE scheme satisfying this security notion immediately implies a TDF with one-wayness under correlated products.

Definition 5 (Oracle Distribution for Separation [21]). *Consider an oracle $\mathbf{O}$ consisting of the suboracles $(\mathbf{g}, \mathbf{e}, \mathbf{d}, \mathbf{w}, \mathbf{u})$ that are defined for each length parameter $n \in \mathbb{N}$ and satisfy the following syntax[5]:*

$\mathbf{g} : \{0,1\}^n \rightarrow \{0,1\}^{3n}$**:** *This is an injective function. This oracle can be thought of as the key generation process that takes a secret key $\mathsf{sk} \in \{0,1\}^n$ as input and outputs a public key $\mathsf{pk} \in \{0,1\}^{3n}$.*

$\mathbf{e} : \{0,1\}^{3n} \times \{0,1\} \times \{0,1\}^n \rightarrow \{0,1\}^{3n}$**:** *For each $\mathsf{pk} \in \{0,1\}^{3n}$, $\mathbf{e}(\mathsf{pk}, \cdot, \cdot) : \{0,1\} \times \{0,1\}^n \rightarrow \{0,1\}^{3n}$ is an injective function. This oracle can be thought of as the encryption process that takes a public key $\mathsf{pk} \in \{0,1\}^{3n}$, a plaintext $\mathsf{m} \in \{0,1\}$, and a randomness $\mathsf{r} \in \{0,1\}^n$ as input, and outputs a ciphertext $\mathsf{ct} \in \{0,1\}^{3n}$.*

$\mathbf{d} : \{0,1\}^n \times \{0,1\}^{3n} \rightarrow \{0,1,\bot\}$**:** *This oracle takes $\mathsf{sk} \in \{0,1\}^n$ and $\mathsf{ct} \in \{0,1\}^{3n}$ as input, and if there exists $(\mathsf{pk}, \mathsf{m}, \mathsf{r}) \in \{0,1\}^{3n} \times \{0,1\} \times \{0,1\}^n$ such that $\mathsf{pk} = \mathbf{g}(\mathsf{sk})$ and $\mathsf{ct} = \mathbf{e}(\mathsf{pk}, \mathsf{m}, \mathsf{r})$, then it outputs m. Otherwise, this oracle outputs $\bot$. This oracle can be thought of as the decryption process.*

$\mathbf{w} : \{0,1\}^{3n} \times \{0,1\}^n \rightarrow \{0,1\}^{3n \times n} \cup \{\bot\}$**:** *This oracle is associated with a "randomness deriving" function $F_{\mathbf{w}} : \{0,1\}^{3n} \times \{0,1\}^n \rightarrow \{0,1\}^{n \times n}$.[6] This oracle takes $\mathsf{pk} \in \{0,1\}^{3n}$ and an index $z \in \{0,1\}^n$ as input, and if there exists no $\mathsf{sk} \in \{0,1\}^n$ such that $\mathsf{pk} = \mathbf{g}(\mathsf{sk})$, then the oracle outputs $\bot$. Otherwise, let $\mathsf{sk} = (\mathsf{s}_1, \ldots, \mathsf{s}_n) \in \{0,1\}^n$ be such that $\mathsf{pk} = \mathbf{g}(\mathsf{sk})$. The oracle computes $(\mathsf{r}_1, \ldots, \mathsf{r}_n) \leftarrow F_{\mathbf{w}}(\mathsf{pk}, z)$, and then $\mathsf{ct}_i \leftarrow \mathbf{e}(\mathsf{pk}, \mathsf{s}_i, \mathsf{r}_i)$ for every $i \in [n]$. Finally, the oracle outputs $(\mathsf{ct}_i)_{i \in [n]}$. This oracle is a "weakening" oracle that helps breaking the IND-CCA1 security of any shielding construction.*

$\mathbf{u} : \{0,1\}^{3n} \times \{0,1\}^{3n} \rightarrow \{\top, \bot\}$**:** *This oracle takes $\mathsf{pk} \in \{0,1\}^{3n}$ and $\mathsf{ct} \in \{0,1\}^{3n}$ as input, and if there exists $(\mathsf{sk}, \mathsf{m}, \mathsf{r}) \in \{0,1\}^n \times \{0,1\} \times \{0,1\}^n$ such that $\mathsf{pk} = \mathbf{g}(\mathsf{sk})$ and $\mathsf{ct} = \mathbf{e}(\mathsf{pk}, \mathsf{m}, \mathsf{r})$, then the oracle outputs $\top$. Otherwise, the oracle outputs $\bot$. This oracle can be thought of as the validity checking process of a ciphertext ct with respect to a public key pk.*

We define the distribution Φ of an oracle $\mathbf{O} = (\mathbf{g}, \mathbf{e}, \mathbf{d}, \mathbf{w}, \mathbf{u})$ as follows: For each $n \in \mathbb{N}$, pick $\mathbf{g}$, $\mathbf{e}$, and $F_{\mathbf{w}}$ uniformly at random, and then define $\mathbf{d}$, $\mathbf{w}$, and $\mathbf{u}$ satisfying the above syntax.[7]

Note that $(\mathbf{g}, \mathbf{e}, \mathbf{d})$ in $\mathbf{O}$ naturally constitutes a 1-bit PKE scheme. Gertner et al. [21] showed the following result, which states that with high probability over $\mathbf{O} \leftarrow \Phi$, the IND-CCA1 security of any candidate shielding black-box construction from the PKE $(\mathbf{g}, \mathbf{e}, \mathbf{d})$ (defined in $\mathbf{O}$) is broken with more than a constant advantage by some adversary making polynomially many queries.

Theorem 5 (Corollary of Theorem 2 in [21]). *Let $\mathsf{PKE} = (\mathsf{KG}, \mathsf{Enc}, \mathsf{Dec})$ be a shielding construction of a 1-bit PKE scheme based on another 1-bit PKE*

---

[5] Among $\mathbf{O} = (\mathbf{g}, \mathbf{e}, \mathbf{d}, \mathbf{w}, \mathbf{u})$, $(\mathbf{g}, \mathbf{e}, \mathbf{d})$ (resp. $(\mathbf{w}, \mathbf{u})$) corresponds to $\mathbf{O}_1$ (resp. $\mathbf{O}_2$) in the above explanation.

[6] The purpose of $F_{\mathbf{w}}$ is to make $\mathbf{w}$ deterministic (after chosen according to the distribution Φ). When an oracle $\mathbf{O}$ is chosen from Φ, $F_{\mathbf{w}}$ will work as a truly random function. This treatment is done implicitly in [21].

[7] Note that the behavior of $\mathbf{O}$ is completely determined by $\mathbf{g}$, $\mathbf{e}$, and $F_{\mathbf{w}}$ used in $\mathbf{w}$.

scheme. For each $\mathbf{O} = (\mathbf{g}, \mathbf{e}, \mathbf{d}, \mathbf{w}, \mathbf{u}) \in \mathsf{Sup}(\Phi)$, *let* $\mathsf{PKE}^{\mathbf{g},\mathbf{e},\mathbf{d}} := (\mathsf{KG}^{\mathbf{g},\mathbf{e},\mathbf{d}}, \mathsf{Enc}^{\mathbf{g},\mathbf{e},\mathbf{d}}, \mathsf{Dec}^{\mathbf{g},\mathbf{d}})$. *Then, there exists a computationally unbounded adversary* $\mathcal{A}$ *that makes at most polynomially many queries and satisfies the following for all sufficiently large* $\lambda \in \mathbb{N}$:

$$\Pr_{\mathbf{O}=(\mathbf{g},\mathbf{e},\mathbf{d},\mathbf{w},\mathbf{u})\leftarrow\Phi}\left[\mathsf{Adv}_{\mathsf{PKE}^{\mathbf{g},\mathbf{e},\mathbf{d}},\mathcal{A}^{\mathbf{O}}}^{\mathsf{cca1}}(\lambda) \geq \frac{1}{2}\right] \geq 1 - \frac{4}{\lambda}.$$

We now show our theorem, which states that with overwhelming probability over the choice of $\mathbf{O} \leftarrow \Phi$, $(\mathbf{g}, \mathbf{e}, \mathbf{d})$ constitutes a 1-bit $\mathcal{P}$-KDM secure PKE scheme (secure in the presence of multiple KDM-encryption queries). Since the bit-by-bit encryption preserves $\mathcal{P}$-KDM security, the existence of a 1-bit (many-time) $\mathcal{P}$-KDM secure PKE scheme implies a $\mathcal{P}$-KDM secure PKE scheme that can encrypt plaintexts of arbitrary length in the black-box sense.

Theorem 6. *For any computationally unbounded adversary* $\mathcal{A}$ *that makes at most polynomially many queries, there exist negligible functions* $\mu(\cdot)$ *and* $\mu'(\cdot)$ *such that for all sufficiently large* $\lambda \in \mathbb{N}$, *we have*

$$\Pr_{\mathbf{O}=(\mathbf{g},\mathbf{e},\mathbf{d},\mathbf{w},\mathbf{u})\leftarrow\Phi}\left[\mathsf{Adv}_{(\mathbf{g},\mathbf{e},\mathbf{d}),\mathcal{P},\mathcal{A}^{\mathbf{O}}}^{\mathsf{kdm}}(\lambda) \leq \mu(\lambda)\right] \geq 1 - \mu'(\lambda).$$

We remark that Theorems 5 and 6 imply Theorem 4 via a standard technique in black-box separation results (using the Borel-Cantelli lemma) (see, e.g. [25]).

Due to the space limitation, the proof of Theorem 4 is given in the full version of this paper [29], and here we give its overview. We call the $\mathcal{P}$-KDM security experiment of the PKE scheme $(\mathbf{g}, \mathbf{e}, \mathbf{d})$ that takes into account the choice $\mathbf{O} = (\mathbf{g}, \mathbf{e}, \mathbf{d}, \mathbf{w}, \mathbf{u}) \leftarrow \Phi$ the *extended KDM security experiment*. Let $\mathcal{A}$ be any computationally unbounded adversary that makes $q = q(\lambda) = \mathsf{poly}(\lambda)$ queries. To prove the theorem, it is sufficient to show that the advantage of $\mathcal{A}^{\mathbf{O},\mathcal{O}_{\mathsf{kdm}}}$ in the extended KDM security experiment is negligible. This is shown by two steps. In the first step, we show that among the suboracles given access to $\mathcal{A}$, $\mathbf{d}$, $\mathbf{w}$, and $\mathbf{u}$ do not help $\mathcal{A}$ much. More specifically, we essentially show that for $\mathcal{A}^{\mathbf{O},\mathcal{O}_{\mathsf{kdm}}}$, there exists another computationally unbounded adversary $\mathcal{B}^{\mathbf{g},\mathbf{e},\mathcal{O}_{\mathsf{kdm}}}$ that make at most $\mathsf{poly}(q)$ queries and whose advantage in the extended KDM experiment is negligibly close to that of $\mathcal{A}$'s. Then, in the second step, we show that the advantage of $\mathcal{B}^{\mathbf{g},\mathbf{e},\mathcal{O}_{\mathsf{kdm}}}$ in the extended KDM experiment is negligible by relying on the property that the suboracles $\mathbf{g}(\cdot)$ and $\mathbf{e}(\mathsf{pk}, \cdot, \cdot)$ for each pk are random (almost) length-tripling injective functions when chosen according to Φ.

6   TDF via KDM Security

In this section, we show our proposed TDF with adaptive one-wayness, which is an extension of our IND-CCA secure KEM presented in Sect. 4.

Construction. Let $\ell = \ell(\lambda)$ be a polynomial. Our TDF uses the building blocks KEM, SKE, and Hash with the following properties:

- $\mathsf{KEM} = (\mathsf{KKG}, \mathsf{Encap}, \mathsf{Decap})$ is a KEM such that (1) its session key space is $\{0,1\}^{3\lambda}$, (2) the randomness space of Encap is $\{0,1\}^{\lambda}$, and (3) the ciphertext space $\mathcal{C}$ forms an abelian group (where we use the additive notation) and satisfies $|\mathcal{C}| \geq 2^{2\lambda}$.
- $\mathsf{SKE} = (\mathsf{K}, \mathsf{E}, \mathsf{D})$ is an SKE scheme such that (1) it has the randomness-recovering decryption property (with the randomness-recovering decryption algorithm RD), (2) its secret key space is $\{0,1\}^n$ for some polynomial $n = n(\lambda)$, and (3) the plaintext space is $\{0,1\}^{n\cdot\lambda+\ell}$.
  We denote the randomness space of E by $\mathcal{R}_{\mathsf{SKE}}$.
- $\mathsf{Hash} = (\mathsf{HKG}, \mathsf{H})$ is a keyed hash function such that the range of H is $\{0,1\}^{\lambda}$, which we are going to assume to be target collision resistant.

Using these building blocks, the proposed TDF $\mathsf{TDF} = (\mathsf{Setup}, \mathsf{Samp}, \mathsf{Eval}, \mathsf{Inv})$ is constructed as described in Fig. 4. The domain $\mathcal{X}$ of TDF is $\mathcal{X} = \{0,1\}^n \times \{0,1\}^{n\cdot\lambda} \times \{0,1\}^{\ell} \times \mathcal{R}_{\mathsf{SKE}}$.

For the correctness and security of TDF, the following theorems hold.

$\mathsf{Setup}(1^{\lambda})$:	$\mathsf{Samp}(1^{\lambda})$:
$\forall v \in \{0,1\} : (\mathsf{pk}^v, \mathsf{sk}^v) \leftarrow \mathsf{KKG}(1^{\lambda})$	$\mathsf{s} = (\mathsf{s}_1, \ldots, \mathsf{s}_n) \leftarrow \mathsf{K}(1^{\lambda})$
$A_1, \ldots, A_n, B \xleftarrow{r} \{0,1\}^{3\lambda}$	$r_1^{\mathsf{s}_1}, \ldots, r_n^{\mathsf{s}_n} \xleftarrow{r} \{0,1\}^{\lambda}$
$C_1, \ldots, C_n \xleftarrow{r} \mathcal{C}$	$\mathsf{k} \xleftarrow{r} \{0,1\}^{\ell}$
$\mathsf{hk} \leftarrow \mathsf{HKG}(1^{\lambda})$	Sample $r_{\mathsf{SKE}} \in \mathcal{R}_{\mathsf{SKE}}$
$\mathsf{ek} \leftarrow (\mathsf{pk}^0, \mathsf{pk}^1, (A_i, C_i)_{i \in [n]}, B, \mathsf{hk})$	$\qquad\qquad$ in the same way as in E.
$\mathsf{td} \leftarrow (\mathsf{sk}^0, \mathsf{ek})$	Return $\mathsf{x} \leftarrow (\mathsf{s}, (r_i^{\mathsf{s}_i})_{i \in [n]}, \mathsf{k}, r_{\mathsf{SKE}})$.
Return $(\mathsf{ek}, \mathsf{td})$.	
$\mathsf{Eval}(\mathsf{ek}, \mathsf{x})$:	$\mathsf{Inv}(\mathsf{td}, \mathsf{y})$:
$(\mathsf{pk}^0, \mathsf{pk}^1, (A_i, C_i)_{i \in [n]}, B, \mathsf{hk}) \leftarrow \mathsf{ek}$	$(\mathsf{sk}^0, \mathsf{ek}) \leftarrow \mathsf{td}$
$(\mathsf{s} = (\mathsf{s}_1, \ldots, \mathsf{s}_n), (r_i^{\mathsf{s}_i})_{i \in [n]}, \mathsf{k}, r_{\mathsf{SKE}}) \leftarrow \mathsf{x}$	$(\mathsf{pk}^0, \mathsf{pk}^1, (A_i, C_i)_{i \in [n]}, B, \mathsf{hk}) \leftarrow \mathsf{ek}$
$\mathsf{ct}_{\mathsf{SKE}} \leftarrow \mathsf{E}(\mathsf{s}, (r_i^{\mathsf{s}_i})_{i \in [n]} \| \mathsf{k}; r_{\mathsf{SKE}})$	$((\mathsf{ct}_i, T_i)_{i \in [n]}, \mathsf{ct}_{\mathsf{SKE}}) \leftarrow \mathsf{y}$
$\forall i \in [n] :$	$h \leftarrow \mathsf{H}(\mathsf{hk}, (\mathsf{ct}_i)_{i \in [n]} \| \mathsf{ct}_{\mathsf{SKE}})$
$\quad (\mathsf{ct}_i^{\mathsf{s}_i}, k_i^{\mathsf{s}_i}) \leftarrow \mathsf{Encap}(\mathsf{pk}^{\mathsf{s}_i}; r_i^{\mathsf{s}_i})$	$\forall i \in [n] :$
$\quad \mathsf{ct}_i \leftarrow \mathsf{ct}_i^{\mathsf{s}_i} + \mathsf{s}_i \cdot C_i \quad$ (‡)	$\quad \mathsf{s}_i \leftarrow 1 - (\mathsf{Decap}(\mathsf{sk}^0, \mathsf{ct}_i) \stackrel{?}{=} T_i) \quad$ (⋆)
$\qquad = \begin{cases} \mathsf{ct}_i^0 & \text{if } \mathsf{s}_i = 0 \\ \mathsf{ct}_i^1 + C_i & \text{if } \mathsf{s}_i = 1 \end{cases}$	$\qquad = \begin{cases} 0 & \text{if } \mathsf{Decap}(\mathsf{sk}^0, \mathsf{ct}_i) = T_i \\ 1 & \text{otherwise} \end{cases}$
$h \leftarrow \mathsf{H}(\mathsf{hk}, (\mathsf{ct}_i)_{i \in [n]} \| \mathsf{ct}_{\mathsf{SKE}})$	$\mathsf{s} \leftarrow (\mathsf{s}_1, \ldots, \mathsf{s}_n) \in \{0,1\}^n$
$\forall i \in [n] :$	$(m, r_{\mathsf{SKE}}) \leftarrow \mathsf{RD}(\mathsf{s}, \mathsf{ct}_{\mathsf{SKE}})$
$\quad T_i \leftarrow k_i^{\mathsf{s}_i} + \mathsf{s}_i \cdot (A_i + B \cdot h) \quad$ (†)	Parse m as $(r_i^{\mathsf{s}_i})_{i \in [n]} \in \{0,1\}^{n\cdot\lambda}$
$\qquad = \begin{cases} k_i^0 & \text{if } \mathsf{s}_i = 0 \\ k_i^1 + A_i + B \cdot h & \text{if } \mathsf{s}_i = 1 \end{cases}$	$\qquad\qquad$ and $\mathsf{k} \in \{0,1\}^{\ell}$.
Return $\mathsf{y} \leftarrow ((\mathsf{ct}_i, T_i)_{i \in [n]}, \mathsf{ct}_{\mathsf{SKE}})$.	$\mathsf{x} \leftarrow (\mathsf{s}, (r_i^{\mathsf{s}_i})_{i \in [n]}, \mathsf{k}, r_{\mathsf{SKE}})$
	If $\mathsf{Eval}(\mathsf{ek}, \mathsf{x}) = \mathsf{y}$
	$\qquad$ then return x else return $\bot$.

Fig. 4. The proposed TDF TDF. (†) $h \in \{0,1\}^{\lambda}$ is treated as an element of $\{0,1\}^{3\lambda}$ by some canonical injective encoding (say, putting the prefix $0^{2\lambda}$), and the arithmetic is done over $\mathrm{GF}(2^{3\lambda})$ where we identify $\{0,1\}^{3\lambda}$ with $\mathrm{GF}(2^{3\lambda})$. (‡) The addition is done over $\mathcal{C}$. (⋆) We call this step the *find step*.

Theorem 7. *Let* $\epsilon = \epsilon(\lambda) \in [0,1]$. *If* KEM *is* ϵ-*almost-all-keys correct and* SKE *has the randomness-recovering decryption property, then* TDF *is* $(\epsilon + n \cdot 2^{-\lambda})$-*almost-all-keys correct.*

Theorem 8. *Assume that* KEM *satisfies the pseudorandom ciphertext property and almost-all-keys correctness,* SKE *is one-time* $\mathcal{P}$-*KDM secure, and* Hash *is target collision resistant. Then,* TDF *is adaptively one-way.*

The proofs of Theorems 7 and 8 are given in the full version [29]. Other than using additional properties of the building blocks, the proofs for the above theorems go similarly to those for our IND-CCA secure KEM in Sect. 4.

Adaptively One-Way TDFs Based on the LPN Assumptions. By instantiating the building blocks in our construction TDF properly, we obtain the first adaptively one-way TDF based on the sub-exponential hardness of the *constant-noise* LPN problem. We note that previously, even a TDF with ordinary one-wayness was not known based on the constant-noise LPN assumption. Specifically, the following LPN-based building blocks can be used.

- For KEM, we use the KEM-analogue of the IND-CPA secure PKE scheme based on the sub-exponential hardness of the constant-noise LPN problem proposed by Yu and Zhang [42]. Their security analysis in fact shows that it satisfies the pseudorandom ciphertext property. However, the scheme does not satisfy almost-all-keys correctness as it is. Thus, we apply the transformation by Dwork, Naor, and Reingold [18] that transforms any PKE scheme whose correctness is imperfect into one with almost-all-keys correctness. (This transformation preserves the pseudorandom ciphertext property of the underlying scheme.)
- For SKE, we can use the $\mathcal{P}$-KDM secure SKE scheme proposed by Applebaum et al. [3] based on the (polynomial) hardness of the constant-noise LPN problem. Their scheme clearly admits the randomness-recovering decryption property. In particular, whenever a plaintext is recovered in the decryption, the decryptor can also compute the "noise" used in the encryption process, which is the only encryption randomness of this scheme. In addition, their scheme can be easily made perfectly correct.

Moreover, we can also obtain the first adaptively one-way TDF based on the (polynomial) hardness of the *low-noise* LPN problem, by replacing the Yu-Zhang scheme in the above instantiation with the existing PKE schemes based on the low-noise LPN assumption [1,17,26] (which all satisfy the pseudorandom ciphertext property). Previously, a TDF satisfying ordinary one-wayness based on the low-noise LPN assumption was proposed by Kiltz, Masny, and Pietrzak [26].

Flexible Hard-Core Bits k. We note that $k \in \{0,1\}^{\ell}$ can be directly used as hardcore bits of an input $x = (s = (s_1, \ldots, s_n), (r_i^{s_i})_{i \in [n]}, k, r_{SKE})$, even in the presence of the inversion oracle. Its proof is a straightforward extension of the proof of

Theorem 8, and thus omitted. Since an adaptively one-way TDF with ℓ-bit hard-core bits can be seen as an IND-CCA secure KEM with session-key space $\{0,1\}^\ell$, TDF can be viewed as an IND-CCA secure KEM in which the randomness used to generate a ciphertext is fully recovered during the decapsulation.

Additional Remarks. We remark that due to the structural similarity of our construction TDF to $\mathsf{KEM_{cca}}$, several properties satisfied by $\mathsf{KEM_{cca}}$ are inherited to TDF. Specifically, as in the case of our IND-CCA secure KEM $\mathsf{KEM_{cca}}$, if we adopt the syntax that allows a system-wide public parameter shared by all users, pk^1, $(\mathsf{A}_i)_{i \in [n]}$, $(\mathsf{C}_i)_{i \in [n]}$, B, and hk in ek can be put in it, so that an evaluation key/trapdoor pair of each user consists only of $(\mathsf{pk}^0, \mathsf{sk}^0)$ of the underlying KEM KEM. Moreover, we can consider another variant of TDF in which the underlying $\mathcal{P}$-KDM secure SKE scheme is replaced with a hinting PRG, in a similar manner it is used in the Koppula-Waters construction [30].

Unlike $\mathsf{KEM_{cca}}$, however, we can*not* make TDF perfectly correct even if we replace the underlying KEM KEM with the combination of a PKE scheme and a PRG. This is because the standard correctness of PKE does not guarantee anything about the decryption result of an element chosen randomly from the ciphertext space, which naturally occurs in the inversion process of TDF.

Acknowledgments. A part of this work was supported by NTT Secure Platform Laboratories, JST OPERA JPMJOP1612, JST CREST JPMJCR14D6 and JPMJCR19F6, and JSPS KAKENHI JP16H01705 and JP17H01695.

References

1. Alekhnovich, M.: More on average case vs approximation complexity. In: FOCS, pp. 298–307 (2003)
2. Applebaum, B.: Key-dependent message security: generic amplification and completeness. In: Paterson, K.G. (ed.) EUROCRYPT 2011. LNCS, vol. 6632, pp. 527–546. Springer, Heidelberg (2011). https://doi.org/10.1007/978-3-642-20465-4_29
3. Applebaum, B., Cash, D., Peikert, C., Sahai, A.: Fast cryptographic primitives and circular-secure encryption based on hard learning problems. In: Halevi, S. (ed.) CRYPTO 2009. LNCS, vol. 5677, pp. 595–618. Springer, Heidelberg (2009). https://doi.org/10.1007/978-3-642-03356-8_35
4. Bellare, M., Boldyreva, A., O'Neill, A.: Deterministic and efficiently searchable encryption. In: Menezes, A. (ed.) CRYPTO 2007. LNCS, vol. 4622, pp. 535–552. Springer, Heidelberg (2007). https://doi.org/10.1007/978-3-540-74143-5_30
5. Bellare, M., Boldyreva, A., Staddon, J.: Randomness re-use in multi-recipient encryption schemeas. In: Desmedt, Y.G. (ed.) PKC 2003. LNCS, vol. 2567, pp. 85–99. Springer, Heidelberg (2003). https://doi.org/10.1007/3-540-36288-6_7
6. Bellare, M., Halevi, S., Sahai, A., Vadhan, S.: Many-to-one trapdoor functions and their relation to public-key cryptosystems. In: Krawczyk, H. (ed.) CRYPTO 1998. LNCS, vol. 1462, pp. 283–298. Springer, Heidelberg (1998). https://doi.org/10.1007/BFb0055735
7. Bellare, M., Rogaway, P.: Random oracles are practical: A paradigm for designing efficient protocols. In: CCS, pp. 62–73 (1993)

8. Birrell, E., Chung, K.-M., Pass, R., Telang, S.: Randomness-dependent message security. In: Sahai, A. (ed.) TCC 2013. LNCS, vol. 7785, pp. 700–720. Springer, Heidelberg (2013). https://doi.org/10.1007/978-3-642-36594-2_39

9. Black, J., Rogaway, P., Shrimpton, T.: Encryption-scheme security in the presence of key-dependent messages. In: Nyberg, K., Heys, H. (eds.) SAC 2002. LNCS, vol. 2595, pp. 62–75. Springer, Heidelberg (2003). https://doi.org/10.1007/3-540-36492-7_6

10. Bleichenbacher, D.: Chosen ciphertext attacks against protocols based on the RSA encryption standard PKCS #1. In: Krawczyk, H. (ed.) CRYPTO 1998. LNCS, vol. 1462, pp. 1–12. Springer, Heidelberg (1998). https://doi.org/10.1007/BFb0055716

11. Boneh, D., Halevi, S., Hamburg, M., Ostrovsky, R.: Circular-secure encryption from decision Diffie-Hellman. In: Wagner, D. (ed.) CRYPTO 2008. LNCS, vol. 5157, pp. 108–125. Springer, Heidelberg (2008). https://doi.org/10.1007/978-3-540-85174-5_7

12. Brakerski, Z., Goldwasser, S.: Circular and leakage resilient public-key encryption under subgroup indistinguishability - (or: Quadratic residuosity strikes back). In: Rabin, T. (ed.) CRYPTO 2010. LNCS, vol. 6223, pp. 1–20. Springer, Heidelberg (2010). https://doi.org/10.1007/978-3-642-14623-7_1

13. Brakerski, Z., Lombardi, A., Segev, G., Vaikuntanathan, V.: Anonymous IBE, leakage resilience and circular security from new assumptions. In: Nielsen, J.B., Rijmen, V. (eds.) EUROCRYPT 2018. LNCS, vol. 10820, pp. 535–564. Springer, Cham (2018). https://doi.org/10.1007/978-3-319-78381-9_20

14. Camenisch, J., Lysyanskaya, A.: An efficient system for non-transferable anonymous credentials with optional anonymity revocation. In: Pfitzmann, B. (ed.) EUROCRYPT 2001. LNCS, vol. 2045, pp. 93–118. Springer, Heidelberg (2001). https://doi.org/10.1007/3-540-44987-6_7

15. Dolev, D., Dwork, C., Naor, M.: Non-malleable cryptography (extended abstract). In: STOC, pp. 542–552 (1991)

16. Döttling, N., Garg, S., Hajiabadi, M., Masny, D.: New constructions of identity-based and key-dependent message secure encryption schemes. In: Abdalla, M., Dahab, R. (eds.) PKC 2018. LNCS, vol. 10769, pp. 3–31. Springer, Cham (2018). https://doi.org/10.1007/978-3-319-76578-5_1

17. Döttling, N., Müller-Quade, J., Nascimento, A.C.A.: IND-CCA secure cryptography based on a variant of the LPN problem. In: Wang, X., Sako, K. (eds.) ASIACRYPT 2012. LNCS, vol. 7658, pp. 485–503. Springer, Heidelberg (2012). https://doi.org/10.1007/978-3-642-34961-4_30

18. Dwork, C., Naor, M., Reingold, O.: Immunizing encryption schemes from decryption errors. In: Cachin, C., Camenisch, J.L. (eds.) EUROCRYPT 2004. LNCS, vol. 3027, pp. 342–360. Springer, Heidelberg (2004). https://doi.org/10.1007/978-3-540-24676-3_21

19. Fujisaki, E., Okamoto, T.: How to enhance the security of public-key encryption at minimum cost. In: Imai, H., Zheng, Y. (eds.) PKC 1999. LNCS, vol. 1560, pp. 53–68. Springer, Heidelberg (1999). https://doi.org/10.1007/3-540-49162-7_5

20. Garg, S., Gay, R., Hajiabadi, M.: New techniques for efficient trapdoor functions and applications. In: Ishai, Y., Rijmen, V. (eds.) EUROCRYPT 2019. LNCS, vol. 11478, pp. 33–63. Springer, Cham (2019). https://doi.org/10.1007/978-3-030-17659-4_2

21. Gertner, Y., Malkin, T., Myers, S.: Towards a separation of semantic and CCA security for public key encryption. In: Vadhan, S.P. (ed.) TCC 2007. LNCS, vol. 4392, pp. 434–455. Springer, Heidelberg (2007). https://doi.org/10.1007/978-3-540-70936-7_24

22. Gertner, Y., Malkin, T., Reingold, O.: On the impossibility of basing trapdoor functions on trapdoor predicates. In: FOCS, pp. 126–135 (2001)
23. Goldwasser, S., Micali, S.: Probabilistic encryption and how to play mental poker keeping secret all partial information. In: STOC, pp. 365–377 (1982)
24. Hajiabadi, M., Kapron, B.M.: Reproducible circularly-secure bit encryption: applications and realizations. In: Gennaro, R., Robshaw, M. (eds.) CRYPTO 2015. LNCS, vol. 9215, pp. 224–243. Springer, Heidelberg (2015). https://doi.org/10.1007/978-3-662-47989-6_11
25. Hsiao, C.-Y., Reyzin, L.: Finding collisions on a public road, or do secure hash functions need secret coins? In: Franklin, M. (ed.) CRYPTO 2004. LNCS, vol. 3152, pp. 92–105. Springer, Heidelberg (2004). https://doi.org/10.1007/978-3-540-28628-8_6
26. Kiltz, E., Masny, D., Pietrzak, K.: Simple chosen-ciphertext security from low-noise LPN. In: Krawczyk, H. (ed.) PKC 2014. LNCS, vol. 8383, pp. 1–18. Springer, Heidelberg (2014). https://doi.org/10.1007/978-3-642-54631-0_1
27. Kiltz, E., Mohassel, P., O'Neill, A.: Adaptive trapdoor functions and chosen-ciphertext security. In: Gilbert, H. (ed.) EUROCRYPT 2010. LNCS, vol. 6110, pp. 673–692. Springer, Heidelberg (2010). https://doi.org/10.1007/978-3-642-13190-5_34
28. Kitagawa, F., Matsuda, T.: CPA-to-CCA transformation for KDM security. IACR Cryptology ePrint Archive, 2019:609
29. Kitagawa, F., Matsuda, T., Tanaka, K.: CCA security and trapdoor functions via key-dependent-message security. IACR Cryptology ePrint Archive, 2019:291
30. Koppula, V., Waters, B.: Realizing chosen ciphertext security generically in attribute-based encryption and predicate encryption. IACR Cryptology ePrint Archive, 2018:847. To appear in CRYPTO 2019
31. Lombardi, A., Quach, W., Rothblum, R.D., Wichs, D., Wu, D.J.: New constructions of reusable designated-verifier NIZKs. IACR Cryptology ePrint Archive, 2019:242. (Dated on Feb 27, 2019.) To appear in CRYPTO 2019
32. Lombardi, A., Quach, W., Rothblum, R.D., Wichs, D., Wu, D.J.: New constructions of reusable designated-verifier NIZKs. IACR Cryptology ePrint Archive, 2019:242. (Dated on May 23, 2019.) To appear in CRYPTO 2019
33. Matsuda, T., Hanaoka, G.: Constructing and understanding chosen ciphertext security via puncturable key encapsulation mechanisms. In: Dodis, Y., Nielsen, J.B. (eds.) TCC 2015. LNCS, vol. 9014, pp. 561–590. Springer, Heidelberg (2015). https://doi.org/10.1007/978-3-662-46494-6_23
34. Peikert, C., Waters, B.: Lossy trapdoor functions and their applications. In: STOC, pp. 187–196 (2008)
35. Rackoff, C., Simon, D.R.: Non-interactive zero-knowledge proof of knowledge and chosen ciphertext attack. In: Feigenbaum, J. (ed.) CRYPTO 1991. LNCS, vol. 576, pp. 433–444. Springer, Heidelberg (1992). https://doi.org/10.1007/3-540-46766-1_35
36. Reingold, O., Trevisan, L., Vadhan, S.: Notions of reducibility between cryptographic primitives. In: Naor, M. (ed.) TCC 2004. LNCS, vol. 2951, pp. 1–20. Springer, Heidelberg (2004). https://doi.org/10.1007/978-3-540-24638-1_1
37. Rompel, J.: One-way functions are necessary and sufficient for secure signatures. In: STOC, pp. 387–394 (1990)
38. Rosen, A., Segev, G.: Chosen-ciphertext security via correlated products. In: Reingold, O. (ed.) TCC 2009. LNCS, vol. 5444, pp. 419–436. Springer, Heidelberg (2009). https://doi.org/10.1007/978-3-642-00457-5_25

39. Wee, H.: KDM-security via homomorphic smooth projective hashing. In: Cheng, C.-M., Chung, K.-M., Persiano, G., Yang, B.-Y. (eds.) PKC 2016. LNCS, vol. 9615, pp. 159–179. Springer, Heidelberg (2016). https://doi.org/10.1007/978-3-662-49387-8_7

40. Yao, A.C.-C.: Theory and applications of trapdoor functions (extended abstract). In: FOCS, pp. 80–91 (1982)

41. Yao, A.C.-C.: How to generate and exchange secrets (extended abstract). In: FOCS, pp. 162–167 (1986)

42. Yu, Y., Zhang, J.: Cryptography with auxiliary input and trapdoor from constant-noise LPN. In: Robshaw, M., Katz, J. (eds.) CRYPTO 2016. LNCS, vol. 9814, pp. 214–243. Springer, Heidelberg (2016). https://doi.org/10.1007/978-3-662-53018-4_9

Zero Knowledge I

Zero-Knowledge Proofs on Secret-Shared Data via Fully Linear PCPs

Dan Boneh[1(✉)], Elette Boyle[2(✉)], Henry Corrigan-Gibbs[1], Niv Gilboa[3], and Yuval Ishai[4]

[1] Stanford University, Stanford, USA
{dabo,henrycg}@cs.stanford.edu
[2] IDC Herzliya, Herzliya, Israel
eboyle@alum.mit.edu
[3] Ben-Gurion University, Be'er Sheva, Israel
gilboan@bgu.ac.il
[4] Technion, Haifa, Israel
yuvali@cs.technion.ac.il

Abstract. We introduce and study the notion of *fully linear* probabilistically checkable proof systems. In such a proof system, the verifier can make a small number of linear queries that apply *jointly* to the input and a proof vector.

Our new type of proof system is motivated by applications in which the input statement is not fully available to any single verifier, but can still be efficiently accessed via linear queries. This situation arises in scenarios where the input is partitioned or secret-shared between two or more parties, or alternatively is encoded using an additively homomorphic encryption or commitment scheme. This setting appears in the context of secure messaging platforms, verifiable outsourced computation, PIR writing, private computation of aggregate statistics, and secure multiparty computation (MPC). In all these applications, there is a need for fully linear proof systems with *short proofs*.

While several efficient constructions of fully linear proof systems are implicit in the interactive proofs literature, many questions about their complexity are open. We present several new constructions of fully linear *zero-knowledge* proof systems with *sublinear* proof size for "simple" or "structured" languages. For example, in the *non-interactive* setting of fully linear PCPs, we show how to prove that an input vector $x \in \mathbb{F}^n$, for a finite field $\mathbb{F}$, satisfies a single degree-2 equation with a proof of size $O(\sqrt{n})$ and $O(\sqrt{n})$ linear queries, which we show to be optimal. More generally, for languages that can be recognized by systems of constant-degree equations, we can reduce the proof size to $O(\log n)$ at the cost of $O(\log n)$ rounds of interaction.

We use our new proof systems to construct new short zero-knowledge proofs on distributed and secret-shared data. These proofs can be used to improve the performance of the example systems mentioned above.

Finally, we observe that zero-knowledge proofs on distributed data provide a general-purpose tool for protecting MPC protocols against malicious parties. Applying our short fully linear PCPs to "natural"

© International Association for Cryptologic Research 2019
A. Boldyreva and D. Micciancio (Eds.): CRYPTO 2019, LNCS 11694, pp. 67–97, 2019.
https://doi.org/10.1007/978-3-030-26954-8_3

MPC protocols in the honest-majority setting, we can achieve unconditional protection against malicious parties with sublinear additive communication cost. We use this to improve the communication complexity of recent honest-majority MPC protocols. For instance, using any pseudorandom generator, we obtain a 3-party protocol for Boolean circuits in which the amortized communication cost is only *one bit* per AND gate per party (compared to 10 bits in the best previous protocol), matching the best known protocols for semi-honest parties.

1   Introduction

In this work, we develop new techniques for proving in zero knowledge statements that are *distributed* (i.e., partitioned or secret-shared) across two or more verifiers. Recall that in a standard interactive proof system [8,10,14,53] a verifier holds an input $x \in \{0,1\}^*$ and a prover tries to convince the verifier that x is a member of some language $\mathcal{L} \subseteq \{0,1\}^*$. We consider instead the setting in which there are *multiple* verifiers, and each verifier holds only a piece of the input, such as a share of x generated using a linear secret-sharing scheme. Critically, no single verifier holds the entire input x. The prover, who holds the entire input x, must convince the verifiers, who only hold pieces of x, that $x \in \mathcal{L}$. At the same time, we require that the proof system be *strongly zero knowledge*: every proper subset of the verifiers should learn nothing about x, apart from the fact that $x \in \mathcal{L}$.

Special cases of this type of proof system appear in existing systems for anonymous messaging [38], verifiable function secret sharing [30], and systems for the private computation of aggregate statistics [37]. We observe that such proof systems also provide a powerful tool for protecting protocols for *secure multiparty computation* over *point-to-point channels* against malicious parties, analogous to the role that standard zero-knowledge proofs play in the GMW compiler [50]. Indeed, in protocols that involve point-to-point communication, the task of proving compliance with the protocol exactly requires executing a zero-knowledge proof on distributed data.

We introduce the central new abstraction of a *fully linear proof system*. Such proof systems apply not only to efficiently proving (in zero-knowledge) statements on distributed or secret-shared data, but also to data that is encrypted or committed using a linearly homomorphic system. While several efficient constructions of fully linear proof systems are implicit in the literature on interactive and probabilistically checkable proofs (in particular, the linear PCPs from [6,49] and the interactive proofs from [52,76] can be cast as such proof systems), many questions about their complexity are open. We present several new constructions of fully linear zero-knowledge proof systems that achieve *sublinear* proof size for "simple" or "structured" languages. Finally, we present several applications of such proof systems in the context of the motivating applications discussed above.

We now give a more detailed overview of our contributions.

Contribution I: Fully Linear Proof Systems. We begin by introducing the notion of a *fully linear proof system*, which captures the information-theoretic object at the core of all of our constructions. We consider the non-interactive variant of such proof systems, called *fully linear PCPs*, and then we describe a natural extension to the interactive setting.

A fully linear PCP is a refinement of linear PCPs [6,23,58]. Recall that in a standard linear PCP over a finite field $\mathbb{F}$, a polynomial-time verifier holds an input $x \in \mathbb{F}^n$ and a prover produces a proof $\pi \in \mathbb{F}^m$ to the assertion that $x \in \mathcal{L}$, for some language $\mathcal{L} \subseteq \mathbb{F}^n$. The verifier checks the proof by reading x and making *linear queries* (i.e., inner-product queries) to the proof π. In particular, the verifier can make a bounded number of queries to the proof of the form $q_j \in \mathbb{F}^m$, and receives answers $a_j = \langle q_j, \pi \rangle \in \mathbb{F}$.

In a fully linear PCP, we further restrict the verifier: the verifier cannot read the entire input x directly, but only has access to it via linear queries. Concretely, the verifier in a fully linear PCP makes linear queries q_j to the concatenated input-proof vector $(x \| \pi) \in \mathbb{F}^{n+m}$ and must accept or reject the assertion that $x \in \mathcal{L}$ based on the answers a_j to these linear queries. Motivated by the applications we consider, we would also like fully linear PCPs to satisfy the following *strong zero-knowledge* requirement: the queries q_j together with the answers a_j reveal no additional information about x other than the fact that $x \in \mathcal{L}$. This is stronger than the standard notion of zero-knowledge proofs in which x is essentially public and the interaction need not hide x. See Sect. 3 for formal definitions of fully linear PCPs and their strong zero knowledge variant.

The full linearity restriction is naturally motivated by applications in which the input statement is not fully available to any single verifier, but can still be efficiently accessed via linear queries. This situation arises in scenarios where the input x is distributed or secret-shared between two or more parties, or alternatively is encoded using an additively homomorphic encryption or commitment scheme. In these scenarios, verifiers can readily compute answers to public linear queries via *local* computations on their view of x. While fully linear PCPs can be meaningfully applied in all of the above scenarios, we will primarily focus on their applications to proofs on distributed or secret-shared data.

We stress again that in a fully linear PCP, the verifier only has *linear query access* to x. An interesting consequence is that even if $\mathcal{L}$ is an easy language that can be decided in polynomial time, a verifier making a bounded (e.g., constant) number of such queries typically cannot decide whether $x \in \mathcal{L}$ without the aid of a proof, even if the verifier can run in unbounded time. This makes the existence of fully linear proof systems with good parameters meaningful even for finite languages and even if, say, P = PSPACE.[1] The same fact makes possible a connection between fully linear PCPs and communication complexity [3,64,66].

---

[1] This is akin to *proofs of proximity* [21], which place a more stringent restriction on the verifier's access to the input. However, unlike proofs of proximity, in fully linear PCPs the verifier is guaranteed that the input is actually in the language rather than being "close" to some input the language. Another related notion is that of a *holographic proof* [9,57], where the verifier gets oracle access to an *encoding* of the input using an arbitrary error-correcting code.

Using this connection, we prove unconditional lower bounds on the efficiency properties of fully linear PCPs.

Different kinds of linear PCPs were used, either explicitly or implicitly, in the vast literature on succinct arguments for NP (see [22,23,25,29,49,55,58, 68,75,77,78,83,86] and references therein). These linear PCPs, including the "Hadamard PCP" [6,58] and ones obtained from quadratic span programs or quadratic arithmetic programs [23,49,74], can be cast into the fully linear framework. This fact was implicitly used in previous proof systems on committed or secret-shared data [11,37,39]. Our notion of fully linear PCPs provides a convenient abstraction of the properties on which such systems can be based.

Contribution II: Shorter Proofs for Structured and Simple Languages. When using fully linear PCPs to build zero-knowledge proof systems on distributed or secret-shared data, as discussed in Contribution IV below, the *proof length* determines the number of bits that the prover must send to the verifiers. As such, we aim to design short proofs. This goal is especially important when many different assertions are proved about the same input statement x. In such a scenario, the initial setup cost of distributing x is amortized away. Having short fully linear PCPs yields similar efficiency benefits in the settings of encryption and commitments.

These applications motivate the need for fully linear PCPs with *short proofs*. For general NP relations, all known linear PCPs have size at least *linear* in the size of an arithmetic circuit recognizing the relation. In Sect. 4, we achieve significant length savings by designing new *sublinear* sized fully linear PCPs for languages recognized by deterministic circuits with repeated sub-structures (Theorem 11) or by a degree-2 polynomial (Corollary 13). In the latter case, we can even prove that the $O(\sqrt{n})$ complexity of our construction is optimal up to low-order terms (see full version). These and other proof systems constructed in this work satisfy the notion of strong zero knowledge discussed above.

Theorem 1 (Informal - short fully linear PCP for a degree-2 polynomial). *If membership in $\mathcal{L} \subseteq \mathbb{F}^n$ can be recognized by a single degree-2 polynomial, then $\mathcal{L}$ admits a fully linear PCP with strong zero knowledge that has proof length and query complexity $\tilde{O}(\sqrt{n})$ and soundness error $O(\sqrt{n}/|\mathbb{F}|)$. Furthermore, there exists a language $\mathcal{L}$ as above such that the sum of the proof length and query complexity must be $\Omega(\sqrt{n})$, even when we allow constant soundness error and do not require zero knowledge.*

See Corollary 13 for a more precise and general statement.

Contribution III: Reducing Proof Size by Interaction. To further drive down the proof length, we consider a generalization of fully linear PCPs that allows multiple rounds of interaction between the prover and verifier. These *fully linear interactive oracle proofs*, or fully linear IOPs, are the linear analogue of interactive oracle proofs (IOP) [20], also known as probabilistically checkable interactive proofs [76]. We note that without the zero-knowledge requirement, several existing interactive proof systems from the literature, including the GKR protocol [51], the CMT protocol [35], and the RRR protocol [76] can be viewed as fully linear IOPs.

For the case of "well-structured" languages, we show in Sect. 5 that interaction can dramatically shrink the proof size, while maintaining the required strong zero-knowledge property. In particular, any language whose membership can be verified by a system of constant-degree equations over a finite field admits a fully linear IOP with strong zero-knowledge in $O(\log n)$ rounds and only $O(\log n)$ proof length, provided that the underlying field is sufficiently large. Even for degree-2 languages, this provably gives an exponential reduction in proof size over the non-interactive case.

Theorem 2 (Informal - fully linear zero-knowledge IOPs for low-degree languages). *Suppose $\mathcal{L} \subseteq \mathbb{F}^n$ can be recognized by a system of constant-degree equations. Then, $\mathcal{L}$ admits a fully linear IOP with strong zero knowledge, $O(\log n)$ rounds, and proof length and query complexity $O(\log n)$.*

See Theorem 15 for a more precise and general statement, including an extension to rings.

Contribution IV: Zero-Knowledge Proofs on Distributed or Secret-Shared Data. The primary motivation for our new types of proof systems is the fact that in many cases, data can be efficiently accessed via linear queries. This includes several different scenarios, but our main focus in this work is on the case of *distributed* or *secret-shared* data. (See full version for application to proofs on *encrypted* or *committed* data.) More precisely, the prover knows x in its entirety and each of k verifiers $V_1, \ldots, V_k$ only has a piece (or a secret share) of x.

In the full version we show that any fully linear PCP and IOP can be compiled into a zero-knowledge proof system on distributed or secret-shared data in the following natural way. Instead of sending a proof vector π to a single verifier, the prover P secret-shares the proof vector π between the k verifiers using a linear secret-sharing scheme. The verifiers can now locally apply each linear query to the concatenation of their share of the input x and their share of π, and exchange the resulting answer shares with the other verifiers. The verifiers then reconstruct the answers to the linear queries and apply the decision predicate to decide to accept or reject x. We present different variants of this compiler that further optimize this approach and that achieve zero-knowledge even when up to $k-1$ verifiers are malicious.

Theorem 3 (Informal - distributed zero-knowledge proofs for low-degree languages on secret-shared data: malicious prover *or* verifiers). *Suppose $\mathcal{L} \subseteq \mathbb{F}^n$ can be recognized by a system of constant-degree equations. Then, assuming ideal coin-tossing, there is an $O(\log n)$-round distributed zero-knowledge protocol for proving that $x \in \mathcal{L}$, where x is additively shared between k verifiers, with communication complexity $O(k \log n)$. The protocol is sound against a malicious prover and is strongly zero-knowledge against $t = k - 1$ malicious verifiers.*

We also give a Fiat-Shamir-style compiler that uses a random oracle to collapse multiple rounds of interaction into a single message sent by P to each V_j over a private channel, followed by a single message by each V_j.

Given a robust encoding (or robust secret sharing) of the input x, we present distributed zero-knowledge protocols that maintain their soundness even when a malicious prover colludes with $t < k/2$ malicious verifiers. In contrast, we note that previous sublinear proof systems on secret-shared data either do not attempt to protect against malicious verifiers [30], or assume a majority of honest verifiers [38]. Neither considers soundness against a malicious prover colluding with malicious verifiers.

Table 1 summarizes the communication and round complexity of the proof systems on secret-shared data for languages that frequently come up in practice, for example in the Prio system [37] for privately aggregating data, and in the Riposte [38] system for anonymous communication. The table illustrates the strong benefits of interactive fully linear proof systems over non-interactive ones.

We note that interactive proofs with distributed verifiers were recently studied in [65,71] for the purpose of proving properties of a communication graph

Table 1. Communication and round complexity for proof systems where the input data is secret shared among a number of parties. We assume the proofs are over a finite field $\mathbb{F}$ with $|\mathbb{F}| \gg n$. Prio [37] is a system for private data aggregation that uses proofs on secret shared data for data integrity. Riposte [38] is a system for anonymous communication that uses proofs on secret shared data to prevent data corruption. Verifiable function secret sharing (FSS) [30] enables secret sharing of simple functions.

Language	Proof system	Comm. complexity	Rounds
Hamming weight 1:	Prio [37]	$O(n)$	1
$\bar{x} \in \mathbb{F}^n$, weight$(\bar{x}) = 1$	Theorem 15	$O(\sqrt{n})$	2
	Theorem 15	$O(\log n)$	$O(\log n)$
	Implicit in [41]	$O(1)$	2
	Riposte** [38]	$O(\sqrt{n})$	1
	Verifiable FSS** [30]	$O(1)$	1
$\bar{x} \in \{0,\dots,B\}^n \subseteq \mathbb{F}^n$	Prio [37]	$O(B \cdot n)$	1
	Theorem 15	$O(B \cdot \sqrt{n})$	2
	Theorem 15	$O(B \cdot \log n)$	$O(\log n)$
n Beaver triples:	Prio [37]	$O(n)$	1
$\bar{x}, \bar{y}, \bar{z} \in \mathbb{F}^n$ where	Theorem 15	$O(\sqrt{n})$	2
$x_i \cdot y_i = z_i$ for all $i \in [n]$	GKR [52]	$O(\log^2 n)$	$O(\log^2 n)$
	Theorem 15	$O(\log n)$	$O(\log n)$
Arbitrary circuit C, $C(\bar{x}) = 1$	Prio [37]	$O(n)$	1
(size n, depth d, fan-in 2)	GKR [52]	$O(d \log n)$	$O(d \log n)$

** All systems in the table, except Riposte, verifiable FSS, and GKR, maintain zero knowledge when all but one of the verifiers are malicious. In contrast, 3-server Riposte tolerates only one corruption. Verifiable FSS tolerates only semi-honest verifiers and GKR does not provide zero-knowledge.

connecting a large number of verifiers. The relevance of the interactive proofs of GKR [51] and RRR [76] to this setting has been observed in [71]. Our focus here is quite different; we are motivated by the goal of proving in zero knowledge simple properties of data distributed among a small set of verifiers. As a result, our abstractions, constructions, and applications are very different from those in prior work [65, 71].

Contribution V: Applications to Honest-Majority MPC. We next demonstrate applications of our zero-knowledge fully linear proof systems for protecting protocols for secure multiparty computation (MPC) in the honest-majority setting against *malicious* parties, with vanishing amortized communication overhead, and without resorting to the heavy machinery of succinct (two-party) zero-knowledge argument systems for NP.

COMPILING "NATURAL" HONEST-MAJORITY PROTOCOLS. Dating back to the work of Goldreich, Micali, and Wigderson (GMW) [50], the standard approach to secure protocol design begins by attaining semi-honest (passive) security, then compiling the protocol in some way to enforce semi-honest behavior. The GMW compiler relies on standard zero-knowledge proofs, which apply to *public* statements. As a result, it does not apply directly to the case of protocols that employ communication over secure point-to-point channels. To get around this limitation, we employ our distributed zero-knowledge proofs in the following way.

As observed in recent works, the vast majority of semi-honest MPC protocols from the literature share the following natural form:

- Up to the final exchange of messages, the protocol reveals *no* information about parties' inputs, even if parties act maliciously.
- The messages sent by a party P_i in each round are *degree-2* functions (or, more generally, low-degree functions) of messages received in previous rounds.

The first property means that parties can safely execute all but the final round of the underlying protocol unchanged, and then simultaneously verify that in all prior rounds the parties acted semi-honestly. The second property means that this verification can be expressed as satisfaction of a collection of several degree-2 constraints on parties' incoming and outgoing messages. More concretely, each party P_i must convince the remaining parties in zero knowledge that the statement M_i consisting of all his round-by-round incoming and outgoing messages—and which is *distributed* across the remaining parties—is indeed contained within some appropriate language $\mathcal{L}_i$ verifiable by a degree-2 circuit. This is precisely the setting of our zero knowledge proofs on distributed data.

We demonstrate an approach for compiling semi-honest protocols of the above "natural" form (formally defined in the full version) in the honest-majority setting, to *malicious* security with abort, with *sublinear additive communication overhead*. This is achieved by adding a phase in the penultimate round of the base protocol, in which each party P_i executes a single interactive proof on distributed data that the *entire* interaction thus far has been performed honestly. The necessary zero-knowledge protocols that we develop induce communication that is sublinear in the circuit size.

Note that while many efficient MPC protocols from the literature implement batch-verification of shared secrets by revealing random linear combinations, this technique only applies to checking *linear* relations between the secrets. Fully linear proof systems provide a powerful extension of this approach to batch-verification of *non-linear* relations with sublinear communication cost.

THE CASE OF 3-PARTY COMPUTATION. A specific motivated setting is that of 3-party computation with 1 malicious corruption (and security with abort). The task of minimizing communication in such protocols has attracted a significant amount of research effort (e.g., [4,5,34,44,48,54,67,70,72]). To date, the best protocols communicate: 2 field elements per multiplication gate per party over large fields (size comparable to 2^σ for statistical security parameter σ) [34,72], or alternatively 10 bits per multiplication gate per party over Boolean circuits [48].

Applying our compiler to a 3-party semi-honest protocol of Katz et al. [62][2] (see also [5,40,43]), we obtain a 3-party protocol guaranteeing security with abort against 1 malicious party, with *1 ring element* communicated per party per multiplication (amortized over large circuit size). Our result holds over any finite field or modular arithmetic ring $\mathbb{Z}_w$; in particular, also for Boolean circuits.

Theorem 4 (Informal - Malicious 3PC, 1 ring element/gate/party).
There exists a 3-party protocol for securely computing any R-arithmetic circuit C (for R field of arbitrary size or $R = \mathbb{Z}_w$) with the following features:

- *The protocol makes black-box use of any pseudorandom generator. If R is a field, it also makes a black-box use of R.*
- *The protocol is computationally secure with abort against one malicious party.*
- *The communication complexity is $|C| + o(|C|)$ elements of R per party, where $|C|$ denotes the number of multiplication and input gates in C.*

We also describe an application of a variant of our compiler in the more general honest majority case where $t < n/2$ for constant n, building from a semi-honest protocol à la Damgård and Nielsen [42]. Overall, our resulting protocol achieves malicious security with $3t/(2t + 1)$ (always ≤ 1.5) ring elements communicated per gate per party.

2 A Taxonomy of Information-Theoretic Proof Systems

One of the contributions of this work is to introduce and formalize the notions of *fully linear* PCPs and IOPs. To situate these new types of proof systems in the context of prior work, we briefly survey the landscape of existing systems. This discussion will be relatively informal; see Sect. 3 for formal definitions of linear and fully linear proof systems.

---

[2] Our compiler can analogously apply to the 3-party semi-honest protocol of Araki et al. [5]. We build on the protocol from [62] since its dealer-party structure offers a slightly simpler description within our framework and the advantage of lower online (input-dependent) cost.

A tremendously successful paradigm for the construction of cryptographic proof systems is the following: First, construct a proof system that provides security guarantees (soundness and possibly zero-knowledge) against *computationally unbounded* parties. We will refer to this as an "information-theoretic proof system," or sometimes as a probabilistically checkable proof (PCP). This information-theoretic system is often useless as a standalone object, since it typically makes idealized assumptions (such as independence between two messages or restricted access to the proof) that are difficult to enforce. Next, use cryptographic assumptions and/or an augmented model of computation (e.g., the random-oracle model [12]) to "compile" the information-theoretic proof system into one that can be directly implemented. This compiler may also provide extra desirable properties, such eliminating interaction, improved communication complexity, or sometimes even an extra zero knowledge property, at the possible cost of security against *computationally bounded* prover and/or verifier. We refer to this type of compiler as a "cryptographic compiler."

Different kinds of information-theoretic proof systems call for different cryptographic compilers. The main advantage of this separation is modularity: information-theoretic proof systems can be designed, analyzed and optimized independently of the cryptographic compilers, and their security properties (soundness and zero-knowledge) do not depend on any cryptographic assumptions. It may be beneficial to apply different cryptographic compilers to the same information-theoretic proof system, as different compilers may have incomparable efficiency and security features. For instance, they may trade succinctness for better computational complexity or post-quantum security or, more relevant to this work, apply to different representations of the input statement.

To give just a few examples of this methodology: Micali [69] uses a random oracle to compile any classical PCP into a *succinct* non-interactive argument system for NP. As another example, Ben-Or et al. [13] compile any interactive proof system into a *zero-knowledge* interactive proof system using cryptographic commitments. Finally, Bitansky et al. [23] compile a linear PCP into a succinct non-interactive argument of knowledge (SNARK) using either a "linear-only encryption" for the designated-verifier setting or a "linear-only one-way encoding," instantiated via bilinear groups, for the public verification setting.[3] In this work we compile *fully linear* PCPs and IOPs into proofs on distributed, secret-shared, encrypted, or committed data.

2.1 Comparison with Other Proof Systems

In the following we survey some information-theoretic proof systems used in prior work. For simplicity, we ignore the zero-knowledge feature that is typically added to all proof systems.

---

[3] For instantiating the publicly verifiable variant with bilinear groups, the linear PCP needs to have a verification predicate of algebraic degree 2. Such linear PCPs can be obtained either directly or via quadratic span programs or quadratic arithmetic programs [23, 49, 74].

Let $\mathcal{L} \subseteq \{0,1\}^*$ be a language. Speaking informally, a proof system for $\mathcal{L}$ is a pair of (possibly interactive) algorithms (P, V). Both the prover P and verifier V take a string $x \in \{0,1\}^*$ as input (e.g., a SAT formula), and the prover's task is to convince the verifier that $x \in \mathcal{L}$ (e.g., that x is satisfiable). We sometimes view x as a vector over a finite field $\mathbb{F}$. We require the standard notions of *completeness* and *soundness*.

In the simplest such proof system, the prover sends the verifier a single proof string π of size $\mathsf{poly}(|x|)$, the verifier reads x and π, and accepts or rejects. When the verifier is randomized and efficient, this setting corresponds to a Merlin-Arthur proof system [8]. There are a number of modifications to this basic paradigm that yield interesting alternative proof systems. In particular, we can:

- *Allow interaction between the prover and verifier.* In an interactive proof, the prover and verifier exchange many messages, after which the verifier must accept or reject. Allowing interaction may increase the power of the proof system [81] and makes it possible to provide zero-knowledge [53] in the plain model. (Alternatively, a common reference string is sufficient [24].)
- *Restrict the verifier's access to the proof.* Another way to modify the basic paradigm is to restrict the means by which the verifier interacts with the proof. In particular, we can view the proof as an oracle, and only allow the verifier to make a bounded (e.g., constant) number of queries to the proof oracle.

  In the classical PCP model [7,45,46], the proof is a string $\pi \in \Sigma^m$, for some finite alphabet Σ, and the verifier can only read a small number of symbols from the proof. On input i, the oracle returns the ith bit of the proof string π. (We call these "point queries.")

  In the linear PCP model [23,58], the proof is a vector $\pi \in \mathbb{F}^m$, for some finite field $\mathbb{F}$, and the verifier can only make a small number of "linear queries" to the proof. That is, the proof oracle takes as input a vector $q \in \mathbb{F}^m$ and returns the inner-product $\langle \pi, q \rangle \in \mathbb{F}$.
- *Restrict the verifier's access to the input.* Yet another way to modify the basic paradigm is to restrict the verifier's access to the input x. In particular, we can view the *input* as an oracle, and only allow the verifier to make a bounded (e.g., constant) number of queries to the input oracle. The strong motivation for this is explained later in this section. We consider two variants.

  The model in which we view the input as a string, and only allow the verifier to make a limited number of point queries to the input, corresponds to a PCP of proximity [21]. With a few point queries, it is not possible to distinguish between an input $x \in \mathcal{L}$, and an input x "close to $\mathcal{L}$" (in Hamming distance). For this reason, PCPs of proximity necessarily provide only a relaxed notion of soundness: if x is "far from $\mathcal{L}$," then the verifier will likely reject.

  Alternatively, we can view the input as a vector $x \in \mathbb{F}^n$, for some finite field $\mathbb{F}$, and only allow the verifier to make a small number of linear queries to the input x. That is, the input oracle takes as input a vector $q \in \mathbb{F}^n$ and returns the inner-product $\langle x, q \rangle \in \mathbb{F}$. We show that this notion, introduced and studied in this work, is sufficient to provide a standard notion of soundness (unlike the relaxed notion of soundness provided by PCPs of proximity).

We now have three attributes by which we can classify information-theoretic proof systems: interactivity (yes/no), proof query type (read all/point/linear), and input query type (read all/point/linear). Taking the Cartesian product of these attributes yields 18 different possible proof systems, and we list ten of particular interest in Table 2.

Table 2. A comparison of information-theoretic proof systems. The **bolded** proof system models are ones that we introduce explicitly in this work. "Read all" refers to reading the entire data field, "Point" refers to reading a small number of cells of the data, and "Linear" refers to a small number of linear queries to the data.

	Proof type	Queries to input	Queries to proof	Representative compilers
Non-interactive	Classical (MA) [8]	Read all	Read all	
	PCP [6,7]	Read all	Point	Kilian [63], Micali [69]
	Linear PCP [58]	Read all	Linear	IKO [58], Pepper [80], GGPR [49], PHGR [74, 75], BCIOP [23]
	PCP of proximity [21]	Point	Point	Kalai & Rothblum [60]
	Fully linear PCP	Linear	Linear	*This paper*
Interactive	Interactive proof (IP) [53]	Read all	Read all	Ben Or et al. [13]
	IOP [20]	Read all	Point	BCS [20]
	Linear IOP	Read all	Linear	
	IOP of proximity [16,17]	Point	Point	
	Fully linear IOP	Linear	Linear	*This paper*, Hyrax [83], vSQL [85,86]

For example, interactive oracle proofs (IOPs) are interactive proofs in which the verifier has unrestricted access to the input but may make only point queries to proof strings [20]. Ben-Sasson et al. [20] show how to compile such proofs into SNARGs in the random-oracle model and recent hash-based SNARGs, including Ligero [2], STARK [15], and Aurora [19] are built using this technique.

Why Fully Linear Proof Systems? It is often the case that the verifier only has access to an additively homomorphic *encoding* of a statement x, and the prover convinces the verifier that the encoded statement is true. For example the verifier may be given an additively homomorphic commitment or encryption of the statement x. Or the verifier may be implemented as a set of two or more servers who have a linear secret sharing of the statement x, or who hold different parts of x.

In all these settings, the verifiers can easily compute an *encoding* of the inner product of the statement x with a known query vector q. In some cases (such as the case of encrypted or committed data), the verifiers may need the prover's help to "open" the resulting inner products.

When we compile fully linear PCPs into proof systems on shared, encrypted, or committed data, our compilers have the same structure: the prover sends an additively homomorphic encoding of the proof to the verifier. The verifier makes linear queries to the proof and input, and (if necessary) the prover provides "openings" of these linear queries to the verifier. The verifier checks that the openings are consistent with the encodings it was given, and then runs the fully linear PCP verifier to decide whether to accept or reject the proof.

The Need for New Constructions. In current applications of PCPs and linear PCPs, the length of the proof is not a complexity metric of much relevance. For example, in the BCIOP compiler [23] for compiling a linear PCP into a succinct non-interactive argument of knowledge (SNARK), the size of the proof corresponds to the prover's running time.

If the language $\mathcal{L}$ in question is decided by circuits of size $|C|$, then having proofs of size $|C|$ is acceptable, since the prover must run in time $\Omega(|C|)$ no matter what. A similar property holds for Micali's CS proofs [69], Kilian's PCP compiler [63], the BCS compiler [20] of interactive oracle proofs, and so on.

In our compilers, the prover must materialize the entire fully linear PCP proof, encode it, and send it to the verifier. For us, the size of the fully linear PCP proof not only dictates the running time of the prover, but also dictates the number of bits that the prover must communicate to the verifier. For this reason, in our setting, minimizing the proof size is an important goal.

Furthermore, when compiling linear PCPs into SNARKs using the existing compilers [23,56,75] it is critical that the linear PCP verifier be expressible as an arithmetic circuit of degree two. This is because the linear PCP verification checks are essentially run "in the exponent" of a bilinear group. In contrast, the settings we consider allow for more flexibility: the arithmetic degree of the verifier typically does not play a role in the final applications, except perhaps for a possible influence on proof verification time.

Relating Fully Linear PCPs to Streaming Proof Systems. The setting of *stream annotations* [33], introduced by Chakrabarti, Cormode, McGregor, and Thaler, restricts not only the verifier's access to the input and proof, but also the space usage of the verifier. In this model, the verifier is a space-bounded streaming algorithm: it may take a single pass over the input and proof, and must decide whether to accept or reject. For example, the verifier might be allowed only $O(\sqrt{n})$ bits of working space to decide inputs of length n. The *streaming interactive proof* model [36] is a generalization in which the prover and verifier may interact.

Fully linear interactive proofs naturally give rise to stream annotation proof systems. The reason is that if a fully linear PCP verifier makes q_π linear proof queries and q_x linear input queries, then the verifier can compute the responses to all of its queries by taking a single streaming pass over the input and proof while using $(q_x + q_\pi) \log_2 |\mathbb{F}|$ bits of space. Thus, fully linear PCPs with small proof size and query complexity give rise to stream annotation proof systems with small proof and space requirements. Similarly, fully linear IOPs give rise to streaming interactive proofs.

The implication in the other direction does not always hold, however, since stream annotation systems do not always give rise to fully linear PCPs with good parameters. The reason is that a streaming verifier may, in general, compute some non-linear function of the input that is difficult to simulate with linear queries.

Other Proof Systems. We briefly mention a number of other important classes of proof systems in the literature that are out of scope of this discussion. *Linear interactive proofs* are a model of interactive proof in which each message that the prover sends is an affine function of all of the verifier's previous messages (but is not necessarily an affine function of the input) [23].

The fully linear PCP model is well matched to the problem of proving statements on data encoded with an additively homomorphic encoding, such as Paillier encryption [73] or a linear secret-sharing scheme. A different type of encoding is a *succinct* encoding, in which the prover can commit to a vector in $\mathbb{F}^m$ with a string of size sublinear in m [32,61]. Bootle et al. [28] introduce the "Ideal Linear Commitment" (ILC) model as an abstraction better suited to this setting. In the ILC proof model, the prover sends the verifier *multiple* proofs vectors $\pi_1, \ldots, \pi_k \in \mathbb{F}^m$ in each round. The verifier is given a proof oracle that takes as input a vector $q \in \mathbb{F}^k$ and returns the linear combination $q^T \cdot (\pi_1 \ \ldots \ \pi_k) \in \mathbb{F}^m$. It is possible to translate linear IOP proofs into ILC proofs (and vice versa) up to some looseness in the parameters. A linear IOP in which the prover sends a length-m proof in each round implies an ILC proof with the same query complexity in which the prover sends m proofs of length 1 in each round. An ILC proof in which the prover sends k proofs of length m and makes ℓ queries in each round implies a linear IOP with proof length $k \cdot m$ and query complexity $\ell \cdot m$. ILC-type proofs underlie the recent succinct zero-knowledge arguments of Bootle et al. [27] and Bünz et al. [31], whose security is premised on the hardness of the discrete-log problem.

Finally, another related notion from the literature is that of a *holographic proof* [9,57], where the verifier gets oracle access to an *encoding* of the input using an arbitrary error-correcting code, typically a Reed-Muller code. Our notion of fully linear PCPs can be viewed as a variant of this model where the input is (implicitly) encoded by the Hadamard code and the proof can be accessed via *linear* queries (as opposed to point queries). In fact, our model allows a single linear query to apply *jointly* to the input and the proof.

We have not discussed multi-prover interactive proofs [14], in which multiple non-colluding provers interact with a single verifier, or more recently, multi-prover proofs in which a verifier gets access to multiple (possibly linear) proof oracles [26,58].

"Best-of-Both-Worlds" Proof Systems. To conclude this section, we point to an interesting direction for future work on proof systems. A very desirable type of proof system, which is *not* listed in Table 2, would be one in which the verifier makes *linear* queries to the input and *point* queries to the proof. This type of proof system, which we call a *strongly linear* proof, achieves in some sense the "best of both worlds:" the verifier has restricted access to the input (as in a

PCP of proximity or fully linear PCP) and yet achieves the standard notion of soundness (as in a classical PCP). While it is possible in principle to construct such strongly linear PCPs and IOPs by combining standard PCPs or IOPs of proximity [17,21] with linear error-correcting codes, this generic combination may not yield the best achievable parameters.

3   Definitions

Notation. For $n \in \mathbb{N}$, let $[n] = \{1, \ldots, n\}$. Let $\|$ denote concatenation, $\langle \cdot, \cdot \rangle$ inner product and $\perp$ the empty string. When C is an arithmetic circuit over a finite field $\mathbb{F}$, we use $|C|$ to denote the number of multiplication gates in the circuit. When $|\mathbb{F}| > n$, we let $1, 2, \ldots, n$ denote distinct nonzero field elements.

On Concrete vs. Asymptotic Treatment. Since our new types of proof systems are meaningful even when all of algorithms involved are computationally unbounded, our definitions refer to languages and NP-relations as finite objects and do not refer to running time of algorithms. All of our definitions can be naturally extended to the standard asymptotic setting of infinite languages and relations with polynomial-time verifiers, honest provers, simulators, and knowledge extractors. Our positive results satisfy these asymptotic efficiency requirements.

Fully Linear PCPs. Our new notion of *fully* linear PCPs build upon the definitions of standard linear PCPs from Ishai et al. [58] and Bitansky et al. [23]. We start by recalling the original notion.

Definition 5 (Linear PCP). Let $\mathbb{F}$ be a finite field and let $\mathcal{R} \subseteq \mathbb{F}^n \times \mathbb{F}^h$ be a binary relation. A linear probabilistically checkable proof system for $\mathcal{R}$ over $\mathbb{F}$ with proof length m, soundness error ϵ, and query complexity ℓ is a pair of algorithms $(P_{\mathsf{LPCP}}, V_{\mathsf{LPCP}})$ with the following properties:

- For every $(x, w) \in \mathcal{R}$, the prover $P_{\mathsf{LPCP}}(x, w)$ outputs a proof $\pi \in \mathbb{F}^m$.
- The verifier V_{LPCP} consists of a query algorithm Q_{LPCP} and a decision algorithm D_{LPCP}. The query algorithm Q_{LPCP} takes no input and outputs ℓ queries $q_1, \ldots, q_\ell \in \mathbb{F}^m$ and state information st. The decision algorithm D_{LPCP} takes as input the state st, the statement x, and the ℓ answers $\langle \pi, q_1 \rangle, \ldots, \langle \pi, q_\ell \rangle \in \mathbb{F}$ to Q_{LPCP}'s queries. It outputs "accept" or "reject."

The algorithms additionally satisfy the following requirements:

- **Completeness.** For all $(x, w) \in \mathcal{R}$, the verifier accepts a valid proof:

$$\Pr\left[D_{\mathsf{LPCP}}(\mathsf{st}, x, \langle \pi, q_1 \rangle, \ldots, \langle \pi, q_\ell \rangle) = \text{``accept''} : \begin{matrix} \pi \leftarrow P_{\mathsf{LPCP}}(x, w) \\ (\mathsf{st}, q_1, \ldots, q_\ell) \leftarrow Q_{\mathsf{LPCP}}() \end{matrix} \right] = 1.$$

- **Soundness.** For all $x^* \notin \mathcal{L}(\mathcal{R})$, and for all false proofs $\pi^* \in \mathbb{F}^m$, the probability that the verifier accepts is at most ϵ:

$$\Pr\left[D_{\mathsf{LPCP}}(\mathsf{st}, x^*, \langle \pi^*, q_1 \rangle, \ldots, \langle \pi^*, q_\ell \rangle) = \text{``accept''} : (\mathsf{st}, q_1, \ldots, q_\ell) \leftarrow Q_{\mathsf{LPCP}}() \right] \leq \epsilon.$$

In some applications, one also needs a **knowledge** property [23]: there exists an extractor E_{LPCP} such that if $V_{\mathsf{LPCP}}(x)$ accepts a proof π, then E_{LPCP} on input π outputs a witness w such that $(x, w) \in \mathcal{R}$. The linear PCPs we introduce in this work satisfy this property, though we only prove the simpler soundness property.

Remark (Linear PCPs for languages). On occasion we refer to linear PCPs for a *language* $\mathcal{L} \subseteq \mathbb{F}^n$, rather than for a binary relation $\mathcal{R} \subseteq \mathbb{F}^n \times \mathbb{F}^h$. This will typically be the case when $\mathcal{L}$ is efficiently recognizable, in which case the prover does not require an additional witness w. Essentially the same notions of completeness and soundness apply in this setting: if $x \in \mathcal{L}$, the verifier always accepts and for all $x \notin \mathcal{L}$ the verifier rejects except with at most ϵ probability.

We now define our main new notion of *fully linear PCPs* and their associated *strong zero knowledge* property.

Definition 6 (Fully linear PCP - FLPCP). We say that a linear PCP is *fully linear* if the decision predicate D_{LPCP} makes only linear queries to both the statement x and to the proof π. More formally, the query algorithm Q_{LPCP} outputs queries $q_1, \ldots, q_\ell \in \mathbb{F}^{m+n}$, and state information st. The decision algorithm D_{LPCP} takes as input the query answers $a_1 = \langle (x\|\pi), q_1 \rangle, \ldots, a_\ell = \langle (x\|\pi), q_\ell \rangle$, along with the state st, and outputs an accept/reject bit.

Remark. If we do not restrict the running time of the linear PCP verifier and we do not restrict the manner in which the verifier can access the statement x, then all relations have trivial a linear PCPs: an inefficient linear PCP verifier can simply iterate over every possible witness w and test whether $(x, w) \in \mathcal{R}$. To make the definition non-trivial, the standard notion of PCPs [82] (and also linear PCPs [23,58]) restricts the verifier to run in polynomial time. In contrast, a fully linear PCP restricts the *verifier's access to the statement* x by permitting the verifier to make a bounded number of linear queries to x. This restriction makes the definition non-trivial: even if the verifier can run in unbounded time, it cannot necessarily decide whether $x \in \mathcal{L}(\mathcal{R})$ without the help of a proof π.

Definition 7 (Strong zero-knowledge fully linear PCPs). A fully linear PCP is *strong honest-verifier zero knowledge* (strong HVZK) if there exists a simulator S_{LPCP} such that for all $(x, w) \in \mathcal{R}$, the following distributions are identical:

$$S_{\mathsf{LPCP}}() \equiv \left\{ \begin{array}{c} (q_1, \ldots, q_\ell) \\ (\langle (x\|\pi), q_1 \rangle, \ldots, \langle (x\|\pi), q_\ell \rangle) \end{array} : \begin{array}{c} \pi \leftarrow P_{\mathsf{LPCP}}(x, w) \\ (q_1, \ldots, q_\ell) \leftarrow Q_{\mathsf{LPCP}}() \end{array} \right\}.$$

Remark. The strong zero-knowledge property here departs from the traditional zero-knowledge notion in that it essentially requires that an honest verifier learn *nothing* about the statement x by interacting with the prover, except that $x \in \mathcal{L}(\mathcal{R})$. This notion is meaningful in our applications, since the statement x could be encrypted or secret-shared (for example), and thus it makes sense for a verifier to learn that $x \in \mathcal{L}(\mathcal{R})$ without learning anything else about x.

Fully Linear Interactive Oracle Proofs. In a linear PCP, the interaction between the prover and verifier is "one-shot:" the prover produces a proof π, the verifier makes queries to the proof, and the verifier either accepts or rejects the proof. We define *fully linear interactive oracle proofs* ("fully linear IOPs"), generalizing linear PCPs to several communication rounds. This sort of linear proof system is inspired by the notion of IOPs from [20,76] (generalizing an earlier notion of interactive PCPs [59]) that use point queries instead of linear queries.

In the ith round of a linear IOP interaction, the prover sends the verifier a proof $\pi_i \in \mathbb{F}^m$, where $\mathbb{F}$ is a finite field and m is a proof length parameter. The verifier issues linear queries to the proof π_i and then sends a challenge $r_i \in \{0,1\}^*$ to the prover. The verifier's queries in round i, along with the challenges it produces, may depend on all of the messages it has seen thus far. The prover's next proof π_{i+1} may depend on the challenge r_i, and all of the messages it has seen so far.

As with a linear PCP, we also introduce the notion of *fully linear IOPs*, in which the verifier makes only linear queries to the input, and define the strong zero-knowledge property in a natural way. The fully linear IOPs constructed in this work are all *public-coin* in the following sense.

Definition 8 (Public-coin fully linear IOP). We say that a t-round ℓ-query fully linear IOP is *public coin* if it satisfies the following additional properties:

1. In every round $i \in \{1, \ldots, t\}$ of interaction, first the prover provides a proof π_i and then a *public* random challenge r_i is picked uniformly at random from a finite set $\mathcal{S}_i$. (The choice of r_i is made independently of the proof π_i of the same round.) The public randomness r_i can influence all proofs generated by the prover in the following rounds. Following the final round, ℓ queries $(q_1, \ldots, q_\ell)$ (made to $x\|\pi_1\|\ldots\|\pi_t$) are determined by the random challenges $(r_1, \ldots, r_t)$.
2. The verifier's decision predicate is a function only of the public random challenges $(r_1, \ldots, r_t)$ and the answers to the verifier's queries $(q_1, \ldots, q_\ell)$.

When the first round does not involve a proof but only a random challenge π_i, we deduct $1/2$ from the number of rounds. In particular, a 1.5-round public-coin fully linear IOP is one that involves (in this order): a random challenge r, a proof π (that may depend on r), queries $(q_1, \ldots, q_\ell)$ to $x\|\pi$ that may depend on fresh public randomness r', and decision based on r, r' and the answers to the queries.

4   Constructions: Fully Linear PCPs

In this section we first show how to construct fully linear PCPs from existing linear PCPs. Next, we introduce a new fully linear PCP that yields shorter proofs for languages that are recognized by arithmetic circuits with certain repeated structure; the only cost is an increase in the algebraic degree of the verifier, which is irrelevant for the main applications we consider. This new fully linear PCP is used by our fully linear IOP constructions in Sect. 5.

We begin by observing that the Hadamard [6,23] and GGPR-style linear PCPs [18,23,49,79], as described in the work of Bitansky et al. [23, Appendix A], satisfy our new notions of full linearity and strong zero knowledge (Table 3).

Table 3. A comparison of existing and new fully linear PCP constructions for satisfiability of an arithmetic circuit $C : \mathbb{F}^n \to \mathbb{F}$. Proof length measures the number of field elements in $\mathbb{F}$. For the G-gates construction, $G : \mathbb{F}^L \to \mathbb{F}$ is an arithmetic circuit of degree $\deg G$ and M is the number of G-gates in the circuit C.

Linear PCP	Proof length	Queries	Verifier deg	Soundness error
Hadamard LPCP [6,23]	$O(|C|^2)$	3	2	$O(1)/|\mathbb{F}|$
GGPR-style [49]	$O(|C|)$	4	2	$O(|C|)/|\mathbb{F}|$
G-gates (Theorem 11)	$M \cdot \deg G$	$L + 2$	$\deg G$	$M \cdot \deg G/(|\mathbb{F}| - M)$
Degree-two (Corollary 13)	$O(\sqrt{|C|})$	$O(\sqrt{|C|})$	2	$O(\sqrt{|C|})/|\mathbb{F}|$

Claim 9 (Informal). The Hadamard linear PCP and the GGPR-based linear PCP are constant-query *fully* linear PCPs, in the sense of Definition 6. Moreover, they yield fully linear PCPs with *strong* HVZK.

We now describe a fully linear PCP for arithmetic circuit satisfiability, for circuits C with a certain type of repeated structure. When applied to arithmetic circuits of size $|C|$, it can yield proofs of length $o(|C|)$ field elements. In contrast, the existing general-purpose linear PCPs in Claim 9 have proof size $\Omega(|C|)$.

This new linear PCP construction applies to circuits that contain many instances of the same subcircuit, which we call a "G-gate." If the arithmetic degree of the G-gate is small, then the resulting linear PCP is short. More formally, we define:

Definition 10 (Arithmetic circuit with G-gates). We say that a gate in an arithmetic circuit is an *affine gate* if (a) it is an addition gate, or (b) it is a multiplication gate in which one of the two input is a constant. Let $G : \mathbb{F}^L \to \mathbb{F}$ be an arithmetic circuit composed of affine gates and multiplication gates. An *arithmetic circuit with G-gates* is an arithmetic circuit composed of affine gates and G-gates.

The following theorem is the main result of this section. Recall that $|G|$ refers to the number of non-constant multiplication gates in the arithmetic circuit for G.

Theorem 11. *Let C be an arithmetic circuit with G-gates over $\mathbb{F}$ such that:*

(a) the gate $G : \mathbb{F}^L \to \mathbb{F}$ has arithmetic degree $\deg G$,
(b) the circuit C consists of M instances of a G-gate and any number of affine gates, and

(c) the field $\mathbb{F}$ is such that $|\mathbb{F}| > M \deg G$.

Then, there exists a fully linear PCP with strong HVZK for the relation $\mathcal{R}_C = \{(x, w) \in \mathbb{F}^n \times \mathbb{F}^h \mid C(x, w) = 0\}$ that has:

- *proof length $h + L + M \deg G + 1$ elements of $\mathbb{F}$, where h is the witness length and L is the arity of the G-gate,*
- *query complexity $L + 2$,*
- *soundness error $M \deg G / (|\mathbb{F}| - M)$, and*
- *a verification circuit of degree $\deg G$ containing $|G|$ multiplication gates.*

Furthermore, if we require a fully linear PCP that is not necessarily strong HVZK, then the proof length decreases to $h + (M - 1) \deg G + 1$ elements of $\mathbb{F}$ and the soundness error decreases to $M \deg G / |\mathbb{F}|$.

The proof of Theorem 11 uses the following simple fact about the linearity of polynomial interpolation and evaluation.

Fact 12. *Let $\mathbb{F}$ be a finite field and let $\pi \in \mathbb{F}^m$. For some integer $n < |\mathbb{F}|$, let $A_1, \ldots, A_n$ be affine functions that map $\mathbb{F}^m$ to $\mathbb{F}$. Define f to be the polynomial of lowest-degree such that $f(i) = A_i(\pi)$ for all $i \in \{1, \ldots, n\}$. Then for all $r \in \mathbb{F}$ and all choices of the A_i, there exists a vector $\lambda_r \in \mathbb{F}^m$ and scalar $\delta_r \in \mathbb{F}$, such that $f(r) = \langle \lambda_r, \pi \rangle + \delta_r$ for all $\pi \in \mathbb{F}^m$.*

Fact 12 says that given the values of a polynomial f at the points $1, \ldots, n$ as affine functions of a vector $\pi \in \mathbb{F}^m$, we can express $f(r)$ as an affine function of π, and this affine function is independent of π. This follows from the fact that polynomial interpolation applied to the n points $\{(i, A_i(\pi))\}_{i=1}^{n}$ followed by polynomial evaluation at the point r is an affine function of π.

Proof of Theorem 11. The construction that proves Theorem 11 is a generalization of the linear PCP implicit in the construction used in the Prio system [37] and is closely related to a Merlin-Arthur proof system of Williams for batch verification of circuit evaluation [84]. Figure 1 gives an example of the proof construction, applied to a particular simple circuit.

Label the G-gates of the circuit C in topological order from inputs to outputs; there are M such gates in the circuit. Without loss of generality, we assume that the output of the circuit C is the value on the output wire of the last G-gate in the circuit.

FLPCP Prover. On input $(x, w) \in \mathbb{F}^n \times \mathbb{F}^h$, the prover evaluates the circuit $C(\cdot, \cdot)$ on the pair (x, w). The prover then defines L polynomials $f_1, \ldots, f_L \in \mathbb{F}[X]$ such that, for every $i \in \{1, \ldots, L\}$,

(i) the constant term $f_i(0)$ is a value chosen independently and uniformly at random from $\mathbb{F}$, and
(ii) for all $j \in \{1, \ldots, M\}$, $f_i(j) \in \mathbb{F}$ is the value on the i-th input wire to the j-th G-gate when evaluating the circuit C on the input-witness pair (x, w).

Furthermore, the prover lets $f_1, \ldots, f_L$ be the polynomials of lowest degree that satisfy these relations. Observe that each of the polynomials $f_1, \ldots, f_L$ has degree at most M.

Next, the prover constructs a proof polynomial $p = G(f_1, \ldots, f_L) \in \mathbb{F}[X]$. By construction of p, we know that, for $j \in \{1, \ldots, M\}$, $p(j)$ is the value on the output wire from the j-th G-gate in the evaluation of $C(x, w)$. Moreover, $p(M) = C(x, w)$. Let d be the degree of the polynomial p and let $c_p \in \mathbb{F}^{d+1}$ be the vector of coeffcients of $p \in \mathbb{F}[X]$. By construction, the degree of p satisfies $d \leq M \deg G$.

The prover outputs $\pi = (w, \ f_1(0), \ldots, f_L(0), \ c_p) \in \mathbb{F}^{h+L+d+1}$ as the linear PCP proof.

(*Note:* If we do not require strong HVZK to hold, then the prover need not randomize the constant terms of the polynomials $f_1, \ldots, f_L$. In this case, the prover does not include the values $f_1(0), \ldots, f_L(0)$ in the proof, and the degree of the polynomial p decreases to $(M-1) \deg G$. Thus, if we do not require strong HVZK, the proof length falls to $h + (M-1) \deg G + 1$.)

FLPCP Queries. We can parse the (possibly maliciously crafted) proof $\pi \in \mathbb{F}^{h+L+d+1}$ as: a purported witness $w' \in \mathbb{F}^h$, the values $(z'_1, \ldots, z'_L) \in \mathbb{F}^L$ representing the constant terms of some polynomials $f'_1, \ldots, f'_L$, and the coefficients $c'_p \in \mathbb{F}^{d+1}$ of a polynomial $p' \in \mathbb{F}[X]$ of degree at most d. If the proof is well-formed, the polynomial p' is such that $p'(j)$ encodes the output wire of the jth G-gate in the circuit $C(\cdot, \cdot)$ when evaluated on the pair (x, w').

Given p', we define L polynomials $f'_1, \ldots, f'_L \in \mathbb{F}[X]$ such that:

(i) the constant term satisfies $f'_i(0) = z'_i$, where z'_i is the value included in the proof π', and

(ii) $f'_i(j) \in \mathbb{F}$ is the value on the i-th input wire to the j-th G-gate in the circuit, under the purported assignment of values to the output wires of the G-gates implied by the polynomial p' and witness w'.

More precisely, we define $f'_i(j)$ inductively: The value on the ith input wire to the jth G-gate in the circuit $C(x, w')$ is some affine function A_{ij} of

 – the input $x \in \mathbb{F}^n$,
 – the purported witness $w' \in \mathbb{F}^h$, and
 – the purported outputs of the first $j-1$ G-gates in the circuit: $p'(1), \ldots, p'(j-1) \in \mathbb{F}$.

So, for all $i \in \{1, \ldots, L\}$, we define f'_i to be the polynomial of least degree satisfying:

$$f'_i(0) = z'_i$$
$$f'_i(j) = A_{ij}(x, w', p'(1), \ldots, p'(j-1)) \qquad \text{for} \quad 1 \leq j \leq M,$$

where A_{ij} is a fixed affine function defined by the circuit C.

The verifier's goal is to check that:

1. $p' = G(f'_1, \ldots, f'_L)$, and,
2. the circuit output $p'(M)$ satisfies $p'(M) = 0$.

As we argue below, the first condition ensures that $p'(M)$ is equal to the output of the circuit $C(x, w')$. The second check ensures that the output is 0.

To implement the first check, the verifier samples a random point $r \xleftarrow{\text{R}} \mathbb{F} \setminus \{1, \ldots, M\}$ and outputs query vectors that allow evaluating p' and $f'_1, \ldots, f'_L$ at the point r. (For the honest-verifier zero knowledge property to hold, it is important that we exclude the set $\{1, \ldots, M\}$ from the set of choices for r.) The verifier has linear access to the input x, witness w', constant terms $z' = (z'_1, \ldots, z'_L)$, and the coefficients $c'_p \in \mathbb{F}^{d+1}$ of the polynomial p'. Hence, using Fact 12, it follows that the query algorithm can compute vectors $\lambda_1, \ldots, \lambda_L \in \mathbb{F}^{n+h+L+d+1}$ and scalars $\delta_1, \ldots, \delta_L \in \mathbb{F}$ such that $f'_i(r) = \langle \lambda_i, (x \| w' \| z' \| c') \rangle + \delta_i$ for $i = 1, \ldots, L$, where $r \in \mathbb{F}$ is the random point chosen above. Similarly, the query algorithm can compute a vector $\lambda \in \mathbb{F}^{n+h+L+d+1}$ such that $p'(r) = \langle \lambda, (x \| w' \| z' \| c') \rangle$.

The verifier can execute the second check, to ensure that $p'(M) = 0$, with a single linear query.

FLPCP Decision. The decision algorithm takes as input the state value $r \in \mathbb{F} \setminus \{1, \ldots, M\}$, along with the query answers $a, a_1, \ldots, a_L, b \in \mathbb{F}$, where $a = p'(r)$, $a_i = f'_i(r)$ for $i \in \{1, \ldots, \ell\}$, and $b = p'(M)$. The verifier accepts if $a = G(a_1, \ldots, a_L)$ and $b = 0$.

Security Arguments. We show completeness, soundness, and strong HVZK.

Completeness. If the prover is honest, then $p' = G(f'_1, \ldots, f'_L)$ and $p'(M) = 0$ by construction. The verifier will always accept in this case.

Soundness. Fix a circuit C, a statement $x \in \mathbb{F}^n$, and a proof $\pi' \in \mathbb{F}^{h+L+d+1}$. We show that if $x \notin \mathcal{L}(\mathcal{R}_C)$ then the verifier accepts with probability at most $M \deg G / (|\mathbb{F}| - M)$.

As in the description of the query algorithm, we can view:

- the first h elements of the proof as a witness $w' \in \mathbb{F}^h$,
- the next L elements of the proof as constant terms $z'_1, \ldots, z'_L \in \mathbb{F}$, and
- the latter elements as the coefficients of a polynomial p' of degree at most $d \leq M \deg G$.

We may assume that $p'(M) = 0$, since otherwise the verifier always rejects. In the discussion that follows, let the polynomials $f'_1, \ldots, f'_L$ be the ones defined in the description of the linear PCP query algorithm.

We claim that if for all $j \in \{1, \ldots, M\}$, it holds that $p'(j) = G(f'_1(j), \ldots, f'_L(j))$, then for all $j \in \{1, \ldots, M\}$, $p'(j)$ encodes the value of the output wire of the jth G-gate in the circuit C when evaluated on input (x, w').

We prove this claim by induction on j:

- *Base case $(j = 1)$.* The values $(f'_1(1), \ldots, f'_L(1))$ depend only on the pair (x, w'). By construction, the values $(f'_1(1), \ldots, f'_L(1))$ are exactly the values of the input wires to the first G-gate in the evaluation of $C(x, w')$. Then if $p'(1) = G(f'_1(1), \ldots, f'_L(1))$, $p'(1)$ encodes the value on the output wire of the first G-gate.

- *Induction step.* Assume that, for all $k \in \{1, \ldots, j - 1\}$, $p'(k) = G(f'_1(k), \ldots, f'_L(k))$. Then, by the induction hypothesis, $(p'(1), \ldots, p'(j-1))$ are the values on the output wires of the first $j - 1$ G-gates of C, when evaluated on (x, w').

  The values $(f'_1(j), \ldots, f'_L(j))$ are affine functions of x, w' and the values $p'(1), \ldots, p'(j - 1)$. Then, by construction of the polynomials $(f'_1, \ldots, f'_L)$, the values $(f'_1(j), \ldots, f'_L(j))$ encode the values on the input wires to the j-th G-gate in the evaluation of the circuit $C(x, w')$. Finally, if we assume that $p'(j) = G(f'_1(j), \ldots, f'_L(j))$, then $p'(j)$ must be the value on the output wire of the jth G-gate.

  We have thus proved the induction step.

This completes the proof of the claim.

If $p'(M) = 0$ (as we have assumed), but there exists no witness w' such that $C(x, w') = 0$, then $p'(M)$ does not encode the output value of the Mth G-gate in the evaluation of the circuit $C(x, w')$. By the claim just proved, this implies that for some $j^* \in \{1, \ldots, M\}$, $p'(j^*) \neq G(f'_1(j^*), \ldots, f'_L(j^*))$. Thus, when we view $p', f'_1, \ldots, f'_L \in \mathbb{F}[X]$ as univariate polynomials, we have that $p' \neq G(f'_1, \ldots, f'_L)$.

Now, if $p' \neq G(f'_1, \ldots, f'_L)$ then $p' - G(f'_1, \ldots, f'_L) \in \mathbb{F}[X]$ is a non-zero univariate polynomial of degree at most $M \deg G$. Such a polynomial can have at most $M \deg G$ roots over $\mathbb{F}$. Therefore the probability, over the verifier's random choice of $r \xleftarrow{\text{R}} \mathbb{F}\backslash\{1, \ldots, M\}$, that $p'(r) - G(f'_1(r), \ldots, f'_L(r)) = 0$ is at most $M \deg G/(|\mathbb{F}| - M)$. We conclude that the verifier accepts a false proof with probability at most $M \deg G/(|\mathbb{F}| - M)$.

See full version for a proof that the construction satisfies strong HVZK. $\quad\square$

If we define the G-gate to be a multiplication gate, so that $\deg G = 2$, then the construction of Theorem 11 matches the complexity of the GGPR-based linear PCP [49,79] and provides what is essentially an alternative formulation of that proof system. In contrast, if $\deg G \ll |G|$, then this construction can yield significantly shorter proofs than the GGPR-based linear PCP, at the cost of increasing the algebraic degree of the verifier from 2 to $\deg G$.

Remark. We can generalize Theorem 11 to handle circuits with many distinct repeated subcircuits $G_1, \ldots, G_q$ with M_i instances of each gate $G_i : \mathbb{F}^{L_i} \to \mathbb{F}$, for $i \in \{1, \ldots, q\}$. The resulting fully linear PCP with strong HVZK has proof length at most $h + (\sum_{i=1}^{q} L_i) + (\sum_{i=1}^{q} M_i \deg G_i) + q$ elements of $\mathbb{F}$, query complexity $1 + \sum_{i=1}^{q}(L_i + 1)$, a verifier of algebraic degree $\max_i \deg G_i$, and soundness error $\sum_{i=1}^{q} (M_i \deg G_i/(|\mathbb{F}| - M_i))$.

Remark. To get good soundness when applying the proof system of Theorem 11, the field $\mathbb{F}$ must be such that $|\mathbb{F}| \gg M \deg G$. In many applications, the input $x \in \mathbb{F}^n$ is a vector in a small field, such as the binary field $\mathbb{F}_2$. In this case, we apply Theorem 11 by lifting x into an extension field $\tilde{\mathbb{F}}$ of $\mathbb{F}$, and carrying out the linear PCP operations in the extension.

The randomization technique we use to achieve honest-verifier zero-knowledge in Theorem 11 is inspired by the one that appears in the work of Bitansky et al. [23] for achieving HVZK in the Hadamard linear PCP construction.

Application: Short Proofs for Degree-Two Relations. As an application of Theorem 11 we demonstrate a special-purpose fully linear PCP for relations recognized by arithmetic circuits of degree two. When applied to an arithmetic circuit $C : \mathbb{F}^n \times \mathbb{F}^h \to \mathbb{F}$, we obtain a proof that consists of only $O(h + \sqrt{n})$ field elements and whose query complexity is only $O(\sqrt{n+h})$. For general-purpose

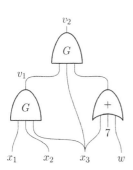

Circuit. An example circuit $C(x_1, x_2, x_3, w)$ using an arbitrary three-input G-gate. The circuit takes as input the vector $(x_1, x_2, x_3) \in \mathbb{F}^3$, and a witness $w \in \mathbb{F}$. The circuit C outputs v_2, the value on the output wire of the topologically last G-gate.

Linear PCP proof. Using Theorem 11, we construct a fully linear PCP proof π that the input $(x_1, x_2, x_3) \in \mathbb{F}^3$ is in the language recognized by C. That is, the prover asserts that there exists a witness $w \in \mathbb{F}$ such that $C(x_1, x_2, x_3, w) = 0 \in \mathbb{F}$.

The prover first constructs three polynomials f_1, f_2, f_3. The value $f_i(j)$ encodes the value on the i-th input to the j-th G-gate, in topological order from inputs to outputs. The constant terms are random elements $z_1, z_2, z_3 \xleftarrow{\text{R}} \mathbb{F}$. That is:

$$f_1(0)=z_1 \qquad f_2(0)=z_2 \qquad f_3(0)=z_3$$
$$f_1(1)=x_1 \qquad f_2(1)=x_2 \qquad f_3(1)=x_3$$
$$f_1(2)=v_1=G(x_1,x_2,x_3) \qquad f_2(2)=x_3 \qquad f_3(2)=x_3+w+7$$

Next, the prover constructs the polynomial p, which satisfies $p = G(f_1, f_2, f_3)$, and which has degree at most $d = 2 \deg G$. Notice that for $j \in \{1,2\}$, $p(j)$ is the value on the output wire of the j-th G-gate. Letting $d = 3 \deg G$, we can write the values of p as:

$$p(0)=G(f_1(0),f_2(0),f_3(0))=G(z_1,z_2,z_3)$$
$$p(1)=G(f_1(1),f_2(1),f_3(1))=v_1=G(x_1,x_2,x_3)$$
$$p(2)=G(f_1(2),f_2(2),f_3(2))=v_2=G(v_1,x_3,x_3+w+7)$$
$$p(3)=G(f_1(3),f_2(3),f_3(3))$$
$$\vdots$$
$$p(d)=G(f_1(d),f_2(d),f_3(d))$$

The linear PCP proof π consists of the elements: $(w, z_1, z_2, z_3, \bar{p}) \in \mathbb{F}^{L+d+2}$, where $\bar{p} \in \mathbb{F}^{d+1}$ is the vector of coefficients of the polynomial p.

Fig. 1. An example of the fully linear PCP proof of Theorem 11.

linear PCPs, such as the Hadamard or GGPR-based linear PCPs, the proof length plus query complexity is much larger: $\Omega(n + h)$.

A special case of this proof yields a linear PCP for the language of vectors whose inner product is equal to a certain value. To give one application of such a proof system: Given encryptions of two sets, represented by their characteristic vectors, this proof system would allow a prover to succinctly show that the sets are disjoint.

This construction also reveals the close connection between fully linear PCPs and communication complexity. Without zero knowledge, this proof protocol boils down to the Merlin-Arthur communication complexity protocol of Aaronson and Wigderson [1]. Furthermore, as we show in the full version of this work, we can use lower bounds on the communication complexity of inner-product to show that this fully linear PCP construction has essentially optimal parameters.

Corollary 13 (FLPCP for degree-two circuits). *Let $\mathbb{F}$ be a finite field, let $C : \mathbb{F}^n \times \mathbb{F}^h \to \mathbb{F}$ be an arithmetic circuit of degree two, and let $\mathcal{R}_C = \{(x, w) \in \mathbb{F}^n \times \mathbb{F}^h \mid C(x, w) = 0\}$. There is a fully linear PCP with strong HVZK for $\mathcal{R}_C$ that has proof length $h + O(\sqrt{n + h})$ elements of $\mathbb{F}$, query complexity $O(\sqrt{n + h})$, a verifier of algebraic degree 2, and soundness error $\frac{O(\sqrt{n+h})}{|\mathbb{F}| - \lceil\sqrt{n+h}\rceil}$.*

The idea of Corollary 13 is that any degree-two circuit $C : \mathbb{F}^n \to \mathbb{F}$ can be expressed as a circuit that computes an inner-product of dimension-n vectors, along with some number of affine gates. This property is special to degree-two circuits—the idea does not easily generalize to circuits of higher constant degree.

Proof of Corollary 13. Without loss of generality we can assume that C implements a quadratic form $C(x, w) = (x\|w)^T \cdot A \cdot (x\|w)$ for some matrix $A \in \mathbb{F}^{(n+h) \times (n+h)}$. Indeed, a proof system for quadratic forms yields a proof system for any circuit of degree 2. We can re-write $C(x, w)$ as the inner-product of the vectors $y = (x\|w)$ and $z = A \cdot (x\|w)$ in $\mathbb{F}^{n+h}$. Hence, it suffices to design a fully linear PCP for the inner-product relation $\mathcal{R}'_C = \{(x, w) \in \mathbb{F}^n \times \mathbb{F}^h \mid \langle (x\|w) , A \cdot (x\|w) \rangle = 0\}$.

Let L^2 be the closest perfect square greater than or equal to $n + h$, and pad the vectors $y = (x\|w)$ and $z = A(x\|w)$ with zeros so that both are in $\mathbb{F}^{(L^2)}$. Next, arrange the vector y into a matrix $Y \in \mathbb{F}^{L \times L}$, and arrange z into a matrix $Z \in \mathbb{F}^{L \times L}$ in the same way. Then $C(x, w) = \langle y, z \rangle = \text{trace}(Y \cdot Z^T)$.

Because the trace is a linear function, we can compute $C(x, w)$ using a circuit C' consisting of only addition gates and a total of L gates $G : \mathbb{F}^L \times \mathbb{F}^L \to \mathbb{F}$ defined as $G(u, v) = \langle u, v \rangle$ for $u, v \in \mathbb{F}^L$. Clearly $\deg G = 2$ and $L = O(\sqrt{n + h})$. Applying Theorem 11 to this G-gate circuit gives a fully linear PCP for $\mathcal{R}_{C'}$ with strong HVZK with the parameters stated in the corollary, as required. The proof needs at most $2L$ additional linear queries to verify that the padding in y and z is all zero, but this does not change the parameters in the corollary.   □

Remark. A simple extension of Corollary 13 yields a two-round (in fact, 1.5-round) fully linear IOP for relations recognized by general degree-two circuits

$C : \mathbb{F}^n \times \mathbb{F}^h \to \mathbb{F}^k$, for $k \geq 1$. To sketch the idea behind this extension, write the circuit C as $C(x) = (C_1(x), C_2(x), \ldots, C_k(x)) \in \mathbb{F}^k$, where each C_i is a degree-two circuit. In the first round of the protocol, the verifier sends a random value $r \in \mathbb{F}$. Then the prover and verifier define the degree-two circuit $C_r(x) = \sum_{i=1}^{k} r^i \cdot C_i(x) \in \mathbb{F}$. The prover then uses the fully linear PCP of Corollary 13 to convince the verifier that C_r accepts the input $x \in \mathbb{F}^n$. The efficiency parameters match those of the corollary, except that the soundness error increases by an additive term $k/|\mathbb{F}|$ to account for the failure event that some $C_i(x)$ outputs a non-zero value and yet the sum $C_r(x)$ is zero. See Theorem 15 for a more general version of this protocol.

Application: Short Proofs for Parallel-Sum Circuits. As a second application of Theorem 11, we give a special-purpose fully linear PCP for languages recognized by circuits that take as input a vector $x \in \mathbb{F}^n$ and:

- apply an affine transformation to the input,
- apply the same sub-circuit $C : \mathbb{F}^L \to \mathbb{F}$ in parallel to each block of L values,
- sum the outputs of the C circuits.

More formally, let $C : \mathbb{F}^L \to \mathbb{F}$ be an arithmetic circuit. Let $A : \mathbb{F}^n \to \mathbb{F}$ and $A_1, \ldots, A_M : \mathbb{F}^n \to \mathbb{F}^L$ be affine functions. This linear PCP construction applies to the language of values $x \in \mathbb{F}^n$ such that $\sum_{i=1}^{M} C(A_i(x)) = A(x)$.

Corollary 14 (FLPCP for parallel-sum circuits). *Let $C : \mathbb{F}^L \to \mathbb{F}$ be an arithmetic circuit over $\mathbb{F}$ that has arithmetic degree $\deg C$. Let $A : \mathbb{F}^n \to \mathbb{F}$ and $A_1, \ldots, A_M \in \mathbb{F}^n \to \mathbb{F}^L$ be affine functions. Then, there exists a strong HVZK fully linear PCP for the language $\mathcal{L}_{C,A,A_1,\ldots,A_M} = \{x \in \mathbb{F}^n \mid \sum_{i=1}^{M} C(A_i(x)) = A(x)\}$ that has:*

- *proof length $O(\sqrt{M} \cdot (L + \deg C))$ elements of $\mathbb{F}$,*
- *query complexity $O(\sqrt{M} \cdot L)$,*
- *soundness error $\frac{\sqrt{M} \cdot \deg C}{|\mathbb{F}| - \sqrt{M}}$, and*
- *an arithmetic verification circuit of degree $\deg C$ containing $O(\sqrt{M} \cdot |C|)$ multiplication gates.*

Proof of Corollary 14. We define an appropriate G-gate and then invoke Theorem 11. Assume that M is a perfect square, since otherwise we can pad M up to the nearest square. The gadget $G : \mathbb{F}^{\sqrt{M}L} \to \mathbb{F}$ applies the circuit C to $\sqrt{M}$ blocks of L inputs. So, on input $(\bar{x}_1, \ldots, \bar{x}_{\sqrt{M}}) \in \mathbb{F}^{\sqrt{M}L}$, where $\bar{x}_j \in \mathbb{F}^L$ for all $j \in \{1, \ldots, \sqrt{M}\}$, the G-gate outputs:

$$G(\bar{x}_1, \ldots, \bar{x}_{\sqrt{M}}) \overset{\text{def}}{=} \sum_{j=1}^{\sqrt{M}} C(\bar{x}_j) \quad \in \mathbb{F}. \tag{1}$$

Then the language $\mathcal{L}_{C,A,A_1,\ldots,A_M}$ is recognized by a circuit containing $M' = \sqrt{M}$ instances of the G-gate, along with some number of affine gates. Applying Theorem 11 using this G-gate yields a fully linear PCP as required. □

5   Constructions: Fully Linear Interactive Oracle Proofs

In this section, we describe an extension of our fully linear PCPs to fuller linear interactive oracle proofs (linear IOPs). These extra rounds of interaction can buy efficiency improvements in total proof length and verifier time.

For example, a corollary of our general construction gives an $O(\log n)$ round strong HVZK fully linear IOP for proving that a vector $x \in \mathbb{F}^n$ consists entirely of $0/1$ entries, where the proof size is only $O(\log n)$ field elements. In comparison, linear PCPs yield proofs of size $\Omega(n)$.

Several protocols from the literature, including notably the "Muggles" protocol of Goldwasser, Kalai, and Rothblum [51,52] are implicitly linear IOPs. See full version for connections between our notion and these protocols.

A Recursive Linear IOP for Parallel-Sum Circuits. Corollary 14 gives a linear PCP for "parallel-sum" circuits whose length grows as the square root of the degree of parallelism. Here, we show that by increasing the number of rounds between the prover and verifier, we can decrease the proof size to *logarithmic* in the degree of parallelism. The key observation is that in Corollary 14, the linear PCP verifier is itself a parallel-sum circuit. So rather than having the verifier evaluate this circuit on its own, the verifier can outsource the work of evaluating the verification circuit to the prover. The prover then uses a secondary linear PCP to convince the verifier that it executed this step correctly.

To get the optimal bounds we rebalance the parameters used in the proof of Corollary 14. Instead of a G-gate containing $\sqrt{M}$ copies of C, as in (1), we use a G-gate containing $M/2$ copies of C, and then recursively verify one input/output pair for that G-gate.

A useful application of this technique is to the case of "low-degree languages," namely languages in which membership can be checked by a system of low-degree equations. The following theorem, whose proof appears in the full version, describes fully linear IOPs for such low-degree languages, over both finite fields and rings of the form $R = \mathbb{Z}_w$.

Theorem 15 (ZK-FLIOP for low-degree languages). *Let R be a ring, let $C : R^n \to R^m$ be an arithmetic multi-output circuit of degree d defined by $C(x) = (C_1(x), \ldots, C_m(x))$ and let M be the number of distinct monomials in the representation of $C_1, \ldots, C_m$ as polynomials. Let $\mathcal{L}_C = \{x \in R^n \mid C(x) = 0^m\}$ and let ϵ be a required soundness error bound. Then, there is a fully linear IOP Π over R with strong HVZK for the language $\mathcal{L}_C$ that has the following efficiency features.*

- **Degree $d = 2$, constant rounds:** *If $d = 2$ then Π has 1.5 rounds, proof length $O(\eta\sqrt{n})$, challenge length $O(\eta)$, and query complexity $O(\sqrt{n})$, where $\eta = \log_{|R|}((m + \sqrt{n})/\epsilon)$ if R is a finite field or $\eta = \log_2((m + \sqrt{n})/\epsilon)$ if $R = \mathbb{Z}_{2^k}$. The computational complexity is $\tilde{O}(M)$*
- **Degree d, logarithmic rounds:** *If $d \geq 2$ then Π has $O(\log M)$ rounds, proof length $O(\eta d \log M)$, challenge length $O(\eta)$, and query complexity $O(\log M)$,*

where $\eta = \log_{|R|}((m + d \log M)/\epsilon)$ if R is a finite field or $\eta = \log_2((m + d \log M)/\epsilon)$ if $R = \mathbb{Z}_{2^k}$. The computational complexity is $\tilde{O}(dM)$.

Trading Communication for Computation. Most of our motivating applications involve low-degree verification circuits that have constant output locality. For instance, this is the case for checking that $x \in \{0, 1\}^n$ or for languages corresponding to standard MPC protocols (e.g., checking Beaver triples). In this case, we can reduce computational cost while maintaining sublinear communication via the following simple tradeoff technique. Chop the m outputs into blocks of size ℓ, viewing each block as a low-degree circuit with $O(\ell)$ inputs and ℓ outputs, and apply a separate FLIOP to each block. This gives a smooth tradeoff between communication and computation, which may be useful for tuning concrete efficiency depending on the available bandwidth and computational power.

6   Conclusions

We have demonstrated that fully linear proof systems capture many existing techniques for zero-knowledge proof on secret-shared, encrypted, or committed data. We presented new constructions of zero-knowledge fully linear PCPs and IOPs for "simple" languages with sublinear proof size, and demonstrated the usefulness of such proof systems to protecting secret-sharing based MPC protocols against malicious parties with low communication overhead.

Despite some progress obtained in this work and in prior related works, there is a lot more to understand about the power of (fully) linear PCPs and their interactive variants. We mention a couple of concrete open questions:

- To what extent are the tradeoffs we obtain for low-degree languages optimal? In particular, is there a linear PCP of size $o(n)$ for the language $\mathcal{L}_{\{0,1\}^n} \stackrel{\text{def}}{=} \{x \in \mathbb{F}^n \mid x \in \{0,1\}^n\}$? Our sublinear constructions require interaction.
- Are there linear PCPs for general arithmetic circuit satisfiability with constant query complexity and proof size sublinear in the circuit size? In the full version, we show a lower bound result that unconditionally rules out such succinct *fully* linear PCPs. *Standard* PCPs with succinctness properties cannot exist unless the polynomial hierarchy collapses [47]. Does the same restriction apply to general linear PCPs?

Acknowledgments. We thank Shai Halevi, Ariel Nof, Ron Rothblum, David J. Wu, and Eylon Yogev for helpful discussions and comments. Justin Thaler gave us many useful references to related work on sum-check-based proof protocols and helped us understand the relationship between those protocols and our own.

E. Boyle, N. Gilboa, and Y. Ishai supported by ERC grant 742754 (project NTSC). E. Boyle additionally supported by ISF grant 1861/16 and AFOSR Award FA9550-17-1-0069. N. Gilboa additionally supported by ISF grant 1638/15, and a grant by the BGU Cyber Center. Y. Ishai additionally supported by ISF grant 1709/14, NSF-BSF grant 2015782, and a grant from the Ministry of Science and Technology, Israel and Department of Science and Technology, Government of India. D. Boneh and H. Corrigan-Gibbs are supported by NSF, ONR, DARPA, the Simons Foundation, CISPA, and a Google faculty fellowship.

References

1. Aaronson, S., Wigderson, A.: Algebrization: a new barrier in complexity theory. ACM Trans. Comput. Theory (TOCT) **1**(1), 2 (2009)
2. Ames, S., Hazay, C., Ishai, Y., Venkitasubramaniam, M.: Ligero: lightweight sublinear arguments without a trusted setup. In: CCS (2017)
3. Andrew, C.C.Y.: Some complexity questions related to distributed computing. In: STOC (1979)
4. Araki, T., et al.: Optimized honest-majority MPC for malicious adversaries - breaking the 1 billion-gate per second barrier. In: IEEE Symposium on Security and Privacy (2017)
5. Araki, T., Furukawa, J., Lindell, Y., Nof, A., Ohara, K.: High-throughput semi-honest secure three-party computation with an honest majority. In: ACM CCS (2016)
6. Arora, S., Lund, C., Motwani, R., Sudan, M., Szegedy, M.: Proof verification and the hardness of approximation problems. J. ACM **45**(3), 501–555 (1998)
7. Arora, S., Safra, S.: Probabilistic checking of proofs: a new characterization of NP. J. ACM **45**(1), 70–122 (1998)
8. Babai, L.: Trading group theory for randomness. In: STOC (1985)
9. Babai, L., Fortnow, L., Levin, L.A., Szegedy, M.: Checking computations in polylogarithmic time. In: STOC (1991)
10. Babai, L., Moran, S.: Arthur-Merlin games: a randomized proof system, and a hierarchy of complexity classes. J. Comput. Syst. Sci. **36**(2), 254–276 (1988)
11. Backes, M., Barbosa, M., Fiore, D., Reischuk, R.M.: ADSNARK: nearly practical and privacy-preserving proofs on authenticated data. In: 2015 IEEE Symposium on Security and Privacy, SP 2015, San Jose, CA, USA, 17–21 May 2015 (2015)
12. Bellare, M., Rogaway, P.: Random oracles are practical: a paradigm for designing efficient protocols. In: CCS (1993)
13. Ben-Or, M., et al.: Everything provable is provable in zero-knowledge. In: Goldwasser, S. (ed.) CRYPTO 1988. LNCS, vol. 403, pp. 37–56. Springer, New York (1990). https://doi.org/10.1007/0-387-34799-2_4
14. Ben-Or, M., Goldwasser, S., Kilian, J., Wigderson, A.: Multi-prover interactive proofs: how to remove intractability assumptions. In: STOC (1988)
15. Ben-Sasson, E., Bentov, I., Horesh, Y., Riabzev, M.: Scalable, transparent, and post-quantum secure computational integrity. Cryptology ePrint Archive, Report 2018/046 (2018)
16. Ben-Sasson, E., Chiesa, A., Forbes, M.A., Gabizon, A., Riabzev, M., Spooner, N.: On probabilistic checking in perfect zero knowledge. In: Electronic Colloquium on Computational Complexity (ECCC), no. 156 (2016)
17. Ben-Sasson, E., Chiesa, A., Gabizon, A., Riabzev, M., Spooner, N.: Interactive oracle proofs with constant rate and query complexity. In: ICALP (2017)
18. Ben-Sasson, E., Chiesa, A., Genkin, D., Tromer, E., Virza, M.: SNARKs for C: verifying program executions succinctly and in zero knowledge. In: Canetti, R., Garay, J.A. (eds.) CRYPTO 2013. LNCS, vol. 8043, pp. 90–108. Springer, Heidelberg (2013). https://doi.org/10.1007/978-3-642-40084-1_6
19. Ben-Sasson, E., Chiesa, A., Riabzev, M., Spooner, N., Virza, M., Ward, N.P.: Aurora: transparent succinct arguments for R1CS. Cryptology ePrint Archive, Report 2018/828 (2018). https://eprint.iacr.org/2018/828
20. Ben-Sasson, E., Chiesa, A., Spooner, N.: Interactive oracle proofs. In: Hirt, M., Smith, A. (eds.) TCC 2016. LNCS, vol. 9986, pp. 31–60. Springer, Heidelberg (2016). https://doi.org/10.1007/978-3-662-53644-5_2

21. Ben-Sasson, E., Goldreich, O., Harsha, P., Sudan, M., Vadhan, S.: Robust PCPs of proximity, shorter PCPs, and applications to coding. SIAM J. Comput. **36**(4), 889–974 (2006)

22. Bitansky, N., Canetti, R., Chiesa, A., Tromer, E.: From extractable collision resistance to succinct non-interactive arguments of knowledge, and back again. In: Innovations in Theoretical Computer Science 2012, Cambridge, MA, USA, 8–10 January 2012 (2012)

23. Bitansky, N., Chiesa, A., Ishai, Y., Paneth, O., Ostrovsky, R.: Succinct non-interactive arguments via linear interactive proofs. In: Sahai, A. (ed.) TCC 2013. LNCS, vol. 7785, pp. 315–333. Springer, Heidelberg (2013). https://doi.org/10.1007/978-3-642-36594-2_18

24. Blum, M., Feldman, P., Micali, S.: Non-interactive zero-knowledge and its applications (extended abstract). In: Proceedings of the 20th Annual ACM Symposium on Theory of Computing, Chicago, Illinois, USA, 2–4 May 1988 (1988)

25. Boneh, D., Ishai, Y., Sahai, A., Wu, D.J.: Lattice-based SNARGs and their application to more efficient obfuscation. In: Coron, J.-S., Nielsen, J.B. (eds.) EUROCRYPT 2017. LNCS, vol. 10212, pp. 247–277. Springer, Cham (2017). https://doi.org/10.1007/978-3-319-56617-7_9

26. Boneh, D., Ishai, Y., Sahai, A., Wu, D.J.: Quasi-optimal SNARGs via linear multi-prover interactive proofs. In: Nielsen, J.B., Rijmen, V. (eds.) EUROCRYPT 2018. LNCS, vol. 10822, pp. 222–255. Springer, Cham (2018). https://doi.org/10.1007/978-3-319-78372-7_8

27. Bootle, J., Cerulli, A., Chaidos, P., Groth, J., Petit, C.: Efficient zero-knowledge arguments for arithmetic circuits in the discrete log setting. In: Fischlin, M., Coron, J.-S. (eds.) EUROCRYPT 2016. LNCS, vol. 9666, pp. 327–357. Springer, Heidelberg (2016). https://doi.org/10.1007/978-3-662-49896-5_12

28. Bootle, J., Cerulli, A., Ghadafi, E., Groth, J., Hajiabadi, M., Jakobsen, S.K.: Linear-time zero-knowledge proofs for arithmetic circuit satisfiability. In: Takagi, T., Peyrin, T. (eds.) ASIACRYPT 2017. LNCS, vol. 10626, pp. 336–365. Springer, Cham (2017). https://doi.org/10.1007/978-3-319-70700-6_12

29. Bootle, J., Groth, J.: Efficient batch zero-knowledge arguments for low degree polynomials. In: Abdalla, M., Dahab, R. (eds.) PKC 2018. LNCS, vol. 10770, pp. 561–588. Springer, Cham (2018). https://doi.org/10.1007/978-3-319-76581-5_19

30. Boyle, E., Gilboa, N., Ishai, Y.: Function secret sharing: improvements and extensions. In: CCS (2016)

31. Bünz, B., Bootle, J., Boneh, D., Poelstra, A., Wuille, P., Maxwell, G.: Bulletproofs: efficient range proofs for confidential transactions. Cryptology ePrint Archive, Report 2017/1066 (2017)

32. Catalano, D., Fiore, D.: Vector commitments and their applications. In: Kurosawa, K., Hanaoka, G. (eds.) PKC 2013. LNCS, vol. 7778, pp. 55–72. Springer, Heidelberg (2013). https://doi.org/10.1007/978-3-642-36362-7_5

33. Chakrabarti, A., Cormode, G., McGregor, A., Thaler, J.: Annotations in data streams. ACM Trans. Algorithms **11**(1), 7 (2014)

34. Chida, K., et al.: Fast large-scale honest-majority MPC for malicious adversaries. In: Shacham, H., Boldyreva, A. (eds.) CRYPTO 2018. LNCS, vol. 10993, pp. 34–64. Springer, Cham (2018). https://doi.org/10.1007/978-3-319-96878-0_2

35. Cormode, G., Mitzenmacher, M., Thaler, J.: Practical verified computation with streaming interactive proofs. In: ITCS (2012)

36. Cormode, G., Thaler, J., Yi, K.: Verifying computations with streaming interactive proofs. Proc. VLDB Endow. **5**(1), 25–36 (2011)

37. Corrigan-Gibbs, H., Boneh, D.: Prio: private, robust, and scalable computation of aggregate statistics. In: NSDI (2017)
38. Corrigan-Gibbs, H., Boneh, D., Mazières, D.: Riposte: an anonymous messaging system handling millions of users. In: Symposium on Security and Privacy (2015)
39. Costello, C., et al.: Geppetto: versatile verifiable computation. In: 2015 IEEE Symposium on Security and Privacy, SP 2015, San Jose, CA, USA, 17–21 May 2015 (2015)
40. Couteau, G.: A note on the communication complexity of multiparty computation in the correlated randomness model. IACR Cryptology ePrint Archive 2018, 465 (2018)
41. Damgård, I., Luo, J., Oechsner, S., Scholl, P., Simkin, M.: Compact zero-knowledge proofs of small hamming weight. In: Abdalla, M., Dahab, R. (eds.) PKC 2018. LNCS, vol. 10770, pp. 530–560. Springer, Cham (2018). https://doi.org/10.1007/978-3-319-76581-5_18
42. Damgård, I., Nielsen, J.B.: Scalable and unconditionally secure multiparty computation. In: Menezes, A. (ed.) CRYPTO 2007. LNCS, vol. 4622, pp. 572–590. Springer, Heidelberg (2007). https://doi.org/10.1007/978-3-540-74143-5_32
43. Damgård, I., Nielsen, J.B., Nielsen, M., Ranellucci, S.: The tinytable protocol for 2-party secure computation, or: gate-scrambling revisited. In: Katz, J., Shacham, H. (eds.) CRYPTO 2017. LNCS, vol. 10401, pp. 167–187. Springer, Cham (2017). https://doi.org/10.1007/978-3-319-63688-7_6
44. Eerikson, H., Orlandi, C., Pullonen, P., Puura, J., Simkin, M.: Use your brain! Arithmetic 3PC for any modulus with active security. IACR Cryptology ePrint Archive 2019, 164 (2019)
45. Feige, U., Goldwasser, S., Lovász, L., Safra, S., Szegedy, M.: Approximating clique is almost NP-complete. In: FOCS (1991)
46. Fortnow, L., Rompel, J., Sipser, M.: On the power of multi-prover interactive protocols. Theor. Comput. Sci. 134(2), 545–557 (1994)
47. Fortnow, L., Santhanam, R.: Infeasibility of instance compression and succinct PCPs for NP. In: STOC (2008)
48. Furukawa, J., Lindell, Y., Nof, A., Weinstein, O.: High-throughput secure three-party computation for malicious adversaries and an honest majority. In: Coron, J.-S., Nielsen, J.B. (eds.) EUROCRYPT 2017. LNCS, vol. 10211, pp. 225–255. Springer, Cham (2017). https://doi.org/10.1007/978-3-319-56614-6_8
49. Gennaro, R., Gentry, C., Parno, B., Raykova, M.: Quadratic span programs and succinct NIZKs without PCPs. In: Johansson, T., Nguyen, P.Q. (eds.) EUROCRYPT 2013. LNCS, vol. 7881, pp. 626–645. Springer, Heidelberg (2013). https://doi.org/10.1007/978-3-642-38348-9_37
50. Goldreich, O., Micali, S., Wigderson, A.: How to play any mental game or a completeness theorem for protocols with honest majority. In: STOC (1987)
51. Goldwasser, S., Kalai, Y.T., Rothblum, G.N.: Delegating computation: interactive proofs for muggles. In: STOC (2008)
52. Goldwasser, S., Kalai, Y.T., Rothblum, G.N.: Delegating computation: interactive proofs for muggles. J. ACM 62(4), 27 (2015)
53. Goldwasser, S., Micali, S., Rackoff, C.: The knowledge complexity of interactive proof systems. SIAM J. Comput. 18(1), 186–208 (1989)
54. Gordon, S.D., Ranellucci, S., Wang, X.: Secure computation with low communication from cross-checking. IACR Cryptology ePrint Archive 2018, 216 (2018)
55. Groth, J.: Short pairing-based non-interactive zero-knowledge arguments. In: Abe, M. (ed.) ASIACRYPT 2010. LNCS, vol. 6477, pp. 321–340. Springer, Heidelberg (2010). https://doi.org/10.1007/978-3-642-17373-8_19

56. Groth, J.: On the size of pairing-based non-interactive arguments. In: Fischlin, M., Coron, J.-S. (eds.) EUROCRYPT 2016. LNCS, vol. 9666, pp. 305–326. Springer, Heidelberg (2016). https://doi.org/10.1007/978-3-662-49896-5_11

57. Gur, T., Rothblum, R.D.: A hierarchy theorem for interactive proofs of proximity. In: 8th Innovations in Theoretical Computer Science Conference, ITCS 2017, Berkeley, CA, USA, 9–11 January 2017 (2017)

58. Ishai, Y., Kushilevitz, E., Ostrovsky, R.: Efficient arguments without short PCPs. In: Conference on Computational Complexity (2007)

59. Kalai, Y.T., Raz, R.: Interactive PCP. In: Aceto, L., Damgård, I., Goldberg, L.A., Halldórsson, M.M., Ingólfsdóttir, A., Walukiewicz, I. (eds.) ICALP 2008. LNCS, vol. 5126, pp. 536–547. Springer, Heidelberg (2008). https://doi.org/10.1007/978-3-540-70583-3_44

60. Kalai, Y.T., Rothblum, R.D.: Arguments of proximity. In: Gennaro, R., Robshaw, M. (eds.) CRYPTO 2015. LNCS, vol. 9216, pp. 422–442. Springer, Heidelberg (2015). https://doi.org/10.1007/978-3-662-48000-7_21

61. Kate, A., Zaverucha, G.M., Goldberg, I.: Constant-size commitments to polynomials and their applications. In: Abe, M. (ed.) ASIACRYPT 2010. LNCS, vol. 6477, pp. 177–194. Springer, Heidelberg (2010). https://doi.org/10.1007/978-3-642-17373-8_11

62. Katz, J., Kolesnikov, V., Wang, X.: Improved non-interactive zero knowledge with applications to post-quantum signatures. Technical report, Cryptology ePrint Archive, Report 2018/475 (2018)

63. Kilian, J.: A note on efficient zero-knowledge proofs and arguments. In: STOC (1992)

64. Klauck, H.: Rectangle size bounds and threshold covers in communication complexity. In: Conference on Computational Complexity (2003)

65. Kol, G., Oshman, R., Saxena, R.R.: Interactive distributed proofs. In: Proceedings of the 2018 ACM Symposium on Principles of Distributed Computing, PODC 2018, Egham, United Kingdom, 23–27 July 2018 (2018)

66. Kushilevitz, E.: Communication complexity. Adv. Comput. 44, 331–360 (1997)

67. Lindell, Y., Nof, A.: A framework for constructing fast MPC over arithmetic circuits with malicious adversaries and an honest-majority. In: ACM SIGSAC Conference on Computer and Communications Security, CCS (2017)

68. Lipmaa, H.: Progression-free sets and sublinear pairing-based non-interactive zero-knowledge arguments. In: Cramer, R. (ed.) TCC 2012. LNCS, vol. 7194, pp. 169–189. Springer, Heidelberg (2012). https://doi.org/10.1007/978-3-642-28914-9_10

69. Micali, S.: CS proofs. In: FOCS (1994)

70. Mohassel, P., Rosulek, M., Zhang, Y.: Fast and secure three-party computation: the garbled circuit approach. In: ACM SIGSAC Conference on Computer and Communications Security, CCS (2015)

71. Naor, M., Parter, M., Yogev, E.: The power of distributed verifiers in interactive proofs. http://arxiv.org/abs/1812.10917 (2018)

72. Nordholt, P.S., Veeningen, M.: Minimising communication in honest-majority MPC by batchwise multiplication verification. In: Preneel, B., Vercauteren, F. (eds.) ACNS 2018. LNCS, vol. 10892, pp. 321–339. Springer, Cham (2018). https://doi.org/10.1007/978-3-319-93387-0_17

73. Paillier, P.: Public-key cryptosystems based on composite degree residuosity classes. In: Stern, J. (ed.) EUROCRYPT 1999. LNCS, vol. 1592, pp. 223–238. Springer, Heidelberg (1999). https://doi.org/10.1007/3-540-48910-X_16

74. Parno, B., Howell, J., Gentry, C., Raykova, M.: Pinocchio: nearly practical verifiable computation. In: Symposium on Security and Privacy (2013)

75. Parno, B., Howell, J., Gentry, C., Raykova, M.: Pinocchio: nearly practical verifiable computation. Commun. ACM **59**(2), 103–112 (2016)
76. Reingold, O., Rothblum, G.N., Rothblum, R.D.: Constant-round interactive proofs for delegating computation. In: Proceedings of the Forty-Eighth Annual ACM Symposium on Theory of Computing (2016)
77. Rothblum, G.N., Vadhan, S.P.: Are PCPs inherent in efficient arguments? Comput. Complex. **19**(2), 265–304 (2010)
78. Sasson, E.B., et al.: Zerocash: decentralized anonymous payments from bitcoin. In: Symposium on Security and Privacy (2014)
79. Setty, S., Braun, B., Vu, V., Blumberg, A.J., Parno, B., Walfish, M.: Resolving the conflict between generality and plausibility in verified computation. In: EuroSys (2013)
80. Setty, S.T., McPherson, R., Blumberg, A.J., Walfish, M.: Making argument systems for outsourced computation practical (sometimes). In: NDSS (2012)
81. Shamir, A.: IP = PSPACE. J. ACM **39**(4), 869–877 (1992)
82. Sudan, M.: Probabilistically checkable proofs. Commun. ACM **52**(3), 76–84 (2009)
83. Wahby, R.S., Tzialla, I., Shelat, A., Thaler, J., Walfish, M.: Doubly-efficient zkSNARKs without trusted setup (2018)
84. Williams, R.: Strong ETH breaks with Merlin and Arthur: short non-interactive proofs of batch evaluation. arXiv preprint arXiv:1601.04743 (2016)
85. Zhang, Y., Genkin, D., Katz, J., Papadopoulos, D., Papamanthou, C.: vSQL: verifying arbitrary SQL queries over dynamic outsourced databases. In: Symposium on Security and Privacy (2017)
86. Zhang, Y., Genkin, D., Katz, J., Papadopoulos, D., Papamanthou, C.: A zero-knowledge version of vSQL. Cryptology ePrint Archive, Report 2017/1146 (2017)

Non-Uniformly Sound Certificates with Applications to Concurrent Zero-Knowledge

Cody Freitag$^{(\boxtimes)}$, Ilan Komargodski, and Rafael Pass

Cornell Tech, New York, NY 10044, USA
{cfreitag,rafael}@cs.cornell.edu, komargodski@cornell.edu

Abstract. We introduce the notion of non-uniformly sound certificates: succinct single-message (unidirectional) argument systems that satisfy a "best-possible security" against non-uniform polynomial-time attackers. In particular, no polynomial-time attacker with s bits of non-uniform advice can find significantly more than s accepting proofs for false statements. Our first result is a construction of non-uniformly sound certificates for all **NP** in the random oracle model, where the attacker's advice can depend arbitrarily on the random oracle.

We next show that the existence of non-uniformly sound certificates for **P** (and collision resistant hash functions) yields a *public-coin constant-round* fully concurrent zero-knowledge argument for **NP**.

1 Introduction

We consider the following compression task for a language L in **NP**. An efficient prover holds an input x and a witness w to the fact that $x \in L$ and wishes to send to a verifier a "short" *certificate* π testifying to the validity of x. The length of the certificate should be independent of the length of the statement x, the witness w, and the time needed to verify that w is a witness for x. In other words, the same proof length n can be used for every **NP** language L and all statements x with arbitrary polynomial length in n. The verifier should be able to determine whether π is a valid certificate for a statement x in time polynomial in $|x|, |\pi|$. We refer to this "witness compression" task as a *succinct* certificate system, or simply a certificate system.

By the result of Goldreich and Håstad [29], certificate systems for **NP** with statistical soundness (i.e., soundness against unbounded provers) imply that **NP** can be decided in subexponential time, and thus are unlikely to exist. Even for **P**, certificate systems imply that non-determinism can speed up arbitrary polynomial-time computation, contradicting widely believed derandomization assumptions (e.g., Barak et al. [4,5]). Thus, we are interested in certificate systems with *computational* soundness, where soundness holds against efficient

Supported in part by NSF Award CNS-1561209, NSF Award SATC-1617676, NSF Award SATC-1704788, and AFOSR Award FA9550-15-1-0262.

A. Boldyreva and D. Micciancio (Eds.): CRYPTO 2019, LNCS 11694, pp. 98–127, 2019.
https://doi.org/10.1007/978-3-030-26954-8_4

attackers. Note that the notion of SNARGs (succinct non-interactive arguments) [26,45] satisfies our efficiency and soundness requirements, but are actually not "unidirectionally" non-interactive: rather, the verifier (or some other trusted entity) must first generate and send a public parameter (which can be reused over multiple proofs) to the prover which the prover can use to produce its proof. Rather, in a certificate system, there is no *a priori* agreed-upon public parameters and no communication from the verifier to the prover.

The problem in such a fully non-interactive setting is that the standard notion of computational soundness (against non-uniform polynomial-time attackers) trivially collapses down to the notion of statistical soundness: if a cheating certificate π exists for some statement x (violating statistical soundness), then an efficient non-uniform attacker can simply get the pair (x, π) as non-uniform advice and consequently break computational soundness. Note that this attack is no longer possible for SNARGs when the non-uniform advice cannot be chosen as a function of the public parameters.

On Best-Possible Security. One approach to overcome the above problem is to settle for soundness against only *uniform* polynomial-time attackers. Certificate systems satisfying such a uniform notion of soundness were considered for **P** under the name **P**-certificates by Chung, Lin, and Pass [14]. They also observed that Micali's CS-proofs [45] satisfy uniform soundness in the random oracle model. But, there is a reason security against non-uniform attackers has become the standard notion of security in the cryptographic literature: it captures the natural idea that an adversary may have been designed to attack specific instances, guaranteeing security against an expensive preprocessing stage or any unknown future attacks.

Of course, s bits of non-uniform advice can be used to encode roughly s accepting proofs for false statements. But can they be used to encode much more? This motivates the following definition of *best-possible soundness* in the language of computational Kolmogorov complexity: the computational Kolmogorov complexity of K accepting proofs of different false statements cannot be significantly smaller than K. In other words, false certificates are "incompressible."

Equivalently, in a more complexity-theoretic language, we consider a notion of "multi-statement" soundness which requires that no non-uniform polynomial-time adversary having non-uniform advice of length s can produce accepting certificates for significantly more than s false statement. For a class of problems $\mathcal{C}$, we call argument systems that satisfy such a notion as *non-uniformly sound certificates for $\mathcal{C}$*, or nuCerts for $\mathcal{C}$ in short.

On the Existence of nuCerts. We initiate the study of nuCerts. We first note that whereas [14] observed that Micali's CS-proofs are uniformly sound in the random-oracle model, they do *not* satisfy multi-statement soundness. In fact, an efficient cheating prover with just polynomially-many bits of advice about the random oracle can produce proofs for *exponentially* many false statements! The same happens for other SNARG constructions which use only a random string as a public parameter (and for SNARGs that use a non-random public parameter, it is not clear how to turn them into certificates).

Our first main result is a construction of nuCerts in the random oracle model. Formally, we prove that our construction satisfies multi-statement soundness in the auxiliary-input random oracle model. The auxiliary-input random oracle model (AI-ROM), introduced by Unruh [55], captures preprocessing attacks, where the non-uniform advice string given to the attacker can depend arbitrarily on the random oracle.

Theorem 1 (Informal). *There exist* nuCerts *for **NP** in the auxiliary-input random oracle model.*

At a very high level, we present a construction which mimics Micali's construction of CS-proofs. Micali's construction works as follows: (1) start off with an efficient multi-round argument systems for **NP** and next (2) collapse the rounds to make it non-interactive using the Fiat-Shamir heuristic [22] (i.e., use the random oracle to generate verifier messages for the interactive protocol). Whereas the Fiat-Shamir heuristic indeed leads to a sound round reduction for uniform attackers in the random oracle model, in general it does not for non-uniform ones (where a non-uniform attacker can perform unbounded preprocessing on the random oracle). Indeed, as mentioned above, Micali's CS-proofs do not satisfy multi-statement soundness w.r.t. non-uniform attackers. As a warm-up, we show that if the underlying interactive proofs system has 3 rounds and has *statistical soundness*, then Fiat-Shamir with a minor modification in fact works. Unfortunately, this modification of Fiat-Shamir does not suffice for making *any* argument non-interactive. Rather, we present a different variant of Kilian's efficient arguments for **NP** and prove that for this *particular* argument system, the Fiat-Shamir paradigm does lead to a multi-statement sound non-interactive proof (although it does not work for Kilian's original argument). Our proof relies on a quite interesting compression argument which we believe may be of independent interest.

Application: Public-Coin Constant-Round Concurrent Zero-Knowledge. Given a language $L \in$ **NP** and an instance x, zero-knowledge (ZK) proofs [30] allow (paradoxically) for a prover to convince a verifier of the validity of a mathematical statement $x \in L$, while providing zero additional knowledge to the verifier. This is formalized by requiring that the view of every efficient adversarial verifier interacting with the honest prover be *simulated* by an efficient machine called the simulator. *Concurrent* ZK models the (realistic) asynchronous and concurrent setting, where a single adversary can "attack" the prover by acting as a verifier in many *concurrent* executions. Starting with the original work of Dwork, Naor, and Sahai [19], there has been a long line of constructions of concurrent ZK protocols. These include constructions with black-box simulation (e.g., [40,53,54]) nearly matching the almost logarithmic-round lower bound of [11] (by [51], these protocols are inherently private-coin), constructions based on different setup assumptions (e.g., [10,17,20,28,32,50]) and constructions in alternative less standard models (e.g., super-polynomial-time simulation [48,52] or based on knowledge assumptions [33]).

Using nuCerts for **P**, we give a public-coin, constant-round, (fully) concurrent ZK argument for **NP**. Public-coin protocols are ones where the verifier's messages are simply random coin tosses. This is a natural and appealing property of a protocol, which is useful in various applications such as public verifiability, leakage resilience [24], constructing resettably-sound protocols [3,51], and many more. The security of our construction relies on the following assumptions: the existence of a nuCert for **P** and a family of collision resistant hash functions (both with slightly super-polynomial security).

Theorem 2 (Informal). *Assume the existence of families of collision-resistant hash functions, and the existence of a* nuCert *for* ***P*** *(both with slightly super-polynomial security). Then, there exists a public-coin constant-round concurrent ZK argument for* ***NP***.

Barak's breakthrough work [1] gives a public-coin constant-round protocol but with *bounded* concurrency. Canetti, Lin, and Paneth [12] achieve full concurrency but require $O(\log^{1+\epsilon} n)$ rounds in the global hash model, and similarly Goyal [31] requires $O(n^\epsilon)$ rounds based on more standard assumptions (where in both n is the security parameter and $\epsilon > 0$ is an arbitrary small constant). Chung, Lin, and Pass [14] achieve constant rounds assuming **P**-certificates but only with a less standard notion of soundness (*uniform* soundness).

We stress that the construction from Theorem 2 is in the standard model assuming the existence of collision resistant hash functions and nuCerts for **P**. Using Theorem 1, we can instantiate nuCerts for **P** using a (non-programmable) random oracle and get a public-coin constant-round concurrent ZK argument for **NP**.

Corollary 1. *In the auxiliary-input random oracle model, there exists a public-coin constant-round concurrent zero-knowledge argument for* ***NP***.

Note that our protocol comes with an explicit ZK simulator. For the instantiation in the random oracle model, only soundness relies on the random oracle while ZK holds with any concrete function. Prior to this work, there were no public-coin constant-round constructions that provably satisfy concurrent ZK and even heuristically satisfy non-uniform soundness.

Lastly, even ignoring the public-coin aspect of our protocol, our result is meaningful: The only previously known (private-coin) constant-round fully concurrent ZK protocols rely on obfuscation-type assumptions (Chung, Lin, and Pass [15] rely on indistinguishability obfuscation and Pandey, Prabhakaran and Sahai [47] rely on differing-input obfuscation). Based on the protocol of Chung et al. [15], Chongchitmate, Ostrovsky, and Visconti [13] show a transformation to achieve simultaneously resettable ZK [3,10] in constant rounds based on the same assumptions (including indistinguishability obfuscation). Since our protocol is public-coin, we immediately get a constant-round simultaneously-resettable ZK protocol using known transformations [3,18,51] based on nuCerts for **P** (and hence also in the auxiliary-input random oracle model).

Paper Organization. In Sect. 2, we give an overview of our main techniques. In Sect. 3, we provide preliminary definitions and standard notation. In Sect. 4, we formally define nuCerts, and in Sect. 5, we present our candidate nuCert construction. Lastly, in Sect. 6, we show how to use nuCerts for **P** to get a public-coin constant-round concurrent zero-knowledge protocol.

1.1 Related Work

The idea to define the best-possible security for setup-free non-interactive primitives is inspired by the work of Bitansky, Kalai, and Paneth [7] that considered keyless multi-collision resistant hash functions. These are compressing functions where it is assumed that no efficient adversary with s bits of non-uniform advice can find significantly more than s values all of which collide relative to a fixed hash function. They used such functions to shave off one round of communication in various zero-knowledge protocols. Multi-collision resistant hashing [6,7,41–43] was also studied in the keyed setting as a relaxation of plain collision resistance.

In a recent work, Bitansky and Lin [8] considered one-message zero-knowledge arguments, where the soundness guarantee is that the number of false statements that an efficient non-uniform adversary can convince the verifier to accept is not much larger than the size of its non-uniform advice. They constructed such zero-knowledge arguments based on keyless collision resistant hash functions. Note that their construction is not succinct and thus cannot be used in place of our non-uniform certificates.

2 Technical Overview

In this section we provide a high-level overview of our constructions. We start with the non-uniformly sound certificates and then present our concurrent zero-knowledge protocol.

2.1 Non-uniformly Sound Certificates

Let us start with a more elaborate description of Micali's CS-proofs [45] and why they give only *uniformly* sound certificates [14]. Micali's protocol is obtained by applying the Fiat-Shamir heuristic [22] to Kilian's 4-round argument system [38]. In Kilian's protocol, the verifier sends a description of a collision resistant hash function to the prover. Using this hash function, the prover computes a Merkle hash a of a PCP proof for the statement q and sends it back to the verifier. The verifier then sends b, defining a set of PCP challenge queries, and the prover replies with the authentication paths c in the Merkle tree for all openings in the PCP proof specified by b. Micali's protocol collapses Kilian's protocol to one message by using a random oracle to compute the Merkle tree with root a, then uses the random oracle on a to derive the challenge b specifying openings with authentication paths c. The final proof $\pi = (a, b, c)$ is sent to the verifier to be checked.

One way to argue uniform soundness of Micali's non-interactive protocol is to reduce the security to Kilian's interactive protocol (using the same random oracle for the Merkle tree). Basically, we receive a random challenge b from the interactive protocol and then simulate the non-interactive cheating prover. When the cheating prover queries the random oracle for the value b', we respond instead with the challenge b. (We identify the query for b' by just guessing, which is okay since there are polynomially-many queries.) Since the adversary is uniform, it cannot distinguish b from b', so with noticeable probability, it will output accepting authentication paths, which we forward to the interactive verifier.

The above proof fails to go through when the adversary has non-uniform advice depending on the random oracle. The query for b' is not necessarily random, so the adversary may be able to distinguish b from b' and as a result will fail to output accepting authentication paths. Concretely, a non-uniform attacker for the non-interactive protocol can have hardwired a triple (a, b, c) which causes the verifier to accept for a fixed random oracle. In this case, we cannot change the value of b to make the above reduction go through. But, could it be the case that if the adversary needs to come up with *many* accepting proofs for false statements, at least one will have a random b value? The answer is "no." When the adversary has unbounded preprocessing time, there are many more cheating strategies. For example, the adversary may have hardcoded collisions relative to the random oracle that allow him to explain the root value of the Merkle tree of the statement in exponentially many ways.

Multi-statement Sound Fiat-Shamir. A natural first question is to understand how to modify the Fiat-Shamir heuristic to get multi-statement soundness. As a warm-up, let us start with a 3-message, public-coin, succinct *proof* system. Can we make it non-interactive and multi-statement sound? The security guarantee of this protocol is that for any false instance and every message a from the prover, there is a small set of b values that will allow the prover to come up with a c message which causes the verifier to accept. A first attempt to make it non-interactive is to use the random oracle to derive the b value given the a value, $b = \mathcal{O}(a)$. This is completely insecure as it could be the case that there is a b message which always causes the verifier to accept, so all the cheating prover has to do is to find one a that is mapped to b (which it can do in the preprocessing stage). The natural fix is to index the random oracle $\mathcal{O}$ with the statement q, $\mathcal{O}(q, \cdot)$. Then, intuitively, if he wishes to cheat on many statements by sending the bad b message, it needs to find many statements q' with corresponding a' values such that for all pairs, it holds that $\mathcal{O}(q', a') = b$.

Regarding security, we need to prove that our construction has defended against *all possible attacks* in the auxiliary-input random oracle model. The first proof approach to consider in this model is using the bit-fixing random oracle model of Unruh [55] (see also Coretti et al. [16]). At a high level, this approach says that any result in the "uniform" random oracle model can be translated into a hybrid model where some of the locations of the random oracle have been fixed but the rest are lazily sampled. Then, as long as we can show the adversary will likely query outside the set of fixed points, we can argue soundness just as in the uniform setting. This elegant model unfortunately does not work in the fully non-interactive setting where there is no high entropy setup *independent* of the adversary's advice. Thus, the adversary may only query fixed points for which it has encoded information.

Our proof of security is done via a compression argument, à la Gennaro and Trevisan [25]. We show that if an adversary with only s bits of non-uniform advice can come up with significantly more than s accepting proofs for false statements, then we can use the adversary to *compress* the random oracle. The idea in the proof, at a very high level, is to carefully map all possible ways the adversary can cheat to first encode the random oracle $\mathcal{O}$ in a way that we can still answer all of the adversary's queries. Then, we can run the adversary to uniquely reconstruct $\mathcal{O}$. If the encoding has been compressed more than the adversary's advice, then the adversary can succeed only on a small fraction of random oracles. In the compression argument, we crucially use the fact that the protocol is statistically sound and that we can uniquely extract the statement corresponding to each query in order to enumerate the small set of accepting b values (which is limited by soundness).

Caveat 1: While it may seem like we are done, there is a significant caveat in the above scheme. The issue is that we cannot use the statement q itself to index the random oracle $\mathcal{O}$ since q has no *a priori* size bound. The most we could hope for is to use a *short commitment* to the statement as an index to the random oracle. One could try to use a Merkle tree to implement this approach, i.e., index $\mathcal{O}$ with $\tilde{q} = \mathsf{MerHash}^{\mathcal{O}(\cdot)}(q)$, but it is again completely insecure – a cheating prover can simply encode collisions and use a mix-and-match attack to find exponentially different statements with the same hash value.

Solution 1: A similar issue came up in recent works on domain extension of multi-collision resistant hash functions [7,42]. In both works, they propose to encode the input using a specific code before hashing via a Merkle tree. Following [42], we use *list-recoverable codes* (LRC) to encode each statement before applying a Merkle tree to hash the statement to a short value. That is, for a statement q, we compute $\tilde{q} = \mathsf{MerHash}^{\mathcal{O}(\cdot)}(\mathsf{LRC}(q))$. The LRC guarantees that if the adversary can open each leaf in the Merkle tree to only a polynomial number of values, then there are only a polynomial (rather than exponential) number of possible statements with valid codewords. It follows that the prover can cheat on only a bounded number of hash values and can find only a bounded number of statements per hash value.

Caveat 2: Recall that our compression argument requires us to know how to map each oracle query for b back to the statement q. However, the solution to the previous problem, was to index the queries only with a short commitment to the statement $b = \mathcal{O}(\tilde{q}, a)$. So, we need a way to map this commitment $\tilde{q}$ to a unique statement q (in the proof).

Solution 2: We append to the proof a Merkle hash of the statement using the random oracle $\mathcal{O}(\tilde{q}, \cdot)$ indexed by $\tilde{q}$: $\hat{q} = \mathsf{MerHash}^{\mathcal{O}(\tilde{q}, \cdot)}(q)$. Additionally, we derive b by indexing $\mathcal{O}$ with both $\tilde{q}$ and $\hat{q}$: $b = \mathcal{O}(\tilde{q}, \hat{q}, a)$. Then, in our compression argument, we try to use the adversary's queries to $\mathcal{O}(\tilde{q}, \cdot)$ (which it must make to compute $\hat{q}$) to reconstruct the statement q and be able to compress the possible b values by statistical soundness. In doing so, we will compress the random oracle in one of three ways. Either:

1. there is a unique way to reconstruct q, so we can use statistical soundness to compress the oracle query for $b = \mathcal{O}(\tilde{q}, \hat{q}, a)$;
2. there is more than one way to reconstruct q, so the adversary must have found a collision in $\mathcal{O}(\tilde{q}, \cdot)$; or
3. there is no way to reconstruct q, so the adversary must "know" the preimage of some point in $\mathcal{O}(\tilde{q}, \cdot)$.

In summary, the variant of Fiat-Shamir we introduce is to first encode the statement q with a good list-recoverable code $\mathsf{LRC}(q)$ and hash it down to get $\tilde{q} = \mathsf{MerHash}^{\mathcal{O}(\cdot)}(\mathsf{LRC}(q))$. Then, hash down the statement using a random oracle that is indexed by $\tilde{q}$ to get $\hat{q} = \mathsf{MerHash}^{\mathcal{O}(\tilde{q}, \cdot)}(q)$. Then, compute $b = \mathcal{O}(\tilde{q}, \hat{q}, a)$ with a random oracle indexed by $\tilde{q}$ and $\hat{q}$.

Multi-statement Soundness for Arguments. While the above approach works for proof systems, it does not hold generically for arguments (by the same reason that the original Fiat-Shamir heuristic fails on Barak's protocol [1]). However, we show that it does work for Kilian's protocol [38] relying on some specific properties of this protocol.

Our main idea is to leverage the soundness of the underlying PCP proof system. By PCP soundness, for any statement q and any fixed PCP proof string $\Pi = \mathsf{PCP}(q)$, the number of accepting b values must be small. The main technical difficulty is that to use PCP soundness, we need to make sure the adversary is bound to a single PCP proof Π, which we need to know to determine the accepting b values. We use the same compression idea as before in order to extract the statement. Namely, we compute $a = \mathsf{MerHash}^{\mathcal{O}(\tilde{q}, \cdot)}(\Pi)$. Then, in the compression argument, either (1) we can uniquely extract a PCP proof string Π from the prover's queries and can compress the query for $b = \mathcal{O}(\tilde{q}, \hat{q}, a)$ by PCP soundness; (2) we reconstruct more than one PCP proof string, so the adversary must know a collision in $\mathcal{O}(\tilde{q}, \cdot)$; or (3) we cannot reconstruct a valid PCP proof, so the adversary must know some preimage for $\mathcal{O}(\tilde{q}, \cdot)$. We show that this covers all possibilities, and for each commitment value $\tilde{q}$ that the adversary cheats on, we will compress the random oracle at a new point.

In summary, our construction consists of a prover and verifier with the following strategies. The prover's strategy given a statement q is:

- Encode the statement with a good list-recoverable code $\mathsf{LRC}(q)$ and hash it down to get $\tilde{q} = \mathsf{MerHash}^{\mathcal{O}(\cdot)}(\mathsf{LRC}(q))$.
- Hash down the statement using a random oracle that is indexed by $\tilde{q}$ to get $\hat{q} = \mathsf{MerHash}^{\mathcal{O}(\tilde{q}, \cdot)}(q)$.
- Compute a commitment to a PCP of q using a random oracle indexed by $\tilde{q}$ and $\hat{q}$: $a = \mathsf{MerHash}^{\mathcal{O}(\tilde{q}, \hat{q}, \cdot)}(\mathsf{PCP}(q))$.
- Compute $b = \mathcal{O}(\tilde{q}, \hat{q}, a)$ with a random oracle indexed by $\tilde{q}$ and $\hat{q}$.
- Let c be the authentication paths corresponding to the indices given by b.

– **Output:** The certificate is $\pi = (a, b, c)$.

The verifier on input $\pi = (a, b, c)$ and q first computes $\tilde{q}$ and $\hat{q}$ in the same way as the prover (this is allowed since the LRC is efficient and the verifier can run in time polynomial in $|q|$). Then it checks that $b = \mathcal{O}(\tilde{q}, \hat{q}, a)$ and checks the validity of all authentications paths in c using the PCP verifier. We refer to Sect. 5 for the full details.

2.2   Concurrent Zero-Knowledge

Let us first explain at a very high-level the challenges that we are faced with. In Barak's protocol [1], if one tries to obtain unbounded concurrency, the simulation overhead grows polynomially with every nested execution. The idea of Chung, Lin, and Pass [14] was to leverage **P**-certificates, i.e., succinct non-interactive proofs, to shortcut some of the nested computations. Particularly, **P**-certificates allowed them to reuse proofs that some computation was done correctly without the need to recompute it. This makes sense in the uniform setting where we assume that no false **P**-certificates can be found. However, using nuCerts in the non-uniform setting, it seems to be a problem because—intuitively—false nuCerts can be combined to get many more false proofs: a false proof that A implies B can be combined with a correct proof that B implies C to get a false proof that A implies C. The way we overcome this is by combining the proofs and the statements that we prove in a sequence such that if the adversary comes up with a false proof for one statement, it changes the entire sequence and forces the adversary to come up with many false proofs for new statements. In what follows, we discuss in detail the shortcomings with the protocols of Barak [1] and of Chung et al. [14], and then we explain how we avoid the aforementioned mix-and-match attack using nuCerts.

Barak's Protocol. We recall Barak's non-black-box constant-round zero-knowledge protocol [1] that achieves bounded concurrency. On common input 1^n and $x \in \{0, 1\}^{\mathsf{poly}(n)}$, the Prover P and Verifier V, proceed in two phases. In phase 1, P sends a commitment $c \in \{0, 1\}^n$ of 0^n to V, and V replies with a challenge $r \in \{0, 1\}^{2n}$. In phase 2, P shows (using a witness indistinguishable argument of knowledge) that either x is true, or there exists a "short" string $\sigma \in \{0, 1\}^n$ such that c is a commitment to a program M such that $M(\sigma) = r$. Soundness follows from the fact that even if a malicious prover P^* tries to commit to some program M (instead of committing to 0^n), with high probability, the string r sent by V will be different from $M(\sigma)$ for every string $\sigma \in \{0, 1\}^n$. This relies on the fact that r is longer than σ. To prove ZK, consider the non-black-box simulator S that commits to the code of the malicious verifier V^*; note that by definition it thus holds that $M(c) = r$, and the simulator can use $\sigma = c$ as a "fake" witness in the final proof. To formalize this approach, the witness indistinguishable argument in Stage 2 must be a witness indistinguishable universal argument (WIUA) [2,45] since the statement "c is a commitment to a program M of arbitrary polynomial size and $M(c) = r$ within some arbitrary polynomial time," is not in **NP**.

To show (bounded) concurrency, we need to simulate the view of a verifier that has $m = \mathsf{poly}(n)$ concurrent executions of the protocol. The above simulator no longer works in this setting: the problem is that the verifier's code is now a function of all the prover messages sent in different executions. So one solution is to increase the length of r in the above protocol to depend on the number of concurrent sessions, then we would be done by a similar argument. However, such an approach can handle only an *a priori* bounded number of sessions. A natural idea is to let the simulator commit not only to the code of V^*, but also to a program M that generates all other prover messages. Implementing this idea naively results with exponential blowup in the running time of the simulation since the verifier may nest concurrent sessions [49].

Uniform Soundness via P-certificate. The main idea of Chung, Lin, and Pass [14] is to use **P**-certificates to overcome this blowup to achieve *unbounded* concurrency. At a very high level, their idea is that once the simulator has generated a **P**-certificate π to certify some partial computation performed by S in one session i, then the same certificate may be reused (without any additional cost) to certify the same computation also in other sessions $i' \neq i$, providing a "shortcut" for the simulator. It is crucial that the **P**-certificates are both fully non-interactive and succinct. Without the former, the certificates cannot be reused, and without the latter, we will not gain anything by reusing proofs.

Chung et al. [14] define a sequence of protocols $\Pi_1, \Pi_2, \ldots$, where protocol Π_k satisfies zero-knowledge for n^k concurrent sessions. The "trapdoor" for the simulation in Π_1, in contrast to Barak's protocol, now only requires that the a cheating prover can open the commitment to a machine M_1 and provide a **P**-certificate π_1 certifying that M_1 outputs the challenge r. However, we have not really gained anything over Barak's protocol yet since the challenge r can depend on the **P**-certificates in all previous sessions. Protocol Π_k uses k "levels" of **P**-certificates in a tree structure, where each higher level **P**-certificate certifies the correct generation of n lower level **P**-certificates. Then in protocol Π_k, the trapdoor requires that a cheating prover can open the commitment to a sequence of $M_1, \ldots, M_k$ such that: (1) for $i > 1$, the cheating prover can provide a **P**-certificate π_i certifying that M_i (given all higher level **P**-certificates) outputs the certified level $i - 1$ **P**-certificates, and (2) π_1 certifies that M_1 outputs r (again given all higher level **P**-certificates). The challenge r then only needs to depend on the non-certified **P**-certificates, which, because of the tree structure, is significantly smaller (and in particular apriori bounded) than the number of concurrent session.

Achieving Non-uniform Soundness via nuCerts for P. For security, the resulting concurrent zero-knowledge protocol shares the soundness guarantee of the underlying **P**-certificates. As we previously discussed, **P**-certificates can only satisfy uniform soundness (under standard assumptions), so our approach to overcome this is to replace **P**-certificates with nuCerts for **P**, which guarantee non-uniform soundness at the cost of allowing the adversary to cheat on a bounded number of statements. To argue soundness, we need to use a cheating prover in the zero-knowledge protocol to extract many false nuCerts. We can rewind the cheating prover many times until we extract a large collection of accepting proofs for false statements. While seemingly simple, there are several technicalities with this argument.

First, the adversary may be able to use different false proofs per statement and mix-and-match statements to cheat in an exponential number of ways. In general, this indeed seems like an unavoidable problem. Chung et al. [14] suggested a way around it if one assumes a strong version of **P**-certificates, called *unique* **P**-certificates, which guarantee that every statement has *at most* one accepting proof. Using indistinguishablity obfuscation, Chung et al. [15] constructed a slightly weaker primitive, called delegatable unique **P**-certificates, and modified the protocol of [14] to work with this object (at the cost of making it private-coin).

We get around this by noticing that this is not a problem for us! In short, the thing that saves us is that we require the entire *sequence* of proofs to be certified (not just individually, thus the order matters). If the adversary tries to use a different false proof at any level, it yields an entirely new sequence that it must cheat on. In more detail, recall that the construction consists of a tree of nuCerts that certify the whole computation. At level 1 (the leaves), we have a sequence of n^k "certified" nuCerts λ_1. At level 2, we have a sequence of n^{k-1} nuCerts λ_2, and so on until level k when we don't have any certified nuCerts. As the name suggests, the role of each level i is to certify the total computation that happens below level i, and level 1 certifies the randomness r. So, π_1 is a nuCert certifying that there is a (deterministic) machine M_1 such that M_1 on input $\lambda_{\geq 1}$ outputs r, where $\lambda_{\geq 1}$ consists of all certificates at or above level 1. π_2 certifies that M_2 on input $\lambda_{\geq 2}$ outputs λ_1. π_3 certifies that M_3 on input $\lambda_{\geq 3}$ outputs λ_2, and so on until π_k, which certifies that M_k on a short input outputs λ_{k-1}.

The machines $M_1, \ldots, M_k$ are deterministic and are committed to by the adversary before seeing r. So, even though there could be a single certificate that explains multiple values of r, when we fix the machines ahead of time it can only output one of them. Namely, the adversary can come up with many inputs for M_1 that output any value of r just by having many "options" for the sequence λ_1. Since there are many choices for λ_1 and M_2 is deterministic, either the adversary has many accepting proofs π_2 for false statements that look like "M_2 on input $\lambda_{\geq 2}$ outputs λ_1" with a small set of $\lambda_{\geq 2}$, or the statements are in fact true and there are many different sequences $\lambda_{\geq 2}$ explaining them. In the former case, we are done as we can extract these proofs from the adversary. In the latter case, we must have many different sequences $\lambda_{\geq 2}$. We can continue with the same argument in level 3 that should output and explain all options for λ_2, and so on until the root of the tree at level k. At this point, we have that a short input is used to explain many possible random outputs, which is information theoretically impossible unless the adversary knows many accepting proofs for false statements. We formalize this intuition by a compression argument, and we refer to Sect. 6 for the full details of the argument.

3   Preliminaries

For a distribution X we denote by $x \leftarrow X$ the process of sampling a value x from the distribution X. We use $\mathbb{N}$ to denote the set of positive integers and $[n]$ to denote the set $\{1, 2, \ldots, n\}$.

We consider interactive Turing machines, denoted ITM, and interactive protocols. Given a pair of ITMs, A and B, we denote by $(A(x), B(y))(z)$ the random variable representing the (local) output of B on common input z and private input y, when interacting with A on private input x, when the random tape of each machine is uniformly and independently chosen. We also let $\mathsf{View}_B(A(x), B(y))(z)$ be the random variable representing B's view in such an interaction.

The term *negligible* is used for denoting functions that are asymptotically smaller than any inverse polynomial. We say that an event happens with *noticeable* probability if it happens with non-negligible probability, i.e. greater than $1/p(\cdot)$ probability for polynomial p. We say that an event happens with *overwhelming* probability if it occurs with all but negligible probability, i.e. at least $1 - \nu(\cdot)$ probability for negligible ν.

(Non)-uniformity. We use the acronym PPT for *probabilistic polynomial-time*. A uniform PPT machine can be thought of as a fixed Turing machine that has access to an input tape and performs some computation on the given input. If the computation is randomized, the machine has access to a random tape as well. A non-uniform machine can be thought of as a family of machines, one for each input length. Equivalently, one can think of a non-uniform machine as a single machine for all input lengths that has access to an advice string which might be different for every input length.

Witness Relations for NP. We recall the definition of a witness relation for an **NP** language [27]. A *witness relation* for a language $L \in$ **NP** is a binary relation $\mathbf{R}_L$ that is polynomially bounded, polynomial time recognizable, and characterizes L by $L = \{x : \exists w \text{ s.t. } (x, w) \in \mathbf{R}_L\}$. We say that w is a witness for the membership $x \in L$ if $(x, w) \in \mathbf{R}_L$. We also let $\mathbf{R}_L(x)$ denote the set of witnesses for the membership $x \in L$, i.e. $\mathbf{R}_L(x) = \{w : (x, w) \in \mathbf{R}_L\}$.

Commitments and Collision Resistant Hashing. Commitment protocols allow a *sender* to commit itself to a value while keeping it secret from the *receiver*; this property is called *hiding*. At a later time, the commitment can only be opened to a single value as determined during the commitment protocol; this property is called *binding*. We consider non-interactive, computationally-hiding, statistically-binding commitment schemes. Such commitment schemes can be based on one-way functions [37,46] in the common random string (CRS) model, but we ignore this for simplicity as the CRS can be generated honestly by the receiver.

We also consider families of collision resistant hash functions. A family of functions $F = \{F_n \colon \{0,1\}^{2n} \to \{0,1\}^n\}$ is collision resistant if for any non-uniform PPT adversary, the probability (over a random function in the family) that it can output a collision is negligible. It is known that a secure fixed-length hash function family can be used to obtain a secure variable-input-length hash function family, i.e., we can hash arbitrarily long inputs while guaranteeing collision resistance.

We say that a commitment scheme or a collision resistant hash function family is T-secure if every non-uniform $\mathsf{poly}(T)$-time attacker can break the corresponding security property with at most negligible in T probability.

3.1   Interactive Protocols

We define interactive proofs [30] and arguments systems (a.k.a. computationally sound proofs) [9]. In our definition of arguments, we distinguish between uniform soundness, where soundness only needs to hold against a uniform PPT adversary, and non-uniform soundness, where it holds against non-uniform polynomial-time algorithms. Typically, in the literature on zero-knowledge arguments, non-uniform soundness is more commonly used.

Definition 1 (Interactive Proof System). *A pair of interactive machines (P, V) is called an* interactive proof system *for a language L if there is a negligible function $\nu(\cdot)$ such that the following two conditions hold:*

- Completeness: *For every $n \in \mathbb{N}$, $x \in L$ and every $w \in \mathbf{R}_L(x)$,*

$$\Pr[(P(w), V)(1^n, x) = 1] = 1.$$

- Soundness: *For every machine P^* and every $n \in \mathbb{N}$,*

$$\Pr[(x, z) \leftarrow P^*(1^n) : x \notin L \wedge (P^*(z), V)(1^n, x) = 1] \leq \nu(n).$$

If the soundness condition only holds against all non-uniform PPT (resp. uniform PPT) machines P^*, the pair (P, V) is called a non-uniformly sound (resp. uniformly sound) *interactive argument system.*

Witness Indistinguishability. An interactive protocol is *witness indistinguishable* (WI) [21] if the verifier's view is "independent" of the witness used by the prover for proving the statement.

Definition 2 (Witness Indistinguishability). *An interactive protocol (P, V) for $L \in \mathbf{NP}$ is* witness indistinguishable *for $\mathbf{R}_L$ if for every PPT adversarial verifier V^*, and for every two sequences $\{w^1_{n,x}\}_{n \in \mathbb{N}, x \in L \cap \{0,1\}^{\mathsf{poly}(n)}}$ and $\{w^2_{n,x}\}_{n \in \mathbb{N}, x \in L \cap \{0,1\}^{\mathsf{poly}(n)}}$ such that $w^1_{n,x}, w^2_{n,x} \in \mathbf{R}_L(x)$ for every $n \in \mathbb{N}$ and $x \in L \cap \{0,1\}^{\mathsf{poly}(n)}$, the following ensembles are computationally indistinguishable over $\mathbb{N}$:*

- $\{\mathsf{View}_{V^*}(P(w^1_{n,x}), V^*(z))(1^n, x)\}_{n \in \mathbb{N}, x \in L \cap \{0,1\}^{\mathsf{poly}(n)}, z \in \{0,1\}^*}$
- $\{\mathsf{View}_{V^*}(P(w^2_{n,x}), V^*(z))(1^n, x)\}_{n \in \mathbb{N}, x \in L \cap \{0,1\}^{\mathsf{poly}(n)}, z \in \{0,1\}^*}$

Universal Arguments. Universal arguments, introduced by Barak and Goldreich [2], are used in order to provide "efficient" proofs to statements of the universal language $L_\mathcal{U}$ with witness relation $\mathbf{R}_\mathcal{U}$ defined in [2]. This notion is closely related to the notion of CS-proofs [45]. A triplet $q = (M, x, t)$ is in $L_\mathcal{U}$ if the non-deterministic machine M accepts input x within $t < T(|x|)$ steps, for a slightly super-polynomial function $T(n) = n^{\log \log n}$. We denote by $T_M(x, w)$ the running time of M on input q using the witness w. Notice that every language in **NP** is linear time reducible to $L_\mathcal{U}$. Thus, a proof system for $L_\mathcal{U}$ allows us to handle all **NP**-statements.

Definition 3 (Universal Argument [2]**).** *A pair of interactive Turing machines* (P, V) *is called a* universal argument system *if it satisfies the following properties:*

- Efficient verification: *There exists a polynomial* p_V *such that for any* $q = (M, x, t)$, *the total time spent by the (probabilistic) verifier strategy* V, *on common input* 1^n, q, *is at most* $p_V(n + |q|)$. *In particular, all messages exchanged in the protocol have length smaller than* $p_V(n + |q|)$.
- Completeness by a relatively efficient prover: *For every* $n \in \mathbb{N}$, $q = (M, x, t) \in L_\mathcal{U}$, *and* $w \in \mathbf{R}_\mathcal{U}(q)$,

$$\Pr[(P(w), V)(1^n, q) = 1] = 1.$$

Furthermore, there exists a polynomial p_P *such that the total time spent by* $P(w)$, *on common inputs* 1^n *and* (M, x, t), *is at most* $p_P(n + |q| + t)$.
- Computational soundness: *For every non-uniform PPT algorithm* $P^* = \{P_n^*\}_{n \in \mathbb{N}}$, *there is a negligible function* negl, *such that, for every* $n \in \mathbb{N}$ *and every triplet* $(M, x, t) \in \{0, 1\}^{\mathsf{poly}(n)} \backslash L_\mathcal{U}$,

$$\Pr[(P_n^*, V)(1^n, q) = 1)] \leq \mathsf{negl}(n).$$

- Global proof of knowledge: *For every polynomial* p_1 *there exists a polynomial* p_2 *and a probabilistic oracle machine* $E^{(\cdot)}$ *such that the following holds: for every non-uniform PPT algorithm* $P^* = \{P_n^*\}_{n \in \mathbb{N}}$, *every sufficiently large* $n \in \mathbb{N}$, *and every* $q = (M, x, t) \in \{0, 1\}^{\mathsf{poly}(n)}$, *if* $\Pr[(P_n^*, V)(1^n, q) = 1] \geq 1/p_1(n)$, *then*

$$\Pr_r[\exists w \in \mathbf{R}_\mathcal{U}(q), E_r^{P_n^*}(1^n, q) = w] \geq 1/p_2(n),$$

where $E_r^{P_n^*}$ *runs in time* $\mathsf{poly}(n, t)$, *uses randomness fixed to* r, *and has oracle access to* P_n^*.

The notion of witness indistinguishability of universal argument for $\mathbf{R}_\mathcal{U}$ is defined similarly as that for interactive proofs/argument for **NP** relations; we refer the reader to [2] for a formal definition. [2] (based on [39, 45]) presents a witness indistinguishable universal argument based on the existence of families of collision resistant hash functions.

3.2 List-Recoverable Codes

List-recoverable codes were introduced Guruswami and Sudan [34] to handle a setting where an adversary is allowed to submit a set $S \subseteq \mathbb{F}$ (where $\mathbb{F}$ is the alphabet of the code) of possible symbols and then construct any codeword using only those symbols. In this model, it is impossible to completely recover a codeword given the lists, but these codes guarantee that there is only a small list of codewords that are consistent with all the lists.

More precisely, a mapping $\mathsf{LRC} \colon \mathbb{F}^v \to \mathbb{F}^m$ from length v messages to length m codewords, is called (α, ℓ, L)-*list-recoverable* if there is a procedure that is given a set S of size ℓ, is able to output all messages $x \in \mathbb{F}^v$ such that $\mathsf{LRC}(x)_i \notin S$ for at most $1 - \alpha$ fraction of the coordinates $i \in [n]$. The code guarantees that there are at most L such messages. For our purposes, we need a list-recoverable code with $\alpha = 1$, which we refer to as an (ℓ, L)-list-recoverable code, defined formally as follows.

Definition 4 (List-Recoverable Codes). *We say that a tuple $x \in (\{0,1\}^k)^m$ is* consistent *with sets $S_1, \ldots, S_m \subseteq \{0,1\}^k$ if $x_i \in S_i$ for all $i \in [m]$.*

A function $\mathsf{LRC} \colon \{0,1\}^v \to (\{0,1\}^k)^m$ is (ℓ, L)-list-recoverable, if for any sets $S_1, \ldots, S_m \subseteq \{0,1\}^k$ each of size at most ℓ, there are at most L strings $x \in \{0,1\}^v$ such that $\mathsf{LRC}(x)$ is consistent with $S_1, \ldots, S_m$. The strings in the image of LRC are referred to as codewords.

It is well-known (see e.g., [36]) that the notion of list-recoverable codes is equivalent to unbalanced expanders with a certain expansion property. The left set of vertices in the graph is $\{0,1\}^v$, the right set of vertices is $\{0,1\}^k$ and the left degree is m. This graph naturally induces a mapping $\mathsf{LRC} \colon \{0,1\}^v \to (\{0,1\}^k)^m$ which on input $x \in \{0,1\}^v$ (left vertex) outputs n neighbors (right vertices). The mapping LRC is (ℓ, L)-list-recoverable if and only if for every set $S \subseteq \{0,1\}^k$ of size larger than L of nodes on the right, the set of left neighbors of S is of size larger than ℓ.

The following instantiation of locally-recoverable codes based on the explicit construction of unbalanced expanders of [35] is taken (with minor modifications) from [36].

Theorem 3 ([35,36]). *For every $k < v \in \mathbb{N}$, there exists a $\mathsf{poly}(v)$-time computable function $\mathsf{LRC}_v \colon \{0,1\}^v \to (\{0,1\}^k)^{v^2 k^3}$ that defines an (ℓ, L)-list-recoverable code for any $L \geq \ell^2$ such that $L \leq 2^{k/2}$. The list-recovery algorithm runs in time $\mathsf{poly}(v, \ell)$.*

3.3 Concurrent Zero-Knowledge

An interactive proof is said to be *zero-knowledge*, denoted as ZK, if it yields nothing beyond the validity of the statement being proved [30].

Definition 5 (Zero-Knowledge). *An interactive protocol (P, V) for language L is* zero-knowledge *if for every PPT adversarial verifier V^*, there exists a PPT simulator S such that the following ensembles are computationally indistinguishable over $n \in \mathbb{N}$:*

- $\{\mathsf{View}_{V^*}(P(w), V^*(z))(1^n, x)\}_{n \in \mathbb{N}, x \in L \cap \{0,1\}^{\mathsf{poly}(n)}, w \in \mathbf{R}_L(x), z \in \{0,1\}^{\mathsf{poly}(n)}}$
- $\{S(1^n, x, z)\}_{n \in \mathbb{N}, x \in L \cap \{0,1\}^{\mathsf{poly}(n)}, w \in \mathbf{R}_L(x), z \in \{0,1\}^{\mathsf{poly}(n)}}$

In this work, we consider the setting of concurrent composition. Given an interactive protocol (P, V) and a polynomial m, an m-session *concurrent adversarial verifier* V^* is a PPT machine that, on common input x and auxiliary input z, interacts with up to $m(|x|)$ independent copies of P concurrently. The different interactions are called sessions. There are no restrictions on how V^* schedules the messages among the different sessions, and V^* may choose to abort some sessions but not others. For convenience of notation, we overload the notation $\mathsf{View}_{V^*}(P, V^*(z))(1^n, x)$ to represent the view of the cheating verifier V^* in the above mentioned concurrent execution, where V^*'s auxiliary input is z, both parties are given common input $1^n, x \in L$, and the honest prover has a valid witness w of x.

Definition 6 (Concurrent Zero-Knowledge [19]). *An interactive protocol (P, V) for language L is* concurrent zero-knowledge *if for every concurrent adversarial verifier V^* (i.e. any m-session concurrent adversarial verifier for any polynomial m), there exists a PPT simulator S such that the following two ensembles are computationally indistinguishable over $n \in \mathbb{N}$:*

- $\{\mathsf{View}_{V^*}(P(w), V^*(z))(1^n, x)\}_{n \in \mathbb{N}, x \in L \cap \{0,1\}^{\mathsf{poly}(n)}, w \in \mathbf{R}_L(x), z \in \{0,1\}^{\mathsf{poly}(n)}}$
- $\{S(1^n, x, z)\}_{n \in \mathbb{N}, x \in L \cap \{0,1\}^{\mathsf{poly}(n)}, w \in \mathbf{R}_L(x), z \in \{0,1\}^{\mathsf{poly}(n)}}$

4 Non-uniformly Sound Certificates

We give a definition of a certificate system that captures non-uniform attackers. Roughly speaking, a certificate system, (P, V), is a non-interactive (unidirectional) argument system (i.e., the prover send a single message to the verifier, who either accepts or rejects) such that (1) P can efficiently convince V the validity of some statement $x \in L$ using a "certificate" π of fixed polynomial length *independent* of the statement and (2) V can efficiently check the validity of π in fixed polynomial time in the statement size yet independent of the language's verification time. To capture non-uniform attackers, we additionally require (3) that no non-uniform cheating prover P^* should be able to falsely convince V of the validity of substantially more statements than the size of P^*'s non-uniform advice. In what follows, we first formalize these requirements for **P** and later discuss (in Remark 1) how to generalize them to **NP**.

Following Micali's CS-proofs [45], we first define the efficiency properties required for any certificate system for **P**. We consider a canonical language L_c for $\mathsf{TIME}(n^c)$: for every constant $c \in \mathbb{N}$, let L_c be the language that consists of triples (M, x, y) such that machine M on input x outputs y when executed for $|x|^c$ steps. That is,

$$L_c = \{(M, x, y) \colon M(x) = y \text{ within } |x|^c \text{ steps}\}.$$

Let $T_M(x)$ denote the running time of M on input x.

Definition 7 (Certificates for P). *Let (P, V) be a pair of probabilistic inter-active Turing machines in a non-interactive protocol. We say that (P, V) is a* certificate system for **P** *if it satisfies the following two efficiency conditions:*

– Completeness by a relatively-efficient prover: *There exist polynomials g_P, ℓ such that for every $c, n \in \mathbb{N}$ and every $q = (M, x, y) \in L_c$, it holds that*

$$\Pr[\pi \leftarrow P(c, 1^n, q) : V(c, 1^n, q, \pi) = 1] = 1.$$

Furthermore, P on input $(c, 1^n, q)$ outputs a certificate π of length $\ell(n)$ in time bounded by $g_P(n + |q| + T_M(x))$.
– Efficient verification: *There exists a polynomial g_V such that for every $c, n \in \mathbb{N}$, $q = (M, x, y) \in L_c$ and $\pi \in \{0, 1\}^*$, the running time of $V_{\mathsf{nu}}(c, 1^n, q, \pi)$ is bounded by $g_V(n + |q|)$.*

Best-Possible Soundness. At a high level, we require non-uniformly sound certificates to achieve the *best-possible soundness* against non-uniform attackers. This means that our notion of soundness allows the adversary to come up with *some* accepting certificates for false statements, but not too many more than the size of its advice. We formalize this intuition with the notion of (K, T)-soundness, which intuitively says that a non-uniform adversary running in time T cannot output false proofs for more than K statements. We define this as follows.

Definition 8 ((K, T)-soundness). *Let $K, T \colon \mathbb{N} \to \mathbb{N}$ be functions. We say that a certificate system for **P**, (P, V), is (K, T)-sound if there exists a function $B(n) \in \omega(1)$ such that the following holds:*
For every probabilistic algorithm P^* and any sequence of polynomial-size advice $\{z_n\}_{n \in \mathbb{N}}$ where $P^*(1^n, z_n)$ runs in time at most $T(n)$, there exists a negligible function $\mathsf{negl}(\cdot)$ such that for every $n \in \mathbb{N}$, letting $K = K(n)$,

$$\Pr\left[\{(c_i, q_i, \pi_i)\}_{i \in [K]} \leftarrow P^*(1^n, z_n) : \begin{array}{c} \forall i \neq j \colon q_i \neq q_j, \\ \forall i \in [K] \colon c_i \leq B(n) \,\wedge \\ q_i \notin L_{c_i} \wedge \\ V(c_i, 1^n, q_i, \pi_i) = 1 \end{array}\right] \leq \mathsf{negl}(n).$$

We are now ready to define non-uniformly sound certificates (nuCerts) for **P**. Intuitively, we require that no non-uniform cheating prover with polynomial-size advice can output a super-polynomial number of accepting proofs for false statements where we allow the cheating prover to run in super-polynomial time per false proof it outputs.

Definition 9 (nuCerts for P). *Let (P, V) be a pair of probabilistic interactive Turing machines in a non-interactive protocol. We say that (P, V) is a non-uniformly sound certificate system (nuCert) for **P** if it is a certificate system for **P** and is (K, T)-sound for some $K(n) \in n^{\omega(1)}$ and $T(n) \in K(n) \cdot n^{\omega(1)}$.*

Some remarks are in order.

Remark 1. *The above definition generalizes to **NP** by considering non-deterministic languages L_c corresponding to $\mathsf{NTIME}(n^c)$ where we provide the prover with a witness w and let $T_M(x)$ be the time to verify that $(x, w) \in \mathbf{R}_L$.*

Remark 2. *The notion of (K, T)-sound certificate systems for **P** is a generalization of strong **P**-certificates (of Chung et al. [14]) as they coincide when the number of false proofs is just one, i.e., $K(n) = 1$, and the running time of the adversary is a (slightly) super-polynomial function, i.e., $T(n) \in n^{\omega(1)}$.*

Remark 3. *The definition of (K, T)-soundness as defined can only be achieved for super-polynomial $K(n) \in n^{\omega(1)}$. This notion is sufficient for our concurrent zero-knowledge protocol given in Sect. 6. However, one can consider a more fine-grained notion where we allow the number of false proofs to depend on the size of the advice and accepting statements. We actually achieve this (stronger) notion in our nuCerts construction in Sect. 5.*

Remark 4. *The size of accepting statements $q = (M, x, y)$ for L_c must be bounded by $O(|x|^c)$ without loss of generality since V would not accept q for the language L_c if $|y| > |x|^c$.*

Remark 5. *We could consider an alternative definition of (K, T)-soundness where we remove the restriction that statements are unique and just require that the proofs are. These notions are equivalent up to a factor that depends exponentially on the certificate size for K.*

In more detail, one trivial way to bound the number of false proofs in general is to bound the number of false proofs for specific statements. In the worst case, if you can find a false proof for an accepting statement, then all proofs for that statement may be accepted. So, if a (K, T)-sound certificate system has proofs π with length bounded by $\ell_\pi(n)$, this implies it is $(K \cdot 2^{\ell_\pi(n)}, T)$-sound when the statements need not be unique.

Relation to Kolmogorov Complexity. Our definition has a natural interpretation in the language of computational Kolmogorov complexity. Recall that the Kolmogorov function $C(x)$ is the length of the smallest program generating x. Namely, $C(x) = \min_p \{|p| : U(p) = x\}$, where U is a universal machine. There are many resource-bounded variants to Kolmogorov complexity [23]. Our definition is parametrized by an efficiently recognizable set X and a time bound t. We define $C^t(X)$ as the smallest machine that runs in time t and outputs an element in X. Namely,

$$C^t(X) = \min_p \{|p| : U(p) \text{ outputs } x \in X \text{ in } t(|x|) \text{ steps}\}.$$

Claim 1. *Let (P, V) be a certificate system, $K \in n^{\omega(1)}$, $T \in K(n) \cdot n^{\omega(1)}$, and let X be a set of sets such that every set is a collection of accepting proofs for K false statements. (P, V) is (K, T)-sound if and only if $C^T(X) \in n^{\omega(1)}$.*

Proof. Assume for contradiction that $C^T(X) \in \mathsf{poly}(n)$. This means there is a polynomial size encoding that in time T can be used to generate K accepting proofs for false statements, contradicting (K, T)-soundness of (P, V). In the other direction, assume that (P, V) satisfies (K, T)-soundness. Then, there is a cheating prover with polynomial-size advice running in time T that is able to find K accepting proofs for false statements. This implies a machine of polynomial size that encodes an element in X, contradicting $C^T(X) \in n^{\omega(1)}$.

5   The Construction

In this section, we give a construction of a nuCert system for **P** as defined in Sect. 4. Our construction is in the auxiliary input random oracle model, introduced by Unruh [55]. In this model all parties have access to a public random function. Additionally, the adversary has an unbounded preprocessing stage (the offline phase where he can compute arbitrarily an advice string for the online phase where he attacks the system. The output of the offline phase can be thought of as the process that generates the non-uniform advice. In the online phase, the adversary can use the advice string and a bounded number of queries (though his running time is unbounded).

Theorem 4. *In the auxiliary-input random oracle model, there exists a certificate system for* **P** *that satisfies (K, T)-soundness for any $K(n) \geq (3s)^{25\alpha}$ and $T(n) \leq 2^{n/6}$ against non-uniform adversaries with advice $\{z_n\}_n$ of size $s = s(n)$ that output accepting statements of size at most n^α.*

The protocol we present is actually a nuCert for **NP** (with essentially the same proof). In Sect. 6, we will use the result only for **P** so we focus on this setting here.

We note that if the adversary outputs statements of super-polynomial size, we may assume that they will not be accepted by a verifier for the universal language for **P**. Still, the adversary may output accepting statements of arbitrary polynomial size, so without assuming anything about the adversary, the theorem holds for any slightly super-constant $\alpha \in \omega(1)$. In this case, we guarantee that no adversary can output a slightly super-polynomial number of accepting proofs for unique false statements, e.g., $K(n) = n^{\log \log n}$. Additionally, we can set $T(n) = n^{\log n}$ so that $T(n) \in K(n) \cdot n^{\omega(1)}$. Thus, we get the following corollary to Theorem 4 by Definition 9.

Theorem 5 *(Restatement of Theorem 1).* *In the auxiliary-input random oracle model, there exists a nuCert system for* **P**.

We devote the rest of this section to the proof of Theorem 4 which is based on a compression technique (à la Gennaro and Trevisan [25]). In Sect. 5.1 we describe our nuCert construction and then prove security in the auxiliary-input random oracle model in Sect. 5.2.

5.1   Construction

Our nuCert system, denoted (P_{nu}, V_{nu}), builds off of Micali's CS-proofs but makes significant modifications. Recall that in Micali's protocol, the prover uses a random oracle to compute a Merkle hash a of a PCP proof for the statement q. The prover then uses a random oracle to compute b, defining a set of PCP challenge queries. Finally, it computes the authentication paths c in the Merkle tree for all openings in the PCP proof specified by b. The final proof $\pi = (a, b, c)$ is sent to the verifier to be checked.

Merkle Trees and PCPs. In the construction, we will use Merkle trees and probabilistic checkable proofs (PCPs).

A Merkle tree [44] is a method to succinctly commit on a string while allowing to open a specific location without revealing the whole input string. The latter property is called *local opening*. The security of the commitment is based on the existence of a collision resistant hash function family. More precisely, a Merkle tree procedure $\mathsf{MT}^{f(\cdot)}$ has oracle access to a compressing function $f \colon \{0,1\}^\lambda \to \{0,1\}^n$, which it uses to hash a long string into a short one. This is done by "breaking" the input into blocks of the right size and hasing each consecutive pair using the hash function. We continue this recursively in a tree-like fashion until we are left with a single string of size n.

A PCP system is a proof system that allows for local verification of a language. It consists of two algorithms (PCP.Prove, PCP.Ver). PCP.Prove(x) is a deterministic algorithm that takes as input a statement x from some language L and computes a proof Π to the fact that $x \in L$. PCP.Ver$^\Pi(x, r)$ is a randomized algorithm using r as its randomness source that takes as input a statement x and has query access to a (possibly partial) PCP proof Π and outputs a bit b.

The Construction. We split (P_{nu}, V_{nu}) into two different phases: a commitment and a proof phase. The commitment phase forces P_{nu} to succinctly commit to the statement it is proving. The proof phase is exactly as Micali's CS-proofs with the modification that the random oracles used are indexed by the statement's commitment.

In more detail, the commitment consists of two parts. The first part, which we denote by $\tilde{q}$, is a Merkle hash of a list-recoverable code encoding of q. The list-recoverable code provides a weak binding property for any particular commitment; no non-uniform adversary can find too many statements consistent with $\tilde{q}$. In the second part of the commitment, which we denote by $\hat{q}$, the prover Merkle hashes q using a random oracle indexed by $\tilde{q}$. $\hat{q}$ guarantees that a cheating prover that provides an accepting proof of a false statement q either uses specific knowledge that depends on $\tilde{q}$ or can be used to extract q.

The proof phase computes $\pi = (a, b, c)$ as in Micali's CS-proofs except that we index both the Merkle tree and FS-heuristic random oracles with the commitment $(\tilde{q}, \hat{q})$. This guarantees that each false proof with a unique commitment requires the adversary to use fresh information about the random oracle. The full description of the non-interactive protocol, (P_{nu}, V_{nu}), is given in Fig. 1.

A nuCert SYSTEM (P_{nu}, V_{nu})

Common Input: Security parameter 1^n, time bound c, and a statement $q = (M, x, y)$ for the language L_c.

Common Oracles: $\mathcal{O}_1 \colon \{0,1\}^{n^2} \rightarrow \{0,1\}^n$, $\mathcal{O}_2 \colon \{0,1\}^{n+n^2} \rightarrow \{0,1\}^n$, $\mathcal{O}_3 \colon \{0,1\}^{2n+n^2} \rightarrow \{0,1\}^n$, $\mathcal{O}_4 \colon \{0,1\}^{3n} \rightarrow \{0,1\}^{\ell_b}$.

Subroutines: PCP system PCP $=$ (Prove, Ver) with soundness error 2^{-n} using $\ell_b \in O(n \log n)$ bits of randomness, a Merkle tree algorithm $\mathsf{MT}^{(\cdot)}$, and collection of codes $\mathsf{LRC}_v \colon \{0,1\}^v \rightarrow (\{0,1\}^{n^2})^{v^2 n^6}$ that satisfies (ℓ, L)-list-recoverability for any $L \leq 2^{n^2/2}$ such that $L \geq \ell^2$.

Prover $P_{nu}(1^n, q)$:

  Commitment phase:

    1. Compute $\tilde{q} \leftarrow \mathsf{MT}^{\mathcal{O}_1(\cdot)}(\mathsf{LRC}_{|q|}(q))$.
    2. Compute $\hat{q} \leftarrow \mathsf{MT}^{\mathcal{O}_2(\tilde{q},\cdot)}(q)$.

  Proof phase:

    3. Compute $\Pi \leftarrow \mathsf{PCP}.\mathsf{Prove}(q)$. Compute $a \leftarrow \mathsf{MT}^{\mathcal{O}_3(\tilde{q},\hat{q},\cdot)}(\Pi)$.
    4. Compute $b \leftarrow \mathcal{O}_4(\tilde{q}, \hat{q}, a)$.
    5. Let I be the set of indices queried by $\mathsf{PCP}.\mathsf{Ver}^\Pi(q; b)$. Let c be the authentication paths for indices I in the Merkle tree of Π.
    6. Send $\pi = (a, b, c)$ to V_{nu}.

Verifier $V_{nu}(1^n, q, \pi)$:

  Commitment verification:

    1. Compute $\tilde{q} \leftarrow \mathsf{MT}^{\mathcal{O}_1(\cdot)}(\mathsf{LRC}_{|q|}(q))$.
    2. Compute $\hat{q} \leftarrow \mathsf{MT}^{\mathcal{O}_2(\tilde{q},\cdot)}(q)$.

  Proof verification:

    3. Parse $\pi = (a, b, c)$. Verify $b = \mathcal{O}_3(\tilde{q}, \hat{q}, a)$.
    4. Construct a partial PCP proof Π with openings from c.
    5. Let I be the set of indices queried by $\mathsf{PCP}.\mathsf{Ver}^\Pi(q; b)$. Verify the authentication paths c given the indices I and the Merkle hash root a.
    6. Accept if and only if $\mathsf{PCP}.\mathsf{Ver}^\Pi(q; b)$ accepts.

Fig. 1. A nuCert for **P** defined in the auxiliary-input random oracle model.

Efficiency and Completeness. We first argue that (P_{nu}, V_{nu}) is a valid certificate system for **P** by showing the *completeness by a relatively efficient prover* and *efficient verification* properties.

Completeness follows from the completeness of the underlying PCP proof system. For prover efficiency, note that computing $\tilde{q}$ and $\hat{q}$ in the commitment phase only takes time polynomial in the statement size. This uses the efficiency of the list-recoverable code. Recall that a proof $\pi = (a, b, c)$ consists of a n bit Merkle tree root, the randomness for the PCP proof, and the authentication paths for locations specified by the PCP proof. In order to compute a, the prover computes the PCP proof for q, which takes time polynomial in the machine's running time. Since the protocol uses a PCP proof system with soundness error 2^{-n}, the prover has to open and authenticate $O(n)$ bits using $O(\log n)$ bits of randomness per location, which takes polynomial time only in the security parameter n. Each authentication path in the Merkle tree has size $O(n \log n)$. This implies a polynomial length bound of $\ell_\pi(n) \in O(n^2 \log n)$.

The verifier also needs to compute $\tilde{q}$ and $\hat{q}$, but does not need to compute the PCP proof for q. Thus, the verifier's running time is independent of the machine's running time, and depends only polynomially on the statement size $|q|$ and the proof length $\ell_\pi(n)$.

5.2   Proof of Theorem 4

The proof of (K, T)-soundness proceeds in two steps. We first show that a non-uniform adversary can only find a bounded number of statements per $\tilde{q}$ value in the commitment. Then we show that a non-uniform adversary cannot come up with a false proof for too many $\tilde{q}$ values.

Bounding Statements Per $\tilde{q}$. Recall that $\tilde{q}$ is a Merkle hash of a list-recoverable code encoding of some statement q. We show that a non-uniform cheating prover cannot find too many statements that yield the same $\tilde{q}$ value.

Lemma 1. *Let $\mathcal{O}$ be a random function from n^2 to n bits. For any functions $K, s \colon \mathbb{N} \to \mathbb{N}$ and sequence of advice $\{z_n\}_{n \in \mathbb{N}}$ of size $s = s(n) \geq 4$, let $\mathcal{A}^{\mathcal{O}}$ be a non-uniform algorithm that on input $(1^n, z_n)$ makes at most $2^{n/2}$ queries and outputs $K = K(n)$ unique statements $q_1, \ldots, q_K$. Define $N = (3s)^{24 \cdot \alpha}$ where α satisfies $|q_i| \leq n^\alpha$ for all $i \in [K]$, and define $\tilde{q}_i = \mathsf{MT}^{\mathcal{O}(\cdot)}(\mathsf{LRC}_{|q_i|}(q_i))$. Then, for every $n \in \mathbb{N}$, it holds that*

$$\Pr_{\mathcal{O}} \left[(q_1, \ldots, q_K) \leftarrow \mathcal{A}^{\mathcal{O}}(1^n, z_n) : \begin{array}{c} \forall i \neq j \in [K] \colon q_i \neq q_j \\ |\{\tilde{q}_i : i \in [K]\}| \leq K/N \end{array} \right] \leq 2^{-n}.$$

The proof of this lemma appears in the full version.

Bounding False Proofs Per $\tilde{q}$. We show that if a cheating prover comes up with a false proof for a statement with a new $\tilde{q}$ value, it must have used some knowledge to either find (1) a new collision, (2) a new pre-image of a previously queried point, or (3) a new challenge message b that comes from a small set. We use each scenario to compress the random oracle's description on some input, which bounds the number of oracles a cheating prover can succeed on. We note that we can use a single oracle $\mathcal{O}$ with large enough domain and range to represent all four oracles defined in Fig. 1. We can simply modify each query to first specify an index for which oracle it wants to query and then restrict the input and output to the correctly defined length. We formalize this compression-style argument in the following lemma.

Lemma 2. *Let $(P_{\mathsf{nu}}, V_{\mathsf{nu}})$ be the nuCert system from Fig. 1 with random oracle $\mathcal{O} = (\mathcal{O}_1, \mathcal{O}_2, \mathcal{O}_3, \mathcal{O}_4)$. For any functions $K, s \colon \mathbb{N} \to \mathbb{N}$ and sequence of advice $\{z_n\}_{n \in \mathbb{N}}$ of size $s = s(n)$, let $\mathcal{A}^{\mathcal{O}}$ be a non-uniform algorithm that on input $(1^n, z_n)$ makes T oracle queries and outputs $(C_1, q_1, \pi_1), \ldots, (C_K, q_K, \pi_K)$ where $K = K(n)$. Then, for every $n \in \mathbb{N}$, it holds that*

$$\Pr_{\mathcal{O}}\left[\{(C_i, q_i, \pi_i)\}_{i \in [K]} \leftarrow \mathcal{A}^{\mathcal{O}}(1^n, z_n) : \begin{array}{l} \forall i \neq j \in [K] : \tilde{q}_i \neq \tilde{q}_j \\ \wedge\, q_i \neq q_j, \\ \forall i \in [K] : q_i \notin L_{C_i} \\ \wedge\, V_{\mathsf{nu}}(C_i, 1^n, q_i, \pi_i) = 1 \end{array}\right] \leq 2^{-K(n - 3\log T) + s}.$$

Proof. For each proof that $\mathcal{A}^{\mathcal{O}}(1^n, z_n)$ outputs, parse $\pi_i = (a_i, b_i, c_i)$. We assume without loss of generality that $\mathcal{A}^{\mathcal{O}}(1^n, z_n)$ makes every query that V_{nu} checks exactly once. Otherwise, we can modify $\mathcal{A}^{\mathcal{O}}$ to make all such queries at the end and never make the same query twice, which uses at most $K \cdot \mathsf{poly}(n)$ extra queries by the efficiency of V_{nu}. Let $Q_1, \ldots, Q_T$ be the unique random oracle queries that $\mathcal{A}^{\mathcal{O}}(1^n, z_n)$ makes.

Before explicitly defining our representation of $\mathcal{O}$, we introduce some notation. For every statement q and PCP proof Π, we define $B(q, \Pi)$ to be the set of all b values for which $\mathsf{PCP.Ver}^{\Pi}(q, b)$ accepts, i.e.,

$$B(q, \Pi) = \{b \mid \mathsf{PCP.Ver}^{\Pi}(q; b) = 1\}.$$

By the 2^{-n} soundness error of the underlying PCP proof system, $|B(q, \Pi)| \leq 2^{\ell_b - n}$ for all statements q not in the specified language where recall ℓ_b is the length of b. When we refer to the mth element of the set $B(q, \Pi)$, we mean the mth element in the lexicographic enumeration of the set, which is uniquely defined.

We now define a procedure to generate a representation of a particular random oracle $\mathcal{O}$ using $\mathcal{A}^{\mathcal{O}}(1^n, z_n)$. We assume for simplicity that z_n starts with the description of $\mathcal{A}$.

1. Initialize lists L_{col}, L_{pre}, L_{pcp}, L_{query}, and L_{other} to be empty.
2. Run $\mathcal{A}^{\mathcal{O}}(1^n, z_n)$ to get false proofs $\pi_i = (a_i, b_i, c_i)$ for statements q_i with unique $\tilde{q}_i$ values for $i \in [K]$.
3. For each query Q_j in order, do exactly one the following.
   (a) If $\mathcal{O}(Q_j) = \mathcal{O}(Q_m)$ for $m < j$, add (j, m) to L_{col}.
   (b) If $\mathcal{O}(Q_j) = Q_m[\mathsf{pos} \cdot n + 1 : (\mathsf{pos} + 1) \cdot n]$ (where $Q_m[i_1 : i_2]$ is the substring from index i_1 to i_2 inclusive) for $m < j$ and $\mathsf{pos} \in \{0, \ldots, n + 1\}$, add (j, m, pos) to L_{pre}.
   (c) If the following conditions hold, add (j, m) to L_{pcp}.
      i. $Q_j = (\tilde{q}, \hat{q}, a_i)$ and $\mathcal{O}_4(\tilde{q}, \hat{q}, a_i) = b_i$ for some $i \in [K]$.
      ii. It is possible to uniquely extract a statement q that Merkle hashes to $\hat{q}$ using only previous $\mathcal{O}_2(\tilde{q}, \cdot)$ queries.
      iii. It is possible to uniquely extract a partial PCP proof Π that Merkle hashes to a_i using only previous $\mathcal{O}_3(\tilde{q}, \hat{q}, \cdot)$ queries.
      iv. b_i is the mth element of $B(q_i, \Pi)$.
   (d) Otherwise, add $\mathcal{O}(Q_j)$ to L_{query}.
4. For all other inputs x, add $\mathcal{O}(x)$ to L_{other} in lexicographic order.
5. Output $z_n, L_{\mathsf{col}}, L_{\mathsf{pre}}, L_{\mathsf{pcp}}, L_{\mathsf{query}}, L_{\mathsf{other}}$ as the representation.

Using only the representation, we define a procedure to compute all $\mathcal{O}$ queries.

1. Run $\mathcal{A}^{(\cdot)}(1^n, z_n)$ and simulate its queries to $\mathcal{O}$.
2. On the jth query Q_j, do the following.
   (a) If (j, m) is in L_{col} for $m < j$, output $\mathcal{O}(Q_m)$.
   (b) If (j, m, pos) is in L_{pre} for $m < j$ and $\mathsf{pos} \in \{0, \dots, n+1\}$, output $Q_m[\mathsf{pos} \cdot n + 1 : (\mathsf{pos} + 1) \cdot n]$.
   (c) If (j, m) is in L_{pcp}, do the following.
      i. Parse $Q_j = (\tilde{q}, \hat{q}, a)$.
      ii. Extract a statement q that Merkle hashes to $\hat{q}$ using only previous queries to $\mathcal{O}_2(\tilde{q}, \cdot)$.
      iii. Extract a partial PCP proof Π that Merkle hashes to a using only previous queries to $\mathcal{O}_3(\tilde{q}, \hat{q}, \cdot)$.
      iv. Output the mth element of $B(q, \Pi)$.
   (d) Otherwise, output the next value in the list L_{query}.
3. Compute all other outputs for $\mathcal{O}$ using L_{other}.

In the following claim, we prove that for any machine $\mathcal{A}^{\mathcal{O}}(1^n, z_n)$, the above procedure defines a valid and unique representation for $\mathcal{O}$.

Claim 2. *For every machine $\mathcal{A}^{\mathcal{O}}(1^n, z_n)$, the representation of $\mathcal{O}$ defined above is correct and unique.*

The proof of this claim appears in the full version.

We next show that the representation of $\mathcal{O}$ is actually compressing when $\mathcal{A}^{\mathcal{O}}(1^n, z_n)$ succeeds. Note that all random oracle outputs are added to exactly one of the lists L_{col}, L_{pre}, L_{pcp}, L_{query}, or L_{other}. Any output that is added to L_{col}, L_{pre}, or L_{pcp} requires fewer bits to represent than the full output. At a high level, we argue that at least K outputs will be added to these lists.

Claim 3. *Suppose that $\mathcal{A}^{\mathcal{O}}(1^n, z_n)$ outputs a false proof $\pi = (a, b, c)$ for a statement q mapping to $\tilde{q}$. Then, there is some query unique to $\tilde{q}$ that was added to either L_{col}, L_{pre}, or L_{pcp} in the representation defined above.*

Proof. Suppose there is no query of the form $(\tilde{q}, \cdot)$ or $(\tilde{q}, \hat{q}, \cdot)$ added to L_{col} or L_{pre}. It suffices to prove there is some query Q_j of the form $(\tilde{q}, \hat{q}, a)$ that is added to L_{pcp}. Recall that we assume $\mathcal{A}^{\mathcal{O}}(1^n, z_n)$ queries everything checked by V_{nu}. This implies that $\mathcal{A}^{\mathcal{O}}(1^n, z_n)$ queries $Q_j = (\tilde{q}, \hat{q}, a)$ at some point. We show that each of the conditions required for Q_j to be added to L_{pcp} hold. Namely, it is possible to uniquely extract q and Π such that $b = \mathcal{O}(\tilde{q}, \hat{q}, a)$ is contained in $B(q, \Pi)$.

First suppose it is not possible to uniquely extract q using previous queries to $\mathcal{O}_2(\tilde{q}, \cdot)$. We have assumed the entire Merkle tree computing $\mathsf{MT}^{\mathcal{O}_2(\tilde{q}, \cdot)}(q)$ is queried at some point. If we are not able to extract the correct statement q, then some query in the Merkle tree must be made after query Q_j. This would require that some pre-image will be queried using $\mathcal{O}_2(\tilde{q}, \cdot)$, which contradicts the assumption that no query containing $\tilde{q}$ is added to L_{pre}. If it is possible to extract the statement q but it is not unique, then there must be some collision queried in the Merkle tree using $\mathcal{O}_2(\tilde{q})$, but this contradicts that no query of the form $(\tilde{q}, \cdot)$ was added to L_{col}. Thus, we must be able to uniquely extract q when query Q_j is made.

Similarly, we must be able to use previous queries to $\mathcal{O}_3(\tilde{q}, \hat{q}, \cdot)$ to uniquely reconstruct a partial PCP proof Π. If it is not unique, there must be a collision in $\mathcal{O}_3(\tilde{q}, \hat{q}, \cdot)$, which is a contradiction. If all authenticating paths are not queried before Q_j, there will be some pre-image queried with $\mathcal{O}_3(\tilde{q}, \hat{q}, \cdot)$, which again is a contradiction.

Lastly, because (a, b, c) is an accepting proof for the statement q, b must be in the set $B(q, \Pi)$, which has bounded size since q is not in the specified language. We conclude that Q_j must be added to L_{pcp}.

By the above claim, we add at least one query to L_{col}, L_{pre}, or L_{pcp} for each unique $\tilde{q}$ value. Each query added to L_{col} uses at most $2 \log T$ bits to represent, L_{pre} uses at most $2 \log T + \log(n+2)$ bits, and L_{pcp} uses at most $\log T + \ell_b - n$ bits to represent a value of size ℓ_b. Since $A^{\mathcal{O}}$ queries everything that V_{nu} queries, T is at least $n + 2$, so $\log(n+2) \le \log T$. This implies that we compress by at least $n - 3 \log T$ bits per query added to L_{col}, L_{pre}, or L_{pcp}. The total representation in bits in this case is at most

$$n \cdot (2^{2n} + 2^{3n} + 2^{4n}) + \ell_b \cdot 2^{3n} + s - K(n - 3 \log T).$$

Because the representation is unique, this bounds the total number of oracles that $\mathcal{A}^{\mathcal{O}}(1^n, z_n)$ succeeds by $2^{n \cdot (2^{2n} + 2^{3n} + 2^{4n}) + \ell_b \cdot 2^{3n} + s - K(n - 3 \log T)}$ but there are $2^{n \cdot (2^{2n} + 2^{3n} + 2^{4n}) + \ell_b \cdot 2^{3n}}$ oracles in total. So the probability $\mathcal{A}^{\mathcal{O}}(1^n, z_n)$ succeeds on a randomly chosen oracle is at most $2^{-K(n - 3 \log T) + s}$.

We finish the proof of Theorem 4 next.

Proof (of Theorem 4). Let $P^{*\mathcal{O}}(1^n, z_n)$ be a non-uniform cheating prover that makes T queries to the random oracle and outputs $(C_1, q_1, \pi_1), \ldots, (C_K, q_K, \pi_K)$ for unique statements. We will show that

$$\Pr_{\mathcal{O}}\left[\{(C_i, q_i, \pi_i)\}_{i \in [K]} \leftarrow P^{*\mathcal{O}}(1^n, z_n) : \begin{array}{l} \forall i \ne j \in [K]: q_i \ne q_j, \\ \forall i \in [K]: q_i \notin L_{C_i} \\ \wedge V_{\text{nu}}(C_i, 1^n, q_i, \pi_i) = 1 \end{array} \right] \le 2^{-n+1}.$$

Let SUCC be the event that $P^{*\mathcal{O}}(1^n, z_n)$ succeeds, i.e., the condition above holds.

Consider an execution of $P^{*\mathcal{O}}(1^n, z_n)$ for a random function $\mathcal{O}$ that outputs $(C_1, q_1, \pi_1), \ldots, (C_K, q_K, \pi_K)$. Define α to be the smallest constant such that such that $|q_i| \le n^\alpha$ for all $i \in [K]$, and define $N = (3s)^{24 \cdot \alpha}$. Let BAD be the event that $|\{\tilde{q}_i = \text{MT}^{\mathcal{O}}(\text{LRC}_{|q_i|}(q_i)) : i \in [K]\}| \le K/N$. Since $\Pr[\text{SUCC}] \le \Pr[\text{BAD}] + \Pr[\text{SUCC} \mid \neg\text{BAD}]$, it suffices to bound each term separately.

By Lemma 1, $\Pr[\text{BAD}] \le 2^{-n}$. Given that BAD does not occur, we can find a set of statements $X \subseteq \{q_1, \ldots, q_K\}$ with false proofs and with a unique $\tilde{q}$ value where $|X| = K/N$. By Lemma 2, this can succeed with probability at most $2^{-(K/N) \cdot (n - 3 \log T) + s}$ over the choice of $\mathcal{O}$. When $K/N = 3s$ and $T \le 2^{n/6}$, this is at most 2^{-n}. In this case, $K = (3s)^{24\alpha + 1} \le (3s)^{25 \cdot \alpha}$, and $\Pr[\text{SUCC}] \le 2^{-n+1}$.

Remark 6. *As discussed in Remark 5, Theorem 4 immediately implies a corollary for a definition of (K, T)-soundness where the statements do not need* *to be unique. Specifically, we argued in Sect. 5.1 that $(P_{\mathsf{nu}}, V_{\mathsf{nu}})$ has a proof length bound of $\ell_\pi = O(n^2 \log n)$. It follows that $(P_{\mathsf{nu}}, V_{\mathsf{nu}})$ is (K', T)-sound for $K' = (3s)^{25\alpha} \cdot n^{n^2}$ in the case where only the proofs need to be unique rather than the statements.*

6   Concurrent Zero-Knowledge Protocol

In this section, we present our concurrent zero-knowledge protocol and prove that it satisfies *non-uniform* soundness when instantiated with our notion of nuCerts for **P**.

Theorem 6 (Restatement of Theorem 2). *Suppose there exist super-polynomially-secure families of collision resistant hash functions and* nuCerts *for* **P**. *Then, there exists a public-coin constant-round concurrent zero-knowledge protocol for* **NP** *with non-uniform soundness and an explicit simulator.*

We recall from Theorem 5 that we construct a nuCert for **P** in the auxiliary-input random oracle model. By a similar compression argument as in Sect. 5, it is easy to show that a compressing random oracle is a secure collision resistant hash function even in the auxiliary-input random oracle model. Thus, we get the following corollary to Theorems 5 and 6.

Corollary 2 (Restatement of Corollary 1). *In the auxiliary-input random oracle model, there exists a public-coin constant-round concurrent zero-knowledge protocol for* **NP**.

Our protocol is very similar to that of Chung et al. [14] which, in turn, is a variant of Barak's [1] constant-round (bounded concurrency) zero-knowledge protocol. At a very high level, Barak's simulator uses the verifier's code as a trapdoor to convince the verifier of the validity of the statement at hand. The simulator of Chung et al. instead uses to a succinct proof to certify that it knows a program that does the required task. To be able to provide such proofs for concurrent verifiers that may start nested sessions, rather than redoing computation multiple times, they design a way to provide succinct proofs to "shortcut" some of the computation. Specifically, they use k levels of uniformly sound certificates for **P** (**P**-certificates). The first layer of **P**-certificates is used to certify the verifier's messages in its interaction with the prover, and all above layers certify the correct generation of lower level **P**-certificates in a tree-like fashion.

In our construction, we use nuCerts for **P** in place of the **P**-certificates of [14]. We describe a sequence of protocols $\Pi_1, \Pi_2, \dots$, where protocol Π_k uses k levels of nuCerts and allows us to simulate n^k concurrent sessions. Thus, to capture full concurrency, our final instantiation is Π_k for any $k \in \omega(1)$.

We proceed with the description of our protocol $\Pi_k = (P_k, V_k)$ for a language $L \in \mathbf{NP}$. We present the protocol assuming that , is non-interactive, statistically binding commitment scheme, but this can be naturally replaced by any constant-round commitment scheme (for example, the scheme of Naor [37,46] which consists of two rounds and relies on the existence of one-way functions).

We further assume $\mathcal{H}_n = \{h\colon \{0,1\}^{\mathsf{poly}(n)} \to \{0,1\}^n\}$ is a family of collision resistant hash functions mapping strings of arbitrary polynomial length to strings of length n. We can instantiate this using a Merkle tree based on any family of compressing collision resistant hash functions. Lastly, we assume nuCerts for $\mathbf{P}$ with length bounded by $\ell(n) \in \mathsf{poly}(n)$.

Let 1^n and x be common inputs to (P_k, V_k) and w be a private input to P_k such that $(x, w) \in \mathbf{R}_L$. The protocol proceeds in two phases. In the first phase, the prover commits to a message before receiving a "challenge" r from the verifier. In the second phase, the prover provides a WIUA proving either that x is in the **NP** language or that the message it committed to in phase 1 was actually a sequence of machines that outputs r. We summarize this protocol Π_k as follows:

Phase 1: P_k and V_k exchange the following three messages.

1. V_k chooses a randomly sampled hash function $h \xleftarrow{\$} \mathcal{H}_n$ and sends h to P_k.
2. P_k sends a commitment to 0^n using , with randomness ρ.
3. V_k replies with a random "challenge" $r \xleftarrow{\$} \{0,1\}^{6\ell nk}$.

Phase 2: P_k provides a WIUA of the statement that either $x \in L$ OR there exists $\langle \vec{M}, j, \vec{s}, \vec{\pi}, \vec{\sigma}, \vec{\lambda}, \rho \rangle$ such that:

1. **Commitment Consistency:** c is a commitment to $h(\vec{M})$ using randomness ρ,

2. **Input Certification:**
   (a) $|\vec{\sigma}| \leq \ell nk$.
   (b) For $2 \leq i \leq k$, π_i certifies that $M_i(1^n, \zeta(j, i), s_i, ([\lambda_{\geq i}]_{\leq \zeta(j,i)}, [\sigma_{\geq i}]_{\leq \zeta(j,i)})) = \lambda_{i-1}$.

3. **Prediction Correctness:** π_1 certifies that $M_1(1^n, j, s_1, ([\lambda_{\geq 1}]_{\leq j}, [\sigma_{\geq 1}]_{\leq j})) = r$.

We define $\zeta(j, i) \triangleq j - (j \bmod n^{i-1})$, $\gamma_{\geq i} = (\gamma_i, \gamma_{i+1}, \ldots)$, and $[\gamma]_{\leq j} \triangleq \{(j', \cdot, \cdot) \in \gamma : j' \leq j\}$. These are used to "filter out" all unnecessary messages from future rounds.

There are two things we need to show: (1) there exists a simulator that can communicate with a cheating verifier in arbitrarily (yet polynomial) number of concurrent sessions and be able to convince it that the instance is in the language, even without having the witness, and (2) any *non-uniform* efficient cheating prover cannot convince the verifier the validity of a false statement. For (1), the ZK simulator is identical to [14] as nuCerts for $\mathbf{P}$ and $\mathbf{P}$-certificates have the same completeness and efficiency guarantees. We refer to the full version of the paper for the proof of (2) and hence Theorem 6.

References

1. Barak, B.: How to go beyond the black-box simulation barrier. In: 42nd Annual Symposium on Foundations of Computer Science, FOCS, pp. 106–115 (2001)
2. Barak, B., Goldreich, O.: Universal arguments and their applications. SIAM J. Comput. **38**(5), 1661–1694 (2008)

3. Barak, B., Goldreich, O., Goldwasser, S., Lindell, Y.: Resettably-sound zero-knowledge and its applications. In: 42nd Annual Symposium on Foundations of Computer Science, FOCS, pp. 116–125 (2001)
4. Barak, B., Lindell, Y., Vadhan, S.P.: Lower bounds for non-black-box zero knowledge. J. Comput. Syst. Sci. **72**(2), 321–391 (2006)
5. Barak, B., Ong, S.J., Vadhan, S.P.: Derandomization in cryptography. SIAM J. Comput. **37**(2), 380–400 (2007)
6. Berman, I., Degwekar, A., Rothblum, R.D., Vasudevan, P.N.: Multi-collision resistant hash functions and their applications. In: Nielsen, J.B., Rijmen, V. (eds.) EUROCRYPT 2018. LNCS, vol. 10821, pp. 133–161. Springer, Cham (2018). https://doi.org/10.1007/978-3-319-78375-8_5
7. Bitansky, N., Kalai, Y.T., Paneth, O.: Multi-collision resistance: a paradigm for keyless hash functions. In: 50th Annual ACM SIGACT Symposium on Theory of Computing, STOC, pp. 671–684 (2018)
8. Bitansky, N., Lin, H.: One-message zero knowledge and non-malleable commitments. In: Beimel, A., Dziembowski, S. (eds.) TCC 2018. LNCS, vol. 11239, pp. 209–234. Springer, Cham (2018). https://doi.org/10.1007/978-3-030-03807-6_8
9. Brassard, G., Chaum, D., Crépeau, C.: Minimum disclosure proofs of knowledge. J. Comput. Syst. Sci. **37**(2), 156–189 (1988)
10. Canetti, R., Goldreich, O., Goldwasser, S., Micali, S.: Resettable zero-knowledge (extended abstract). In: 32nd Annual ACM Symposium on Theory of Computing, STOC, pp. 235–244 (2000)
11. Canetti, R., Kilian, J., Petrank, E., Rosen, A.: Black-box concurrent zero-knowledge requires (almost) logarithmically many rounds. SIAM J. Comput. **32**(1), 1–47 (2002)
12. Canetti, R., Lin, H., Paneth, O.: Public-coin concurrent zero-knowledge in the global hash model. In: Sahai, A. (ed.) TCC 2013. LNCS, vol. 7785, pp. 80–99. Springer, Heidelberg (2013). https://doi.org/10.1007/978-3-642-36594-2_5
13. Chongchitmate, W., Ostrovsky, R., Visconti, I.: Resettably-sound resettable zero knowledge in constant rounds. In: Kalai, Y., Reyzin, L. (eds.) TCC 2017. LNCS, vol. 10678, pp. 111–138. Springer, Cham (2017). https://doi.org/10.1007/978-3-319-70503-3_4
14. Chung, K., Lin, H., Pass, R.: Constant-round concurrent zero knowledge from p-certificates. In: 54th Annual IEEE Symposium on Foundations of Computer Science, FOCS, pp. 50–59 (2013)
15. Chung, K.-M., Lin, H., Pass, R.: Constant-round concurrent zero-knowledge from indistinguishability obfuscation. In: Gennaro, R., Robshaw, M. (eds.) CRYPTO 2015. LNCS, vol. 9215, pp. 287–307. Springer, Heidelberg (2015). https://doi.org/10.1007/978-3-662-47989-6_14
16. Coretti, S., Dodis, Y., Guo, S., Steinberger, J.P.: Random oracles and non-uniformity. In: Nielsen, J.B., Rijmen, V. (eds.) EUROCRYPT 2018. LNCS, vol. 10820, pp. 227–258. Springer, Cham (2018). https://doi.org/10.1007/978-3-319-78381-9_9
17. Damgård, I.: Efficient concurrent zero-knowledge in the auxiliary string model. In: Preneel, B. (ed.) EUROCRYPT 2000. LNCS, vol. 1807, pp. 418–430. Springer, Heidelberg (2000). https://doi.org/10.1007/3-540-45539-6_30
18. Deng, Y., Goyal, V., Sahai, A.: Resolving the simultaneous resettability conjecture and a new non-black-box simulation strategy. In: 50th Annual IEEE Symposium on Foundations of Computer Science, FOCS, pp. 251–260 (2009)
19. Dwork, C., Naor, M., Sahai, A.: Concurrent zero-knowledge. J. ACM (JACM) **51**(6), 851–898 (2004)

20. Dwork, C., Sahai, A.: Concurrent zero-knowledge: reducing the need for timing constraints. In: Krawczyk, H. (ed.) CRYPTO 1998. LNCS, vol. 1462, pp. 442–457. Springer, Heidelberg (1998). https://doi.org/10.1007/BFb0055746

21. Feige, U., Shamir, A.: Witness indistinguishable and witness hiding protocols. In: Proceedings of the Twenty-Second Annual ACM Symposium on Theory of Computing, pp. 416–426. ACM (1990)

22. Fiat, A., Shamir, A.: How to prove yourself: practical solutions to identification and signature problems. In: Odlyzko, A.M. (ed.) CRYPTO 1986. LNCS, vol. 263, pp. 186–194. Springer, Heidelberg (1987). https://doi.org/10.1007/3-540-47721-7_12

23. Fortnow, L.: Kolmogorov complexity and computational complexity. Complexity of Computations and Proofs. Quaderni di Matematica, vol. 13 (2004)

24. Garg, S., Jain, A., Sahai, A.: Leakage-resilient zero knowledge. In: Rogaway, P. (ed.) CRYPTO 2011. LNCS, vol. 6841, pp. 297–315. Springer, Heidelberg (2011). https://doi.org/10.1007/978-3-642-22792-9_17

25. Gennaro, R., Trevisan, L.: Lower bounds on the efficiency of generic cryptographic constructions. In: 41st Annual Symposium on Foundations of Computer Science, FOCS, pp. 305–313 (2000)

26. Gentry, C., Wichs, D.: Separating succinct non-interactive arguments from all falsifiable assumptions. In: 43rd ACM Symposium on Theory of Computing, STOC, pp. 99–108 (2011)

27. Goldreich, O.: The Foundations of Cryptography - Volume 1, Basic Techniques. Cambridge University Press, Cambridge (2001)

28. Goldreich, O.: Concurrent zero-knowledge with timing, revisited. In: 34th Annual ACM Symposium on Theory of Computing, STOC, pp. 332–340 (2002)

29. Goldreich, O., Håstad, J.: On the complexity of interactive proofs with bounded communication. Inf. Process. Lett. **67**(4), 205–214 (1998)

30. Goldwasser, S., Micali, S., Rackoff, C.: The knowledge complexity of interactive proof systems. SIAM J. Comput. **18**(1), 186–208 (1989)

31. Goyal, V.: Non-black-box simulation in the fully concurrent setting. In: Symposium on Theory of Computing Conference, STOC, pp. 221–230. ACM (2013)

32. Goyal, V., Jain, A., Ostrovsky, R., Richelson, S., Visconti, I.: Constant-round concurrent zero knowledge in the bounded player model. In: Sako, K., Sarkar, P. (eds.) ASIACRYPT 2013. LNCS, vol. 8269, pp. 21–40. Springer, Heidelberg (2013). https://doi.org/10.1007/978-3-642-42033-7_2

33. Gupta, D., Sahai, A.: On constant-round concurrent zero-knowledge from a knowledge assumption. In: Meier, W., Mukhopadhyay, D. (eds.) INDOCRYPT 2014. LNCS, vol. 8885, pp. 71–88. Springer, Cham (2014). https://doi.org/10.1007/978-3-319-13039-2_5

34. Guruswami, V., Sudan, M.: Improved decoding of Reed-Solomon and algebraic-geometry codes. IEEE Trans. Inf. Theory **45**(6), 1757–1767 (1999)

35. Guruswami, V., Umans, C., Vadhan, S.P.: Unbalanced expanders and randomness extractors from parvaresh-vardy codes. J. ACM **56**(4), 20:1–20:34 (2009)

36. Haitner, I., Ishai, Y., Omri, E., Shaltiel, R.: Parallel hashing via list recoverability. In: Gennaro, R., Robshaw, M. (eds.) CRYPTO 2015. LNCS, vol. 9216, pp. 173–190. Springer, Heidelberg (2015). https://doi.org/10.1007/978-3-662-48000-7_9

37. Håstad, J., Impagliazzo, R., Levin, L.A., Luby, M.: A pseudorandom generator from any one-way function. SIAM J. Comput. **28**(4), 1364–1396 (1999)

38. Kilian, J.: A note on efficient zero-knowledge proofs and arguments. In: Proceedings of the Twenty-Fourth Annual ACM Symposium on Theory of Computing, pp. 723–732. ACM (1992)

39. Kilian, J.: Improved efficient arguments. In: Coppersmith, D. (ed.) CRYPTO 1995. LNCS, vol. 963, pp. 311–324. Springer, Heidelberg (1995). https://doi.org/10.1007/3-540-44750-4_25

40. Kilian, J., Petrank, E.: Concurrent and resettable zero-knowledge in polyloalgorithm rounds. In: 33rd Annual ACM Symposium on Theory of Computing, STOC, pp. 560–569 (2001)

41. Komargodski, I., Naor, M., Yogev, E.: White-box vs. black-box complexity of search problems: Ramsey and graph property testing. In: 58th IEEE Annual Symposium on Foundations of Computer Science, FOCS, pp. 622–632 (2017)

42. Komargodski, I., Naor, M., Yogev, E.: Collision resistant hashing for paranoids: dealing with multiple collisions. In: Nielsen, J.B., Rijmen, V. (eds.) EUROCRYPT 2018. LNCS, vol. 10821, pp. 162–194. Springer, Cham (2018). https://doi.org/10.1007/978-3-319-78375-8_6

43. Komargodski, I., Yogev, E.: On distributional collision resistant hashing. In: Shacham, H., Boldyreva, A. (eds.) CRYPTO 2018. LNCS, vol. 10992, pp. 303–327. Springer, Cham (2018). https://doi.org/10.1007/978-3-319-96881-0_11

44. Merkle, R.C.: A certified digital signature. In: Brassard, G. (ed.) CRYPTO 1989. LNCS, vol. 435, pp. 218–238. Springer, New York (1990). https://doi.org/10.1007/0-387-34805-0_21

45. Micali, S.: Computationally sound proofs. SIAM J. Comput. **30**(4), 1253–1298 (2000)

46. Naor, M.: Bit commitment using pseudorandomness. J. Cryptol. **4**(2), 151–158 (1991)

47. Pandey, O., Prabhakaran, M., Sahai, A.: Obfuscation-based non-black-box simulation and four message concurrent zero knowledge for NP. In: Dodis, Y., Nielsen, J.B. (eds.) TCC 2015. LNCS, vol. 9015, pp. 638–667. Springer, Heidelberg (2015). https://doi.org/10.1007/978-3-662-46497-7_25

48. Pass, R.: Simulation in quasi-polynomial time, and its application to protocol composition. In: Biham, E. (ed.) EUROCRYPT 2003. LNCS, vol. 2656, pp. 160–176. Springer, Heidelberg (2003). https://doi.org/10.1007/3-540-39200-9_10

49. Pass, R., Rosen, A., Tseng, W.D.: Public-coin parallel zero-knowledge for NP. J. Cryptol. **26**(1), 1–10 (2013)

50. Pass, R., Tseng, W.D., Venkitasubramaniam, M.: Concurrent zero knowledge, revisited. J. Cryptol. **27**(1), 45–66 (2014)

51. Pass, R., Tseng, W.D., Wikström, D.: On the composition of public-coin zero-knowledge protocols. SIAM J. Comput. **40**(6), 1529–1553 (2011)

52. Pass, R., Venkitasubramaniam, M.: On constant-round concurrent zero-knowledge. In: Canetti, R. (ed.) TCC 2008. LNCS, vol. 4948, pp. 553–570. Springer, Heidelberg (2008). https://doi.org/10.1007/978-3-540-78524-8_30

53. Prabhakaran, M., Rosen, A., Sahai, A.: Concurrent zero knowledge with logarithmic round-complexity. In: 43rd Symposium on Foundations of Computer Science FOCS, pp. 366–375. IEEE Computer Society (2002)

54. Richardson, R., Kilian, J.: On the concurrent composition of zero-knowledge proofs. In: Stern, J. (ed.) EUROCRYPT 1999. LNCS, vol. 1592, pp. 415–431. Springer, Heidelberg (1999). https://doi.org/10.1007/3-540-48910-X_29

55. Unruh, D.: Random oracles and auxiliary input. In: Menezes, A. (ed.) CRYPTO 2007. LNCS, vol. 4622, pp. 205–223. Springer, Heidelberg (2007). https://doi.org/10.1007/978-3-540-74143-5_12

On Round Optimal Statistical Zero Knowledge Arguments

Nir Bitansky[1(✉)] and Omer Paneth[2(✉)]

[1] Tel Aviv University, Tel Aviv-Yafo, Israel
nbitansky@gmail.com
[2] MIT and Northeastern University, Cambridge, USA
omerpa@gmail.com

Abstract. We construct the first three message statistical zero knowledge arguments for all of NP, matching the known lower bound. We do so based on keyless multi-collision resistant hash functions and the Learning with Errors assumption—the same assumptions used to obtain round optimal computational zero knowledge.

The main component in our construction is a statistically witness indistinguishable argument of knowledge based on a new notion of statistically hiding commitments with subset opening.

1 Introduction

Since their introduction three decades ago [GMR89], the concept of zero knowledge protocols has played a central role in the development of modern cryptography. Different flavors of zero knowledge protocols have been studied according to the level of soundness and zero knowledge achieved. Either property can be *statistical* or *computational*, meaning that it holds against unbounded or computationally bounded adversaries, respectively. Protocols that satisfy both properties statistically, known as *statistical zero knowledge proofs*, are only possible for languages in $\mathbf{AM} \cap \mathbf{coAM}$ [For89, AH91]; however, once either property is relaxed to computational, protocols for all of $\mathbf{NP}$ can be constructed assuming one way functions [GMW91, Nao91, BCC88, NOVY98, HNO+09].

In this work, we focus on *statistical zero knowledge arguments* for $\mathbf{NP}$; namely, computationally sound protocols where the view of any efficient verifier can be efficiently simulated up to a negligible statistical difference. Such protocols are especially appealing due to their *everlasting zero knowledge guarantee*—even if the verifier stores conversations with the prover and post-processes them for as long as it wants, it does not learn anything that cannot be simulated efficiently.

N. Bitansky—Member of the Check Point Institute of Information Security. Supported by ISF grant 18/484, the Alon Young Faculty Fellowship, and by Len Blavatnik and the Blavatnik Family Foundation.

O. Paneth—Supported by NSF Grants CNS-1413964, CNS-1350619 and CNS-1414119, and the Defense Advanced Research Projects Agency (DARPA) and the U.S. Army Research Office under contracts W911NF-15-C-0226 and W911NF-15-C-0236.

© International Association for Cryptologic Research 2019
A. Boldyreva and D. Micciancio (Eds.): CRYPTO 2019, LNCS 11694, pp. 128–156, 2019.
https://doi.org/10.1007/978-3-030-26954-8_5

A foundational question is the round complexity of such protocols. Four message protocols can be constructed based on collision resistant hash functions [BJY97]. In terms of lower bounds, at least three messages are necessary even for computational zero knowledge [GO94]. Constructing zero knowledge arguments with matching round complexity has so far appeared more difficult in the statistical setting than in the computational one. Computational zero knowledge in three messages has been long known under unfalsifiable knowledge assumptions [HT98,BP04,CD09,BCC+14] and recently also under a falsifiable multi-collision resistance assumption on keyless hash functions [BKP18]. In contrast, three message statistical zero knowledge has been out of reach (even under knowledge assumptions).

The difference between the statistical and computational settings seems to run somewhat deeper, and manifests itself even in *witness indistinguishability*, a relaxation of zero knowledge. While computational witness indistinguishability has been long known in three [GMW91,FLS99], two [DN07], or even one message [BOV07,GOS12], statistical witness indistinguishability in less than four messages has only been very recently achieved [KKS18]. In fact, *witness indistinguishable arguments of knowledge*, which are essential in the constructions of three message computational zero knowledge, are still not known in less than four messages in the statistical setting.

All and all, we are faced with the question:

What is the round complexity of statistical zero knowledge arguments?

1.1   Results

We construct the first round optimal statistical zero knowledge argument under the same assumptions on which computational zero knowledge arguments are currently known.

Theorem 1.1 (Informal). *Assuming keyless multi-collision resistant hash functions and LWE, both quasi-polynomially hard, there exist three message statistical zero knowledge arguments.*[1]

Keyless multi-collision resistant hash functions, introduced in [BKP18], are functions $H : \{0,1\}^{2\lambda} \to \{0,1\}^{\lambda}$ guaranteeing that no efficient adversary with non-uniform description of polynomial size S can find more than $\text{poly}(S)$ elements that collide under H. Here poly is some fixed polynomial and the adversary's running time may be an arbitrarily larger polynomial, or even quasipolynomial (as required in the above theorem). While at this point non-standard, multi-collision resistance of keyless hash functions is a falsifiable and relatively simple assumption, which plausibly holds for existing keyless hash functions (see discussion in [BKP18]).

Four Message Protocols from Weaker Assumptions. When considering keyed hash functions, multi-collision resistance becomes a standard assumption

---

[1] Here LWE is used to realize several generic primitives, which we address in the body.

that relaxes the classical notion of collision resistance. A recent line of work explores such hash functions demonstrating that their power goes beyond one-way functions to achieve some of the applications of collision resistance [BDRV18, BKP18,KNY17,KNY18,BHKY19]. Our second result is along this vein showing that four message statistical zero knowledge arguments can be based on (keyed) multi-collision resistance instead of full fledged collision resistance.

Theorem 1.2 (Informal). *Assuming (keyed) multi-collision resistant hash functions, there exist four message statistical zero knowledge arguments.*

A main building block in both of the above results is a new statistically witness indistinguishable argument of knowledge, which was so far known from collision resistance in four messages.

Theorem 1.3 (Informal). *Assuming multi-collision resistant hash functions, there exist four message statistically witness indistinguishable arguments of knowledge. If the hash functions are keyless the arguments have three messages.*

Most of the technical effort in this work is devoted toward proving this theorem.

1.2   Technical Overview

We now provide an overview of the main ideas and techniques behind our results. We start with our construction of statistically witness indistinguishable arguments of knowledge and then move on to explain how they are used to construct statistical zero knowledge arguments.

Classical Witness Indistinguishable Protocols from Bit Commitments. To understand the challenge, let us recall how classical witness indistinguishable arguments of knowledge are designed. Such protocols traditionally involve three basic steps: a prover commitment, a verifier challenge, and a prover decommitment. The prover commitment consists of multiple bit commitments, a subset of which are opened in the decommitment step according to the challenge given by the verifier. For instance, in Blum's Hamiltonicity protocol [Blu86], the prover commits to the entries of the adjacency matrix of a graph and then, according to the challenge, either opens a subset of edges corresponding to a Hamiltonian cycle or the entire graph. This is repeated in parallel to decrease the soundness error to negligible. (The protocol contains additional details that we omit.)

Indeed, given statistically hiding bit commitments, such protocols can be shown to be statistically witness indistinguishable. However, focusing on round complexity, such commitments inherently require at least two messages—if the commitment was non-interactive, a cheating prover could have equivocal openings for some commitments non-uniformly hardwired into its code; such openings always exist due to statistical hiding.

Weakly Binding Commitments. While standard binding cannot be achieved non-interactively for statistically hiding bit commitments, keyless multi-collision resistant hash functions are known to imply non-interactive statistically hiding commitments with *weak binding* [BKP18]. Weak binding says that an attacker could only ever open a given commitment to values from some polynomial-size set. Intuitively, this means that even if it has equivocal openings of some commitment hardwired in its code, these cannot be used to sample more openings (except with negligible probability). Weak binding, however, is only meaningful in commitments for long strings and is completely meaningless for bit commitments, where the prover can open commitments to both zero and one. Accordingly, it is not clear how to use it in classical witness indistinguishable protocols that are all based on bit commitments.

An analogous problem is encountered in the work of [BKP18]. They define commitments for long strings with a subset opening property that enables to open only a given subset of bits, without having to open the entire string. While traditionally we require that every individual bit is fixed by the commitment, they suggest a relaxed definition suited for the setting of weak binding. They require that for any fixed adversary, a commitment to a long string $X \in \{0,1\}^L$ fixes a *global* set of strings $\mathbf{X} \subseteq \{0,1\}^L$ of polynomial size K, so that whenever the adversary opens some subset of bits $I \subseteq [L]$, they must all be *simultaneously consistent* with one string in the set $\mathbf{X}$ (except with negligible probability over the adversary's coins).

Our first observation is that commitments with subset opening and the above weak, but global, binding guarantee is sufficient for establishing soundness and also knowledge extraction in classical protocols. Roughly speaking, this is because for any prover that convinces the verifier of accepting with noticeable probability ε, there must be a single string $X \in \mathbf{X}$, such that with probability ε/K, the prover convinces the verifier *while answering consistently with X*. Since ε/K is still noticeable, soundness and knowledge extraction essentially reduce to those of the original protocol in the fully binding setting.

The work of [BKP18] constructs commitments with subset opening that fall short of achieving statistical hiding (indeed they focus on succinctness rather than hiding). In their construction, an opening of a given subset also reveals information regarding unopened bits, thus making them unfit for instantiating witness indistinguishable protocols. At high level, the reason they do not achieve statistical hiding is that to enforce consistency, subsets of bits are always opened in a correlated way and the correlations also pertain to unopened bits (this will become more clear below when we describe our construction).

Statistically Hiding Commitments with Subset Opening. We provide a construction that also achieves statistical hiding. Specifically, commitments to any two vectors X, X' are statistically indistinguishable, even given an opening of any subset of entries where X and X' agree. Our construction combines ideas from [BKP18] along with new ideas aimed toward statistical hiding.

The construction is based on statistically hiding weakly binding string commitments (with no subset opening) and Shamir secret sharing [Sha79]. At abstract level, Shamir secret sharing with parameters (n, d) allows to sample an encoding $\hat{b} \in \Sigma^n$ over some alphabet Σ of a secret bit $b \in \{0,1\}$, so that two properties are guaranteed. First, any two encodings $\hat{0}$ and $\hat{1}$ of zero and one agree on at most d entries. Second, any d entries of a random encoding $\hat{b}$ perfectly hide the bit b.

The commitment scheme works as follows:

- **Commitment:** to commit to a string $X \in \{0,1\}^L$, we sample encodings $\widehat{X}_i$ for all bits X_i of X. Then, considering the matrix $\widehat{X} = \left(\widehat{X}_{i,j}\right)$ whose rows are the encodings $\widehat{X}_i$, we compute a statistically hiding weakly-binding commitment to each row and each column of the matrix $\widehat{X}$.
- **Opening:** opening a subset of entries $I \subseteq [L]$ consists of two messages: a receiver challenge C, and a corresponding decommitment. The challenge consists of d random indices $C \subseteq [n]$. A decommitment involves opening the commitments to all rows $i \in I$ and all columns $j \in C$. The receiver verifies that the individual decommitments are valid and are consistent (on the intersection of corresponding rows and columns).

Let us explain at high level how the scheme satisfies statistical hiding and (global) weak binding. To show that any unopened entry $i \notin I$ remains statistically hidden, we rely on the fact that the commitment corresponding to its row $\widehat{X}_i$ is statistically hiding and never opened. Since only d column commitments are opened, only d entries of $\widehat{X}_i$ are revealed and thus the Shamir hiding property guarantees that the bit X_i remains statistically hidden.

Proving weak (global) binding is inspired by ideas from [BKP18]. Roughly speaking, the weak binding of individual row commitments guarantees that for every row i, the sender can only ever open the corresponding commitment to encodings $\widehat{X}_i$ from some fixed set $\mathbf{S}_i$ of polynomial size $K = \mathrm{poly}(\lambda)$ in the security parameter λ. We then use the fact that encodings of two distinct bits are far apart to argue that with overwhelming probability the answers to the random challenge (columns) uniquely fix all the bits of the string X. We further show that due to the individual weak binding of column commitments, these answers come from a polynomial set, and accordingly the string X determined by these answers must also come from a polynomial-size set $\mathbf{X}$.

In a bit more detail, we choose the parameters (n, d) of Shamir secret sharing so that the relative agreement of encodings of distinct bits is polynomially small $d/n < \lambda^{-\Omega(1)}$. Then choosing a large enough constant τ such that

$$L \cdot K^2 \cdot (d/n)^\tau \ll 1$$

guarantees that for τ random locations $T \subseteq [n]$, for all bits $i \in [L]$, any two encodings in $\mathbf{S}_i$ that agree on T must encode the same bit.

By the weak binding of column commitments, any opened column $j \in T$ is taken from a fixed set $\mathbf{S}'_j$ of polynomial size K, which means that all opened bits must simultaneously be consistent with some X taken from a set $\mathbf{X}_T$ of polynomial size K^τ. The actual construction chooses d random challenges C for super-logarithmic d, so that with overwhelming probability they include a fixing set $T \subseteq C$, and the set $\mathbf{X}$ is the union of all corresponding sets $\mathbf{X}_T$ (the number of which is at most d^τ and thus polynomial).

Statistical Zero Knowledge. We now explain how the statistical zero knowledge protocols behind Theorems 1.1 and 1.2 is obtained. The four message protocol from (keyed) multi-collision resistance is obtained in a black-box way by replacing the statistically witness indistinguishable argument of knowledge (from collision resistance) in the protocol of [BJY97] with our witness indistinguishable argument from multi-collision resistance. We focus on explaining how three-message statistical zero knowledge is obtained from keyless multi-collision resistant hashing.

Our starting point is the three-message *computational* zero knowledge argument of [BBK+16] and its subsequent extension in [BKP18] based on multi-collision resistant hash functions. At high level, their protocol follows the recipe of Barak's non-black-box simulation technique [Bar01]. To prove an **NP** statement $x \in \mathcal{L}$, the prover sends a shrinking commitment cmt to the code of some (potentially long) program Π and the verifier responds with a random string r. Then, the prover gives a succinct witness indistinguishable argument of knowledge proving that either $x \in \mathcal{L}$ or that the committed program $\Pi(\text{cmt})$ outputs r. At high level, by committing to the code of the verifier itself, a non-black-box simulator is able to produce an accepting transcript without using the witness, while a cheating prover, who does not know the verifier's randomness r, can only commit to such a program with negligible probability.

In [BBK+16, BKP18], the succinct witness indistinguishable argument of knowledge is constructed from a (non-succinct) witness indistinguishable argument of knowledge, a *secure function evaluation scheme*, and a *weak memory delegation scheme*, which they construct based on keyless multi-collision resistant hashing. Upgrading the protocol from computational zero knowledge to statistical zero knowledge requires two main changes. First, the prover commitment cmt is replaced with a statistically hiding commitment that is weakly binding, which as already observed in [BKP18] is sufficient. Second, the succinct witness indistinguishable argument of knowledge is replaced with a statistically witness indistinguishable one.

To obtain the succinct witness indistinguishable argument, we replace the (computationally) witness indistinguishable argument with our statistically witness indistinguishable argument. In addition, need the secure function evaluation scheme to satisfy statistical function hiding, which can be achieved assuming LWE [OPP14, BD18]. The actual construction requires that the witness indistinguishable argument possesses additional properties, such as adaptive witness indistinguishability and adaptive argument of knowledge, when the statement proven is adversarially chosen after the first two messages of the protocol. The protocol we construct is a slightly tweaked version of the protocol described in this introduction that satisfies these properties.

1.3   More Related Work

We next address additional related work in more detail.

More on Statistical Zero Knowledge Arguments. From the early constructions of zero knowledge protocols [GMW91, BCC88] it was evident that statistically hiding commitments are sufficient to obtain statistically zero knowledge arguments in a super logarithmic number of rounds. (See [HNO+09] for a survey on statistically hiding commitments.) Early constant round constructions [BCY91] were based on specific number theoretic assumptions. The work of Bellare, Jakobson, and Yung constructed computational zero knowledge arguments in four messages from one-way functions; however, their construction in fact uses a four message witness indistinguishable argument of knowledge in a generic manner. Using two-message statistically hiding commitments [DPP93,HM96], such arguments can be obtained from collision resistant hashing.

The Round Complexity of Zero Knowledge Proofs. This paper focuses on the notion of (statistical zero knowledge) arguments. The round complexity of zero-knowledge proofs (which are statistically sound) for **NP** has also been studied extensively. Four-message proofs are impossible to achieve via black-box simulation, except for languages in **NP ∩ coAM** [Kat12]. Four message proofs with non-black-box simulation are only known assuming multi-collision-resistance keyless hash functions [BKP18]. Recent evidence [FGJ18] suggests that, differently from zero-knowledge arguments, zero-knowledge proofs may be impossible to achieve in three messages (even with non-black-box simulation).

The Black Box Barrier. Goldreich and Krawczyk show that three message computational (let alone, statistical) zero knowledge arguments cannot be achieved with black box simulation [GK96]. The seminal work of Barak was the first to show that *non-black-box simulation* could potentially cross such black box barriers [Bar01]. Works of Bitansky et al. [BCPR14,BBK+16] obtain three message (computational) zero knowledge arguments in case where either the (adversarial) verifier or prover have an a-priori bounded description (and arbitrary polynomial running time). Following, the work of [BKP18] obtains such arguments also against non-uniform verifiers and provers relying on keyless multi-collision resistance.

A Stronger Notion of Statistical Zero Knowledge. The literature (e.g. [HNO+09]) also considers a stronger form of statistical zero knowledge than the one presented in this introduction where the simulator is not only required to statistically simulate the view of efficient verifiers, but also of inefficient ones, given oracle access to the verifier. We note that this notion is outright impossible in three messages where black box simulation is impossible [GK96]. Our four message protocol, in fact, does achieve this stronger notion.

2   Preliminaries

We rely on the standard computational concepts and notation:

- A PPT is a probabilistic polynomial-time algorithm.
- A uniform algorithm is T-time if it runs in time polynomial in T. (T may be super-polynomial in its input size.)

- We follow the standard habit of modeling any efficient adversary strategy as a family of polynomial-size circuits. For an adversary $\mathcal{A}$ corresponding to a family of polynomial-size circuits $\{\mathcal{A}_\lambda\}_{\lambda \in \mathbb{N}}$, we often omit the subscript λ, when it is clear from the context.
- We say that a function $f : \mathbb{N} \to \mathbb{R}$ is negligible if for all constants $c > 0$, there exists $N \in \mathbb{N}$ such that for all $n > N$, $f(n) < n^{-c}$. We sometimes denote negligible functions by negl.
- We say that a function $f : \mathbb{N} \to \mathbb{R}$ is noticeable if there exists a constant $c > 0$ and $N \in \mathbb{N}$ such that for all $n > N$, $f(n) \geq n^{-c}$.
- We denote statistical distance by **SD**.
- For two random variables X, Y and $\varepsilon \in [0, 1]$, we write $X \approx_\varepsilon Y$ to denote the fact that $\mathbf{SD}(X, Y) \leq \varepsilon$.
- For two ensembles $\mathcal{X} = \{X_\lambda\}_{\lambda \in \mathbb{N}}$ and $\mathcal{Y} = \{Y_\lambda\}_{\lambda \in \mathbb{N}}$, we say that $\mathcal{X}$ and $\mathcal{Y}$ are statistically indistinguishable if there exists a negligible $\mu(\cdot)$, such that for all λ, $X_\lambda \approx_{\mu(\lambda)} Y_\lambda$. We denote this by $\mathcal{X} \approx_s \mathcal{Y}$.
- For a string X of length n, and a subset $I \subseteq [n]$, we denote by $X|_I$ its restriction to the entries in I.

2.1 Statistical Zero-Knowledge Arguments

In what follows, we denote by $\langle \mathsf{P} \leftrightarrows \mathsf{V} \rangle$ a protocol between two parties P and V. For input w for P, and common input x, we denote by $\langle \mathsf{P}(w) \leftrightarrows \mathsf{V} \rangle(x)$ the output of V in the protocol. For honest verifiers this output will be a single bit indicating acceptance (or rejection), whereas malicious verifiers output their entire view. Throughout, we assume that honest parties in all protocols are uniform PPT algorithms.

Definition 2.1. *A protocol $\langle \mathsf{P} \leftrightarrows \mathsf{V} \rangle$ for an* **NP** *relation $\mathcal{R}(x, w)$ is a statistical zero-knowledge argument if it satisfies:*

Completeness: *For any $\lambda \in \mathbb{N}, x \in \mathcal{L}(\mathcal{R}) \cap \{0, 1\}^\lambda$, $w \in \mathcal{R}(x)$:*

$$\Pr\left[\langle \mathsf{P}(w) \leftrightarrows \mathsf{V} \rangle(x) = 1\right] = 1.$$

Computational Soundness: *For every polynomial-size circuit family of provers $\mathsf{P}^* = \{\mathsf{P}^*_\lambda\}_\lambda$, there exists a negligible function μ, such that for any $x \in \{0, 1\}^\lambda \setminus \mathcal{L}(\mathcal{R})$,*

$$\Pr\left[\langle \mathsf{P}^*_\lambda \leftrightarrows \mathsf{V} \rangle(x) = 1\right] \leq \mu(\lambda).$$

Statistical Zero-Knowledge: *There exists a PPT simulator S such that for every polynomial-size circuit family $\mathsf{V}^* = \{\mathsf{V}^*_\lambda\}_\lambda$:*

$$\{\langle \mathsf{P}(w) \leftrightarrows \mathsf{V}^*_\lambda \rangle(x)\}_{\substack{(x,w) \in \mathcal{R} \\ |x| = \lambda}} \approx_s \{\mathsf{S}(x, \mathsf{V}^*_\lambda)\}_{\substack{(x,w) \in \mathcal{R} \\ |x| = \lambda}}.$$

2.2 Weakly Binding Commitments and Multi-collision Resistant Hash Functions

We define weakly-binding statistically-hiding commitments [BKP18]. The definition addresses both the setting of keyed hash functions as well as keyless ones.

Syntax: A commitment scheme is associated with an input length function $\ell(\lambda)$ and polynomial-time algorithms SHC = (SHC.Gen, SHC.Com) with the following syntax:

- pk $\leftarrow$ SHC.Gen(1^λ): a probabilistic algorithm that takes the security parameter 1^λ and outputs a key pk $\in \{0,1\}^\lambda$. In the keyless setting, this algorithm is deterministic and outputs a fixed key pk $\equiv 1^\lambda$.
- cmt $\leftarrow$ SHC.Com(X; pk): a probabilistic algorithm that takes the key pk and an input $X \in \{0,1\}^{\ell(\lambda)}$ and outputs a commitment cmt. When we want to be explicit about the randomness r used by the algorithm, we may write SHC.Com(X; pk, r).

Definition 2.2 (Weakly-Binding Statistically-Hiding Commitments). *For a polynomial $\ell(\cdot)$, a weakly-binding statistically-hiding commitment SHC = (SHC.Gen, SHC.Com), for messages of length ℓ, satisfies:*

Statistical Hiding: *For any key and any two plaintexts, the corresponding commitments are statistically close:*

$$\{\text{SHC.Com}(X; \text{pk})\}_{\substack{\lambda \in \mathbb{N}, \text{pk} \in \{0,1\}^\lambda, \\ X, X' \in \{0,1\}^{\ell(\lambda)}}} \approx_{2^{-\lambda}} \{\text{SHC.Com}(X'; \text{pk})\}_{\substack{\lambda \in \mathbb{N}, \text{pk} \in \{0,1\}^\lambda, \\ X, X' \in \{0,1\}^{\ell(\lambda)}}} .$$

Weak Binding: *For any non-uniform polynomial-size probabilistic $\mathcal{A} = \{\mathcal{A}_\lambda^1, \mathcal{A}_\lambda^2\}_\lambda$ there exists a polynomial $K(\cdot)$ and a negligible $\mu(\cdot)$, such that for all $\lambda \in \mathbb{N}$,*

$$\Pr_{\substack{\text{pk} \leftarrow \text{SHC.Gen}(1^\lambda) \\ (\text{cmt}, \text{st}) \leftarrow \mathcal{A}_\lambda^1(\text{pk})}} \left[\begin{array}{l} \exists \mathbf{X} \text{ of size } K(\lambda): \\ \Pr_{(X,r) \leftarrow \mathcal{A}_\lambda^2(\text{st})} \left[\begin{array}{l} \text{cmt} = \text{SHC.Com}(X; \text{pk}, r) \\ X \notin \mathbf{X} \end{array} \right] \leq \mu(\lambda) \end{array} \right] \geq 1 - \mu(\lambda).$$

Multi-collision Resistance. We also define multi-collision resistant hash functions [BKP18], which are similar to weakly binding commitments, only that the hiding requirement is replaced with the requirement that they shrink their input (accordingly, they are also deterministic).

Syntax: A hashing scheme is associated with an input length function $\ell(\lambda)$ and polynomial-time algorithms H = (H.Gen, H.Hash) with the following syntax:

- pk $\leftarrow$ H.Gen(1^λ): a probabilistic algorithm that takes the security parameter 1^λ and outputs a key pk $\in \{0,1\}^\lambda$. In the keyless setting, this algorithm is deterministic and outputs a fixed key pk $\equiv 1^\lambda$.
- $Y \leftarrow$ H.Hash(X; pk): a deterministic algorithm that takes the key pk and an input $X \in \{0,1\}^{\ell(\lambda)}$ and outputs a hash value Y.

Definition 2.3 (Multi-collision Resistant Hash). *For a polynomial $\ell(\cdot)$, a multi-collision resistant hash* $\mathsf{H} = (\mathsf{H.Gen}, \mathsf{H.Hash})$*, for messages of length ℓ, satisfies:*

Compression: *$\ell(\lambda) > \lambda$ and $|\mathsf{H.Hash}(X)| = \lambda$ for all $\lambda \in \mathbb{N}$, key $\mathsf{pk} \in \{0,1\}^\lambda$, and $X \in \{0,1\}^{\ell(\lambda)}$. If $\ell = \lambda \cdot (1 + \Omega(1))$ we say that H is linearly compressing and if $\ell = \lambda^{1+\Omega(1)}$ we say that H is polynomially compressing.*

Multi-collision Resistance: *For any non-uniform polynomial-size probabilistic $\mathcal{A} = \{\mathcal{A}_\lambda^1, \mathcal{A}_\lambda^2\}_\lambda$ there exists a polynomial K and a negligible $\mu(\cdot)$, such that for all $\lambda \in \mathbb{N}$,*

$$\Pr_{\substack{\mathsf{pk} \leftarrow \mathsf{SHC.Gen}(1^\lambda) \\ (Y,\mathsf{st}) \leftarrow \mathcal{A}_\lambda^1(\mathsf{pk})}} \left[\begin{array}{l} \exists \mathbf{X} \text{ of size } K(\lambda) : \\ \Pr_{X \leftarrow \mathcal{A}_\lambda^2(\mathsf{st})} [Y = \mathsf{H.Hash}(X; \mathsf{pk}) \wedge X \notin \mathbf{X}] \leq \mu(\lambda) \end{array} \right] \geq 1 - \mu(\lambda).$$

We also consider a generalized notion of T-secure multi-collision resistant hashing that allows addressing attackers that run in super-polynomial time. The constructions in this paper all rely on the above polynomial notion. Quasipolynomial security is used in [BKP18] to construct weak memory delegation as defined in Sect. 2.3. We state the definition here for completeness.

T-Secure Multi-collision Resistance: *For any non-uniform polynomial-size probabilistic $\mathcal{A} = \{\mathcal{A}_\lambda^1\}$ and any uniform T-time $\mathcal{A}_2$ there exists a polynomial K and a negligible $\mu(\cdot)$, such that for all $\lambda \in \mathbb{N}$,*

$$\Pr_{\substack{\mathsf{pk} \leftarrow \mathsf{SHC.Gen}(1^\lambda) \\ (Y,\mathsf{st}) \leftarrow \mathcal{A}_\lambda^1(\mathsf{pk})}} \left[\begin{array}{l} \exists \mathbf{X} \text{ of size } K(\lambda) : \\ \Pr_{X \leftarrow \mathcal{A}^2(\mathsf{st})} [Y = \mathsf{H.Hash}(X; \mathsf{pk}) \wedge X \notin \mathbf{X}] \leq \mu(\lambda) \end{array} \right] \geq 1 - \mu(\lambda).$$

Remark 2.1. Note that for polynomial $T(\lambda) = \mathrm{poly}(\lambda)$, T-security coincides with (plain) security. Indeed, the non-uniformity of $\mathcal{A}^2$ can always be pushed to $\mathcal{A}^1$ who passes a state to $\mathcal{A}^2$.

In [BKP18], it is shown that multi-collision resistant hashing implies weakly binding string commitments.

Theorem 2.1 ([BKP18]). *Assuming a multi-collision-resistant keyless hash that is either:*

- *polynomially compressing*
- *or, linearly compressing and* quasipoly(λ)*-secure*

there exist, for every polynomial $L(\cdot)$, a weakly-binding statistically-hiding commitment and multi-collision-resistant keyless hash, both for messages of length L.

2.3 Weak Memory Delegation

The notion of weak memory delegation was defined in [BKP18] as a relaxation of memory delegation [CKLR11, KP16]. In a two-message memory delegation scheme, an untrusted server provides the client a short commitment or *digest* dig of a large memory D. The client can then delegate any arbitrary deterministic computation M to be executed over the memory. The server responds with the computation's output y, as well as a short proof of correctness that can be verified by the client in time that is independent of that of the delegated computation and the size of the memory.

In the definition of memory delegation in [KP16], the soundness requirement says that having provided the digest dig, a cheating prover should not be able to prove that a given computation M results in more than a single outcome y. In weak memory delegation, the prover should not be able to prove consistency with *too many* outcomes y.

Syntax: A two-message memory delegation scheme is associated with polynomial-time algorithms
    (MD.Mem, MD.Query, MD.Prove, MD.Ver) with the following syntax:

- dig ← MD.Mem($1^\lambda, D$): a deterministic polynomial-time algorithm that given the security parameter 1^λ and memory D, outputs a digest dig $\in \{0,1\}^\lambda$ of the memory.
- (q, vst) ← MD.Query(1^λ): a randomized polynomial-time algorithm that given the security parameter 1^λ, outputs a query q and a secret state vst.
- π ← MD.Prove($1^\lambda, D, (M, 1^t, y), q$): a deterministic algorithm that takes the security parameter 1^λ, a memory string D, a (deterministic) Turing machine M, an output string y, and time bound 1^t such that $|D| \le t \le 2^\lambda$ and $M(D)$ outputs y within t steps. It outputs a proof π.
- b ← MD.Ver(1^λ, dig, (M, t, y), vst, π): a deterministic polynomial time oracle algorithm that takes the security parameter 1^λ, a digest dig, a (deterministic) Turing machine M, a time bound t, an output string y, a secret state vst and a proof π. It outputs an acceptance bit b.

Definition 2.4 (Entropic Distribution Ensemble). *We say that an efficiently samplable distribution ensemble* $\{Y_\lambda\}_{\lambda \in \mathbb{N}}$ *is entropic if*

$$H_\infty(Y_\lambda) := -\log \max_{y \in \text{supp}(Y_\lambda)} \Pr[Y_\lambda = y] = \Omega(\lambda).$$

Definition 2.5 (Weak Memory Delegation). *A two-message delegation scheme*
MD = (MD.Mem, MD.Query, MD.Prove, MD.Ver) *satisfies:*

Efficiency: *There exists a polynomial p such that for every $\lambda \in \mathbb{N}$ and D such that $|D| \le 2^\lambda$, MD.Mem($1^\lambda, D$) outputs a digest dig of length at most $p(\lambda)$.*

Correctness: *For every security parameter $\lambda \in \mathbb{N}$, every $(M, t, y) \in \{0,1\}^\lambda$, and every D such that $M(D)$ outputs y within t steps, and $|D| \le t \le 2^\lambda$:*

$$\Pr\left[\text{MD.Ver}(1^\lambda, \text{dig}, (M, t, y), \text{vst}, \pi) = 1 \,\middle|\, \begin{array}{l} \text{dig} \leftarrow \text{MD.Mem}(1^\lambda, D) \\ (\text{q}, \text{vst}) \leftarrow \text{MD.Query}(1^\lambda) \\ \pi \leftarrow \text{MD.Prove}(1^\lambda, D, (M, 1^t, y), \text{q}) \end{array} \right] = 1.$$

Weak Soundness for Time-T: *For every non-uniform polynomial-size proba-bilistic $(\mathcal{A}_1, \mathcal{A}_2)$, there exists a negligible function μ, such that for every ensemble of samplable entropic distributions $\{Y_\lambda\}_{\lambda \in \mathbb{N}}$, $\lambda \in \mathbb{N}$ and $t \leq T(\lambda)$:*

$$\Pr\left[\mathsf{MD.Ver}(1^\lambda, \mathsf{dig}, (M, t, y), \mathsf{vst}, \pi) = 1 \,\middle|\, \begin{array}{l} (\mathsf{dig}, M, \mathsf{st}) \leftarrow \mathcal{A}_1(1^\lambda) \\ (\mathsf{q}, \mathsf{vst}) \leftarrow \mathsf{MD.Query}(1^\lambda) \\ y \leftarrow Y_\lambda \\ \pi \leftarrow \mathcal{A}_2(\mathsf{q}, y; \mathsf{st}) \end{array} \right] \leq \mu(\lambda).$$

Theorem 2.2 ([BKP18]). *Assuming a linearly compressing* quasipoly(λ)-*secure multi-collision-resistant keyless hash and* quasipoly(λ)-*secure fully-homomorphic encryption, there exists a two-message memory-delegation scheme with weak soundness for time-*quasipoly(λ).

2.4   Function Hiding Secure Function Evaluation

We define two-message secure function evaluation protocols with statistical func-tion hiding.

Syntax: Let $\mathcal{C} = \{\mathcal{C}_\lambda\}_\lambda$ be a family of circuits. A two-message secure func-tion evaluation protocol for $\mathcal{C}$ is associated with polynomial-time algorithms (SFE.Enc, SFE.Eval, SFE.Dec) with the following syntax:

- $(\mathsf{sk}, \mathsf{ct}) \leftarrow \mathsf{SFE.Enc}(1^\lambda, x)$: a probabilistic algorithm that takes a security parameter 1^λ and a string $x \in \{0, 1\}^*$ and outputs a secret key sk and a ciphertext ct.
- $\widehat{\mathsf{ct}} \leftarrow \mathsf{SFE.Eval}(C, \mathsf{ct})$: a probabilistic algorithm that takes a circuit $C \in \mathcal{C}$ and a ciphertext ct and outputs an evaluated ciphertext $\widehat{\mathsf{ct}}$.
- $\widehat{x} \leftarrow \mathsf{SFE.Dec}(\widehat{\mathsf{ct}}; \mathsf{sk})$: a deterministic algorithm that takes a ciphertext $\widehat{\mathsf{ct}}$ and the secret key sk and outputs a string $\widehat{x}$.

Definition 2.6. *A two-message secure function evaluation protocol* (SFE.Enc, SFE.Eval, SFE.Dec) *for a family of circuits* $\mathcal{C} = \{\mathcal{C}_\lambda\}_\lambda$ *satisfies:*

- **Perfect Correctness:** *For any* $\lambda \in \mathbb{N}$, $x \in \{0, 1\}^*$ *and circuit* $C \in \mathcal{C}_\lambda$

$$\Pr\left[\mathsf{SFE.Dec}(\widehat{\mathsf{ct}}; \mathsf{sk}) = C(x) \,\middle|\, \begin{array}{l} (\mathsf{sk}, \mathsf{ct}) \leftarrow \mathsf{SFE.Enc}(x; 1^\lambda) \\ \widehat{\mathsf{ct}} \leftarrow \mathsf{SFE.Eval}(C, \mathsf{ct}) \end{array} \right] = 1.$$

- **Semantic Security:** *For any polynomial* $\ell(\lambda)$ *and non-uniform polynomial-size probabilistic* $\mathcal{A} = \{\mathcal{A}_\lambda\}_\lambda$, *there exists a negligible function* ν *such that every* $\lambda \in \mathbb{N}$, *and pair of messages* $x_0, x_1 \in \{0, 1\}^{\ell(\lambda)}$:

$$\Pr\left[\mathcal{A}_\lambda(\mathsf{ct}) = b \,\middle|\, \begin{array}{l} b \leftarrow \{0, 1\} \\ (\mathsf{sk}, \mathsf{ct}) \leftarrow \mathsf{SFE.Enc}(x_b; 1^\lambda) \end{array} \right] \leq \frac{1}{2} + \mu(\lambda).$$

- **Statistical Circuit Privacy:** *There exist unbounded algorithms* Sim, Ext *such that:*

$$\left\{\mathsf{SFE.Eval}(C, \mathsf{ct}^*)\right\}_{\substack{\lambda \in \mathbb{N}, C \in \mathcal{C}_\lambda \\ \mathsf{ct}^* \in \{0,1\}^{\mathrm{poly}(\lambda)}}} \approx_s \left\{\mathsf{Sim}(C(\mathsf{Ext}(\mathsf{ct}^*; 1^\lambda)); 1^\lambda)\right\}_{\substack{\lambda \in \mathbb{N}, C \in \mathcal{C}_\lambda \\ \mathsf{ct}^* \in \{0,1\}^{\mathrm{poly}(\lambda)}}}.$$

Such secure function evaluation schemes are known based on LWE [OPP14, BV11, BD18].

2.5   Shamir Secret Sharing

We define Shamir secret sharing schemes.

Syntax: A Shamir secret sharing scheme is associated with functions $\delta(\lambda), n(\lambda)$, a field $\mathbb{F}_\lambda$ and a probabilistic polynomial-time encoding algorithm $\widehat{S} \leftarrow$ SSS.Enc$(S; 1^\lambda)$ that takes a secret $S \in \mathbb{F}$ and a parameter 1^λ and outputs an encoding $\widehat{S} \in \mathbb{F}^n$.

Definition 2.7 (Shamir Secret Sharing). *For polynomials* $\delta(\cdot), n(\cdot)$ *A Shamir secret sharing encoding* SSS.Enc *satisfies:*

Perfect Hiding: *Any* δ *coordinates in the encoding are perfectly hiding:*

$$\Big\{\text{SSS.Enc}(S_0; 1^\lambda)|_I\Big\}_{\substack{\lambda \in \mathbb{N}, \\ S_0, S_1 \in \mathbb{F}, \\ I \in \binom{[n]}{\delta}}} \equiv \Big\{\text{SSS.Enc}(S_1; 1^\lambda)|_I\Big\}_{\substack{\lambda \in \mathbb{N}, \\ S_0, S_1 \in \mathbb{F}, \\ I \in \binom{[n]}{\delta}}},$$

where $\binom{[n]}{\delta}$ *denotes the collection of subsets* $I \subseteq [n]$ *of size* δ.

Distance: *For any* $\lambda \in \mathbb{N}$ *and distinct secrets* $S_0, S_1 \in \mathbb{F}$,

$$\Delta(\text{SSS.Enc}(S_0; 1^\lambda), \text{SSS.Enc}(S_1; 1^\lambda)) \geq 1 - \delta/n,$$

where Δ *denotes the relative hamming distance over* $\mathbb{F}^n$.

Shamir secret sharing schemes are known to exist unconditionally [Sha79].

3   Weakly-Binding Commitments with Subset Opening

In this section, we define and construct weakly-binding statistically hiding commitments with subset opening.

3.1   Definition

The definition addresses both the setting of keyed hash functions as well as keyless ones.

Syntax: A commitment with subset opening is associated with a length function $L(\lambda)$ and polynomial-time algorithms SHC $=$ (CSO.Gen, CSO.Com, CSO.Chal, CSO.Open, CSO.Ver) with the following syntax:

- pk $\leftarrow$ CSO.Gen(1^λ): a probabilistic algorithm that takes the security parameter 1^λ and outputs a key pk $\in \{0,1\}^\lambda$. In the keyless setting, this algorithm is deterministic and outputs a fixed key pk $\equiv 1^\lambda$.
- (cmt, st) $\leftarrow$ CSO.Com$(X; \text{pk})$: a probabilistic algorithm that takes the key pk and a string $X \in \{0,1\}^{L(\lambda)}$ and outputs a commitment cmt and private state st.
- $C \leftarrow$ CSO.Chal(pk): a probabilistic algorithm that takes the key pk and outputs a challenge C.

- $d \leftarrow$ CSO.Open(I, C, st): a deterministic algorithm that takes an index set I, a challenge C and private state st and outputs a decommitment d.
- $b \leftarrow$ CSO.Ver$(\mathsf{cmt}, \alpha, I, C, d)$: a deterministic algorithm that takes a commitment cmt, an index set I, an assignment $\alpha : I \rightarrow \{0, 1\}$, and decommitment d and outputs an acceptance bit b.

Definition 3.1 (Weakly-Binding Statistically-Hiding Commitments with Subset Opening). *For a polynomial $L(\cdot)$, a weakly-binding statistically-hiding commitment with subset opening* CSO $=$ (CSO.Gen, CSO.Com, CSO.Chal, CSO.Open, CSO.Ver)*, for strings of length L, satisfies:*

Subset Statistical Hiding: *There exists a negligible $\mu(\cdot)$ such that for all $\lambda \in \mathbb{N}$, no unbounded adversary $\mathcal{A}$ wins the following game with probability greater than $1/2 + \mu(\lambda)$:*

1. *$\mathcal{A}$ submits to a challenger $\mathsf{pk} \in \{0, 1\}^{\lambda}$, $X_0, X_1 \in \{0, 1\}^{L(\lambda)}$.*
2. *The challenger samples a random $b \leftarrow \{0, 1\}$ and $(\mathsf{cmt}_b, \mathsf{st}_b) \leftarrow$ CSO.Com$(X_b; \mathsf{pk})$, and gives cmt_b to $\mathcal{A}$.*
3. *$\mathcal{A}$ submits a commitment challenge C.*
4. *The challenger computes $d =$ CSO.Open(I, C, st) where $I = \{i \in [L] : X_0[i] = X_1[i]\}$ is the set of indices on which the strings X_0, X_1 agree.*
5. *$\mathcal{A}$ wins if it correctly guesses the bit b.*

Weak Binding: *For any non-uniform polynomial-size probabilistic $\mathcal{A} = \{\mathcal{A}_\lambda^1, \mathcal{A}_\lambda^2\}_\lambda$ there exists a polynomial $K(\cdot)$ and a negligible $\mu(\cdot)$, such that for all $\lambda \in \mathbb{N}$,*

$$\Pr_{\substack{\mathsf{pk} \leftarrow \mathsf{CSO.Gen}(1^\lambda) \\ (\mathsf{cmt}, \mathsf{st}) \leftarrow \mathcal{A}_\lambda^1(\mathsf{pk})}} \left[\begin{array}{l} \exists \mathbf{X} \text{ of size } K(\lambda) : \\ \Pr_{\substack{C \leftarrow \mathsf{CSO.Chal}(1^\lambda) \\ (\alpha, I, d) \leftarrow \mathcal{A}_\lambda^2(C; \mathsf{st})}} \left[\begin{array}{l} \mathsf{CSO.Ver}(\mathsf{cmt}, \alpha, I, C, d) = 1 \\ \alpha \notin \mathbf{X}_I \end{array} \right] \leq \mu(\lambda) \end{array} \right]$$
$$\geq 1 - \mu(\lambda),$$

where $\mathbf{X}_I$ denotes the set of assignments $X|_I : I \rightarrow \{0, 1\}$ to indices in I induced by every $X \in \mathbf{X}$.

Succinct Commitment: *$|\mathsf{cmt}| = \lambda$ for any $\mathsf{pk} \in \{0, 1\}^\lambda$ and any cmt in the support of* CSO.Com$(\cdot; \mathsf{pk})$.

In the remainder of this section we construct weakly-binding statistically hiding commitments with subset opening.

Theorem 3.1. *Assuming a polynomially compressing multi-collision-resistant keyless hash there exists a weakly-binding statistically-hiding commitment with subset opening for strings of length L for any polynomial L.*

3.2   Construction

We provide a construction of weakly-binding statistically-hiding commitments with subset opening from (plain) weakly-binding statistically-hiding commitments and multi-collision resistant hash functions.

Ingredients

- SSS.Enc a Shamir secret sharing encoding with parameters $\delta(\lambda) = \sqrt{\lambda}$, $n(\lambda) = \lambda$, and field $\mathbb{F} = \{\mathbb{F}_\lambda\}_\lambda$.
- SHC a weakly binding statistically hiding commitment for strings of length $\ell = |\mathbb{F}_\lambda| \cdot \max(L, n)$. We denote the size of commitment in this scheme by $t(\lambda)$.
- H a multi-collision resistant hash for strings of length $\ell' = (L + n) \cdot t$.

The Scheme CSO

- CSO.Gen(1^λ): Runs the key generator for the underlying commitment $\mathsf{pk}_1 \leftarrow$ CSO.Gen(1^λ) and hash $\mathsf{pk}_2 \leftarrow$ H.Gen(1^λ), and outputs $\mathsf{pk} = (\mathsf{pk}_1, \mathsf{pk}_2)$.
- CSO.Com($X; \mathsf{pk}$):
  - For $i \in [L]$, compute an encoding $\widehat{X}_i \leftarrow$ SSS.Enc($X_i; 1^\lambda$).
  - Consider the matrix $\widehat{X} = \left(\widehat{X}_{i,j} \right)_{i \in [L], j \in [n]}$.
  - Compute commitments to the rows $\mathsf{rowcmt}_i \leftarrow$ SHC.Com($\widehat{X}_{i,1}, \ldots, \widehat{X}_{i,n}; \mathsf{pk}_1$).
  - Compute commitments to the columns $\mathsf{colcmt}_j \leftarrow$ SHC.Com($\widehat{X}_{1,j}, \ldots, \widehat{X}_{L,j}; \mathsf{pk}_1$).
  - Compute a hash of all of the above commitments $Y \leftarrow$ H.Hash($(\mathsf{rowcmt}_i)_i, (\mathsf{colcmt}_j)_j; \mathsf{pk}_2$) and output $\mathsf{cmt} = Y$ as the commitment.
  - Output as the state st all the commitments $(\mathsf{rowcmt}_i)_i, (\mathsf{colcmt}_j)_j$, all the randomness $(\hat{r}_i)_i, (\mathsf{rr}_i)_i, (\mathsf{rc}_j)_j$ used to generate the encodings $\widehat{X}_i$ and commitments $\mathsf{rowcmt}_i, \mathsf{colcmt}_j$, respectively, and the encoding $\widehat{X}_i$ themselves.
- CSO.Chal(pk_1): sample δ random column indices $j_1, \ldots, j_\delta \leftarrow [n]$ and output $C = (j_i)_{i \in [\delta]}$.
- CSO.Open(I, C, st): output as the decommitment information d all the commitments $(\mathsf{rowcmt}_i)_i, (\mathsf{colcmt}_j)_j$, the randomness $(\hat{r}_i, \mathsf{rr}_i)_{i \in I}$ used to compute the encodings and commitments corresponding to all rows $i \in I$, the randomness $(\mathsf{rc}_j)_{j \in C}$ and the columns $\left(\widehat{X}_{1,j}, \ldots, \widehat{X}_{L,j} \right)_{j \in C}$ themselves, corresponding to all challenge columns $j \in C$.
- CSO.Ver($\mathsf{cmt}, \alpha, I, C, d$):
  - Parse d as $(\mathsf{rowcmt}_i)_i, (\mathsf{colcmt}_j)_j, (\mathsf{rr}_i, \hat{r}_i)_{i \in I}, (\mathsf{rc}_j, \widehat{X}_{1,j}, \ldots, \widehat{X}_{L,j})_{j \in C}$.
  - Verify that $\mathsf{cmt} =$ H.Hash($((\mathsf{rowcmt}_i)_i, (\mathsf{colcmt}_j)_j); \mathsf{pk}_2$).
  - For every $i \in I$, compute $\hat{\alpha}_i :=$ SSS.Enc($\alpha(i); \hat{r}_i$) and verify that $\mathsf{rowcmt}_i =$ SHC.Com($\hat{\alpha}_i; \mathsf{pk}_1, \mathsf{rr}_i$).
  - For every $j \in C$, verify that $\mathsf{colcmt}_j =$ SHC.Com($\widehat{X}_{1,j}, \ldots, \widehat{X}_{L,j}; \mathsf{pk}_1, \mathsf{rc}_j$) and that for every $i \in I$, $\alpha_{i,j} = \widehat{X}_{i,j}$.

3.3   Analysis

We now analyze the construction. We first prove subset statistical hiding and then prove weak binding.

Proposition 3.1. *The construction is subset statistically hiding.*

Proof. We first claim that statistical hiding holds for any fixed challenge set C.

Claim 3.2. *Fix any* pk *and* $C \in [n]^{\delta}$, *and set of indices* $I \subseteq [n]$. *There exists a simulator S such that for any $X \in \{0,1\}^L$,*

$$\mathsf{cmt}, d \approx_{2^{-\Omega(\lambda)}} S(X|_I),$$

where $(\mathsf{cmt}, \mathsf{st}) \leftarrow \mathsf{CSO.Com}(X; \mathsf{pk})$ *and* $d \leftarrow \mathsf{CSO.Open}(I, C, \mathsf{st})$.

Proof. We describe how the simulator samples the commitments $\mathsf{rowcmt}_i, \mathsf{colcmt}_j$:

- For every $i \in I$, compute an encoding $\widehat{X}_i$ of X_i, and sample a commitment rowcmt_i to this encoding.
- For every $i \notin I$, sample a commitment rowcmt_i to the all-zero string. Also sample an encoding $\widehat{Y}_i$ of for an arbitrary bit Y, and store $\widehat{Y}_i$.
- For every $j \in C$, sample a commitment colcmt_j to the j-th column of the matrix whose rows are given by the encodings $\widehat{X}_i$ for $i \in I$ and by the encodings $\widehat{Y}_i$ for $i \notin I$.
- For every $j \notin C$ sample a commitment colcmt_j to the all-zero string.

We now argue that the commitments $\mathsf{rowcmt}_i, \mathsf{colcmt}_j$ produced above along with an opening with respect to I, C are $2^{-\Omega(\lambda)}$-close to their distribution in a commitment to X.

Consider a hybrid distribution cmt^*, d^* where we change the distribution of commitments to X as follows. For all unopened rows $i \notin I$, we change the commitment rowcmt_i from a commitment to $\widehat{X}_i$ to a commitment to an all-zero string, and for all unopened columns $j \notin C$, we change the commitment colcmt_j from a commitment to the j-column of the matrix $(\widehat{X}_{i,j})_{i,j}$ to a commitment to the all zero string.

Then by the statistical hiding of the underlying commitment SHC,

$$\mathsf{cmt}, d \quad \approx_{2^{-\lambda \cdot (L+n)}} \quad \mathsf{cmt}^*, d^*,$$

where $2^{-\lambda}(L + n) \leq 2^{-\Omega(\lambda)}$.

Next, note that the only difference between the hybrid distribution cmt^*, d^* and the simulated distribution $S(X|_I)$ is in the commitments to the columns $j \in C$. In the first, the plaintexts are the columns of the matrix $\left(\widehat{X}_{ij}\right)_{i \in [L], j \in C}$, whereas in the second its the concatenation of $\left(\widehat{X}_{ij}\right)_{i \in I, j \in C}$ and $\left(\widehat{Y}_{ij}\right)_{i \in [L] \setminus I, j \in C}$. However, since $|C| \leq \delta$, the perfect hiding of the Shamir secret sharing implies that these two matrices are identically distributed.

Now fix any key pk and any two $X, X' \in \{0,1\}^L$, and let $I \subseteq [L]$ be the set of indices on they agree. Then by Claim 3.2, for any fixed challenge C, the distributions cmt, d and cmt', d' corresponding to X and X', respectively, are $2^{-\Omega(\lambda)}$-close.

To complete the proof, we now show that they remain close also when C is chosen adaptively.

Claim 3.3. *For any (unbounded) adversary $\mathcal{A}$,*

$$\mathsf{cmt}, C, d \quad \approx_{2^{\Omega(\lambda)}} \mathsf{cmt}', C', d',$$

where $(\mathsf{cmt}, \mathsf{st}) \leftarrow \mathsf{CSO.Com}(X; \mathsf{pk})$, $C \leftarrow \mathcal{A}(\mathsf{cmt})$ *and* $d \leftarrow \mathsf{CSO.Open}(I, C, \mathsf{st})$, *and* cmt', C', d' *is sampled similarly with respect to* X'.

Proof.

$$\mathbf{SD}((\mathsf{cmt}, C, d), (\mathsf{cmt}', C', d')) =$$

$$\sum_{\alpha, \beta, \gamma} |\Pr\left[(\mathsf{cmt}, C, d) = (\alpha, \beta, \gamma)\right] - \Pr\left[(\mathsf{cmt}', C', d') = (\alpha, \beta, \gamma)\right]| \leq$$

$$\sum_{\beta \in [n]^\delta} 2^{-\Omega(\lambda)} = \lambda^{\sqrt{\lambda}} \cdot 2^{-\Omega(\lambda)} \leq 2^{-\Omega(\lambda)},$$

where the first inequality follows from Claim 3.2.

This completes the proof of Proposition 3.1.

Proposition 3.2. *The construction is weakly binding.*

Proof. Fix a polynomial-size adversary $\mathcal{A} = \{\mathcal{A}_\lambda^1, \mathcal{A}_\lambda^2\}_\lambda$ against the commitment. The proof is divided to two main claims. We first prove a (computational) claim attesting that with overwhelming probability $\mathcal{A}$'s commitment fixes a polynomial-size set of strings $\mathbf{S}$, such that any valid opening of the underlying weakly-binding commitment is to a string from $\mathbf{S}$. This claim relies on the weak binding of the underlying commitment and the multi-collision resistance of the hash function. Then we prove an information-theoretic claim that shows that provided the restriction to the set $\mathbf{S}$ there also exists a polynomial-size global set of strings $\mathbf{X}$, such that any opening of some subset must be consistent with one of the strings in $\mathbf{X}$.

The following claim asserts that a commitment from the adversary $\mathcal{A}$, fixes a polynomial-size set of strings $\mathbf{S} \subseteq \{0,1\}^\ell$, such that the adversary can only open any commitments $\mathsf{rowcmt}_i, \mathsf{colcmt}_j$ to a string from $\mathbf{S}$.

Claim 3.4. *There exist a polynomial $K(\cdot)$ and a negligible function $\mu(\cdot)$ such that for all $\lambda \in \mathbb{N}$, except with probability $\mu(\lambda)$ over $\mathsf{pk} \leftarrow \mathsf{CSO.Gen}(1^\lambda)$ and $(\mathsf{cmt}, \mathsf{st}) \leftarrow \mathcal{A}_\lambda^1(\mathsf{pk})$ there exists a set $\mathbf{S} \subseteq \{0,1\}^\ell$ of size $K(\lambda)$ such that*

$$\Pr_{\substack{C \leftarrow \mathsf{CSO.Chal}(1^\lambda) \\ (\alpha, I, d) \leftarrow \mathcal{A}_\lambda^2(C; \mathsf{st})}} \left[\mathsf{CSO.Ver}(\mathsf{cmt}, \alpha, I, C, d) = 1 \wedge \widehat{X}(\alpha, I, d) \not\subseteq \mathbf{S}\right] \leq \mu(\lambda),$$

where $\widehat{X}(\alpha, I, d) \subseteq \{0,1\}^\ell$ *is the set of rows and columns of the matrix* $(\widehat{X})_{ij}$, *which $\mathcal{A}$ opens in its decommitment.*

Proof. Assume toward contradiction that for any polynomial K, there exists a noticeable function ε, such that for infinitely many $\lambda \in \mathbb{N}$, with probability $\varepsilon(\lambda)$ over $\mathsf{pk} \leftarrow \mathsf{CSO.Gen}(1^\lambda)$ and $(\mathsf{cmt}, \mathsf{st}) \leftarrow \mathcal{A}^1_\lambda(\mathsf{pk})$ for any set $\mathbf{S} \subseteq \{0,1\}^\ell$ of size $K(\lambda)$

$$\Pr_{\substack{C \leftarrow \mathsf{CSO.Chal}(1^\lambda) \\ (\alpha, I, d) \leftarrow \mathcal{A}^2_\lambda(C; \mathsf{st})}} \left[\mathsf{CSO.Ver}(\mathsf{cmt}, \alpha, I, C, d) = 1 \wedge \widehat{X}(\alpha, I, d) \not\subseteq \mathbf{S} \right] \geq \varepsilon(\lambda).$$

We consider two complementary cases:

1. For infinitely many λ, except with probability $\varepsilon/2$ over $\mathsf{pk}, \mathsf{cmt}, \mathsf{st}$ there exists a set $\mathbf{S}' \subseteq \{0,1\}^{\ell'}$ of size $\sqrt{K}$ such that except with probability $\varepsilon/2$, $\mathcal{A}$ never opens the hash value cmt to $S = ((\mathsf{rowcmt}_i)_i, (\mathsf{colcmt}_j)_j) \notin \mathbf{S}'$.
2. For infinitely many λ, with probability at least $\varepsilon/2$ over $\mathsf{pk}, \mathsf{cmt}, \mathsf{st}$ for any set $\mathbf{S}' \subseteq \{0,1\}^\ell$ of size $\sqrt{K}$, with probability $\varepsilon/2$, $\mathcal{A}$ opens the hash value cmt to $S = ((\mathsf{rowcmt}_i)_i, (\mathsf{colcmt}_j)_j) \notin \mathbf{S}'$.

First, note that the second case implies that $\mathcal{A}$ breaks the multi-collision resistance of the underlying hash H. Thus, we can assume that the first case holds. It follows that

Claim 3.5. *For infinitely many λ, with probability at least $\varepsilon/2$ over $\mathsf{pk}, \mathsf{cmt}, \mathsf{st}$, there exists a set $\mathbf{S}' \subseteq \{0,1\}^{\ell'}$ of size $\sqrt{K}$ as required by the first condition, but for any set $\mathbf{S}$ of size K and with probability $\varepsilon/2$ over the decommitment phase $\widehat{X}(\alpha, I, d) \not\subseteq \mathbf{S}$ whereas the opened $S = ((\mathsf{rowcmt}_i)_i, (\mathsf{colcmt}_j)_j) \in \mathbf{S}'$.*

Proof. This follows directly from our assumption toward contradiction and the fact that the first case above holds.

From hereon fix $\mathsf{pk}, \mathsf{cmt}, \mathsf{st}$ such that Claim 3.5 holds. We next argue that

Claim 3.6. *There exists $S' = ((\mathsf{rowcmt}_i)_i, (\mathsf{colcmt}_j)_j) \in \mathbf{S}'$ and $\mathsf{cmt}' \in S'$ such that for any set $\mathbf{X} \subseteq \{0,1\}^\ell$ of size $\sqrt{K}/(L+n)$, with probability $\varepsilon/2(L+n)\sqrt{K}$ over the decommitment phase cmt is opened to S', but cmt' is opened to $X \notin \mathbf{X}$.*

Proof. Otherwise, for each $S' \in \mathbf{S}'$ and $\mathsf{cmt}' \in S'$, we can choose $\mathbf{X}(S', \mathsf{cmt}')$ such that the above does not hold, and obtain

$$\mathbf{S} = \bigcup_{S' \in \mathbf{S}, \mathsf{cmt}' \in S'} \mathbf{X}(S', \mathsf{cmt}')$$

of size K, which violates Claim 3.5.

We now obtain an adversary $\mathcal{B} = \{\mathcal{B}^1_\lambda, \mathcal{B}^2_\lambda\}_\lambda$ that breaks the weak binding of the commitment SHC. $\mathcal{B}^1_\lambda(\mathsf{pk}_1)$ first samples $\mathsf{pk}_2 \leftarrow \mathsf{H.Gen}(1^\lambda)$, sets $\mathsf{pk} = (\mathsf{pk}_1, \mathsf{pk}_2)$, runs $\mathcal{A}^1_\lambda(\mathsf{pk})$ and obtains a state st, it then simulates a random challenge $C \leftarrow C(1^\lambda)$ and runs $\mathcal{A}^2_\lambda(C; \mathsf{st})$. It then takes the set of commitments $S' = (\mathsf{rowcmt}_i)_{i \in L}, (\mathsf{colcmt}_j)_{j \in [n]}$ and outputs a random commitment $\mathsf{cmt}' \in S'$ along with the state st. $\mathcal{B}^2_\lambda(\mathsf{st})$ samples a new random challenge C' and runs $\mathcal{A}^2_\lambda(C'; \mathsf{st})$, and outputs whatever opening $\mathcal{A}^2_\lambda$ outputs for cmt', or $\perp$ if there is no such opening.

Claim 3.7. $\mathcal{B}$ *breaks weak binding.*

Proof. By construction and Claims 3.5 and 3.6, with probability at least $\frac{\varepsilon}{2} \cdot \frac{\varepsilon}{2(L+n)\sqrt{K}}$ over the commitment phase of $\mathcal{B}_\lambda^1$, for any set $\mathbf{X} \subseteq \{0,1\}^\ell$ of size $\sqrt{K}/(L+n)$, $\mathcal{B}_\lambda^2$ opens that commitment to a value $X \notin \mathbf{X}$ with probability at least $\varepsilon/2(L+n)\sqrt{K}$.

This complete the proof of Claim 3.4.

We now proceed to prove the binding property of the scheme. The following claim asserts that whenever all strings $\widehat{X}$ are consistent with some set $\mathbf{S}$, there exists a polynomial-size set of strings $\mathbf{X} \subseteq \{0,1\}^L$ such that all openings are consistent with $\mathbf{X}$, which will conclude the proof.

Claim 3.8. *Let K be the polynomial given by Claim 3.4 and let τ be a constant such that $\tau > 2\log_\lambda(2K^2)$. Fix λ, pk, cmt, st such that Claim 3.4 holds with respect to a set $\mathbf{S}$. Then there exists $\mathbf{X} \subseteq \{0,1\}^L$ of size $K' = (nK)^\tau$ such that*

$$\Pr_{\substack{C \leftarrow \mathsf{CSO.Chal}(1^\lambda) \\ (\alpha,I,d) \leftarrow \mathcal{A}_\lambda^2(C;\mathsf{st})}} [\mathsf{CSO.Ver}(\mathsf{cmt}, \alpha, I, C, d) = 1 \wedge \alpha \notin \mathbf{X}|_I] \leq \mu(\lambda).$$

Proof. We first argue that random τ locations fix at most a single encoding in $\mathbf{S}$.

Claim 3.9. *Let $T \subseteq [n]$ be a set of τ indices chosen independently at random, then*

$$\Pr_T \left[\exists \widehat{S}_0, \widehat{S}_1 \in \mathbf{S} \text{ such that } \widehat{S}_0|_T = \widehat{S}_1|_T \,\middle|\, \begin{array}{c} \widehat{S}_b \in \mathsf{SSS.Enc}(S_b) \\ S_0 \neq S_1 \end{array} \right] \leq 1/2.$$

We call any set T as above fixing.

Proof. The proof follows directly from the distance of Shamir encodings, the bound K on the size of $\mathbf{S}$, and the definition of τ. Specifically the above can be bounded by

$$|\mathbf{S}|^2 \left(\frac{\delta}{n}\right)^\tau \leq K^2 \left(\frac{\sqrt{\lambda}}{\lambda}\right)^{2\log_\lambda(2K^2)} = \frac{1}{2}.$$

Now, let T be any fixing set and consider any set of τ columns

$$Q = \{(Q_{1,j}, \ldots, Q_{L,j}) : j \in [T]\}.$$

Then, T, Q fix a unique string $X(T,Q) \in \{0, 1, \bot\}^L$ defined as follows:

- If T is not fixing, set $X(T,Q) = \bot$. Otherwise, proceed to the following.
- For any $i \in [L]$, if for some $b \in \{0,1\}$, there exists a Shamir encoding $\widehat{X}_i \in \mathsf{SSS.Enc}(b; 1^\lambda)$ such that $\widehat{X}_i \in \mathbf{S}$ and $\widehat{X}_{i,j} = Q_{i,j}$ for all $j \in T$, set $X_i(T,Q) = b$. Otherwise, set $X_i(T,Q) = \bot$.
  (Since T is fixing, there exists at most a single $b \in \{0,1\}$ that satisfies the condition.)

We now define the set $\mathbf{X}$ as follows:

$$\mathbf{X} := \{X(T, Q) \mid T \in [n]^\tau, Q \in \mathbf{S}^\tau\}.$$

First, note that $\mathbf{X}$ is of size at most $(n \cdot |\mathbf{S}|)^\tau = (nK)^\tau$, which is polynomial in λ. We now argue that

$$\Pr_{\substack{C \leftarrow \mathsf{CSO.Chal}(1^\lambda) \\ (\alpha, I, d) \leftarrow \mathcal{A}_\lambda^2(C; \mathsf{st})}} [\mathsf{CSO.Ver}(\mathsf{cmt}, \alpha, I, C, d) = 1 \wedge \alpha \notin \mathbf{X}|_I] \leq \mu(\lambda).$$

Recall that $C \subseteq [n]$ consists of λ indices chosen independently at random. In particular, by Claim 3.9, C contains a fixing set T except with probability $(1/2)^{\delta/\tau} = 2^{-\tilde{\Omega}(\sqrt{\lambda})}$. Recall that except with negligible probability all row and column commitments opened by $\mathcal{A}$ are consistent with some string in $\mathbf{S}$. From hereon we assume that the latter occurs and that C contains a fixing T.

Then when $\mathsf{CSO.Ver}(\mathsf{cmt}, \alpha, I, C, d) = 1$, $\mathcal{A}$ opens the columns in T to some $Q = (Q_{1,j}, \ldots, Q_{L,j})_{j \in [T]} \in \mathbf{S}^\tau$. Also the assignment $\alpha : I \to \{0, 1\}$ is such that for every $i \in I$, there exists an encoding $\hat{\alpha}_i \in \mathsf{SSS.Enc}(\alpha_i; 1^\lambda) \in \mathbf{S}$ and $\hat{\alpha}$ is consistent with Q. By definition, it follows that for every $i \in I$, $\alpha_i = X_i(T, Q)$; namely, $\alpha \in \mathbf{X}|_I$ as required.

This completes the proof of Claim 3.8.

This completes the proof of Proposition 3.2.

4 Offline-Online Statistically WI Arguments of Knowledge

In this section, we define and construct offline-online statistically witness indistinguishable arguments of knowledge.

4.1 Definition

In offline-online statistically WI arguments of knowledge, the protocol $\langle \mathsf{P} \leftrightarrows \mathsf{V} \rangle$ can be divided to:

- an offline protocol $\langle \mathsf{OffP} \leftrightarrows \mathsf{OffV} \rangle(1^\lambda, 1^\ell)$, where the parties take as common input the security parameter 1^λ and an input size 1^ℓ and output each a state $\mathsf{st_P}, \mathsf{st_V}$.
- an online protocol $\langle \mathsf{OnP}(\mathsf{st_P}, w) \leftrightarrows \mathsf{OnV}(\mathsf{st_V}) \rangle(x)$, where the parties, in addition to their previous state, take as common input an instance $x \in \mathcal{L} \cap \{0, 1\}^\ell$ and the prover obtains also obtain as input a witness $w \in \mathcal{R}_\mathcal{L}(x)$.

We now formally define the properties that such systems are required to satisfy.

Definition 4.1 (Offline-Online SWIAOK). $\langle \mathsf{P} \leftrightarrows \mathsf{V} \rangle$ *is an offline-online statistically witness indistinguishable argument of knowledge for $\mathcal{L}$ if it satisfies:*

Completeness: *For any* $\ell, \lambda \in \mathbb{N}$, $x \in \mathcal{L} \cap \{0,1\}^\ell$, *and* $w \in \mathcal{R}_\mathcal{L}(x)$:

$$\Pr\left[\begin{array}{l} \langle \mathsf{OffP} \leftrightarrows \mathsf{OffV}\rangle(1^\lambda, 1^\ell) = (\mathsf{st_P}, \mathsf{st_V}) \\ \langle \mathsf{OnP}(\mathsf{st_P}, w) \leftrightarrows \mathsf{OnV}(\mathsf{st_V})\rangle(x) = 1 \end{array}\right] = 1.$$

Adaptive Statistical Witness Indistinguishability: *For any polynomial* $\ell(\cdot)$ *and unbounded verifier* V^*, *there exists a negligible function* $\mu(\cdot)$ *such that for all* $\lambda \in \mathbb{N}$:

$$\Pr\left[\langle \mathsf{OnP}(\mathsf{st_P}, w_b) \leftrightarrows \mathsf{OnV}^*(\mathsf{st_V})\rangle(x) = b \mid \right.$$
$$\langle \mathsf{OffP} \leftrightarrows \mathsf{OffV}^*\rangle(1^\lambda, 1^{\ell(\lambda)}) = (\mathsf{st_P}, (\mathsf{st_V}, x, w_0, w_1))$$
$$\left. b \leftarrow \{0,1\} \right] \le \frac{1}{2} + \mu(\lambda),$$

where $x \in \mathcal{L} \cap \{0,1\}^{\ell(\lambda)}$ *and* $w_0, w_1 \in \mathcal{R}_\mathcal{L}(x)$.

Adaptive Proof of Knowledge: *There is a uniform* ***PPT*** *extractor* $\mathcal{E}$ *such that for any polynomial* $\ell(\cdot)$ *and any non-uniform polynomial-size prover* $\mathsf{P}^* = \{\mathsf{P}^*_\lambda\}_{\lambda \in \mathbb{N}}$ *there is a polynomial* $K(\cdot)$ *and a negligible* $\mu(\cdot)$ *such that for all* $\lambda \in \mathbb{N}$:

if
$$\Pr\left[\langle \mathsf{OnP}^*_\lambda(\mathsf{st_P}) \leftrightarrows \mathsf{OnV}(\mathsf{st_V})\rangle(x) = 1 \mid \right.$$
$$\left. \langle \mathsf{OffP}^* \leftrightarrows \mathsf{OffV}\rangle(1^\lambda, 1^{\ell(\lambda)}) = ((\mathsf{st_P}, x), \mathsf{st_V})\right] = \varepsilon,$$

then
$$\Pr\left[\begin{array}{l} \langle \mathsf{OnP}^*_\lambda(\mathsf{st_P}) \leftrightarrows \mathsf{OnV}(\mathsf{st_V})\rangle(x) = 1 \\ w \leftarrow \mathcal{E}^{\mathsf{P}^*_\lambda}(x, \mathsf{st_P}, \mathsf{st_V}) \\ w \in \mathcal{R}_\mathcal{L}(x) \\ \langle \mathsf{OffP}^* \leftrightarrows \mathsf{OffV}\rangle(1^\lambda, 1^{\ell(\lambda)}) = ((\mathsf{st_P}, x), \mathsf{st_V}) \end{array}\right]$$
$$\ge \operatorname{poly}\left(\frac{\varepsilon}{K(\lambda)}\right) - \mu(\lambda),$$

where $x \in \{0,1\}^{\ell(\lambda)}$.

Offline Succinctness: *All messages sent by* OffP *in the offline stage are of length* λ *(independently of* ℓ).

In the remainder of this section we construct offline-online statistically witness indistinguishable arguments of knowledge.

Theorem 4.1. *Assuming a polynomially-compressing multi-collision-resistant keyless hash there exists an offline-online statistically witness indistinguishable argument of knowledge for* **NP** *with two messages in the offline part and one message in the online part.*

4.2   A Protocol for Hamiltonicity

We now give an offline-online protocol for the NP complete problem of Hamiltonicity. The protocol is essentially the Lapidot-Shamir protocol [LS90a] whereas instead of using standard (binding) commitments, we rely on the notion of weakly-binding commitments with subset opening from the previous section.

Ingredients and Notation

- Let $n(\cdot)$ be a polynomial and let (CSO.Gen, CSO.Com, CSO.Chal, CSO.Open) be a weakly binding statistically hiding commitment with subset opening for strings of length $n^2 \cdot \lambda$.
- A graph G with n nodes will be represented by its $n \times n$ adjacency matrix. Sometimes we may think of G as a string in the natural way.
- Let G, H be two graphs on the same set of nodes $[n]$ and let $\varphi : [n] \rightarrow [n]$ be a permutation. We write $H \subseteq G$ to denote the fact that H's set of edges is contained in G's set of edges. We write $\varphi(G) = H$ to denote the fact that $H_{\varphi(i),\varphi(j)} = G_{i,j}$ for every $i, j \in [n]$.
- A Hamiltonian cycle graph H is a graph that consists of a Hamiltonian cycle (and no additional edges).

4.3   Analysis

The offline succinctness property follows directly from the succinct commitment property of the underlying commitment with subset opening. We focus on proving the argument of knowledge and the statistical witness indistinguishability properties.

Proposition 4.1. *Protocol 1 is an adaptive argument of knowledge.*

Proof. Fix a non-uniform polynomial-size prover $\mathsf{P}^* = \{\mathsf{P}^*_\lambda\}_{\lambda \in \mathbb{N}}$ such that

$$\Pr\left[\langle \mathsf{OnP}^*_\lambda(\mathsf{st_P}) \leftrightarrows \mathsf{OnV}(\mathsf{st_V})\rangle(x) = 1 \ \middle| \ \langle \mathsf{OffP}^* \leftrightarrows \mathsf{OffV}\rangle(1^\lambda, 1^\ell) = ((\mathsf{st_P}, x), \mathsf{st_V})\right] = \varepsilon.$$

We now describe how the witness extractor $\mathcal{E}(\mathsf{P}^*_\lambda, x, \mathsf{st_P}, \mathsf{st_V})$ operates. $\mathcal{E}$ first emulates the last prover message corresponding to the state of the offline phase it is given. It obtains $(\mathbf{I}, \mathbf{H}|_{\mathbf{I}}, \varphi)$. $\mathcal{E}$ then rewinds the prover P^*_λ back to the offline phase, and sends it a fresh random challenge σ', C'. It then obtains in the online phase corresponding $(\mathbf{I}', \mathbf{H}'|_{\mathbf{I}'}, \varphi')$. $\mathcal{E}$ now looks for an $i \in [\lambda]$ such that $\sigma_i = $ antiedges and $\sigma'_i = $ cycle, and returns the cycle $\varphi_i^{-1}(H'_i)$. If any of the above fail, it aborts (Fig. 1).

Claim 4.2. *There exists a polynomial $K(\cdot)$ and a negligible $\mu(\cdot)$ such that*

$$\Pr\left[\begin{array}{l} \langle \mathsf{OnP}^*_\lambda(\mathsf{st_P}) \leftrightarrows \mathsf{OnV}(\mathsf{st_V})\rangle(x) = 1 \\ w \leftarrow \mathcal{E}(\mathsf{P}^*_\lambda, x, \mathsf{st_P}, \mathsf{st_V}) \\ w \in \mathcal{R}_\mathcal{L}(x) \end{array} \ \middle| \ \langle \mathsf{OffP}^* \leftrightarrows \mathsf{OffV}\rangle(1^\lambda, 1^{\ell(\lambda)}) = ((\mathsf{st_P}, x), \mathsf{st_V})\right] \geq \frac{\varepsilon^3}{8K^2(\lambda)} - \mu(\lambda).$$

Proof. First, by an averaging argument with probability at least $\varepsilon/2$ over the choice of the first two messages in the protocol, namely the key pk and commitment cmt, it holds that with probability at least $\varepsilon/2$ over the rest of the protocol the prover convinces the verifier of accepting. In addition, by the weak binding property of the underlying commitment with subset opening, there exists a

---

Protocol 1

Offline:

Common Input: $(1^\lambda, 1^n)$.

1. OffV samples a key $\mathsf{pk} \leftarrow \mathsf{CSO.Gen}(1^\lambda)$ for a weakly-binding commitment with length parameter $L = n^2 \cdot \lambda$, and sends pk. (In a keyless scheme, $\mathsf{pk} \equiv 1^\lambda$, and this message is skipped).
2. OffP computes
   - λ random Hamiltonian cycle graphs $\mathbf{H} = (H_1, \ldots, H_\lambda) \in \{0, 1\}^{n^2 \times \lambda}$.
   - a commitment with subset opening $(\mathsf{cmt}, \mathsf{st}) \leftarrow \mathsf{CSO.Com}(\mathbf{H}; \mathsf{pk})$.

   It sends cmt.
3. OffV computes
   - a commitment challenge $C \leftarrow \mathsf{CSO.Chal}(\mathsf{pk})$,
   - λ random challenges $\boldsymbol{\sigma} = (\sigma_1, \ldots, \sigma_\lambda) \leftarrow \{\text{cycle}, \text{antiedges}\}^\lambda$.

   It sends $(C, \boldsymbol{\sigma})$.
4. OffP and OffV output $\mathsf{st_P} = (\mathsf{pk}, \mathbf{H}, \mathsf{st}, C, \boldsymbol{\sigma})$ and $\mathsf{st_V} = (\mathsf{pk}, \mathsf{cmt}, C, \boldsymbol{\sigma})$.

Online:

Common Input: A graph $G \in \{0, 1\}^{n \times n}$.
Prover Input: A Hamiltonian cycle graph $H \subseteq G$ and the state $\mathsf{st_P}$.
Verifier Input: state $\mathsf{st_V}$.

5. OnP computes
   - for every $j \in [\lambda]$,
     - If $\sigma_j = \text{cycle}$, let $I_j = (j-1)n^2 + [n^2]$ be the set of all indices corresponding to H_j.
     - If $\sigma_j = \text{antiedges}$, sample a random permutation φ_j such that $\varphi(H) = H_j$. Let $I_j \subset (j-1)n^2 + [n^2]$ be the set of indices corresponding to anti-edges in $\varphi_j(G)$.
   - $\mathbf{I} = \bigcup_{j \in [\lambda]} I_j$, $\boldsymbol{\varphi} = (\varphi_j)_j$.
   - $d \leftarrow \mathsf{CSO.Open}(\mathbf{I}, C, \mathsf{st})$.

   and sends $(\mathbf{I}, \mathbf{H}|_{\mathbf{I}}, \boldsymbol{\varphi}, d)$.
6. OnV verifies that:
   - $\mathsf{CSO.Ver}(\mathsf{cmt}, \mathbf{H}|_{\mathbf{I}}, \mathbf{I}, C, d) = 1$,
   - the sets $I_j \in \mathbf{I}$ are defined consistently with σ_j and φ_j.
   - $\mathbf{H}_{I_j}$ represents a Hamiltonian cycle graph, if $\sigma_j = \text{cycle}$,
   - $\mathbf{H}_{I_j} \equiv 0$ if $\sigma_j = \text{antiedges}$.

Fig. 1. A 3-message **SWI** argument of knowledge for Hamiltonicity.

polynomial K, such that except with negligible probability $\nu(\lambda)$ over the first two messages, there exists a set $\mathbf{X}$ of size at most K, consisting of strings $\mathbf{H} \in \{0, 1\}^{n^2 \times \lambda}$, such that except with negligible probability $\nu(\lambda)$, any valid opening of the commitment by the prover is consistent with some $\mathbf{H} \in \mathbf{X}$. Also, note that for two random challenges $\boldsymbol{\sigma}, \boldsymbol{\sigma}'$ there exists some i such that $\sigma_i = \text{antiedges}$ and $\sigma_i' = \text{cycle}$ except with probability $(3/4)^\lambda$.

It follows that with probability at least $\varepsilon/2 - \nu$ over the choice of the first two messages, there exists a single string $\mathbf{H}^* \in \mathbf{X}$, such that with probability at least $(\varepsilon/2K)^2 - (3/4)^\lambda$, in both executions performed by $\mathcal{E}$:

1. The prover convinces the verifier.
2. Both openings $\mathbf{H}|_{\mathbf{I}}$ and $\mathbf{H}'|_{\mathbf{I}'}$ obtained by $\mathcal{E}$ are consistent with $\mathbf{H}$.
3. For some i, $\sigma_i = $ antiedges and $\sigma_i' = $ cycle.

Since the verifier accepts in the second execution, H_i is a Hamiltonian cycle graph. Since the verifier accepts in the first execution, and H_i is a Hamiltonian cycle, $\varphi_i^{-1}(H_i)$ is a Hamiltonian cycle in G, since all anti-edges in G are mapped to anti-edges in H_i.

Overall, the extractor succeeds with probability at least $\varepsilon^3/8K^2 - \lambda^{-\omega(1)}$.

Proposition 4.2. *Protocol 1 satisfies adaptive statistical witness indistinguishability.*

The proof of witness indistinguishability is similar to that of the original Lapidot-Shamir protocol [LS90a]. The main difference is that there it is convenient to first prove WI for a single instance (with a single challenge σ) and then rely on a generic hybrid argument, whereas in our protocol the commitment with subset opening correlates the λ instances. The proof accordingly proceeds via a slightly less generic hybrid argument. The proof the proposition can be found in the full version of this work.

5   A Three Message Statistical Zero Knowledge Argument

In this section, we construct a three message statistical zero knowledge argument.

Theorem 5.1. *Assuming a linearly compressing* quasipoly(λ)-*secure multi-collision-resistant keyless hash, a* quasipoly(λ)-*secure fully-homomorphic encryption, and a two-message secure function evaluation protocol with statistical function hiding, there exists a statistical zero knowledge argument for* **NP** *with three messages.*

Ingredients and Notation

- A two-message weak memory delegation scheme (MD.Mem, MD.Query, MD.Prove, MD.Ver) with weak soundness for time-T for $T = $ quasipoly(λ), as in Definition 2.5.
- A two-message secure function evaluation protocol (SFE.Enc, SFE.Eval, SFE.Dec) with statistical function hiding as in Definition 2.6.
- An offline-online statistically witness indistinguishable argument of knowledge $\langle \mathsf{P} \leftrightarrows \mathsf{V} \rangle$ where the offline part of the protocol $\langle \mathsf{OffP} \leftrightarrows \mathsf{OffV} \rangle$ consists of two messages and the online part of the protocol $\langle \mathsf{OnP} \leftrightarrows \mathsf{OnV} \rangle$ consists of one message. Such a protocol is defined and constructed in Sect. 4.
- A weakly-binding statistically-hiding keyless commitment SHC.Com as in Definition 2.2.
- For a string x, denote by $\mathcal{M}_x$ a Turing machine that given memory $D = \mathsf{V}^*$, emulates the Turing machine encoded by V^* on the input x, parses the result as $(u, \mathsf{wi}_2, \mathsf{q}, \widehat{\mathsf{ct}}_\tau)$, and outputs u.

- Denote by $\mathcal{V}_{\mathsf{param}}$ a circuit that has the string param hardcoded and operates as follows. Given as input a secret state vst for the delegation scheme:
  - parse $\mathsf{param} = (x, \mathsf{q}, u, \mathsf{dig}, t, \pi)$,
  - return 1 ("accept") if either of the following occurs:
    * the delegation verifier accepts: $\mathsf{MD.Ver}(1^\lambda, \mathsf{dig}, (\mathcal{M}_x, t, u), \mathsf{vst}, \pi) = 1$,
    * the query and secret state are inconsistent: $(\mathsf{q}, \mathsf{vst}) \notin \mathsf{MD.Query}(1^\lambda)$.
    (We can assume without loss of generality that the state vst contains the random coins of $\mathsf{MD.Query}$ and, therefore, consistency can be tested efficiently.)
  In words, $\mathcal{V}_{\mathsf{param}}$, given the secret state vst, first verifies the proof π that "$\mathcal{M}_x(D) = (u, \cdots)$" where D is the database corresponding to the digest dig. In addition, it verifies that q is truly consistent with the coins vst.
- Denote by $\mathbf{1}$ a circuit of the same size as $\mathcal{V}_{\mathsf{param}}$ that always returns 1.

We describe our three-message zero-knowledge protocol in Fig. 2.

Proposition 5.1. *Protocol 2 is a statistical zero-knowledge argument.*

Proof (Sketch). As explained in the introduction, the protocol is based on the zero-knowledge protocols in [BBK+16, BKP18]. In particular, Bitansky et al. [BBK+16] show a three-message computational zero knowledge protocol in the *global hash model*, where parties have access to a collision-resistant hash function sampled during a setup phase. The main differences between our protocol and theirs is:

- Their two-message memory delegation scheme has full soundness instead of weak soundness.
- Their secure function evaluation has computational function-hiding instead of statistical.
- Their offline-online argument of knowledge is computationally witness indistinguishable instead of statistically.
- The non-interactive commitment is perfectly binding and computationally hiding instead of weakly binding and statistically hiding.

Next we outline the analysis of [BBK+16] and explain how to modify it for our protocol.

Soundness. Assuming that $x \notin \mathcal{L}$, in order to pass the witness indistinguishable argument of knowledge with respect to an evaluated cipher $\widehat{\mathsf{ct}}$ that decrypts to 1, the prover must know a proof $\pi \in \{0, 1\}^\lambda$ and an opening of cmt to a digest $\mathsf{dig} \in \{0, 1\}^\lambda$ and a time bound $t \leq T(\lambda)$ such that $\mathcal{V}_{\mathsf{param}}(\mathsf{vst}) = 1$. This, by definition, means that (dig, π, t) are such that the delegation verifier $\mathsf{MD.Ver}$ is convinced that the digest dig corresponds to a machine V^* such that $\mathsf{V}^*(\mathsf{wi}_1, \mathsf{cmt}) = (u, \dots)$.

By the weak binding of cmt, the prover can only open the commitment to a polynomial number of different digests. Therefore, there must exist one digest dig for which the prover can convince delegation verifier $\mathsf{MD.Ver}$ with high probability for an output u with high entropy, contradicting the weak soundness of

---

Protocol 2

Common Input: an instance $x \in \mathcal{L} \cap \{0,1\}^\lambda$, for security parameter λ.
P: a witness $w \in \mathcal{R}_\mathcal{L}(x)$.

1. P computes
   - wi_1, the first message of the offline prover $\mathsf{OffP}(1^\lambda, 1^{\ell_\Psi(\lambda)})$ where ℓ_Ψ is the length of the statement Ψ defined in Step 3 below,
   - $\mathsf{cmt} \leftarrow \mathsf{SHC.Com}(0^{2\lambda}; 1^\lambda)$, a commitment to the all zero string,

   and sends $(\mathsf{wi}_1, \mathsf{cmt})$.

2. V computes
   - st_V and wi_2, the state and the second message of the offline verifier $\mathsf{OffV}(1^\lambda, 1^{\ell_\Psi(\lambda)})$ after receiving the message wi_1.
   - $(\mathsf{q}, \mathsf{vst}) \leftarrow \mathsf{MD.Query}(1^\lambda)$, a query and secret state for the delegation scheme,
   - $(\mathsf{ct}_\mathsf{vst}, \mathsf{sk}) \leftarrow \mathsf{SFE.Enc}(1^\lambda, \mathsf{vst})$, an encryption of the secret state,
   - $u \leftarrow \{0,1\}^\lambda$, a uniformly random string,

   and sends $(u, \mathsf{wi}_2, \mathsf{q}, \mathsf{ct}_\mathsf{vst})$.

3. P computes
   - $\widehat{\mathsf{ct}} \leftarrow \mathsf{SFE.Eval}(1, \mathsf{ct}_\mathsf{vst})$, an evaluation of the constant one function,
   - st_P, the state of the offline prover $\mathsf{OffP}(1^\lambda, 1^{\ell_\Psi(\lambda)})$ after receiving the message wi_2.
   - wi_3, the message for online prover OnP given the state st_P, the statement $\Psi = \Psi_1(x) \vee \Psi_2(\mathsf{wi}_1, \mathsf{cmt}, \mathsf{q}, u, \mathsf{ct}_\mathsf{vst}, \widehat{\mathsf{ct}})$ of length $\ell_\Psi(\lambda)$ given by:

   $$\left\{ \exists w \,\middle|\, (x,w) \in \mathcal{R}_\mathcal{L} \right\} \bigvee$$

   $$\left\{ \exists \begin{matrix} \mathsf{dig}, \pi, r_\mathsf{cmt}, r_{\widehat{\mathsf{ct}}} \in \{0,1\}^{\mathrm{poly}(\lambda)} \\ t \leq T(\lambda) \end{matrix} \,\middle|\, \begin{matrix} \mathsf{cmt} = \mathsf{Com}(\mathsf{dig}, t; r_\mathsf{cmt}) \\ \mathsf{param} = ((\mathsf{wi}_1, \mathsf{cmt}), \mathsf{q}, u, \mathsf{dig}, t, \pi) \\ \widehat{\mathsf{ct}} = \mathsf{SFE.Eval}(\mathcal{V}_\mathsf{param}, \mathsf{ct}_\mathsf{vst}, r_{\widehat{\mathsf{ct}}}) \end{matrix} \right\} ,$$

   and the witness $w \in \mathcal{R}_\mathcal{L}(x)$ for Ψ_1,

   and sends $(\widehat{\mathsf{ct}}, \mathsf{wi}_3)$.

4. V verifies that $\mathsf{SFE.Dec}(\widehat{\mathsf{ct}}; \mathsf{sk}) = 1$ and that the online verifier OnP with state st_V and the statement Ψ accepts after receiving the message wi_3.

Fig. 2. A three-message statistical **ZK** argument of knowledge for **NP**.

the delegation scheme. In order to break the underlying delegation scheme we also rely on the semantic security of the encryption scheme to hide the secret verification state vst from the prover.

Statistical Zero Knowledge. To show statistical zero knowledge, we construct a non-black-box simulator following the simulator of Barak [Bar01]. At high-level, the simulator uses the code of the (malicious) verifier V^* as the memory for the delegation scheme, and completes the witness indistinguishable argument of knowledge using a witness for the trapdoor statement Ψ_2. The witness consists of (dig, π, t) where dig is the digest corresponding to V^*, $t \approx |\mathsf{V}^*|$ and π is the corresponding delegation proof that $V^*(wi_1, cmt) = (u, \ldots)$, which is now true by definition.

By the perfect completeness of the delegation scheme, we know that for any encrypted secret state vst, given a query q that is consistent with vst, the delegation verifier MD.Ver will accept the corresponding proof. Thus, the perfect function hiding of the secure function evaluation (which holds also if the verifier produces a malformed ciphertext) guarantees that the evaluated ciphertext $\widehat{ct}$ in the simulated proof is statistically close to that computed in the real proof where the prover actually evaluates the constant 1 circuit.

Relying also on the statistical witness indistinguishability of the argument of knowledge and the statistical hiding of cmt we deduce that V^*'s view in the real proof and the simulated view are statistically close.

References

[AH91]   Aiello, W., Håstad, J.: Statistical zero-knowledge languages can be recognized in two rounds. J. Comput. Syst. Sci. **42**(3), 327–345 (1991)

[Bar01]   Barak, B.: How to go beyond the black-box simulation barrier. In: 42nd Annual Symposium on Foundations of Computer Science, FOCS 2001, Las Vegas, Nevada, USA, 14–17 October 2001, pp. 106–115 (2001)

[BBK+16]   Bitansky, N., Brakerski, Z., Kalai, Y.T., Paneth, O., Vaikuntanathan, V.: 3-message zero knowledge against human ignorance. In: Hirt, M., Smith, A. (eds.) TCC 2016, Part I. LNCS, vol. 9985, pp. 57–83. Springer, Heidelberg (2016). https://doi.org/10.1007/978-3-662-53641-4_3

[BCC88]   Brassard, G., Chaum, D., Crépeau, C.: Minimum disclosure proofs of knowledge. J. Comput. Syst. Sci. **37**(2), 156–189 (1988)

[BCC+14]   Bitansky, N., et al.: The hunting of the SNARK. IACR Cryptology ePrint Archive, 2014:580 (2014)

[BCPR14]   Bitansky, N., Canetti, R., Paneth, O., Rosen, A.: On the existence of extractable one-way functions. In: Symposium on Theory of Computing, STOC 2014, New York, NY, USA, 31 May–03 June 2014, pp. 505–514 (2014)

[BCY91]   Brassard, G., Crépeau, C., Yung, M.: Constant-round perfect zero-knowledge computationally convincing protocols. Theoret. Comput. Sci. **84**(1), 23–52 (1991)

[BD18]   Brakerski, Z., Döttling, N.: Two-message statistically sender-private OT from LWE. In: Beimel, A., Dziembowski, S. (eds.) TCC 2018, Part II. LNCS, vol. 11240, pp. 370–390. Springer, Cham (2018). https://doi.org/10.1007/978-3-030-03810-6_14

[BDRV18]   Berman, I., Degwekar, A., Rothblum, R.D., Vasudevan, P.N.: Multi-collision resistant hash functions and their applications. In: Nielsen, J.B., Rijmen, V. (eds.) EUROCRYPT 2018, Part II. LNCS, vol. 10821, pp. 133–161. Springer, Cham (2018). https://doi.org/10.1007/978-3-319-78375-8_5

[BHKY19]   Bitansky, N., Haitner, I., Komargodski, I., Yogev, E.: Distributional collision resistance beyond one-way functions. In: Ishai, Y., Rijmen, V. (eds.) EUROCRYPT 2019. LNCS, vol. 11478, pp. 667–695. Springer, Cham (2019). https://doi.org/10.1007/978-3-030-17659-4_23

[BJY97]   Bellare, M., Jakobsson, M., Yung, M.: Round-optimal zero-knowledge arguments based on any one-way function. In: Fumy, W. (ed.) EUROCRYPT 1997. LNCS, vol. 1233, pp. 280–305. Springer, Heidelberg (1997). https://doi.org/10.1007/3-540-69053-0_20

[BKP18]   Bitansky, N., Kalai, Y.T., Paneth, O.: Multi-collision resistance: a paradigm for keyless hash functions. In: Proceedings of the 50th Annual ACM SIGACT Symposium on Theory of Computing, STOC 2018, Los Angeles, CA, USA, 25–29 June 2018, pp. 671–684 (2018)

[Blu86]   Blum, M.: How to prove a theorem so no one else can claim it (1986)

[BOV07]   Barak, B., Ong, S.J., Vadhan, S.P.: Derandomization in cryptography. SIAM J. Comput. 37(2), 380–400 (2007)

[BP04]   Bellare, M., Palacio, A.: The knowledge-of-exponent assumptions and 3-round zero-knowledge protocols. In: Franklin, M. (ed.) CRYPTO 2004. LNCS, vol. 3152, pp. 273–289. Springer, Heidelberg (2004). https://doi.org/10.1007/978-3-540-28628-8_17

[BV11]   Brakerski, Z., Vaikuntanathan, V.: Efficient fully homomorphic encryption from (standard) LWE. In: IEEE 52nd Annual Symposium on Foundations of Computer Science, FOCS 2011, Palm Springs, CA, USA, 22–25 October 2011, pp. 97–106 (2011)

[CD09]   Canetti, R., Dakdouk, R.R.: Towards a theory of extractable functions. In: Reingold, O. (ed.) TCC 2009. LNCS, vol. 5444, pp. 595–613. Springer, Heidelberg (2009). https://doi.org/10.1007/978-3-642-00457-5_35

[CKLR11]   Chung, K.-M., Kalai, Y.T., Liu, F.-H., Raz, R.: Memory delegation. In: Rogaway, P. (ed.) CRYPTO 2011. LNCS, vol. 6841, pp. 151–168. Springer, Heidelberg (2011). https://doi.org/10.1007/978-3-642-22792-9_9

[DN07]   Dwork, C., Naor, M.: Zaps and their applications. SIAM J. Comput. 36(6), 1513–1543 (2007)

[DPP93]   Damgård, I.B., Pedersen, T.P., Pfitzmann, B.: On the existence of statistically hiding bit commitment schemes and fail-stop signatures. In: Stinson, D.R. (ed.) CRYPTO 1993. LNCS, vol. 773, pp. 250–265. Springer, Heidelberg (1994). https://doi.org/10.1007/3-540-48329-2_22

[FGJ18]   Fleischhacker, N., Goyal, V., Jain, A.: On the existence of three round zero-knowledge proofs. IACR Cryptology ePrint Archive, 2018:167 (2018)

[FLS99]   Feige, U., Lapidot, D., Shamir, A.: Multiple noninteractive zero knowledge proofs under general assumptions. SIAM J. Comput. 29(1), 1–28 (1999)

[For89]   Fortnow, L.: The complexity of perfect zero-knowledge. Adv. Comput. Res. 5, 327–343 (1989)

[GK96]   Goldreich, O., Kahan, A.: How to construct constant-round zero-knowledge proof systems for NP. J. Cryptol. 9(3), 167–190 (1996)

[GMR89]   Goldwasser, S., Micali, S., Rackoff, C.: The knowledge complexity of interactive proof systems. SIAM J. Comput. 18(1), 186–208 (1989)

[GMW91]   Goldreich, O., Micali, S., Wigderson, A.: Proofs that yield nothing but their validity for all languages in NP have zero-knowledge proof systems. J. ACM 38(3), 691–729 (1991)

[GO94]   Goldreich, O., Oren, Y.: Definitions and properties of zero-knowledge proof systems. J. Cryptol. 7(1), 1–32 (1994)

[GOS12]   Groth, J., Ostrovsky, R., Sahai, A.: New techniques for noninteractive zero-knowledge. J. ACM 59(3), 11 (2012)

[HM96]   Halevi, S., Micali, S.: Practical and provably-secure commitment schemes from collision-free hashing. In: Koblitz, N. (ed.) CRYPTO 1996. LNCS, vol. 1109, pp. 201–215. Springer, Heidelberg (1996). https://doi.org/10.1007/3-540-68697-5_16

[HNO+09] Haitner, I., Nguyen, M.-H., Ong, S.J., Reingold, O., Vadhan, S.P.: Statistically hiding commitments and statistical zero-knowledge arguments from any one-way function. SIAM J. Comput. 39(3), 1153–1218 (2009)

[HT98]   Hada, S., Tanaka, T.: On the existence of 3-round zero-knowledge protocols. In: Krawczyk, H. (ed.) CRYPTO 1998. LNCS, vol. 1462, pp. 408–423. Springer, Heidelberg (1998). https://doi.org/10.1007/BFb0055744

[Kat12] Katz, J.: Which languages have 4-round zero-knowledge proofs? J. Cryptol. 25(1), 41–56 (2012)

[KKS18] Kalai, Y.T., Khurana, D., Sahai, A.: Statistical witness indistinguishability (and more) in two messages. In: Nielsen, J.B., Rijmen, V. (eds.) EUROCRYPT 2018, Part III. LNCS, vol. 10822, pp. 34–65. Springer, Cham (2018). https://doi.org/10.1007/978-3-319-78372-7_2

[KNY17] Komargodski, I., Naor, M., Yogev, E.: White-box vs. black-box complexity of search problems: Ramsey and graph property testing. In: 58th IEEE Annual Symposium on Foundations of Computer Science, FOCS 2017, Berkeley, CA, USA, 15–17 October 2017, pp. 622–632 (2017)

[KNY18] Komargodski, I., Naor, M., Yogev, E.: Collision resistant hashing for paranoids: dealing with multiple collisions. In: Nielsen, J.B., Rijmen, V. (eds.) EUROCRYPT 2018, Part II. LNCS, vol. 10821, pp. 162–194. Springer, Cham (2018). https://doi.org/10.1007/978-3-319-78375-8_6

[KP16]   Kalai, Y.T., Paneth, O.: Delegating RAM computations. In: Hirt, M., Smith, A. (eds.) TCC 2016, Part II. LNCS, vol. 9986, pp. 91–118. Springer, Heidelberg (2016). https://doi.org/10.1007/978-3-662-53644-5_4

[LS90a] Lapidot, D., Shamir, A.: Publicly verifiable non-interactive zero-knowledge proofs. In: Menezes, A.J., Vanstone, S.A. (eds.) CRYPTO 1990. LNCS, vol. 537, pp. 353–365. Springer, Heidelberg (1991). https://doi.org/10.1007/3-540-38424-3_26

[Nao91] Naor, M.: Bit commitment using pseudorandomness. J. Cryptol. 4(2), 151–158 (1991)

[NOVY98] Naor, M., Ostrovsky, R., Venkatesan, R., Yung, M.: Perfect zero-knowledge arguments for NP using any one-way permutation. J. Cryptol. 11(2), 87–108 (1998)

[OPP14] Ostrovsky, R., Paskin-Cherniavsky, A., Paskin-Cherniavsky, B.: Maliciously circuit-private FHE. In: Garay, J.A., Gennaro, R. (eds.) CRYPTO 2014, Part I. LNCS, vol. 8616, pp. 536–553. Springer, Heidelberg (2014). https://doi.org/10.1007/978-3-662-44371-2_30

[Sha79] Shamir, A.: How to share a secret. Commun. ACM 22(11), 612–613 (1979)

Signatures and Messaging

It Wasn't Me!
Repudiability and Claimability of Ring Signatures

Sunoo Park[1] and Adam Sealfon[2(✉)]

[1] MIT and Harvard, Cambridge, USA
[2] MIT, Cambridge, USA
asealfon@mit.edu

Abstract. Ring signatures, introduced by [RST01], are a variant of digital signatures which certify that *one among a particular set* of parties has endorsed a message while hiding *which* party in the set was the signer. Ring signatures are designed to allow *anyone* to attach anyone else's name to a signature, as long as the signer's own name is also attached. But what guarantee do ring signatures provide if a purported signatory wishes to denounce a signed message—or alternatively, if a signatory wishes to later come forward and claim ownership of a signature? Prior security definitions for ring signatures do not give a conclusive answer to this question: under most existing definitions, the guarantees could go either way. That is, it is consistent with some standard definitions that a non-signer might be able to *repudiate* a signature that he did not produce, or that this might be impossible. Similarly, a signer might be able to later convincingly claim that a signature he produced is indeed his own, or not. Any of these guarantees might be desirable. For instance, a whistleblower might have reason to want to later claim an anonymously released signature, or a person falsely implicated in a crime associated with a ring signature might wish to denounce the signature that is framing them and damaging their reputation. In other circumstances, it might be desirable that even under duress, a member of a ring cannot produce proof that he did or did not sign a particular signature. In any case, a *guarantee* one way or the other seems highly desirable.

In this work, we formalize definitions and give constructions of the new notions of *repudiable*, *unrepudiable*, *claimable*, and *unclaimable* ring signatures. Our repudiable construction is based on VRFs, which are implied by several number-theoretic assumptions (including strong RSA or bilinear maps); our claimable construction is a black-box transformation from any standard ring signature scheme to a claimable one; and our unclaimable construction is derived from the lattice-based ring signatures of [BK10], which rely on hardness of SIS. Our repudiable construction also provides a new construction of standard ring signatures.

1 Introduction

Ring signatures, introduced by [RST01], are a variant of digital signatures which certify that *one among a particular set* of parties has signed a particular message,

© International Association for Cryptologic Research 2019
A. Boldyreva and D. Micciancio (Eds.): CRYPTO 2019, LNCS 11694, pp. 159–190, 2019.
https://doi.org/10.1007/978-3-030-26954-8_6

without revealing which specific party is the signer. This set is called a "ring." Ring signatures can be useful, for example, to certify that certain leaked information comes from a privileged set of government or company officials without revealing the identity of the whistleblower, to issue important orders or directives without setting up the signer to be a scapegoat for repercussions, or to enable untraceable transactions in cryptocurrencies (as in Monero [Mon]).

In a ring signature scheme, just as in a traditional digital signature scheme, any party can create a key pair for signing and verification, and publish the verification key. Signers can produce signatures that verify with respect to any set of verification keys that includes their own, and unforgeability guarantees that no party can produce a valid signature with respect to a set of verification keys without possessing a corresponding secret key.

But what guarantee does a ring signature scheme provide if a purported signatory wishes to denounce a signed message—or alternatively, if a signatory wishes to later come forward and *claim* ownership of a signature? Given the motivation of anonymity behind the notion of a ring signature, a natural first intuition might be that parties should be able neither to denounce nor to claim a signature in a convincing way. However, depending on the threat model, we believe that the opposite guarantees—that is, to guarantee the ability to denounce or claim signatures—may be useful too, as elaborated below. Furthermore, whatever one's preference, a guarantee one way or the other seems more desirable than no guarantee either way.

Prior security definitions for ring signatures do not conclusively provide these guarantees one way or the other. That is, a non-signer might be able to *repudiate* a signature that he did not produce ("repudiability"), or this might be impossible ("unrepudiability"). Similarly, a signer might be able to later convincingly claim that a signature he produced is indeed his own ("claimability"), or be unable to do so ("unclaimability").

The most detailed taxonomy of security definitions for ring signatures was given by [BKM09], which presents a series of anonymity guarantees of increasing strength. A natural anonymity guarantee defined by [BKM09], called "anonymity against adversarially chosen keys," is informally described as follows: an adversary who controls all but $t \geq 2$ parties in a ring, and who may produce his own malformed key pairs as well as corrupt honest parties' keys, must have negligible advantage at guessing which of the t honest parties produced a given signature. This anonymity definition might allow a party to ascertain whether a given signature was produced by her own signing key, and perhaps also to convince others of this fact—but it does not *guarantee* or *prohibit* either of these capabilities.

On the other hand, the strongest of the anonymity definitions of [BKM09] (called "anonymity against full key exposure") requires that even if an adversary compromises every single party in a ring, the adversary cannot identify the signers of past signatures. It is relatively straightforward to see that under such a strong anonymity guarantee, Alice would have no way to convince anyone that she did not produce the objectionable message; indeed, she herself cannot tell the difference between a signature produced using her own signing key and one produced using someone else's.

The ability to identify whether one's own signing key was used to produce a particular signature can be a feature or a bug. To protect anonymity of past signatures against a very strong adversary who might compromise all the secret keys in a ring, it seems desirable to prevent distinguishing one's own signatures from those generated by someone else. On the other hand, without the ability to distinguish, it would be virtually impossible to tell if someone had stolen your signing key. Moreover, as discussed below, it could be beneficial in certain circumstances for members of a ring to have the ability to disown signatures of messages that they have strong reasons to denounce; and conversely, in some circumstances the signer of a message might later wish to prove to the world that he was the one who produced a particular signature in the past.

We have now identified four potentially useful notions for ring signatures: *repudiability*, *unrepudiability*, *claimability*, and *unclaimability*. The main contributions in this paper consist both of new definitions and constructions of each of these notions. Before diving into an overview of definition and constructions, we provide some discussion of why each of these notions—some of which directly oppose each other—may be meaningful and desirable: the following scenarios explore a few of the circumstances in which various of the above guarantees might be appropriate. Though some of the scenarios are phrased somewhat whimsically, we believe that each scenario illustrates a meaningful threat model motivating the definition concerned.

Scenario 1 (Repudiability). Let us consider a hypothetical tale, wherein two candidates Alice and Bob are running for president in the land of Oz. Oz is notorious for its petty partisan politics and its tendency to prefer whomever appears friendlier in a series of nationally televised grinning contests between the main-party candidates. At the peak of election season, a disgruntled citizen Eve decides to help out her preferred candidate Bob by publishing the following message, which goes viral on the social networks of Bob supporters:

> *I created a notorious terrorist group and laundered lots of money!*
> *Signed: Alice or Eve or Alice's campaign chairman.*

Of course, the virally publicized message does not actually incriminate Alice at all, since any one of the signatories could have produced it. However, perhaps there is nothing that Alice can do to allay the doubt in the minds of her suspicious detractors. As mentioned above, ring signatures are deliberately designed to allow *anyone* to attach anyone else's name to a signature, without the latter's knowledge or consent. Despite this, there could be realistic situations in which non-signing members of a ring associated with a particular message could suffer serious consequences through no fault of their own, perhaps due to the real signer adversarially trying to damage their reputation. In light of this, perhaps it would be desirable in some contexts for the owner of a verification key to be able to denounce messages, e.g., to clear her name of a crime or hate speech accusation that might otherwise impact her life in terms of reputation, job prospects, or incarceration.

Scenario 2 (Claimability). Our next story concerns a talented brewery employee who developed new statistical techniques to test the quality of beers. Naturally, his employer was protective of its competitive advantage since other breweries at the time may not have been using similar statistical methods. Yet, in the interest of science, they allowed him to publish his results—on condition of anonymity.[1] A credible way to prove authorship at a later date, after the need for anonymity has ceased to exist, might be very useful—especially in case of competing claims by impostors. As we see here, claiming authorship of an anonymous work may become appropriate after a passage of time. The next example illustrates quite a different type of situation in which claimability at the signer's discretion may be valuable.

Consider an employee Emily who is concerned about unethical practices at her company, and takes it upon herself to expose what is going on and publish a critical commentary. Concerned about her job security and possible retribution, as well as the credibility of her allegations, she maintains her anonymity using ring signatures. It emerges, in fact, that similar practices are prevalent across the industry: related revelations drive a wider movement of reform. Some time later, after her company has substantially reformed its practices and her fears of retribution have been allayed—perhaps by her promotion, or by a change in leadership—Emily seeks to reveal her identity and add her voice to the growing movement, providing her solidarity, legitimation, and follow-up story. In addition, if following the reforms, those involved in the earlier unethical practices were subject to stigma or even prosecution, claimability of her earlier ring signatures would allow Emily to exculpate herself.

Scenario 3 (Unrepudiability and Unclaimability). Let us return to the government of the fictional country of Oz. The parliament of Oz is mired in partisan gridlock, with legislators from each party ruthlessly voting down any bills, however reasonable, proposed by members of the opposing party—preventing any laws at all from being enacted and effectively shutting down the government, which is in no party's interest. Suppose that instead of directly proposing a new law, a legislator of Oz anonymously publishes the text of the proposed bill using a ring signature scheme:

> *Proposed: that free ice cream shall be provided every Tuesday.*[2]
> *Signed: a member of the Parliament of Oz.*

If the signer used an unclaimable ring signature scheme, then she could not decide to reveal her identity upon a later change of heart, allowing legislators of both parties to support or oppose the bill on its merits without worrying about purely political considerations.

---

[1] This is the true story of William Sealy Gosset's invention of the Student's *t*-test at Guinness Brewery in 1908 [Man00].

[2] Even if each party might support this legislation, they may be unwilling to do so if it were proposed by the other party, decrying their respective opponents as either fiscally irresponsible or in the pocket of Big Ice Cream.

Unclaimability and unrepudiability may be particularly useful guarantees in scenarios where the placement of whole groups of people under duress is a substantial concern. For instance, in circumstances where an employer or authoritarian government may coercively compel individuals to provide a repudiation or proof of authorship (e.g. signing randomness) for a signature, the provable inability to do so convincingly may be essential. Unrepudiability may also be desirable in situations in which members of a ring are likely to have conflicting individual incentives but there is a possibility of collective benefit in case of cooperation, as in a prisoner's dilemma scenario.

Summary of Technical Contributions. We formalize *repudiability, unrepudiability, claimability,* and *unclaimability* of ring signatures, as well as strengthened anonymity and unforgeability definitions which are compatible with each of these notions. We show that *unclaimability* implies *unrepudiability* (intuitively, because a failed repudiation can be used as a claim). Anonymity against adversarially chosen keys is the strongest anonymity notion compatible with *repudiability* and *claimability*, and anonymity against full key exposure is implied by *unclaimability* and equivalent to *unrepudiability*.

We provide three constructions based on different assumptions, one for each of the three notions of *repudiability, claimability,* and *unclaimability*. Perhaps the most surprising of these is *unclaimability*, which guarantees that the signer cannot later credibly convince others that she produced a particular signature. A natural first intuition is that meaningful notions of unclaimability might be impossible to achieve, since a signer can always remember the signing randomness (and later present it as "proof" of having produced a signature). The key insight for our definition and construction of unclaimable ring signatures is that the signing randomness does not constitute a convincing claim if *anyone in the ring can also produce credible signing randomness* for any signature in which they are implicated. Our construction of *unclaimable* ring signatures is an augmentation of the lattice-based ring signature scheme of [BK10] that adds additional algorithms allowing anyone in the ring to generate credible signing randomness; this capability is achieved via lattice trapdoors.

Our construction of *repudiable* ring signatures is based on verifiable random functions (VRFs), which are implied by either the (strong) RSA assumption, assumptions on bilinear maps, or NIWIs and commitments; see [Bit17, GHKW17] and references therein for more detailed discussion of the assumptions that imply VRFs. Our construction does not use standard ring signatures as a building block, and as such can also be viewed as a new construction of standard ring signatures. Our construction of *claimable* ring signatures, on the other hand, is a simple and generic black-box transformation from any standard ring signature scheme to a claimable one. We overview our contributions in more detail below.

1.1 Definitional Contributions

Repudiability. We define a *repudiable ring signature scheme* as a ring signature scheme that is equipped with additional algorithms Repudiate and VerRepud as follows. Repudiate takes as input a signing key sk, a ring signature σ, and a "ring" R (i.e., a set of verification keys), and outputs a *repudiation* ξ. VerRepud takes as input a ring R, a signature σ, a repudiation ξ, and a verification key vk, and outputs a single bit indicating whether or not ξ is a valid repudiation attesting that σ was not produced by vk. The two requirements for a ring signature scheme to be *repudiable* are, informally, as follows.

1. *Correctness:* Any member of a ring must be able to produce valid repudiations of any signature that he did not produce.
2. *Soundness:* A cheating signer must not be able to produce a valid signature with respect to a ring, and also be able to produce valid repudiations of that signature under every verification key in that ring that he owns.

Once a ring signature scheme is equipped with these additional repudiation algorithms, the standard definitions of *unforgeability* and *anonymity* against adversarially chosen keys are insufficient to capture the natural guarantees that would be desired for a repudiable ring signature scheme: we need the release of repudiations not to compromise the unforgeability or anonymity of any future signatures. Accordingly, we modify the definitions of unforgeability and anonymity for repudiable ring signatures (Definitions 12 and 13), by additionally giving the adversary access to a *repudiation oracle*. This ensures that repudiations of past signatures do not affect the security guarantees of future signatures. See Sect. 3.1 for formal definitions of repudiability.

Claimability. We define a *claimable ring signature scheme* as a ring signature scheme equipped with additional algorithms Claim and VerClaim as follows. Claim takes as input a signing key sk, a signature σ, and a ring R, and outputs a claim ζ. VerClaim takes a input a ring R, a verification key vk, a signature σ, and a claim ζ, and outputs a single bit indicating whether or not ζ is a valid claim attesting that σ was produced by vk. The three requirements for a claimable ring signature scheme are, informally, as follows.

1. *Correctness:* Any honest signer must be able to produce a valid claim with respect to any signature that he produced.
2. *Soundness:* No adversary can produce a valid claim with respect to a signature produced by an honest signer, even if the adversary can choose the message and ring with respect to which the signature is produced, and can insert malformed verification keys into the ring.
3. *No framing:* No adversary can produce a signature together with a valid claim of that signature on behalf of an honest (non-signing) party.

As above, once a ring signature scheme is equipped with these additional claiming algorithms, the standard definitions of *unforgeability* and *anonymity* against adversarially chosen keys are insufficient. We modify the definitions of anonymity and unforgeability for claimable ring signatures (Definitions 18 and 19), by additionally giving the adversary access to a *claim oracle*. See Sect. 3.3 for formal definitions of repudiability.

Repudiability and *claimability* are compatible, i.e., a ring signature scheme can be both repudiable and claimable. Indeed, our repudiable and claimable constructions together give rise to such a scheme. Notably, the unforgeability and anonymity definitions corresponding to the natural notion of a repudiable-and-claimable ring signature scheme are *not* the conjunction of unforgeability and anonymity for repudiable ring signatures and for claimable ring signatures. Rather, the unforgeability and anonymity definitions for a repudiable-and-claimable ring signature scheme involve a stronger adversary which is simultaneously given access to both a repudiation oracle and a claim oracle. See Sect. 3.5 for further discussion on repudiable-and-claimable schemes.

Unclaimability. We also introduce *unclaimable* ring signature schemes, in which the signer *provably cannot* convincingly claim that she was the one who produced the signature. As briefly mentioned above, while the signer can always save the signing randomness and reveal it along with her secret key in an attempt to claim authorship of a signature, it is not always true that this constitutes a convincing claim. In particular, such a claim is not credible if *any* member of the ring can take a valid signature and produce fake randomness that produces the desired signature using her own signing key.

The idea that a non-signer can adaptively produce fake randomness is reminiscent of deniable encryption [CDNO97], in which an encryptor and/or recipient is required to produce fake randomness "explaining" that a particular ciphertext is an encryption of an adversarially chosen message.

We define an *unclaimable* ring signature scheme to capture just this requirement: that is, any member of the ring must be able to produce fake signing randomness for a signature that is distributed indistinguishably from real signing randomness. Intuitively, the only information potentially possessed by a signer but not by the other members of the ring is the signing randomness, so non-signers that can generate convincing simulated signing randomness can also convincingly simulate any additional information that might be released by the signer in an attempt to claim the signature. We consider a strong flavor of this definition in which the indistinguishability property, described informally below, is statistical.

1. *Indistinguishability:* Any member of a ring must be able to produce fake signing randomness given a signature. The signature and fake signing randomness must be distributed statistically close to an honestly generated signature and corresponding signing randomness used by that individual to sign the same message, even given all verification keys and signing keys.

Remark 1. Even under this definition, if the signer chooses a message to sign that corresponds to a secret known only to herself, then she may still be able to convince others that she was the signer. For instance, if the signed message is the output of a one-way function, she may be able to convince others that she was the signer by subsequently revealing the preimage. Even more flagrantly, the signed message could contain a signature using a standard (non-ring) signature scheme, directly identifying the signer. This property is rather inherent: if knowledge of

Repudiable	VRF (Section 4)
Unrepudiable	RS anonymous against FKE (Section 3.2)
Claimable	Transformation from any RS (Section 5)
Unclaimable	SIS (Section 6)

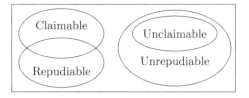

Fig. 1. Summary of our results and assumptions relied on. VRF = verifiable random function, RS = ring signature, FKE = full key exposure, SIS = short integer solution problem.

the contents of the message itself at the time of signing are enough to identify the signer, then no security property on the signature scheme can enforce that the signer remains hidden, since the identification of the signer is unrelated to the signature and based only on the signed message (Fig. 1).

Indeed, ring signatures were not designed to provide anonymity for signers who *want* to identify themselves, but rather for those who desire anonymity. Similarly, our unclaimability definition does not guarantee unclaimability for those who *want* to identify themselves, but rather provides credibility for a signer who *wants* to later be able to claim (e.g., under duress) that she could not convincingly claim the signature even if she wanted to. In particular, even an adversary with unlimited computational power who obtains the secret keys belonging to every member of the ring and a purported signing randomness from an alleged signer, he still will not be convinced of the identity of the signer, since fake signing randomness from the right distribution can be produced for every member of the ring.

Unrepudiability. Unclaimability intuitively guarantees that no member of the ring can convincingly prove that she was the signer. A related, weaker notion that might be desirable in some circumstances is that of *unrepudiability*, which guarantees that no member of the ring can convincingly prove that she was *not* the signer. Unrepudiability is equivalent to anonymity against full key exposure and is implied by unclaimability.

1.2   Overview of Our Constructions

Our Repudiable Construction. Our construction relies on ZAPs (two-round public-coin witness-indistinguishable proofs) and verifiable random functions (VRFs) as building blocks.[3] Our building blocks have some overlap with those of the ring signature construction of [BKM09], which uses ZAPs, public-key encryption (PKE), and a digital signature scheme. Both our scheme and theirs use ZAPs to achieve anonymity of the ring signatures, but with different approaches: the statements proven by the ZAPs are quite unrelated in the two constructions.

---

[3] VRFs imply ZAPs, so it suffices to assume VRFs [GO92,DN07].

Moreover, in our scheme, we do not need PKE or signature schemes, and instead use VRFs directly to achieve unforgeability and repudiability. The structure of our construction is thus very different from that of [BKM09].

At a very high level, each signing key in our construction contains a tuple of four VRF keys. A signature consists of the output of each of the signer's VRFs on the message, along with a ZAP proof that (several of) the VRF values in the signature are correct w.r.t. the VRF verification key of some member of the ring. A repudiation for individual i consists of a ZAP proof that some of the VRF values in the signature are different from the correct values for party i's VRFs evaluated at the message. One complication arises because we must guarantee that the release of a repudiation for individual i on a message does not subsequently allow a different member of the ring to produce a signature on the message that cannot be repudiated by individual i. We overcome this difficulty by relying on the witness indistinguishability property of the ZAP and ensuring that the repudiation does not reveal the actual VRF outputs of the repudiator; that is, the ZAP proof is produced with the VRF proof as a *witness*. The specific statement proven by the ZAPs is that some specific combination of at least two of the purported VRF outputs is correct. Although in the honest usage of the scheme, all four are produced correctly, we design the specific structure of the statements proved in order to allow a hybrid argument to argue indistinguishability between signatures of different signers in a ring. This scheme of proving the correctness of VRF outputs turns out also to imply unforgeability, not only repudiability, so we do not need to rely on any underlying signature scheme as building block. (In other words, our scheme can also be seen as a new construction of standard ring signatures based on VRFs.)

Our Claimable Construction. We give a generic transformation from any standard ring signature scheme RS to a claimable one. The transformation uses commitment schemes, standard signatures, and PRFs (which are all achievable from one-way functions). The basic idea is to take a signature σ_{RS} under RS and append to it a *commitment* c to (vk, σ_{RS}) where vk is the verification key of the signer. The verification algorithm simply checks whether σ_{RS} verifies. The claim consists of a decommitment revealing that c is a commitment to (vk, σ_{RS}). Intuitively, by the hiding property of the commitment scheme, the identity of the signer is hidden until he chooses to publish a claim.

The simple transformation just described runs into a couple of problems when examined in detail. First, what if a signer commits to (σ_{RS}, vk') where vk' is not his own key but that of someone else in the ring? This ability would violate Eq. (6) of Definition 17 (claimability). To prevent such behavior, our construction actually commits to a *standard (non-ring) signature* on (vk, σ_{RS}). The unforgeability property of standard signatures then guarantees, intuitively, that a signer cannot convincingly make a claim with respect to any verification key unless he knows a corresponding signing key.

A second issue encountered by the scheme thus far described is that the signer must remember the commitment randomness in order to produce a claim. It is preferable that the signer not be stateful between signing and claiming; indeed,

Definition 17 requires this. To resolve this, our construction derives commitment randomness from a PRF. For similar reasons, the signing randomness for the standard (non-ring) signature in our construction is also derived from a PRF.

Remark 2. Among the constructions presented in this paper, claimability is by far the simplest. Moreover, as a generic transformation, it has the advantage of adding minimal efficiency overhead to the existing state of the art in ring signatures. The simplicity of achieving claimability is perhaps unsurprising in light of the natural intuition that claiming should be possible simply by remembering the signing randomness. As evidenced by *un*claimability, this intuition is not strictly true in general, as in certain schemes, producing signing randomness may not prove authorship. In a nutshell, our generic transformation ensures that signing randomness is indeed a convincing proof of authorship in the resulting scheme, and moreover builds into the scheme a simple method of efficiently recovering the signing randomness without storing it explicitly.

Our Unclaimable Construction. Our construction of unclaimable ring signatures is an extension of the SIS-based ring signature scheme of Brakerski and Kalai [BK10]. The construction is based on trapdoor sampling. In this overview, we describe a simplified version of the scheme. The full scheme is described in Sect. 6. The basic idea for obtaining unclaimability is that each identity corresponds to a public matrix $A_i \in \mathbb{Z}_q^{n \times m}$ sampled together with a secret trapdoor T_i. A signature will consist of short vectors $x_i \in \mathbb{Z}_q^m$ such that

$$\sum_i A_i x_i = y,$$

where y is a target value. For this overview, we can think of y as the output of a random oracle on the message; in the actual construction, y will be obtained as the sum of additional matrix-vector products. In order to sign the message, signer i first samples short vectors x_j for each $j \neq i$. Then, using the lattice trapdoor T_i, he samples a short vector x_i such that the equation

$$x_i = y - \sum_{j \neq i} A_j x_j$$

is satisfied. The signature is the list of vectors $\sigma = (x_i)_i$. Using properties of lattice trapdoors, it follows that the distribution over $(x_i)_i$ can be made statistically close no matter which trapdoor was used to produce the signature. Moreover, given a vector x^* to be produced, we can sample random coins that will yield that vector under either the ordinary sampling algorithm or the trapdoor sampling algorithm. Consequently, we obtain an algorithm that can produce explanatory randomness for a signature under any identity in the ring.

Removing the random oracle to obtain ring signatures in the plain model (and unclaimable ones) requires several complications. [BK10] first describes a basic ring signature scheme with weaker unforgeability properties, in which the target vector y is determined using additional matrix-vector products for matrices that depend on the bits of the message. They then amplify the security of the scheme through a sequence of transformations that ultimately yield a scheme with full unforgeability. In Sect. 6, we first define an algorithm for producing explanatory randomness for their basic scheme, and then describe how to modify this algorithm for each modification of the basic scheme, ultimately yielding an unclaimable ring signature scheme based on the SIS assumption.

Remark 3. The idea that a non-signer of a given signature can adaptively produce fake signing randomness is reminiscent of deniable encryption [CDNO97], in which an encryptor of a given ciphertext can adaptively produce fake randomness consistent with it being an encryption of a different message. In this context, it may seem somewhat surprising that our construction relies on a relatively standard assumption (SIS) while many natural definitions of deniable encryption are not known to be achievable without heavier assumptions such as indistinguishability obfuscation [SW14, CPP18]. A subtle difference that is significant here is that a deniably encrypted message must still be recoverable by the honest decryptor, while in the unclaimable ring signature setting, the signer's identity need not be recoverable by anyone.

1.3   Other Related Work

Several constructions of ring signatures based on lattice assumptions have been proposed (e.g., [BK10, MBB+13, BLO18]). The only other construction of ring signatures based on ZAPs is [BKM09], to our knowledge. Numerous other ring signature constructions have been proposed, mostly based on various assumptions on bilinear maps, many but not all of which are in the random oracle model (e.g., [Ngu05, SS10, BCC+15]).

Two additional works in the lattice trapdoor literature bear mentioning: the seminal [Ajt99], and the more recent [MP12]. The latter is more recent than [GPV08], whose trapdoors our unclaimable construction relies on (this reliance is carried over from the [BK10] construction).

Ring Signatures with Additional Guarantees. Since the original proposal of ring signatures by [RST01], various variant definitions have been proposed. For example, *linkable* ring signatures [LWW04] allow identification of signatures that were produced by the same signer, without compromising the anonymity of the signer within the ring. An enhancement to this notion called *designated linkability* [LSW06] does not allow linkability by default, but instead allows links to be revealed at will by a designated party. Another notion called *traceable* ring signatures [FS07] considers a setting where signatures are generated with respect to "tags" and each member may sign at most a single message (say, a vote) with respect to a particular tag, or else his identity will be revealed. *Accountable* ring signatures [XY04, BCC+15] allow a signer to assign the power to de-anonymize her signature to a specific publicly identified party.

It may seem that some of these variants of ring signature schemes have properties that would be useful for constructing *claimable* ring signatures as introduced in this paper. This implication is unsurprising in the context of our results: *all* of the above types of ring signature schemes in fact imply claimable ring signatures, since our construction of claimable ring signatures is a generic transformation from *any* ring signature scheme. It is unclear if leveraging the additional features of variant schemes would be more desirable than applying our generic transformation, which has very low overhead and moreover can be applied to a simpler, more efficient ring signature scheme that may lack these additional properties.

Group Signatures. Group signatures [CvH91] are a different type of signature that allow signing w.r.t. a set of verification keys and provide anonymity of the signer within that set. This concept differs most strikingly from ring signatures in that there is a central authority that (1) sets up the group (i.e., set of signers) and issues keys to members of the group and (2) has the power to revoke the anonymity of the signer of a signature. Notions such as (un)linkability, described above, have been applied to the group signature setting as well. Notably, there has also been proposed a notion of *deniable group signatures* [IEH+16], in which the group manager may issue proofs that a particular group member did *not* sign a particular signature. This bears a little resemblance to our notion of *repudiability* in ring signatures; however, the presence of a central authority in the group signature setting means these problems are technically rather disparate. [LNWX17] construct lattice-based deniable group signatures; however, their technique for deniability is very different from ours, and relies on zero-knowledge proofs of plaintext inequality for LWE ciphertexts, which do not suffice in our setting.

2   Anonymity and Unforgeability of Ring Signatures

This section overviews standard ring signature definitions: syntax, correctness, anonymity, and unforgeability. We express the anonymity and unforgeability definitions differently from prior work, as explained in their respective subsections. However, our definitions are equivalent to the correspondingly named definitions from prior work. Throughout the paper, k denotes the security parameter.

Definition 1 (Ring signature). *A* ring signature scheme *is a triple of PPT algorithms* $\mathsf{RS} = (\mathsf{Gen}, \mathsf{Sign}, \mathsf{Verify})$, *satisfying the three properties of* correctness *(Definition 2),* anonymity *(Definitions 5 and 6), and* unforgeability *(Definition 8). The syntax of* Gen, Sign, *and* Verify *follows.*

- $\mathsf{Gen}(1^k)$ *takes k as input and outputs* verification key vk *and* signing key sk.
- $\mathsf{Sign}(R, sk, m)$ *takes as input a signing key sk, a message m, and a set of verification keys $R = \{vk_1, \ldots, vk_N\}$, and outputs a signature σ. The set R is also known as a "ring."*
- $\mathsf{Verify}(R, \sigma, m)$ *takes as input a set R of verification keys, a signature σ, and a message m, and outputs a single bit indicating whether or not σ is a valid signature on m w.r.t. R.*

Where it may not be clear from context, we sometimes write RS.Gen, RS.Sign, RS.Verify *to denote the* Gen, Sign, Verify *algorithms belonging to* RS.

Definition 2 (Correctness). *A ring signature scheme* RS = (Gen, Sign, Verify) *satisfies* correctness *if there is a negligible function* ε *s.t. for any* $N = \mathsf{poly}(k)$, *any* $(vk_1, sk_1), \ldots, (vk_N, sk_N) \leftarrow \mathsf{Gen}(1^k)$, *any* $i \in [N]$, *and any message* m,

$$\Pr\left[\mathsf{Verify}(R, \mathsf{Sign}(R, sk_i, m), m) = 1\right] = 1 - \varepsilon(k), \tag{1}$$

where $R = \{vk_1, \ldots, vk_N\}$. RS *satisfies* perfect correctness *if* (1) *holds for* $\varepsilon = 0$.

2.1 Anonymity

Prior work, notably [RST01,BKM09], has presented several ring signature anonymity definitions. Two of the definitions from prior work are relevant to this paper: anonymity against adversarially chosen keys and against full key exposure.

This section presents a new, generalized anonymity definition parametrized by *oracle sets*, and expresses the two relevant anonymity definitions as instantiations of the generalized definition. This generalized definition is useful to consolidate the existing definitions and make clear their relationship to one another; it captures not only the two definitions we rely on here, but also others from prior work. Moreover, the generalized definition will be essential to concisely express the new anonymity definitions that we introduce in later sections for anonymity of *repudiable* and *claimable* ring signature schemes (in Sects. 3.1 and 3.3 respectively). In a nutshell, this is because the new definitions need to allow the adversary access to additional oracles related to repudiation and/or claiming.

The generalized definition follows. It is parametrized by sets of oracles $\mathcal{O}_1, \mathcal{O}_2$ and an additional parameter $\alpha \in \{0, 1, 2\}$ that limits the adversary's corruptions.

Definition 3 (($\mathcal{O}_1, \mathcal{O}_2, \alpha$)-anonymity). *Let* $\mathcal{O}_1, \mathcal{O}_2$ *be sets of oracles, where each oracle in the set is parametrized by a list of key-pairs. Define* $\mathsf{Corr}_{(vk_1, sk_1), \ldots, (vk_N, sk_N)}$ *to take as input* $i \in [N]$ *and output* $\omega_i \leftarrow \mathsf{Gen}^{-1}(vk_i, sk_i)$.[4]

A ring signature scheme RS = (Gen, Sign, Verify) *satisfies* ($\mathcal{O}_1, \mathcal{O}_2, \alpha$)-*anonymity if for any PPT adversary* $\mathcal{A}$ *and any polynomial* $N = \mathsf{poly}(k)$, $\Pr[b' = b]$ *in the above game is negligibly close to* $1/2$. *That is, formally,* $\forall$ *PPT* $\mathcal{A} = (\mathcal{A}_1, \mathcal{A}_2)$, $N = \mathsf{poly}(k)$, *there is a negligible function* ε *such that*

---

[4] The function Gen^{-1} takes as input a verification key vk and signing key sk produced by Gen, and produces the randomness used by Gen to produce this key pair. That is, it samples from the set $\{\omega : \mathsf{Gen}(1^k; \omega) = (vk, sk)\}$. In practice we will only ever invoke Gen^{-1} on a key pair produced by Gen, so we could invert efficiently by simply remembering the randomness used by Gen, but for the purposes of this definition we will describe it as a sampling procedure. Upon the first invocation on an input i, Corr samples $\omega_i \leftarrow \mathsf{Gen}^{-1}(vk_i, sk_i)$, stores it, and outputs it. If Corr is queried twice on the same input i then it outputs the same ω_i that was previously stored.

$$\Pr\left[\begin{array}{l}(vk_1, sk_1), \ldots, (vk_N, sk_N) \leftarrow \mathsf{Gen}(1^k) \\ ((m^*, i_0^*, i_1^*, R^*), \mathfrak{s}) \leftarrow \mathcal{A}_1^{\mathcal{O}_1, \mathsf{Corr}}(vk_1, \ldots, vk_N) \\ b \leftarrow \{0, 1\} \\ \sigma \leftarrow \mathsf{Sign}(R^* \cup \{vk_{i_0^*}, vk_{i_1^*}\}, sk_{i_b^*}, m^*) \\ b' \leftarrow \mathcal{A}_2^{\mathcal{O}_2, \mathsf{Corr}}(\mathfrak{s}, \sigma)\end{array} : b' = b \wedge |\{i_0^*, i_1^*\} \cap I| \leq \alpha\right] < \frac{1}{2} + \varepsilon(k), \quad (2)$$

where I is the set of queries to the corruption oracle; and the notation $\mathcal{A}^{\mathcal{O}, \mathsf{Corr}}$ means that for each oracle O in $\mathcal{O}$, $\mathcal{A}$ has oracle access to $O_{(vk_1, sk_1), \ldots, (vk_N, sk_N)}$, and $\mathcal{A}$ also has oracle access to $\mathsf{Corr}_{(vk_1, sk_1), \ldots, (vk_N, sk_N)}$.

Definitions 5 and 6 are instantiations of Definition 3. They are equivalent to the correspondingly named definitions in [BKM09].

Definition 4 (Signing oracle OSign). *For a ring signature scheme* RS, *the oracle* $\mathsf{OSign}_{(vk_1, sk_1), \ldots, (vk_N, sk_N)}$ *is defined to take as input* $i \in [n]$, *a message* m, *and a set* R, *and output* $\mathsf{RS.Sign}(R \cup \{vk_i\}, sk_i, m)$. *When the oracle is invoked with respect to a single key pair (i.e.,* $\mathsf{OSign}_{(vk, sk)}$*), we treat the oracle as taking only two inputs,* m *and* R, *since* i *is superfluous in this case.*

Definition 5 (Anonymity against adversarially chosen keys). *A ring signature scheme* RS $=$ (Gen, Sign, Verify) *satisfies* anonymity against adversarially chosen keys *if it is* ({OSign}, ∅, 0)-*anonymous. Moreover,* RS *satisfies* adaptive anonymity against adversarially chosen keys *if it is* ({OSign}, {OSign}, 0)-*anonymous.*

Definition 5 captures the guarantee that as long as there are at least two honest parties in a ring (represented by i_0^*, i_1^*), even if all other parties in the ring are corrupted by an adversary, the adversary cannot tell which of the honest parties produced a signature. One can also consider an even stronger definition where the adversary may corrupt *all but one* or even *all* of the parties in the ring, as in Definition 6.

Definition 6 (Anonymity against full key exposure). *A ring signature scheme* RS $=$ (Gen, Sign, Verify) *satisfies* anonymity against full key exposure *if it is* ({OSign}, ∅, 2)-*anonymous.*

Remark 4. Adaptive variants of anonymity were not discussed in prior work. In this paper, we refer primarily to *adaptive anonymity against adversarially chosen keys*: this is the strongest notion compatible with repudiability and claimability. Definition 6 does not include an adaptive version because adaptivity does not give the adversary any additional power when he can corrupt all the keys.

2.2 Unforgeability

The first unforgeability definition that follows is parametrized by an oracle set, taking a similar approach to our anonymity definitions above. In this section, we only give one instantiation of the parametrized definition of unforgeability. We will give other instantiations of Definition 7 in Sects. 3.1 and 3.3.

Definition 7 ($\mathcal{O}$-unforgeability). *Let $\mathcal{O}$ be a set of oracles, where each oracle in the set is parametrized by a list of key-pairs. A ring signature scheme $\mathsf{RS} = (\mathsf{Gen}, \mathsf{Sign}, \mathsf{Verify})$ is $\mathcal{O}$-unforgeable if for any PPT $\mathcal{A}$ and any $N = \mathsf{poly}(k)$, there is a negligible function ε such that*

$$\Pr\left[\begin{array}{l}(vk_1, sk_1), \ldots, (vk_N, sk_N) \leftarrow \mathsf{Gen}(1^k) \\ (R^*, m^*, \sigma^*) \leftarrow \mathcal{A}^{\mathcal{O},\mathsf{OSign},\mathsf{Corr}}(vk_1, \ldots, vk_N) \\ b \leftarrow \mathsf{Verify}(R^*, \sigma^*, m^*)\end{array} : \begin{array}{l}b = 1 \wedge R^* \subseteq \{vk_1, \ldots, vk_N\} \setminus I \\ \wedge Q \cap \{(\cdot, m^*, R^*)\} = \varnothing\end{array}\right] < \varepsilon(k),$$

where the notation $\mathcal{A}^{\mathcal{O},\mathsf{OSign},\mathsf{Corr}}$ is defined as in Definition 3, and I and Q are the sets of queries made to the corruption and signing oracles respectively.

We refer to the event that the conditions on the right-hand side of the colon in the above probability expression are met as a "successful forgery."

Definition 8 (Unforgeability of ring signatures). *A ring signature scheme $\mathsf{RS} = (\mathsf{Gen}, \mathsf{Sign}, \mathsf{Verify})$ is unforgeable if it is $\varnothing$-unforgeable.*

3   New Definitions: (Un)repudiability and (Un)claimability

3.1   Repudiable Ring Signatures

Repudiability addresses the question of whether ring members can prove that they did *not* sign a particular message (when they in fact did not sign it).

Definition 9 (Repudiable ring signature). *A repudiable ring signature scheme is a ring signature scheme with an additional pair of algorithms (Repudiate, VerRepud), satisfying the four properties of correctness (Definition 2), repudiability (Definition 11), anonymity (Definition 12), and unforgeability (Definition 13). The syntax of Repudiate and VerRepud follows.*

- Repudiate(R, sk, σ) *takes as input a signing key sk, a ring signature σ, and a set of verification keys $R = \{vk_1, \ldots, vk_N\}$, and outputs a repudiation ξ.*
- VerRepud(R, vk, σ, ξ) *takes as input a set R of verification keys, a signature σ, a repudiation ξ, and an identity vk, and outputs a single bit indicating whether or not ξ is a valid repudiation of signature σ for identity vk.*

Definition 10 (Repudiation oracle ORpd). *For a repudiable ring signature scheme RS, the oracle $\mathsf{ORpd}_{(vk_1,sk_1),\ldots,(vk_N,sk_N)}$ is defined to take as input $i \in [n]$, a signature σ, and a set R, and output $\mathsf{RS}.\mathsf{Repudiate}(R \cup \{vk_i\}, sk_i, \sigma)$. When the oracle is invoked with respect to a single key pair (i.e., $\mathsf{ORpd}_{(vk,sk)}$), we treat the oracle as taking only two inputs, σ and R, since i is superfluous in this case.*

Additionally, we define the oracle $\mathsf{ORpd}_{(vk_1,sk_1),\ldots,(vk_N,sk_N)}^{\langle \sigma^* \rangle}$ to output $\perp$ when it receives the signature σ^* as input, and otherwise to give the same response as $\mathsf{ORpd}_{(vk_1,sk_1),\ldots,(vk_N,sk_N)}$.

Repudiability requires two conditions, expressed by Eqs. (3) and (4) below. Intuitively, (3) captures the requirement "good people can repudiate," i.e., that for any (possibly maliciously generated) signature, an honest party who did not produce it should be able to successfully repudiate. (4) captures the requirements that "bad people cannot repudiate a signature they produced," i.e., addressing the case where the malicious signature and repudiation are both produced using the key being verified, and thus we want the signer to be unable to produce a valid repudiation.

Definition 11 (Repudiability). *A ring signature scheme* Σ = (Gen, Sign, Verify) *satisfies* repudiability *if equipped with algorithms* (Repudiate, VerRepud) *such that the following conditions hold.*

1. (Non-signers can repudiate). *Let* $\mathcal{O} = \{\text{OSign}\}$. *For any (possibly adversarial) PPT signing algorithm* $\mathcal{A}_{\text{Sign}}$, *there exists a negligible function* ε *such that*

$$\Pr\left[\begin{array}{l} (vk, sk) \leftarrow \text{Gen}(1^k) \\ (\sigma, m, R') \leftarrow \mathcal{A}_{\text{Sign}}^{\mathcal{O}, \text{ORpd}_{(vk,sk)}}(vk) \\ \xi \leftarrow \text{Repudiate}(R', sk, \sigma) \\ b \leftarrow \text{VerRepud}(R', vk, \sigma, \xi) \\ b' \leftarrow \text{Verify}(R', \sigma, m) \end{array} : \begin{array}{l} b = 1 \vee b' = 0 \\ \vee Q \cap \{(\cdot, m, R')\} \neq \varnothing \end{array}\right] > 1 - \varepsilon(k). \quad (3)$$

2. (Signer cannot repudiate). *For any (possibly adversarial) sign-and-repudiate algorithm* $\mathcal{A}_{\text{S\&R}}$, *there is a negligible function* ε *such that for any* $N = \text{poly}(k)$,

$$\Pr\left[\begin{array}{l} (vk_1, sk_1), \ldots, (vk_N, sk_N) \leftarrow \text{Gen}(1^k) \\ (\sigma, R', m, \{\xi_{vk}\}_{vk \in R' \setminus R}) \leftarrow \mathcal{A}_{\text{S\&R}}^{\mathcal{O}}(R) \\ \forall vk \in R' \setminus R, \; b_{vk} \leftarrow \text{VerRepud}(R', vk, \sigma, \xi_{vk}) \\ b' \leftarrow \text{Verify}(R', \sigma, m) \end{array} : \begin{array}{l} R' \cap R = \varnothing \vee \bigvee_{vk \in R' \setminus R} b_{vk} = 0 \\ \vee b' = 0 \vee Q \cap \{(\cdot, m, R')\} \neq \varnothing \end{array}\right] > 1 - \varepsilon(k), \quad (4)$$

where $R = \{vk_1, \ldots, vk_N\}$, $\mathcal{O} = \{\text{OSign}, \text{ORpd}\}$, *and* Q *is the set of* OSign *queries.*

Remark 5. Equation 4 guarantees that a party possessing a set of signing keys cannot repudiate under all of these keys, *as long as some key in the ring is honestly generated.* If the adversary generates all keys in the ring, then he may be able to produce a repudiation under every key in the ring. However, this does not undermine the purpose of repudiability: indeed, if presented with repudiations under every key in a ring, one can confidently conclude that all keys in the ring were generated dishonestly, and thus that all parties in the ring effectively colluded to produce each signature under that ring. Similarly, given repudiations for a subset of the identities in a ring, one can conclude that *either* one of the remaining identities in the ring produced the signature *or* all of the remaining identities in the ring colluded maliciously to produce the signature. That is, either way, at least one of the remaining identities is responsible for the signature.

Anonymity and Unforgeability of Repudiable Ring Signatures. The definitions of anonymity and unforgeability need to be adapted for repudiable ring signature schemes, to incorporate a repudiation oracle as described next.

Definition 12 (Anonymity of repudiable ring signatures). *A repudiable ring signature scheme* $(\mathsf{Gen}, \mathsf{Sign}, \mathsf{Verify}, (\mathsf{Repudiate}, \mathsf{VerRepud}))$ *satisfies* anonymity against adversarially chosen keys *if* $(\mathsf{Gen}, \mathsf{Sign}, \mathsf{Verify})$ *is* $(\{\mathsf{OSign}, \mathsf{ORpd}\}, \varnothing, 0)$-*anonymous (Definition 3) Moreover, it satisfies* adaptive anonymity against adversarially chosen keys *if* $(\mathsf{Gen}, \mathsf{Sign}, \mathsf{Verify})$ *is* $(\{\mathsf{OSign}, \mathsf{ORpd}\}, \{\mathsf{OSign}, \mathsf{ORpd}^{\langle \sigma \rangle}\}, 0)$-*anonymous, where* σ *is the challenge signature in Eq. 2.*

Recall from Remark 4 that adaptive anonymity against adversarially chosen keys is the strongest anonymity notion compatible with repudiability.

Definition 13 (Unforgeability of repudiable ring signatures). *A repudiable ring signature scheme* $(\mathsf{Gen}, \mathsf{Sign}, \mathsf{Verify}, (\mathsf{Repudiate}, \mathsf{VerRepud}))$ *is unforgeable if* $(\mathsf{Gen}, \mathsf{Sign}, \mathsf{Verify})$ *is* $\{\mathsf{ORpd}\}$-*unforgeable (Definition 7).*

3.2 Unrepudiable Ring Signatures

We next consider a notion where it is *not* possible for a party to prove to others that he did not produce a particular signature. In fact, though it may not be immediately apparent, a natural formalization of this notion is expressed by the definition of *anonymity against full key exposure* (Definition 6): that is, the strongest of the anonymity definitions given in Sect. 2. The following paragraphs justify this claim with detailed intuition.

Recall that anonymity against full key exposure (FKE) preserves signer anonymity even against an adversary that obtains all of the secret keys of all members of a ring. A ring signature scheme that satisfies repudiability could not also satisfy anonymity against FKE, because of the following attack: the adversary obtains all secret keys in the ring, attempts to repudiate using each secret key, and identifies as the signer the one secret key with respect to which the repudiation algorithm does not produce a valid repudiation. With overwhelming probability, by definition of repudiability, there is exactly one such secret key.

This informal argument establishes that anonymity against FKE must imply any reasonable notion of unrepudiability. Then are the two notions equivalent? While there arguably exist meaningful definitions of unrepudiability that are weaker than anonymity against FKE, we believe anonymity against FKE is the most reasonable definition of unrepudiability, as explained next.

Any reasonable definition of unrepudiability should capture the intuitive requirement that non-signers cannot behave distinguishably from signers. A little more precisely, for any protocol that could be executed by a non-signer Nancy with respect to a signature σ and her verification key vk', the signer Sigmund of that signature must be able to engage in the same protocol with respect to his own verification key vk and behave indistinguishably from Nancy. In other words, we require that if Nancy's secret key were stolen, the thief would be unable to tell whether σ was produced by Nancy or by someone else. Indeed, if Nancy were stateless and did not remember what signatures she had produced in the past, or simply lent her secret key to someone else who used it to produce signatures, then she herself would not be able to tell. The definition of anonymity against FKE embodies almost exactly this requirement—but instead of requiring anonymity against the thief who steals just Nancy's key, the definition makes the stronger requirement that anonymity must hold even against a thief who has every secret key in the ring corresponding to σ.

Is a weaker definition, which only rules out *unilateral* repudiations by a single party, a meaningful definition of unrepudiability? Perhaps. However, it is more in keeping with the intuitive goals and standard properties of ring signatures to protect against adversaries that may have many or all secret keys in a ring: that is, to rule out even the possibility of multiple ring members *colluding* to produce a repudiation for some ring member. Thus we arrive at the following definition.

Definition 14 (Unrepudiable ring signature scheme). *A ring signature scheme is* unrepudiable *if it satisfies anonymity against full key exposure.*

3.3 Claimable Ring Signatures

Claimability addresses whether the actual signer can prove later that they were the signer, without remembering the signing randomness.

Definition 15 (Claimable ring signature). *A* claimable ring signature scheme *is a ring signature scheme with an additional pair of algorithms* (Claim, VerClaim), *satisfying the four properties of* correctness *(Definition 2),* claimability *(Definition 17),* anonymity *(Definition 18), and* unforgeability *(Definition 19). The syntax of* Claim *and* VerClaim *follows.*

- Claim(R, sk, σ) *takes as input a signing key sk, a ring signature σ, and a set of verification keys $R = \{vk_1, \ldots, vk_N\}$, and outputs a claim ζ.*
- VerClaim(R, vk, σ, ζ) *takes as input a set R of verification keys, a signature σ, a claim ζ, and an identity vk, and outputs a single bit indicating whether or not ζ is a valid claim of signature σ for identity vk.*

Definition 16 (Claim oracle OClaim). *For a claimable ring signature scheme* RS, *the oracle* $\mathsf{OClaim}_{(vk_1, sk_1), \ldots, (vk_N, sk_N)}$ *is defined to take as input $i \in [n]$, a set R, and a signature σ, and output* RS.Claim(R, sk, σ). *When the oracle is invoked with respect to a single key pair (i.e.,* $\mathsf{OClaim}_{(vk, sk)}$*), we treat the oracle as taking only two inputs, R and σ, since i is superfluous in this case.*

Additionally, we define the oracle $\mathsf{OClaim}^{\langle \sigma^* \rangle}_{(vk_1, sk_1), \ldots, (vk_N, sk_N)}$ *to output $\perp$ when it receives the signature σ^* as input, and otherwise to give the same response as* $\mathsf{OClaim}_{(vk_1, sk_1), \ldots, (vk_N, sk_N)}$.

Claimability requires three conditions, expressed by Eqs. (5), (6), and (7) below. Informally, (5) requires that honest signers can successfully claim their signatures, (6) requires that adversarial parties cannot successfully claim a signature that they did not produce, and (7) requires that adversarial parties cannot produce a signature along with a claim that appears to be produced by an honest party (that is, falsely framing the honest party as the signer).[5]

Definition 17 (Claimability). *A ring signature scheme* $(\mathsf{Gen}, \mathsf{Sign}, \mathsf{Verify})$ *is* claimable *if equipped with algorithms* $(\mathsf{Claim}, \mathsf{VerClaim})$ *such that the following conditions hold.*

1. *(Honest signer can claim). There exists a negligible function ε such that for any $N = \mathsf{poly}(k)$ and $(vk_1, sk_1), \ldots, (vk_N, sk_N) \leftarrow \mathsf{Gen}(1^k)$ and any $i \in [N]$, it holds for any message m that*

$$\Pr\left[\sigma \leftarrow \mathsf{Sign}(R, sk_i, m) : \mathsf{VerClaim}(R, vk_i, \sigma, \mathsf{Claim}(R, sk_i, \sigma)) = 1\right] > 1 - \varepsilon(k), \quad (5)$$

   where $R = \{vk_1, \ldots, vk_N\}$.

2. *(Non-signers cannot claim). Let $\mathcal{O} = \{\mathsf{OSign}\}$. For any (possibly adversarial) PPT sampling-and-claiming algorithm $\mathcal{A}_{\mathsf{Claim}} = (\mathcal{A}_1, \mathcal{A}_2)$, there exists a negligible function ε such that*

$$\Pr\left[\begin{array}{l} (vk, sk) \leftarrow \mathsf{Gen}(1^k) \\ (R', m, \mathfrak{s}) \leftarrow \mathcal{A}_1^{\mathcal{O}, \mathsf{OClaim}_{(vk, sk)}}(vk) \\ \sigma \leftarrow \mathsf{Sign}(R' \cup \{vk\}, sk, m) \\ (\zeta, vk') \leftarrow \mathcal{A}_2^{\mathcal{O}, \mathsf{OClaim}_{(vk, sk)}}(R' \cup \{vk\}, \sigma, \mathfrak{s}) \\ b \leftarrow \mathsf{VerClaim}(R' \cup \{vk\}, vk', \sigma, \zeta) \\ b' \leftarrow \mathsf{Verify}(R' \cup \{vk\}, \sigma, m) \end{array} : \begin{array}{l} b = 1 \wedge b' = 1 \\ \wedge vk' \neq vk \end{array}\right] < \varepsilon(k). \quad (6)$$

3. *(Malicious signer cannot frame an honest party). For any PPT adversary $\mathcal{A}_{\mathsf{S\&C}}$, there exists a negligible function ε such that*

$$\Pr\left[\begin{array}{l} (vk, sk) \leftarrow \mathsf{Gen}(1^k) \\ (R', m, \sigma, \zeta) \leftarrow \mathcal{A}_{\mathsf{S\&C}}^{\mathcal{O}, \mathsf{OClaim}_{(vk, sk)}}(vk) \\ b \leftarrow \mathsf{VerClaim}(R' \cup \{vk\}, vk, \sigma, \zeta) \\ b' \leftarrow \mathsf{Verify}(R' \cup \{vk\}, \sigma, m) \end{array} : \begin{array}{l} b = 1 \wedge b' = 1 \\ \wedge Q \cap \{(\cdot, \sigma)\} = \varnothing \end{array}\right] < \varepsilon(k). \quad (7)$$

where $\mathcal{O} = \{\mathsf{OSign}\}$ and Q is the set of queries made to oracle $\mathsf{OClaim}_{vk, sk}$.

Anonymity and Unforgeability of Claimable Ring Signatures. The definitions of anonymity and unforgeability must be adapted for claimable ring signature schemes, to allow the adversary a claim oracle as described next.

Definition 18 (Anonymity of claimable ring signatures). *A claimable ring signature scheme $(\mathsf{Gen}, \mathsf{Sign}, \mathsf{Verify}, (\mathsf{Claim}, \mathsf{VerClaim}))$ satisfies anonymity against adversarially chosen keys if $(\mathsf{Gen}, \mathsf{Sign}, \mathsf{Verify})$ is $(\{\mathsf{OSign}, \mathsf{OClaim}\}, \varnothing, 0)$-anonymous (Definition 3). Moreover, the repudiable ring signature satisfies adaptive anonymity against adversarially chosen keys if $(\mathsf{Gen}, \mathsf{Sign}, \mathsf{Verify})$ is*

$$(\{\mathsf{OSign}, \mathsf{OClaim}\}, \{\mathsf{OSign}, \mathsf{OClaim}^{\langle \sigma \rangle}\}, 0)\text{-anonymous},$$

---

[5] Our definition does not guarantee that all signatures that verify (possibly a superset of all honestly generated signatures) can be claimed by someone; requiring this could be a reasonable alternative definition. See the full version [PS19] for more discussion.

where σ is the challenge signature in the anonymity experiment (Eq. (2)).

Recall from Remark 4 that adaptive anonymity against adversarially chosen keys is the strongest anonymity notion compatible with claimability.

Definition 19 (Unforgeability of claimable ring signatures). *A claimable ring signature scheme* (Gen, Sign, Verify, (Claim, VerClaim)) *is unforgeable if* (Gen, Sign, Verify) *is* {OClaim}-*unforgeable (Definition 7).*

3.4   Unclaimable Ring Signatures

An unclaimable ring signature scheme has the property that the signer cannot later convince anyone of her identity. That is, for any function that the true signer can compute given the signing randomness and the secret key, any other member of the ring can compute an indistinguishable function. The result is that even an adversary holding all ring members under duress cannot figure out who produced a given signature. This is true even if the ring members under duress attempt to cooperate with the adversary.

To achieve this, it suffices for any member of the ring to be able to extract signing randomness distributed indistinguishably from true signing randomness, that would produce the given signature under their secret key. More formally, the following guarantee should hold.

Definition 20 (Unclaimable ring signatures). *A* unclaimable *ring signature scheme is a ring signature scheme augmented with an additional algorithm* ExtractRandomness *as follows.*

- ExtractRandomness(R, sk, σ, m) *takes as input a ring R, a secret key sk, a signature σ and a message m. If sk is one of the secret keys for ring R, and σ is a signature on m with respect to R, then it outputs randomness ρ.*

ExtractRandomness *must satisfy the following condition.*

- (Statistical unclaimability). *Let $\mathcal{R}$ be the distribution of signing randomness. For any $N = $ poly(k) there is a negligible function ϵ such that the following holds. Let $(vk_1, sk_1), (vk_2, sk_2) \leftarrow $ Gen(1^k). For any message m and any $vk_3, \ldots, vk_N$ and $sk_3, \ldots, sk_N$, let $R = \{vk_1, \ldots, vk_N\}$ and $S = \{(i, vk_i, sk_i)\}_{i \in [N]}$. Let $\rho \leftarrow \mathcal{R}$, $\sigma_1 \leftarrow $ Sign$(R, sk_1, m; \rho)$, and $\rho_1 \leftarrow $ ExtractRandomness(R, sk_2, σ_1, m). Let $\rho_2 \leftarrow \mathcal{R}$ and $\sigma_2 \leftarrow $ Sign$(R, sk_2, m; \rho_2)$. Then $(S, \rho_1, \sigma_1) \approx_\epsilon (S, \rho_2, \sigma_2)$.*

Definition 20 is unusual among the definitions in this paper, in that it gives a statistical rather than a computational guarantee. We opted to give the statistical definition because it is simpler, it is a stronger guarantee, and our construction in this case achieves the statistical guarantee. One could also consider a computational definition.

Remark 6 (Claimability is not the opposite of unclaimability). According to these definitions, unclaimability is *not* technically the opposite of claimability (even when ignoring the fact that the formal definitions give a statistical guarantee for unclaimability but a computational guarantee for claimability). Claimability requires the ability to "voluntarily claim" a signature *without remembering the signing randomness*, whereas unclaimability rules out the ability to "claim under duress" *even given the signing randomness*. For voluntary claims, the natural and stronger definition is to guarantee the ability to claim adaptive, without "planning ahead" and without the storage requirement of remembering the signing randomness. In contrast, when considering attempts to claim under duress, the natural and stronger definition is to rule out the possibility of successful claims even in the presence of the signing randomness.

Remark 7 (Unclaimability protects honest *signers).* An adversarial signer who *wants* to claim can devise ways of credibly later claiming a ring signature, even when using an unclaimable ring signature scheme.[6] This does not decrease the utility of an unclaimable ring signature scheme for honest signers who *want* their signatures to be unclaimable.

Unclaimability Implies Unrepudiability. Any unclaimable ring signature scheme is also unrepudiable. Recall that the definition of unclaimability captures the idea that for any function that the true signer can compute given the signing randomness and the secret key, any other member of the ring can compute an indistinguishable function. Intuitively, the implication follows from the fact that repudiation would require a non-signer to behave in a way that *distinguishable* from any possible behavior of the actual signer.

Theorem 1. *Any unclaimable ring signature scheme is also unrepudiable.*

3.5 Repudiable-and-Claimable Ring Signatures

Suppose that (Gen, Sign, Verify) is a ring signature scheme, and there are algorithms Repudiate, VerRepud, Claim, and VerClaim such that, taken together with (Gen, Sign, Verify), they form a repudiable ring signature scheme and a claimable ring signature scheme respectively. The seven algorithms together do *not* necessarily satisfy the natural notion of a "repudiable-and-claimable" scheme. This is not only syntactic: in certain cases, security might in fact not hold in the 7-algorithm scheme. The natural security definition for a repudiable-and-claimable ring signature scheme is to include both repudiation and claim oracles throughout the repudiability, claimability, anonymity, and unforgeability definitions. More discussion and formal definitions are given in the full version.

---

[6] For example, an adversarial signer might use a PRG output as his signing randomness, or append it to his message, and remember the preimage. If he later revealed the preimage, it would likely serve as a credible claim to authorship of the signature.

4   Repudiable Construction

Due to space constraints, all proofs are deferred to the full version [PS19]. We begin by defining the building blocks.

ZAPs are two-message public coin witness indistinguishable proofs [DN07].

Definition 21 (ZAP). *A ZAP for an NP language L with witness relation $\mathcal{R}_L$ is a triple of algorithms $\mathsf{ZAP}_L = (\mathsf{ZAP.Setup}_L, \mathsf{ZAP.Prove}_L, \mathsf{ZAP.Verify}_L)$, where $\mathsf{ZAP.Setup}$ and $\mathsf{ZAP.Prove}$ are PPT and $\mathsf{ZAP.Verify}$ is polynomial-time and deterministic, satisfying the following properties.*

> ***Public coin.*** *For some polynomial $\ell = \ell(k)$, $\mathsf{ZAP.Setup}$ is the algorithm that on input 1^k, outputs a uniformly random element of $\{0,1\}^\ell$.*
> ***Completeness.*** *For any $(x,w) \in \mathcal{R}_L$, $\rho \in \{0,1\}^{\ell(k)}$, we have $\Pr_{\pi \leftarrow \mathsf{ZAP.Prove}(\rho,x,w)}[\mathsf{ZAP.Verify}(\rho,\pi,x) = 1] = 1$.*
> ***Adaptive soundness.*** *There exists a negligible function ϵ such that $\Pr_{\rho \leftarrow \mathsf{ZAP.Setup}(1^k)}[\exists(x,\pi) : x \notin L \wedge \mathsf{ZAP.Verify}(\rho,\pi,x)] \le \epsilon(k)$.*
> ***Witness indistinguishability.*** *For any sequences $\{\rho_k\}_{k\in\mathbb{N}}$, $\{x_k\}_{k\in\mathbb{N}}$, $\{w_{0,k}\}_{k\in\mathbb{N}}$, $\{w_{1,k}\}_{k\in\mathbb{N}}$, where for all k, $\rho_k \in \{0,1\}^{\ell(k)}$, $x_k \in L$ and $(x_k, w_{0,k}), (x_k, w_{1,k}) \in \mathcal{R}_L$, the following pair of ensembles is computationally indistinguishable: $\{\mathsf{ZAP.Prove}(\rho_k, x_k, w_{0,k})\}_{k\in\mathbb{N}} \stackrel{c}{\approx} \{\mathsf{ZAP.Prove}(\rho_k, x_k, w_{1,k})\}_{k\in\mathbb{N}}$.*

In this work, for simplicity, we will assume use of a ZAP for some NP-complete language L_{NP} (with witness relation $\mathcal{R}_{L_{\mathrm{NP}}}$) and for any $L \in$ NP with witness relation $\mathcal{R}_L$, we define $\mathsf{ZAP.Prove}_L$ and $\mathsf{ZAP.Verify}_L$ as follows.

- $\mathsf{ZAP.Prove}_L$ takes as input a triple (ρ, x, w). If $(x, w) \notin \mathcal{R}_L$, then output $\bot$. Otherwise, use an NP reduction on (x, w) to get a pair $(x_{\mathrm{NP}}, w_{\mathrm{NP}}) \in \mathcal{R}_{L_{\mathrm{NP}}}$, and output $\mathsf{ZAP.Prove}(\rho, x, w)$.
- $\mathsf{ZAP.Verify}_L$ takes as input a triple (ρ, π, x), uses the same NP reduction to obtain x_{NP} (which is in L_{NP} iff $x \in L$), and outputs $\mathsf{ZAP.Verify}(\rho, \pi, x)$.

Next, we recall the definition of verifiable random functions (VRFs) [MRV99].

Definition 22 (VRF). *A* verifiable random function *(VRF) is a tuple of algorithms $\mathsf{VRF} = (\mathsf{VRF.Gen}, \mathsf{VRF.Eval}, \mathsf{VRF.Prove}, \mathsf{VRF.Verify})$, where Gen and Verify are PPT and Eval and Prove are polynomial time and deterministic, satisfying:*

> ***Complete provability.*** *With probability at least $1 - 2^{-\Omega(k)}$ over $(pk, sk) \leftarrow \mathsf{VRF.Gen}(1^k)$, we have for all inputs x that $\Pr[\mathsf{VRF.Verify}(pk, x, \mathsf{VRF.Eval}(sk, x), \mathsf{VRF.Prove}(sk, x)) = 1] > 1 - 2^{-\Omega(k)}$.*
> ***Unique provability.*** *For all $pk, x, y_1, y_2, \tau_1, \tau_2$ with $y_1 \ne y_2$, for either $i = 1$ or $i = 2$ it holds that $\Pr[\mathsf{VRF.Verify}(pk, x, y_i, \tau_i) = 1] < 2^{-\Omega(k)}$.*
> ***Residual pseudorandomness.*** *Let $\mathcal{A} = (\mathcal{A}_1, \mathcal{A}_2)$ be a PPT adversary, where both $\mathcal{A}_1$ and $\mathcal{A}_2$ get oracle access to the VRF evaluation and prove algorithms. Let $(pk, sk) \leftarrow \mathsf{VRF.Gen}(1^k)$, and let $(x, \mathsf{s}) \leftarrow$*

$\mathcal{A}_1^{\mathsf{VRF.Eval}(sk,\cdot),\mathsf{VRF.Prove}(sk,\cdot)}(1^k, pk)$. Let $b \leftarrow \{0,1\}$, and let v be either $\mathsf{VRF.Eval}(sk, x)$ or uniformly random, depending on the choice bit b. Let $b' = \mathcal{A}_2^{\mathsf{VRF.Eval}(sk,\cdot),\mathsf{VRF.Prove}(sk,\cdot)}(1^k, v, \mathfrak{s})$. Then there is a negligible function ϵ such that $\Pr[b = b' \text{ and } x \notin Q] < 1/2 + \epsilon(k)$, where Q is the set of oracle queries made by $\mathcal{A}$ to either oracle.

For simplicity, we assume that Eval takes inputs x of any length, i.e., $x \in \{0,1\}^*$.

Definition 23. *The* verification failure probability *of a VRF* VRF *is*

$$\Pr\left[\begin{array}{c} (pk, sk) \leftarrow \mathsf{VRF.Gen}(1^k) \\ b \leftarrow \mathsf{VRF.Verify}(pk, x, \mathsf{VRF.Eval}(sk, x), \mathsf{VRF.Prove}(sk, x)) \end{array} : b = 0 \right].$$

The residual pseudorandomness property still holds even if the adversary queries many key pairs at once, and may adaptively learn some of the secret keys (then, residual pseudorandomness holds for the uncorrupted keys only).

Lemma 1 (Parallel VRF Game). *Let* VRF *be a a VRF. Then* $\forall$ *PPT* $\mathcal{A} = (\mathcal{A}_1, \mathcal{A}_2)$ *and all* $N = \mathsf{poly}(k)$, *there is a negligible function* ε *such that*

$$\Pr\left[\begin{array}{l} (pk_1, sk_1), \ldots, (pk_N, sk_N) \leftarrow \mathsf{VRF.Gen}(1^k) \\ (m^*, \mathfrak{s}) \leftarrow \mathcal{A}_1^{\mathcal{V},\mathsf{Corr}}(vk_1, \ldots, vk_N) \\ \forall i \in [N], y_{i,0} \leftarrow \mathsf{VRF.Eval}(sk_i, m^*) \\ \forall i \in [N], y_{i,1} \leftarrow \$ \\ b \leftarrow \{0,1\} \\ b' \leftarrow \mathcal{A}_2(\mathfrak{s}, (y_{i,b})_{i \in [N] \setminus C}) \end{array} : b = b' \land \forall i \in [N] \setminus C, (i, m^*) \notin Q \right] < 1/2 + \varepsilon(k), \quad (8)$$

where oracle $\mathcal{V}$ *maps* (i, m) *to* $(y, \tau) = (\mathsf{VRF.Eval}(sk_i, m), \mathsf{VRF.Prove}(sk_i, m))$, *oracle* Corr *maps* i *to* sk_i, *and* C, Q *are the sets of queries to* Corr, $\mathcal{V}$ *respectively.*

4.1 Construction

Construction 1. *Our construction* R-RS *is parametrized by* ZAP, VRF, *and* M, *where:* ZAP *is a ZAP;* VRF *is a VRF with input domain* $\{0,1\}^*$, *whose* Verify *algorithm takes* ν *bits of randomness and whose verification failure probability (Definition 23) is* ε; *and* M *is a polynomial satisfying* $M \geq (\nu + k)/\log_2(1/\varepsilon)$.[7]

R-RS.Gen(1^k)
1. $(vk_{\mathsf{VRF}}^1, sk_{\mathsf{VRF}}^1), \ldots, (vk_{\mathsf{VRF}}^4, sk_{\mathsf{VRF}}^4) \leftarrow \mathsf{VRF.Gen}(1^k)$.
   Let $\boldsymbol{vk}_{\mathsf{VRF}} = (vk_{\mathsf{VRF}}^1, \ldots, vk_{\mathsf{VRF}}^4)$ and $\boldsymbol{sk}_{\mathsf{VRF}} = (sk_{\mathsf{VRF}}^1, \ldots, sk_{\mathsf{VRF}}^4)$.
2. $\rho \leftarrow \mathsf{ZAP.Setup}(1^k)$.
3. $\boldsymbol{\alpha} = (\alpha_1, \ldots, \alpha_M) \leftarrow (\{0,1\}^\nu)^M$.
4. Output $vk = (\boldsymbol{vk}_{\mathsf{VRF}}, \rho, \boldsymbol{\alpha})$ and $sk = (\boldsymbol{sk}_{\mathsf{VRF}}, vk)$.

   Hereafter, we (implicitly) use the following convention to parse a ring R.

Write $R = \{vk_1, \ldots, vk_N\}$.
For each $i \in [N]$, write $vk_i = (\boldsymbol{vk}_{\mathsf{VRF}}^i = (vk_{\mathsf{VRF}}^{i,1}, \ldots, vk_{\mathsf{VRF}}^{i,4}), \rho_i, \boldsymbol{\alpha}_i = (\alpha_1^i, \ldots, \alpha_M^i))$.

$$(9)$$

---

[7] As explained in the full version, a satisfactory value of M can be set even without knowledge of ε. If ε happens to be known, a smaller value of M can be chosen.

Definition 24. *Let L be the following NP language.*

$$\{(R, m, \varphi, (y_1, y_2, y_3, y_4)) : \exists i^*, \tau_1, \tau_2, \tau_3, \tau_4, \gamma \ s.t. \ (b_1 \vee b_2) \wedge (b_3 \vee b_4)$$

$$where \ \forall \eta \in \{1, 2, 3, 4\}, b_\eta = \bigwedge_{i \in [N], j \in [M]} \mathsf{VRF.Verify}(vk_{\mathsf{VRF}}^{i^*, \eta}, (R, m, \varphi), y_\eta, \tau_\eta; \alpha_j^i \oplus \gamma)\}.$$

We now present the Sign and Verify algorithms of our construction.

R-RS.Sign(R, sk, m)

1. *Parse R as described above and $sk = ((sk_{\mathsf{VRF}}^1, \ldots, sk_{\mathsf{VRF}}^4), vk)$.*
2. *If $vk \notin R$ output $\perp$ and halt.*
3. *Define $i^* \in [N]$ such that $vk_{i^*} = vk$.*
4. *$\gamma \leftarrow \{0, 1\}^\nu$. (This is used as part of the ZAP witness in Step 6.)*
5. *$\varphi \leftarrow \{0, 1\}^k$. (This is used as a salt for the VRF input in Step 7, and output in Step 8.)*
6. *For $\eta \in \{1, 2, 3, 4\}$, let $y_\eta = \mathsf{VRF.Eval}(sk_{\mathsf{VRF}}^\eta, (R, m, \varphi))$ and $\tau_\eta = \mathsf{VRF.Prove}(sk_{\mathsf{VRF}}^\eta, (R, m, \varphi))$. Let $\boldsymbol{y} = (y_1, \ldots, y_4)$.*
7. *For each $i \in [N]$, let $\pi_i \leftarrow \mathsf{ZAP.Prove}_L(\rho_i, (R, m, \varphi, \boldsymbol{y}), (i^*, \tau_1, \perp, \tau_3, \perp, \gamma))$. Let $\boldsymbol{\pi} = (\pi_1, \ldots, \pi_N)$.*
8. *Output $\sigma = (\boldsymbol{\pi}, \boldsymbol{y}, \varphi)$.*

R-RS.Verify(R, σ, m)

1. *Parse R as above and $\sigma = ((\pi_1, \cdots, \pi_N), \boldsymbol{y}, \varphi)$.*
2. *Output $\bigwedge_{i \in [N]} \mathsf{ZAP.Verify}_L(\rho_i, \pi_i, (R, m, \varphi, \boldsymbol{y}))$.*

Next, we describe the repudiation algorithms for R-RS.

Definition 25. *Let L' be the following NP language:*

$$\left\{ (R, m, \varphi, (y_1, \ldots, y_4), vk = (\boldsymbol{vk}_{\mathsf{VRF}}, \rho, \boldsymbol{\alpha})) : \exists i^*, y_1', \ldots, y_4', \tau_1', \ldots, \tau_4', \gamma \ s.t. \right.$$

$$((b_1' \wedge b_2') \vee (b_3' \wedge b_4')) \wedge vk = vk_{i^*}, \ where \ \forall \eta \in \{1, 2, 3, 4\},$$

$$\left. b_\eta' = \left(y_\eta' \neq y_\eta \wedge \bigwedge_{i \in [N], j \in [M]} \mathsf{VRF.Verify}(vk_{\mathsf{VRF}}^{i^*, \eta}, (R, m, \varphi), y_\eta', \tau_\eta'; \alpha_j^i \oplus \gamma) \right) \right\}.$$

R-RS.Repudiate(R, sk, σ)

1. *Parse R as above, $sk = ((sk_{\mathsf{VRF}}^1, \ldots, sk_{\mathsf{VRF}}^4), vk)$, and $\sigma = (\boldsymbol{\pi}, \boldsymbol{y}, \varphi)$.*
2. *If $vk \notin R$ output $\perp$ and halt.*
3. *Define $i^* \in [N]$ such that $vk_{i^*} = vk$.*
4. *For $\eta \in \{1, 2\}$: let $y_\eta' = \mathsf{VRF.Eval}(sk_{\mathsf{VRF}}^\eta, (R, m, \varphi))$ and let $\tau_\eta' = \mathsf{VRF.Prove}(sk_{\mathsf{VRF}}^\eta, (R, m, \varphi))$.*
5. *$\gamma \leftarrow \{0, 1\}^\nu$. (This is used as part of the ZAP witness in Step 6.)*
6. *For each $i \in [N]$, let $\xi_i \leftarrow \mathsf{ZAP.Prove}_{L'}(\rho_i, (R, m, \varphi, \boldsymbol{y}, vk), (i^*, y_1', y_2', \perp, \perp, \tau_1', \tau_2', \perp, \perp, \gamma))$.*
7. *Output $\xi = (\xi_1, \ldots, \xi_N)$.*

R-RS.VerRepud(R, vk, σ, ξ)

1. *Parse R as above. If $vk \notin R$, output 1 and halt.*
2. *Parse $\sigma = (\boldsymbol{\pi}, \boldsymbol{y}, \varphi)$, and $\xi = (\xi_1, \dots, \xi_N)$.*
3. *Output $\bigwedge_{i \in [N]}$ ZAP.Verify$_{L'}(\rho_i, \xi_i, (R, m, \varphi, \boldsymbol{y}, vk))$.*

Remark 8. As written, the size of the VRF input (R, m, φ) scales with the size of R, and we have assumed that the VRF can take variable-length inputs. When this is not the case, or when a smaller-input VRF is desirable for efficiency reasons, the scheme can be straightforwardly modified using a collision-resistant hash function h, and evaluating the VRF on $h(R, m, \varphi)$.

Theorem 2. *Let VRF be a VRF and ZAP be a ZAP. Then R-RS is a repudiable ring signature scheme.*

Proofs are deferred to the full version [PS19].

5 Claimable Transformation

In this section, we give a simple black-box transformation from any ring signature to a claimable ring signature scheme. If the original scheme is repudiable, the resulting scheme is moreover *claimable-and-repudiable*. We assume familiarity with the standard notions of commitments, standard signatures, and PRFs. We use standard syntax for these; the full version gives detailed syntax definitions.

5.1 The Transformation

Construction 2. *Our transformation C-RS is parametrized by the following: RS, a ring signature scheme; Σ, a standard signature scheme; Com, a commitment scheme; and PRF, a PRF. For convenience, and w.l.o.g., we assume that the randomness of Com and Σ and the output of PRF.Eval are all in $\{0,1\}^\nu$.*

C-RS.Gen(1^k)

1. *Let $(vk_{\mathsf{RS}}, sk_{\mathsf{RS}}) \leftarrow$ RS.Gen(1^k).*
2. *Let $(vk_\Sigma, sk_\Sigma) \leftarrow \Sigma$.Gen$(1^k)$.*
3. *Let $sk_{\mathsf{PRF}} \leftarrow$ PRF.Gen(1^k).*
4. *Output $vk = (vk_{\mathsf{RS}}, vk_\Sigma)$ and $sk = (vk, sk_{\mathsf{RS}}, sk_\Sigma, sk_{\mathsf{PRF}})$.*

Hereafter, we implicitly parse verification and signing keys of C-RS as $vk = (vk_{\mathsf{RS}}, vk_\Sigma)$ and $sk = (vk, sk_{\mathsf{RS}}, sk_\Sigma, sk_{\mathsf{PRF}})$ respectively. Also, for a ring $R = \left(vk_1 = (vk_{\mathsf{RS}}^1, vk_\Sigma^1), \dots, vk_N = (vk_{\mathsf{RS}}^N, vk_\Sigma^N)\right)$, we write RS$(R)$ to denote $(vk_{\mathsf{RS}}^1, \dots, vk_{\mathsf{RS}}^N)$.

C-RS.Sign(R, sk, m)

1. *Let $\sigma_{\mathsf{RS}} \leftarrow$ RS.Sign$(\mathsf{RS}(R), sk_{\mathsf{RS}}, m)$.*
2. *Let $r_\Sigma =$ PRF.Eval$(sk_{\mathsf{PRF}}, (vk, \sigma_{\mathsf{RS}}, 0))$.*
3. *Let $\sigma_\Sigma = \Sigma$.Sign$(sk_\Sigma, (vk, \sigma_{\mathsf{RS}}); r_\Sigma)$.*
4. *Let $r_{\mathsf{Com}} =$ PRF.Eval$(sk_{\mathsf{PRF}}, (vk, \sigma_{\mathsf{RS}}, 1))$.*

5. Let $c = \mathsf{Com}((vk, \sigma_\Sigma); r_{\mathsf{Com}})$.
6. Let $\sigma = (\sigma_{\mathsf{RS}}, c)$.
7. If $\mathsf{C\text{-}RS.VerClaim}(R, vk, \sigma, \mathsf{C\text{-}RS.Claim}(R, sk, \sigma)) = 1$, output σ.
8. Otherwise, output $(\perp, \perp)$.

$\mathsf{C\text{-}RS.Verify}(R, \sigma = (\sigma_{\mathsf{RS}}, c), m)$

1. If $\sigma_{\mathsf{RS}} = \perp$, output 0.
2. Otherwise, output $\mathsf{RS.Verify}(\mathsf{RS}(R), \sigma_{\mathsf{RS}}, m)$.

$\mathsf{C\text{-}RS.Claim}(R, sk, \sigma = (\sigma_{\mathsf{RS}}, c))$

1. Let $r'_\Sigma = \mathsf{PRF.Eval}(sk_{\mathsf{PRF}}, (vk, \sigma_{\mathsf{RS}}, 0))$.
2. Let $r'_{\mathsf{Com}} = \mathsf{PRF.Eval}(sk_{\mathsf{PRF}}, (vk, \sigma_{\mathsf{RS}}, 1))$.
3. Let $\sigma'_\Sigma = \Sigma.\mathsf{Sign}(sk_\Sigma, (vk, \sigma_{\mathsf{RS}}); r'_\Sigma)$.
4. If $c \neq \mathsf{Com}(\sigma'_\Sigma, r'_{\mathsf{Com}})$, output $\zeta = \perp$.
5. Otherwise, output $\zeta = (r'_{\mathsf{Com}}, \sigma'_\Sigma)$.

$\mathsf{C\text{-}RS.VerClaim}(R, vk, \sigma = (\sigma_{\mathsf{RS}}, c), \zeta = (r'_{\mathsf{Com}}, \sigma'_\Sigma))$

1. Let $c' = \mathsf{Com}((vk, \sigma'_\Sigma); r'_{\mathsf{Com}})$.
2. Output $(c = c') \wedge \Sigma.\mathsf{Verify}(vk_\Sigma, \sigma'_\Sigma, (vk, \sigma_{\mathsf{RS}}))$.

If RS is a *repudiable ring signature scheme* then we additionally define $\mathsf{C\text{-}RS.Repudiate}$ and $\mathsf{C\text{-}RS.VerRepud}$ *as follows.*

$\mathsf{C\text{-}RS.Repudiate}(R, sk, \sigma = (\sigma_{\mathsf{RS}}, c))$
1. Output $\mathsf{RS.Repudiate}(\mathsf{RS}(R), sk, \sigma_{\mathsf{RS}})$.

$\mathsf{C\text{-}RS.VerRepud}(R, vk, \sigma = (\sigma_{\mathsf{RS}}, c), \xi)$
1. Output $\mathsf{RS.VerRepud}(\mathsf{RS}(R), sk, \sigma_{\mathsf{RS}}, \xi)$.

Theorem 3. C-RS *is a claimable ring signature scheme. Moreover, if* RS *is a repudiable ring signature scheme, then* C-RS *is repudiable-and-claimable.*

6   Unclaimable Construction

In this section we show how to construct unclaimable ring signatures from lattice assumptions. The scheme is exactly the SIS-based ring signature scheme of Brakerski and Kalai [BK10], augmented with an additional algorithm ExtractRandomness.

6.1 Lattice Trapdoor Sampling

We first give a very brief summary of necessary background on lattice trapdoors; see [GPV08] and the full version [PS19] for details Let $q \in \mathbb{N}$, $m' \in \mathbb{N}$, and $\beta \in \mathbb{Z}$ be functions of security parameter n. The (inhomogeneous, average-case) *short integer solution* ($\mathsf{SIS}_{q,m,\beta}$) assumption states that given $A \leftarrow \mathbb{Z}_q^{n \times m'}$, $v \leftarrow \mathbb{Z}_q^n$, it is computationally hard to find $x \in \mathbb{Z}_q^{m'}$ such that $Ax = v$ and $\|x\| \le \beta$. For polynomial m', β and prime $q \ge \beta \cdot \omega(\sqrt{n \log n})$, the SIS problem is known to be as hard as approximating worst-case lattice problems, in particular the Shortest Independent Vectors Problem (SIVP), to within a factor of $\beta \cdot \tilde{O}(\sqrt{n})$ [MR07, GPV08].

Let $D_{\Lambda,s,c}$ denote the discrete Gaussian distribution over n-dimensional lattice Λ, centered at $c \in \mathbb{R}^n$ and with parameter s. We note the existence of the following algorithms, described in [GPV08].

- There is an algorithm TrapdoorSamp that on input a security parameter 1^n produces a matrix $A \in \mathbb{Z}_q^n$ and a trapdoor T, where A is statistically close to uniform and T is a short basis for the lattice $\Lambda^\perp(A)$.
- There is an algorithm SampleDist sampling from the discrete Gaussian $D_{\mathbb{Z}^{m'},s,0}$.
- There is an algorithm SampleCond that on input a matrix A, trapdoor T, parameter s and vector u, produces a sample x distributed statistically close to the discrete Gaussian distribution $D_{\mathbb{Z}^{m'},s,0}$ conditioned on $Ax = u$. We have that $\|x\|_2 \le s\sqrt{n}$ with probability 1.

We will also require additional algorithms that given output values of the algorithms SampleDist and SampleCond, respectively, sample randomness under which the algorithm produces the desired output.

- There is an algorithm ExplainDist that on input an image vector x and parameter s, samples from the distribution $\{\rho | \mathsf{SampleDist}(s; \rho) = x\}$.
- There is an algorithm ExplainCond that on input matrix A, trapdoor T, parameter s, vector u and image vector x, samples randomness ρ that yields output x under algorithm SampleCond with inputs (A, T, s, u), i.e. samples from the distribution $\{\rho | \mathsf{SampleCond}(A, T, s, u; \rho) = x\}$.

We describe the algorithms ExplainDist and ExplainCond in the full version. We will use a slight modification of the SampleCond algorithm of [GPV08] that uses the basis randomization technique of [CHKP10]. We need the following lemma.

Lemma 2. *Let (A_1, T_1) and (A_2, T_2) be sampled from TrapdoorSamp, let $y \in \mathbb{Z}_q^n$, and let $s \ge \max(\|\tilde{T}_1\|, \|\tilde{T}_2\|) \cdot \omega(\sqrt{\log n})$, where the tilde denotes Gram-Schmidt orthogonalization. Sample vectors x_1 and x_2' from SampleDist. Let $x_2 \leftarrow \mathsf{SampleCond}(A_2, T_2, s, y - A_1 x_1)$, and let $x_1' \leftarrow \mathsf{SampleCond}(A_1, T_1, s, y - A_2 x_2')$. Then $(A_1, T_1, A_2, T_2, x_1, x_2)$ and $(A_1, T_1, A_2, T_2, x_1', x_2')$ are statistically close.*

Intuitively, this lemma says that the two trapdoors induce the same distribution on sampled vectors. This follows immediately from Lemma 3.3 of [CHKP10].

6.2   The Basic Construction of [BK10]

We now describe the construction of [BK10], which first constructs a "basic" scheme, then augments it to fully secure ring signatures in a series of steps.

Let the message space be $\{0,1\}^\ell$, and let $X = \{x \in \mathbb{Z}_q^{m'} : \|x\|_2 \le s\sqrt{m'}\}$ for some $s = \omega(\sqrt{n \log n \log q})$ be the set of "short" vectors.

The key generation algorithm samples a matrix with an SIS trapdoor, and an additional set of 2ℓ matrices, two corresponding to each bit of the message. It additionally samples a target vector y, and outputs the matrices and target vector as the verification key and the trapdoor as the signing key.

BK-RS.Gen(1^k)
1. Let $(A, T) \leftarrow \mathsf{TrapdoorSamp}(1^k)$.
2. For $(i, b) \in [\ell] \times \{0, 1\}$, let $A_{i,b} \leftarrow \mathbb{Z}_q^{n \times m'}$.
3. Let $y \leftarrow \mathbb{Z}_q^n$.
4. Output $vk = (A, (A_{j,b})_{(j,b)\in[\ell]\times\{0,1\}}, y)$ and $sk = (vk, T)$.

The signing algorithm proceeds as follows. A target vector y is selected from the lexicographically first verification key. For each identity in the ring, short vectors are sampled for matrices corresponding to each bit of the message to be signed, as well as the additional matrix. Finally, the trapdoor is used to obtain a short vector sampled from the same distribution conditioned on Eq. 10. The signature consists of the list of short vectors.

BK-RS.Sign$(R, sk, m; \rho)$
1. Parse $R = (vk_1, \dots, vk_N)$ and $sk = (vk, T)$.
2. For $i \in [N]$, parse $vk_i = (A_i, (A_{j,b}^{(i)})_{(j,b)\in[\ell]\times\{0,1\}}, y_i)$.
3. Let $y = y_i$, where $i \in [N]$ is such that vk_i is lexicographically first.
4. If $vk \notin R$, output $\perp$ and halt.
5. Define $i^* \in [N]$ be such that $vk_{i^*} = vk$.
6. Using trapdoor T_A for A_{i^*}, we can sample $(x_j^{(i)})_{i\in[N], j\in\{0\}\cup[\ell]}$ such that

$$\sum_{i\in[N]} A_i x_0^{(i)} + \sum_{\substack{i\in[N] \\ j\in[\ell]}} A_{j,m_j}^{(i)} x_j^{(i)} = y. \tag{10}$$

That is, for $(i, j) \in [N] \times \{0\} \cup [\ell]$ other than the pair $(i^*, 0)$, we invoke algorithm $\mathsf{SampleDist}$ to sample $x_j^{(i)} \in$ independently from the discrete Gaussian distribution X. Finally, we invoke algorithm $\mathsf{SampleCond}$ use the trapdoor T for A_{i^*} to sample $x_0^{(i^*)}$ from a distribution statistically close to the distribution X conditioned on Eq. 10 being satisfied.
7. Output $\sigma = (x_j^{(i)})_{i\in[N], j\in\{0\}\cup[\ell]}$.

The verification procedure simply checks that each vector in the signature has short entries and that Eq. 10 is satisfied.

BK-RS.Verify(R, σ, m)

1. Parse $R = (vk_1, \ldots, vk_N)$.
2. For $i \in [N]$, parse $vk_i = (A_i, (A^{(i)}_{j,b})_{(j,b)\in[\ell\times\{0,1\}}, y_i)$.
3. Parse $\sigma = (x^{(i)}_j)_{i\in[N], j\in\{0\}\cup[\ell]}$.
4. For each $x^{(i)}_j$ for $i \in [N], j \in \{0\} \cup [\ell]$, if $x^{(i)}_j \notin X$ then immediately reject.
5. Let $y = y_i$, where $i \in [N]$ is such that A_{i^*} is lexicographically first.
6. Accept if Eq. 10 above is satisfied, and otherwise reject.

We now augment the basic [BK10] ring signature scheme with additional algorithm ExtractRandomness that produces "explaining randomness." The algorithms ExplainDist and ExplainCond referenced below are described in the full version.

BK-RS.ExtractRandomness(R, sk, σ, m)

1. Parse $R = (vk_1, \ldots, vk_N)$ and $sk = (vk, T)$.
2. For $i \in [N]$, parse $vk_i = (A_i, (A^{(i)}_{j,b})_{(j,b)\in[\ell\times\{0,1\}}, y_i)$.
3. Parse $\sigma = (x^{(i)}_j)_{i\in[N], j\in\{0\}\cup[\ell]}$.
4. If $vk \notin R$, output $\perp$ and halt.
5. Define $i^* \in [N]$ be such that $vk_{i^*} = vk$.
6. For $(i, j) \in [N] \times \{0\} \cup [\ell]$ s.t. $(i, j) \neq (i^*, 0)$, run ExplainDist to sample randomness $\rho^{(i)}_j$ giving output $x^{(i)}_j$ from discrete Gaussian sampling.
7. Run ExplainCond to sample random coins $\rho^{(i^*)}_0$ that produce output $x^{(i^*)}_0$ under the conditional random sampling algorithm using trapdoor T.
8. Output $(\rho^{(i)}_j)$.

Theorem 4. *Under the* SIS$_{q,m',\beta}$ *assumption,* BK-RS *is a unclaimable ring signature scheme satisfying a weak notion of unforgeability in which the challenge is sampled at random at the beginning of the experiment.*

6.3   Unclaimability for the Full Ring Signature Scheme of [BK10]

The ring signature scheme above satisfies a weak notion of unforgeability, in which the forgery message is sampled at random by the challenger and sent to the forger in the beginning of the experiment. To achieve full unforgeability, [BK10] provide a sequence of four reductions to construct schemes satisfying successively stronger notions of unforgeability. We give a brief overview of these reductions and the corresponding modifications of the ExtractRandomness algorithm.

The first modified scheme appends a description of the ring to the message to be signed, so ExtractRandomness is simply invoked on a different message.

The second modification is the most complicated, and introduces a variant of chameleon hash functions. A chameleon hash function h is sampled during Gen and is included in the verification key vk. During Sign, randomness r is sampled from a certain distribution, and a value $y = h(m, r)$ is computed, where m is the message to be signed and h is the hash function corresponding to the lexicographically first identity in the ring. The previous signature scheme is invoked on $y = h(m, r)$, where m is the message and h is the hash function for the lexicographically first identity in the ring; then, r is appended to the resulting signature. Now the only randomness to explain is r and the previous signature scheme's randomness. So the only change to ExtractRandomness is that it now also gives random coins resulting in a particular r, which is straightforward.

The third modification simply computes a signature under the previous scheme of every prefix of the message, and outputs these $|m|$ signatures as its signature. The final modification has Gen additionally output a random pad α, and computes a signature on $m \oplus \alpha_1$ where α_1 is the pad for the lexicographically first identity in the ring. For each of these we simply invoke the previous ExtractRandomness algorithm on a different message. This yields the following.

Theorem 5. *Assuming* $\mathsf{SIS}_{q,m',\beta}$, *[BK10] ring signatures augmented with the above* ExtractRandomness *algorithm is an unclaimable ring signature scheme.*

Acknowledgements. We thank Yael Tauman Kalai for advice on an earlier draft, and anonymous reviewers for their comments. Both authors' research was supported by the following grants: NSF MACS (CNS-1413920), DARPA IBM (W911NF-15-C-0236), Simons Investigator award agreement dated June 5th, 2012, and the Center for Science of Information (CSoI), an NSF Science and Technology Center, under grant agreement CCF-0939370. Sunoo Park was additionally supported by the MIT Media Lab's Digital Currency Initiative. Adam Sealfon was additionally supported by a DOE CSGF fellowship, DARPA/NJIT Palisade 491512803, Sloan/NJIT 996698, and MIT/IBM W1771646.

References

[Ajt99]   Ajtai, M.: Generating hard instances of the short basis problem. In: Wiedermann, J., van Emde Boas, P., Nielsen, M. (eds.) ICALP 1999. LNCS, vol. 1644, pp. 1–9. Springer, Heidelberg (1999). https://doi.org/10.1007/3-540-48523-6_1

[BCC+15]   Bootle, J., Cerulli, A., Chaidos, P., Ghadafi, E., Groth, J., Petit, C.: Short accountable ring signatures based on DDH. In: Pernul, G., Ryan, P.Y.A., Weippl, E. (eds.) ESORICS 2015. LNCS, vol. 9326, pp. 243–265. Springer, Cham (2015). https://doi.org/10.1007/978-3-319-24174-6_13

[Bit17]   Bitansky, N.: Verifiable random functions from non-interactive witness-indistinguishable proofs. In: Kalai, Y., Reyzin, L. (eds.) TCC 2017. LNCS, vol. 10678, pp. 567–594. Springer, Cham (2017). https://doi.org/10.1007/978-3-319-70503-3_19

[BK10]   Brakerski, Z., Kalai, Y.T.: A framework for efficient signatures, ring signatures and identity based encryption in the standard model. IACR Cryptology ePrint Archive 2010/086 (2010)

[BKM09]   Bender, A., Katz, J., Morselli, R.: Ring signatures: stronger definitions, and constructions without random oracles. J. Cryptol. **22**(1), 114–138 (2009)

[BLO18]   Baum, C., Lin, H., Oechsner, S.: Towards practical lattice-based one-time linkable ring signatures. Cryptology ePrint Archive 2018/107 (2018)

[CDNO97] Canetti, R., Dwork, C., Naor, M., Ostrovsky, R.: Deniable encryption. In: Kaliski, B.S. (ed.) CRYPTO 1997. LNCS, vol. 1294, pp. 90–104. Springer, Heidelberg (1997). https://doi.org/10.1007/BFb0052229

[CHKP10] Cash, D., Hofheinz, D., Kiltz, E., Peikert, C.: Bonsai trees, or how to delegate a lattice basis. In: Gilbert, H. (ed.) EUROCRYPT 2010. LNCS, vol. 6110, pp. 523–552. Springer, Heidelberg (2010). https://doi.org/10.1007/978-3-642-13190-5_27

[CPP18] Canetti, R., Park, S., Poburinnaya, O.: Fully bideniable interactive encryption. IACR Cryptology ePrint Archive, 2018:1244 (2018)

[CvH91] Chaum, D., van Heyst, E.: Group signatures. In: Davies, D.W. (ed.) EUROCRYPT 1991. LNCS, vol. 547, pp. 257–265. Springer, Heidelberg (1991). https://doi.org/10.1007/3-540-46416-6_22

[DN07] Dwork, C., Naor, M.: Zaps and their applications. SIAM J. Comput. **36**(6), 1513–1543 (2007)

[FS07] Fujisaki, E., Suzuki, K.: Traceable ring signature. In: Okamoto, T., Wang, X. (eds.) PKC 2007. LNCS, vol. 4450, pp. 181–200. Springer, Heidelberg (2007). https://doi.org/10.1007/978-3-540-71677-8_13

[GHKW17] Goyal, R., Hohenberger, S., Koppula, V., Waters, B.: A generic approach to constructing and proving verifiable random functions. In: Kalai, Y., Reyzin, L. (eds.) TCC 2017. LNCS, vol. 10678, pp. 537–566. Springer, Cham (2017). https://doi.org/10.1007/978-3-319-70503-3_18

[GO92] Goldwasser, S., Ostrovsky, R.: *Invariant* signatures and non-interactive zero-knowledge proofs are equivalent (extended abstract). In: Brickell, E.F. (ed.) CRYPTO 1992. LNCS, vol. 740, pp. 228–245. Springer, Heidelberg (1993). https://doi.org/10.1007/3-540-48071-4_16

[GPV08] Gentry, C., Peikert, C., Vaikuntanathan, V.: Trapdoors for hard lattices and new cryptographic constructions. In: STOC (2008)

[IEH+16] Ishida, A., Emura, K., Hanaoka, G., Sakai, Y., Tanaka, K.: Group signature with deniability: how to disavow a signature. In: Foresti, S., Persiano, G. (eds.) CANS 2016. LNCS, vol. 10052, pp. 228–244. Springer, Cham (2016). https://doi.org/10.1007/978-3-319-48965-0_14

[LNWX17] Ling, S., Nguyen, K., Wang, H., Xu, Y.: Lattice-based group signatures: achieving full dynamicity with ease. In: Gollmann, D., Miyaji, A., Kikuchi, H. (eds.) ACNS 2017. LNCS, vol. 10355, pp. 293–312. Springer, Cham (2017). https://doi.org/10.1007/978-3-319-61204-1_15

[LSW06] Liu, J.K., Susilo, W., Wong, D.S.: Ring signature with designated linkability. In: Yoshiura, H., Sakurai, K., Rannenberg, K., Murayama, Y., Kawamura, S. (eds.) IWSEC 2006. LNCS, vol. 4266, pp. 104–119. Springer, Heidelberg (2006). https://doi.org/10.1007/11908739_8

[LWW04] Liu, J.K., Wei, V.K., Wong, D.S.: Linkable spontaneous anonymous group signature for ad hoc groups (extended abstract). In: Wang, H., Pieprzyk, J., Varadharajan, V. (eds.) ACISP 2004. LNCS, vol. 3108, pp. 325–335. Springer, Heidelberg (2004). https://doi.org/10.1007/978-3-540-27800-9_28

[Man00] Mankiewicz, R.: The Story of Mathematics. Princeton University Press, Princeton (2000)

[MBB+13] Aguilar Melchor, C., Bettaieb, S., Boyen, X., Fousse, L., Gaborit, P.: Adapting Lyubashevsky's signature schemes to the ring signature setting. In: Youssef, A., Nitaj, A., Hassanien, A.E. (eds.) AFRICACRYPT 2013. LNCS, vol. 7918, pp. 1–25. Springer, Heidelberg (2013). https://doi.org/10.1007/978-3-642-38553-7_1

[Mon]   Monero. Monero: private digital currency. https://www.getmonero.org

[MP12]   Micciancio, D., Peikert, C.: Trapdoors for lattices: simpler, tighter, faster, smaller. In: Pointcheval, D., Johansson, T. (eds.) EUROCRYPT 2012. LNCS, vol. 7237, pp. 700–718. Springer, Heidelberg (2012). https://doi.org/10.1007/978-3-642-29011-4_41

[MR07]   Micciancio, D., Regev, O.: Worst-case to average-case reductions based on Gaussian measures. SIAM J. Comput. **37**(1), 267–302 (2007)

[MRV99] Micali, S., Rabin, M.O., Vadhan,S.P.: Verifiable random functions. In: FOCS (1999)

[Ngu05] Nguyen, L.: Accumulators from bilinear pairings and applications. In: Menezes, A. (ed.) CT-RSA 2005. LNCS, vol. 3376, pp. 275–292. Springer, Heidelberg (2005). https://doi.org/10.1007/978-3-540-30574-3_19

[PS19]   Park, S., Sealfon, A.: It wasn't me! Repudiability and unclaimability of ring signatures. IACR Cryptology ePrint Archive, 2019:135 (2019)

[RST01] Rivest, R.L., Shamir, A., Tauman, Y.: How to leak a secret. In: Boyd, C. (ed.) ASIACRYPT 2001. LNCS, vol. 2248, pp. 552–565. Springer, Heidelberg (2001). https://doi.org/10.1007/3-540-45682-1_32

[SS10]   Schäge, S., Schwenk, J.: A CDH-based ring signature scheme with short signatures and public keys. In: Sion, R. (ed.) FC 2010. LNCS, vol. 6052, pp. 129–142. Springer, Heidelberg (2010). https://doi.org/10.1007/978-3-642-14577-3_12

[SW14]   Sahai, A., Waters, B.: How to use indistinguishability obfuscation: deniable encryption, and more. In: STOC, pp. 475–484 (2014)

[XY04]   Xu, S., Yung, M.: Accountable ring signatures: a smart card approach. In: Quisquater, J.J., Paradinas, P., Deswarte, Y., El Kalam, A.A. (eds.) CARDIS 2004. IFIPAICT, vol. 153, pp. 271–286. Springer, Boston (2004). https://doi.org/10.1007/1-4020-8147-2_18

Two-Party ECDSA from Hash Proof Systems and Efficient Instantiations

Guilhem Castagnos[1(✉)], Dario Catalano[2(✉)], Fabien Laguillaumie[3],
Federico Savasta[2,4], and Ida Tucker[3]

[1] Université de Bordeaux, Inria, CNRS, IMB UMR 5251, F-33405 Talence, France
guilhem.castagnos@math-u.bordeaux.fr
[2] Università di Catania, Catania, Italy
catalano@dmi.unict.it
[3] Univ Lyon, EnsL, UCBL, CNRS, Inria, LIP, F-69342 Lyon Cedex 07, France
[4] Scuola Superiore di Catania, Catania, Italy

Abstract. ECDSA is a widely adopted digital signature standard. Unfortunately, efficient distributed variants of this primitive are notoriously hard to achieve and known solutions often require expensive zero knowledge proofs to deal with malicious adversaries. For the two party case, Lindell [Lin17] recently managed to get an efficient solution which, to achieve simulation-based security, relies on an interactive, non standard, assumption on Paillier's cryptosystem. In this paper we generalize Lindell's solution using hash proof systems. The main advantage of our generic method is that it results in a simulation-based security proof without resorting to non-standard interactive assumptions.

Moving to concrete constructions, we show how to instantiate our framework using class groups of imaginary quadratic fields. Our implementations show that the practical impact of dropping such interactive assumptions is minimal. Indeed, while for 128-bit security our scheme is marginally slower than Lindell's, for 256-bit security it turns out to be better both in key generation and signing time. Moreover, in terms of communication cost, our implementation significantly reduces both the number of rounds and the transmitted bits without exception.

1 Introduction

Threshold cryptography [Des88, DF90, GJKR96, SG98, Sho00, Boy86, CH89, MR04] allows n users to share a common key in such a way that any subset of t parties can use this key to decrypt or sign, while any coalition of less than t can do nothing. The key feature of this paradigm is that it allows to use the shared key without explicitly reconstructing it in the clear. This means a subset of t parties have to actively participate in the protocol whenever the secret key is used.

Applications of threshold cryptography range from contexts where many signers need to agree to sign one common document to distributed scenarios where sensitive documents should become accessible only by a quorum. This versatility sparked intense research efforts that, mainly in the decade from the early 1990s

© International Association for Cryptologic Research 2019
A. Boldyreva and D. Micciancio (Eds.): CRYPTO 2019, LNCS 11694, pp. 191–221, 2019.
https://doi.org/10.1007/978-3-030-26954-8_7

to the early 2000s, produced efficient threshold versions of most commonly used cryptographic schemes. Recent years have seen renewed interest in the field (e.g. [GGN16, Lin17, GG18, DKLs18, LN18, GG18, DKLs19]) for several reasons. First a number of start-up companies are using this technology to protect keys in real life applications [Ser, Unb, Sep]. Moreover, Bitcoin and other cryptocurrencies – for which security breaches can result in concrete financial losses – use ECDSA as underlying digital signature scheme. While multisignature-based countermeasures are built-in to Bitcoin, they offer less flexibility and introduce anonymity and scalability issues (see [GGN16]). Finally, some of the schemes developed twenty years ago are not as efficient as current applications want them to be. This is the case, for instance, for ECDSA/DSA signatures. Indeed, while for many other schemes fast threshold variants are known (e.g. RSA decryption/signing and ECIES decryption) constructing efficient threshold variant of these signatures proved to be much harder. The main reason for this unfair distribution seems to result from the inversion step that requires one to compute $k^{-1} \bmod q$ from an unknown k. To explain why this is the case, let us first briefly recall how ECDSA actually works[1]. The public key is an elliptic curve point Q and the signing key is x, such that $Q \leftarrow xP$, where P is a generator of the elliptic curve group of points of order q. To sign a message m one first hashes it using some suitable hash function H and then proceeds according to the following algorithm

1. Choose k random in $\mathbf{Z}/q\mathbf{Z}$
2. Compute $R \leftarrow kP$
3. Let $r \leftarrow r_x \bmod q$ where $R = (r_x, r_y)$
4. Set $s \leftarrow k^{-1}(H(m) + rx) \bmod q$
5. Output (r, s)

Now, the natural approach to make the above algorithm distributed would be to share x additively among the participants and then start a multiparty computation protocol to produce the signature. In the two party case, this means that players start with shares x_1 and x_2 such that $Q = (x_1 + x_2)P$. The players can then proceed by generating random shares k_1, k_2 such that $R = (k_1 + k_2)P$. At this point, however, it is not clear how to compute, efficiently, shares k'_1, k'_2 such that $k'_1 + k'_2 = k'^{-1} \bmod q$.

Starting from [MR04] two party ECDSA signature protocols started adopting a less common *multiplicative* sharing both for x and k. The basic idea of these constructions is very simple. Players start holding shares x_1, x_2 such that $Q = x_1 x_2 P = xP$. Whenever a new signature has to be generated they generate random k_1, k_2 such that $R = k_1 k_2 P = kP$. This immediately allows to get shares of the inverse k' as clearly $(k_1)^{-1}(k_2)^{-1} = (k_1 k_2)^{-1} \bmod q$. As a final ingredient, the parties use Paillier's homomorphic encryption to secretly add their shares and complete the signature. For instance, player P_1 computes $c_1 \leftarrow \mathsf{Enc}((k_1)^{-1}H(m))$ and $c_2 \leftarrow \mathsf{Enc}((k_1)^{-1}x_1 r)$. P_2 can then complete the signature,

---

[1] From now on we will focus on the elliptic curve variant of the scheme, as this is the most commonly used scheme in applications. We stress that our reasoning apply to the basic DSA case as well.

using the homomorphic properties of the scheme as follows

$$c \leftarrow c_1^{k_2^{-1}} c_2^{k_2^{-1} x_2} = \mathsf{Enc}(k^{-1}H(m))\mathsf{Enc}(k^{-1}xr) = \mathsf{Enc}(k^{-1}(H(m) + xr))$$

P_2 concludes the protocol by sending back c to P_1. Now, if P_1 also knows the decryption key, he can extract the signature $s \leftarrow k^{-1}(H(m) + xr))$ from c.

However, proving that each party followed the protocol correctly turns out to be hard. Initial attempts [MR04] addressed this via expensive zero knowledge proofs. More recently Lindell in [Lin17] managed to provide a much simpler and efficient protocol. The crucial idea of Lindell's protocol is the observation that, in the above two party ECDSA signing protocol, dishonest parties can create very little trouble. Indeed, if in a preliminary phase P_2 receives both Paillier's encryption key *and* an encryption $\mathsf{Enc}(x_1)$ of P_1's share of the secret signing key, essentially, all a corrupted P_1 can do is participate in the generation of $R \leftarrow k_1 k_2 P$. Notice however that the latter is just the well established Diffie-Hellman protocol for which very efficient and robust protocols exist.

On the other hand, if P_2 is corrupted all she can do (except again participate in the generation of R) is to create a bad c as a final response for P_1. However, while P_2 can certainly try that, this would be easy to detect by simply checking the validity of the resulting signature.

Turning this nice intuition into a formal proof induces some caveats though. A first problem comes from the fact that Paillier's plaintexts space is $\mathbf{Z}/N\mathbf{Z}$ (N is a large composite) whereas ECDSA signatures live in $\mathbf{Z}/q\mathbf{Z}$ (q is prime). Thus to avoid inconsistencies one needs to make sure that N is taken large enough so that no wraps around occur during the whole signature generation process. This also means that, when sending $\mathsf{Enc}(x_1)$ to P_2, P_1 needs to prove that the plaintext x_1 is in the right range (*i.e.*, sufficiently small).

A more subtle issue arises from the use of Paillier's encryption in the proof. Indeed, if one wants to use the scheme to argue indistinguishability of an adversary's view in real and simulated executions, it seems necessary to set up a reduction to the indistinguishability of Paillier's cryptosystem. This means one must design a proof technique that manages to successfully use Paillier's scheme *without* knowing the corresponding secret key. In Lindell's protocol the issue arises when designing the simulator's strategy against a corrupted player P_2. In such a case, P_2 might indeed send a wrong ciphertext c (*i.e.*, one that does not encrypt a signature) that the simulator simply cannot recognize as bad.

Lindell [Lin17] proposes two alternative proofs to overcome this. The first one relies on a game-based definition and avoids the problem by simply allowing the simulator to abort with a probability that depends on the number of issued signatures q_s. This results in a proof of security that is not tight (as the reduction actually looses a factor q_s). The second proof is simulation based, avoids the aborts, but requires the introduction of a new (interactive) non standard assumption regarding Paillier's encryption. Thus, it is fair to say that, in spite of recent progress in the area, the following question remains open.

Is it possible to devise a two party ECDSA signing protocol which is practical (both in terms of computational efficiency and in terms of bandwidth consumption), does not require interactive assumptions and allows for a tight security reduction?[2]

1.1 Our Contribution

In this paper we provide a positive answer to the question above. In this sense, our contribution is twofold.

First, we provide a generic construction for two-party ECDSA signing from hash proof systems (HPS). Our solution can be seen as a generalization of Lindell's scheme [Lin17] to the general setting of HPSs that are homomorphic in the sense of [HO09]. This generic solution is not efficient enough for practical applications as, for instance, it employs general purpose zero knowledge as underlying building block. Still, beyond providing a clean, general framework which is of interest in its own right, it allows us to abstract away the properties we want to realize. In particular, our new protocol allows for a proof of security that is tight and does not require artificial interactive assumptions when proving simulation security. Indeed, in encryption schemes based on HPSs, indistinguishability of ciphertexts is not compromised by the challenger knowing the scheme's secret keys as it relies on a computational assumption and a statistical argument.

The correctness of our protocol follows from homomorphic properties that we require of the underlying HPS. We define the notion of *homomorphically-extended projective hash families* which ensure the homomorphic properties of the HPS hold for any public key sampled from an efficiently recognisable set, thus no zero-knowledge proofs are required for the public key.

Towards efficient solutions, we then show how to instantiate our (homomorphic) HPS construction using class groups of imaginary quadratic fields. Although the devastating attack from [CL09] shows that large families of protocols built over such groups are insecure, Castagnos and Laguillaumie [CL15] showed that, if carefully designed, discrete logarithm based cryptosystems within such groups are still possible and allow for very efficient solutions. Algorithms to compute discrete logarithms in such groups have been extensively studied since the 80's and the best ones known to date have a subexponential complexity[3] of $\mathcal{O}(L[1/2, o(1)])$ (compared to an $\mathcal{O}(L[1/3, o(1)])$ complexity for factorisation or discrete logarithm computation in finite fields). In [BH03], Bauer and Hamdy also showed that, for the specific case of imaginary quadratic fields, better complexities seem unlikely. Thus, the resulting schemes benefit from (asymptotically) shorter keys. Moreover, interest in the area has recently been renewed as it allows versatile and efficient solutions such as encryption switching protocols [CIL17], inner product functional encryption [CLT18] or verifiable delay functions [BBBF18, Wes19].

---

[2] We note here that the very recent two party protocol of [DKLs18] is very fast in signing time and only relies on the ECDSA assumption. However its bandwidth consumption is much higher than [Lin17].

[3] $L[\alpha, c]$ denotes $L_{\alpha,c}(x) := \exp(c \log(x)^\alpha \log(\log(x))^{1-\alpha})$.

Concretely, the main feature of the Castagnos and Laguillaumie cryptosystem and its variants (CL from now on) is that they rely on the existence of groups with associated easy discrete log subgroups, for which hard decision problems can be defined. More precisely, in [CL15] there exist a cyclic group $G := \langle g \rangle$ of order qs where s is unknown, q is prime and $\gcd(q, s) = 1$, and an associated cyclic subgroup of order q, $F := \langle f \rangle$. Denoting with $G^q := \langle g_q \rangle$ the subgroup of q-th powers in G (of unknown order s), one has $G = F \times G^q$, and one can define an hard subgroup membership problem. Informally, and deferring for later the necessary mathematical details, this allows to build a linearly homomorphic encryption scheme where the plaintext space is $\mathbf{Z}/q\mathbf{Z}$ for arbitrarily large q. This also means that if one uses the very same q underlying the ECDSA signature, one gets a concrete instantiation of our general protocol which naturally avoids all the inefficiencies resulting from N and q being different!

We remark that, similarly to Lindell's solution, our schemes require P_2 to hold an encryption $\mathsf{Enc}(x_1)$ of P_1's share of the secret key. As for Lindell's case, this imposes a somewhat heavy key registration phase in which P_1 has to prove, among other things, that the public key is correctly generated. While, in our setting we can achieve this without resorting to expensive range proofs, difficulties arise from the fact that (1) we work with groups of unknown order and (2) we cannot assume that all ciphertexts are valid (*i.e.*, actually encrypt a message)[4]. We address this by developing a new proof that solves both issues at the same time. Our proof is inspired by the Girault *et al.* [GPS06] identification protocol but introduces new ideas to adapt it to our setting and to make it a proof of knowledge. As for Lindell's case, it uses a binary challenge, which implies that the proof has to be repeated t times to get soundness error 2^t. We believe that it should be possible to enlarge the challenge space using techniques similar to those [CKY09] adapted to work in the context of class groups. Exploring the actual feasibility of this idea is left as a future work. Clearly, advances in this direction would lead to substantial efficiency improvements.

As final contribution, we propose a C implementation of our protocol[5]. Our results show that our improved security guarantees come almost at no additional cost. Indeed, while our scheme is slightly slower (by a factor 1.5 for key generation and 3.5 for signing) for 128-bit security level, we are actually better for larger parameters: for 256-bit security, we are more efficient both in terms of key generation and signing time (by respective factors of 4.2 and 1.3).

Intuitively, this behavior is due to the fact that our interactive key generation requires fewer exponentiations than that of Lindell's protocol (160 vs. 360), but an exponentiation in a class group is more expensive than an exponentiation in $\mathbf{Z}/n\mathbf{Z}$. The effect of the $L_{1/2}$ complexity and the fewer number of exponentiations starts at 192 bit of security. In terms of bandwidth, our protocol dramatically improves the communication cost by *factors varying from 5 (112 bit security) to 10 (256 bit security)* for key generation, and from 1.2 to 2.1 for signatures. It reduces the number of rounds from 175 (in Lindell's protocol) to 126 for the

---

[4] For Paillier's scheme, used in [Lin17], this is not an issue: every ciphertext is valid.
[5] We also re-implemented Lindell's protocol to ensure a fair comparison.

key generation process (the two signatures have the same number of rounds). We refer to Sect. 5 for precise implementation considerations and timings.

As a final remark, our HPS methods also allow a concrete implementation based on Paillier's decisional composite residuosity assumption, competitive with Lindell's for 112 and 128 bits of security as detailed in [CCLST19, Sect. 6].

2   Preliminaries

Notations. For a distribution $\mathcal{D}$, we write $d \hookleftarrow \mathcal{D}$ to refer to d being sampled from $\mathcal{D}$ and $b \xleftarrow{\$} B$ if b is sampled uniformly in the set B. In an interactive protocol IP, between parties P_1 and P_2, we denote by $\mathsf{IP}\langle x_1; x_2 \rangle \to \langle y_1; y_2 \rangle$ the joint execution of parties $\{P_i\}_{i \in \{1,2\}}$ in the protocol, with respective inputs x_i, and where P_i's private output at the end of the execution is y_i.

The Elliptic Curve Digital Signature Algorithm. ECDSA is the elliptic curve analogue of the Digital Signature Algorithm (DSA). It was put forth by Vanstone [Van92] and accepted as ISO, ANSI, IEEE and FIPS standards. It works in a group $(\mathbb{G}, +)$ of prime order q (of say μ bits) of points of an elliptic curve over a finite field, generated by P and consists of the following algorithms.

$\mathsf{KeyGen}(\mathbb{G}, q, P) \to (x, Q)$ where $x \xleftarrow{\$} \mathbf{Z}/q\mathbf{Z}$ is the secret signing key and $Q \leftarrow xP$ is the public verification key.

$\mathsf{Sign}(x, m) \to (r, s)$ where r and s are computed as follows:
  1. Compute m': the μ leftmost bits of $\mathsf{SHA256}(m)$ where m is to be signed.
  2. Sample $k \xleftarrow{\$} (\mathbf{Z}/q\mathbf{Z})^*$ and compute $R \leftarrow kP$; denote $R = (r_x, r_y)$ and let $r \leftarrow r_x \mod q$. If $r = 0$ chose another k.
  3. Compute $s \leftarrow k^{-1} \cdot (m' + r \cdot x) \mod q$

$\mathsf{Verif}(Q, m, (r, s)) \to \{0, 1\}$ indicating whether or not the signature is accepted.

Two-Party ECDSA. This consists of the following interactive protocols:

$\mathsf{IKeyGen}\langle (\mathbb{G}, q, P); (\mathbb{G}, q, P) \rangle \to \langle (x_1, Q); (x_2, Q) \rangle$ such that $\mathsf{KeyGen}(\mathbb{G}, q, P) \to (x, Q)$ where x_1 and x_2 are shares of x.

$\mathsf{ISign}\langle (x_1, m); (x_2, m) \rangle \to \langle \emptyset; (r, s) \rangle$ **or** $\langle (r, s); \emptyset \rangle$ **or** $\langle (r, s); (r, s) \rangle$ where $\emptyset$ is the empty output, signifying that one of the parties may have no output and $\mathsf{Sign}(x, m) \to (r, s)$.

The verification algorithm is non interactive and identical to that of ECDSA.

Interactive Zero-Knowledge Proof Systems. A zero-knowledge proof system (P, V) for a language $\mathcal{L}$ is an interactive protocol between two probabilistic algorithms: a prover P and a polynomial-time verifier V. Informally P, detaining a witness for a given statement, must convince V that it is true without revealing anything other to V. See [Gol01] for interactive proofs and [GMR89] for zero-knowledge.

Simulation-Based Security and Ideal Functionalities. To prove a protocol is secure, one must first define what *secure* means. Basically, the Ideal/Real paradigm is to imagine what properties one would have in an ideal world; then if a real world (constructed) protocol has similar properties it is considered secure. We consider static adversaries, that choose which parties are corrupted before the protocol begins. [Lin16] provides a detailed explanation of the simulation paradigm.

We will use ideal functionalities for commitments, zero-knowledge proofs of knowledge (ZKPoK) and commitments to non interactive zero-knowledge (NIZK) proofs of knowledge between two parties P_1 and P_2. We give the intuition behind these ideal functionalities with the example of ZKPoK. We consider the case of a prover P_i with $i \in \{1, 2\}$ who wants to prove the knowledge of a witness w for an element x which ensures that (x, w) satisfy the relation R, *i.e.* $(x, w) \in$ R. In an ideal world we can imagine an honest and trustful third party, which can communicate with both P_i and P_{3-i}. In this ideal scenario, P_i could give (x, w) to this trusted party, the latter would then check if $(x, w) \in$ R and tell P_{3-i} if this is true or false. In the real world we do not have such trusted parties and must substitute them with a cryptographic protocol between P_1 and P_2. Roughly speaking, the Ideal/Real paradigm requires that whatever information an adversary $\mathcal{A}$ (corrupting either P_1 or P_2) could recover in the real world, it can also recover in the ideal world. The trusted third party can be viewed as the ideal functionality and we denote it by $\mathcal{F}$. If some protocol satisfies the above property regarding this functionality, we call it secure.

Formally, we denote $\mathcal{F}\langle x_1; x_2 \rangle \rightarrow \langle y_1; y_2 \rangle$ the joint execution of the parties via the functionality $\mathcal{F}$, with respective inputs x_i, and respective private outputs at the end of the execution y_i. Each transmitted message is labelled with a session identifier *sid*, which identifies an iteration of the functionality. The *ideal ZKPoK functionality* [HL10, Sect. 6.5.3], denoted $\mathcal{F}_{zk}$, is defined for a relation R by $\mathcal{F}_{zk}\langle (x, w); \emptyset \rangle \rightarrow \langle \emptyset; (x, \mathsf{R}(x, w)) \rangle$, where $\emptyset$ is the empty output, signifying that the first party receives no output (cf. Fig. 1).

- Upon receiving (**prove**, *sid*, x, w) from a party P_i (for $i \in \{1, 2\}$): if $(x, w) \notin$ R or *sid* has been previously used then ignore the message. Otherwise, send (**proof**, *sid*, x) to party P_{3-i}

Fig. 1. The $\mathcal{F}_{zk}^{\mathsf{R}}$ functionality

The *ideal commitment functionality*, denoted $\mathcal{F}_{com}$, is depicted in Fig. 2. We also use an ideal functionality $\mathcal{F}_{com-zk}^{\mathsf{R}}$ for *commitments to NIZK proofs* for a relation R (cf. Fig. 3). Essentially, this is a commitment functionality, where the committed value is a NIZK proof.

The Ideal Functionality for Two-Party ECDSA. The ideal functionality $\mathscr{F}_{ECDSA}$ (cf. Fig. 4) consists of two functions: a key generation function, called once, and a signing function, called an arbitrary number of times with the generated keys.

- Upon receiving (commit, sid, x) from party P_i (for $i \in \{1, 2\}$), record (sid, i, x) and send (receipt, sid) to party P_{3-i}. If some (commit, $sid, *$) is already stored, then ignore the message.
- Upon receiving (decommit, sid) from party P_i , if (sid, i, x) is recorded then send (decommit, sid, x) to party P_{3-i}.

Fig. 2. The $\mathscr{F}_{com}$ functionality

- Upon receiving (com $-$ prove, sid, x, w) from a party P_i (for $i \in \{1, 2\}$): if $(x, w) \notin$ R or sid has been previously used then ignore the message. Otherwise, store (sid, i, x) and send (proof $-$ receipt, sid) to P_{3-i}.
- Upon receiving (decom $-$ proof, sid) from a party P_i (for $i \in \{1, 2\}$): if (sid, i, x) has been stored then send (decom $-$ proof, sid, x) to P_{3-i}

Fig. 3. The $\mathscr{F}_{com-zk}^{R}$ functionality

Consider an Elliptic-curve group $\mathbb{G}$ of order q with generator a point P, then:
- Upon receiving KeyGen($\mathbb{G}, P, q$) from both P_1 and P_2:
    1. Generate an *ECDSA* key pair (Q, x), where $x \xleftarrow{\$} (\mathbf{Z}/q\mathbf{Z})^*$ is chosen randomly and Q is computed as $Q \leftarrow x \cdot P$.
    2. Choose a hash function $H_q : \{0, 1\}^* \to \{0, 1\}^{\lfloor \log |q| \rfloor}$, and store $(\mathbb{G}, P, q, H_q, x)$.
    3. Send Q (and H_q) to both P_1 and P_2.
    4. Ignore future calls to KeyGen.
- Upon receiving Sign(sid, m) from both P_1 and P_2, where keys have already been generated from a call to Keygen and sid has not been previously used, compute an *ECDSA* signature (r, s) on m, and send it to both P_1 and P_2. (To do this, choose a random $k \xleftarrow{\$} (\mathbf{Z}/q\mathbf{Z})^*$, compute $(r_x, r_y) \leftarrow k \cdot P$ and set $r \leftarrow r_x \mod q$. Finally, compute $s \leftarrow k^{-1}(H_q(m) + rx)$ and output (r, s).)

Fig. 4. The $\mathscr{F}_{ECDSA}$ functionality

3   Two-Party ECDSA from Hash Proof Systems

In this section we provide a generic construction for two-party ECDSA signing from hash proof systems (HPS) which we prove secure in the simulation based model. Throughout the section we consider the group of points of an elliptic curve $\mathbb{G}$ of order q, generated by P. In Subsect. 3.1, we first recall some basic definitions on the HPS framework from [CS02], before defining the specific properties we require for our construction in Subsect. 3.2, in particular, to guarantee correctness of the protocol (in order for party P_2 to be able to perform homomorphic operations on ciphertexts provided by P_1, which are encryptions of elements in $\mathbf{Z}/q\mathbf{Z}$) the HPS must be homomorphic; and for security to hold against malicious adversaries we also require that the subset membership problem underlying the HPS be hard, and that the HPS be smooth. We note that diverse group systems (often used as a foundation for constructions of HPSs) imply all the aforementioned properties. Such HPSs define linearly homomorphic encryption schemes as described in Subsect. 3.3. Finally, before presenting the overall two party signing protocol and proving its security, we describe the zero-knowledge proofs (ZKP) related to the aforementioned HPSs, and justify that they fulfil the $\mathcal{F}_{com}/\mathcal{F}_{com-zk}$ hybrid model.

3.1 Background on Hash Proof Systems

Hash proof systems were introduced in [CS02] as a generalisation of the techniques used in [CS98] to design chosen ciphertext secure public-key encryption schemes. Consider a set of words $\mathcal{X}$, an NP language $\mathcal{L} \subset \mathcal{X}$ s.t. $\mathcal{L} := \{x \in \mathcal{X} \mid w \in \mathcal{W} : (x,w) \in R\}$ where R is the relation defining the language, $\mathcal{L}$ is the language of true statements in $\mathcal{X}$, and for $(x,w) \in R$, $w \in \mathcal{W}$ is a witness for $x \in \mathcal{L}$. The set $(\mathcal{X}, \mathcal{L}, \mathcal{W}, R)$ defines an instance of a subset membership problem, i.e. the problem of deciding if an element $x \in \mathcal{X}$ is in $\mathcal{L}$ or in $\mathcal{X} \backslash \mathcal{L}$.

A HPS associates a projective hash family (PHF) to such a subset membership problem. The PHF defines a key generation algorithm PHF.KeyGen which outputs a secret hashing key hk sampled from distribution of hashing keys $\mathcal{D}_{hk}$ over a hash key space K_{hk}, and a public projection key $hp \leftarrow \alpha(hk)$ in projection key space K_{hp} (where $\alpha : K_{hk} \mapsto K_{hp}$ is an efficient auxiliary function). The secret hashing key hk defines a hash function $\mathcal{H}_{hk} : \mathcal{X} \mapsto \Pi$, and hp allows for the (public) evaluation of the hash function on words $x \in \mathcal{L}$, i.e. $\mathcal{H}_{hp}(x,w) = \mathcal{H}_{hk}(x)$ for $(x,w) \in R$. A projective hash family PHF is thus defined by $\mathsf{PHF} := (\{\mathcal{H}_{hk}\}_{hk \in K_{hk}}, K_{hk}, \mathcal{X}, \mathcal{L}, \Pi, K_{hp}, \alpha)$.

3.2 Required Properties

δ_s-*Smoothness.* The standard *smoothness* property of a PHF requires that for any $x \notin \mathcal{L}$, the value $\mathcal{H}_{hk}(x)$ be uniformly distributed knowing hp. In this work messages will be encoded in a subgroup $\mathcal{F}$ of Π of order q, indeed, for integration with ECDSA it must hold that the group in which the message is encoded has order q, since the message space is dictated by the order of the elliptic curve group $\mathbb{G}$. In some instantiations $\mathcal{F} = \Pi$, but $\mathcal{F}$ may also be a strict subgroup of Π. For $m \in \mathbf{Z}/q\mathbf{Z}$ we denote $\mathsf{Encode}(m)$ the encoding of m in $\mathcal{F}$, where $\mathsf{Encode} : (\mathbf{Z}/q\mathbf{Z}, +) \mapsto (\mathcal{F}, \cdot)$ is an efficient isomorphism. We denote Decode the inverse isomorphism, which must also be efficiently computable.

If $\mathcal{F} \subsetneq \Pi$, we require smoothness over $\mathcal{X}$ on $\mathcal{F}$ [CS02, Subsect. 8.2.4]. A PHF is δ_s-smooth over $\mathcal{X}$ on $\mathcal{F}$ if for any $x \in \mathcal{X} \backslash \mathcal{L}$, a random $\pi \in \mathcal{F}$ and a randomly sampled hashing key $\mathsf{hk} \hookleftarrow \mathcal{D}_{\mathsf{hk}}$, the distributions $\mathcal{U} := \{x, \alpha(\mathsf{hk}), \pi \cdot \mathcal{H}_{\mathsf{hk}}(x)\}$ and $\mathcal{V} := \{x, \alpha(\mathsf{hk}), \mathcal{H}_{\mathsf{hk}}(x)\}$ are δ_s-close.

$\delta_{\mathcal{L}}-Hard\ Subset\ Membership\ Problem.$ For security to hold $(\mathcal{X}, \mathcal{L}, \mathcal{W}, \mathsf{R})$ must be an instance of a hard subset membership problem, i.e. no polynomial time algorithm can distinguish random elements of $\mathcal{X} \backslash \mathcal{L}$ from those of $\mathcal{L}$ with significant advantage. We say $(\mathcal{X}, \mathcal{L}, \mathcal{W}, \mathsf{R})$ is a $\delta_{\mathcal{L}}-$hard subset membership problem if $\delta_{\mathcal{L}}$ is the maximal advantage of any polynomial time adversary in distinguishing random elements of $\mathcal{X} \backslash \mathcal{L}$ from those of $\mathcal{L}$.

Linearly Homomorphic PHF. In order for the homomorphic operations performed by P_2 to hold in the two party ECDSA protocol, we require that the PHF also be homomorphic as defined in [HO09].

Definition 1 ([HO09]). *The family* $\mathsf{PHF} := (\{\mathcal{H}_{\mathsf{hk}}\}_{\mathsf{hk} \in K_{\mathsf{hk}}}, K_{\mathsf{hk}}, \mathcal{X}, \mathcal{L}, \Pi, K_{\mathsf{hp}}, \alpha)$ *is homomorphic if* $(\mathcal{X}, \star)$ *and* $(\Pi, \cdot)$ *are groups, and for all* $\mathsf{hk} \in K_{\mathsf{hk}}$, *and* $u_1, u_2 \in \mathcal{X}$, *we have* $\mathcal{H}_{\mathsf{hk}}(u_1) \cdot \mathcal{H}_{\mathsf{hk}}(u_2) = \mathcal{H}_{\mathsf{hk}}(u_1 \star u_2)$, *that is to say* $\mathcal{H}_{\mathsf{hk}}$ *is a homomorphism for each* hk.

This clearly implies that for $\mathsf{hp} \leftarrow \alpha(\mathsf{hk})$ the public projective hash function is linearly homomorphic with respect to elements $u_1, u_2 \in \mathcal{L}$.

Homomorphically Extended PHF. Note that the co-domain of α, which specifies the set of valid projection keys, may not be efficiently recognisable. Though we do not require – as did the protocol of [Lin17] – a costly ZKPoK of the secret key associated to the public key, it is essential in our protocol that even if a public key is chosen maliciously (i.e. there does not exist $\mathsf{hk} \in K_{\mathsf{hk}}$ such that $\mathsf{hp} \leftarrow \alpha(\mathsf{hk})$, which may go unnoticed to honest parties in the protocol), the homomorphic properties of the public projective hash function still hold. We thus require that the co-domain of α, which defines valid projection keys, be contained in an *efficiently recognisable* space K'_{hp}, such that for all $\mathsf{hp}' \in K'_{\mathsf{hp}}$, $\mathcal{H}_{\mathsf{hp}'}$ is a homomorphism (respectively to its inputs in $\mathcal{L}$).

Definition 2 (Homomorphically extended PHF). *We say that the family* $\mathsf{PHF} := (\{\mathcal{H}_{\mathsf{hk}}\}_{\mathsf{hk} \in K_{\mathsf{hk}}}, K_{\mathsf{hk}}, \mathcal{X}, \mathcal{L}, \Pi, K_{\mathsf{hp}}, K'_{\mathsf{hp}}, \alpha)$ *is homomorphically extended if* $\mathsf{PHF} := (\{\mathcal{H}_{\mathsf{hk}}\}_{\mathsf{hk} \in K_{\mathsf{hk}}}, K_{\mathsf{hk}}, \mathcal{X}, \mathcal{L}, \Pi, K_{\mathsf{hp}}, \alpha)$ *is a homomorphic PHF and that there exists an efficiently recognizable space* $K'_{\mathsf{hp}} \supseteq K_{\mathsf{hp}}$ *such that for any* $\mathsf{hp}' \in K'_{\mathsf{hp}}$, *the projective hash function associated to* hp' *is a homomorphism (respectively to its inputs in* $\mathcal{L}$).

ECDSA-Friendly HPS. We here define the notion of an ECDSA-friendly HPS, essentially it is a HPS which meets all of the aforementioned properties, and which suffices to ensure simulation based security in the protocol of Subsect. 3.5.

Definition 3 ($\delta_s/\delta_{\mathcal{L}}-$**ECDSA-friendly HPS**). *Let* $\mathcal{X}, \Pi$ *and* $\mathcal{F}$ *be groups such that* $\mathcal{F}$ *is a subgroup of* Π *of prime order* q, *and such that there exists* *an efficient isomorphism* Encode : $(\mathbf{Z}/q\mathbf{Z}, +) \mapsto (\mathcal{F}, \cdot)$, *whose inverse* Decode *is also efficiently computable. A* $\delta_s/\delta_{\mathcal{L}}-ECDSA$-friendly HPS is a HPS which *associates to a* $\delta_{\mathcal{L}}-hard$ *subset membership problem a homomorphically extended projective hash family* $\mathsf{PHF} := (\{\mathcal{H}_{\mathsf{hk}}\}_{\mathsf{hk} \in K_{\mathsf{hk}}}, K_{\mathsf{hk}}, \mathcal{X}, \mathcal{L}, \Pi, K_{\mathsf{hp}}, K'_{\mathsf{hp}}, \alpha)$ *which is* $\delta_s-smooth$ *over* $\mathcal{X}$ *on* $\mathcal{F}$.

3.3 Resulting Encryption Scheme

We use the standard chosen plaintext attack secure encryption scheme which results from a HPS [CS02]. The key generation algorithm simply runs PHF.KeyGen and sets $\mathsf{hk} \in K_{\mathsf{hk}}$ as the secret key, and the associated public key is $\mathsf{hp} \leftarrow \alpha(\mathsf{hk})$. Encryption of a plaintext message m in $\mathbf{Z}/q\mathbf{Z}$ is done by sampling a random pair $(u, w) \in \mathsf{R}$ and computing $\mathsf{Enc}(\mathsf{hp}, m) \leftarrow (u, \mathcal{H}_{\mathsf{hp}}(u, w) \cdot \mathsf{Encode}(m))$. To specify the randomness used in the encryption algorithm, we sometimes use the notation $\mathsf{Enc}((u, w); (\mathsf{hp}, m))$. To decrypt a ciphertext $(u, e) \in \mathcal{X} \times \Pi$ with secret key hk do: $\mathsf{Dec}(\mathsf{hk}, (u, e)) \leftarrow \mathsf{Decode}(\frac{e}{\mathcal{H}_{\mathsf{hk}}(u)})$. The scheme is indistinguishable under chosen plaintext attacks assuming both the smoothness of the HPS and the hardness of the underlying subset membership problem.

Homomorphic Properties. Given encryptions (u_1, e_1) and (u_2, e_2) of respectively m_1 and m_2, and $a \in \mathbf{Z}$, we require that there exist two procedures EvalSum and EvalScal such that $\mathsf{Dec}(\mathsf{hk}, \mathsf{EvalSum}(\mathsf{hp}, (u_1, e_1), (u_2, e_2))) = m_1 + m_2$ and $\mathsf{Dec}(\mathsf{hk}, \mathsf{EvalScal}(\mathsf{hp}, (u_1, e_1), a)) = a \cdot m_1$; which is the case if the PHF is homomorphic.

3.4 Zero-Knowledge Proofs

Proofs of Knowledge. We use the $\mathcal{F}_{\mathsf{zk}}$, $\mathcal{F}_{\mathsf{com-zk}}$ hybrid model. Ideal ZK functionalities are used for the following relations, were the parameters of the elliptic curve $(\mathbb{G}, P, q)$ are implicit public inputs:

1. $R_{DL} := \{(Q, w) | Q = wP\}$, proves the knowledge of the discrete log of an elliptic curve point.
2. $R_{\mathsf{HPS-DL}} := \{(\mathsf{hp}, (c_1, c_2), Q_1); (x_1, w) | (c_1, c_2) = \mathsf{Enc}((u, w); (\mathsf{hp}, x_1)) \wedge (c_1, w) \in \mathsf{R} \wedge Q_1 = x_1 P\}$, proves the knowledge of the randomness used for encryption, and of the value x_1 which is both encrypted in the ciphertext (c_1, c_2) and the discrete log of the elliptic curve point Q_1.

The functionalities $\mathcal{F}_{\mathsf{zk}}^{R_{DL}}$, $\mathcal{F}_{\mathsf{com-zk}}^{R_{DL}}$ can be instantiated using Schnorr proofs [Sch91]. For the $R_{\mathsf{HPS-DL}}$ proof, Lindell in [Lin17] uses a proof of language membership as opposed to a proof of knowledge. Though his technique is quite generic, it cannot be used in our setting. Indeed, his approach requires that the ciphertext be *valid*, which means that the element c must be decryptable. As Lindell uses Paillier's encryption scheme, any element of $(\mathbf{Z}/N^2\mathbf{Z})^{\times}$ is a valid ciphertext. This is not the case for a HPS-based encryption scheme, since it incorporates redundancy so that any pair in $\mathcal{X} \times \Pi$ is not a valid ciphertext.

For our instantiations, we will introduce specific and efficient proofs. Note that in any case, we needn't prove that $x_1 \in \mathbf{Z}/q\mathbf{Z}$ since both the message space of our encryption scheme and the elliptic curve group $\mathbb{G}$ are of order q.

3.5 Two-Party ECDSA Signing Protocol with Simulation-Based Security

We here provide our generic construction for two-party ECDSA signing from HPSs (Fig. 5), along with a proof that the protocol is secure in the Ideal/Real paradigm (Theorem 1). To this end, we must argue the indistinguishability of an adversary's view – corrupting either party P_1 or P_2 – in real and simulated executions. In Cramer-Shoup like encryption schemes (resulting from HPSs as described in Subsect. 3.3), the chosen plaintext attack indistinguishability of ciphertexts allows for the challenger in the security game to sample the secret hashing key hk, and compute the resulting projection key hp. Thus hk is *known* to the challenger. Indeed here, in order to prove indistinguishability, the challenger first replaces the random masking element $u \in \mathcal{L}$ in the original encryption scheme with an element sampled outside the language $u' \in \mathcal{X} \backslash \mathcal{L}$. Note that in order to perform this change the challenger *must* know the secret hashing key. The hardness of the subset membership problem ensures this goes unnoticed to any polynomial time adversary. Then the smoothness of the PHF allows one to replace the plaintext value by some random element from the plaintext space, thus guaranteeing the indistinguishability of the resulting encryption scheme. We insist on this point since in Lindell's protocol [Lin17], many issues arise from the use of Paillier's cryptosystem, for which the indistinguishability of ciphertexts no longer holds if the challenger knows the secret key. In particular this implies that in Lindell's game based proof, instead of letting the simulator use the Paillier secret key to decrypt the incoming ciphertext (and check the corrupted party P_2 did not send a different ciphertext c than that prescribed by the protocol), the simulator *guesses* when the adversary may have cheated by simulating an abort with a probability depending on the number of issued signatures. This results in a proof of security which is not tight.

Moreover, though this technique suffices for a game-based definition, it does not for simulation-based security definitions. Thus, in order to be able to prove their protocol using simulation, they use a rather non-standard assumption, called Paillier-EC assumption [Lin17, Appendix A]. Thanks to the framework we have chosen to adopt, we are able to avoid such an artificial interactive assumption. Moreover, should one write a game based proof for our construction, the security loss present in [Lin17] would not appear.

Finally we note that the correctness of our protocol follows from the fact Encode is an efficient isomorphism, and from the fact the hash function is linearly homomorphic for any public key in the efficiently recognisable space K'_{hp}.

Theorem 1. *Assume* HPS *is a* $\delta_s/\delta_{\mathcal{L}}-ECDSA\text{-}friendly$ *HPS then the protocol of Fig. 5 securely computes* $\mathcal{F}_{ECDSA}$ *in the* $(\mathcal{F}_{\mathsf{zk}}, \mathcal{F}_{\mathsf{com-zk}})$-*hybrid model in the presence of a malicious static adversary (under the ideal/real definition). Indeed there exists a simulator for the scheme such that no polynomial time adversary – having corrupted either* P_1 *or* P_2 *– can distinguish a real execution of the protocol from a simulated one with probability greater than* $2\delta_{\mathcal{L}} + \delta_s$.

Proof. In this proof, the simulator $\mathcal{S}$ only has access to an ideal functionality $\mathcal{F}_{ECDSA}$ for computing ECDSA signatures, so all it learns in the ideal world is the public key Q which it gets as output of the KeyGen phase from $\mathcal{F}_{ECDSA}$ and signatures (r, s) for messages m of its choice as output of the Sign phase. However in the real world, the adversary, having either corrupted P_1 or P_2 will also see all the interactions with the non corrupted party which lead to the computation of a signature. Thus $\mathcal{S}$ must be able to simulate $\mathcal{A}$'s view of these interactions, while only knowing the expected output. To this end $\mathcal{S}$ must set up with $\mathcal{A}$ the same public key Q that it received from $\mathcal{F}_{ECDSA}$, in order to be able to subsequently simulate interactively signing messages with $\mathcal{A}$, using the output of $\mathcal{F}_{ECDSA}$ from the Sign phase.

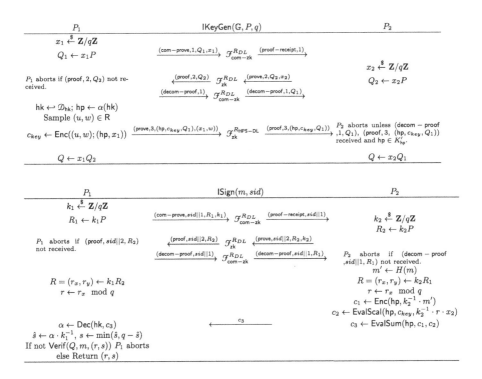

Fig. 5. Two-party ECDSA key generation and signing protocols from HPSs

$\mathcal{S}$ *Simulates* P_2 – *Corrupted* P_1: We first show that if an adversary $\mathcal{A}_1$ corrupts P_1, one can construct a simulator $\mathcal{S}$ s.t. the output distribution of $\mathcal{S}$ is indistinguishable from $\mathcal{A}_1$'s view in an interaction with an honest party P_2. The main difference here with the proof of [Lin17] arises from the fact we no longer use a ZKP from which $\mathcal{S}$ can extract the encryption scheme's secret key. Instead, $\mathcal{S}$ extracts the randomness used for encryption and the plaintext x_1 from the ZKPoK for $R_{\mathsf{HPS-DL}}$, which allows it to recompute the ciphertext and verify it obtains the expected value c_{key}. Moreover since the message space of our encryption scheme is $\mathbf{Z}/q\mathbf{Z}$, if $\mathscr{A}_1$ does not cheat in the proofs (which is guaranteed by the $(\mathscr{F}_{\mathsf{zk}}, \mathscr{F}_{\mathsf{com-zk}})$-hybrid model), the obtained distributions are identical in the ideal and real executions (as opposed to statistically close as in [Lin17]).

Key Generation Phase

1. Given input $\mathsf{KeyGen}(\mathbb{G}, P, q)$, the simulator $\mathscr{S}$ sends $\mathsf{KeyGen}(\mathbb{G}, P, q)$ to the ideal functionality $\mathscr{F}_{ECDSA}$ and receives back a public key Q.
2. $\mathscr{S}$ invokes $\mathscr{A}_1$ on input $\mathsf{IKeyGen}(\mathbb{G}, P, q)$ and receives the commitment to a proof of knowledge of x_1 such that $Q_1 = x_1 P$ denoted $(\mathsf{com - prove}, 1, Q_1, x_1)$ as $\mathscr{A}_1$ intends to send to $\mathscr{F}^{R_{DL}}_{\mathsf{com-zk}}$, such that $\mathscr{S}$ can extract x_1 and Q_1.
3. Using the extracted value x_1, $\mathscr{S}$ verifies that $Q_1 = x_1 P$. If so, it computes $Q_2 \leftarrow x_1^{-1} Q$ (using the value Q received from $\mathscr{F}_{ECDSA}$); otherwise $\mathscr{S}$ samples a random Q_2 from $\mathbb{G}$.
4. $\mathscr{S}$ sends $(\mathsf{proof}, 2, Q_2)$ to $\mathscr{A}_1$ as if sent by $\mathscr{F}^{R_{DL}}_{\mathsf{zk}}$ thereby $\mathscr{S}$ simulating a proof of knowledge of x_2 s.t. $Q_2 = x_2 P$.
5. $\mathscr{S}$ receives $(\mathsf{decom - proof}, 1)$ as $\mathscr{A}_1$ intends to send to $\mathscr{F}^{R_{DL}}_{\mathsf{com-zk}}$ and simulates P_2 aborting if $Q_1 \neq x_1 P$. $\mathscr{S}$ also receives $(\mathsf{prove}, 3, (\mathsf{hp}, c_{key}, Q_1), (x_1, w))$ as $\mathscr{A}_1$ intends to send to $\mathscr{F}^{R_{HPS-DL}}_{\mathsf{zk}}$.
6. $\mathscr{S}$ computes u from w such that $(u, w) \in \mathsf{R}$, and using the extracted value x_1 verifies that $c_{key} = \mathsf{Enc}((u, w); (\mathsf{hp}, x_1))$, and simulates P_2 aborting if not.
7. $\mathscr{S}$ sends $\mathsf{continue}$ to $\mathscr{F}_{ECDSA}$ for P_2 to receive output, and stores (x_1, Q, c_{key}).

When taking $\mathscr{F}_{\mathsf{zk}}$ and $\mathscr{F}_{\mathsf{com-zk}}$ as ideal functionalities, the only difference between the real execution as ran by an honest P_2, and the ideal execution simulated by $\mathscr{S}$ is that in the former $Q_2 \leftarrow x_2 P$ where $x_2 \xleftarrow{\$} \mathbf{Z}/q\mathbf{Z}$, whereas in the latter $Q_2 \leftarrow x_1^{-1} Q$, where Q is the public key returned by the ideal functionality $\mathscr{F}_{ECDSA}$. However since $\mathscr{F}_{ECDSA}$ samples Q uniformly at random from $\mathbb{G}$, the distribution of Q_2 in both cases is identical.

Signing Phase

1. Upon input $\mathsf{Sign}(sid, m)$, simulator $\mathscr{S}$ sends $\mathsf{Sign}(sid, m)$ to $\mathscr{F}_{ECDSA}$ and receives back a signature (r, s).
2. $\mathscr{S}$ computes the elliptic curve point $R = (r, r_y)$ using the ECDSA verification algorithm.
3. $\mathscr{S}$ invokes $\mathscr{A}_1$ with input $\mathsf{ISign}(sid, m)$ and simulates the first three interactions such that $\mathscr{A}_1$ computes R. The strategy is similar to that used to compute Q, in brief, it proceeds as follows:
   (a) $\mathscr{S}$ receives $(\mathsf{com - prove}, sid\|1, R_1, k_1)$ from $\mathscr{A}_1$.
   (b) If $R_1 = k_1 P$ then $\mathscr{S}$ sets $R_2 \leftarrow k_1^{-1} R$; otherwise it chooses R_2 at random. $\mathscr{S}$ sends $(\mathsf{proof}, sid\|2, R_2)$ to $\mathscr{A}_1$.
   (c) $\mathscr{S}$ receives $(\mathsf{decom - proof}, sid\|1)$ from $\mathscr{A}_1$. If $R_1 \neq k_1 P$ then $\mathscr{S}$ simulates P_2 aborting and instructs the trusted party computing $\mathscr{F}_{ECDSA}$ to abort.
4. $\mathscr{S}$ computes $c_3 \leftarrow \mathsf{Enc}_{pk}(k_1 \cdot s \mod q)$, where s was received from $\mathscr{F}_{ECDSA}$, and sends c_3 to $\mathscr{A}_1$.

As with the computation of Q_2 in the key generation phase, R_2 is distributed identically in the real and ideal executions since R is randomly generated by $\mathcal{F}_{ECDSA}$. The zero-knowledge proofs and verifications are also identically distributed in the $\mathcal{F}_{zk}$, $\mathcal{F}_{com-zk}$-hybrid model. Thus, the only difference between a real execution and the simulation is the way that c_3 is computed. In the simulation it is an encryption of $k_1 \cdot s = k_1 \cdot k^{-1}(m' + r \cdot x) = k_2^{-1} \cdot (m' + r \cdot x)$ mod q, whereas in a real execution c_3 is computed from c_{key}, using the homomorphic properties of the encryption scheme. However, notice that as long as there exist (u, w) such that $c_{key} = \mathsf{Enc}((u, w); (\mathsf{hp}, x_1))$ where $Q = x_1 P$ – which is guaranteed by the ideal functionality $\mathcal{F}_{zk}^{R_{HPS-DL}}$ – and as long as the homomorphic operations hold – which is guaranteed for any hp in the efficiently verifiable ensemble K'_{hp} (cf. Subsect. 3.2) – the c_3 obtained in the real scenario is also an encryption of $s' = k_2^{-1} \cdot (m' + r \cdot x)$ mod q. Thus c_3 is distributed identically in both cases.

This implies that the view of a corrupted P_1 is identical in the real and ideal executions of the protocol (in the $\mathcal{F}_{zk}$, $\mathcal{F}_{com-zk}$-hybrid model), *i.e.*, the simulator perfectly simulates the real environment, which completes the proof of this simulation case.

$\mathcal{S}$ *Simulates* P_1 – *Corrupted* P_2: We now suppose an adversary $\mathcal{A}_2$ corrupts P_2 and describe the ideal execution of the protocol. We demonstrate via a sequence of games – where the first game is a real execution and the last game is a simulated execution – that both executions are indistinguishable. This proof methodology differs considerably to that of [Lin17] since the main differences between a real and simulated execution are due to the ciphertext c_{key}, so the indistinguishability of both executions reduces to the ind-cpa security of the underlying encryption scheme. The necessity for the properties required of HPS will thus here become apparent. We first describe an ideal execution of the protocol:

Key Generation Phase

1. Given input $\mathsf{KeyGen}(\mathbb{G}, P, q)$, the simulator $\mathcal{S}$ sends $\mathsf{KeyGen}(\mathbb{G}, P, q)$ to the functionality $\mathcal{F}_{ECDSA}$ and receives back Q.
2. $\mathcal{S}$ invokes $\mathcal{A}_2$ upon input $\mathsf{IKeyGen}(\mathbb{G}, P, q)$ and sends $(\mathsf{proof} - \mathsf{receipt}, 1)$ as $\mathcal{A}_2$ expects to receive from $\mathcal{F}_{com-zk}^{R_{DL}}$.
3. $\mathcal{S}$ receives $(\mathsf{prove}, 2, Q_2, x_2)$ as $\mathcal{A}_2$ intends to send to $\mathcal{F}_{zk}^{R_{DL}}$.
4. Using the extracted value x_2, $\mathcal{S}$ verifies that Q_2 is a non zero point on the curve and that $Q_2 = x_2 P$. If so it computes $Q_1 \leftarrow (x_2)^{-1} Q$ and sends $(\mathsf{decom} - \mathsf{proof}, 1, Q_1)$ to $\mathcal{A}_2$ as it expects to receive from $\mathcal{F}_{com-zk}^{R_{DL}}$. If not it simulates P_1 aborting and halts.
5. $\mathcal{S}$ samples $\mathsf{hk} \hookleftarrow \mathcal{D}_{\mathsf{hk}}$ and computes $\mathsf{hp} \leftarrow \alpha(\mathsf{hk})$. It also samples $\tilde{x}_1 \xleftarrow{\$} \mathbf{Z}/q\mathbf{Z}$ and $(u, w) \in \mathsf{R}$ and computes $c_{key} \leftarrow \mathsf{Enc}((u, w); (\mathsf{hp}, \tilde{x}_1))$.
6. $\mathcal{S}$ sends $(\mathsf{proof}, 3, (\mathsf{hp}, c_{key}, Q_1))$ to $\mathcal{A}_2$, as $\mathcal{A}_2$ expects to receive from $\mathcal{F}_{zk}^{R_{HPS-DL}}$.
7. $\mathcal{S}$ sends $\mathsf{continue}$ to $\mathcal{F}_{ECDSA}$ for P_1 to receive output, and stores Q.

Signing Phase

1. Upon input $\mathsf{Sign}(sid, m)$, simulator $\mathcal{S}$ sends $\mathsf{Sign}(sid, m)$ to $\mathcal{F}_{ECDSA}$ and receives back a signature (r, s).
2. $\mathcal{S}$ computes the point $R = (r, r_y)$ using the ECDSA verification algorithm.
3. $\mathcal{S}$ invokes $\mathcal{A}_2$ with input $\mathsf{ISign}(sid, m)$ and sends $(\mathsf{proof} - \mathsf{receipt}, sid\|1)$ as $\mathcal{A}_2$ expects to receive from $\mathcal{F}_{\mathsf{com}-\mathsf{zk}}^{R_{DL}}$.
4. $\mathcal{S}$ receives $(\mathsf{prove}, sid\|2, R_2, k_2)$ as $\mathcal{A}_2$ intends to send to $\mathcal{F}_{\mathsf{zk}}^{R_{DL}}$.
5. Using the extracted value k_2, $\mathcal{S}$ verifies that R_2 is a non zero point and that $R_2 = k_2 P$. If so it computes $R_1 \leftarrow k_2^{-1} R$ and sends $(\mathsf{decom} - \mathsf{proof}, sid\|1, R_1)$ to $\mathcal{A}_2$ as it expects to receive from $\mathcal{F}_{\mathsf{com}-\mathsf{zk}}^{R_{DL}}$. If not it simulates P_1 aborting and instructs the trusted party computing $\mathcal{F}_{ECDSA}$ to abort.
6. $\mathcal{S}$ receives $c_3 = (\bar{u}, \bar{e})$ from $\mathcal{A}_2$, which it can decrypt using hk, i.e. $\alpha \leftarrow \mathsf{Decode}\left(\dfrac{\bar{e}}{\mathcal{H}_{\mathsf{hk}}(\bar{u})}\right)$. If $\alpha = k_2^{-1} \cdot (m' + r \cdot x_2 \cdot \tilde{x}_1) \bmod q$ then $\mathcal{S}$ sends $\mathsf{continue}$ to the trusted party $\mathcal{F}_{ECDSA}$, s.t. the honest party P_1 receives output. Otherwise it instructs $\mathcal{F}_{ECDSA}$ to abort.

We now describe the sequence of games. Game_0 is the real execution of the protocol, and we finish in Game_6 which is the ideal simulation described above. In the following intermediary games, only the differences in the steps performed by $\mathcal{S}$ are depicted.

Game_0	Game_1	Game_2
$Q \leftarrow x_1 x_2 P$	$Q \leftarrow x_1 x_2 P$	$Q \leftarrow x_1 x_2 P$
$\vdots$	$\vdots$	$\vdots$
$\mathsf{hk} \hookleftarrow \mathcal{D}_{\mathsf{hk}}$	$\mathsf{hk} \hookleftarrow \mathcal{D}_{\mathsf{hk}}$	$\mathsf{hk} \hookleftarrow \mathcal{D}_{\mathsf{hk}}$
$\mathsf{hp} \leftarrow \alpha(\mathsf{hk})$	$\mathsf{hp} \leftarrow \alpha(\mathsf{hk})$	$\mathsf{hp} \leftarrow \alpha(\mathsf{hk})$
	$\mathsf{Sample}\ (u, w) \in \mathsf{R}$	$\tilde{u} \overset{\$}{\leftarrow} \mathcal{X} \backslash \mathcal{L}$
$c_{key} \leftarrow \mathsf{Enc}(\mathsf{hp}, x_1)$	$c_{key} \leftarrow (u, \mathcal{H}_{\mathsf{hk}}(u) \cdot \mathsf{Encode}(x_1))$	$c_{key} \leftarrow (\tilde{u}, \mathcal{H}_{\mathsf{hk}}(\tilde{u}) \cdot \mathsf{Encode}(x_1))$
$\vdots$	$\vdots$	$\vdots$
$R \leftarrow k_1 k_2 P$	$R \leftarrow k_1 k_2 P$	$R \leftarrow k_1 k_2 P$

We now demonstrate that the previous games are indistinguishable from the view of $\mathcal{A}_2$. Intuitively, in Game_1 the simulator uses the secret hashing key hk instead of the public projection key hp to compute c_{key}. Though the values are computed differently, they are distributed identically, and are perfectly indistinguishable. Next in Game_2 we replace the first element of the ciphertext (in Game_1 this is $u \in \mathcal{L}$) with an element $\tilde{u} \in \mathcal{X} \backslash \mathcal{L}$. By the hardness of the subset membership problem Game_1 and Game_2 are indistinguishable. Next in Game_3 we multiply the second element of the ciphertext by a random element of the subgroup group $\mathcal{F}$ in which messages are encoded (or equivalently, add a random element of $\mathbf{Z}/q\mathbf{Z}$ to x_1 such that this sum will be encoded in $\mathcal{F}$), under

Game₃	Game₄
$Q \leftarrow x_1 x_2 P$	$Q \leftarrow x_1 x_2 P$
$\vdots$	$\vdots$
$\mathsf{hk} \hookleftarrow \mathcal{D}_{\mathsf{hk}}$	$\mathsf{hk} \hookleftarrow \mathcal{D}_{\mathsf{hk}}$
$\mathsf{hp} \leftarrow \alpha(\mathsf{hk})$	$\mathsf{hp} \leftarrow \alpha(\mathsf{hk})$
$\tilde{u} \xleftarrow{\$} \mathcal{X} \backslash \mathcal{L},\ \gamma \xleftarrow{\$} \mathbf{Z}/q\mathbf{Z}$	Sample $(u,w) \in \mathsf{R},\ \gamma \xleftarrow{\$} \mathbf{Z}/q\mathbf{Z}$
$c_{key} \leftarrow (\tilde{u}, \mathcal{H}_{\mathsf{hk}}(\tilde{u}) \cdot \mathsf{Encode}(x_1 + \gamma))$	$c_{key} \leftarrow (u, \mathcal{H}_{\mathsf{hk}}(u) \cdot \mathsf{Encode}(x_1 + \gamma))$
$\vdots$	$\vdots$
$R \leftarrow k_1 k_2 P$	$R \leftarrow k_1 k_2 P$

Game₅	Game₆
$Q \leftarrow x_1 x_2 P$	$Q \leftarrow \mathcal{F}_{ECDSA}$
$\vdots$	$\vdots$
$\mathsf{hk} \hookleftarrow \mathcal{D}_{\mathsf{hk}}$	$\mathsf{hk} \hookleftarrow \mathcal{D}_{\mathsf{hk}}$
$\mathsf{hp} \leftarrow \alpha(\mathsf{hk})$	$\mathsf{hp} \leftarrow \alpha(\mathsf{hk})$
Sample $\gamma \xleftarrow{\$} \mathbf{Z}/q\mathbf{Z}$	Sample $\gamma \xleftarrow{\$} \mathbf{Z}/q\mathbf{Z}$
$c_{key} \leftarrow \mathsf{Enc}(\mathsf{hp}, x_1 + \gamma))$	$c_{key} \leftarrow \mathsf{Enc}(\mathsf{hp}, x_1 + \gamma))$
$\vdots$	$\vdots$
$R \leftarrow k_1 k_2 P$	$R \leftarrow \mathcal{F}_{ECDSA}$

the assumption that the HPS is δ_s–smooth over $\mathcal{X}$ in $\mathcal{F}$, the obtained distributions of the public key and ciphertext (as seen by an adversary) are δ_s–close. So both games are indistinguishable. We then again use the hardness of the subset membership problem underlying the hash proof to hop from Game₃ to Game₄, such that in the latter the first element of the ciphertext is once again in $\mathcal{L}$; and again Game₄ to Game₅ are identical from an adversary's point of view since we simply use the public evaluation function of the hash function $\mathcal{H}$ instead of the private one. And finally in Game₆ we change the way R and Q are generated.

We denote by E_i the probability that an algorithm interacting with the simulator in Game$_i$ outputs 1. Thus by demonstrating that $|\Pr[\mathsf{E}_0] - \Pr[\mathsf{E}_6]|$ is negligible, we demonstrate that – from $\mathcal{A}_2$'s view, the real and ideal executions are indistinguishable.

Invalid Ciphertexts: We define the notion of invalid ciphertexts as these will be useful in our game steps. A ciphertext is said to be *invalid* if it is of the form $(u', e') := (u', \mathcal{H}_{\mathsf{hk}}(u') \cdot \mathsf{Encode}(m'))$ where $u' \in \mathcal{X} \backslash \mathcal{L}$. Note that one can compute such a ciphertext using the secret hashing key hk, but not the public projection key hp; that the decryption algorithm applied to (u', e') with secret key hk recovers m'; and that an invalid ciphertext is indistinguishable of a valid one under the hardness of the subset membership problem.

Homomorphic Properties over Invalid Ciphertexts: It is easy to verify that homomorphic operations hold even if a ciphertext is invalid, whether this be between two invalid ciphertexts of between a valid and invalid ciphertext. This is true since the homomorphic properties we required of the hash family hold over the whole group $\mathcal{X}$ (and not only in $\mathcal{L}$).

Game_0 *to* Game_1. In Game_0 and in Game_1, Q and R are computed in the same way. The only difference between Game_0 and Game_1 is the way c_{key} is computed, namely we use the secret hashing key hk instead of the public projection key hp and the witness w to compute c_{key}. Though the values are computed differently, they are distributed identically, and are perfectly indistinguishable from an adversary's point of view: $|\Pr[\mathsf{E}_1] - \Pr[\mathsf{E}_0]| = 0$.

Game_1 *to* Game_2. Suppose that $\mathcal{D}$ is able to distinguish, with non negligible advantage, between the distribution generated in Game_1 from that generated in Game_2. Then we can devise $\hat{\mathcal{S}}$ that can use $\mathcal{D}$ to break the hard subset membership assumption, *i.e.*, distinguish random elements of $\mathcal{L}$ from those of $\mathcal{X} \backslash \mathcal{L}$. The input of $\hat{\mathcal{S}}$ is a hard subset membership challenge x^* which is either an element in $\mathcal{L}$ or an element of $\mathcal{X} \backslash \mathcal{L}$. Precisely $\hat{\mathcal{S}}$ works as $\mathcal{S}$ would in Game_1, interacting with the distinguisher $\mathcal{D}$ instead of $\mathcal{A}_2$, the only difference being that instead of sampling $(u, w) \in \mathsf{R}$ it sets $u := x^*$ and computes $c_{key} \leftarrow (u, \mathcal{H}_{hk}(u) \cdot \mathsf{Encode}(x_1))$. When $\mathcal{D}$ returns a bit b (relative to Game_{b+1}), $\hat{\mathcal{S}}$ returns the same bit, where 0 represents the case $x^* \in \mathcal{L}$ and 1 represents the case $x^* \in \mathcal{X} \backslash \mathcal{L}$.

Analysis – Case $x^* \in \mathcal{L}$: There exists $w \in \mathcal{W}$ such that $(x^*, w) \in \mathsf{R}$ and $\mathcal{H}_{hp}(x^*, w) = \mathcal{H}_{hk}(x^*)$. So $c_{key} = (u, e)$ is an encryption of x_1 as computed in Game_1. *Case* $x^* \in \mathcal{X} \backslash \mathcal{L}$: The ciphertext is $(x^*, \mathcal{H}_{hk}(x^*) \cdot \mathsf{Encode}(x_1))$, which is exactly the distribution obtained in Game_2. So the advantage of $\hat{\mathcal{S}}$ in breaking the hard subset membership assumption is at least that of $\mathcal{D}$ in distinguishing both games. Thus: $|\Pr[\mathsf{E}_2] - \Pr[\mathsf{E}_1]| \leq \delta_{\mathcal{L}}$.

Game_2 *to* Game_3. Let us denote $\tilde{x}_1 := x_1 + \gamma \mod q$. Under the assumption that the HPS is δ_s-smooth over $\mathcal{X}$ in $\mathcal{F}$ (i.e. the co-domain of Encode), it holds that the distribution of $(x^*, \mathcal{H}_{hk}(x^*) \cdot \mathsf{Encode}(x_1))$ and of $(x^*, \mathcal{H}_{hk}(x^*) \cdot \mathsf{Encode}(x_1) \cdot \mathsf{Encode}(\gamma) = \mathcal{H}_{hk}(x^*) \cdot \mathsf{Encode}(\tilde{x}_1))$ for some random $\tilde{x}_1 \in \mathbf{Z}/q\mathbf{Z}$ are δ_s-close. Thus replacing $(x^*, \mathcal{H}_{hk}(x^*) \cdot \mathsf{Encode}(x_1))$ by $(x^*, \mathcal{H}_{hk}(x^*) \cdot \mathsf{Encode}(\tilde{x}_1))$ – as is done from Game_2 to Game_3 – cannot be noticed by any PT adversary with advantage greater than δ_s and: $|\Pr[\mathsf{E}_3] - \Pr[\mathsf{E}_2]| \leq \delta_s$.

Game_3 *to* Game_4. The change here is exactly that between Game_1 and Game_2, thus both games are indistinguishable under the hardness of the subset membership problem on which relies the HPS and: $|\Pr[\mathsf{E}_4] - \Pr[\mathsf{E}_3]| \leq \delta_{\mathcal{L}}$.

Game_4 *to* Game_5. The change here is exactly that between Game_0 and Game_1, thus both games are perfectly indistinguishable, even for an unbounded adversary, thus: $|\Pr[\mathsf{E}_5] - \Pr[\mathsf{E}_4]| = 0$.

Game_5 *to* Game_6. The only differences between Game_5 and Game_6 are the ways Q and R are generated. In Game_5, Q and R derive from a Diffie-Hellman

Key Exchange, which can be simulated. Moreover, since the ideal functionality $\mathcal{F}_{ECDSA}$ samples Q and R uniformly at random from the group $\mathbb{G}$, it holds that $x_2^{-1}Q$ and x_1P have the same distribution, as do $k_2^{-1}R$ and k_1P. All other steps of Game_5 and Game_6 are identical. We conclude that, in the $\mathcal{F}_{zk}$, $\mathcal{F}_{com-zk}$ hybrid model, Game_5 and Game_6 are identical from $\mathcal{A}_2$'s view, and so: $|\Pr[\mathsf{E}_6] - \Pr[\mathsf{E}_5]| = 0$.

Real/Ideal Executions. Putting together the above probabilities, we get that: $|\Pr[\mathsf{E}_6] - \Pr[\mathsf{E}_0]| \leq 2\delta_{\mathcal{L}} + \delta_s$, and so, assuming the hardness of the subset membership problem underlying HPS, and assuming the smoothness of HPS, it holds that the real and ideal executions are computationally indistinguishable from $\mathcal{A}_2$'s view, which concludes the proof of the theorem.   □

4 Instantiation in Class Groups of an Imaginary Quadratic Field

In this section, we give an instantiation of a hash proof system with the required properties in order to apply the generic construction of the previous section. For that we will use a linearly homomorphic encryption scheme modulo a prime number, denoted CL in the following, introduced in [CL15] using a group with an easy Dlog subgroup, with a concrete instantiation using class groups of quadratic fields. In order to define a HPS, we use the recent results of [CLT18] that enhance the CL framework by introducing a hard subgroup membership assumption (HSM). We first give the definition of this assumption in the context of a group with an easy Dlog subgroup, then the instantiation with class groups, and then define a HPS from HSM and prove that it has the required properties to instantiate the generic construction in Sect. 3.

4.1 A Hard Subgroup Membership Assumption

To start with, we explicitly define the generator GenGroup used in the framework of a group with an easy Dlog subgroup introduced in [CL15] and enhanced in [CLT18], with small modifications as discussed below.

Definition 4. *Let* GenGroup *be a pair of algorithms* (Gen, Solve). *The* Gen *algorithm is a group generator which takes as inputs a parameter λ and a prime q and outputs a tuple $(\tilde{s}, g, f, g_q, \widehat{G}, G, F, G^q)$. The set $(\widehat{G}, \cdot)$ is a finite abelian group of order $q \cdot \widehat{s}$ where the bitsize of $\widehat{s}$ is a function of λ and $\gcd(q, \widehat{s}) = 1$. The algorithm* Gen *only outputs an upper bound $\tilde{s}$ of $\widehat{s}$. It is also required that one can efficiently recognise valid encodings of elements in $\widehat{G}$. The set $(F, \cdot)$ is the unique cyclic subgroup of $\widehat{G}$ of order q, generated by f. The set $(G, \cdot)$ is a cyclic subgroup of $\widehat{G}$ of order $q \cdot s$ where s divides $\widehat{s}$. By construction $F \subset G$, and, denoting $G^q := \{x^q, x \in G\}$ the subgroup of order s of G, it holds that $G = G^q \times F$. The algorithm* Gen *outputs f, g_q and $g := f \cdot g_q$ which are respective generators of F, G^q and G. Moreover, the Dlog problem is easy in F, which* *means that the* Solve *algorithm is a deterministic polynomial time algorithm that solves the discrete logarithm problem in* F:

$$\Pr\big[x = x^\star : (\tilde{s}, g, f, g_q, \widehat{G}, G, F, G^q) \leftarrow \mathsf{Gen}(1^\lambda, q), x \xleftarrow{\$} \mathbf{Z}/q\mathbf{Z}, X \leftarrow f^x,$$
$$x^\star \leftarrow \mathsf{Solve}(q, \tilde{s}, g, f, g_q, \widehat{G}, G, F, G^q, X)\big] = 1.$$

Remark 1. In this definition, there are a few modifications compared to the definition of [CLT18]. Namely we take as input the prime q instead of having Gen generating it, and we output the group $\widehat{G}$ from which the group G with an easy Dlog subgroup F is produced. In practice, with the concrete instantiation with class groups, this is a just a matter of rewriting: the prime q was generated independently of the rest of the output in [CL15,CLT18] so it can be an input of the algorithm, and the group $\widehat{G}$ would be the class group which was implicitly defined by its discriminant. We note that it is easy to recognise valid encodings of $\widehat{G}$ while it will be not so for elements of $G \subset \widehat{G}$. This is an important difference with Paillier's encryption, and one of the reason why Lindell's L_{PDL} proof does not work in our setting.

We recall here the definition of a hard subgroup membership (HSM) problem within a group with an easy Dlog subgroup as defined in [CLT18]. HSM is closely related to Paillier's DCR assumption. Such hard subgroup membership problems are based on a long line of assumptions on the hardness of distinguishing powers in groups. In short, DCR and HSM are essentially the same assumption but in different groups, hence there is no direct reduction between them. We emphasise that this assumption is well understood both in general, and for the specific case of class groups of quadratic fields, which we will use to instantiate GenGroup. It was first used by [CLT18] within class groups, this being said, cryptography based on class groups is now well established, and is seeing renewed interest as it allows versatile and efficient solutions such as encryption switching protocols [CIL17], inner product functional encryption [CLT18] or verifiable delay functions [BBBF18,Wes19].

In Definition 4, one has $G = F \times G^q$. The assumption is that it is hard to distinguish the elements of G^q in G.

Definition 5 (HSM assumption). *We say that* GenGroup *is the generator of a* HSM *group with easy Dlog subgroup* F *if it holds that the* HSM *problem is hard even with access to the* Solve *algorithm. Let* $\mathcal{D}$ *(resp.* $\mathcal{D}_q$) *be a distribution over the integers such that the distribution* $\{g^x, x \hookleftarrow \mathcal{D}\}$ *(resp.* $\{g_q^x, x \hookleftarrow \mathcal{D}_q\}$) *is at distance less than* $2^{-\lambda}$ *from the uniform distribution in* G *(resp. in* G^q). *Let* $\mathcal{A}$ *be an adversary for the* HSM *problem, its advantage is defined as:*

$$\mathsf{Adv}_{\mathcal{A}}^{\mathsf{HSM}}(\lambda) = \Big| 2 \cdot \Pr\big[b = b^\star : (\tilde{s}, g, f, g_q, \widehat{G}, G, F, G^q) \leftarrow \mathsf{Gen}(1^\lambda, q),$$
$$x \hookleftarrow \mathcal{D}, x' \hookleftarrow \mathcal{D}_q, b \xleftarrow{\$} \{0,1\}, Z_0 \leftarrow g^x, Z_1 \leftarrow g_q^{x'},$$
$$b^\star \leftarrow \mathcal{A}(q, \tilde{s}, g, f, g_q, \widehat{G}, G, F, G^q, Z_b, \mathsf{Solve}(.))\big] - 1 \Big|$$

The HSM *problem is said to be hard in* G *if for all probabilistic polynomial time attacker* $\mathcal{A}$, $\mathsf{Adv}_{\mathcal{A}}^{\mathsf{HSM}}(\lambda)$ *is negligible.*

Class Groups. Our instantiation makes use of class groups of orders of imaginary quadratic fields. We refer the interested reader to [BH01] for background on this algebraic object and its early use in cryptography. We here briefly sketch an instantiation of algorithm GenGroup in Definition 4, following [CL15, Fig. 2]. The formal description is given in Fig. 6 below and concrete details can be found in [CL15]. Let q be a prime. We construct a fundamental discriminant $\Delta_K := -q \cdot \tilde{q}$ where $\tilde{q}$ is a prime such that $q \cdot \tilde{q} \equiv -1 \pmod{4}$ and $(q/\tilde{q}) = -1$. We then consider the non-maximal order of discriminant $\Delta_q := q^2 \cdot \Delta_K$ and its class group $\widehat{G} := Cl(\Delta_q)$ whose order is $h(\Delta_q) = q \cdot h(\Delta_K)$ where $h(\Delta_K)$ is the class number, *i.e.*, the order of $Cl(\Delta_K)$, the class group of fundamental discriminant Δ_k. This number is known to satisfy the following inequality (see [Coh00, p. 295] for instance): $h(\Delta_K) < \frac{1}{\pi} \log |\Delta_K| \sqrt{|\Delta_K|}$ which is the bound we take for $\tilde{s}$ (a slightly better bound can be computed from the analytic class number formula).

Elements of $\widehat{G}$ are classes of ideals of the order of discriminant Δ_q. Such classes can be represented by a unique reduced ideal. Moreover, ideals can be represented using the so-called two elements representation which correspond to their basis as a lattice of dimension two. Informally, classes can be uniquely represented by two integers (a, b), $a, b < \sqrt{|\Delta_q|}$ and one can efficiently verify that this indeed defines an element of $\widehat{G}$ (by checking if $b^2 \equiv \Delta_q \pmod{4a}$). The arithmetic in class groups (which corresponds to reduction and composition of quadratic forms) is very efficient: the algorithms have a quasi linear time complexity using fast arithmetic (see [Coh00]).

Following [CL15, Fig. 2], we build a generator g_q of a cyclic subgroup of q-th powers of $\widehat{G}$, and denote $G^q := \langle g_q \rangle$. Then we build a generator f for the subgroup F of order q, and then set $g := f \cdot g_q$ as a generator of a cyclic subgroup G of $Cl(\Delta_q)$ of order $q \cdot s$, where s is unknown. Computing discrete logarithms is easy in F thanks to the following facts. We denote the surjection $\bar{\varphi}_q : Cl(\Delta_q) \longrightarrow Cl(\Delta_K)$. From [CL09, Lemma 1], its kernel is cyclic of order q and is generated by f represented by (q^2, q). Moreover, if $1 \leqslant m \leqslant q - 1$ then, once reduced, f^m is of the form $(q^2, L(m)q)$ where $L(m)$ is the odd integer in $[-q, q]$ such that $L(m) \equiv 1/m \pmod{q}$, which gives the efficient algorithm to compute discrete logarithms in $\langle f \rangle$.

Note that following [CL15] the bit size of q must have at least λ bits, where λ is the security parameter, which is the case for ECDSA: q will be the order of the elliptic curve. The size $\eta(\lambda)$ of Δ_K is chosen to resist the best practical attacks, which consists in computing discrete logarithms in $Cl(\Delta_K)$ (or equivalently the class number $h(\Delta_K)$). An index-calculus method to solve the Dlog problem in a class group of imaginary quadratic field of discriminant Δ_K was proposed in [Jac00]. It is conjectured in [BJS10] that a state of the art implementation of this algorithm has complexity $\mathcal{O}(L_{|\Delta_K|}[1/2, o(1)])$, which allows to use asymptotically shorter keys compared to protocols using classical problems that

$\mathsf{Gen}(1^\lambda, q)$

1. Let μ be the bit size of q. Pick $\tilde{q}$ a random $\eta(\lambda) - \mu$ bits prime such that $q\tilde{q} \equiv -1 \pmod 4$ and $(q/\tilde{q}) = -1$.
2. $\Delta_K \leftarrow -q\tilde{q}$, $\Delta_q \leftarrow q^2 \Delta_K$ and $\widehat{G} \leftarrow Cl(\Delta_q)$
3. $f \leftarrow [(q^2, q)]$ in $Cl(\Delta_q)$ and $F := \langle f \rangle$
4. $\tilde{s} \leftarrow \lceil \frac{1}{\pi} \log |\Delta_K| \sqrt{|\Delta_K|} \rceil$
5. Let r be a small prime, with $r \neq q$ and $\left(\frac{\Delta_K}{r}\right) = 1$, set $\mathfrak{r}$ an ideal lying above r.
6. Set $g_q \leftarrow [\varphi_q^{-1}(\mathfrak{r}^2)]^q$ in $C(\Delta_q)$ and $G^q \leftarrow \langle g_q \rangle$
7. Set $g \leftarrow g_p \cdot f$ and $G \leftarrow \langle g \rangle$
8. Return $(\tilde{s}, g, f, g_q, \widehat{G}, G, F, G^q)$

Fig. 6. Group generator Gen

are solved in subexponential complexity $\mathcal{O}(L[1/3, o(1)])$ (see Sect. 5 for concrete sizes for η).

4.2   A Smooth Homomorphic Hash Proof System from HSM

We set $\mathcal{X} := G$ and $\mathcal{L} := G^q$ then $\mathcal{X} \cap \mathcal{L} = G^q$ and the HSM assumption states that it is hard to distinguish random elements of G from those of G^q. This clearly implies the hardness of the subset membership problem, *i.e.*, it is hard to distinguish random elements of $G \backslash G^q$ from those of G^q.

Let $\mathcal{D}$ be a distribution over the integers such that the distribution $\{g^w, w \hookleftarrow \mathcal{D}\}$ is at distance $\delta_{\mathcal{D}} \leq 2^{-\lambda}$ of the uniform distribution in G.

Associated Projective Hash Family. Let PHF be the projective hash family associated to the above subset membership problem, the description of which specifies:

- A hash key space $K := \mathbf{Z}$.
- A keyed hash function, with input and output domain G, s.t., for $\mathsf{hk} \hookleftarrow \mathcal{D}$, and for $x \in G$, $\mathcal{H}_{\mathsf{hk}}(x) := x^{\mathsf{hk}}$.
- An auxiliary function $\alpha : K \mapsto G^q$ such that for $\mathsf{hk} \in K$, $\alpha(\mathsf{hk}) := \mathcal{H}_{\mathsf{hk}}(g_q) = g_q^{\mathsf{hk}}$. Notice that for a hash key hk, and for $x \in G^q$, the knowledge of $\alpha(\mathsf{hk})$ completely determines the value $\mathcal{H}_{\mathsf{hk}}(x)$.
- An efficient public evaluation function, such that, for $x \in G^q$ with witness w such that $x = g_q^w$ one can efficiently compute $\mathcal{H}_{\mathsf{hk}}(x) = \alpha(\mathsf{hk})^w = x^{\mathsf{hk}}$ knowing only the value of the auxiliary function $\alpha(\mathsf{hk})$ (but not hk).

Lemma 1 (Smoothness). *The projective hash family* PHF *is δ_s-smooth over G in F, with $\delta_s \leqslant 2\delta_{\mathcal{D}}$, i.e., for any $x \in G \backslash G^q$, $\pi \leftarrow f^\gamma \in F \subset G$ where $\gamma \overset{\$}{\leftarrow} \mathbf{Z}/q\mathbf{Z}$ and $k \hookleftarrow \mathcal{D}$, the distributions $\mathcal{D}_1 := \{x, g_q^k, \pi \cdot x^k\}$ and $\mathcal{D}_2 := \{x, g_q^k, x^k\}$ are less than $2\delta_{\mathcal{D}}$-close.*

Proof. For $x \in G \backslash G^q$, there exist $a \in \mathbf{Z}/s\mathbf{Z}$ and $b \in (\mathbf{Z}/q\mathbf{Z})^*$ such that $x = g_q^a f^b$. Thus we can write $\mathcal{D}_1 = \{g_q^a f^b, g_q^k, g_q^{a \cdot k} f^{b \cdot k + \gamma}\}$ and $\mathcal{D}_2 = \{g_q^a f^b, g_q^k, g_q^{a \cdot k} f^{b \cdot k}\}$. It remains to study the statistical distance of the third coordinates of the two distributions, given the two first coordinates, *i.e*, if $(a \mod s)$, $(b \mod q)$, and $(k \mod s)$ are fixed. This is the statistical between $X := b \cdot k + \gamma$ and $Y := b \cdot k$ in $\mathbf{Z}/q\mathbf{Z}$. Since γ is uniform in $\mathbf{Z}/q\mathbf{Z}$, X is the uniform distribution. As $\mathcal{D}$ is by definition at statistical distance $\delta_{\mathcal{D}}$ from the uniform distribution modulo $q \cdot s$, and $\gcd(q, s) = 1$, one can prove (cf. [CCLST19, Appendix 2]) that even knowing $(k \mod s)$, the distribution of $(k \mod q)$ is at distance less than $2\delta_{\mathcal{D}}$ from the uniform distribution over $\mathbf{Z}/q\mathbf{Z}$. As a result, the distance between X and Y is bounded by $2\delta_{\mathcal{D}}$, which concludes the proof.   □

Linearly Homomorphic. For all $\mathsf{hk} \in \mathbf{Z}$, and $u_1, u_2 \in G$, $\mathcal{H}_{\mathsf{hk}}(u_1) \cdot \mathcal{H}_{\mathsf{hk}}(u_2) = u_1^{\mathsf{hk}} \cdot u_2^{\mathsf{hk}} = (u_1 \cdot u_2)^{\mathsf{hk}} = \mathcal{H}_{\mathsf{hk}}(u_1 \cdot u_2)$. Thus $\mathcal{H}_{\mathsf{hk}}$ is a homomorphism for each hk.

Resulting Encryption Scheme. A direct application of Subsect. 3.3 using the above HPS results in the encryption scheme called HSM-CL in [CLT18], which is linearly homomorphic modulo q and $\mathsf{ind - cpa}$ under the HSM assumption. We describe this scheme in Fig. 7 for completeness. Note that here the secret key x (and the randomness r) is drawn with a distribution $\mathcal{D}_q$ such that $\{g_q^x, x \hookleftarrow \mathcal{D}_q\}$ is at distance less than $2^{-\lambda}$ from the uniform distribution in G^q, this does not change the view of the attacker. Let $S := 2^{\lambda - 2} \cdot \tilde{s}$. In practice, we will use for $\mathcal{D}_q$ the uniform distribution on $\{0, \dots, S\}$.

4.3   A Zero-Knowledge Proof for $R_{\mathsf{CL - DL}}$

We describe here the ZKPoK for $R_{\mathsf{HPS - DL}}$ used for our instantiation with the encryption scheme of Fig. 7 and denote it $R_{\mathsf{CL - DL}}$. It relies on the Schnorr-like GPS (statistically) zero-knowledge identification scheme [GPS06] that we turn into a zero-knowledge proof of knowledge of the randomness used for encryption and of the discrete logarithm of an element on an elliptic curve, using a binary challenge. This proof is partly performed in a group of unknown order.

Algorithm KeyGen$(1^\lambda, q)$

1. $(\tilde{s}, g, f, g_q, \widehat{G}, G, F, G^q) \leftarrow \mathsf{Gen}(1^\lambda, q)$
2. Pick $x \hookleftarrow \mathcal{D}_q$ and $h \leftarrow g_q^x$
3. Set $pk \leftarrow (\tilde{s}, g_q, f, p, h)$
4. Set $sk \leftarrow x$
5. Return (pk, sk)

Algorithm Enc(pk, m)

1. Pick $r \hookleftarrow \mathcal{D}_q$
2. Return $(g_q^r, f^m h^r)$

Algorithm Dec$(sk, (c_1, c_2))$

1. Compute $M \leftarrow c_2/c_1^x$
2. Return $\mathsf{Solve}(M)$

Fig. 7. Description of the HSM-CL encryption scheme

We denote $c_{key} := (c_1, c_2)$. If c_{key} is a valid encryption of x_1 under public key pk it holds that $c_{key} = (g_q^r, f^{x_1}\mathsf{pk}^r)$ for some $r \in \{0, \ldots, S\}$. The protocol $R_{\mathsf{CL-DL}}$ provides a ZKPoK for the following relation:

$$R_{\mathsf{CL-DL}} := \{(\mathsf{pk}, (c_1, c_2), Q_1); (x_1, r) \mid c_1 = g_q^r \wedge c_2 = f^{x_1}\mathsf{pk}^r \wedge Q_1 = x_1 G\}.$$

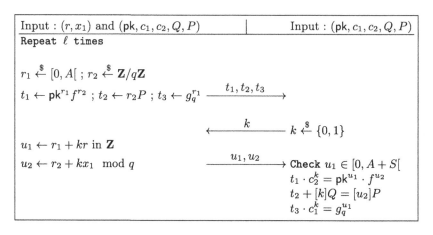

Fig. 8. The zero-knowledge proof of knowledge $R_{\mathsf{CL-DL}}$

Theorem 2, whose proof is given in the full version of the paper [CCLST19, Appendix 3], states the security of the zero-knowledge proof of knowledge $R_{\mathsf{CL-DL}}$.

Theorem 2. *The protocol described in Fig. 8 is a statistical zero-knowledge proof of knowledge with soundness $2^{-\ell}$, as long as ℓ is polynomial and $\ell S/A$ is negligible, where A is a positive integer.*

4.4 Two-Party Distributed ECDSA Protocol from HSM

The protocol results from a direct application of Subsect. 3.5 using the HPS defined in Subsect. 4.2, an the $R_{\mathsf{CL-DL}}$ proof of the previous subsection. Therefore we defer the detailed protocol to the full version [CCLST19, Appendix 4], and simply state the following theorem.

Theorem 3. *Assuming GenGroup is the generator of a HSM group with easy Dlog subgroup F, then the generic construction of Fig. 5, instantiated with the HSM-based PHF of Subsect. 4.2 securely computes $\mathcal{F}_{ECDSA}$ in the $(\mathcal{F}_{zk}, \mathcal{F}_{com-zk})$-hybrid model in the presence of a malicious static adversary (under the ideal/real definition).*

5 Implementation and Efficiency Comparisons

In this section we compare an implementation of our protocol with Lindell's protocol of [Lin17]. For fair comparison, we implement both protocols with the Pari C Library ([PAR18]), as this library handles arithmetic in class groups, $\mathbf{Z}/n\mathbf{Z}$ and elliptic curves. In particular, in this library, exponentiations in $\mathbf{Z}/n\mathbf{Z}$ and in class groups both use the same sliding window method. The running times are measured on a single core of an Intel(R) Core(TM) i7-7700 CPU @ 3.60 GHz (even if key generation can easily be parallelized). We do not implement commitments (this does not bias the comparison as they appear with equal weight in both schemes), and we only measure computation time and do not include communication (again this is fair as communication is similar).

As in [Lin17], we ran our implementation on the standard NIST curves P-256, P-384 and P-521, corresponding to levels of security 128, 192 and 256. For the encryption scheme, we start with a 112 bit security, as in [Lin17], but also study the case where its level of security matches the security of the elliptic curves.

Again as in [Lin17], we fixed the number of rounds in zero knowledge proofs to reach a statistical soundness error of 2^{-40}. For the distributions we also set the parameters to get statistical error of 2^{-40}. The zero knowledge proofs for R_{DL} are implemented with the Schnorr protocol.

In the following, we review the theoretical complexity and experimental results of both schemes, before comparing them. In terms of theoretical complexity, exponentiations in the encryption schemes dominate the computation as elliptic curve operations are much cheaper. Thus, we only count these exponentiations; we will see this results in an accurate prediction of experimental timings.

5.1 Lindell's Protocol with Paillier's Encryption Scheme

The key generation uses on average 360 Paillier exponentiations (of the form $r^N \bmod N^2$) but not all of them are full exponentiations. The signing phase uses only 2 Paillier exponentiations.

The timings corresponds to the mean of several experiments (30 to 1000 depending on the security level). The timings are quite stable other than the generation of the RSA modulus in the key generation. We use standard RSA integers (*i.e.*, not strong prime factors) as this would be too slow for high security levels. For example, for 256 bits security (15360 bits modulus), the generation of the modulus takes 95 s (mean of 30 experiments) with a standard deviation of 56 s. For the rest of the protocol the experimental timings are roughly equal to the number of exponentiations multiplied by the cost of one exponentiation.

The result are summarized in Fig. 9a. Timings are given in milliseconds and sizes in bits. The columns corresponds to the elliptic curve used for ECDSA, the security parameter in bits for the encryption scheme, the corresponding modulus bit size, the timings of one Paillier exponentiation, of the key generation and of the signing phase and the total communication in bits for two phases. Modulus sizes are set according to the NIST recommendations.

Note that for the first line, we use a 2048 bits modulus as in [Lin17] and we obtain a similar experimental result.

Curve	Sec. Param.	Modulus	Expo. (ms)	Keygen (ms)	Signing (ms)	Keygen (b)	Signing (b)
P-256	112	2048	**7**	**2 133**	20	881 901	5 636
P-256	128	3072	**22**	**6 340**	49	1 317 101	7 684
P-384	192	7680	214	65 986	**437**	3 280 429	17 668
P-521	256	15360	1196	429 965	2 415	6 549 402	33 832

(a) Lindell's Protocol with Paillier

Curve	Sec. Param.	Discriminant	Expo. (ms)	Keygen (ms)	Signing (ms)	Keygen (b)	Signing (b)
P-256	112	1348	32	5 521	101	**178 668**	**4 748**
P-256	128	1827	55	9 350	170	**227 526**	**5 706**
P-384	192	3598	**212**	**35 491**	649	**427 112**	**10 272**
P-521	256	5971	**623**	**103 095**	1 888	**688 498**	**16 078**

(b) Our Protocol with HSM-CL

Fig. 9. Experimental results (timings in ms, sizes in bits)

5.2 Our Protocol with HSM-CL Encryption Scheme

The key generation uses a total of 160 class group exponentiations (of the form g_q^r in the class group of discriminant $\Delta_q = -q^3 \cdot \tilde{q}$). This corresponds to the 40 rounds of the $R_{\text{CL}-\text{DL}}$ zero-knowledge proof of knowledge of Fig. 8. Note that exponentiations in $\langle f \rangle$ are almost free as seen in Subsect. 4.1. Signing uses 3 class group exponentiations (one encryption and one decryption).

We use the same number of experiments as for Lindell's protocol. Here timings are very stable. Indeed during key generation, we only compute the public key $h \leftarrow g_q^x$ with one exponentiation, as the output of Gen (mainly the discriminant Δ_q of the class group and the generator g_q) is a common public parameter that only depends on the cardinality q of the elliptic curve. As a result this can be considered as an input of the protocol, as the same group can be used by all users. Moreover, doing this does not change the global result of the comparison with Lindell's protocol: the running time of Gen is dominated by the generation of $\tilde{q}$, a prime of size much smaller than the factor of the RSA modulus. So even if we add this running time in the Keygen column, this does not affect the results of our comparisons for any of the considered security levels.

The results are summarized in Fig. 9b. Timings are in milliseconds and sizes in bits. The columns correspond to the elliptic curve used for ECDSA, the security parameter in bits for the encryption scheme, the corresponding fundamental discriminant $\Delta_K = -q \cdot \tilde{q}$ bit size, the timings of one class group exponentiation, of the key generation and of the signing phase and the total communication in bits for two phases. The discriminant sizes are chosen according to [BJS10].

5.3   Comparison

Figure 9 shows that Lindell's protocol is faster for both key generation and signing for standard security levels for the encryption scheme (112 and 128 bits of security) while our solution remains of the same order of magnitude. However for high security levels, our solution becomes faster (in terms of key generation from a 192-bits security level and for both key generation and signing from a 256-bits security level).

In terms of communications, our solution outperforms the scheme of Lindell at all level of security by a factor 5 to 10 for Keygen. For Signing, we gain 15% for basic security to a factor 2 at 256-bits security level. In terms of rounds, our protocol uses 126 rounds for Keygen and Lindell's protocol uses 175 rounds, so we get a 28% gain. Both protocol use 7 rounds for Signing.

This situation can be explained by the following facts. Firstly we use less than half the number of exponentiations in the key generation as we do not need a range proof: our message space is $\mathbf{Z}/q\mathbf{Z}$ as the CL encryption scheme is homomorphic modulo a prime. Secondly, with class groups of quadratic fields we can use lower parameters than with $\mathbf{Z}/n\mathbf{Z}$ (as shown in the introduction, the best algorithm against the discrete logarithm problem in class groups has complexity $\mathcal{O}(L[1/2, o(1)])$ compared to an $\mathcal{O}(L[1/3, o(1)])$ for factoring). However, the group law is more complex in class groups. By comparing the Expo. time columns in the tables, we see that exponentiations in class groups are cheaper from the 192 bits level. So even if we use half as many exponentiations, the key generation for our solution only takes less time from that level (while being of the same order of magnitude below this level). For signing, we increase the cost by one exponentiation due to the Elgamal structure of the CL encryption scheme. However, one can note that we can pre process this encryption by computing (g_q^τ, h^τ) in an offline phase and computing $c_1 \leftarrow (g_q^\tau, h^\tau f^{k_2^{-1}m'})$ which results in only one multiplication in the online phase (cf. the description of the protocol in the full version [CCLST19, Appendix V]). As a result we will have only one exponentiation in the online signing for the decryption operation. The same holds for Lindell's protocol with Paillier. Using that both protocols take the same time for signing at the 192 bits level.

Obtaining a 2^{-60} Soundness Error. Increasing the number of rounds only impacts KeyGen, where Lindell's scheme and ours both use 40 iterations of ZK proofs to achieve a 2^{-40} soundness error. Lindell's protocol performs 9 exponentiations per iteration while ours performs 4. All timings will thus be multiplied by 3/2 to achieve a 2^{-60} soundness error, and indeed this is what we observe in practice. Complexity is linear in the number of iterations and the ratio between our timings and those of [Lin17] remains constant.

6   Conclusion

Inspired by Lindell's scheme, we have provided the first generic construction for two-party ECDSA signing from hash proof systems which are homomorphic modulo a prime number. Theoretically, our construction allows for a simulation-based proof of security that is both tight and requires no artificial interactive assumptions, due to the structure of the underlying semantically secure homomorphic encryption schemes. Practically, we provide a detailed instantiation, and C implementation, from class groups of imaginary quadratic fields using the CL framework. This yields a better performance than Lindell's Paillier-based scheme for high levels of security, and same order of magnitude for standard levels. Our solution becomes faster than Lindell's from 192-bits of security upwards. Improvements could come from advances in ideal arithmetic in imaginary quadratic fields (see [IJS10] for instance). Recent proposals of verifiable delay functions based on class groups should also motivate research in this area (for example the Chia Network [Chi] has opened a competition for this).

Moreover, the bottleneck of our instantiation is the use of binary challenges in a zero knowledge proof of knowledge, used during key generation, in order to cope with the fact we are working in a cyclic subgroup of a group of unknown order and that we can not check that elements belong to the subgroup. There have been many proposals to deal with generalized Schnorr proofs in groups of unknown order (see for instance the framework of [CKY09] using safeguard groups, or [TW12]). For the case of subgroups of $(\mathbf{Z}/n\mathbf{Z})^{\times}$, efficient solutions for this type of proofs enlarge the challenge space, and rely on variants of the strong RSA assumption. For class groups, there have been informal proposals (see [DF02] for instance). However, computing square roots or finding elements of order 2 can be done efficiently in class groups knowing the factorization of the discriminant (which is public in our case). Moreover, as suggested in [BBF18], there may be other approaches to find low order elements in class groups. Advances in our understanding of class groups would lead to substantial efficiency improvements in several areas of cryptography.

Last but not least, our work focuses on the two party case. We believe that the ideas of our generic construction will lead to improvements in the general case of threshold ECDSA signatures. We leave this for future work.

Acknowledgements. The authors would like to thank Benoît Libert for fruitful discussions. This work was supported by the Universita' degli Studi di Catania, "Piano della Ricerca 2016/2018 Linea di intervento 2", and the French ANR ALAMBIC project (ANR-16-CE39-0006).

References

[BBBF18] Boneh, D., Bonneau, J., Bünz, B., Fisch, B.: Verifiable delay functions. In: Shacham, H., Boldyreva, A. (eds.) CRYPTO 2018, Part I. LNCS, vol. 10991, pp. 757–788. Springer, Cham (2018). https://doi.org/10.1007/978-3-319-96884-1_25

[BBF18] Boneh, D., Bünz, B., Fisch, B.: A survey of two verifiable delay functions. Cryptology ePrint Archive, Report 2018/712 (2018). https://eprint.iacr.org/2018/712

[BH01] Buchmann, J., Hamdy, S.: A survey on IQ cryptography. In: Proceedings of Public Key Cryptography and Computational Number Theory (2001)

[BH03] Bauer, M.L., Hamdy, S.: On class group computations using the number field sieve. In: Laih, C.-S. (ed.) ASIACRYPT 2003. LNCS, vol. 2894, pp. 311–325. Springer, Heidelberg (2003). https://doi.org/10.1007/978-3-540-40061-5_19

[BJS10] Biasse, J.-F., Jacobson, M.J., Silvester, A.K.: Security estimates for quadratic field based cryptosystems. In: Steinfeld, R., Hawkes, P. (eds.) ACISP 2010. LNCS, vol. 6168, pp. 233–247. Springer, Heidelberg (2010). https://doi.org/10.1007/978-3-642-14081-5_15

[Boy86] Boyd, C.: Digital multisignature. In: Baker, H., Piper, F. (eds.) Cryptography and Coding, pp. 241–246. Clarendon Press (1989)

[CCLST19] Castagnos, G., Catalano, D., Laguillaumie, F., Savasta, F., Tucker, I.: Two-party ECDSA from hash proof systems and efficient instantiations. Cryptology ePrint Archive, Report 2019/503 (2019). https://eprint.iacr.org/2019/503

[CH89] Croft, R.A., Harris, S.P.: Public-key cryptography and reusable shared secrets. In: Baker, H., Piper, F. (eds.) Cryptography and Coding, pp. 189–201. Clarendon Press, Oxford (1989)

[Chi] Chia. https://www.chia.net/

[CIL17] Castagnos, G., Imbert, L., Laguillaumie, F.: Encryption switching protocols revisited: switching modulo p. In: Katz, J., Shacham, H. (eds.) CRYPTO 2017. LNCS, vol. 10401, pp. 255–287. Springer, Cham (2017). https://doi.org/10.1007/978-3-319-63688-7_9

[CKY09] Camenisch, J., Kiayias, A., Yung, M.: On the portability of generalized schnorr proofs. In: Joux, A. (ed.) EUROCRYPT 2009. LNCS, vol. 5479, pp. 425–442. Springer, Heidelberg (2009). https://doi.org/10.1007/978-3-642-01001-9_25

[CL09] Castagnos, G., Laguillaumie, F.: On the security of cryptosystems with quadratic decryption: the nicest cryptanalysis. In: Joux, A. (ed.) EUROCRYPT 2009. LNCS, vol. 5479, pp. 260–277. Springer, Heidelberg (2009). https://doi.org/10.1007/978-3-642-01001-9_15

[CL15] Castagnos, G., Laguillaumie, F.: Linearly homomorphic encryption from DDH. In: Nyberg, K. (ed.) CT-RSA 2015. LNCS, vol. 9048, pp. 487–505. Springer, Cham (2015). https://doi.org/10.1007/978-3-319-16715-2_26

[CLT18] Castagnos, G., Laguillaumie, F., Tucker, I.: Practical fully secure unrestricted inner product functional encryption modulo p. In: Peyrin, T., Galbraith, S. (eds.) ASIACRYPT 2018, Part II. LNCS, vol. 11273, pp. 733–764. Springer, Cham (2018). https://doi.org/10.1007/978-3-030-03329-3_25

[Coh00] Cohen, H.: A Course in Computational Algebraic Number Theory. Springer, Heidelberg (2000)

[CS98] Cramer, R., Shoup, V.: A practical public key cryptosystem provably secure against adaptive chosen ciphertext attack. In: Krawczyk, H. (ed.) CRYPTO 1998. LNCS, vol. 1462, pp. 13–25. Springer, Heidelberg (1998). https://doi.org/10.1007/BFb0055717

[CS02] Cramer, R., Shoup, V.: Universal hash proofs and a paradigm for adaptive chosen ciphertext secure public-key encryption. In: Knudsen, L.R. (ed.) EUROCRYPT 2002. LNCS, vol. 2332, pp. 45–64. Springer, Heidelberg (2002). https://doi.org/10.1007/3-540-46035-7_4

[CS03] Camenisch, J., Shoup, V.: Practical verifiable encryption and decryption of discrete logarithms. In: Boneh, D. (ed.) CRYPTO 2003. LNCS, vol. 2729, pp. 126–144. Springer, Heidelberg (2003). https://doi.org/10.1007/978-3-540-45146-4_8

[Des88] Desmedt, Y.: Society and group oriented cryptography: a new concept. In: Pomerance, C. (ed.) CRYPTO 1987. LNCS, vol. 293, pp. 120–127. Springer, Heidelberg (1988). https://doi.org/10.1007/3-540-48184-2_8

[DF90] Desmedt, Y., Frankel, Y.: Threshold cryptosystems. In: Brassard, G. (ed.) CRYPTO 1989. LNCS, vol. 435, pp. 307–315. Springer, New York (1990). https://doi.org/10.1007/0-387-34805-0_28

[DF02] Damgård, I., Fujisaki, E.: A statistically-hiding integer commitment scheme based on groups with hidden order. In: Zheng, Y. (ed.) ASIACRYPT 2002. LNCS, vol. 2501, pp. 125–142. Springer, Heidelberg (2002). https://doi.org/10.1007/3-540-36178-2_8

[DKLs18] Doerner, J., Kondi, Y., Lee, E., Shelat, A.: Secure two-party threshold ECDSA from ECDSA assumptions. In: 2018 IEEE Symposium on Security and Privacy, pp. 980–997. IEEE Computer Society Press (2018)

[DKLs19] Doerner, J., Kondi, Y., Lee, E., Shelat, A.: Threshold ECDSA from ECDSA assumptions: the multiparty case. In: 2019 IEEE Symposium on Security and Privacy, pp. 980–997. IEEE Computer Society Press (2019)

[GG18] Gennaro, R., Goldfeder, S.: Fast multiparty threshold ECDSA with fast trustless setup. In: ACM CCS 2018. ACM Press (2018)

[GGN16] Gennaro, R., Goldfeder, S., Narayanan, A.: Threshold-optimal DSA/ECDSA signatures and an application to bitcoin wallet security. In: Manulis, M., Sadeghi, A.-R., Schneider, S. (eds.) ACNS 2016. LNCS, vol. 9696, pp. 156–174. Springer, Cham (2016). https://doi.org/10.1007/978-3-319-39555-5_9

[GJKR96] Gennaro, R., Jarecki, S., Krawczyk, H., Rabin, T.: Robust threshold DSS signatures. In: Maurer, U. (ed.) EUROCRYPT 1996. LNCS, vol. 1070, pp. 354–371. Springer, Heidelberg (1996). https://doi.org/10.1007/3-540-68339-9_31

[GMR89] Goldwasser, S., Micali, S., Rackoff, C.: The knowledge complexity of interactive proof systems. SIAM J. Comput. 18, 186–208 (1989)

[Gol01] Goldreich, O.: Foundations of Cryptography: Basic Tools. Cambridge University Press, Cambridge (2001)

[GPS06] Girault, M., Poupard, G., Stern, J.: On the fly authentication and signature schemes based on groups of unknown order. J. Cryptol. 19, 463–487 (2006)

[HL10] Hazay, C., Lindell, Y.: Efficient Secure Two-Party Protocols: Techniques and Constructions, 1st edn. Springer, Heidelberg (2010). https://doi.org/10.1007/978-3-642-14303-8

[HO09] Hemenway, B., Ostrovsky, R.: Lossy trapdoor functions from smooth homomorphic hash proof systems. In: Electronic Colloquium on Computational Complexity (ECCC), vol. 16, no. 127 (2009). 01

[IJS10] Imbert, L., Jacobson Jr., M.J., Schmidt, A.: Fast ideal cubing in imaginary quadratic number and function fields. Adv. Math. Commun. 4, 237–260 (2010)

[Jac00] Jacobson Jr., M.J.: Computing discrete logarithms in quadratic orders. J. Cryptol. 13, 473–492 (2000). https://doi.org/10.1007/s001450010013. Springer, Heidelberg

[Lin16] Lindell, Y.: How to simulate it - a tutorial on the simulation proof technique. Cryptology ePrint Archive, Report 2016/046 (2016). http://eprint.iacr.org/2016/046

[Lin17] Lindell, Y.: Fast secure two-party ECDSA signing. In: Katz, J., Shacham, H. (eds.) CRYPTO 2017, Part II. LNCS, vol. 10402, pp. 613–644. Springer, Cham (2017). https://doi.org/10.1007/978-3-319-63715-0_21

[LN18] Lindell, Y., Nof, A.: Fast secure multiparty ECDSA with practical distributed key generation and applications to cryptocurrency custody. In: ACM CCS 2018, pp. 1837–1854. ACM Press, October 2018

[MR04] MacKenzie, P.D., Reiter, M.K.: Two-party generation of DSA signatures. Int. J. Inf. Secur. **2**, 218–239 (2004). https://doi.org/10.1007/s10207-004-0041-0

[PAR18] PARI Group, University Bordeaux. PARI/GP version 2.11.1 (2018). http://pari.math.u-bordeaux.fr/

[Sch91] Schnorr, C.-P.: Efficient signature generation by smart cards. J. Cryptol. **4**, 161–174 (1991)

[Sep] Sepior. http://www.sepior.com

[Ser] I. D. P. Services. https://security.intuit.com/

[SG98] Shoup, V., Gennaro, R.: Securing threshold cryptosystems against chosen ciphertext attack. In: Nyberg, K. (ed.) EUROCRYPT 1998. LNCS, vol. 1403, pp. 1–16. Springer, Heidelberg (1998). https://doi.org/10.1007/BFb0054113

[Sho00] Shoup, V.: Practical threshold signatures. In: Preneel, B. (ed.) EUROCRYPT 2000. LNCS, vol. 1807, pp. 207–220. Springer, Heidelberg (2000). https://doi.org/10.1007/3-540-45539-6_15

[TW12] Terelius, B., Wikström, D.: Efficiency limitations of $\sum$-protocols for group homomorphisms revisited. In: Visconti, I., De Prisco, R. (eds.) SCN 2012. LNCS, vol. 7485, pp. 461–476. Springer, Heidelberg (2012). https://doi.org/10.1007/978-3-642-32928-9_26

[Unb] Unboundtech. https://www.unboundtech.com/

[Van92] Vanstone, S.: Responses to NIST's proposal. Commun. ACM **35**, 50–52 (1992). Communicated by John Anderson

[Wes19] Wesolowski, B.: Efficient verifiable delay functions. In: Ishai, Y., Rijmen, V. (eds.) EUROCRYPT 2019. LNCS, vol. 11478, pp. 379–407. Springer, Cham (2019). https://doi.org/10.1007/978-3-030-17659-4_13

Asymmetric Message Franking: Content Moderation for Metadata-Private End-to-End Encryption

Nirvan Tyagi[1(✉)], Paul Grubbs[1(✉)], Julia Len[1], Ian Miers[1,2], and Thomas Ristenpart[1]

[1] Cornell Tech, New York City, USA
{nt355,pag225,jl3836,imiers,ristenpart}@cornell.edu
[2] University of Maryland, College Park, USA

Abstract. Content moderation is crucial for stopping abusive and harassing messages in online platforms. Existing moderation mechanisms, such as message franking, require platform providers to be able to associate user identifiers to encrypted messages. These mechanisms fail in *metadata-private* messaging systems, such as Signal, where users can hide their identities from platform providers. The key technical challenge preventing moderation is achieving cryptographic accountability while preserving deniability.

In this work, we resolve this tension with a new cryptographic primitive: *asymmetric message franking* (AMF) schemes. We define strong security notions for AMF schemes, including the first formal treatment of deniability in moderation settings. We then construct, analyze, and implement an AMF scheme that is fast enough to use for content moderation of metadata-private messaging.

Keywords: Message franking · Designated verifier signatures · Deniability · End-to-end encryption · Content moderation

1 Introduction

Billions of users communicate via private messaging on platforms like Facebook, Twitter, and Signal. Their success means these platforms are increasingly used for large-scale spam, harassment, and propagation of misinformation. One way platform operators address these threats is via *content moderation*: the receiver of a message can report it to a moderator. If the moderator determines (via human judgment, machine learning algorithm, or both) that the message violated the platform's policies, the platform can ban its sender.

To ensure moderation is not itself abused, the platform must be able to verify both the content of the reported message and associated metadata, e.g. the sender and receiver identity. Doing this is challenging for end-to-end (E2E) encrypted messaging because the platform does not see the cleartext messages. In

© International Association for Cryptologic Research 2019
A. Boldyreva and D. Micciancio (Eds.): CRYPTO 2019, LNCS 11694, pp. 222–250, 2019.
https://doi.org/10.1007/978-3-030-26954-8_8

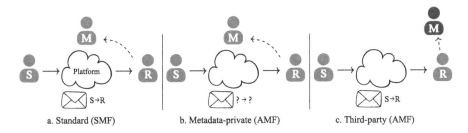

a. Standard (SMF)   b. Metadata-private (AMF)   c. Third-party (AMF)

Fig. 1. Settings for content moderation of messaging. The solid arrow denotes sending a message across the platform and the dashed arrow denotes reporting a message to the moderator. In the standard setting, messages sent across the platform are associated with sender and receiver identities and the platform is the moderator. In the metadata-private setting, the associated sender and receiver identities of messages are hidden from the platform, and by extension, the moderator. In the third-party setting, the moderator is separate from the platform, and thus also cannot associate sender and receiver identities to messages. Our AMF primitive targets the latter two settings.

practice, moderating E2E encrypted messaging has been done via *message franking* [34,39]. Message franking has two main components. First, the E2E encryption uses specially-constructed ciphertexts that include a compact commitment to the plaintext. Second, the platform cryptographically binds the sender and receiver identities to the ciphertexts using a reporting tag (concretely, a MAC over the relevant metadata and the commitment). Because this approach only uses symmetric-key cryptography, we call it *symmetric* message franking (SMF).

SMF carefully navigates the three security requirements of content moderation for E2E encrypted messaging. First, messages not included in reports should remain private. Second, moderation should achieve *accountability*: given a reported message and sender identity, the moderator should always be able to verify the sender sent that message. Finally, moderation for E2E-encrypted messages should be *deniable*: only the moderator should be able to verify the report. This protects users from backlash or embarrassment if their messages are posted publicly after a compromise. Deniability was an explicit goal of Facebook's SMF-based moderation system [34]. If implemented correctly, SMF meets these goals because the commitments are hiding and binding and the identities are bound to the reporting tag.

There are settings, however, where it is impossible to associate identities to encrypted messages and SMF cannot be used for moderation. One such setting is *metadata-private* messaging, depicted in the middle diagram of Fig. 1. Metadata-private messaging systems not only use E2E encryption, but also hide the sender and/or receiver identities of messages from the platform. (In these systems the platform knows the identities of all registered parties but does not learn those identities during communication.) For example, Signal's recent sealed sender feature, which hides the sender identity, now accounts for over 80% of all Signal traffic [5,55]. Achieving even stronger metadata privacy, such as also hiding the receiver identity, is an active research area [7,28,29,41,47–49,52,53,62,71].

Similarly, one may consider decentralized or federated settings where the moderator is decoupled from the platform. (See the right-hand diagram of Fig. 1; more detail on this setting is given below.)

A naive solution for moderation in these settings is per-message digital signatures. These provide accountability even if the moderator cannot see metadata or messages, but not deniability: anyone can verify signatures, not just the moderator. Indeed, this and other approaches based on existing primitives fail because of a fundamental tension between accountability and deniability. To make moderation a reality for metadata-private messaging and other settings, new cryptography is needed.

Asymmetric Message Franking. This work defines and constructs asymmetric message franking (AMF) schemes. AMF schemes are special signatures in which a sender signs a message so that only one of two designated parties, the receiver or the moderator, can verify it. The signature also proves to the receiver that the signature can be verified by the moderator. AMF schemes are deniable and do not require the platform to associate identities with encrypted messages. Thus, AMF schemes resolve the main technical barrier to content moderation for metadata-private messaging.

Using AMF schemes in moderation involves three parties: the *sender*, *receiver*, and *moderator* (or *judge*). Each one has a key pair and knows the public keys of the other two (we assume a PKI is available). The sender of a message uses the AMF scheme's franking algorithm Frank to generate a signature on the message. Then the sender E2E-encrypts the message and the signature and sends the ciphertext to the receiver. The receiver first decrypts the ciphertext then verifies the signature using the receiver verification algorithm Verify. To make a report, the receiver sends the message and signature to the moderator, who verifies using the moderator verification algorithm Judge. The receiver and moderator verification algorithms are different because the receiver and moderator have independent secret keys. Next, we explain security for AMF schemes along two axes: accountability and deniability.

AMF Accountability. For accountability, we want that a malicious sender cannot bypass moderation and a malicious receiver cannot report a message it did not receive. To formalize this we give three security notions for AMF schemes: *sender binding*, *receiver binding*, and *unforgeability*.

Sender binding requires that an attacker who can choose a sender key pair and adaptively query Verify and Judge oracles cannot create a message and signature pair the receiver will accept but the moderator will not. An attacker that can do this can essentially bypass moderation entirely. Similar attacks arise in practice: for example, Dodis et al. demonstrated how to bypass Facebook's SMF scheme [33]. Receiver binding is a complementary notion that requires that no adversary can trick the moderator into accepting a message not actually sent to its designated receiver, even if the adversary can choose the receiver's keys. Unforgeability requires that an attacker that only knows public keys cannot output a forged message and signature pair that fools the receiver. In our full version [72], we prove unforgeability is implied by the combination of receiver binding and sender binding.

AMF Deniability. Deniability guarantees that convincing-looking forgeries can be created even if some parties are compromised or malicious. Our threat model for deniability is very strong: we allow all keys to be compromised (even the moderator's). Providing meaningful deniability definitions for AMF schemes in the context of moderation is challenging as deniability can often contradict accountability. Prior work in this area [34, 39] did not attempt to formalize their deniability guarantees, despite deniability being an explicit goal. Take, for example, a deniability definition which requires that an adversary can produce a signature indistinguishable from a legitimate one, given just the public keys of sender, receiver, and moderator. This contradicts unforgeability, since it suggests that anyone can generate signatures that a receiver and moderator would accept as valid.

We navigate this tension between deniability and accountability by equipping AMF schemes with three forgery algorithms (Forge, RForge, and JForge) and three associated security definitions: *universal deniability, receiver compromise deniability,* and *judge compromise deniability.* The three forgery algorithms are not intended to be run by legitimate users: instead, the existence of each of the three algorithms guarantees deniability in a particular compromise scenario formalized in its associated definition.

We limit our first deniability definition, universal deniability, to hold against everyone except the receiver and moderator. Meeting this goal guarantees the outputs of Forge and Frank are indistinguishable to everyone except those two parties. But this leaves open another way to render AMF signatures undeniable: a receiver (or the moderator) could post their secret key to the internet along with a received message and AMF signature, allowing anyone to run Judge or Verify and rule out a forgery. This could serve as undeniable cryptographic evidence that the sender authored the message.

Because of this, we introduce two additional deniability notions: receiver compromise deniability and judge compromise deniability. Meeting these notions implies deniability holds even if the receiver and/or moderator are compromised or malicious. The former definition corresponds to the case where the receiver's secret key is known and the latter the case where both the receiver and moderator's keys are known. The forgeries generated (by RForge and JForge, respectively) should be indistinguishable from the output of Frank, even to a distinguisher that knows the receiver or both the receiver and moderator's secret keys. This means that a receiver or the moderator cannot offer an undeniable proof that a sender sent a message simply by disclosing their secrets: they could equally well have just generated a forgery.

These three deniability definitions are not the only ones possible, and there exists a large space of possible definitions, though many are at odds with accountability. We explore this broader landscape in more detail in our full version [72], and discuss how our deniability targets compare to others in Sect. 2.

Constructing AMFs. We build a practical AMF scheme that meets the above definitions. As described above, we want to be able to sign messages so that only the receiver and moderator can verify them. Thus, a natural starting point is (strong) designated verifier signatures [44], in which a sender signs a message so that only a particular recipient can verify it. We designate the moderator as one verifier, and extend to allow a receiver (with its own key pair separate from the moderator's) to be a second designated verifier. However, designated verifier signatures alone do not suffice: the receiver (without the moderator's secret key) must be able to verify that the moderator can verify the signature. If this is missing, the scheme would not be sender binding.

Our eventual construction is based on a non-interactive zero-knowledge proof-of-knowledge of a carefully crafted language that balances the needed verification properties with the ability to forge required for deniability. The formal analysis is non-trivial: our definitions give the adversary oracle access to Judge and Verify, both of which need secret keys. In some of our reductions the output of these oracles must be simulated without secret keys, necessitating both standard assumptions like discrete log and the knowledge-of-exponent assumption (KEA), a more exotic (but nevertheless well-studied) assumption [9,30]. In [72], we show a variation of our scheme (with slightly larger signatures) can be proven secure using the standard Gap Diffie-Hellman assumption [14].

We prototype our AMF construction to demonstrate its practicality. Our AMF signatures are relatively compact, requiring less than 500 bytes. Even in our unoptimized implementation, signing and verification (by a receiver or the moderator) takes 7.3 ms or less. We plan to make our AMF implementations open source to support development of new moderation tools.

Other Applications. AMF schemes may prove useful in settings beyond metadata-private encrypted messaging. As described above, existing moderation tools based on SMF cannot support *third-party* moderation, which decouples the platform and moderator (see Fig. 1, right diagram). Third-party moderation is necessary in decentralized or federated messaging systems like Matrix [4] or Mastodon [3]. In such systems no single party operates the platform, so the moderator must be distinct. Even in centralized systems like Twitter, third-party moderation is advantageous if the platform cannot adequately moderate messages, or if sub-communities want to enforce their own content policies. Allowing the moderator to be distinct can also enable cross-platform moderation of multiple messaging systems.

Similarly to the metadata-private setting, a third-party moderator does not learn the needed sender and receiver identities associated with messages. In metadata-private settings, this information is cryptographically hidden, whereas in third-party settings it is simply unavailable because the moderator doesn't run the identity infrastructure. Because AMF schemes are public-key, they can be used in conjunction with PKI to build third-party moderation.

Summary. This work makes the following contributions:

- We highlight the need for content moderation for metadata-private messaging, and identify a key cryptographic challenge: balancing accountability with deniability.
- We introduce and formalize a new cryptographic primitive called asymmetric message franking that simultaneously provides the needed authenticity properties for content moderation, while ensuring cryptographic deniability.
- We show how to build an efficient AMF scheme and formally analyze its security. A prototype implementation indicates that our AMF scheme is practical.

2   Deniability in Messaging

We want AMFs to provide deniability in the event that keys or messages are posted publicly after a compromise. Our setting is therefore most similar to the deniability guarantees sought for designated verifier signatures and proofs [44], but different than settings that allow one to deny encrypted message contents even to an eavesdropper that sees all traffic [21]. An adversary that observes the actual transmission of a message or ciphertext is totally convinced of its origin in our setting. Instead, our concern is not this adversary's conviction, but its ability to convince others. As long as the attacker cannot use what it learns through network manipulation or endpoint compromise to convince others, we have achieved deniability.

The types of deniability guarantees we target have long been a goal in various contexts [23, 25], including messaging [34]. The inability to prevent major compromises has made lack of deniability an increasingly pressing concern. In the 2016 United States' and 2017 French presidential elections, certain candidates' systems were compromised and sensitive data was dumped publicly online. DKIM email signatures prevented the Clinton campaign from denying authorship for hacked emails posted by Wikileaks in 2016 [58]. In contrast, in 2017 the Macron campaign was able to effectively deny the authenticity of leaked messages by including decoy messages as a countermeasure [60]. This defense was only possible because of a lack of cryptographic evidence. One result of these breaches is that politicians and others increasingly use E2E encrypted messaging systems that provide deniability [67]. If E2E encryption provides deniability, the cryptography used for moderation must preserve this deniability. This is a crucial reason why AMFs must be deniable.

These examples additionally demonstrate that deniability in messaging is practically important: it is necessary, but not always sufficient, for (what we call) social deniability, i.e., that people are convinced by a denial. Our goal is to ensure that whatever prior belief people have about the likelihood a message is valid should remain unchanged by the use of cryptography, and to have a system that works with other techniques for increasing the success of social deniability (e.g., use of decoys). We do note that because of pervasive propaganda campaigns an awareness has developed among the general public that malicious parties will try to influence popular sentiment by forging content. This would seem to make social deniability more feasible, as people are unlikely to be convinced by an unverified attribution in the era of "fake news".

An important implication of all this is that, to issue a denial that will convince the general public, it is not sufficient to demonstrate the (perhaps non-constructive) *existence* of a forger who *could* have forged a message—there must exist concrete and runnable forgery algorithms that could have been used by influence campaigns or other adversaries. Our eventual construction has three such implemented algorithms for different compromise scenarios; see Sect. 4 for more details.

3   Syntax and Security Notions

We introduce a new primitive, *asymmetric message franking* (AMF), that provides the cryptographic algorithms needed for secure metadata-private moderation. We will present the algorithms and security definitions of an AMF scheme in three parts. First, we present a brief preliminary on key generation. Then, we describe the accountability algorithms and definitions. Finally, we present the three algorithms used for deniability and definitions.

As you will see, we choose to decouple our security treatment of AMFs from the accompanying end-to-end (E2E) encryption scheme to simplify and modularize the analysis. Indeed in the applications we envision, the accountability and deniability of the system would be determined by the composition of AMFs with an E2E encryption scheme, which we discuss further in Sect. 7.

Formally, an asymmetric message franking scheme AMF = (KeyGen, Frank, Verify, Judge, Forge, RForge, JForge) is a tuple of seven algorithms. An AMF scheme is associated with a public key space $\mathcal{PK}$, secret key space $\mathcal{SK}$, message space $\mathcal{M}$, and signature space Σ. To simplify notation of inputs in the algorithms, we assume all pk inputs are in $\mathcal{PK}$, all sk inputs are in $\mathcal{SK}$, all msg inputs are in $\mathcal{M}$, and all σ inputs are in Σ.

AMF Key Generation. AMF key generation, $(pk, sk) \leftarrow\!\!{\scriptstyle\$}\, \mathsf{KeyGen}$, is a randomized key generation algorithm which outputs a public key pair $(pk, sk) \in \mathcal{PK} \times \mathcal{SK}$. We assume the public key pk can be uniquely recovered from the private key sk. Our schemes have this property. We also assume for simplicity that the judge, senders, and receivers all use the same key generation algorithm.

We will assume that key pairs can be confirmed to be valid. More precisely, we will use later a deterministic algorithm $\mathsf{WellFormed}: \mathcal{PK} \times \mathcal{SK} \to \{0, 1\}$ which takes as input a key pair $(pk, sk) \in \mathcal{PK} \times \mathcal{SK}$ and outputs a bit b denoting whether the key pair is a valid pair $(b = 1)$ or not $(b = 0)$. The purpose of this procedure is to verify that a (possibly adversarially chosen) key pair is *well-formed* relative to some relationship between pk and sk. In our schemes this will be a single exponentiation.

Our formalization of AMFs excludes deployment considerations such as the public key infrastructure and identity-to-public key mappings: see Sects. 6 and 7 for more discussion.

3.1   AMF Algorithms and Security Notions: Accountability

For an AMF = (KeyGen, Frank, Verify, Judge, Forge, RForge, JForge), the three accountability algorithms are Frank, Verify, and Judge. These algorithms are used for creating and verifying signatures. We explain the syntax of each algorithm in turn, then describe the corresponding accountability security notions.

- $\sigma \leftarrow_{\$} \mathsf{Frank}(sk_s, pk_r, pk_j, msg)$: The (randomized) message signing or *franking* algorithm takes as input a receiver public key pk_r, a judge public key pk_j, a sender secret key sk_s, and a message msg. It outputs a signature σ.
- $b \leftarrow \mathsf{Verify}(pk_s, sk_r, pk_j, msg, \sigma)$: The deterministic receiver verification algorithm takes as input a sender public key pk_s, receiver secret key sk_r, judge public key pk_j, message msg, and signature σ, then outputs a bit. The receiver runs this to ensure the message, signature pair (msg, σ) is well-formed and reportable to the judge.
- $b \leftarrow \mathsf{Judge}(pk_s, pk_r, sk_j, msg, \sigma)$: The deterministic judge authentication algorithm takes as input a sender public key pk_s, receiver public key pk_r, judge secret key sk_j, message msg, and signature σ, then outputs a bit. This algorithm is used by the judge to check the authenticity of reported messages, ensuring the message was really sent from the sender and was meant for the recipient.

This formalization restricts attention to non-interactive schemes for which franking, verification, and judging requires sending just a single message. Such non-interactive schemes have important practical benefits, but it is conceivable that there might be some benefits of generalizing our treatment to include interactive schemes, which we leave for future work.

Correctness. Informally, we require AMF signatures created by the franking algorithm are both verified and judged successfully. Formally, for all messages, msg, and for all pairs of public keys, $(pk_{\{s,r,j\}}, sk_{\{s,r,j\}})$, it holds that

$$\Pr \left[\mathsf{Verify}(pk_s, sk_r, pk_j, msg, \mathsf{Frank}(sk_s, pk_r, pk_j, msg)) = 1 \right] = 1$$

and

$$\Pr \left[\mathsf{Judge}(pk_s, pk_r, sk_j, msg, \mathsf{Frank}(sk_s, pk_r, pk_j, msg)) = 1 \right] = 1$$

where the probabilities are taken over the random coins used in Frank.

Security Notions for Accountability. First and foremost an AMF scheme should prevent a party from impersonating a sender to a receiver. This goal, which we call *unforgeability*, is a lifting of standard digital signature unforgeability to the setting of AMF schemes. As discussed above, AMFs should also (1) prevent any sender from creating a signature that can be verified by the receiver but not the moderator, and (2) prevent any receiver from framing a sender by creating a signature on a message that wasn't sent. Following the terminology used in symmetric message franking [39] we refer to these goals as *sender binding* and *receiver binding*, respectively.

$$
\begin{array}{ll}
\hline
\text{r-BIND}^{\mathcal{A}}_{\text{AMF}}: & \text{s-BIND}^{\mathcal{A}}_{\text{AMF}}: \\
(pk_s, sk_s) \leftarrow\!\!\$\ \mathsf{KeyGen} & (pk_r, sk_r) \leftarrow\!\!\$\ \mathsf{KeyGen} \\
(pk_j, sk_j) \leftarrow\!\!\$\ \mathsf{KeyGen} & (pk_j, sk_j) \leftarrow\!\!\$\ \mathsf{KeyGen} \\
(pk_r, msg, \sigma) \leftarrow \mathcal{A}^{\mathcal{O}}(pk_s, pk_j) & (pk_s, msg, \sigma) \leftarrow \mathcal{A}^{\mathcal{O}}(pk_r, pk_j) \\
\text{if } (pk_r, pk_j, msg) \in Q: & b_v \leftarrow \mathsf{Verify}(pk_s, sk_r, pk_j, msg, \sigma) \\
\quad\text{return } 0 & b_j \leftarrow \mathsf{Judge}(pk_s, pk_r, sk_j, msg, \sigma) \\
\text{return } \mathsf{Judge}(pk_s, pk_r, sk_j, msg, \sigma) & \text{return } b_v \wedge \neg b_j \\
 & \\
\mathcal{O}^{\mathsf{Frank}}(pk'_r, pk'_j, msg): & \mathcal{O}^{\mathsf{Verify}}(pk'_s, pk'_j, msg, \sigma): \\
 & \\
Q \leftarrow Q \cup \{(pk'_r, pk'_j, msg)\} & \text{return } \mathsf{Verify}(pk'_s, sk_r, pk'_j, msg, \sigma) \\
\text{return } \mathsf{Frank}(sk_s, pk'_r, pk'_j, msg) & \\
 & \mathcal{O}^{\mathsf{Judge}}(pk'_s, pk'_r, msg, \sigma): \\
\mathcal{O}^{\mathsf{Judge}}(pk'_s, pk'_r, msg, \sigma): & \\
\text{return } \mathsf{Judge}(pk'_s, pk'_r, sk_j, msg, \sigma) & \text{return } \mathsf{Judge}(pk'_s, pk'_r, sk_j, msg, \sigma) \\
\hline
\end{array}
$$

Fig. 2. Accountability games for AMF schemes: receiver binding (left) and sender binding (right).

It turns out sender binding and receiver binding together imply unforgeability. In this section, we proceed by formalizing the sender binding and receiver binding accountability notions. The formalization of unforgeability along with its reduction to receiver binding and sender binding is deferred to [72].

We formalize security using the code-based game approach of Bellare and Rogaway [11]. We will use a concrete security approach in which we account for adversarial resources explicitly in theorem statements, rather than defining security asymptotically. Asymptotic notions can be derived from our treatment in a straightforward way.

Receiver binding is specified formally in game r-BIND on the left-hand side of Fig. 2. The adversary plays the role of a reciever and attempts to create a signature that from a sender pk_s to an adversarially chosen pk_r that correctly judges by pk_j. The adversary is given a Frank oracle for some (honest) sender, to which it can query messages signed to chosen receiver and judge public keys. We also give the adversary access to a Judge oracle to query chosen message and signature pairs. It tries to output a message and signature, distinct from all Frank oracle outputs, for which Judge outputs 1. For an adversary $\mathcal{A}$ and message franking scheme AMF we define the r-BIND advantage of $\mathcal{A}$ against AMF as

$$
\mathbf{Adv}^{\text{r-bind}}_{\text{AMF}}(\mathcal{A}) = \Pr\left[\, \text{r-BIND}^{\mathcal{A}}_{\text{AMF}} \Rightarrow 1 \,\right],
$$

where the probability here (and for subsequent use of games) is over all the random coins used in the game, including those of the adversary.

Sender binding is specified formally in game s-BIND on the right-hand side of Fig. 2. The adversary plays the role of a sender and its goal is to generate, for some adversarially chosen pk_s, an AMF signature that Verify validates but Judge rejects with pk_r and pk_j. The adversary is given a pair of oracles for Verify and Judge to which it can query message and signature pairs. For an adversary

$\mathcal{A}$ and message franking scheme AMF we define the s-BIND advantage of $\mathcal{A}$ against AMF as

$$\mathbf{Adv}_{\mathrm{AMF}}^{\mathrm{s\text{-}bind}}(\mathcal{A}) = \Pr\left[\,\mathrm{s\text{-}BIND}_{\mathrm{AMF}}^{\mathcal{A}} \Rightarrow 1\,\right].$$

3.2   AMF Algorithms and Security Notions: Deniability

To support deniability, we equip AMF schemes with three deniability algorithms and associate to each a security notion. We include the forging algorithms as part of the scheme to emphasize their importance in providing practically-meaningful deniability guarantees. They will be efficient to execute and as easy to implement as the other algorithms. The deniability algorithms for an AMF scheme AMF = (KeyGen, Frank, Verify, Judge, Forge, RForge, JForge) are Forge, RForge, and JForge. We give a formal description of each along with some intuition about the deniability setting they correspond to.

Universal deniability requires that any non-participating party (no access to sender, receiver, or judge secret keys) can forge a signature that is indistinguishable from honestly-generated signatures to other non-participating parties. Intuitively, this allows the sender to claim a message originated from any non-participating party. This is the purpose of the Forge algorithm of an AMF scheme.

- $\sigma \leftarrow_{\$} \mathsf{Forge}(pk_s, pk_r, pk_j, msg)$: The forge algorithm takes a sender public key pk_s, receiver public key pk_r, a judge public key pk_j, and a message msg, then outputs a "forged" AMF signature σ.

We formalize universal deniability in game UnivDen, the leftmost in Fig. 3. The adversary is given access to a frank oracle that outputs a signature created from Frank or Forge depending on a challenge bit that is the adversary's goal to guess. In this deniability game and all subsequent deniability games, the adversary is given access to the sender's secret key sk_s to model sender compromise. For an adversary $\mathcal{A}$ and asymmetric message franking scheme AMF we define the UnivDen advantage of $\mathcal{A}$ against AMF as

$$\mathbf{Adv}_{\mathrm{AMF}}^{\mathrm{univ\text{-}den}}(\mathcal{A}) = \left|\,\Pr\left[\,\mathrm{UnivDen}_{\mathrm{AMF}}^{\mathcal{A},0} \Rightarrow 1\,\right] - \Pr\left[\,\mathrm{UnivDen}_{\mathrm{AMF}}^{\mathcal{A},1} \Rightarrow 1\,\right]\,\right|.$$

Receiver compromise deniability requires that a party with access to the receiver's secret key can forge a signature that is indistinguishable from honestly-generated signatures to other parties with access to the receiver's secret key. This captures deniability in the case where the receiver's secret key is compromised, and allows the sender to claim a message originates from a compromising party or malicious receiver. The RForge algorithm is used for receiver compromise deniability.

- $\sigma \leftarrow_{\$} \mathsf{RForge}(pk_s, sk_r, pk_j, msg)$: The receiver forge algorithm takes a sender public key pk_s, receiver secret key sk_r, a judge public key pk_j, and a message msg, then outputs a "forged" AMF signature σ.

UnivDen$_{\mathrm{AMF}}^{\mathcal{A},b}$:	RecCompDen$_{\mathrm{AMF}}^{\mathcal{A},b}$:	JudgeCompDen$_{\mathrm{AMF}}^{\mathcal{A},b}$:
$(pk_s, sk_s) \leftarrow\!\!\$ \ \mathsf{KeyGen}$	$(pk_s, sk_s) \leftarrow\!\!\$ \ \mathsf{KeyGen}$	$(pk_s, sk_s) \leftarrow\!\!\$ \ \mathsf{KeyGen}$
$(pk_r, sk_r) \leftarrow\!\!\$ \ \mathsf{KeyGen}$	$(pk_j, sk_j) \leftarrow\!\!\$ \ \mathsf{KeyGen}$	$(pk_r, sk_r, pk_j, sk_j, aux) \leftarrow \mathcal{A}_1(pk_s)$
$(pk_j, sk_j) \leftarrow\!\!\$ \ \mathsf{KeyGen}$	$(pk_r, sk_r, aux) \leftarrow \mathcal{A}_1(pk_s, pk_j)$	$b_{\mathrm{wf}}^r \leftarrow \mathsf{WellFormed}(pk_r, sk_r)$
$b' \leftarrow \mathcal{A}^{\mathcal{O}^{\mathsf{Frank}}}(sk_s, pk_r, pk_j)$	$b_{\mathrm{wf}}^r \leftarrow \mathsf{WellFormed}(pk_r, sk_r)$	$b_{\mathrm{wf}}^j \leftarrow \mathsf{WellFormed}(pk_j, sk_j)$
return b'	**if** $b_{\mathrm{wf}}^r \neq 1$:	**if** $b_{\mathrm{wf}}^r \wedge b_{\mathrm{wf}}^j \neq 1$:
	return 0	**return** 0
$\mathcal{O}^{\mathsf{Frank}}(msg)$:	$b' \leftarrow \mathcal{A}_2^{\mathcal{O}^{\mathsf{Frank}}}(sk_s, sk_r, pk_j, aux)$	$b' \leftarrow \mathcal{A}_2^{\mathcal{O}^{\mathsf{Frank}}}(sk_s, sk_r, sk_j, aux)$
	return b'	**return** b'
$\sigma_0 \leftarrow \mathsf{Frank}(sk_s, pk_r, pk_j, msg)$		
$\sigma_1 \leftarrow \mathsf{Forge}(pk_s, pk_r, pk_j, msg)$	$\mathcal{O}^{\mathsf{Frank}}(msg)$:	$\mathcal{O}^{\mathsf{Frank}}(msg)$:
return σ_b		
	$\sigma_0 \leftarrow \mathsf{Frank}(sk_s, pk_r, pk_j, msg)$	$\sigma_0 \leftarrow \mathsf{Frank}(sk_s, pk_r, pk_j, msg)$
	$\sigma_1 \leftarrow \mathsf{RForge}(pk_s, sk_r, pk_j, msg)$	$\sigma_1 \leftarrow \mathsf{JForge}(pk_s, pk_r, sk_j, msg)$
	return σ_b	**return** σ_b

Fig. 3. Deniability security games for AMF schemes: universal deniability (left), receiver compromise deniability (middle), and judge compromise deniability (right).

We formalize receiver compromise deniability in two-stage game RecCompDen, the middle game in Fig. 3. The second-stage adversary $\mathcal{A}_2$ is given access to a frank oracle that outputs a signature created from Frank or RForge depending on a challenge bit. The goal is to guess the challenge bit given the sender and receiver secret keys, sk_s and sk_r. We strengthen the definition by answering the frank oracle queries using a public key pair for the receiver generated in the first stage by adversary $\mathcal{A}_1$. For an adversary $\mathcal{A} = (\mathcal{A}_1, \mathcal{A}_2)$ and message franking scheme AMF, we define the RecCompDen advantage of $\mathcal{A}$ against AMF as

$$\mathbf{Adv}_{\mathrm{AMF}}^{\mathrm{r\text{-}den}}(\mathcal{A}) = \Big| \Pr\Big[\mathrm{RecCompDen}_{\mathrm{AMF}}^{\mathcal{A},0} \Rightarrow 1 \Big]$$
$$- \Pr\Big[\mathrm{RecCompDen}_{\mathrm{AMF}}^{\mathcal{A},1} \Rightarrow 1 \Big] \Big|.$$

Judge compromise deniability requires that a party with access to the judge's secret key can forge a signature that is indistinguishable from honestly-generated signatures to other parties even with access to the judge's secret key and receiver's secret key. This captures deniability in the case where the judge's secret key has become compromised, and allows the sender to claim a message originates from a compromising party or malicious judge. Our definition maintains deniability even in the case where the receiver's secret key is compromised as well. We discuss alternate, weaker deniability notions at the end of this section. The JForge algorithm is used for judge compromise deniability.

- $\sigma \leftarrow\!\!\$ \ \mathsf{JForge}(pk_s, pk_r, sk_j, msg)$: The judge forge algorithm takes a sender public key pk_s, receiver public key pk_r, a judge secret key sk_j, and a message msg, then outputs a "forged" AMF signature σ.

We formalize judge compromise deniability in two-stage game JudgeCompDen, the right-most game in Fig. 3. The second-stage adversary $\mathcal{A}_2$ is given access to a frank oracle that outputs a signature created from Frank or JForge depending on a challenge bit. In contrast to receiver compromise deniability, $\mathcal{A}_1$ generates the judge public key pair in addition to the receiver public key pair and $\mathcal{A}_2$ is given access to all secret keys. For an adversary $\mathcal{A} = (\mathcal{A}_1, \mathcal{A}_2)$ and message franking scheme AMF we define the JudgeCompDen advantage of $\mathcal{A}$ against AMF as

$$\mathbf{Adv}_{\mathrm{AMF}}^{\mathrm{j\text{-}den}}(\mathcal{A}) = \left| \Pr \left[\mathrm{JudgeCompDen}_{\mathrm{AMF}}^{\mathcal{A},0} \Rightarrow 1 \right] \right.$$
$$\left. - \Pr \left[\mathrm{JudgeCompDen}_{\mathrm{AMF}}^{\mathcal{A},1} \Rightarrow 1 \right] \right|.$$

Random Oracle Model. Looking ahead, we will prove security in the random oracle model. In this model, to each definition we add another procedure $\mathcal{O}_{\mathrm{ro}}$. The adversary $\mathcal{A}$ and algorithms Forge, Verify, Judge, Forge, JForge, RForge all have access to it as an oracle. The oracle accepts queries on arbitrary length bit strings m and returns a random bit string r of length hlen. It stores r in a table T indexed by m to answer future queries consistently. In some security proofs we will use a technique referred to as programming the random oracle (setting certain RO outputs to values in a way advantageous to a reduction). Importantly, however, our definitions ensure that the AMF forging algorithms only have access to the oracle (as does the adversary), forcing them to forge without modifying the RO mapping. This means that when we apply the ROM heuristic, instantiating the RO with a hash function such as SHA-256, the forge algorithms can still be executed. This is essential for social deniability.

Space of Deniability Definitions. Notice that our deniability definitions are implicitly parameterized by the combination of secrets keys given to the forger and the combination of secret keys given to the distinguisher, i.e., who is able to fool whom. In this work, we target three specific deniability definitions within this space that we believe have real-world significance. However, this is not the only set of meaningful deniability definitions that one might desire from a scheme. Consider the following two examples. First, our definitions give the distinguisher access to the sender's secret key which models deniability in the face of sender compromise. An alternative definition may dispense with this goal in favor of an accountability notion, disavowability, in which a sender has the ability to cryptographically prove forged signatures were not created using their sender secret key, i.e., disavow forgeries. Second, our judge compromise deniability definition conflicts with strong authentication between sender and receiver—forgeries by the moderator cannot be detected by the receiver. Instead, a stronger unforgeability definition could be satisfied in which the judge's secret key alone is not sufficient to forge messages accepted by the receiver.

Ultimately, there exist many different trade-offs between deniability and accountability within this definition space. We provide a more detailed exploration of the space of possible deniability definitions along with their relationships to various accountability notions in [72].

4   Construction

In this section, we present our construction for building an asymmetric message franking scheme. First, we give intuition for our approach by drawing connections to the literature on designated verifier signatures [44]. Then, we describe our particular instantiation built using signatures of knowledge [19] and detailed in Fig. 5.

4.1   Intuition: AMF from Designated Verifiers

Designating the Moderator as Verifier. The tension between accountability and deniability arises from the desire for franking signatures to be forgeable (deniability) as well as verifiable by certain special parties, e.g. the moderator (accountability). This suggests *designated verifier* signatures [44] as a natural starting point from which to build asymmetric message franking. The sender would designate the moderator as a verifier for a signature of the message.

A designated verifier signature or, more generally, a designated verifier proof system allows a prover to provide a proof of a statement that convinces a designated verifier but no one else. The designated verifier can efficiently forge the proof such that the forged proof is indistinguishable from a real proof even with access to the designated verifier's secret key. This security property, known as non-transferability, ensures there are two possible parties that could have created the signature, the alleged sender or the (compromised) moderator. It matches closely to receiver compromise deniability and judge compromise deniability for AMFs which extends the idea of non-transferability to relationships between three parties.

Universal Deniability from Strong Designated Verifiers. To expand the set of possible forgers to any non-participating party, i.e. universal deniability, we additionally make use of a strong deniability property of *strong designated verifier* signatures [42,44,68]. This property allows anyone to forge a signature between two parties such that the resulting forgery is indistinguishable from real signatures to anyone without secret key access. Without care, universal deniability poses a problem for accountability. Consider a franking signature that consists of the sender creating a strong designated verifier signature for the moderator. A sender can send an abusive message and sign with a universal forgery. If the recipient of the message attempts to report to the moderator, the moderator will not be convinced the message was sent by the sender. This violates sender binding.

Chaining Designated Verifier Proofs. To achieve sender binding, the receiver must have some way of verifying whether messages it receives are reportable to the moderator. Specifically, the receiver must be able to verify the sender's strong designated verifier signature for the moderator is well-formed and not a forgery. This leads us to the final step: the sender can attach a strong designated verifier proof for the receiver *proving* that the strong designated verifier signature for the moderator is well-formed. By using a strong designated verifier proof for this step, the deniability goals are preserved.

The challenge in building AMFs with this approach is in instantiating schemes such that the signing algorithm of the strong designated verifier signature falls into a language compatible with the strong designated verifier proof system. Existing strong designated verifier signatures [42,44,68] do not appear to have this desired structure-preserving property [6] that would lend to using efficient proof systems. Additionally, we are not aware of any general-purpose strong designated verifier proof systems for arbitrary languages. While such a proof system can presumably be constructed using non-interactive zero knowledge proof systems for arbitrary languages [38], such a solution would likely be prohibitively expensive for low latency messaging. Despite these challenges, the question of building AMFs from designated verifier primitives remains interesting and we discuss such a generic construction in [72]. We next turn to building practical AMFs.

4.2   AMF from Signatures of Knowledge

While we do not build off the abstraction of designated verifiers, our construction is modeled off the intuition that an AMF can be composed of a strong designated verifier proof to the receiver of the well-formedness of a strong designated signature to the moderator. Our construction is inspired by the strong designated verifier signature scheme of Huang et al. built using signatures of knowledge [42], which we modify to allow for proofs of well-formedness.

Our construction can be based on any suitable cyclic group. In the following we let $\mathbb{G}$ be a group, let p be its order, and g be a generator for $\mathbb{G}$. We use multiplicative notation, though note that we use elliptic curve groups in our implementation (Sect. 6). Secret keys are uniformly chosen from $\mathcal{SK} = \mathbb{Z}_p$, and public keys are set to be $pk = g^{sk}$. We denote this key generation as PKKeyGen. Note that it is easy to check the well-formedness of such keys.

Signatures of Knowledge. First, we introduce our treatment of signatures of knowledge. These can be thought of as a cross between non-interactive proofs of knowledge and digital signatures. We use a standard Fiat-Shamir signature scheme [36] in which we can produce signatures of knowledge from basic Sigma protocols by including the message in the hash producing the challenge. Our construction uses Schnorr proofs of knowledge of discrete logarithm [69] and Chaum-Pedersen proofs of equality of discrete log [26], extended with conjunctions and disjunctions (logical ANDs and ORs) [15].

Our notation follows closely to that of Camenisch [19]. A signature of knowledge scheme $\mathsf{SPoK}^{\mathcal{R}} = (\mathsf{prove}, \mathsf{verify})$ is a pair of algorithms associated with a witness-statement relation $\mathcal{R}$. A relation $\mathcal{R} \subseteq \mathcal{X} \times \mathcal{Y}$ is defined relative to a set $\mathcal{X}$ called the witness space and set $\mathcal{Y}$ called the statement space. The randomized proving algorithm, prove, outputs a signature proof of the statement for a message given a witness, $\pi \leftarrow_{\$} \mathsf{SPoK}^{\mathcal{R}}.\mathsf{prove}(msg, x)$. The proving algorithm should return a dedicated symbol $\perp$ if $(x, y) \notin \mathcal{R}$ though for brevity we exclude such checks from pseudocode. The deterministic verification algorithm, verify, takes as input a message, signature proof, and statement, then returns a bit indicating whether verification is successful, $b \leftarrow \mathsf{SPoK}^{\mathcal{R}}.\mathsf{verify}(msg, \pi, y)$. As an example, this allows us to create signature proofs of the form: $\mathcal{R} = \{((\alpha, \beta), (g, A, B)) : A = g^{\alpha} \vee B = g^{\beta}\}$, which can be proved with knowledge of either α or β with

Alg.	Security notion	How to prove first clause? $(pk_s = g^t \vee J = g^u)$	How to prove second clause? $((J = (pk_j)^v \wedge E_J = g^v) \vee R = g^w)$	Verify?	Judge?
Frank	Correctness	$\alpha \leftarrow\!\!^\$ \mathbb{Z}_p;\ J \leftarrow (pk_j)^\alpha;\ t = sk_s$	$\beta \leftarrow\!\!^\$ \mathbb{Z}_p;\ R \leftarrow (pk_r)^\beta;\ v = \alpha$	✓	✓
Forge	Univ. den.	$\gamma \leftarrow\!\!^\$ \mathbb{Z}_p;\ J \leftarrow g^\gamma;\ u = \gamma$	$\delta \leftarrow\!\!^\$ \mathbb{Z}_p;\ R \leftarrow g^\delta;\ w = \delta$	✗	✗
RForge	R. comp. den.	$\gamma \leftarrow\!\!^\$ \mathbb{Z}_p;\ J \leftarrow g^\gamma;\ u = \gamma$	$\beta \leftarrow\!\!^\$ \mathbb{Z}_p;\ R \leftarrow (pk_r)^\beta;\ w = \beta \cdot sk_r$	✓	✗
JForge	J. comp. den.	$\alpha \leftarrow\!\!^\$ \mathbb{Z}_p;\ J \leftarrow (pk_j)^\alpha;\ u = \alpha \cdot sk_j$	$\beta \leftarrow\!\!^\$ \mathbb{Z}_p;\ R \leftarrow (pk_r)^\beta;\ v = \alpha$	✓	✓

Fig. 4. Summary of how AMF signing and forging algorithms construct signatures. The rightmost columns indicate with a checkmark (✓) which verification algorithms accept that signature and with a cross (×) which will reject that signature.

witnesses $(\alpha, \bot)$ or $(\bot, \beta)$ respectively. Note that the inclusion of $\bot$ symbols in the witness explicitly indicates which side of the disjunction is satisfied.

We will utilize two security properties of the Sigma protocols from which we derive our Fiat-Shamir signatures of knowledge: *knowledge soundness* and *honest-verifier zero knowledge*. Briefly, knowledge soundness ensures that a prover that generates a valid signature proof for a message must actually "know" a witness for the statement. A scheme being zero knowledge ensures that verification of a proof does not reveal anything about the witness to the verifier other than if it is valid or not. The complete descriptions for constructing signatures of knowledge from Sigma protocols along with formalizations of these security properties are deferred to [72].

Overview of Construction. Consider the strong designated verifier signature (between sender and moderator) derived as a signature of knowledge from the following relation:

$$\mathcal{R}_{\mathsf{SDVS}} = \{((t,\ u),\ (g,\ pk_s,\ J)) : pk_s = g^t \vee J = g^u\},$$

in which an honest sender will construct Diffie-Hellman value $J = (pk_j)^\alpha$ for random choice of $\alpha \leftarrow\!\!^\$ \mathbb{Z}_p$, and send ephemeral value $E_J = g^\alpha$ along with the $\mathsf{SPoK}^{\mathcal{R}_{\mathsf{SDVS}}}$ signature proof, where pk_s and pk_j are the public keys of the sender and moderator, respectively. If J is indeed constructed in this manner, $J = g^u = g^{\alpha \cdot sk_j}$, then knowledge of u cannot be proved by anyone who does not know the moderator's secret key sk_j. This means a moderator that receives a valid signature and well-formed J will be convinced that the signature comes from a sender with knowledge of $t = sk_s$.

On the other hand, anyone can create a valid signature of $\mathsf{SPoK}^{\mathcal{R}_{\mathsf{SDVS}}}$ by using a malformed J set as a random group element, $J = g^\gamma$ for $\gamma \leftarrow\!\!^\$ \mathbb{Z}_p$, proving knowledge of $u = \gamma$, and sending $E_J = g^\alpha$ for independent $\alpha \leftarrow\!\!^\$ \mathbb{Z}_p$. Importantly, only the moderator has the ability to distinguish between well-formed and malformed J, by using the secret key sk_j to check whether (pk_j, E_J, J) forms a valid Diffie-Hellman triple $(J \stackrel{?}{=} E_J^{sk_j})$. This means that anyone can create a forged signature that is indistinguishable from a valid sender signature to everyone but the moderator.

Following the intuition from the previous section, to achieve accountability, the sender must prove to the receiver that the strong designated verifier signature

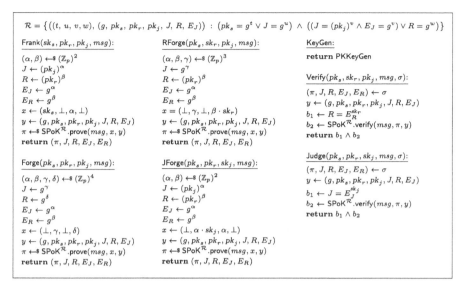

Fig. 5. Algorithms for our deniable AMF scheme. The relation $\mathcal{R}$ defining our SPoK is depicted at the top.

for the moderator is well-formed. This corresponds to proving that J is well-formed, i.e., (pk_j, E_J, J) form a Diffie-Hellman triple. Putting it together, our final AMF construction is the signature of knowledge derived from the following relation:

$$\mathcal{R} = \Big\{ \big((t,\, u,\, v, w),\, (g,\, pk_s,\, pk_r,\, pk_j,\, J,\, R,\, E_J)\big) :$$
$$\big(pk_s = g^t \vee J = g^u\big) \wedge \big((J = (pk_j)^v \wedge E_J = g^v) \vee R = g^w\big)\Big\}.$$

An honest sender constructs $J = (pk_j)^\alpha$ and $R = (pk_r)^\beta$ for $(\alpha, \beta) \leftarrow\!\!{}_\$ (\mathbb{Z}_p)^2$, and sends ephemeral values $(E_J = g^\alpha, E_R = g^\beta)$ along with the $\mathsf{SPoK}^{\mathcal{R}}$ signature, where pk_r is the public key of the receiver. The first conjunction clause represents the strong designated verifier signature to the moderator and the second conjunction clause represents the strong designated proof to the receiver that the first clause is constructed properly. Forgeries for universal deniability are created with malformed J and R, forgeries for receiver compromise deniability with malformed J, and forgeries for judge compromise deniability do not use any malformed elements. Lastly, the receiver's public key is added to the statement even though it does not appear in the proof relation, so that it is bound by the Fiat-Shamir hash challenge. This prevents certain types of identity misbinding attacks. A complete summary of how different signatures and forgeries are proved is given in Fig. 4 and our full construction is detailed in pseudocode in Fig. 5.

5 Security Analysis

We now explore the security of our deniable AMF scheme, arguing it achieves the accountability and deniability properties detailed in Sect. 3. We treat each set of properties in turn.

5.1 Accountability

As we discussed in the last section, the accountability properties intuitively follow from the underlying signature of knowledge's soundness properties: demonstrating forgeries that fool the recipient (unforgeability or sender binding) or the judge (receiver binding) implies the ability to generate a proof without a witness. However, it is not clear how to modularly define a suitably strong knowledge soundness property of the signature of knowledge underlying our construction. Our analyses therefore take a different tack, reducing to the soundness properties of the underlying Sigma protocol.

We discuss receiver binding, which shares the same high level strategy as sender binding. Our strategy is to show a winning adversary $\mathcal{A}$ breaks the one-wayness of the witness-statement relation $\mathcal{R}$, which we can use to build a discrete log adversary $\mathcal{B}$ extracting secret keys from the witness. The approach of the proof uses some techniques related to the proof of existential unforgeability under chosen message attack (EUF-CMA) for Fiat-Shamir-derived signatures (c.f., [15]), but the need of $\mathcal{B}$ to simulate $\mathcal{A}$'s oracle queries requires a more nuanced analysis. In fact performing this simulation leads us to make an additional knowledge-of-exponent assumption (KEA) assumption [9] about $\mathbb{G}$. We detail the needed KEA assumption in [72]. The full theorem is given below.

Theorem 1. *Let* AMF *be the asymmetric message franking scheme using signature of knowledge* SPoK *defined in Fig. 5, where* SPoK *is derived using the Fiat-Shamir heuristic as described in [72] using hash function* $\mathcal{H}$. *If* $\mathcal{H}$ *is modeled as a random oracle, for any* r-BIND *adversary* $\mathcal{A}$ *making at most* Q_{Frank} *franking oracle queries,* Q_{Judge} *judge oracle queries, and* Q_{ro} *random oracle queries, we give adversaries* $\mathcal{B}$ *and* $\mathcal{C}$ *such that*

$$\mathbf{Adv}_{\mathrm{AMF}}^{\mathrm{r\text{-}bind}}(\mathcal{A}) \leq \frac{Q_{\mathsf{Frank}}(Q_{\mathsf{Frank}} + Q_{ro} + 1)}{p^4} + (Q_{\mathsf{Judge}} + 1) \cdot \mathbf{Adv}_{\mathbb{G},g}^{\mathrm{kea}}(\mathcal{C}, \mathcal{E}_{\mathcal{C}})$$

$$+ \frac{Q_{ro} + 1}{p} + \sqrt{2(Q_{ro} + 1) \cdot \mathbf{Adv}_{\mathbb{G},g}^{\mathrm{dl}}(\mathcal{B})}$$

where p *is the order of* $\mathbb{G}$ *and if* $\mathcal{A}$ *runs in time* T *and KEA extractor* $\mathcal{E}_{\mathcal{C}}$ *runs in time* $t_{\mathcal{E}}$, *then* $\mathcal{B}$ *runs in time* $T' \approx 2T + 2(Q_{\mathsf{Judge}} + 1) \cdot t_{\mathcal{E}}$ *and* $\mathcal{C}$ *runs in time* $T' \approx T$.

We use $\approx$ above to hide small constants. We give a proof sketch here. The theorem statements and proofs for sender binding and unforgeability are similar. We defer the full proof details for all three accountability properties to [72].

Proof sketch: Our proof proceeds via a sequence of games. The first set of game hops show how the game can be modified to answer $\mathcal{A}$'s franking queries without using the sender's secret key sk_s. Similarly to proving non-interactive zero knowledge for Fiat-Shamir-derived proofs [15, Theorem 20.3], this is done by programming the random oracle $\mathcal{H}$ to be consistent with the commitments used in the underlying Sigma protocol. This programming fails if a (randomly chosen) commitment collides with a value previously used as input to the random oracle. This happens with low probability as commitments are four uniformly chosen group elements. The birthday-bound term accounts for the probability of such a commitment collision.

The second set of game hops handles simulating the judge oracle without the judge's secret key. To do so we argue that one can simulate the queries using KEA extractors and, if that fails, we can build an adversary $\mathcal{C}$ that violates the KEA. In fact this step uses a hybrid argument which gradually replaces each oracle call with an extractor-utilizing simulation of the check. This accounts for the second term of the theorem's advantage bound.

Finally we are in a game now in which the only use of the judge and sender secret keys is to define the public keys. We use a rewinding lemma [15, Lemma 19.2]. If $\mathcal{A}$ succeeds at forging in one execution against a particular message, we can rerun $\mathcal{A}$ ("rewind" it) with a different random oracle output for that message. The rewinding lemma lower bounds the probability that $\mathcal{A}$ succeeds twice in a row by the probability that it succeeds once. In turn, if one can forge twice with different hash outputs, this allows extracting a witness from the Fiat-Shamir proof of knowledge. The last step involves a case analysis over the relation $\mathcal{R}$ to show that extracting a witness implies learning sk_s or sk_j, which we use to build our desired discrete log adversary $\mathcal{B}$. A subtlety in this final step is that extracting a witness implies learning $u = sk_j \cdot \alpha$, but not sk_j directly. We use a KEA extractor again to extract α, and thus complete the proof. This accounts for the final two terms of the advantage relation.

Replacing KEA with Gap-CDH. The KEA [9] is a somewhat exotic assumption, and a natural question to ask is if we can prove our scheme secure without it. By extending our franking signature by two group elements and reducing to Gap-CDH instead of DL, we can dispense with KEA. The assumption is used in two places in our proof while building DL adversary $\mathcal{B}$, (1) to answer judge oracle queries, and (2) to learn sk_j from the witness. In our alternate proof, the Gap-CDH oracle is used to answer judge oracle queries, and the extended franking signature directly proves knowledge of α and β so KEA is not needed to learn sk_j from the witness. This gives us the following theorem:

Theorem 2. *Let* AMF *be the asymmetric message franking scheme using signature of knowledge* SPoK *defined in Fig. 5 over relation* $\mathcal{R}'$ *defined in [72], where* SPoK *is derived using the Fiat-Shamir heuristic as described in [72] using hash function* $\mathcal{H}$. *If* $\mathcal{H}$ *is modeled as a random oracle, for any* r-BIND *adversary* $\mathcal{A}$ *making at most* Q_{Frank} *franking oracle queries,* Q_{Judge} *judge oracle queries, and* Q_{ro} *random oracle queries, we give adversary* $\mathcal{B}$ *and* $\mathcal{C}$ *such that*

$$\mathbf{Adv}_{\mathrm{AMF}}^{\mathrm{r\text{-}bind}}(\mathcal{A}) \leq \frac{Q_{\mathsf{Frank}}(Q_{\mathsf{Frank}} + Q_{ro} + 1)}{p^4} + \frac{Q_{ro} + 1}{p}$$
$$+ \sqrt{2(Q_{ro} + 1) \cdot \mathbf{Adv}_{\mathbb{G},g}^{\mathrm{gapcdh}}(\mathcal{B})}$$

where p is the order of $\mathbb{G}$ and if $\mathcal{A}$ runs in time T, then $\mathcal{B}$ runs in time $T' \approx 2T$.

We provide the theorem statements for the other two accountability properties, as well as assumption definitions and proof details in [72].

5.2 Deniability

Intuitively, the deniability properties fall out of the non-interactive zero knowledge property of the signature proofs of knowledge. Our signature proof of knowledge is carefully designed so that a variety of different witnesses can satisfy the statement relation $\mathcal{R}$ (as laid out in Fig. 4). This allows forgers to create signatures that can only be caught by checking well-formedness of the statement using secret keys.

In more detail, the deniability proofs all follow the same outline. First notice that there are two high level differences between the frank algorithm and the forge algorithms: (1) the witnesses used to prove the statement are different, and (2) how the elements of the statement are formed is different. Different witnesses are handled by using the zero-knowledge property of the signature proof to switch between witnesses by hopping to a simulated proof and back. In fact, for judge compromise deniability, witness indistinguishability [35] is all that is needed since elements of the statement are well-formed and identical in Frank and JForge. Extra care needs to be taken for Forge and RForge, since some elements of the statement are malformed. Well-formed means, for example, that J is constructed as $J \leftarrow (pk_j)^\alpha$ forming a Diffie-Hellman triple, $(pk_j = g^{sk_j}, E_J = g^\alpha, J = g^{\alpha \cdot sk_j})$. While malformed means $J \leftarrow g^\gamma$ is constructed as a random group element. In RForge, J is malformed, while in Forge both J and R are malformed. This leads to an additional DDH term to bound the advantage of an adversary in distinguishing between each well-formed and malformed statement elements.

The theorem statement for universal deniability is given below. The first term of the advantage comes from hopping between two witnesses through a simulator. The second term of the advantage comes from a decisional Diffie-Hellman hop for each of the two malformed elements of Forge.

Theorem 3. *Let* AMF *be the asymmetric message franking scheme defined in Fig. 5 using signature of knowledge* SPoK *defined in [72]. For all simulators* $\mathcal{S}$ *for* SPoK, *for any* UnivDen *adversary* $\mathcal{A}$, *we give adversaries* $\mathcal{B}$ *and* $\mathcal{C}$ *such that*

$$\mathbf{Adv}_{\mathrm{AMF}}^{\mathrm{univ\text{-}den}}(\mathcal{A}) \leq 2 \cdot \mathbf{Adv}_{\mathsf{SPoK},\mathcal{S}}^{\mathrm{nizk}}(\mathcal{B}) + 2 \cdot \mathbf{Adv}_{\mathbb{G},g}^{\mathrm{ddh}}(\mathcal{C}).$$

where if $\mathcal{A}$ *runs in time* T *and makes at most* Q *queries to the frank oracle, then* $\mathcal{B}$ *and* $\mathcal{C}$ *run in time* $T' \approx T$ *and* $\mathcal{B}$ *makes at most* Q *queries to its proof oracle.*

The advantage terms for receiver compromise deniability and judge compromise deniability follow a similar structure. The full proofs for all deniability properties are deferred to [72].

5.3 Measuring Concrete Security

Performing a concrete security analysis allows us to verify the efficiency of our reductions and inform parameter choices. The full details of our analysis are given in [72]. The reductions for accountability are not tight, due both to inheriting the quadratic loss seemingly fundamental to Schnorr-based Sigma protocols (c.f., [10]) and use of a KEA extractor to respond to each oracle query. The KEA poses a challenge for interpreting the concrete security analyses since the extractor is not concretely instantiated.

Strictly interpreted, our analysis suggests that we need a group $\mathbb{G}$ of more than twice the recommended size—i.e., > 512 bit elliptic curve groups to achieve about 128 bits of security. That said, we are not aware of any attacks against our schemes better than solving a discrete log, which is the same situation for standard Schnorr signatures and other uses of Fiat-Shamir. Therefore, in our implementations we also evaluate using 256-bit groups. This is standard in related settings (see [12,18]). It remains a long-standing open question to understand if this heuristic is dangerous, i.e., if one can show an attack against Schnorr signatures (or similar) built from groups with conjectured 128-bit hardness that succeeds in time closer to 2^{64}.

6 Implementation and Evaluation

To evaluate our protocol, we implemented our signature proof of knowledge construction in Python 3 using the petlib [32] library which relies on OpenSSL for elliptic curve operations. Our implementation consists of a generic interface for implementing and composing Sigma protocols that may be of independent interest. For our AMF construction, we implemented the Schnorr protocol, Chaum-Pedersen protocol, and conjunction and disjunction protocols, as well as a Fiat-Shamir transform to create non-interactive proofs from the generic Sigma protocol interface.

We aim to evaluate the practicality of integrating our AMF scheme into existing messaging platforms. First, we are interested in the timing overhead in creating franking signatures as well as the space overhead in the signatures themselves. To this end, we present microbenchmarks to evaluate the overhead costs in our scheme. Second, we discuss what the deployment of an end-to-end moderation system incorporating asymmetric message franking would look like and present one such proof-of-concept for direct messaging on the Twitter platform. The AMF library as well as the deployment prototype are available open source at https://github.com/julialen/asymmetric-message-franking.

Benchmarks. We present timing and size benchmarks for our implementation of the signature of knowledge AMF construction. These experiments were conducted on an AWS `t3.small` EC2 virtual machine running Ubuntu 18.04 on a 2.5 GHz Intel Scalable Processor using the NIST elliptic curve groups P-256 and P-521 and the hash function SHA-256.

Algorithm	Measured time (ms)		Group operations		
	P-256	P-521	Mul	Add	Inv
Schnorr sig.	0.7 ± 0.12	2.4 ± 0.04	1	0	0
Frank	7.3 ± 0.95	28.3 ± 0.16	11	2	2
Verify	6.6 ± 0.90	29.1 ± 2.5	11	5	0
Judge	6.6 ± 0.16	32.0 ± 1.4	11	5	0
Forge	6.7 ± 0.11	32.0 ± 3.5	12	3	3
RForge	7.2 ± 0.12	34.2 ± 1.7	12	3	3
JForge	6.7 ± 0.11	31.6 ± 4.0	11	2	2

Fig. 6. Measured timing statistics and group operation accounting for the AMF algorithms from Fig. 5 including a baseline comparison to a (undeniable) Schnorr signature. The measured times show the average and standard deviation over 1000 runs using a message size of 4 KB instantiated over NIST elliptic curve groups P-256 and P-521. The group operations give the count of scalar multiplications (Mul), group additions (Add), and group inversions (Inv).

The table in Fig. 6 shows the measured time in milliseconds to run each of the algorithms from Fig. 5. The measured times are the average over 1000 runs using a message size of 4 KB. We compare to a baseline of a basic Schnorr signature of sk_s, which is undeniable. These numbers are as expected—our algorithms perform about ten times as many group operations as a Schnorr signature, and take roughly ten times as long. Though our scheme is slower, it is still fast enough to be used in practical settings where network latency dominates communication cost. We also provide the number of group operations (scalar multiplications, group additions, and group inversions) performed in each algorithm. These experiments were conducted using a fixed message size of 4 KB, but we note that the only message-size dependent operation is a single hash for the Fiat-Shamir signature.

The size of an AMF signature is not message-dependent. Our algorithms all output nine group elements (i.e., elliptic curve points) and six scalars in $\mathbb{Z}_p$. In our implementation, AMF signatures are 489 bytes in size for elliptic curve group P-256 and 795 bytes in size for elliptic curve group P-521. In contrast, a Schnorr signature is one group element and one scalar and is 65 bytes in size for P-256 and 99 bytes in size for P-521.

Deployment. We build a proof-of-concept third-party moderation system using AMFs which we can test by integrating it over already existing messaging platforms. Instantiating a third-party moderation system with asymmetric message franking involves three main services: (1) a judging service that receives and arbitrates abuse reports from users, (2) a publish-subscribe service to maintain an up-to-date community membership list amid new user enrollment and abusive user blocks, and (3) a public key infrastructure (PKI) to map platform identities to public keys. A user registers by enrolling with the membership service and delivering their public key to the PKI. To bind a platform identity to a key, the PKI should check some kind of proof-of-ownership of both the account and the secret key. This can be done using a challenge-response protocol, where the PKI delivers a random challenge to the user, who must sign the challenge with their private key and post the signed challenge on the platform. This will prevent rogue-key attacks that utilize malformed keys (q.v., [65]). Our proof-of-concept interfaces with Keybase [1] which provides the PKI service as described above.

The judging service can be performed by human moderators, automated tools, or some combination of the two. In our proof-of-concept, judging abuse reports is automated through the use of the Perspective conversation API [2] which uses machine learning to assign a "toxicity" score to a message; users are blocked based on a threshold of the score. We note that in a production deployment, use of automated moderation tools would need to be carefully tuned and likely also paired with human decision-making. Finally, we provide a client with a command-line interface to allow users to send, receive, and report direct messages on Twitter. The client automatically creates, appends, and parses franking signatures, as well as filters messages that are malformed or sent from a blocked user.

Lastly, we find that the cryptographic overhead of creating and verifying franking signatures is dwarfed by the overhead incurred by the rest of the infrastructure needed for moderation, e.g. PKI; sending a message over Twitter in our proof-of-concept takes ≈ 0.5 s. Much of this identity-binding infrastructure is needed for any moderation service—augmenting cryptographic verification using asymmetric message franking is not a significant overhead.

7   Discussion

Here we discuss some limitations of the use of AMF schemes.

Strong Authentication. Our scheme does not ensure forgeries by the moderator can be detected by the receiver, and so the receiver cannot rely on AMF signatures alone to authenticate authorship if there is risk of the moderator being malicious. This is fundamental given our strong deniability notions (specifically, judge compromise deniability rules it out). One might weaken our deniability goals to achieve this, however. We explore such an alternate deniability target in [72] and informally present a modification to our scheme that achieves it.

Alternatively, one could rely on the accompanying E2E encryption scheme to provide strong authentication. To preserve deniability properties, the E2E encryption should itself be deniable (otherwise a receiver could potentially convince others that a message was sent by providing a transcript of E2E ciphertexts and keys). Some E2E encryption systems appear to have the requisite deniability properties, such as Signal based on 3DH (Triple Diffie-Hellman) key exchange [45,56]. Others have slightly weaker deniability properties, such as Signal's newer handshake X3DH which extends 3DH with signed prekeys [57]. That said we have not provided a formal treatment of E2E encryption and future work could build off ours to do so.

Transcript Consistency. In Facebook's current moderation solution [34], an abuse report contains context of surrounding messages sent by *both* users. In metadata-private moderation, it is difficult to ensure the moderator, sender, and receiver all have a consistent view of an interleaved message transcript because the moderator does not know what was sent or when. We might include sequence numbers and acknowledgment receipts to protect ordering. However, such techniques should be introduced with care so as not to obviate the system's deniability properties.

Moderator Accountability via Thresholding. Another issue is that our deniability goals may make holding moderators accountable for their actions more difficult. A fundamental property of asymmetric message franking is that the moderator cannot prove someone authored a message. At best they can prove a message was authored *either* by them *or* by the sender. As a result, the moderator cannot prove they had a valid reason for banning someone.

One potential mitigation for this would be to split the moderator's functionality across multiple parties. To do so, the key would need to be shared and a secure multi-party protocol used to test well-formedness of J in the franking signature, which can be done using techniques from verifiable secret sharing [61,63,70]. With threshold moderation, it takes the parties holding some t out of n moderator key shares to invoke Judge. This makes the moderator functionality more robust to accusations of unfair treatment, since t of them would need to act unfairly to falsely accuse someone. This also provides a natural defense against moderator key compromise, since to reconstruct the moderator key, t distinct parties would need to be breached.

Deniable Channels. Finally, care must be taken when composing our AMF scheme with other cryptographic primitives, as those primitives may compromise or prevent deniability. In particular, one might worry about the deniability of the underlying authenticated channels, like TLS, through which AMF signed messages are sent. In general, if the sender uses one-way authentication for TLS, a TLS transcript is (cryptographically) universally deniable. In this authentication mode, the server is authenticated and the client generates and sends a randomly chosen ephemeral prekey to the server from which a session key is derived. Any party can create a session key with the platform server and use that session key to create a forged transcript. The IP address of the sender is learned by the platform server at the time of sending, but any transcript recording the IP address is unconvincing since it is not bound to the client-chosen randomness. Thus while there exist stronger notions of deniable channels [64,73], it seems TLS channels preserve universal deniability for arbitrary message platforms.

Yet, messaging platforms presumably perform their own user authentication *on top* of TLS, and this may be problematic for receiver compromise deniability in some scenarios. Due to the deniability properties of TLS described above, a transcript of messages served by the platform would be unconvincing. However, instead, if the receiver were to reveal their platform credentials, someone can use those credentials to retrieve the messages directly from the platform. This interaction would convince someone that the messages were sent by the sender, given they trust the platform's underlying user authentication. One way to prevent this breach in deniability is if the platform does not serve archived messages.

Platforms such as Signal, WhatsApp, and Facebook secret conversations do not back-up messages, and thus, already fit this model.

8 Related Work

Message Franking Schemes. Symmetric message franking has been studied in several works [27,33,34,39,43]. All of these schemes consider the symmetric setting where a centralized server holds a MAC key that authenticates the ciphertext, sender, recipient tuple. They do not transfer to settings where this communication metadata is not available. Moreover, while deniability is the motivating goal, the actual studied primitive is compactly committing authenticated encryption [39]. They do not formalize deniability.

Special Purpose Signature Schemes. A variety of special purpose signature schemes have been proposed that do not work in our setting. In undeniable signatures [23,25], verification requires interacting with the signer precisely to prevent them from denying messages they wrote. This is the same limitation as designated confirmer signatures [24], with the added problem that any compromise of the confirmer—who holds keys which can confirm but not issue signatures—removes any doubt about the authenticity of a signature.

Group signatures [8,13,17,20] allow members of a specified group to sign messages indicating they are a part of the group without revealing the individual signer's identity. Group membership is determined by a group coordinator who has the additional capability of learning the individual signer from a signature. One can imagine a moderation protocol built from group signatures in which all users are part of the "global" group and the moderator is the group coordinator. Other than the efficiency issues of maintaining a global group with dynamic joins and revocations, these schemes do not achieve judge compromise deniability for the group coordinator's secret key. Ring signatures [66] similarly allow verification of group membership, but are not applicable to moderation, since they do not provide a way for the moderator to learn individual signer identities.

Designated verifier signatures [44,46,50,54], in particular, strong designated verifier signatures [42,68] provide nearly the functionality we need, but do not alone capture the relationship between the moderator and recipient parties. We informally describe an AMF construction (see Sect. 4.1 and [72]) consisting of a strong designated verifier proof [22,31] to the receiver of the well-formedness of a strong designated verifier signature to the moderator. This approach can also be considered as a new variant of multi-designated verifier signatures [51] with a special relationship between designated verifiers, moderator and receiver.

Anonymous Blacklisting Systems. An anonymous blacklisting scheme [40] allows a user to produce a series of unlinkable tokens from a private key. To send a message, they provide a fresh token and prove that no tokens linked to their private key are on some blacklist. In this manner, moderators can blacklist sender tokens without learning the sender's identity—different from AMF where the sender's identity is learned by the moderator. However, the need for the sender to be able to identify and disavow tokens on the blacklist means that there is no deniability in the case an attacker compromises the sender (e.g., as in the DNC email breach). Our scheme, in contrast, protects the user's deniability even if their key is compromised.

Other Work in Deniability. Deniability has also been considered in other cryptographic contexts. Canetti et al. proposed *deniable encryption* [21], which allows the denial of contents of a ciphertext by giving a different opening of it. This doesn't deal with authorship or authentication and hence is not applicable. Borisov et al. [16] explored deniability as a feature for messaging systems. Deployed in OTR [16] and Signal [56], deniable messaging protocols ensure that messages can be authenticated by the receiver but not by third parties. On their own, they do not allow for moderation because the deniability is too strong: no one can authenticate the message, including the moderator. They can be combined with an AMF scheme to get an end-to-end encrypted and moderatable messaging scheme.

Automated Moderation Systems. A variety of works have explored ad-hoc moderation [37] and automated moderation systems [59]. We do not attempt to provide an exhaustive list here. One of the more notable projects is Google Jigsaw's Perspective API [59], which aims to build automated moderation tools to combat toxicity. While these works are promising, they cannot be used effectively if messages cannot be properly attributed to users.

9   Conclusion

In this paper, we investigated moderation for metadata-private messaging systems like Signal. Because user identities are hidden from the platform, existing moderation tools (including symmetric message franking) cannot be used. Other seeming solutions break deniability. Similar issues prevent third-party moderation, in which the messaging platform and moderator are decoupled.

We showed that the main technical challenge is cryptographic: how to balance the need for accountability in abuse reporting with the desire for deniability. We resolved this tension by introducing a new cryptographic primitive called asymmetric message franking (AMF), and showed how to construct one efficient enough for practice.

Acknowledgments. This work was supported in part by NSF awards DGE-1650441, CNS-1704296, and CNS-1558500.

References

1. Keybase (2014). https://keybase.io/docs/server_security
2. Perspective API (2017). https://www.perspectiveapi.com/
3. Mastodon social network (2018). https://joinmastodon.org/

4. Matrix: an open network for secure, decentralized communication (2018). https://matrix.org/
5. Sealed sender represents 80% of signal traffic (2019). https://twitter.com/signalapp/status/1075918894521495552
6. Abe, M., Fuchsbauer, G., Groth, J., Haralambiev, K., Ohkubo, M.: Structure-preserving signatures and commitments to group elements. In: Rabin, T. (ed.) CRYPTO 2010. LNCS, vol. 6223, pp. 209–236. Springer, Heidelberg (2010). https://doi.org/10.1007/978-3-642-14623-7_12
7. Angel, S., Setty, S.T.: Unobservable communication over fully untrusted infrastructure. In: OSDI (2016)
8. Bellare, M., Micciancio, D., Warinschi, B.: Foundations of group signatures: formal definitions, simplified requirements, and a construction based on general assumptions. In: Biham, E. (ed.) EUROCRYPT 2003. LNCS, vol. 2656, pp. 614–629. Springer, Heidelberg (2003). https://doi.org/10.1007/3-540-39200-9_38
9. Bellare, M., Palacio, A.: The knowledge-of-exponent assumptions and 3-round zero-knowledge protocols. In: Franklin, M. (ed.) CRYPTO 2004. LNCS, vol. 3152, pp. 273–289. Springer, Heidelberg (2004). https://doi.org/10.1007/978-3-540-28628-8_17
10. Bellare, M., Poettering, B., Stebila, D.: From identification to signatures, tightly: a framework and generic transforms. In: Cheon, J.H., Takagi, T. (eds.) ASIACRYPT 2016. LNCS, vol. 10032, pp. 435–464. Springer, Heidelberg (2016). https://doi.org/10.1007/978-3-662-53890-6_15
11. Bellare, M., Rogaway, P.: The security of triple encryption and a framework for code-based game-playing proofs. In: Vaudenay, S. (ed.) EUROCRYPT 2006. LNCS, vol. 4004, pp. 409–426. Springer, Heidelberg (2006). https://doi.org/10.1007/11761679_25
12. Bernstein, D.J., Duif, N., Lange, T., Schwabe, P., Yang, B.Y.: High-speed high-security signatures. J. Crypt. Eng. **2**, 77–89 (2012)
13. Boneh, D., Boyen, X., Shacham, H.: Short group signatures. In: Franklin, M. (ed.) CRYPTO 2004. LNCS, vol. 3152, pp. 41–55. Springer, Heidelberg (2004). https://doi.org/10.1007/978-3-540-28628-8_3
14. Boneh, D., Lynn, B., Shacham, H.: Short signatures from the weil pairing. In: Boyd, C. (ed.) ASIACRYPT 2001. LNCS, vol. 2248, pp. 514–532. Springer, Heidelberg (2001). https://doi.org/10.1007/3-540-45682-1_30
15. Boneh, D., Shoup, V.: A Graduate Course in Applied Cryptography (2017). Version 0.4
16. Borisov, N., Goldberg, I., Brewer, E.: Off-the-record communication, or, why not to use PGP. In: ACM WPES (2004)
17. Boyen, X., Waters, B.: Compact group signatures without random oracles. In: Vaudenay, S. (ed.) EUROCRYPT 2006. LNCS, vol. 4004, pp. 427–444. Springer, Heidelberg (2006). https://doi.org/10.1007/11761679_26
18. Bünz, B., Bootle, J., Boneh, D., Poelstra, A., Wuille, P., Maxwell, G.: Bulletproofs: Short proofs for confidential transactions and more. In: IEEE S&P (2018)
19. Camenisch, J.: Group signature schemes and payment systems based on the discrete logarithm problem. Ph.D. thesis, ETH Zurich, Zürich, Switzerland (1998)
20. Camenisch, J., Stadler, M.: Efficient group signature schemes for large groups. In: Kaliski, B.S. (ed.) CRYPTO 1997. LNCS, vol. 1294, pp. 410–424. Springer, Heidelberg (1997). https://doi.org/10.1007/BFb0052252
21. Canetti, R., Dwork, C., Naor, M., Ostrovsky, R.: Deniable encryption. In: Kaliski, B.S. (ed.) CRYPTO 1997. LNCS, vol. 1294, pp. 90–104. Springer, Heidelberg (1997). https://doi.org/10.1007/BFb0052229

22. Chaidos, P., Couteau, G.: Efficient designated-verifier non-interactive zero-knowledge proofs of knowledge. In: Nielsen, J.B., Rijmen, V. (eds.) EUROCRYPT 2018. LNCS, vol. 10822, pp. 193–221. Springer, Cham (2018). https://doi.org/10.1007/978-3-319-78372-7_7

23. Chaum, D.: Zero-knowledge undeniable signatures. In: Damgård, I.B. (ed.) EUROCRYPT 1990. LNCS, vol. 473, pp. 458–464. Springer, Heidelberg (1991). https://doi.org/10.1007/3-540-46877-3_41

24. Chaum, D.: Designated confirmer signatures. In: De Santis, A. (ed.) EUROCRYPT 1994. LNCS, vol. 950, pp. 86–91. Springer, Heidelberg (1995). https://doi.org/10.1007/BFb0053427

25. Chaum, D., van Antwerpen, H.: Undeniable signatures. In: Brassard, G. (ed.) CRYPTO 1989. LNCS, vol. 435, pp. 212–216. Springer, New York (1990). https://doi.org/10.1007/0-387-34805-0_20

26. Cham, D., Pederson, T.P.: Wallet databases with observers. In: Brickell, E.F. (ed.) CRYPTO 1992. LNCS, vol. 740. Springer, Berlin (1993). https://doi.org/10.1007/3-540-48071-4_7

27. Chen, L., Tang, Q.: People who live in glass houses should not throw stones: targeted opening message franking schemes. Cryptology ePrint Archive, Report 2018/994 (2018)

28. Corrigan-Gibbs, H., Boneh, D., Mazieres, D.: Riposte: An anonymous messaging system handling millions of users. In: IEEE S&P (2015)

29. Corrigan-Gibbs, H., Ford, B.: Dissent: accountable anonymous group messaging. In: ACM CCS (2010)

30. Damgård, I.: Towards practical public key systems secure against chosen ciphertext attacks. In: Feigenbaum, J. (ed.) CRYPTO 1991. LNCS, vol. 576, pp. 445–456. Springer, Heidelberg (1992). https://doi.org/10.1007/3-540-46766-1_36

31. Damgård, I., Fazio, N., Nicolosi, A.: Non-interactive zero-knowledge from homomorphic encryption. In: Halevi, S., Rabin, T. (eds.) TCC 2006. LNCS, vol. 3876, pp. 41–59. Springer, Heidelberg (2006). https://doi.org/10.1007/11681878_3

32. Danezis, G.: Petlib library (2018). https://github.com/gdanezis/petlib

33. Dodis, Y., Grubbs, P., Ristenpart, T., Woodage, J.: Fast message franking: from invisible salamanders to encryptment. In: Shacham, H., Boldyreva, A. (eds.) CRYPTO 2018. LNCS, vol. 10991, pp. 155–186. Springer, Cham (2018). https://doi.org/10.1007/978-3-319-96884-1_6

34. Facebook: Messenger secret conversations technical whitepaper (2017). https://fbnewsroomus.files.wordpress.com/2016/07/messenger-secret-conversations-technical-whitepaper.pdf

35. Feige, U., Shamir, A.: Witness indistinguishable and witness hiding protocols. In: STOC (1990)

36. Fiat, A., Shamir, A.: How to prove yourself: practical solutions to identification and signature problems. In: Odlyzko, A.M. (ed.) CRYPTO 1986. LNCS, vol. 263, pp. 186–194. Springer, Heidelberg (1987). https://doi.org/10.1007/3-540-47721-7_12

37. Geiger, R.S.: Bot-based collective blocklists in twitter: the counterpublic moderation of harassment in a networked public space. Inf. Commun. Soc. **19**, 787–803 (2016)

38. Goldreich, O., Micali, S., Wigderson, A.: Proofs that yield nothing but their validity for all languages in NP have zero-knowledge proof systems. J. ACM **38**, 690–728 (1991)

39. Grubbs, P., Lu, J., Ristenpart, T.: Message franking via committing authenticated encryption. In: Katz, J., Shacham, H. (eds.) CRYPTO 2017. LNCS, vol. 10403, pp. 66–97. Springer, Cham (2017). https://doi.org/10.1007/978-3-319-63697-9_3

40. Henry, R., Goldberg, I.: Formalizing anonymous blacklisting systems. In: IEEE S&P (2011)

41. van den Hooff, J., Lazar, D., Zaharia, M., Zeldovich, N.: Vuvuzela: scalable private messaging resistant to traffic analysis. In: SOSP (2015)

42. Huang, Q., Yang, G., Wong, D.S., Susilo, W.: Efficient strong designated verifier signature schemes without random oracle or with non-delegatability. Int. J. Inf. Secur. **10**, 373 (2011)

43. Huguenin-Dumittan, L., Leontiadis, I.: A message franking channel. Cryptology ePrint Archive, Report 2018/920 (2018)

44. Jakobsson, M., Sako, K., Impagliazzo, R.: Designated verifier proofs and their applications. In: Maurer, U. (ed.) EUROCRYPT 1996. LNCS, vol. 1070, pp. 143–154. Springer, Heidelberg (1996). https://doi.org/10.1007/3-540-68339-9_13

45. Kudla, C., Paterson, K.G.: Modular security proofs for key agreement protocols. In: Roy, B. (ed.) ASIACRYPT 2005. LNCS, vol. 3788, pp. 549–565. Springer, Heidelberg (2005). https://doi.org/10.1007/11593447_30

46. Kudla, C., Paterson, K.G.: Non-interactive designated verifier proofs and undeniable signatures. In: Smart, N.P. (ed.) Cryptography and Coding 2005. LNCS, vol. 3796, pp. 136–154. Springer, Heidelberg (2005). https://doi.org/10.1007/11586821_10

47. Kwon, A., Corrigan-Gibbs, H., Devadas, S., Ford, B.: Atom: horizontally scaling strong anonymity. In: SOSP (2017)

48. Kwon, A., Lazar, D., Devadas, S., Ford, B.: Riffle. PoPETs **2016**, 115–134 (2016)

49. Kwon, A., Lu, D., Devadas, S.: XRD: scalable messaging system with cryptographic privacy. arXiv preprint arXiv:1901.04368 (2019)

50. Laguillaumie, F., Vergnaud, D.: Designated verifier signatures: anonymity and efficient construction from *Any* bilinear map. In: Blundo, C., Cimato, S. (eds.) SCN 2004. LNCS, vol. 3352, pp. 105–119. Springer, Heidelberg (2005). https://doi.org/10.1007/978-3-540-30598-9_8

51. Laguillaumie, F., Vergnaud, D.: Multi-designated verifiers signatures. In: Lopez, J., Qing, S., Okamoto, E. (eds.) ICICS 2004. LNCS, vol. 3269, pp. 495–507. Springer, Heidelberg (2004). https://doi.org/10.1007/978-3-540-30191-2_38

52. Lazar, D., Gilad, Y., Zeldovich, N.: Karaoke: distributed private messaging immune to passive traffic analysis. In: OSDI (2018)

53. Lazar, D., Zeldovich, N.: Alpenhorn: bootstrapping secure communication without leaking metadata. In: OSDI (2016)

54. Lipmaa, H., Wang, G., Bao, F.: Designated verifier signature schemes: attacks, new security notions and a new construction. In: Caires, L., Italiano, G.F., Monteiro, L., Palamidessi, C., Yung, M. (eds.) ICALP 2005. LNCS, vol. 3580, pp. 459–471. Springer, Heidelberg (2005). https://doi.org/10.1007/11523468_38

55. Lund, J.: Technology preview: sealed sender for Signal (2018). https://signal.org/blog/sealed-sender/

56. Marlinspike, M.: Simplifying OTR deniability (2013). https://signal.org/blog/simplifying-otr-deniability/

57. Marlinspike, M., Perrin, T.: The X3DH key agreement protocol (2016). https://signal.org/docs/specifications/x3dh/

58. Masnick, M.: The Clinton campaign should stop denying that the Wikileaks emails are valid; they are and they're real (2016). https://www.techdirt.com/articles/20161024/22533835878/clinton-campaign-should-stop-denying-that-wikileaks-emails-are-valid-they-are-theyre-real.shtml

59. Mullin, B.: The New York Times is teaming up with Alphabet's Jigsaw to expand its comments (2017). https://www.poynter.org/news/new-york-times-teaming-alphabets-jigsaw-expand-its-comments

60. Nossiter, A., Sanger, D.E., Perlroth, N.: Hackers Came, but the French were prepared (2017). https://www.nytimes.com/2017/05/09/world/europe/hackers-came-but-the-french-were-prepared.html

61. Pedersen, T.P.: Non-interactive and information-theoretic secure verifiable secret sharing. In: Feigenbaum, J. (ed.) CRYPTO 1991. LNCS, vol. 576, pp. 129–140. Springer, Heidelberg (1992). https://doi.org/10.1007/3-540-46766-1_9

62. Piotrowska, A.M., Hayes, J., Elahi, T., Meiser, S., Danezis, G.: The loopix anonymity system. In: USENIX Security (2017)

63. Rabin, T., Ben-Or, M.: Verifiable secret sharing and multiparty protocols with honest majority (extended abstract). In: STOC (1989)

64. Raimondo, M.D., Gennaro, R., Krawczyk, H.: Deniable authentication and key exchange. In: CCS (2006)

65. Ristenpart, T., Yilek, S.: The power of proofs-of-possession: securing multiparty signatures against rogue-key attacks. In: Naor, M. (ed.) EUROCRYPT 2007. LNCS, vol. 4515, pp. 228–245. Springer, Heidelberg (2007). https://doi.org/10.1007/978-3-540-72540-4_13

66. Rivest, R.L., Shamir, A., Tauman, Y.: How to leak a secret. In: Boyd, C. (ed.) ASIACRYPT 2001. LNCS, vol. 2248, pp. 552–565. Springer, Heidelberg (2001). https://doi.org/10.1007/3-540-45682-1_32

67. Roose, K.: As elites switch to texting, watchdogs fear loss of transparency (2017). https://www.nytimes.com/2017/07/06/business/as-elites-switch-to-texting-watchdogs-fear-loss-of-transparency.html

68. Saeednia, S., Kremer, S., Markowitch, O.: An efficient strong designated verifier signature scheme. In: Lim, J.-I., Lee, D.-H. (eds.) ICISC 2003. LNCS, vol. 2971, pp. 40–54. Springer, Heidelberg (2004). https://doi.org/10.1007/978-3-540-24691-6_4

69. Schnorr, C.P.: Efficient identification and signatures for smart cards. In: Brassard, G. (ed.) CRYPTO 1989. LNCS, vol. 435, pp. 239–252. Springer, New York (1990). https://doi.org/10.1007/0-387-34805-0_22

70. Stadler, M.: Publicly verifiable secret sharing. In: Maurer, U. (ed.) EUROCRYPT 1996. LNCS, vol. 1070, pp. 190–199. Springer, Heidelberg (1996). https://doi.org/10.1007/3-540-68339-9_17

71. Tyagi, N., Gilad, Y., Leung, D., Zaharia, M., Zeldovich, N.: Stadium: a distributed metadata-private messaging system. In: SOSP (2017)

72. Tyagi, N., Grubbs, P., Len, J., Miers, I., Ristenpart, T.: Asymmetric message franking: content moderation for metadata-private end-to-end encryption. Cryptology ePrint Archive, Report 2019/565 (2019)

73. Unger, N., Goldberg, I.: Deniable key exchanges for secure messaging. In: CCS (2015)

Obfuscation

Statistical Zeroing Attack: Cryptanalysis of Candidates of BP Obfuscation over GGH15 Multilinear Map

Jung Hee Cheon[1,2,3], Wonhee Cho[1], Minki Hhan[1], Jiseung Kim[1(✉)], and Changmin Lee[4]

[1] Department of Mathematical Sciences, SNU, Seoul, Republic of Korea
{jhcheon,wony0404,hhan_,tory154}@snu.ac.kr
[2] Research Institute of Mathematics (RIM), SNU, Seoul, Republic of Korea
[3] Cryptolab, Seoul, Republic of Korea
[4] ENS de Lyon, Laboratoire LIP (U. Lyon, CNRS, ENSL, INRIA, UCBL),
Lyon, France
changmin.lee@ens-lyon.fr

Abstract. We present a new cryptanalytic algorithm on obfuscations based on GGH15 multilinear map. Our algorithm, *statistical zeroing attack*, directly distinguishes two distributions from obfuscation while it follows the zeroing attack paradigm, that is, it uses evaluations of zeros of obfuscated programs.

Our attack breaks the recent indistinguishability obfuscation candidate suggested by Chen *et al.* (CRYPTO'18) for the optimal parameter settings. More precisely, we show that there are two functionally equivalent branching programs whose CVW obfuscations can be efficiently distinguished by computing the sample variance of evaluations.

This statistical attack gives a new perspective on the security of the indistinguishability obfuscations: we should consider the shape of the distributions of evaluation of obfuscation to ensure security.

In other words, while most of the previous (weak) security proofs have been studied with respect to algebraic attack model or ideal model, our attack shows that this algebraic security is not enough to achieve indistinguishability obfuscation. In particular, we show that the obfuscation scheme suggested by Bartusek *et al.* (TCC'18) does not achieve the desired security in a certain parameter regime, in which their algebraic security proof still holds.

The correctness of statistical zeroing attacks holds under a mild assumption on the preimage sampling algorithm with a lattice trapdoor. We experimentally verify this assumption for implemented obfuscation by Halevi *et al.* (ACM CCS'17).

Keywords: Cryptanalysis · Indistinguishability obfuscation · Multilinear map

© International Association for Cryptologic Research 2019
A. Boldyreva and D. Micciancio (Eds.): CRYPTO 2019, LNCS 11694, pp. 253–283, 2019.
https://doi.org/10.1007/978-3-030-26954-8_9

1   Introduction

Indistinguishability obfuscation (iO) is one of the most powerful tools used to construct many cryptographic applications such as non-interactive multiparty key exchange and functional encryption [5,18,34]. While constructing a general-purpose iO has been posed as a longstanding open problem, Garg *et al.* [18] first proposed a plausible candidate for the general-purpose iO exploiting a multilinear map in 2013. Starting from this work, many subsequent studies have proposed plausible constructions of iO upon candidate multilinear maps [1–3,6,18,19,25–28,31,32,36].

However, all of the current constructions of multilinear map, essentially classified as GGH13, CLT13 and GGH15 [16,17,20], are merely candidates. These constructions are not known to have the desired security of the multilinear map due to the first class of zeroizing attacks, such as the CHLRS attack and Hu-Jia attack [11,15,26]; these attacks commonly exploits several encodings of zero to show the multi-party key exchange protocol instantiated by candidate multilinear maps are not secure.

On the other hand, the first class of zeroizing attacks does not damage the security of current iO constructions from the candidate multilinear maps. It later turns out that most candidates iO fail to achieve the desired security due to subsequent works, *the second class of zeroizing attacks* [9,10,12–15,33], which employs algebraic relations of the top level encodings of zero. In this light, many researches focus on algebraic security of obfuscation using the weak multilinear map models [4,19,29] to capture the currently known techniques to analyze obfuscations and multilinear map itself.

Recently, GGH15 multilinear map has been in the spotlight because it is shown that GGH15 and its variants can be exploited to construct provable secure special-purpose obfuscations and other cryptographic applications including constraint pseudorandom functions under the hardness of LWE and its variants [7,8,10,22,35]. Therefore, the GGH15 multilinear map has been believed to be the most plausible candidate for constructing the general-purpose obfuscation.

In this respect, Chen *et al.* [10] proposed a new iO candidate over GGH15, called CVW obfuscation, to be secure against all known attacks. Then, Bartusek *et al.* [4] provided a new candidate over GGH15, called BGMZ obfuscation, which is provably secure against generalized algebraic zeroizing attacks. The security of these two schemes in more general setting remains as an open problem.

1.1   Our Result

We give a new polynomial time cryptanalysis, *statistical zeroizing attack*, on the candidates of iO based on the GGH15 multilinear map. This attack directly distinguishes the distributions from zeros of obfuscated programs instead of finding algebraic relations of evaluations. We particularly exploit the sample variance as a distinguisher of the distributions, while this attack introduces wide class of distinguishing methods. In particular, under an assumption on lattice preimage sampling algorithm with a trapdoor, our attack breaks the security of

- CVW obfuscation for the optimal parameter choice. Further, our attack still works for the relatively small variance σ^2 of Gaussian distribution such as $\sigma = \mathsf{poly}(\lambda)$ for the security parameter λ, and
- BGMZ obfuscation for large variance of Gaussian distribution, e.g. $\sigma = 2^\lambda$, which still enables the security proof in the weak GGH15 multilinear map model.[1]

This result refutes the open problem posed in [10] in a certain parameter regime: the CVW obfuscation is not secure even when the adversary gets oracle access to the honest evaluations as matrix products instead of obfuscated program.

Our attack leads a new perspective to the study of iO: we should focus on the statistical properties such as shapes of distributions as well to achieve indistinguishability obfuscation. In particular, the distributions of evaluations should be (almost) the same regardless of the choice of target branching program. Previously, most attacks and constructions only focused on the algebraic structure of evaluations.

Attack Overview. Suppose that the adversary has two functionally equivalent branching programs $\mathbf{M}$ and $\mathbf{N}$, and an obfuscated program $\mathcal{O}(\mathbf{P})$ where $\mathbf{P} = \mathbf{M}$ or $\mathbf{N}$. The purpose of the adversary is to determine whether $\mathbf{P} = \mathbf{M}$ or $\mathbf{N}$. Note that the recent obfuscation constructions compute its output via two processes: the first step is to compute a value, we call *evaluation* here according to the evaluating rules, which is usually to compute a product of given matrices. The second step is to determine the *output* from the size of the evaluation in the first step.

The basic form of statistical zeroizing attack is incredibly simple; just compute the evaluation of obfuscated program (right before computing output) and check if an entry is larger than a threshold value. Since two evaluations of obfuscated programs $\mathcal{O}(\mathbf{M})$ and $\mathcal{O}(\mathbf{N})$ have the different variance, this attack may work.

Technically speaking, we consider a bit complex form of statistical zeroizing attack in this paper to give a rigorous analysis. The above form is simple, but it is hard to check the correctness of attack.[2] Thus we consider the multiple-sample problem instead of one evaluation, and then compute the sample variance. Then we determine $\mathbf{P}$ by checking the inequality of the sample variance and a threshold value. Note that these distributions of evaluations are polynomial-time constructible, i.e. the sampling algorithm is done in polynomial time, since every parameter to do obfuscation process is given to adversary. Therefore the distinguishing algorithm of two distributions implies the distinguishability of two corresponding evaluations by the standard hybrid argument.

Though the attack is conceptually simple, it is difficult to verify that the attack works well for certain obfuscation schemes, and this verification requires

---

[1] That is, our attack is lying outside the considered attack class in [4].

[2] The difference of variance is even not enough to distinguish. For example, the distributions that 0 with overwhelming probability cannot be efficiently distinguished though these can have any variance.

several complex computational tasks. Thus we give the sufficient conditions that attack works well using sample variance for a simpler description of the attack. And we assign many pagesost papers including appendix and technical computations, which can be found in the full version of this paper [11], to show that those conditions hold under an assumption, dealing with many random variables that might be dependent themselves. We derive many lemmas to deal with such intertwined random variables.

Assumption on Lattice Preimage Sampling. The analysis of attack requires an assumption on lattice preimage sampling algorithm. This assumption states that the variance and kurtosis of products of matrices from preimage sampling have almost the same size as one assumed the independency of those matrices. This assumption is experimentally verified for matrices used in implemented obfuscation scheme [23]. For more detailed description, see Assumption 1 and Appendix C.

Example of Statistical Zeroizing Attack. We give an example to show how our attack intuitively works. We consider a simple construction of GGH15-obfuscation without all safeguards. For brevity we only give the result of evaluation. A detailed description of this simple obfuscation is given in Appendix A. We also do not give a computational analysis of the attack here, but this example still is enough to shows that the two distributions of evaluations from different branching programs may have quite different shape.

We consider two functionally equivalent branching programs

$$\mathbf{M} = \{\mathbf{M}_{i,b}\}_{i\in[h],b\in\{0,1\}} \quad and \quad \mathbf{N} = \{\mathbf{N}_{i,b}\}_{i\in[h],b\in\{0,1\}}$$

where

$$\mathbf{M}_{i,b} = \mathbf{0}^{w\times w} \text{ for all } i,b \text{ and } \mathbf{N}_{i,b} = \begin{cases} \mathbf{I}^{w\times w} & \text{if } i=1 \\ \mathbf{0}^{w\times w} & \text{otherwise} \end{cases}.$$

For these BPs, the evaluations are of the form

$$\mathcal{O}(\mathbf{M})(\mathbf{x}) = \mathbf{E}_{1,x_{\mathsf{inp}(1)}} \cdot \prod_{k=2}^{h} \mathbf{D}_{k,x_{\mathsf{inp}(k)}} \text{ and}$$

$$\mathcal{O}(\mathbf{N})(\mathbf{x}) = \mathbf{E}_{1,x_{\mathsf{inp}(1)}} \cdot \prod_{k=2}^{h} \mathbf{D}_{k,x_{\mathsf{inp}(k)}} + \mathbf{I} \cdot \mathbf{E}_{2,x_{\mathsf{inp}(2)}} \cdot \prod_{k=3}^{h} \mathbf{D}_{k,x_{\mathsf{inp}(k)}}.$$

Here $\mathbf{D}$'s are preimage-sampled matrices and $\mathbf{E}$'s are error matrices, whose entries are all following discrete Gaussian distribution.

If we choose polynomial-size variances for those matrices, these two distributions have noticeably different shape. Therefore one can hope to distinguish two distribution; indeed, the sample variance will be served as a distinguisher in this paper. Or, more efficiently, one can distinguish them by looking at the size of sample, but this is not easy to show the correctness as noted in above without strong assumption on shape of distributions.

Applicability and Limitation. The class of branching programs constructed from CNF formulas, suggested in [10, Construction 6.4], is in the range of our attack as well. For example, as we choose two branching programs $\mathbf{N} = \{\mathbf{N}_{i,b}\}$ and $\mathbf{M} = \{\mathbf{M}_{i,b}\}$ as follows: $\mathbf{N}_{1,b}$ as the identity matrix with $w \times w$ size and all other matrices of $\mathbf{M}$ and $\mathbf{N}$ as the zero matrix. These two branching programs $\mathbf{M}$ and $\mathbf{N}$ correspond to some CNF formulas following the construction. This is exactly the same to the target branching programs described in Sect. 4.2 as an attack example.

On the other hand, there is a class of branching programs that seems robust against our attack: permutation matrix branching programs. For this class of branching programs, the distributions of evaluations except bookend vectors are the same for any choice of permutation branching program $\mathbf{M}$ in many obfuscation constructions (under the assumption on trapdoor matrices). Interestingly, (a variant of) the first candidate iO over the GGH15 multilinear map [18, 20] has targeted such branching programs so it is robust against our attack.

Further, the obfuscation schemes over the CLT13 or GGH13 multilinear maps seems to be secure against statistical zeroizing attack. This is due to the structure of those schemes; encodings CLT13 and GGH13 have large randomness in the zero-testing results compared to the message-dependent parts. In other words, the randomness dominates the zero-testing values and the message only gives negligible perturbation on the zero-testing distributions.

Counter Measures. There are two countermeasures on our attack: (1) modifying construction to obfuscate permutation branching programs and (2) adjusting parameters to rule out our attack. We remark that both countermeasures are plausibly blocking the attack but not in the provable security level.

As noted above, we can simply use the known obfuscations to obfuscate permutation branching programs only. Unfortunately, CVW and BGMZ obfuscations in the suggested form are not appropriate to obfuscate the permutation branching programs.[3] We can modify CVW obfuscation to obfuscate the permutation branching programs; this modified construction is secure against all existing attacks including the attack suggested in this paper. This can be done by choosing the bookends appropriately for permutations. A more precise description is placed in Appendix B. The similar modification works well in BGMZ obfuscation.

Another simple countermeasure for our attack is to take another parameter choice for variance σ, especially to adjust the variance of several discrete Gaussian distributions appropriately. For example, one can consider the following modifications.

---

[3] Though there is a general transformation from permutation branching program into Type I branching program [10, Claim 6.2], this induces the bookend vector of the form $(\mathbf{v}|-\mathbf{v})$ rather than the implicitly supposed bookend $\mathbf{1}^{1 \times w}$ in CVW obfuscation. If we directly obfuscate permutation branching programs, the functionality of them is all-rejection. Indeed, if we obfuscate permutation branching programs using CVW obfuscation as this trivial functionality (without transformation), the iO security for these trivial BPs can be proven by the proof technique of [7].

- For CVW obfuscation, the condition of our attack (using sample variance) does not hold for large σ^2, e.g. $\sigma^2 = \Omega(m^\ell)$ for the sampled dimension m of preimage sampling and the length ℓ of branching program.
- For BGMZ obfuscation, the small choice of σ, e.g. $\sigma^2 = O(\nu)$ for the size bound of the bookend vector's entry ν.

Both countermeasures yield the exponential bound in the first attack condition (See Proposition 3.1). We remark that the preimage sampling procedure with large σ can be done in polynomial time using [21].

It is interesting that the large σ yields countermeasure on CVW obfuscation while it allows the attack on BGMZ obfuscation. This difference comes from the structure of scheme, or the dominating term of evaluation's variance. More precisely, the main parts to induce the difference are

- In BGMZ obfuscation, there are auxiliary random matrices terms, which flood other terms. For large σ, a dominating term moves to the message dependent terms.
- In CVW obfuscation, auxiliary random matrices are only larger than the message dependent terms up to polynomial factor, which gives the enough difference to distinguish. When σ is increased, the ratio is going to exponential and yields noise-flooding.

Open Questions. We also leave some open problems:

1. The presented attack shows some weakness of obfuscation for non-permutation branching program, while this class of branching programs is known to have several advantages compared to permutation branching programs including efficiency [10]. Can we construct a provably secure obfuscation against all zeroizing attack without choosing the permutation branching programs?
2. On the other hand, can we extend the zeroizing attack to more general obfuscation or branching programs such as evasive functions or permutation branching programs? Can we derive a new attack that combines algebraic and statistical structure of evaluations?
3. The candidate witness encryption in [10] shares almost the same structure with the CVW obfuscation but we do not know whether it is secure or not.

Organization. In Sect. 2, we introduce preliminary related to the branching program, iO, and lattices. We describe the statistical zeroizing attack in Sect. 3. In Sect. 4, we briefly describe CVW obfuscation and its cryptanalysis. In addition, we review BGMZ obfuscation and its cryptanalysis in Sect. 5.

2   Preliminaries

Notations. $\mathbb{N}, \mathbb{Z}, \mathbb{R}$ denote the sets of natural numbers, integers, and real numbers, respectively. For an integer $q \geq 2$, $\mathbb{Z}_q$ is the set of integers modulo q.

Elements are in $\mathbb{Z}_q$ are usually considered as integers in $[-q/2, q/2)$. We denote the set $\{1, 2, \cdots, h\}$ by $[h]$ for a natural number h.

Lower bold letters means row vectors and capital bold letters denote matrices. In addition, capital italic letters denote random matrices or random variables. For a random variable X, we let $E(X)$ be the expected value of X, $Var(X)$ the variance of X.

The n-dimensional identity matrix is denoted by $\mathbf{I}^{n \times n}$. For a row vector $\mathbf{v}$, a i-th component of $\mathbf{v}$ is denoted by v_i, and for a matrix $\mathbf{A}$, a (i, j)-th entry of a matrix $\mathbf{A}$ is denoted by $a_{i,j}$, respectively. A notation $\mathbf{1}^{a \times b}$ means a $a \times b$ matrix such that all entries are 1. The ℓ_p norm of a vector $\mathbf{v} = (v_i)$ is denoted by $\|\mathbf{v}\|_p = (\sum_i |v_i|^p)^{1/p}$. We denote $\|\mathbf{A}\|_\infty$ by the infinity norm of a matrix $\mathbf{A}$, $\|\mathbf{A}\|_\infty = \max_{i,j} a_{i,j}$ with $\mathbf{A} = (a_{i,j})$.

We use a notation $\mathbf{x} \leftarrow \chi$ to denote the operation of sampling element $\mathbf{x}$ from the distribution χ. Especially, if χ is the uniform distribution on a finite set $\mathbf{X}$, we denote $\mathbf{x} \leftarrow U(\mathbf{X})$.

For two matrices $\mathbf{A} = (a_{i,j}) \in \mathbb{R}^{n \times m}$, $\mathbf{B} \in \mathbb{R}^{k \times \ell}$, the tensor product of matrix $\mathbf{A}$ and $\mathbf{B}$ is defined as

$$\mathbf{A} \otimes \mathbf{B} := \begin{pmatrix} a_{1,1} \cdot \mathbf{B} & \cdots & a_{1,m} \cdot \mathbf{B} \\ \vdots & \ddots & \vdots \\ a_{n,1} \cdot \mathbf{B}, & \cdots, & a_{n,m} \cdot \mathbf{B} \end{pmatrix}.$$

For four matrices $\mathbf{A}, \mathbf{B}, \mathbf{C}, \mathbf{D}$ such that one can form products $\mathbf{A} \cdot \mathbf{C}$ and $\mathbf{B} \cdot \mathbf{D}$, the equation $(\mathbf{A} \otimes \mathbf{B}) \cdot (\mathbf{C} \otimes \mathbf{D}) = (\mathbf{A} \cdot \mathbf{C}) \otimes (\mathbf{B} \cdot \mathbf{D})$ holds.

2.1   Matrix Branching Program

A matrix branching program (BP) is the set which consists of an index-to-input function and several matrix chains.

Definition 2.1. *A width w, length h, and a s-ary matrix branching program* $\mathbf{P}$ *over a ℓ-bit input is a set which consists of index-to-input maps* $\{\mathsf{inp}_\mu : [h] \to [\ell]\}_{\mu \in [s]}$, *sequences of matrices, and two disjoint sets of target matrices.*

$$\mathbf{P} = \{(\mathsf{inp}_\mu)_{\mu \in [s]}, \{\mathbf{P}_{i,b} \in \{0,1\}^{w \times w}\}_{i \in [h], b \in \{0,1\}^s}, \mathcal{P}_0, \mathcal{P}_1 \subset \mathbb{Z}^{w \times w}\}.$$

The evaluation of $\mathbf{P}$ *on input* $\mathbf{x} = (x_i)_{i \in [\ell]} \in \{0,1\}^\ell$ *is computed by*

$$\mathbf{P}(\mathbf{x}) = \begin{cases} 0 & \text{if } \prod_{i=1}^h \mathbf{P}_{i,(x_{\mathsf{inp}_\mu(i)})_{\mu \in [s]}} \in \mathcal{P}_0 \\ 1 & \text{if } \prod_{i=1}^h \mathbf{P}_{i,(x_{\mathsf{inp}_\mu(i)})_{\mu \in [s]}} \in \mathcal{P}_1 \end{cases}.$$

When $s = 1$ ($s = 2$), the BP is called a single-input (dual-input) BP. In this paper, we usually use $\mathcal{P}_0 = \mathbf{0}^{w \times w}$ and $\mathcal{P}_1$ is the set of all nonzero matrices in $\mathbb{Z}^{w \times w}$. Also, we call $\{\mathbf{P}_{i,b}\}_{b \in \{0,1\}^s}$ the i-th layer of the BP. Remark that CVW obfuscation and BGMZ obfuscation take as input different BP type (e.g. single and dual BP) and the required properties of BP for each obfuscation are different. Therefore, we mention the required properties used to construct an obfuscation again before describing each obfuscation.

2.2 Indistinguishability Obfuscation

Definition 2.2 (Indistinguishability Obfuscation). *A probabilistic polynomial time machine $\mathcal{O}$ is an indistinguishability obfuscation for a circuit class $\mathcal{C} = \{\mathcal{C}_\lambda\}$ if the following conditions are satisfied:*

- *For all security parameters $\lambda \in \mathbb{N}$, for all circuits $C \in \mathcal{C}_\lambda$, for all inputs $\mathbf{x}$, the following probability holds:*

$$\Pr\left[C'(\mathbf{x}) = C(\mathbf{x}) : C' \leftarrow \mathcal{O}(\lambda, C)\right] = 1.$$

- *For any p.p.t distinguisher D, there exists a negligible function α satisfying the following statement: For all security parameters $\lambda \in \mathbb{N}$ and all pairs of circuits C_0, $C_1 \in \mathcal{C}_\lambda$, $C_0(\mathbf{x}) = C_1(\mathbf{x})$ for all inputs $\mathbf{x}$ implies*

$$\left|\Pr\left[D(\mathcal{O}(\lambda, C_0)) = 1\right] - \Pr\left[D(\mathcal{O}(\lambda, C_1)) = 1\right]\right| \leq \alpha(\lambda).$$

2.3 Lattice Trapdoor Background

A lattice $\mathcal{L}$ of dimension n is a discrete additive subgroup of $\mathbb{R}^n$. If $\mathcal{L}$ is generated by the set $\{\mathbf{b}_1, \cdots, \mathbf{b}_n\}$, all elements in $\mathcal{L}$ are of the form $\sum_{i=1}^n x_i \cdot \mathbf{b}_i$ for some integers x_i's. In this case, the lattice $\mathcal{L}$ is called the full rank lattice. Throughout this paper, we only consider the full rank lattice. Now we give several definitions and lemmas used in this paper.

For any $\sigma > 0$, the Gaussian function on $\mathbb{R}^n$ centered at $\mathbf{c}$ with parameter σ is defined as

$$\rho_{\sigma, \mathbf{c}}(\mathbf{x}) = e^{-\pi \|\mathbf{x} - \mathbf{c}\| / \sigma^2} \text{ for all } \mathbf{x} \in \mathbb{R}^n.$$

Definition 2.3 (Discrete Gaussian Distribution on Lattices). *For any element $\mathbf{c} \in \mathbb{R}^n$, $\sigma > 0$ and any full rank lattice $\mathcal{L}$ of $\mathbb{R}^n$, the discrete Gaussian distribution over $\mathcal{L}$ is defined as*

$$D_{\mathcal{L}, \sigma, \mathbf{c}}(\mathbf{x}) = \frac{\rho_{\sigma, \mathbf{c}}(\mathbf{x})}{\rho_{\sigma, \mathbf{c}}(\mathcal{L})} \text{ for all } \mathbf{x} \in \mathcal{L}$$

where $\rho_{\sigma, \mathbf{c}}(\mathcal{L}) = \sum_{\mathbf{x} \in \mathcal{L}} \rho_{\sigma, \mathbf{c}}(\mathbf{x})$.

Lemma 2.4 ([30]). *For integers $n \geq 1$, $q \geq 2$ and $m \geq 2n \log q$, there is a p.p.t algorithm $\mathsf{TrapSam}(1^n, 1^m, q)$ that outputs a matrix $\mathbf{A} \in \mathbb{Z}_q^{n \times m}$ and a trapdoor τ such that $\mathbf{A}$ is statistically indistinguishable from $U(\mathbb{Z}_q^{n \times m})$ with a trapdoor τ.*

Lemma 2.5 ([21]). *There is a p.p.t. algorithm $\mathsf{Sample}(\mathbf{A}, \tau, \mathbf{y}, \sigma)$ that outputs a vector $\mathbf{d}$ from a distribution $D_{\mathbb{Z}^m, \sigma}$. Moreover, if $\sigma \geq 2\sqrt{n \log q}$, then with all but negligible probability, we have*

$$\{\mathbf{A}, \mathbf{d}, \mathbf{y} : \mathbf{y} \leftarrow U(\mathbb{Z}_q^n), \mathbf{d} \leftarrow \mathsf{Sample}(\mathbf{A}, \tau, \mathbf{y}, \sigma)\} \approx_s \{\mathbf{A}, \mathbf{d}, \mathbf{y} : \mathbf{d} \leftarrow D_{\mathbb{Z}^m, \sigma}, \mathbf{A}\mathbf{d} = \mathbf{y}\}.$$

3   Statistical Zeroizing Attack

In this section, we introduce our attack, *statistical zeroizing attack*. We give an abstract model for branching program obfuscation and the attack description in this model. In this attack, we are given two functionally equivalent branching programs $\mathbf{M}$ and $\mathbf{N}$, which will be specified later, and an obfuscated program $\mathcal{O}(\mathbf{P})$ for $\mathbf{P} = \mathbf{M}$ or $\mathbf{N}$. Our purpose is to distinguish whether $\mathbf{P} = \mathbf{M}$ or $\mathbf{P} = \mathbf{N}$. The targeted branching programs of the obfuscation output 0 when the product corresponding to input is zero. The obfuscated program $\mathcal{O}(\mathbf{P})$ consists of

$$\left\{ \mathbf{S}, \{\mathbf{D}_{i,b}\}_{1\leq i\leq h, b\in\{0,1\}^s}, \mathbf{T}, \mathsf{inp} = (\mathsf{inp}_1, \cdots, \mathsf{inp}_s) : [h] \to [\ell]^s, B \right\}$$

where every element is a matrix over $\mathbb{Z}_q$ (possibly identity) except the input function inp. The output of the obfuscated program at $\mathbf{x} = (x_1, \cdots, x_\ell) \in \{0,1\}^\ell$ is computed by considering the value

$$\mathcal{O}(\mathbf{P})(\mathbf{x}) = \mathbf{S} \cdot \prod_{i=1}^{h} \mathbf{D}_{i,\mathbf{x}_{\mathsf{inp}(i)}} \cdot \mathbf{T}$$

where $\mathbf{x}_{\mathsf{inp}(i)} = (x_{\mathsf{inp}_1(i)}, \cdots, x_{\mathsf{inp}_s(i)})$. Note that $\mathcal{O}(\mathbf{P})(\mathbf{x})$ can be a matrix, vector or an element (over $\mathbb{Z}_q$). Regard it as matrix/vector/integer over $\mathbb{Z}$ and check the value: if $\|\mathcal{O}(\mathbf{P})(\mathbf{x})\|_\infty < B < q$ then it outputs 0, otherwise outputs 1. We call $\mathcal{O}(\mathbf{P})(\mathbf{x})$ the *evaluation* of the obfuscated program (at $\mathbf{x}$). We also call $\mathcal{O}(\mathbf{P})(\mathbf{x})$ evaluation of zero if $\mathbf{P}(\mathbf{x}) = 0$ in the plain program. We stress that the *output* and *evaluation* of the obfuscated program is different; the output of the obfuscated program is the same to output of original program, and the evaluation is the value $\mathcal{O}(\mathbf{P})(\mathbf{x})$, which is computed right before determining the output.

To distinguish two different obfuscated programs, we see the distribution of valid evaluations of zero of $\mathcal{O}(\mathbf{M})$ and $\mathcal{O}(\mathbf{N})$. For the evaluation of zero, the size of these products is far smaller than q (or B), thus we can obtain the integer value rather than the element in $\mathbb{Z}_q$. Now, if the evaluation is of the matrix or vector form, we consider only the first entry, namely $(1,1)$ entry of the matrix or the first entry of the vector, in the whole procedure of the attack. We call all of these entries by *the first entry* of the evaluation, including the case of the evaluation is just a real value.

Our strategy is to compute the sample variance of the first entries of many independent evaluations which follow the same distribution. The key of the attack is that this variance heavily depends on the plain program of the obfuscated program and the variance is sufficiently different to distinguish for two certain programs. Therefore, from the variance of the several evaluations, we can decide that the obfuscated program is from which program.

Note that one can sample an element following the distribution of obfuscation or its evaluation at fixed point $\mathbf{x} = \mathbf{x}_0$ in polynomial time when the corresponding program is given, since there is no private key in the obfuscation procedure. In this regard, we consider a more general problem which is easier to analyze: Given two polynomial-time constructible distribution $\mathcal{D}_\mathbf{M}$ and

$\mathcal{D}_\mathbf{N}$ and x sampled from one of them, determine that the sample is from which distribution. In our scenario, $\mathcal{D}_\mathbf{M}$ and $\mathcal{D}_\mathbf{N}$ are the distribution of $\mathcal{O}(\mathbf{M})(\mathbf{x})$ and $\mathcal{O}(\mathbf{N})(\mathbf{x})$, respectively where the distribution is over all randomness to construct obfuscations.

Since the adversary has one sample in our setting, the actual algorithm proceeds by sampling multiple evaluations itself as follows.

Data: $\mathcal{D}_\mathbf{M}, \mathcal{D}_\mathbf{N}, x, \kappa$

1. set $B = (\sigma_\mathbf{M}^2 + \sigma_\mathbf{N}^2)/2$ for $\sigma_\mathbf{M}^2 = Var(\mathcal{D}_\mathbf{M})$ and $\sigma_\mathbf{N}^2 = Var(\mathcal{D}_\mathbf{N})$
2. $i \leftarrow [\kappa]$ and let $s_i = x$
3. sample $\{s_j\}_{j \in [i-1]}$ from $\mathcal{D}_\mathbf{M}$ and $\{s_j\}_{i+1 \leq j \leq \kappa}$ from $\mathcal{D}_\mathbf{N}$
4. compute the sample variance S^2 of $\{s_j\}_{j \in [\kappa]}$
5. if $S^2 < B$, decides $\mathcal{D}_\mathbf{M}$, otherwise $\mathcal{D}_\mathbf{N}$.

The choice of κ is specified later in Proposition 3.1. We also remark that the overall time complexity of algorithm is $O(\kappa \cdot T_{\mathsf{sample}})$ plus small computation for sample variance, where T_{sample} is the time complexity for sampling algorithms. The advantage of this algorithm is, by the standard hybrid argument, $\mathsf{adv_{mult}}/\kappa$ where $\mathsf{adv_{mult}} = 0.98$ is the advantage of distinguishing algorithm by sample variance when κ samples are given as inputs instead of one sample as in Proposition 3.1.

In the next subsection, we analyze the distinguishing algorithm using sample variance for general distributions instead of iO when the multiple samples are given. Then we go back to the actual attack for iO for the concrete obfuscations in Sects. 4 and 5 by showing the attack conditions hold well.

3.1 Distinguishing Distributions Using Sample Variance

Now we give the detailed analysis of distinguishing by sample variance. In this algorithm, we compute the variance of the samples, and check whether the distance between the sample variance and the expected variance of $\mathcal{D}_\mathbf{M}$ and $\mathcal{D}_\mathbf{N}$. If the distance from the sample variance to the variance of $\mathcal{D}_\mathbf{M}$ is less than the distance to the variance of $\mathcal{D}_\mathbf{N}$, we decide the given samples are from $\mathcal{D}_\mathbf{M}$. Otherwise we decide the samples are from $\mathcal{D}_\mathbf{N}$. The result of this method is stated in the following proposition.

Proposition 3.1. *Suppose that two random variables $X_\mathbf{M}$ and $X_\mathbf{N}$ that follow polynomial time constructible distributions $\mathcal{D}_\mathbf{N}$ and $\mathcal{D}_\mathbf{M}$ and have the means $\mu_\mathbf{M}$ and $\mu_\mathbf{N}$ and the variances $\sigma_\mathbf{N}^2$ and $\sigma_\mathbf{M}^2$, respectively. For the security parameter λ and polynomials $p, q, r = \mathsf{poly}(\lambda)$, there is a polynomial time algorithm that distinguishes $\mathcal{D}_\mathbf{M}$ and $\mathcal{D}_\mathbf{N}$ with non-negligible advantage when $O(p \cdot (\sqrt{q} + \sqrt{r})) = \mathsf{poly}(\lambda)$ independent samples from $\mathcal{D}_\mathbf{P}$ are given and the following conditions hold:*

$$\left| \frac{\max(\sigma_\mathbf{N}^2, \sigma_\mathbf{M}^2)}{\sigma_\mathbf{N}^2 - \sigma_\mathbf{M}^2} \right| \leq p \quad \left| \frac{E[(X_\mathbf{N} - \mu_\mathbf{N})^4]}{\sigma_\mathbf{N}^4} \right| \leq q, \text{ and } \left| \frac{E[(X_\mathbf{M} - \mu_\mathbf{M})^4]}{\sigma_\mathbf{M}^4} \right| \leq r.$$

In other words, if two known distributions satisfy the conditions, we can solve the distinguishing problem of two distribution with multiple samples. Thus to cryptanalyze the concrete obfuscation schemes, it suffice to show the conditions in Proposition 3.1. We conclude this section by giving the proof of this proposition.

Proof (Proposition 3.1). We call a definition and useful lemmas first.

Lemma 3.2 (Chebyshev's inequality). *Let X be a random variable with a finite expected value μ and a finite variance $\sigma^2 > 0$. Then, it holds that*

$$\Pr[|X - \mu| \geq k\sigma] \leq 1/k^2$$

for any real number $k > 0$.

Definition 3.3 (Sample variance). *Given random n samples $x_1, x_2, \cdots, x_n$ of $\mathcal{D}$, the sample variance of $\mathcal{D}$ is defined by*

$$S^2 = \frac{1}{n-1} \sum_{i=1}^{n} (x_i - \bar{x})^2$$

where $\bar{x} = \frac{1}{n} \sum_{i=1}^{n} x_i$ is the sample mean.

Definition 3.4 (Kurtosis). *Let X be a random variable with a finite expected value μ and a finite variance $\sigma^2 > 0$. The kurtosis of X is defined by*

$$Kurt[X] = \frac{E[(X - \mu)^4]}{E[(X - \mu)^2]^2} = \frac{E[(X - \mu)^4]}{\sigma^4}.$$

Lemma 3.5. *Let S^2 be the sample variance of size κ samples of a distribution $\mathcal{D}$. Let X be a random variable following $\mathcal{D}$ and $\mu_n = E[(X - E[X])^n]$ be the n-th central moment. Then the variance of S^2 satisfies*

$$Var(S^2) = \frac{1}{\kappa} \left(\mu_4 - \frac{\kappa - 3}{\kappa - 1} \mu_2^2 \right).$$

Now we return to the proof. Suppose that all of the conditions hold for polynomials $p, q, r \in \text{poly}(\lambda)$ and $\sigma_{\mathbf{M}}^2 < \sigma_{\mathbf{N}}^2$. By Lemmas 3.2 and 3.5, we compute the 99% confidence interval of variance of S^2 as follows

$$\Pr\left[|S^2 - \sigma_P^2| \geq 10 \cdot \sqrt{\frac{1}{\kappa} \cdot \left(E[(X_P - \mu_P)^4] - \frac{\kappa - 1}{\kappa - 3} \cdot \sigma_P^4 \right)} \right] \leq \frac{1}{100}$$

with κ number of samples. If κ is sufficiently large, the two intervals of sample variance for $\mathbf{M}$ and $\mathbf{N}$ are disjoint. So we can distinguish two distributions by checking the size of sample variance.

More precisely, if $\kappa \geq 100 \cdot (p \cdot \sqrt{q} + p \cdot \sqrt{r})^2$ that is $\text{poly}(\lambda)$, we have $\sigma_{\mathbf{M}}^2 +$

$$10\sigma_{\mathbf{M}}^2 \cdot \sqrt{\frac{1}{\kappa} \cdot \left(\frac{E[(X_{\mathbf{M}} - \mu_{\mathbf{M}})^4]}{\sigma_{\mathbf{M}}^4} - \frac{\kappa - 1}{\kappa - 3} \right)} < \sigma_{\mathbf{N}}^2 - 10\sigma_{\mathbf{N}}^2 \cdot \sqrt{\frac{1}{\kappa} \cdot \left(\frac{E[(X_{\mathbf{N}} - \mu_{\mathbf{N}})^4]}{\sigma_{\mathbf{N}}^4} - \frac{\kappa - 1}{\kappa - 3} \right)}.$$

Thus the algorithm decides the answer by checking if the sample variance is included in which interval; we do not care the case that it is not included both. This algorithm succeeds with probability at least 0.99 for each input, i.e. the advantage of algorithm is at least 0.98. Note that this algorithm only does the polynomial number of sampling and computing the variance, thus the running time is polynomial.   □

4   Cryptanalysis of CVW Obfuscation

In this section, we briefly describe the construction of CVW obfuscation scheme and show that the statistical zeroizing attack works well for CVW obfuscation.

4.1   Construction of CVW Obfuscation

Chen, Vaikuntanathan and Wee proposed a new candidate of iO which is robust against all existing attacks. We here give a brief description of the candidate scheme. For more details, we refer to original paper [10].

First, we start with the description of BPs they used. The authors use single-input binary BPs, *i.e.*, $\mathsf{inp} = \mathsf{inp}_1$. They employ a new function, called an input-to-index map $\bar{\omega}: \{0,1\}^\ell \to \{0,1\}^h$ such that $\bar{\omega}(\mathbf{x})_i = \mathbf{x}_{\mathsf{inp}(i)}$ for all $i \in [h]$, $\mathbf{x} \in \{0,1\}^\ell$. As used in the paper [10], we denote the $\prod_{i=1}^h \mathbf{M}_{i,\bar{\omega}(\mathbf{x})_i}$ by $\mathbf{M}_{\bar{\omega}(\mathbf{x})}$ or simply $\mathbf{M}_\mathbf{x}$. We sometimes abuse the notion $\mathbf{M}_{i,x_i}$ to denote $\mathbf{M}_{i,\bar{\omega}(\mathbf{x})_i}$.

A target BP $\mathbf{P} = \{\mathsf{inp}, \{\mathbf{P}_{i,b}\}_{i\in[h],b\in\{0,1\}}, \mathcal{P}_0, \mathcal{P}_1\}$, which is called *Type I* BP in the original paper, satisfies the following conditions.

1. All the matrices $\mathbf{P}_{i,b}$ are $w \times w$ matrices.
2. For a vector $\mathbf{v} = \mathbf{1}^{1\times w}$, the target sets $\mathcal{P}_0, \mathcal{P}_1$ satisfies $\mathbf{v} \cdot \mathcal{P}_0 = \{\mathbf{0}^{1\times w}\}$, $\mathbf{v} \cdot \mathcal{P}_1 \neq \{\mathbf{0}^{1\times w}\}$.[4]
3. An index length h is set to $(\lambda + 1) \cdot \ell$ with the security parameter λ.
4. An index-to-input function satisfies $\mathsf{inp}(i) = (i \mod \ell)$. Thus, index-to-input function iterates $\lambda + 1$ times.

Construction. CVW obfuscation is a probabilistic polynomial time algorithm which takes as input a BP $\mathbf{P}$ with an input length ℓ, and outputs an obfuscated program preserving the functionality. The algorithm process consists of the following steps. Here we use new parameters $n, m, q, t := (w + 2n\ell) \cdot n, \sigma$ for the construction. We will specify the parameter settings later.

- Sample bundling matrices $\{\mathbf{R}_{i,b} \in \mathbb{Z}^{2n\ell \times 2n\ell}\}_{i\in[h],b\in\{0,1\}}$ such that $(\mathbf{1}^{1\times 2\ell} \otimes \mathbf{I}^{n\times n}) \cdot \mathbf{R}_{\mathbf{x}'} \cdot (\mathbf{1}^{2\ell\times 1} \otimes \mathbf{I}^{n\times n}) = \mathbf{0} \iff \mathbf{x}' \in \bar{\omega}(\{0,1\}^\ell)$ for all $\mathbf{x}' \in \{0,1\}^h$.

---

[4] As noted in the remark of introduction, it is assumed implicitly that $\mathbf{v} = \mathbf{1}^{1\times w}$ for the targeted BP, while the definition of Type I BP uses $\mathbf{v} \in \{0,1\}^{1\times w}$.

More precisely, $\mathbf{R}_{i,b}$ is a block diagonal matrix $\mathsf{diag}(\mathbf{R}_{i,b}^{(1)}, \mathbf{R}_{i,b}^{(2)}, \cdots, \mathbf{R}_{i,b}^{(\ell)})$. Each $\mathbf{R}_{i,b}^{(k)} \in \mathbb{Z}^{2n \times 2n}$ is one of the following three cases.

$$
\mathbf{R}_{i,b}^{(k)} = \begin{cases} \mathbf{I}^{2n \times 2n} & \text{if inp}(i) \neq k \\[2mm] \begin{pmatrix} \tilde{\mathbf{R}}_{i,b}^{(k)} & \\ & \mathbf{I}^{n \times n} \end{pmatrix}, \tilde{\mathbf{R}}_{i,b}^{(k)} \leftarrow \mathcal{D}_{\mathbb{Z},\sigma}^{n \times n} & \text{if inp}(i) = k \text{ and } i \leq \lambda\ell \\[4mm] \begin{pmatrix} -\mathbf{I}^{n \times n} & \\ & \prod\limits_{j=0}^{\lambda-1} \tilde{\mathbf{R}}_{k+j\ell,b}^{(k)} \end{pmatrix} & \text{if inp}(i) = k \text{ and } i > \lambda\ell \end{cases}
$$

- Sample matrices $\{\mathbf{S}_{i,b} \leftarrow \mathcal{D}_{\mathbb{Z},\sigma}^{n \times n}\}_{i \in [h], b \in \{0,1\}}$ and compute

$$
\mathbf{J} := (\mathbf{1}^{1 \times (w+2n\ell)} \otimes \mathbf{I}^{n \times n}) \in \mathbb{Z}^{n \times t}
$$

$$
\hat{\mathbf{S}}_{i,b} := \begin{pmatrix} \mathbf{P}_{i,b} \otimes \mathbf{S}_{i,b} & \\ & \mathbf{R}_{i,b} \otimes \mathbf{S}_{i,b} \end{pmatrix} \in \mathbb{Z}^{t \times t}
$$

$$
\mathbf{L} := (\mathbf{1}^{(w+2n\ell) \times 1} \otimes \mathbf{I}^{n \times n}) \in \mathbb{Z}^{t \times n}
$$

- Sample $(\mathbf{A}_i, \tau_i) \leftarrow \mathsf{TrapSam}(1^t, 1^m, q)$ for $0 \leq i \leq h-1$, $\mathbf{A}_h \leftarrow U(\mathbb{Z}_q^{n \times n})$, $\{\mathbf{E}_{i,b} \leftarrow \mathcal{D}_{\mathbb{Z},\sigma}^{t \times m}\}_{i \in [h-1], b \in \{0,1\}}$ and $\{\mathbf{E}_{h,b} \leftarrow \mathcal{D}_{\mathbb{Z},\sigma}^{t \times n}\}_{b \in \{0,1\}}$.
- Run Sample algorithms to obtain

$$
\mathbf{D}_{i,b} \in \mathbb{Z}^{m \times m} \leftarrow \mathsf{Sample}(\mathbf{A}_{i-1}, \tau_{i-1}, \hat{\mathbf{S}}_{i,b} \cdot \mathbf{A}_i + \mathbf{E}_{i,b}, \sigma) \text{ for } 1 \leq i \leq h-1,
$$

$$
\mathbf{D}_{h,b} \in \mathbb{Z}^{m \times n} \leftarrow \mathsf{Sample}(\mathbf{A}_{h-1}, \tau_{h-1}, \hat{\mathbf{S}}_{h,b} \cdot \mathbf{L} \cdot \mathbf{A}_h + \mathbf{E}_{h,b}, \sigma).
$$

- Define $\mathbf{A_J}$ as a matrix $\mathbf{J} \cdot \mathbf{A}_0 \in \mathbb{Z}^{n \times m}$ and outputs matrices

$$
\left\{\mathsf{inp}, \mathbf{A_J}, \{\mathbf{D}_{i,b}\}_{i \in [h], b \in \{0,1\}}\right\}.
$$

Evaluation. Evaluation process consists of two steps. The first step is to compute a matrix $\mathbf{A_J} \cdot \mathbf{D}_{\bar{\omega}(\mathbf{x})} \bmod q$. The last step is size comparison: If $\|\mathbf{A_J} \cdot \mathbf{D}_{\bar{\omega}(\mathbf{x})} \bmod q\|_\infty \leq B$, output 0 for some fixed B. Otherwise, output 1.

Parameters. Let λ and λ_{LWE} for the security parameters of obfuscation itself and underlying LWE problem satisfying $\lambda_{LWE} = \mathsf{poly}(\lambda)$ and the following constraints. Set $n = \Omega(\lambda_{LWE} \log q)$ and $\chi = D_{\mathbb{Z}, 2\sqrt{\lambda_{LWE}}}$. Moreover, for the trapdoor functionality, $m = \Omega(t \log q)$ and $\sigma = \Omega(\sqrt{t \log q})$ for $t = (w + 2n\ell) \cdot n$. $B \geq (w + 2n\ell) \cdot h \cdot (m \cdot \sigma^2 \sqrt{n(w+2n\ell)}\sigma)^h$ and $q = B \cdot \omega(\mathsf{poly}(\lambda))$ for correctness, and $q \leq (\sigma/\lambda_{LWE}) \cdot 2^{\lambda_{LWE}^{1-\epsilon}}$ for a fixed $\epsilon \in (0,1)$ for security. For more details, we refer readers to the original paper [10].

Remark 1. The original paper [10] only uses one security parameter λ, but the correctness does not hold in that setting. Instead, the trick that uses two security parameters λ and λ_{LWE} resolves this problem as in [4].

Zerotest Functionality. From the construction of the obfuscation, the following equality always holds, which is essentially what we need.

$$[\mathbf{A_J} \cdot \mathbf{D}_{\bar{\omega}(\mathbf{x})}]_q = \left[\mathbf{J} \cdot \left(\prod_{i=1}^{h} \hat{\mathbf{S}}_{i,x_i} \right) \cdot \mathbf{A}_h + \mathbf{J} \cdot \sum_{j=1}^{h} \left(\left(\prod_{i=1}^{j-1} \hat{\mathbf{S}}_{i,x_i} \right) \cdot \mathbf{E}_{j,x_j} \cdot \prod_{k=j+1}^{h} \mathbf{D}_{k,x_k} \right) \right]_q$$

The honest evaluation with $\mathbf{P_x} = \mathbf{0}^{w \times w}$ gives $\hat{\mathbf{S}}_\mathbf{x} = \mathbf{0}^{t \times t}$ due to the construction of $\mathbf{R}_{i,b}$ is zero for the valid evaluation. Then, the following inequality holds:

$$\|[\mathbf{A_J} \cdot \mathbf{D}_{\bar{\omega}(\mathbf{x})}]_q\|_\infty = \left\| \left[\mathbf{J} \cdot \sum_{j=1}^{h} \left(\left(\prod_{i=1}^{j-1} \hat{\mathbf{S}}_{i,x_i} \right) \cdot \mathbf{E}_{j,x_j} \cdot \prod_{k=j+1}^{h} \mathbf{D}_{k,x_k} \right) \right]_q \right\|_\infty \tag{1}$$

$$\leq \left\| \mathbf{J} \cdot \sum_{j=1}^{h} \left(\left(\prod_{i=1}^{j-1} \hat{\mathbf{S}}_{i,x_i} \right) \cdot \mathbf{E}_{j,x_j} \cdot \prod_{k=j+1}^{h} \mathbf{D}_{k,x_k} \right) \right\|_\infty \tag{2}$$

$$\leq h \cdot \left(\max_{i,b} \|\hat{\mathbf{S}}_{i,b}\| \cdot \sigma \cdot m \right)^h \leq B \tag{3}$$

for all but negligible probability due to the choice of B. If $\mathbf{P_x}$ is not the zero matrix, then $\hat{\mathbf{S}}_\mathbf{x}$ is also not the zero matrix with overwhelming probability. It implies that $\|[\mathbf{A_J} \cdot \mathbf{D}_{\bar{\omega}(\mathbf{x})}]_q\|_\infty$ is larger than B with overwhelming probability because of $\mathbf{A}_h \leftarrow U(\mathbb{Z}_q^{n \times n})$.

4.2   Cryptanalysis of CVW Obfuscation

We apply the statistical zeroizing attack to the CVW obfuscation. As stated in Sect. 3, it is enough to show that the conditions of Proposition 3.1 hold. We only consider small variance σ^2 so that $\sigma = \mathsf{poly}(\lambda)$, and sufficiently large ℓ.[5] This includes the optimal parameter choice as well.

Our targeted two functionally equivalent BPs $\mathbf{M} = \{\mathbf{M}_{i,b}\}_{i \in [h], b \in \{0,1\}}$ and $\mathbf{N} = \{\mathbf{N}_{i,b}\}_{i \in [h], b \in \{0,1\}}$ are of the form

$$\mathbf{M}_{i,b} = \mathbf{0}^{w \times w} \text{ for all } i, b \text{ and } \mathbf{N}_{i,b} = \begin{cases} \mathbf{1}^{w \times w} & \text{if } i = 1 \\ \mathbf{0}^{w \times w} & \text{otherwise} \end{cases}.$$

Suppose that we have an obfuscated program $\mathcal{O}(\mathbf{P})$ for $\mathbf{P} = \mathbf{M}$ or $\mathbf{P} = \mathbf{N}$. Our goal is to determine whether the program $\mathcal{O}(\mathbf{P})$ is an obfuscation of $\mathbf{M}$ or $\mathbf{N}$.

By the standard hybrid argument, it suffices to distinguish the distributions $\mathcal{D}_\mathbf{M}$ or $\mathcal{D}_\mathbf{N}$ where $\mathcal{D}_\mathbf{M}$ and $\mathcal{D}_\mathbf{N}$ is the distributions of the (1,1) entry of evaluation at a fixed vector $\mathbf{x}$ of the obfuscated program of $\mathbf{M}$ or $\mathbf{N}$, respectively. To exploit Proposition 3.1, we transform the CVW construction into the language

---

[5] Indeed, the attack requires the condition $\sigma^4 < m^\ell / n^{\ell+1}$.

of random variables. We denote the random matrix by the capital italic words whose entry follows a distribution that corresponds to the distribution of entry of the bold matrix. For example, the entry of random matrix $E_{i,b}$ follows the distribution $\mathcal{D}_{\mathbb{Z},\sigma}$ since the matrix $\mathbf{E}_{i,b}$ is chosen from $\mathcal{D}_{\mathbb{Z},\sigma}^{t\times m}$ in the CVW construction. More precisely, we define random matrices $\tilde{R}_{i,b}^{(k)}$ following $\mathcal{D}_{\mathbb{Z},\sigma}^{n\times n}$, $S_{i,b}$ following $\mathcal{D}_{\mathbb{Z},\sigma}^{n\times n}$ and A_i as in the trapdoor sampling algorithm. Then we obtain random matrices $\hat{S}_{i,b}^{(\mathbf{P})}$, $R_{i,b}^{(\mathbf{P})}$, $E_{i,b}^{(\mathbf{P})}$ and $D_{i,b}^{(\mathbf{P})}$ as in the construction of CVW obfuscation for the branching programs $\mathbf{P} = \mathbf{M}$ or $\mathbf{N}$. We note that only $\hat{S}_{i,b}^{(\mathbf{P})}$ and $D_{i,b}^{(\mathbf{P})}$ depend on the choice of branching program, but we put $\mathbf{P}$ in some other random variables for convenience of distinction.

Under this setting, it suffices to show the following proposition.

Proposition 4.1. *For a security parameter λ, fix the Gaussian variance parameter $\sigma = \mathsf{poly}(\lambda)$. Then, there are two functionally equivalent branching programs $\mathbf{M}$ and $\mathbf{N}$ with sufficiently large input length ℓ satisfying the following statement: let $Z_{\mathbf{M}}$ and $Z_{\mathbf{N}}$ be random variables satisfying*

$$Z_{\mathbf{M}} = \left[\left(\mathbf{J} \cdot A_0 \cdot D_{\tilde{\omega}(\mathbf{x})}^{(\mathbf{M})}\right)_{(1,1)}\right]_q , \quad Z_{\mathbf{N}} = \left[\left(\mathbf{J} \cdot A_0 \cdot D_{\tilde{\omega}(\mathbf{x})}^{(\mathbf{N})}\right)_{(1,1)}\right]_q$$

where every random matrix is defined as the above. Let $\mu_{\mathbf{M}}$ and $\mu_{\mathbf{N}}$, $\sigma_{\mathbf{M}}^2$ and $\sigma_{\mathbf{N}}^2$ be mean and variance of the random variables of $Z_{\mathbf{M}}$ and $Z_{\mathbf{N}}$, respectively. Then, it holds that

$$\left|\frac{\max(\sigma_{\mathbf{N}}^2, \sigma_{\mathbf{M}}^2)}{\sigma_{\mathbf{N}}^2 - \sigma_{\mathbf{M}}^2}\right| \leq p, \quad \left|\frac{E[(Z_{\mathbf{N}} - \mu_{\mathbf{N}})^4]}{\sigma_{\mathbf{N}}^4}\right| \leq q, \text{ and } \left|\frac{E[(Z_{\mathbf{M}} - \mu_{\mathbf{M}})^4]}{\sigma_{\mathbf{M}}^4}\right| \leq q.$$

for some $p, q = \mathsf{poly}(\lambda)$ under Assumption 1.

We remark that since the random matrices D's are dependent each other, we need to assume the statistical property for verifying conditions of Proposition 4.1 as follows.

Assumption 1. *For an integer $0 \leq k \leq h - 2$ and $\mathbf{P} = \mathbf{M}$ or $\mathbf{N}$, let $\hat{D}_k^{(\mathbf{P})}$ be a random matrix such that $\hat{D}_k^{(\mathbf{P})} = \prod_{i=k+2}^{h} D_i^{(\mathbf{P})}$, where $D_i^{(\mathbf{P})}$ is the random matrix which follows a distribution corresponding preimage-sampled matrix $\mathbf{D}_i^{(\mathbf{P})}$. Then, the following equations hold*

1. *the variance is approximated by the same one assumed that D's are independent Gaussian, that is, it holds that*

$$Var[\hat{D}_k^{(\mathbf{P})}] = \Theta\left(m^{h-k-2}(\sigma^2)^{h-k-1}\right).$$

2. *the kurtosis is bounded by constant, that is, it holds that*

$$\frac{E[(\hat{D}_k^{(\mathbf{P})} - E[\hat{D}_k^{(\mathbf{P})}])^4]}{Var[\hat{D}_k^{(\mathbf{P})}]^2} = O(\mathsf{poly}(\lambda)).$$

We experimentally verify this assumption using the implementation of GGH15 BP obfuscation by Halevi $et\ al.$ [23]. More detailed experimental results are presented in Appendix C. We remark that if we assume that D's are independent matrices that have discrete Gaussian entry with the variance σ^2, the following computations hold:

- the variance of $\hat{D}_k^{(\mathbf{P})}$ is exactly $m^{h-k-2} \cdot (\sigma^2)^{h-k-1}$, and
- the kurtosis of $\hat{D}_k^{(\mathbf{P})}$ is $3 \cdot (1 + 2/m)^{h-k} = \Theta(1)$.

The honest evaluation of the CVW obfuscation $[\mathbf{A_J} \cdot \mathbf{D}_{\bar{\omega}(\mathbf{x})}^{(\mathbf{P})}]_q$ is the matrix of the form

$$
\mathbf{J} \cdot \sum_{j=0}^{h-1} \left(\left(\prod_{i=1}^{j} \hat{\mathbf{S}}_{i,x_i} \right) \cdot \mathbf{E}_{j+1,x_{j+1}} \cdot \prod_{k=j+2}^{h} \mathbf{D}_{k,x_k}^{(\mathbf{P})} \right),
$$

which does not contain the term including the trapdoor matrices $\mathbf{A}_i$ for $i = 0, \cdots, h-1$. Thus, to establish the statistical properties including variance in Proposition 4.1, it suffices to analyze the statistical properties of the random matrices $\hat{S}_{i,b}^{(\mathbf{P})}$, $E_{i,b}^{(\mathbf{P})}$, $D_{i,b}^{(\mathbf{P})}$ and their products.

By the definition of $Z_{\mathbf{P}}$ with $\mathbf{P} = \mathbf{M}$ or $\mathbf{P} = \mathbf{N}$, it is rewritten as

$$
Z_{\mathbf{P}} = \mathbf{J} \cdot \sum_{j=0}^{h-1} \left(\left(\prod_{i=1}^{j} \hat{S}_{i,x_i} \right) \cdot E_{j+1,x_{j+1}} \cdot \prod_{k=j+2}^{h} D_{k,x_k}^{(\mathbf{P})} \right).
$$

Now we give the lemmas to prove Proposition 4.1. The proofs of lemmas can be found in the full version of this paper [11]. The proof of Proposition 4.1 using the lemmas is placed in the concluding part of this section.

For the convenience of the statement, let $(Z_{1,1}^{(\mathbf{M})})_j$ be random variables of $(1,1)$-th entry of the random matrices

$$
\mathbf{J} \cdot \prod_{i=1}^{j} \hat{S}_i^{(\mathbf{M})} \cdot E_{j+1}^{(\mathbf{M})} \cdot \prod_{k=j+2}^{h} D_k^{(\mathbf{M})}
$$

for $j = 0, 1, \cdots, h-1$. In this notation, $Z_{\mathbf{M}}$ is the summation of $(Z_{1,1}^{(\mathbf{M})})_j$ for $j \in \{0, 1, \cdots, h-1\}$. Similarly, we define $(Z_{1,1}^{(\mathbf{N})})_j$ for all $j = 0, \cdots, h-1$. We employ additional notations constants c, d and (possibly polynomial) c_0 such that for all $0 \le k \le h-2$,

$$
c \le \frac{Var[\hat{D}_k^{(\mathbf{P})}]}{m^{h-k-2}(\sigma^2)^{h-k-1}} \le d \quad \text{and} \quad \frac{E[(\hat{D}_k^{(\mathbf{P})} - E[\hat{D}_k^{(\mathbf{P})}])^4]}{Var[\hat{D}_k^{(\mathbf{P})}]^2} \le c_0.
$$

We remark that variances of many terms for $\mathbf{M}$ and $\mathbf{N}$ are $exactly\ the\ same$ since the only $D_1, \hat{S}_1$ are different and the different terms in products of $\hat{S}$ are canceled for $j \ge 2$. Note that most of lemmas hold under Assumption 1, but we omit this repeated statement $under\ Assumption\ 1$ for brevity.

Lemma 4.2. $E[(Z_{1,1}^{(M)})_j] = E[(Z_{1,1}^{(N)})_j] = 0$ for all $j = 0, \cdots, h-1$.

Lemma 4.3. $E[(Z_{1,1}^{(M)})_{\mu_1} \cdot (Z_{1,1}^{(M)})_{\mu_2}] = E[(Z_{1,1}^{(N)})_{\mu_1} \cdot (Z_{1,1}^{(N)})_{\mu_2}] = 0$ for $\mu_1 \neq \mu_2$.

Lemma 4.4. $(j = 0)$ It holds that

$$Var[(Z_{1,1}^{(M)})_0] = Var[(Z_{1,1}^{(N)})_0] = \Theta\left((w + 2n\ell) \cdot m^{h-1} \cdot \sigma^{2h}\right) \text{ and}$$

$$\left|\frac{E[(Z_{1,1}^{(M)})_0^4]}{Var[(Z_{1,1}^{(M)})_0]^2}\right|, \ \left|\frac{E[(Z_{1,1}^{(N)})_0^4]}{Var[(Z_{1,1}^{(N)})_0]^2}\right| \leq 3c_0 \cdot (w + 2n\ell)^2 \cdot m^2 \cdot \left(\frac{d}{c}\right)^2 = \mathsf{poly}(\lambda).$$

Lemma 4.5. $(j = 1)$ It holds that

$$Var[(Z_{1,1}^{(M)})_1] = \Theta\left(\left(n^3\sigma^2 + (2\ell - 1) \cdot n^2\right) \cdot m^{h-2}(\sigma^2)^h\right),$$

$$Var[(Z_{1,1}^{(N)})_1] = \Theta\left(w^3 \cdot n \cdot m^{h-2}(\sigma^2)^h\right) + Var[(Z_{1,1}^{(M)})_1]$$

$$\left|\frac{E[(Z_{1,1}^{(M)})_1^4]}{Var[(Z_{1,1}^{(M)})_1]^2}\right|, \ \left|\frac{E[(Z_{1,1}^{(N)})_1^4]}{Var[(Z_{1,1}^{(N)})_1]^2}\right| \leq 27c_0 \cdot (w + 2n\ell)^4 n^2 m^2 \cdot \left(\frac{d}{c}\right)^2 = \mathsf{poly}(\lambda).$$

Lemma 4.6. $(1 < j \leq \lambda \cdot \ell)$ Let j be a fixed integer with $j = \ell \cdot j_1 + j_2 > 1$ for $0 \leq j_2 < \ell$ and $2 \leq j \leq \lambda \cdot \ell$. Then, it holds that

$$Var[(Z_{1,1}^{(M)})_j] = Var[(Z_{1,1}^{(N)})_j]$$
$$= \Theta\left(\left(j_2 n^{j+j_1+2}(\sigma^2)^{j_1+1} + (\ell - j_2)n^{j+j_1+1}(\sigma^2)^{j_1} + \ell n^{j+1}\right)m^{h-j-1}(\sigma^2)^h\right).$$

Moreover, it holds that

$$\left|\frac{E[(Z_{1,1}^{(M)})_j^4]}{Var[(Z_{1,1}^{(M)})_j]^2}\right|, \ \left|\frac{E[(Z_{1,1}^{(N)})_j^4]}{Var[(Z_{1,1}^{(N)})_j]^2}\right| \leq 27c_0(w + 2n\ell)^4 n^2 m^2 \left(1 + \frac{2}{n}\right)^{j_1+j-1}\left(\frac{d}{c}\right)^2$$
$$= \mathsf{poly}(\lambda).$$

Lemma 4.7. $(j > \lambda \cdot \ell)$ Let j be a fixed integer with $j = \ell \cdot j_1 + j_2 > 1$ for $0 \leq j_2 < \ell$ and $j > \lambda \cdot \ell$. Then, it holds that

$$Var[(Z_{1,1}^{(M)})_j] = Var[(Z_{1,1}^{(N)})_j]$$
$$= \Theta\left(\left((\ell + j_2) \cdot n^{\lambda+j+1} \cdot (\sigma^2)^\lambda + (\ell - j_2) \cdot n^{j+1}\right) \cdot m^{h-j-1} \cdot (\sigma^2)^h\right).$$

In addition, it holds that

$$\left|\frac{E[(Z_{1,1}^{(M)})_j^4]}{Var[(Z_{1,1}^{(M)})_j]^2}\right|, \ \left|\frac{E[(Z_{1,1}^{(N)})_j^4]}{Var[(Z_{1,1}^{(N)})_j]^2}\right| \leq 27c_0(w + 2n\ell)^4 n^2 m^2 \left(1 + \frac{2}{n}\right)^{\lambda+j-2}\left(\frac{d}{c}\right)^2$$
$$= \mathsf{poly}(\lambda).$$

Now we give a proof of the Proposition 4.1 using above lemmas.

Proof (of Proposition 4.1). Fix ℓ be a sufficiently large so that $\sigma^4 < m^\ell/n^{\ell+1}$ and choose BP **M** and **N** as the given in the first page of this section. These two branching programs have the same functionality and length.

Using the results of lemmas, we can prove the proposition by analyzing the summation of random matrices. We first verify the results for $Z_{\mathbf{M}}$. The similar result holds for $Z_{\mathbf{N}}$ since the bounds of lemmas are almost same.

From Lemmas 4.2, 4.3 and the definition of $Z_{\mathbf{M}}$, we have

$$Var[Z_{\mathbf{M}}] = E\left[(\sum_{j=0}^{h-1}(Z_{1,1}^{(\mathbf{M})})_j)^2\right] = E\left[\sum_{j=0}^{h-1}(Z_{1,1}^{(\mathbf{M})})_j^2\right] = \sum_{j=0}^{h-1} Var[(Z_{1,1}^{(\mathbf{M})})_j].$$

On the other hands, applying to the Cauchy-Schwarz inequality, it also holds

$$E[Z_{\mathbf{M}}^4] = E\left[(\sum_{j=0}^{h-1}(Z_{1,1}^{(\mathbf{M})})_j)^4\right] \leq E\left[h^3 \cdot (\sum_{j=0}^{h-1}(Z_{1,1}^{(\mathbf{M})})_j^4)\right].$$

When dividing both sides by $Var[Z_{\mathbf{M}}]^2$, we obtain the inequality

$$\left|\frac{E[Z_{\mathbf{M}}^4]}{Var[Z_{\mathbf{M}}]^2}\right| \leq \left|\frac{E[h^3 \cdot (\sum_{j=0}^{h-1}(Z_{1,1}^{(\mathbf{M})})_j^4)]}{Var[Z_{\mathbf{M}}]^2}\right| = h^3 \cdot \left|\frac{E[\sum_{j=0}^{h-1}(Z_{1,1}^{(\mathbf{M})})_j^4]}{Var[Z_{\mathbf{M}}]^2}\right|$$

$$= h^3 \cdot \sum_{j=0}^{h-1}\left|\frac{E[(Z_{1,1}^{(\mathbf{M})})_j^4]}{Var[Z_{\mathbf{M}}]^2}\right| \leq h^3 \cdot \sum_{j=0}^{h-1}\left|\frac{E[(Z_{1,1}^{(\mathbf{M})})_j^4]}{Var[(Z_{1,1}^{(\mathbf{M})})_j]^2}\right|.$$

By Lemmas 4.4, 4.5, 4.6 and 4.7, $\left|\dfrac{E[(Z_{1,1}^{(\mathbf{M})})_j^4]}{Var[(Z_{1,1}^{(\mathbf{M})})_j]^2}\right|$ is bounded by poly(λ) for all $j = 0, 1, \cdots, h-1$. Therefore, the following inequality holds.

$$\left|\frac{E[Z_{\mathbf{M}}^4]}{Var[Z_{\mathbf{M}}]^2}\right| \leq \mathsf{poly}(\lambda) =: q(\lambda)$$

The same holds for **N** as well.

Moreover, $Var[Z_{\mathbf{N}}] - Var[Z_{\mathbf{M}}] = \Theta\left(w^3 \cdot n \cdot m^{h-2}(\sigma^2)^h\right)$ holds by Lemma 4.5. Then the values $\left|Var[(Z_{1,1}^{(\mathbf{M})})_j]/(Var[Z_{\mathbf{N}}] - Var[Z_{\mathbf{M}}])\right|$ is bounded by poly(λ) for every j since $\sigma^4 < m^\ell/n^{\ell+1}$. This implies the first condition also holds. □

Remark 2. In the original paper [10], the authors give two different choice of the distributions of $\mathbf{E}_{i,b}$; $\mathcal{D}_{\mathbb{Z},\sigma}$ with corresponding dimension in Sect. 11, and $\chi = \mathcal{D}_{\mathbb{Z},2\sqrt{\lambda_{LWE}}}$ with appropriate dimension in Sect. 5. This paper focus on $\mathcal{D}_{\mathbb{Z},\sigma}$ but the result still holds for $\chi = \mathcal{D}_{\mathbb{Z},2\sqrt{\lambda_{LWE}}}$ with slight modification.

5   Cryptanalysis of BGMZ Obfuscation

In this section, we briefly review the BGMZ obfuscation and apply the statistical zeroizing attack on BGMZ obfuscation for exponentially large variance σ. Note that the security proof of BGMZ obfuscation under GGH15 zeroizing model (and underlying BPUA assumption) is independent of the parameter σ, so our attack implies that the algebraic security proof is not enough to achieve the ideal security of iO.

5.1   Construction of BGMZ Obfuscation

Bartusek *et al.* proposed a new candidate of iO which is provably secure in the GGH15 zeroizing model. We briefly review the construction of this scheme. For more detail, we refer to the original paper [4].

We start with the conditions of BP they used. The authors use a dual-input binary BP's. *i.e.*, $\mathsf{inp}(i) = (\mathsf{inp}_1(i), \mathsf{inp}_2(i))$. For simplicity, they use the notation $\boldsymbol{x}(i) = (x_{\mathsf{inp}_1(i)}, x_{\mathsf{inp}_2(i)})$. Moreover, they employ the new parameter $\eta = \mathsf{poly}(\ell, \lambda)$ with $\eta \geq \ell^4$ which decides the minimum number of the BP layer for the security parameter λ and input length ℓ.

The targeted BP $\mathbf{P}$ also satisfies the following conditions.

1. All the matrices $\{\mathbf{P}_{i,b}\}_{i \in [h], b \in \{0,1\}^2}$ are $w \times w$ matrices.
2. $\prod_{i=1}^{h} \mathbf{P}_{i,\boldsymbol{x}(i)} = \mathbf{0}^{w \times w}$.
3. Each pair of input bits (j, k) is read in at least $4\ell^2$ different layers of branching program.
4. There exist layers $i_1 < i_2 < \cdots < i_\eta$ such that $\mathsf{inp}_1(i_1), \cdots, \mathsf{inp}_1(i_\eta)$ cycles η/ℓ times through $[\ell]$.

To obfuscate a branching program that does not satisfy the condition 3 or 4, one pads the identity matrices to satisfy the conditions while preserving the functionality.

Remark 3. The original construction consider the straddling set and asymmetric level structures to prohibit *invalid* evaluations. The description below omitted them because our attack only exploits the valid evaluations whose results are the same regardless of them.

Construction. BGMZ obfuscation is a probabilistic polynomial time algorithm which takes as input a BP $\mathbf{P}$ with a length h, and outputs an obfuscated program with the same functionality. We use several parameter such as $n, m, q, t := (w + 1) \cdot n, \sigma, \nu, g$ in the construction. We will describe the setting for new parameters such as g, ν later.

The obfuscation procedure consists of the following steps.

- Sample $(\mathbf{A}_i, \tau_i) \leftarrow \mathsf{TrapSam}(1^t, 1^m, q)$ for $0 \leq i \leq h - 1$, $\mathbf{A}_h \leftarrow U(\mathbb{Z}_q^{t \times m})$, $\{\mathbf{E}_{i,b} \leftarrow \chi^{t \times m}\}_{i \in [h-1], b \in \{0,1\}^2}$ and $\mathbf{E}_h \leftarrow \chi^{t \times m}$ where $t := (w + 1) \cdot n$.

- Sample matrices $\mathbf{B}_{i,b} \in \mathbb{Z}_\nu^{g \times g}$ and invertible matrices $\mathbf{R}_i \in \mathbb{Z}_q^{(m+g) \times (m+g)}$ randomly.
- Sample matrices $\{\mathbf{S}_{i,b} \leftarrow \mathcal{D}_{\mathbb{Z},\sigma}^{n \times n}\}_{i \in [h-1], b \in \{0,1\}^2}$ and a final encoding $\mathbf{D}_h$ as

$$\mathbf{D}_h \in \mathbb{Z}^{m \times m} \leftarrow \mathsf{Sample}\left(\mathbf{A}_{h-1}, \tau_{h-1}, \begin{pmatrix} \mathbf{I}^{wn \times wn} \\ \mathbf{0}^{n \times n} \end{pmatrix} \cdot \mathbf{A}_h + \mathbf{E}_h, \sigma\right),$$

and compute bookend vectors $\mathbf{v}$ and $\mathbf{w}$ as

$$\mathbf{v} = [\mathbf{v}' \cdot \mathbf{J} \cdot \mathbf{A}_0 \mid \mathbf{b}_v] \cdot \mathbf{R}_1,$$

$$\hat{\mathbf{S}}_{i,b} := \begin{pmatrix} \mathbf{P}_{i,b} \otimes \mathbf{S}_{i,b} \\ & \mathbf{S}_{i,b} \end{pmatrix} \in \mathbb{Z}^{t \times t}$$

$$\mathbf{w}^T = \mathbf{R}_h^{-1} \cdot \begin{pmatrix} \mathbf{D}_h \cdot \mathbf{w}'^T \\ \mathbf{b}_w^T \end{pmatrix}$$

where $\mathbf{v}' \leftarrow \mathcal{D}_{\mathbb{Z},\sigma}^n$, $\mathbf{w}' \leftarrow \mathcal{D}_{\mathbb{Z},\sigma}^m$, $\mathbf{b}_v, \mathbf{b}_w \leftarrow U(\mathbb{Z}_\nu^k)$ and $\mathbf{J} := [\mathbf{J}' | \mathbf{I}^{n \times n}]$ with a randomly chosen matrix $\mathbf{J}' \leftarrow \{0,1\}^{n \times wn}$.
- Compute matrices

$$\mathbf{D}_{i,} \in \mathbb{Z}^{m \times m} \leftarrow \mathsf{Sample}(\mathbf{A}_{i-1}, \tau_{i-1}, \hat{\mathbf{S}}_{i,b} \cdot \mathbf{A}_i + \mathbf{E}_{i,b}, \sigma) \text{ with } 1 \le i \le h-1,$$

and $\mathbf{C}_{i,b} = \mathbf{R}_i^{-1} \cdot \begin{pmatrix} \mathbf{D}_{i,b} \\ & \mathbf{B}_{i,b} \end{pmatrix} \cdot \mathbf{R}_{i+1}$ with $i = 1, \cdots, h-1$.

Evaluation. Outputs 0 if $|\mathbf{v} \cdot \prod_{i=1}^{h-1} \mathbf{C}_{i,\mathbf{x}(i)} \cdot \mathbf{w}^T| \le B$. Otherwise, outputs 1.

Parameters. We first consider several security parameters. Let λ and $\lambda_{LWE} = \mathsf{poly}(\lambda)$ be security parameters depending on the obfuscation itself and the hardness of LWE satisfying following constraints, respectively. Set $n = \Omega(\lambda_{LWE} \log q)$, $\chi = \mathcal{D}_{\mathbb{Z},s}$ with $s = \Omega(\sqrt{n})$. Moreover, for the trapdoor functionality, we set $m = \Omega(t \log q)$ and $\sigma = \Omega(\sqrt{t \log q})$. In addition, they use parameters $g = 5$ and $\nu = 2^\lambda$. For correctness we set zerotest bound $B = (m \cdot \beta \cdot \sigma \cdot \sqrt{t})^{h+1} + (k \cdot \nu)^{h+1}$ and $B \cdot \omega(\mathsf{poly}(\lambda)) \le q \le (\sigma/\lambda_{LWE}) \cdot 2^{\lambda_{LWE}^{1-\epsilon}}$ for some fixed $\epsilon \in (0,1)$. For more detail we refer readers to the original paper [4].

Zerotest Functionality. From the construction of obfuscation, the following equality always holds if $\mathbf{C} := \prod_{i=1}^{h-1} \mathbf{C}_{i,\mathbf{x}(i)}$ is an encoding of zero computed by honest evaluation.

$$\|[\mathbf{v} \cdot \mathbf{C} \cdot \mathbf{w}^T]_q\|_\infty$$

$$= \left\| \left[\mathbf{v}' \cdot \mathbf{J} \cdot \sum_{j=1}^{h} \left(\left(\prod_{i=1}^{j-1} \hat{\mathbf{S}}_{i,\mathbf{x}(i)}\right) \cdot \mathbf{E}_{j,\mathbf{x}(j)} \cdot \prod_{k=j+1}^{h} \mathbf{D}_{k,\mathbf{x}(k)} \cdot \mathbf{w}'^T + \mathbf{b}_v \cdot \prod_{i=1}^{h-1} \mathbf{B}_{i,\mathbf{x}(i)} \cdot \mathbf{b}_w^T \right] \right\|_{q \, \infty}$$

$$\le \left\| \mathbf{v}' \cdot \mathbf{J} \cdot \sum_{j=1}^{h} \left(\left(\prod_{i=1}^{j-1} \hat{\mathbf{S}}_{i,\mathbf{x}(i)}\right) \cdot \mathbf{E}_{j,\mathbf{x}(j)} \cdot \prod_{k=j+1}^{h} \mathbf{D}_{k,\mathbf{x}(k)} \cdot \mathbf{w}'^T + \mathbf{b}_v \cdot \prod_{i=1}^{h-1} \mathbf{B}_{i,\mathbf{x}(i)} \cdot \mathbf{b}_w^T \right\|_\infty$$

$$\le \sigma^2 \cdot m^2 \cdot (m \cdot \beta \cdot \sigma \cdot \sqrt{t})^{h-1} + (k \cdot \nu)^{h+1}$$

Since $\|[\mathbf{v}\cdot\mathbf{C}\cdot\mathbf{w}^T]_q\|_\infty$ is bounded by $\sigma^2\cdot m^2\cdot(m\cdot\beta\cdot\sigma\cdot\sqrt{t})^{h-1}+(k\cdot\nu)^{h+1}\le B$ for all but negligible probability. Moreover, if $\prod_{i=1}^{h}\mathbf{P}_{i,\mathbf{x}(i)}$ is a nonzero matrix, then $\prod_{i=1}^{h}\hat{\mathbf{S}}_{i,\mathbf{x}(i)}$ is also nonzero matrix. Thus, $\|[\mathbf{v}\cdot\mathbf{C}\cdot\mathbf{w}^T]_q\|_\infty$ is larger than B with overwhelming probability because of $\mathbf{A}_h\leftarrow U(\mathbb{Z}_q^{t\times m})$.

5.2   Cryptanalysis of BGMZ Obfuscation

In this section, we analyze the conditions for the statistical zeroizing attack on the BGMZ obfuscation when we assume $\sigma\ge\nu=2^\lambda$. (More precisely, the same result holds when $\sigma^2\ge\nu^2 g/12m$). As in Sect. 4.2, the notation written in the capital italic words are regarded as the random matrix whose entry follows a distribution that corresponds to the distribution of entry of the bold-written matrix.

The targeted BPs are $\mathbf{M}=\{\mathbf{M}_{i,b}\}_{i\in[h],b\in\{0,1\}^2}$ and $\mathbf{N}=\{\mathbf{N}_{i,b}\}_{i\in[h],b\in\{0,1\}^2}$ such that

$$\mathbf{M}_{i,b}=\mathbf{0}^{w\times w}\text{ for all }i,b\text{ and }\mathbf{N}_{i,b}=\begin{cases}\mathbf{I}^{w\times w}&\text{if }i=1\\\mathbf{0}^{w\times w}&\text{otherwise}\end{cases}.$$

Note that two branching programs always output zero. Now we suppose that we have polynomially many samples from the one of two distributions $\mathcal{D}_\mathbf{M}$ and $\mathcal{D}_\mathbf{N}$, where $\mathcal{D}_\mathbf{M}$ and $\mathcal{D}_\mathbf{N}$ are the distributions of the evaluations of obfuscations of $\mathbf{M}$ and $\mathbf{N}$.

Then our purpose is to distinguish whether the samples come from $\mathcal{D}_\mathbf{M}$ or $\mathcal{D}_\mathbf{N}$ by Proposition 3.1. We obtain random matrices $S_{i,\mathbf{b}}^{(\mathbf{P})}$, $E_{i,\mathbf{b}}^{(\mathbf{P})}$, $D_{i,\mathbf{b}}^{(\mathbf{P})}$ and $C_{i,\mathbf{b}}^{(\mathbf{P})}$ as in the construction of BGMZ obfuscation for branching programs $\mathbf{P}=\mathbf{M}$ or $\mathbf{N}$. Thus, it suffices to prove the following proposition.

Proposition 5.1. *Let λ be a security parameter and σ the Gaussian variance parameter satisfying $\sigma^2\ge\nu^2 g/12m$ for parameters m,ν and g of BGMZ obfuscation. Then, there are two functionally equivalent branching programs $\mathbf{M}$ and $\mathbf{N}$ satisfying the following statement: let $Z_\mathbf{M}$ and $Z_\mathbf{N}$ be random variables satisfying*

$$Z_\mathbf{M}=\left[v\cdot\prod_{i=1}^{h-1}C_{i,\mathbf{x}(i)}^{(\mathbf{M})}\cdot w^T\right]_q\text{ and }Z_\mathbf{N}=\left[v\cdot\prod_{i=1}^{h-1}C_{i,\mathbf{x}(i)}^{(\mathbf{N})}\cdot w^T\right]_q.$$

where every random matrix is defined as the above. Let $\mu_\mathbf{M}$ and $\mu_\mathbf{N}$, $\sigma_\mathbf{M}^2$ and $\sigma_\mathbf{N}^2$ be mean and variance of the random variables of $Z_\mathbf{M}$ and $Z_\mathbf{N}$, respectively. Then, it holds that

$$\left|\frac{\max(\sigma_\mathbf{N}^2,\sigma_\mathbf{M}^2)}{\sigma_\mathbf{N}^2-\sigma_\mathbf{M}^2}\right|\le p,\quad\left|\frac{E[(Z_\mathbf{N}-\mu_\mathbf{N})^4]}{\sigma_\mathbf{N}^4}\right|\le q,\text{ and }\left|\frac{E[(Z_\mathbf{M}-\mu_\mathbf{M})^4]}{\sigma_\mathbf{M}^4}\right|\le q.$$

for some $p,q=\mathsf{poly}(\lambda)$ under Assumption 1.

Note that Assumption 1 (for BGMZ obfuscation) is also needed to verify the proposition. With the honest evaluation $\left[\mathbf{v} \cdot \prod_{i=1}^{h-1} \mathbf{C}_{i,\boldsymbol{x}(i)} \cdot \mathbf{w}^T \right]_q$ of the BGMZ obfuscation, we obtain the integer of the form

$$
\mathbf{v}' \cdot \mathbf{J} \sum_{j=1}^{h} \left(\prod_{i=1}^{j-1} \hat{\mathbf{S}}_{i,\boldsymbol{x}(i)} \right) \mathbf{E}_{j,\boldsymbol{x}(j)} \prod_{k=j+1}^{h} \mathbf{D}_{k,\boldsymbol{x}(k)} \cdot \mathbf{w}'^T + \mathbf{b}_v \cdot \prod_{i=1}^{h-1} \mathbf{B}_{i,\boldsymbol{x}(i)} \cdot \mathbf{b}_w^T
$$

which does not contain the term including trapdoor matrices $\mathbf{A}_i$'s. Thus, similarly to the CVW obfuscation case, we need to analyze the statistical properties of the random vectors $v'^{(\mathbf{P})}, w'^{(\mathbf{P})}, b_v^{(\mathbf{P})}, b_w^{(\mathbf{P})}$ and random matrices $\hat{S}_{i,b}^{(\mathbf{P})}, E_{i,b}^{(\mathbf{P})}, D_{i,b}^{(\mathbf{P})}$ and their products to prove the statistical properties including the variance in Proposition 5.1.

The proof of Proposition 5.1 is based on the following lemmas and placed in the concluding part of this section. All proofs of these lemmas can be found in the full version [11]. Note that most lemmas in this section also hold under Assumption 1 as the Sect. 4.2, so we omit repeated *under Assumption 1* in statements. Notations c_0, c, and d are similarly defined as Sect. 4.

For $j = 0, 1, \cdots, h - 1$, let $(Z^{(\mathbf{M})})_j$ be a random variable of the form

$$
v'^{(\mathbf{M})} \cdot J^{(\mathbf{M})} \cdot \prod_{i=1}^{j} \hat{S}_{i,\boldsymbol{x}(i)}^{(\mathbf{M})} \cdot E_{j+1,\boldsymbol{x}(j+1)}^{(\mathbf{M})} \cdot \prod_{k=j+2}^{h} D_{k,\boldsymbol{x}(k)}^{(\mathbf{M})} \cdot w'^{(\mathbf{M})^T},
$$

and for $j = h$, $(Z^{(\mathbf{M})})_h$ a random variable of the form

$$
b_v^{(\mathbf{M})} \cdot \prod_{i=1}^{h-1} B_{i,\boldsymbol{x}(i)}^{(\mathbf{M})} \cdot b_w^{(\mathbf{M})^T}.
$$

We similarly define $(Z^{(\mathbf{N})})_j$ for $j = 0, 1, \cdots, h$, and $Z_{\mathbf{P}} = \sum_{i=0}^{h} (Z^{(\mathbf{P})})_j$ for $\mathbf{P} = \mathbf{M}$ and $\mathbf{N}$.

Lemma 5.2. $E[(Z^{(\mathbf{M})})_j] = E[(Z^{(\mathbf{N})})_j] = 0$ *for all* $j = 0, 1, \cdots, h$.

Lemma 5.3. $E[(Z^{(\mathbf{M})})_{\mu_1} \cdot (Z^{(\mathbf{M})})_{\mu_2}] = E[(Z^{(\mathbf{N})})_{\mu_1} \cdot (Z^{(\mathbf{N})})_{\mu_2}] = 0$ *for* $\mu_1 \neq \mu_2$.

Lemma 5.4. $(j = 0)$ *It holds that*

$$
Var[(Z^{(\mathbf{M})})_0] = Var[(Z^{(\mathbf{N})})_0] = \Theta \left(wn \cdot m^h \cdot (\sigma^2)^{h+1} \cdot s^2 \right),
$$

$$
\left| \frac{E[(Z^{(\mathbf{M})})_0^4]}{Var[(Z^{(\mathbf{M})})_0]^2} \right|, \quad \left| \frac{E[(Z^{(\mathbf{N})})_0^4]}{Var[(Z^{(\mathbf{N})})_0]^2} \right| \leq 108 c_0 (w+1)^2 \cdot n^2 m^4 \cdot \left(\frac{d}{c} \right)^2 = \mathsf{poly}(\lambda).
$$

Lemma 5.5. $(j = 1)$ *It holds that*

$$
Var[(Z^{(\mathbf{M})})_1] = \Theta \left(n^2 m^{h-1} \cdot (\sigma^2)^{h+1} \cdot s^2 \right),
$$
$$
Var[(Z^{(\mathbf{N})})_1] = \Theta \left(wn^3 m^{h-1} \cdot (\sigma^2)^{h+1} \cdot s^2 \right) + Var[(Z^{(\mathbf{M})})_1]
$$

Moreover, it holds that

$$\left|\frac{E[(Z^{(\mathbf{M})})_1^4]}{Var[(Z^{(\mathbf{M})})_1]^2}\right| \le 81c_0 \cdot n^4 m^4 \cdot \left(\frac{d}{c}\right)^2 = \mathsf{poly}(\lambda),$$

$$\left|\frac{E[(Z^{(\mathbf{N})})_1^4]}{Var[(Z^{(\mathbf{N})})_1]^2}\right| \le 324c_0(w+1)^2 \cdot n^6 m^4 \cdot \left(\frac{d}{c}\right)^2 = \mathsf{poly}(\lambda).$$

Lemma 5.6. $(2 \le j \le h-1)$ *It holds that*

$$Var[(Z^{(\mathbf{M})})_j] = Var[(Z^{(\mathbf{N})})_j] = \Theta\left(n^{j+1} m^{h-j} \cdot (\sigma^2)^{h+1} \cdot s^2\right).$$

Moreover, it holds that

$$\left|\frac{E[(Z^{(\mathbf{M})})_j^4]}{Var[(Z^{(\mathbf{M})})_j]^2}\right|, \left|\frac{E[(Z^{(\mathbf{N})})_j^4]}{Var[(Z^{(\mathbf{N})})_j]^2}\right| \le 81c_0 \cdot n^4 m^4 \left(1 + \frac{2}{n}\right)^{j-1} \left(\frac{d}{c}\right)^2 = \mathsf{poly}(\lambda).$$

Lemma 5.7. $(j = h)$ *It holds that*

$$Var[(Z^{(\mathbf{M})})_h] = Var[(Z^{(\mathbf{N})})_h] = g^h \cdot \left\{\frac{1}{12} \cdot \nu(\nu+2)\right\}^{h+1}.$$

Moreover, it holds that

$$E[(Z^{(\mathbf{M})})_h^4], E[(Z^{(\mathbf{N})})_h^4] \le 27 \cdot (g^2)^4 \cdot \{g(g+2)\}^{h-2} \cdot \left\{\frac{1}{12} \cdot \nu(\nu+2)\right\}^{2(h+1)}.$$

Now we give a proof of the Proposition 5.1 using the above lemmas.

Proof (of Proposition 5.1). Choose BPs $\mathbf{M}$ and $\mathbf{N}$ as given in the first page of this section. They have the same functionality and length.

Note that elements $(Z^{(\mathbf{M})})_j$ in the above Lemmas are of the form

$$(Z^{(\mathbf{M})})_j = v'^{(\mathbf{M})} \cdot J^{(\mathbf{M})} \cdot \prod_{i=1}^{j} \hat{S}_{i,x(i)}^{(\mathbf{M})} \cdot E_{j+1,x(j+1)}^{(\mathbf{M})} \cdot \prod_{k=j+2}^{h} D_{k,x(k)}^{(\mathbf{M})} \cdot w'^{(\mathbf{M})^T} \quad \text{for } j < h$$

$$(Z^{(\mathbf{M})})_h = b_v^{(\mathbf{M})} \cdot \prod_{i=1}^{h-1} B_{i,x(i)}^{(\mathbf{M})} \cdot b_w^{(\mathbf{M})^T}$$

Let $Z_{\mathbf{M}}$ be the summation of $(Z^{(\mathbf{M})})_j$ for $j \in \{0, 1, \cdots, h\}$. From Lemma 5.3, we have

$$Var[Z_{\mathbf{M}}] = E\left[\left(\sum_{i=0}^{h}(Z^{(\mathbf{M})})_i\right)^2\right] = E\left[\sum_{i=0}^{h}(Z^{(\mathbf{M})})_i^2\right] = \sum_{i=0}^{h} Var[(Z^{(\mathbf{M})})_i],$$

$$E[Z_{\mathbf{M}}^4] = E\left[\left(\sum_{i=0}^{h}(Z^{(\mathbf{M})})_i\right)^4\right] \le E\left[(h+1)^3 \cdot \left(\sum_{i=0}^{h}(Z^{(\mathbf{M})})_i^4\right)\right].$$

After dividing both sides by $Var[Z_{\mathbf{M}}]^2$, we obtain the following inequality

$$\left|\frac{E[Z_{\mathbf{M}}^4]}{Var[Z_{\mathbf{M}}]^2}\right| \leq \left|\frac{E[(h+1)^3 \cdot (\sum_{i=0}^{h}(Z^{(\mathbf{M})})_i^4)]}{Var[Z_{\mathbf{M}}]^2}\right| = (h+1)^3 \cdot \left|\frac{E[\sum_{i=0}^{h}(Z^{(\mathbf{M})})_i^4]}{Var[Z_{\mathbf{M}}]^2}\right|$$

$$= (h+1)^3 \cdot \sum_{i=0}^{h} \left|\frac{E[(Z^{(\mathbf{M})})_i^4]}{Var[Z_{\mathbf{M}}]^2}\right|$$

$$\leq (h+1)^3 \cdot \left(\sum_{i=0}^{h-1} \left|\frac{E[(Z^{(\mathbf{M})})_i^4]}{Var[(Z^{(\mathbf{M})})_i]^2}\right| + \left|\frac{E[(Z^{(\mathbf{M})})_h^4]}{Var[Z_{\mathbf{M}}]^2}\right|\right)$$

By Lemmas 5.4, 5.5, 5.6 and 5.7, $\left|\dfrac{E[(Z^{(\mathbf{M})})_i^4]}{Var[(Z^{(\mathbf{M})})_i]^2}\right|$ is bounded by $\mathsf{poly}(\lambda)$ for all $i = 0, 1, \cdots, h-1$ regardless of $\mathbf{P} = \mathbf{M}$ or $\mathbf{P} = \mathbf{N}$. Since $\sigma^2 \geq \nu^2 g/12m$, we obtain the following upper bound.

$$\left|\frac{E[(Z^{(\mathbf{M})})_h^4]}{Var[Z_{\mathbf{M}}]^2}\right| \leq \left|\frac{E[(Z^{(\mathbf{M})})_h^4]}{Var[(Z^{(\mathbf{M})})_0]^2}\right|$$

$$= O\left((g^2)^4 \cdot \left(\frac{g(g+2)}{m^2}\right)^{h-2} \cdot \left(\frac{\nu(\nu+2)}{12\sigma^2}\right)^{h+1}\right)$$

$$= \mathsf{poly}(\lambda)$$

Thus the kurtosis is bounded by polynomial of security parameter λ.

Moreover, by the definition of $Z_{\mathbf{N}}$ and $Z_{\mathbf{M}}$ and lemmas, we obtain the equality $|\sigma_{\mathbf{N}}^2 - \sigma_{\mathbf{M}}^2| = \Theta\left(wn^3m^{h-1} \cdot (\sigma^2)^{h+1} \cdot s^2\right)$. Using lemmas, $\left|\dfrac{\max(\sigma_{\mathbf{N}}^2, \sigma_{\mathbf{M}}^2)}{\sigma_{\mathbf{N}}^2 - \sigma_{\mathbf{M}}^2}\right|$ is bounded by $\mathsf{poly}(\lambda)$. □

Acknowledgments. We sincerely thank to James Bartusek, Fermi Ma and anonymous reviewers of Eurocrypt 2019 for noting the errors in the earlier version of this paper. We also thank to the anonymous reviewers of Crypto 2019 for their careful comments.

The authors of Seoul National University were supported by Institute for Information & communication Technology Promotion (IITP) grant funded by the Korea government (MSIT) (No. 2016-6-00598, The mathematical structure of functional encryption and its analysis), and the ARO and DARPA under Contract No. W911NF-15-C-0227. The author of ENS de Lyon was supported by the LABEX MILYON (ANR-10-LABX-0070) of Université de Lyon, within the program "Investissements d'Avenir" (ANR-11-IDEX-0007) operated by the French National Research Agency (ANR).

A   Simple GGH15 Obfuscation

We briefly describe the construction of single input BP obfuscation based GGH15 without safeguard.

For an index to input function $\mathsf{inp} : [h] \rightarrow [\ell]$, let

$$\mathbf{P} = \big\{ \mathsf{inp}, \{\mathbf{P}_{i,b} \in \{0,1\}^{w \times w}\}_{i \in [h], b \in \{0,1\}}, \mathcal{P}_0 = \mathbf{0}^{w \times w}, \mathcal{P}_1 = \mathbb{Z}^{w \times w} \setminus \mathcal{P}_0 \big\}$$

be a single input BP.

For parameters $w, m, q, B \in \mathbb{N}$ and $\sigma \in \mathbb{R}^+$, the BP obfuscation based GGH15 consists of the matrices and input function, namely

$$\mathcal{O}(\mathbf{P}) = \big\{ \mathsf{inp}, \mathbf{A}_0, \{\mathbf{D}_{i,b} \in \mathbb{Z}^{m \times m}\}_{i \in [h], b \in \{0,1\}} \big\}.$$

In this case, the matrix $\mathbf{T}$ in the abstract model is the identity matrix and $\mathbf{S} = \mathbf{A}_0$. The output of the obfuscation at $\mathbf{x}$ is computed as follows: compute the matrix $\mathbf{A}_0 \cdot \prod_{i=1}^{h} \mathbf{D}_{i,x_{\mathsf{inp}(i)}} \bmod q$ and compare its $\| \cdot \|_\infty$ to a zerotest bound B. If it is less than B, outputs zero. Otherwise, outputs 1.

The algorithm to construct an obfuscated program $\mathcal{O}(\mathbf{P})$ proceeds as follows:

- Sample matrices $(\mathbf{A}_i, \tau_i) \leftarrow \mathsf{TrapSam}(1^w, 1^m, q)$ for $i = 0, 1, \cdots, h-1$, $\mathbf{A}_h \leftarrow U(\mathbb{Z}_q^{w \times m})$ and $\mathbf{E}_{i,b} \leftarrow \chi^{w \times m}$ where χ is a distribution related to the hardness of LWE problem.
- By using the trapdoor τ_i, sample matrices

$$\mathbf{D}_{i,b} \in \mathbb{Z}^{m \times m} \leftarrow \mathsf{Sample}(\mathbf{A}_{i-1}, \tau_{i-1}, \mathbf{P}_{i,b} \cdot \mathbf{A}_i + \mathbf{E}_{i,b}, \sigma) \text{ with } 1 \le i \le h.$$

- Output matrices $\{\mathbf{A}_0, \{\mathbf{D}_{i,b} \in \mathbb{Z}^{m \times m}\}_{i \in [h], b \in \{0,1\}}\}$.

Then, we observe the product $\mathcal{O}(\mathbf{P})(\mathbf{x}) = [\mathbf{A}_0 \cdot \prod_{i=1}^{h} \mathbf{D}_{i,x_{\mathsf{inp}(i)}}]_q$ is equal to

$$\prod_{i=1}^{h} \mathbf{P}_{i,x_{\mathsf{inp}(i)}} \cdot \mathbf{A}_h + \sum_{j=1}^{h} \left(\left(\prod_{i=1}^{j-1} \mathbf{P}_{i,x_{\mathsf{inp}(i)}} \right) \cdot \mathbf{E}_{j,x_{\mathsf{inp}(j)}} \cdot \prod_{k=j+1}^{h} \mathbf{D}_{i,x_{\mathsf{inp}(k)}} \right)$$

over $\mathbb{Z}_q$. If $\prod_{i=1}^{h} \mathbf{P}_{i,x_{\mathsf{inp}(i)}} = \mathbf{0}^{w \times w}$, then $\mathcal{O}(\mathbf{P})(\mathbf{x})$ can be regarded as a summation of matrices over integers instead of $\mathbb{Z}_q$ under the certain choice of parameters as follows

$$\mathcal{O}(\mathbf{P})(\mathbf{x}) = \left[\mathbf{A}_0 \cdot \prod_{i=1}^{h} \mathbf{D}_{i,x_{\mathsf{inp}(i)}} \right]_q = \sum_{j=1}^{h} \left(\left(\prod_{i=1}^{j-1} \mathbf{P}_{i,x_{\mathsf{inp}(i)}} \right) \cdot \mathbf{E}_{j,x_{\mathsf{inp}(j)}} \cdot \prod_{k=j+1}^{h} \mathbf{D}_{i,x_{\mathsf{inp}(k)}} \right)$$

since the infinity norm of the above matrix is less than $B \ll q$. Note that the evaluation values only rely on the matrices $\mathbf{P}_{i,b}$, $\mathbf{E}_{i,b}$ and $\mathbf{D}_{i,b}$. Thus, the evaluation result depends on the message matrices $\mathbf{P}_{i,b}$.

Suppose that we have two functionally equivalent BPs $\mathbf{M} = \{\mathbf{M}_{i,b}\}_{i \in [h], b \in \{0,1\}}$ and $\mathbf{N} = \{\mathbf{N}_{i,b}\}_{i \in [h], b \in \{0,1\}}$ satisfies

$$\mathbf{M}_{i,b} = \mathbf{0}^{w \times w} \text{ for all } i, b \text{ and } \mathbf{N}_{i,b} = \begin{cases} \mathbf{I}^{w \times w} & \text{if } i = 1 \\ \mathbf{0}^{w \times w} & \text{otherwise} \end{cases},$$

and an obfuscated program $\mathcal{O}(\mathbf{P})$. The goal of adversary is to determine whether $\mathbf{P}$ is $\mathbf{M}$ or not. For all $\mathbf{x} \in \{0,1\}^\ell$, the evaluation of the obfuscation is of the form

$$\mathcal{O}(\mathbf{M})(\mathbf{x}) = \mathbf{E}_{1,x_{\mathsf{inp}(1)}} \cdot \prod_{k=2}^{h} \mathbf{D}_{k,x_{\mathsf{inp}(k)}} \text{ and}$$

$$\mathcal{O}(\mathbf{N})(\mathbf{x}) = \mathbf{E}_{1,x_{\mathsf{inp}(1)}} \cdot \prod_{k=2}^{h} \mathbf{D}_{k,x_{\mathsf{inp}(k)}} + \mathbf{I} \cdot \mathbf{E}_{2,x_{\mathsf{inp}(2)}} \cdot \prod_{k=3}^{h} \mathbf{D}_{k,x_{\mathsf{inp}(k)}}.$$

Note that they correspond to the distributions $\mathcal{D}_\mathbf{M}$ and $\mathcal{D}_\mathbf{N}$ for a fixed vector $\mathbf{x}$. These equations show the difference of two distributions in this case.

B   Modified CVW Obfuscation

We give a modification of CVW obfuscation, which can obfuscate the permutation matrix branching programs. This modification is, as far as we know, robust against all existing attacks. We first describe the transformation of branching programs. Then, we describe the modification of CVW obfuscation.

B.1   Transformation of Branching Programs

We first introduce the transformation from single-input permutation matrix branching programs to *Type I* BP. This transformation is applicable to BPs which outputs 0 when the product of BP matrices is the identity matrix. The output of transformation is a new branching program that outputs 0 when the product of BP matrices is the zero matrix. Through this transformation, the width of branching program is doubled. Note that this is adapted version of [10, Claim 6.2].

We are given a branching program with input size ℓ

$$\mathbf{P} = \{\{\mathbf{P}_{i,b} \in \{0,1\}^{w \times w}\}_{i \in [h], b \in \{0,1\}}, \mathsf{inp} : [h] \to [\ell]\}$$

where the evaluation of $\mathbf{P}$ at $\mathbf{x} \in \{0,1\}^\ell$ is computed by

$$\mathbf{P}(\mathbf{x}) = \begin{cases} 0 & \text{if } \prod_{i=1}^{h} \mathbf{P}_{i,(x_{\mathsf{inp}(i)})} = \mathbf{I}_w \\ 1 & \text{otherwise} \end{cases}$$

Then the transformation is done by changing branching program matrices as

$$\mathbf{P}' = \left\{ \left\{ \mathbf{P}'_{i,b} = \begin{pmatrix} \mathbf{P}_{i,b} & \mathbf{0} \\ \mathbf{0} & \mathbf{I}_w \end{pmatrix} \in \{0,1\}^{2w \times 2w} \right\}_{i \in [h], b \in \{0,1\}}, \mathsf{inp} : [h] \to [\ell] \right\}$$

and the evaluation is similar but uses new vectors $\mathbf{v}' = (\mathbf{v} | -\mathbf{v})$ and $\mathbf{w}' = (\mathbf{w} | \mathbf{w})$ for $\mathbf{v}, \mathbf{w} \in \mathbb{Z}^w$:

$$\mathbf{P}'(\mathbf{x}) = \begin{cases} 0 & \text{if } \mathbf{v}' \cdot \prod_{i=1}^{h} \mathbf{P}'_{i,(x_{\mathsf{inp}(i)})} \cdot \mathbf{w}'^T = 0 \\ 1 & \text{otherwise} \end{cases}$$

We will choose $\mathbf{v}$ and $\mathbf{w}$ as random Gaussian vectors. Note that the resulting branching program is also a permutation BP.

B.2 Modification of CVW Obfuscation

We give here how to modify the CVW obfuscation to be applicable to the resulting permutation BPs of the above transform. We also assume that the index length $h = (\lambda + 1) \cdot \ell$ and the index-to-input function satisfies $\mathsf{inp}(i) = (i \mod \ell)$ as in the CVW obfuscation. We also assume that the BP is $(\lambda + 1)$-input repetition BP as in the original construction. The changed parts are written in red. Note that the targeted BPs have width $2w$. Thus we set $t := (2w + 2n\ell) \cdot n$.

- Sample bundling matrices $\{\mathbf{R}_{i,b} \in \mathbb{Z}^{2n\ell \times 2n\ell}\}_{i \in [h], b \in \{0,1\}}$ such that $(1^{1 \times 2\ell} \otimes \mathbf{I}^{n \times n}) \cdot \mathbf{R}_{\mathbf{x}'} \cdot (1^{2\ell \times 1} \otimes \mathbf{I}^{n \times n}) = \mathbf{0} \iff \mathbf{x}' \in \bar{\omega}(\{0,1\}^\ell)$ for all $\mathbf{x}' \in \{0,1\}^h$. More precisely, $\mathbf{R}_{i,b}$ is a block diagonal matrix $\mathsf{diag}(\mathbf{R}_{i,b}^{(1)}, \mathbf{R}_{i,b}^{(2)}, \cdots, \mathbf{R}_{i,b}^{(\ell)})$. Each $\mathbf{R}_{i,b}^{(k)} \in \mathbb{Z}^{2n \times 2n}$ is one of the following three cases.

$$
\mathbf{R}_{i,b}^{(k)} = \begin{cases} \mathbf{I}^{2n \times 2n} & \text{if } \mathsf{inp}(i) \neq k \\ \begin{pmatrix} \tilde{\mathbf{R}}_{i,b}^{(k)} & \\ & \mathbf{I}^{n \times n} \end{pmatrix}, \tilde{\mathbf{R}}_{i,b}^{(k)} \leftarrow \mathcal{D}_{\mathbb{Z},\sigma}^{n \times n} & \text{if } \mathsf{inp}(i) = k \text{ and } i \leq \lambda\ell \\ \begin{pmatrix} -\mathbf{I}^{n \times n} & \\ & \prod_{j=0}^{\lambda-1} \tilde{\mathbf{R}}_{k+j\ell,b}^{(k)} \end{pmatrix} & \text{if } \mathsf{inp}(i) = k \text{ and } i > \lambda\ell \end{cases}
$$

- Sample matrices $\{\mathbf{S}_{i,b} \leftarrow \mathcal{D}_{\mathbb{Z},\sigma}^{n \times n}\}_{i \in [h], b \in \{0,1\}}$, bookend vectors $\mathbf{v} \leftarrow \mathcal{D}_{\mathbb{Z},\sigma}^{w}$ and $\mathbf{w} \leftarrow \mathcal{D}_{\mathbb{Z},\sigma}^{w}$ and compute

$$
\mathbf{J} := ((\mathbf{v}| - \mathbf{v}|1^{1 \times 2n\ell}) \otimes \mathbf{I}^{n \times n}) \in \mathbb{Z}^{n \times t}
$$

$$
\hat{\mathbf{S}}_{i,b} := \begin{pmatrix} \mathbf{P}_{i,b} \otimes \mathbf{S}_{i,b} & \\ & \mathbf{R}_{i,b} \otimes \mathbf{S}_{i,b} \end{pmatrix} \in \mathbb{Z}^{t \times t}
$$

$$
\mathbf{L} := ((\mathbf{w}|\mathbf{w}|1^{1 \times 2n\ell})^T \otimes \mathbf{I}^{n \times n}) \in \mathbb{Z}^{t \times n}
$$

- Sample $(\mathbf{A}_i, \tau_i) \leftarrow \mathsf{TrapSam}(1^t, 1^m, q)$ for $0 \leq i \leq h - 1$, $\mathbf{A}_h \leftarrow U(\mathbb{Z}_q^{n \times n})$, $\{\mathbf{E}_{i,b} \leftarrow \mathcal{D}_{\mathbb{Z},\sigma}^{t \times m}\}_{i \in [h-1], b \in \{0,1\}}$ and $\{\mathbf{E}_{h,b} \leftarrow \mathcal{D}_{\mathbb{Z},\sigma}^{t \times n}\}_{b \in \{0,1\}}$.
- Run Sample algorithms to obtain

$$
\mathbf{D}_{i,b} \in \mathbb{Z}^{m \times m} \leftarrow \mathsf{Sample}(\mathbf{A}_{i-1}, \tau_{i-1}, \hat{\mathbf{S}}_{i,b} \cdot \mathbf{A}_i + \mathbf{E}_{i,b}, \sigma) \text{ for } 1 \leq i \leq h - 1,
$$

$$
\mathbf{D}_{h,b} \in \mathbb{Z}^{m \times n} \leftarrow \mathsf{Sample}(\mathbf{A}_{h-1}, \tau_{h-1}, \hat{\mathbf{S}}_{h,b} \cdot \mathbf{L} \cdot \mathbf{A}_h + \mathbf{E}_{h,b}, \sigma).
$$

- Define $\mathbf{A}_{\mathbf{J}}$ as a matrix $\mathbf{J} \cdot \mathbf{A}_0 \in \mathbb{Z}^{n \times m}$ and outputs matrices

$$
\{\mathsf{inp}, \mathbf{A}_{\mathbf{J}}, \{\mathbf{D}_{i,b}\}_{i \in [h], b \in \{0,1\}}\}.
$$

We omit the procedure and correctness of evaluation that are almost the same as the original one.

C   Assumptions of Lattice Preimage Sampling

In this section we provide the experimental results of Assumption 1. Our experiments are built upon the preimage sampling algorithm in the [24], an implementation of BP obfuscation [23].[6] The results imply that the variance and kurtosis move almost the same as one assumed independency, the correctness of attack only requires much relaxed assumption (Table 1).

Table 1. Experiment results on statistical value of preimage sampling. #products stands for the number of producted preimage matrices, σ_x^2 the variance of preimage sampling, S^2 the sample variance, $E[X^4]/\sigma^4$ the sample kurtosis and σ^2 the expected variance. Every experiment is done using 100 samples. The expected variance is computed under the assumption on independency of D's. Every expected kurtosis assuming independency of D's is about 3.

Parameters			Experiments		Expected
#products	m	$\log_2 \sigma_x^2$	$\log_2 S^2$	$E[X^4]/\sigma^4$	$\log_2 \sigma^2$
2	2191	34.9	80.8	2.937	80.8
2	2771	35.2	81.4	2.702	81.7
2	3352	35.4	82.4	2.677	82.5
3	2771	35.2	128.7	3.025	128.4
4	3352	35.4	177.0	2.900	176.8
5	3932	35.6	225.9	3.068	225.9
7	5621	36.1	328.1	3.210	327.5

References

1. Ananth, P.V., Gupta, D., Ishai, Y., Sahai, A.: Avoiding Barrington's theorem: optimizing obfuscation. In: ACM CCS 2014, pp. 646–658 (2014)
2. Badrinarayanan, S., Miles, E., Sahai, A., Zhandry, M.: Post-zeroizing obfuscation: new mathematical tools, and the case of evasive circuits. In: Fischlin, M., Coron, J.-S. (eds.) EUROCRYPT 2016. LNCS, vol. 9666, pp. 764–791. Springer, Heidelberg (2016). https://doi.org/10.1007/978-3-662-49896-5_27
3. Barak, B., Garg, S., Kalai, Y.T., Paneth, O., Sahai, A.: Protecting obfuscation against algebraic attacks. In: Nguyen, P.Q., Oswald, E. (eds.) EUROCRYPT 2014. LNCS, vol. 8441, pp. 221–238. Springer, Heidelberg (2014). https://doi.org/10.1007/978-3-642-55220-5_13

---

[6] We also verify the correctness of the attack itself for [23], but with *large entry* BPs. It requires very large number of samples (say 2^{20} but polynomially many) to verify the attack with binary entry BPs, which is not easy to experiment because the obfuscation/evaluation of [23] takes long time (say few minutes to obtain one evaluation).

4. Bartusek, J., Guan, J., Ma, F., Zhandry, M.: Return of GGH15: provable security against zeroizing attacks. In: Beimel, A., Dziembowski, S. (eds.) TCC 2018. LNCS, vol. 11240, pp. 544–574. Springer, Cham (2018). https://doi.org/10.1007/978-3-030-03810-6_20

5. Boneh, D., Zhandry, M.: Multiparty key exchange, efficient traitor tracing, and more from indistinguishability obfuscation. Algorithmica **79**(4), 1233–1285 (2017)

6. Brakerski, Z., Rothblum, G.N.: Virtual black-box obfuscation for all circuits via generic graded encoding. In: Lindell, Y. (ed.) TCC 2014. LNCS, vol. 8349, pp. 1–25. Springer, Heidelberg (2014). https://doi.org/10.1007/978-3-642-54242-8_1

7. Brakerski, Z., Vaikuntanathan, V., Wee, H., Wichs, D.: Obfuscating conjunctions under entropic ring LWE. In: ITCS 2016, pp. 147–156 (2016)

8. Canetti, R., Chen, Y.: Constraint-hiding constrained PRFs for NC^1 from LWE. In: Coron, J.-S., Nielsen, J.B. (eds.) EUROCRYPT 2017. LNCS, vol. 10210, pp. 446–476. Springer, Cham (2017). https://doi.org/10.1007/978-3-319-56620-7_16

9. Chen, Y., Gentry, C., Halevi, S.: Cryptanalyses of candidate branching program obfuscators. In: Coron, J.-S., Nielsen, J.B. (eds.) EUROCRYPT 2017. LNCS, vol. 10212, pp. 278–307. Springer, Cham (2017). https://doi.org/10.1007/978-3-319-56617-7_10

10. Chen, Y., Vaikuntanathan, V., Wee, H.: GGH15 beyond permutation branching programs: proofs, attacks, and candidates. In: Shacham, H., Boldyreva, A. (eds.) CRYPTO 2018. LNCS, vol. 10992, pp. 577–607. Springer, Cham (2018). https://doi.org/10.1007/978-3-319-96881-0_20

11. Cheon, J.H., Cho, W., Hhan, M., Kim, J., Lee, C.: Statistical zeroizing attack: cryptanalysis of candidates of BP obfuscation over GGH15 multilinear map (2018). Full version of this paper: https://eprint.iacr.org/2018/1081

12. Cheon, J.H., Hhan, M., Kim, J., Lee, C.: Cryptanalyses of branching program obfuscations over GGH13 multilinear map from the NTRU problem. In: Shacham, H., Boldyreva, A. (eds.) CRYPTO 2018. LNCS, vol. 10993, pp. 184–210. Springer, Cham (2018). https://doi.org/10.1007/978-3-319-96878-0_7

13. Cheon, J.H., Hhan, M., Kim, J., Lee, C.: Cryptanalysis on the HHSS obfuscation arising from absence of safeguards. IEEE Access **6**, 40096–40104 (2018)

14. Coron, J.-S., et al.: Zeroizing without low-level zeroes: new MMAP attacks and their limitations. In: Gennaro, R., Robshaw, M. (eds.) CRYPTO 2015. LNCS, vol. 9215, pp. 247–266. Springer, Heidelberg (2015). https://doi.org/10.1007/978-3-662-47989-6_12

15. Coron, J.-S., Lee, M.S., Lepoint, T., Tibouchi, M.: Zeroizing attacks on indistinguishability obfuscation over CLT13. In: Fehr, S. (ed.) PKC 2017. LNCS, vol. 10174, pp. 41–58. Springer, Heidelberg (2017). https://doi.org/10.1007/978-3-662-54365-8_3

16. Coron, J.-S., Lepoint, T., Tibouchi, M.: Practical multilinear maps over the integers. In: Canetti, R., Garay, J.A. (eds.) CRYPTO 2013. LNCS, vol. 8042, pp. 476–493. Springer, Heidelberg (2013). https://doi.org/10.1007/978-3-642-40041-4_26

17. Garg, S., Gentry, C., Halevi, S.: Candidate multilinear maps from ideal lattices. In: Johansson, T., Nguyen, P.Q. (eds.) EUROCRYPT 2013. LNCS, vol. 7881, pp. 1–17. Springer, Heidelberg (2013). https://doi.org/10.1007/978-3-642-38348-9_1

18. Garg, S., Gentry, C., Halevi, S., Raykova, M., Sahai, A., Waters, B.: Candidate indistinguishability obfuscation and functional encryption for all circuits. In: 54th FOCS, pp. 40–49 (2013)

19. Garg, S., Miles, E., Mukherjee, P., Sahai, A., Srinivasan, A., Zhandry, M.: Secure obfuscation in a weak multilinear map model. In: Hirt, M., Smith, A. (eds.) TCC 2016. LNCS, vol. 9986, pp. 241–268. Springer, Heidelberg (2016). https://doi.org/10.1007/978-3-662-53644-5_10

20. Gentry, C., Gorbunov, S., Halevi, S.: Graph-induced multilinear maps from lattices. In: Dodis, Y., Nielsen, J.B. (eds.) TCC 2015. LNCS, vol. 9015, pp. 498–527. Springer, Heidelberg (2015). https://doi.org/10.1007/978-3-662-46497-7_20

21. Gentry, C., Peikert, C., Vaikuntanathan, V.: Trapdoors for hard lattices and new cryptographic constructions. In: 40th STOC, pp. 197–206 (2008)

22. Goyal, R., Koppula, V., Waters, B.: Lockable obfuscation. In: 58th FOCS, pp. 612–621 (2017)

23. Halevi, S., Halevi, T., Shoup, V., Stephens-Davidowitz, N.: Implementing BP-obfuscation using graph-induced encoding. In: ACM CCS 2017, pp. 783–798. ACM (2017)

24. Halevi, S., Halevi, T., Shoup, V., Stephens-Davidowitz, N.: Implementing BP-obfuscation using graph-induced encoding (2017). https://github.com/shaih/BPobfus

25. Lin, H.: Indistinguishability obfuscation from constant-degree graded encoding schemes. In: Fischlin, M., Coron, J.-S. (eds.) EUROCRYPT 2016. LNCS, vol. 9665, pp. 28–57. Springer, Heidelberg (2016). https://doi.org/10.1007/978-3-662-49890-3_2

26. Lin, H.: Indistinguishability obfuscation from SXDH on 5-linear maps and locality-5 PRGs. In: Katz, J., Shacham, H. (eds.) CRYPTO 2017. LNCS, vol. 10401, pp. 599–629. Springer, Cham (2017). https://doi.org/10.1007/978-3-319-63688-7_20

27. Lin, H., Tessaro, S.: Indistinguishability obfuscation from trilinear maps and block-wise local PRGs. In: Katz, J., Shacham, H. (eds.) CRYPTO 2017. LNCS, vol. 10401, pp. 630–660. Springer, Cham (2017). https://doi.org/10.1007/978-3-319-63688-7_21

28. Lin, H., Vaikuntanathan, V.: Indistinguishability obfuscation from DDH-like assumptions on constant-degree graded encodings. In: 57th FOCS, pp. 11–20 (2016)

29. Ma, F., Zhandry, M.: The MMap strikes back: obfuscation and new multilinear maps immune to CLT13 zeroing attacks. In: Beimel, A., Dziembowski, S. (eds.) TCC 2018. LNCS, vol. 11240, pp. 513–543. Springer, Cham (2018). https://doi.org/10.1007/978-3-030-03810-6_19

30. Micciancio, D., Peikert, C.: Trapdoors for lattices: simpler, tighter, faster, smaller. In: Pointcheval, D., Johansson, T. (eds.) EUROCRYPT 2012. LNCS, vol. 7237, pp. 700–718. Springer, Heidelberg (2012). https://doi.org/10.1007/978-3-642-29011-4_41

31. Miles, E., Sahai, A., Weiss, M.: Protecting obfuscation against arithmetic attacks. IACR Cryptology ePrint Archive 2014:878 (2014)

32. Pass, R., Seth, K., Telang, S.: Indistinguishability obfuscation from semantically-secure multilinear encodings. In: Garay, J.A., Gennaro, R. (eds.) CRYPTO 2014. LNCS, vol. 8616, pp. 500–517. Springer, Heidelberg (2014). https://doi.org/10.1007/978-3-662-44371-2_28

33. Pellet-Mary, A.: Quantum attacks against indistinguishablility obfuscators proved secure in the weak multilinear map model. In: Shacham, H., Boldyreva, A. (eds.) CRYPTO 2018. LNCS, vol. 10993, pp. 153–183. Springer, Cham (2018). https://doi.org/10.1007/978-3-319-96878-0_6

34. Sahai, A., Waters, B.: How to use indistinguishability obfuscation: deniable encryption, and more. In: STOC 2014, pp. 475–484 (2014)

35. Wichs, D., Zirdelis, G.: Obfuscating compute-and-compare programs under LWE. In: 58th FOCS, pp. 600–611 (2017)
36. Zimmerman, J.: How to obfuscate programs directly. In: Oswald, E., Fischlin, M. (eds.) EUROCRYPT 2015. LNCS, vol. 9057, pp. 439–467. Springer, Heidelberg (2015). https://doi.org/10.1007/978-3-662-46803-6_15

Indistinguishability Obfuscation Without Multilinear Maps: New Paradigms via Low Degree Weak Pseudorandomness and Security Amplification

Prabhanjan Ananth[1]($\boxtimes$), Aayush Jain[2]($\boxtimes$), Huijia Lin[3], Christian Matt[4], and Amit Sahai[2]

[1] MIT, Cambridge, USA
prabhanjan@csail.mit.edu
[2] UCLA, Los Angeles, USA
{aayushjain,sahai}@cs.ucla.edu
[3] University of Washington, Seattle, USA
rachel@cs.washington.edu
[4] Concordium, Zurich, Switzerland
cm@concordium.com

Abstract. The existence of secure indistinguishability obfuscators ($i\mathcal{O}$) has far-reaching implications, significantly expanding the scope of problems amenable to cryptographic study. All known approaches to constructing $i\mathcal{O}$ rely on d-linear maps. While secure *bilinear maps* are well established in cryptographic literature, the security of candidates for $d > 2$ is poorly understood.

We propose a new approach to constructing $i\mathcal{O}$ for general circuits. Unlike all previously known realizations of $i\mathcal{O}$, we avoid the use of d-linear maps of degree $d \geq 3$.

At the heart of our approach is the assumption that a new *weak* pseudorandom object exists. We consider two related variants of these objects, which we call *perturbation resilient generator* (ΔRG) and *pseudo flawed-smudging generator* (PFG), respectively. At a high level, both objects are polynomially expanding functions whose outputs partially hide (or smudge) small noise vectors when added to them. We further require that they are computable by a family of degree-3 polynomials over $\mathbb{Z}$. We show how they can be used to construct functional encryption schemes with weak security guarantees. Finally, we use novel amplification techniques to obtain full security.

As a result, we obtain $i\mathcal{O}$ for general circuits assuming:

- Subexponentially secure LWE
- Bilinear Maps
- poly(λ)-secure 3-block-local PRGs
- ΔRGs or PFGs

This paper is a merge of two independent works, one by Ananth, Jain, and Sahai [AJS18], and the other by Lin and Matt [LM18].

A. Boldyreva and D. Micciancio (Eds.): CRYPTO 2019, LNCS 11694, pp. 284–332, 2019.
https://doi.org/10.1007/978-3-030-26954-8_10

1 Introduction

Program obfuscation considers the problem of building an efficient randomized compiler that takes as input a computer program P and outputs an equivalent program $O(P)$ such that any secrets present within P are "as hard as possible" to extract from $O(P)$. This property can be formalized by the notion of indistinguishability obfuscation (iO) [BGI+01, GR07]. Formally, iO requires that given any two equivalent programs P_1 and P_2 of the same size, it is not possible for a computationally bounded adversary to distinguish between the obfuscated versions of these programs. Recently, starting with the works of [GGH+13b, SW14], it has been shown that iO would have far-reaching applications, significantly expanding the scope of problems to which cryptography can be applied (e.g., [SW14, KLW15, GGHR14, CHN+16, GPS16, HSW14, BPR15, GGG+14, HJK+16, BFM14]).

The work of [GGH+13b] gave the first mathematical candidate iO construction, and since then more than a dozen candidates have been proposed and studied [GGH13a, CLT13a, GGH15a, CLT15a, Hal15, BR14a, BGK+14a, PST14a, AGIS14a], [BMSZ16, CHL+15, BWZ14, CGH+15, HJ15, BGH+15, Hal15, CLR15, MF15, MSZ16, DGG+16a]. Furthermore, more recent candidates [Lin16a, LV16, AS17, LT17] based iO on simple primtives and assumptions. However, all these iO constructions rely on multi-linear maps with degree at least 3. Unfortunately, all known candidates for degree-3 multilinear maps [GGH13a, CLT13a, GGH15a] have poorly understood security properties, and even security models [MSZ16, BGMZ18, MZ18].

Our Results in a Nutshell. Securely building iO remains a central challenge in cryptography. In this paper, we report on the works of [AJS18, LM18], in which we develop new techniques that enables building iO without multilinear maps of degree ≥ 3. Instead, we rely on (relatively) standard assumptions including (subexponentnailly secure) *bilinear maps*, LWE, and block-local PRGs [LT17] (a relaxation of local PRGs, a.k.a. Goldreich's PRGs [Gol00]), as well as new types of "weak" pseudo-randomness generators with certain "simple" structures— either perturbation resilient generators [AJS18] or pseudo flawed-smudging generators [LM18]. We now elaborate.

Along the way, we study the notion of Functional Encryption, which was introduced by [SW05], and formalized by [BSW11, O'N10]. We provide new general security amplification theorems for amplifying Functional Encryption with $(1/\lambda^c)$-indistinguishability-based security to Functional Encryption with standard security [AJS18], and security amplification for amplifying certain leaky forms of Functional Encryption to standard security [LM18]. We now elaborate.

Prior iO from Multilinear Maps with Degree $\geq$ 3. The first-generation iO constructions [GGH+13b, BR14a, BGK+14a, PST14a, AGIS14a, GLSW14, Zim15, AB15, GMM+16a, DGG+16a] rely on polynomial-degree *multilinear maps* or *graded encodings*. An L-linear map [BS02] essentially allows to evaluate degree-L polynomials on secret encoded values, and to test whether the output of such polynomials is zero or not. While bilinear maps (i.e., $L = 2$) can be efficiently instantiated from elliptic curves, instantiation of L-linear maps for $L \geq 3$ has remained elusive—While candidate constructions of such graded encoding schemes exist [CLT13a, LSS14, GGH15a, CLT15a], their security is poorly understood due to several known explicit attacks on certain distributions of encoded values [CHL+15, BWZ14, CGH+15, HJ15, BGH+15, Hal15, CLR15, MF15, MSZ16][1].

A line of recent works [Lin16a, LV16, Lin17, AS17] aimed at finding the minimal degree of multilinear maps sufficient for constructing $i\mathcal{O}$, and has successfully reduced the required degree to $L = 3$. A key ingredient in these second-generation constructions are PRGs with *small locality*[2]. They showed that to construct $i\mathcal{O}$, it suffices to have multilinear maps with degree matching exactly the locality of the PRG [Lin16a, AS17], or even the relaxed notion of *block locality* [LT17]. These constructions essentially use degree-L multilinear maps to evaluate a PRG with (block-)locality L, and then bootstrap from there to hide arbitrary complex computation. Unfortunately, the locality of a PRG cannot be smaller than 5 [CM01, MST03], and recent attacks [LV17, BBKK18] showed that block-locality cannot be smaller than 3.[3] This raises the following natural question:

> *Can we build $i\mathcal{O}$ without cryptographic multilinear maps of degree ≥ 3?*
> *Are there new types of simple and weak pseudo-randomness generators*
> *that can help?*

Our Simple and Weak Pseudorandomness Generators. We answer the above questions positively, relying on either the new notion of *perturbation-resilient generators*, ΔRG for short, proposed by [AJS18] (AJS), or *pseudo flawed-smuding generators*, PFG for short, proposed by [LM18] (LM). They are weak pseudo-randomness generators with the same simple structure, and similar intuitive security guarantees. However, their concrete security formalizations are very different, requiring different techniques of using them in $i\mathcal{O}$ constructions as done in [AJS18, LM18].

We start with explaining their shared simple structure. A ΔRG/PFG is given by a polynomially expanding function G from n input (or seed) elements to $m = n^{1+\alpha}$ output elements in $\mathbb{Z}_p$, together with a seed distribution $\mathcal{S}$ over $\mathbb{Z}_p^n$ that samples a pair $\mathbf{s} = (\mathbf{s}_1, \mathbf{s}_2)$ of public and private seeds[4]. G has the simple structure that *(1)* it is a degree 3 polynomial over $\mathbb{Z}_p$ with degree 1 in the public

---

[1] Note that this does not necessarily mean that the resulting $i\mathcal{O}$ constructions are insecure; in particular, there have been efforts (e.g., [GMM+16a]) in constructing $i\mathcal{O}$ in more complex security models for multilinear maps (e.g. [MSZ16]) that have resisted polynomial-time attacks. There have also been several other $i\mathcal{O}$ candidates proposed which are not known to polynomial-time broken (e.g. [CVW18, BGMZ18]).

[2] A function has locality ℓ if every output element depends on at most ℓ input elements.

[3] The attacks actually leave open a very small window of expansion. Nevertheless, they have weakened our confidence on the security of PRGs with block-locality 2.

[4] n, m, p are parameterized by the security parameter λ.

seed $\mathbf{s}_1$ and degree 2 in the private seed $\mathbf{s}_2$, and *(2)* its output distribution $G(\mathcal{S})$ is polynomially bounded. At a very high-level, these two structural properties ensure that we can essentially compute G in the exponent of bilinear pairing groups (property 1) and extract the output in the clear via brute force discrete logarithm (property 2). An acute reader may be curious about the purpose of the public seed $\mathbf{s}_1$. In short, it is a relaxation to requiring G having total degree 2, and as we shall see later, is crucial for the security of the instantiation of G.

Intuitively, the security of $\Delta RG/PFG$ guarantees that its output when added to a small noise vector, producing $G(\mathbf{s}) + \mathbf{e}$, *weakly* "smudge" or "hide" $\mathbf{e}$. In the literature, noise smudging (or noise flooding) is a commonly used technique for hiding small noises in LWE samples, which is also our purpose. However, to completely hide the noise vector $\mathbf{e}$, the smudging noises must be super-polynomially large. This stands in contrast with the fact that $G(\mathbf{s})$ is polynomially bounded. To circumvent this, ΔRG and PFG formalizes different weakly hiding requirements:

- ΔRG guarantees that the distributions $\Delta RG(\mathbf{s})$ and $(\Delta RG(\mathbf{s}) + \mathbf{e})$ are *somewhat* hard to distinguish as long as the perturbation $\mathbf{e}$ is relatively small. More specifically, it suffices if efficient adversaries fail to distinguish these two distributions with at least some fixed $1/\text{poly}(\lambda)$ probability. Thus, a candidate ΔRG would be secure, for instance, if an adversary could distinguish between $\Delta RG(\mathbf{s})$ and $(\Delta RG(\mathbf{s}) + \mathbf{e})$ with probability 99%, but no adversary could distinguish with probability over 99.5%.
- PFG guarantees that $G(\mathbf{s})$ is computationally indistinguishable to a so-called, *flawed-smudging distribution* $\mathbf{Y} \leftarrow \mathcal{Y}$, satisfying that given $\mathbf{Y} + \mathbf{e}$, the values of $\mathbf{e}$ at a few $o(\lambda)$ coordinates are revealed, while the values at the rest coordinates are hidden.

We elaborate on the security definitions of these generators, and possible instantiations, in Sect. 2.

Hardness of Polynomials over the Reals. The security of our candidate $\Delta RGs/PFGs$ crucially relies on the hardness of solving certain over-determinined systems of degree-3 polynomial equations over the reals, and a LWE leakage assumption. Solving systems of polynomials over the reals has been studied by mathematicians, scientists, and engineers for hundreds of years. This is precisely why we are taking this approach: we want to relate $i\mathcal{O}$ to simple-to-state problems related to areas of mathematics with long histories of study. Aside from that, our work also fundamentally diversifies the kinds of assumptions from which $i\mathcal{O}$ can be constructed.

In Sect. 2.4, we describe specific candidates suggested in follow-up work by [BHJ+19] that were inspired by the hardness of RANDOM 3-SAT. We hope that our work will motivate further cryptanalytic study of simple pseudorandom objects.

Using respectively ΔRG and PFG, we show how to construct $i\mathcal{O}$ without multilinear maps of degree ≥ 3 in two concurrent works [AJS18,LM18]. Next, we describe the results in each work slightly more formally.

Results in AJS in More Detail. AJS constructs $i\mathcal{O}$ based on bilinear maps, LWE, ΔRG, and block-locality 3 PRG. For the latter, in fact AJS require only a weakened forms of 3-blockwise-local PRGs [LT17] where efficient adversaries fail to distinguish the PRG output distribution from the uniformly random distribution with some polynomial probability[5].

Theorem 1 (AJS Main Theorem, Informal). *For every constants c, there is a construction of indistinguishability obfuscation for all polynomial-sized circuits from,*

- $\left(1 - \frac{1}{\lambda^c}\right)$-*indistinguishable perturbation-resilient generators with aforementioned structure and security against sub-exponential size adversaries,*
- $\frac{1}{2\lambda^c}$-*indistinguishable three-block-local pseudorandom generators [LT17] with polynomial stretch and security against sub-exponential size adversaries,*
- *learning with errors secure against sub-exponential size adversaries, and*
- *assumptions on bilinear maps secure against sub-exponential size adversaries (that hold unconditionally in the generic bilinear map model).*

Here κ-indistinguishability refers to security where the distinguishing advantage of such adversaries is bounded by κ. Thus, standard security would be $\mathsf{negl}(\lambda)$-security, where negl is a negligible function. In contrast $(1 - p)$-security allows for an adversary that fails to distinguish only with probability p.

Along the way to proving the result above, AJS also obtains a security amplification theorem for functional encryption:

Theorem 2 (AJS security amplification theorem, informal). *Assume there exists a constant $c > 0$, and*

- $(1 - 1/\lambda^c)$-*indistinguishable sublinearly compact secret key FE schemes for polynomial size circuits of depth λ, and*
- *learning with errors secure against sub-exponential size adversaries.*

There exists sublinearly compact secret key FE schemes for polynomial size circuits of depth λ with $\mathsf{negl}(\lambda)$-indistinguishability.

Note that the amplification theorem above relies only on subexponential LWE, and no new assumptions. Moreover, if we assume the underlying FE schemes to be secure against subexponential size, then the resulting schemes satisfy subexponential security. Please refer [AJS18] for a complete formulation.

Results in LM in More Detail. LM constructs $i\mathcal{O}$ based on bilinear maps, LWE, PFGs, and constant block-local PRGs.

Theorem 3 (LM Main Theorem, informal). *There is a construction of indistinguishability obfuscation for all polynomial-sized circuits from,*

---

[5] There is be a tradeoff between how much AJS can weaken the indistinguishability requirements of the ΔRG and the 3-block-local PRG.

- *pseudo flawed-smudging generators with aforementioned structure and security against sub-exponential size adversaries,*
- *constant-block-local pseudorandom generators* [LT17] *with mild structural properties described in Remark 1, and security against sub-exponential size adversaries,*
- *learning with errors secure against sub-exponential size adversaries, and*
- *the SXDH assumption on bilinear maps secure against sub-exponential size adversaries.*

Remark 1. The block-local PRGs used in LM map n bits to $n^{1+\alpha}$ bits for an arbitrarily small constant α, where every PRG is defined by a predicate P and an input-output dependency graph G, such that the i'th output bit $y_i = P(\mathsf{Seed}_{G(i)})$ is computed by evaluating the predicate P on a subset of seed bits $\mathsf{Seed}_{G(i)}$ specified by $G(i)$. LM requires the output locality (i.e., $\max_i |G(i)|$) to be a constant, and the input locality (i.e., the maximal number of output bits that an input bit influences) to be bounded by $o(n^{1-\alpha})$. Most candidate constant-locality PRGs [Gol00, MST03, OW14, AL16] satisfy these structural properties. In particular, the input-output dependency graph is often chosen at random in which case the input locality is indeed bounded by $o(n^{1-\alpha})$. The security of local PRGs, especially ones with large constant locality, has been studied extensively, for instance in [CM01, MST03, CEMT09, BQ12, OW14, AL16].

Partially Hiding Functional Encryption. In order to evaluate ΔRGs/PFGs using bilinear map, we develop the primitive of Partially Hiding Functional Encryption schemes (PHFE), introduced under the name 3-restricted FE by [AJS18]. The notion of PHFE is a natural modification of partially-hiding Predicate Encryption (PE) of [GVW15] by strengthening the security requirement from that of PE to FE. PHFE schemes can evaluate functions of the form $g(\mathbf{x}, \mathbf{y})$ and guarantee that ciphertexts and secret keys reveal only the outputs and part of its input $\mathbf{x}$, referred to as the *public input*, while hiding the remaining part $\mathbf{y}$, referred to as the *private input*. Partially-hiding FE naturally interpolates attribute-based encryption and functional encryption: if the public input $\mathbf{x}$ is empty, it is equivalent to functional encryption, and if g is such that it outputs $\mathbf{y}$ when some predicate on $\mathbf{x}$ evaluates to 1, then it corresponds to attribute-based encryption.

In the literature, there are constructions of secret-key FE schemes for quadratic polynomials from bilinear map groups [Lin17, BCFG17]. In AJS and LM, we extend these constructions to allow for additional linear computation on a public input.

Theorem 4 (PHFE in AJS and LM, Informal). *There are constructions of secret-key partially-hiding FE schemes for computing multilinear cubic polynomials $g(\mathbf{x}, (\mathbf{y}, \mathbf{z}))$ over $\mathbb{Z}_p$ with polynomially bounded outputs and $\mathbf{x}$ as the public input, from bilinear pairing groups of order p. The schemes have linear encryption time $\mathrm{poly}(\lambda)N$ in the input length $N = \max(|\mathbf{x}|, |\mathbf{y}|, |\mathbf{z}|)$.*

The constructions of PHFE in AJS and LM differ in details. The scheme originally developed in AJS, referred to as 3-restricted FE there, follows the semifunctional FE framework and is based on assumptions over bilinear maps that hold unconditionally in the generic bilinear map model. The scheme subsequently developed in LM, referred to as degree-(1,2) PHFE there, satisfies simulation security for one ciphertext (meaning that the outputs evaluated on one encryption input can be programmed) and is based on SXDH.

Finally, we mention that in followup works, our approach has been extended to *(i)* use ΔRGs/PFGs implementable by polynomials of any *constant*-degree [JLMS19], *(ii)* remove the need for block-local PRGs completely [JLS19], and *(iii)* construct PHFE supporting NC_1 public computation and degree 2 private computation [JLS19].

1.1 History

We provide a timeline describing how the results were conceived, to clarify how this line of work has developed.

06/17/2018: [AJS18] **Received by Eprint (2018/615)**
[AJS18] introduced ΔRGs, 3-restricted FE, and a new general FE amplification theorem.

Historical notes: Earlier weaker versions of [AJS18] were submitted to EC 2018 (on 9/19/2017) and Crypto 2018 (on 2/13/2018). These earlier versions contained the notions of 3-restricted FE, and Tempered Cubic Encoding. However, they did not contain either the notion of ΔRG nor the FE amplification theorem. The authors of [AJS18] were not aware of the relevant concurrent work by [Agr18a] or [LM18] until seeing Eprint papers appear.

06/17/2018: [Agr18a] **Received by Eprint (2018/633)**
To hide decryption noises, [Agr18a] introduced different notions of (smudging) noise generators, which all *perfectly* hides the noises. Hence [Agr18a] did not develop any FE security amplification technique. In terms of instantiation, [Agr18a] proposed using MQ or 2 block-local PRG as degree 2 candidates and used off-the-shelf deg 2 FE to evaluate them. [Agr18a] contains a gap in the construction: It proposes to use known deg 2 FE to compute the noise generator. Known deg 2 FE restricts the outputs of the noise generator to be poly-large. On the other hand, [Agr18a] needs the noise generator to perfectly hide the HE decryption noise e, which requires the outputs to be super-poly large. (Note: this is why [AJS18]'s ΔRG and [LM18]'s PFG only provide weak guarantees. This allows for having poly-large outputs, but opens many challenges in order to deal with the weak guarantees.)

07/02/2018: [LM18] **Received by Eprint (2018/646)**
In Aug 2017, Lin discussed with Agrawal about her ideas and Agrawal shared a manuscript. After the discussion, Agrawal and Lin proceeded independently. Since the shared manuscript has large overlap with the later posted [Agr18a, LM18] simply treats entire [Agr18a] as prior work for clarity.

Prior to posting, [LM18] has developed for over a year. [LM18] introduced the notion of Pseudo Flawed-smudging Generator (PFG) and the leakage-based security amplification technique. They analyzed PFG properties and proposed using deg 2 polynomials sampled from a special distribution as the candidates.

07/08/2018: [AJS18] Updated on Eprint (2018/615)
Added explicit degree 3 ΔRG candidate and associated explicit ΔRG assumption.

08/17/2018: [Agr18a] Updated on Eprint (2018/633)
[Agr18a] cites [AJS18] for fixing the aforementioned gap. This means using the notion of ΔRG and the FE security amplification theorem of [AJS18].

08/19/2018: [BHJ+19] Announced at "Beyond Crypto" Workshop at CRYPTO 2018
This work gave empirical and theoretical evidence of polynomial-time attacks on all known explicit degree-2 candidates considered in [AJS18, Agr18a, LM18]. It is explicitly noted that the attacks do not extend to the degree 3 ΔRG candidate of [AJS18].

10/4/2018: [JS18, BHJ+19] Submitted to Eurocrypt 2019
[JS18] showed how to construct constant-restricted FE for any constant (i.e., (deg-$O(1)$, deg (2)-PHFE) assuming SXDH. This enables using constant degree candidates, for any constant. [JS18] is clearly marked as a follow-up work to [AJS18, Agr18a, LM18].

10/9/2018: The Second Version of [LM18] was Updated on Eprint (2018/646). Added construction of (deg 1, deg 2)-PHFE, which is a variant of 3-restricted FE, and proposed to use the degree 3 candidate of [AJS18] as candidate PFGs, which are not subject to [BHJ+19] attacks. This updated [LM18] clearly cites [AJS18] for this candidate and the idea of using weak deg-3 FE to evaluate it. However, note that this just replaces the previous deg 2 candidate and deg 2 FE in [LM18], which are very simple and not the main technical contributions of [LM18].

In this update, there is also a construction of PHFE able to handle public computation of poly degree, but subject to certain size constraints. This construction does not appear in this current paper for two reasons: (1) Lin and Matt were added as authors to [JS18] in credit for this concurrent PHFE construction, and (2) it is later superseded by a full (NC1, deg 2) PHFE construction in a follow-up [JLS19].

10/11/2018: [JS18] Received by Eprint (2018/973)

02/01/2019: [JS18, BHJ+19] Accepted at Eurocrypt 2019
The authors of [JS18] emailed Chairs to add Lin and Matt as authors, resulting in publication [JLMS19]. The paper [JLMS19] is clearly marked as a follow-up work to [AJS18, Agr18a, LM18].

1.2 Comparison of Techniques

We provide a detailed comparison of the works of [AJS18, LM18, Agr18b, BHJ+19, JLMS19].

Comparison of the Works of [AJS18] *and* [LM18]. We first start by comparing the notions of PFGs and ΔRGs. Both notions are geared for the purpose of generating a smudging noise $\mathbf{Y}$ to hide a small polynomially bounded noise $\mathbf{e}$, however, with different guarantees. The output $\mathbf{O}$ of PFGs is *computationally indistinguishable* to flawed smudging noises $\mathbf{Y}$ such that $(\mathbf{e}, \mathbf{Y}+\mathbf{e})$ and $(\mathbf{e}', \mathbf{Y}+\mathbf{e})$ are statistically close with probability δ. On the other hand, the output $\mathbf{O}$ of ΔRGs directly guarantees that $(\mathbf{e}, \mathbf{O}+\mathbf{e})$ and $(\mathbf{e}', \mathbf{O}+\mathbf{e})$ are computationally indistinguishable up to advantage $1-\delta$. Furthermore, in the good case with probability δ, the output of PFGs may still reveal $\mathbf{e}$ at a few coordinates (i.e., $\mathbf{e}$ and $\mathbf{e}'$ agree at a few coordinates), whereas ΔRG ask for weak indistinguishability between the two cases (i.e. $\mathbf{e}$ and $\mathbf{e}'$).

Besides the use of different weak notions of randomness generators, other differences between [AJS18] and [LM18] include: *(i)* [LM18] rely on constant-locality PRGs with mild structural properties, while [AJS18] use block-locality 3 PRGs. *(ii)* [AJS18] first showed security in the generic bilinear map model, subsequently [LM18] relied on the SXDH assumption over bilinear pairing groups.

In terms of techniques, both works start with constructing some weak notions of FE: [LM18] construct FE for constant-degree polynomials that may leak a small portion of the input, whereas [AJS18] construct FE for degree 3 polynomials that bounds the adversarial advantage only by $1 - 1/\mathrm{poly}(\lambda)$. Both works then design different methods to amplify their respective weak FE to full-fledged FE. The amplification techniques are similar in parts, for instance, both works use threshold FHE, but also have differences, for instance, while [LM18] relies on the use of random permutations and a careful analysis to ensure that the effect of compromising a few bits of the seed of a constant-locality PRG can be "controlled". On the other hand, [AJS18] use techniques from the dense model theorem to give a general security amplification for Functional Encryption with weak distinguishing advantage, into Functional Encryption satisfying the standard notion of security.

Comparison of [AJS18, LM18] *with the Work of Agrawal* [Agr18a]. Following [AR17], to obtain compact ciphertexts, Agrawal [Agr18b] (*as mentioned in the timeline, an early version of* [Agr18a] *was shared by the author of* [Agr18b] *with the authors of* [LM18]) proposed the approach of using a noise generator to generate $\mathbf{Y}$. As an abstraction of that, they introduced the notion of *noisy linear functional encryption* that adds the smudging noises $\mathbf{Y}$ to the outputs. The noise generator in [Agr18b] is able to produce super-polynomially large smudging noises, and they propose a constant degree FE scheme supporting super-polynomially large outputs from a new assumption on NTRU Rings. The works of [AJS18] and [LM18] explore what happens when $\mathbf{Y}$ is polynomially bounded and $\mathbf{e}$ may be leaked, which allows us to use FE schemes supporting only polynomially large outputs from multilinear maps.

Subsequent to [AJS18], Agrawal notes that their construction is compatible with the approach of [AJS18] using ΔRG with polynomially large outputs and weak security, and later amplifying the security of FE in a black-box way. Thus, the construction in the updated version can use known constructions of FE schemes with restricted output size.

Comparison with the Work by Jain, Lin, Matt and Sahai [JLMS19]. As a follow-up to [AJS18, LM18, Agr18a], Jain, Lin, Matt and Sahai [JLMS19] construct FE schemes for degree $d + 2$ functions multilinear in their inputs $\mathbf{x}_1, \ldots, \mathbf{x}_d, \mathbf{y}, \mathbf{z}$, where $\mathbf{x}_1, \ldots, \mathbf{x}_d$ are public, $\mathbf{y}$ and $\mathbf{z}$ are private, and d can be any constant. They further improve upon [AJS18] by only relying on the SXDH assumption instead of the generic bilinear map model. Moreover, their work provides new candidates of ΔRGs that can be computed by their FE schemes. Similar to [AJS18, LM18], their candidates hide the public inputs as noises in LWE samples.

Comparison of [AJS18, LM18] *and* [GKP+13, GVW15, BTVW17, AR17]. Both the works of [AJS18, LM18] use a homomorphic encryption scheme (HE) in conjunction with the newly introduced pseudorandom generators to construct FE. This approach of using a homomorphic encryption scheme to construct FE is not new has already been explored in several works [GVW12, GKP+13, GVW15, BTVW17, AR17, Agr18a]. The challenges to build FE from HE are twofold: *(1) privacy*—decrypt a ciphertext $\mathsf{CT}_{f,x}$ encrypting an output $f(x) = \mathbf{y}$ securely revealing only $\mathbf{y}$, and *(2) integrity*—enforce that only ciphertexts for "legitimate" functions f (ones for which secret keys are generated) can be decrypted. Below, we briefly discuss how this approach was adopted in previous works.

The work of Goldwasser et al. [GKP+13] use the above template to build a single-functional encryption scheme. They use an attribute-based encryption scheme to ensure integrity and garbled circuits to ensure privacy. Then they combine both these tools along with HE to achieve their result.

Gorbunov, Vaikuntanathan, and Wee [GVW15], also using the above approach, construct a predicate encryption scheme based on learning with errors; recall that predicate encryption is a weaker form of functional encryption. They propose a novel primitive, called partial-hiding predicate encryption scheme and then combine it with HE to obtain a predicate encryption scheme. Their notion of partial-hiding predicate encryption scheme incorporates both the privacy and the integrity properties. In terms of techniques, the starting point to their construction of partial-hiding predicate encryption scheme is the observation that the HE decryption corresponds to computing an inner product followed by a threshold function. Moreover, there are lattice-based constructions of predicate encryption schemes for threshold of inner product [AFV11, GMW15]. They then propose a novel method to combine a lattice-based predicate encryption for threshold of inner product with a lattice-based attribute-based encryption scheme to achieve a partial-hiding predicate encryption scheme. Natural attempts to extend their construction to achieve functional encryption have been shown to be broken [Agr17a].

In [AR17], to ensure privacy of HE decryption, they use an FE scheme to perform linear HE half-decryption and add super-polynomially large smudging noises $\mathbf{Y}$ to hide the decryption noise $\mathbf{e}$. In their scheme, the smudging noises $\mathbf{Y}$ are sampled and encoded into the ciphertext. As a result, the ciphertext size grows with the output length of the computation, which is non-compact. In addition, they also developed a new approach to ensure integrity. Instead of relying on primitives like attribute based encryption or PHFE to ensure integrity as in [GVW12, GKP+13, GVW15], they employ a special HE scheme whose decryption equation has the form $\mathbf{y} + \mathbf{e} = \mathbf{c}_f - \mathbf{A}_f\mathbf{s}$, where $\mathbf{A}_f$ depends only on the public and reusable random matrix $\mathbf{A}$ in LWE samples and the evaluated function f. Thus, to ensure integrity, it suffices to enforce that only linear functions $\mathbf{A}_f\mathbf{s}$ for legitimate f can be evaluated on $\mathbf{s}$. The work of [LM18] follows their approach for integrity. The work of [AJS18], however, takes a different path, by introducing the notion of 3-restricted FE (that we call partially hiding functional encryption here).

1.3   Open Questions

Our work opens many interesting questions. First, we call for more study of the candidate ΔRGs/PFGs. Studying their security as well as finding new candidates may build interesting connection with algorithm and complexity theory as already demonstrated in the attack by [BHJ+19] using SOS algorithms.

   Secondly, can we further strengthen the construction of FE or $i\mathcal{O}$ in order to further weaken the requirements on the structure and security of ΔRGs/PFGs? Follow-up works show how to construct PHFE schemes that can perform constant-degree [JLMS19] computation or even up to NC_1 computation [JLS19] in the public input, instead of just linear (still quadratic in the private input). Such scheme allows for having more candidate ΔRGs/PFGs.

   Thirdly, the reason that we can only work with polynomially bounded smudging noises is because we do not have constant-degree FE schemes that support super-polynomially large outputs from multilinear maps and/or standard assumptions. For instance, can we build a quadratic FE scheme for super-polynomially large outputs from standard assumptions? That would lead to a significant simplification of our construction of NC^1-FE as there would be no more leakage.

2   New PRG Assumptions

This section is organized as follows. In Sect. 2.1 we define the notion of perturbation resilient generator ΔRG proposed by [AJS18]. In Sect. 2.2 we define pseudo-flawed smudging generators (PFGs) proposed by [LM18]. Then, in Sect. 2.3 we give an algorithmic framework to realise ΔRG and PFG. Both of them are PRGs which has seed consisting of one public input and two secret input. These PRGs evaluate degree-3 multilinear polynomials over $\mathbb{Z_p}$ over these inputs. In the same section, we give an intuition as to why this structure can be realised using bilinear maps. In Sect. 2.4 we give candidate polynomials which can be used to instantiate these primitives. In Sect. 2.5, we illustrate a *single* assumption which will imply the notion of a perturbation resilient generator sufficient to build $i\mathcal{O}$ [AJS18]. In Sect. 2.6 we present the state of art in cryptanalysis of the candidate polynomials.

2.1   Perturbation Resilient Generator

A perturbation-resilient generator, denoted by ΔRG, consists of the following algorithms:

- **Setup, Setup$(1^\lambda, 1^n, B)$:** On input security parameter λ, the length parameter n and a polynomial $B = B(\lambda)$, it outputs a seed Seed and public parameters pp.
- **Evaluation, Eval(pp, Seed):** It takes as input public parameters pp, seed Seed and outputs a vector $(h_1, ..., h_\ell) \in \mathbb{Z}^\ell$. The parameter ℓ is defined to be the stretch of ΔRG.

The following properties are associated with a ΔRG scheme.

Efficiency: The following conditions need to be satisfied.

- The time taken to compute Setup$(1^\lambda, 1^n, B)$ is $n \cdot \text{poly}(\lambda)$ for some fixed polynomial poly.
- For all $i \in [\ell]$, $|h_i| = \text{poly}(\lambda, n)$. That is, the norm of each component h_i in $\mathbb{Z}$ is bounded by some polynomial in λ and n.

Perturbation Resilience: For every polynomial $B(\lambda)$, for every large enough polynomial $n = n(\lambda)$ and for all large enough λ, the following holds: for every $a_1, ..., a_\ell \in \mathbb{Z}$, with $|a_i| \leq B(\lambda)$, we have that for any distinguisher D of size 2^λ,

$$\left| \Pr_{x \xleftarrow{\$} \mathcal{D}_1} [1 \leftarrow D(x)] - \Pr_{x \xleftarrow{\$} \mathcal{D}_2} [1 \leftarrow D(x)] \right| < 1 - 1/\lambda,$$

where the sampling algorithms of $\mathcal{D}_1$ and $\mathcal{D}_2$ are defined as follows:

- Distribution $\mathcal{D}_1$: Compute (pp, Seed) $\leftarrow$ Setup$(1^\lambda, 1^n, B)$ and $(h_1, ..., h_\ell) \leftarrow$ Eval(pp, Seed). Output (pp, $h_1, ..., h_\ell$).
- Distribution $\mathcal{D}_2$: Compute (pp, Seed) $\leftarrow$ Setup$(1^\lambda, 1^n, B)$ and $(h_1, ..., h_\ell) \leftarrow$ Eval(pp, Seed). Output (pp, $h_1 + a_1, ..., h_\ell + a_\ell$).

Note that as is, we are not able to use the notion of a ΔRG to construct iO. We now define the notion of a perturbation-resilient generator implementable by a three-restricted FE scheme (3ΔRG for short). This notion turns out to be useful for our construction of iO.

ΔRG Implementable by Three-Restricted FE. A ΔRG scheme implementable by Three-Restricted FE (3ΔRG for short) is a perturbation resilient generator with some additional structural properties. We describe syntax again for a complete specification.

- Setup$(1^\lambda, 1^n, B) \rightarrow$ (pp, Seed). The setup algorithm takes as input a security parameter λ, the length parameter 1^n and a polynomial $B = B(\lambda)$ and outputs a seed Seed and public parameters pp. Here, Seed = (Seed.pub, Seed.priv(1), Seed.priv(2)) is a vector on $\mathbb{Z}_{\mathbf{p}}$ for a modulus $\mathbf{p}$, which is also the modulus used in three-restricted FE scheme. There are three components of this vector, where one of the component is public and two components are private, each in $\mathbb{Z}_\mathbf{P}^{n\text{poly}(\lambda)}$. Also each part can be partitioned into sub-components as follows. $\mathsf{Seed.pub} = (\mathsf{Seed}_{\mathsf{pub},1}, ..., \mathsf{Seed}_{\mathsf{pub},n})$, $\mathsf{Seed.priv}(1) = (\mathsf{Seed}_{\mathsf{priv}(1),1}, ..., \mathsf{Seed}_{\mathsf{priv}(1),n})$ and $\mathsf{Seed.priv}(2) = (\mathsf{Seed}_{\mathsf{priv}(2),1}, ..., \mathsf{Seed}_{\mathsf{priv}(2),n})$. Here, each sub component is in $\mathbb{Z}_\mathbf{P}^{\text{poly}(\lambda)}$ for some fixed polynomial poly independent of n. Also, $\mathsf{pp} = (\mathsf{Seed.pub}, q_1, .., q_\ell)$ where each q_i is a cubic multilinear polynomial described in the next algorithm. We require syntactically there exists two algorithms SetupSeed and SetupPoly such that Setup can be decomposed follows:

1. $\mathsf{SetupSeed}(1^\lambda, 1^n, B) \to \mathsf{Seed}$. The SetupSeed algorithm outputs the seed.
2. $\mathsf{SetupPoly}(1^\lambda, 1^n, B) \to q_1, ..., q_\ell$. The SetupPoly algorithm outputs $q_1, .., q_\ell$.

- $\mathsf{Eval}(\mathsf{pp}, \mathsf{Seed}) \to (h_1, ..., h_\ell)$, evaluation algorithm output a vector $(h_1, ..., h_\ell) \in \mathbb{Z}^\ell$. Here for $i \in [\ell]$, $h_i = q_i(\mathsf{Seed})$ and ℓ is the stretch of 3$\mathit{\Delta}$RG. Here q_i is a cubic polynomial which is multilinear in public and private components of the seed.

The security and efficiency requirements are same as before.

Remark 2. To construct iO we need the stretch of 3$\mathit{\Delta}$RG to be equal to $\ell = n^{1+\epsilon}$ for some constant $\epsilon > 0$.

We can construct 3$\mathit{\Delta}$RG from a succinctly stated, instance independent and a falsifiable assumption stated in Sect. 2.5.

2.2   Pseudo-Flawed Smudging Generators

In this section, we first define what it means for a distribution over $\mathbb{Z}^\ell$ to be smudging and flawed-smudging, and then introduce pseudo flawed-smudging generators.

First, the distribution of a random variable X is smudging if the statistical distance between X and $X + e$ is small for all e with bounded magnitude.

Definition 1 (Smudging distributions). *Let ℓ be a positive integer, let $\varepsilon \in [0, 1]$, and let B either be a positive integer or an ℓ-dimensional vector of positive integers. We say a distribution $\mathcal{X}$ over $\mathbb{Z}^\ell$ is (B, ε)-smudging if for $X \leftarrow \mathcal{X}$ and for all B-bounded $e \in \mathbb{Z}^\ell$, we have $\delta(X, X + e) \le \varepsilon$.*

We next define distributions obtained by fixing some positions in the output of a distribution. This will be used for defining flawed-smudging distributions.

Definition 2 (Bit-fixing distributions). *Let $\mathcal{D}$ be a distribution over strings in Δ^ℓ for some set Δ and some integer ℓ. Let $I \subseteq [\ell]$ be a set of indices, and x an arbitrary string in $\Delta^{|I|}$. Define $\mathcal{D}|_{x,I}$ to be the distribution of sampling $\bar{x}$ from $\mathcal{D}$ conditioned on $\bar{x}_I = x$. For convenience, we sometimes also write I as its characteristic vector v, where $v_i = 1$ iff $i \in I$.*

We say that $\mathcal{D}$ is bit-fixing efficiently samplable if $\mathcal{D}|_{x,I}$ is efficiently samplable for any x, I.

We now define flawed-smudging distributions. On a high level, the distribution of X is flawed-smudging for a random variable E if there are a few "bad" coordinates such that $X + E$ "hides" E at all coordinates that are not bad. This means, given $X + E$ and which coordinates are bad, one cannot distinguish E from $\overline{E}$, where $\overline{E}$ is a fresh sample conditioned on agreeing with E on the bad coordinates.

Definition 3 (Flawed-smudging distributions). *Let ℓ be a positive integer and let $\mathcal{X}$ and $\mathcal{E}$ be distributions over $\mathbb{Z}^\ell$. Further let $K \in \mathbb{N}$ and $\mu \in [0,1]$. We say that $\mathcal{X}$ is (K, μ)-flawed-smudging for $\mathcal{E}$ if there exist randomized predicates $\{\mathrm{BAD}_i \colon \mathbb{Z}^{\ell+1} \to \{0,1\}\}_{i \in [\ell]}$ such that the following two distributions are identical:*

$$
\mathcal{D}_1 = \left\{
\begin{array}{c}
E \leftarrow \mathcal{E} \\
X \leftarrow \mathcal{X} \\
\mathrm{bad} = \big(\mathrm{bad}_i \leftarrow \mathrm{BAD}_i(E_i, X)\big)_{i \in [\ell]}
\end{array}
\quad : \quad (E, \ X + E, \ \mathrm{bad})
\right\},
$$

$$
\mathcal{D}_2 = \left\{
\begin{array}{c}
E \leftarrow \mathcal{E} \\
X \leftarrow \mathcal{X} \\
\mathrm{bad} = \big(\mathrm{bad}_i \leftarrow \mathrm{BAD}_i(E_i, X)\big)_{i \in [\ell]} \\
\overline{E} \leftarrow \mathcal{E}|_{E_{\mathrm{bad}}, \mathrm{bad}}
\end{array}
\quad : \quad (\overline{E}, \ X + E, \ \mathrm{bad})
\right\},
$$

and in addition, with probability at least $1 - \mu$, the 1-norm of bad is bounded by $|\mathrm{bad}|_1 \le K$.

We say the distribution $\mathcal{X}$ is (K, μ)-flawed-smudging for B-bounded distributions if it is (K, μ)-flawed-smudging for every B-bounded distribution $\mathcal{E}$, where B can either be a positive integer or a vector in $\mathbb{Z}^\ell$.

Remark 3. A more direct generalization of the definition of smudging distributions (see Definition 1) would be that for all e, the distribution of $X + e$ is equal (or statistically close) to the distribution of Y, where $Y_i = X_i + e_i$ for all bad i, and $Y_i = X_i$ for non-bad i. This is, however, not sufficient for our purposes: We need that no information about the non-bad coordinates is leaked. While X_i itself does not leak anything about e_i, the fact that i is not a bad coordinate can leak something about e_i, since the predicate BAD depends on e_i. Definition 3 resolves this issue by sampling the non-bad coordinates freshly after sampling bad.

Pseudo Flawed-Smudging Generators. We now define pseudo flawed-smudging generators (PFGs). A PFG is a distribution of efficiently computable functions and seeds for which the output of the functions is indistinguishable from a flawed-smudging distribution.

Definition 4. *(Pseudo Flawed-Smudging Generator) Let n, m, K, B be polynomials. A family of (K, μ)-pseudo flawed-smudging generators $((K, \mu)$-PFG) for B-bounded distributions is an ensemble of distributions $\mathcal{PFG} = \{\mathcal{PFG}_\lambda\}_{\lambda \in \mathbb{N}}$ satisfying the following properties:*

Syntax: *For every $\lambda \in \mathbb{N}$, every $(\text{PFG}, \mathcal{D}^{sd})$ in the support of $\mathcal{PFG}_\lambda$ defines a function $\text{PFG}: \mathbb{Z}^{n(\lambda)} \to \mathbb{Z}^{m(\lambda)}$ and a distribution $\mathcal{D}^{sd}$ over seeds.*

Efficiency: *There is a uniform Turing machine M satisfying that for every $\lambda \in \mathbb{N}$, every $(\text{PFG}, \mathcal{D}^{sd}) \in \text{Support}(\mathcal{PFG}_\lambda)$ and $\text{Seed} \in \text{Support}(\mathcal{D}^{sd})$, $M(\text{PFG}, \text{Seed})$ runs in time $\text{poly}(\lambda)$ and we have $M(\text{PFG}, \text{Seed}) = \text{PFG}(\text{Seed})$. Furthermore, $\mathcal{PFG}$ and all $\mathcal{D}^{sd}$ in the support of $\mathcal{PFG}_\lambda$ are efficiently samplable.*

(K, μ)-pseudo-flawed-smudging for B-bounded distributions: *There exists an ensemble $\{\mathcal{X}_\lambda\}$ of distributions, such that the distribution $\mathcal{X}_\lambda$ is $(K(\lambda), \mu(\lambda))$-flawed-smudging for all $B(\lambda)$-bounded distributions, and the following ensembles are μ-indistinguishable:*

$$\left\{ (\text{PFG}, \mathcal{D}^{sd}) \leftarrow \mathcal{PFG}_\lambda; \text{Seed} \leftarrow \mathcal{D}^{sd} : (\text{PFG}, \text{PFG}(\text{Seed})) \right\}_{\lambda \in \mathbb{N}},$$

$$\left\{ (\text{PFG}, \mathcal{D}^{sd}) \leftarrow \mathcal{PFG}_\lambda; X \leftarrow \mathcal{X}_\lambda : (\text{PFG}, X) \right\}_{\lambda \in \mathbb{N}}.$$

Degree 3 PFG with Partial Public Input. As mentioned in the introduction and as described w.r.t. ΔRG, it suffices if our PFG has the simple structure that every function PFG sampled from $\mathcal{PFG}_\lambda$ is a degree 2 polynomial over $\mathbb{Z}_p$, where p is a modulus that eventually matches the modulus that our PHFE supports, which in turn is the modulus associated with the bilinear maps. However, so far, we do not know how to instantiate a truly degree 2 PFG. Instead, we can work with the following slightly weaker structure, where the PFG is a degree 3 multilinear polynomial, and the first input vector can be made public, more specifically:

Structure: *For every λ, every $(\text{PFG}, \mathcal{D}^{sd}) \in \mathcal{PFG}_\lambda$ satisfies that $\mathcal{D}^{sd}$ is a distribution over $(\mathbf{x}, \mathbf{y}, \mathbf{z}) \in \mathbb{Z}_p^3$ for some modulus p, and $\text{PFG}(\mathbf{x}, \mathbf{y}, \mathbf{z})$ is a multilinear degree 3 polynomial over $\mathbb{Z}_p^3$.*

Security with partial public input: *The security in Definition 4 is strengthened so that the following distributions are indistinguishable:*

$$\left\{ (\text{PFG}, \mathcal{D}^{sd}) \leftarrow \mathcal{PFG}_\lambda; \text{Seed} = (\mathbf{x}, \mathbf{y}, \mathbf{z}) \leftarrow \mathcal{D}^{sd} : (\text{PFG}, \mathbf{x}, \text{PFG}(\text{Seed})) \right\}_{\lambda \in \mathbb{N}},$$

$$\left\{ (\text{PFG}, \mathcal{D}^{sd}) \leftarrow \mathcal{PFG}_\lambda; \text{Seed} = (\mathbf{x}, \mathbf{y}, \mathbf{z}) \leftarrow \mathcal{D}^{sd}; X \leftarrow \mathcal{X}_\lambda : (\text{PFG}, \mathbf{x}, X) \right\}_{\lambda \in \mathbb{N}}.$$

Weaker Variant: Flawed-Smudging with $1/\text{poly}(\lambda)$ Probability. In the full version [LM18], we show how to further weaken the requirements on PFGs. Roughly speaking, the PFG outputs are indistinguishable to a flawed-smudging distribution only with some $1/\text{poly}(\lambda)$ probability. We show that using essentially the same technique for handling the partial hiding guarantee of PFG can also be used to handle this weakening. We omit details here; see [LM18] for more details.

Properties of (Flawed-)Smudging Distributions. In the full version [LM18], we prove some properties of smudging and of flawed-smudging distributions. More specifically, we show the following:

- Polynomially bounded distributions cannot be smudging with negligible ε. More precisely, if $\mathcal{X}$ is B-bounded and (B', ε)-smudging, then $\varepsilon \geq \frac{1}{2B+1}$.
- Adding independent values preserves the (flawed-)smudging property, i.e., if X and Y are independent and the distribution of X is (flawed-)smudging, then the distribution of $X + Y$ is (flawed-)smudging with the same parameters.
- Probabilistically mixing (flawed-)smudging distributions yields a (flawed-) smudging distribution. That is, if the distributions of X_i are (B, ε_i)-smudging (or (K, μ_i)-flawed-smudging) and $\alpha_i \in [0, 1]$ such that $\sum_i \alpha_i = 1$, then the distribution of X with $\Pr[X = x] = \sum_i \alpha_i \Pr[X_i = x]$ is $(B, \sum_i \alpha_i \varepsilon_i)$-smudging (or $(K, \sum_i \alpha_i \mu_i)$-flawed-smudging).
- The joint distribution of mutually independent smudging distributions is flawed-smudging. More precisely, we show that if $\mathcal{X}$ is a distribution over $\mathbb{Z}^\ell$ such that for $(X_1, \ldots, X_\ell) \leftarrow \mathcal{X}$, $X_1, \ldots, X_\ell$ are mutually independent and the distribution of each X_i is (B, ε)-smudging for $\varepsilon \leq \frac{K+1}{2 \cdot 2\ell \cdot (2B+1)}$, then $\mathcal{X}$ is $(K, 2^{-K})$-flawed-smudging for B-bounded distributions.
- The product of flawed-smudging distributions is flawed-smudging. That is, for distributions $\mathcal{X}^{(1)}$ and $\mathcal{X}^{(2)}$ such that $\mathcal{X}^{(i)}$ is $(K^{(i)}, \mu^{(i)})$-flawed-smudging, we have that $\mathcal{X}^{(1)} \times \mathcal{X}^{(2)}$ is $(K^{(1)} + K^{(2)}, \mu^{(1)} + \mu^{(2)})$-flawed-smudging.
- If the distribution of X is flawed-smudging for the distribution of E and $E = E(V)$ is a function of some random vector V such that each coordinate of $E(V)$ depends only on a few coordinates of V, then $E(V) + X$ hides V at all but a few locations.

2.3 Framework for Algorithms of 3ΔRG and PFG

We now describe a framework of algorithms that can be used to instantiate ΔRG and PFG. However for the sake of succinctness and clarity we describe it in terms of a perturbation resilient generator 3ΔRG. For concreteness, we use a large enough prime modulus $\mathbf{p} = O(2^\lambda)$, which is the same as the modulus used by 3$-$restricted FE/(1,2)-PHFE, let χ be a distribution used to sample input elements over $\mathbb{Z}$. Let Q denote a polynomial sampler. Next we describe the algorithms in terms of χ and Q but give concrete instantiations later in Sect. 2.4.

- Setup$(1^\lambda, 1^n, B) \rightarrow (\mathsf{pp}, \mathsf{Seed})$. Sample a secret $\mathbf{s} \leftarrow \mathbb{Z}_\mathbf{p}^{1 \times \mathsf{d}}$ for $\mathsf{d} = \mathrm{poly}(\lambda)$ such that $\mathsf{LWE}_{\mathsf{d}, n \cdot \mathsf{d}, \mathbf{p}, \chi}$ holds. Here χ is a bounded distribution with bound $\mathrm{poly}(\lambda)$. Let $\mathcal{Q}$ denote an efficiently samplable distribution of homogeneous degree 3 polynomials (instantiated later). Then proceed with SetupSeed as follows:
  1. Sample $\mathbf{a}_i \leftarrow \mathbb{Z}_\mathbf{p}^{1 \times \mathsf{d}}$ for $i \in [n]$ along with $e_i, y_i, z_i \leftarrow \chi$ for $i \in [n]$.
  2. Compute LWE samples $\mathbf{w}_i = (\mathbf{a}_i, r_i = \langle \mathbf{a}_i, \mathbf{s} \rangle + e_i \mod \mathbf{p})$ for $i \in [n]$.
  3. Output Seed.pub$(i) = \mathbf{w}_i$ for $i \in [n]$, Seed.priv$(1, j) = y_i \otimes (-\mathbf{s}, 1)$ for $j \in [n]$ and Seed.priv$(2, k) = z_k$ for $k \in [n]$.

- SetupPoly : Now we describe SetupPoly. Fix $\eta = n^{1+\epsilon}$.
    1. Sample polynomials q'_ℓ for $\ell \in [\eta]$ as follows. $q'_\ell(e_1, ..., e_n, y_1, ..., y_n, z_1, ..., z_n) = \Sigma_{\mathbf{I}=(i,j,k)} c_{\mathbf{I}} e_i \cdot y_j \cdot z_k$ where coefficients $c_{\mathbf{I}}$ are bounded by $\mathrm{poly}(\lambda)$. These polynomials $\{q'_\ell\}$ are sampled according to $\mathcal{Q}$
    2. Define q_i be a multilinear homogeneous degree 3 polynomial takes as input $\mathsf{Seed} = (\{\mathbf{w}_i\}_{i\in[n]}, \mathbf{y}'_1, ..., \mathbf{y}'_n, \mathbf{z})$. Then it computes each monomial $c_{\mathbf{I}} e_i y_j \cdot z_k$ as follows and then adds all the results:
        - Compute $c_{\mathbf{I}} \langle \mathbf{w}_i, (-\mathbf{s}, 1) \rangle \cdot y_j \cdot z_k$. This step requires $\mathbf{y}'_i = y_i \otimes (-\mathbf{s}, 1)$ to perform this computation.
    3. Output $q_1, ..., q_\eta$. Observe that $q_i(\mathsf{Seed}) = q'_i(\mathbf{e}, \mathbf{y}, \mathbf{z})$ for all i.
- $\mathsf{Eval}(\mathsf{pp}, \mathsf{Seed}) \rightarrow (h_1, ..., h_\eta)$, evaluation algorithm output a vector $(h_1, ..., h_\eta) \in \mathbb{Z}^\eta$. Here for $i \in [\eta]$, $h_i = q_i(\mathsf{Seed})$ and η is the stretch of $3\varDelta\mathsf{RG}$. Here q_i is a degree 3 homogenenous multilinear polynomial (defined above) which is degree 1 in public and 2 in private components of the seed.

We prove that the above candidate satisfies the efficiency property of a perturbation-resilient generator.

Efficiency:

1. Note that Seed contains n LWE samples $\mathbf{w}_i$ for $i \in [n]$ of dimension d. Along with the samples, it contains elements $\mathbf{y}'_i = y_i \otimes \mathbf{t}$ for $i \in [n]$ and elements z_i for $i \in [n]$. Note that the size of these elements are bounded by $\mathrm{poly}(\lambda)$ and is independent of n.
2. The values $h_i = q_i(\mathsf{Seed}) = \Sigma_{\mathbf{I}=(i,j,k)} c_{\mathbf{I}} e_i \cdot y_j \cdot z_k$. Since χ is a bounded distribution, bounded by $\mathrm{poly}(\lambda, n)$, and coefficients $c_{\mathbf{I}}$ are also polynomially bounded, each $|h_i| < \mathrm{poly}(\lambda, n)$ for $i \in [m]$.

Intuition Behind Candidate with Partially-Public Inputs. Starting from a cubic multilinear candidate $g(\mathbf{x}, \mathbf{y}, \mathbf{z})$ where all inputs are private, and the first input $\mathbf{x}$ is from a distribution that can be used as LWE noises, we transform it into another function $h(\mathbf{C}, \mathbf{y}', \mathbf{z})$ where the first input can be made public. The key idea is hiding $\mathbf{x}$ in LWE samples $\mathbf{C} = (\mathbf{A}, \mathbf{A}\mathbf{s}' + \mathbf{x}) \bmod p$ as the noise terms. Then computing g translates into computing another function h where $\mathbf{x}$ is replaced with $\mathbf{C}\mathbf{s} \bmod p$ for $\mathbf{s} = (-\mathbf{s}'||1)$,

$$h(\mathbf{C}, \ \mathbf{y}' = (\mathbf{y} \otimes \mathbf{s}), \ \mathbf{z}) := \sum_j g(\mathbf{C}[\star, j], \ s_j \mathbf{y}, \ \mathbf{z}) = g(\mathbf{C}\mathbf{s}, \mathbf{y}, \mathbf{z}) = g(\mathbf{x}, \mathbf{y}, \mathbf{z}) \pmod{p},$$

where $\mathbf{C}[\star, j]$ is the vector containing the j'th element of all LWE samples. Now $\mathbf{C}$ is the public input of h. By providing the tensor $\mathbf{y} \otimes \mathbf{s}$ as input, the polynomial h is multilinear. For h to be secure when $\mathbf{C}$ is public, the output of g needs to be indistinguishable from a pseudo flawed-smudging distribution, say $\mathcal{D}$, even when its first input is hidden in some LWE samples,

$$\{g(\mathbf{x}, \mathbf{y}, \mathbf{z}), \ \mathbf{C} = (\mathbf{A}, \mathbf{A}\mathbf{s}' + \mathbf{x})\} \approx \{\varDelta \leftarrow \mathcal{D}, \ \mathbf{C} = (\mathbf{A}, \mathbf{A}\mathbf{s}' + \mathbf{x})\}.$$

The family of cubic polynomials with partially-public input of [AJS18] corresponds exactly to h obtained by applying the above transformation to the degree

$d = 3$ candidates $g(\mathbf{x}, \mathbf{y}, \mathbf{z}) = \sum_{i_1, i_2, i_3} c_{i_1, i_2, i_3} x_{i_1} y_{i_2} z_{i_3}$ with small inputs and coefficients described in Instantiation 1. We observe that for every fixed public input $\mathbf{C}$, the function h is quadratic in $\mathbf{y}$ and $\mathbf{z}$, but its computation over $\mathbb{Z}_p$ does not degenerate to computation over $\mathbb{Z}$, as it does trigger wrap-around modulo p due to LWE "decryption".

2.4   Our Instantiation of Polynomials for ΔRG and PFG

We now give various instantiations of Q. Let χ be the discrete gaussian distribution with 0 mean and standard deviation n. The following candidate is proposed by [BHJ+19] and [AJS18] based on the investigation of the hardness of families of expanding polynomials over the reals. For any vector $\mathbf{v}$, denote by $\mathbf{v}[i]$, the ith component of the vector.

Instantiation: 3XOR Based Candidate. Let $t = B^2 \lambda$. Sample each polynomial q'_i for $i \in [\eta]$ as follows. $q'_i(\mathbf{x}_1, \ldots, \mathbf{x}_t, \mathbf{y}_1, \ldots, \mathbf{y}_t, \mathbf{z}_1, \ldots, \mathbf{z}_t) = \sum_{j \in [t]} q'_{i,j}(\mathbf{x}_j, \mathbf{y}_j, \mathbf{z}_j)$. Here $\mathbf{x}_j \in \chi^{d \times n}$ and $\mathbf{y}_j, \mathbf{z}_j \in \chi^n$ for $j \in [t]$. In other words, q'_i is a sum of t polynomials $q'_{i,j}$ over t disjoint set of variables.

Now we describe how to sample $q'_{i,j}$ for $j \in [\eta]$.

1. To sample $q'_{i,j}$ do the following. Sample three indices randomly and independently $i_1, i_2, i_3 \leftarrow [n]$.
2. Set $q'_{i,j}(\mathbf{x_j}, \mathbf{y_j}, \mathbf{z_j}) = \mathbf{x_j}[i_1] \cdot \mathbf{y_j}[i_2] \cdot \mathbf{z_j}[i_3]$

Remark: The candidate above was generalised to have a constant degree d in a followup. This can be found in [JLMS19]. One could also consider arithmetic versions of various boolean predicates. For example, any clause of the form $a_1 \vee a_2 \vee a_3$ can be written as $1 - (1 - a_1)(1 - a_2)(1 - a_3)$ over integers where a_1, a_2, a_3 are literals in first case and take values in $\{0, 1\}$, and thus any random satisfiable 3SAT formula can be converted to polynomials in this manner.

2.5   Pseudorandomness Assumption in Ananth-Jain-Sahai

Below we describe the actual hardness assumption needed by [AJS18], when combined with subexponentially secure LWE, bilinear maps, and 3-block-local PRGs, to imply $i\mathcal{O}$.

The AJS Assumption. This assumption states the following. There exists a polynomially bounded distribution χ over the integers, and there exists a polynomial sampler Q over families of multilinear degree-3 polynomials. Let $\delta_i \in \mathbb{Z}$ be output by the adversary given only the parameters $(1^\lambda, 1^n)$, such that for all $i \in [n^{1+\epsilon}]$, we have that $|\delta_i| < \lambda^c$ for some constant c. Then consider the following two distributions:

Distribution $\mathcal{D}_1$: Fix a prime modulus $\mathbf{p} = O(2^\lambda)$. Run $Q(n, \lambda^c, \epsilon)$ to obtain polynomials $(q_1, ..., q_{\lfloor n^{1+\epsilon} \rfloor})$. Sample a secret $\mathbf{s} \leftarrow \mathbb{Z}_p^\lambda$ and sample $\mathbf{a}_i \leftarrow \mathbb{Z}_p^\lambda$ for

$i \in [n]$. Finally, for every $i \in [n]$, sample $e_i, y_i, z_i \leftarrow \chi$, and write $\mathbf{e} = (e_1, \ldots, e_n)$, $\mathbf{y} = (y_1, \ldots, y_n)$, $\mathbf{z} = (z_1, \ldots, z_n)$. Output:

$$\{\mathbf{a}_i, \langle \mathbf{a}_i, \mathbf{s} \rangle + e_i \bmod p\}_{i \in [n]}$$

along with

$$\{q_k, q_k(\mathbf{e}, \mathbf{y}, \mathbf{z})\}_{k \in [n^{1+\epsilon}]}$$

Distribution $\mathcal{D}_2$ is the same as $\mathcal{D}_1$, except that we consider polynomial evaluations perturbed with δ_i. The output is now

$$\{\mathbf{a}_i, \langle \mathbf{a}_i, \mathbf{s} \rangle + e_i \bmod p\}_{i \in [n]}$$

along with

$$\{q_k, q_k(\mathbf{e}, \mathbf{y}, \mathbf{z}) + \delta_k\}_{k \in [n^{1+\epsilon}]}$$

Then we require that for all subexponential-time adversary $\mathcal{A}$ it holds that:

$$\left| \Pr_{Z \overset{\$}{\leftarrow} \mathcal{D}_1} [\mathcal{A}(Z) = 1] - \Pr_{Z \overset{\$}{\leftarrow} \mathcal{D}_2} [\mathcal{A}(Z) = 1] \right| \leq 1 - 1/\lambda$$

Remark 4. For concreteness, the candidate for the sampler Q can be found in Sect. 2.4.

Decomposing the Assumption into Two Parts. To help understand the assumption above, next we make the following observation. The assumption described above is sufficient to build $i\mathcal{O}$ and it turns out the assumption above is true if the following two simpler assumptions are true. This implication is one sided and indeed it may be true that one of the two assumptions below is false but the assumption above still holds. We present the assumptions below only to help the reader conceptually understand the assumption above. The first assumption called "Weak LWE with Leakage" states that given the polynomial samples, it is computationally hard to determine whether the LWE sample is chosen with the same error over which the polynomials are evaluated or a completely independently chosen error.

Explaining the AJS Assumption, Part 1. Weak LWE with Leakage. This assumption states that there exists a polynomially bounded distribution χ over the integers, and there exists a polynomial sampler Q over families of multilinear degree-3 polynomials such that the following two distributions are weakly indistinguishable (specified later).

Distribution $\mathcal{D}_1$: Fix a prime modulus $\mathbf{p} = O(2^\lambda)$. Run $Q(n, \lambda^c, \epsilon)$ to obtain polynomials $(q_1, ..., q_{\lfloor n^{1+\epsilon} \rfloor})$ for some constant $c > 0$. Sample a secret $\mathbf{s} \leftarrow \mathbb{Z}_p^\lambda$ and sample $\mathbf{a}_i \leftarrow \mathbb{Z}_p^\lambda$ for $i \in [n]$. Finally, for every $i \in [n]$, sample $e_i, y_i, z_i \leftarrow \chi$, and write $\mathbf{e} = (e_1, \ldots, e_n)$, $\mathbf{y} = (y_1, \ldots, y_n)$, $\mathbf{z} = (z_1, \ldots, z_n)$. Output:

$$\{\mathbf{a}_i, \langle \mathbf{a}_i, \mathbf{s} \rangle + e_i \bmod p\}_{i \in [n]}$$

along with

$$\{q_k, q_k(\mathbf{e}, \mathbf{y}, \mathbf{z})\}_{k \in [n^{1+\epsilon}]}$$

Distribution $\mathcal{D}_2$ is the same as $\mathcal{D}_1$, except that we additionally sample $e'_j \leftarrow \chi$ for $i \in [n]$. The output is now

$$\{\mathbf{a}_i, \langle \mathbf{a}_i, \mathbf{s} \rangle + e'_i \bmod p\}_{i \in [n]}$$

along with

$$\{q_k, q_k(\mathbf{e}, \mathbf{y}, \mathbf{z})\}_{k \in [n^{1+\epsilon}]}$$

Then it holds that for any adversary $\mathcal{A}$ of subexponential size:

$$\left| \Pr_{Z \xleftarrow{\$} \mathcal{D}_1} [\mathcal{A}(Z) = 1] - \Pr_{Z \xleftarrow{\$} \mathcal{D}_2} [\mathcal{A}(Z) = 1] \right| \leq 1/\lambda$$

We can think of the polynomials $q_k(\mathbf{e}, \mathbf{y}, \mathbf{z})$ as "leaking" some information about the LWE errors e_i. The assumption above states that such leakage provides only a limited advantage to the adversary. Critically, the fact that there are $n^2 > n^{1+\epsilon}$ quadratic monomials involving just $\mathbf{y}$ and $\mathbf{z}$ above, which are not used in the LWE samples at all, is crucial to avoiding linearization attacks over $\mathbb{Z}_p$ in the spirit of Arora-Ge [AG11]. For more discussion of the security of the above assumption in the context of $D = 3$, see [BHJ+19].

The second assumption deals only with expanding degree-3 polynomials over the reals, and requires that these polynomials are weakly perturbation resilient.

Explaining the AJS Assumption, Part 2. Weak Perturbation-Resilience. This assumption states that for the same distribution of polynomials and inputs as above the following distributions are weakly indistinguishable. Let $\delta_i \in \mathbb{Z}$ be output by the adversary given only the parameters $(1^\lambda, 1^n)$, such that for all $i \in [n^{1+\epsilon}]$, we have that $|\delta_i| < \lambda^c$ for some constant c. Consider the following two distributions:

Distribution $\mathcal{D}_1$ consists of the evaluated polynomial samples. That is, we output:

$$\{q_k, q_k(\mathbf{e}, \mathbf{y}, \mathbf{z})\}_{k \in [n^{1+\epsilon}]}$$

Distribution $\mathcal{D}_2$ consists of the evaluated polynomial samples with added perturbations δ_i for $i \in [n^{1+\epsilon}]$. That is, we output:

$$\{q_k, q_k(\mathbf{e}, \mathbf{y}, \mathbf{z}) + \delta_k\}_{k \in [n^{1+\epsilon}]}$$

Then it holds that for any adversary $\mathcal{A}$ of subexponential size:

$$\left| \Pr_{Z \xleftarrow{\$} \mathcal{D}_1} [\mathcal{A}(Z) = 1] - \Pr_{Z \xleftarrow{\$} \mathcal{D}_2} [\mathcal{A}(Z) = 1] \right| \leq 1 - 3/\lambda$$

2.6   Known Cryptanalysis

Now, we discuss various preliminary cryptanalysis attempts made on these candidates. These attacks can be categorised in the following categories:

Linearisation Attacks: The system of degree-3 polynomials described above can be converted to a degree-2 system over $\mathbb{Z}_p$ by performing back substitution of e_i, from the LWE sample $(a_i, \langle a_i, s \rangle + e_i \mod \mathbf{p})$. However, the resulting system has about $\Omega(n)$ variables $\mathbf{y} \otimes \mathbf{s}$ and $\mathbf{z}$, but only about $n^{1+\epsilon}$ equations. Thus, all known linearization attack fail. This was considered in the work of [BHJ+19].

Sum-of-Squares Attacks: [BHJ+19] systematically studies SDP attacks on such system and they gave an evidence why the assumptions above instantiated using degree-2 polynomials over reals is unlikely to be true. However, they also conjecture that for degree-3 and higher, these systems exhibit SoS lower bounds (at least, the lower bounds are known to hold in the case when inputs are chosen from $\{-1, 1\}$ [Gri01, Sch08]). The lower bounds hold when number of equations $m \leq n^{d/2}$ for a general degree $d \geq 3$. Thus for our case when $m = n^{1+\epsilon}$ for any $\epsilon > 0$, the SoS algorithm is unlikely to attack such systems in polynomial time. Please refer [BHJ+19] for further details.

Gradient Descent: We implemented gradient descent to cryptanalyze all our candidates. It seems like given the signs of the planted inputs, gradient descent was able to recover the planted inputs in most cases. For degree-2 candidates, gradient descent was able to recover the planted inputs even with random starting points (even with no information on the signs). For degree-3 and higher, our implementation of gradient descent did not yield any attack starting from random signs. This matches our intuition developed in SoS literature, since the lower bounds hold when inputs are sampled from $\{+1, -1\}$ (thus implying finding signs is hard).

3   Technical Overview of Ananth-Jain-Sahai 18

We now begin with a very high-level overview of our techniques in [AJS18].

The Story So Far. Prior work, culminating in the most recent works of [AS17, Lin17, LT17] showed us that the powerful primitive of indistinguishability obfuscation can be based on trilinear maps and (sub-exponential) 3-block-local pseudorandom generators. Importantly for us, these works also (implicitly) demonstrate that in order to achieve indistinguishability obfuscation, it suffices to construct (sub-exponentially secure) secret-key sublinear FE for cubic polynomials, satisfying semi-functional security. Unfortunately, these prior approaches necessarily relied on multilinear maps with degree at least 3 to build such a cubic FE scheme.

That is because intuitively such a cubic FE scheme guarantees a way to evaluate a cubic polynomial on encrypted inputs without revealing any information about the input except the evaluation of the polynomial. In other words, such a scheme provides a way to output the decryption of a degree-3 polynomial evaluated "homomorphically" on encoded inputs. However, we seek to accomplish this without the use of degree-3 maps.

Since we seek to operate homomorphically on encoded values, a natural starting idea is to use fully homomorphic encryption (for concreteness and simplicity, in this paper we rely on the GSW fully homomorphic encryption scheme [GSW13]) with polynomially bounded error in order to perform cubic evaluations on encrypted inputs. The main challenge, however, is to reveal the output of cubic evaluation without compromising security.

Initial Approach. Our first observation is that computing the inner product $\langle \mathsf{GSW.sk}, \mathsf{GSW.CT} \rangle$ of a GSW secret key with a GSW ciphertext encrypting message M, outputs $(M \cdot \lfloor q/2 \rfloor + e)$ where the LWE modulus is q and e is a small error. With the assistance of a bilinear map, this inner product can be carried out via pairings, such that the output $(M \cdot \lfloor q/2 \rfloor + e)$ appears as an exponent in the target group. Next, one can hope to test whether the message M is zero by computing a discrete logarithm by brute-force checking all possible values, provided the output range is polynomial, which would happen if $M = 0$.

A reader familiar with GSW will observe that this approach already runs into major hurdles. The first problem is that brute-force computing the message M also reveals the error e to a potential adversary, which is problematic when we try to invoke the semantic security of GSW. In fact, recent work shows how knowledge of such error can be used to build devastating attacks [Agr17a]. We will crucially deal with this issue, but before we tackle this, let us first consider how we can force the adversary to obtain only inner products $\langle \mathsf{GSW.sk}, \mathsf{GSW.CT} \rangle$ where the messages correspond to cubic computations that the adversary is allowed to obtain.

3-Restricted FE. To accomplish this, we first define a *restricted* version of functional encryption (FE) – which allows for the computation of multilinear cubic polynomials of three inputs, where one remains unencoded and is called the public component and the other two are encoded; these are the private components. In other words, our restricted FE is a *partially hiding* FE, or PHFE for short. The input to the encryption algorithm is split into three parts $\mathbf{x}, \mathbf{y}$, and $\mathbf{z}$, where $\mathbf{x}$ is not hidden by the encryption, but $\mathbf{y}$ and $\mathbf{z}$ are kept hidden.

One of our key technical contributions is to achieve a new way of (indistinguishably) enforcing the output of such a 3-restricted FE scheme, despite the fact that one of the encodings is publicly known to the adversary. We use these techniques to achieve security for this 3-restricted variant of FE relying solely on asymmetric bilinear maps. While we only need the resulting 3-restricted FE to be sublinear, our construction in fact achieves compactness, where the size of encoding is only linear in the input length.

Constructing Three-Restricted FE. Before getting to 3 restricted FE, let's first recap how secret key quadratic functional encryption schemes [AS17, Lin17] work at a high level. Let's say that the encryptor wants to encrypt $\mathbf{y}, \mathbf{z} \in \mathbb{Z}_\mathbf{p}^n$. The master secret key consists of two secret random vectors $\beta, \gamma \in \mathbb{Z}_\mathbf{p}^n$ that are used for enforcement of computations done on $\mathbf{y}$ and $\mathbf{z}$ respectively. The idea is that the encryptor encodes $\mathbf{y}$ and β using some randomness r, and similarly encodes $\mathbf{z}$ and γ together as well. These encodings are created using bilinear maps in one of the two base groups. These encodings are constructed so that the decryptor can compute an encoding of $[g(\mathbf{y}, \mathbf{z}) - rg(\beta, \gamma)]_t$ in the target group for *any* quadratic function g. The function key for the given function f is constructed in such a manner that it allows the decryptor to compute the encoding $[rf(\beta, \gamma)]_t$ in the target group. Thus the output $[f(\mathbf{y}, \mathbf{z})]_t$ can be recovered in the exponent by computing the sum of $[rf(\beta, \gamma)]_t$ and $[f(\mathbf{y}, \mathbf{z}) - rf(\beta, \gamma)]_t$ in the exponent. As long as $f(\mathbf{y}, \mathbf{z})$ is polynomially small, this value can then be recovered efficiently.

Clearly the idea above only works for degree-2 computations, if we use bilinear maps. However, we build upon this idea nevertheless to construct a 3-restricted FE scheme. Recall, in a 3-restricted FE one wants to encrypt three vectors $\mathbf{x}, \mathbf{y}, \mathbf{z} \in \mathbb{Z}_\mathbf{p}^n$. While $\mathbf{y}$ and $\mathbf{z}$ are required to be hidden, $\mathbf{x}$ is not required to be hidden.

Now, in addition to $\beta, \gamma \in \mathbb{Z}_\mathbf{p}^n$ in case of a quadratic FE, another vector $\alpha \in \mathbb{Z}_\mathbf{p}^n$ is also sampled that is used to enforce the correctness of the $\mathbf{x}$ part of the computation. As before, given the ciphertext one can compute $[\mathbf{y}[j]\mathbf{z}[k] - r\beta[j]\gamma[k]]_t$ for $j, k \in [n]$. But this is clearly not enough, as these encodings do not involve $\mathbf{x}$ in any way. Thus, in addition, an encoding of $r(\mathbf{x}[i] - \alpha[i])$ is also given in the ciphertext for $i \in [n]$. Inside the function key, there are corresponding encodings of $\beta[j]\gamma[k]$ for $j, k \in [n]$ which the decryptor can pair with encoding of $r(\mathbf{x}[i] - \alpha[i])$ to form the encoding $[r(\mathbf{x}[i] - \alpha[i])\beta[j]\gamma[k]]_t$ in the target group. Now observe that,

$$\mathbf{x}[i] \cdot \big(\mathbf{y}[j]\mathbf{z}[k] - r\beta[j]\gamma[k]\big) + r(\mathbf{x}[i] - \alpha[i]) \cdot \beta[j]\gamma[k]$$
$$= \mathbf{x}[i]\mathbf{y}[j]\mathbf{z}[k] - r\alpha[i]\beta[j]\gamma[k]$$

Above, since $\mathbf{x}[i]$ is public, the decryptor can herself take $(\mathbf{y}[j]\mathbf{z}[k] - r\beta[j]\gamma[k])$, which she already has, and multiply it with $\mathbf{x}[i]$ in the exponent. This allows her to compute encoding of $[\mathbf{x}[i]\mathbf{y}[j]\mathbf{z}[k] - r\alpha[i]\beta[j]\gamma[k]]_t$. Combining these encodings appropriately, she can obtain $[g(\mathbf{x}, \mathbf{y}, \mathbf{z}) - rg(\alpha, \beta, \gamma)]_t$ for any degree-3 multilinear function g. Given the function key for f and the ciphertext, one can compute $[rf(\alpha, \beta, \gamma)]_t$ which can be used to unmask the output. This is because the ciphertext contains an encoding of r in one of the base groups and the function key contains an encoding of $f(\alpha, \beta, \gamma)$ in the other group and pairing them results in $[rf(\alpha, \beta, \gamma)]_t$.

In full version [AJS18], we provide details of our 3-restricted FE; specifically, we define a notion of semi-functional security [AS17] (variant of function-hiding) associated with a three-restricted FE scheme. Once we have such a restricted FE, making the leap to cubic FE would require us to also keep the public encoding hidden. Therefore, it is not clear whether we have achieved anything meaningful yet.

Applying Three-Restricted FE. One way that we can hope to protect or hide the input that goes into the public component of the 3-restricted FE, is to let this component itself be a GSW-based fully homomorphic encryption of the input. We can then rely on 3-restricted FE to homomorphically evaluate the cubic function itself and obtain a GSW encryption of the output of cubic evaluation. Note, however, that releasing such a GSW encryption by itself is useless, because it does not allow even an honest evaluator to recover the output of cubic evaluation.

At this point, let us go back to the initial approach described at the beginning of this section. Notice that instead of relying on 3-restricted FE to *only* homomorphically evaluate the cubic function itself, we can also perform a GSW decryption via 3-restricted FE. The secret key for GSW decryption can be embedded as input into one of the private components of the 3-restricted FE. We show how this can be carefully done via degree three operations only, to obtain output the GSW plaintext with some added error, that is, we obtain out $= \mu \lfloor \frac{q}{2} \rfloor + e$. Our actual method of bootstrapping three-restricted FE to sublinear FE for cubic polynomials involves additional subtleties, and in particular, we define and construct what we call *tempered cubic encodings* that serve as a useful abstraction in this process. We now further discuss one of the main technical issues that arises in this process.

Because the error e is sampled from a (bounded) polynomial-sized domain, it is possible to iterate, in polynomial time, over all possible values of out corresponding to $\mu = 0$ and $\mu = 1$, and therefore recover μ. Unfortunately, this process also reveals the error e, which can be devastating as we noted before.

Preventing the Revelation of Error Terms. To prevent this issue, we will reveal the value out $= \mu \lfloor \frac{q}{2} \rfloor + e$ but with some added noise, so as to hide the error e via noise flooding. Unfortunately, this idea still suffers from two major drawbacks:

- How should we generate such noise? A natural idea is to rely a pseudorandom generator that can be computed via quadratic operations only. However, this is exactly the reason why previous approaches from the literature could not rely on bilinear maps – in fact, the recent works of [LV17,BBKK17] showed that such PRGs are quite difficult to construct. To overcome this problem, we introduce and rely on a very weak variant of a pseudorandom object, that instead of guaranteeing pseudorandomness, only guarantees perturbation resilience. Furthermore, we will implement this object with degree-3 polynomials. We will soon explain this object in more detail.
- For an honest evaluator to recover μ by iterating over all possible values of out $= \mu \lfloor \frac{q}{2} \rfloor + e$, we crucially require the added noise be sampled from a polynomial-sized domain. But such noise appears to be insufficient for security, in particular, an adversary would have advantage at least $\frac{1}{\text{poly}(\lambda)}$ in distinguishing a message with added noise from a message without noise. Another key technical contribution of our work is to find a way to *amplify security*, via tools inspired by the dense model theorem. In the next two bullets, we describe these ideas in additional detail.

The Challenge of Constructing Degree-3 Pseudorandomness: A Barrier at Degree 2. As we've outlined above, we need a way to create pseudorandomness to (at least partially) hide noise values. The most straightforward way to do this would be to build a degree-2 pseudorandom generator (PRG) whose output is indistinguishable from some nice m-dimensional distribution, like a discrete gaussian. Intuitively, if such a degree-2 object existed, a bilinear map would be sufficient to implement it. However, the works of [BBKK17,LV17] showed that there are fundamental barriers to constructing such PRGs due to attacks arising from the Sum of Squares paradigm. Because we will propose a direction to overcome this barrier, we now review how these attacks work at a high level.

For simplicity, let's restrict our attention to polynomials where every monomial is of degree exactly 2. We can represent any such polynomial p as a symmetric n-by-n matrix P, where $P_{i,j} = P_{j,i}$ is equal to half the coefficient of the monomial $x_i x_j$ if $i \neq j$, and $P_{i,i}$ is equal to the coefficient of the monomial x_i^2. Then we observe that $p(x) = x^\top P x$. Suppose, then, we have a candidate PRG consisting of m degree-2 polynomials that we represent by matrices $M_1, \ldots, M_m$. Thus, to sample from this PRG, we sample a seed vector x from a bounded-norm distribution, and obtain the outputs $y_i = x^\top M_i x$. The goal of an attack would be to distinguish such outputs from a set of independent random values $r_1, \ldots, r_m$, say from a discrete gaussian distribution centered around zero.

The works of [BBKK17,LV17] suggest the following attack approach: Suppose we receive values $z_1, \ldots, z_m$. Then we construct the matrix

$$M = \sum_{i=1}^{m} z_i M_i$$

Observe now, that if $z_i = y_i$ corresponding to some seed vector x, then we have:

$$x^\top M x = \sum_{i=1}^{m} y_i x^\top M_i x = \sum_{i=1}^{m} y_i^2$$

Intuitively, because the above sum is a sum of squares, this will be a quite large positive value, showing that there exists x of bounded norm such that $x^\top M x$ can be quite large.

However, if the $z_i = r_i$, then the entries of the matrix M arise from a "random walk," and thus intuitively, the matrix M should behave a lot like a random matrix. However a random matrix has bounded eigenvalues, and thus we expect that there should not exist any x of bounded norm such that $x^\top M x$ is large. Indeed, this intuition can be made formal and gives rise to actual attacks on many degree-2 PRGs [BBKK17,LV17]. The attack above was generalized further in a followup work to this paper [BHJ+19], showing that several families of degree-2 pseudorandom objects cannot exist. While there are still potential caveats to known degree-2 attacks, we propose a different, more conservative, way forward:

Perturbation-Resilient Generators (ΔRG). We observe that even though the most natural way to "drown out" the GSW error term above is by adding some nice noise distribution, all we actually need is something we will call a perturbation-resilient generator (ΔRG): Informally speaking, we want that for every polynomial bound $B(\lambda)$, there should exist a low-degree[6] ΔRG using polynomially bounded seeds and coefficients, such that for any perturbation vector $a \in [-B, B]^m$, it should be true that all efficient adversaries must fail to distinguish between the distributions $\Delta RG(x)$ and $(\Delta RG(x) + a)$ with probability at least $1/poly(\lambda)$, which is a fixed inverse polynomial in the security parameter. We stress again that we are not seeking a ΔRG with standard negligible security, but only some low level of security. Indeed, even if an efficient adversary could distinguish between $\Delta RG(x)$ and $(\Delta RG(x) + a)$ with probability $1 - 1/poly(\lambda)$, but still fail to distinguish on at least $1/poly(\lambda)$ probability mass, our approach will succeed due to amplification (see below).

Crucially, instead of requiring the ΔRG to be computable via polynomials of degree two, we define a notion of ΔRG implementable by degree three polynomials via our notion of 3-restricted FE.

The seed for a ΔRG consists of one public and two private components, and perturbation-resilience is required even when the adversary has access to the public component of the seed. Furthermore, the use of cubic (as opposed to quadratic) polynomials gives reason to hope that our ΔRGs do not suffer from inversion attacks and achieve the weak form of security described above. Further in-depth research is certainly needed to explore our new assumptions. Indeed, we see our work as strongly motivating the systematic exploration of the limits of various types of low degree pseudorandom objects over $\mathbb{Z}$ using the Sum of Squares paradigm and beyond. Indeed, our work reveals a fascinating connection between achieving $i\mathcal{O}$ and studying distributions of expanding low-degree polynomials over the reals that are hard to solve. We refer the reader to [BHJ+19] for further discussion on this topic.

Implementing Degree-3 ΔRGs. Having constructed a three-restricted FE scheme, we now describe how to implement the degree-3 ΔRG as described above. Let $\mathbf{e} = (e_1, \ldots, e_n)$, $\mathbf{y} = (y_1, \ldots, y_n)$ and $\mathbf{z} = (z_1, ..., z_n)$ and we want to compute degree three polynomials of the form $q_\ell(\mathbf{e}, \mathbf{y}, \mathbf{z}) = \Sigma_{\mathbf{I}=(i,j,k)} c_{\mathbf{I}} \cdot e_i \cdot y_j \cdot z_k$ where $\ell \in [\eta]$ is the stretch. Here all variables and coefficients are polynomially bounded in absolute value.

At first glance, one could think to could encrypt $\mathbf{e}$ in the public component and $\mathbf{y}, \mathbf{z}$ in the private component of the three restricted FE scheme. Then, one could issue function keys for polynomials q_ℓ for $\ell \in [\eta]$. However, such a scheme would essentially yield a degree 2 system of polynomials in $\mathbf{y}$ and $\mathbf{z}$ as $\mathbf{e}$ is public, and not provide any additional security beyond using degree-2 polynomials. In order to fix this issue, we take a different approach.

Encrypting $\mathbf{e}$ as an LWE-Style Error. Instead, we sample a secret $\mathbf{s} \in \mathbb{Z}_\mathbf{p}^\mathsf{d}$ where d is some polynomial in the security parameter. We also sample vectors $\mathbf{a_i} \leftarrow \mathbb{Z}_\mathbf{p}^\mathsf{d}$

---

[6] In an earlier version of this paper, this overview focused on constructing degree-2 ΔRGs. However, as we describe now, our technical approach is more general, and we describe it in greater generality here.

for $i \in [n]$. Then we compute $r_i = \langle \mathbf{a_i}, \mathbf{s} \rangle + e_i$. Let $\mathbf{w_i} = (\mathbf{a_i}, r_i)$ for $i \in [n]$. Thus we have encrypted $\mathbf{e}$ using the secret $\mathbf{s}$. Now to implement degree-3 randomness generator we consider the polynomial:

$$q_\ell(\mathbf{e}, \mathbf{y}, \mathbf{z}) = \Sigma_{\mathbf{I}=(i,j,k)} c_{\mathbf{I}} \cdot e_i \cdot y_j \cdot z_k$$

This polynomial can be re-written as:

$$q_\ell(\mathbf{e}, \mathbf{y}, \mathbf{z}) = \Sigma_{\mathbf{I}=(i,j,k)} c_{\mathbf{I}} \cdot (r_i - \langle \mathbf{a_i}, \mathbf{s} \rangle) \cdot y_j \cdot z_k$$

Now suppose in the private component that contained $\mathbf{y}$, we also put $\mathbf{y} \otimes \mathbf{s}$ (where $\otimes$ denotes the tensor operation). Then observe that if $\mathbf{w}_i$ for $i \in [n]$ are all public values, then the entire polynomial can now be computed using a three-restricted FE scheme.

For this approach to be secure, intuitively we want that $\mathbf{e}$ is sampled from an "error" distribution with respect to which the LWE assumption holds. (For simplicity, we can think of $\mathbf{y}$ and $\mathbf{z}$ also being sampled from such a distribution.) The security of our ΔRG would then rely on a variant of the LWE assumption. Experience teaches that one should be cautious when considering the security of variants of LWE, and our case is no exception. This variant was studied in a follow-up work of [BHJ+19], where several unsuccessful attacks were considered. We briefly review one of these now. The most common source of devastating attacks to LWE variants is linearization. However, a key barrier to such attacks in our setting is the fact that the LWE-based public values $\mathbf{w}_i$ contain *no information whatsoever* about $\mathbf{y}$ and $\mathbf{z}$. Thus, over $\mathbb{Z}_\mathbf{p}$, we would obtain a set of roughly $n^{1+\epsilon}$ quadratic equations in $\mathbf{y} \otimes \mathbf{s}$ and $\mathbf{z}$, but crucially with *large* coefficients in $\mathbb{Z}_\mathbf{p}$. These large coefficients would arise from the fact that r_i and $\mathbf{a}_i$ are large values. Such systems, called MQ systems, have been widely studied cryptanalytically and are widely believed to be hard to solve [Wol02, KS99] in general. We again refer the reader to [BHJ+19] for further discussion. Specific candidates for the degree-3 polynomials q_ℓ above, inspired by the hardness of RANDOM 3-SAT and suggested by [BHJ+19], are also given in Sect. 2.

Security Amplification. Crucially, we want allow an adversary to have a very large distinguishing advantage when attempting to distinguish between $\Delta RG(x)$ and $(\Delta RG(x) + a)$, since this is a new assumption. For simplicity for this technical overview, we will assume that the ΔRG we introduce above is $\frac{1}{\lambda}$-secure. (More generally, we can tolerate any fixed inverse polynomial in the security parameter).

Using ideas already discussed above, it is possible to show (as we do in our technical sections) that relying on $\frac{1}{\lambda}$-secure ΔRG in the approach outlined above, allows us to achieve a "weak" form of sublinear FE (sFE), that only bounds adversarial advantage by $\frac{1}{\lambda}$. Unfortunately, such an FE scheme it not known to yield $i\mathcal{O}$, and for our approach to succeed, we must find a way to amplify security of sublinear FE.

How should we amplify security? An initial idea is to implement a direct-product type theorem for functional encryption. However, a simple XOR trick does not suffice: since we are trying to amplify security of a complex primitive like FE while retaining correctness, we will additionally need to rely on a special kind of secure computation. More precisely, we will use (subexponentially secure) n-out-of-n threshold fully homomorphic encryption (TFHE [MW16, BGG+18]), that is known to exist based on LWE [Reg05]. Recall that such a threshold (public key) fully homomorphic encryption scheme allows to encrypt a ciphertext in such a way that all secret key holders can *partially* decrypt the ciphertext, and then can recover the plaintext by combining these partial decryptions. However, any coalition of secret key holders of size at most $n - 1$ learns no information about the message.

A simplified overview of our scheme, that makes use of $t = \lambda^2$ weak sublinear FEs, is as follows:

- The setup algorithm outputs the master secret keys msk_i for all weak sublinear FEs.
- In order to generate the encryption of a plaintext M, generate a public key TFHE.pk and t fresh secret keys TFHE.sk_i for a threshold FHE, and encrypt M using the public key for threshold FHE to obtain ciphertext TFHE.ct. Additionally, for all i, encrypt (TFHE.ct, TFHE.sk_i) using the master secret key msk_i for the ith weak sublinear FE.
- To generate a function secret key for circuit C, generate t function secret keys for the sFEs, each of which computes the output of the ith TFHE partial decryption of the result of homomorphic evaluation of the circuit C on TFHE.ct.
- Finally, to evaluate a functional secret key for circuit C on a ciphertext, combine the results of the TFHE threshold decryptions obtained via the t outputs of sFE evaluation of the t function secret keys.

The correctness of our scheme follows immediately from the correctness properties of the TFHE scheme. *Intuitively*, security seems to hold because of the following argument. Upon combining λ^2 independent, random instances of the weak sFE, with overwhelming probability, at least one must remain secure. As long as a single instance remains secure, the corresponding secret key for TFHE will remain hidden from the adversary. Now, TFHE guarantees semantic security against any adversary that fails to obtain even one secret key, and as a result, the resulting FE scheme should be secure. While this intuition sounds deceptively simple, many of these intuitive leaps assume information-theoretic security. Thus, this template evades a formal proof in the computational setting, and we must work harder to obtain our proof of security, as we now sketch.

From a cryptographic point of view, one of the early hurdles when trying to obtain such a proof is the following. A reduction must rely on an adversary that breaks security of the final FE scheme with *any* noticeable probability, in order to break $\frac{1}{\lambda}$ security of one of the λ^2 "weak" FEs. However, the reduction does not know which of the λ^2 repetitions is secure, and therefore does not directly know where to embed an external challenge. To deal with this, we rely on the concept of a *hardcore measure* [Imp95, MT10]. Roughly speaking, we obtain measures of probability mass roughly $\frac{1}{\lambda}$ over the randomness of the sFE schemes, such that no efficient adversary can break the security of the sFE scheme even with some inverse subexponential probability.

However, unfortunately these hardcore measures can depend on other parameters in our system, such as the TFHE public key. And unfortunately, this dependence is via extreme inefficiency; the hardcore measure is not efficiently sampleable. This means that, for example, the hardcore measure could in principle contain information about the TFHE master secret key. If this information is leaked to the adversary, this would destroy the security of our scheme.

We overcome this issue through the following idea, which can be made formal via the work on simulating auxiliary input [JP14, CCL18]. Because the hardcore measure has reasonable probability mass $\frac{1}{\lambda}$, it cannot *verifiably* contain useful information to the adversary. For example, even if the hardcore distribution revealed the first few bits of the TFHE master secret key, the adversary could not *know* for sure that these bits were in fact the correct bits. Indeed, we use the works of [JP14, CCL18] to make this idea precise, and show that the hardcore measures can be simulated in a way that fools all efficient adversaries, with a simulation that runs in subexponential time.

Finally, using complexity leveraging, we can set the security of the TFHE scheme to be such that its security holds against adversaries whose running time exceeds this simulation. Thus, for example, even if the original hardcore measure was revealing partial information about the TFHE master secret key, we show that we can give the adversary access to a simulated hardcore measure that provably does not reveal any useful information about the TFHE master secret key, and the adversary can't tell the difference!

In this way, we accomplish security amplification for sFE, which allows us to achieve $i\mathcal{O}$ for general circuits when combined with previous work [AS17, LT17]. Along the way, our amplification technique also shows that we can weaken the security requirement on the relatively new notion of a 3-block-local PRG due to [LT17], in a way that still allows us to achieve $i\mathcal{O}$. Our amplification result can be stated as the following theorem.

Theorem 5. *Assuming there exists a constant $c > 0$ and there exists:*

- $(2^{\lambda^c}, \mathsf{adv} = 1 - 1/\lambda)$-*secure sublinear semi-functional FE scheme for $\mathcal{C}_{n',s'}$.*
- $(2^{\lambda^c}, 2^{-\lambda^c})$-*secure threshold homomorphic encryption scheme.*
- $(2^{\lambda^c}, 2^{-\lambda^c})$-*secure PRFs in NC^1.*
- $(2^{\lambda^c}, 2^{-\lambda^c})$-*secure statistically binding commitments.*

There exists a sublinear secret key FE scheme for circuit class $\mathcal{C}_{n,s}$ with $(2^{\lambda^{c'}}, 2^{-\lambda^{c'}})$ security for some constant $c' > 0$.

Combining these ideas, we obtain the following result.

Theorem 6. *Assuming*

- *LWE secure against subexponential sized circuits.*
- *Secure Three restricted FE scheme.*
- *PRGs with*

- Stretch of $k^{1+\epsilon}$ (length of input being k bits) for some constant $\epsilon > 0$.
- Block locality three.
- Security with negl distinguishing gap against adversaries of subexponential size.

- Perturbation resilient generators implementable by three restricted FE scheme with:
  - Stretch of $k^{1+\epsilon}$ for some $\epsilon > 0$.
  - Security with distinguishing gap $1 - 1/\lambda$ against adversaries of subexponential size.

there exists a secure iO scheme for P/poly.

In a follow-up to our work [JLMS19] showed a construction of a d-restricted FE scheme for any constant $d \geq 3$ from SXDH over bilinear maps.

Theorem 7 ([JS18, LM18, JLMS19]). *Assuming SXDH over bilinear maps, there exists a construction of a three-restricted FE scheme.*

Thus, in full generality we can prove the following result.

Theorem 8. *Let* $\mathsf{adv}_1, \mathsf{adv}_2$ *be two distinguishing gaps such that* $\mathsf{adv}_1 + \mathsf{adv}_2 \leq 1 - 1/p(\lambda)$ *for any fixed polynomial* $p(\lambda) > 1$. *Then assuming,*

- LWE secure against adversaries of subexponential size.
- SXDH secure against adversaries of subexponential size.
- PRGs with
  - Stretch of $k^{1+\epsilon}$ (length of input being k bits) for some constant $\epsilon > 0$.
  - Block locality three.
  - Security with distinguishing gap bounded by adv_1 against adversaries of subexponential size.
- Perturbation resilient generators implementable by three restricted FE scheme with:
  - Stretch of $k^{1+\epsilon}$ for some $\epsilon > 0$.
  - Security with distinguishing gap adv_2 against adversaries of subexponential size.

there exists a secure iO scheme for P/poly.

3.1   Reader's Guide

In the technical overview and the introduction, we have already described our notions of three restricted FE scheme and perturbation resilient generator (ΔRG). In the sequel, for clarity, we will denote by 3ΔRG a ΔRG that is implementable by three restricted FE. Below we give a high level description of various terms used above that we have not already discussed.

Tempered Cubic Encoding: Tempered cubic encoding is a natural abstraction encapsulating a 3ΔRG and cubic homomorphic evaluation. This framework is compatible with our notion of a three restricted FE scheme and is used to build Functional Encryption for cubic polynomials.

Semi-Functional FE for Cubic Polynomials. A semi-functional FE scheme for cubic polynomials (FE_3 for short) is a secret key functional encryption scheme supporting evaluation for cubic polynomials where the size of the ciphertext is linear in the number of inputs. It satisfies semi-functional security: where you can hard code secret values in the function key which will be decrypted only using a single special ciphertext (known as a semi-functional ciphertext). Note that all our primitives satisfy $1 - 1/\text{poly}(\lambda)$ security. They are finally amplified to construct fully secure primitives.

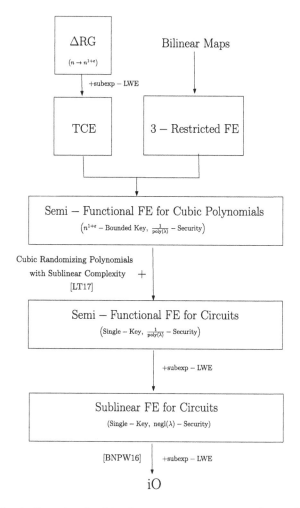

Fig. 1. Steps involved in the construction of $i\mathcal{O}$ in [AJS18].

Semi-Functional FE for Circuits. A semi-functional FE scheme for circuits is a secret key functional encryption scheme supporting evaluation of circuits where

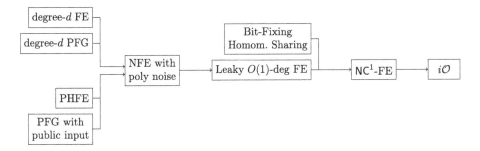

Fig. 2. Overview of constructions in [LM18] leading to $i\mathcal{O}$.

the size of the ciphertext is sublinear in the maximum size of circuit supported. This notion also satisfies semi-functional security.

We present a diagrammatic view of construction of $i\mathcal{O}$ in Fig. 1.

4 Technical Overview of Lin-Matt 18

We now describe techniques in [LM18] in more detail. An overview is depicted in Fig. 2.

NC^1-FE from PFGs and FE that Computes Them. It is known that to construct $i\mathcal{O}$, it suffices to construct secret-key FE schemes for computing NC^1 circuits that have *sublinearly compact* ciphertexts of size polynomial in the security parameter λ and input length N, and sublinear in the size S of the circuits computed. Towards constructing functional encryption schemes for NC^1, we follow the same two-step approach as previous works [Lin16a, LV16, Lin17, AS17]: They showed that the task of constructing NC^1-FE can be reduced to the task of constructing FE for computing NC^0 functions, i.e., constant-degree constant-locality polynomials, by converting any NC^1 function into a NC^0 function using randomized encoding and a low locality PRG. In this work, we develop a new technique for constructing constant-degree FE and a new bootstrapping method to NC^1-FE that is "leakage resilient".

Basic Ideas: Constant-degree FE via HE and Noisy Linear FE. Existing compact constant-degree FE schemes [GGHZ16, AS17, Lin17] use multilinear map groups to directly compute the constant-degree polynomial in the exponent. We here explore a different natural approach, that has already appeared in the literature [GVW12, GVW15, BTVW17, GKP+13, AR17, Agr18b] and that performs the computation homomorphically over the encrypted input via an HE scheme. The output ciphertext is eventually decrypted using multilinear maps.

The rough template is as follows: Let the FE scheme encrypt an input $\mathbf{x}$ using an HE scheme and a secret vector $\mathbf{s}$ to obtain a ciphertext $\mathbf{c}$. To compute a function f on $\mathbf{x}$, the decryptor can homomorphically evaluate f on $\mathbf{c}$ and obtain a ciphertext CT_f encrypting the output $\mathbf{y} = f(\mathbf{x})$. The two challenges are

- **privacy**—how to decrypt CT_f in a secure way that reveals only $\mathbf{y}$ and hides all other information about $\mathbf{x}$, and
- **integrity**—how to enforce that only ciphertexts associated with a "legitimate" function f (ones for which secret keys have been generated) can be decrypted.

Previous works [GVW12, GKP+13, GVW15, BTVW17, AR17, Agr18b] developed novel techniques for achieving privacy and integrity, using various tools from garbled circuits, partially hiding predicate encryption, to noisy linear FE. But the resulting schemes either achieve weaker security guarantees as in Predicate Encryption [GVW15, BTVW17], or lose ciphertext compactness [GKP+13, AR17], or make use of strong primitives that are themselves hard to instantiate [GVW12, Agr18b]. Building upon their techniques, we propose new ones toward solving the challenges.

Observe that the decryption of most HE schemes, such as [BV11, BGV12] based on LWE, involves *(i)* a linear operation, $L_{\text{dec}}(\mathsf{CT}_f, \mathbf{s})$ (e.g., $\langle \mathsf{CT}_f, \mathbf{s} \rangle$), which produces an *approximate* output, $\mathbf{y} + 2\mathbf{e}$, perturbed by a small noise vector $\mathbf{e}$, referred to as "half-decrypt", *(ii)* followed by a threshold function (complex, in NC^1) to remove the noise. Privacy entails that we must hide the secret $\mathbf{s}$ and the noise $\mathbf{e}$. Hiding the secret is relatively easy as we have FE schemes for computing a linear function, here L, over a secret, here $\mathbf{s}$, from various assumptions (e.g., DDH, LWE, Paillier). However, the output of the linear FE would be the approximate output $\mathbf{y} + 2\mathbf{e}$, and the noise $\mathbf{e}$ is *sensitive*, revealing information about the input $\mathbf{x}$, the noises used for generating the original ciphertext $\mathbf{c}$ encrypting $\mathbf{x}$, and (indirectly) the secret $\mathbf{s}$. On the other hand, removing the noise $\mathbf{e}$ requires a high-degree computation (such as $\bmod\, 2$). The works of [AR17, Agr18b] propose to hide $\mathbf{e}$ using another bigger smudging noise—compute instead the approximate output $\mathbf{y} + 2\mathbf{e} + 2\mathbf{Y}$ further shifted by a large noise $\mathbf{Y}$ that hides $\mathbf{e}$. Agrawal [Agr18b] further encapsulated the task to be done in a primitive called *noisy linear FE*, which performs a linear computation, here the half-decrypt, and adds a *fresh* noise to the decrypted output of every pair of ciphertext and secret key. Let us now delve deeper into noisy linear FE.

4.1 Noisy Linear Functional Encryption

Noisy secret-key FE schemes have the same syntax as regular secret-key FE schemes, but decrypting a ciphertext nct of $\mathbf{v}$ with a secret key nsk_L for a linear function L yields a perturbed output $L(\mathbf{v}) + \mathbf{Y}$ (over $\mathbb{Z}_p$ for some modulus p), where the noise $\mathbf{Y}$ is distributed indistinguishably to a distribution η—we call such a scheme a η-noisy linear FE. We further only require weak correctness in the sense that decryption only needs to succeed if all coordinates of $L(\mathbf{v})$ lie in a polynomially sized range, and $\mathbf{Y}$ is polynomially bounded.

In terms of security, we require a notion of 1-ciphertext simulation security in the sense that the simulator is required to be able to "program" the output of computation on the encrypted input of a challenge ciphertext. More specifically, there exists a simulator that can simulate a secret key nsk_L and a ciphertext $\mathsf{nct}^\star$ for input $\mathbf{v}^\star$ given only L and $L(\mathbf{v}^\star) + \mathbf{Y}$, where $\mathbf{Y}$ is sampled from η. However, in the secret key setting, adversaries cannot produce ciphertexts on their own and we must directly model security when multiple ciphertexts are available. On the other hand, is well know that simulation security is impossible when the number of ciphertexts is unbounded and ciphertexts are sublinearly compact. Instead, we do not require the simulator to "program" the outputs for all encrypted input, it only needs to do so for one challenge ciphertexts, and is given with the actual encrypted inputs for all other ciphertexts—hence the name 1-ciphertext simulation security. Note that this notion is not new, as many works achieve indistinguishability based security via showing such 1-ciphertext simulation security. More precisely, we require

$$\left\{ \mathsf{nsk}_L, \ \mathsf{nct}^\star, \ \{\mathsf{nct}_i\}_{i \in [t]} \right\} \approx \left\{ \mathbf{e} \leftarrow \eta \ : \ \mathsf{Sim}\Big(L, \ L(\mathbf{x}^\star) + \mathbf{e}, \ \{\mathbf{x}_i\}_{i \in [t]}\Big) \right\}.$$

where nsk_f and $\mathsf{nct}^\star$ are the challenge key and ciphertext and every nct_i is an honestly generated ciphertext for an arbitrary input x_i, which is given to the simulator.

Compared to noisy linear function encryption by Agrawal [Agr18a], our notion differs in three points: First, we parametrize the notion by the noise distribution η, while Agrawal's notion is parametrized by a bound on the decryption error and distributions restricting the adversary's challenge messages. Secondly, we only require weak correctness. And thirdly, we consider simulation-security, whereas Agrawal defines indistinguishability-based security.

Construction from PHFE and Noise Generator. There is a simple construction of an η-noisy secret-key linear FE scheme if there is a PHFE scheme for a function class $\mathcal{G}$ and a noise generator G in the same class whose outputs are indistinguishable to η. Take for example our PHFE scheme from bilinear map (Theorem 4) for computing multilinear cubic polynomials $g(\mathbf{z}_1, \mathbf{z}_2, \mathbf{z}_3)$ in $\mathbb{Z}_p$ with $\mathbf{z}_1$ public and $\mathbf{z}_2, \mathbf{z}_3$ private. Assume there is a family of noise generators and seed distributions $(G, \mathcal{D}^{sd}) \leftarrow \mathcal{N}\mathcal{G}$ observing the same structure, whose output distribution $G(\mathbf{s}_1, \mathbf{s}_2, \mathbf{s}_3)$ with $(\mathbf{s}_1, \mathbf{s}_2, \mathbf{s}_3 \leftarrow \mathcal{D}^{sd})$ is indistinguishable to η when $\mathbf{s}_1$ is made public. We can construct η-noisy linear FE as follows:

- To encrypt a vector $\mathbf{v}$, the encryptor samples a seed $(\mathbf{s}_1, \mathbf{s}_2, \mathbf{s}_3)$ and encrypts $\mathbf{z}_1 = \mathbf{s}_1$ as the public input, and $\mathbf{z}_2 = (\mathbf{v}\|\mathbf{s}_2), \mathbf{z}_3 = \mathbf{s}_3$ as the private inputs.
- To generate a key for a function f, it generates a key for the function $g(\mathbf{z}_1, \mathbf{z}_2, \mathbf{z}_3) = L(\mathbf{v}) + \mathbf{Y}$ where $\mathbf{Y} = G(\mathbf{s}_1, \mathbf{s}_2, \mathbf{s}_3)$.

Decryption clearly recovers $L(\mathbf{v}) + \mathbf{Y}$, where by the property of the noise generator G, $\mathbf{Y}$ is distributed indistinguishably to η. For the 1-ciphertext simulation security to hold, we correspondingly need the underlying PHFE to satisfy 1-ciphertext simulation security (defined similarly that a simulator can "program" the output for a single challenge ciphertext), which our construction achieves.

Finally, observe that the ciphertexts are sublinear compact, as long as G has superlinear stretch. We provide a formal description and proofs of the construction in the full version [LM18].

Back to Constant-Degree FE. Recall that we want to use a noisy linear FE scheme to perform the linear half decryption on the output ciphertext CT_f, $L_{\mathrm{dec}}(\mathsf{CT}_f, \mathbf{s})$, and obtain $\mathbf{y} + 2\mathbf{e} + 2\mathbf{Y}$ (think of η as a distribution over $2\mathbf{Y}$). We still face two challenges:

- **privacy:** Our PHFE from bilinear maps (and all known sublinearly compact degree-d FE from degree-d multilinear maps) only allows decryption if outputs reside in a polynomially sized range. (This is because computation is performed in the exponent, and outputs are extracted via brute force discrete logarithm.) This means $\mathbf{y} + 2\mathbf{e} + 2\mathbf{Y}$ must be polynomially bounded. However, as argued in the introduction, a polynomially-bounded $\mathbf{Y}$ cannot hide $\mathbf{e}$ entirely. But revealing $\mathbf{e}$ at even *one* coordinate potentially reveals information about $\mathbf{x}$.
- **integrity:** How can we ensure that only output ciphertexts CT_f for legitimate constant-degree polynomials f can be decrypted? To ensure that, we would like to give out a noisy linear FE secret key nsk for the function $L_{\mathrm{dec}}(\mathsf{CT}_f, \star)$ and ciphertext nct encrypting the HE secret key $\mathbf{s}$. However, the key generator has no idea what CT_f is.

For the privacy problem, we weaken the requirements on the noise generators, formulating PFG, so that outputs are polynomially bounded and $\mathbf{e}$ is guaranteed to be partially hidden; then, we manage the leakage on $\mathbf{e}$ to still achieve meaningful security. For the integrity problem, we follow the approach of [AR17, Agr18a] of using special (1-time) HE that has a special decryption equation. We elaborate in the next section.

4.2 Weak and Leaky Constant-Degree FE

Let's first consider the privacy problem: How to manage leakage of the value $\mathbf{e}_i$'s at a few coordinates i's? Since $\mathbf{e}_i$ does depend on $\mathbf{x}$, some information of $\mathbf{x}$ is for sure leaked. Hence, we aim for what is the best possible: ensuring that revealing $\mathbf{e}$ at *a few* coordinates translates to revealing $\mathbf{x}$ at *a few* coordinates, if the function computed has *small locality*. We show that this can be done, and construct constant-degree FE with (1-key) *weak and leaky* 1-ciphertext simulation security. Roughly speaking, it guarantees that for every distribution of $f \leftarrow \mathcal{FN}$ and every distribution of $\mathbf{x} \leftarrow \mathcal{X}$, the secret key sk_f for f and the ciphertext $\mathsf{CT}_\mathbf{x}$ for $\mathbf{x}$ can be simulated a simulator Sim using the output $y = f(x)$, as well as the value of $\mathbf{x}$ at a few coordinates. In addition, in the multi-ciphertext setting, the adversaries also see a set of additional ciphertexts $\mathsf{CT}_{\mathbf{x}_i}$ for arbitrary inputs $\mathbf{x}_i$, and the simulator is required to simulate them given the actual inputs $\mathbf{x}_i$. More precisely, there is correlated random variables K and x^* representing the set of leaked coordinates and their values, such that $|x^*| = |K| = o(\lambda)$ and

$$\{x, \ sk_f, \mathsf{CT}_x, \ \{\mathsf{CT}_{x_i}\}\} \ \approx \ \{x, \ \mathsf{Sim}\,((x^*, K), \ f, \ y = f(x), \ \{x_i\})\},$$
$$\text{where } (x^*, K) \leftarrow \mathsf{Fix}, \text{ and } x \leftarrow \mathcal{X}|_{x^*, K}.$$

In other words, given sk_f, CT_x, and many other ciphertexts the encrypted input x appears random up to a few coordinates being fixed and the output being y.

We now give some intuition on why weak and leaky simulation security is achievable. Assume that $\mathbf{Y} + \mathbf{e}$ reveals a few coordinates of $\mathbf{e}$, say with index set J, and hides all other coordinates. We carefully analyze what information $\mathbf{e}_J$ depends on: if the function computed has small locality, output elements in J depend only on *a few* input elements at coordinates J'. Suppose an ideal case where the HE scheme satisfies the following properties:

HE properties:

1. *Preserving locality:* the homomorphic evaluation preserves this locality and $\mathbf{e}_J$ depends only on ciphertexts $\mathbf{c}_{J'}$ encrypting $\mathbf{x}_{J'}$,
2. *Preserving entropy:* revealing information related to a few ciphertexts $\mathbf{c}_{J'}$ only reduces the entropy of $\mathbf{s}$ by a small amount, and
3. *Robustness:* the HE scheme used is *robust to small leakage of the secret key.*

We can assert that ciphertexts encrypting other coordinates of $\mathbf{x}$ outside J' remain hiding, and hence only a few coordinates of $\mathbf{x}$ at J' are leaked.

For the above argument to go through, we need a slightly stronger version of the flawed-smudging property: For any B-bounded noise vector distribution $\chi = e(\mathcal{R})$, where the noise $\mathbf{e}$ is the output of a local function over another distributional secret $\mathbf{w} \leftarrow \mathcal{R}$, there is a correlated random variable I such that

$$\{I, \ \mathbf{w}, \ \mathbf{Y} + e(\mathbf{w})\} \approx \{I, \ \mathbf{w}', \ \mathbf{Y} + e(\mathbf{w})\}, \text{ where } \mathbf{w}' \leftarrow \chi|_{\mathbf{w}_I, I}.$$

This means given $\mathbf{Y} + e(\mathbf{w})$, only a few coordinates of $\mathbf{w}$ get fixed and leaked. In our construction, $\mathbf{w}$ depends on the input $\mathbf{x}$, the HE secret $\mathbf{s}$, and the noises used originally for encrypting $\mathbf{x}$. The above property then allows us to bound what information of them is leaked through $\mathbf{e}$. We further show that this stronger flawed-smudging property is in fact implied by the normal flawed-smudging property that is agnostic of how $\mathbf{e}$ is generated.

Let us now consider the integrity problem: How can we ensure only CT_f for the right f is decrypted? The works of [AR17, Agr18b] presented HE schemes whose ciphertexts $\mathbf{c}_\mathbf{x}$ consists of $\mathbf{A}, \mathsf{hCT}_\mathbf{x}$, where $\mathbf{A}$ is public and independent of the input $\mathbf{x}$ (e.g., $\mathbf{A}$ could be LWE matrices, or RLWE scalars) and only $\mathsf{hCT}_\mathbf{x}$ depends on $\mathbf{x}$. Furthermore, homomorphic evaluation operates on $\mathbf{A}$ and $(\mathbf{A}, \mathsf{hCT}_\mathbf{x})$ respectively to obtain $\mathbf{A}_f$ and hCT_f, and decryption does[7]:

---

[7] The schemes in [AR17, Agr18a] has more complicated decryption equation, where the decryption noise is of form $\sum_i p_i \mathbf{e}_i$ where $\{p_i\}$ is a set of increasing moduli. Here we omit this complexity.

4. *Special decryption equation:*

$$\mathbf{s}_f = L_{\text{dec}}(\mathbf{A}_f, \mathbf{s}), \qquad \mathsf{hCT}_f + \mathbf{s}_f = f(\mathbf{x}) + 2\mathbf{e} \qquad (\text{mod } p)$$

We can view $\mathbf{s}_f$ as a decryption key for f and it is computed from $\mathbf{s}$ independently of hCT_f! We can now ensure integrity as follows:

- Fix $\mathbf{A}$ at set-up time. This means the same $\mathbf{A}$ is reused for all HE ciphertexts.
- The key generator publishes a noisy linear FE key nsk for $L_{\text{dec}}(\mathbf{A}_f, \star)$
- The encryptor publishes $\mathsf{hCT}_{\mathbf{x}}$ encrypting $\mathbf{x}$ using secret $\mathbf{s}$ and generates a noisy linear FE ciphertext nct encrypting $\mathbf{s}$.
- The decryptor decrypts $\mathsf{nct}, \mathsf{nsk}$ to obtain $\mathbf{s}_f + 2\mathbf{Y}$, and computes hCT_f from hCT, from which $\mathbf{y} + 2\mathbf{e} + 2\mathbf{Y}$ is revealed.

Note that since $\mathbf{A}$ is fixed and reused for all HE ciphertext, each secret key $\mathbf{s}$ can only be used once. This is not a problem as the encryptor can sample a fresh secret key $\mathbf{s}$ for each encryption.

Instantiating the HE Scheme. The question now is whether there is a HE scheme that simultaneously has the special decryption equation (property 4) and is robust to leakage (properties 1–3). The schemes in [AR17, Agr18a] unfortunately are complicated and we do not know how to analyze their robustness to leakage. Nevertheless, we manage to construct a HE scheme satisfying all 4 properties, based on the simple HE scheme by [BV11] from LWE. We sketch our design. First, it was shown in [GKPV10, AKPW13], that the LWE assumption is robust, in the sense that when the LWE secret $\mathbf{s}$ comes from a small domain (e.g., $[-1, 0, 1]^\lambda$), the hardness of LWE holds as long as $\mathbf{s}$ has sufficient entropy. Thus, it is easy to observe that the HE schemes of [BV11, BGV12] are robust. Furthermore, the simple BV-scheme without relinearization, which can already handle constant-degree computations, also satisfies properties *(1)* and *(2)*.

However, the simple-BV scheme does not have the special decryption equation. Inspired by [AR17, Agr18a], we use a recursive construction to homomorphically evaluate the BV-decryption itself similar to bootstrapping, but for a different purpose. In slightly more details, we can decompose the BV evaluation-and-decryption procedure $\mathsf{HE.Dec}(\mathbf{s}, \mathsf{HE.Eval}(f, \mathsf{hCT}))$ into a public part Pub that does not depend on the secret key $\mathbf{s}$ and a private part Priv that depends on $\mathbf{s}$.

$$\mathsf{CT}_f = \mathsf{Pub}(f, \mathsf{hCT}, \mathbf{A}) \qquad \mathbf{s}_f = \mathsf{Priv}(f, \mathbf{A}, \mathsf{hCT}, \mathbf{s})$$
$$\mathsf{CT}_f + \mathbf{s}_f = f(\mathbf{x}) + 2\mathbf{e}$$

A wishful thinking is giving out noisy linear FE key nsk for $\mathsf{Priv}(f, \mathbf{A}, \star, \star)$ and ciphertext nct for $(\mathsf{hCT}, \mathbf{s})$, to enable computing $\mathbf{s}_f$. This does not work as Priv has degree d in $\mathbf{s}$ and degree $d - 1$ in hCT, where d is the degree of f. The high degree in $\mathbf{s}$ can be dealt with as the encryptor can compute all degree d monomials in $\mathbf{s}$ and encrypt them, and there are only n^d of them where $n = |\mathbf{s}| = \text{poly}(\lambda)$. But, the same cannot be applied to hCT which is long (length $S^{1-\epsilon}$, where S is the output length of L) and encrypting even the quadratic monomials would make the ciphertexts non-compact. However, the good news is that the degree in hCT is $d-1$—one less than the degree of the computation f. Therefore, by recursively encrypting $((\mathsf{hCT},1)\otimes(\mathbf{s},1)\otimes(\mathbf{s},1))$ in a ciphertext hCT' using an independent secret key $\mathbf{s}'$, we can compute $\mathbf{s}_f$ by homomorphically evaluating Priv on hCT' in degree $d-1$ and then decrypt. The key observation is that the new private computation $\mathsf{Priv}'(\mathsf{Priv},\mathbf{A}',\mathsf{hCT}',\mathbf{s}')$ now has only degree $d-2$ in hCT'. Thus, we can recursively reduce the degree of private computation, till we obtain a scheme whose Priv is linear in its ciphertext hCT and degree 2 in its secret key $\mathbf{s}$. Hence,

$$\mathsf{Priv}(f,\mathbf{A},\mathsf{hCT},\mathbf{s}) = L_{f,\mathbf{A}}((\mathsf{hCT},1)\otimes(\mathbf{s},1)\otimes(\mathbf{s},1))$$

where the total the number of monomials to be encrypted is $|\mathsf{hCT}|n^2$, keeping sublinear compactness. In summary, our weak and leaky FE for local constant degree computation operates as follows:

- Fix $\mathbf{A}$ at set-up time.
- The key generator publishes a noisy linear FE key nsk for $L_{f,\mathbf{A}}$.
- The encryptor publishes a ciphertext hCT encrypting $\mathbf{x}$ under secret key $\mathbf{s}$ using our recursively constructed HE scheme, and generates a noisy linear FE ciphertext nct encrypting $(\mathsf{hCT},1)\otimes(\mathbf{s},1)\otimes(\mathbf{s},1)$.
- The decryptor decrypts $\mathsf{nct},\mathsf{nsk}$ to obtain $\mathbf{s}_f + 2\mathbf{Y}$ and computes $\mathsf{hCT}_f = \mathsf{Pub}(f,\mathsf{hCT},\mathbf{A})$, from which $\mathbf{y}+2\mathbf{e}+2\mathbf{Y}$ is revealed.

The above description is simplified; please see the full paper [LM18] for a formal description and analysis of our constant degree FE scheme.

4.3 New Bootstrapping to FE for NC_1

We next present a new bootstrapping technique to FE for NC^1 from weak and leaky constant-degree FE. Our bootstrapping follows the same paradigm as previous works [Lin16a, LV16, Lin17, AS17, LV17]: it uses a randomized encoding [IK02, AIK04] to transform an NC^1 computation $g(v)$ into a simple constant-degree constant-locality polynomial $\hat{g}(v;r)$, and uses a constant locality PRG to supply pseudorandom coins $r = \mathsf{PRG}(\mathsf{Seed})$ needed for the randomized encoding. The fact that the underlying constant-degree FE is weak and leaky means both the input v, as well as the PRG seed Seed may be fixed and leaked at a few coordinates. To deal with this, we introduce a new primitive called *Bit-Fixing Homomorphic Sharing* in order to make the original computation g robust.

Our (T, t_1, t_2)-bit-fixing homomorphic sharing resembles the recent new concept of Homomorphic Secret Sharing (HSS) [BGI15] in syntax, but differs in security and efficiency requirements. It enables compiling a single computation $g(v)$ into a collection of computations $o_1 = h_1(x_1),\ldots,o_T = h_T(x_T)$ that operate on a secret sharing $x_1,\ldots,x_T$ of the original input v, and from the collection of output shares $o_1,\ldots,o_T$, the original output $g(v)$ can be reconstructed. Security ensures that the original input v remains hidden, given all output shares $o_1,\ldots,o_T$ and a subset of t_2 input shares. Moreover, the security is robust to a few t_1 bits in the input shares being fixed. In terms of efficiency, we allow the output share size to scale with the size of the computation g, however, it should not depend on the number of computations to be preformed—in other words, the shares are reusable.

In comparison, HSS shares need to be succinct and output reconstruction needs to be simple, which are not required here. In terms of security, HSS is secure against an adversary seeing a subset of the input shares only. From these input shares, the adversaries can always derive the corresponding output shares, but not all output shares. In contrast, our bit-fixing homomorphic sharing is secure against adversaries seeing all output shares. Note, however, HSS with additive reconstruction i.e., $o = \sum_i o_i$, does satisfy this stronger security, since the adversaries knowing the output o can easily reverse sample the missing additive output shares[8].

We give a construction of bit-fixing homomorphic sharing BF from multi-key FHE with threshold decryption as constructed in [MW16], which roughly works as follows:

- BFsetup samples a CRS crs for the multi-key FHE.
- BFshare shares a string v as follow: It additively shares v into $v = \text{ss}_1 \oplus \ldots \oplus \text{ss}_T$, generates T key-pairs (PK_i, sk_i) of the multi-key FHE scheme, and encrypts the ith share ss_i under PK_i to obtain ciphertext CT_i. It additionally samples a PRF key K_i. Finally, the i'th share is set to

$$x_i = \left\{ \{\text{CT}_i, \text{PK}_i\}_{i \in [T]}, sk_i, K_i \right\}$$

- BFeval on input crs, x_i, i, g evaluates g on the i'th share as follows: It homomorphically evaluates the function g on all ciphertexts $\text{CT}_1, \ldots, \text{CT}_T$ obtaining CT_f. By properties of the multi-key FHE scheme, this output ciphertexts can be decrypted in a distributed way using each secret key sk_i independently. Hence, the i'th output share o_i is set to the value decrypted from CT_g by sk_i. (The decryption procedure of MKFHE is actually randomized. BFeval uses the PRF K_i to generate the pseudorandom coins).
- BFdec reconstructs the final output o from $o_1, \cdots, o_T$ using the reconstruction procedure of the multi-key FHE.

Security of this scheme follows simply from the security of the multi-key FHE scheme and the fact that less than T additive shares ss_i reveal nothing about v.

Next, to construct FE for NC_1, instead of using our weak and leaky constant-degree FE to compute the randomized encodings $\{\text{RE}(g_j, v; \text{PRG}_j(\text{Seed}))\}_j$ for each output bit $g_j(v)$ directly, where $\text{PRG}_i(\text{Seed})$ denotes the j'th chunk of output bits of PRG, we compute the randomized encodings $\{\text{RE}(\text{BFeval}, (\text{crs}, x_i, i, g_j); \text{PRG}_{i,j}(\text{Seed}))\}_{i \in [T], j}$ for evaluating each g_j on each input share x_i. By the weak and leaky security of constant-degree FE, only a few coordinates of its encrypted input, here $\{(\text{crs}x_i, i, g)\}$ and Seed, are leaked. Small leakage on $\{(\text{crs}x_i, i, g)\}$ alone is harmless, as the security of bit-fixing

---

[8] Thanks Yuval Ishai and Elette Boyal for pointing this out.

homomorphic sharing ensures that the original input v would remain hidden under such leakage.

However, small leakage on Seed is problematic. Consider a typical local PRG where every output bit depends on $O(1)$ randomly chosen seed bits. Since PRG maps $S^{1-\alpha}$ bits to S bits where S is proportional the size of g, each seed bit Seed_k influences a large number, S^ϵ on average, of output bits. If Seed_k is leaked, all these output bits are no longer pseudorandom—call them corrupted. In turn, all the randomized encodings that use these output bits are no longer hiding, which may leak all input shares x_i. To circumvent this, instead of having only a single set of shares $\{x_i\}_{i\in[T]}$, we will have $M = S^{1-\alpha}$ sets of shares $\{x_i^t\}_{t\in[M],i\in[T]}$. We divide the output bits of g into M chunks, each containing S^α bits, and the t'th chunk is computed using the t'th set of input shares as described above. Why does this help? Suppose that the locations of the corrupted PRG output bits are distributed randomly. Since there are only about $\mathrm{poly}(\lambda)S^\alpha$ corrupted output bits, whereas way more $M = S^{1-\alpha}$ chunks, with overwhelming probability, no chunk ends up using more than λ corrupted PRG output bits. As a result, for each set of input shares $\{x_i^t\}$, at most λ input shares are leaked, and the security of bit fixing homomorphic sharing kicks in again, and hence v is hidden. To ensure that corrupted PRG output bits indeed distribute randomly, we apply a random permutation π to the output of the PRG. In other words, the i'th pseudorandom bit is the $\pi(i)$'th PRG output bit.

In summary, our FE scheme for NC^1 depth Dep proceeds as follows: DFE is our weak and leaky FE for local constant degree computation.

FE.Setup(1^λ): Generate a DFE master secret key DMSK, and a CRS for the bit-fixing homomorphic sharing scheme crs. Output $\mathsf{MSK} = (\mathsf{DMSK}, \mathrm{crs})$.

FE.KeyGen(MSK, g): g is a NC_1 function with input-length N, output-length S, and depth Dep. Assume w.l.o.g. that every output bit g_i is computable in some fixed polynomial size $= \mathrm{poly}(\lambda)$.[9]

– Generate a polynomial f as follows:
  - Divide the output bits of g into $M = S^{1-\alpha}$ (assume for convenience that M divides S) consecutive chunks $I_1, \ldots, I_M$, where chunk I_j includes output bits $(j-1)S/M + 1, \ldots, jS/M$. For every $j \in [M]$, let $g_{I_j} = \{g_k\}_{k\in I_j}$ denote the collection of circuits that computes output bits in chunk I_j.
  - For every $j \in [M]$ and $i \in [\lambda]$, let D_i^j be the circuit that on input the i'th share x_i^j of the j'th sharing $\mathbf{x}^j$ of v, homomorphically evaluates g_{I_j}, i.e.,

$$D_i^j(x_i^j) = \mathsf{BFeval}(\mathrm{crs}, x_i^j, i, g_{I_j}) = o_i^j.$$

  - Choose a random permutation $\pi \colon [\lambda] \times [M] \times [\phi] \to [\lambda M \phi]$. For every $j \in [M]$ and $i \in [\lambda]$, let f_i^j be the following function:

$$f_i^j(x_i^j, \mathsf{Seed}) = \mathsf{REnc}\big(D_i^j, x_i^j \; ; \; \mathsf{PRG}_{\Pi_i^j}(\mathsf{Seed})\big).$$

---

[9] If not, one can always use garbled circuits to turn g into another circuit where every output bit is computable in size $\mathrm{poly}(\lambda)$, at the cost of increasing the size, input length, and output length of the circuit by a multiplicative $\mathrm{poly}(\lambda)$ factor.

Above, $\mathsf{PRG}_{\Pi_i^j}(\mathsf{Seed})$ contains PRG output bits at locations $\{\pi(i,j,k)\}_{k \in [\phi]}$ determined by the random permutation π and is sufficiently long for supplying the random coins needed for computing the randomized encoding. Finally, set

$$f\left(\left\{\mathbf{x}^j = \{x_i^j\}_{i \in [\lambda]}\right\}_{j \in [M]}, \mathsf{Seed}\right) := \left\{f_i^j(x_i^j, \mathsf{Seed})\right\}_{j,i}.$$

- Generate a DFE secret key of f, $\mathsf{D}sk \leftarrow \mathsf{DFE.KeyGen}(\mathsf{DMSK}, f)$.
  This can be done since by the efficiency of the bit-fixing homomorphic sharing and randomized encoding, the input length and size of f is $N' = |\{x_i^j\}| + |\mathsf{Seed}| = \mathrm{poly}(\lambda, s)\lambda M + \mathrm{poly}(\lambda)S^{1-\alpha} = \mathrm{poly}(\lambda)S^{1-\alpha}$ and $S' = |f_i^j|\lambda M = \mathrm{poly}(\lambda)S$. Since the AIK randomized encoding algorithm REnc and PRG both have constant locality, f also has constant locality ℓ. Moreover, over the field $\mathbb{Z}_2$, it has at most degree ℓ.

Output $sk = \mathsf{D}sk$.
  $\mathsf{FE.Enc}(\mathsf{MSK}, v)$: On input $\mathsf{MSK} = (\mathsf{DMSK}, \mathrm{crs})$ and $v \in \{0,1\}^N$, do:

- For every $j \in [M]$, generate the j'th BF sharing of v, $\mathbf{x}^j = \{x_i^j\}_{i \in [\lambda]} \leftarrow \mathsf{BFshare}(\mathrm{crs}, v)$.
- Sample randomly a PRG seed Seed.
- Encrypt $X = (\{\mathbf{x}^j\}_j, \mathsf{Seed})$ using DFE, $\mathsf{DCT} \leftarrow \mathsf{DFE.Enc}(\mathsf{DMSK}, X)$.

Output $\mathsf{CT} = \mathsf{DCT}$.
  $\mathsf{FE.Dec}(sk, \mathsf{CT})$: On input $sk = \mathsf{D}sk$ and $\mathsf{CT} = \mathsf{DCT}$, do

- Decrypt the DFE ciphertext DCT with the secret key $\mathsf{D}sk$ to obtain $y = f(X) = \mathsf{DFE.Dec}(\mathsf{D}sk, \mathsf{DCT})$.
- Parse $y = \{y_i^j\}$, and for every $j \in [M]$ and $i \in [\lambda]$, decode y_i^j using REval to obtain $o_i^j = \mathsf{REval}(y_i^j)$.
- For every $j \in [M]$, decode the output shares $\{o_i^j\}_{i \in [\lambda]}$ to obtain the actual output $u^j = \mathsf{BFdec}(\mathrm{crs}, \{o_i^j\})$.

Output $u = \{u^j\}$.
  Correctness of the construction can be shown as follows: By the correctness of DFE, we have

$$y = f(X) = \left\{y_i^j = f_i^j(x_i^j, \mathsf{Seed})\right\}_{j,i},$$
$$y_i^j = \mathsf{REnc}(D_i^j, x_i^j \ ; \ \mathsf{PRG}_{\Pi_i^j}(\mathsf{Seed})).$$

By the correctness of RE, we have that

$$o_i^j = \mathsf{REval}(y_i^j) = D_i^j(x_i^j) = \mathsf{BFeval}(\mathrm{crs}, x_i^j, i, g_{I_j}) = o_i^j.$$

By the correctness of BF, we have that $u^j = g_{I_j}(v)$.
  In the full version [LM18], we formally prove that the above construction is a sublinearly compact secret key FE scheme for NC_1 satisfying standard indistinguishability-based security, which implies $i\mathcal{O}$.

Acknowledgments. Huijia Lin and Christian Matt thank Shweta Agrawal for sharing an early version of [Agr18a], and Stefano Tessaro for many general discussions. This work was done in part when both of these two authors were at the University of California, Santa Barbara.

Prabhanjan Ananth, Aayush Jain and Amit Sahai thank Dakshita Khurana for collaboration in the initial stages of this research, for contributing to the writeup, and for countless discussions and comments supporting this work and improving the write up. Eventually, the current set of authors had to reluctantly agree to Dakshita's repeated requests to not be listed in the set of authors, and hence she is in these acknowledgements instead. We thank Boaz Barak, Sam Hopkins and Pravesh Kothari for insights and extremely helpful suggestions about how attacks based on the Sum of Squares paradigm could impact our new assumptions on perturbation-resilient generators.

Huijia Lin and Christian Matt were supported by NSF grants CNS-1528178, CNS-1514526, CNS-1652849 (CAREER), a Hellman Fellowship, the Defense Advanced Research Projects Agency (DARPA) and Army Research Office (ARO) under Contract No. W911NF-15-C-0236, and a subcontract No. 2017-002 through Galois. The views expressed are those of the authors and do not reflect the official policy or position of the Department of Defense, the National Science Foundation, or the U.S. Government.

Prabhanjan Ananth, Aayush Jain and Amit Sahai were supported in part from a DARPA/ARL SAFEWARE award, NSF Frontier Award 1413955, and NSF grant 1619348, BSF grant 2012378, a Xerox Faculty Research Award, a Google Faculty Research Award, an equipment grant from Intel, and an Okawa Foundation Research Grant. Aayush Jain is also supported by a Google PhD fellowship award in Privacy and Security. This material is based upon work supported by the Defense Advanced Research Projects Agency through the ARL under Contract W911NF-15-C- 0205. The views expressed are those of the authors and do not reflect the official policy or position of the Department of Defense, the National Science Foundation, the U.S. Government or Google.

References

[AB15]   Applebaum, B., Brakerski, Z.: Obfuscating circuits via composite-order graded encoding. In: Dodis, Y., Nielsen, J.B. (eds.) TCC 2015. LNCS, vol. 9015, pp. 528–556. Springer, Heidelberg (2015). https://doi.org/10.1007/978-3-662-46497-7_21

[AFV11] Agrawal, S., Freeman, D.M., Vaikuntanathan, V.: Functional encryption for inner product predicates from learning with errors. In: Lee, D.H., Wang, X. (eds.) ASIACRYPT 2011. LNCS, vol. 7073, pp. 21–40. Springer, Heidelberg (2011). https://doi.org/10.1007/978-3-642-25385-0_2

[AG11]   Arora, S., Ge, R.: New algorithms for learning in presence of errors. In: Aceto, L., Henzinger, M., Sgall, J. (eds.) ICALP 2011. LNCS, vol. 6755, pp. 403–415. Springer, Heidelberg (2011). https://doi.org/10.1007/978-3-642-22006-7_34

[AGIS14a] Ananth, P., Gupta, D., Ishai, Y., Sahai, A.: Optimizing obfuscation: avoiding Barrington's theorem. In: Proceedings of the 2014 ACM SIGSAC Conference on Computer and Communications Security, CCS 2014, pp. 646–658. ACM, New York (2014)

[Agr17a] Agrawal, S.: Stronger security for reusable garbled circuits, general definitions and attacks. In: Katz, J., Shacham, H. (eds.) CRYPTO 2017. LNCS, vol. 10401, pp. 3–35. Springer, Cham (2017). https://doi.org/10.1007/978-3-319-63688-7_1

[Agr18a] Agrawal, S.: New methods for indistinguishability obfuscation: bootstrapping and instantiation. Cryptology ePrint Archive, Report 2018/633 (2018). https://eprint.iacr.org/2018/633

[Agr18b] Agrawal, S.: Personal communication and a previous version of eprint report 2018/633 (2018)

[AIK04] Applebaum, B., Ishai, Y., Kushilevitz, E.: Cryptography in NC0. In: 45th Annual IEEE Symposium on Foundations of Computer Science, pp. 166–175, October 2004

[AJS18] Ananth, P., Jain, A., Sahai, A.: Indistinguishability obfuscation without multilinear maps: iO from LWE, bilinear maps, and weak pseudorandomness. Cryptology ePrint Archive, Report 2018/615 (2018). https://eprint.iacr.org/2018/615

[AKPW13] Alwen, J., Krenn, S., Pietrzak, K., Wichs, D.: Learning with rounding, revisited. In: Canetti, R., Garay, J.A. (eds.) CRYPTO 2013. LNCS, vol. 8042, pp. 57–74. Springer, Heidelberg (2013). https://doi.org/10.1007/978-3-642-40041-4_4

[AL16] Applebaum, B., Lovett, S.: Algebraic attacks against random local functions and their countermeasures. In: Proceedings of the Forty-Eighth Annual ACM Symposium on Theory of Computing, STOC 2016, pp. 1087–1100. ACM, New York (2016)

[AR17] Agrawal, S., Rosen, A.: Functional encryption for bounded collusions, revisited. In: Kalai, Y., Reyzin, L. (eds.) TCC 2017. LNCS, vol. 10677, pp. 173–205. Springer, Cham (2017). https://doi.org/10.1007/978-3-319-70500-2_7

[AS17] Ananth, P., Sahai, A.: Projective arithmetic functional encryption and indistinguishability obfuscation from degree-5 multilinear maps. In: Coron, J.-S., Nielsen, J.B. (eds.) EUROCRYPT 2017. LNCS, vol. 10210, pp. 152–181. Springer, Cham (2017). https://doi.org/10.1007/978-3-319-56620-7_6

[BBKK17] Barak, B., Brakerski, Z., Komargodski, I., Kothari, P.: Limits on low-degree pseudorandom generators (or: sum-of-squares meets program obfuscation). Electron. Colloq. Comput. Complex. (ECCC) 24, 60 (2017)

[BBKK18] Barak, B., Brakerski, Z., Komargodski, I., Kothari, P.K.: Limits on low-degree pseudorandom generators (or: sum-of-squares meets program obfuscation). In: Nielsen, J.B., Rijmen, V. (eds.) EUROCRYPT 2018. LNCS, vol. 10821, pp. 649–679. Springer, Cham (2018). https://doi.org/10.1007/978-3-319-78375-8_21

[BCFG17] Baltico, C.E.Z., Catalano, D., Fiore, D., Gay, R.: Practical functional encryption for quadratic functions with applications to predicate encryption. In: Katz, J., Shacham, H. (eds.) CRYPTO 2017. LNCS, vol. 10401, pp. 67–98. Springer, Cham (2017). https://doi.org/10.1007/978-3-319-63688-7_3

[BFM14] Brzuska, C., Farshim, P., Mittelbach, A.: Indistinguishability obfuscation and UCEs: the case of computationally unpredictable sources. In: Garay, J.A., Gennaro, R. (eds.) CRYPTO 2014. LNCS, vol. 8616, pp. 188–205. Springer, Heidelberg (2014). https://doi.org/10.1007/978-3-662-44371-2_11

[BGG+18] Boneh, D., et al.: Threshold cryptosystems from threshold fully homo-morphic encryption. In: Shacham, H., Boldyreva, A. (eds.) CRYPTO 2018. LNCS, vol. 10991, pp. 565–596. Springer, Cham (2018). https://doi.org/10.1007/978-3-319-96884-1_19

[BGH+15] Brakerski, Z., Gentry, C., Halevi, S., Lepoint, T., Sahai, A., Tibouchi, M.: Cryptanalysis of the quadratic zero-testing of GGH. Cryptology ePrint Archive, Report 2015/845 (2015). http://eprint.iacr.org/

[BGI+01] Barak, B., et al.: On the (im)possibility of obfuscating programs. In: Kilian, J. (ed.) CRYPTO 2001. LNCS, vol. 2139, pp. 1–18. Springer, Heidelberg (2001). https://doi.org/10.1007/3-540-44647-8_1

[BGI15] Boyle, E., Gilboa, N., Ishai, Y.: Function secret sharing. In: Oswald, E., Fischlin, M. (eds.) EUROCRYPT 2015. LNCS, vol. 9057, pp. 337–367. Springer, Heidelberg (2015). https://doi.org/10.1007/978-3-662-46803-6_12

[BGK+14a] Barak, B., Garg, S., Kalai, Y.T., Paneth, O., Sahai, A.: Protecting obfuscation against algebraic attacks. In: Nguyen, P.Q., Oswald, E. (eds.) EUROCRYPT 2014. LNCS, vol. 8441, pp. 221–238. Springer, Heidelberg (2014). https://doi.org/10.1007/978-3-642-55220-5_13

[BGMZ18] Bartusek, J., Guan, J., Ma, F., Zhandry, M.: Return of GGH15: provable security against zeroizing attacks. In: Beimel, A., Dziembowski, S. (eds.) TCC 2018. LNCS, vol. 11240, pp. 544–574. Springer, Cham (2018). https://doi.org/10.1007/978-3-030-03810-6_20

[BGV12] Brakerski, Z., Gentry, C., Vaikuntanathan, V.: (Leveled) fully homo-morphic encryption without bootstrapping. In: Proceedings of the 3rd Innovations in Theoretical Computer Science Conference, ITCS 2012, pp. 309–325. ACM, New York (2012)

[BHJ+19] Barak, B., Hopkins, S.B., Jain, A., Kothari, P., Sahai, A.: Sum-of-squares meets program obfuscation, revisited. In: Ishai, Y., Rijmen, V. (eds.) EUROCRYPT 2019. LNCS, vol. 11476, pp. 226–250. Springer, Cham (2019). https://doi.org/10.1007/978-3-030-17653-2_8

[BMSZ16] Badrinarayanan, S., Miles, E., Sahai, A., Zhandry, M.: Post-zeroizing obfuscation: new mathematical tools, and the case of evasive circuits. In: Fischlin, M., Coron, J.-S. (eds.) EUROCRYPT 2016. LNCS, vol. 9666, pp. 764–791. Springer, Heidelberg (2016). https://doi.org/10.1007/978-3-662-49896-5_27

[BPR15] Bitansky, N., Paneth, O., Rosen, A.: On the cryptographic hardness of finding a nash equilibrium. In: FOCS (2015)

[BQ12] Bogdanov, A., Qiao, Y.: On the security of Goldreich's one-way function. Comput. Complex. **21**(1), 83–127 (2012)

[BR14a] Brakerski, Z., Rothblum, G.N.: Virtual black-box obfuscation for all circuits via generic graded encoding. In: Lindell, Y. (ed.) TCC 2014. LNCS, vol. 8349, pp. 1–25. Springer, Heidelberg (2014). https://doi.org/10.1007/978-3-642-54242-8_1

[BS02] Boneh, D., Silverberg, A.: Applications of multilinear forms to cryptog-raphy. Contemp. Math. **324**, 71–90 (2002)

[BSW11] Boneh, D., Sahai, A., Waters, B.: Functional encryption: definitions and challenges. In: Ishai, Y. (ed.) TCC 2011. LNCS, vol. 6597, pp. 253–273. Springer, Heidelberg (2011). https://doi.org/10.1007/978-3-642-19571-6_16

[BTVW17] Brakerski, Z., Tsabary, R., Vaikuntanathan, V., Wee, H.: Private constrained PRFs (and more) from LWE. In: Kalai, Y., Reyzin, L. (eds.) TCC 2017. LNCS, vol. 10677, pp. 264–302. Springer, Cham (2017). https://doi.org/10.1007/978-3-319-70500-2_10

[BV11] Brakerski, Z., Vaikuntanathan, V.: Efficient fully homomorphic encryption from (standard) LWE. In: 2011 IEEE 52nd Annual Symposium on Foundations of Computer Science, pp. 97–106, October 2011

[BWZ14] Boneh, D., Wu, D.J., Zimmerman, J.: Immunizing multilinear maps against zeroizing attacks. IACR Cryptology ePrint Archive 2014:930 (2014)

[CCL18] Chen, Y.-H., Chung, K.-M., Liao, J.-J.: On the complexity of simulating auxiliary input. IACR Cryptology ePrint Archive 2018:171 (2018)

[CEMT09] Cook, J., Etesami, O., Miller, R., Trevisan, L.: Goldreich's one-way function candidate and myopic backtracking algorithms. In: Reingold, O. (ed.) TCC 2009. LNCS, vol. 5444, pp. 521–538. Springer, Heidelberg (2009). https://doi.org/10.1007/978-3-642-00457-5_31

[CGH+15] Coron, J.-S., et al.: Zeroizing without low-level zeroes: new MMAP attacks and their limitations. In: Gennaro, R., Robshaw, M. (eds.) CRYPTO 2015. LNCS, vol. 9215, pp. 247–266. Springer, Heidelberg (2015). https://doi.org/10.1007/978-3-662-47989-6_12

[CHL+15] Cheon, J.H., Han, K., Lee, C., Ryu, H., Stehlé, D.: Cryptanalysis of the multilinear map over the integers. In: Oswald, E., Fischlin, M. (eds.) EUROCRYPT 2015. LNCS, vol. 9056, pp. 3–12. Springer, Heidelberg (2015). https://doi.org/10.1007/978-3-662-46800-5_1

[CHN+16] Cohen, A., Holmgren, J., Nishimaki, R., Vaikuntanathan, V., Wichs, D.: Watermarking cryptographic capabilities. In: STOC (2016)

[CLR15] Cheon, J.H., Lee, C., Ryu, H.: Cryptanalysis of the new CLT multilinear maps. Cryptology ePrint Archive, Report 2015/934 (2015). http://eprint.iacr.org/

[CLT13a] Coron, J.-S., Lepoint, T., Tibouchi, M.: Practical multilinear maps over the integers. In: Canetti, R., Garay, J.A. (eds.) CRYPTO 2013. LNCS, vol. 8042, pp. 476–493. Springer, Heidelberg (2013). https://doi.org/10.1007/978-3-642-40041-4_26

[CLT15a] Coron, J.-S., Lepoint, T., Tibouchi, M.: New multilinear maps over the integers. In: Gennaro, R., Robshaw, M. (eds.) CRYPTO 2015. LNCS, vol. 9215, pp. 267–286. Springer, Heidelberg (2015). https://doi.org/10.1007/978-3-662-47989-6_13

[CM01] Cryan, M., Miltersen, P.B.: On pseudorandom generators in NC^0. In: Sgall, J., Pultr, A., Kolman, P. (eds.) MFCS 2001. LNCS, vol. 2136, pp. 272–284. Springer, Heidelberg (2001). https://doi.org/10.1007/3-540-44683-4_24

[CVW18] Chen, Y., Vaikuntanathan, V., Wee, H.: GGH15 beyond permutation branching programs: proofs, attacks, and candidates. In: Shacham, H., Boldyreva, A. (eds.) CRYPTO 2018. LNCS, vol. 10992, pp. 577–607. Springer, Cham (2018). https://doi.org/10.1007/978-3-319-96881-0_20

[DGG+16a] Döttling, N., Garg, S., Gupta, D., Miao, P., Mukherjee, P.: Obfuscation from low noise multilinear maps. IACR Cryptology ePrint Archive, Report 2016/599 (2016). https://eprint.iacr.org/2016/599

[GGG+14] Goldwasser, S., et al.: Multi-input functional encryption. In: Nguyen, P.Q., Oswald, E. (eds.) EUROCRYPT 2014. LNCS, vol. 8441, pp. 578–602. Springer, Heidelberg (2014). https://doi.org/10.1007/978-3-642-55220-5_32

[GGH13a] Garg, S., Gentry, C., Halevi, S.: Candidate multilinear maps from ideal lattices. In: Johansson, T., Nguyen, P.Q. (eds.) EUROCRYPT 2013. LNCS, vol. 7881, pp. 1–17. Springer, Heidelberg (2013). https://doi.org/10.1007/978-3-642-38348-9_1

[GGH+13b] Garg, S., Gentry, C., Halevi, S., Raykova, M., Sahai, A., Waters, B.: Candidate indistinguishability obfuscation and functional encryption for all circuits. In: 54th Annual IEEE Symposium on Foundations of Computer Science, FOCS 2013, Berkeley, CA, USA, 26–29 October 2013, pp. 40–49. IEEE Computer Society (2013)

[GGH15a] Gentry, C., Gorbunov, S., Halevi, S.: Graph-induced multilinear maps from lattices. In: Dodis, Y., Nielsen, J.B. (eds.) TCC 2015. LNCS, vol. 9015, pp. 498–527. Springer, Heidelberg (2015). https://doi.org/10.1007/978-3-662-46497-7_20

[GGHR14] Garg, S., Gentry, C., Halevi, S., Raykova, M.: Two-round secure MPC from indistinguishability obfuscation. In: Lindell, Y. (ed.) TCC 2014. LNCS, vol. 8349, pp. 74–94. Springer, Heidelberg (2014). https://doi.org/10.1007/978-3-642-54242-8_4

[GGHZ16] Garg, S., Gentry, C., Halevi, S., Zhandry, M.: Functional encryption without obfuscation. In: Kushilevitz, E., Malkin, T. (eds.) TCC 2016. LNCS, vol. 9563, pp. 480–511. Springer, Heidelberg (2016). https://doi.org/10.1007/978-3-662-49099-0_18

[GKP+13] Goldwasser, S., Kalai, Y.T., Popa, R.A., Vaikuntanathan, V., Zeldovich, N.: Reusable garbled circuits and succinct functional encryption. In: Boneh, D., Roughgarden, T., Feigenbaum, J. (eds.) Symposium on Theory of Computing Conference, STOC 2013, Palo Alto, CA, USA, 1–4 June 2013, pp. 555–564. ACM (2013)

[GKPV10] Goldwasser, S., Kalai, Y.T., Peikert, C., Vaikuntanathan, V.: Robustness of the learning with errors assumption. In: Proceedings of the Innovations in Computer Science - ICS 2010, Tsinghua University, Beijing, China, 5–7 January 2010, pp. 230–240 (2010)

[GLSW14] Gentry, C., Lewko, A.B., Sahai, A., Waters, B.: Indistinguishability obfuscation from the multilinear subgroup elimination assumption. IACR Cryptology ePrint Archive 2014:309 (2014)

[GMM+16a] Garg, S., Miles, E., Mukherjee, P., Sahai, A., Srinivasan, A., Zhandry, M.: Secure obfuscation in a weak multilinear map model. In: Hirt, M., Smith, A. (eds.) TCC 2016. LNCS, vol. 9986, pp. 241–268. Springer, Heidelberg (2016). https://doi.org/10.1007/978-3-662-53644-5_10

[GMW15] Gay, R., Méaux, P., Wee, H.: Predicate encryption for multi-dimensional range queries from lattices. In: Katz, J. (ed.) PKC 2015. LNCS, vol. 9020, pp. 752–776. Springer, Heidelberg (2015). https://doi.org/10.1007/978-3-662-46447-2_34

[Gol00] Goldreich, O.: Candidate one-way functions based on expander graphs. Electron. Colloq. Comput. Compl. (ECCC) 7(90) (2000)

[GPS16] Garg, S., Pandey, O., Srinivasan, A.: Revisiting the cryptographic hardness of finding a nash equilibrium. In: Robshaw, M., Katz, J. (eds.) CRYPTO 2016. LNCS, vol. 9815, pp. 579–604. Springer, Heidelberg (2016). https://doi.org/10.1007/978-3-662-53008-5_20

[GR07] Goldwasser, S., Rothblum, G.N.: On best-possible obfuscation. In: Vadhan, S.P. (ed.) TCC 2007. LNCS, vol. 4392, pp. 194–213. Springer, Heidelberg (2007). https://doi.org/10.1007/978-3-540-70936-7_11

[Gri01] Grigoriev, D.: Linear lower bound on degrees of positivstellensatz calculus proofs for the parity. Theor. Comput. Sci. **259**(1–2), 613–622 (2001)

[GSW13] Gentry, C., Sahai, A., Waters, B.: Homomorphic encryption from learning with errors: conceptually-simpler, asymptotically-faster, attribute-based. In: Canetti, R., Garay, J.A. (eds.) CRYPTO 2013. LNCS, vol. 8042, pp. 75–92. Springer, Heidelberg (2013). https://doi.org/10.1007/978-3-642-40041-4_5

[GVW12] Gorbunov, S., Vaikuntanathan, V., Wee, H.: Functional encryption with bounded collusions via multi-party computation. In: Safavi-Naini, R., Canetti, R. (eds.) CRYPTO 2012. LNCS, vol. 7417, pp. 162–179. Springer, Heidelberg (2012). https://doi.org/10.1007/978-3-642-32009-5_11

[GVW15] Gorbunov, S., Vaikuntanathan, V., Wee, H.: Predicate encryption for circuits from LWE. In: Gennaro, R., Robshaw, M. (eds.) CRYPTO 2015. LNCS, vol. 9216, pp. 503–523. Springer, Heidelberg (2015). https://doi.org/10.1007/978-3-662-48000-7_25

[Hal15] Halevi, S.: Graded encoding, variations on a scheme. IACR Cryptology ePrint Archive 2015:866 (2015)

[HJ15] Hu, Y., Jia, H.: Cryptanalysis of GGH map. IACR Cryptology ePrint Archive 2015:301 (2015)

[HJK+16] Hofheinz, D., Jager, T., Khurana, D., Sahai, A., Waters, B., Zhandry, M.: How to generate and use universal samplers. In: Cheon, J.H., Takagi, T. (eds.) ASIACRYPT 2016. LNCS, vol. 10032, pp. 715–744. Springer, Heidelberg (2016). https://doi.org/10.1007/978-3-662-53890-6_24

[HSW14] Hohenberger, S., Sahai, A., Waters, B.: Replacing a random oracle: full domain hash from indistinguishability obfuscation. In: Nguyen, P.Q., Oswald, E. (eds.) EUROCRYPT 2014. LNCS, vol. 8441, pp. 201–220. Springer, Heidelberg (2014). https://doi.org/10.1007/978-3-642-55220-5_12

[IK02] Ishai, Y., Kushilevitz, E.: Perfect constant-round secure computation via perfect randomizing polynomials. In: Widmayer, P., Eidenbenz, S., Triguero, F., Morales, R., Conejo, R., Hennessy, M. (eds.) ICALP 2002. LNCS, vol. 2380, pp. 244–256. Springer, Heidelberg (2002). https://doi.org/10.1007/3-540-45465-9_22

[Imp95] Impagliazzo, R.: Hard-core distributions for somewhat hard problems. In: FOCS, pp. 538–545 (1995)

[JLMS19] Jain, A., Lin, H., Matt, C., Sahai, A.: How to leverage hardness of constant-degree expanding polynomials over $\mathbb{R}$ to build $i\mathcal{O}$. In: Ishai, Y., Rijmen, V. (eds.) EUROCRYPT 2019. LNCS, vol. 11476, pp. 251–281. Springer, Cham (2019). https://doi.org/10.1007/978-3-030-17653-2_9

[JLS19] Jain, A., Lin, H., Sahai, A.: Removing the need block-local PRGs to build iO. IACR Cryptology ePrint Archive 2019 (2019)

[JP14] Jetchev, D., Pietrzak, K.: How to fake auxiliary input. In: Lindell, Y. (ed.) TCC 2014. LNCS, vol. 8349, pp. 566–590. Springer, Heidelberg (2014). https://doi.org/10.1007/978-3-642-54242-8_24

[JS18] Jain, A., Sahai, A.: How to leverage hardness of constant-degree polynomials over R to build iO. IACR Cryptology ePrint Archive 2018:973 (2018)

[KLW15] Koppula, V., Lewko, A.B., Waters, B.: Indistinguishability obfuscation for turing machines with unbounded memory. In: STOC (2015)

[KS99] Kipnis, A., Shamir, A.: Cryptanalysis of the HFE public key cryptosystem by relinearization. In: Wiener, M. (ed.) CRYPTO 1999. LNCS, vol. 1666, pp. 19–30. Springer, Heidelberg (1999). https://doi.org/10.1007/3-540-48405-1_2

[Lin16a] Lin, H.: Indistinguishability obfuscation from constant-degree graded encoding schemes. In: Fischlin, M., Coron, J.-S. (eds.) EUROCRYPT 2016. LNCS, vol. 9665, pp. 28–57. Springer, Heidelberg (2016). https://doi.org/10.1007/978-3-662-49890-3_2

[Lin17] Lin, H.: Indistinguishability obfuscation from SXDH on 5-linear maps and locality-5 PRGs. In: Katz, J., Shacham, H. (eds.) CRYPTO 2017. LNCS, vol. 10401, pp. 599–629. Springer, Cham (2017). https://doi.org/10.1007/978-3-319-63688-7_20

[LM18] Lin, H., Matt, C.: Pseudo flawed-smudging generators and their application to indistinguishability obfuscation. IACR Cryptology ePrint Archive 2018:646 (2018)

[LSS14] Langlois, A., Stehlé, D., Steinfeld, R.: GGHLite: more efficient multilinear maps from ideal lattices. In: Nguyen, P.Q., Oswald, E. (eds.) EUROCRYPT 2014. LNCS, vol. 8441, pp. 239–256. Springer, Heidelberg (2014). https://doi.org/10.1007/978-3-642-55220-5_14

[LT17] Lin, H., Tessaro, S.: Indistinguishability obfuscation from trilinear maps and block-wise local PRGs. In: Katz, J., Shacham, H. (eds.) CRYPTO 2017. LNCS, vol. 10401, pp. 630–660. Springer, Cham (2017). https://doi.org/10.1007/978-3-319-63688-7_21

[LV16] Lin, H., Vaikuntanathan, V.: Indistinguishability obfuscation from DDH-like assumptions on constant-degree graded encodings. In: FOCS, pp. 11–20. IEEE (2016)

[LV17] Lombardi, A., Vaikuntanathan, V.: Limits on the locality of pseudorandom generators and applications to indistinguishability obfuscation. In: Kalai, Y., Reyzin, L. (eds.) TCC 2017. LNCS, vol. 10677, pp. 119–137. Springer, Cham (2017). https://doi.org/10.1007/978-3-319-70500-2_5

[MF15] Minaud, B., Fouque, P.-A.: Cryptanalysis of the new multilinear map over the integers. Cryptology ePrint Archive, Report 2015/941 (2015). http://eprint.iacr.org/

[MST03] Mossel, E., Shpilka, A., Trevisan, L.: On e-biased generators in NC0. In: Proceedings of the 44th Annual IEEE Symposium on Foundations of Computer Science, pp. 136–145, October 2003

[MSZ16] Miles, E., Sahai, A., Zhandry, M.: Annihilation attacks for multilinear maps: cryptanalysis of indistinguishability obfuscation over GGH13. In: Robshaw, M., Katz, J. (eds.) CRYPTO 2016. LNCS, vol. 9815, pp. 629–658. Springer, Heidelberg (2016). https://doi.org/10.1007/978-3-662-53008-5_22

[MT10] Maurer, U., Tessaro, S.: A hardcore lemma for computational indistinguishability: security amplification for arbitrarily weak PRGs with optimal stretch. In: Micciancio, D. (ed.) TCC 2010. LNCS, vol. 5978, pp. 237–254. Springer, Heidelberg (2010). https://doi.org/10.1007/978-3-642-11799-2_15

[MW16] Mukherjee, P., Wichs, D.: Two round multiparty computation via multi-key FHE. In: Fischlin, M., Coron, J.-S. (eds.) EUROCRYPT 2016. LNCS, vol. 9666, pp. 735–763. Springer, Heidelberg (2016). https://doi.org/10.1007/978-3-662-49896-5_26

[MZ18] Ma, F., Zhandry, M.: The MMap strikes back: obfuscation and new multilinear maps immune to CLT13 zeroizing attacks. In: Beimel, A., Dziembowski, S. (eds.) TCC 2018. LNCS, vol. 11240, pp. 513–543. Springer, Cham (2018). https://doi.org/10.1007/978-3-030-03810-6_19

[O'N10] O'Neill, A.: Definitional issues in functional encryption. IACR Cryptology ePrint Archive 2010:556 (2010)

[OW14] O'Donnell, R., Witmer, D.: Goldreich's PRG: evidence for near-optimal polynomial stretch. In: 2014 IEEE 29th Conference on Computational Complexity (CCC), pp. 1–12, June 2014

[PST14a] Pass, R., Seth, K., Telang, S.: Indistinguishability obfuscation from semantically-secure multilinear encodings. In: Garay, J.A., Gennaro, R. (eds.) CRYPTO 2014. LNCS, vol. 8616, pp. 500–517. Springer, Heidelberg (2014). https://doi.org/10.1007/978-3-662-44371-2_28

[Reg05] Regev, O.: On lattices, learning with errors, random linear codes, and cryptography. In: STOC, pp. 84–93 (2005)

[Sch08] Schoenebeck, G.: Linear level lasserre lower bounds for certain k-CSPs. In: 49th Annual IEEE Symposium on Foundations of Computer Science, FOCS 2008, Philadelphia, PA, USA, 25–28 October 2008, pp. 593–602 (2008)

[SW05] Sahai, A., Waters, B.: Fuzzy identity-based encryption. In: Cramer, R. (ed.) EUROCRYPT 2005. LNCS, vol. 3494, pp. 457–473. Springer, Heidelberg (2005). https://doi.org/10.1007/11426639_27

[SW14] Sahai, A., Waters, B.: How to use indistinguishability obfuscation: deniable encryption, and more. In Shmoys, D.B. (ed) Symposium on Theory of Computing, STOC 2014, 31 May–03 June 2014, pp. 475–484. ACM, New York (2014)

[Wol02] Wolf, C.: "Hidden field equations" (HFE) - variations and attacks. Master's thesis, Universität Ulm, December 2002. http://www.christopher-wolf.de/dpl

[Zim15] Zimmerman, J.: How to obfuscate programs directly. In: Oswald, E., Fischlin, M. (eds.) EUROCRYPT 2015. LNCS, vol. 9057, pp. 439–467. Springer, Heidelberg (2015). https://doi.org/10.1007/978-3-662-46803-6_15

Watermarking

Watermarking PRFs from Lattices: Stronger Security via Extractable PRFs

Sam Kim[1(✉)] and David J. Wu[2]

[1] Stanford University, Stanford, CA, USA
`skim13@cs.stanford.edu`
[2] University of Virginia, Charlottesville, VA, USA
`dwu4@virginia.edu`

Abstract. A software watermarking scheme enables one to embed a "mark" (i.e., a message) within a program while preserving the program's functionality. Moreover, there is an extraction algorithm that recovers an embedded message from a program. The main security goal is that it should be difficult to remove the watermark without destroying the functionality of the program. Existing constructions of watermarking focus on watermarking cryptographic functions like pseudorandom functions (PRFs); even in this setting, realizing watermarking from standard assumptions remains difficult. The first lattice-based construction of secret-key watermarking due to Kim and Wu (CRYPTO 2017) only ensures mark-unremovability against an adversary who does not have access to the mark-extraction oracle. The construction of Quach et al. (TCC 2018) achieves the stronger notion of mark-unremovability even if the adversary can make extraction queries, but has the drawback that the watermarking authority (who holds the watermarking secret key) can break pseudorandomness of all PRF keys in the family (including *unmarked* keys).

In this work, we construct new lattice-based secret-key watermarking schemes for PRFs that both provide unremovability against adversaries that have access to the mark-extraction oracle and offer a strong and meaningful notion of pseudorandomness even against the watermarking authority (i.e., the outputs of unmarked keys are pseudorandom almost everywhere). Moreover, security of several of our schemes can be based on the hardness of computing *nearly polynomial* approximations to worst-case lattice problems. This is a qualitatively weaker assumption than that needed for existing lattice-based constructions of watermarking (that support message-embedding), all of which require quasi-polynomial approximation factors. Our constructions rely on a new cryptographic primitive called an *extractable PRF*, which may be of independent interest.

1 Introduction

A software watermarking scheme enables a user or an authority to embed a "mark" within a program in a way that the marked program behaves almost

---

The full version of this paper is available at https://eprint.iacr.org/2018/986.pdf.

D.J. Wu—Part of this work was done while a student at Stanford University.

© International Association for Cryptologic Research 2019
A. Boldyreva and D. Micciancio (Eds.): CRYPTO 2019, LNCS 11694, pp. 335–366, 2019.
https://doi.org/10.1007/978-3-030-26954-8_11

identically to the original program. It should be difficult to remove the watermark from a marked program without significantly altering the program's behavior, and moreover, it should be difficult to create new (or malformed) programs that are considered to be watermarked. The first property of *unremovability* is useful for proving ownership of software (e.g., in applications to digital rights management) while the second property of *unforgeability* is useful for authenticating software (e.g., for proving that the software comes from a trusted distributor).

1.1 Background and Motivation

Barak et al. [9,10] and Hopper et al. [35] introduced the first rigorous mathematical framework for software watermarking. Realizing the strong security requirements put forth in these works has been difficult. Early works [42,43,51] made partial progress by considering weaker security models and imposing restrictions on the adversary's capabilities. This changed with the work of Cohen et al. [27], who gave the first positive construction of software watermarking (for classes of cryptographic functionalities) that achieved unremovability against *arbitrary* adversarial strategies from indistinguishability obfuscation.

More formally, a software watermarking scheme consists of two main algorithms. First, the marking algorithm takes a circuit C and outputs a "marked" circuit C' with the property that C' and C agree almost everywhere. Second, a verification algorithm takes a circuit C and outputs MARKED or UNMARKED. In the message-embedding setting, the marking algorithm also takes a message m in addition to the circuit and embeds the message m within the circuit as the watermark. In this case, we replace the verification algorithm with a mark-extraction algorithm that takes a circuit as input and which outputs either the embedded message or UNMARKED. A watermarking scheme is robust against *arbitrary* removal strategies if the adversary is given complete flexibility in crafting a circuit $\tilde{C}'$ that mimics the behavior of a marked circuit C', but does not contain the watermark. This most directly captures our intuitive notions of unremovability and is the setting that we focus on in this work.

Since the work of Cohen et al., there has been many works on building stronger variants of software watermarking [49,50] and constructing watermarking (and variants) from simpler assumptions [5,16,38,45]. While this latter line of work has made tremendous progress and has yielded constructions of watermarking from standard lattice assumptions [38], CCA-secure encryption [45], and even public-key encryption (in the stateful setting) [5], these gains have come at the price of relaxing the watermarking security requirements. As such, there is still a significant gap between the security and capabilities of the Cohen et al. construction [27] from indistinguishability obfuscation and the best schemes we have from standard assumptions. In this work, we narrow this gap and introduce a new lattice-based software watermarking scheme for pseudorandom functions (PRFs) that satisfies stronger security and provides more functionality than the previous constructions from standard assumptions.

Watermarking PRFs. While the notion of software watermarking is well-defined for general functionalities, Cohen et al. [27] showed that watermarking is impossible for any class of learnable functions. Consequently, research on watermarking has focused on cryptographic functions like PRFs. In their work, Cohen et al. gave the first constructions of watermarking for PRFs (as well as several public-key primitives) from indistinguishability obfuscation. The Cohen et al. watermarking construction has the appealing property in that the scheme supports *public mark-extraction* (i.e., anyone is able to extract the embedded message from a watermarked program). The main drawback though is their reliance on strong (and non-standard) assumptions. Subsequently, Boneh et al. [16] introduced the concept of a private puncturable PRF and showed how to construct *secretly-extractable* watermarking schemes from a variant of private puncturable PRFs (called private programmable PRFs). Building on the Boneh et al. framework, Kim and Wu [38] showed that a relaxation of private programmable PRFs also sufficed for watermarking, and they gave the first construction of watermarking from standard lattice assumptions. Neither of these constructions support public extraction, and constructing watermarking schemes that support public extraction from standard assumptions remains a major open problem.

Towards Publicly-Extractable Watermarking. Not only did the schemes in [16,38] not support public extraction, they had the additional drawback that an adversary who only has access to the extraction oracle for the watermarking scheme can easily remove the watermark from a marked program (using the algorithm from [27, §2.4]). Thus, it is unclear whether these schemes bring us any closer to a watermarking scheme with public extraction. A stepping stone towards a publicly-extractable watermarking scheme is to construct a secretly-extractable watermarking scheme, except we give the adversary access to the extraction oracle. The difficulty in handling extraction queries is due to the "verifier rejection" problem that also arises in similar settings such as constructing designated-verifier proof systems or CCA-secure encryption. Namely, the adversary can submit carefully-crafted circuits to the extraction oracle and based on the oracle's responses, learn information about the secret watermarking key.

Recently, Quach et al. [45] gave an elegant and conceptually-simple construction of secretly-extractable watermarking that provided unremovability in this stronger model where the adversary has access to the extraction oracle. Moreover, their scheme also supports *public marking*: namely, anyone is able to take a PRF and embed a watermark within it. The basic version of their scheme is mark-embedding (i.e., programs are either marked or unmarked) and can be instantiated from any CCA-secure public-key encryption scheme. To support full message-embedding, their construction additionally requires private puncturable PRFs (and thus, the only standard-model instantiation today relies on lattices). In both cases, however, their scheme has the drawback in that the holder of the watermarking secret key completely compromises pseudorandomness of all PRF keys in the family (including *unmarked* keys). In particular, given even two evaluations of a PRF (on distinct points), the watermarking authority in the scheme of [45] can already distinguish the evaluations from random. While it might be reasonable to trust the watermarking authority, we note here that users must *fully* trust the authority (even if they generate a PRF key only for themselves and never interact with the watermarking authority). Even if the authority *passively* observes PRF evaluations (generated by honest users), it is able to tell those evaluations apart from truly random values. As we discuss below, this is a significant drawback of their construction and limits its applicability. Previous constructions [16,27,38] did not have this drawback.

Security Against the Watermarking Authority. Intuitively, it might seem like in any secret-key watermarking scheme, users implicitly have to trust the watermarking authority (either to mark their keys, or to verify their keys, or both), and so, there is no reason to require security against the watermarking authority. However, we note that this is not the case. For example, the marking and extraction algorithms can always be implemented by a two-party computation between the watermarking authority and the user, in which case the watermarking authority *never* sees any of the users' keys in the clear, and yet, the users still enjoy all of the protections of a watermarking scheme. In existing schemes that do not provide security against the watermarking authority [45], the PRF essentially has a "backdoor" and the watermarking authority is able to distinguish *every* evaluation or *every* PRF in the family from random. This is a significant increase in the amount of trust the user now has to place in the watermarking authority. The constructions we provide in this work provide a meaningful notion of security even against the watermarking authority. Namely, as long as the users never evaluate the PRF on a restricted set of points (which is a sparse subset of the domain and statistically hidden from the users), then the input/output behavior of both unmarked and marked keys remain pseudorandom even against the watermarking authority.

More generally, as noted above, a watermarking scheme that supports extraction queries is an intermediate primitive between secretly-extractable watermarking and publicly-extractable watermarking. If the intermediate scheme is insecure in the presence of a party who can extract, then the techniques used in that scheme are unlikely to extend to the public-key setting (where *everyone* can extract). Handling extraction queries (with security against the authority) is closer to publicly-extractable watermarking compared to notions from past works. We believe our techniques bring us closer towards publicly-extractable watermarking from standard assumptions.

1.2   Our Contributions

In this work and similar to [45], we study secretly-verifiable watermarking schemes for PRFs that provide unremovability (and unforgeability) against adversaries that have access to both the marking and the extraction oracles. Our goal is to achieve these security requirements while maintaining security even against the watermarking authority. We provide several new constructions of secretly-verifiable watermarking schemes for PRFs from standard lattice

Table 1. Comparison of our watermarkable family of PRFs to previous constructions. We focus exclusively on *message-embedding* constructions. For each scheme, we indicate whether it supports public marking and public extraction, whether mark-unremovability holds in the presence of an extraction oracle, whether unmarked keys remain pseudorandom against the watermarking authority, and the hardness assumption each scheme is based on. In the above, "iO" denotes indistinguishability obfuscation and "RO" denotes a random oracle

Scheme	Public Marking	Public Extraction	Extraction Oracle	PRF Security (Authority)	Hardness Assumption
Cohen et al. [27]	✗	✓	✓	✓	iO
Boneh et al. [16]	✗	✗	✗	✓	iO
Kim-Wu [38]	✗	✗	✗	✓	LWE*
Quach et al. [45]	✓	✗	✓	✗	LWE*
Yang et al. [50]	✗	✓	✓	✓	iO
This Work	✗	✗	✓	✓†	LWE‡
	✓	✗	✓	✓†	LWE‡ + RO

*LWE with a quasi-polynomial modulus-to-noise ratio (i.e., $2^{\log^c n}$ for constant $c > 1$).
†Our construction provides a weaker notion of *restricted* pseudorandomness against the watermarking authority.
‡ LWE with a nearly polynomial modulus-to-noise ratio (i.e., $n^{\omega(1)}$).

assumptions where the adversary has access to the extraction oracle. Moreover, we show that all of our constructions achieve a relaxed (but still meaningful) notion of pseudorandomness for unmarked keys even in the presence of the watermarking authority. Our constructions also simultaneously achieve unremovability and unforgeability (with parameters that match the lower bounds in Cohen et al. [27]). In fact, we show that meaningful notions of unforgeability (that capture the spirit of unforgeability and software authentication as discussed in [27,35,50]) are even possible for schemes that support public marking. Our constructions are the first to provide all of these features. Moreover, we are able to realize these new features while relying on *qualitatively weaker* lattice-based assumptions compared to all previous watermarking constructions from standard assumptions (specifically, on the hardness of computing *nearly polynomial* (i.e., $n^{\omega(1)}$) approximations to worst-case lattice problems as opposed to computing *quasi-polynomial* (i.e., $2^{\log^c(n)}$ for constant $c > 1$) approximations; see Remark 4.13). We provide a comparison of our new watermarking construction to previous schemes in Table 1, and also summarize these results below.

Extractable PRFs. The key cryptographic building block we introduce in this work is the notion of an *extractable PRF*. An extractable PRF is a standard PRF family $\mathsf{F} \colon \mathcal{K} \times \mathcal{X} \to \mathcal{Y}$ outfitted with an extraction trapdoor td. The extractability property says that given any circuit that computes $\mathsf{F}(k, \cdot)$, the holder of the trapdoor td can recover the PRF key k (with overwhelming probability). In fact, the extraction process is *robust* in the following sense: given any circuit $C\colon \mathcal{X} \to \mathcal{Y}$ whose behavior is "close" to $\mathsf{F}(k, \cdot)$, the extraction algorithm still extracts the PRF key k. The notion of closeness that we use is ε-closeness: we say that two circuits C_0 and C_1 are ε-close if C_0 and C_1 only differ on at most an ε-fraction of the domain. Of course, for extraction to be well-defined, it must be the case that for any pair of distinct keys k_1, k_2, the functions $\mathsf{F}(k_1, \cdot)$ and $\mathsf{F}(k_2, \cdot)$ are far apart. We capture this by imposing a statistical requirement on the PRF family called key-injectivity,[1] which requires that $\mathsf{F}(k_1, \cdot)$ and $\mathsf{F}(k_2, \cdot)$ differ on at least an ε'-fraction of points where $\varepsilon' \gg \varepsilon$. This ensures that if C is ε-close to some PRF $\mathsf{F}(k, \cdot)$, then k is unique (and extraction recovers k). In Sect. 2, we provide a detailed technical overview on how to construct extractable PRFs from standard lattice assumptions. We give the formal definition, construction, and security analysis in Sect. 4.

From Extractable PRFs to Watermarking. The combination of extractability and key-injectivity gives a natural path for constructing a secret-key watermarking scheme for PRFs. We begin with a high-level description of our basic mark-embedding construction which illustrates the main principles. First, we will need to extend our extractable PRF family to additionally support puncturing. In a puncturable PRF [18,19,37], the holder of a PRF key k can puncture k at a point x^* to derive a "punctured key" k_{x^*} with the property that k_{x^*} can be used to evaluate the PRF on all points $x \neq x^*$. Moreover, given the punctured key k_{x^*}, the value of the PRF $\mathsf{F}(k, x^*)$ at x^* is still indistinguishable from a uniformly random value.

Suppose now that we have an extractable PRF where the PRF keys can be punctured. To construct a mark-embedding watermarkable family of PRFs $\mathsf{F}\colon \mathcal{K} \times \mathcal{X} \to \mathcal{Y}$, we take the watermarking secret key to be the trapdoor for the extractable PRF family. To mark a PRF key $k \in \mathcal{K}$, the watermarking authority derives a special point $x^{(k)} \in \mathcal{X}$ from k (using a PRF key that is also part of the watermarking secret key), and punctures k at $x^{(k)}$ to obtain the punctured key $k_{x^{(k)}}$. The watermarked program just implements PRF evaluation using the punctured key $k_{x^{(k)}}$. To check whether a circuit $C\colon \mathcal{X} \to \mathcal{Y}$ is marked, the watermarking authority applies the extraction algorithm to C to obtain a key $k \in \mathcal{K}$ (or $\bot$ if extraction does not output a key). If the extraction algorithm outputs a key $k \in \mathcal{K}$, the verification algorithm computes the special point $x^{(k)}$ from k and outputs MARKED if $C(x^{(k)}) \neq \mathsf{F}(k, x^{(k)})$ and UNMARKED otherwise. If the extraction algorithm outputs $\bot$, the algorithm outputs UNMARKED.

Unremovability of this construction essentially reduces to puncturing security. By robust extractability (and key-injectivity), if the adversary only corrupts a small number of points in a marked key (within the unremovability threshold), then the extraction algorithm successfully recovers k (with overwhelming probability). To remove the watermark, the adversary's task is to "fix" the value of the PRF at the punctured point $x^{(k)}$. Any adversary that succeeds to do so

---

[1] Key-injectivity also played a role in previous watermarking constructions, though in a different context [27,38].

breaks puncturing security (in particular, the adversary must be able to recover the real value of the PRF at the punctured point given only the punctured key). Note that here, we do require that the range $\mathcal{Y}$ of the PRF be super-polynomial (if the range was polynomial, then the adversary can guess the correct value of the PRF at $x^{(k)}$ with noticeable probability and remove the watermark). Note that this basic scheme neither provides unforgeability (i.e., it is easy to construct circuits that are considered MARKED even without the watermarking key) nor supports message-embedding. As we discuss in greater detail below, both of these properties can be achieved with additional work.

Handling Extraction Queries. A primary objective of this work is to construct a watermarking scheme for PRFs where unremovability holds even against an adversary that has access to the extraction oracle. At first glance, our marking algorithm may appear very similar to that in [16, 38], since all of these constructions rely on some form of puncturable PRFs. These previous constructions do not satisfy unremovability in the presence of an extraction oracle because they critically rely on the adversary not being able to identify the special point $x^{(k)}$. Namely, in these constructions, to check whether a circuit C is marked or not, the authority derives the special point $x^{(k)}$ from the input/output behavior of C and then checks whether $C(x^{(k)})$ has a *specific* structure. If the adversary is able to learn the point $x^{(k)}$, then it can tweak the value of the marked circuit at $x^{(k)}$ and remove the watermark. In fact, even if the puncturable PRF completely hides the special point $x^{(k)}$, the binary search attack from Cohen et al. [27] allows the adversary to use the extraction oracle to recover $x^{(k)}$, and thus, defeat the watermarking scheme.

In our construction, to decide whether a circuit C is marked or not, the authority first extracts a key k and checks whether $C(x^{(k)}) = \mathsf{F}(k, x^{(k)})$. Therefore, in order to remove the watermark, it is not enough for the adversary to just recover the special point $x^{(k)}$ via the extraction oracle (in fact, the special point $x^{(k)}$ is public). To succeed, the adversary has to recover the original *value* of the PRF at $x^{(k)}$, which is hard when the PRF has a super-polynomial range and the PRF satisfies puncturing security. The fact that we do *not* rely on the unpredictability of the special point for security is a subtle but important distinction in our construction. In Sect. 5, we show that assuming the underlying PRF provides robust extractability (and key-injectivity), the adversary can simulate for itself the behavior of the extraction oracle. Thus, the presence of the extraction oracle cannot help the adversary break unremovability.

Unforgeability and Message-Embedding via Multi-puncturing. While the basic construction above provides unremovability, it is easy to forge watermarked programs. Namely, an adversary can simply take a circuit that implements a PRF $\mathsf{F}(k, \cdot)$ and randomly corrupt a $(1/\mathsf{poly}(\lambda))$-fraction of the output (where λ is a security parameter). Then, with noticeable probability, the adversary will corrupt the PRF at the special point $x^{(k)}$ associated with k, thereby causing the verification algorithm to conclude that the circuit is marked. This is easily prevented by puncturing k at λ points $x_1^{(k)}, \ldots, x_\lambda^{(k)}$. We now say that a circuit C is marked only if $C(x_i^{(k)}) \neq \mathsf{F}(k, x_i^{(k)})$ for all $i \in [\lambda]$. Of course, this modification does not affect unremovability. Now, to forge a watermarked program, the adversary has to construct a circuit C whose behavior closely resembles $\mathsf{F}(k, \cdot)$, and yet, C and $\mathsf{F}(k, \cdot)$ disagree on *all* of the special points $x_1^{(k)}, \ldots, x_\lambda^{(k)}$, which are derived pseudorandomly from the key k. This means that unless the adversary previously made a request to mark k (in which case its circuit C would no longer be considered a forgery), the points $x_1^{(k)}, \ldots, x_\lambda^{(k)}$ associated with k look uniformly random to $\mathcal{A}$. But now, if C and $\mathsf{F}(k, \cdot)$ are close, they will not differ on λ random points, except with negligible probability. We formalize this argument in Sect. 5.2.

The same technique of puncturing at multiple points also enables us to extend our basic mark-embedding watermarking scheme into a scheme that supports message-embedding. We take a basic bit-by-bit approach similar in spirit to the ideas taken in [38,43,45]. Specifically, to support embedding messages of length t in a PRF key k, we first derive from k a collection of λ pseudorandom points for each index and each possible bit: $S_{i,b}^{(k)} = \{x_{i,b,1}^{(k)}, \ldots, x_{i,b,\lambda}^{(k)}\}$ for all $i \in [t]$ and $b \in \{0,1\}$. To embed a message $m \in \{0,1\}^t$ in the key k, the marking algorithm punctures k at all of the points in the sets $S_{i,m_i}^{(t)}$ for $i \in [t]$. To recover the watermark, the extraction algorithm proceeds very similarly as before. Specifically, on input a circuit C, the extraction algorithm uses the trapdoor for the underlying extractable PRF to obtain a candidate key k (or outputs UNMARKED if no key is extracted). Given a candidate key k, the extraction algorithm derives the sets $S_{i,b}^{(k)}$ for each index $i \in [t]$ and bit $b \in \{0,1\}$. For each index, the algorithm counts the number of points in $S_{i,0}^{(k)}$ and $S_{i,1}^{(k)}$ on which C and $\mathsf{F}(k, \cdot)$ disagree. For correctly-watermarked keys, C and $\mathsf{F}(k, \cdot)$ will disagree on all of the points in one of the sets and none of the points in the other set. This difference in behavior allows the extraction algorithm to recover the bit at index i. We provide the full description and analysis in the full version of this paper [39].

Public Marking in the Random Oracle Model. In the mark-embedding and message-embedding watermarking constructions we have described so far, both marking and extraction require knowledge of the watermarking secret key. If we look more closely at the marking algorithm, however, we see that the only time the watermarking key is used during marking is to derive the set of points to be punctured (specifically, the set of points to be punctured is derived by evaluating a PRF on the key k). Critically, we do *not* require that the set of punctured points be hidden from the adversary (and indeed, the watermarked key completely reveals the set of punctured points), but only that they are unpredictable (without knowledge of k). Thus, instead of using a PRF to derive the points to be punctured, we can use a random oracle. This gives a construction of a message-embedding watermarking scheme that supports *public marking*. We provide the full description and analysis of this scheme in the full version of this paper [39]. We note that Quach et al. [45] were the first to give a watermarking scheme that supported public marking *without* random oracles (for mark-embedding, they only needed CCA-secure public-key encryption while for full message-embedding, they relied on lattices). However, as noted before, their scheme does not provide any security against a malicious watermarking authority (or provide unforgeability, which we discuss below).

Unforgeability and Public Marking. Recall that unforgeability for a watermarking scheme says that no efficient adversary should be able to construct a marked circuit that is significantly different from marked circuits it already received. This property seems at odds with the semantics of a watermarking scheme that supports public marking, since in the latter, anyone can mark programs of their choosing. However, we can still capture the following spirit of unforgeability by requiring that the only marked circuits that an adversary can construct are those that are close to circuits that are contained in the function class. In the case of watermarking PRFs, this means that the only circuits that would be considered to be watermarked are those that are functionally close to a legitimate PRF. This property is useful in scenarios where the presence of a watermark is used to argue *authenticity* of software (e.g., to prove to someone that the software implements a specific type of computation). In this work, we introduce a weaker notion of unforgeability that precisely captures this authenticity property. We then show that our watermarking construction supports public-marking while still achieving this form of weak unforgeability. The only previous candidate of software watermarking that supports public marking [45] does not satisfy this property, and indeed, in their scheme, it is easy to construct functions that are constant everywhere (which are decidedly *not* pseudorandom), but nonetheless would be considered to be marked.

Optimal Bounds for Unremovability and Unforgeability. We say that a watermarking scheme is ε-unremovable if an adversary who only changes an ε-fraction of the values of a marked circuit cannot remove the watermark,[2] and that it is δ-unforgeable if an adversary cannot create a new marked program that differs on at least a δ-fraction of points from any marked circuits it was given. Conceptually, larger values of ε means that the watermark remains intact even if the adversary can corrupt the behavior of the marked program on a larger fraction of inputs, while smaller values of δ means that the adversary's forgery is allowed to agree on a larger fraction of the inputs of a marked program. Previously, Cohen et al. [27] showed that any message-embedding watermarking scheme can at best achieve $\varepsilon = 1/2 - 1/\mathsf{poly}(\lambda)$ and $\delta = \varepsilon + 1/\mathsf{poly}(\lambda)$. Our constructions in this work achieve both of these bounds (for any choice of $\mathsf{poly}(\lambda)$ factors). Previous constructions like [27,45] did not provide unforgeability while [16,38] could only tolerate $\varepsilon = \mathsf{negl}(\lambda)$ (and any $\delta = 1/\mathsf{poly}(\lambda)$).

---

[2] This definition is the complement of the definition from previous works on watermarking [16,27,38,45,49,50], but we adopt this to maintain consistency with our definition for robust extractability.

Security Against the Watermarking Authority. The key property of extractable PRFs that underlies our watermarking constructions is that there is an extraction trapdoor td that can be used to extract the original PRF key k from any circuit whose behavior is sufficiently similar to that of $\mathsf{F}(k, \cdot)$. In the case of watermarking, the watermarking authority must hold the trapdoor to use it to extract watermarks from marked programs. This raises a new security concern as the watermarking authority can now break security of *all* PRFs in the family, including *unmarked* ones. As discussed in Sect. 1.1, this was the main drawback of the Quach et al. [45] watermarking construction.

Due to our reliance on extractable PRFs, our watermarkable family of PRFs also cannot satisfy full pseudorandomness against the watermarking authority. However, we can show a weaker property against the watermarking authority we call T-restricted pseudorandomness. Namely, we can associate a set $S \subseteq \mathcal{X}$ of size at most T with our watermarkable family of PRFs such that any adversary (even if they have the extraction trapdoor) is unable to break pseudorandomness of any (unmarked) PRF, provided that they do not query the function on points in S. The distinguisher is also provided the set S. In other words, our family of PRFs still provides pseudorandomness everywhere except S. In our concrete constructions (Construction 4.5), the restricted set S consists of λ *randomly-chosen* points in $\mathcal{X}$. This means that if the domain of the PRF is super-polynomial, our notion of T-restricted pseudorandomness strictly interpolates between weak pseudorandomness (or even non-adaptive pseudorandomness)[3] and strong pseudorandomness. It is also worth noting that from the perspective of a user who does not hold the watermarking secret key, the points in S are *statistically hidden*. This means that in any standard usage of the PRF between honest users, with overwhelming probability, the PRF would never be evaluated on one of the restricted points. Equivalently, if the watermarking authority only sees passive evaluations of the PRF, then it will not be able to break pseudorandomness of the underlying PRF. This notion of "passive" security against the watermarking authority strictly improves upon the lattice-based message-embedding watermarking construction in [45]. In their setting, the watermarking authority is able to break pseudorandomness given *any* two (distinct) evaluations of the PRF; that is, their scheme does not even satisfy weak pseudorandomness against the watermarking authority. It is an interesting and important question to obtain watermarking with security in the presence of an extraction oracle and which retrains full pseudorandomness even against the watermarking authority. The only constructions that satisfy this notion rely on obfuscation.

Watermarking *Without* Private Puncturing. All existing constructions of message-embedding watermarking from standard assumptions have relied

---

[3] In the weak pseudorandomness game, the adversary is given outputs of the PRF on random inputs, while in the non-adaptive pseudorandomness game, the adversary must declare *all* of its evaluation queries before seeing any evaluations of the PRF or the public parameters.

on *private* puncturable PRFs[4] in some form [38,45]. Our message-embedding watermarking construction is the first that does *not* rely on private puncturing; standard puncturing in conjunction with key-extractability suffices. While this might seem like a minor distinction, we note that constrained PRFs can be constructed from weaker assumptions. For instance, puncturable PRFs can be built from one-way functions [18,19,30,37] while the simplest constructions of private puncturable PRFs rely on lattice-based assumptions [14,21,25,26,44]. If we just consider lattice-based constrained PRFs, the Brakerski-Vaikuntanathan puncturable PRF [23] can be based on the (polynomial) hardness of solving worst-case lattice problems with a *nearly polynomial* approximation factor (i.e., $n^{\omega(1)}$),[5] while constructions of private puncturable PRFs from lattices [14,21,25,26,44] can only be based on the hardness of solving worst-case lattice problems with a *quasi-polynomial* approximation factor (i.e., $2^{\log^c n}$ for some constant $c > 1$). Since all of the existing constructions of message-embedding watermarking from standard assumptions rely on private puncturing in some form, they can only be reduced to worst-case lattice problems with quasi-polynomial approximation factors at best. In this work, we show that a variant of our construction (satisfying a relaxed notion of unforgeability as in [38]) can be based solely on worst-case lattice problems with a nearly polynomial approximation factor (Remark 4.13). Concretely, we give the first (message-embedding) watermarking scheme whose security can be based on computing nearly polynomial approximations to worst-case lattice problems (Corollary 5.4).

1.3   Additional Related Work

We now survey some additional works that use similar techniques as those in our construction.

Lattice-Based PRFs. The study of lattice-based PRFs started with the seminal work of Banerjee et al. [8]. Subsequently, [7,15] constructed the first lattice-based key-homomorphic PRFs. The first circuit-constrained PRFs were constructed in [6,23] and were later extended to private constrained PRFs in [14,21,25,26,44].

Matrix Embeddings. The matrix embedding techniques used in this work build on a series of works in the areas of attribute-based encryption [47] and predicate encryption [17,36] from LWE. These include the attributed-based

---

[4] A private puncturable PRF [16] is a puncturable PRF where the punctured key also *hides* the punctured point. There are several lattice-based constructions of private puncturable PRFs (and more generally, private constrained PRFs) [14,21,25,26,44].

[5] While the general construction described in [23] relies on worst-case lattice problems with sub-exponential approximation factors, when restricted to just puncturing constraints (which can be computable by *log-depth* circuits), it can be based on worst-case lattice problems with a nearly polynomial approximation factor by leveraging the techniques for branching program evaluation [22].

encryption constructions of [1,12,20,24,31,33] and the (one-sided) predicate encryption constructions of [2,21,28,32,34,48].

2   Technical Overview

In this section, we provide a technical overview of our construction of extractable PRFs from standard lattice assumptions. As described in Sect. 1.2, this is the key cryptographic primitive we rely on in our watermarking constructions (described formally in Sect. 5). We believe that the algebraic techniques we develop for constructing our extractable PRF are general and will find applications beyond the study of PRFs and watermarking. We highlight the core principles and techniques here, but defer the formal definitions, constructions, and analysis to Sect. 4.

The LWE Assumption. The learning with errors (LWE) assumption [46], parameterized by n, m, q, χ, states that for a uniformly random vector $\mathbf{s} \in \mathbb{Z}_q^n$, a uniformly random matrix $\mathbf{A} \in \mathbb{Z}_q^{n \times m}$, and a noise vector $\mathbf{e}$ sampled from a (low-norm) error distribution χ, the distribution $(\mathbf{A}, \mathbf{s} \cdot \mathbf{A} + \mathbf{e})^6$ is computationally indistinguishable from the uniform distribution over $\mathbb{Z}_q^{n \times m} \times \mathbb{Z}_q^m$. Equivalently, rather than explicitly adding noise, the LWE assumption can instead be defined with respect to a rounding modulus $p < q$ and the component-wise rounding operation $\lfloor \cdot \rceil_p : \mathbb{Z}_q \to \mathbb{Z}_p$ [8]. This variant of the LWE assumption states that the distribution $(\mathbf{A}, \lfloor \mathbf{s} \cdot \mathbf{A} \rceil_p)$ is computationally indistinguishable from the uniform distribution over $\mathbb{Z}_q^{n \times m} \times \mathbb{Z}_p^m$; this is also known as the *learning with rounding* (LWR) assumption [8]. For the parameter setting we consider in this work, hardness of LWE implies hardness of LWR [8].

Lattice-Based PRFs. A natural way to construct a pseudorandom function $\mathsf{F} \colon \mathcal{K} \times \mathcal{X} \to \mathcal{Y}$ from the LWE assumption is to take the PRF key $k \in \mathcal{K}$ to be the LWE secret $\mathbf{s} \in \mathbb{Z}_q^n$ and define $\mathsf{F}(\mathbf{s}, x)$ to output an LWE sample $\lfloor \mathbf{s} \cdot \mathbf{A}_x \rceil_p$ for a matrix $\mathbf{A}_x$ that is uniquely determined by the input $x \in \mathcal{X}$. Note that when the domain $\mathcal{X}$ is super-polynomial, the matrix $\mathbf{A}_x$ cannot be a uniformly random matrix as required by the LWE assumption since $\mathsf{F}(\mathbf{s}, \cdot)$ must be an (efficiently-computable) deterministic function. Constructing a PRF from LWE thus amounts to designing a suitable mapping $x \mapsto \mathbf{A}_x$ such that the vector $\lfloor \mathbf{s} \cdot \mathbf{A}_x \rceil_p$ is still pseudorandom under LWE.

Nearly all existing LWE-based PRF constructions follow this general blueprint; we refer to Sect. 1.3 for a more comprehensive discussion of related work. Specifically, these PRF families are defined with respect to a set of public matrices $\mathsf{pp} = (\mathbf{A}_1, \ldots, \mathbf{A}_\rho)$ and an input-to-matrix mapping $\mathsf{Eval}_{\mathsf{pp}} \colon \mathcal{X} \to \mathbb{Z}_q^{n \times m}$ (that implements the mapping $x \mapsto \mathbf{A}_x$) such that the outputs of

$$\mathsf{F}(\mathbf{s}, x) := \lfloor \mathbf{s} \cdot \mathbf{A}_x \rceil_p \text{ where } \mathbf{A}_x \leftarrow \mathsf{Eval}_{\mathsf{pp}}(x) \tag{2.1}$$

---

[6] For notational simplicity, we drop the transpose notation when it is clear from context.

are computationally indistinguishable from uniform vectors over $\mathbb{Z}_p^n$ under the LWE assumption. In this overview, rather than focusing on a particular PRF construction, we show how to obtain an extractable PRF from any lattice-based PRF family that follows this blueprint.

Key Extraction Via Lattice Trapdoors. Recall from Sect. 1 that in an extractable PRF family, the holder of a trapdoor td (for the PRF family) can recover the PRF key $k \in \mathcal{K}$ given only oracle access to the PRF $\mathsf{F}(k, \cdot)$. Using the basic structure of lattice-based PRF candidates from Eq. (2.1), a natural starting point is to design the mapping $\mathsf{Eval}_{\mathsf{pp}} \colon \mathcal{X} \to \mathbb{Z}_q^{n \times m}$ such that for a special input $x^* \in \mathcal{X}$, the matrix $\mathbf{D} \leftarrow \mathsf{Eval}_{\mathsf{pp}}(x^*)$ has a known (lattice) trapdoor $\mathsf{td}_{\mathbf{D}}$, which can be included as part of the trapdoor for the extractable PRF family (together with the special input x^*).

A lattice trapdoor $\mathsf{td}_{\mathbf{D}}$ for a matrix $\mathbf{D} \in \mathbb{Z}_q^{n \times m}$ enables sampling short preimages under the matrix $\mathbf{D}$ [3,4,29,40,41]. Specifically, given an arbitrary target matrix $\mathbf{T} \in \mathbb{Z}_q^{n \times m}$, the trapdoor $\mathsf{td}_{\mathbf{D}}$ enables sampling a short matrix $\mathbf{R}_{\mathbf{T}} \in \mathbb{Z}_q^{m \times m}$ such that $\mathbf{D} \cdot \mathbf{R}_{\mathbf{T}} = \mathbf{T}$. Additionally, the trapdoor for $\mathbf{D}$ can be used to solve the search version of the LWE problem: given an LWE instance $(\mathbf{D}, \lfloor \mathbf{s} \cdot \mathbf{D} \rceil_p)$, one first computes a short matrix $\mathbf{R}_{\mathbf{G}}$ using the trapdoor $\mathbf{D}$ and then derive the vector

$$\lfloor \mathbf{s} \cdot \mathbf{D} \rceil_p \cdot \mathbf{R}_{\mathbf{G}} = \lfloor \mathbf{s} \cdot \mathbf{D} \cdot \mathbf{R}_{\mathbf{G}} \rceil_p + \mathsf{noise} = \lfloor \mathbf{s} \cdot \mathbf{G} \rceil_p + \mathsf{noise} \in \mathbb{Z}_p^m,$$

where noise is a small error vector that occurs from the modular rounding and $\mathbf{G} \in \mathbb{Z}_q^{n \times m}$ is the standard powers-of-two gadget matrix [41]. Since $\mathbf{G}^T$ is the generator matrix for a linear error-correcting code, recovering $\mathbf{s}$ form $\lfloor \mathbf{s} \cdot \mathbf{G} \rceil_p + \mathsf{noise}$ is straightforward (c.f., [41]).

Given the trapdoor $\mathsf{td}_{\mathbf{D}}$, it is straightforward to implement the Extract algorithm. Namely, Extract first queries $\mathsf{F}(\mathbf{s}, \cdot)$ on the special point $x^* \in \mathcal{X}$ to obtain the output $\lfloor \mathbf{s} \cdot \mathbf{D} \rceil_p$. It then uses the trapdoor information $\mathsf{td}_{\mathbf{D}}$ to recover the secret key $\mathbf{s}$.

Programming the Trapdoor. The problem of constructing an extractable PRF family now boils down to generating a set of public parameters pp and a suitable mapping $\mathsf{Eval}_{\mathsf{pp}} \colon \mathcal{X} \to \mathbb{Z}_q^{n \times m}$ such that the matrix $\mathbf{A}_{x^*} \leftarrow \mathsf{Eval}_{\mathsf{pp}}(x^*)$ can be programmed to be a trapdoor matrix $\mathbf{D}$. At the same time, $\mathsf{Eval}_{\mathsf{pp}}$ must be designed so that the basic blueprint from Eq. (2.1) still satisfies pseudorandomness. The concept of programming the output of a PRF was previously explored in the context of constrained PRFs [16,25,38,44]. These works study the notion of a *private programmable PRF* where *constrained keys* can be programmed to a specific value at a particular point (or set of points). However, the techniques used in these works do not directly apply to our setting as our goal is fundamentally different. To construct an extractable PRF, we need a PRF family such that the evaluation of *every* PRF key from the family is programmed to a trapdoor matrix. In fact, our notion is completely independent of constraining, and an extractable PRF family need not even support constraining. In other words, we

want programmability with respect to the public parameters of the PRF family
rather than just an individual PRF key.

The way we construct the function $\mathsf{Eval}_{\mathsf{pp}}$ is quite simple and general. We
take any existing PRF construction $\mathsf{F}' \colon \mathbb{Z}_q^m \times \mathcal{X} \to \mathbb{Z}_p^m$ following the blueprint
from Eq. (2.1) that is defined respect to a set of matrices $\mathsf{pp}' = (\mathbf{A}_1, \ldots, \mathbf{A}_\rho)$
and mapping $\mathsf{Eval}'_{\mathsf{pp}'} \colon \mathcal{X} \to \mathbb{Z}_q^{n \times m}$, and define a new *shifted* mapping

$$\mathsf{Eval}_{\mathsf{pp}}(x) := \mathsf{Eval}'_{\mathsf{pp}'}(x) + \mathbf{W} = \mathbf{A}_x + \mathbf{W},$$

for some shift matrix $\mathbf{W} \in \mathbb{Z}_q^{n \times m}$ and a new set of public matrices $\mathsf{pp} = (\mathbf{A}_1, \ldots, \mathbf{A}_\rho, \mathbf{W})$. First, observe that given a point $x^* \in \mathcal{X}$ and a trapdoor matrix
$\mathbf{D}$, it is easy to generate a programmed set of public parameters:

1. Generate the matrices $\mathbf{A}_1, \ldots, \mathbf{A}_\rho \in \mathbb{Z}_q^{n \times m}$ as in the original PRF family.
2. Set $\mathbf{W} = \mathbf{D} - \mathbf{A}_{x^*}$ where $\mathbf{A}_{x^*} \leftarrow \mathsf{Eval}'_{\mathsf{pp}'}(x^*)$.

It is easy to see that security of the original PRF family is preserved. Specifically,
we now have

$$\mathsf{F}(\mathbf{s}, x) = \lfloor \mathbf{s} \cdot (\mathbf{A}_x + \mathbf{W}) \rceil_p \approx \lfloor \mathbf{s} \cdot \mathbf{A}_x \rceil_p + \lfloor \mathbf{s} \cdot \mathbf{W} \rceil_p = \mathsf{F}'(\mathbf{s}, x) + \lfloor \mathbf{s} \cdot \mathbf{W} \rceil_p, \quad (2.2)$$

Since a randomly sampled trapdoor matrix $\mathbf{D}$ is statistically close to uniform, the
matrix $\mathbf{W}$ is also statistically close to uniform. This means that the additional
vector offset $\mathbf{w} = \lfloor \mathbf{s} \cdot \mathbf{W} \rceil_p$ introduced by $\mathbf{W}$ looks indistinguishable from a
uniformly random vector under LWE. Moreover,

$$\mathsf{F}(\mathbf{s}, x^*) = \lfloor \mathbf{s} \cdot (\mathbf{A}_{x^*} + \mathbf{W}) \rceil_p = \lfloor \mathbf{s} \cdot \mathbf{D} \rceil_p,$$

so given the trapdoor $\mathsf{td}_{\mathbf{D}}$, it is easy to recover the key $\mathbf{s}$.

2.1   Robust Extractability

The PRF family $\mathsf{F} \colon \mathbb{Z}_q^n \times \mathcal{X} \to \mathbb{Z}_p^n$ defined in Eq. (2.2) already satisfies a basic
notion of key-extractability. Namely, any authority who holds the trapdoor infor-
mation $(x^*, \mathsf{td}_{\mathbf{D}})$ is able to extract the PRF key given just oracle access to the
function $\mathsf{F}(\mathbf{s}, \cdot)$; moreover, $\mathsf{F}(\mathbf{s}, \cdot)$ remains pseudorandom to anyone who does not
possess the trapdoor. To support watermarking, however, we require a stronger
security property called *robust extractability* (Definition 4.3).

Robustness and Key-Injectivity. At a high level, robust extractability says
that the Extract algorithm should successfully recover the PRF key even if it is
just given access to a function (modeled as a circuit) whose behavior is "close"
to $\mathsf{F}(\mathbf{s}, \cdot)$. In fact, even if the adversary has oracle access to Extract, it should not
be able to produce a circuit C whose behavior is sufficiently "close" to $\mathsf{F}(\mathbf{s}, \cdot)$
for some key $\mathbf{s} \in \mathbb{Z}_q^n$, and for which, the extraction algorithm fails to extract $\mathbf{s}$
from C. The closeness metric that we use in this work is ε-closeness; namely, we
say that two circuits C and C' are ε-close if they agree on all but an ε-fraction

of elements in the domain. In all of our constructions, $\varepsilon = 1/\mathsf{poly}(\lambda)$. Of course, for the extractability property to be well-defined, it should be the case that for distinct keys $\mathbf{s}_1, \mathbf{s}_2 \in \mathbb{Z}_q^n$, $\mathsf{F}(\mathbf{s}_1, \cdot)$ and $\mathsf{F}(\mathbf{s}_2, \cdot)$ should be "far" apart. As discussed in Sect. 1.2, we capture this by defining a notion of *key-injectivity* similar in flavor to previous definitions from [27,38], and then show (Theorem 4.8) that over the randomness used to sample the public parameters, the basic construction in Eq. (2.2) satisfies our key-injectivity property. Thus, in the subsequent discussion, we assume without loss of generality that if a circuit C is ε-close to $\mathsf{F}(\mathbf{s}, \cdot)$ for any $\varepsilon = 1/\mathsf{poly}(\lambda)$, then $\mathbf{s}$ is unique.

The basic PRF construction from Eq. (2.2) does *not* satisfy robust extractability (for *any* closeness parameter $\varepsilon = 1/\mathsf{poly}(\lambda)$). Specifically, the adversary can recover the special point $x^* \in \mathcal{X}$ using binary search. To mount the attack, the adversary first chooses a key $\mathbf{s} \in \mathbb{Z}_q^n$, and constructs the circuit $\mathsf{F}(\mathbf{s}, \cdot)$. The adversary then (arbitrarily) partitions the domain into two halves $\mathcal{X}_1$ and $\mathcal{X}_2$ and queries the extraction oracle on a circuit C that agrees with $\mathsf{F}(\mathbf{s}, \cdot)$ on $\mathcal{X}_1$ and outputs $\perp$ on $\mathcal{X}_2$. Depending on whether the extraction algorithm succeeds in recovering $\mathbf{s}$ or not, the adversary learns which of $\mathcal{X}_1$ or $\mathcal{X}_2$ contains the special point x^*. After a polynomial number of queries, the adversary learns x^*. Once the adversary learns the special point x^*, it can always cause extraction to fail on a circuit by simply having the circuit output $\perp$ on x^* (and $\mathsf{F}(\mathbf{s}, x)$ on all $x \neq x^*$). Moreover, this circuit agrees with $\mathsf{F}(\mathbf{s}, \cdot)$ on all but a single point (i.e., they agree on all but a negligible fraction of the domain when $|\mathcal{X}|$ is super-polynomial), which breaks robust extractability.

Defending Against Binary Search. Effectively, the binary search attack relies on the fact that the adversary can easily construct circuits C such that the behavior of $\mathsf{Extract}$ on C (specifically, whether $\mathsf{Extract}$ succeeds or not) is correlated with the secret extraction trapdoor (specifically, the point x^*). To defend against this, we develop a way to ensure that the behavior of $\mathsf{Extract}$ on a circuit C depends *only* on properties of the circuit C (and *not* on the extraction trapdoor). If this is the case, then the extraction oracle does not leak information about the extraction trapdoor, and in turn, robust extractability holds. We note that this type of approach is conceptually very similar to the notion of *strong soundness* in the context of constructing *multi-theorem* argument systems in the designated-verifier setting [11,13].[7] To achieve this, we proceed in two steps.

---

[7] In designated-verifier argument systems, an adversary who has oracle access to the verifier can observe the verifier's behavior on different statements and proof strings. When the verifier's responses are correlated with its secret verification state, the prover can potentially leverage the leakage and compromise soundness. This is the so-called "verifier rejection" problem. Strong soundness is a property that says that the responses of the verifier depend only on the statement or proof string, and *not* on the secret verification state (the analog in our setting is that the behavior of the extraction oracle only depends on the input circuit and not the extraction trapdoor). This property is very useful for arguing soundness in the presence of a verification oracle for designated-verifier argument systems.

First, we modify the Extract algorithm to force the adversary to only submit circuits that are very close to an actual PRF circuit $F(\mathbf{s}, \cdot)$. Then, we tweak the construction to ensure that extraction queries on circuits C that are too close to a real PRF circuit are not helpful to the adversary. We describe this below.

- **Testing for closeness.** After the Extract algorithm recovers a candidate key $\mathbf{s} \in \mathbb{Z}_q^n$ from a circuit C, it additionally checks whether the behavior of the circuit C and $F(\mathbf{s}, \cdot)$ are "similar." While computing the exact distance between C and $F(\mathbf{s}, \cdot)$ cannot be done in polynomial time, it is straightforward to construct a randomized algorithm that accepts (with overwhelming probability) whenever C and $F(\mathbf{s}, \cdot)$ are ε_1-close and rejects (with overwhelming probability) whenever C and $F(\mathbf{s}, \cdot)$ are ε_2-far, for any choice of $\varepsilon_2 > \varepsilon_1 + 1/\mathsf{poly}(\lambda)$. This can be done by sampling random points $x_1, \ldots, x_\xi \xleftarrow{\text{R}} \mathcal{X}$ and counting the number of inputs where $C(x_i) = F(\mathbf{s}, x_i)$. If the number of points on which the two circuits differ is greater than $\xi \cdot (\varepsilon_1 + \varepsilon_2)/2$, then the Extract algorithm outputs $\perp$. By choosing $\xi = \mathsf{poly}(\lambda)$ accordingly, we can appeal to standard concentration bounds and show that Extract will only output a candidate key when C and $F(\mathbf{s}, \cdot)$ are at least ε_2-close. When applied to watermarking, the parameter ε_1 corresponds to the unremovability threshold while the parameter ε_2 corresponds to the unforgeability threshold.
- **Embedding multiple trapdoors.** The closeness test prevents the adversary from querying the extraction oracle on circuits that are more than ε_2-far from valid PRF circuits $F(\mathbf{s}, \cdot)$, since the output of Extract on these queries is $\perp$ with overwhelming probability. However, since $\varepsilon_2 = 1/\mathsf{poly}(\lambda)$, the adversary can still query the extraction oracle on circuits that are ε_2-close to the real PRF circuit $F(\mathbf{s}, \cdot)$. In this case, each query still (roughly) allows the adversary to rule out at least an ε_2-fraction of the domain, and so, in time $\mathsf{poly}(1/\varepsilon_2) = \mathsf{poly}(\lambda)$, the adversary is again able to extract the special point x^* for the PRF family.

The second ingredient in our construction is to embed *multiple* trapdoors. Specifically, instead of just embedding a single lattice trapdoor at x^*, we instead embed λ distinct trapdoors at λ special points $x_1^*, \ldots, x_\lambda^* \xleftarrow{\text{R}} \mathcal{X}$. Now, on input a circuit C, the Extract algorithm evaluates C at each special point x_i^*, and use the lattice trapdoor inversion algorithm to obtain candidate keys $\mathbf{s}_i$. It performs the closeness test described above on each candidate key $\mathbf{s}_i$ and outputs $\mathbf{s}_i$ if the closeness test succeeds, and $\perp$ if none succeed. By key-injectivity, there can only be one key $\mathbf{s}$ where $F(\mathbf{s}, \cdot)$ is ε_2-close to C whenever $\varepsilon_2 < 1/2$. At a very high level, the benefit of having multiple trapdoors is that the adversary has to corrupt the value at all of the trapdoors in order to cause the output of the Extract algorithm to differ (in a manner that is correlated with the secret extraction state). Since the special points $x_1^*, \ldots, x_\lambda^*$ are independently and uniformly distributed, and the adversary is effectively constrained to choosing circuits C which are ε_2-close to some $F(\mathbf{s}, \cdot)$, the probability that the adversary succeeds in constructing such a circuit is $\varepsilon_2^\lambda = \mathsf{negl}(\lambda)$. We refer to Sect. 4.2 and Theorem 4.12 for the formal analysis.

2.2 Puncturing and Pseudorandomness Given the Trapdoor

Recall from Sect. 1.2 that to obtain a watermarking scheme from an extractable PRF, we additionally require that the extractable PRFs support puncturing constraints. Since our techniques for building extractable PRFs are broadly applicable to many lattice-based PRFs, we can take an existing candidate with the structure from Eq. (2.1) and derive from it an extractable PRF. In particular, we can apply our general construction to the Brakerski-Vaikuntanathan constrained PRF [23], and obtain a puncturable extractable PRF. To achieve the stronger security notion of (T-restricted) pseudorandomness against an authority that holds the extraction trapdoor, we have to develop new techniques. We discuss the challenges below.

Security Against the Authority. As discussed in Sect. 1.2, a key contribution of our work is showing that the keys in our watermarkable PRF family still provide a relaxed form of pseudorandomness even against the holder of the watermarking secret key. This property amounts to showing that the underlying extractable PRF satisfies T-restricted pseudorandomness against an adversary who is given the extraction trapdoor. Specifically, we show that as long as the adversary (who has the trapdoor) is not allowed to query the PRF on the special points $x_1^*, \ldots, x_\lambda^*$, then pseudorandomness holds. This set of special points constitute the *restricted set* in the T-restricted pseudorandomness experiment. First, recall from Eq. (2.2) that

$$\mathsf{F}(\mathbf{s}, x) = \lfloor \mathbf{s} \cdot (\mathbf{A}_x + \mathbf{W}) \rceil_p \approx \mathsf{F}'(\mathbf{s}, x) + \lfloor \mathbf{s} \cdot \mathbf{W} \rceil_p,$$

where $\mathsf{F}'(\mathbf{s}, x)$ is the existing PRF (specifically, the Brakerski-Vaikuntanathan PRF [23]). At first glance, one might be tempted to believe that T-restricted pseudorandomness against the authority follows immediately from the security of F' since the value $\mathsf{F}(\mathbf{s}, x)$ is just $\mathsf{F}'(\mathbf{s}, x)$ shifted by $\lfloor \mathbf{s} \cdot \mathbf{W} \rceil_p$ where $\mathbf{W} = \mathbf{D} - \mathbf{A}_{x^*}$. Without the extraction trapdoor, $\mathbf{D}$ is statistically close to uniform, so we can appeal to LWE to argue that the shift $\lfloor \mathbf{s} \cdot \mathbf{W} \rceil_p$ is uniformly random (and looks independent of $\mathsf{F}'(\mathbf{s}, x)$). But given the trapdoor matrix $\mathbf{D}$, this is no longer the case; the shift $\lfloor \mathbf{s} \cdot \mathbf{W} \rceil_p$ is *correlated* with the PRF key $\mathbf{s}$, and not easily simulated without knowing $\mathbf{s}$ itself. Thus, it is unclear how to directly reduce security of F to security of the underlying PRF F'.

Consider a potential reduction algorithm $\mathcal{B}$ that uses an adversary for F in the T-restricted pseudorandomness security game to break the security of F'. In this case, $\mathcal{B}$ is given the extraction trapdoor. If the reduction algorithm $\mathcal{B}$ is able to correctly simulate the evaluation $\mathsf{F}(\mathbf{s}, x)$ on all points $x \in \mathcal{X}$, then it can use its trapdoor information $\mathsf{td}_\mathbf{D}$ to extract $\mathbf{s}$ and break security of F' itself. Thus, for the proof to go through, we minimally need to rely on some type of "puncturing" argument (c.f., [23]). A possible starting point is to give the reduction algorithm $\mathcal{B}$ a punctured key k_S' for F' that enables evaluation of F' at all points except the restricted points $S = (x_1^*, \ldots, x_\lambda^*)$. Then, $\mathcal{B}$ can simulate the correct PRF evaluations at all non-restricted points, but it is unable to compute the evaluations at the special points for itself.

Unfortunately, this basic puncturing approach is still insufficient to prove security. Namely, even if the reduction algorithm can simulate the non-shifted PRF evaluation $\mathsf{F}'(\mathbf{s}, x)$ at all of the non-restricted points, it must still simulate the shift $\lfloor \mathbf{s} \cdot \mathbf{W} \rceil_p$ *without* knowledge of the key $\mathbf{s}$. To address this, we additionally need to "program" the evaluations of the punctured key k_S at the non-punctured points. Specifically, we program the key k_S to introduce a shift by the key-dependent vector $\lfloor \mathbf{s} \cdot \mathbf{W} \rceil_p$ at all of the non-punctured points. This latter step relies on an adaptation of the technique of *programmable matrix embeddings* from [38]. This enables $\mathcal{B}$ to simulate the full PRF evaluation $\mathsf{F}(\mathbf{s}, x) = \mathsf{F}'(\mathbf{s}, x) + \lfloor \mathbf{s} \cdot \mathbf{W} \rceil_p$ for the adversary. We refer to Sect. 4.2 for the full details of the construction and security analysis.

3   Preliminaries

We begin by introducing some of the notation we use in this work. For an integer $n \geq 1$, we write $[n]$ to denote the set of integers $\{1, \ldots, n\}$. For a distribution $\mathcal{D}$, we write $x \leftarrow \mathcal{D}$ to denote that x is sampled from $\mathcal{D}$; for a finite set S, we write $x \xleftarrow{\mathrm{R}} S$ to denote that x is sampled uniformly from S.

Unless specified otherwise, we use λ to denote the security parameter. We say a function $f(\lambda)$ is negligible in λ, denoted by $\mathsf{negl}(\lambda)$, if $f(\lambda) = o(1/\lambda^c)$ for all $c \in \mathbb{N}$. We say that an event happens with overwhelming probability if its complement happens with negligible probability. We say an algorithm is efficient if it runs in probabilistic polynomial time in the length of its input. We use $\mathsf{poly}(\lambda)$ to denote a quantity whose value is bounded by a fixed polynomial in λ. For two families of distributions $\mathcal{D}_1$ and $\mathcal{D}_2$, we write $\mathcal{D}_1 \overset{s}{\approx} \mathcal{D}_2$ if the two distributions are statistically indistinguishable (i.e., the statistical distance between $\mathcal{D}_1$ and $\mathcal{D}_2$ is negligible). We now define the circuit-similarity metric we use in this work.

Definition 3.1 (Circuit Similarity). *Fix a circuit class $\mathcal{C}$ on ρ-bit inputs. For two circuits $C, C' \in \mathcal{C}$ and for a non-decreasing function $\varepsilon \colon \mathbb{N} \to \mathbb{N}$, we write say that C is ε-close to C', denoted $C \sim_\varepsilon C'$, if C and C' agree on all but an ε-fraction of inputs. More precisely, we write*

$$C \sim_\varepsilon C' \iff \Pr[x \xleftarrow{\mathrm{R}} \{0,1\}^\rho : C(x) \neq C'(x)] \leq \varepsilon.$$

Similarly, we write $C \not\sim_\varepsilon C'$ to denote that C and C' differ on at least an ε-fraction of inputs.

We provide additional background on lattice-based cryptography in the full version of this paper [39].

4   Extractable PRF

In this section, we introduce the core notion of an extractable PRF that we use throughout this work. Due to space limitations, we just present our definition of *robust extractability*. In the full version of this paper [39], we provide the formal definitions of both pseudorandomness as well as our relaxed notion of T-restricted pseudorandomness from Sect. 1, where pseudorandomness holds on all but a small number (i.e., up to T) points.

Definition 4.1 (Extractable PRF). *An* extractable PRF *with key-space $\mathcal{K}$, domain $\mathcal{X}$, and range $\mathcal{Y}$ consists of a tuple of efficient algorithms $\Pi_{\mathsf{EPRF}} = (\mathsf{PrmsGen}, \mathsf{SampleKey}, \mathsf{Eval}, \mathsf{Extract})$ with the following syntax:*

- $\mathsf{PrmsGen}(1^\lambda) \to (\mathsf{pp}, \mathsf{td})$: *On input the security parameter λ, the parameter-generation algorithm outputs a set of public parameters pp and a trapdoor td.*
- $\mathsf{SampleKey}(\mathsf{pp}) \to k$: *On input the public parameters pp, the key-generation algorithm outputs a PRF key $k \in \mathcal{K}$.*
- $\mathsf{Eval}(\mathsf{pp}, k, x) \to y$: *On input the public parameters pp, a PRF key $k \in \mathcal{K}$, and input $x \in \mathcal{X}$, the PRF evaluation algorithm outputs a value $y \in \mathcal{Y}$.*
- $\mathsf{Extract}(\mathsf{pp}, \mathsf{td}, C) \to k/\bot$: *On input the public parameters pp, the trapdoor td, and a circuit $C \colon \mathcal{X} \to \mathcal{Y}$, the extraction algorithm outputs a key $k \in \mathcal{K} \cup \{\bot\}$. Without loss of generality, the $\mathsf{Extract}$ algorithm can also be defined to take a circuit whose domain is any* superset *of the PRF domain $\mathcal{X}$.*

The public parameters pp of an extractable PRF induces a PRF family $\mathsf{F}_{\mathsf{pp}} \colon \mathcal{K} \times \mathcal{X} \to \mathcal{Y}$ where $\mathsf{F}_{\mathsf{pp}}(k, x) := \mathsf{Eval}(\mathsf{pp}, k, x)$ and $\mathsf{F}_{\mathsf{pp}}.\mathsf{KeyGen}(1^\lambda)$ computes and returns $k \leftarrow \mathsf{SampleKey}(\mathsf{pp})$. Note that the description of the induced PRF family F does not *include the trapdoor td.*

Definition 4.2 (Extract-and-Test). *An extractable PRF $\Pi_{\mathsf{EPRF}} = (\mathsf{PrmsGen}, \mathsf{SampleKey}, \mathsf{Eval}, \mathsf{Extract})$ with key-space $\mathcal{K}$ has an "extract-and-test" extraction algorithm if $\mathsf{Extract}$ can additionally be decomposed into two algorithms $(\mathsf{ExtractCandidates}, \mathsf{TestCandidate})$ with the following properties:*

- $\mathsf{ExtractCandidates}(\mathsf{pp}, \mathsf{td}, C) \to S$: *On input the public parameters pp, the trapdoor td, and a circuit C, the candidate extraction algorithm outputs a (possibly empty) set $S \subseteq \mathcal{K}$ of candidate keys, where $|S| = \mathsf{poly}(\lambda)$.*
- $\mathsf{TestCandidate}(\mathsf{pp}, \mathsf{td}, C, k) \to b$: *On input the public parameters pp, the trapdoor td, a circuit $C \colon \mathcal{X} \to \mathcal{Y}$, and a candidate key $k \in \mathcal{K}$, the test candidate algorithm outputs a bit $b \in \{0, 1\}$. Note that we allow $\mathsf{TestCandidate}$ to be a randomized algorithm.*

Moreover, the $\mathsf{Extract}(\mathsf{pp}, \mathsf{td}, C)$ algorithm can be written as follows:

- $\mathsf{Extract}(\mathsf{pp}, \mathsf{td}, C)$: *First invoke $\mathsf{ExtractCandidates}(\mathsf{pp}, \mathsf{td}, C)$ to obtain a set $S \subseteq \mathcal{K}$ of candidate keys. For each $k \in S$, compute $b_k \leftarrow \mathsf{TestCandidate}(\mathsf{pp}, \mathsf{td}, C, k)$. Output any $k \in S$ where $b_k = 1$. If $b_k = 0$ for all $k \in S$, output $\bot$.*

Definition 4.3 (Robust Extractability). *Fix a security parameter λ and closeness parameters $\varepsilon_1, \varepsilon_2$. Let $\Pi_{\mathsf{EPRF}} = (\mathsf{PrmsGen}, \mathsf{SampleKey}, \mathsf{Eval}, \mathsf{Extract})$ be* *an extractable pseudorandom function with key-space* $\mathcal{K}$, *domain* $\mathcal{X}$, *and range* $\mathcal{Y}$. *Suppose* Π_{EPRF} *has an extract-and-test extraction algorithm where for* $(\mathsf{pp}, \mathsf{td}) \leftarrow \mathsf{PrmsGen}(1^\lambda)$ *and* $\varepsilon_1 < \varepsilon_2$, *the* TestCandidate *algorithm satisfies the following two properties:*

- *For all* $k \in \mathcal{K}$ *and* $C(\cdot) \sim_{\varepsilon_1} \mathsf{Eval}(\mathsf{pp}, k, \cdot)$, $\Pr[\mathsf{TestCandidate}(\mathsf{pp}, \mathsf{td}, C, k) = 1] = 1 - \mathsf{negl}(\lambda)$.
- *For all* $k \in \mathcal{K}$ *and* $C(\cdot) \not\sim_{\varepsilon_2} \mathsf{Eval}(\mathsf{pp}, k, \cdot)$, $\Pr[\mathsf{TestCandidate}(\mathsf{pp}, \mathsf{td}, C, k) = 1] = \mathsf{negl}(\lambda)$.

Next, for an adversary $\mathcal{A}$, *we define two experiments* $\mathsf{ExtReal}_{\mathcal{A}}(\lambda, \varepsilon_1, \varepsilon_2)$ *and* $\mathsf{ExtIdeal}_{\mathcal{A}}(\lambda, \varepsilon_1, \varepsilon_2)$:

- **Setup phase:** *At the start of both experiments, the challenger samples* $(\mathsf{pp}, \mathsf{td}) \leftarrow \mathsf{PrmsGen}(1^\lambda)$ *and gives* pp *to* $\mathcal{A}$.
- **Query phase:** *Adversary* $\mathcal{A}$ *can issue any (polynomial) number of extraction queries to the challenger. On an extraction oracle query* $C \colon \mathcal{X} \to \mathcal{Y}$, *the challenger in the two experiments responds as follows:*
  - $\mathsf{ExtReal}$: *In the real experiment, the challenger replies with* $\mathsf{Extract}(\mathsf{pp}, \mathsf{td}, C)$.
  - $\mathsf{ExtIdeal}$: *In the ideal experiment, the challenger proceeds as follows:*
    - *If there exists a* unique $k \in \mathcal{K}$ *where* $C(\cdot) \sim_{\varepsilon_2} \mathsf{Eval}(\mathsf{pp}, k, \cdot)$, *the challenger computes* $b_k \leftarrow \mathsf{TestCandidate}(\mathsf{pp}, \mathsf{td}, C, k)$. *It replies with* k *if* $b_k = 1$ *and* $\perp$ *if* $b_k = 0$.
    - *Otherwise, the challenger replies with* $\perp$.
- **Output phase:** *Once the adversary* $\mathcal{A}$ *is done making queries, it outputs a bit* $b \in \{0, 1\}$. *This is the output of the experiment.*

We say that Π_{EPRF} *satisfies* $(\varepsilon_1, \varepsilon_2)$-*robust extractability if for all (possibly unbounded) adversaries* $\mathcal{A}$ *making any polynomial number* $Q = \mathsf{poly}(\lambda)$ *queries, we have that*

$$\left| \Pr\left[\mathsf{ExtReal}_{\mathcal{A}}(\lambda, \varepsilon_1, \varepsilon_2) = 1 \right] - \Pr\left[\mathsf{ExtIdeal}_{\mathcal{A}}(\lambda, \varepsilon_1, \varepsilon_2) = 1 \right] \right| = \mathsf{negl}(\lambda).$$

Remark 4.4 (Generalized Candidate Testing). In our constructions, we will require a generalized version of TestCandidate with the following properties:

- The TestCandidate algorithm is *publicly-computable*; namely, TestCandidate does *not* depend on the trapdoor td. To make this explicit, in the case where TestCandidate is publicly-computable, we write the algorithm as $\mathsf{TestCandidate}(\mathsf{pp}, C, k)$.
- If C_1, C_2 satisfy $C_1 \sim_\varepsilon C_2$ for some $\varepsilon = \mathsf{negl}(\lambda)$, then for all pp and all $k \in \mathcal{K}$,

$$\Pr[\mathsf{TestCandidate}(\mathsf{pp}, C_1, k) \neq \mathsf{TestCandidate}(\mathsf{pp}, C_2, k)] = \mathsf{negl}(\lambda).$$

- Instead of taking as input a candidate key $k \in \mathcal{K}$ as input, the TestCandidate can also take as input an arbitrary circuit $C' \colon \mathcal{X} \to \mathcal{Y}$, with the property that for $(\mathsf{pp}, \mathsf{td}) \leftarrow \mathsf{PrmsGen}(1^\lambda)$ and $k \leftarrow \mathsf{SampleKey}(\mathsf{pp})$, and any circuit $C' \colon \mathcal{X} \to \mathcal{Y}$ where $C' \sim_\varepsilon \mathsf{Eval}(\mathsf{pp}, k, \cdot)$ and $\varepsilon = \mathsf{negl}(\lambda)$,

$$\{\mathsf{TestCandidate}(\mathsf{pp}, C, k)\} \overset{s}{\approx} \{\mathsf{TestCandidate}(\mathsf{pp}, C, C')\},$$

where the randomness is taken over the random coins in $\mathsf{PrmsGen}$, $\mathsf{SampleKey}$, and $\mathsf{TestCandidate}$.

Key-Injectivity. As discussed in Sect. 2, a property that is often useful in conjunction with robust extractability is key-injectivity. We give the formal definition in the full version of this paper [39].

4.1 Puncturable Extractable PRFs

In a puncturable PRF [18,19,37], the PRF key k can be used to derive a punctured key k_{x^*} that can be used to evaluate the PRF everywhere *except* the punctured point $x^* \in \mathcal{X}$. Moreover, the actual PRF value $\mathsf{F}(k, x^*)$ remains pseudorandom even given the punctured key. More generally, we can consider puncturing the PRF at a set $S \subseteq \mathcal{X}$. In this case, the punctured key k_S can be used to evaluate the PRF at all points in $\mathcal{X} \setminus S$, while the PRF values at points in S remain pseudorandom. This is also called a *constrained PRF* [18]. In our setting, we primarily consider puncturing at sets containing up to $\mathsf{poly}(\lambda)$ elements. We review the formal definitions in the full version of this paper [39].

4.2 Constructing Extractable PRFs

In this section, we present our extractable PRF family from standard lattice assumptions. Although our construction follows the main ideas that we outlined in Sect. 2, implementing these ideas algebraically is non-trivial. We begin with a brief algebraic overview of our construction.

Construction Overview. As discussed in Sect. 2, our PRF family is defined with respect to a set of public matrices in $\mathbb{Z}_q^{n \times m}$, which we denote by $(\mathbf{A}_j)_{j \in [\rho]}$, $(\widetilde{\mathbf{A}}_{\alpha,\beta})_{\alpha \in [n], \beta \in [m]}$, $(\mathbf{B}_{i,j})_{i \in [t], j \in [\rho]}$, $(\mathbf{C}_j)_{j \in [\rho]}$, $\mathbf{V}$, and $\mathbf{W}$. Here, n, m, q are lattice parameters, t is the number of punctured points, and ρ is the bit-length of the PRF input. These matrices can be logically partitioned into three sets of matrices that handle different correctness or security goals.

- The matrices $(\mathbf{A}_j)_{j \in [\rho]}$, $(\widetilde{\mathbf{A}}_{\alpha,\beta})_{\alpha \in [n], \beta \in [m]}$ are used for the T-restricted pseudorandomness proof. As discussed in Sect. 2.2, handling the evaluation queries in T-restricted pseudorandomness requires generating a punctured key that is specifically programmed to enable simulation of the key-dependent shift (i.e., the $\lfloor \mathbf{s} \cdot \mathbf{W} \rceil_p$ term in Eq. (2.2)).
- The matrices $(\mathbf{B}_{i,j})_{i \in [t], j \in [\rho]}$, $(\mathbf{C}_j)_{j \in [\rho]}$, $\mathbf{V}$ implement the constrained PRF construction of [23].

- The matrix $\mathbf{W}$ is the shift matrix. As described in Sect. 2, matrix $\mathbf{W}$ is generated by first evaluating $\mathsf{Eval}_{\mathsf{pp}}$ on the rest of the matrices $(\mathbf{A}_j)_{j\in[\rho]}$, $(\widetilde{\mathbf{A}}_{\alpha,\beta})_{\alpha\in[n],\beta\in[m]}$, $(\mathbf{B}_{i,j})_{i\in[t],j\in[\rho]}$, $(\mathbf{C}_j)_{j\in[\rho]}$, $\mathbf{V}$, and then defining it as a corresponding shifted matrix from a trapdoor matrix $\mathbf{D}$.

As discussed in Sect. 2.1, to achieve robust extractability, we need to embed multiple trapdoors. We support this by simply concatenating together multiple copies of the PRF, where each copy is associated with one of the trapdoors. We now give the formal construction.

Construction 4.5 (Puncturable Extractable PRFs). Let λ be a security parameter, and $\varepsilon_1, \varepsilon_2$ be distance parameters where $0 < \varepsilon_1 < \varepsilon_2 < 1/2$, and $\varepsilon_2 \geq \varepsilon_1 + 1/\mathsf{poly}(\lambda)$. We define the following scheme parameters:

- (n, m, q, χ_B) – lattice parameters, where χ_B is a B-bounded distribution,
- p – the rounding modulus,
- t – a bound on the number of points to be punctured (indexed by i),
- ρ – the bit-length of the PRF input (indexed by j),
- η – the number of special points where we embed the extraction trapdoor (indexed by ℓ).

Throughout this section and in the analysis, we will assume that $n, m, t, \rho, \eta = \mathsf{poly}(\lambda)$. Let $(\mathsf{TrapGen}, \mathsf{Invert})$ be the lattice trapdoor algorithms (see full version of this paper [39]). For an input $x \in \{0,1\}^\rho$, we define the equality function $f_x^{\mathsf{eq}}: \{0,1\}^\rho \to \{0,1\}$ where

$$f_x^{\mathsf{eq}}(x^*) = \begin{cases} 1 & \text{if } x = x^* \\ 0 & \text{otherwise.} \end{cases}$$

More generally, for a set of points $S \subseteq \{0,1\}^\rho$ of size t (represented as a concatenation of the bit-strings in S), we define the containment function $f_x^{\mathsf{con}}: \{0,1\}^{t\rho} \to \{0,1\}$ where

$$f_x^{\mathsf{con}}(S) = \begin{cases} 1 & \text{if } x \in S \\ 0 & \text{otherwise.} \end{cases}$$

Note that both the equality circuit f_x^{eq} and the containment circuit f_x^{con} for any $x \in \{0,1\}^\rho$ can be computed by a circuit of depth $d = O(\log \rho + \log t) = O(\log \lambda)$. Our (puncturable) extractable PRF $\Pi_{\mathsf{PRF}} = (\mathsf{PrmsGen}, \mathsf{SampleKey}, \mathsf{Eval}, \mathsf{Extract}, \mathsf{Puncture}, \mathsf{PunctureEval})$ with key-space $\mathcal{K} = [-B, B]^n$, domain $\mathcal{X} = \{0,1\}^\rho \backslash \{\mathbf{0}\}$, and range $\mathcal{Y} = \mathbb{Z}_p^{\eta m}$ is defined as follows:[8]

- $\mathsf{PrmsGen}(1^\lambda)$: On input the security parameter λ, the $\mathsf{PrmsGen}$ algorithm begins by sampling $(\mathbf{A}_j^{(\ell)})_{j\in[\rho]}$, $(\widetilde{\mathbf{A}}_{\alpha,\beta}^{(\ell)})_{\alpha\in[n],\beta\in[m]}$, $(\mathbf{B}_{i,j}^{(\ell)})_{i\in[t],j\in[\rho]}$, $(\mathbf{C}_j^{(\ell)})_{j\in[\rho]}$, $\mathbf{V}^{(\ell)}$ uniformly at random from $\mathbb{Z}_q^{n\times m}$ for every $\ell \in [\eta]$. It also samples a set of η special points $h^{(\ell)} \xleftarrow{\text{R}} \{0,1\}^\rho$ along with trapdoor matrices $(\mathbf{D}^{(\ell)}, \mathsf{td}_{\mathbf{D}^{(\ell)}}) \leftarrow \mathsf{TrapGen}(1^\lambda)$ for all $\ell \in [\eta]$. Then, for all $\ell \in [\eta]$, it computes

---

[8] We refer to the full version of this paper [39] for the specification of the $\mathsf{Eval}_{\mathsf{pk}}$, $\mathsf{Eval}_{\mathsf{ct}}$, $\mathsf{EvalP}_{\mathsf{pk}}$, and $\mathsf{EvalP}_{\mathsf{ct}}$ algorithms for computing on matrix embeddings [12,38].

- $\mathbf{A}^{(\ell)}_{h^{(\ell)}} \leftarrow \mathsf{EvalP}_{\mathsf{pk}}\left(f^{\mathsf{eq}}_{h^{(\ell)}}, (\mathbf{A}^{(\ell)}_j)_{j \in [\rho]}, (\widetilde{\mathbf{A}}^{(\ell)}_{\alpha,\beta})_{\alpha \in [n], \beta \in [m]}\right)$,
- $\mathbf{B}^{(\ell)}_{h^{(\ell)}} \leftarrow \mathsf{Eval}_{\mathsf{pk}}\left(f^{\mathsf{con}}_{h^{(\ell)}}, (\mathbf{B}^{(\ell)}_{i,j})_{i \in [t], j \in [\rho]}\right)$,
- $\mathbf{C}^{(\ell)}_{h^{(\ell)}} \leftarrow \mathsf{Eval}_{\mathsf{pk}}\left(f^{\mathsf{eq}}_{h^{(\ell)}}, (\mathbf{C}^{(\ell)}_j)_{j \in [\rho]}\right)$,

and defines the matrix

$$\mathbf{W}^{(\ell)} = \mathbf{A}^{(\ell)}_{h^{(\ell)}} + \mathbf{B}^{(\ell)}_{h^{(\ell)}} \mathbf{G}^{-1}(\mathbf{C}^{(\ell)}_{h^{(\ell)}}) \mathbf{G}^{-1}(\mathbf{V}^{(\ell)}) + \mathbf{D}^{(\ell)} \in \mathbb{Z}_q^{n \times m}. \qquad (4.1)$$

Finally, it outputs

$$\mathsf{pp} = \left(\mathbf{W}^{(\ell)}, (\mathbf{A}^{(\ell)}_j)_{j \in [\rho]}, (\widetilde{\mathbf{A}}^{(\ell)}_{\alpha,\beta})_{\alpha \in [n], \beta \in [m]}, (\mathbf{B}^{(\ell)}_{i,j})_{i \in [t], j \in [\rho]}, (\mathbf{C}^{(\ell)}_j)_{j \in [\rho]}, \mathbf{V}^{(\ell)}\right)_{\ell \in [\eta]}, \qquad (4.2)$$

and $\mathsf{td} = \left(h^{(\ell)}, \mathsf{td}_{\mathbf{D}^{(\ell)}}\right)_{\ell \in [\eta]}$.

- SampleKey(pp): On input the public parameters pp, the key-generation algorithm samples a key $\mathbf{s} \leftarrow \chi^n$, and outputs the PRF key $k = \mathbf{s}$.
- Eval(pp, k, x): On input the public parameters pp (as specified in Eq. (4.2)), a PRF key $k = \mathbf{s}$, and an input $x \in \{0,1\}^\rho \setminus \{\mathbf{0}\}$, the evaluation algorithm first computes the matrices
  - $\mathbf{A}^{(\ell)}_x \leftarrow \mathsf{EvalP}_{\mathsf{pk}}\left(f^{\mathsf{eq}}_x, (\mathbf{A}^{(\ell)}_j)_{j \in [\rho]}, (\widetilde{\mathbf{A}}^{(\ell)}_{\alpha,\beta})_{\alpha \in [n], \beta \in [m]}\right)$,
  - $\mathbf{B}^{(\ell)}_x \leftarrow \mathsf{Eval}_{\mathsf{pk}}\left(f^{\mathsf{con}}_x, (\mathbf{B}^{(\ell)}_{i,j})_{i \in [t], j \in [\rho]}\right)$,
  - $\mathbf{C}^{(\ell)}_x \leftarrow \mathsf{Eval}_{\mathsf{pk}}\left(f^{\mathsf{eq}}_x, (\mathbf{C}^{(\ell)}_j)_{j \in [\rho]}\right)$,

  for all $\ell \in [\eta]$. Then, it sets

$$\mathbf{Z}^{(\ell)}_x = \mathbf{A}^{(\ell)}_x + \mathbf{B}^{(\ell)}_x \mathbf{G}^{-1}(\mathbf{C}^{(\ell)}_x) \mathbf{G}^{-1}(\mathbf{V}^{(\ell)}), \qquad (4.3)$$

  for all $\ell \in [\eta]$, and computes the vector

$$\widetilde{\mathbf{y}}_x = \mathbf{s}\left(\mathbf{W}^{(1)} - \mathbf{Z}^{(1)}_x \mid \cdots \mid \mathbf{W}^{(\eta)} - \mathbf{Z}^{(\eta)}_x\right) \in \mathbb{Z}_q^{\eta m}. \qquad (4.4)$$

  Finally, it outputs the rounded vector $\mathbf{y}_x = \lfloor \widetilde{\mathbf{y}} \rceil_p \in \mathbb{Z}_p^{\eta m}$.
- Extract(pp, td, C): The extraction algorithm is defined with respect to two sub-algorithms ExtractCandidates and TestCandidate (as in Definition 4.2) that are defined as follows:
  - ExtractCandidates(pp, td, C): On input the public parameters pp (as specified in Eq. (4.2)), a trapdoor $\mathsf{td} = \left(h^{(\ell)}, \mathsf{td}_{\mathbf{D}^{(\ell)}}\right)_{\ell \in [\eta]}$, and a circuit $C: \{0,1\}^\rho \to \mathbb{Z}_p^{\eta m}$, the candidate extraction algorithm evaluates the circuit on the test points to get $\mathbf{y}^{(\ell)} \leftarrow C(h^{(\ell)})$ for all $\ell \in [\eta]$. Then, for all $\ell \in [\eta]$, it parses the vector $\mathbf{y}^{(\ell)} = (\mathbf{y}^{(\ell)}_1 \mid \cdots \mid \mathbf{y}^{(\ell)}_\eta)$ where each $\mathbf{y}^{(\ell)}_1, \ldots, \mathbf{y}^{(\ell)}_\eta \in \mathbb{Z}_p^m$. Then, it extracts $\mathbf{s}^{(\ell)} \leftarrow \mathsf{Invert}(\mathsf{td}_{\mathbf{D}^{(\ell)}}, \mathbf{y}^{(\ell)}_\ell)$ and outputs the set of all $\mathbf{s}^{(\ell)}$ for which $\mathbf{s}^{(\ell)} \neq \bot$ and $\mathbf{s}^{(\ell)} \in [-B, B]^n$.
  - TestCandidate(pp, C, k): Let $\delta = (\varepsilon_2 - \varepsilon_1)/2 = 1/\mathsf{poly}(\lambda)$, $\varepsilon = \varepsilon_1 + \delta$, and $\xi = \lambda/\delta^2 = \mathsf{poly}(\lambda)$. On input the public parameters pp, a key $k = \mathbf{s}$, and a circuit $C: \{0,1\}^\rho \to \mathbb{Z}_p^{\eta m}$, the test candidate algorithm samples

$x_1^*, \ldots, x_\xi^* \xleftarrow{\text{R}} \{0,1\}^\rho$ and computes the number $N_{\mathbf{s}}$ of indices $i \in [\xi]$ where $C(x_i^*) \neq \mathsf{Eval}(\mathsf{pp}, \mathbf{s}, x_i^*)$. If $N_{\mathbf{s}} \leq \varepsilon\xi$, then output 1. Otherwise, output 0. Note that $\mathsf{TestCandidate}$ is *publicly-computable* (it does not require a trapdoor).

The full extraction algorithm follows the extract-and-test procedure described in Definition 4.2.

- $\mathsf{Puncture}(\mathsf{pp}, k, S)$: On input the public parameter pp (as specified in Eq. (4.2)), a PRF key $k = \mathbf{s}$, and a set of points to be punctured $S = \{x_i\}_{i \in [t]}$, the $\mathsf{Puncture}$ algorithm first samples error vectors $\mathbf{e}_{\mathbf{A},j}^{(\ell)}, \mathbf{e}_{\tilde{\mathbf{A}},\alpha,\beta}^{(\ell)}, \mathbf{e}_{\mathbf{B},i,j}^{(\ell)}, \mathbf{e}_{\mathbf{W}}^{(\ell)} \leftarrow \chi^m$ for all $i \in [t]$, $j \in [\rho]$, $\alpha \in [n]$, $\beta \in [m]$, and $\ell \in [\eta]$. Then, for each $\ell \in [\eta]$ it defines the vectors
  - $\mathbf{a}_j^{(\ell)} = \mathbf{s}\mathbf{A}_j^{(\ell)} + \mathbf{e}_{\mathbf{A},j}^{(\ell)}$ for all $j \in [\rho]$,
  - $\tilde{\mathbf{a}}_{\alpha,\beta}^{(\ell)} = \mathbf{s}\tilde{\mathbf{A}}_{\alpha,\beta}^{(\ell)} + \mathbf{e}_{\tilde{\mathbf{A}},\alpha,\beta}^{(\ell)}$ for all $\alpha \in [n]$ and $\beta \in [m]$,
  - $\mathbf{b}_{i,j}^{(\ell)} = \mathbf{s}(\mathbf{B}_{i,j}^{(\ell)} + x_{i,j} \cdot \mathbf{G}) + \mathbf{e}_{\mathbf{B},i,j}^{(\ell)}$ for all $i \in [t]$ and $j \in [\rho]$,
  - $\mathbf{w}^{(\ell)} = \mathbf{s}\mathbf{W}^{(\ell)} + \mathbf{e}_{\mathbf{W}}^{(\ell)}$.

  Finally, it outputs the punctured key

$$k_S = \left(S, \left(\mathbf{w}^{(\ell)}, (\mathbf{a}_j^{(\ell)})_{j\in[\rho]}, (\tilde{\mathbf{a}}_{\alpha,\beta}^{(\ell)})_{\alpha\in[n],\beta\in[m]}, (\mathbf{b}_{i,j}^{(\ell)})_{i\in[t],j\in[\rho]} \right)_{\ell\in[\eta]} \right). \quad (4.5)$$

- $\mathsf{PunctureEval}(\mathsf{pp}, k_S, x)$: On input the public parameters pp (as specified in Eq. (4.2)), the punctured key k_S (as specified in Eq. (4.5)), and an input $x \in \{0,1\}^\rho \setminus \{\mathbf{0}\}$, the punctured evaluation algorithm computes the following for each $\ell \in [\eta]$:
  - $\mathbf{a}_x^{(\ell)} \leftarrow \mathsf{EvalP}_{\mathsf{ct}}\left(f_x^{\mathsf{eq}}, \mathbf{0}, (\mathbf{A}_j^{(\ell)})_{j\in[\rho]}, \quad (\tilde{\mathbf{A}}_{\alpha,\beta}^{(\ell)})_{\alpha\in[n],\beta\in[m]}, \quad (\mathbf{a}_j^{(\ell)})_{j\in[\rho]}, (\tilde{\mathbf{a}}_{\alpha,\beta}^{(\ell)})_{\alpha\in[n],\beta\in[m]} \right)$,
  - $\mathbf{b}_x^{(\ell)} \leftarrow \mathsf{Eval}_{\mathsf{ct}}\left(f_x^{\mathsf{con}}, S, (\mathbf{B}_{i,j}^{(\ell)})_{i\in[t],j\in[\rho]}, (\mathbf{b}_{i,j}^{(\ell)})_{i\in[t],j\in[\rho]} \right)$,
  - $\mathbf{C}_x^{(\ell)} \leftarrow \mathsf{Eval}_{\mathsf{pk}}\left(f_x^{\mathsf{eq}}, (\mathbf{C}_j^{(\ell)})_{j\in[\rho]} \right)$.

  Then, for each $\ell \in [\eta]$, it sets

$$\mathbf{z}_x^{(\ell)} = \mathbf{a}_x^{(\ell)} + \mathbf{b}_x^{(\ell)} \mathbf{G}^{-1}(\mathbf{C}_x^{(\ell)}) \mathbf{G}^{-1}(\mathbf{V}^{(\ell)}), \quad (4.6)$$

  and computes the vector

$$\mathbf{y}_x = (\mathbf{w}^{(1)} - \mathbf{z}_x^{(1)} \mid \cdots \mid \mathbf{w}^{(\eta)} - \mathbf{z}_x^{(\eta)}) \in \mathbb{Z}_q^{\eta m}. \quad (4.7)$$

Finally, it outputs the rounded vector $\mathbf{y}_x = \lfloor \tilde{\mathbf{y}}_x \rceil_p \in \mathbb{Z}_p^{\eta m}$.

Security Analysis. We now show that under the LWE and 1D-SIS-R [14, 23] assumptions (with suitable parameters),[9] the puncturable extractable PRF construction from Construction 4.5 satisfies correctness, puncturing security, and robust extractability. We give the formal theorem statements here, but defer the formal proofs to the full version of this paper [39]. We also discuss adaptive security in the full version.

---

[9] We refer to full version of this paper [39] for the formal statements of these assumptions.

Theorem 4.6 (Perfect Correctness for Most Keys). *Fix a security parameter λ and lattice parameters n, m, q, p, B. Suppose $m = \Omega(n \log q)$, $q = \Omega(np\sqrt{\log q})$, and $2^{\rho}B \cdot m^{O(\log \lambda)} \cdot p/q = \mathsf{negl}(\lambda)$. Then, the extractable PRF Π_{EPRF} from Construction 4.5 satisfies perfect correctness for most keys.*

Theorem 4.7 (Almost-Functionality-Preserving for All Keys). *Fix a security parameter λ and lattice parameters n, m, q, p, B. Suppose $m = \Omega(n \log q)$, $q = \Omega(np\sqrt{\log q})$, and $\rho = \omega(\log \lambda)$. Then, under the 1D-SIS-R$_{m',p,q,E}$ assumption for $m' = nm\eta$ and $E = B \cdot m^{O(\log \lambda)}$, the extractable PRF Π_{EPRF} from Construction 4.5 is almost-functionality-preserving for all keys.*

Theorem 4.8 (Key-Injectivity). *Fix a security parameter λ and lattice parameters n, m, q, p, B. Suppose $m = \Omega(n \log q)$, $q = \Omega(np\sqrt{\log q})$, and $2^{\rho}(4B+1)^n/p^{nm} = \mathsf{negl}(\lambda)$. Then, the extractable PRF Π_{EPRF} from Construction 4.5 satisfies key-injectivity.*

Theorem 4.9 (Puncturing Security). *Fix a security parameter λ and lattice parameters n, m, q, p, B. Suppose $m = \Omega(n \log q)$, $q = \Omega(np\sqrt{\log q})$, and $2^{\rho}B \cdot m^{O(\log \lambda)} \cdot p/q = \mathsf{negl}(\lambda)$. Then, under the $\mathsf{LWE}_{n,m',q,\chi}$ assumption for $m' = \eta m(nm + (t+2)\rho + 1) + \eta m$, the extractable PRF Π_{EPRF} from Construction 4.5 satisfies selective puncturing security.*

Corollary 4.10 (Pseudorandomness). *Fix a security parameter λ and lattice parameters n, m, q, p, B. Suppose the conditions in Theorem 4.9 hold. Then, the extractable PRF Π_{EPRF} from Construction 4.5 satisfies selective pseudorandomness.*

Theorem 4.11 (T-Restricted Psueodrandomness). *Fix a security parameter λ and lattice parameters n, m, q, p, B. Suppose $m = \Omega(n \log q)$ and $q = \Omega(np\sqrt{\log q})$ and $2^{\rho}B \cdot m^{O(\log \lambda)} \cdot p/q = \mathsf{negl}(\lambda)$. Then, under the $\mathsf{LWE}_{n,m',q,\chi}$ assumption for $m' = \eta m(nm + \rho(t+2)) + \eta m$, the extractable PRF Π_{EPRF} from Construction 4.5 satisfies selective T-restricted pseudorandomness for $T = \eta$.*

Theorem 4.12 (Robust Extractability). *Fix a security parameter λ and lattice parameters n, m, q, p, B. Take any $0 < \varepsilon_1 < \varepsilon_2 < 1/2$ where $\varepsilon_2 - \varepsilon_1 \geq 1/\mathsf{poly}(\lambda)$. Let Π_{EPRF} be the extractable PRF from Construction 4.5. Suppose $m = \Omega(n \log q)$, $q = \Omega(np\sqrt{\log q})$, $m \geq 2n \log q$, $\lceil q/p \rceil \leq q/4$, and $\eta = \omega(\log \lambda)$, and that Π_{EPRF} satisfies key-injectivity. Then, Π_{EPRF} satisfies $(\varepsilon_1, \varepsilon_2)$-robust extractability (Definition 4.3). Moreover, the $\mathsf{TestCandidate}$ algorithm in Construction 4.5 satisfies the generalized candidate testing properties from Remark 4.4.*

4.3 Concrete Parameter Instantiations

In the full version of this paper [39], we describe one possible instantiation for the parameters of the extractable PRF scheme in Construction 4.5. We choose our parameters so that the underlying LWE and 1D-SIS assumptions that we rely on reduce to approximating worst-case lattice problems to within a sub-exponential factor $2^{\tilde{O}(n^{1/c})}$ for some constant c where n is the lattice dimension.

Remark 4.13 (Extractable PRFs from Weaker Lattice Assumptions). If we relax the requirements on the extractable PRF and only require the standard notion of correctness (Theorem 4.6), then it is possible to instantiate the parameters such that all of the remaining properties only rely on the hardness of solving worst-case lattice problems with a *nearly polynomial* approximation factor. We provide more details in full version of this paper [39].

5 Watermarking from Puncturable Extractable PRFs

In this section, we show how to use our extractable PRF to construct a mark-embedding watermarking scheme in the secret-key setting. In the full version of this paper [39], we show how to extend this construction to obtain *message-embedding watermarking* from the same assumptions. We also show to obtain a scheme that supports *public marking* in the random oracle model.

5.1 Watermarking PRFs

We begin by formally introducing the notion of a watermarkable PRF family.

Definition 5.1 (Watermarkable Family of PRFs). *Fix a security parameter λ and a message space $\mathcal{M}$. A secretly-extractable, message-embedding watermarkable family of PRFs with key-space $\mathcal{K}$, a domain $\mathcal{X}$, and a range $\mathcal{Y}$ is a tuple of algorithms $\Pi_{\mathsf{WM}} = (\mathsf{Setup}, \mathsf{Mark}, \mathsf{Extract})$ with the following properties:*

- $\mathsf{Setup}(1^\lambda) \to (\mathsf{pp}, \mathsf{wsk})$: *On input the security parameter λ, the setup algorithm outputs public parameters pp and the watermarking secret key wsk.*
- $\mathsf{Mark}(\mathsf{wsk}, k, m) \to C$: *On input the watermarking secret key wsk, a PRF key $k \in \mathcal{K}$, and a message $m \in \mathcal{M}$, the mark algorithm outputs a circuit $C \colon \mathcal{X} \to \mathcal{Y}$.*
- $\mathsf{Extract}(\mathsf{wsk}, C) \to m$: *On input the watermarking secret key wsk and a circuit $C \colon \mathcal{X} \to \mathcal{Y}$, the extraction algorithm outputs a string $m \in \mathcal{M} \cup \{\bot\}$.*

Moreover, Π_{WM} includes the description of a PRF family $\mathsf{F} \colon \mathcal{K} \times \mathcal{X} \to \mathcal{Y}$. The description of the PRF family may include the public parameters pp for the watermarkable PRF family, as sampled by the Setup algorithm. We often refer to Π_{WM} as a watermarking scheme for the PRF family $\mathsf{F} \colon \mathcal{K} \times \mathcal{X} \to \mathcal{Y}$.

Remark 5.2 (Mark-Embedding Watermarking). To simplify the description of our construction (and just focus on the main ideas), we also consider the weaker notion of *mark-embedding* watermarking where programs are either considered to be MARKED or UNMARKED. Equivalently, this corresponds to Definition 5.1 where $\mathcal{M} = \{\text{MARKED}\}$. When describing a mark-embedding watermarking scheme, we simplify the Mark algorithm to only take in two parameters: the watermarking secret key wsk and the PRF key k. In this case, we will also often write UNMARKED in place of $\bot$.

Correctness. The two correctness requirements on a software watermarking scheme are that the watermarked keys (approximately) implement the same functionality as the original key. Moreover, the extraction algorithm should successfully extract the embedded message from a marked key. We give the formal definitions and some discussion in the full version of this paper [39].

Pseudorandomness. The second property we require on a watermarkable family of PRFs is the usual notion of pseudorandomness for the PRF family. As discussed in Sect. 1, we also consider a stronger notion where pseudorandomness should hold even against the watermarking authority (i.e., the holder of the watermarking secret key). While many existing watermarking schemes based on obfuscation or lattices [16,27,38] naturally satisfy this property, both our scheme and that of Quach et al. [45] do not provide full pseudorandomness. However, in our case, we can achieve the weaker notion of T-restricted pseudorandomness against the watermarking authority. Intuitively, this means that pseudorandomness is ensured even against the watermarking authority provided that the authority does not see the PRF evaluations on any of T "special" points. We define this formally in the full version of this paper [39].

Unforgeability and Unremovability. The main security notions for a cryptographic watermarking scheme we consider are unremovability and unforgeability. Conceptually, unremovability says that an efficient adversary cannot should not be able to remove a watermark from a marked program while unforgeability says that an adversary should not be able to construct a new marked program. We provide the formal definitions in the full version of this paper [39].

5.2 Mark-Embedding Watermarking

In this section, we present our basic construction of a mark-embedding watermarkable family of PRFs (in the secret-key setting) from extractable PRFs. We refer to Sect. 1.2 for a high-level overview of this construction. In the full version of this paper [39], we build upon this construction to obtain message-embedding watermarking (and, in the random oracle model, message-embedding watermarking with public marking).

Construction 5.3 (Mark-Embedding Watermarkable PRFs). Let λ be a security parameter. Our *mark-embedding* watermarkable PRF relies on the following primitives:

- Let $\Pi_{\mathsf{EPRF}} = (\mathsf{EX.PrmsGen}, \mathsf{EX.SampleKey}, \mathsf{EX.Eval}, \mathsf{EX.Extract}, \mathsf{EX.Puncture}, \mathsf{EX.PunctureEval})$ be a puncturable extractable PRF with key-space $\mathcal{K}_{\mathsf{EPRF}}$, domain $\mathcal{X}$, and range $\mathcal{Y}$.
- Let $\mathsf{PRF} \colon \mathcal{K}_{\mathsf{PRF}} \times \mathcal{K}_{\mathsf{EPRF}} \to \mathcal{X}^\lambda$ be a pseudorandom function.

We construct a watermarkable PRF $\Pi_{\mathsf{WM}} = (\mathsf{Setup}, \mathsf{Mark}, \mathsf{Extract})$ as follows:

- Setup(1^λ): On input the security parameter λ, the setup algorithm samples a PRF key $k_{\mathsf{PRF}} \xleftarrow{\text{R}} \mathcal{K}_{\mathsf{PRF}}$, and parameters for the extractable PRF $(\mathsf{pp}, \mathsf{td}) \leftarrow$ EX.PrmsGen(1^λ). It outputs the public parameters pp and the watermarking secret key $\mathsf{wsk} = (k_{\mathsf{PRF}}, \mathsf{pp}, \mathsf{td})$.

- Mark(wsk, k): On input the watermarking secret key $\mathsf{wsk} = (k_{\mathsf{PRF}}, \mathsf{pp}, \mathsf{td})$, and a key $k \in \mathcal{K}_{\mathsf{EPRF}}$, the marking algorithm derives points $(x_1^*, \ldots, x_\lambda^*) \leftarrow$ PRF(k_{PRF}, k) and a punctured key $k' \leftarrow$ EX.Puncture($\mathsf{pp}, k, (x_1^*, \ldots, x_\lambda^*)$). It outputs the circuit $C \colon \mathcal{X} \to \mathcal{Y}$ that implements the punctured evaluation algorithm EX.PunctureEval($\mathsf{pp}, k', \cdot$).

- Extract(wsk, C): On input the watermarking secret key $\mathsf{wsk} = (k_{\mathsf{PRF}}, \mathsf{pp}, \mathsf{td})$, and a circuit $C \colon \mathcal{X} \to \mathcal{Y}$, the extraction algorithm first extracts a key $k \leftarrow$ EX.Extract($\mathsf{pp}, \mathsf{td}, C$). If $k = \bot$, output UNMARKED. Otherwise, it computes $(x_1^*, \ldots, x_\lambda^*) \leftarrow$ PRF(k_{PRF}, k). If $C(x_i^*) \neq$ EX.Eval(pp, k, x_i^*) for all $i \in [\lambda]$, then output MARKED. Otherwise, output UNMARKED.

The underlying PRF family $\mathsf{F} \colon \mathcal{K}_{\mathsf{EPRF}} \times \mathcal{X} \to \mathcal{Y}$ (induced by the public parameters pp for the watermarking scheme) is defined as $\mathsf{F}(k, x) := \mathsf{Eval}(\mathsf{pp}, k, x)$ and F.KeyGen simply returns EX.SampleKey(pp). Note that the description of the PRF family F includes the public parameters pp, but not the other components in the watermarking secret key wsk.

In the full version of this paper [39], we show that assuming Π_{EPRF} is a puncturable extractable PRF and PRF is a secure pseudorandom function, then Π_{WM} from Construction 5.3 is a mark-embedding watermarking scheme that provides unremovability, unforgeability, and T-restricted pseudorandomness against the watermarking authority.

5.3   Watermarking Instantiations from Lattices

In this section, we summarize our main results on constructing new lattice-based watermarking schemes from our puncturable extractable PRF. We refer to the full version of this paper [39] for the full details of our constructions (as well as extensions to the main construction).

Corollary 5.4 (Message-Embedding Watermarking from Lattices). *Fix a security parameter λ. Take any $0 < \varepsilon < \delta < 1/2$ where $\delta > \varepsilon + 1/\mathsf{poly}(\lambda)$. Then, assuming it is difficult to approximate to worst-case lattice problems (e.g., GapSVP or SIVP) with a nearly polynomial approximation factor, there exists a secret-key message-embedding watermarking scheme that satisfies ε-unremovability, a relaxed version of δ-unforgeability (see the full version of this paper [39]), and T-restricted pseudorandomness against the watermarking authority for $T = \lambda$. Assuming hardness of approximating worst-case lattice problems with a sub-exponential approximation factor, the resulting watermarking scheme satisfies the standard notion of δ-unforgeability. Moreover, under the same assumptions in the random oracle model, we obtain watermarking schemes that satisfy weak δ-unforgeability (and all of the other properties) that additionally supports public marking.*

Acknowledgments. We thank Willy Quach, Sina Shiehian, Daniel Wichs, and Giorgos Zirdelis for many insightful conversations. We thank the anonymous CRYPTO reviewers for helpful feedback on the presentation. This work was funded by NSF, DARPA, a grant from ONR, and the Simons Foundation. Opinions, findings and conclusions or recommendations expressed in this material are those of the authors and do not necessarily reflect the views of DARPA.

References

1. Agrawal, S., Boneh, D., Boyen, X.: Efficient lattice (H)IBE in the standard model. In: Gilbert, H. (ed.) EUROCRYPT 2010. LNCS, vol. 6110, pp. 553–572. Springer, Heidelberg (2010). https://doi.org/10.1007/978-3-642-13190-5_28

2. Agrawal, S., Freeman, D.M., Vaikuntanathan, V.: Functional encryption for inner product predicates from learning with errors. In: Lee, D.H., Wang, X. (eds.) ASIACRYPT 2011. LNCS, vol. 7073, pp. 21–40. Springer, Heidelberg (2011). https://doi.org/10.1007/978-3-642-25385-0_2

3. Ajtai, M.: Generating hard instances of the short basis problem. In: Wiedermann, J., van Emde Boas, P., Nielsen, M. (eds.) ICALP 1999. LNCS, vol. 1644, pp. 1–9. Springer, Heidelberg (1999). https://doi.org/10.1007/3-540-48523-6_1

4. Alwen, J., Peikert, C.: Generating shorter bases for hard random lattices. In: STACS (2009)

5. Baldimtsi, F., Kiayias, A., Samari, K.: Watermarking public-key cryptographic functionalities and implementations. In: Nguyen, P., Zhou, J. (eds.) ISC 2017. Lecture Notes in Computer Science, vol. 10599. Springer, Cham (2017). https://doi.org/10.1007/978-3-319-69659-1_10

6. Banerjee, A., Fuchsbauer, G., Peikert, C., Pietrzak, K., Stevens, S.: Key-homomorphic constrained pseudorandom functions. In: Dodis, Y., Nielsen, J.B. (eds.) TCC 2015. LNCS, vol. 9015, pp. 31–60. Springer, Heidelberg (2015). https://doi.org/10.1007/978-3-662-46497-7_2

7. Banerjee, A., Peikert, C.: New and improved key-homomorphic pseudorandom functions. In: Garay, J.A., Gennaro, R. (eds.) CRYPTO 2014. LNCS, vol. 8616, pp. 353–370. Springer, Heidelberg (2014). https://doi.org/10.1007/978-3-662-44371-2_20

8. Banerjee, A., Peikert, C., Rosen, A.: Pseudorandom functions and lattices. In: Pointcheval, D., Johansson, T. (eds.) EUROCRYPT 2012. LNCS, vol. 7237, pp. 719–737. Springer, Heidelberg (2012). https://doi.org/10.1007/978-3-642-29011-4_42

9. Barak, B., et al.: On the (Im)possibility of obfuscating programs. In: Kilian, J. (ed.) CRYPTO 2001. LNCS, vol. 2139, pp. 1–18. Springer, Heidelberg (2001). https://doi.org/10.1007/3-540-44647-8_1

10. Barak, B., et al.: On the (im)possibility of obfuscating programs. J. ACM **59**(2), 6 (2012)

11. Bitansky, N., Chiesa, A., Ishai, Y., Paneth, O., Ostrovsky, R.: Succinct non-interactive arguments via linear interactive proofs. In: Sahai, A. (ed.) TCC 2013. LNCS, vol. 7785, pp. 315–333. Springer, Heidelberg (2013). https://doi.org/10.1007/978-3-642-36594-2_18

12. Boneh, D., et al.: Fully key-homomorphic encryption, arithmetic circuit ABE and compact garbled circuits. In: Nguyen, P.Q., Oswald, E. (eds.) EUROCRYPT 2014. LNCS, vol. 8441, pp. 533–556. Springer, Heidelberg (2014). https://doi.org/10.1007/978-3-642-55220-5_30

13. Boneh, D., Ishai, Y., Sahai, A., Wu, D.J.: Lattice-based SNARGs and their application to more efficient obfuscation. In: Coron, J.-S., Nielsen, J.B. (eds.) EUROCRYPT 2017. LNCS, vol. 10212, pp. 247–277. Springer, Cham (2017). https://doi.org/10.1007/978-3-319-56617-7_9

14. Boneh, D., Kim, S., Montgomery, H.W.: Private puncturable PRFs from standard lattice assumptions. In: Coron, J.-S., Nielsen, J.B. (eds.) EUROCRYPT 2017. LNCS, vol. 10210, pp. 415–445. Springer, Cham (2017). https://doi.org/10.1007/978-3-319-56620-7_15

15. Boneh, D., Lewi, K., Montgomery, H.W., Raghunathan, A.: Key homomorphic PRFs and their applications. In: Canetti, R., Garay, J.A. (eds.) CRYPTO 2013. LNCS, vol. 8042, pp. 410–428. Springer, Heidelberg (2013). https://doi.org/10.1007/978-3-642-40041-4_23

16. Boneh, D., Lewi, K., Wu, D.J.: Constraining pseudorandom functions privately. In: Fehr, S. (ed.) PKC 2017. LNCS, vol. 10175, pp. 494–524. Springer, Heidelberg (2017). https://doi.org/10.1007/978-3-662-54388-7_17

17. Boneh, D., Waters, B.: Conjunctive, subset, and range queries on encrypted data. In: Vadhan, S.P. (ed.) TCC 2007. LNCS, vol. 4392, pp. 535–554. Springer, Heidelberg (2007). https://doi.org/10.1007/978-3-540-70936-7_29

18. Boneh, D., Waters, B.: Constrained pseudorandom functions and their applications. In: Sako, K., Sarkar, P. (eds.) ASIACRYPT 2013. LNCS, vol. 8270, pp. 280–300. Springer, Heidelberg (2013). https://doi.org/10.1007/978-3-642-42045-0_15

19. Boyle, E., Goldwasser, S., Ivan, I.: Functional signatures and pseudorandom functions. In: Krawczyk, H. (ed.) PKC 2014. LNCS, vol. 8383, pp. 501–519. Springer, Heidelberg (2014). https://doi.org/10.1007/978-3-642-54631-0_29

20. Brakerski, Z., Cash, D., Tsabary, R., Wee, H.: Targeted homomorphic attribute-based encryption. In: Hirt, M., Smith, A. (eds.) TCC 2016. LNCS, vol. 9986, pp. 330–360. Springer, Heidelberg (2016). https://doi.org/10.1007/978-3-662-53644-5_13

21. Brakerski, Z., Tsabary, R., Vaikuntanathan, V., Wee, H.: Private constrained PRFs (and More) from LWE. In: Kalai, Y., Reyzin, L. (eds.) TCC 2017. LNCS, vol. 10677, pp. 264–302. Springer, Cham (2017). https://doi.org/10.1007/978-3-319-70500-2_10

22. Brakerski, Z., Vaikuntanathan, V.: Lattice-based FHE as secure as PKE. In: ITCS, pp. 1–12 (2014)

23. Brakerski, Z., Vaikuntanathan, V.: Constrained key-homomorphic PRFs from standard lattice assumptions. In: Dodis, Y., Nielsen, J.B. (eds.) TCC 2015. LNCS, vol. 9015, pp. 1–30. Springer, Heidelberg (2015). https://doi.org/10.1007/978-3-662-46497-7_1

24. Brakerski, Z., Vaikuntanathan, V.: Circuit-ABE from LWE: unbounded attributes and semi-adaptive security. In: Robshaw, M., Katz, J. (eds.) CRYPTO 2016. LNCS, vol. 9816, pp. 363–384. Springer, Heidelberg (2016). https://doi.org/10.1007/978-3-662-53015-3_13

25. Canetti, R., Chen, Y.: Constraint-hiding constrained PRFs for NC^1 from LWE. In: EUROCRYPT (2017)

26. Chen, Y., Vaikuntanathan, V., Wee, H.: GGH15 beyond permutation branching programs: proofs, attacks, and candidates. In: Shacham, H., Boldyreva, A. (eds.) CRYPTO 2018. LNCS, vol. 10992, pp. 577–607. Springer, Cham (2018). https://doi.org/10.1007/978-3-319-96881-0_20

27. Cohen, A., Holmgren, J., Nishimaki, R., Vaikuntanathan, V., Wichs, D.: Watermarking cryptographic capabilities. In: STOC (2016)

28. Gay, R., Méaux, P., Wee, H.: Predicate encryption for multi-dimensional range queries from lattices. In: Katz, J. (ed.) PKC 2015. LNCS, vol. 9020, pp. 752–776. Springer, Heidelberg (2015). https://doi.org/10.1007/978-3-662-46447-2_34

29. Gentry, C., Peikert, C., Vaikuntanathan, V.: Trapdoors for hard lattices and new cryptographic constructions. In: STOC (2008)

30. Goldreich, O., Goldwasser, S., Micali, S.: How to construct random functions (extended abstract). In: FOCS (1984)

31. Gorbunov, S., Vaikuntanathan, V., Wee, H.: Attribute-based encryption for circuits. In: STOC (2013)

32. Gorbunov, S., Vaikuntanathan, V., Wee, H.: Predicate encryption for circuits from LWE. In: Gennaro, R., Robshaw, M. (eds.) CRYPTO 2015. LNCS, vol. 9216, pp. 503–523. Springer, Heidelberg (2015). https://doi.org/10.1007/978-3-662-48000-7_25

33. Gorbunov, S., Vinayagamurthy, D.: Riding on asymmetry: efficient ABE for branching programs. In: Iwata, T., Cheon, J.H. (eds.) ASIACRYPT 2015. LNCS, vol. 9452, pp. 550–574. Springer, Heidelberg (2015). https://doi.org/10.1007/978-3-662-48797-6_23

34. Goyal, R., Koppula, V., Waters, B.: Lockable obfuscation. In: FOCS (2017)

35. Hopper, N., Molnar, D., Wagner, D.A.: From weak to strong watermarking. In: Vadhan, S.P. (ed.) TCC 2007. LNCS, vol. 4392, pp. 362–382. Springer, Heidelberg (2007). https://doi.org/10.1007/978-3-540-70936-7_20

36. Katz, J., Sahai, A., Waters, B.: Predicate encryption supporting disjunctions, polynomial equations, and inner products. In: EUROCRYPT (2008)

37. Kiayias, A., Papadopoulos, S., Triandopoulos, N., Zacharias, T.: Delegatable pseudorandom functions and applications. In: ACM CCS (2013)

38. Kim, S., Wu, D.J.: Watermarking cryptographic functionalities from standard lattice assumptions. In: Katz, J., Shacham, H. (eds.) CRYPTO 2017. LNCS, vol. 10401, pp. 503–536. Springer, Cham (2017). https://doi.org/10.1007/978-3-319-63688-7_17

39. Kim, S., Wu, D.J.: Watermarking prfs from lattices: stronger security via extractable prfs. IACR Cryptology ePrint Archive 2018: 986 (2018)

40. Lyubashevsky, V., Wichs, D.: Simple lattice trapdoor sampling from a broad class of distributions. In: Katz, J. (ed.) PKC 2015. LNCS, vol. 9020, pp. 716–730. Springer, Heidelberg (2015). https://doi.org/10.1007/978-3-662-46447-2_32

41. Micciancio, D., Peikert, C.: Trapdoors for lattices: simpler, tighter, faster, smaller. In: Pointcheval, D., Johansson, T. (eds.) EUROCRYPT 2012. LNCS, vol. 7237, pp. 700–718. Springer, Heidelberg (2012). https://doi.org/10.1007/978-3-642-29011-4_41

42. Naccache, D., Shamir, A., Stern, J.P.: How to copyright a function? In: Imai, H., Zheng, Y. (eds.) PKC 1999. LNCS, vol. 1560, pp. 188–196. Springer, Heidelberg (1999). https://doi.org/10.1007/3-540-49162-7_14

43. Nishimaki, R.: How to watermark cryptographic functions. In: Johansson, T., Nguyen, P.Q. (eds.) EUROCRYPT 2013. LNCS, vol. 7881, pp. 111–125. Springer, Heidelberg (2013). https://doi.org/10.1007/978-3-642-38348-9_7

44. Peikert, C., Shiehian, S.: Privately constraining and programming PRFs, the LWE way. In: Abdalla, M., Dahab, R. (eds.) PKC 2018. LNCS, vol. 10770, pp. 675–701. Springer, Cham (2018). https://doi.org/10.1007/978-3-319-76581-5_23

45. Quach, W., Wichs, D., Zirdelis, G.: Watermarking PRFs under standard assumptions: public marking and security with extraction queries. In: Beimel, A., Dziembowski, S. (eds.) TCC 2018. LNCS, vol. 11240, pp. 669–698. Springer, Cham (2018). https://doi.org/10.1007/978-3-030-03810-6_24

46. Regev, O.: On lattices, learning with errors, random linear codes, and cryptography. In: STOC (2005)
47. Sahai, A., Waters, B.: Fuzzy identity-based encryption. In: Cramer, R. (ed.) EUROCRYPT 2005. LNCS, vol. 3494, pp. 457–473. Springer, Heidelberg (2005). https://doi.org/10.1007/11426639_27
48. Wichs, D., Zirdelis, G.: Obfuscating compute-and-compare programs under LWE. In: FOCS (2017)
49. Yang, R., Au, M.H., Lai, J., Xu, Q., Yu, Z.: Collusion resistant watermarking schemes for cryptographic functionalities. IACR Cryptology ePrint Archive (2017)
50. Yang, R., Au, M.H., Lai, J., Xu, Q., Yu, Z.: Unforgeable watermarking schemes with public extraction. In: Catalano, D., De Prisco, R. (eds.) SCN 2018. LNCS, vol. 11035, pp. 63–80. Springer, Cham (2018). https://doi.org/10.1007/978-3-319-98113-0_4
51. Yoshida, M., Fujiwara, T.: Toward digital watermarking for cryptographic data. IEICE Trans. **94**(A(1)), 270–272 (2011)

Watermarking Public-Key Cryptographic Primitives

Rishab Goyal[1]([envelope]), Sam Kim[2]([envelope]), Nathan Manohar[3], Brent Waters[1,4], and David J. Wu[5]

[1] UT Austin, Austin, TX, USA
{rgoyal,bwaters}@cs.utexas.edu
[2] Stanford University, Stanford, CA, USA
skim13@cs.stanford.edu
[3] UCLA, Los Angeles, CA, USA
nmanohar@cs.ucla.edu
[4] NTT Research, East Palo Alto, CA, USA
[5] University of Virginia, Charlottesville, VA, USA
dwu4@virginia.edu

Abstract. A software watermarking scheme enables users to embed a message or mark within a program while preserving its functionality. Moreover, it is difficult for an adversary to remove a watermark from a marked program without corrupting its behavior. Existing constructions of software watermarking from standard assumptions have focused exclusively on watermarking pseudorandom functions (PRFs).

In this work, we study watermarking public-key primitives such as the signing key of a digital signature scheme or the decryption key of a public-key (predicate) encryption scheme. While watermarking public-key primitives might intuitively seem more challenging than watermarking PRFs, our constructions only rely on simple assumptions. Our watermarkable signature scheme can be built from the minimal assumption of one-way functions while our watermarkable public-key encryption scheme can be built from most standard algebraic assumptions that imply public-key encryption (e.g., factoring, discrete log, or lattice assumptions). Our schemes also satisfy a number of appealing properties: public marking, public mark-extraction, and collusion resistance. Our schemes are the first to simultaneously achieve all of these properties.

The key enabler of our new constructions is a relaxed notion of functionality-preserving. While traditionally, we require that a marked program (approximately) preserve the *input/output* behavior of the original program, in the public-key setting, preserving the "functionality" does not necessarily require preserving the *exact* input/output behavior. For instance, if we want to mark a signing algorithm, it suffices that the marked algorithm still output valid signatures (even if those signatures might be different from the ones output by the unmarked algorithm). Similarly, if we want to mark a decryption algorithm, it suffices that the marked algorithm correctly decrypt all valid ciphertexts (but may behave differently from the unmarked algorithm on invalid or malformed ciphertexts). Our relaxed notion of functionality-preserving captures the

A. Boldyreva and D. Micciancio (Eds.): CRYPTO 2019, LNCS 11694, pp. 367–398, 2019.
https://doi.org/10.1007/978-3-030-26954-8_12

essence of watermarking and still supports the traditional applications, but provides additional flexibility to enable new and simple realizations of this powerful cryptographic notion.

1   Introduction

Watermarking is a way to embed special information called a "mark" into digital objects such as images, videos, audio, or software so that the marked object has the same appearance or behavior of the original object. Moreover, it should be difficult for an adversary to remove the mark without damaging the object itself. Watermarking is a useful tool both for protecting ownership and for preventing unauthorized distribution of digital media.

Software Watermarking. In this work, we focus on software watermarking for cryptographic functionalities. Barak et al. [8,9] and Hopper et al. [35] provided the first rigorous mathematical framework for software watermarking. Very briefly, a software watermarking scheme consists of two main algorithms. First, there is a *marking* algorithm that takes as input a program, modeled as a Boolean circuit C, and outputs a new marked circuit C' with the property that C and C' agree almost everywhere. Second, there is an *extraction* algorithm that takes as input a circuit C and outputs a bit indicating whether the program is marked or not. In the case of message-embedding watermarking, the marking algorithm additionally takes a message τ as input, and the extraction algorithm will either output the mark τ or a special symbol $\perp$ to indicate an unmarked program. The primary security requirement is unremovability, which says that given a marked circuit C' with an embedded message τ, no efficient adversary can construct a new circuit $\tilde{C}'$ that has roughly the same behavior as C', and yet the extraction algorithm on $\tilde{C}'$ fails to output τ. Notably, there are no restrictions on the circuit the adversary can output (other than the requirement that the adversary be efficient). This notion of security is often referred to as security against *arbitrary removal strategies* and captures the intuitive notion of watermarking where an adversary cannot replicate a program's functionality without also preserving the watermark.

Realizing the strong security requirements put forth in the early works on cryptographic watermarking [8,9,35] has proven challenging. In fact, Barak et al. showed an impossibility result (under indistinguishability obfuscation) on the existence of watermarking schemes that are *perfectly functionality-preserving* (i.e., schemes where the input/output behavior of the marked function is identical to that of the original function). In light of this lower bound, early works [44,48,60] provided partial results for watermarking specific classes of cryptographic functionalities by imposing limitations on the adversary's ability to modify the program and remove the watermark.

The first positive result on constructing watermarking schemes with security against *arbitrary* adversarial strategies was due to Cohen et al. [27] who showed that if we relax the perfect functionality-preserving requirement to only require *statistical* functionality-preserving (i.e., the marked function only has to implement the original function almost everywhere), then watermarking is possible. Moreover, Cohen et al. showed how to watermark several classes of cryptographic primitives, including pseudorandom functions (PRFs) and public-key encryption, with strong security from indistinguishability obfuscation. Since the seminal work of Cohen et al., a number of works have studied how to build watermarkable families of PRFs from weaker assumptions such as lattice-based assumptions [37,38] or CCA-secure encryption [52].

Watermarking Public-Key Primitives. Existing constructions of software watermarking from standard cryptographic assumptions all focus on watermarking symmetric primitives, notably, PRFs [37,38,52]. The one exception is the work of Baldimtsi et al. [6], who showed how to watermark public-key cryptographic primitives, but in a stateful setting, and under a modified security model where a trusted watermarking authority generates *both* unmarked and marked keys.[1] Our focus in this work is constructing software watermarking schemes for two classes of public-key cryptographic primitives: digital signatures and (CPA-secure) public-key encryption (and more generally, public-key predicate encryption [19,36,55]).

1.1   Our Contributions

In this work, we show how to construct a watermarkable signature scheme, where the signing functionality can be marked, as well as a watermarkable public-key (predicate) encryption scheme, where the decryption functionality can be marked. Moreover, all of our constructions are based on very weak assumptions: namely, our watermarkable signature scheme can be constructed based on any vanilla signature scheme (say, from one-way functions [31]), and our watermarkable public-key predicate encryption scheme can be based on any public-key encryption scheme together with a low-complexity pseudorandom generator (implied by most standard intractability assumptions [7,45–47]). One caveat is that our watermarkable predicate encryption scheme is only bounded-collusion secure.

Relaxing Functionality-Preserving. In spite of the recent progress in realizing new constructions of cryptographic watermarking from standard assumptions, watermarking remains a challenging notion to realize. Existing constructions of watermarking [37,38,52] from standard assumptions do not support properties like collusion resistance (where the watermark remains unremovable even if a user sees multiple marked versions of the program) or public verifiability (where anyone is able to tell if a program is marked). Moreover, these constructions rely on heavy cryptographic machinery, such as fully homomorphic encryption, even to watermark a PRF.

Our starting point, in this work, is to take a step back and revisit some of the definitions underlying software watermarking. Much like Cohen et al. [27] started by relaxing perfect functionality-preserving to statistical functionality-preserving and used that as the basis for obtaining the first positive results on watermarking, we also start by identifying another meaningful relaxation of the functionality-preserving requirement. As discussed above, functionality-preserving is typically

---

[1] In the standard watermarking model, anyone can generate keys (without going through or trusting the watermarking authority), and at a later time, decide if they want to mark the keys or not.

synonymous with preserving a program's input/output behavior: namely the input/output behavior of a marked circuit C' should be almost identical to that of the original circuit C. In many settings, such as when C implements a PRF, this is indeed the most natural notion of functionality-preserving. However, when considering the signing functionality of a signature scheme or the decryption functionality of an encryption scheme, there is additional flexibility:

- Suppose the circuit C implements the signing algorithm for a signature scheme. The functionality we care about is that on input a message m, $C(m)$ outputs a valid signature (with respect to the verification key vk). In this case, we can preserve this functionality *without* preserving the exact input/output behavior. Namely, we can allow the marked circuit C' to behave differently from C, as long as $C'(m)$ still outputs a valid signature (under vk) on the message m. In particular, the marked circuit is just as good as the original signing circuit even if they do not have identical input/output behavior. For instance, if we are watermarking the signing key used in a signature-based challenge-response authentication scheme, it suffices that the marked key still produces valid signatures, even if those signatures are not exactly the same as the ones output by an unmarked key.
- Suppose the circuit C implements the decryption algorithm for a public-key encryption scheme. In this case, the functionality we care about is that on input a valid ciphertext ct (i.e., one output by the encryption algorithm), $C(\text{ct})$ outputs the underlying message m. In this case, the set of valid ciphertexts (i.e., those in the support of the honest encryption algorithm) might form a sparse subset of a larger space. In this case, we can define our functionality-preserving requirement to just require the marked circuit C' to correctly decrypt the set of valid ciphertexts. If we invoke C' on an invalid or malformed ciphertext, then C' and C are allowed to disagree. Analogous to the case with the signature scheme, the marked circuit C' is just as useful as a decryption circuit. Since the behavior of the decryption algorithm on a malformed ciphertext is usually unspecified, preserving this behavior seems non-essential for most applications. For example, if we are watermarking the decryption key (e.g., for a Blu-Ray player), it suffices that the marked key correctly decrypts *valid* ciphertexts.

To summarize, in the public-key setting, we can capture the spirit of "functionality-preserving" watermarking without requiring that the marked circuit and the unmarked circuit have identical input/output behaviors. It turns out that this added degree of freedom enables new constructions of software watermarking from simple assumptions (e.g., one-way functions or public-key encryption) that also satisfy a number of desirable properties that have eluded all existing watermarking constructions: collusion resistance, public marking, and public extraction. We discuss these properties in greater detail below and then comment more broadly on their implications.

Our Results. By working with our relaxed notion of functionality-preserving, we construct watermarkable signatures and watermarkable public-key predicate encryption schemes that *simultaneously* achieve *all* of the following properties:

- **Collusion resistance:** Existing constructions of watermarking [14,27,37,38, 52] only provide unremovability against adversaries that see a *single* marked key. While this is the natural notion in the setting where programs are either marked or unmarked, this is not true in the message-embedding case. In fact, in all the aforementioned constructions, an adversary that obtains two copies of a key marked with different messages $\tau \neq \tau'$ can efficiently construct a new program that is functionally-similar to the marked program, and yet does not contain the watermark. Such watermarking schemes are not *collusion resistant*. We say that a watermarking scheme is collusion resistant if an adversary who sees marked versions of a circuit C with marks $\tau_1, \ldots, \tau_n$ cannot construct a new circuit C' that is functionally-close to C and yet, on input C', the extraction algorithm fails to produce one of $\tau_1, \ldots, \tau_n$.[2] In applications where keys are watermarked with different identities (for instance, when the decryption key embedded in a Blu-Ray player is marked with the owner's name), collusion resistant unremovability is a critical property. In this work, we construct a watermarkable signature scheme that is fully collusion resistant (i.e., collusion resistant against an adversary who can see an arbitrary polynomial of marked circuits) and a watermarkable public-key predicate encryption scheme that provides bounded-collusion resistance.
- **Public marking:** A watermarking scheme supports public marking if anyone is able to run the marking algorithm. Conversely, a scheme supports secret marking if only the holder of a secret watermarking key is able to watermark programs. Public marking is a desirable feature because users are able to watermark their secret keys without having to share them with a watermarking authority. Several previous watermarking schemes for PRFs [38,52] provided public marking, but at the expense of giving the watermarking authority a trapdoor that allows it to break security of all of the keys in the system (including *unmarked* keys). Our schemes naturally support public marking without this drawback (and, in fact, our schemes do not require the existence of a central watermarking authority at all).
- **Public extraction:** A watermarking scheme supports public mark-extraction if anyone can run the extraction algorithm and obtain the watermark within a piece of software. This is useful if users want to directly prove software ownership (or authenticity) without going through a trusted watermarking authority. Obtaining watermarkable PRFs with public extraction from standard assumptions remains a major open problem, and existing watermarking schemes with this property [27] all rely on indistinguishability obfuscation. In this work, all of our schemes support public mark-extraction.
- **Security against a malicious watermarking authority:** A watermarking scheme that supports public marking and public mark-extraction is very appealing because users do *not* need to trust a central watermarking authority for marking or extraction. Our schemes give the first watermarking scheme that supports public marking and public extraction. This resolves a key open ques-

---

[2] This is conceptually very similar to the closely-related cryptographic primitive of traitor tracing, and we discuss the similarities and differences in greater detail later in this section and in Sect. 1.2.

tion in the work of Cohen et al. [27], although under a relaxed (but still meaningful) notion of functionality-preserving. In fact, our schemes remain secure even if the public parameters of the watermarking scheme are chosen maliciously.

Our relaxed notion of functionality-preserving is certainly much weaker than the more stringent requirement of preserving input/output behavior. But, as we discussed above, our relaxed notion still seems to capture the essence of the requirement in the context of watermarking signatures and encryption schemes. By relaxing this functionality-preserving requirement, we are able to achieve stronger security notions from weaker cryptographic assumptions. At a philosophical level, our work highlights the need to further explore and identify the "right" set of definitions for software watermarking that enable useful and meaningful constructions from simple assumptions while still supporting the standard applications of software watermarking.

Watermarking Digital Signatures. Our watermarkable digital signature scheme relies on constrained signatures (also known as policy-based signatures) [10,59]. In a constrained signature scheme over a message space $\mathcal{M}$, the signing key sk can be used to derive a constrained signing key sk_f for a particular predicate $f \colon \mathcal{M} \to \{0, 1\}$ with the property that the constrained key sk_f can be used to sign all messages m where $f(m) = 1$. The security property is that an adversary who is given constrained keys $\mathsf{sk}_1, \ldots, \mathsf{sk}_n$ for functions $f_1, \ldots, f_n$ cannot produce a valid signature on any message m where $f_i(m) = 0$ for all $i \in [n]$. It is straightforward to construct constrained signatures from any standard signature scheme using certificates [10], and we briefly recall this basic construction in Sect. 3.3.

A constrained signature scheme that supports the class of "prefix-based" constraints immediately gives rise to a watermarkable signature scheme. In more detail, if we want to construct a watermarkable signature with message space $\mathcal{M}$ and mark space $\mathcal{T}$, we use a prefix-constrained signature scheme with message space $\mathcal{T} \times \mathcal{M}$. Signing and verification keys for the watermarkable signature directly correspond to signing and verification keys for the underlying prefix-constrained signature scheme. A signature on a message m consists of a tuple $\sigma_m = (\bot, \sigma')$ where σ' is a signature on $(\bot, m)$. To verify a signature $\sigma = (\tau, \sigma')$ on a message m, the verification algorithm checks that σ' is a valid signature on the pair (τ, m). Now, to mark a signing key with mark $\tau^* \in \mathcal{T}$, the user constrains the signing key sk to the prefix-based constraint $f_{\tau^*} \colon \mathcal{T} \times \mathcal{M} \to \{0, 1\}$ where $f_{\tau^*}(\tau, x) = 1$ if $\tau^* = \tau$ and 0 otherwise. The marked circuit C_{τ^*} is a circuit that takes as input a message m and outputs (τ^*, σ'), where σ' is a signature on (τ^*, m) using the constrained key sk_{τ^*}. To extract a watermark from a candidate circuit C', simply sample a random message $m \xleftarrow{\mathrm{R}} \mathcal{M}$,[3] compute

---

[3] More generally, we can consider a stronger notion of unremovability where we replace the uniform distribution over $\mathcal{M}$ with *any* (adversarially-chosen) efficiently-sampleable distribution over $\mathcal{M}$ where the circuit succeeds in generating valid signatures with non-negligible probability. Notably, the support of this distribution may have negligible density in $\mathcal{M}$. We provide more details in the full version of this paper.

$(\tau, \sigma') \leftarrow C'(m)$, and output τ if σ' is a valid signature on (τ, m). Note that if C' only succeeds in producing valid signatures with ε probability (for non-negligible ε), then this procedure can be repeated λ/ε times. If no marks are extracted after λ/ε iterations, then output $\perp$ (to indicate an unmarked circuit).

By correctness of the underlying constrained signature scheme, the marked circuit C_{τ^*} outputs valid signatures on all messages $m \in \mathcal{M}$, so the marked circuit is functionality-preserving (even though the signatures output by C are noticeably different than the signatures output by the original signing algorithm). Unremovability follows from security of the underlying constrained signature. Namely, an adversary who only has signing circuits marked with $\tau_1, \ldots, \tau_n$ should only be able to compute signatures on tuples of the form (τ_i, m) for $i \in [n]$. Thus, if the extraction algorithm outputs some $\tau' \neq \tau_i$ for all $i \in [n]$, then the adversary's circuit must have forged a valid signature on (τ', m) for some message $m \in \mathcal{M}$, which breaks security of the underlying constrained signature scheme. In addition, if the underlying constrained signature scheme is collusion resistant (i.e., security holds against adversaries that obtain an a priori unbounded polynomial number of constrained keys), then the resulting watermarkable signature scheme is also collusion resistant. We describe this construction and its security analysis in greater detail in Sect. 3.

Watermarking Public-Key Encryption and Traitor Tracing. Turning now to (CPA-secure) public-key encryption, we first describe a correspondence between watermarkable public-key encryption and traitor tracing [24]. In traitor tracing, there is a set of n honest users, each associated with a numeric identity $i \in [n]$. In addition, there is a central authority that generates a public key pk for the scheme as well as secret decryption keys sk_i for each user $i \in [n]$. Anyone can encrypt a message under the public key pk, and each legitimate user is able to decrypt the resulting ciphertext using their individual secret key sk_i. The tracing property says that there is an efficient tracing algorithm that, given black-box access to any valid decryption circuit, is able to recover at least one of the secret decryption keys sk_i that went into constructing the private decoder. As noted by Nishimaki et al. [49], a collusion resistant watermarkable public-key encryption scheme can be used to build a traitor tracing scheme: namely, the secret decryption keys for each user would correspond to watermarked decryption keys, where the watermark is the user's index.

With a few syntactic changes, the converse also holds; namely, any traitor tracing scheme that supports *public* tracing also implies a watermarkable public-key encryption scheme under our relaxed notion of functionality-preserving. Typically, in a traitor tracing scheme, there is a central authority that generates the public key and *all* of the decryption keys at the same time. In watermarking, however, anyone should be able to sample a public/private key-pair and, later on, have the ability to watermark their decryption key. However, this distinction is superficial, as we can always take the master secret key of the traitor tracing scheme to be the setup randomness and let that be the secret key in the watermarkable public-key encryption scheme. To mark the secret key with an identity $i \in [n]$, the marking algorithm would run the setup algorithm of the traitor tracing scheme and output decryption key sk_i. Unremovability of the scheme follows directly from the traceability of the underlying traitor tracing scheme.[4]

Watermarking Advanced Public-Key Functionalities. Having established a correspondence between traitor tracing schemes with public tracing and watermarkable public-key encryption schemes, we ask whether we can watermark more complex public-key functionalities like identity-based encryption [13,26,54], attribute-based encryption [34,53], or predicate encryption [19,36,55]. In the following description, we focus on predicate encryption, the most general notion among these primitives. In a (key-policy) predicate encryption scheme, ciphertexts are associated with an attribute x as well as a message m, while secret keys are associated with functions or predicates f. A secret key sk_f for a predicate f can decrypt all ciphertexts encrypted with respect to an attribute x where $f(x) = 1$. The security property is that an adversary who has keys $sk_1, \ldots, sk_n$ for predicates $f_1, \ldots, f_n$ cannot learn anything about ciphertexts encrypted to an attribute x where $f_i(x) = 0$ for all $i \in [n]$. Moreover, in a predicate encryption scheme, the ciphertexts *hide* the attribute x (whereas in the similar setting of attribute-based encryption, the attribute is public).

The question we ask is whether we can watermark the decryption keys sk_f in a predicate encryption scheme. As an example application, imagine an organization that uses a predicate encryption scheme for enforcing access control (e.g., ciphertexts are tagged with different classification levels), and it wants to issue decryption keys to different clients, each marked with the client's identity. Then, if a client uses their key to construct an unauthorized decryption device, it is possible to identify the identity of the client (by extracting the watermark).

Constructing a Watermarkable Predicate Encryption Scheme. In this work, we show that a generalization of the traitor tracing scheme by Nishimaki et al. [49] in combination with a hierarchical functional encryption scheme [22] gives a watermarkable (bounded-collusion) predicate encryption scheme based only on public-key encryption and the existence of pseudorandom generators (PRGs) computable in NC^1 (which follow from standard intractability assumptions such as factoring, discrete log, or lattice-based assumptions [7,45–47]). This notion is conceptually similar to the notion of attribute-based traitor tracing, and we compare and contrast the two notions in Sect. 1.1. In contrast to the setting of watermarking public-key encryption, watermarking predicate encryption does not appear to follow from attribute-based traitor tracing (although the converse does follow).

The starting point of our construction is the classic approach for constructing traitor tracing via a *private linear broadcast encryption* (PLBE) introduced by

---

[4] Traditionally, in a traitor tracing scheme, the tracing algorithm requires a secret tracing key output by the tracing algorithm [16,23,30,33]. A traitor tracing scheme supports public tracing [2,18,49] if the tracing algorithm does not depend on any secret information. In this simple construction of watermarkable public-key encryption from traitor tracing, the extraction algorithm would not have access to the tracing key, so instantiating this basic blueprint will require a traitor tracing scheme that supports public tracing.

Boneh et al. [16]. In a PLBE scheme with n users, each associated with an index $i \in [n]$, it is possible to construct a ciphertext that can only be decrypted by users whose index $i < T$ is smaller than some threshold T. Moreover, ciphertexts encrypted to two different thresholds $T < T'$ are only distinguishable if a user possesses a secret key for an index $i \in \{T, T+1, \ldots, T'-1\}$. A PLBE scheme that supports n users implies a traitor tracing scheme with identity space $[n]$: namely, to trace a circuit C, the tracing algorithm encrypts (random) messages to indices $i = 0, 1, \ldots, n$, and tests whether C correctly decrypts the ciphertext or not. When $i = 0$, decryption always fails, while at $i = n$, decryption should succeed with noticeable probability. Thus, there must be some index i where there is a "big jump" in the decryption success probability, which corresponds to the user possessing the decryption key for index i. When n is polynomial, the tracing algorithm can simply do a linear scan over the entire identity space to identify the big jumps. Nishimaki et al. [49] show how to generalize this approach to the setting where the identity space is exponential (which allows embedding arbitrary information in the decryption keys).

As described above, a traitor tracing scheme that supports public tracing directly implies a watermarkable public-key encryption scheme. To extend this to the setting of watermarking a predicate encryption scheme, we use a hierarchical functional encryption scheme. In a standard functional encryption (FE) scheme [17,50], encryption keys are associated with functions f, and decrypting a ciphertext encrypting a value x with a function key sk_f for f yields the value $f(x)$. It is not difficult to see that a FE scheme can be used to build a predicate encryption scheme as well as a PLBE scheme (this is the approach taken by Nishimaki et al. [49] in their traitor-tracing construction). In a hierarchical FE scheme [22], there is an additional delegation function that allows one to take a function key sk_f for a function f and delegate it to a key $\mathsf{sk}_{g \circ f}$ for the function $g \circ f$. At a high-level, our construction of a watermarkable predicate encryption scheme relies on a two-level hierarchical FE scheme, where the ordinary function keys are used to implement a predicate encryption scheme, while the marked keys consist of a delegated key that embeds a PLBE functionality (used to embed the watermark).

In more detail, to encrypt a message m with attribute x, we construct an FE encryption of the triple $(x, m, 1)$, where the last component is a special flag (used for mark extraction). A predicate encryption key for the predicate f consists of an FE key for the associated function g_f where

$$g_f(x, m, b) = \begin{cases} (x, m) & b = 0 \\ (0^\ell, 0^n) & b = 1 \text{ and } f(x) = 0 \\ (1^\ell, m) & b = 1 \text{ and } f(x) = 1. \end{cases}$$

By construction, decrypting an honestly-generated ciphertext with attribute x and message m with a key f where $f(x) = 1$ will always yield the pair $(1^\ell, m)$, from which the message can be recovered. Now, to mark a key sk_f with a mark $\tau \in \{0,1\}^\ell \setminus \{1^\ell\}$, we take sk_f and use the delegation mechanism to issue a function key for the function $h_\tau \circ g_f$ where

$$h_\tau(x, m) = \begin{cases} (0^\ell, 0^n) & x \leq \tau \\ (1^\ell, m) & x > \tau, \end{cases}$$

where we interpret $x, \tau \in \{0, 1\}^\ell$ as the binary representation of an ℓ-bit integer. We make two observations. First, the marked key can still be used to decrypt all honestly-generated ciphertexts (namely, ciphertexts where the flag is set to 1). However, notice that when the flag $b = 0$, the marked key can only decrypt ciphertexts where the encrypted attribute x exceeds the threshold τ associated with the marked key. This precisely coincides with the semantics of a PLBE scheme. We can now apply the techniques developed by Nishimaki et al. [49] to extract the associated identity τ, thereby recovering the watermark. We provide the full description of this scheme and its analysis in Sect. 4. Overall, we show that we can obtain a bounded-collusion resistant watermarkable family of predicate encryption schemes from public-key encryption and low-complexity PRGs; both of these assumptions can be instantiated by most assumptions that imply public-key encryption (e.g., factoring, discrete log, or lattice-based assumptions [7, 45–47]).

The parameter sizes of the resulting bounded-collusion watermarkable predicate encryption scheme are directly inherited from those of the underlying bounded-collusion hierarchical functional encryption scheme, which can in turn be built from a standard bounded-collusion functional encryption scheme [22]. For instance, instantiating the underlying functional encryption scheme with [32] yields a watermarkable predicate encryption scheme where the ciphertext size scales with $O(Q^4)$, where Q is the collusion bound. Alternatively, with the FE scheme from [3], the ciphertext size scales with $O(Q^2)$ and with the scheme from [5], the ciphertext size scales with $O(Q)$.

1.2   Additional Related Work

In this section, we survey some additional related work as well as compare our new watermarking notions to related notions studied in prior work.

Constrained Signatures. Numerous works [10, 21, 43, 59] have studied constructing constrained signatures (and variants thereof) together with properties like privacy, anonymity, succinct keys, or succinct signatures.

Traitor Tracing. Since the work of Chor et al. [24], there have been a vast number of constructions of fully collusion resistant traitor tracing from combinatorial constructions [15, 56], pairing-based assumptions [16, 18, 29, 30, 41, 42], lattice-based assumptions [23, 33], and indistinguishability obfuscation [20, 49]. With the exception of [49], the existing constructions only support efficient tracing over a polynomial-size identity space (this is referred to as "flexible" traitor tracing [49]). There are also numerous constructions that provide security in the bounded-collusion setting [1, 2, 11, 12, 24, 25, 28, 39, 40, 51, 57, 58].

Attribute-Based Traitor Tracing. Directly relevant to our notion of watermarkable predicate encryption is the notion of attribute-based traitor tracing

[1,23,41,42], which is a hybrid of attribute-based encryption and traitor tracing. The main difference between these two notions is that in the traitor-tracing setting, the marking and key-generation algorithms are combined (namely, the key-generation algorithm takes as input the function together with the mark). In watermarking, we have the additional flexibility that we can embed the watermark *after* issuing the key as well as support watermarking *adversarially-chosen* keys. When considering the simpler notion of watermarkable public-key encryption and traitor tracing, we can equate these two notions with a suitable redefinition of the traitor tracing schema (assuming that the traitor tracing scheme supports a *public* tracing algorithm). However, this equivalence does not seem to extend to the setting of attribute-based encryption or predicate encryption. Another key difference is that existing constructions of attribute-based traitor tracing from standard assumptions only support tracing over a polynomial-size identity space, while in the standard notions of message-embedding watermarking, the identity space is exponential. Note that since a watermarkable predicate encryption scheme implies an attribute-based traitor tracing scheme, our results give a bounded-collusion attribute-based traitor tracing scheme that supports an exponential number of possible identities.

2   Preliminaries

We begin by introducing the notation that we use in this work. We use λ (often implicitly) to denote the security parameter. We write $\mathsf{poly}(\lambda)$ to denote a quantity that is bounded by a fixed polynomial in λ and $\mathsf{negl}(\lambda)$ to denote a function that is $o(1/\lambda^c)$ for all $c \in \mathbb{N}$. We say that an event occurs with overwhelming probability if its complement occurs with negligible probability. We say an algorithm is efficient if it runs in probabilistic polynomial time in the length of its input. For two families of distributions $\mathcal{D}_1 = \{\mathcal{D}_{1,\lambda}\}_{\lambda \in \mathbb{N}}$ and $\mathcal{D}_2 = \{\mathcal{D}_{2,\lambda}\}_{\lambda \in \mathbb{N}}$, we write $\mathcal{D}_1 \overset{c}{\approx} \mathcal{D}_2$ if the two distributions are computationally indistinguishable (i.e., no efficient algorithm can distinguish distribution $\mathcal{D}_1$ from $\mathcal{D}_2$ except with negligible probability), and $\mathcal{D}_1 \overset{s}{\approx} \mathcal{D}_2$ if the two distributions are statistically indistinguishable (i.e., the statistical distance between $\mathcal{D}_1$ and $\mathcal{D}_2$ is $\mathsf{negl}(\lambda)$).

For an integer $n \geq 1$, we write $[n]$ to denote the set of integers $\{1, \ldots, n\}$. For integers $n \geq m \geq 1$, we write $[m, n]$ to denote the set of integers $\{m, m+1, \ldots, n\}$, and $[m, n]_{\mathbb{R}}$ to denote the closed interval between m and n (inclusive) over the real numbers. For a distribution $\mathcal{D}$, we write $x \leftarrow \mathcal{D}$ to denote that x is drawn from $\mathcal{D}$. For a finite set S, we write $x \xleftarrow{\mathbb{R}} S$ to denote that x is drawn uniformly at random from S. For sets $\mathcal{X}$ and $\mathcal{Y}$, we write $\mathsf{Funs}[\mathcal{X}, \mathcal{Y}]$ to denote the set of all functions from $\mathcal{X}$ to $\mathcal{Y}$. In the the full version of this paper, we also recall the definition of a digital signature scheme and a public-key predicate encryption scheme.

3   Watermarking Digital Signatures

In this section, we show how to watermark a digital signature scheme. We begin by formally introducing the notion of a watermarkable signature scheme. Our definitions are based on adaptations of existing definitions of watermarking PRFs [14,27,37,38,52] as well as the candidate definitions for watermarking public-key functionalities put forward in the work of Cohen et al. [27]. We present our construction in the fully public-key setting (namely, both marking and extraction are public operations, and there is no watermarking secret key).

Definition 3.1 (Watermarkable Signature). *A watermarkable digital signature scheme with message space $\mathcal{M}$ and mark space $\mathcal{T}$ is a tuple of algorithms* (Setup, KeyGen, Sign, Verify, Mark, Extract) *with the following properties:*

- Setup(1^λ) $\rightarrow$ wpp*: On input the security parameter λ, the setup algorithm outputs a set of watermarking public parameters* wpp.
- *The public parameters* wpp *induce a digital signature scheme* (KeyGen, Sign, Verify) *with message space $\mathcal{M}$, verification key space $\mathcal{VK}$, signing key space $\mathcal{SK}$, and signature space $\mathcal{SIG}$. Note that we implicitly allow* KeyGen, Sign, *and* Verify *to take* wpp *as input.*
- Mark(wpp, sk, τ) $\rightarrow C$*: On input the watermarking parameters* wpp*, a signing key* sk $\in \mathcal{SK}$*, and a mark $\tau \in \mathcal{T}$, the marking algorithm outputs a circuit $C \colon \mathcal{M} \rightarrow \mathcal{SIG}$.*
- Extract(wpp, vk, C) $\rightarrow \tau/\bot$*: On input the watermarking parameters* wpp*, a verification key* vk $\in \mathcal{VK}$*, and a circuit $C \colon \mathcal{M} \rightarrow \mathcal{SIG}$, the extraction algorithm either outputs a mark $\tau \in \mathcal{T}$ or a special symbol $\bot$.*

Remark 3.2 (Comparison with Cohen et al. [27]). There are several differences between our watermarking schema and that introduced by Cohen et al. [27]. We summarize these below:

- **Extraction semantics:** Our extraction algorithm Extract additionally takes the verification key associated with the signing circuit as an additional input. This does not seem like a substantial limitation to the usefulness of the scheme since in most applications, the verification key associated with a signature scheme is assumed to be publicly known.
- **Independent key-generation and marking algorithms:** In addition, we have *independent* key-generation and marking algorithms. The schema from Cohen et al. for public-key primitives introduced an additional restriction that the watermark is generated at the same time as the signing key, while in our scheme, the signing key can be generated independently, and later on, a user can decide to mark the key. Thus, our schema provides additional flexibility in how keys are generated and marked. In particular, our definition allows a user to take the same signing key and mark it with different messages (for instance, to give to different users). This definition is more similar to existing definitions for watermarking secret-key primitives, which consider independent key-generation and marking algorithms.

  We additionally note that if we allow the verification key to depend on the mark (i.e., as in the Cohen et al. construction), there is a simple way to satisfy their definition.[5] In particular, we simply include the mark τ as part of the signing key and verification key. A signature on a message m is just the pair (τ, σ), where σ is a vanilla signature on m. Verification first affirms that the first component of the signature is the mark τ and then checks σ as usual. If the adversary constructs a circuit that outputs valid signatures with probability better than $\varepsilon > 1/2 + 1/\mathsf{poly}(\lambda)$,[6] then the output of the circuit contains the mark τ on a majority of inputs. In this case, the extraction algorithm can evaluate the circuit on $\mathsf{poly}(\lambda)$ random inputs and output the majority tag. This basic construction does not apply in our setting because we require that the signing/verification keys be generated *independently* of the mark.

- **Collusion resistance:** Since our definition separates the key-generation and marking algorithms, the *same* signing key can be marked with different messages. Correspondingly, we can define a notion of *collusion resistant* watermarking, where unremovability holds even if the adversary sees the same signing key marked with *distinct* messages. This is a critical property for any realistic application of watermarking where a single key might be marked with multiple identities.

Correctness. Next, we introduce the correctness requirements of a watermarking scheme. There are three main properties we care about. The first is the usual notion of extraction correctness, which says that the extraction algorithm should successfully recover the watermark from an honestly-marked key. The second property is a "meaningfulness" or "non-triviality" property, which says that most circuits should not be marked. Finally, the third property is functionality-preserving. As noted in Sect. 1.1, one of the main differences between this work and previous works on software watermarking is we consider a relaxed notion of functionality-preserving, where we require that a marked signing key can sign arbitrary messages (that verify with respect to the *same* verification key), but we allow the resulting signatures to be different from the signatures output by the original signing key. In other words, the marked key implements a perfectly valid signing algorithm, but it does not have to preserve the exact input/output behavior of the unmarked signing key. We give the precise definition below:

Definition 3.3 (Correctness). *Let* $\Pi_{\mathsf{WM}} = (\mathsf{Setup}, \mathsf{KeyGen}, \mathsf{Sign}, \mathsf{Verify}, \mathsf{Mark}, \mathsf{Extract})$ *be a watermarkable signature scheme with message space* $\mathcal{M}$, *signature space* $\mathcal{SIG}$, *and verification key space* $\mathcal{VK}$. *Then,* Π_{WM} *is correct if for all* $\mathsf{wpp} \leftarrow$

---

[5] This basic construction also directly extends to their notion of watermarkable public-key encryption, which considers the analogous restriction where the encryption/decryption keys are sampled jointly with the watermark.

[6] As noted in Remark 3.9, the unremovability definition in Cohen et al. [27] (for message-embedding watermarking) is satisfiable only when the adversary is restricted to constructing circuits that agree with the marked circuit on strictly more than half of the inputs. This coincides with the setting where our simple construction applies.

Setup(1^λ), *the induced signature scheme* (KeyGen, Sign, Verify) *is correct, and the following properties also hold:*

- **Extraction correctness:** *For all marks* $\tau \in \mathcal{T}$,

$$\Pr[(\mathsf{vk}, \mathsf{sk}) \leftarrow \mathsf{KeyGen}(1^\lambda, \mathsf{wpp}) : \mathsf{Extract}(\mathsf{wpp}, \mathsf{vk}, \mathsf{Mark}(\mathsf{wpp}, \mathsf{sk}, \tau)) \neq \tau] = \mathsf{negl}(\lambda).$$

- **Meaningfulness:** *For all fixed circuits* $C \colon \mathcal{M} \to \mathcal{SIG}$ *(independent of the public parameters* wpp*) and all verification keys* $\mathsf{vk} \in \mathcal{VK}$,

$$\Pr[\mathsf{Extract}(\mathsf{wpp}, \mathsf{vk}, C) \neq \bot] = \mathsf{negl}(\lambda),$$

and for $(\mathsf{vk}, \mathsf{sk}) \leftarrow \mathsf{KeyGen}(\mathsf{wpp})$,

$$\Pr[\mathsf{Extract}(\mathsf{wpp}, \mathsf{vk}, \mathsf{Sign}(\mathsf{wpp}, \mathsf{sk}, \cdot)) \neq \bot] = \mathsf{negl}(\lambda).$$

- **Functionality-preserving:** *For all marks* $\tau \in \mathcal{T}$ *and all messages* $m \in \mathcal{M}$, *if we take* $(\mathsf{vk}, \mathsf{sk}) \leftarrow \mathsf{KeyGen}(1^\lambda, \mathsf{wpp})$ *and* $C \leftarrow \mathsf{Mark}(\mathsf{wpp}, \mathsf{sk}, \tau)$,

$$\Pr[\mathsf{Verify}(\mathsf{wpp}, \mathsf{vk}, m, C(m)) \neq 1] = \mathsf{negl}(\lambda).$$

Remark 3.4 (Unique Signature Schemes and Functionality-Preserving). We note that if we have a *unique* signature scheme (i.e., a signature scheme where for every message $m \in \mathcal{M}$, there is a unique signature σ that verifies with respect to the verification key), then our notion of functionality-preserving precisely coincides with preserving the input/output behavior of the original signing circuit. We do not know how to watermark a unique signature scheme and leave this as an intriguing open problem.

Security of the Underlying Signature Scheme. The first security requirement is that the underlying signature scheme associated with a watermarkable signature scheme satisfies the usual notion of unforgeability. In fact, we would like the stronger property that even if the watermarking parameters wpp are chosen in a malicious manner, the resulting signature scheme remains secure (i.e., provides unforgeability). Recent constructions of watermarking for PRFs [38,52] have the drawback that even a semi-honest watermarking authority is able to break security of the *unmarked* keys in the system (and previous constructions from standard assumptions [37] become insecure if the watermarking authority generates the parameters maliciously). Our security notion ensures that a malicious party cannot generate the parameters in such a way as to embed a "trapdoor" into the signature scheme. In fact, since our watermarking scheme supports both public marking and public verification, this property means that users can use the scheme without needing to trust any central authority; this is an appealing property that is not satisfied by *any* existing watermarking scheme.

Definition 3.5 (Signature Unforgeability). *Let* $\Pi_{\mathsf{WM}} = $ (Setup, KeyGen, Sign, Verify, Mark, Extract) *be a watermarkable signature scheme. We say that* Π_{WM} *satisfies signature unforgeability if the induced signature scheme* (KeyGen,

Sign, Verify) *satisfies unforgeability. We say that* Π_{WM} *satisfies* signature unforgeability in the presence of a malicious authority *if the induced signature scheme satisfies unforgeability even if the adversary can choose the public parameters* wpp *for* Π_{WM}.

Unremovability. The main security requirement we require from a watermarking scheme is unremovability: namely, an adversary that obtains one or more marked keys cannot produce a new key that preserves the same functionality as the original key and, yet, does not contain the watermark. Our definition is the direct generalization of the corresponding notion of unremovability in the setting of watermarking PRFs [14, 27], with the following differences:

- First, we use the same relaxation of functionality-preserving discussed above: namely, the adversary is allowed to construct any circuit that outputs valid signatures with noticeable probability (that verify under the signature scheme's verification key); it does not have to preserve the input/output behavior of the marked circuits it is given. This gives the adversary *more* power, but is consistent with our relaxed view of what it means to be "functionality-preserving" in the public-key setting.
- Second, we allow the adversary to make multiple marking queries: namely, the adversary can see the same signing key marked with different and adversarially-chosen identities, and, even then, we require that the adversary cannot produce a new circuit whose watermark is not one of the ones corresponding to a signing circuit already given to the adversary. Namely, if an adversary sees a signing key marked with identities τ_1 and τ_2, it cannot create a new functional signing circuit where the watermark is not one of τ_1 or τ_2. We discuss this notion of *collusion resistance* in greater detail in Remark 3.8.
- Finally, because of our relaxed notion of functionality-preserving, signatures output by the unmarked key can look different from signatures output by the marked key, so we additionally give the adversary access to the signing oracle with the unmarked key.

We give our formal definition below:

Definition 3.6 (Watermarking Signatures Security Experiment). *Let* $\Pi_{\mathsf{WM}} = (\mathsf{Setup}, \mathsf{KeyGen}, \mathsf{Sign}, \mathsf{Verify}, \mathsf{Mark}, \mathsf{Extract})$ *be a watermarkable signature scheme with message space* $\mathcal{M}$, *mark space* $\mathcal{T}$, *and signature space* $\mathcal{SIG}$. *Then, for an adversary* $\mathcal{A}$, *we define the watermarking signatures security experiment as follows:*

1. *The challenger begins by sampling* $\mathsf{wpp} \leftarrow \mathsf{Setup}(1^\lambda)$ *and* $(\mathsf{vk}, \mathsf{sk}) \leftarrow \mathsf{KeyGen}(1^\lambda, \mathsf{wpp})$. *The challenger gives* $(\mathsf{wpp}, \mathsf{vk})$ *to the adversary.*
2. *The adversary is now given access to the following oracles:*
   - *Marking oracle: On input a mark* $\tau \in \mathcal{T}$, *the challenger replies with* $C_\tau \leftarrow \mathsf{Mark}(\mathsf{wpp}, \mathsf{sk}, \tau)$.
   - *Signing oracle: On input a message* $m \in \mathcal{M}$, *the challenger replies with* $\sigma \leftarrow \mathsf{Sign}(\mathsf{sk}, m)$.

3. *The adversary outputs a circuit* $C^* \colon \mathcal{M} \to \mathcal{SIG}$.

The output of the experiment, denoted $\mathsf{ExptWM}_{\mathsf{Sig}}[\lambda, \mathcal{A}]$ *is* $\mathsf{Extract}(\mathsf{wpp}, \mathsf{vk}, C^*)$.

Definition 3.7 (ε-Unremovability). *Let Π_{WM} be a watermarkable signature scheme with message space $\mathcal{M}$ and signature space $\mathcal{SIG}$. We say an adversary $\mathcal{A}$ is ε-unremovable admissible if the adversary's circuit $C^* \colon \mathcal{M} \to \mathcal{SIG}$ in the watermarking signatures security experiment satisfies*

$$\Pr[m \xleftarrow{\text{\tiny R}} \mathcal{M} : \mathsf{Verify}(\mathsf{wpp}, \mathsf{vk}, m, C^*(m)) = 1] \geq \varepsilon.$$

In the watermarking signatures security experiment, let $\mathcal{Q} \subseteq \mathcal{T}$ be the set of marks the adversary submitted to the marking oracle. Then, Π_{WM} satisfies ε-unremovability if for all efficient and ε-unremovability admissible adversaries $\mathcal{A}$, $\Pr[\mathsf{ExptWM}_{\mathsf{Sig}}[\lambda, \mathcal{A}] \notin \mathcal{Q}] = \mathsf{negl}(\lambda)$.

Remark 3.8 (Collusion Resistance). We say that a watermarking scheme is *fully collusion resistant* if unremovability holds against all efficient adversaries that can make any a priori unbounded $\mathsf{poly}(\lambda)$ queries to the marking oracle. We say that it is q-bounded collusion resistant if unremovability hold only against efficient adversaries that make at most q marking queries. Existing watermarking schemes for cryptographic functionalities from standard assumptions are only 1-collusion resistant [37,38,52].

Remark 3.9 (Small Unremovability Thresholds). Previously, Cohen et al. [27] showed that message-embedding watermarking schemes satisfying ε-unremovability are possible only when $\varepsilon \geq 1/2 + 1/\mathsf{poly}(\lambda)$. This lower bound does not apply to our notion of ε-unremovability (Definition 3.7). In fact, our constructions satisfy ε-unremovability for *any* non-negligible $\varepsilon = 1/\mathsf{poly}(\lambda)$. The reason is that our mark-extraction algorithm takes in the verification key as input, while the Cohen et al. definition does not (i.e., their extraction algorithm only takes the circuit as input).

To provide some additional detail, we first recall the attack from Cohen et al. when $\varepsilon = 1/2$. Let C be the challenge circuit marked with a message m in the unremovability security game, and let C' be an arbitrary circuit (for a different function) marked with a message $m' \neq m$. In both the secret and public marking setting, the adversary can generate C' by either using the marking oracle (secret-marking setting) or using the public marking algorithm (public-marking setting). To carry out the attack, the adversary constructs a challenge circuit C^* that agrees with C on half of the points (chosen randomly) and agrees with C' on the other half. By symmetry, the extraction algorithm on C^* outputs m and m' with equal probability, where the probability is taken over the coins of the Extract algorithm and the adversary's randomness used to determine m, m', and C^*. This means that the probability that the extraction algorithm outputs m is at most $1/2$, and so the adversary succeeds with probability at least $1/2$.

The above attack critically relies on the fact that the adversary is able to obtain a marked circuit C' where the extraction algorithm on C' outputs $m' \neq m$. In order to mount the same attack in our setting, the adversary needs to be able to obtain a circuit C' such that $\mathsf{Extract}(\mathsf{wpp}, \mathsf{vk}, C') = m'$, where vk is the verification key chosen by the challenger. In the security game, there is no mechanism for the adversary to obtain a marked circuit with respect to vk other than by making a marking query on m'. If the adversary makes a marking query on m', then as long as the extraction algorithm recovers *either* m or m', the adversary does not break unremovability. Observe that if, on the contrary, vk is not provided as input to $\mathsf{Extract}$, then the adversary can easily construct a circuit with an embedded mark m' (by marking an arbitrary key of its choosing) and mount the Cohen et al. attack. This distinction, where the extraction algorithm is defined with respect to a *specific* verification key, enables us to circumvent the lower bound for ε-unremovability when $\varepsilon \leq 1/2$.

3.1 Building Block: Constrained Signatures

As discussed in Sect. 1.1, the main building block we use to construct a watermarkable signature scheme is a prefix-constrained signature (which can be built generically from any signature scheme, or more generally, any one-way function). We recall the formal definition below:

Definition 3.10 (Constrained Signatures [10,59]). *A constrained signature scheme with message space $\mathcal{M}$ and constraint family $\mathcal{F} \subseteq \mathsf{Funs}[\mathcal{M}, \{0,1\}]$ is a tuple of algorithm $\Pi_{\mathsf{CSig}} = (\mathsf{Setup}, \mathsf{Sign}, \mathsf{Verify}, \mathsf{Constrain}, \mathsf{ConstrainSign})$ with the following properties:*

- $\mathsf{Setup}(1^\lambda) \to (\mathsf{vk}, \mathsf{msk})$: *On input the security parameter λ, the setup algorithm outputs the verification key and the master secret key msk.*
- $\mathsf{Sign}(\mathsf{msk}, m) \to \sigma$: *On input the master signing key msk and a message $m \in \mathcal{M}$, the signing algorithm outputs a signature σ.*
- $\mathsf{Verify}(\mathsf{vk}, m, \sigma) \to b$: *On input the verification key vk, a message $m \in \mathcal{M}$, and a signature σ, the verification algorithm outputs a bit $b \in \{0,1\}$.*
- $\mathsf{Constrain}(\mathsf{msk}, f) \to \mathsf{sk}_f$: *On input the master signing key msk and a function $f \in \mathcal{F}$, the constrain algorithm outputs a constrained key sk_f.*
- $\mathsf{ConstrainSign}(\mathsf{sk}_f, m) \to \sigma$: *On input a constrained key sk_f and a message $m \in \mathcal{M}$, the signing algorithm outputs a signature σ.*

Definition 3.11 (Correctness). *A constrained signature scheme $\Pi_{\mathsf{CSig}} = (\mathsf{Setup}, \mathsf{Sign}, \mathsf{Verify}, \mathsf{Constrain}, \mathsf{ConstrainSign})$ with message space $\mathcal{M}$ and constraint family $\mathcal{F}$ is correct if for all messages $m \in \mathcal{M}$ and taking $(\mathsf{vk}, \mathsf{msk}) \leftarrow \mathsf{Setup}(1^\lambda)$,*

$$\Pr[\mathsf{Verify}(\mathsf{vk}, m, \mathsf{Sign}(\mathsf{msk}, m)) = 1] = 1.$$

In addition, for all constraints $f \in \mathcal{F}$ where $f(m) = 1$, if we compute $\mathsf{sk}_f \leftarrow \mathsf{Constrain}(\mathsf{msk}, f)$,

$$\Pr[\mathsf{Verify}(\mathsf{vk}, m, \mathsf{ConstrainSign}(\mathsf{sk}_f, m)) = 1] = 1.$$

Definition 3.12 (Constrained Unforgeability). *Let* $\Pi_{\mathsf{CSig}} = (\mathsf{Setup}, \mathsf{Sign},$ $\mathsf{Verify}, \mathsf{Constrain}, \mathsf{ConstrainSign})$ *be a constrained signature scheme with message space* $\mathcal{M}$ *and constraint family* $\mathcal{F}$. *We define the constrained unforgeability experiment between an adversary* $\mathcal{A}$ *and a challenger as follows:*

1. *At the beginning of the experiment, the challenger samples* $(\mathsf{vk}, \mathsf{msk}) \leftarrow$ $\mathsf{Setup}(1^\lambda)$ *and gives* vk *to the adversary.*
2. *The adversary is then given access to the following oracles:*
   - **Constrain oracle:** *On input a function* $f \in \mathcal{F}$, *the challenger replies with* $\mathsf{sk}_f \leftarrow \mathsf{Constrain}(\mathsf{msk}, f)$.
   - **Signing oracle:** *On input a message* $m \in \mathcal{M}$, *the challenger replies with a signature* $\sigma \leftarrow \mathsf{Sign}(\mathsf{msk}, m)$.
   - *At the end of the game, the adversary outputs a message-signature pair* (m^*, σ^*).

The output of the experiment, denoted $\mathsf{ExptCSig}[\mathcal{A}, \lambda]$ *is* 1 *if the following conditions hold:*

- *The adversary did not make a signing query on message* m^*.
- *The adversary did not make a constrain query on any function* $f \in \mathcal{F}$ *where* $f(m^*) = 1$.
- $\mathsf{Verify}(\mathsf{vk}, m^*, \sigma^*) = 1$.

We say that Π_{CSig} *is secure if for all efficient adversaries* $\mathcal{A}$, $\Pr[\mathsf{ExptCSig}[\mathcal{A}, \lambda] = 1] = \mathsf{negl}(\lambda)$.

3.2   Watermarking Signatures from Constrained Signatures

In this section, we show how to construct a fully collusion-resistant watermarking scheme for digital signatures from prefix-constrained signatures.

Construction 3.13 (Watermarkable Signatures from Prefix-Constrained Signatures). *Fix a message space* $\mathcal{M}$ *and a mark space* $\mathcal{T}$. *Let* $\varepsilon = 1/\mathsf{poly}(\lambda)$ *be an unremovability parameter. We define the following primitives:*

- *Let* $\mathcal{Z}$ *be a tag space, and let* $\mathcal{T}' = \mathcal{T} \cup \{\bot\}$.
- *For a mark* $\tau^* \in \mathcal{T}$, *let* $f_{\tau^*} \colon \mathcal{T}' \times \mathcal{M} \to \{0, 1\}$ *be the function where* $f_{\tau^*}(\tau, m) = 1$ *if* $\tau = \tau^*$ *and* 0 *otherwise.*
- *Let* $\Pi_{\mathsf{CSig}} = (\mathsf{CSig.Setup}, \mathsf{CSig.Sign}, \mathsf{CSig.Verify}, \mathsf{CSig.Constrain}, \mathsf{CSig.Constrain}$ $\mathsf{Sign})$ *be a constrained signature scheme with message space* $\mathcal{M}' = \mathcal{T}' \times \mathcal{M}$ *and function class* $\mathcal{F} = \{\tau^* \in \mathcal{T} \colon f_{\tau^*}\}$. *Let* $\mathcal{SIG}'$ *be the signature space of* Π_{CSig}.

We construct a watermarkable signature scheme $\Pi_{\mathsf{WM}} = (\mathsf{Setup}, \mathsf{KeyGen}, \mathsf{Sign},$ $\mathsf{Verify}, \mathsf{Mark}, \mathsf{Extract})$ *with signature space* $\mathcal{SIG} = \mathcal{Z} \times \mathcal{T}' \times \mathcal{SIG}'$ *as follows:*

- $\mathsf{Setup}(1^\lambda) \to \mathsf{wpp}$: *On input the security parameter* λ, *sample* $z \xleftarrow{\mathrm{R}} \mathcal{Z}$, *and output* $\mathsf{wpp} = z$.

- KeyGen$(1^\lambda, \text{wpp}) \to (\text{vk}, \text{sk})$: *On input the security parameter λ and public parameters* $\text{wpp} = z$, *the key-generation algorithm outputs a signing/verification key-pair* $(\text{vk}, \text{sk}) \leftarrow \text{CSig.Setup}(1^\lambda)$.
- Sign$(\text{wpp}, \text{sk}, m) \to \sigma$: *On input the public parameters* $\text{wpp} = z$, *a signing key* sk, *and a message* $m \in \mathcal{M}$, *the signing algorithm signs* $\sigma' \leftarrow \text{CSig.Sign}(\text{sk}, (\bot, m))$, *and outputs the signature* $\sigma = (z, \bot, \sigma')$.
- Verify$(\text{wpp}, \text{vk}, m, \sigma) \to b$: *On input the public parameters* $\text{wpp} = z$, *a verification key* vk, *a message* $m \in \mathcal{M}$, *and a signature* $\sigma = (z', \tau', \sigma')$, *the verification algorithm outputs 0 if* $z' \neq z$, *and, otherwise, it outputs the bit* $b \leftarrow \text{CSig.Verify}(\text{vk}, (\tau', m), \sigma')$.
- Mark$(\text{wpp}, \text{sk}, \tau) \to C$: *On input the public parameters* $\text{wpp} = z$, *a signing key* sk, *and a mark* $\tau \in \mathcal{T}$, *the marking algorithm computes* $\text{sk}_\tau \leftarrow \text{CSig.Constrain}(\text{sk}, f_\tau)$ *and outputs a circuit* $C_\tau \colon \mathcal{M} \to \mathcal{SIG}$ *where* $C_\tau(\cdot) := (z, \tau, \text{CSig.ConstrainSign}(\text{sk}_\tau, (\tau, \cdot)))$.
- Extract$(\text{wpp}, \text{vk}, C) \to \tau/\bot$: *On input the public parameters* $\text{wpp} = z$, *a verification key* vk, *and a circuit* $C \colon \mathcal{M} \to \mathcal{SIG}$, *the extraction algorithm performs the following procedure* $T = \lambda/\varepsilon = \text{poly}(\lambda)$ *times:*
  - *For* $i \in [T]$, *sample* $m_i \xleftarrow{\text{R}} \mathcal{M}$ *and compute* $(z_i', \tau_i', \sigma_i') \leftarrow C(m)$. *If* $z_i' = z$ *and* $\text{CSig.Verify}(\text{vk}, (\tau_i', m_i), \sigma_i') = 1$, *abort and output* τ_i'.
  If the above procedure does not abort with some output τ, *then output* $\bot$.

Correctness and Security Analysis. We now state our correctness and security theorems, but defer their formal analysis to the full version of this paper.

Theorem 3.14 (Correctness). *Suppose* $1/|\mathcal{Z}| = \text{negl}(\lambda)$ *and* Π_{CSig} *is correct. Then, the watermarkable signature scheme* Π_{WM} *from Construction 3.13 is correct (Definition 3.3).*

Theorem 3.15 (Signature Unforgeability). *If* Π_{CSig} *satisfies constrained unforgeability (Definition 3.12), then the watermarkable signature scheme* Π_{WM} *from Construction 3.13 satisfies signature unforgeability in the presence of a malicious watermarking authority (Definition 3.5).*

Theorem 3.16 (Unremovability). *Take any* $\varepsilon = 1/\text{poly}(\lambda)$. *If* $1/|\mathcal{M}| = \text{negl}(\lambda)$ *and* Π_{CSig} *satisfies constrained unforgeability (Definition 3.12), then the watermarkable signature scheme* Π_{WM} *from Construction 3.13 is* ε-*unremovable.*

3.3   Instantiations and Extensions

As noted by Bellare and Fuchsbauer [10], fully collusion resistant constrained signatures (for arbitrary circuit constraints) satisfying unforgeability follow immediately from any standard signature scheme (which can in turn be based on one-way functions [31]). We briefly recall the "certificate-based" construction here. The public parameters for the constrained signature scheme is a verification key vk for a standard signature scheme, and the master secret key is the associated signing key sk. To issue a constrained key for a function f, the authority generates a fresh pair of signing and verification keys (vk', sk'), and constructs a signature ("certificate") σ on (vk', f) with the master signing key sk. The constrained key is the tuple $(\mathsf{vk}', \mathsf{sk}', f, \sigma)$. A signature on m using the constrained key consists of a signature σ' on m using sk' together with the tuple $(\mathsf{vk}', f, \sigma)$. To verify, one checks that σ is a valid signature on (vk', f) with respect to the master verification key vk, that $f(m) = 1$, and that σ' is a valid signature on m with respect to vk'. From this construction, we obtain the following corollary:

Corollary 3.17 (Watermarkable Signatures from One-Way Functions). *Take any $\varepsilon = 1/\mathsf{poly}(\lambda)$ and mark space $\mathcal{T} = \{0,1\}^\ell$, where $\ell = \mathsf{poly}(\lambda)$. Assuming one-way functions exist, there exists a fully collusion resistant watermarkable family of signatures with mark space $\mathcal{T}$ that satisfies ε-unremovability (Definition 3.7) and where the underlying signature scheme is unforgeable even against a malicious authority (Definition 3.5).*

In the full version of this paper, we describe a variant of our watermarkable signature scheme that achieves mark-unforgeability in the secret-marking setting (i.e., no efficient adversary is able to come up with a marked circuit of its own).

4   Watermarking Public-Key Predicate Encryption

In this section, we show how to watermark a public-key predicate encryption scheme. In particular, this notion implies watermarking for simpler classes of public-key primitives like public-key encryption,[7] identity-based encryption, and attribute-based encryption. We begin by formally introducing the notion of watermarking public-key predicate encryption schemes. Our definitions have a very similar flavor to our corresponding definitions for watermarking digital signature schemes from Sect. 3 and the previous definitions of Cohen et al. [27].

Definition 4.1 (Watermarkable Public-Key Predicate Encryption). *A watermarkable public-key predicate encryption scheme with message space $\mathcal{M}$, attribute space $\mathcal{X}$, function space $\mathcal{F} \subseteq \mathsf{Funs}[\mathcal{X}, \{0,1\}]$, and mark space $\mathcal{T}$ is a tuple of algorithms* (WMSetup, PESetup, KeyGen, Encrypt, Decrypt, Mark, Extract) *with the following properties:*

- WMSetup$(1^\lambda) \to$ wpp: *On input the security parameter λ, the watermarking setup algorithm outputs a set of watermarking public parameters* wpp.
- *The watermarking parameters* wpp *induces a public-key predicate-encryption scheme* (PESetup, KeyGen, Encrypt, Decrypt) *with message space $\mathcal{M}$, attribute space $\mathcal{X}$, and function space $\mathcal{F}$. We implicitly allow* PESetup, KeyGen, Encrypt, *and* Decrypt *to take the watermarking parameters* wpp *as input. Let $\mathcal{PK}$ denote the space of master public keys, $\mathcal{SK}$ denote the space of function keys, and $\mathcal{CT}$ denote the ciphertext space of the induced predicate encryption scheme.*

---

[7] As noted in Sect. 1.1, a traitor-tracing scheme that supports public tracing (e.g., [2,18,49]) directly gives a watermarkable public-key encryption scheme.

– Mark(wpp, sk, τ) → C_τ: *On input the watermarking parameters* wpp, *a secret key* sk ∈ $\mathcal{SK}$, *and a mark* τ ∈ $\mathcal{T}$, *the marking algorithm outputs a circuit* $C_\tau : \mathcal{CT} \rightarrow \mathcal{M} \cup \{\bot\}$.

– Extract(wpp, mpk, C) → $\tau/\bot$: *On input the watermarking parameters* wpp, *a master public key* mpk ∈ $\mathcal{PK}$ *and a circuit* $C : \mathcal{CT} \rightarrow \mathcal{M} \cup \{\bot\}$, *the extraction algorithm either outputs a mark* τ ∈ $\mathcal{T}$ *or a special symbol* $\bot$.

Definition 4.2 (Correctness). *Let* Π_{WM} = (WMSetup, PESetup, KeyGen, Encrypt, Decrypt, Mark, Extract) *be a watermarkable predicate encryption scheme for function family* $\mathcal{F}$. *Then,* Π_{WM} *is correct if for* wpp ← Setup(1^λ), *the induced public-key predicate encryption scheme* (PESetup, KeyGen, Encrypt, Decrypt) *is correct and the following properties also hold:*

– ***Extraction correctness:*** *For all marks* τ ∈ $\mathcal{T}$ *and all functions* f ∈ $\mathcal{F}$, *if we take* (mpk, msk) ← PESetup(1^λ, wpp) *and* sk_f ← KeyGen(wpp, msk, f), *then*

$$\Pr[\text{Extract}(\mathsf{wpp}, \mathsf{mpk}, \text{Mark}(\mathsf{wpp}, \mathsf{sk}_f, \tau)) \neq \tau] = \text{negl}(\lambda).$$

– ***Meaningfulness:*** *For all fixed circuits* $C : \mathcal{CT} \rightarrow \mathcal{M} \cup \{\bot\}$ *(independent of the public parameters* wpp*) and all master public keys* mpk ∈ $\mathcal{PK}$,

$$\Pr[\text{Extract}(\mathsf{wpp}, \mathsf{mpk}, C) \neq \bot] = \text{negl}(\lambda),$$

and for all functions f ∈ $\mathcal{F}$, (mpk, msk) ← PESetup(1^λ, wpp), *and* sk_f ← KeyGen(wpp, msk, f),

$$\Pr[\text{Extract}(\mathsf{wpp}, \mathsf{mpk}, \text{Decrypt}(\mathsf{wpp}, \mathsf{sk}_f, \cdot)) \neq \bot] = \text{negl}(\lambda).$$

– ***Functionality-preserving:*** *For all marks* τ ∈ $\mathcal{T}$, *all messages* m ∈ $\mathcal{M}$, *all attributes* x ∈ $\mathcal{X}$, *and all functions* f ∈ $\mathcal{F}$ *where* $f(x) = 1$, *if we take* (mpk, msk) ← PESetup(1^λ, wpp), sk_f ← KeyGen(wpp, mpk, f) *and* C ← Mark(wpp, sk_f, τ), *we have that*

$$\Pr[C(\text{Encrypt}(\mathsf{wpp}, \mathsf{mpk}, x, m)) \neq m] = \text{negl}(\lambda).$$

Definition 4.3 (Security). *Let* Π_{WM} = (WMSetup, PESetup, KeyGen, Encrypt, Decrypt, Mark, Extract) *be a watermarkable predicate encryption scheme. Then,* Π_{WM} *is secure if the induced predicate encryption scheme* (PESetup, KeyGen, Encrypt, Decrypt) *is secure. We say that* Π_{WM} *satisfies security in the presence of a malicious authority if the induced predicate encryption scheme is secure even if the adversary is allowed to choose the watermarking parameters* wpp.

Definition 4.4 (Watermarking PE Security Experiment). *Let* Π_{WM} = (WMSetup, PESetup, KeyGen, Encrypt, Decrypt, Mark, Extract) *be a watermarkable predicate encryption scheme with message space* $\mathcal{M}$, *attribute space* $\mathcal{X}$, *function space* $\mathcal{F} \subseteq$ Funs[$\mathcal{X}$, {0, 1}], *and mark space* $\mathcal{T}$. *Let* $\mathcal{CT}$ *denote the ciphertext space for* Π_{WM}. *For an adversary* $\mathcal{A}$, *we define the watermarking PE security experiment as follows:*

1. *The challenger begins by sampling* wpp $\leftarrow$ WMSetup(1^λ) *and* (mpk, msk) $\leftarrow$ KeyGen$(1^\lambda,$ wpp$)$. *It gives* (wpp, mpk) *to the adversary* $\mathcal{A}$.
2. *The adversary specifies a function* $f \in \mathcal{F}$ *it would like to target. The challenger computes a secret key* sk$_f$ $\leftarrow$ KeyGen(wpp, msk, f), *but does not give* sk$_f$ *to the adversary.*
3. *The adversary can then make marking oracle queries. On each marking query, the adversary specifies a mark* $\tau \in \mathcal{T}$, *and the challenger replies with the circuit* $C_\tau \leftarrow$ Mark(wpp, sk$_f$, τ).
4. *At the end of the experiment, the adversary outputs a circuit* $C^* : \mathcal{CT} \rightarrow \mathcal{M} \cup \{\bot\}$ *and an attribute* $x \in \mathcal{X}$.

The output of the experiment, denoted ExptWM$_{\mathsf{PE}}(\lambda, \mathcal{A})$, *is* Extract(wpp, mpk, C').

Definition 4.5 (ε-Unremovability). *Let* Π_{WM} *be a watermarkable public-key encryption scheme with message space* $\mathcal{M}$ *and ciphertext space* $\mathcal{CT}$. *We say an adversary* $\mathcal{A}$ *is* ε-*unremovable admissible if the adversary in the watermarking security game outputs an attribute* $x \in \mathcal{X}$ *and a circuit* $C^* : \mathcal{CT} \rightarrow \mathcal{M} \cup \{\bot\}$ *where*

$$\Pr[m \xleftarrow{\text{R}} \mathcal{M} : C^*(\mathsf{Encrypt}(\mathsf{wpp}, \mathsf{mpk}, x, m)) = m] \geq \varepsilon.$$

In the watermarking PE security experiment, let $\mathcal{Q} \subseteq \mathcal{T}$ *be the set of marks the adversary submitted to the marking oracle. Then,* Π_{WM} *satisfies* ε-*unremovability if for all efficient and* ε-*unremovability admissible adversaries* $\mathcal{A}$, $\Pr[\mathsf{ExptWM}_{\mathsf{PE}}[\lambda, \mathcal{A}] \notin \mathcal{Q}] = \mathsf{negl}(\lambda)$.

Remark 4.6 (Collusion Resistance). We say that a watermarkable predicate encryption scheme Π_{WM} is $(q_{\mathsf{key}}, q_{\mathsf{mark}})$-collusion resistant if the induced predicate encryption scheme is q_{key}-bounded collusion resistant and the watermarking adversary in the unremovability game can make at most q_{mark} marking queries. When q_{key} and q_{mark} can be arbitrary and a priori unbounded polynomials, we say Π_{WM} is *fully* collusion resistant.

Remark 4.7 (Stronger Notions of Unremovability). Our definitions of unremovability (Definitions 4.4 and 4.5) only allows the adversary to request (multiple) marked version of a *single* predicate encryption key sk$_f$. A stronger notion would allow the adversary to specify both a decryption function f as well as a mark τ on each marking oracle query. Such a scheme would then be secure even if an adversary could obtain marked versions of different decryption keys. Our construction does not achieve this stronger notion and we leave this as an open problem.

Remark 4.8 (Watermarking Functional Encryption). A further generalization of watermarking predicate encryption is to watermark the decryption keys in a *functional encryption* scheme. One challenge here is characterizing the set of decryption keys that can be marked. For example, it is not possible to watermark a decryption key for a constant-valued function, since the adversary can implement the decryption functionality with a circuit that just computes the constant function (which, of course, removes the watermark). It seems plausible that we can watermark decryption keys corresponding to functions with "high min-entropy:" namely, functions $f \colon \mathcal{X} \to \mathcal{Y}$ where for any $y \in \mathcal{Y}$, $\Pr[x \xleftarrow{\text{R}} \mathcal{X} : f(x) = y] = \mathsf{negl}(\lambda)$. While it is straightforward to modify our construction of watermarkable predicate encryption to support marking function keys of this form, in the resulting construction, we would additionally have to provide the Extract algorithm a description of the function f associated with a particular decryption circuit. Whether this a reasonable modeling assumption will depend on the particular application. It is an interesting question to both develop a better understanding of the types of function families that can be watermarked as well as identify a suitable schema for watermarking general functional encryption schemes.

4.1 Building Blocks: Functional Encryption and Traitor Tracing

In this section, we review the main building blocks we use to construct our scheme for watermarking predicate encryption.

Hierarchical Functional Encryption. Our main building block for constructing a watermarkable predicate encryption scheme is a general-purpose hierarchical functional encryption scheme. Below, we recall the formal definition from [4,22]:

Definition 4.9 (Hierarchical Functional Encryption [4,22]). *A hierarchical functional encryption (FE) scheme with domain* $\mathcal{X}$*, range* $\mathcal{Y}$*, and function space* $\mathcal{F}$ *is a tuple of algorithms* $\Pi_{\mathsf{HFE}} = (\mathsf{Setup}, \mathsf{KeyGen}, \mathsf{Encrypt}, \mathsf{Decrypt},$ $\mathsf{Delegate})$ *with the following properties:*

- $\mathsf{Setup}(1^\lambda) \to (\mathsf{mpk}, \mathsf{msk})$*: On input the security parameter* λ*, the setup algorithm outputs the master public key* mpk *and the master secret key* msk*.*
- $\mathsf{KeyGen}(\mathsf{msk}, f) \to \mathsf{sk}_f$*: On input the master secret key* msk *and a function* $f \in \mathcal{F}$*, the key-generation algorithm outputs a secret key* sk_f*.*
- $\mathsf{Encrypt}(\mathsf{mpk}, x) \to \mathsf{ct}_x$*: On input the master public key* mpk *and an input* $x \in \mathcal{X}$*, the encryption algorithm outputs a ciphertext* ct_x*.*
- $\mathsf{Decrypt}(\mathsf{sk}, \mathsf{ct}) \to y/\bot$*: On input a secret key* sk *and a ciphertext* ct*, the decryption algorithm either outputs a value* $y \in \mathcal{Y}$ *or a special symbol* $\bot$*.*
- $\mathsf{Delegate}(\mathsf{sk}_f, g) \to \mathsf{sk}_{g \circ f}$*: On input a secret key* sk_f *and a function* $g \in \mathcal{F}$*, the delegate algorithm outputs a secret key* $\mathsf{sk}_{g \circ f}$*.*

A hierarchical functional encryption scheme should satisfy the following properties:

- ***Correctness:*** *For all* $x \in \mathcal{X}$ *and functions* $f \in \mathcal{F}$*, if we sample* $(\mathsf{mpk}, \mathsf{msk}) \leftarrow$ $\mathsf{Setup}(1^\lambda)$*,* $\mathsf{sk}_f \leftarrow \mathsf{KeyGen}(\mathsf{msk}, f)$*, and* $\mathsf{ct}_x \leftarrow \mathsf{Encrypt}(\mathsf{mpk}, x)$*, then*

$$\Pr[\mathsf{Decrypt}(\mathsf{sk}_f, \mathsf{ct}_x) = f(x)] = 1.$$

– **Delegation correctness:** *For all $x \in \mathcal{X}$ and functions $f, g \in \mathcal{F}$ where $g \circ f \in \mathcal{F}$, if we sample* $(\mathsf{mpk}, \mathsf{msk}) \leftarrow \mathsf{Setup}(1^\lambda)$, $\mathsf{sk}_f \leftarrow \mathsf{KeyGen}(\mathsf{msk}, f)$, $\mathsf{sk}_{g \circ f} \leftarrow \mathsf{Delegate}(\mathsf{sk}_f, g)$, *and* $\mathsf{ct}_x \leftarrow \mathsf{Encrypt}(\mathsf{mpk}, x)$, *then*

$$\Pr[\mathsf{Decrypt}(\mathsf{sk}_{g \circ f}, \mathsf{ct}_x) = g(f(x))] = 1.$$

Note that this definition only considers correctness for single-hop *delegation. We can define a corresponding notion of multi-hop delegation correctness. However, single-hop delegation already suffices for our construction.*

– **Security:** *Due to space limitations, we defer the security definition of hierarchical functional encryption to the full version of this paper.*

Remark 4.10 (Collusion Resistance). We say that a (hierarchical) functional encryption scheme Π_{HFE} is q-bounded collusion resistant if the security property holds against all efficient adversaries that make at most q key-generation queries and that it is fully collusion resistant if security holds against all adversaries that can make an a priori unbounded polynomial number of key-generation queries.

The Jump-Finding Problem. We recall the jump-finding problem introduced in the work of Nishimaki et al. [49] for constructing flexible traitor tracing schemes (i.e., traitor tracing schemes where the space of identities that can be traced is exponential). We rely on similar techniques to watermark the decryption keys in a predicate encryption scheme.

Definition 4.11 (Noisy Jump Finding Problem [49, Definition 3.6]). *The $(N, q, \delta, \varepsilon)$-jump-finding problem is defined as follows. An adversary chooses a set $C \subseteq [N]$ of q unknown points. Then, the adversary provides an oracle $P \colon [0, N] \to [0, 1]_{\mathbb{R}}$ with the following properties:*

– $|P(N) - P(0)| \geq \varepsilon$.
– *For any $x, y \in [0, N]$ where $x < y$ and $[x+1, y] \cap C = \varnothing$, then $|P(y) - P(x)| < \delta$.*

The $(N, q, \delta, \varepsilon)$-jump finding problem is to interact with the oracle P and output an element in C. In the $(N, q, \delta, \varepsilon)$-noisy jump finding problem, the oracle P is replaced with a randomized oracle $Q \colon [0, N] \to \{0, 1\}$ where on input $x \in [0, N]$, $Q(x)$ outputs 1 with probability $P(x)$. A fresh independent draw is chosen for each query to $Q(x)$.

Theorem 4.12 (Noisy Jump Finding Algorithm [49, Theorem 3.7]). *There is an efficient algorithm $\mathsf{QTrace}^Q(\lambda, N, q, \delta, \varepsilon)$ that runs in time $t = \mathsf{poly}(\lambda, \log N, q, 1/\delta)$ and makes at most t queries to Q that solves the $(N, q, \delta, \varepsilon)$-noisy-jump-finding problem whenever $\varepsilon > \delta(5 + 2(\lceil \log N - 1 \rceil)q)$. In particular, $\mathsf{QTrace}^Q(\lambda, N, q, \delta, \varepsilon)$ will output at least one element in C with probability $1 - \mathsf{negl}(\lambda)$ and will never output an element outside C. Moreover, any element x output by $\mathsf{QTrace}^Q(\lambda, N, q, \delta, \varepsilon)$ has the property that $P(x) - P(x - 1) > \delta$, where $P(x) = \Pr[Q(x) = 1]$.*

4.2 Watermarking Predicate Encryption from Hierarchical FE

In this section, we show how to construct a (bounded) collusion resistant watermarkable predicate encryption scheme for general predicates from any (bounded) collusion resistant hierarchical functional encryption scheme for general circuits.

Construction 4.13 (Watermarkable PE from Hierarchical FE). *Let* $\mathcal{M} = \{0,1\}^n$ *be a message space,* $\mathcal{X} = \{0,1\}^\ell \setminus \{1^\ell\}$ *be an attribute space,* $\mathcal{F} \subseteq \mathsf{Funs}[\{0,1\}^\ell, \{0,1\}]$ *be a class of predicates, and* $\mathcal{T} \subseteq \mathcal{X} = \{0,1\}^\ell \setminus \{1^\ell\}$ *be a mark space. Let* $\varepsilon = 1/\mathsf{poly}(\lambda)$ *be an unremovability parameter. We rely on the following ingredients:*

- *Let* $\mathcal{Z} = \mathcal{M} = \{0,1\}^n$ *be a tag space.*
- *Let* $q_{\mathsf{mark}} = \mathsf{poly}(\lambda)$ *be a bound on the number of marking oracle queries the watermarking adversary is allowed to make. In Remark 4.17, we describe a simple adaptation of the extraction algorithm that achieves full collusion resistance (assuming a fully collusion resistant hierarchical FE scheme)*
- *For a function* $f \in \mathcal{F}$, *let* $g_f \colon \{0,1\}^{\ell+n+1} \to \{0,1\}^{\ell+n}$ *be the function defined as follows:*

$$g_f(x, m, b) = \begin{cases} (x, m) & b = 0 \\ (0^\ell, 0^n) & b = 1 \text{ and } f(x) = 0 \\ (1^\ell, m) & b = 1 \text{ and } f(x) = 1, \end{cases} \tag{4.1}$$

  where $x \in \{0,1\}^\ell$, $m \in \{0,1\}^n$, *and* $b \in \{0,1\}$. *Define the function class* $\mathcal{G} = \{f \in \mathcal{F} : g_f\}$.
- *For a mark* $\tau \in \{0,1\}^\ell$, *define the function* $h_\tau \colon \{0,1\}^{\ell+n} \to \{0,1\}^{\ell+n}$ *as follows:*

$$h_\tau(x, m) = \begin{cases} (0^\ell, 0^n) & x \leq \tau \\ (1^\ell, m) & x > \tau, \end{cases} \tag{4.2}$$

  where $x \in \{0,1\}^\ell$ *and* $m \in \{0,1\}^n$, *and are interpreted as values in* $[0, 2^\ell - 1]$ *and* $[0, 2^n - 1]$, *respectively.*
- *Let* $\Pi_{\mathsf{HFE}} = $ (HFE.Setup, HFE.KeyGen, HFE.Encrypt, HFE.Decrypt, HFE. Delegate) *be a hierarchical FE scheme with domain* $\{0,1\}^{\ell+n+1}$, *range* $\{0,1\}^{\ell+n}$, *and function class* $\mathcal{G}$. *Let* $\mathcal{CT}$ *be the space of ciphertexts for* Π_{HFE}.

We construct a watermarkable predicate encryption scheme $\Pi_{\mathsf{WM}} = $ (WMSetup, PESetup, KeyGen, Encrypt, Decrypt, Mark, Extract) *as follows:*

- WMSetup(1^λ) $\to$ wpp: *On input the security parameter* λ, *sample* $z \xleftarrow{\text{R}} \{0,1\}^n$ *and output* wpp $= z$.
- PESetup(1^λ, wpp) $\to$ (mpk, msk): *On input the security parameter* λ *and the watermarking parameters* wpp $= z$, *the key-generation algorithm outputs a key-pair* (mpk, msk) $\leftarrow$ HFE.Setup(1^λ).
- KeyGen(wpp, msk, f) $\to$ sk$_f$: *On input the watermarking parameters* wpp $= z$, *a master secret key* msk, *and a function* $f \in \mathcal{F}$, *the key-generation algorithm outputs a secret key* sk$_f$ $\leftarrow$ HFE.KeyGen(msk, g_f), *where* g_f *is defined in Eq. (4.1).*

- Encrypt(wpp, mpk, x, m) $\rightarrow$ ct$_{x,m}$: *On input the watermarking parameters* wpp $= z$, *a master public key* mpk, *an attribute* $x \in \{0,1\}^\ell$, *and a message* $m \in \{0,1\}^n$, *the encryption algorithm outputs a ciphertext* ct$_{x,m}$ $\leftarrow$ HFE.Encrypt(mpk, $(x, m \oplus z, 1)) \in \mathcal{CT}$.

- Decrypt(wpp, sk, ct) $\rightarrow m/\bot$: *On input the watermarking parameter* wpp $= z$, *a secret key* sk, *and a ciphertext* ct, *the decryption algorithm computes* $y \leftarrow$ HFE.Decrypt(sk, ct). *If* $y = \bot$, *then output* $\bot$. *Otherwise, it parses* $y = (x, m')$ *where* $x \in \{0,1\}^\ell$ *and* $m' \in \{0,1\}^n$. *It outputs* $m' \oplus z$ *if* $x = 1^\ell$ *and* $\bot$ *otherwise.*

- Mark(wpp, sk, τ) $\rightarrow C_\tau$: *On input the watermarking parameters* wpp $= z$, *a secret key* sk, *and a mark* $\tau \in \{0,1\}^t$, *the marking algorithm constructs a new key* sk$_\tau$ $\leftarrow$ HFE.Delegate(sk, h_τ), *where* h_τ *is defined in Eq. (4.2). Finally, it outputs the circuit* $C \colon \mathcal{CT} \rightarrow \mathcal{M} \cup \{\bot\}$ *that computes the marked function* $P[z, \text{sk}_\tau]$ *defined as follows (Fig. 1):*

On input a ciphertext ct $\in \mathcal{CT}$:

1. *Compute* $y \leftarrow$ HFE.Decrypt(sk$_\tau$, ct). *If* $y = \bot$, *output* $\bot$.
2. *Otherwise, parse* $y = (x, m')$, *where* $x \in \{0,1\}^\ell$ *and* $m' \in \{0,1\}^n$. *Output* $m' \oplus z$ *if* $x = 1^\ell$ *and* $\bot$ *otherwise.*

Fig. 1. The marked function $P[z, \text{sk}_\tau]$

- Extract(wpp, mpk, C) $\rightarrow \tau/\bot$: *On input the watermarking parameters* wpp $= z$, *a master public key* mpk, *and a circuit* $C \colon \mathcal{CT} \rightarrow \mathcal{M} \cup \{\bot\}$, *the extraction algorithm first performs the following decryption check* $T = \lambda/\varepsilon = \text{poly}(\lambda)$ *times:*
  - *For each* $i \in [T]$, *sample* $m_i \overset{\text{R}}{\leftarrow} \mathcal{M}$ *and compute the ciphertext* ct$_i$ $\leftarrow$ HFE.Encrypt(mpk, $(1^\ell, m_i \oplus z, 0))$ *and* $y_i \leftarrow C(\text{ct}_i)$.

  If for all $i \in [T]$, $y_i \neq m_i$, *then output* $\bot$. *Otherwise, the extraction algorithm constructs the following function* $Q_C \colon \{0,1\}^\ell \rightarrow \{0,1\}$ *(Fig. 2):*

On input an input $x \in \{0,1\}^\ell$ *(interpreted as a value in* $[0, 2^\ell - 1]$):

  - *Sample a random* $m \overset{\text{R}}{\leftarrow} \{0,1\}^n$ *and construct the ciphertext* ct $\leftarrow$ HFE.Encrypt(mpk, $(x, m \oplus z, 0))$.
  - *Compute* $m' \leftarrow C(\text{ct})$ *and output* 1 *if* $m = m'$ *and* 0 *otherwise.*

Fig. 2. The extraction test function Q_C

Let $\delta = \varepsilon/(5 + 2(\ell-1)q_{mark})$ and compute $\tau \leftarrow \mathsf{QTrace}^{Q_C}(\lambda, 2^\ell - 1, q_{mark}, \delta, \varepsilon)$. If $\tau = 1^\ell$, then output $\perp$. Otherwise, output τ. In Remark 4.17, we describe a variant of the Extract *algorithm that does not require an explicit bound q_{mark} to be provided as input.*

Correctness and Security Analysis. We now state our correctness and security theorems, but defer their formal analysis to the full version of this paper.

Theorem 4.14 (Correctness). *Suppose $1/\varepsilon = \mathsf{poly}(\lambda)$, $1/|\mathcal{M}| = \mathsf{negl}(\lambda)$, and Π_{HFE} is correct and secure (Definition 4.9). Then, the watermarkable predicate encryption scheme Π_{WM} from Construction 4.13 is correct.*

Theorem 4.15 (Predicate Encryption Security). *If Π_{HFE} is secure (Definition 4.9), then Construction 4.13 is secure even in the presence of a malicious authority (Definition 4.3).*

Theorem 4.16 (ε-Unremovability). *Take any $\varepsilon = 1/\mathsf{poly}(\lambda)$. If $1/|\mathcal{M}| = \mathsf{negl}(\lambda)$ and Π_{HFE} is secure (Definition 4.9), then the watermarkable predicate encryption scheme Π_{WM} from Construction 4.13 is ε-unremovable.*

Remark 4.17 (Extraction Without an A Priori Bound). As described, the Extract algorithm in Construction 4.13 assumes there is an a priori bound q_{mark} on the number of marked keys the adversary sees (and this bound is provided as an input to the Extract algorithm). It is straightforward to extend Extract to operate when no explicit bound is provided. Namely, instead of running QTrace^Q with $q = q_{mark}$, the algorithm instead runs QTrace on successive powers of two $q = 2^0, 2^1, 2^2, \ldots, 2^\ell$ where $\delta = \varepsilon/(5 + 2(\ell - 1)q))$. By Theorem 4.12, if QTrace^Q succeeds, it produces a $\tau \in \{0,1\}^\ell$ such that $|\Pr[Q(\tau) = 1] - \Pr[Q(\tau - 1) = 1]| > \delta$. Moreover, we can show that for all efficiently-computable $\tau \notin Q$, we have that $\Pr[Q(\tau) = 1] - \Pr[Q(\tau - 1) = 1] = \mathsf{negl}(\lambda)$. Thus, if QTrace^Q outputs a mark τ, then $\tau \in Q$, as required. Moreover, once $q > q_{mark}$, we can appeal to Theorem 4.12 to conclude that with overwhelming probability, the extraction algorithm will output a τ such that this condition holds. This algorithm will terminate after at most $O(\log q_{mark}) = \mathsf{poly}(\lambda)$ iterations.

4.3   Instantiations and Extensions

In the full version of this paper, we describe two ways to instantiate our watermarkable predicate encryption scheme: one secure against bounded collusions based on the existence of public-key encryption and low-depth pseudorandom generators (PRGs)[8] and one secure against unbounded collusions based on indistinguishability obfuscation (and one-way functions). We also describe a simple variant of our construction that provides watermarking unforgeability in the secret-marking setting. We state the main conclusions below:

---

[8] These are known to follow from most algebraic cryptographic assumptions such as the hardness of factoring, the discrete log assumption, or standard lattice assumptions [7,45–47].

Corollary 4.18 (Bounded Collusion-Resistant Watermarkable Predicate Encryption). *Take any* $\varepsilon = 1/\mathsf{poly}(\lambda)$, *any fixed polynomials* $q, q_{\mathsf{key}}, q_{\mathsf{mark}} = \mathsf{poly}(\lambda)$, *and mark space* $\mathcal{T} = \{0,1\}^\ell$, *where* $\ell = \mathsf{poly}(\lambda)$. *Assuming public-key encryption and a PRG computable in* NC^1, *there exists a* $(q_{\mathsf{key}}, q_{\mathsf{mark}})$-*bounded collusion resistant watermarkable family of predicate encryption schemes with mark space* $\mathcal{T}$ *that satisfies* ε-*unremovability (Definition 4.5, Remark 4.6). Moreover, the associated predicate encryption scheme is* q-*bounded collusion resistant and remains secure even in the presence of a malicious watermarking authority (Definition 4.3).*

Corollary 4.19 (Fully Collusion-Resistant Watermarkable Predicate Encryption). *Take any* $\varepsilon = 1/\mathsf{poly}(\lambda)$ *and mark space* $\mathcal{T} = \{0,1\}^\ell$. *Assuming indistinguishability obfuscation and the existence of one-way functions, there exists a fully collusion resistant watermarkable family of predicate encryption schemes with mark space* $\mathcal{T}$ *that provides* ε-*unremovability (Definition 4.5) and where the associated predicate encryption scheme is fully collusion resistant and secure even in the presence of a malicious watermarking authority (Definition 4.3).*

Acknowledgments. We thank Aayush Jain for helpful discussions on this work and the anonymous CRYPTO reviewers for useful feedback on the presentation. R. Goyal was supported by an IBM PhD fellowship. S. Kim was supported by NSF, DARPA, a grant from ONR, and the Simons Foundation. N. Manohar was supported in part by a DARPA/ARL SAFEWARE award, NSF Frontier Award 1413955, NSF grants 1619348, 1228984, 1136174, and 1065276, and BSF grant 2012378. B. Waters was supported by NSF CNS-1908611, CNS-1414082, a DARPA/ARL SAFEWARE award and a Packard Foundation Fellowship. Opinions, findings and conclusions or recommendations expressed in this material are those of the authors and do not necessarily reflect the official policy or position of the Department of Defense, the National Science Foundation, or the U.S. Government.

References

1. Abdalla, M., Dent, A.W., Malone-Lee, J., Neven, G., Phan, D.H., Smart, N.P.: Identity-based traitor tracing. In: Okamoto, T., Wang, X. (eds.) PKC 2007. LNCS, vol. 4450, pp. 361–376. Springer, Heidelberg (2007). https://doi.org/10.1007/978-3-540-71677-8_24

2. Agrawal, S., Bhattacherjee, S., Phan, D.H., Stehlé, D., Yamada, S.: Efficient public trace and revoke from standard assumptions: extended abstract. In: ACM CCS, pp. 2277–2293 (2017)

3. Agrawal, S., Rosen, A.: Functional encryption for bounded collusions, revisited. In: Kalai, Y., Reyzin, L. (eds.) TCC 2017. LNCS, vol. 10677, pp. 173–205. Springer, Cham (2017). https://doi.org/10.1007/978-3-319-70500-2_7

4. Ananth, P., Boneh, D., Garg, S., Sahai, A., Zhandry, M.: Differing-inputs obfuscation and applications. IACR Cryptology ePrint Archive 2013 (2013)

5. Ananth, P., Vaikuntanathan, V.: Optimal bounded-collusion secure functional encryption. IACR Cryptology ePrint Archive 2019, 314 (2019)

6. Baldimtsi, F., Kiayias, A., Samari, K.: Watermarking public-key cryptographic functionalities and implementations. In: Nguyen, P., Zhou, J. (eds.) ISC 2017. LNCS, vol. 10599, pp. 173–191. Springer, Cham (2017). https://doi.org/10.1007/978-3-319-69659-1_10

7. Banerjee, A., Peikert, C., Rosen, A.: Pseudorandom functions and lattices. In: Pointcheval, D., Johansson, T. (eds.) EUROCRYPT 2012. LNCS, vol. 7237, pp. 719–737. Springer, Heidelberg (2012). https://doi.org/10.1007/978-3-642-29011-4_42

8. Barak, B., et al.: On the (im)possibility of obfuscating programs. In: Kilian, J. (ed.) CRYPTO 2001. LNCS, vol. 2139, pp. 1–18. Springer, Heidelberg (2001). https://doi.org/10.1007/3-540-44647-8_1

9. Barak, B., et al.: On the (im)possibility of obfuscating programs. J. ACM **59**(2), 1–48 (2012). Article no. 6

10. Bellare, M., Fuchsbauer, G.: Policy-based signatures. In: Krawczyk, H. (ed.) PKC 2014. LNCS, vol. 8383, pp. 520–537. Springer, Heidelberg (2014). https://doi.org/10.1007/978-3-642-54631-0_30

11. Billet, O., Phan, D.H.: Efficient traitor tracing from collusion secure codes. In: Safavi-Naini, R. (ed.) ICITS 2008. LNCS, vol. 5155, pp. 171–182. Springer, Heidelberg (2008). https://doi.org/10.1007/978-3-540-85093-9_17

12. Boneh, D., Franklin, M.K.: An efficient public key traitor tracing scheme. In: Wiener, M. (ed.) CRYPTO 1999. LNCS, vol. 1666, pp. 338–353. Springer, Heidelberg (1999). https://doi.org/10.1007/3-540-48405-1_22

13. Boneh, D., Franklin, M.K.: Identity-based encryption from the Weil pairing. In: Kilian, J. (ed.) CRYPTO 2001. LNCS, vol. 2139, pp. 213–229. Springer, Heidelberg (2001). https://doi.org/10.1007/3-540-44647-8_13

14. Boneh, D., Lewi, K., Wu, D.J.: Constraining pseudorandom functions privately. In: Fehr, S. (ed.) PKC 2017. LNCS, vol. 10175, pp. 494–524. Springer, Heidelberg (2017). https://doi.org/10.1007/978-3-662-54388-7_17

15. Boneh, D., Naor, M.: Traitor tracing with constant size ciphertext. In: ACM CCS (2008)

16. Boneh, D., Sahai, A., Waters, B.: Fully collusion resistant traitor tracing with short ciphertexts and private keys. In: Vaudenay, S. (ed.) EUROCRYPT 2006. LNCS, vol. 4004, pp. 573–592. Springer, Heidelberg (2006). https://doi.org/10.1007/11761679_34

17. Boneh, D., Sahai, A., Waters, B.: Functional encryption: definitions and challenges. In: Ishai, Y. (ed.) TCC 2011. LNCS, vol. 6597, pp. 253–273. Springer, Heidelberg (2011). https://doi.org/10.1007/978-3-642-19571-6_16

18. Boneh, D., Waters, B.: A fully collusion resistant broadcast, trace, revoke system. In: ACM CCS (2006)

19. Boneh, D., Waters, B.: Conjunctive, subset, and range queries on encrypted data. In: Vadhan, S.P. (ed.) TCC 2007. LNCS, vol. 4392, pp. 535–554. Springer, Heidelberg (2007). https://doi.org/10.1007/978-3-540-70936-7_29

20. Boneh, D., Zhandry, M.: Multiparty key exchange, efficient traitor tracing, and more from indistinguishability obfuscation. In: Garay, J.A., Gennaro, R. (eds.) CRYPTO 2014. LNCS, vol. 8616, pp. 480–499. Springer, Heidelberg (2014). https://doi.org/10.1007/978-3-662-44371-2_27

21. Boyle, E., Goldwasser, S., Ivan, I.: Functional signatures and pseudorandom functions. In: Krawczyk, H. (ed.) PKC 2014. LNCS, vol. 8383, pp. 501–519. Springer, Heidelberg (2014). https://doi.org/10.1007/978-3-642-54631-0_29

22. Brakerski, Z., Chandran, N., Goyal, V., Jain, A., Sahai, A., Segev, G.: Hierarchical functional encryption. In: ITCS (2017)

23. Chen, Y., Vaikuntanathan, V., Waters, B., Wee, H., Wichs, D.: Traitor-tracing from LWE made simple and attribute-based. In: Beimel, A., Dziembowski, S. (eds.) TCC 2018. LNCS, vol. 11240, pp. 341–369. Springer, Cham (2018). https://doi.org/10.1007/978-3-030-03810-6_13

24. Chor, B., Fiat, A., Naor, M.: Tracing traitors. In: Desmedt, Y.G. (ed.) CRYPTO 1994. LNCS, vol. 839, pp. 257–270. Springer, Heidelberg (1994). https://doi.org/10.1007/3-540-48658-5_25

25. Chor, B., Fiat, A., Naor, M., Pinkas, B.: Tracing traitors. IEEE Trans. Inf. Theory **46**(3), 893–910 (2000)

26. Cocks, C.C.: An identity based encryption scheme based on quadratic residues. In: Honary, B. (ed.) Cryptography and Coding 2001. LNCS, vol. 2260, pp. 360–363. Springer, Heidelberg (2001). https://doi.org/10.1007/3-540-45325-3_32

27. Cohen, A., Holmgren, J., Nishimaki, R., Vaikuntanathan, V., Wichs, D.: Watermarking cryptographic capabilities. In: STOC (2016)

28. Fazio, N., Nicolosi, A., Phan, D.H.: Traitor tracing with optimal transmission rate. In: Garay, J.A., Lenstra, A.K., Mambo, M., Peralta, R. (eds.) ISC 2007. LNCS, vol. 4779, pp. 71–88. Springer, Heidelberg (2007). https://doi.org/10.1007/978-3-540-75496-1_5

29. Freeman, D.M.: Converting pairing-based cryptosystems from composite-order groups to prime-order groups. In: Gilbert, H. (ed.) EUROCRYPT 2010. LNCS, vol. 6110, pp. 44–61. Springer, Heidelberg (2010). https://doi.org/10.1007/978-3-642-13190-5_3

30. Garg, S., Kumarasubramanian, A., Sahai, A., Waters, B.: Building efficient fully collusion-resilient traitor tracing and revocation schemes. In: ACM CCS (2010)

31. Goldreich, O.: The Foundations of Cryptography - Volume 2, Basic Applications. Cambridge University Press, Cambridge (2004)

32. Gorbunov, S., Vaikuntanathan, V., Wee, H.: Functional encryption with bounded collusions via multi-party computation. In: Safavi-Naini, R., Canetti, R. (eds.) CRYPTO 2012. LNCS, vol. 7417, pp. 162–179. Springer, Heidelberg (2012). https://doi.org/10.1007/978-3-642-32009-5_11

33. Goyal, R., Koppula, V., Waters, B.: Collusion resistant traitor tracing from learning with errors. In: STOC (2018)

34. Goyal, V., Pandey, O., Sahai, A., Waters, B.: Attribute-based encryption for fine-grained access control of encrypted data. In: ACM CCS (2006)

35. Hopper, N., Molnar, D., Wagner, D.A.: From weak to strong watermarking. In: Vadhan, S.P. (ed.) TCC 2007. LNCS, vol. 4392, pp. 362–382. Springer, Heidelberg (2007). https://doi.org/10.1007/978-3-540-70936-7_20

36. Katz, J., Sahai, A., Waters, B.: Predicate encryption supporting disjunctions, polynomial equations, and inner products. In: Smart, N. (ed.) EUROCRYPT 2008. LNCS, vol. 4965, pp. 146–162. Springer, Heidelberg (2008). https://doi.org/10.1007/978-3-540-78967-3_9

37. Kim, S., Wu, D.J.: Watermarking cryptographic functionalities from standard lattice assumptions. In: Katz, J., Shacham, H. (eds.) CRYPTO 2017. LNCS, vol. 10401, pp. 503–536. Springer, Cham (2017). https://doi.org/10.1007/978-3-319-63688-7_17

38. Kim, S., Wu, D.J.: Watermarking PRFs from lattices: Stronger security via extractable PRFs. In: Boldyreva, A., Micciancio, D. (eds.) CRYPTO 2019. LNCS, vol. 11694, pp. 335–366. Springer, Cham (2019)

39. Kurosawa, K., Desmedt, Y.: Optimum traitor tracing and asymmetric schemes. In: Nyberg, K. (ed.) EUROCRYPT 1998. LNCS, vol. 1403, pp. 145–157. Springer, Heidelberg (1998). https://doi.org/10.1007/BFb0054123

40. Ling, S., Phan, D.H., Stehlé, D., Steinfeld, R.: Hardness of k-LWE and applications in traitor tracing. In: Garay, J.A., Gennaro, R. (eds.) CRYPTO 2014. LNCS, vol. 8616, pp. 315–334. Springer, Heidelberg (2014). https://doi.org/10.1007/978-3-662-44371-2_18

41. Liu, Z., Cao, Z., Wong, D.S.: Blackbox traceable CP-ABE: how to catch people leaking their keys by selling decryption devices on eBay. In: ACM CCS (2013)

42. Liu, Z., Wong, D.S.: Practical ciphertext-policy attribute-based encryption: traitor tracing, revocation, and large universe. In: Malkin, T., Kolesnikov, V., Lewko, A.B., Polychronakis, M. (eds.) ACNS 2015. LNCS, vol. 9092, pp. 127–146. Springer, Cham (2015). https://doi.org/10.1007/978-3-319-28166-7_7

43. Maji, H.K., Prabhakaran, M., Rosulek, M.: Attribute-based signatures. In: Kiayias, A. (ed.) CT-RSA 2011. LNCS, vol. 6558, pp. 376–392. Springer, Heidelberg (2011). https://doi.org/10.1007/978-3-642-19074-2_24

44. Naccache, D., Shamir, A., Stern, J.P.: How to copyright a function? In: Imai, H., Zheng, Y. (eds.) PKC 1999. LNCS, vol. 1560, pp. 188–196. Springer, Heidelberg (1999). https://doi.org/10.1007/3-540-49162-7_14

45. Naor, M., Reingold, O.: Synthesizers and their application to the parallel construction of pseudo-random functions. In: FOCS (1995)

46. Naor, M., Reingold, O.: Number-theoretic constructions of efficient pseudo-random functions. In: FOCS, pp. 458–467 (1997)

47. Naor, M., Reingold, O., Rosen, A.: Pseudo-random functions and factoring (extended abstract). In: STOC, pp. 11–20 (2000)

48. Nishimaki, R.: How to watermark cryptographic functions. In: Johansson, T., Nguyen, P.Q. (eds.) EUROCRYPT 2013. LNCS, vol. 7881, pp. 111–125. Springer, Heidelberg (2013). https://doi.org/10.1007/978-3-642-38348-9_7

49. Nishimaki, R., Wichs, D., Zhandry, M.: Anonymous traitor tracing: how to embed arbitrary information in a key. In: Fischlin, M., Coron, J.-S. (eds.) EUROCRYPT 2016. LNCS, vol. 9666, pp. 388–419. Springer, Heidelberg (2016). https://doi.org/10.1007/978-3-662-49896-5_14

50. O'Neill, A.: Definitional issues in functional encryption. IACR Cryptology ePrint Archive 2010 (2010)

51. Phan, D.H., Safavi-Naini, R., Tonien, D.: Generic construction of hybrid public key traitor tracing with full-public-traceability. In: Bugliesi, M., Preneel, B., Sassone, V., Wegener, I. (eds.) ICALP 2006. LNCS, vol. 4052, pp. 264–275. Springer, Heidelberg (2006). https://doi.org/10.1007/11787006_23

52. Quach, W., Wichs, D., Zirdelis, G.: Watermarking PRFs under standard assumptions: public marking and security with extraction queries. In: Beimel, A., Dziembowski, S. (eds.) TCC 2018. LNCS, vol. 11240, pp. 669–698. Springer, Cham (2018). https://doi.org/10.1007/978-3-030-03810-6_24

53. Sahai, A., Waters, B.: Fuzzy identity-based encryption. In: Cramer, R. (ed.) EUROCRYPT 2005. LNCS, vol. 3494, pp. 457–473. Springer, Heidelberg (2005). https://doi.org/10.1007/11426639_27

54. Shamir, A.: Identity-based cryptosystems and signature schemes. In: Blakley, G.R., Chaum, D. (eds.) CRYPTO 1984. LNCS, vol. 196, pp. 47–53. Springer, Heidelberg (1985). https://doi.org/10.1007/3-540-39568-7_5

55. Shi, E., Bethencourt, J., Chan, H.T., Song, D.X., Perrig, A.: Multi-dimensional range query over encrypted data. In: IEEE S&P (2007)

56. Sirvent, T.: Traitor tracing scheme with constant ciphertext rate against powerful pirates. IACR Cryptology ePrint Archive 2006 (2006)

57. Staddon, J., Stinson, D.R., Wei, R.: Combinatorial properties of frameproof and traceability codes. IEEE Trans. Inf. Theory **47**(3), 1042–1049 (2001)

58. Stinson, D.R., Wei, R.: Combinatorial properties and constructions of traceability schemes and frameproof codes. SIAM J. Discrete Math. **11**(1), 41–53 (1998)
59. Tsabary, R.: An equivalence between attribute-based signatures and homomorphic signatures, and new constructions for both. In: Kalai, Y., Reyzin, L. (eds.) TCC 2017. LNCS, vol. 10678, pp. 489–518. Springer, Cham (2017). https://doi.org/10.1007/978-3-319-70503-3_16
60. Yoshida, M., Fujiwara, T.: Toward digital watermarking for cryptographic data. IEICE Trans. **94-A**(1), 270–272 (2011)

Secure Computation

SpOT-Light: Lightweight Private Set Intersection from Sparse OT Extension

Benny Pinkas[1]([⊠]), Mike Rosulek[2], Ni Trieu[2], and Avishay Yanai[1]([⊠])

[1] Bar-Ilan University, Ramat Gan, Israel
benny@pinkas.net, ay.yanay@gmail.com
[2] Oregon State University, Corvallis, USA
{rosulekm,trieun}@oregonstate.edu

Abstract. We describe a novel approach for two-party private set intersection (PSI) with semi-honest security. Compared to existing PSI protocols, ours has a more favorable balance between communication and computation. Specifically, our protocol has the *lowest monetary cost* of any known PSI protocol, when run over the Internet using cloud-based computing services (taking into account current rates for CPU + data). On slow networks (e.g., 10 Mbps) our protocol is actually the *fastest*.

Our novel underlying technique is a variant of oblivious transfer (OT) extension that we call *sparse OT extension*. Conceptually it can be thought of as a communication-efficient multipoint oblivious PRF evaluation. Our sparse OT technique relies heavily on manipulating high-degree polynomials over large finite fields (i.e. elements whose representation requires hundreds of bits). We introduce extensive algorithmic and engineering improvements for interpolation and multi-point evaluation of such polynomials, which we believe will be of independent interest.

Finally, we present an extensive empirical comparison of state-of-the-art PSI protocols in several application scenarios and along several dimensions of measurement: running time, communication, peak memory consumption, and—arguably the most relevant metric for practice—monetary cost.

1 Introduction

Private set intersection (PSI) allows two parties, who each hold a set of items, to learn the intersection of their sets without revealing anything else about the items. PSI has many privacy-preserving applications: e.g., private contact discovery [8,15,47][1], DNA testing and pattern matching [51], remote diagnostics [5], record linkage [25], and measuring the effectiveness of online advertising [30].

---

[1] See also https://whispersystems.org/blog/contact-discovery/.

B. Pinkas—Supported by the BIU Center for Research in Applied Cryptography and Cyber Security in conjunction with the Israel National Cyber Bureau in the Prime Minister's Office, and by a grant from the Israel Science Foundation.
M. Rosulek—Partially supported by NSF award 1617197, a Google faculty award, and a Visa faculty award.

© International Association for Cryptologic Research 2019
A. Boldyreva and D. Micciancio (Eds.): CRYPTO 2019, LNCS 11694, pp. 401–431, 2019.
https://doi.org/10.1007/978-3-030-26954-8_13

Over the last several years PSI has become truly practical with extremely fast implementations [7,8,11,12,16,20,24,35,36,45,47,48] that can process millions of items in seconds.

In this paper we focus on **two-party** PSI with **semi-honest** security (with one variant of our protocol achieving malicious security for one party). While we describe our protocols in terms of any number of items, our evaluation focuses on the case where the two parties have **sets of the same size.** We discuss the setting of unequal set sizes in the full version.

1.1   What Should We Value in a PSI Protocol?

The standard ways to measure the cost of a protocol are running time and communication. Depending on which of these metrics is prioritized, a different protocol will be preferred.

Minimizing Time. The fastest known PSI protocols are all based on efficient oblivious transfers (OT). The idea is to reduce the PSI computation to many instances of oblivious transfer. This approach is the fastest because modern OT extension protocols [1,3,31,34] use only a small (fixed) number of public-key operations (e.g., elliptic curve multiplications) but otherwise use only *cheap symmetric-key operations*. The approach to PSI was introduced by Pinkas et al. [45] and refined in a sequence of works [35,44]. The state-of-the-art protocol [35] computes an intersection of million-item sets in about 4 s.

Minimizing Communication. To the best of our knowledge, the PSI protocol with lowest communication in this setting is due to Ateniese et al. [2]. This protocol requires communication that is only marginally more than a naïve and *insecure* protocol (in which one party sends just a short hash of each item), and also has the nice property of hiding the size of the input set. However, the protocol requires at least $n \log n$ RSA exponentiations (for PSI of n items). These requirements make the protocol prohibitively expensive in practice.[2]

A more popular (as well as the earliest) approach to low-communication PSI is based on the commutative property of Diffie-Hellman key agreement (DH-PSI), and appears in several works [28,39,50]. The idea is for the parties to compute the intersection of $\{(H(x)^\alpha)^\beta) \mid x \in X\}$ and $\{(H(y)^\beta)^\alpha) \mid y \in Y\}$ in the clear, where α and β are secrets known by Alice and Bob, respectively. The DH-PSI protocol strikes a more favorable balance between communication and computation than the RSA-based protocol. It requires n exponentiations in a Diffie-Hellman group, which are considerably cheaper than RSA exponentiations but considerably more expensive than the symmetric-key operations used in OT extension. In terms of communication, it requires less than 3 group elements per item. When instantiated with compact elliptic curve groups (ECDH-PSI), the communication complexity is very small. For example, Curve25519 [4] provides 128-bit security with only 256-bit group elements (around 600 bits of communication per item).

---

[2] We are not aware of any prior implementation of this protocol, but estimated the running time through benchmark RSA exponentiations. For the set sizes we consider in this work, the protocol would require many hours or even a day.

An Ideal Balance. Communication cost and overall running time are clearly both important, but which metric best reflects the balance between the two costs, and the true suitability of a protocol for practice? We argue that the most appropriate metric which balances the two costs is the **monetary cost to run the protocol on a cloud computing service.** First, a typical real-world application of PSI is likely to use such a service rather than in-house computing. Second, the pricing model of such services already takes into account the difference in cost to send a bit vs. perform a CPU clock cycle.

1.2 Our Contributions

We present a new PSI protocol paradigm that is secure against semi-honest adversaries under standard-model assumptions. We offer two variants of our protocol: one is optimized for low communication and the other for fast computation. The variant that is optimized for low communication is also secure against a malicious sender in the (non-programmable) random oracle model.

Better Balance of Computation and Communication. Compared to DH-PSI and RSA-based PSI [2], both of our protocol variants have much faster running time, since ours are based on OT extension (i.e., dominated by cheap symmetric-key operations). The low-communication variant has smaller communication overhead than DH-PSI (even on a 256-bit elliptic curve) while the fast-computation variant has about the same communication cost as DH-PSI.

Compared to [35], both of our protocol variants require much less communication. Our protocols perform more computation in the form of finite field operations, making our protocols slower over high-bandwidth networks. However, the variant optimized for fast computation has a competitive running time and is the fastest over low-bandwidth networks (e.g., 30 Mbps and less).

Extensive Cost Comparison. In Sect. 6 we perform an extensive benchmark of state-of-the-art PSI protocols for various set sizes and bandwidth configurations. To the best of our knowledge, our analysis is the first to assess PSI protocols in terms of their monetary costs. Our experiments show that in *all* settings we considered, the fast variant of our protocol has the **least monetary cost** of all protocols—up to 40% less in some cases. A summary of the state of the art (including this work) is depicted in Fig. 1.

Sparse OT Extension Technique. Our main technique, which we call *sparse OT extension*, is a novel twist on oblivious transfer (OT) extension. Roughly speaking, the idea allows the receiver to obliviously pick up a chosen subset of k out of N random secrets (where N may be exponential), with communication cost proportional only to k.

The concept is similar to an oblivious PRF [19] on which the receiver can evaluate k chosen points. Other PSI protocols like [35,44] can also be expressed as a construction of OPRF from OT extension. However, these involve an OPRF that the receiver can evaluate *on only a single value*, resulting in significantly more effort to build PSI. This qualitative difference in OPRF flavor is the main source of our performance improvements.

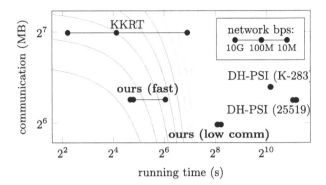

Fig. 1. Communication and running time for different PSI protocols, with $n = 2^{20}$ items, on 3 network configurations. Curved lines are lines of equal monetary cost on a representative AWS configuration (see Sect. 6).

New Hashing Techniques. It is common in PSI literature to assign items randomly to bins, and then perform a PSI within each bin. For security reasons, it is necessary to add dummy items to each bin. With existing techniques, dummy items account for 20–80% of the protocol cost! Our speed-optimized protocol variant is the first to use a kind of 2-choice hashing [49] that requires almost no dummy items (e.g., 2.5%). This 2-choice hashing technique requires placing many items per bin, while previous PSI techniques are only efficient with 1 item per bin (due to their qualitatively different OPRF flavor). Hence, this hashing technique does not immediately benefit existing PSI protocols.

New Polynomial Interpolation Techniques. Our communication-optimized protocol variant requires interpolation and multi-point evaluation of a polynomial, which turns out to be the main bottleneck for the following reasons: (1) The polynomial is over a large field of $\gg 2^{400}$ elements, since the polynomial encodes values related to an underlying OT-extension protocol. (2) The number of interpolation points depend on the parties' set size, which could be in the millions. (3) The best algorithms, which incur $O(n \log n)$ field operations, require a special set of interpolation points, namely, the x-values should be the roots of unity of the field or have a special algebraic structure. In contrast, in the context of our protocol the interpolation points (the x-values) are the parties PSI input items, which are arbitrary. The best algorithms with an arbitrary set of interpolation points incur $O(n \log^2 n)$ field operations [40].

We develop and demonstrate new techniques, called *Slice & Stream* and *Subproduct-Tree Reuse*, to speed up the concrete efficiency of these tasks by up to 2× for the special case in which the x and y-coordinates of the points are drawn from the domains $\mathcal{D}_x$ and $\mathcal{D}_y$ where $|\mathcal{D}_x| \ll |\mathcal{D}_y|$. We believe those techniques could have a general interest (even outside of the field of cryptography).

1.3   Related Work and Comparison

We compare our results to relevant related work here, focusing on qualitative differences between the protocols. A quantitative comparison is given later in Sect. 6.

DH-PSI. Our protocol uses less communication than DH-PSI, even when the latter is instantiated with the most compact elliptic curve known. In terms of computation, our protocol uses only symmetric-key operations (apart from a fixed number of base OTs). Its main computational bottleneck is computing polynomial interpolation, requiring either $O(n \log^2 \lambda)$ or $O(n \log^2 n)$ finite field operations (i.e., multiplications), depending on the variant, where n is the set size and λ is the statistical security parameter. The DH-PSI protocol computes $O(n)$ exponentiations (or elliptic curve multiplications, which are each computed using $\log |\mathbb{G}|$ multiplication operations in the underlying cyclic group $\mathbb{G}$). If we consider the basic unit of computation to be a multiplication in the underlying field/group, then our protocol uses at most $O(n \log^2 n)$ multiplications whereas DH-PSI uses $O(n \log |\mathbb{G}|)$ multiplications. The experiments that we describe in Sect. 6 demonstrate that our protocol is substantially faster than DH-PSI for all realistic set sizes and on all network configurations.

Our communication-optimized protocol variant has security against one malicious party. In contrast, DH-PSI is not easily adapted to malicious security, even against just one party.[3] In order to harden DH-PSI against malicious parties, the leading protocol of De Cristofaro et al. [12] requires *both parties* to run zero-knowledge proofs involving all of their input items. Thus, even one-sided malicious security requires significant overhead to the semi-honest protocol.

While we do not formally consider security against quantum adversaries, we do point out that our protocol exclusively uses primitives that can be instantiated with post-quantum security (OT, PRFs, and hash functions). DH-PSI on the other hand is trivially broken against quantum adversaries.

Protocols Based on an RSA Accumulator. The protocol of [2] has a very low communication overhead of roughly $\lambda + \log^2 n$ bits per item, which may even be optimal (even for an insecure protocol). On the other hand, it computes $O(n \log n)$ RSA exponentiations, and as such is slower than DH-PSI by at least an order of magnitude (due to the $\log n$ factor, and to RSA exponentiations being slower than elliptic curve multiplications). Our protocols are substantially faster than both of these protocols (see Sect. 6). This protocol also requires a random oracle, whereas for semi-honest security ours is in the standard model.

OT-Based Protocols. Our protocol requires 40–50% less communication compared to [35] and is the fastest over low-bandwidth networks (30 Mbps and lower). Over high-bandwidth networks, even though our protocol is slower than [35], ours still requires less monetary cost (see Sect. 6).

---

[3] The main challenge is that a simulator would have to extract effective inputs $\{x_1, \dots, x_n\}$ from a corrupt party, seeing only $\{H(x_1)^\alpha, \dots, H(x_n)^\alpha\}$.

Independently, Lambæk [37] and Patra et al. [43] showed how to enhance the protocols of [35,45] with a security against a *malicious receiver* with almost no additional overhead. Interestingly, our protocol naturally provides security against a *malicious sender*. In both of these protocols, if the parties have sets of very different sizes then the party with more items should play the role of sender. Providing a different flavor of one-sided malicious security is therefore potentially valuable.

Ghosh and Nilges [22] proposed a PSI protocol based on oblivious linear function evaluation (OLE). This protocol requires $2n$ passive OLE invocations, polynomial interpolations at 3 times (one of degree n, and two of degree $2n$), and polynomial evaluation on $2n + 1$ points at 4 times. In terms of communication, the required passive OLE instances [21,32] require $8(n + 1)$ elements sent from the receiver to the sender to create a noisy encoding, and the cost of doing $4n$-out-of-$8(n + 1)$ OT which incurs an overhead of at least $8(n + 1)$ on the number of Correlated OT. Hence, this OLE-based PSI protocol requires at least $8(n+1)(\kappa + 2\ell)$ bits communication, where ℓ is bit-length of item. For example, when $\ell = 128$, our protocols show a factor of $4.8 - 6.3\times$ improvement in terms of communication.

Recently, Falk, Noble and Ostrovsky [18] presented a protocol for PSI that achieves linear communication complexity relying on standard assumption (i.e. in the OT-hybrid model, assuming the existence of correlation robust hash and one-way functions) and in the standard model (i.e. without a random oracle). This is in contrast to previous protocols that achieve linear communication but rely on stronger assumptions (like [12,13] that are based on the one-more RSA assumption and a random oracle); and to previous OT-based protocols that achieve only super-linear communication complexity due to the stash handling. In the protocol of [18], just like previous OT-based protocols, Bob maps his n items to $O(n)$ bins using a Cuckoo hashing, hence, it has at most one item in each bin. Bob also maintains a special bin for items that could not be mapped to the 'regular' bins, this special bin is called the *stash* and it contains $\omega(1)$ items. Alice maps her items to $O(n)$ bins using simple hashing, hence, she has at most $O(\log n/\log \log n)$ items in each bin with high probability. Then, Bob can obtain the intersection between items in its 'regular' bins and Alice's set using the BaRK-OPRF technique of [35] with communication complexity $O(n \cdot \kappa)$ (where κ is the computational security parameter). It remains to compare the items in Bob's stash to all Alice's items; since the stash is of size $\omega(1)$ this comparison would naively require $\omega(n \cdot \kappa)$ communication overall. However, the observation in [18] is that this comparison can be performed using a separate PSI protocol that is specialized for *unbalanced* set sizes in which Alice has much more items than Bob; such a protocol can achieve communication complexity that depends only on the larger set size, therefore, the overall communication complexity of [18] is $O(n \cdot \kappa)$ rather than $\omega(n \cdot \kappa)$. We note that in concurrent to their work, in this paper we achieve the same (linear) communication complexity, under the same standard assumptions and without a random oracle, using a new primitive, namely the *Sparse OT Extension*.

Other Paradigms. Other approaches for PSI have been proposed, including ones based on Bloom filters [16] and generic MPC [27]. Pinkas et al. [44,45] performed a comprehensive comparison of semi-honest PSI techniques and found the OT-extension paradigm to strictly dominate others in terms of performance. They found that the best Bloom-filter approach is 2× worse in runtime, 4× worse in communication; best generic-MPC-based approach is 100× worse in runtime and 10× worse in communication. For this reason, we do not include these protocol paradigms in further comparisons.

Asymmetric Set Sizes. Several recent PSI protocols are optimized specifically for the case of highly asymmetric set sizes [8,33,44,47]. We discuss these protocols in the full version.

Other Related Work. One way of viewing our new technique is that we covertly embed some protocol messages into a polynomial. Similar ideas appear in [9,38]. In particular, [9] explicitly propose to embed private equality-test protocol messages into a polynomial, to yield a PSI protocol. Their protocol is based on the DH paradigm, and therefore requires a linear number of exponentiations. They also achieve a stronger *covertness* property (participants cannot distinguish other participants from random noise, until the protocol terminates). In our case, we look inside IKNP OT extension and identify the minimal part of the protocol that needs to be covertly embedded into a polynomial, in order to achieve *standard* (semi-honest or malicious) security.

2   Technical Preliminaries

2.1   Notation

Throughout the paper we use the following notation: We let κ, λ denote the computational and statistical security parameters, respectively. We write $[m]$ to denote a set $\{1, \ldots, m\}$. The notation $d_H(\boldsymbol{x}, \boldsymbol{y},)$ denotes the Hamming distance between bit vectors (strings) $\boldsymbol{x}$ and $\boldsymbol{y}$ of the same length and $w_H(\boldsymbol{x}) = d_H(\boldsymbol{x}, \boldsymbol{0})$ denotes the Hamming weight of $\boldsymbol{x}$. For a bit vector $\boldsymbol{v}$ we let v_i denote the bit in the ith coordinate. If $\boldsymbol{a} = a_1 \| \cdots \| a_p$ and $\boldsymbol{b} = b_1 \| \cdots \| b_p$ are two vectors, the notation $\boldsymbol{a} \oplus \boldsymbol{b}$ denotes the vector $(a_1 \oplus b_1) \| \cdots \| (a_p \oplus b_p)$. Similarly, the notation $\boldsymbol{a} \cdot \boldsymbol{b}$ represents the bitwise-AND of vectors: $(a_1 \cdot b_1) \| \cdots \| (a_p \cdot b_p)$.

2.2   Oblivious Transfer

Oblivious Transfer (OT) is a central cryptographic primitive in the area of secure computation, which was introduced by Rabin [46]. 1-out-of-2 OT [17] refers to the setting where a sender with two input strings $(\boldsymbol{m_0}, \boldsymbol{m_1})$ interacts with a receiver who has a input choice bit b. As the result, the receiver learns $\boldsymbol{m_b}$ without learning anything about $\boldsymbol{m_{1-b}}$, while the sender learns nothing about b. Rabin OT protocol requires expensive public-key operations. In 2003, Ishai et al. [31] proposed a construction of OT extension (refer as IKNP) that allows a large

PARAMETERS: Sender $\mathcal{S}$, receiver $\mathcal{R}$, length κ

FUNCTIONALITY:

- Wait for an input $b \leftarrow \{0, 1\}$ from the receiver $\mathcal{R}$.
- Choose $m_0, m_1 \leftarrow \{0, 1\}^\kappa$, and give both to sender $\mathcal{S}$.
- Give m_b to receiver $\mathcal{R}$.

Fig. 2. The $\mathcal{F}_{\mathsf{ROT}}^\kappa$ ideal functionality for Random Oblivious Transfer.

number of OTs executions at the cost of computing a small number of expensive OTs [41]. Later, Kolesnikov and Kumaresan [34] improved IKNP for short secrets. It gives $O(\log(\kappa))$ factor performance improvement in communication and computation. In the same year, [1] presented several IKNP optimizations and several weaker variants of OT. In Random OT (ROT), the sender's OT inputs (m_0, m_1) are chosen at random, therefore, it allows the protocol itself to give him the values (m_0, m_1) randomly. With ROT, the bandwidth requirement is significantly reduced since the sender sends nothing to receiver. In our construction, we require this weaker variant, random OT, whose functionality is described in Fig. 2.

2.3 (Hamming) Correlation Robustness

Our PSI construction is proven secure under a *correlation robust* assumption which was introduced for IKNP OT extension [31] and later generalized in [35] to the version we use in this work.

Definition 1 [35]. *Let H be a function with input length n. Then H is d-**Hamming correlation robust function** (CRF) if, for any $a_1, \ldots, a_m, b_1, \ldots, b_m$ with $a_i, b_i \in \{0, 1\}^n$ and $w_H(b_i) \geq d$ for all $i \in [m]$, the following distribution, induced by random sampling of $s \leftarrow \{0, 1\}^n$, is pseudorandom:*

$$H(a_1 \oplus [b_1 \wedge s]), \ldots, H(a_m \oplus [b_m \wedge s])$$

The IKNP protocol uses this assumption with $n = d = \kappa$. In that case, the only valid choice for b_i is 1^κ, and the distribution simplifies to $H(a_1 \oplus s), \ldots, H(a_m \oplus s)$. In our case, we use $n > d = \kappa$, so other choices for the b_i values are possible.

2.4 Private Set Intersection

PSI is a special case of secure two-party computation, and we use the standard security definitions for two-party computation in this work. The guarantees of PSI are captured in the ideal functionality $\mathcal{F}_{\mathsf{PSI}}$ defined in Fig. 3. For security against malicious parties, we use the framework of universal composability (UC) [6].

PARAMETERS: Sender $\mathcal{S}$, receiver $\mathcal{R}$, set sizes n_1, n_2.

FUNCTIONALITY:

- Wait for input $X = \{x_1, \ldots, x_{n_1}\} \subseteq \{0,1\}^*$ from sender $\mathcal{S}$.
- Wait for input $Y = \{y_1, \ldots, y_{n_2}\} \subseteq \{0,1\}^*$ from receiver $\mathcal{R}$.
- Give output $X \cap Y$ to receiver $\mathcal{R}$.

Fig. 3. PSI ideal functionality $\mathcal{F}_{\mathsf{PSI}}$.

PARAMETERS:

- A PRG $G : \{0,1\}^\kappa \to \{0,1\}^N$
- A κ-Hamming CRF $H : \{0,1\}^\kappa \to \{0,1\}^\kappa$.

INPUT OF SENDER ALICE: none.

INPUT OF RECEIVER BOB: an N-bit string $\boldsymbol{r}$.

PROTOCOL:

1. Alice chooses $\boldsymbol{s} \leftarrow \{0,1\}^\kappa$ uniformly at random.
2. Alice and Bob invoke κ instances of Random OT $\mathcal{F}_{\mathsf{ROT}}^\kappa$. In the i-th instance:
   - Alice acts as *receiver* with input s_i.
   - Bob acts as *sender*, and receives outputs $\boldsymbol{t}_i, \boldsymbol{u}_i \in \{0,1\}^\kappa$.
   - Alice receives output $\boldsymbol{q}_i$.
3. Bob computes the following $N \times \kappa$ matrices:
   - T whose ith column is $G(\boldsymbol{t}_i)$
   - U whose ith column is $G(\boldsymbol{u}_i)$
   - C whose ith **row** is 0^κ if $r_i = 0$ and 1^κ if $r_i = 1$

   Bob sends the matrix $P = T \oplus U \oplus C$ to Alice. For each $i \in [N]$, Bob outputs $\boldsymbol{m}_i^* = H(T(i))$, where $T(i)$ denotes the ith **row** of T.
4. Alice computes an $N \times \kappa$ matrix Q whose ith column is $G(\boldsymbol{q}_i)$. Now let $Q(i)$ denote the ith **row** of this matrix, and let $P(i)$ denote the ith **row** of P. For each $i \in [N]$, Alice outputs:

$$\boldsymbol{m}_{i,0} = H(Q(i) \oplus \boldsymbol{s} \cdot P(i))$$
$$\boldsymbol{m}_{i,1} = H(Q(i) \oplus \boldsymbol{s} \cdot P(i) \oplus \boldsymbol{s})$$

Fig. 4. The IKNP protocol for OT extension.

2.5   The IKNP OT Extension: A Reminder

It is well-known that oblivious transfer cannot be obtained from scratch using only symmetric-key primitives [29]. OT extension [3] refers to the idea that parties can perform only a small number κ of OTs (using public-key primitives), and then, *using only symmetric-key operations thereafter*, obtain $N \gg \kappa$ effective instances of OT. Modern OT extension protocols follow the overall structure of the IKNP protocol [31]. In Fig. 4 we review the variant of the IKNP protocol where the sender's OT payloads are chosen uniformly.

From the correctness of the base OTs, we have that:

$$q_i = t_i \oplus s_i \cdot (t_i \oplus u_i) = \begin{cases} t_i & \text{if } s_i = 0 \\ u_i & \text{if } s_i = 1 \end{cases}$$

This relationship can be extended across the rows of the $N \times \kappa$ matrices to obtain: $Q(i) = T(i) \oplus s \cdot (T(i) \oplus U(i))$, where $T(i)$ and $U(i)$ correspond to the rows of T and U. Then:

$$Q(i) \oplus s \cdot P(i) = \Big(T(i) \oplus s \cdot (T(i) \oplus U(i)) \Big) \oplus s \cdot (T(i) \oplus U(i) \oplus C(i))$$

$$= T(i) \oplus s \cdot C(i) = \begin{cases} T(i) & \text{if } r_i = 0 \\ T(i) \oplus s & \text{if } r_i = 1 \end{cases}$$

From this we can deduce that Bob's output is $m_i^* = m_{i,r_i}$, whereas $m_{i,1-r_i} = H(T(i) \oplus s)$. From the correlation-robust property of H, this value is pseudorandom from Bob's perspective.

3 Our Main Protocol

3.1 A Conceptual Overview: PSI from a Multi-point OPRF

A conceptually simple way to realize PSI is with an **oblivious PRF** (OPRF) [19,23], which allows a sender Alice to learn a [pseudo]random function F, and allows the receiver Bob to learn $F(y_i)$ for each chosen item in his set $\{y_1, \ldots, y_n\}$. If Alice has items $\{x_1, \ldots, x_n\}$, she can send $F(x_1), \ldots, F(x_n)$ to Bob. If the output of F is sufficiently long, then except with negligible probability we have $F(x_i) = F(y_j)$ if and only if $x_i = y_j$. Hence, Bob can deduce the intersection of the two sets. The fact that F is pseudorandom ensures that for any item $x_i \notin \{y_1, \ldots, y_n\}$, the corresponding $F(x_i)$ looks random to Bob. Hence, no information about such items is leaked to Bob.

Sparse OT Extension: Key Idea. We can interpret IKNP OT extension (Fig. 4) as an OPRF as follows: Define the function $F(i) = m_{i,0}$. Clearly the sender who knows the key of F can compute $F(i)$ for any i. The receiver can set his i'th choice bit in the OT to be $r_i = 0$ if he chooses to learn $F(i)$ (in this case he learns $m_{i,0}$), and use $r_i = 1$ if he chooses not to learn $F(i)$ (now he learns $m_{i,1}$). To learn k OPRF outputs, the receiver includes k 0s among his choice bits. The security of OT extension implies that the receiver learns nothing about $F(i)$ whenever $r_i = 1$, and the sender learns nothing about the r_i bits.

This yields an OPRF of the form $F : [N] \to \{0,1\}^\kappa$, where N is the number of rows in the OT extension matrix. To be useful for PSI, N should be exponentially large, making this simple approach extremly inefficient. The following two key observations allow us to make the above approach efficient:

1. The parties require only *random access* to the large OT extension matrices. In the PSI application, they only read the $n \ll N$ rows indexed by their

PSI inputs. While IKNP defines the matrices T, U, Q by expanding base OT values via a PRG, we instead expand with a PRF^4.

2. Besides the base OTs, the only communication in IKNP is when Bob sends the $N \times \kappa$ matrix P. In PSI, Bob only has knowledge of the $n \ll N$ rows of P indexed by his PSI input. Yet he must not let Alice identify the indices of these rows. Our idea is to have Bob interpolate a degree-n polynomial P where $P(y)$ is the correct "target row" of the IKNP OT extension matrix, for each y in his PSI input set. He then **sends this polynomial P instead of a huge matrix**. This change reduces Bob's communication from $O(N\kappa)$ to $O(n\kappa)$, allowing N to be exponential.

The polynomial P is distributed as a random polynomial (hiding Bob's inputs) since all rows of the IKNP matrix are pseudorandom from Alice's point of view. The more important concern is whether Bob learns too much. For example, suppose Bob interpolates P on points $\{y_1, \ldots, y_n\}$, but P happens to match the correct "IKNP target value" on some other $y^* \notin \{y_1, \ldots, y_n\}$ as well. This would allow Bob to learn whether Alice holds y^*, violating privacy. We argue that: (1) When the OT extension matrix is sufficiently wide, all relevant values $P(y^*)$ are sufficiently far in Hamming distance from their "target value". (2) When this is true, then Bob gets no information about Alice's items not in the intersection.

Comparison to Other PSI Paradigms. Other state-of-the-art PSI protocols (e.g., [35,45]) can also be interpreted as constructing an OPRF from OT extension ([35] is explicitly described this way). These works construct an OPRF that the receiver can evaluate on *only one point,* and use various hashing tricks to reduce PSI to many independent instances of such an OPRF. In contrast, we construct a single instance of an OPRF where the receiver can evaluate *many points.* With such a multi-point OPRF it is trivial to achieve PSI, as illustrated above.

3.2   Protocol Details, Correctness, Performance

The formal details of our protocol are given in Fig. 5. We use n_1 for the size of Alice's set and n_2 for the size of Bob's. We write $\mathsf{Interp}_{\mathbb{F}}(\{(x_1, y_1), \ldots, (x_d, y_d)\})$ to denote the unique polynomial P over field $\mathbb{F}$ of degree less than d where $P(x_i) = y_i$. In IKNP, the width of the matrices (and number of base OTs) is κ whereas the width in our instantiation is $\ell > \kappa$, where ℓ is determined by the security analysis.

Costs. The main computational cost is evaluating the degree-n_2 polynomial for Alice and interpolating the polynomial for Bob. In the case of $n_1 = n_2 = n$ this can be done with $O(n \log^2 n)$ field operations (details in Sect. 5.1).

---

[4] In [26, Sect. 3.2] they also use a PRF rather than PRG, but for a completely different purpose: random access to the OT extension matrix was used to parallelize OT extension and reduce memory footprint.

INPUT OF SENDER ALICE: $X = \{x_1, \ldots, x_{n_1}\} \subseteq [N]$
INPUT OF RECEIVER BOB: $Y = \{y_1, \ldots, y_{n_2}\} \subseteq [N]$
PARAMETERS:

- The size $\ell := \log_2 |\mathbb{F}|$ as defined in Fig.6
- A κ-Hamming CRF $H : \{0,1\}^\ell \rightarrow \{0,1\}^{\lambda + \log(n_1 n_2)}$
- A PRF $F : \{0,1\}^\kappa \times [N] \rightarrow \{0,1\}$

PROTOCOL:

1. Alice chooses $s \leftarrow \{0,1\}^\ell$ uniformly at random.
2. Alice and Bob invoke ℓ instances of Random OT $\mathcal{F}_{\mathsf{ROT}}^\kappa$. In the i-th instance:
   - Alice acts as *receiver* with input s_i.
   - Bob acts as *sender*, and receives outputs $t_i, u_i \in \{0,1\}^\kappa$.
   - Alice receives output q_i.
3. For $y \in Y$, Bob computes $R(y) = T(y) \oplus U(y)$, where:

$$T(y) := F(t_1, y) \| F(t_2, y) \| \cdots \| F(t_\ell, y)$$
$$U(y) := F(u_1, y) \| F(u_2, y) \| \cdots \| F(u_\ell, y)$$

4. Bob computes a polynomial $P := \mathsf{Interp}_{\mathbb{F}}(\{y, R(y)\}_{y \in Y})$, and sends its coefficients to Alice
5. Alice defines Q as follows:

$$Q(x) := F(q_1, x) \| F(q_2, x) \| \cdots \| F(q_\ell, x)$$

   and sends $\mathcal{O} = \{H(Q(x) \oplus s \cdot P(x)) \mid x \in X\}$ randomly permuted to Bob
6. Bob outputs $\{y \in Y \mid H(T(y)) \in \mathcal{O}\}$

Fig. 5. Our PSI protocol.

In the communication costs of the protocol, we exclude the cost of the base OTs. These are fixed and don't depend on the parties' set sizes. Bob sends $n_2 \ell$ bits, while Alice sends $n_1(\lambda + \log(n_1 n_2))$ bits. Generally speaking, ℓ is much larger than $\lambda + \log(n_1 n_2)$, which suggests that the party with more items should play the role of Alice. Concrete values are discussed later in Sect. 6.

Correctness. The idea behind the protocol is that for every row which Bob uses to interpolate the polynomial P (namely, a row corresponding to an input of Bob), Alice sends a value which is equal to the corresponding hash value that Bob computes in the last step of the protocol.

Namely, following the discussion of IKNP, we can see that

$$Q(x) = T(x) \oplus s \cdot (T(x) \oplus U(x)) = T(x) \oplus s \cdot R(x)$$

and therefore in Step 5 Alice computes:

$$Q(x) \oplus s \cdot P(x) = T(x) \oplus s \cdot (P(x) \oplus R(x)) \tag{1}$$

Now, consider the case that both parties have a common item x^*. Bob constructs P so that $P(x^*) = R(x^*)$. Alice computes $H(Q(x^*) \oplus s \cdot P(x^*))$ which from Eq. 1 gives Alice $H(T(x^*))$. Hence, Bob will include x^* in his output.

In case that $x \notin Y$, $P(x)$ and $R(x)$ will be different in at least κ bits with overwhelming probability (see the analysis below). Therefore, $H\big(Q(x) \oplus \boldsymbol{s} \cdot P(x)\big)$ is pseudorandom from Bob's view, under the Hamming correlation robust assumption. If σ is the output length of H, then the probability that this random value equals $H(T(y))$ for some $y \in Y$ is $n_2 2^{-\sigma}$. By a union bound over the items of $X \setminus Y$, the overall probability of Bob including an incorrect value in the output is at most $n_1 n_2 2^{-\sigma}$. Hence, choosing $\sigma = \lambda + \log_2(n_1 n_2)$ ensures that this error probability is negligible $(2^{-\lambda})$.

3.3   Properties of Polynomials

We first prove some simple lemmas about polynomials that are used in the security proof of our PSI protocol.

Hiding Bob's Input. For security against a corrupt sender Alice, we simply need Bob's polynomial to hide his input:

Proposition 1. *If $z_1, \ldots, z_d$ are uniformly distributed over $\mathbb{F}$, then for all distinct $x_1, \ldots, x_d$, the output of $\mathsf{Interp}_{\mathbb{F}}(\{(x_1, z_1), \ldots, (x_d, z_d)\})$ is uniformly distributed. In particular, the distribution does not depend on the x_i's.*

Proof. Viewing polynomial interpolation as a linear operation, we have the following, where $p_0, \ldots, p_{d-1}$ are the coefficients of the polynomial.

$$
\begin{bmatrix} p_0 \\ p_1 \\ \vdots \\ p_{d-1} \end{bmatrix} = \begin{bmatrix} 1 & x_1 & x_1^2 & \cdots & x_1^{d-1} \\ 1 & x_2 & x_2^2 & \cdots & x_2^{d-1} \\ \vdots & \vdots & \vdots & \ddots & \vdots \\ 1 & x_d & x_d^2 & \cdots & x_d^{d-1} \end{bmatrix}^{-1} \times \begin{bmatrix} z_1 \\ z_2 \\ \vdots \\ z_d \end{bmatrix}
$$

Since the polynomial is computed as a nonsingular matrix times a uniform vector, the polynomial's distribution is also uniform. ∎

Security for Alice. In our protocol, Bob generates a polynomial P such that $P(y) = R(y)$ for his input points $y \in Y$. The security of the protocol relies on the property that for *all other* points $x \notin Y$, $P(x)$ is far from $R(x)$ in Hamming distance (with very high probability).

Definition 2. (Bad polynomial). *Let $\mathsf{BadPoly}_{\mathbb{F}}^R(X, Y)$ be the procedure defined as follows:*

1. $P := \mathsf{Interp}_{\mathbb{F}}(\{(y, R(y)) \mid y \in Y\})$
2. *Output 1 iff $\exists x \in X \setminus Y$ s.t. $d_H(P(x), R(x)) < \kappa$*

Proposition 2. *The probability that a polynomial interpolated over points in Y also passes "too close" to another point in X is bounded by $\frac{n_1}{|\mathbb{F}|} \sum_{i < \kappa} \binom{\log_2 |\mathbb{F}|}{i}$. Formally, for all X, Y with $|X| = n_1$,*

$$
\Pr[\mathsf{BadPoly}_{\mathbb{F}}^R(X, Y) = 1] \leq \frac{n_1}{|\mathbb{F}|} \sum_{i < \kappa} \binom{\log_2 |\mathbb{F}|}{i},
$$

where the probability is over choice of random function $R : \mathbb{F} \to \mathbb{F}$.

					n_1:			
Pr[BadPoly]	2^{10}	2^{12}	2^{14}	2^{16}	2^{18}	2^{20}	2^{22}	2^{24}
2^{-40}	416	420	424	428	432	436	440	444
2^{-80}	491	495	498	502	505	509	512	515

Fig. 6. Field size $\log_2 |\mathbb{F}|$ for our protocol, with $\kappa = 128$.

Proof. For a fixed element $v \in \mathbb{F}$, the probability of a uniformly chosen element $u \leftarrow \mathbb{F}$ being closer than Hamming distance κ to v is $\sum_{i<\kappa} \binom{\log_2 |\mathbb{F}|}{i}/|\mathbb{F}|$. This is the case when entering to the second step of the procedure in Definition 2, where each $P(x)$ is already fixed and $R(x)$ is uniform in $\mathbb{F}$. The claim follows by a union bound over the (at most n_1) items in $X \setminus Y$. ∎

On the Communication Complexity of the Protocol. Let $\ell = \log_2 |\mathbb{F}|$. In our protocol a small ℓ leads to a bad event where two terms are close in Hamming distance. Since this bad event is a *one-time* event, it suffices to bound its probability by the statistical security parameter λ. Since the bad event involves a union bound over n, the concrete analysis involves both λ and n.

However, we could also just compute ℓ assuming the worst case $n = 2^\kappa$ (where κ is the computational security parameter), and we would get $\ell = \mathsf{poly}(\kappa)$ and a bad-event probability of $\mathsf{poly}(\mathsf{n})/2^\kappa$. For our specific protocol/analysis, $\ell = 4.3 \cdot \kappa$ appears sufficient to achieve bad event probability $n/2^\kappa$ (robust to a wide range of κ). As an analogy: in *any* OPRF-based PSI protocol, receiver learns $F(y_1), F(y_2), \ldots$ and sender sends $F(x_1), F(x_2), \ldots$. For correctness it suffices to truncate F to $\lambda + 2log(n)$ bits, but of course it is quite enough to let F have $O(\kappa)$ bits.

In summary, asymptotically $O(n \cdot \kappa)$ bits do suffice for correctness/security, but so do $O(n \cdot \ell)$ bits, where ℓ is some function of λ, κ, n. The more fine-grained analysis of ℓ leads to less concrete communication, and that is why our concrete analysis displays a dependency of ℓ on n.

Hence, given a desired κ, n_1, and Pr[BadPoly] one can solve for the smallest compatible field size. A table of such field sizes is provided in Fig. 6.

3.4 Semi-honest Security

Theorem 1. *The protocol in Fig. 5 securely realizes the PSI functionality of Fig. 3 in a semi-honest setting, when F is a pseudo-random function, H is a κ-Hamming correlation robust (Definition 1), and the parameter ℓ is chosen according to the table in Fig. 6.*

Proof. Due to space limitation we only sketch here the simulators for the two cases of corrupt Alice and corrupt Bob. The full security proof including (via hybrid arguments) is defered to the full version.

Corrupt Alice. The simulator observes Alice's inputs to the $\mathcal{F}_{\mathsf{ROT}}$ primitive and gives random $\boldsymbol{q}_i$ as OT outputs in Step 2. The only other message Alice receives is the polynomial P in Step 4. Instead of $P := \mathsf{Interp}_{\mathbb{F}}(\{y, R(y)\}_{y \in Y})$, the simulator sends a uniformly random polynomial to Alice.

Briefly, this simulation is indistinguishable for the following reasons: $R(y)$ is pseudorandom from Alice's view (by the security of the PRF which defines the conceptual OT-extension matrices). Hence, the polynomial P is distributed uniformly (from Proposition 1).

Corrupt Bob. The simulator for a corrupt Bob first obtains $X \cap Y$ from the ideal PSI functionality. It simulates random outputs t_i, q_i from $\mathcal{F}_{\mathsf{ROT}}$. The only other message received by Bob is the set $\mathcal{O}$ in Step 5. To simulate this message, the simulator computes $n' = n_1 - |X \cap Y|$ and uniformly samples values $z_1, \ldots, z_{n'}$. It then simulates $\mathcal{O} = \{H(T(x)) \mid x \in X \cap Y\} \cup \{z_1, \ldots, z_{n'}\}$.

This simulation is indistinguishable because $P(x)$ and $R(x)$ will differ in at least κ bits for every $x \in X \setminus Y$ (Proposition 2), and as long as that is true, the corresponding outputs of H will be pseudorandom (Definition 1).

3.5 Optimizations: Reducing Alice's Communication

Recall that Alice's communication consists of n_1 OPRF outputs, each of length $\lambda + \log(n_1 n_2)$. In the full version, we discuss techniques to reduce this cost to roughly $\lambda + \log n_1$ bits per item.

3.6 Security Against Malicious Sender

Our protocol is secure against a malicious sender if F is modeled as a non-programmable random oracle. (In the full version we show that our protocol is *insecure* against a malicious receiver.)

Theorem 2. *The protocol in Fig. 5 securely realizes the PSI functionality of Fig. 3 against a malicious sender Alice, when F is modeled as a (non-programmable) random oracle.*

Proof (Proof Sketch). The simulator plays the role of honest receiver Bob and the ideal $\mathcal{F}_{\mathsf{ROT}}$ functionalities in steps 1 and 2, observing Alice's $\mathcal{F}_{\mathsf{ROT}}$-input s and generating random outputs $\{q_i\}_{i \in [\ell]}$. Throughout the protocol, the simulator also observes all of Alice's queries to the random oracle F. Without loss of generality, we can assume that whenever Alice makes a query of the form $F(q_i, x)$ to the random oracle, where q_i is one of the $\mathcal{F}_{\mathsf{ROT}}$-outputs, it also queries $F(q_j, x)$ for *all* $j \in [\ell]$. The simulator observes Alice's oracle queries and maintains a list

$$C = \{x \mid \text{Alice queried } F \text{ on some } F(q_i, x)\}.$$

In step 4, the simulator sends a random polynomial P. In step 5, the simulator receives a set $\mathcal{O}$ from the corrupt Alice and computes

$$\widetilde{X} = \{x \in C \mid H(Q(x) + s \cdot P(x)) \in \mathcal{O}\},$$

and finally sends $\widetilde{X}$ to the PSI ideal functionality.

In the full version we use a hybrid argument to formally prove the indistinguishability of this simulator. $\square$

4   The Fast Protocol Variant

The biggest performance bottleneck in our protocol is interpolating and evaluating extremely high-degree (e.g., $d = 2^{20}$) polynomials over large (e.g., $|\mathbb{F}| > 2^{64}$) finite fields. To reduce this computational cost, we employ a technique of hashing the items into bins, and performing PSI (involving lower-degree polynomials) within each bin. This general technique is quite common in the PSI literature, and two different types of hashing have been suggested in previous work. However, we introduce a new hashing technique that (to the best of our knowledge) has not been suggested previously for PSI. As we illustrate, previous protocols are not able to immediately benefit from this new hashing technique—only our approach enjoys the advantages of this new approach.

4.1   Previous Hashing Techniques

In **simple hashing**, parties choose a random hash function $h : \{0,1\}^* \to [m]$ and assign each item x to bin with index $h(x)$. Since if Alice and Bob have the same item they both map it to the same bin, then they can perform a separate PSI within each bin. The load of each bin leaks information (i.e., it cannot be simulated just given the intersection), and therefore the parties must pad each bin up to a maximum size with dummy items. For example, with n items and $m = O(n/\log n)$ bins, the expected load of each bin is $n/m = O(\log n)$ and the maximum load B is $O(\log n)$ with high probability. In practice, B may be 4 to 5 times higher than n/m, meaning that **about 80% of the items are dummies.**

In **Cuckoo hashing** (used in [35,45]), the parties choose two hash function $h_1, h_2 : \{0,1\}^* \to [m]$. The receiver Bob places his items into m bins so that x is placed in either $h_1(x)$ or $h_2(x)$, and each bin contains at most one item. Alice places each of her items x in *both* locations $h_1(x)$ and $h_2(x)$. As above, Bob must pad each bin with dummy items to contain *exactly* one item (we can avoid dummy items for Alice). The parties perform a PSI in each bin. Cuckoo hashing leads to roughly **20% dummy items** (this is for Cuckoo hashing with three hash functions; Cuckoo hashing with two hash functions has even more dummy items), not to mention extra protocol costs associated with the stash (a special bin for items that cannot find a home in the Cuckoo hashing).

4.2   Our High-Level Approach

An important feature of Cuckoo hashing is that it results in at most one item per bin for Bob. This situation is the ideal fit for the underlying OPRF primitive of [35,45], which allows the receiver (Bob in this case) to evaluate the OPRF on *a single value*. With Cuckoo hashing, the PSI performed in each bin can be achieved with such an OPRF.

But our sparse OT extension technique results in a multi-point OPRF primitive that allows the receiver to evaluate on many values. Hence we have no need to constrain the receiver Bob to have only one item per bin. We propose to use a generalization of Cuckoo hashing called **2-choice hashing**. Similar to Cuckoo hashing, there are two hash functions h_1 and h_2, and item x can be placed in either $h_1(x)$ or $h_2(x)$. Unlike Cuckoo hashing, there is no restriction on the number of items per bin.

Cuckoo hashing is also often synonymous with an *online* hashing procedure, where all the items are processed in a single pass. For the application to PSI, though, all items are known upfront. We are free to make the best assignment of items to bins, taking into account global information about all items.[5]

These facts about 2-choice hashing indeed lead to much better performance (in terms of dummy items). The following theorem of Czumaj, Riley, and Scheideler [14] shows that when the bins are allowed to contain significantly many items, *no dummy items are needed at all!*

Theorem 3 ([14]). *Let $h_1, h_2 : \{0,1\}^* \to [m]$ be two random functions. Suppose there are n items and m bins, where each item x can be placed in either $h_1(x)$ or $h_2(x)$. Let $L = \lceil n/m \rceil$. If $n = \Omega(m \log m)$ then with high probability there exists an **optimal assignment**, where each bin contains no more than L items.*

The proof uses an explicit randomized algorithm to generate an optimal assignment. However, we found that the algorithm takes prohibitively long to converge. Also, its analysis of error probability is not concrete. However, if we are willing to settle for merely an "almost optimal" assignment of items to bins, the following theorem of Sanders, Egner, and Korst [49] suggests that one can be found quite efficiently:

Theorem 4 ([49]). *Let n, m, h_1, h_2 be as above, with $L = \lceil n/m \rceil$. There is a deterministic algorithm running in time $O(n \log n)$ that assigns at most $L + 1$ items to each bin, with probability $1 - O(1/m)^L$ over the choice of h_1, h_2.*

We propose the two-pass heuristic in Algorithm 1 for assigning items to bins. This very simple, **linear time** algorithm seems to perform well. In our experience, it never fails to find a near-optimal assignment with maximum load $L + 1 = \lceil n/m \rceil + 1$, for the parameters we use. In the rare event that it *does* fail, more iterations of the final loop are likely to succeed.

Algorithm 1. FindAssignment(X, m, h_1, h_2)

1: **for** $x \in X$ **do**
2:     Assign item x to bin $h_1(x)$
3: **for** $x \in X$ **do**
4:     Assign item x to whichever of $h_1(x), h_2(x)$ currently has fewest items
---

With such a near-optimal assignment, we can see that for each of the n/m bins there is only one dummy item. In practice, we set n/m to be the statistical security parameter λ so that an assignment exists with overwhelming probability. Setting $n/m = \lambda = 40$ leads to the most dummy items one would ever consider for our protocol, but still there are **only 2.5% ($= 1/40$) dummy items.**

---
[5] This observation was concurrently and independently noted in [18]; however, their focus is exclusively on Cuckoo hashing, with at most one item per bin. They do not consider our generalized 2-choice hashing.

INPUT OF SENDER ALICE: $X = \{x_1, \ldots, x_{n_1}\} \subseteq [N]$
INPUT OF RECEIVER BOB: $Y = \{y_1, \ldots, y_{n_2}\} \subseteq [N]$
PARAMETERS: (same as Figure 5, except ℓ is chosen to be compatible with $2n_1$ rather than n_1 — see text for discussion)
PROTOCOL: (steps 1–3 are the same as Figure 5)

4. Bob sets $m = n_2/\lambda$, chooses random functions $h_1, h_2 : [N] \to [m]$, and sends them to Alice. Then Bob assigns its items using FindAssignment(Y, m, h_1, h_2) (from Alg. 1) and adds dummy items so that each bin has exactly $\lceil n_2/m \rceil + 1$ items. Write $y\|b \in \mathcal{B}_i$ to mean that y was assigned to bin i by hash h_b. For each bin i, Alice computes a polynomial $P_i := \mathsf{Interp}_{\mathbb{F}}(\{y\|b, R(y\|b)\}_{y\|b \in \mathcal{B}_i})$, and sends its coefficients to Alice.

5. Alice defines Q as in Figure 5 and defines the sets:

$$\mathcal{O}_1 = \Big\{ H\big(Q(x\|1) \oplus s \cdot P_{h_1(x)}(x\|1)\big) \ \Big| \ x \in X \Big\}$$

$$\mathcal{O}_2 = \Big\{ H\big(Q(x\|2) \oplus s \cdot P_{h_2(x)}(x\|2)\big) \ \Big| \ x \in X \Big\}$$

She permutes each one randomly and sends them to Bob.

6. Bob outputs $\{y \mid y\|b \in \bigcup_i \mathcal{B}_i \text{ and } H(T(y\|b)) \in \mathcal{O}_b\}$

Fig. 7. PSI protocol using 2-choice hashing optimization.

In the overall PSI protocol, Bob will send a polynomial of degree $\lceil n/m \rceil + 1$ for each bin. For each item of Alice $x \in X$, she considers both locations $h_1(x)$ and $h_2(x)$ and derives an OT-extension/OPRF output for both possibilities. She then sends these 2 outputs for each item.

4.3 Protocol Details

The details of the protocol are given in Fig. 7. It mostly follows the outline given above, with one important exception. Most of the time, Alice computes two distinct mask values for each $x \in X$: one for $h_1(x)$ and one for $h_2(x)$. But $h_1(x) = h_2(x)$ is possible with probability $1/m$. In that case, depending on how one specifies this edge case, Alice will either send a repeated mask or send less masks overall. Either way, this event leaks to Bob that Alice holds such an item satisfying $h_1(x) = h_2(x)$. This issue is common to all PSI protocols that use Cuckoo hashing as well.

To address this issue, we let Bob append to each item y a bit $b \in \{1, 2\}$ indicating which hash function h_b was used to assign it to this bin. If $h_1(y) = h_2(y)$ we just choose b arbitrarily. Then the OT extension & polynomials are done with respect to these "extended" values. Now in the case of $h_1(y) = h_2(y)$, Bob will only learn the OT-extension output for one variant $y\|b$, but Alice (if she has such an item) will still be able to compute two distinct OT-extension outputs for the two variants.

Theorem 5. *The protocol in Fig. 7 securely realizes the PSI functionality of Fig. 3 in a semi-honest setting, with F, H as in Theorem 1 and ℓ according to the column indexed by $2n_1$ in Table Fig. 6.*

The semi-honest security of the modified protocol follows with a very similar proof as the original protocol, therefore we omit it for the sake of space. Unlike the original protocol, this new one is *not secure* against malicious adversaries (details are given in the full version).

Efficiency. Theorem 4 suggests that a near-optimal assignment of items to bins exists with probability at least $1 - 2^{-n_2/m}$. Hence, we must have $n_2/m \geq \lambda$, the statistical security parameter, to ensure that Bob's hashing step succeeds with overwhelming probability. Setting $m = n_2/\lambda$, the cost of all interpolations is now $m \cdot O(\lambda \log^2 \lambda) = O(n_2 \log^2 \lambda)$ field operations if using the asymptotically efficient algorithm, or $m \cdot O(\lambda^2) = O(n_2\lambda)$ using the simpler quadratic interpolation algorithm (which is indeed faster in practice for such small polynomials). In either case, this is a **significant** improvement over $O(n_2 \log^2 n_2)$ of the basic protocol (not to mention that distinct bins allow for easy parallelization). The cost of Alice's polynomial evaluation is similarly improved.

No matter what m we choose (assuming n_2/m is an integer), there will always be exactly m dummy items for Bob. The percentage of dummy items is m/n_2, so Alice's communication will increase by a multiplicative factor of $(1 + m/n_2)$. We suggest $m = n_2/\lambda$, so Alice's communication increases by a $(1 + 1/\lambda)$ factor. As mentioned above, for $\lambda = 40$, this increase is only 2.5%.

Recall from Sect. 3.3 that the parameter ℓ (width of OT extension matrix) depends on the number of rows of the OT extension matrix that Alice accesses. With this new optimization, she accesses twice as many rows (rows $x\|1$ and $x\|2$ for every $x \in X$). This leads to a slight increase in ℓ. For the concrete parameters we consider (see Fig. 6), ℓ must increase by only 2 bits.

5   Optimizations for High-Degree Polynomials

Despite using fast polynomial algorithms, having one party (the *interpolating party*) interpolating the huge-degree polynomial leads to a long idle time by the other party (*evaluating party*), which implies a serious computational bottleneck. In this section we show that in case that the x and y coordinates of the interpolation points are drawn from the domains $\mathcal{D}_x$ and $\mathcal{D}_y$, respectively, such that $\mathcal{D}_x \ll \mathcal{D}_y$, the idle time can be significantly shrinked. To this end, we developed new techniques, namely, *slice & stream* and *sub-product tree reuse* that allow a significant reduction of the overall time of the protocol. The former technique means that we "slice" the interpolation points into several parts, then we can interpolated each part over a smaller field and hence faster; when a slice is ready it is sent immediately to the other party for evaluation (i.e. streaming of polynomials). The latter technique is based on our observation that one sub-algorithm that constructs a sub-product tree (which is used both in interpolation and evaluation) depends only on the x-values of the interpolation points. Since all polynomial slices use the same x-values and differ only on their y-values we can reuse the same sub-product tree for all slices! We believe our techniques are valuable for other applications that require an implementation of high-degree polynomial algorithms over large fields. As demonstrated in Sect. 5.2, our techniques reduce the overall interpolation and evaluation time by up to 60%.

In Sect. 5.1 we give an overview on known polynomial algorithms and in Sect. 5.2 we introduce our techniques in detail.

5.1   Background: Interpolation and Multi-point Evaluation

Trivial implementations of polynomial interpolation and multi-point evaluation of *arbitrary* points adopt the $O(n^2)$ algorithms as they are sufficient for the typical use cases of low-degree polynomials. However, in our case the degree is in the millions, so the $O(n^2)$ algorithms are completely impractical. Faster algorithms, by Moenck and Borodin from 1972 [40], achieve computational complexity of $O(n \log^2 n)$. In the following we present a high level overview on the algorithms, while a detailed description is given in the full version.

Let $X = \{x_1, \ldots, x_n\} \subset \{0, 1\}^\alpha$ and $Y = \{y_1, \ldots, y_n\} \subset \{0, 1\}^\beta$.

- Given X and Y, the problem of *polynomial interpolation* is to find the unique $(n-1)$-degree polynomial P that passes through the points $\{(x_i, y_i)\}_{i \in [n]}$.
- Given X and an $(n-1)$-degree polynomial Q, the problem of *multi-point evaluation* is to compute $Q(X) = \{Q(x_i)\}_{i \in [n]}$.

Algorithms for both problems follow the divide-and-conquer approach such that in every iteration the problem is reduced to two half-size problems. Combining the solutions of the half-size problems to a solution of the full-size problem has a computational complexity of $O(n \log n)$. Formally, let $T(n)$ be the time to solve the interpolation and multi-point evaluation problems for $|X| = |Y| = n$, then the recurrence relation is: $T(n) = 2 \cdot T\left(\frac{n}{2}\right) + O(n \log n) = O(n \log^2 n)$ where the second equality follows from the Master theorem [10, Chap. 4].

The evaluation and interpolation algorithms are separated to two and four sub-procedures, respectively, as follows.

Evaluation.   Algorithm MULTIPOINTEVALUATE(Q, X) invokes $M \leftarrow$ BUILDTREE(X) and outputs $Y \leftarrow$ EVALUATE(Q, M).

- BUILDTREE(X) constructs and outputs a binary tree of polynomials, denoted M. Its leaves are the 1-degree polynomials $\{(x - a)\}_{a \in X}$ and each node is the multiplication of its two children. Thus, if the degrees of the childs are d_1 and d_2 then the node's degree is $d_1 \cdot d_2$. If n is a power of 2 then the degree of M's root is n.
- EVALUATE(Q, M) evaluates the polynomial Q on X, note that X is implicitly "encoded" within M. The idea is that for every node $m \in M$ (recall that m is a polynomial), if $(x - a)$ divides m then $Q(a) = R(a)$ where $R = Q \mod m$

(i.e. it is the remainder of the division of Q by m). To obtain $Q(a)$ we replace each node m with $(\text{PARENT}(m) \bmod m)$ and finally output the result on that leaf. The remainder is computed in $O(n \log n)$ arithmetic operations in the underlying field.

Interpolation. Algorithm $\text{INTERPOLATE}(X, Y)$ invokes $M \leftarrow \text{BUILDTREE}(X)$ as described above. Let M_0 be M's root, it computes M_0's derivative by $M_0' \leftarrow \text{DERIVATIVE}(M_0)$ and then evaluates M_0' over X by $A \leftarrow \text{MULTIPOINTEVALUATE}(M_0', X)$. Finally it invokes $P \leftarrow \text{INTERNALINTERPOLATE}(M, A)$ and outputs P. The purpose of the sub-algorithms is to enable the division of a n-size problem to two $\frac{n}{2}$-size problems. Note that within $\text{MULTIPOINTEVALUATE}$ there is a construction of the same sub-product tree as in BUILDTREE, therefore we can skip this and construct M only once. The time of the algorithm is the sum of the times of these four sub-algorithms, $T_{\text{INTERPOLATE}}(n) = T_{\text{BUILDTREE}}(n) + T_{\text{DERIVATIVE}}(n) + T_{\text{MULTIPOINTEVALUATE}}(n) + T_{\text{INTERNALINTERPOLATE}}(n) = O(n \log^2 n) + O(n) + O(n \log^2 n) + O(n \log^2 n) = O(n \log^2 n)$.

5.2 Polynomial Slicing and Streaming

Let $x_1, \ldots, x_n \in \{0, 1\}^\alpha$ and $y_1, \ldots, y_n \in \{0, 1\}^\beta$ (where $\beta > \alpha$) then we interpolate the polynomial P using points $\{(x_i, y_i)\}_{i \in [n]}$ over a field $\mathbb{F}$ where $|\mathbb{F}| = 2^\beta$. For the sake of exposition suppose that α divides β and let $\rho = \frac{\beta}{\alpha}$. For each i we define y_i^j for $j \in [\rho]$ such that $|y_i^j| = \alpha$ and $y_i = y_i^1 || \ldots || y_i^\rho$. We can "cut" P into ρ slices $P_1, \ldots, P_\rho$ such that for every x_i it holds that $P(x_i) = P_1(x_i) || \ldots || P_\rho(x_i)$. This is done by interpolating the polynomial P_j (for $j \in [\rho]$) using the points $\{(x_i, y_i^j)\}_{i \in [n]}$. This requires a smaller field, i.e. we need that $|\mathbb{F}| = 2^\alpha$, hence P_j is produced in a shorter time.

To demonstrate the above let us fix some parameters. Assume that the parties' only task is to interpolate P using $n = 2^{20}$ points and then perform a multi-point evaluation of n points; also assume an ideal network with zero latency. Consider first performing this task directly to a "single-slice" polynomial over a field of size 2^β where $\beta = 512$. Interpolation and multi-point evaluation take $233 + 167 = 400$ s (detailed measurements are given in the full version. We ignore milliseconds here and in the following). Utilizing the slicing technique with $\alpha = 128$ we have $\rho = \frac{\beta}{\alpha} = \frac{512}{128} = 4$ slices. This means that the interpolating party produces the sliced polynomials one after the other and sends them immediately (i.e. without waiting until for all polynomials to be ready) and the evaluating party evaluates them one by one upon reception. This leads to $67 \cdot 4 + 49 = 317$ s which is 81% of the trivial implementation.

Further Utilizing the Slicing Technique. As shown above, the slicing and streaming technique leads to an improvement over the trivial implementation. The following observation significantly pushes forward the slicing technique:

Building the polynomials tree M in the evaluation process depends only on $x_1, \ldots, x_n$, which means this can be performed *only once for all slices*. Similarly, in the interpolation algorithm the tasks of building the polynomials tree, calculating the derivative and evaluating it depends only on $x_1, \ldots, x_n$ and can be performed once and for all slices. Thus, taking $\beta = 512$, $\alpha = 128$ and $n = 2^{20}$ the one-time tasks of building the sub-product tree, calculating the derivative and evaluating it takes $12889 + 86 + 33144 = 46119$ ms. The one-time task of the evaluating party (building the sub-product tree) takes 13959 ms and can surely be done simultaneously. Then the interpolating party produces 4 polynomial slices, each takes 19471 ms, and the evaluating party evaluates them upon reception. Since the evaluation task is more expensive than the interpolating task (the part being performed for each slice) the total running time is $46119 + 4 \cdot 35835 = 189459$ ms. This is less than 60% of the initial slicing technique and 48% of the trivial implementation. Both of our optimizations, together with the trivial implementation are illustrated in Fig. 8.

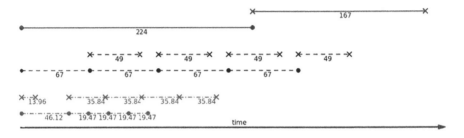

Fig. 8. Illustrating the slicing technique. The lines between •'s represent the interpolating party and the lines between the ✗'s represent the evaluating party. Solid (blue) lines illustrate the trivial implementation (overall 400 s), dashed (black) lines illustrate the initial slicing technique (overall 317 s) and dotted-dashed (red) lines illustrate the final optimization (overall 189 s). (Color figure online)

Communication. Observe that this technique *does not increase* the communication complexity of the protocol. This is due to the fact that instead of sending 2^n coefficients of P, each of size β, we send 2^n coefficients of P_j, each of size α, for every j. This leads to exactly same communication size of $2^n \cdot \alpha \cdot \rho = 2^n \cdot \beta$.

6   Implementation and Performance Comparison

Recall that we have presented two variants of our protocol. In this section we will refer to them as:

spot-low: the communication-optimized variant presented in Fig. 5, in which Bob sends one large polynomial and Alice sends one OPRF output per item.

spot-fast: the speed-optimized variant presented in Fig. 7, in which Bob uses 2-choice hashing and Alice sends two OPRF outputs per item.

Table 1. Theoretical communication costs of PSI protocols (in bits), calculated using computational security $\kappa = 128$ and statistical security $\lambda = 40$. Ignores cost of base OTs (in our protocol and KKRT) which are independent of input size. ϕ is the size of elliptic curve group elements (256 is used here). ℓ is width of OT extension matrix (depends on n_1 and protocol).

Protocol	Communication	$n = n_1 = n_2$		
		2^{16}	2^{20}	2^{24}
KKRT	$(3+s)(\lambda + \log(n_1 n_2))n_1 + 1.2\ell n_2$	$1042n$	$1018n$	$978n$
DH-PSI	$\phi n_1 + (\phi + \lambda + \log(n_1 n_2))n_2$	$584n$	$592n$	$600n$
spot-low	$1.02(\lambda + \log_2(n_2) + 2)n_1 + \ell n_2$	$488n$	$500n$	$512n$
spot-fast	$2(\lambda + \log(n_1 n_2))n_1 + \ell(1 + 1/\lambda)n_2$	$583n$	$609n$	$634n$

We also compare our protocols to the following:

KKRT: the leading OT-extension-based protocol from [35].
DH-PSI: Diffie-Hellman-based PSI, instantiated with either Koblitz-283 (K283) or Curve25519 (25519) elliptic curves.

Our focus in this section is on the case where $n_1 = n_2$, i.e., the parties have sets of equal size. We report some findings also for the case of unequal set sizes in the full version. Our complete implementation is available on GitHub: https://github.com/osu-crypto/SpOT-PSI.

6.1 Theoretical Analysis of Communication

We first compare the *theoretical* communication complexity of protocols (Table 1). This measures how much communication the protocols require on an idealized network where we do not care about protocol metadata, realistic encodings, byte alignment, etc. In practice, data is split up into multiples of bytes (or CPU words), and different data is encoded with headers, etc.—empirical measurements of such real-world costs are given later in Table 2.

For set sizes in the range 2^{16} to 2^{24}, our spot-low variant has the least communication of any of the protocols we consider: $\sim$15% less than DH-PSI and $\sim$50% less than KKRT. Our spot-fast variant uses up to $\sim$5% more communication than DH-PSI but 35–43% less than KKRT.

We note that KKRT uses a parameter ℓ similar to ours (corresponding to the width of the OT extension matrix), but their parameter is always slightly larger. This is because (as in our protocol) ℓ depends on how many rows of the OT matrix the sender accesses, which is more than in ours ($(3+s)n_1$ in KKRT).

The communication optimization (described in Sect. 3.5) can indeed be applied to other protocols as well (DH-PSI, KKRT, and spot-fast). For example, when $n = 2^{20}$ it saves 16 bits per item (only 2.6 MB in total), so the effect does not have significant impact on any comparisons. However, the optimization would be much more expensive or cumbersome to implement since it requires all

OPRF outputs to be computed and sorted, but without this optimization they can be sent as they are computed.

6.2 Experimental Comparison

We now present a comparison based on implementations of all protocols.

Implementation Details. We used the implementation of KKRT provided by the authors. We implemented DH-PSI using the Miracl library implementations of Koblitz K-283 and Curve25519 elliptic curves.

For our own protocols, we implemented the polynomial interpolation and evaluation algorithms using a field of prime order p, where p is the smallest prime greater than 2^ℓ and ℓ is bit length of the output of our sparse-OT extension (the ℓ in Fig. 6). We discuss this choice in the full version. The polynomial operations are implemented using the NTL library v10.5.0.

Note that both KKRT and our protocols require the same underlying primitives: a Hamming correlation-robust function H, a pseudorandom function F, and base OTs for OT extension. We instantiated these primitives exactly as KKRT: both H and F instantiated using AES, and base OTs instantiated using Naor-Pinkas [42]. We use the implementation of base OTs from the libOTe library[6].

All protocols use a computational security $\kappa = 128$ bits and a statistical security $\lambda = 40$ bits.

Experimental Setup: AWS Benchmark. We performed a series of benchmarks on the Amazon web services (AWS) EC2 cloud computing service. We use the M5.large machine class, which is classified as the current state-of-the-art "general purpose" instance. These machines have 2 vCPU (2.5 GHz Intel Xeon) and 8 GB RAM. We considered other kinds of instances, but ultimately rejected

		1	2	3	4	5	6
Virginia	1	9.6	0.17	1.08	0.063	0.068	0.084
Oregon	2			0.18	0.053	0.072	0.058
Ohio	3				0.058	0.069	0.078
Mumbai	4					0.050	0.034
Sidney	5						0.031
Sao-paolo	6						

Fig. 9. Gbps between AWS sites.

them. The cheaper T2 class ("burstable") was found to be too unstable for our workloads, while the more expensive C5 class ("compute-optimized") resulted in more monetary cost than M5 in all cases.

Based on the geographic region of the two parties, we can realize different network speeds, as illustrated in Fig. 9. The network speeds given in the table were measured using the iperf3 command.[7] This collection of AWS sites was chosen to give a large range of bandwidth performance.

---

[6] https://github.com/osu-crypto/libOTe.
[7] See https://iperf.fr/iperf-download.php.

Experimental Setup: Local Benchmark. The AWS benchmarks use a real network connection which is sometimes unpredictable. For a highly controlled experimental network, we benchmarked protocols on a single machine: Intel Xeon 2.30 GHz, 256 GB RAM, 36 physical cores (note that all implementations are single-threaded unless otherwise indicated). We simulated a network connection using the Linux tc command, communicating via localhost network. We simulated a LAN setting with 10 Gbps network bandwidth and 0.2 ms round-trip latency, and various WAN settings with 100 Mpbs, 10 Mpbs, 1 Mpbs and 80 ms round-trip latency.

AWS Pricing Scheme. Part of our motivation for evaluating protocols on AWS is to report and compare their real-world monetary costs. Hence we describe now the pricing scheme for AWS at the time of our comparison.[8] Costs are associated with both *running time* and *data transfer*, and both depend on the data center (geographic location) at which the instance runs.

The running-time cost per hour (in USD) for our instance type M5.large is 0.096 (USA), 0.101 (Mumbai), 0.12 (Sydney), 0.153 (Sao Paolo).

The data transfer cost differ depending on whether both endpoints are within AWS, and the data-center of the endpoints. We consider two network settings:

- In a **business-to-business (B2B)** setting between two fixed organizations that want to regularly perform PSI on their dynamic data, both endpoints may be within the AWS network.
- In an **internet** setting where one organization wishes to regularly perform PSI with a dynamically changing partner, only one party may be within the AWS network.

These considerations have the following effect on the cost of data transfer on AWS:

- Inbound data transfer from the Internet to EC2 is free.
- Outbound data transfer from EC2 to the Internet incurs the highest cost. Rates in USD per 1 GB are 0.09 (USA), 0.1093 (Mumbai), 0.114 (Sydney), 0.25 (Sao Paolo).
- Outbound data transfer between two instance at the same site cost 0.01 USD/GB per direction.
- Outbound data transfer to another AWS site costs (in USD/GB): 0.02 (USA), 0.086 (Mumbai), 0.14 (Sydney) and 0.16 (Sao Paolo)
- Additional cost is for using a public IP address, which is indeed required for the scenarios we consider; this costs 0.01 USD/GB for all sites.

We compute the total monetary cost of a protocol execution as follows. Let T be the runtime in hours of the protocol; let X_1 and X_2 be the outbound communication of the first and second parties, resp.; let C_{T1}, C_{T2} be the uptime

---

[8] The pricing can be found in https://aws.amazon.com/ec2/pricing/on-demand/.

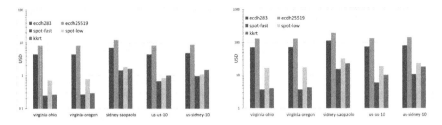

Fig. 10. Monetary cost (in USD) per 1000 runs of PSI on 2^{16} (left) and 2^{20} (right) items, in the B2B network scenario.

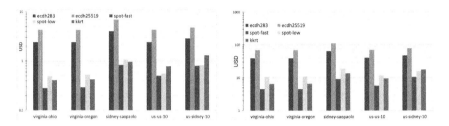

Fig. 11. Monetary cost (in USD) per 1000 runs of PSI on 2^{16} (left) and 2^{20} (right) items, in the 'Internet' network scenario.

rate of the machines run by the parties; and let C_{X1}, C_{X2} be the outbound data transfer rates for the machines/regions of the parties. The cost in USD is then:

$$\mathsf{TotalCost} = \mathsf{T} \cdot (\mathsf{C_{T1}} + \mathsf{C_{T2}}) + \mathsf{X_1} \cdot \mathsf{C_{X1}} + \mathsf{X_2} \cdot \mathsf{C_{X2}} + 0.01 \cdot (\mathsf{X_1} + \mathsf{X_2})$$

6.3   Experimental Results

AWS Monetary Cost. To limit the number of protocol executions performed on AWS, we focus on set sizes of 2^{16} and 2^{20} as they are representative of realistic set sizes for aformentioned applications of PSI.

The monetary cost of PSI protocols is presented in Figs. 10 and 11. We see that our spot-fast protocol variant is the cheapest protocol in all of the settings we consider. In the B2B scenarios it is 4%–35% for PSI of 2^{16} items and 10%–40% cheaper for PSI of 2^{20} items, compared to the second cheapest protocol (KKRT). In the 'Internet' scenarios it is 13%–38% cheaper for PSI of 2^{16} items and 30%–40% cheaper for 2^{20} items. The numerical costs can be found in the full version.

Break-Even Point with KKRT. Our protocol has less communication than the faster KKRT protocol. As the network becomes slower, the protocol becomes more network-bound and our advantage in communication eventually leads to

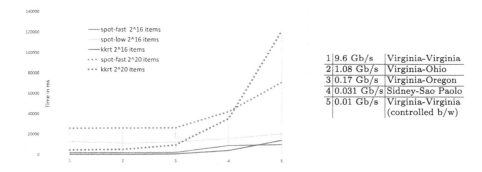

1	9.6 Gb/s	Virginia-Virginia
2	1.08 Gb/s	Virginia-Ohio
3	0.17 Gb/s	Virginia-Oregon
4	0.031 Gb/s	Sidney-Sao Paolo
5	0.01 Gb/s	Virginia-Virginia (controlled b/w)

Fig. 12. Evaluated run times over AWS EC2 with descending bandwidth. Solid and dotted lines are for PSI over 2^{16} and 2^{20} items respectively. The 1–5 numbers at the x-axis of the figure represent the configurations 1–5 described in the table to the right.

Table 2. Total communication cost in MB and running time in seconds comparing our protocol to [35] and HD-PSI, with $T \in \{1, 4\}$ threads; each item has 128-bit length. 10 Gbps network assumes 0.2 ms RTT, and others use 80 ms RTT. Cells with "—" denote setting not supported or program out of memory.

Params.		Protocol	Comm.	Total time (seconds)							
n_1	n_2		(MB)	10 Gbps		100 Mbps		10 Mbps		1 Mbps	
				$T = 1$	4	1	4	1	4	1	4
2^{24}	2^{24}	DH-PSI (K-283)	—	—	—	—	—	—	—	—	—
		DH-PSI (25519)	—	—	—	—	—	—	—	—	—
		KKRT	1955.2	**63.3**	—	**261.9**	—	1852.1	—	—	—
		spot-low	—	—	—	—	—	—	—	—	—
		spot-fast	1254.5	440.1	146.1	474.6	173.3	**1071.8**	**1062.8**	—	—
2^{20}	2^{20}	DH-PSI (K-283)	84.0	1141.8	338.5	1152.5	336.9	1158.2	334.2	1472.4	854.3
		DH-PSI (25519)	76.1	2110.6	632.8	2290.5	634.5	2325.7	673.0	2497.8	1014.0
		KKRT	127	**4.61**	—	**17.47**	—	120.1	—	1154.5	—
		spot-low	**63.1**	270.3	179.2	273.4	185.3	299.6	206.67	687.2	**311.16**
		spot-fast	76.4	25.6	**7.6**	27.8	**10.53**	**66.2**	**66.0**	646.3	645.3
2^{16}	2^{16}	DH-PSI (K-283)	5.2	69.8	20.20	70.77	21.93	71.10	22.8	80.1	44.4
		DH-PSI (25519)	4.7	136.9	39.4	140.4	40.1	142.8	40.8	151.3	48.2
		KKRT	8.06	**0.43**	—	**1.99**	—	8.4	—	74.5	—
		spot-low	**3.9**	12.8	8.8	13.7	9.8	15.1	10.9	41.1	**39.1**
		spot-fast	4.71	1.90	**0.77**	2.91	**2.02**	**5.46**	**5.36**	40.19	40.08
2^{12}	2^{12}	DH-PSI (K-283)	0.32	4.59	1.87	4.65	1.67	4.82	1.56	5.18	**2.75**
		DH-PSI (25519)	0.29	8.72	2.58	8.90	27.5	9.10	2.80	9.59	2.98
		KKRT	0.53	**0.22**	—	**0.87**	—	1.24	—	5.7	—
		spot-low	**0.25**	0.87	0.61	1.4	1.2	1.4	13.23	3.17	3.0
		spot-fast	0.3	0.4	**0.21**	1.14	**0.99**	**1.16**	**1.01**	**3.58**	3.51

faster performance than KKRT. We compared the running time of the PSI protocols on networks of different speeds, in order to identify the "break-even point" where our protocol (spot-fast) becomes faster than KKRT.

From the running times in Fig. 12, we find that the spot-fast variant overtakes KKRT as the fastest PSI protocol when network bandwidth drops below the 10–30 Mbps range. The concrete times are detailed in the full version.

Detailed, Controlled Local Benchmarks. A more detailed benchmark for set sizes $2^{12} - 2^{24}$ and controlled network configurations is given in Table 2. We also considered the effect of multi-threading on protocol performance, with $T \in \{1, 4\}$ threads. The implementation of KKRT does not support multi-threading.

The communication of our protocol is approximately $2\times$ smaller than that of [35]. For example, computing the intersection of sets of size $n = 2^{20}$, spot-fast and spot-low variants require 76.43 MB and 63.18 MB respectively, whereas [35] requires 127 MB of communication, (a $1.7 - 2.0\times$ improvement).

In a single-threaded LAN setting, spot-fast variant is several times slower than KKRT, requiring 25.62 s with $n = 2^{20}$. Applying the same parameters to [35] results in a running time of 4.1 s. The running time of spot-fast variant is improved significantly by multi-threading, improving to 7.61 s when utilizing 4 threads.

In the WAN setting, spot-fast becomes the fastest protocol on slow (10 Mbps and 1 Mbps) network, due to its lower communication cost. For example, in the 10 Mpbs network, for sets of size $n = 2^{20}$, spot-fast takes 66.2 s, while [35] requires 120.13 s, a $1.8\times$ improvement.

Both of our protocols outperformed DH-PSI. For example, spot-low requires 63 MB while DH-PSI (Curve25519) requires 76 MB, a $\sim$12% improvement.

In terms of computation, even our slower spot-low variant is based on symmetric-key operations, and is significantly faster than DH-PSI. We also examined the effect of multi-threading. Similar to DH-PSI, spot-fast variant is extremely amenable to parallelization. Concretely, we parallelize our algorithm at the level of bins. Both DH-PSI and spot-fast yield a similar speedup of about $3.5\times$ by using 4 threads.

References

1. Asharov, G., Lindell, Y., Schneider, T., Zohner, M.: More efficient oblivious transfer and extensions for faster secure computation. In: ACM CCS, pp. 535–548 (2013)
2. Ateniese, G., De Cristofaro, E., Tsudik, G.: (If) size matters: size-hiding private set intersection. In: Catalano, D., Fazio, N., Gennaro, R., Nicolosi, A. (eds.) PKC 2011. LNCS, vol. 6571, pp. 156–173. Springer, Heidelberg (2011). https://doi.org/10.1007/978-3-642-19379-8_10
3. Beaver, D.: Correlated pseudorandomness and the complexity of private computations. In: STOC, pp. 479–488 (1996)
4. Bernstein, D.J.: Curve25519: new Diffie-Hellman speed records. In: Yung, M., Dodis, Y., Kiayias, A., Malkin, T. (eds.) PKC 2006. LNCS, vol. 3958, pp. 207–228. Springer, Heidelberg (2006). https://doi.org/10.1007/11745853_14
5. Brickell, J., Porter, D.E., Shmatikov, V., Witchel, E.: Privacy-preserving remote diagnostics. In: ACM CCS, pp. 498–507 (2007)

6. Canetti, R.: Universally composable security: a new paradigm for cryptographic protocols. In: FOCS, pp. 136–145 (2001)
7. Cerulli, A., De Cristofaro, E., Soriente, C.: Nothing refreshes like a RePSI: reactive private set intersection. In: Preneel, B., Vercauteren, F. (eds.) ACNS 2018. LNCS, vol. 10892, pp. 280–300. Springer, Cham (2018). https://doi.org/10.1007/978-3-319-93387-0_15
8. Chen, H., Laine, K., Rindal, P.: Fast private set intersection from homomorphic encryption. In: ACM CCS 2017, pp. 1243–1255 (2017)
9. Cho, C., Dachman-Soled, D., Jarecki, S.: Efficient concurrent covert computation of string equality and set intersection. In: Sako, K. (ed.) CT-RSA 2016. LNCS, vol. 9610, pp. 164–179. Springer, Cham (2016). https://doi.org/10.1007/978-3-319-29485-8_10
10. Cormen, T.H., Leiserson, C.E., Rivest, R.L., Stein, C.: Introduction to Algorithms, 3rd edn. MIT Press, Cambridge (2009)
11. De Cristofaro, E., Gasti, P., Tsudik, G.: Fast and private computation of cardinality of set intersection and union. In: Pieprzyk, J., Sadeghi, A.-R., Manulis, M. (eds.) CANS 2012. LNCS, vol. 7712, pp. 218–231. Springer, Heidelberg (2012). https://doi.org/10.1007/978-3-642-35404-5_17
12. De Cristofaro, E., Kim, J., Tsudik, G.: Linear-complexity private set intersection protocols secure in malicious model. In: Abe, M. (ed.) ASIACRYPT 2010. LNCS, vol. 6477, pp. 213–231. Springer, Heidelberg (2010). https://doi.org/10.1007/978-3-642-17373-8_13
13. De Cristofaro, E., Tsudik, G.: Experimenting with fast private set intersection. In: Katzenbeisser, S., Weippl, E., Camp, L.J., Volkamer, M., Reiter, M., Zhang, X. (eds.) Trust 2012. LNCS, vol. 7344, pp. 55–73. Springer, Heidelberg (2012). https://doi.org/10.1007/978-3-642-30921-2_4
14. Czumaj, A., Riley, C., Scheideler, C.: Perfectly balanced allocation. In: Arora, S., Jansen, K., Rolim, J.D.P., Sahai, A. (eds.) APPROX/RANDOM -2003. LNCS, vol. 2764, pp. 240–251. Springer, Heidelberg (2003). https://doi.org/10.1007/978-3-540-45198-3_21
15. Demmler, D., Rindal, P., Rosulek, M., Trieu, N.: PIR-PSI: scaling private contact discovery. Proc. Priv. Enhancing Technol. **2018**(4), 159–178 (2018)
16. Dong, C., Chen, L., Wen, Z.: When private set intersection meets big data: an efficient and scalable protocol. In: ACM CCS 2013, pp. 789–800 (2013)
17. Even, S., Goldreich, O., Lempel, A.: A randomized protocol for signing contracts. Commun. ACM **28**, 637–647 (1985)
18. Falk, B.H., Noble, D., Ostrovsky, R.: Private set intersection with linear communication from general assumptions. ePrint Archive, Report 2018/238 (2018)
19. Freedman, M.J., Ishai, Y., Pinkas, B., Reingold, O.: Keyword search and oblivious pseudorandom functions. In: Kilian, J. (ed.) TCC 2005. LNCS, vol. 3378, pp. 303–324. Springer, Heidelberg (2005). https://doi.org/10.1007/978-3-540-30576-7_17
20. Ghosh, S., Nielsen, J.B., Nilges, T.: Maliciously secure oblivious linear function evaluation with constant overhead. Cryptology ePrint Archive, Report 2017/409 (2017). http://eprint.iacr.org/2017/409
21. Ghosh, S., Nielsen, J.B., Nilges, T.: Maliciously secure oblivious linear function evaluation with constant overhead. In: Takagi, T., Peyrin, T. (eds.) ASIACRYPT 2017, Part I. LNCS, vol. 10624, pp. 629–659. Springer, Cham (2017). https://doi.org/10.1007/978-3-319-70694-8_22
22. Ghosh, S., Nilges, T.: An algebraic approach to maliciously secure private set intersection. In: Ishai, Y., Rijmen, V. (eds.) EUROCRYPT 2019. LNCS, vol. 11478, pp. 154–185. Springer, Cham (2019). https://doi.org/10.1007/978-3-030-17659-4_6

23. Hazay, C., Lindell, Y.: Efficient protocols for set intersection and pattern matching with security against malicious and covert adversaries. In: Canetti, R. (ed.) TCC 2008. LNCS, vol. 4948, pp. 155–175. Springer, Heidelberg (2008). https://doi.org/10.1007/978-3-540-78524-8_10

24. Hazay, C., Venkitasubramaniam, M.: Scalable multi-party private set-intersection. In: Fehr, S. (ed.) PKC 2017, Part I. LNCS, vol. 10174, pp. 175–203. Springer, Heidelberg (2017). https://doi.org/10.1007/978-3-662-54365-8_8

25. He, X., Machanavajjhala, A., Flynn, C.J., Srivastava, D.: Composing differential privacy and secure computation: a case study on scaling private record linkage. In: ACM CCS, pp. 1389–1406 (2017)

26. Henecka, W., Schneider, T.: Faster secure two-party computation with less memory. In: ASIA CCS, pp. 437–446 (2013)

27. Huang, Y., Evans, D., Katz, J.: Private set intersection: are garbled circuits better than custom protocols? In: NDSS (2012)

28. Huberman, B.A., Franklin, M.K., Hogg, T.: Enhancing privacy and trust in electronic communities. In: EC, pp. 78–86 (1999). https://dblp.org/rec/conf/sigecom/HubermanFH99

29. Impagliazzo, R., Rudich, S.: Limits on the provable consequences of one-way permutations. In: Goldwasser, S. (ed.) CRYPTO 1988. LNCS, vol. 403, pp. 8–26. Springer, New York (1990). https://doi.org/10.1007/0-387-34799-2_2

30. Ion, M., et al.: Private intersection-sum protocol with applications to attributing aggregate ad conversions. ePrint Archive 2017/738 (2017)

31. Ishai, Y., Kilian, J., Nissim, K., Petrank, E.: Extending oblivious transfers efficiently. In: Boneh, D. (ed.) CRYPTO 2003. LNCS, vol. 2729, pp. 145–161. Springer, Heidelberg (2003). https://doi.org/10.1007/978-3-540-45146-4_9

32. Ishai, Y., Prabhakaran, M., Sahai, A.: Secure arithmetic computation with no honest majority. In: Reingold, O. (ed.) TCC 2009. LNCS, vol. 5444, pp. 294–314. Springer, Heidelberg (2009). https://doi.org/10.1007/978-3-642-00457-5_18

33. Kiss, Á., Liu, J., Schneider, T., Asokan, N., Pinkas, B.: Private set intersection for unequal set sizes with mobile applications. PoPETs **2017**(4), 177–197 (2017)

34. Kolesnikov, V., Kumaresan, R.: Improved OT extension for transferring short secrets. In: Canetti, R., Garay, J.A. (eds.) CRYPTO 2013. LNCS, vol. 8043, pp. 54–70. Springer, Heidelberg (2013). https://doi.org/10.1007/978-3-642-40084-1_4

35. Kolesnikov, V., Kumaresan, R., Rosulek, M., Trieu, N.: Efficient batched OPRF with applications to PSI. In: ACM CCS (2016)

36. Kolesnikov, V., Matania, N., Pinkas, B., Rosulek, M., Trieu, N.: Practical multiparty private set intersection from symmetric-key techniques. In: Thuraisingham, B.M., Evans, D., Malkin, T., Xu, D. (eds.) ACM CCS 17, pp. 1257–1272. ACM Press (2017)

37. Lambæk, M.: Breaking and fixing private set intersection protocols. Master's thesis, Aarhus University (2016)

38. Manulis, M., Pinkas, B., Poettering, B.: Privacy-preserving group discovery with linear complexity. In: Zhou, J., Yung, M. (eds.) ACNS 2010. LNCS, vol. 6123, pp. 420–437. Springer, Heidelberg (2010). https://doi.org/10.1007/978-3-642-13708-2_25

39. Meadows, C.: A more efficient cryptographic matchmaking protocol for use in the absence of a continuously available third party. In: IEEE S&P (1986)

40. Moenck, R., Borodin, A.: Fast modular transforms via division. In: Switching and Automata Theory, pp. 90–96 (1972)

41. Naor, M., Pinkas, B.: Oblivious transfer and polynomial evaluation. In: 31st ACM STOC, pp. 245–254. ACM Press, May 1999

42. Naor, M., Pinkas, B.: Efficient oblivious transfer protocols. In: Kosaraju, S.R. (ed.) 12th SODA, pp. 448–457. ACM-SIAM (2001)
43. Patra, A., Sarkar, P., Suresh, A.: Fast actively secure OT extension for short secrets. In: NDSS (2017)
44. Pinkas, B., Schneider, T., Segev, G., Zohner, M.: Phasing: private set intersection using permutation-based hashing. In: USENIX 2015 (2015)
45. Pinkas, B., Schneider, T., Zohner, M.: Faster private set intersection based on OT extension. In: USENIX 2014, pp. 797–812 (2014)
46. Rabin, M.O.: How to exchange secrets with oblivious transfer. ePrint Archive 2005/187, (2005)
47. Resende, A.C.D., Aranha, D.F.: Unbalanced approximate private set intersection. ePrint Archive 2017/677 (2017)
48. Rindal, P., Rosulek, M.: Malicious-secure private set intersection via dual execution. In: Thuraisingham, B.M., Evans, D., Malkin, T., Xu, D. (eds.) ACM CCS 17, pp. 1229–1242. ACM Press (2017)
49. Sanders, P., Egner, S., Korst, J.: Fast concurrent access to parallel disks. Algorithmica **35**(1), 21–55 (2003)
50. Shamir, A.: On the power of commutativity in cryptography. In: de Bakker, J., van Leeuwen, J. (eds.) ICALP 1980. LNCS, vol. 85, pp. 582–595. Springer, Heidelberg (1980). https://doi.org/10.1007/3-540-10003-2_100
51. Troncoso-Pastoriza, J.R., Katzenbeisser, S., Celik, M.U.: Privacy preserving error resilient DNA searching through oblivious automata. In: ACM CCS, pp. 519–528 (2007)

Universally Composable Secure Computation with Corrupted Tokens

Nishanth Chandran[1]([⊠]), Wutichai Chongchitmate[2]([⊠]), Rafail Ostrovsky[3], and Ivan Visconti[4]

[1] Microsoft Research India, Bengaluru, India
nichandr@microsoft.com
[2] Department of Mathematics and Computer Science, Faculty of Science, Chulalongkorn University, Bangkok, Thailand
wutichai.ch@chula.ac.th
[3] Department of Computer Science and Department of Mathematics, University of California, Los Angeles, CA, USA
rafail@cs.ucla.edu
[4] DIEM, University of Salerno, Fisciano, Italy
visconti@unisa.it

Abstract. We introduce the *corrupted token model*. This model generalizes the *tamper-proof token model* proposed by Katz (EUROCRYPT '07) relaxing the trust assumption on the honest behavior of tokens. Our model is motivated by the real-world practice of outsourcing hardware production to possibly corrupted manufacturers. We capture the malicious behavior of token manufacturers by allowing the adversary to corrupt the tokens of honest players at the time of their creation.

We show that under minimal complexity assumptions, i.e., the existence of one-way functions, it is possible to UC-securely realize (a variant of) the tamper-proof token functionality of Katz in the corrupted token model with n stateless tokens assuming that the adversary corrupts at most $n - 1$ of them (for any $n > 0$). We apply this result to existing multi-party protocols in Katz's model to achieve UC-secure MPC in the corrupted token model assuming only the existence of one-way functions. Finally, we show how to obtain the above results using tokens of small size that take only short inputs. The technique in this result can also be used to improve the assumption of UC-secure hardware obfuscation recently proposed by Nayak *et al.* (NDSS '17). While their construction

W. Chongchitmate—Work done while the author was at Department of Computer Science, University of California, Los Angeles.

R. Ostrovsky—Research supported in part by NSF-BSF grant 1619348, DARPA SafeWare subcontract to Galois Inc., DARPA SPAWAR contract N66001-15-C-4065, US-Israel BSF grant 2012366, JP Morgan Faculty Award, OKAWA Foundation Research Award, IBM Faculty Research Award, Xerox Faculty Research Award, B. John Garrick Foundation Award, Teradata Research Award, and Lockheed-Martin Corporation Research Award. The views expressed are those of the authors and do not reflect position of the Department of Defense or the U.S. Government.

I. Visconti—Work done in part while the author was visiting UCLA.

A. Boldyreva and D. Micciancio (Eds.): CRYPTO 2019, LNCS 11694, pp. 432–461, 2019.
https://doi.org/10.1007/978-3-030-26954-8_14

requires the existence of collision-resistant hash functions, we can obtain the same result from only one-way functions. Moreover using our main result we can improve the trust assumption on the tokens as well.

1   Introduction

UC-secure MPC. Secure multi-party computation [27] (MPC) allows mutually distrustful parties to jointly compute a function f, while preserving the privacy of their inputs/outputs. Canetti [8] introduced the notion of universal composability (UC) to model secure MPC in an environment where multiple concurrent executions of different protocols take place. Unfortunately UC security is significantly harder to achieve than plain secure computation. In fact, in the plain model (i.e., without trusted set-up assumptions, physical assumptions, superpolynomial-time simulation and so on) most functionalities can not be UC-realized [11,13]. Impossibility results exist even for the basic case of self-concurrent composition with static inputs [1,4,25].

In light of these impossibility results, various trust assumptions have been studied in order to obtain UC-secure constructions. Among these, one of the most studied is that of tamper-proof hardware tokens. Hofheinz *et al.* [32], considered the notion of "tamper-proof devices" in the form of signature cards in order to realize UC-secure protocols. They show how to construct UC-secure commitment and zero-knowledge arguments using tamper-proof signature cards as the setup assumption. The more general formalization of tamper-proof hardware tokens was given by Katz [35]. Katz's tamper-proof token functionality abstractly captures a physical tamper-proof hardware token that is created and sent by a sender to a receiver. The receiver can use the token to execute the program stored in it multiple times as a black-box, on inputs of his choice. Tokens can be either *stateful* (i.e., they retain an updatable memory between executions; this is a stronger trust assumption because it additionally assumes a tamper-proof updatable memory) or *stateless* (i.e., all executions start with the same configuration). Motivated by the practical relevance of the model, as well as the challenging open questions on the feasibility of protocols in this model, UC-security with tamper-proof tokens has been widely explored with a focus on the more challenging case of stateless tokens [5,14,15,17,20,29,31,36,39].

Token Manufacturing. Assuming that tokens are honestly generated is clearly a very demanding assumption that essentially requires honest players to rely on the honesty of a token manufacturer that they trust. Hence, while the tamper-proof token model works as a physical assumption in theory, in practice it degenerates into a model where the security of an honest player depends on the honest behavior of an external player chosen by the honest player[1]. All prior works that consider hardware-based security critically rely on the honest player being able to reliably construct tamper-proof tokens. An attempt to relax this assumption was

---

[1] A similar question for the case of Common Reference String (CRS) generation was answered in the multi-string model [30].

done in [23] focusing only on the set intersection functionality, without considering UC security. More recently, [2] considered the problem of outsourcing circuit fabrication where a given circuit is compiled into smaller components, each of which can be outsourced to a possibly malicious manufacturer. The components (both honestly and maliciously manufactured) are then re-assembled honestly to get a "secure hardware token". Their (stand-alone) security model only allows an adversary black-box access to the rebuilt circuit, and not the individual components and additionally also requires one "small" tamper-proof token that can be generated honestly in a trusted manner. In contrast, we do not wish to make any assumptions on small trusted components and consider composability. The above state of affairs brings us to the following natural question.

> *"Can we obtain UC-secure hardware-based security in a world where most hardware token manufacturers may be corrupt?"*

1.1 Our Results

We resolve the above open problem in the positive under minimal complexity assumptions. We now discuss all our contributions in detail.

The Corrupted Token Model. We consider the concrete scenario where the sender of a token does not have the ability to physically create a tamper-proof token, but instead has to rely on possibly untrusted manufacturers. In case a manufacturer is corrupted (and may be colluding with other parties), the program embedded in the token may be leaked, or replaced in its entirety. In other words, tokens in this model can be tampered arbitrarily at the time of creation.

To model security, we define a functionality for UC security allowing the design of protocols that make use of tokens generated by potentially adversarial manufacturers. In turn, we propose a new model extending the stateless version of Katz's tamper-proof token model in [35], that we call *corrupted token model*. In our new model, the adversary is allowed to corrupt tokens when they are created by honest parties. The attack happens during the token creation phase, and the adversary learns all information that the honest player wanted to store in the token. Moreover the adversary is allowed to replace the token with a different token of its choice, including even a stateful one.

The corrupted token model abstractly represents the process of outsourcing the production of hardware tokens to possibly corrupted manufacturers. This is the reason why we allow corruption to occur only at the time the tokens are created. Our model also allows adaptive corruption of the manufacturers, in the sense that the adversary may choose to corrupt the next request of token generation of an honest player depending on what has been learnt so far. Finally, the adversary can freely decide the content of corrupted tokens and can even make it stateful. This is similar to dealing with a real-world hardware Trojan as described in [21,38] with a few key differences. In the model of [21], there exists an incorruptible "master circuit," whose role is to manage communication between tokens honestly. The model of [38] also has a "controller" circuit, whose role is similar to the master circuit in [21], but is allowed to be compromised. On the other hand, our model does not have a token with a specific role and allows any token to be corrupted. Both [21] and [38] do not consider UC security and additionally the construction of [38] is based on variants of ElGamal public-key encryption and Schnorr signature scheme, whose security are based on hardness of elliptic curve Diffie-Hellman and discrete logarithm, respectively. Our construction is UC-secure and is based on the minimal assumption of OWFs.

Katz's Token Functionality in the Corrupted Token Model. We construct a protocol in the corrupted token model using n tokens that UC-realizes a stronger variant of Katz's tamper-proof token functionality. We call such a variant the *tamper-proof token with abort* functionality. The difference between the tamper-proof token with abort functionality and the original Katz's tamper-proof token functionality is that our variant allows the adversary to learn that a token has been sent (even between honest parties), and can choose to abort and prevent the delivery of that token. This captures the realistic scenario where an adversary physically prevents token delivery and thus stops the protocol that relies on tokens. Still the adversary learns nothing about the program in the uncorrupted token generated by the honest party. The need for abort in the functionality is unavoidable as seen through the following reasoning. Suppose the tamper-proof token functionality (without abort) can be realized by n corruptible tokens. Then, the adversary in the corrupted token model corrupts all but one of the tokens and replaces them with corrupted tokens that do nothing. Now, if the tamper-proof token functionality without abort is realized with the remaining (uncorrupted) token, then this token must hold the complete program and secrets of the honest party (so that it can carry out the computation by itself). However, in an alternate corruption strategy, this token is also susceptible to corruption, and if the adversary had instead corrupted only this token, she would have learnt all secrets of the original honest token in Katz's model resulting in the insecurity of the protocol. Hence, the functionality must allow for aborts.

It is easy to see that this argument extends to the case of any dishonest majority (i.e., even with only $\lfloor n/2 + 1 \rfloor$ corrupted tokens). Our protocol UC-realizes the tamper-proof token with abort functionality assuming that the adversary corrupts at most $n - 1$ tokens where n is the number of token creations invoked by an honest party. We remark that, if we were willing to make the assumption that a majority of token manufacturers were honest, then we can avoid aborting the protocol when the adversary corrupts a (minority) fraction of the tokens.

The notion of token transfer across the environment in various sessions in the Global-UC (GUC) framework has been studied recently by Hazay *et al.* [31]. Obtaining GUC security is more challenging and we leave the question of GUC security in the corrupted token model to future research. Still, we stress that in many natural scenarios, UC security already suffices and achieves a very strong level of security under composition with any other protocol as long as there is a way to avoid the *sharing of the same setup among sessions*.

A Compiler to Reduce Trust in Tokens. As our main result, we show how to transform any protocol in Katz's tamper-proof token model into a protocol in our corrupted token model thereby improving the trust assumption of several hardware token-based protocols. Indeed the transformed protocol remains secure even when $n-1$ out of the n tokens created by honest parties are corrupted at the time of creation. Our transformation preserves UC security and only assumes the existence of one-way functions (OWF). We focus on stateless tokens since this is the milder physical assumption and is the most challenging case. We remark here that requiring one token to be uncorrupted is unavoidable. To see this, suppose for the sake of contradiction, there is a protocol UC-realizing a tamper-proof token functionality using n corruptible tokens that remains secure even when an adversary corrupts all n tokens. Now suppose an adversary in the secure computation protocol corrupts all but one of the parties and corrupts all the tokens manufactured by this party. Now, if the resulting protocol still remains secure, then this would give us a UC-secure MPC protocol (secure against all-but-one corruption) with no trusted setup, as all "trusted" components created by the honest party are corrupted (in more detail, generating and sending a token could then be replaced by sending a message with the description of the program of the token). This contradicts known impossibility results [11,13]. Hence, we must assume that at least one hardware token created by every honest party is uncorrupted. Additionally, the existence of OWFs is the minimal assumption that one can hope for since, as argued in [29], any unbounded adversary can query a stateless tokens exponentially many times to learn the programs embedded.

Our transformation can be applied to existing protocols in the Katz's token model to obtain new results in the corrupted token model. For instance, starting with the recent UC-secure MPC constructions in the tamper-proof token model based on OWFs [31], we get the same results in the corrupted token model assuming only OWFs.

Other Results and Sub-protocols. As an additional result, we improve the result of [39] by removing the need of collision-resistant hash functions, and apply our transformation to obtain an obfuscation protocol in the corrupted token model based solely on OWFs. Moreover, as a building block for our constructions, we present a simultaneous resettable zero-knowledge (sim-res ZK) argument and UC-secure MPC for any well-formed functionality in the correlated randomness (CR) model assuming OWFs only. In the CR model, each party has access to a private, input-independent, honestly generated, string before the execution of the protocol by the correlated randomness functionality. These protocols may be of independent interest. We stress that correlated randomness is not required as a setup for our construction achieving UC security in the corrupted token model and is only used as an intermediate building block.

1.2   High-Level Overview of Our Constructions

Realizing Katz's Token Functionality. We begin by describing how to UC-realize Katz's token functionality in the $(n, n-1)$-token-corruptible hybrid model, (i.e., the model where n tokens are generated by an honest player and at most $n-1$ are corrupted by the adversary at the time of token generation). We refer to the final protocol that realizes Katz's functionality as Π. Protocol Π will make use of a UC-secure n-party protocol Π' and a sim-res ZK argument Π_{rsZK} with straight-line simulator, both in the CR model[2]. At a very high level, we construct Π as follows. Given a description of the program P for Katz's tamper-proof token (such a description is specified by the protocol in Katz's model) we first create n shares of the description of P using an n-out-of-n threshold secret sharing scheme. Then n tokens are created as follows. The program of the i-th token includes: (1) the i-th share; (2) commitments of all shares; (3) decommitment information for the i-th share; (4) correlated randomness to run the n-party UC-secure MPC in the CR model; (5) correlated randomness to run a simultaneous resettable ZK in the CR model; (6) seed for a PRF; and (7) random tape for commitment of the seed.

When a user must query a Katz token implementing program P on input x, he/she must first send each token this input value (a dishonest user may send different values to different tokens). We shall refer to the "version" that the ith token receives by x_i. When queried with an input x_i, the i-th token first commits to its input (i.e., x_i) and to its seed for the PRF (see point 6 above). The randomness used for the first commitment comes from evaluating the PRF using the above seed and the input x_i while the randomness for the second commitment is the string stored in the token (see point 7 above). These commitments provided by all the tokens together is called the determining message. For the remaining execution of Π, each token obtains the random tape needed by Π' and Π_{rsZK} by computing the PRF on the determining message (and a unique ID value) using its seed. The tokens will execute an n-party UC-secure MPC protocol in the CR model, Π' (see point 4 above). More specifically, the i-th token, if honest, will run the code of the i-th player of Π' on input the following pair: the received input (i.e., x_i) and the i-th share of P (see step 1 above). Π' will securely compute the functionality that reconstructs P from the shares that are part of the inputs of the players and then executes P on input x. The reconstruction aborts if $x \neq x_i$ for some i. Each Π' message m sent by the ith token is followed by a simultaneous resettable ZK argument of knowledge (see step 5 above) proving that the message m is computed correctly according to the committed PRF seed and the i-th committed share (see step 2 and 3 above) of P.

The resettable soundness of the ZK argument guarantees that a corrupted token cannot deviate from the underlying MPC protocol Π' even when the adversary can execute any tokens any number of times on any inputs of his choice (even after resetting the state of the honest token several times). Moreover, the security of Π' guarantees that the adversary corrupting all but one token does not learn anything about the inputs of uncorrupted tokens other than x_i he chooses and the output. This means the adversary only learns at most $n - 1$

---

[2] The correlated randomness is the key that allows us to avoid the impossibility of resettably-secure computation in the standard model proven in [25]. However, we stress that correlated randomness is not required by our main theorem for UC security with tamper-proof stateless corruptible tokens from OWFs.

shares of the program P, and thus learns nothing about P by the security of the secret sharing scheme.

Since tokens are stateless, we employ the technique in [39] to encrypt the state of the token and output it along with the message. Each subsequent invocation of the token requires an encrypted previous state as additional input. A symmetric key encryption scheme is used to prevent the adversary to learn or modify states of uncorrupted tokens. This allows us to construct a simulator that simulates both the MPC and ZK messages using their simulators.

Simultaneous Resettable ZK Argument in the CR Model. The above discussion assumed the existence of a sim-res ZK argument Π_{srZK} with straight-line simulator in the CR model. We obtain this result in 2 steps starting from a 3-round public-coin ZK argument Σ, in the CRS model with straight-line simulation based on OWFs (such as the one in [37]).

First, we add the argument of knowledge (AoK) property with straight-line witness extractor to Σ in the CR model. For this, we use a technique similar to the one used in [24] where a prover encrypts a witness, sends the encryption as a message, and then uses Σ to prove that it is the encryption of the right witness. To avoid the use of stronger assumptions than OWFs, we replace a public-key encryption scheme in [24] with a secret-key encryption scheme and a commitment scheme. The commitment of a secret key and its corresponding decommitment information are given to the prover while only the commitment is given to the verifier as part of their correlated randomness. The resulting protocol is still 3-round, public-coin and with straight-line simulation.

In the second step, we add a simultaneous resettable witness indistinguishability (sim-res WI) argument of knowledge from OWFs to construct a simultaneous resettable zero-knowledge argument in the CR model with straight-line simulation. To prevent a malicious prover from resetting, the verifier uses a PRF applied to the statement and the prover's message to generate a string c to play in the second round of Σ instead of uniformly sampling her message. Then, to prevent a malicious verifier from resetting, the verifier runs the prover of the sim-res WI to prove that c is generated honestly or that a given long string d is an output of a PRG on input a short seed. Since d is uniformly chosen as part of the correlated randomness, the verifier cannot maliciously manipulate c. Resettable soundness can then be shown through a hybrid experiment where d is generated from the PRG similarly to [19].

UC-secure n-party Computation in the CR Model. Our main result also assumed Π', i.e., a UC-secure n-party computation protocol in the CR model for any well-formed functionality. We next outline how we construct Π' based on OWFs.

First, we consider UC-secure MPC in the OT-hybrid model against a malicious adversary corrupting all but one party such as the one in [34]. Since OT can be generated using correlated randomness [6], we focus towards obtaining a UC-secure MPC in the CR model. However, we face a new challenge. Since our final protocol can be executed on polynomially many inputs, where the polynomial is not apriori known to the correlated randomness generator, we must be able to produce "different" randomness for any input on which the protocol is generated. This would require a stronger version of the OT extension technique from [7] that allows the extension to super-polynomial number of OTs. This is similar in spirit to constructing a PRF that can generate "super-polynomial" randomness from a short seed (even though it will only be evaluated on polynomially many inputs). In particular, we modify the technique in [7] to construct UC-secure unbounded number of OTs from a small number of OTs distributed as setup in the CR model. We do this as follows. In the OT extension protocol in [7], a sender uses a circuit that first computes a PRG that takes a small input and outputs a large random string and then uses the string to obtain a large number of OTs. The circuit is then garbled using Yao's garbled circuit and sent to a receiver. The receiver then uses a small number of OTs to obtain a garbled input correspond to its small random seed. In our approach, the sender uses a PRF that allows us to generate super-polynomial number of such random strings. While a computationally bounded sender cannot compute a garbled circuit of super-polynomial size, it only needs to send a smaller subcircuit to compute the ith string in each execution. This garbled circuit is of polynomial size as in Beaver's version, computing only the required amount of OTs at a time. This is repeated to give an (apriori) unbounded number of OTs. Composing the UC-secure unbounded number of OTs in the CR model and a UC-secure MPC in the OT-hybrid model, we get UC-secure MPC in the CR model.

Getting Rid of Correlated Randomness. While the building blocks Π' and Π_{rsZK} are in the CR model, our main protocol Π is not. Both subprotocols will be run by n tokens created by a single honest party to emulate the token functionality of a single well-formed token in Katz's model. Therefore, in Π, the party requesting the creation of a token can generate and give the correlated randomness to n different manufacturers. Hence, the correlated randomness is not a setup of our main result, and is computed by an honest player in our protocol to run subprotocols that need it. An adversary can replace the correlated randomness in $n-1$ of those tokens arbitrarily, and still our protocol is secure because Π' and Π_{rsZK} are secure with respect to such behavior. In fact, as a further optimization, if we wish to create tokens that are completely independent of each other, then the honest player in our protocol can create tokens that will only contain private keys to encryption and MAC schemes – the correlated randomness and shares of program required by the token can then be provided as encrypted and MACed input by the honest player to the token when they need to be used.

Reducing the Token Size. In order to ensure that the queries to tokens are short and the size of each token is small, we consider a technique used in [39] where a large input is fed into a token in blocks of small size. To ensure the consistency of the input, in [39] a Merkle's tree based on CRHFs is used to commit to the input beforehand. We improve on this technique by replacing the Merkle's tree with a new construction based on OWFs. At a very high level, we require the user to "commit" to his/her input by feeding the input bit-by-bit into to the token. The token will produce an authentication tag for every bit of the input sequentially, such that the final authentication tag will act as a "commitment" to the user's input. This result is of independent interest as an improvement on the assumption of [39]. We generalize the technique of "bounded-size" tokens to our corrupted token protocol. We first give a variant of corrupted token functionality where the token size is independent of program P and the token can only accept queries of (apriori) fixed, constant size. We then construct a protocol that UC-realizes the corrupted token functionality in the corrupted "bounded-size" token hybrid model using the above technique. Finally, we combine this protocol with our main result to give a protocol that UC-realizes 'standard' tamper-proof token functionality in the corrupted "bounded-size" token hybrid model.

2   Preliminaries

A polynomial-time relation R is a relation for which it is possible to verify in time polynomial in $|x|$ whether $R(x, w) = 1$. Let us consider an $\mathcal{NP}$-language L and denote by R_L the corresponding polynomial-time relation such that $x \in L$ if and only if there exists w such that $R_L(x, w) = 1$. We will call such a w a *valid witness for* $x \in L$. Let λ denote the security parameter. A *negligible* function $\nu(\lambda)$ is a non-negative function such that for any constant $c < 0$ and for all sufficiently large λ, $\nu(\lambda) < \lambda^c$. We will denote by $\Pr_r[X]$ the probability of an event X over coins r, and $\Pr[X]$ when r is not specified. The abbreviation "PPT" stands for probabilistic polynomial time. For a randomized algorithm A, let $A(x; r)$ denote running A on an input x with random coins r. If r is chosen uniformly at random with an output y, we denote $y \leftarrow A(x)$. For a pair of interactive Turing machines (P, V), let $\langle P, V \rangle(x)$ denote V's output after interacting with P upon common input x. We say V accepts if $\langle P, V \rangle(x) = 1$ and rejects if $\langle P, V \rangle(x) = 0$. We denote by $\text{view}_{V(x,z)}^{P(w)}$ the view (i.e., its private coins and the received messages) of V during an interaction with $P(w)$ on common input x and auxiliary input z. We will use the standard notion of computational indistinguishability [28].

2.1   Building Blocks

The main building blocks of our construction include simultaneous resettable ZK arguments and MPC in the CR model. Please see the full version of this paper [9] for various definitions related to interactive argument systems, zero-knowledge arguments of knowledge, witness indistinguishability and resettability in the CR model, adapted from their counterparts [3,12,22] in the plain model. We also present other standard definitions of commitments, secret sharing schemes and pseudorandom functions that we make use of in our construction.

2.2   UC Security in the Correlated Randomness (CR) Model

The correlated randomness (CR) model is an extension of the CRS model where each party has access to a string generated by a trusted third party. Unlike in the CRS model, the strings for parties may be different, but possibly correlated and unlike in the augmented CRS model of [10], honest parties can access their strings privately. Thus, it can be considered as a variant of the key registration (KR) model of [10].

Our CR model is defined to be consistent with the one of [33], taking into account the UC setting. A protocol ϕ in the CR model is defined with the corresponding correlated randomness functionality $\mathcal{F}_{corr}^{\phi}$, which generates a correlated random string for each party in the protocol ϕ independently of the parties' input. Each party can access its string (but not other parties' random strings) by invoking $\mathcal{F}_{corr}^{\phi}$. In the security proof, the ideal world simulator is allowed to obtain the correlated random strings associated to all parties, thereby having an advantage over the real-world adversary.

Let ϕ be n-party protocol in the CR model. Let $\mathcal{D}$ be a distribution on $S_1 \times \ldots \times S_n$ where S_i is the set of possible random strings for party P_i. The correlated randomness functionality $\mathcal{F}_{corr}^{\phi}$ is defined in Fig. 1.

$$\mathcal{F}_{corr}^{\phi}$$

When receiving (sid) from P_i:

1. If there is no tuple of the form $(\mathsf{sid}, \star, \ldots, \star)$,
   (a) Generate $(s_1, \ldots, s_n) \leftarrow \mathcal{D}(1^{\lambda})$.
   (b) Store $(\mathsf{sid}, s_1, \ldots, s_n)$.
   Otherwise, retrieve the stored $(\mathsf{sid}, s_1, \ldots, s_n)$.
2. Send (sid, s_i) to P_i.

Fig. 1. Correlated randomness functionality $\mathcal{F}_{corr}^{\phi}$

Definition 1. *Let $\mathcal{F}$ be an ideal functionality and let ϕ be a multi-party protocol. Then the protocol ϕ UC realizes $\mathcal{F}$ in $\mathcal{F}_{corr}^{\phi}$-hybrid model if $\forall$ PPT hybrid model adversary $\mathcal{A}$, $\exists$ a uniform PPT simulator $\mathcal{S}$ such that for every non-uniform environment $\mathcal{Z}$, the following two ensembles are computationally indistinguishable*

$$\{\mathsf{View}_{\phi, \mathcal{A}, \mathcal{Z}}^{\mathcal{F}_{corr}^{\phi}}(\lambda)\}_{\lambda \in \mathbb{N}} \approx^c \{\mathsf{View}_{\mathcal{F}, \mathcal{S}, \mathcal{Z}}(\lambda)\}_{\lambda \in \mathbb{N}}.$$

3 Simultaneous Resettable ZK from OWFs

In this section, we construct a simultaneous resettable ZK argument in the correlated randomness model with straight-line simulation. The security of our construction relies only on the existence of OWFs. The main building block for our construction is a 3-round public-coin ZK argument system in the CRS model with straight-line simulation based on OWFs (such as in [37]). Using this public-coin argument system, we first construct a zero-knowledge *argument of knowledge* (ZKAoK) in the CR model with straight-line simulation and extraction. We then use this ZKAoK protocol to construct a simultaneously resettable zero-knowledge protocol in the correlated randomness model, based only on OWFs. We do so, in the following way: As part of the correlated randomness, the prover is given the commitment t, to the seed of a PRF, s, as well as a long random string d. The verifier is given the decommitment information (s and randomness) to this commitment t as well as d. Now, we have the verifier prove, using a simultaneous resettable WI (srWI) argument (based on OWFs [16]), that: either the verifier's random message c in the ZKAoK protocol is the output of a PRF (using seed s) on input the transcript so far, or that d is the output of a PRG on input a short string. The prover verifies the srWI argument and if this is successful, will execute the remainder of the ZKAoK taking c as the verifier's message. More details follow.

3.1   ZKAoK in the Correlated Randomness Model from OWFs

We first show how to convert a 3-round public-coin ZK argument system in the CRS model with straight-line simulation (based on OWFs) into one that is also an argument of knowledge (with straight-line simulation and straight-line witness extractor) in the CR model. Let $\Pi_{ZK} = (K, P, V)$ be the ZK argument in the CRS model with a straight-line simulator $\mathcal{S} = (\mathcal{S}_1, \mathcal{S}_2)$ (e.g. [37]). Let (KeyGen, Enc, Dec) be a CPA-secure secret key encryption scheme. Define (K', P', V') in the CR model as in Fig. 2.

Lemma 1. Π_{ZKAoK} *is ZKAoK with straight-line simulator and witness extractor in the correlated randomness model.*

For a proof of the above lemma, please see the full version of this paper [9]. Note that if the protocol Π_{ZK} is 3-round and public-coin, the resulting protocol Π_{ZKAoK} is also 3-round and public-coin.

3.2   Simultaneous Resettable ZK in the CR Model from OWFs

We now construct a simultaneous resettable ZK argument system in the correlated randomness model based on OWFs. Let $\Pi_{ZKAoK} = (K_{ZKAoK}, P_{ZKAoK}, V_{ZKAoK})$ be a 3-round ZK argument of knowledge protocol in the CR model with transcript (m_1, c, m_2) where $c \in \{0,1\}^\lambda$ is chosen uniformly at random, a straight-line simulator $\mathcal{S}_{ZKAoK} = (\mathcal{S}_1, \mathcal{S}_2)$, and a straight-line witness extractor $\mathcal{E}_{ZKAoK} = (\mathcal{E}_1, \mathcal{E}_2)$ from Lemma 1. Let (P_{WI}, V_{WI}) be a srWI argument (e.g. [16]). Let $\{f_s\}_s$ be a family of pseudorandom functions such that for $s \in \{0,1\}^{\ell_0(\lambda)}$, f_s outputs $c \in \{0,1\}^\lambda$. Let $f : \{0,1\}^{\ell_1(\lambda)} \to \{0,1\}^{\ell_2(\lambda)}$ be a PRG. We define Π_{srZK} as in Fig. 3.

The proof of resettable soundness goes as follows. We first consider the experiment with an imaginary protocol Π_F where a truly random function is used

---

$$\Pi_{ZKAoK} = (K', P', V')$$

$K'(1^\lambda)$:

1. $\sigma \leftarrow K(1^\lambda)$, $sk \leftarrow \mathsf{KeyGen}(1^\lambda)$. Let $k = \mathsf{com}(sk)$ and γ_0 be the decommitment information.
2. K' outputs $s_P = (\sigma, sk, k, \gamma_0)$ and $s_V = (\sigma, k)$.

Execution phase: P' on input (x, w) and private string s_P; V' on input x and private string s_V

1. P' parses $s_P = (\sigma, sk, k, \gamma_0)$, computes $e \leftarrow \mathsf{Enc}(sk, w)$ and sends e to V'.
2. V' parses $s_V = (\sigma, k)$.
3. P' and V' run $\langle P(w'), V \rangle(\sigma, x')$ where $x' = (x, e, k)$ and $w' = (w, sk, \gamma_0)$ to prove that there exists w, sk, γ_0 such that $(x, w) \in R_L$ and $w = \mathsf{Dec}(sk, e)$ and k can be decommitted to sk using γ_0.
4. V' outputs the output of V.

Fig. 2. ZKAoK argument protocol Π_{ZKAoK} in the correlated randomness model

instead of the PRF, and the verifier uses an alternate witness for the sim-res WI. We will show that Π_F is resettably sound by contradiction. Finally, we show that the probability that any resetting adversary can prove a false theorem in Π_{srZK} is negligibly close to that of Π_F through a series of hybrids. This implies that Π_{srZK} is also resettably-sound.

Lemma 2. *The protocol Π_{srZK} in the CR model is resettably-sound.*

Lemma 3. *Protocol Π_{srZK} is resettable ZK in the CR model with a straight-line simulator.*

For proofs of the above lemmas, please see the full version of this paper [9]. Lemmas 2 and 3 together gives us the following theorem:

Theorem 4. *Assuming the existence of OWFs, there exists a simultaneous resettable ZK argument protocol in the CR model with a straight-line simulator.*[3]

4   MPC in the Correlated Randomness Model

In this section, we construct a UC-secure MPC protocol in the CR model based on OWFs. The key ingredients are an MPC protocol in the OT-hybrid model UC-secure against an adversary corrupting all but one party, and a protocol UC-realizing unbounded number of OTs in the CR model. In [34], Ishai, Prabhakaran

---

[3] Our ZK argument protocol also has a straight-line witness extractor, but it is not necessary for our applications.

$$\Pi_{srZK} = (K, P, V)$$

$K(1^\lambda)$:

1. $(\sigma_P, \sigma_V) \leftarrow K_{ZKAoK}(1^\lambda)$, $s \leftarrow U_{\ell_0(\lambda)}$, $d \leftarrow U_{\ell_2(\lambda)}$. Let $t = \mathsf{com}(s)$ and γ be the decommitment information.
2. K outputs $s_P = (\sigma_P, t, d)$ and $s_V = (\sigma_V, s, \gamma, t, d)$.

Execution phase: P on input (x, w) and private string s_P; V on input x and private string s_V

1. P parses $s_P = (\sigma_P, t, d)$, runs $P_{ZKAoK}(x, w, \sigma_P)$ to compute m_1, and sends m_1 to V.
2. V parses $s_V = (\sigma_V, s, \gamma, t, d)$, runs $V_{ZKAoK}(x, \sigma_V)$ to sends $c = f_s(x||m_1)$ on behalf of V_{ZKAoK} to P (running P_{ZKAoK}), and runs $P_{WI}(y, (s, \gamma))$, with $y = (t, c, d, x, m_1)$, proving to P running $V_{WI}(y)$ that one of the following statements hold
   - there exists s' and γ such that t can be decommitted to s' using γ and $c = f_{s'}(x||m_1)$.
   - there exists d' such that $d = f(d')$.
3. If V_{WI} accepts, P continues running $P_{ZKAoK}(x, w, \sigma_P)$ to compute m_2 and send it to V.
4. V runs V_{ZKAoK} on (m_1, c, m_2) and outputs the output of V_{ZKAoK}.

Fig. 3. Simultaneous resettable ZK argument protocol Π_{srZK} in the CR model

and Sahai introduce the IPS compiler which combines an MPC with an honest majority and a protocol secure against semi-honest adversary in the OT-hybrid model to get a protocol UC-secure against malicious adversaries in the setting of no honest majority. One of their main applications, by applying the compiler to a variant of the protocol in [18], gives an MPC protocol in the OT-hybrid model that is UC-secure against a malicious adversary corrupting all but one party, assuming only a PRG. Unlike their main result, however, this MPC protocol requires a large number of OTs, proportional to the circuit size.

To address the number of OTs required, we then construct a UC-secure protocol for unbounded number of OTs in the CR model. The first attempt is to use Beaver's OT extension [7] from a bounded number of OTs which can be generated using correlated randomness [6]. The problem with this approach is that we can only get polynomial number (in the number of original OTs) of OTs for some fixed polynomial known in advance. However, in our protocol, we would require (an apriori) unknown number of OTs to be generated from the initial OTs – this is because the number of OTs needed depends on the number of times the hardware token is executed.

To get around this problem, we do as follows. We have the sender construct a super-polynomial size Yao's garbled circuit that computes the OTs. Of course, the sender cannot compute this entire garbled circuit. So, instead of sending the garbled circuit to the receiver, the sender commits to the first layer of the garbled circuit and the seed for the PRF that is used to generate the rest of the garbled circuit. When the receiver queries for the ith OT, the sender sends a section of the garbled circuit that suffices to compute the output followed by the ZK argument that it is consistent with committed values. However, this section of the circuit is now of polynomial size. This technique is similar in spirit to the GGM [26] technique for constructing a PRF. We now present more details.

4.1 Beaver's OT Extension

Before we construct a UC-secure protocol computing unbounded number of OTs, we first recall Beaver's construction [7]. Beaver considers two notions of OT.

- $\frac{1}{2}$OT: the sender S has x_0 and x_1. At the end of the protocol, the receiver learns (b, x_b) for a random bit b, the sender learns nothing about b.
- $\binom{2}{1}$OT: the sender has x_0 and x_1, the receiver has a bit b. At the end of the protocol, the receiver learns x_b, the sender learns nothing about b.

In [6], Beaver shows that $O(n)$ instances of $\binom{2}{1}$OT can be generated from $O(n^2)$ instances of $\frac{1}{2}$OT. In [7], the sender constructs a garbled circuit that takes a short input for a PRG, then expands it to a long string. Each bit of the string is used to select one of each pair of the sender's inputs. In order to get a garbled input corresponding to the receiver's seed and the garbled circuit, the sender and the receiver only need to perform a small number of OTs for each bit of the short input. This OT extension technique extends λ $\binom{2}{1}$OTs to $poly(\lambda)$ $\frac{1}{2}$OTs. This small number of OTs can be precomputed [6] as part of the correlated randomness. While this OT extension results in $\frac{1}{2}$OT, smaller number (but still polynomial) of $\binom{2}{1}$OT can be generated using the same number of starting OTs.

4.2 Unbounded Number of OTs

We now construct a UC-secure protocol computing unbounded number of OTs in the correlated randomness model assuming only OWFs. We consider the following modification to the OT extension above. Instead of a PRG, we use a PRF to generate a pseudorandom r_i for any $i \in \{0,1\}^\lambda$ using seed s_1 given to the sender on input $s_2||i$ where s_2 plays the same role as the seed in Beaver's extension protocol. Each r_i can be used to select the sender's input in the same way as in Beaver's protocol. However, the entire circuit (for all i) will have exponential size. To get around this problem, for each i, the sender only sends a garbled circuit corresponding to a subcircuit that suffices to compute an output based on the sender's ith input and r_i. We also use UC-secure ZK argument and commitment to ensure that malicious parties cannot deviate from the protocol. Since the whole garbled circuit is fixed given the committed values, the sender cannot change the circuit and still successfully provide the ZK argument. Sender security is proved by arguing that the receiver does not learn more than the intended output by the property of the garbled circuits.

$$\mathsf{OT}^{\mathsf{unbounded}} = (K, S, R)$$

$K(1^\lambda)$:

1. $(\sigma_S, \sigma_R) \leftarrow K_0(1^\lambda)$, $\sigma_{ZK} \leftarrow K_{ZK}(1^\lambda)$, $s_1, s_2, s_3 \leftarrow S$. For $i = 1, 2, 3$, let $(c_i, \gamma_i) \leftarrow \mathsf{com}(s_i)$ with decommitment information $\gamma_i \in \{0, 1\}^{\ell(\lambda)}$.
2. K outputs $s_S = (\sigma_S, \sigma_{ZK}, s_1, \gamma_1, s_3, \gamma_3, c_2)$ and $s_R = (\sigma_R, \sigma_{ZK}, s_2, \gamma_2, c_1, c_3)$.

Before 1st Execution phase: S on private string s_S; R on private string s_R

1. S parses $s_S = (\sigma_S, \sigma_{ZK}, s_1, \gamma_1, s_3, \gamma_3, c_2)$. Let $C(s, i) = C_{X, s_1, c_2}(s, i)$ be a circuit that outputs $(r_1, \ldots, r_n) = F_{s_1}(s||i)$. Let $(G, \pi) = \mathsf{GC}(C; f_{s_3}(0))$.
2. R parses $s_R = (\sigma_R, \sigma_{ZK}, s_2, \gamma_2, c_1, c_3)$. R runs $R_0(s_2, \sigma_R)$ to query $\pi(s_2)$ from S running $S_0(\pi, \sigma_S)$. R records the output $\bar{s}$.
3. R runs $P_{ZK}(\sigma_{ZK}, (s_2, \gamma_2))$ to prove to S running $V_{ZK}(\sigma_{ZK})$ that c_2 can be decommitted to s_2 using γ_2 and R queries for s_2. If V_{ZK} rejects, S aborts.

ith Execution phase: S on input $X_i = \{x_0^{i,j}, x_1^{i,j}\}_{j \in [n]}$, where $x_b^{i,j} \in \{0, 1\}$ and private string s_S; R on private string s_R

1. S parses $s_S = (\sigma_S, \sigma_{ZK}, s_1, \gamma_1, s_3, \gamma_3, c_2)$. Let $C_i(s) = C_{i, X, s_1, c_2}(s)$ be a circuit that first computes $r = C(s, i)$, and if $r = (r_1, \ldots, r_n) \neq \bot$, outputs $((r_1, x_{r_1}^{i,1}), \ldots, (r_n, x_{r_n}^{i,n}))$; otherwise, outputs $\bot$. S computes $(G_i, \pi) = \mathsf{GC}(C_i; f_{s_3}(0), f_{s_3}(i))$ such that $f_{s_3}(0)$ is used for input wires (for consistency of π) and $f_{s_3}(i)$ is used for the rest. S sends G_i to R
2. R parses $s_R = (\sigma_R, \sigma_{ZK}, s_2, \gamma_2, c_1, c_3)$; S runs $P_{ZK}(\sigma_{ZK}, (s_1, s_3, \gamma_1, \gamma_3)))$ to prove to R running $V_{ZK}(\sigma_{ZK})$ that G_i is generated using s_1 and s_3, which decommitted to c_1 and c_3 using γ_1 and γ_3, respectively. R aborts if V_{ZK} rejects.
3. R outputs $\mathsf{GE}(G_i, \bar{s})$.

Fig. 4. UC-secure unbounded OT protocol

Let $\mathcal{G} = (\mathsf{GC}, \mathsf{GE})$ be Yao's garbling circuit scheme where each gate and wire are encrypted. For a circuit C, let $(G, \pi) \leftarrow \mathsf{GC}(C)$ consist of a garbled circuit C and garbled input function π such that $\pi(i, x)$ is a garbled input for ith position input $x \in \{0, 1\}$. Let $\mathsf{OT}_0 = (K_0, S_0, R_0)$ be a protocol for λ $\binom{2}{1}$OTs in the CR model. Let $\{f_s\}_{s \in \mathcal{S}}$ be a family of PRFs with seed space $\mathcal{S}$ and $f_s : \{0, 1\}^{2\lambda} \rightarrow \{0, 1\}^{p_1(\lambda)}$ for some polynomial p_1. The unbounded OT protocol construction, $\mathsf{OT}^{\mathsf{unbounded}}$, is provided in Fig. 4. Each execution of $\mathsf{OT}^{\mathsf{unbounded}}$ gives $n = p_1(\lambda)$ $\frac{1}{2}$OTs similar to Beaver's, which can be turned into $p_2(\lambda)$ $\binom{2}{1}$OT for a smaller polynomial p_2. A computational-bounded receiver can execute $\mathsf{OT}^{\mathsf{unbounded}}$ polynomially many times for any polynomial not known at construction time (as long as the polynomial is smaller than 2^λ).

Theorem 5. *Assuming OWFs, the protocol in Fig. 4 is a UC-secure protocol computing unbounded number of OTs in the CR model.*

For a proof of the above theorem, please see the full version of this paper [9].

4.3 MPC in the OT-Hybrid Model

Ishai et al. [34], construct a compiler that turns an MPC protocol that is secure against adversary corrupting less than half of the parties (honest majority) into a UC-secure MPC protocol in the OT-hybrid model. They apply this transformation to a variant of the MPC protocol from [18] to obtain the following:

Theorem 6 (Theorem 3 in [34]). *Assuming a PRG, for any $n \geq 2$, $\exists$ an n-party constant-round MPC protocol in the OT-hybrid model that is UC-secure against an active adversary adaptively corrupting at most $n - 1$ parties.*

Combining this theorem with our UC-secure protocol for unbounded number of OTs in the CR model, we get the following corollary.

Corollary 1. *Assuming OWFs, for any $n \geq 2$, there exists an n-party constant-round MPC protocol in the CR model that is UC-secure against an active adversary adaptively corrupting at most $n - 1$ parties.*

5   Corrupted Token Model

We consider a generalization of the Katz's tamper-proof token model [35] where tokens can be corrupted by adversaries even when they are created by honest parties. Our model is inspired by the real world application where honest users cannot create tokens themselves. They instead rely on a number of manufacturers, some of whom could be malicious. Thus, the secrets embedded in the token description can be revealed to the adversary. Furthermore, the adversary can replace the tokens with ones of its choice.

5.1   Katz's Stateless Tamper-Proof Token Functionality $\mathcal{F}_{\mathsf{token}}$

Our model is based on the stateless version of Katz's tamper-proof token model [35]. In this model, each user can create a stateless token by sending its description to $\mathcal{F}_{\mathsf{token}}$. The token is tamper-proof in the sense that the receiver can only access it through $\mathcal{F}_{\mathsf{token}}$ functionality in a black-box manner. We consider the case of stateless tokens where the tokens do not keep information between each access and use the same random tape. Hence, without loss of generality, we can assume that the function computed by the token is deterministic. In this case, we may represent the function with a circuit.

Our protocol will UC-realize a variant of $\mathcal{F}_{\mathsf{token}}$, called $\mathcal{F}_{\mathsf{token}}^{\mathsf{abort}}$, in which the adversary is notified whenever a party creates a token and can choose to interrupt its delivery. The receiver will not receive the token, but will be notified with the special message interrupted. In such a case, the receiver aborts the protocol. This (otherwise unavoidable) change can be avoided by restricting the adversary to corrupt less than half of the corruptible tokens, which will allow the receiver to compute the output using the remaining uncorrupted tokens, but will weaken the threshold of corruptions tolerated. For formal descriptions of the two functionalities, please see the full version of this paper [9].

5.2   Corruptible Tamper-Proof Token Functionality $\mathcal{F}_{\text{token}}^{\text{corruptible}}$

We generalize the tamper-proof token model to accommodate such a scenario by allowing an adversary to corrupt each token upon its creation. We define corruptible tamper-proof token functionality $\mathcal{F}_{\text{token}}^{\text{corruptible}}$ in Fig. 5 by modifying $\mathcal{F}_{\text{token}}$ as follows. Every time a user sends create command to the functionality $\mathcal{F}_{\text{token}}^{\text{corruptible}}$, it first notifies the adversary and waits for one of two possible responses. The adversary may choose to learn the description of the token, and replace it with another (possibly stateful) token of its choice. We call the token chosen by the adversary a *corrupted* token. Alternately, the adversary may ignore the creation of that token, and therefore, that token creation is completed successfully and in this case, the adversary will not learn the description of the token. After uncorrupted tokens are created, they are tamper-proof in the same sense as in Katz's model. The stateful program for the corrupted token can be represented by a Turing machine.

In the case that the adversary chooses not to corrupt any token created by honest users, our model is identical to the model of Katz. Thus, our model generalizes the standard tamper-proof token model. We show that we can achieve UC-secure 2PC/MPC in the corrupted token model allowing the adversary to corrupt one party and all but one token generated by every honest party.

6   A Compiler to the Corrupted Token Model

6.1   Protocol for Corruptible Tokens

In this section, we describe a multi-party protocol that the n corruptible tokens will run in order to emulate the Katz' stateless token functionality.

Let $(K_{srZK}, P_{srZK}, V_{srZK})$ be a simultaneous resettable ZK argument in the correlated randomness model with straight-line simulator. Let $\mathcal{S} = (\text{share}, \text{recon})$ be an n out of n secret sharing scheme. Let Γ_0 be a UC-secure MPC protocol in the CR model for functionality $\mathcal{F}$ described in Fig. 6.

We define a multi-party protocol $\Gamma = \Gamma(\Pi)$ on input $(x_1, \ldots, x_n)$ to compute $\Pi(x)$ when $x = x_i$ for all $i \in [n]$ in Fig. 7.

6.2   Realizing a Tamper-Proof Token with Corruptible Tokens

Now we are ready to describe our protocol realizing the tamper-proof token with n corruptible tokens. To compute Π, the corruptible tokens are given the setup parameters for the MPC protocol $\Gamma(\Pi)$. Up on execution with input x_i, they will run $\Gamma(\Pi)$ to compute $\Pi(x)$ only if $x = x_i$ for all $i \in [n]$. We let Γ_i be the Turing machine computing messages Party P_i in Γ sends to other P_j, $j \in [n] \setminus \{i\}$ in each round of Γ. Since our token are stateless, Γ_i takes as input a state state_{k-1} which stores internal memory of P_i in round $k - 1$ together with in which consists of all incoming messages P_i receives in round $k - 1$. Γ_i outputs a new state state_k and outgoing messages for round k.

Formally, $\Gamma_i(\text{state}_{k-1}, in_{k-1}) = (\text{state}_k, out_k)$ where state_k is the internal state of P_i in round k and

$$\mathcal{F}_{\text{token}}^{\text{corruptible}}$$

Upon receiving (create, sid, P_j, Π) from P_i with $i \neq j$:

1. If there is no tuple of the form (sid, P_i, P_j, $\star$, $\star$), store (sid, P_i, P_j, Π, creating).
2. Send (create, sid, P_i, P_j) to Adv.

Upon receiving (corrupt, sid, P_i, P_j) from Adv:

1. Find the stored tuple (sid, P_j, P_i, Π, creating). If no such tuple exists, abort.
2. Send Π to Adv.

Upon receiving (replace, sid, P_i, P_j, Π^*, state$_0$) from Adv:

1. Find and remove the unique stored tuple (sid, P_j, P_i, Π, creating). If no such tuple exists, abort.
2. Store (sid, P_i, P_j, Π^*, state$_0$), send (done, sid) to P_i, send (create, sid, P_i) to P_j.

Upon receiving (notcorrupt, sid, P_i, P_j) from Adv:

1. Find and remove the unique stored tuple (sid, P_j, P_i, Π, creating). If no such tuple exists, abort.
2. Store (sid, P_i, P_j, Π, $\perp$), send (done, sid) to P_i and send (create, sid, P_i) to P_j.

Upon receiving (execute, sid, P_i, inp) from P_j with $i \neq j$:

1. Find the stored tuple (sid, P_i, P_j, Π, state). If no such tuple exists, abort.
2. Run Π(state, inp) and let (state$'$, out) be the output. If state $\neq \perp$, set state = state$'$.
3. Send (sid, out) to P_j.

Upon receiving (read, sid, P_i, P_j) from Adv:

1. Find the unique stored tuple (sid, P_j, P_i, P, state). If no such tuple exists, abort.
2. Send (sid, state) to Adv.

Fig. 5. Token functionality $\mathcal{F}_{\text{token}}^{\text{corruptible}}$

- $in_{k-1} = \{m_{j,i,k-1}\}_{j \in [n] \setminus \{i\}}$ where $m_{j,i,k-1}$ is the incoming message from Party P_j to Party P_i in round $k - 1$. $m_{j,i,k-1} = \perp$ if P_i does not receive a message from P_j in round $k - 1$.
- $out_k = \{m_{i,j,k}\}_{j \in [n] \setminus \{i\}}$ where $m_{i,j,k}$ is the outgoing message from Party P_i to Party P_j in round k. $m_{i,j,k} = \perp$ if Party P_i does not send a message to Party P_j in round k.
- Let state$_0 = \perp$ and in_0 be P_i's input for Γ.
- If P_i terminates at the end of round t, $\Gamma_i($state$_t, in_t) = ($done, $output)$ where $output$ is P_i's output for Γ.

$\mathcal{F}$

On input $((\Pi_1, x_1), \ldots, (\Pi_n, x_n))$

1. If $x_i \neq x_j$ for some $i \neq j$, output $\perp$. Otherwise, let x be the common input.
2. $\Pi = \mathsf{recon}(\Pi_1, \ldots, \Pi_n)$.
3. Output $\Pi(x)$.

Fig. 6. Function $\mathcal{F}$

$\Gamma(\Pi)$

Setup:

1. Let $(\Pi_1, \ldots, \Pi_n) \leftarrow \mathsf{share}(\Pi)$. Let $c_i = \mathsf{com}(\Pi_i)$ with decommitment information d_i for $i \in [n]$.
2. For $i \neq j \in [n]$, let $(\sigma_{i,j,P}, \sigma_{i,j,V}) \leftarrow K_{srZK}(1^\lambda)$ be the correlated randomness for the simultaneous resettable ZK argument with prover P_i and verifier P_j.
3. Let $(\sigma_1, \ldots, \sigma_n) \leftarrow \mathsf{SetUp}_{\Gamma_0}(1^\lambda)$ be the correlated randomness for Γ_0.
4. For $i \in [n]$, send $\Sigma_i = (\Pi_i, \sigma_i, c_i, d_i, \{c_j, \sigma_{i,j,P}, \sigma_{j,i,V}\}_{j \in [n] \setminus \{i\}})$ to Party P_i.

Execution: Party P_i on input x_i, correlated string Σ_i and a random tape $R_i = (s_i, r_i)$

1. For each $i \in [n]$, P_i commits to its input x_i and its PRF seed s_i using randomness $r_{i,x} = PRF_{s_i}(x_i)$ and r_i, respectively. P_i sends its *determining message* $M_i = (\mathsf{com}(x_i; r_{i,x}) \| \mathsf{com}(s_i; r_i))$ to all P_j, $j \neq i$.
2. For each $i \in [n]$, P_i computes $R_i' = PRF_{s_i}(M_1 \| \ldots \| M_n)$ consisting of $R_i'[0]$ for running Γ_0 and $R_i'[1]$ for running (P_{srZK}, V_{srZK}).
3. For each $i \in [n]$, P_i executes as the ith party in Γ_0 where P_i follows kth round message $m_{i,k}$ by running P_{srZK} to prove that there exists $\alpha_i = (x_i, s_i)$ and Π_i such that
   (a) $M_i = (M_i[0], M_i[1])$ where $M_i[0]$ can be decommitted to x_i and $M_i[1]$ can be decommitted to s_i;
   (b) c_i can be decommitted to Π_i;
   (c) $m_{i,k}$ is correctly computed using $R_i'[0]$ in Γ_0 with (Π_i, x_i) as an input where $R_i' = PRF_{s_i}(M_1 \| \ldots \| M_n)$.

Fig. 7. Multi-party protocol $\Gamma(\Pi)$ computing Π

In order to protect Γ_i's state state_k when a token is sent to a malicious party, we use a symmetric key encryption scheme with a secret key embedded in the token to encrypt a state state before outputting. Let $\mathbb{S} = (\mathsf{SetUp}, \mathsf{Enc}, \mathsf{Dec})$ be a symmetric key encryption scheme. Let $\overline{\mathsf{state}}$ denote an encryption of state using

$\mathbb{S}$. Let s_i consists of all information embedded in the ith token. Formally, we define $T_i = T(s_i)$ in Fig. 8.

On input $(\mathsf{Initialize}, x_i)$

1. Parse $s_i = (i, sk_i, R_i, \Pi_i, \sigma_i, c_i, d_i, \{c_j, \sigma_{i,j,P}, \sigma_{j,i,V}\}_{j \in [n] \setminus \{i\}})$.
2. Initiate Γ_i on setup parameters $(\Pi_i, \sigma_i, c_i, d_i, \{c_j, \sigma_{i,j,P}, \sigma_{j,i,V}\})_{j \in [n] \setminus \{i\}})$, random tape R_i
3. Let $\Gamma_i(\bot, x_i) = (\mathsf{state}, out)$.
4. Output $(\mathsf{Enc}(sk_i, \mathsf{state}), out)$.

On input $(\overline{\mathsf{state}}, in)$

1. Parse $s_i = (i, sk_i, R_i, \Pi_i, \sigma_i, c_i, d_i, \{c_j, \sigma_{i,j,P}, \sigma_{j,i,V}\}_{j \in [n] \setminus \{i\}})$.
2. Initiate Γ_i on setup parameters $(\Pi_i, \sigma_i, c_i, d_i, \{c_j, \sigma_{i,j,P}, \sigma_{j,i,V}\})_{j \in [n] \setminus \{i\}})$, random tape R_i.
3. Decrypt $\mathsf{state} = \mathsf{Dec}(sk_i, \overline{\mathsf{state}})$, abort if fail.
4. Let $\Gamma_i(\mathsf{state}, in) = (\mathsf{state}', out)$
5. Output $(\mathsf{Enc}(sk_i, \mathsf{state}'), out)$.

Fig. 8. Token $T_i = T(s_i)$

Finally, protocol Λ in $\mathcal{F}_{\mathsf{token}}^{\mathsf{corruptible}}$-hybrid model realizing $\mathcal{F}_{\mathsf{token}}^{\mathsf{abort}}$ is in Fig. 9.

6.3 Proof of Security

Let $\mathcal{S}_{srZK} = (\mathcal{S}_1, \mathcal{S}_2)$ be the straight-line simulator for the simultaneous resettable ZK, and Sim_{MPC} be the UC simulator for the UC-secure MPC.

Let Adv be an adversary corrupting up to $n - 1$ tokens. Let n_c be the number of corrupted tokens, and $n_h = n - n_c$ be the number of honest (uncorrupted) tokens. We construct a UC simulator Sim in Fig. 10 internally running Adv such that any environment $\mathcal{E}$ cannot distinguish between interacting with Adv running Λ in the real world and interacting with Sim running $\mathcal{F}_{\mathsf{token}}^{\mathsf{abort}}$ in the ideal world. Now consider the series of hybrids:

Hybrid H_0: This hybrid is the real world execution.

Hybrid H_1: This hybrid is similar to H_0 except that every message to $\mathcal{F}_{\mathsf{token}}^{\mathsf{corruptible}}$ goes to Sim, and Sim acts honestly on behalf of $\mathcal{F}_{\mathsf{token}}^{\mathsf{corruptible}}$ while recording the messages. This hybrid is identical to H_0.

Let t be the maximum number of call from Adv to execute uncorrupted tokens. Let Hybrid $H_{2.0} = H_1$. For $k = 1, \ldots, t$

Hybrid $H_{2.k}$: This hybrid is similar to $H_{2.(k-1)}$ except that Sim records and replaces the kth encrypted state $\overline{\mathsf{state}}$ from uncorrupted T_l with $\overline{\mathsf{state}}^* =$

Λ

To create a token running Π for P_j, P_i does the following:

1. Generate the setup parameters for $\Gamma(\Pi)$: $(\Pi_k, \sigma_k, c_k, d_k, \{c_l, \sigma_{k,l,P}, \sigma_{l,k,V})\}_{l \in [n]})$ for $k \in [n]$ as defined in Figure 7.
2. Generate secret keys for decrypting share/state $sk_k \leftarrow \mathsf{KeyGen}(1^\lambda)$ for all $k \in [n]$.
3. Let $s_k = (k, sk_k, R_k, \Pi_k, \sigma_k, c_k, d_k, \{c_l, \sigma_{k,l,P}, \sigma_{l,k,V}\}_{l \in [n]})$.
4. Send $(\mathsf{create}, \mathsf{sid}_k, P_j, T_k)$ to $\mathcal{F}_{\mathsf{token}}^{\mathsf{corruptible}}$ where $T_k = T(s_k)$ for $k \in [n]$.

To execute a token running Π sent by P_i, P_j does the following:

1. For $k \in [n]$, initialize T_k by sending $(\mathsf{execute}, \mathsf{sid}_k, S, (\mathsf{initialize}, inp))$ to $\mathcal{F}_{\mathsf{token}}^{\mathsf{corruptible}}$ to compute $T_k(\mathsf{initialize}, inp) = (\overline{\mathsf{state}}_k, out_k)$.
2. While $\overline{\mathsf{state}}_k \neq \mathsf{done}$ for all $k \in [n]$, for $k \in [n]$
   (a) Parse $out_k = \{m_{k,l}\}_{l \neq k}$. Let $in_k = \{m_{l,k}\}_{l \neq k}$.
   (b) Send $(\mathsf{execute}, \mathsf{sid}_k, P_i, (\overline{\mathsf{state}}_k, in_k))$ to $\mathcal{F}_{\mathsf{token}}^{\mathsf{corruptible}}$ to compute $T_k(\overline{\mathsf{state}}_k, in_k) = (\overline{\mathsf{state}}'_k, out'_k)$.
   (c) Replace $\overline{\mathsf{state}}_k$ by $\overline{\mathsf{state}}'_k$ and out_k by out'_k.
3. Let $out = out_k$ for $k \in [n]$ such that $\overline{\mathsf{state}}_k = \mathsf{done}$.

Fig. 9. Protocol Λ in $\mathcal{F}_{\mathsf{token}}^{\mathsf{corruptible}}$-hybrid model UC realizing $\mathcal{F}_{\mathsf{token}}^{\mathsf{abort}}$

$\mathsf{Enc}(sk_l, 0^{|\mathsf{state}|})$ before sending it to Adv and replaces $\overline{\mathsf{state}}^*$ with $\overline{\mathsf{state}}$ before applying T_l. Hybrid $H_{2.(k-1)}$ and $H_{2.k}$ are indistinguishable by the security of the symmetric key encryption $\mathbb{S}$.

Let Hybrid $H_{3.0} = H_{2.t}$. For $k = 1, \ldots, n_h \cdot n_c$,

Hybrid $H_{3.k}$: This hybrid is similar to $H_{3.(k-1)}$ except that Sim uses $\mathcal{S}_1$ to generate $(\sigma_{i,j,P}, \sigma_{i,j,V}, \tau_{i,j})$ instead of K_{srZK} for honest token i and corrupted token j with $k = i(n_c - 1) + j$, and runs $\mathcal{S}_2(\tau_{i,j})$ to generate the sim-res ZK messages for token i by feeding the sim-res ZK messages from corrupted tokens. Sim records the transcript leading to each sim-res ZK session. By the GUC-security of the rZK, this hybrid is indistinguishable from H_1.

Lemma 7. *Hybrid $H_{3.(k-1)}$ and $H_{3.k}$ are indistinguishable.*

Proof. Suppose there exists a poly-time D that can distinguish $H_3.(k-1)$ and $H_3.k$ with non-negligible probability. We construct a distinguisher D' that can distinguish an interaction of P_{srZK} with a resetting verifier V_{srZK}^* and $\mathcal{S}_2(\tau_{i,j})$ for the sim-res ZK as follows. Given setup strings for the sim-res ZK, D' generates the setup for other pairs of tokens and the inputs for $\Gamma(\Pi)$. D' then runs $H_3.(k-1)$ or $H_3.k$ until Adv queries the honest token to prove a statement x using the sim-res ZK. D' runs the interaction and passes the messages from and to Adv as V_{srZK}^*'s messages. When V_{srZK}^* resets P_{srZK} or $\mathcal{S}_2(\tau_{i,j})$, D' queries the token

---

Sim

Whenever Sim receives (create, sid, P_i, P_j) from $\mathcal{F}_{\text{token}}^{\text{abort}}$, Sim does the followings:

1. For each $k \in [n]$, send (create, sid_k, P_i, P_j) to Adv.
2. If Adv replies with (corrupt, sid_k, P_i, P_j) for any $k \in [n]$ or P_j is corrupted,
   (a) Follow the protocol of Λ for creating a token, except that Sim uses zero string $0^{|\Pi|}$ instead of the actual token Π to create secret shares $\Pi_1, \ldots, \Pi_n$, and uses $\mathcal{S}_1$ to generate $(\sigma_{i,j,P}, \sigma_{i,j,V}, \tau_{i,j})$ instead of K_{srZK} and Sim_{MPC} to generate σ_i instead of SetUp_{Γ_0} for the setup parameters of Γ for the corruptible tokens. Sim stores the secret shares for later comparison.
   (b) Send T_k to Adv for each k Adv chose to corrupt.
   (c) Store (replace, $\text{sid}_k, P_i, P_j, T'_k, \text{state}_k$) from Adv.
   (d) Send (interrupt, sid, P_i, P_j) to $\mathcal{F}_{\text{token}}^{\text{abort}}$.
3. Otherwise, send (notinterrupt, sid, P_i, P_j) to $\mathcal{F}_{\text{token}}^{\text{abort}}$.

Whenever Adv runs the protocol for execution that involves both corrupted and uncorrupted tokens, Sim does the following:

1. Sim generates the Γ messages for uncorrupted T_k using $\mathcal{S}_2(\tau_k)$ and Sim_{MPC} as follows:
   (a) Sim generates and commits to α_k honestly as in Γ.
   (b) Sim runs Sim_{MPC} to generate messages for Γ_0.
   (c) Sim For each message generated by Sim_{MPC}, runs $\mathcal{S}_2(\tau_k)$ to generate messages for the following sim-res ZK argument.
   (d) When Sim_{MPC} queries the functionality of the function F on input $((\Pi'_1, x'_1), \ldots, (\Pi'_n, x'_n))$, if x'_k's are all equal to x', send (execute, sid, P_i, x) to $\mathcal{F}_{\text{token}}^{\text{abort}}$ and passes the output to Sim_{MPC}. Otherwise, Sim aborts.
2. Sim records and replaces every encrypted state $\overline{\text{state}}$ from uncorrupted T_k with $\overline{\text{state}}^* = \text{Enc}(sk_l, 0^{|\text{state}|})$ before sending it to Adv and replaces $\overline{\text{state}}^*$ with $\overline{\text{state}}$ before applying T_k.
3. Sim records all inputs/outputs to the tokens. If Adv queries with the same input (state and incoming messages), Sim returns the recorded output (new state and outgoing messages).

Fig. 10. UC Simulator Sim for Λ

using the saved state of the earlier round in the sim-res ZK. Finally, D' outputs the output of D. □

Claim. Fix a combined determining message $M = M_1 || \ldots || M_n$, any polynomial-time resetting machine Adv can find only one transcript of Γ_0 in $\Gamma(\Pi)$ that every following sim-res ZK argument convinces the verifier to accept.

Proof. Suppose not. Let $tr = (\ldots, m_{i,k})$ and $tr' = (\ldots, m'_{i,k})$ be the partial transcripts of Γ_0 generated by Adv up to the differing messages

$m_{i,k}, m'_{i,k}$ with accepting sim-res ZK argument. Note that we cannot have both $(c_i, M_i, M, tr), (c_i, M_i, M, tr') \in R_{rsZK}$. Otherwise, either M_i or c_i can be decommitted to two different values, and thus can be reduced to the security of the commitment scheme. Hence, either $(c_i, M_i, M, tr) \notin R_{rsZK}$ or $(c_i, M_i, M, tr') \notin R_{rsZK}$. Thus, we can construct a resetting prover P^*_{srZK} that can prove a false statement.   □

Let Hybrid $H_{4.0} = H_{3.(n_h \cdot n_c)}$. Let m be the number of distinct sessions of Γ_0 based on combined determining message $M_1 || \ldots || M_n$ generated through Adv querying the tokens. For $k = 1, \ldots, m$,

Hybrid $H_{4.k}$: This hybrid is similar to $H_{4.(k-1)}$ except that Sim runs Sim_{MPC} to generate the MPC messages for uncorrupted tokens by feeding the MPC messages from corrupted tokens in the execution of $\Gamma(\Pi)$ following kth combined determining message.

Lemma 8. *Hybrid $H_{4.(k-1)}$ and $H_{4.k}$ are indistinguishable.*

Proof. Suppose there exists a poly-time D that can distinguish $H_{4.(k-1)}$ and $H_{4.k}$ with non-negligible probability. We construct a distinguisher D' for Sim_{MPC} as follows. Given the correlated randomness for the MPC, D' generates the rest of the setup parameters for $\Sigma(\Pi)$ as in the experiment. D' then passes the MPC messages from Adv to D followed by the srZK messages from Sim_{ZK}. Since the accepting transcript is unique by the claim above, Adv cannot change the messages. D' outputs the output of D.   □

Let Hybrid $H_{5.0} = H_{4.m}$. For $k = 1, \ldots, n$,

Hybrid $H_{5.k}$: This hybrid is similar to $H_{5.(k-1)}$ except that if the kth token is uncorrupted, Sim replaces the PRF in $\Gamma(\Pi)$ with truly random function F.

Lemma 9. *Hybrid $H_{5.(k-1)}$ and $H_{5.k}$ are indistinguishable.*

Proof. Suppose there exists a PPT distinguisher D that can distinguish $H_{5.(k-1)}$ and $H_{5.k}$ with non-negligible probability p. We construct a PPT D' that given function f, it runs $H_{5.(k-1)}$ and outputs the output of D when PRF_{s_i} is replaced by f. By the property of the PRF, p is negligible.   □

Let Hybrid $H_{6.0} = H_{5.n}$. For $k = 1, \ldots, n$,

Hybrid $H_{6.k}$: This hybrid is similar to $H_{6.(k-1)}$ except that if the kth token is uncorrupted, Sim replaces the second half of the determining message M_i in $\Gamma(\Pi)$ with $\text{com}(0^{|s_i|}; r_i)$ where s_i is the PRF seed in $\Gamma(\Pi)$.

Lemma 10. *Hybrid $H_{6.(k-1)}$ and $H_{6.k}$ are indistinguishable.*

Proof. Suppose there exists a PPT distinguisher D that can distinguish $H_{6.(k-1)}$ and $H_{6.k}$ with non-negligible probability p. We construct a PPT D' that given a commitment C of s_i or $0^{|s_i|}$, it runs $H_{6.(k-1)}$ or $H_{6.k}$ and outputs the output of D when the second half of M_i is replaced by C. Since s_i is not used as a witness nor as a PRF seed in $H_{6.(k-1)}$ or $H_{6.k}$, D' can generate the input for D. By the hiding property of com, p is negligible.   □

Hybrid H_7: This is similar to $H_{6.n}$ except that Sim checks if inputs x_k, $k \in [n]$, are the same. If not, Sim records x_k's and replaces outputs of $\Gamma(\Pi)$ by $\perp$.

Lemma 11. *Hybrid $H_{6.n}$ and H_7 are indistinguishable.*

Proof. By the binding of com, Adv cannot find x_k' that $\mathsf{com}(x_k; r)$ (where r is an output of the truly random function f) decommitted to x_k except with negligible probability. In this case, by the soundness of rsZK, the output of $\Gamma(\Pi)$ is $\perp$. $\square$

Hybrid H_8: This hybrid is similar to H_7 except that Sim passes token creation request from honest parties to $\mathcal{F}_{\mathrm{token}}^{\mathrm{abort}}$ and uses it to compute the output for Sim_{MPC}.

Lemma 12. *Hybrid H_7 and H_8 are indistinguishable.*

Proof. Note that if Adv generates messages for the MPC honestly using the same input x_i and the share Π_i given in the setup, then the output from $\mathcal{F}_{\mathrm{token}}^{\mathrm{abort}}$ must be the same as the output of the MPC by the correctness of the MPC. Suppose there exists a poly-time D that can distinguish H_3 and H_4 with non-negligible probability p. There must be at least one MPC message m^* from Adv that is not generated honestly. Thus, we construct a resetting prover P_{srZK}^* for the sim-res ZK argument following m^* by randomly choosing a Γ_0 message and passing the following prover messages to V. When Adv sends a different message using the same token state, P_{srZK}^* resets the verifier. It has at least $1/T$ probability of choosing m^* where T is the number of Γ_0 messages sent by Adv. Thus, it has at least p/T probability of proving a false statement, contradicting the resettable soundness of the sim-res ZK. $\square$

Hybrid H_9: This hybrid is similar to H_8 except that Sim generates secret share of zero string $0^{|\Pi|}$ instead of the one received from an honest party.

Lemma 13. *Hybrid H_8 and H_9 are indistinguishable.*

Proof. Suppose there exists a poly-time D that can distinguish H_8 and H_9 with non-negligible probability. We construct a distinguisher D' for the secret sharing scheme $\mathcal{S}$ as follows. D' runs the experiment for D until it is given Adv shares consisting of less than n shares. D' then continues the experiment and D distinguishes between H_8 and H_9. Using the result of D, D' can distinguish between less than n shares of 0 and some program Π, contradicting the security of $\mathcal{S}$. $\square$

Let Hybrid $H_{10.0} = H_9$. For $k = 1, \ldots, n$,

Hybrid $H_{10.k}$: This hybrid is similar to $H_{10.(k-1)}$ except that if the kth token is uncorrupted, Sim replaces the second half of the determining message M_i in $\Gamma(\Pi)$ with $\mathsf{com}(s_i; r_i)$ where s_i is the PRF seed in R_i. Hybrid $H_{10.(k-1)}$ and $H_{10.k}$ are indistinguishable by similar argument as Lemma 10.

Let Hybrid $H_{11.0} = H_{10.n}$. For $k = 1, \ldots, n$,

Hybrid $H_{11.k}$: This hybrid is similar to $H_{11.(k-1)}$ except that if the kth token is uncorrupted, Sim replaces the truly random function F in $\Gamma(\Pi)$ with PRF_{s_i}. Hybrid $H_{10.(k-1)}$ and $H_{10.k}$ are indistinguishable by similar argument as Lemma 9. This hybrid is the ideal world execution.

Using these, we prove our main theorem below.

Theorem 14. *Assuming an existence of OWFs, there exists a protocol with n corruptible tokens in $\mathcal{F}_{\mathsf{token}}^{\mathsf{corruptible}}$-hybrid model UC-realizing $\mathcal{F}_{\mathsf{token}}^{\mathsf{abort}}$.*

7   RAM Obfuscation and Tokens with Bounded Memory

RAM Obfuscation. We now describe how to obtain program obfuscation with stateless hardware tokens solely from OWFs. This improves the assumption from the work of Nayak *et al.* [39], who additionally also assumed collision-resistant hash functions. At a very high level, the protocol of Nayak *et al.* makes use of OWFs and CRHFs. First, they make use of CRHFs for the authenticated ORAM structure. We observe that we can replace the authenticated ORAM used in Nayak *et al.* with an authenticated ORAM based on OWF (that can be built from the work of Ostrovsky and Goldreich, Ostrovsky). Next, in order to obtain a single starting seed for randomness that depends on the specific execution of the program and input, Nayak *et al.* require the user to first feed in a hash of the input to the token and then use this hash to derive all randomness (along with a unique program id). This gives them a unique execution id. We derive a unique value based on the input and program by having the user feed the input one-by-one to the token. Upon receiving one input, the token will authenticate it and provide an authentication tag (this process is deterministic) that will then allow the user to input the next input. This process continues until the last input is inserted into the token, upon which the authentication tag produced at this stage is a unique id that can be used (in combination with the program id) to derive all randomness needed by the token for program execution. This process is similar in spirit to the GGM construction of deriving a PRF from a PRG.

7.1   High Level Description of the Protocol

Program Authentication. At a high level, the program creation by the sender works as follows. Let the program to be obfuscated be $\mathsf{RAM} := (\mathsf{cpustate}, \mathsf{mem})$ where mem is a list of program instructions and $\mathsf{cpustate}$ is the initial cpu state. Let the program comprise of t instructions. The sender first creates the token containing a hardwired secret key K where $K := (K_e, K_{\mathrm{prf}})$. K_e is used as the encryption key for encrypting state, K_{prf} is used as the key to a pseudorandom function used by the token to generate all randomness needed for executing the ORAM, creating ciphertexts, and so on. The sender creates a unique execution identity $\mathsf{id}_{\mathrm{exec}}$, which is unique for every program created. The sender then encrypts $\mathsf{mem}\|\mathsf{id}_{\mathrm{exec}}\|\mathsf{id}_{\mathrm{instr}}$ (one instruction at a time) to obtain $\overline{\mathsf{mem}}$ ($\overline{\mathsf{mem}}_i$ denotes the ciphertext obtained upon encrypting

$\text{mem}_i \| \text{id}_{\text{exec}} \| i)$. The sender also computes a "tag" of the start ciphertext, $\overline{\text{mem}}_1$, as $\tau_1 = \text{PRF}_{K_{\text{prf}}}(\text{start}, \overline{\text{mem}}_1)$. The sender creates an encrypted program header $\overline{\text{Header}} := \text{Enc}_{K_e}(\text{cpustate}, \text{id}_{\text{exec}}, t)$. The receiver is sent $\overline{\text{mem}}, \overline{\text{mem}}_1^*$ and $\overline{\text{Header}}$ as the obfuscated program.

Program Feed. At a very high level, the receiver will feed in the program, one instruction at a time, to the token, as follows:

1. As the first message, the token receives $(\texttt{programauth}, 1, \overline{\text{mem}}_1,$ $\tau_1, \overline{\text{mem}}_2, \overline{\text{Header}})$. It will check that $\text{PRF}_{K_{\text{prf}}}(\text{start}, \overline{\text{mem}}_1, \overline{\text{Header}}) = \tau_1$ and output $\perp$ otherwise. Similarly, for all $2 \leq i < t - 1$, it receives $(\texttt{programauth}, i, \tau_{i-1}, \overline{\text{mem}}_i, \tau_i, \overline{\text{mem}}_{i+1}, \overline{\text{Header}})$. It will check that $\text{PRF}_{K_{\text{prf}}}(\tau_{i-1}, \overline{\text{mem}}_i, \overline{\text{Header}}) = \tau_i$ and output $\perp$ otherwise.
2. Next, it decrypts $\overline{\text{mem}}_i$ and $\overline{\text{mem}}_{i+1}$ to get mem_i and mem_{i+1}, and id_{exec} as well as decrypt $\overline{\text{Header}}$ to get id_{exec} and t. It will check that $\text{id}_{\text{instr}} = i$ and $i + 1$ respectively (also that these values are $\leq t$) and that the two id_{exec} values are the same and equal to the id_{exec} value in $\overline{\text{Header}}$. If these checks do not pass, it will respond with $\perp$. If the checks pass, the token will output $\tau_{i+1} = \text{PRF}_{K_{\text{prf}}}(\tau_i, \overline{\text{mem}}_{i+1}, \overline{\text{Header}})$.

Input Feed. Let the input to the program be denoted by $x_1, \cdots, x_n$. The receiver will send the following instructions, step-by-step, for every input, to the token.

1. On input, $(\texttt{inputauth}, 1, \tau_{t-1}, \overline{\text{mem}}_t, \tau_t, x_1, n, \overline{\text{Header}})$, it checks that $\text{PRF}_{K_{\text{prf}}}(\tau_{t-1}, \overline{\text{mem}}_t, \overline{\text{Header}}) = \tau_t$, that $\overline{\text{mem}}_t$ is the tth program instruction (by decrypting $\overline{\text{mem}}_t$ to get id_{instr} and $\overline{\text{Header}}$ to get t and comparing) and output $\perp$ otherwise. It outputs $\tau_{t+1} = \text{PRF}_{K_{\text{prf}}}(\tau_t, 1, x_1, n, \overline{\text{Header}})$.
2. On input, $(\texttt{inputauth}, j, \tau_{t+j-2}, x_{j-1}, \tau_{t+j-1}, x_j, n, \overline{\text{Header}})$, for $2 \leq j \leq n$, it checks that $\text{PRF}_{K_{\text{prf}}}(\tau_{t+j-2}, j - 1, x_{j-1}, n, \overline{\text{Header}}) = \tau_{t+j-1}$ and outputs $\perp$ otherwise. It then outputs $\tau_{t+j} = \text{PRF}_{K_{\text{prf}}}(\tau_{t+j-1}, j, x_j, n, \overline{\text{Header}})$.

Program/Input ORAM Insertion. Once the program and input authentication is done, the program and input, henceforth collectively referred to as memory, must be inserted into the Authenticated Oblivious RAM structure. There are t program instructions and n inputs that must be inserted. Let $\ell = t + n$ be the total memory requirement of the program (we can assume this without loss of generality as any additional memory needed by the program can be thought of as dummy program instructions). First, a set of ℓ "zeroes" are inserted into the ORAM structure (i.e., the values of memory in all locations is set to 0)[4]. The insertion of a set of ℓ "zeroes" into the ORAM structure is done as follows:

1. For every memory location $1 \leq i \leq \ell$, the user prepares the message $(\texttt{ORAMsetup}, i, \ell, \tau_{i-1}^{\text{oraminit}}, n, x_n, \overline{\text{Header}}, \tau_i^{\text{oraminit}}, \tau_\ell)$ and gives it to the

---

[4] Whenever, the state of the program (ORAM or otherwise) needs to be modified, this is done by appending encrypted $\texttt{state}$ with $\overline{\text{Header}}$ and then authenticating, similar to Nayak *et al.* [39].

token, with $\tau_1^{\text{oraminit}} = \tau_\ell$ and $\tau_0^{\text{oraminit}} = \tau_{\ell-1}$. The token checks that $\text{PRF}_{K_{\text{prf}}}(\tau_0^{\text{oraminit}}, n, x_n, n, \overline{\text{Header}}) = \tau_1^{\text{oraminit}}$ (for $i = 1$) and $\text{PRF}_{K_{\text{prf}}}(\text{ORAMsetup}, i, \ell, \overline{\text{Header}}, \tau_{i-1}^{\text{oraminit}}, \tau_\ell) = \tau_i^{\text{oraminit}}$ (for all other i) and outputs $\perp$ otherwise.

2. Otherwise, the token derives a key for the ORAM structure – this ORAM key is derived as $K_{\text{oram}} = \text{PRF}_{K_{\text{prf}}}(\text{ORAMKey}, \tau_\ell)$.

   (a) It creates an ORAM initialization structure (that is, creates an initial random mapping of all virtual addresses to their real address); this initialization is done using randomness from the ORAM key K_{oram}.

   (b) In this map let address a_j have been mapped to address i. In this case, the token creates an authenticated encryption of $(a_j, 0)$ (again using keys and randomness derived from K_{oram}) to be inserted into the ORAM structure at virtual address i.

   (c) The token then outputs $\tau_{i+1}^{\text{oraminit}} = \text{PRF}_{K_{\text{prf}}}(\text{ORAMsetup}, i, \ell, \overline{\text{Header}}, \tau_i^{\text{oraminit}}, \tau_\ell)$.

Once all ℓ memory locations have been inserted with 0 values, the user then inserts the real input and program into the ORAM structure. This is done as follows: in the reverse order, starting with the nth input to the first input, and then the tth to the first program instruction. We now describe this process at a high level. For ease of exposition, we shall assume that every ORAM operation is a single step denoted as $\text{oram}_{\sigma, K_{\text{oram}}}(i, v_i, \text{read/write}, \perp/v_i^*)$ (this can be easily extended to the case when the ORAM read/write is a set of operations, similar to Nayak et al. [39]). The protocol is as follows:

1. The user will insert the ith memory location ($\ell \geq i \geq 1$, which is either an input or a program instruction) by sending the message $(\text{MemORAMInsert}, i, \ell, \tau_{2\ell-i}^{\text{oraminit}}, n, x_n, n, \overline{\text{Header}}, \tau_{2\ell-i+1}^{\text{oraminit}}, \tau_i, \tau_{i-1}, w_i)$, where $w_i = (i - t, x_{i-t}, n)$ if the ith location has an input (i.e., $\ell \geq i \geq t+1$) and $w_i = \overline{\text{mem}}_i$ if the ith location has a program instruction (i.e., $t \geq i \geq 1$).

2. If the ith location has an input:

   (a) The token will check that $\tau_i = \text{PRF}_{K_{\text{prf}}}(\tau_{i-1}, i - t, x_{i-t}, n, \overline{\text{Header}})$ and that $\tau_{2\ell-i+1}^{\text{oraminit}} = \text{PRF}_{K_{\text{prf}}}(\text{ORAMsetup}, i, \ell, \overline{\text{Header}}, \tau_{2\ell-i}^{\text{oraminit}}, \tau_\ell)$.

   (b) The token will then execute the ORAM instruction $\text{oram}_{\sigma, K_{\text{oram}}}(i, 0, \text{write}, x_{i-t})$.

   (c) The token then outputs $\tau_{2\ell-i+2}^{\text{oraminit}} = \text{PRF}_{K_{\text{prf}}}(\text{ORAMsetup}, i - 1, \ell, \overline{\text{Header}}, \tau_{2\ell-i+1}^{\text{oraminit}}, \tau_\ell)$.

3. If the ith location has a program instruction:

   (a) The token will check that $\tau_i = \text{PRF}_{K_{\text{prf}}}(\tau_{i-1}, \overline{\text{mem}}_i, \overline{\text{Header}})$ and that $\tau_{2\ell-i+1}^{\text{oraminit}} = \text{PRF}_{K_{\text{prf}}}(\text{ORAMsetup}, i, \ell, \overline{\text{Header}}, \tau_{2\ell-i}^{\text{oraminit}}, \tau_\ell)$.

   (b) The token decrypts $\overline{\text{mem}}_i$ to get $\text{mem}_i\|\text{id}_{\text{exec}}\|i$ and executes the ORAM instruction $\text{oram}_{\sigma, K_{\text{oram}}}(i, 0, \text{write}, \text{mem}_i\|\text{id}_{\text{exec}}\|i)$.

   (c) The token then outputs $\tau_{2\ell-i+2}^{\text{oraminit}} = \text{PRF}_{K_{\text{prf}}}(\text{ORAMsetup}, i - 1, \ell, \overline{\text{Header}}, \tau_{2\ell-i+1}^{\text{oraminit}}, \tau_\ell)$.

Program Execution. The program execution is similar to Nayak et al. [39].

8   Tokens with Small Memory

We consider a variant of $\mathcal{F}_{\text{token}}^{\text{corruptible}}$ in Fig. 5, called $\mathcal{F}_{\text{token}}^{\text{corruptible,short},L_1,L_2}$ where create and execute only take Π and inp of short size. We also allow a token sender to send a message along with the token created through the functionality. This allows the adversary to intercept the message when it chooses to corrupt a token without neither sender nor receiver knowledge. This is unavoidable as we represent a token in the standard corruptible model with both a token and an additional auxiliary string from the sender. We use $\mathcal{F}_{\text{token}}^{\text{corruptible,short}}$ when L_1 and L_2 are clear from the context.

In theory, we would like L_1 and L_2 be of constant size in security parameter. Though [39] suggests using logarithmic size in practice for better performance. We define an implementation Token of $\mathcal{F}_{\text{token}}^{\text{corruptible}}$ in $\mathcal{F}_{\text{token}}^{\text{corruptible,short}}$-hybrid model and prove the following theorem in the full version of this paper [9].

Theorem 15. *The protocol* Token *UC-realizes* $\mathcal{F}_{\text{token}}^{\text{corruptible}}$ *in* $\mathcal{F}_{\text{token}}^{\text{corruptible,short}}$-*hybrid model.*

Combining the above result with the result in Sect. 6 gives:

Corollary 2. *Assuming OWFs, there exists a protocol that UC realizes* $\mathcal{F}_{\text{token}}^{\text{abort}}$ *functionality in* $\mathcal{F}_{\text{token}}^{\text{corruptible,short}}$-*hybrid model using n corruptible tokens with short inputs and small size against an adversary corrupting up to n − 1 tokens.*

References

1. Agrawal, S., Goyal, V., Jain, A., Prabhakaran, M., Sahai, A.: New impossibility results for concurrent composition and a non-interactive completeness theorem for secure computation. In: Safavi-Naini, R., Canetti, R. (eds.) CRYPTO 2012. LNCS, vol. 7417, pp. 443–460. Springer, Heidelberg (2012). https://doi.org/10.1007/978-3-642-32009-5_26

2. Ateniese, G., Kiayias, A., Magri, B., Tselekounis, Y., Venturi, D.: Secure outsourcing of cryptographic circuits manufacturing. In: Baek, J., Susilo, W., Kim, J. (eds.) ProvSec 2018. LNCS, vol. 11192, pp. 75–93. Springer, Cham (2018). https://doi.org/10.1007/978-3-030-01446-9_5

3. Barak, B., Goldreich, O., Goldwasser, S., Lindell, Y.: Resettably-sound zero-knowledge and its applications. In: FOCS 2002, pp. 116–125 (2001)

4. Barak, B., Prabhakaran, M., Sahai, A.: Concurrent non-malleable zero knowledge. In: FOCS 2006, pp. 345–354 (2006)

5. Badrinarayanan, S., Jain, A., Ostrovsky, R., Visconti, I.: Non-interactive secure computation from one-way functions. In: Peyrin, T., Galbraith, S. (eds.) ASIACRYPT 2018. LNCS, vol. 11274, pp. 118–138. Springer, Cham (2018). https://doi.org/10.1007/978-3-030-03332-3_5

6. Beaver, D.: Precomputing oblivious transfer. In: Coppersmith, D. (ed.) CRYPTO 1995. LNCS, vol. 963, pp. 97–109. Springer, Heidelberg (1995). https://doi.org/10.1007/3-540-44750-4_8

7. Beaver, D.: Correlated pseudorandomness and the complexity of private computations. In: STOC 1996, pp. 479–488. ACM (1996)

8. Canetti, R.: Universally composable security: a new paradigm for cryptographic protocols. In: FOCS 2001, pp. 136–145. IEEE (2001)

9. Chandran, N., Chongchitmate, W., Ostrovsky, R., Visconti, I.: Universally composable secure computation with corrupted tokens. Cryptology ePrint Archive, Report 2017/1092 (2017)

10. Canetti, R., Dodis, Y., Pass, R., Walfish, S.: Universally composable security with global setup. In: Vadhan, S.P. (ed.) TCC 2007. LNCS, vol. 4392, pp. 61–85. Springer, Heidelberg (2007). https://doi.org/10.1007/978-3-540-70936-7_4

11. Canetti, R., Fischlin, M.: Universally composable commitments. In: Kilian, J. (ed.) CRYPTO 2001. LNCS, vol. 2139, pp. 19–40. Springer, Heidelberg (2001). https://doi.org/10.1007/3-540-44647-8_2

12. Canetti, R., Goldreich, O., Goldwasser, S., Micali, S.: Resettable zero-knowledge (extended abstract). In: STOC 2000, pp. 235–244 (2000)

13. Canetti, R., Kushilevitz, E., Lindell, Y.: On the limitations of universally composable two-party computation without set-up assumptions. J. Cryptol. **19**(2), 135–167 (2006)

14. Chandran, N., Goyal, V., Sahai, A.: New constructions for UC secure computation using tamper-proof hardware. In: Smart, N. (ed.) EUROCRYPT 2008. LNCS, vol. 4965, pp. 545–562. Springer, Heidelberg (2008). https://doi.org/10.1007/978-3-540-78967-3_31

15. Choi, S.G., Katz, J., Schröder, D., Yerukhimovich, A., Zhou, H.-S.: (Efficient) universally composable oblivious transfer using a minimal number of stateless tokens. In: Lindell, Y. (ed.) TCC 2014. LNCS, vol. 8349, pp. 638–662. Springer, Heidelberg (2014). https://doi.org/10.1007/978-3-642-54242-8_27

16. Chung, K.-M., Ostrovsky, R., Pass, R., Visconti, I.: Simultaneous resettability from one-way functions. In: FOCS 2013, pp. 60–69. IEEE (2013)

17. Dachman-Soled, D., Malkin, T., Raykova, M., Venkitasubramaniam, M.: Adaptive and concurrent secure computation from new adaptive, non-malleable commitments. In: Sako, K., Sarkar, P. (eds.) ASIACRYPT 2013. LNCS, vol. 8269, pp. 316–336. Springer, Heidelberg (2013). https://doi.org/10.1007/978-3-642-42033-7_17

18. Damgård, I., Ishai, Y.: Constant-round multiparty computation using a black-box pseudorandom generator. In: Shoup, V. (ed.) CRYPTO 2005. LNCS, vol. 3621, pp. 378–394. Springer, Heidelberg (2005). https://doi.org/10.1007/11535218_23

19. De Santis, A., Di Crescenzo, G., Ostrovsky, R., Persiano, G., Sahai, A.: Robust noninteractive zero knowledge. In: Kilian, J. (ed.) CRYPTO 2001. LNCS, vol. 2139, pp. 566–598. Springer, Heidelberg (2001). https://doi.org/10.1007/3-540-44647-8_33

20. Döttling, N., Kraschewski, D., Müller-Quade, J., Nilges, T.: General statistically secure computation with bounded-resettable hardware tokens. In: Dodis, Y., Nielsen, J.B. (eds.) TCC 2015. LNCS, vol. 9014, pp. 319–344. Springer, Heidelberg (2015). https://doi.org/10.1007/978-3-662-46494-6_14

21. Dziembowski, S., Faust, S., Standaert, F.-X.: Private circuits iii: hardware trojan-resilience via testing amplification. In: CCS 2016, pp. 142–153. ACM (2016)

22. Feige, U., Shamir, A.: Witness indistinguishable and witness hiding protocols. In: STOC 1990, pp. 416–426 (1990)

23. Fischlin, M., Pinkas, B., Sadeghi, A.-R., Schneider, T., Visconti, I.: Secure set intersection with untrusted hardware tokens. In: Kiayias, A. (ed.) CT-RSA 2011. LNCS, vol. 6558, pp. 1–16. Springer, Heidelberg (2011). https://doi.org/10.1007/978-3-642-19074-2_1

24. Garay, J.A., MacKenzie, P., Yang, K.: Strengthening zero-knowledge protocols using signatures. In: Biham, E. (ed.) EUROCRYPT 2003. LNCS, vol. 2656, pp. 177–194. Springer, Heidelberg (2003). https://doi.org/10.1007/3-540-39200-9_11

25. Garg, S., Kumarasubramanian, A., Ostrovsky, R., Visconti, I.: Impossibility results for static input secure computation. In: Safavi-Naini, R., Canetti, R. (eds.) CRYPTO 2012. LNCS, vol. 7417, pp. 424–442. Springer, Heidelberg (2012). https://doi.org/10.1007/978-3-642-32009-5_25

26. Goldreich, O., Goldwasser, S., Micali, S.: How to construct random functions. J. ACM **33**(4), 792–807 (1986)

27. Goldreich, O., Micali, S., Wigderson, A.: How to play any mental game or a completeness theorem for protocols with honest majority. In: STOC 1987, pp. 218–229 (1987)

28. Goldwasser, S., Micali, S.: Probabilistic encryption. J. Comput. Syst. Sci. **28**(2), 270–299 (1984)

29. Goyal, V., Ishai, Y., Sahai, A., Venkatesan, R., Wadia, A.: Founding cryptography on tamper-proof hardware tokens. In: Micciancio, D. (ed.) TCC 2010. LNCS, vol. 5978, pp. 308–326. Springer, Heidelberg (2010). https://doi.org/10.1007/978-3-642-11799-2_19

30. Groth, J., Ostrovsky, R.: Cryptography in the multi-string model. In: Menezes, A. (ed.) CRYPTO 2007. LNCS, vol. 4622, pp. 323–341. Springer, Heidelberg (2007). https://doi.org/10.1007/978-3-540-74143-5_18

31. Hazay, C., Polychroniadou, A., Venkitasubramaniam, M.: Composable security in the tamper-proof hardware model under minimal complexity. In: Hirt, M., Smith, A. (eds.) TCC 2016. LNCS, vol. 9985, pp. 367–399. Springer, Heidelberg (2016). https://doi.org/10.1007/978-3-662-53641-4_15

32. Hofheinz, D., Müller-Quade, J., Unruh, D.: Universally composable zero-knowledge arguments and commitments from signature cards. In: 5th Central European Conference on Cryptology (2005)

33. Ishai, Y., Kushilevitz, E., Meldgaard, S., Orlandi, C., Paskin-Cherniavsky, A.: On the power of correlated randomness in secure computation. In: Sahai, A. (ed.) TCC 2013. LNCS, vol. 7785, pp. 600–620. Springer, Heidelberg (2013). https://doi.org/10.1007/978-3-642-36594-2_34

34. Ishai, Y., Prabhakaran, M., Sahai, A.: Founding cryptography on oblivious transfer – efficiently. In: Wagner, D. (ed.) CRYPTO 2008. LNCS, vol. 5157, pp. 572–592. Springer, Heidelberg (2008). https://doi.org/10.1007/978-3-540-85174-5_32

35. Katz, J.: Universally composable multi-party computation using tamper-proof hardware. In: Naor, M. (ed.) EUROCRYPT 2007. LNCS, vol. 4515, pp. 115–128. Springer, Heidelberg (2007). https://doi.org/10.1007/978-3-540-72540-4_7

36. Lin, H., Pass, R., Venkitasubramaniam, M.: A unified framework for concurrent security: universal composability from stand-alone non-malleability. In: STOC 2009, pp. 179–188. ACM (2009)

37. MacKenzie, P., Yang, K.: On simulation-sound trapdoor commitments. In: Cachin, C., Camenisch, J.L. (eds.) EUROCRYPT 2004. LNCS, vol. 3027, pp. 382–400. Springer, Heidelberg (2004). https://doi.org/10.1007/978-3-540-24676-3_23

38. Mavroudis, V., Cerulli, A., Svenda, P., Cvrcek, D., Klinec, D., Danezis, G.: A touch of evil: high-assurance cryptographic hardware from untrusted components. In: CCS 2017, pp. 1583–1600. ACM (2017)

39. Nayak, K., et al.: HOP: hardware makes obfuscation practical. In: NDSS 2017 (2017)

Reusable Non-Interactive Secure Computation

Melissa Chase[1], Yevgeniy Dodis[2], Yuval Ishai[3(✉)], Daniel Kraschewski[4],
Tianren Liu[5(✉)], Rafail Ostrovsky[6], and Vinod Vaikuntanathan[5]

[1] Microsoft Research, Redmond, USA
melissac@microsoft.com
[2] New York University, New York, USA
dodis@cs.nyu.edu
[3] Technion, Haifa, Israel
yuvali@cs.technion.ac.il
[4] TNG Technology Consulting GmbH, Unterföhring, Germany
daniel.kraschewski@tngtech.com
[5] MIT, Cambridge, USA
{liutr,vinodv}@mit.edu
[6] UCLA, Los Angeles, USA
rafail@cs.ucla.edu

Abstract. We consider the problem of Non-Interactive Two-Party Secure Computation (NISC), where Rachel wishes to publish an encryption of her input x, in such a way that any other party, who holds an input y, can send her a single message which conveys to her the value $f(x,y)$, and nothing more. We demand security against malicious parties. While such protocols are easy to construct using garbled circuits and general non-interactive zero-knowledge proofs, this approach inherently makes a non-black-box use of the underlying cryptographic primitives and is infeasible in practice.

Ishai et al. (Eurocrypt 2011) showed how to construct NISC protocols that only use parallel calls to an ideal oblivious transfer (OT) oracle, and additionally make only a black-box use of any pseudorandom generator. Combined with the efficient 2-message OT protocol of Peikert et al. (Crypto 2008), this leads to a practical approach to NISC that has been implemented in subsequent works. However, a major limitation of all known OT-based NISC protocols is that they are subject to *selective failure attacks* that allows a malicious sender to entirely compromise the security of the protocol when the receiver's first message is reused.

Motivated by the failure of the OT-based approach, we consider the problem of basing *reusable* NISC on parallel invocations of a standard arithmetic generalization of OT known as oblivious linear-function evaluation (OLE). We obtain the following results:

– We construct an information-theoretically secure reusable NISC protocol for arithmetic branching programs and general zero-knowledge functionalities in the OLE-hybrid model. Our zero-knowledge protocol only makes an absolute constant number of OLE calls per gate in an arithmetic circuit whose satisfiability is being proved. We also get

A. Boldyreva and D. Micciancio (Eds.): CRYPTO 2019, LNCS 11694, pp. 462–488, 2019.
https://doi.org/10.1007/978-3-030-26954-8_15

reusable NISC in the OLE-hybrid model for general Boolean circuits using any one-way function.

- We complement this by a negative result, showing that reusable NISC is impossible to achieve in the OT-hybrid model. This provides a formal justification for the need to replace OT by OLE.
- We build a universally composable 2-message *reusable* OLE protocol in the CRS model that can be based on the security of Paillier encryption and requires only a constant number of modular exponentiations. This provides the first arithmetic analogue of the 2-message OT protocols of Peikert et al. (Crypto 2008).
- By combining our NISC protocol in the OLE-hybrid model and the 2-message OLE protocol, we get protocols with new attractive asymptotic and concrete efficiency features. In particular, we get the first (designated-verifier) NIZK protocols for NP where following a statement-independent preprocessing, both proving and verifying are entirely "non-cryptographic" and involve only a constant computational overhead. Furthermore, we get the first *statistical* designated-verifier NIZK argument for NP under an assumption related to factoring.

1   Introduction

Non-interactive secure computation (NISC) refers to the problem where Rachel wishes to publish an encryption of her input x, in such a way that any other party, who holds an input y, can send her a single message which conveys to her the value $f(x, y)$, and nothing more. In the semi-honest setting, there are several solutions to this problem including (i) garbled circuits [23,29] combined with two-message oblivious transfer (OT) protocols (e.g., [2,24,26]) and (ii) fully homomorphic encryption [9,16,27].

In reality, we care about security against potentially malicious parties and indeed, we have tools to achieve this level of security. For example, one could compile these protocols to be secure against malicious parties by using general non-interactive zero-knowledge (NIZK) proofs in the common reference string (CRS) model [6]. However, this requires making *non-black-box* use of the underlying cryptographic primitives, and is generally infeasible in practice. A recent line of work [1,19] has come up with *efficient* maliciously secure NISC protocols that make oracle calls to an oblivious transfer primitive. This model is referred to as the OT-hybrid model, and we henceforth refer to NISC protocols in the OT-hybrid model succinctly as NISC/OT protocols.

The paradigm of designing protocols in the OT-hybrid model that are either information-theoretically secure or make use of symmetric cryptographic primitives such as a pseudorandom generator, and plugging in fast implementations of OT, has paid great dividends in cryptography for several reasons. First, we have fast OT implementations under standard assumptions. Secondly, OT is self-reducible, so the cryptographic cost of implementing it can be pushed to an offline phase. OT can itself also be implemented with information-theoretic security given correlated randomness. In short, combining efficient NISC/OT protocols with efficient 2-message OT implementations, we can get efficient "public-key" non-interactive variants of secure computation, as was recently accomplished in [1,19]. This approach is beneficial even in simpler special cases such as constructing (designated-verifier) NIZK. For these cases, and more generally for functionalities computed by log-depth circuits or polynomial-size branching programs, such NISC/OT protocols can be made information-theoretically secure (in particular, there is no need for the pseudorandom generator).

Selective Failure Attacks and (Non-)Reusability. The starting point of this work is that this rosy picture belies a major defect of all known NISC/OT protocols. To see this, imagine that Rachel wants to publish a *reusable* encryption of her input x, obtain messages from anyone in the world with inputs y_i, conveying to her the value of $f(x, y_i)$. In the semi-honest setting, any NISC/OT protocol is guaranteed to be reusable, in the sense that if we fix Rachel's OT inputs and let Sam choose fresh OT inputs in each invocation, security still holds. However, in all known NISC/OT protocols (e.g., [1,19]), a malicious Sam can mount a "selective failure attack", feeding malformed OT messages to Rachel, checking whether she aborts or not, and using this information to violate both the secrecy of her input and the correctness of her output. The same holds for the special case of zero-knowledge functionalities, namely for NIZK/OT protocols (e.g., [5,20]). Such attacks have been previously considered in other contexts, such as in the setting of verifiable outsourcing of computation [15], and seem notoriously difficult to eliminate.

1.1   Our Contribution

We start by showing that the above limitation of OT-based protocols is inherent. That is, we show:

Theorem 1.1 (Informal). *There is no information-theoretic and reusably secure implementation of NISC/OT for general functions, or even for NC^1 functions.*

We also prove a similar result for zero-knowledge functionalities, though in a more restricted "black-box" framework that is still broad enough to capture all existing NIZK/OT protocols.

Achieving Reusability with OLE. Towards bypassing this negative result, we make the following key observation: the inherent limitation of OT-based protocols can be overcome if we replace OT by an *arithmetic extension* of OT known as oblivious linear function evaluation (OLE). The OLE functionality maps sender inputs (a, b) and receiver input x to receiver output $ax + b$, where a, b, x are taken from some (typically large) field or ring. The high level intuition is that by making the domain size of the receiver's selections super-polynomial, we can effectively eliminate the correlation between the receiver's OT inputs and the event of the receiver detecting failure. We note that OLE enjoys many of the useful features of OT, including a self-reducibility property that enables shifting almost all of the implementation cost to an offline phase.

Our main result shows that this relaxation from OT to OLE is indeed helpful. We present a general-purpose *reusable* non-interactive secure computation protocol that only makes *parallel OLE calls* over a large field.[1] Here reusability means that the same receiver OLE inputs x_i can be used for polynomially many function evaluations while still ensuring full simulation-based security. This implies in particular that even if the sender learns full or partial information about the receiver's outputs (such as whether the receiver accepts or rejects), the sender cannot obtain more influence on the receiver's outputs than in an ideal function evaluation. We denote such a reusable NISC protocol by rNISC/OLE.

Theorem 1.2. *There exists a statistically secure rNISC/OLE protocol for (arithmetic or boolean) branching programs and* NC^1 *circuits. Evaluating an t-node n-variant branching program costs* $O(nt^3)$ *OLE calls. It comes with an efficient black-box straight-line simulator, the statistical simulation error is* $O(nt^3)/|\mathbb{F}|$.

Our rNISC/OLE protocol for branching programs is information-theoretic and does not rely on any cryptographic assumptions. Its complexity is polynomial in the size of an arithmetic branching program being computed. This is sufficient to capture arithmetic log-depth (NC^1) circuits. In the case of general polynomial-size circuits, we obtain a similar result, except that we also make use of a pseudorandom generator.

Theorem 1.3. *If one-way functions exist, there exists an rNISC/OLE protocol for circuits.*

In the important special case of zero-knowledge functionalities, where verification can always be done by a shallow circuit, our rNISC/OLE protocol is still information-theoretic and only makes a constant number of OLE calls per gate in an arithmetic circuit whose satisfiability is being proved. Even in the single-shot case (without a reusability requirement), and even in the special case of zero-knowledge functionalities, similar NIZK/OLE protocols were not known prior to our work.

Theorem 1.4. *There exists a statistically secure rNIZK/OLE protocol (i.e., rNISC for zero-knowledge functionalities), such that proving the satisfiability of an arithmetic or boolean circuit costs* $O(1)$ *OLE calls per gate. It comes with an efficient black-box straight-line simulator, the statistical simulation error is* $O(circuit\ size)/|\mathbb{F}|$.

We optimize the concrete efficiency of our rNIZK/OLE protocol in the full version, so that proving knowledge of a satisfying assignment of an arithmetic

---

[1] Alternatively, settling for computational security, one can replace a field by a "pseudo-field," namely a ring whose description hides all zero-divisors. A useful example is the ring $\mathbb{Z}_N$ for an RSA modulus N with an unknown factorization.

circuit costs 7 OLE calls per addition gate and 44 OLE calls per multiplication gate. (Minimizing this constant is an interesting future research direction that can be motivated by practical implementations.) We stress that since the protocol is information-theoretic in the OLE-hybrid model, each OLE involves only a small number of field operations (without any exponentiations) in the online phase.

Constructing Reusable OLE. We complement our rNISC/OLE protocol by proposing an efficient secure implementation of the reusable OLE oracle which is compatible with our efficiency goals. Concretely, assuming the security of Paillier's encryption scheme [25], we construct a universally secure 2-message reusable OLE protocol in the CRS model (over the ring $\mathbb{Z}_N$ for an RSA modulus N). The communication cost of the protocol involves a constant number of group elements and its computational cost is dominated by a constant number of exponentiations. This protocol provides the first arithmetic analogue of the 2-message OT protocol of PVW [26], which is commonly used in implementations of secure two-party computation (in particular, it is used by the non-interactive ones from [1]). Our efficient OLE protocol is independently motivated by other applications of OLE in cryptography; see [3,17] and references therein.

Theorem 1.5 (Informal). *Under the Paillier assumption, there is a reusable OLE scheme in the common reference string (CRS) model with a communication complexity of $O(1)$ group elements, and a computational cost of $O(1)$ group exponentiations. Moreover, depending on the CRS distribution, the OLE can be statistically secure against either the sender or the receiver.*

Combining our statistical NIZK/OLE with the OLE protocol in the statistical sender security mode, we get the first statistical NIZK argument for NP under an assumption related to factoring.

Theorem 1.6 (Informal). *Under the Paillier assumption, there exists a* statistical *designated-verifier NIZK argument for NP.*

On the Efficiency Benefits of Switching to OLE. The switch from OT to OLE has some unexpected efficiency benefits. Beyond the reusability issue, OT-based protocols in the malicious security model use a "cut and choose" approach that has considerable (super-constant) overhead in communication and computation. While there are effective techniques for amortizing the communication overhead (cf. [21]), these come at the expense of a super-constant computational overhead and apply only in the Boolean setting. Other approaches that employ OLE and apply to the arithmetic setting, such as the ones from [12,14], are inherently interactive.

The combination of our information-theoretic rNISC/OLE and the Paillier-based OLE implementation yields NISC and designated-verifier NIZK protocols with attractive new efficiency features. As discussed above, for general NISC there was no previous approach that could offer reusable security, even for the case of boolean circuits, without applying general-purpose NIZK on top of a semi-honest secure NISC protocol.

Even for the special case of zero-knowledge, where many other competing approaches are known, our approach is quite unique. In particular, we are the first to construct any kind of (reusable-setup) NIZK protocol where one can push *all of the cryptographic operations* to an offline phase; using the self-reducibility of OLE, we can have an online phase that involves only arithmetic computations in the "plaintext domain" and its security (given the preprocessed information) is unconditional. Moreover, the online phase satisfies a strong notion of *constant computational overhead* in the sense that both the prover and verifier only need to perform a constant number of addition and multiplication operations for each gate of the arithmetic verification circuit, in the same ring $\mathbb{Z}_N$ over which the circuit is defined. As additional bonus features, the preprocessing required for implementing this highly efficient online phase consists only of a constant number of exponentiations per gate, and its security relies on a conservative, "20th century" assumption.

In addition, even in the stand-alone (non-reusable) world, our approach has its benefits. For example, as a corollary of our approach, we show that the satisfiability of an arithmetic circuit of size s can be proved in zero knowledge with soundness error $O(s)/|\mathbb{F}|$ via $O(s)$ parallel calls to (regular, non-reusable) OLE over $\mathbb{F}$. We also get an analogous result for NISC where the number of OLE calls depends polynomially on the arithmetic branching programs size.

1.2   Related Work

We briefly discuss several recent works that are relevant to the asymptotic efficiency features of our protocol. As discussed above, a distinctive efficiency feature of our rNIZK/OLE protocol for arithmetic verification circuits (more generally, rNISC/OLE for constant-depth arithmetic circuits) is that, in an offline-online setting, its online phase is non-cryptographic and has a constant computational overhead. Moreover, the offline phase only requires a constant number of exponentiations per arithmetic gate.

Bootle et al. [7] construct zero-knowledge protocols for arithmetic verification circuits with constant computational overhead in the plain model, i.e., without any offline phase. However, this protocol relies on constant-overhead implementations of cryptographic primitives (a plausible but non-standard assumption), it requires multiple rounds of interaction (but can be made non-interactive via the Fiat-Shamir heuristic) and, most importantly in the context of our work, the cryptographic work in this protocol cannot be preprocessed. Finally, this protocol does not directly apply in the more general setting of secure computation.

Applebaum et al. [3] obtain (again, under plausible but non-standard assumptions) secure two-party protocols for evaluating arithmetic circuits that have constant computational overhead in the plain model. However, these protocols are inherently interactive (even when restricted to constant-depth circuits) and are only secure against semi-honest parties.

Finally, Chaidos and Couteau [11] construct an alternative Paillier-based designated-verifier (reusable) NIZK protocol with a constant number of exponentiations per arithmetic gate. The constant from [11] is significantly smaller than ours and the protocol can be based on more general assumptions. However, whereas for NIZK there are several other competing approaches, including succinct and publicly verifiable protocols, our NISC protocol provides the *first* reusable solution for NISC that is efficient enough to be implemented. Moreover, the NIZK protocol from [11] (which is based on Σ-protocols) does not have the feature of a non-cryptographic online phase that our protocol inherits from the underlying information-theoretic OLE-based protocol.

There has been recent interest in the goal of constructing reusable NIZK protocols with different forms of setup from alternative assumptions such as LWE [10,22,28]. Our work provides a new avenue for constructing such protocols by reducing this goal to the construction of reusable 2-message OLE. The usefulness of our approach has been demonstrated in the recent work of Boyle et al. [8], which constructs (bounded) reusable NIZK with a correlated randomness setup from the Learning Parity with Noise (LPN) assumption over large fields. This construction can rely on a simplified honest-verifier variant of our rNIZK/OLE protocol, as the correlated randomness setup effectively restricts the verifier to be honest.

There are two main qualitative differences between our work and all of the recent NIZK-related works mentioned above. First, we obtain non-trivial (positive and negative) results on NIZK in a natural and well-motivated *information-theoretic* setting, whereas all of the above works are inherently cast in a computational setting. This information-theoretic aspect of our positive results is crucial for obtaining reusable NIZK protocols that have a non-cryptographic online phase given offline preprocessing. Second, our positive results apply to NISC, which is more general than NIZK in a useful way. While many different techniques for constructing NIZK protocols from different assumptions are known, including black-box constructions from cryptographically hard groups, our work provides the first black-box constructions of reusable NISC protocols of any kind.

2   Overview of the Techniques

In this section we provide a high level overview of the proofs of our main results.

2.1   Impossibility of rNISC/OT

We show several negative results, which highlight the hardness of reusable secure computation. The first negative result shows that for non-interactive two-party computation protocols, even perfect security against malicious senders *does not* imply reusable security. In particular, previous works that construct NISC/OT protocols do not immediately imply rNISC/OT.

The second negative result shows that OLE is strictly stronger than OT in the sense that there exists *no* information-theoretic rNISC/OT protocol for the OLE functionality with composable security. Third and finally, assuming the existence of one-way functions, in the OT-hybrid model, we show that there are no general resettably sound, non-interactive zero-knowledge proofs with black-box simulation. We describe below an outline of the second and third impossibility results. For the technical details, we refer the reader to the full version.

OT is Not Sufficient for Reusability. The basic intuition behind the weakness ("non-reusability") of OT is the following: a malicious sender can learn the receiver's choice bits if the receiver uses the same randomness and input in different protocol runs. In particular, suppose the receiver's private OT choice bit has been fixed in a set-up phase. In the first protocol run, a malicious sender feeds (a, b) to the OT. In the second protocol run, the malicious sender feeds (a', b') to the OT where either $a \neq a'$ or $b \neq b'$ (but not both). If the receiver output is different in these two protocol runs, the malicious sender can deduce the receiver's choice bit.

Moreover, imagine implementing a functionality, such as reusable OLE or reusable NIZK, in the OT hybrid model. Such an implementation will involve the receiver calling the OT functionality using a vector of choice bits. Suppose now that the receiver has different outputs in two protocol runs where the sender chooses OT-input strings $(\mathbf{a}, \mathbf{b})$ and $(\mathbf{a}', \mathbf{b}')$ respectively. The malicious sender can now modify $(\mathbf{a}, \mathbf{b})$ to equal $(\mathbf{a}', \mathbf{b}')$ by a sequence of single-bit modifications. By observing the receiver's output when the sender feeds these intermediate OT-input strings, the malicious sender can always learn the sender's j-th choice bit for some j such that $(\mathbf{a}[j], \mathbf{b}[j]) \neq (\mathbf{a}'[j], \mathbf{b}'[j])$.

In the *OLE*-hybrid model, this intuition does not work. Consider a similar scenario: The receiver uses the same randomness and input in two protocol runs, let $\mathbf{x}[i] \in \mathbb{F}$ be the receiver's input in the i-th OLE instance. The malicious sender feeds $(\mathbf{a}[i], \mathbf{b}[i])$ and $(\mathbf{a}'[i], \mathbf{b}'[i])$ to the i-th OLE instance in these two protocol runs respectively. Say the $(\mathbf{a}[j], \mathbf{b}[j]) \neq (\mathbf{a}'[j], \mathbf{b}'[j])$ is the only difference between $(\mathbf{a}, \mathbf{b})$ and $(\mathbf{a}', \mathbf{b}')$ and the receiver outputs differently in these two protocol runs. Given the above information, the malicious sender can only deduce that $\mathbf{x}[j] \neq -\frac{\mathbf{b}[j] - \mathbf{b}'[j]}{\mathbf{a}[j] - \mathbf{a}'[j]}$. Such knowledge contains little information if $\mathbf{x}[j]$ has large min entropy.

We now outline how to translate this intuition into concrete impossibility results for the OLE functionality first, and then the zero-knowledge functionality. Details can be seen in the full version.

First, we outline the impossibility of a statistically reusable non-interactive OLE/OT protocol. The intuition behind our impossibility proof relies on a commitment protocol. There is a statistically reusable commitment protocol in the OLE-hybrid model: The receiver first samples a random $x \in \mathbb{F}$ as his OLE-input. To commit $s_i \in \mathbb{F}$, the sender samples random $r_i \in \mathbb{F}$ and feeds (s_i, r_i) to the OLE oracle, so that the receiver gets OLE-output $y_i = s_i \cdot x + r_i$. To unveil the i-th commitment, send (s_i, r_i) to the receiver. Such a protocol has statistical reusable security in the OLE-hybrid model. We show that in an OT-based implementation of the OLE primitive, a corrupted sender can recover the receiver's private input x after polynomially many rounds. The corrupted sender repeats the following so that either he recovers x or he learns more about receiver's OT choice bits. The sender samples an honest run in which the sender chooses $(s, r, \mathbf{a}, \mathbf{b})$, then samples $(s', r', \mathbf{a}', \mathbf{b}')$ from the same distribution subject to the condition that $(\mathbf{a}', \mathbf{b}')$ agrees with $(\mathbf{a}, \mathbf{b})$ on the *known* receiver choice bits. The sender can test whether (s', r') and (s, r) are consistent with the same x, i.e. whether $s'x + r' = sx + r$, by testing whether the receiver accepts (s', r') as an unveil message when the sender's OT-input strings are $\mathbf{a}, \mathbf{b}$. If so, the sender recovers $x = -\frac{r-r'}{s-s'}$ and thus finish the attack ($s \neq s'$ with high probability because s is statistically hidden in the receiver's view). Otherwise, the receiver would reject (s', r') as an unveil message when the sender's OT-input strings are $\mathbf{a}, \mathbf{b}$, while accept it when the sender's OT-input strings are $\mathbf{a}', \mathbf{b}'$. The sender will be able to learn at least one more receiver's choice bit from such a difference. At the end of this process, the sender learns all the *relevant* choice bits of the receiver, upon which he can sample an (s, r) and (s', r') pair that results in the same commitment $sx + r = s'x + r'$. This, by the calculation above, allows him to extract x.

Also in the full version we show that there is no UC secure rNISC/OT protocol for general zero-knowledge proof functionality. Suppose such protocol exists. This means the sender can prove statements $x \in L$ just by transforming a corresponding witness w into sender's OT-input strings. By assuming the existence of one-way functions, we can define the language such that it is easy to sample a random no instance $y \notin L$ or to sample a random yes instance $x \in L$ together with a witness w, while it's computationally hard to distinguish a random yes instance from a no instance. Now how can a malicious sender (prover) find some $y \notin L$ but still convince the receiver to accept y? He just samples a true statement (x, w) and starts off flipping bits in the corresponding OT-input strings, then checks each time if the receiver still accepts. Of course, the sender only flips the part of OT-input strings where he does not know the receiver's choice bits yet. As soon as the receiver starts rejecting, the malicious prover find out one more receiver's choice bit. This process can be repeated until the malicious prover has learned sufficiently many of the receiver's choice bits. There are so few indices where the malicious prover doesn't know the choice bits—denote these indexes by U—such that even if the OT-input strings are replaced with random bits on indexes in U, the receiver will still accept with high probability. Then by the UC security, if the sender instead samples $y \notin L$, generates OT-input strings using the black-box simulator, and replaces the generated OT-input strings with random bits on indexes in U, the receiver will also accept with high probability, breaking soundness. The details of this impossibility result are in the full version.

2.2 Construction of Information-Theoretic rNISC/OLE

Semi-honest NISC/OLE Our rNISC/OLE construction is a complicated object with many intermediate steps. Let us start with a warm-up question, namely, how to construct NISC with semi-honest security. As a starting point, we present a construction for the semi-honest model from the work of Ishai and Kushilevitz [18]. Then we will outline the main contribution of our work, namely, how to obtain (reusable) security against malicious parties.

Let $\mathbf{x}$ denote the receiver Rachel's input and let $\mathbf{y}$ denote the sender Sam's input. We consider arithmetic functionalities. Namely, both $\mathbf{x}, \mathbf{y}$ are vectors over a given finite field $\mathbb{F}$. The functionality is computed by an *arithmetic branching program*, defined as follows (see [18] for a more formal description). A t-node arithmetic branching program is specified by affine functions $g_{1,1}, g_{1,2}, \ldots, g_{t,t}$. The branching program maps input vectors $\mathbf{x}, \mathbf{y}$ to the determinant of the matrix

$$
G(\mathbf{x}, \mathbf{y}) \stackrel{\triangle}{=}
\begin{bmatrix}
g_{1,1}(\mathbf{x}, \mathbf{y}) & \cdots & & g_{1,t}(\mathbf{x}, \mathbf{y}) \\
-1 & \ddots & & \\
& \ddots & \ddots & \vdots \\
& & -1 & g_{t,t}(\mathbf{x}, \mathbf{y})
\end{bmatrix}.
$$

Branching programs can efficiently simulate arithmetic formulas and arithmetic NC^1 circuits. For example, the formula $x_1 y_1 + x_2 y_2 + x_3 y_3$ can be computed by the branching program

$$
x_1 y_1 + x_2 y_2 + x_3 y_3 = \det
\begin{bmatrix}
x_1 & x_2 & x_3 & \\
-1 & & & y_1 \\
& -1 & & y_2 \\
& & -1 & y_3
\end{bmatrix}.
$$

The technique for securely reducing a branching program computation to parallel OLE calls can be viewed as an arithmetic analogue of Yao's garbled circuit technique [4,29]. In a nutshell, the construction of the two-party protocol works as follows: The sender Sam samples two random upper triangular matrixes R_1, R_2 with an all-one diagonal. Observe that the matrix $R_1 G(\mathbf{x}, \mathbf{y}) R_2$ is a *randomized encoding* of $\det G(\mathbf{x}, \mathbf{y})$ since:

- $\det G(\mathbf{x}, \mathbf{y})$ can be computed from $R_1 G(\mathbf{x}, \mathbf{y}) R_2$ because multiplying by R_1 and R_2 preserves the determinant; and
- the distribution of $R_1 G(\mathbf{x}, \mathbf{y}) R_2$ merely depends on $\det G(\mathbf{x}, \mathbf{y})$ and not on $\mathbf{x}$ and $\mathbf{y}$. (This depends crucially on the structure of G, in particular the fact that the one-off diagonal of $\mathbf{G}$ consists of -1; we refer the reader to [18] for more details.)

Therefore, if the receiver gets only $R_1 G(\mathbf{x}, \mathbf{y}) R_2$, he will learn no information other than $\det G(\mathbf{x}, \mathbf{y})$.

Now to construct a semi-honest NISC/OLE protocol, we use the fact that the OLE functionality allows secure evaluation of affine functions. Therefore, the receiver chooses $\mathbf{x}$ as its input, and the sender feeds the affine function $\mathbf{x} \mapsto R_1 G(\mathbf{x}, \mathbf{y}) R_2$ to the OLE oracle. Let us denote this affine function by G', i.e. $G'(\mathbf{x}) = G'_{R_1, R_2, \mathbf{y}}(\mathbf{x}) := R_1 G(\mathbf{x}, \mathbf{y}) R_2$. Eventually, the receiver gets $R_1 G(\mathbf{x}, \mathbf{y}) R_2$, which leaks $\det G(\mathbf{x}, \mathbf{y})$ but perfectly hides all other information.

Additionally, this NISC/OLE protocol is perfectly secure against *malicious receivers, if the underlying OLE protocol is reusable*. Since this is the first time reusability rears its head, let us explain in a bit more detail why this is the case. The affine function in question can be thought of as

$$\mathbf{x} \mapsto R_1 \mathsf{G}(\mathbf{x}, \mathbf{y}) R_2 := \mathbf{v}_0 + \sum_{i \in [n]} x_i \mathbf{v}_i$$

for some vectors $\mathbf{v}_0, \ldots, \mathbf{v}_n$ chosen by the sender (as functions of $\mathbf{y}$, R_1 and R_2.) Now, it turns out to be easy to create a functionality out of (non-reusable) OLE where the sender inputs $(\mathbf{v}_0[j], \mathbf{v}_1[j], \ldots, \mathbf{v}_n[j])$, the receiver inputs $\mathbf{x} := (x_1, \ldots, x_n)$, and the receiver obtains $\mathbf{v}_0[j] + \sum_{i \in [n]} x_i \mathbf{v}_i[j]$. That is, each coordinate of the computation above can be realized using (non-reusable) OLE. However, using non-reusable OLE to compute the entire output by repeating this process once per co-ordinate runs into a serious issue when the receiver Rachel is malicious: she can feed the different instances of OLE with different values of $\mathbf{x}$. On the other hand, if the underlying OLE functionality is *reusable*, it permits the receiver to send a single message $\mathbf{x}$ that can be used for multiple invocations of OLE, *ipso facto* forcing Rachel to be semi-honest.

However, the protocol is not secure against malicious senders. Indeed, the sender can choose any affine G' so that the receiver will output $\det \mathsf{G}'(\mathbf{x})$. For security against malicious senders, the sender needs to prove that G', the affine function he fed into the OLE satisfies an arithmetic constraint: namely, that the sender knows two upper triangular matrixes R_1, R_2 and an input vector $\mathbf{y}$ such that $\mathsf{G}'(\cdot) \equiv R_1 \mathsf{G}(\cdot, \mathbf{y}) R_2$.

This is *the* key problem that remains to be solved. We now describe how to achieve this goal in a number of steps that make this task successively simpler, eventually reducing everything to reusable OLE.

An Intermediate Primitive: Certified OLE. Certified OLE is a specialized OLE wherein the sender can prove that the coefficients he chose satisfies some arithmetic conditions. More precisely, we define certified OLE as a primitive that allows:

- the receiver to learn the outputs of affine functions, where the inputs are chosen by the receiver and the coefficients are chosen by the sender;
- the sender to convince the receiver that the sender-chosen coefficients satisfy arbitrary arithmetic constraints.

We will implement a CertifiedOLE/OLE construction in the reusable world, whose security is information-theoretic.

An Intermediate Primitive: Replicated OLE. Certified OLE allows the sender to prove that his coefficients satisfy arbitrary arithmetic constraints. In particular, the sender can prove an equality constraint, i.e., prove that two of the coefficients she chose are equal. We isolate this ability into another (weaker) primitive called *replicated OLE*. More precisely, we define replicated OLE as a primitive that allows:

- the receiver to learn the outputs of affine functions, where, as before, the inputs are chosen by the receiver and the coefficients by the sender;
- the sender to convince the receiver that some of the sender-chosen coefficients are equal.

Replicated OLE is not as powerful as certified OLE, yet it is an important stepping stone to our eventual construction. In the corresponding section in the full version, we first construct replicated OLE directly from OLE, then construct certified OLE from replicated OLE[2]. For now, let us assume that we already have reusable replicated OLE, and we will construct (reusable) certified OLE using replicated OLE as a black box.

To begin with, note that to construct certified OLE, it is sufficient to support the following atomic operations.

1. Reveal $ax + b$ to the receiver, where $a, b \in \mathbb{F}$ are coefficients chosen by the sender, $x \in \mathbb{F}$ is an input chosen by the receiver, $\mathbb{F}$ is a finite field.
   In this overview, all coefficients chosen by the sender will be denoted by the first few letters in the alphabet such as a, b, c and inputs chosen by the receiver will be denoted by the last few such as x, y, z.
2. Allow the sender to convince the receiver that two coefficients are equal.
3. Allow the sender to convince the receiver that three coefficients a, b, c satisfies $a + b = c$.
4. Allow the sender to convince the receiver that three coefficients a, b, c satisfies $ab = c$.

The first two atomic operations are already supported by replicated OLE. We will implement latter two using calls to replicated OLE.

The third atomic operation, i.e., proving $a + b = c$, is implemented as the following. The receiver samples an random $x \in \mathbb{F}$ and uses it as an input to OLE. The sender samples random $a', b' \in \mathbb{F}$ and sets $c' = a' + b'$. The replicated OLE is used to reveal $ax + a', bx + b', cx + c'$ to the receiver. Clearly, the receiver cannot cheat; no matter which x be picks, he will receive three values, the first two of which are random and the third is the sum of the first two. How about a cheating sender? Note that the receiver is convinced if and only if $(ax + a') + (bx + b') = (cx + c')$. Since x is randomly chosen by the receiver and hidden from the sender, in case the sender sets $a + b \neq c$ (or $a' + b' \neq c'$), the receiver can detect this with overwhelming probability.

The last atomic operation, i.e., proving $ab = c$, is implemented using a similar idea. The receiver samples random $x, y \in \mathbb{F}$, sets $z = xy$ and uses x, y, z as inputs to an OLE. Note that a malicious receiver might choose $z \neq xy$ and the sender can never detect this. Therefore, we have to design a mechanism that can "enforce" honest receiver behavior. More precisely, our mechanism should prevent the receiver from learning any information in case he chooses $z \neq xy$. We will explain the details of this mechanism later; for now, let us simply assume the receiver chooses $z = xy$.

---

[2] The actual roadmap is somewhat different, and will be gradually revealed in this overview. An impatient reader is referred to Fig. 1 at the end of the overview.

The sender samples random $a', b', c' \in \mathbb{F}$, sets $d = ab', e = a'b$ and samples $d', e' \in \mathbb{F}$ such that $d' + e' = a'b' - c'$. The replicated OLE is used to reveal $ax + a', by + b', cz + c', dx + d', ey + e'$ to the receiver. The receiver is convinced if and only if $(ax + a')(by + b') - (cz + c') - (dx + d') - (ey + e') = 0$. Notice that if both sender and receiver are honest, then

$$(ax + a')(by + b') - (cz + c') = a'by + b'ax + a'b' - c' = (dx + d') + (ey + e').$$

In case the sender behaves maliciously, the receiver will detect this with overwhelming probability. To prove this, we consider $(ax + a')(by + b') - (cxy + c') - (dx + d') - (ey + e')$ as a polynomial in variables x and y, which equals

$$(ab - c)xy + (ab' - d)x + (a'b - e)y + a'b' - c' - d' - e',$$

This turns out to be a non-zero polynomial as long as the sender deviates from the protocol. Thus by sampling random $x, y \in \mathbb{F}$, the receiver will detect cheating with overwhelming probability.

Now, there are two outstanding issues we have not handled: (1) in the description above, we assumed that the receiver chooses x, y, z such that $z = xy$ honestly; and (2) we haven't yet shown how to construct replicated OLE, starting from (reusable) OLE. We will both of these in turn.

An Intermediate Primitive: Half-Replicated OLE. Our replicated OLE is constructed on top of what we call *half-replicated OLE*. In each OLE call, the sender chooses two coefficients. We separate them, and call them the *multiplicative coefficient* and the *additive coefficient* respectively. Half-replicated OLE only supports two operations:

1. Reveal $ax + b$ to the receiver, where $x \in \mathbb{F}$ is an input chosen by the receiver, $a \in \mathbb{F}$ is a multiplicative coefficient chosen by the sender, $b \in \mathbb{F}$ is an additive coefficient chosen by the sender (as before); and
2. Allow the sender to convince the receiver that two *multiplicative* coefficients are equal.

Half-replicated OLE is even weaker than replicated OLE. We first construct replicated OLE on top of half-replicated OLE by the following protocol: The receiver samples random y and sets it as an input to OLE. For each receiver-chosen input x, the receiver let $x' = xy$ and sets it as an extra input to OLE. Notice that as before, the sender cannot detect whether the receiver generated the tuple (x, y, x') honestly. Therefore, we have to design a mechanism that can enforce $x' = xy$. Again, analogous to the construction of certified OLE from replicated OLE, we will defer this to later; for now, just assume the receiver chooses $x' = xy$ honestly.

The sender uses the replicated OLE to reveal $ax + b$ and $ax' + by$ to the receiver. (More precisely, the sender does this by sampling a random c and revealing $ax + b, ax' + c, by - c$ to the receiver.) The receiver then uses the identity $(ax + b) \cdot y = (ax' + c) + (by - c)$ to check whether the sender behaves honestly.

Using a completely analogous argument as before, we can show that the receiver catches a cheating sender with high probability. (For this argument to work, we need the fact that the sender uses the same a in the first two invocations, but we already have this by the half-replicated guarantee since a is a *multiplicative* coefficient.)

At this point, there are *three* outstanding issues we have not handled: (1) in the construction of certified OLE from replicated OLE, we assumed that the receiver chooses x, y, z such that $z = xy$ honestly; (2) in the construction of replicated OLE from half-replicated OLE, we assumed that the receiver chooses x, y, x' such that $x' = xy$ honestly; and (3) we haven't yet shown how to construct half-replicated OLE, starting from (reusable) OLE. (1) and (3) are issues we already saw, but we just added (2) to our list. (In fact, as the reader might observe, (1) and (2) are really the same issue.)

We will first solve issues (1) and (2) by introducing the primitive of half-replicated OLE allowing CDS operations.

An Intermediate Primitive: Half-Replicated OLE Allowing CDS Operations. Our replicated OLE and certified OLE require the receiver to choose three inputs x, y, z such that $z = xy$. Unfortunately, there was no means for the sender to detect whether the receiver behaves honestly, and we left this problem open.

We design a mechanism called *conditional disclosure of secrets (CDS)*, in which the sender can disclose a message to the receiver if and only if the receiver-chosen inputs satisfy some arithmetic constraints. For example, in certified OLE, the sender can encrypt his messages using one-time pad, and disclose the pad if and only if the receiver chooses $z = xy$ honestly.

We now show how to design a half-replicated OLE allowing CDS operations starting from any half-replicated OLE.

As a first try, in order to disclose secret $a \in \mathbb{F}$ to the receiver if and only if $z = xy$, the sender samples random $b, c \in \mathbb{F}$ and uses the half-replicated OLE to disclose

$$\begin{bmatrix} y & z \\ 1 & x \end{bmatrix} \begin{bmatrix} b \\ c \end{bmatrix} + \begin{bmatrix} a \\ 0 \end{bmatrix}$$

to the receiver. (More precisely, this means the sender should also sample random b', c' that $b' + c' = a$, and use the half-replicated OLE to disclose $by + b', cz + c', cx + b$.) If $z = xy$ is satisfied, then the receiver can recover a as

$$(1, -y) \cdot \left(\begin{bmatrix} y & z \\ 1 & x \end{bmatrix} \begin{bmatrix} b \\ c \end{bmatrix} + \begin{bmatrix} a \\ 0 \end{bmatrix} \right) = a.$$

It is not hard to verify security against malicious receiver. When $z \neq xy$, the matrix $\begin{bmatrix} y & z \\ 1 & x \end{bmatrix}$ is invertible, in which case all information about a is erased by one-time padding.

But this protocol is not secure against a malicious sender: As the protocol is built on top of half-replicated OLE, the sender can deviate from the protocol by changing the additive coefficients. In particular, the sender can choose a non-zero

$d \in \mathbb{F}$ and uses the half-replicated OLE to disclose $\left[\begin{smallmatrix} y & z \\ 1 & x \end{smallmatrix}\right]\left[\begin{smallmatrix} b \\ c \end{smallmatrix}\right] + \left[\begin{smallmatrix} a \\ d \end{smallmatrix}\right]$ to the receiver. Then the receiver will recover $(1, -y) \cdot \left(\left[\begin{smallmatrix} y & z \\ 1 & x \end{smallmatrix}\right]\left[\begin{smallmatrix} b \\ c \end{smallmatrix}\right] + \left[\begin{smallmatrix} a \\ d \end{smallmatrix}\right]\right) = a - dy$, which is a function of the receiver's inputs, and constitutes a deviation from the protocol.

An easy way to solve this problem is to rely on the fact that the (honest) receiver samples $y \in \mathbb{F}$ uniformly at random, and we can use this ability to fight against the malicious sender.[3] The sender samples a random a' as an extra coefficient and uses the above insecure CDS protocol (with freshly sampled b' and c' in the place of b and c) to disclose a' if $z = xy$. If the sender is malicious, then the receiver gets $a' - d'y$.

Finally, the receiver can now detect malicious behaviour, by running a third subprotocol: sample a random $w \in \mathbb{F}$ as an extra input and ask the sender to disclose $aw + a'$ using OLE.

In summary, there are three sub-protocols going on here:

1. In sub-protocol 1, the sender inputs (an arbitrary) a and uniformly random b, c and the receiver inputs x, y, z and the receiver gets

$$\left[\begin{smallmatrix} y & z \\ 1 & x \end{smallmatrix}\right]\left[\begin{smallmatrix} b \\ c \end{smallmatrix}\right] + \left[\begin{smallmatrix} a \\ 0 \end{smallmatrix}\right]$$

2. In sub-protocol 2, the sender inputs uniformly random a', b', c' and the receiver inputs (the same) x, y, z and the receiver gets

$$\left[\begin{smallmatrix} y & z \\ 1 & x \end{smallmatrix}\right]\left[\begin{smallmatrix} b' \\ c' \end{smallmatrix}\right] + \left[\begin{smallmatrix} a' \\ 0 \end{smallmatrix}\right]$$

3. In sub-protocol 3, the sender inputs a and a', the receiver inputs a random w and gets $a' + wa$.

The receiver has no cheating room here. The reusability of the underlying (half-replicated) OLE forces her to use the same x, y and z in the subprotocols. Furthermore, if she chooses $z \neq xy$, she gets nothing, as we argued above. Finally, choosing w arbitrarily in the third subprotocol doesn't help her either due to the randomness of a'.

As for a cheating sender, the details of the argument are somewhat more complex but it is very similar in spirit to earlier arguments of the same flavor.

In turn, it is not hard to see that fortifying half-replicated OLE with CDS operations (as we just did) solves both problems (1) and (2) discussed above. It remains to solve (3), namely constructing a (reusable) half-replicated OLE protocol starting from any reusable OLE.

Revisiting Half-Replicated OLE. The last missing piece is to construct half-replicated OLE in the (reusable) OLE-hybrid model. The key idea of the construction is the following.

The receiver samples a random $w \in \mathbb{F}$ and sets w as an input to the OLE. For each multiplicative coefficient $a \in \mathbb{F}$, the sender has to sample a random $a' \in \mathbb{F}$ and use OLE to disclose $aw + a'$. This OLE call works essentially as

---

[3] In the main body, we do not need to assume that y is random. Moreover, we will consider more general arithmetic conditions beyond $z = xy$.

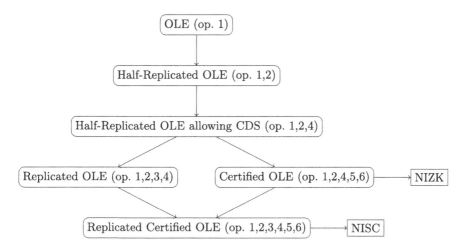

Fig. 1. Primitives (and supported operations – described below in text – in the bracket). We remark that "Replicated OLE" in this figure is only defined and used in the overview. In the main body, our proof follows the other path, directly constructing "Replicated Certified OLE".

a commitment of a. For each half-replicated OLE input $x \in \mathbb{F}$, the receiver translates it into two OLE inputs $y, z \in \mathbb{F}$ such that y is sampled uniformly at random, and $z = x - wy$.

Each half-replicated OLE call $ax + b$ can be translated into three OLE calls using the equation

$$
\begin{aligned}
ax + b &= a(wy + x - wy) + b \\
&= awy + az + b \\
&= y(aw + c) - (cy + d) + (az + b + d),
\end{aligned}
\tag{1}
$$

where c, d are arbitrary numbers. More precisely, the sender should sample random $c, d \in \mathbb{F}$ and use the OLE to disclose $aw + c$, $cy + d$ and $az + b + d$ to the receiver. Finally, the receiver computes the right output using Eq. 1.

We refer to this half-replicated OLE protocol as $\Pi_{\alpha\text{-}\frac{1}{2}\text{repOLE}}$ in the main body. The correctness of such a half-replicated OLE protocol is straight-forward. In this protocol, the sender can cheat without being detected by the receiver. Instead, when the sender deviates from the protocol, the receiver will output a random number. Moreover, as the randomness comes from w and y which are sampled by the receiver, the receiver's output is statistically close to the uniform distribution, even conditioned on the sender's view and x. Therefore it is not hard to embed another mechanism which detects any malicious sender behaviour with overwhelming probability. We leave the details to the full version.

Roadmap. We defer the detailed presentation of the results in this subsection to the full version. There, starting from reusable OLE, we define and construct a sequence of increasingly more powerful primitives, the last of which eventually supports all of the following operations.

1. Reveal $ax + b$ to the receiver, where $x \in \mathbb{F}$ is an input chosen by the receiver, $a \in \mathbb{F}$ is a multiplicative coefficient chosen by the sender, $b \in \mathbb{F}$ is an additive coefficient chosen by the sender.
2. Convince the receiver that two *multiplicative* coefficients are equal.
3. Convince the receiver that two coefficients are equal.
4. Disclose a message to the receiver if receiver-chosen inputs x, y, z satisfies $z = xy$.
5. Convince the receiver that three multiplicative coefficients a, b, c satisfies $a + b = c$.
6. Convince the receiver that three multiplicative coefficients a, b, c satisfies $ab = c$.

Such a primitive readily implies reusable NIZK and reusable NISC. The intermediate primitives are sorted in Fig. 1 by dependence. Each of them only supports a subset of the operations.

A Corollary: Single-Shot (Non-reusable) NISC/OLE and NIZK/OLE. As a corollary of our techniques, we get a (non-reusable) NISC/OLE protocol with interesting features. In particular, we get a single-shot NISC/OLE protocol where the number of OLE calls depends polynomially on the arithmetic branching program size, and the simulation is statistical with an error of poly(branching program size)$/|\mathbb{F}|$. In the special case of the zero-knowledge functionality, we get a single-shot NIZK/OLE protocol which (a) uses $O(1)$ (non-reusable) OLE calls per gate of the verification circuit; and (b) is entirely non-cryptographic in its online phase.

These results are proved by combining the following two facts:

– Our reusable NISC/OLE protocol immediately implies a single-shot NISC protocol in the (non-reusable) *vector-OLE* hybrid model. Vector OLE is a generalization of OLE where the receiver inputs a scalar $x \in \mathbb{F}$ and a number $k \in \mathbb{N}$, the sender gets k and inputs a pair of vectors $(\mathbf{a}, \mathbf{b}) \in (\mathbb{F}^k)^2$, and the receiver obtains $\mathbf{a}x + \mathbf{b} \in \mathbb{F}^k$. Vector OLE can be viewed as reusable OLE under the constraints that the number of OLE calls is known in the choice phase, and all OLE calls are non-adaptive. Our simulator also fits this (non-reusable) protocol.
– The result of Döttling, Kraschewski and Müller-Quade [13] shows an efficient equivalence between OLE and vector OLE. In particular, they show a constant rate statistical vector-OLE protocol in OLE hybrid model. It also comes with an efficient straight-line simulator achieving $O(\text{communication})/|\mathbb{F}|$ statistical soundness error.

Putting these together, we get our single-shot NISC/OLE and NIZK/OLE protocols.

2.3   Paillier-Based 2-Message OLE Protocol

In this subsection, we provide a quick overview of our Paillier-based instantiation of reusable OLE. For more details, we refer the reader to Sect. 4.

Consider a simplified OLE scheme as follows: The CRS will contain an ElGamal public key $(b, B_0 = b^{sk_0})$ in a Paillier group. (Paillier allows us to get additive homomorphism, while ElGamal means that the receiver will be able to construct related key pairs.) On input α, the receiver forms another related public key b, B_1, such that it knows the secret key corresponding to $(b, B_1 B_0^\alpha)$. It sends this key pair to the sender. On input z_0, z_1, the sender encrypts z_0 under (b, B_0) and z_1 under (b, B_1), using the same randomness, and sends both ciphertexts to the receiver. The receiver can then combine the ciphertexts to obtain an encryption of $\alpha z_0 + z_1$ under $(b, B_1 B_0^\alpha)$, which it can decrypt.

Recall that in a Paillier group for $N = (2p' + 1)(2q' + 1)$ all elements can be decomposed into a component in a subgroup of order $2p'q'$, and a component of order N, call them $G_{2p'q'}$ and G_N; the ElGamal encryption will encode the message in the order N component. Intuitively, we can argue the scheme is secure against a corrupt receiver as follows: First the CRS is indistinguishable from one where b is only in $G_{2p'q'}$, but B_0 has a component in G_N. Then suppose that the receiver chooses B_1 whose G_N component is $(1 + N)^\alpha$ (and note that a simulator can recover this α using the factorization of N). The G_N components of the resulting ciphertexts can be shown information theoretically to depend only on $z_0\alpha + z_1$, while the $G_{2p'q'}$ components are independent of z_0, z_1.[4]

Security against a corrupt sender is more challenging, because it could send invalid ciphertexts (i.e., ciphertexts in which decryption produces an element not in G_N). In particular, an adversarial sender could form a pair of ciphertexts that decrypt correctly under a specific α and incorrectly otherwise, and thus perform a selective failure attack. To prevent this, we need a way for the receiver to identify bad ciphertext pairs that can't be predicted based on α. Suppose the receiver runs the scheme twice, once with a random input γ, and once with input $2\alpha - \gamma$, while the sender uses inputs z_0, w for random w in the first instance and $z_0, z_1 - w$ in the second; combining the results of the two schemes would allow the receiver to decrypt $z_0\gamma + w + z_0(\alpha - \gamma) + z_1 - w = z_0\alpha + z_1$. This would prevent the selective failure attack: we argue that (under appropriate, indistinguishable CRS) B_1 information theoretically hides γ, so the probability that the resulting linear combination of two invalid ciphertexts decrypts correctly is negligible.[5] Of course, we must ensure that the malicious sender uses the same z_0 in both instances; thus we require that all the ciphertexts are related, using the same randomness.

---

[4] This is because the first component of the ciphertext, b^r contains no information about $r \mod N$.

[5] There is a minor subtlety here, where because $G_{2p'q'}$ has an order 2 subgroup an extra component in this subgroup might not be detected; to prevent this, we actually square all the elements during decryption to eliminate this subgroup, and then decrypt the final result divided by 2.

3   Preliminaries

We consider sender-receiver functions that take inputs from a sender Sam and a receiver Rachel and deliver the output to Rachel. Two simple but useful examples for such functions are OT and OLE. In this work, we consider the *reusable* extension of such sender-receiver functions, allowing Sam to invoke the function on polynomially many inputs, where Rachel's input is fixed. In each such invocation, Rachel obtains a separate output. We will sometimes use an r-prefix (as in rOT, rOLE, or rNISC) to stress that we consider the reusable variant.

3.1   Sender-Receiver Functions and Reusable Two-Party Computation

In this section we give a generic definition of reusable non-interactive secure computation (rNISC). Our complete rNISC construction for arbitrary functions is quite complex. To make it as modular as possible, we define intermediate functionalities, namely rNISC for arithmetic circuits (see the full version) and linear functions (see Sect. 3.2).

Notation 1 (Sender-receiver functions). *A sender-receiver function is specified by three sets R_{in}, S_{in}, R_{out} and a mapping $f : R_{in} \times S_{in} \to R_{out}$. The intuition is that we have two parties: a receiver Rachel and a sender Sam. Rachel chooses an input $x \in R_{in}$, Sam chooses an input $y \in S_{in}$, and Rachel learns the corresponding output $z := f(x, y) \in R_{out}$.*

Functionality $\mathcal{F}_{rNISC}^{(F)}$

Parametrized by a sender-receiver function $F = (R_{in}, S_{in}, R_{out}, f)$ in the sense of Notation 1.

Choice phase:

- Upon receiving input (sid, x) from Rachel where $x \in R_{in}$ and sid is a session identifier, store (sid, x), send $(sid, \texttt{initialized})$ to the adversary, and ignore any further inputs $(sid, \tilde{x})$ from Rachel with the same session identifier sid.

Send phases:

- Upon receiving input (sid, y, i) from Sam where $(y, i) \in S_{in} \times \mathbb{N}$ and sid is a session identifier, record (sid, y, i), send $(sid, \texttt{sent}, i)$ to the adversary, and ignore any further inputs $(sid, \tilde{y}, i)$ from Sam with the same session identifier sid and the same value of i.
- Upon receiving a message $(sid, \texttt{Delivery}, i)$ from the adversary, verify that there are stored inputs (sid, x) from Rachel and (sid, y, i) from Sam; otherwise ignore that message. Next, compute $z := f(x, y)$, send (sid, z, i) to Rachel, and ignore further messages $(sid, \texttt{Delivery}, i)$ from the adversary with the same session identifier sid and the same value of i.

Fig. 2. Generic ideal functionality for reusable non-interactive secure computation.

We emphasize that it is not enforced that the receiver's input x is fixed before the sender chooses an input y for a corresponding send phase. Neither do we forbid that the receiver provides an input (sid', x) after having learned an output (sid, z, i), as long as $sid \neq sid'$. Our main application just provides a setting where all receiver inputs are chosen before the sender takes any action, but this is not required for the security proofs of our protocols.

The ideal functionality for reusable NISC tailored to arithmetic circuit evaluation is formally defined in the full version.

3.2   Reusable Oblivious Linear Function Evaluation

We aim at an OLE-based implementation of $\mathcal{F}_{\mathrm{rNISC}}^{(\Phi)}$ for arbitrary arithmetic circuits Φ over a given ring $\mathcal{R}$, where the ring size $|\mathcal{R}|$ is determined by a statistical security parameter. More particularly, the security parameter is $\log |\mathcal{R}|$. However, we will need to restrict ourself to circuits Φ that are given as collections of formulas (i.e., the underlying graph G is a forest).

The primitive we take for granted lets Rachel pick an input $x \in \mathcal{R}$ and then Sam send his tuples $(a, b) \in \mathcal{R} \times \mathcal{R}$, such that she learns the corresponding OLE-outputs $a \cdot x + b$. In particular, Sam can send several tuples (a, b) for the same receiver input x. In other words, the ideal functionality for oblivious linear function evaluation with reusable receiver input is another special instance of the functionality $\mathcal{F}_{\mathrm{rNISC}}^{(F)}$ from Fig. 2, namely with $S_{\mathrm{in}} = \mathcal{R} \times \mathcal{R}$, $R_{\mathrm{in}} = R_{\mathrm{out}} = \mathcal{R}$, and $f : R_{\mathrm{in}} \times S_{\mathrm{in}} \to R_{\mathrm{out}}$, $(x, (a, b)) \mapsto a \cdot x + b$ (Fig. 3).

Functionality $\mathcal{F}_{\mathrm{rOLE}}^{(\mathcal{R})}$

Parametrized by a finite ring $\mathcal{R}$.

Setup/choice phase:

- Upon receiving input (sid, x) from Rachel where $x \in \mathcal{R}$ and $sid \in \mathbb{N}$ is a session identifier, store (sid, x), send $(sid, \texttt{initialized})$ to the adversary and ignore any further inputs from Rachel with the same session identifier sid.

Send phases:

- Upon receiving input (sid, a, b, i) from Sam where $(a, b, i) \in \mathcal{R} \times \mathcal{R} \times \mathbb{N}$ and sid is a session identifier, store (sid, a, b, i), send $(sid, \texttt{sent}, i)$ to the adversary, and ignore any further inputs from Sam with the same session identifier sid and the same value of i.
- Upon receiving a message $(sid, \texttt{Delivery}, i)$ from the adversary where $i \in \mathbb{N}$ and sid is a session identifier, verify that there are stored inputs (sid, x) from Rachel and (sid, a, b, i) from Sam; otherwise ignore that message. Next, compute $z := a \cdot x + b$, send (sid, z, i) to Rachel, and ignore further messages $(sid, \texttt{Delivery}, i)$ from the adversary with the same session identifier sid and the same value of i.

Fig. 3. Ideal functionality for reusable oblivious linear function evaluation over a ring $\mathcal{R}$.

4   A Reusable OLE Construction Based on Paillier

In this section, we show a reusable OLE construction Π_{rOLE} based on the Paillier assumption. Our construction proceeds as follows.

- CRSSetup(1^λ): Sample primes p', q' of the appropriate length for security parameter k such that $p = 2p' + 1, q = 2q' + 1$ are also primes. Let $N = pq$, $h = N + 1$ and $T = 2^\lambda N^2$. All operations will be in $\mathbb{Z}_{N^2}$ unless otherwise specified. Sample $w', W_0' \leftarrow \mathbb{Z}_{N^2}^*$ and let $w = (w')^{2N}, W_0 = (W_0')^{2N} h$. Output $crs = (N, h, w, W_0, T)$.
- CRSDualSetup(1^λ): Sample N, h, w, T the same way as in CRSSetup(1^λ). Sample $W_0' \leftarrow \mathbb{Z}_{N^2}^*$ and let $W_0 = (W_0')^{2N}$. Output $crs = (N, h, w, W_0, T)$.
- ReceiverRequest(crs, x): Parse $crs = (N, h, w, W_0, T)$. Sample $sk_1, sk_2, x_1 \leftarrow [T]$, let $x_2 := x - x_1$. Send $W_1 = w^{sk_1} W_0^{-x_1}$ and $W_2 = w^{sk_2} W_0^{-x_2}$ to the sender. Output state (sk_1, sk_2, x_1, x_2).
- SenderResponse($crs, (W_1, W_2), a, b$): Parse $crs = (N, h, w, W_0, T)$. Sample $r \leftarrow [T]$, $b_1 \leftarrow \mathbb{Z}_N$. Let $b_2 := b - b_1$. Send $v = w^r$, $V_0 = W_0^r h^a$, $V_1 = W_1^r h^{b_1}$ and $V_2 = W_2^r h^{b_2}$ to the receiver.
- ReceiverReceive($crs, (v, V_0, V_1, V_2), (sk_1, sk_2, x_1, x_2)$): Compute $Z_1 = V_0^{x_1} V_1/v^{sk_1}$ and $Z_2 = V_0^{x_2} V_1/v^{sk_2}$. If it is not the case that Z_1^2 and Z_2^2 are of the form $1 + z_1 N$ and $1 + z_2 N$ for some $z_1, z_2 \in \mathbb{Z}_N$, then output $\perp$. Otherwise output $z = (z_1 + z_2)/2$.

We first show correctness when both parties are honest. Then the response is computed as follows, for $i \in \{0, 1\}$

$$
\begin{aligned}
Z_i &= V_0^{x_i} V_i / v^{sk_i} && \text{(from ReceiverReceive)} \\
&= (W_0^r h^a)^{x_i} W_i^r h^{b_i}/(w^r)^{sk_i} && \text{(from SenderResponse)} \\
&= (W_0^{x_i} W_i / w^{sk_i})^r h^{ax_i + b_i} \\
&= (w^{sk_i}/w^{sk_i})^r h^{ax_i + b_i} && \text{(from ReceiverRequest)} \\
&= h^{ax_i + b_i}.
\end{aligned}
$$

Note that $(Z_i)^2 = h^{2(ax_i + b_i)} = 1 + 2(ax_i + b_i)N$. So the $z_i = 2(ax_i + b_i)$ and the receiver will output $z = (z_1 + z_2)/2 = a(x_1 + x_2) + (b_1 + b_2) = ax + b \mod N$.

Theorem 4.1. *Π_{rOLE} is a UC-secure realization of the reusable OLE functionality $\mathcal{F}_{\text{rOLE}}$ over the ring $\mathbb{Z}_N$. Moreover, the statistical simulation error against malicious receiver is negligible when the CRS is generated by CRSSetup; the statistical simulation error against malicious sender is negligible when the CRS is generated by CRSDualSetup.*

4.1   Indistinguishability of CRS

Lemma 4.2. *The CRS generated from CRSDualSetup is indistinguishable from the CRS generated by CRSSetup as long as the decisional composite residuosity assumption (DCRA) holds.*

Proof. Let N, h, w, T be generated as in CRSSetup, and W'_0 be sampled uniformly from $\mathbb{Z}^*_{N^2}$. By DCRA, W'_0 and $(W'_0)^N$ are indistinguishable even given N, h, w, T. Therefore, $(W'_0)^2$ and $(W'_0)^{2N}$ are indistinguishable, and $(W'_0)^2h$ and $(W'_0)^{2N}h$ are also indistinguishable. Moreover, $(W'_0)^2$ equals $(W'_0)^2h$ in distribution as $h = h^{N+1} = (h^{\frac{N+1}{2}})^2$ is also a quadratic residue.

In a nutshell,

$$\underbrace{\left[\; W_0 = (W'_0)^{2N} \;\right]}_{\text{generated by CRSDualSetup}} \approx_C \underbrace{\left[W_0 = (W'_0)^2 \right] \overset{d}{=} \left[W_0 = (W'_0)^2 h \right]}_{\text{a random quadratic residue}} \approx_C \underbrace{\left[\; W_0 = (W'_0)^{2N} h \;\right]}_{\text{generated by CRSSetup}}.$$

The CRS distributions produced by CRSSetup and CRSDualSetup are indistinguishable. Thus the statistical UC-security against malicious sender in dual mode implies the computational version of the same security in primal mode; and vice versa, the statistical UC-security against malicious receiver in primal mode implies the computational version of the same security in dual mode. Moreover, the computational UC-security would be preserved if the CRS is sampled from any other computationally indistinguishable distribution.

4.2 Statistical Security Against Malicious Receiver

Let $G_{4p'q'}$ be the subgroup of $\mathbb{Z}^*_{N^2}$ consisting of elements of the form $w = (w')^N$ for $w' \in \mathbb{Z}^*_{N^2}$. $G_{4p'q'}$ is isomorphic to $\mathbb{Z}^*_N$ and $\mathbb{Z}_{p'} \times \mathbb{Z}_2 \times \mathbb{Z}_{q'} \times \mathbb{Z}_2$. Consider the following simulator $\mathcal{S}$.

- CRS is generated as in CRSSetup, but stores the factorization of N.
- When the adversary sends (w, W_1, W_2), the simulator proceeds as follows: Use the factorization of N to compute $U_0, U_1, U_2 \in G_{4p'q'}$ and $\hat{x}_1, \hat{x}_2 \in \mathbb{Z}_N$ such that $W_0 = U_0h$, $W_1 = U_1h^{-\hat{x}_1}$ and $W_2 = U_2h^{-\hat{x}_2}$. Send $\hat{x}_1 + \hat{x}_2$ to $\mathcal{F}$.
- When receive z from $\mathcal{F}$: Sample random $r \leftarrow \mathbb{Z}_{2p'q'}$, $s_0, s_1 \leftarrow \mathbb{Z}_N$, and compute

$$v = w^r,$$
$$V_0 = U_0^r h^{s_0},$$
$$V_1 = U_1^r h^{s_1},$$
$$V_2 = U_2^r h^{z - s_0(\hat{x}_1 + \hat{x}_2) - s_1}.$$

Send (v, V_0, V_1, V_2) to A.

Lemma 4.3. *The environment's view in the real world is statistically close to its view when interacting with simulator $\mathcal{S}$ and functionality $\mathcal{F}$ as defined above.*

Proof. The sender samples $r \leftarrow [T]$ in the real game. Let r' be its mod-$2p'q'$ component and r'' be its mod-N component. Since $T/2p'q'N$ is exponential in the security parameter, the joint distribution of (r', r'') is statistically close to uniform distribution over $\mathbb{Z}_{2p'q'} \times \mathbb{Z}_N$. In the real game, the sender will response

$$v = w^r \qquad\qquad\qquad = w^{r'},$$
$$V_0 = W_0{}^r h^a = U_0^r h^{r+a} \qquad = U_0^{r'} h^{r''+a},$$
$$V_1 = W_1{}^r h^{b_1} = U_1^r h^{-r\hat{x}_1+b_1} \qquad = U_1^{r'} h^{-r''\hat{x}_1+b_1},$$
$$V_2 = W_2{}^r h^{b_2} = U_2^r h^{-r\hat{x}_2+b_2} \qquad = U_2^{r'} h^{-r''\hat{x}_2+b_2}.$$

Now we will argue that the environment's view here is identical to its view when interacting with simulator $\mathcal{S}$ and functionality $\mathcal{F}$. Set $s_0 := r'' + a$ and $s_1 := -r''\hat{x}_1 + b_1$. Then (s_0, s_1) is uniformly random in $\mathbb{Z}_N \times \mathbb{Z}_N$ due to the (uniform) randomness of r'' and b_1. The resulting (v, V_0, V_1, V_2) is as follows:

$$v = w^{r'},$$
$$V_0 = U_0^{r'} h^{r''+a} = U_0^{r'} h^{s_0},$$
$$V_1 = U_1^{r'} h^{-r''\hat{x}_1+b_1} = U_1^{r'} h^{s_1},$$
$$V_2 = U_2^{r'} h^{-r''\hat{x}_2+b_2} = U_2^{r'} h^{-r''\hat{x}_1+b-b_1} = U_2^{r'} h^{-r''(\hat{x}_1+\hat{x}_2)+b-s_1}$$
$$= U_2^{r'} h^{(a-s_0)(\hat{x}_1+\hat{x}_2)+b-s_1} = U_2^{r'} h^{z-s_0(\hat{x}_1+\hat{x}_2)-s_1}$$

for $z := a(\hat{x}_1 + \hat{x}_2) + b$. Finally, note that this is exactly the distribution that would be produced by the simulator.

4.3   Statistical Security Against Malicious Sender in Dual Mode

The group $\mathbb{Z}_{N^2}^*$ is isomorphic to $\mathbb{Z}_N \times (\mathbb{Z}_2)^2 \times \mathbb{Z}_{p'q'}$. Thus it can be decomposed into the following three groups. Let G_N be the subgroup of $\mathbb{Z}_{N^2}^*$ expended by h, which is isomorphic to $\mathbb{Z}_N$. Let G_4 be the subgroup of $\mathbb{Z}_{N^2}^*$ consisting of elements of the form $x = x'^{p'q'N}$ for $x' \in \mathbb{Z}_{N^2}^*$, which is isomorphic to $\mathbb{Z}_2 \times \mathbb{Z}_2$. Let $G_{p'q'}$ be the subgroup of $\mathbb{Z}_{N^2}^*$ consisting of elements of the form $x = x'^{2N}$ for $x' \in \mathbb{Z}_{N^2}^*$, which is isomorphic to $\mathbb{Z}_{p'q'}$. For every element $x \in \mathbb{Z}_{N^2}^*$, there exists an unique decomposition $(a, b, c) \in G_{p'q'} \times G_4 \times \mathbb{Z}_N$ such that $x = ab(1 + cN)$.

Consider the following simulator $\mathcal{S}$.

- To generate the CRS, the simulator generates N, h, w, T as in CRSDualSetup. It then sample random $sk_0 \leftarrow \mathbb{Z}_{p'q'}^*$, let $W_0 = w^{sk_0}$, and outputs $crs = (N, h, w, W_0, T)$.
- The simulator generates W_1, W_2 as follows: sample random $sk_1', sk_2' \leftarrow \mathbb{Z}_{p'q'}$ and send $W_1 = w^{sk_1'}$ and $W_2 = w^{sk_2'}$.
- When the adversary responses (v, V_0, V_1, V_2), proceed as follows: Compute $C_0 = V_0/v^{sk_0}$, $C_1 = V_1/v^{sk_1'}$, and $C_2 = V_2/v^{sk_2'}$. If it is not the case that C_0^2, C_1^2, and C_2^2 are of the form $1 + c_0 N$, $1 + c_1 N$ and $1 + c_2 N$ for some $c_0, c_1, c_2 \in \mathbb{Z}_N$, then send $\perp$ to $\mathcal{F}$. Otherwise send $c_0/2$ and $(c_1 + c_2)/2$ to $\mathcal{F}$.

Lemma 4.4. *The environment's view when interacting with simulator $\mathcal{S}$ and $\mathcal{F}$ as defined above, is statistically close to its view in the real game when the CRS is generated by* CRSDualSetup.

Proof. The CRS produced by the simulator $\mathcal{S}$ is statistically close to the CRS produced by CRSDualSetup. CRSDualSetup generates W_0 as a fresh sample from uniform distribution over $G_{p'q'}$. When w is a generator of $G_{p'q'}$, which happens with overwhelming probability $1 - \frac{1}{p'} - \frac{1}{q'}$, the simulator will also sample W_0 uniformly from $G_{p'q'}$.

We consider a variation of the real game where the receiver samples (sk_1, sk_2, x_1) from $\mathbb{Z}_{p'q'} \times \mathbb{Z}_{p'q'}$ In the real game, the receiver will sends $W_1 = w^{sk_1} W_0^{-x_1} = w^{sk_1 - sk_0 x_1}$ and $W_2 = w^{sk_2} W_0^{-x_2} = w^{sk_2 - sk_0 x_2}$. Let $sk'_1 := sk_1 - sk_0 x_1 \mod p'q'$, $sk'_2 := sk_2 - sk_0 x_2 \mod p'q'$, then (sk'_1, sk'_2, x_1) is statistically close to the uniform distribution over $\mathbb{Z}_{p'q'} \times \mathbb{Z}_{p'q'} \times [T]$, and the receiver will send $W_1 = w^{sk'_1}$ and $W_2 = w^{sk'_2}$, which is the same as what the simulator $\mathcal{S}$ will send.

Finally, the environment responses the receiver with message (v, V_0, V_1, V_2). We show how the receiver's behavior is simulated with negligible statistical error. The simulator defines intermediate variables $C_0 = V_0/v^{sk_0}, C_1 = V_1/v^{sk'_1}, C_2 = V_2/v^{sk'_2}$. The intermediate variables used by the receiver can be expressed as

$$Z_i = V_0^{x_i} V_i / v^{sk_i} = V_0^{x_i} V_i / v^{sk_0 x_i + sk'_i} = (C_0)^{x_i} C_i.$$

The receiver in the real game will abort unless both $(Z_1)^2$ and $(Z_2)^2$ lay inside G_N. We decompose $(C_0)^2, (C_1)^2, (C_2)^2$ into their components in $G_{p'q'}, G_4, G_N$. Let $D_0, D_1, D_2 \in G_{p'q'}$, $c_0, c_1, c_2 \in \mathbb{Z}_N$ be such that $(C_i)^2 = D_i(1 + c_i N)$, note that squaring erases the component in G_4.

In the case when $D_0 = D_1 = D_2 = 1$, the receiver will compute $(Z_1)^2 = 1 + (c_0 x_1 + c_1)N$ and $(Z_2)^2 = 1 + (c_0 x_2 + c_2)N$, then output

$$z = (z_1 + z_2)/2 = \frac{c_0 x_1 + c_1 + c_0 x_2 + c_2}{2} = c_0 x + (c_1 + c_2)/2.$$

In the ideal world, the simulator will feed c_0 and $(c_1 + c_2)/2$ to the functionality $\mathcal{F}$, and the functionality will produce the same output.

In the case when at least one of D_0, D_1, D_2 is not the identity element, the simulator $\mathcal{S}$ will output $\bot$. We show the receiver will also abort with overwhelming probability. W.l.o.g. assume $(D_0, D_1) \neq (1, 1)$, the receiver will abort if $(Z_1)^2 \notin G_N$ where

$$(Z_1)^2 = (C_0)^{2x_i} C_1 = (D_0)^{x_1} D_1 h^{c_0 x_1 + c_1}.$$

This condition is satisfied with overwhelming probability as x_1 is uniformly random in $[T]$.

Acknowledgements. Y. Dodis was supported in part by gifts from VMware Labs, Facebook and Google, and NSF grants 1314568, 1619158, 1815546. Y. Ishai was supported by ERC Project NTSC (742754), ISF grant 1709/14, NSF-BSF grant 2015782, and a grant from the Ministry of Science and Technology, Israel and Department of Science and Technology, Government of India. D. Kraschewski Supported by the European Union's Tenth Framework Programme (FP10/2010-2016) under grant agreement no. 259426 - ERC Cryptography and Complexity. Work mostly done while at the Technion. T. Liu was supported in part by NSF Grants CNS-1350619, CNS-1414119 and CNS-1718161, an MIT-IBM grant and a DARPA Young Faculty Award. R. Ostrovsky was supported by NSF grant 1619348, BSF grant 2015782, DARPA SafeWare subcontract to Galois Inc., DARPA SPAWAR contract N66001-15-C-4065, JP Morgan Faculty Research Award, OKAWA Foundation Research Award, IBM Faculty Research Award, Xerox Faculty Research Award, B. John Garrick Foundation Award, Teradata Research Award, and Lockheed-Martin Corporation Research Award. The views expressed are those of the authors and do not reflect position of the Department of Defense or the U.S. Government. V. Vaikuntanathan was supported in part by NSF Grants CNS-1350619, CNS-1414119 and CNS-1718161, an MIT-IBM grant and a DARPA Young Faculty Award.

References

1. Afshar, A., Mohassel, P., Pinkas, B., Riva, B.: Non-interactive secure computation based on cut-and-choose. In: Nguyen, P.Q., Oswald, E. (eds.) EUROCRYPT 2014. LNCS, vol. 8441, pp. 387–404. Springer, Heidelberg (2014). https://doi.org/10.1007/978-3-642-55220-5_22

2. Aiello, B., Ishai, Y., Reingold, O.: Priced oblivious transfer: how to sell digital goods. In: Pfitzmann, B. (ed.) EUROCRYPT 2001. LNCS, vol. 2045, pp. 119–135. Springer, Heidelberg (2001). https://doi.org/10.1007/3-540-44987-6_8

3. Applebaum, B., Damgård, I., Ishai, Y., Nielsen, M., Zichron, L.: Secure arithmetic computation with constant computational overhead. In: Katz, J., Shacham, H. (eds.) CRYPTO 2017, Part I. LNCS, vol. 10401, pp. 223–254. Springer, Cham (2017). https://doi.org/10.1007/978-3-319-63688-7_8

4. Applebaum, B., Ishai, Y., Kushilevitz, E.: How to garble arithmetic circuits. SIAM J. Comput. **43**(2), 905–929 (2014)

5. Bellare, M., Micali, S., Ostrovsky, R.: The (true) complexity of statistical zero knowledge. In: Ortiz, H. (ed.) Proceedings of the 22nd Annual ACM Symposium on Theory of Computing, Baltimore, Maryland, USA, 13–17 May 1990 (1990)

6. Blum, M., Feldman, P., Micali, S.: Non-interactive zero-knowledge and its applications (extended abstract). In: Simon, J. (ed.) Proceedings of the 20th Annual ACM Symposium on Theory of Computing, Chicago, Illinois, USA, 2–4 May 1988 (1988)

7. Bootle, J., Cerulli, A., Ghadafi, E., Groth, J., Hajiabadi, M., Jakobsen, S.K.: Linear-time zero-knowledge proofs for arithmetic circuit satisfiability. In: Takagi, T., Peyrin, T. (eds.) ASIACRYPT 2017, Part III. LNCS, vol. 10626, pp. 336–365. Springer, Cham (2017). https://doi.org/10.1007/978-3-319-70700-6_12

8. Boyle, E., Couteau, G., Gilboa, N., Ishai, Y.: Compressing vector OLE. In: Proceedings of the 2018 ACM SIGSAC Conference on Computer and Communications Security, CCS 2018, Toronto, ON, Canada, 15–19 October 2018 (2018)

9. Brakerski, Z., Vaikuntanathan, V.: Efficient fully homomorphic encryption from (standard) LWE. In: IEEE 52nd Annual Symposium on Foundations of Computer Science, FOCS 2011, Palm Springs, CA, USA, 22–25 October 2011 (2011)

10. Canetti, R., Chen, Y., Holmgren, J., Lombardi, A., Rothblum, G.N., Rothblum, R.D.: Fiat-Shamir from simpler assumptions. Cryptology ePrint Archive, Report 2018/1004 (2018)

11. Chaidos, P., Couteau, G.: Efficient designated-verifier non-interactive zero-knowledge proofs of knowledge. In: Nielsen, J.B., Rijmen, V. (eds.) EUROCRYPT 2018, Part III. LNCS, vol. 10822, pp. 193–221. Springer, Cham (2018). https://doi.org/10.1007/978-3-319-78372-7_7

12. Döttling, N., Ghosh, S., Nielsen, J.B., Nilges, T., Trifiletti, R.: TinyOLE: efficient actively secure two-party computation from oblivious linear function evaluation. In: CCS 2017 (2017)

13. Döttling, N., Kraschewski, D., Müller-Quade, J.: Statistically secure linear-rate dimension extension for oblivious affine function evaluation. In: Smith, A. (ed.) ICITS 2012. LNCS, vol. 7412, pp. 111–128. Springer, Heidelberg (2012). https://doi.org/10.1007/978-3-642-32284-6_7

14. Genkin, D., Ishai, Y., Prabhakaran, M., Sahai, A., Tromer, E.: Circuits resilient to additive attacks with applications to secure computation. In: STOC 2014 (2014)

15. Gennaro, R., Gentry, C., Parno, B.: Non-interactive verifiable computing: outsourcing computation to untrusted workers. In: Rabin, T. (ed.) CRYPTO 2010. LNCS, vol. 6223, pp. 465–482. Springer, Heidelberg (2010). https://doi.org/10.1007/978-3-642-14623-7_25

16. Gentry, C.: Fully homomorphic encryption using ideal lattices. In: Proceedings of the 41st Annual ACM Symposium on Theory of Computing, STOC 2009, Bethesda, MD, USA, 31 May–2 June 2009 (2009)

17. Ghosh, S., Nielsen, J.B., Nilges, T.: Maliciously secure oblivious linear function evaluation with constant overhead. In: Takagi, T., Peyrin, T. (eds.) ASIACRYPT 2017. LNCS, vol. 10624, pp. 629–659. Springer, Cham (2017). https://doi.org/10.1007/978-3-319-70694-8_22

18. Ishai, Y., Kushilevitz, E.: Perfect constant-round secure computation via perfect randomizing polynomials. In: Widmayer, P., Eidenbenz, S., Triguero, F., Morales, R., Conejo, R., Hennessy, M. (eds.) ICALP 2002. LNCS, vol. 2380, pp. 244–256. Springer, Heidelberg (2002). https://doi.org/10.1007/3-540-45465-9_22

19. Ishai, Y., Kushilevitz, E., Ostrovsky, R., Prabhakaran, M., Sahai, A.: Efficient non-interactive secure computation. In: Paterson, K.G. (ed.) EUROCRYPT 2011. LNCS, vol. 6632, pp. 406–425. Springer, Heidelberg (2011). https://doi.org/10.1007/978-3-642-20465-4_23

20. Ishai, Y., Kushilevitz, E., Ostrovsky, R., Sahai, A.: Zero-knowledge proofs from secure multiparty computation. SIAM J. Comput. **39**(3), 1121–1152 (2009)

21. Ishai, Y., Prabhakaran, M., Sahai, A.: Founding cryptography on oblivious transfer – efficiently. In: Wagner, D.A. (ed.) CRYPTO 2008. LNCS, vol. 5157, pp. 572–591. Springer, Heidelberg (2008). https://doi.org/10.1007/978-3-540-85174-5_32

22. Kim, S., Wu, D.J.: Multi-theorem preprocessing NIZKs from lattices. In: Shacham, H., Boldyreva, A. (eds.) CRYPTO 2018, Part II. LNCS, vol. 10992, pp. 733–765. Springer, Cham (2018). https://doi.org/10.1007/978-3-319-96881-0_25

23. Lindell, Y., Pinkas, B.: A proof of security of Yao's protocol for two-party computation. J. Cryptol. **22**(2), 161–188 (2009)

24. Naor, M., Pinkas, B.: Efficient oblivious transfer protocols. In: Proceedings of the Twelfth Annual Symposium on Discrete Algorithms, Washington, DC, USA, 7–9 January 2001 (2001)

25. Paillier, P.: Public-key cryptosystems based on composite degree residuosity classes. In: Stern, J. (ed.) EUROCRYPT 1999. LNCS, vol. 1592, pp. 223–238. Springer, Heidelberg (1999). https://doi.org/10.1007/3-540-48910-X_16

26. Peikert, C., Vaikuntanathan, V., Waters, B.: A framework for efficient and composable oblivious transfer. In: Wagner, D. (ed.) CRYPTO 2008. LNCS, vol. 5157, pp. 554–571. Springer, Heidelberg (2008). https://doi.org/10.1007/978-3-540-85174-5_31

27. Rivest, R.L., Adleman, L., Dertouzos, M.L.: On data banks and privacy homomorphisms. In: DeMillo, R.A., Dobkin, D.P., Jones, A.K., Lipton, R.J. (eds.) Foundations of Secure Computation (1978)

28. Rothblum, R.D., Sealfon, A., Sotiraki, K.: Towards non-interactive zero-knowledge for NP from LWE. IACR Cryptology ePrint Archive 2018, 240 (2018)

29. Yao, A.C.C.: How to generate and exchange secrets (extended abstract). In: Proceedings of FOCS 1986 (1986)

Efficient Pseudorandom Correlation Generators: Silent OT Extension and More

Elette Boyle[1], Geoffroy Couteau[2(✉)], Niv Gilboa[3], Yuval Ishai[4], Lisa Kohl[2], and Peter Scholl[5(✉)]

[1] IDC Herzliya, Herzliya, Israel
[2] Karlsruhe Institute of Technology, Karlsruhe, Germany
geoffroy.couteau@kit.edu
[3] Ben-Gurion University of the Negev, Beersheba, Israel
[4] Technion, Haifa, Israel
[5] Aarhus University, Aarhus, Denmark
peter.scholl@cs.au.dk

Abstract. Secure multiparty computation (MPC) often relies on correlated randomness for better efficiency and simplicity. This is particularly useful for MPC with no honest majority, where input-independent correlated randomness enables a lightweight "non-cryptographic" online phase once the inputs are known. However, since the amount of randomness typically scales with the circuit size of the function being computed, securely generating correlated randomness forms an efficiency bottleneck, involving a large amount of communication and storage.

A natural tool for addressing the above limitations is a *pseudorandom correlation generator* (PCG). A PCG allows two or more parties to securely generate long sources of useful correlated randomness via a local expansion of correlated short seeds and no interaction. PCGs enable MPC with *silent preprocessing*, where a small amount of interaction used for securely sampling the seeds is followed by silent local generation of correlated pseudorandomness.

A concretely efficient PCG for Vector-OLE correlations was recently obtained by Boyle et al. (CCS 2018) based on variants of the learning parity with noise (LPN) assumption over large fields. In this work, we initiate a systematic study of PCGs and present concretely efficient constructions for several types of useful MPC correlations. We obtain the following main contributions:

- **PCG foundations.** We give a general security definition for PCGs. Our definition suffices for any MPC protocol satisfying a stronger security requirement that is met by existing protocols. We prove that a stronger security requirement is indeed necessary, and justify our PCG definition by ruling out a stronger and more natural definition.
- **Silent OT extension.** We present the first concretely efficient PCG for oblivious transfer correlations. Its security is based on a variant of the binary LPN assumption and any correlation-robust hash function. We expect it to provide a faster alternative to the IKNP OT extension protocol (Crypto 2003) when communication is the

© International Association for Cryptologic Research 2019
A. Boldyreva and D. Micciancio (Eds.): CRYPTO 2019, LNCS 11694, pp. 489–518, 2019.
https://doi.org/10.1007/978-3-030-26954-8_16

bottleneck. We present several applications, including protocols for non-interactive zero-knowledge with bounded-reusable preprocessing from binary LPN, and concretely efficient related-key oblivious pseudorandom functions.

- **PCGs for simple 2-party correlations.** We obtain PCGs for several other types of useful 2-party correlations, including (authenticated) one-time truth-tables and Beaver triples. While the latter PCGs are slower than our PCG for OT, they are still practically feasible. These PCGs are based on a host of assumptions and techniques, including specialized homomorphic secret sharing schemes and pseudorandom generators tailored to their structure.
- **Multiparty correlations.** We obtain PCGs for multiparty correlations that can be used to make the (input-dependent) online communication of MPC protocols scale *linearly* with the number of parties, instead of quadratically.

1   Introduction

Correlated secret randomness is a valuable resource for secure multi-party computation (MPC). A simple example is a common random key that is given to two parties, who can later use it as a one-time pad for secure message transmission. In the context of MPC, a more useful example is a random *oblivious transfer* (OT) correlation, in which one party is given a pair of random bits (more generally, strings) (s_0, s_1) and the other party is given the pair (r, s_r) for a random bit r. The OT correlation can serve as a basis for general MPC protocols with no honest majority [40,49,54]. Other kinds of two-party correlations that are useful for MPC include *oblivious linear-function evaluation* (OLE) correlations [3,50,58], *multiplication triples* (also known as "Beaver triples") [8,10,29], and *one-time truth tables* [28,30,47].

The above types of correlated randomness are commonly used to implement efficient MPC protocols in the *preprocessing model*. Such protocols consist of an offline, input-independent *preprocessing phase*, where many independent instances of the correlated randomness are generated, followed by a fast *online phase* that consumes this correlated randomness for the purpose of securely evaluate a given function of the inputs. In many cases, the online phase is "information-theoretic"[1] and its computational complexity is only a small-constant times higher than that of an insecure function evaluation. Most importantly for the present work, the online phase of such protocols typically outperforms all competing approaches in terms of concrete efficiency.

A major challenge in implementing such offline-online protocols is that the preprocessing phase needs to *securely* generate and store a large amount of correlated randomness. This is typically done by using a special-purpose interactive MPC protocol, which involves a significant amount of communication and computation for each gate of a circuit that should be evaluated in the online phase.

---

[1] This can be formalized by requiring that the joint states of the parties in the end of the offline phase can be swapped by *computationally indistinguishable* states, given which the online protocol is secure against computationally unbounded parties.

A dream goal would be to replace this source of correlated randomness with *short* correlated seeds, which can be "silently" expanded *without any interaction* to produce a large amount of *pseudorandom* correlated randomness. This process should emulate an ideal process for generating the target distribution not only from the point of view of outsiders, but also from the point of view of *insiders* who can observe the correlated seeds. We refer to such an object as a *pseudorandom correlation generator*, or PCG for short.

A bit more precisely, a two-party PCG is defined as follows. Let (R_0, R_1) be a target correlation, defined by some efficient sampling algorithm $\mathcal{C}$ that on input 1^λ outputs a pair of correlated strings (r_0, r_1). For instance, $\mathcal{C}(1^\lambda)$ may output $n = \lambda^3$ independent instances of an OT correlation. A PCG is a pair of efficient algorithms (Gen, Expand) such that:

- Gen samples a pair of short correlated seeds $(k_0, k_1) \xleftarrow{\$} \mathsf{Gen}(1^\lambda)$,
- Expand is a *local* deterministic seed expansion algorithm mapping k_i to $r_i \leftarrow \mathsf{Expand}(i, k_i)$, where $|r_i| > |k_i|$.

We would like the outputs (r_0, r_1) resulting from this process to be "indistinguishable" from an ideal sample (R_0, R_1) generated by $\mathcal{C}(1^\lambda)$, even to a party who receives one of the seeds k_b.

A useful special case of PCG was recently considered by Boyle et al. [14], who constructed (under variants of the Learning Parity with Noise assumption [12]) a concretely efficient PCG for the *vector OLE* (VOLE) correlation. The VOLE correlation over a field $\mathbb{F}$ samples a random scalar $x \in \mathbb{F}$ and vectors $\boldsymbol{u}, \boldsymbol{v} \in \mathbb{F}^n$, and outputs $r_0 = (\boldsymbol{u}, \boldsymbol{v})$ to one party (the "sender") and $r_1 = (x, \boldsymbol{w} = \boldsymbol{u}x + \boldsymbol{v})$ to the other party (the "receiver"). The VOLE correlation is useful for secure computation of functions that employ scalar-vector products over large fields, such as ones arising in the context of linear algebra and keyword search [3].

Designing efficient PCGs for a wider class of correlations is strongly motivated by the goal of improving the efficiency of *general* MPC in the preprocessing model, where the preprocessing phase is used to securely generate the PCG seeds. We refer to this as *MPC with silent preprocessing*. More concretely, such a protocol consists of three phases: (1) an interactive *setup phase* for securely distributing the seed generation algorithm Gen; in the end of this phase, which involves a small amount of communication, only the short seeds are stored for later use; (2) a silent *seed expansion* phase, where the seeds are expanded into long correlated randomness via a local computation of Expand and without any interaction; (3) a final *online phase* where the correlated randomness is consumed to evaluate a given function of the inputs. One could employ Phase 1 when deciding that an MPC interaction *might* take place in the future, Phase 2 when interaction seems likely to take place in the near future, and Phase 3 to carry out the MPC interaction once the inputs are available. The low communication footprint of silent preprocessing can eliminate traffic analysis attacks that aim to anticipate future MPC plans. Finally, another benefit of the PCG-based approach is that it can help reduce the cost of protecting MPC protocols against malicious parties. Indeed, since Phase 2 does not involve any interaction, it suffices to protect Phase 1 and Phase 3 against malicious parties, which is typically much cheaper.

Several different kinds of PCG constructions are implicit in the MPC literature. These include PCGs for simple multi-party linear correlations from any pseudorandom generator [26,38], for general correlations from indistinguishability obfuscation [42,45], for so-called "bilinear" correlations from homomorphic secret sharing [16], for restricted variants of OT correlations from key-homomorphic pseudorandom functions [60] and, most recently, for VOLE correlation from LPN [14]. With the exception of linear multi-party correlations [26,38] and VOLE correlations [14], none of these prior constructions seem appealing from a practical point of view. In particular, there was no prior approach (even a heuristic one) for constructing a concretely efficient PCG for OT correlations.

1.1 Our Contributions

In this work, we initiate a more systematic study of pseudorandom correlation generators. Our contributions are on both the foundational side, where we present new definitions, impossibility results and connections with other primitives, and the applied side, with concretely efficient constructions for commonly used MPC correlations, including OT correlations and others. Our most practical PCG constructions handle restricted (yet still useful) classes of correlations, while our more general constructions can handle much larger classes of correlations, at the expense of a bigger seed size and higher computational costs (and, for some of them, public-key-style assumptions such as lattice-based or pairing-based cryptography).

We now give a more detailed account of our contributions. Unless noted otherwise, we refer to MPC with computational security against semi-honest (i.e., passive) and static (i.e., non-adaptive) adversaries who may corrupt an arbitrary subset of parties.

Foundations of Pseudorandom Correlation Generators. Our first goal is to present a general security definition for the intuitive notion of PCG described above. As pointed out in [38], this is not quite as straightforward as one might imagine, and previous works side-stepped the problem by taking an ad-hoc approach. To motivate our general definition, we start by discussing the most natural alternative.

RULING OUT A SIMULATION-BASED DEFINITION. Recall that the ultimate desire would be that in any protocol, one can securely replace an ideal correlated randomness functionality C with pseudo-randomness obtained from expanding the correlated seeds of a PCG for C. This would indeed follow from a natural simulation-based security definition for PCG as a computationally secure, dealer-assisted protocol for computing the randomized functionality defined by C. Concretely, in the two-party case, the simulation-based definition requires the existence of a simulator S such that the *real* distribution $(k_b, \mathsf{Expand}(k_{1-b}))$, where (k_0, k_1) are generated by Gen (capturing the view of a corrupted party b jointly with the output of the uncorrupted party $1-b$) is computationally indistinguishable from the *ideal* distribution $(S(r_b), r_{1-b})$, where (r_0, r_1) are sampled by $\mathcal{C}$. Unfortunately, we show (building on [45], and extending an informal argument from [38]) that such a definition is impossible to realize even for simple correlations. Intuitively, the impossibility follows from the fact that in the real distribution k_b "explains" the output of the honest party in an efficiently verifiable way, whereas such an explanation of r_{1-b} cannot be generated from r_b in the ideal distribution.

A GENERAL PCG DEFINITION. To get around the above impossibility, we present a relaxed indistinguishability-based definition of PCG security, generalizing the specialized security definition for the VOLE correlation from [14]. Our definition requires that given its PCG key k_b, corrupted party b cannot distinguish the *true* expanded output of the honest party $r_{1-b} = \mathsf{Expand}(1-b, k_{1-b})$ from a *random* output r_{1-b} consistent with the correlation $\mathcal{C}$ and its own expanded output $r_b = \mathsf{Expand}(b, k_b)$. In other words, we replace the ideal distribution in the above simulation-based definition by $(k_b, [r_{1-b} \mid R_b = \mathsf{Expand}(k_b)])$. Note that the latter distribution involves reverse-sampling from R_{1-b} conditioned on a fixed value for R_b, which may not be well-defined. However, in this work we only consider *additive* correlations, where (R_0, R_1) are additive secret shares (over a finite Abelian group) of a sample from some core distribution. For such additive correlations, the reverse-sampling is well-defined and is computationally efficient. More broadly, our general PCG definition is meaningful when this reverse-sampling is efficient.

LIMITATIONS. Our PCG definition is not good enough for generating correlated randomness in *all* applications. Indeed, the impossibility of the simulation-based definition discussed above implies such simple counterexamples for randomized functionalities. Concretely, for any $\mathcal{C}$ to which the impossibility result applies, there is a trivial MPC protocol for $\mathcal{C}$ given correlated randomness from $\mathcal{C}$ in which each party outputs its correlated randomness. However, the impossibility result shows that using *any* PCG for $\mathcal{C}$ would render this simple protocol insecure. We show, under standard cryptographic assumptions, that a similar impossibility holds even if one restricts attention to MPC for *deterministic* functionalities. Concretely, we show a protocol which uses correlated randomness $\mathcal{C}$ to realize a deterministic functionality with statistical security against malicious parties, but which becomes completely *insecure* (even against semi-honest parties) when $\mathcal{C}$ is replaced by a specific PCG for $\mathcal{C}$ that meets our indistinguishability-based definition.

A PLUG-AND-PLAY USE OF PCG. We complement the above negative results by a positive result, showing that our PCG definition does suffice to imply our "ultimate desire" in the context of most applications. Concretely, we put forward a slightly stronger security requirement for MPC with preprocessing, such that in any protocol satisfying this requirement, a PCG can be used as a drop-in replacement for correlated randomness. The stronger security requirement asserts that security still hold even if the ideal correlation functionality (R_0, R_1) is replaced by a *corruptible* functionality that allows corrupted party b to pick its own randomness r_b^*, and then delivers to the uncorrupted party a sample r_{1-b} from the conditional distribution $[r_{1-b} \mid R_b = r_b^*]$. It fortunately turns out that natural MPC protocols in the preprocessing model already satisfy this stronger security requirement. This allows for a plug-and-play use of PCGs in many application scenarios.

RELATION WITH HOMOMORPHIC SECRET SHARING. A (two-party) homomorphic secret sharing (HSS) scheme [18,21] for a function class $\mathcal{F}$ splits a secret x into two shares (x_0, x_1), such that given any $f \in \mathcal{F}$ one can efficiently evaluate *additive* shares of $f(x)$ via local computation on the shares. We show a two-way relation between PCG and HSS. First, we show that a PCG for any *additive* correlation (as defined above) can be reduced to HSS for a related function class $\mathcal{F}$, generalizing and formalizing a previous observation from [16]. In particular, HSS for general circuits implies PCG for all additive correlations, which include most of the useful MPC correlations as special cases. (This is only a feasibility result, which does not directly imply concretely efficient constructions.) Second, we show that some converse is also true: a PCG for the degree-d "tensoring" correlation, obtained by picking a random vector $X \in \mathcal{R}^n$ and outputting additive shares of all products of at most d entries of X, implies HSS for the class $\mathcal{F}$ of degree-d (n-variate) polynomials over $\mathcal{R}^n$, where the share size grows linearly with n and the homomorphic evaluation time grows linearly with n^d.

Silent OT Extension. A central contribution of this work is the first *concretely efficient* construction of PCG for the oblivious transfer (OT) correlation. From an asymptotic point of view, our PCG can achieve an arbitrary polynomial stretch, assuming: (1) The *binary* Learning Parity with Noise (LPN) assumption [12] with a conservative choice of parameters, and (2) A correlation-robust hash function [46]. The hash function primitive, which is only used in a black-box way, can be instantiated in practice by a general-purpose hash function or block cipher. Assuming LPN with a linear number of samples and inverse-polynomial noise rate holds for the dual of a near-linear time encodable code (such as the codes proposed in [1,3,34,44]), which is still a conservative assumption, the *computational* complexity of Expand is nearly linear in the output length.[2]

In a nutshell, our efficient PCG for OT applies the PCG for VOLE from [14] over a large extension field $\mathbb{F}_{2^\lambda}$, except for restricting the sender's output $\boldsymbol{u}$ to be over the base field. This yields n correlated instances of random OT that can be converted into standard OT by using a correlation-robust hash function, as in [46]. See Sect. 2 for more details.

By applying a secure two-party protocol for distributing Gen, we obtain a *silent OT extension* protocol that generates n pseudo-random OT instances using a small number of OTs, with a total of $O(n^\epsilon)$ bits of communication for any $\epsilon > 0$. This should be compared with existing OT extension protocols [9,46] that do not require the LPN assumption but where the communication complexity is bigger than n.

---

[2] In Sect. 1.1 below we describe an alternative LPN-based approach to constructing PCG for OT that dispenses with assumption (2), but requires at least quadratic computation in the output length n.

Concrete Efficiency. Our LPN-based PCG for OT is very attractive in terms of concrete efficiency, and we expect it to outperform state-of-the-art OT extension protocols [7,46,55] in settings where communication is the bottleneck. To give a few data points, our PCG can expand a pair of seeds of length 10KB into a million instances of random 128-bit string-OT, of total size 16 MB (receiver) and 32 MB (sender), in an estimated[3] time of around a second on a single core of a modern CPU. Alternatively, seeds of length 7 KB can be expanded into 65 thousand OTs at roughly half the amortized computational cost. Factoring in the cost of securely distributing Gen (with semi-honest security, building on [32]), the amortized communication complexity of our silent OT extension protocol is 0–3 bits *for each random 128-bit string-OT*. To put that into context, state-of-the-art OT extension protocols [7,46] require 128 bits of communication per random 128-bit string-OT and can generate around 10 million OTs per second [41] over a fast network, so the price we pay for the (much) lower communication complexity seems quite modest. Even for the easier case of random *bit*-OT, the best previous OT extension protocol [55] required roughly 80 bits of communication per OT.

Other PCG Constructions. We present an assortment of practically feasible PCGs for other useful two-party correlations, based on a variety of underlying tools and assumptions.

– *PCG for Constant-Degree Polynomials from LPN.* We show that a generalization of the LPN-based VOLE generator from [14] can be used to obtain a PCG for any constant-degree additive correlation, namely a correlation that additively secret-shares a vector of degree-d polynomials of a random $X \in \mathbb{F}^n$ for some constant $d \geq 2$. This PCG relies on LPN over $\mathbb{F}$ in a similar noise regime as the PCG for OT from Sect. 1.1. In fact, by increasing the computation time (but still keeping it polynomial), one can use the LPN assumption in a parameter regime that is not known to imply public-key encryption [2], let alone OT. The main caveat is that even for generating simple degree-d correlations, such as $\Omega(n)$ Beaver triples ($d = 2$), the *computational* complexity of Expand is bigger than n^d. While much slower than our PCG for OT, this construction may still be practically feasible for $d = 2$ even with reasonably large n. We leave the question of obtaining more efficient variants of this construction to future work.

  As discussed in Sect. 1.1, this PCG construction implies (2-party) HSS schemes for constant-degree polynomials from LPN. By additionally assuming a standard OT protocol, it implies secure two-party computation protocols for constant-degree polynomials in which the communication complexity is nearly linear in the input size. Using the techniques from [18,25], it also implies an "almost-sublinear" general secure computation protocol: for any

---

[3] We caution that we have not implemented our constructions. Our estimates are based on counting basic operations and estimating their cost; the actual running times may vary due to other costs we neglected such as cache misses. We leave the task of optimizing and implementing our constructions to future work.

constant $c > 1$ and layered boolean circuit of size s (and assuming binary LPN and OT), there is a secure two-party computation protocol with polynomial computation and total communication bounded by s/c. We stress again that these are mainly feasibility results because of the high computational cost of this PCG construction.

- *PCG for One-Time Truth Tables from any PRG.* One-time truth tables (OTTT) are a type of correlation that allow secure evaluation of a public lookup table in MPC, on a secret-shared input [28,30,47], and are well-suited to computations such as the S-box of AES. For MPC with active security, the correlation outputs need to be authenticated with information-theoretic MACs, as in the recent TinyTable protocol [28]. We present a very simple PCG for authenticated OTTT using only a distributed point function (DPF) [19,39], which in turn can be efficiently constructed from any pseudorandom generator (PRG). This PCG follows naturally from a building block of the silent OT extension construction (as we explain in Sect. 2). It compresses the storage cost of an authenticated OTTT from $O(\lambda n)$ bits down to $O(\lambda \log n)$ bits, for a table of size n, giving a reduction in size of over 20x for a length-256 table such as the AES S-box. There is a concretely efficient protocol to distribute the seed generator Gen with semi-honest security by using the distributed DPF key generation protocol from [32]. While a similar protocol with malicious security is considerably more expensive, even a naive approach based on general-purpose secure computation (e.g., using recent protocols such as [51]) is feasible in practice, enabling the compressed storage benefit of the PCG-based approach.

- *PCGs from Homomorphic Secret Sharing.* We give practically feasible PCG constructions for OLE and (authenticated) Beaver triple correlations, which are useful for arithmetic MPC protocols such as SPDZ [29]. For these constructions we use HSS based on ring-LWE [22,23,31] and the BGN (pairing-based) cryptosystem [13,16,18]. To expand the seeds, we rely on a multivariate quadratic (MQ) assumption based PRG, which limits the stretch to subquadratic, but allows for reasonable computational efficiency. For example, with our ring-LWE-based PCG we estimate that one should be able to expand a pair of 3 GB seeds into 17 GB of authenticated Beaver triples in a 128-bit field, at a rate of around 6 thousand triples per second; various tradeoffs are possible between seed size and computation time, and we also explore an iterative variant which produces triples in small batches. Securely computing Gen to distribute the seeds is relatively cheap compared to the expansion phase, and the overall performance should be comparable to recent work on actively secure triple generation with much more interaction [53]. With BGN, we estimate around 200 ms for computing an OLE correlation over $\mathbb{Z}_N$ for small N (say, $N < 10$). Although much more expensive than our silent OT extension, an advantage of the ring-LWE-based constructions, beyond the richer class of correlations, is that they can be extended to the *multi-party* setting, as we discuss next.

PCGs for Multi-party Correlations. Finally, we present a general transformation for extending certain classes of PCGs from the 2-party to the multi-party setting. This can be applied to PCGs for simple bilinear correlations, including VOLE and Beaver triples, giving the first non-trivial, efficient PCG constructions in the multi-party setting. The transformation applies to most of our 2-party PCGs, including the LPN-based PCG for constant-degree correlations.

On top of the silent preprocessing feature, an appealing application of our multi-party PCGs is in obtaining secure M-party computation protocols with *total* communication complexity $O(Ms + M^2 \cdot s^\epsilon)$ (for circuit size s and constant $0 < \epsilon < 1$). The $O(Ms)$ term is the cost of the (information-theoretic) online phase, and the $O(M^2 \cdot s^\epsilon)$ term is the cost of distributing the PCG seed generation, which is the only part of the protocol requiring pairwise communication. This should be contrasted with OT-based MPC protocols, which have total communication complexity $\Omega(M^2s)$ [40,43]. Protocols with such communication complexity (without the silent preprocessing feature) could previously be based on different flavors of somewhat homomorphic encryption [27,29,35]. We get the first such protocol that only relies on LPN and OT, and the first practically feasible protocol that has sublinear-communication offline phase and information-theoretic online phase (Table 1).

Table 1. Summary of the New PCG Constructions. Costs are estimated based on one core of a modern laptop.

PCG	Section 5	[15]	[15]	[15]	[15]	[15]
Assumption	LPN	PRG*	LPN	deg-d HSS + MQ/LPN	SXDH + LPN	LWE + MQ
Correlations	OT*	OTTT*	deg-d	deg-$d/2$	deg-2	deg-d
Efficiency	1M OT/s†	-	-	-	5 OLE/s‡	6000/s**
Multiparty (bilinear corr.)	✗	✗	✓	✓	✗	✓

*PRG stands for an arbitrary pseudorandom generator, OT for random oblivious transfer, and OTTT for authenticated one-time truth-table correlation.
†With average communication of 0.2 bits/OT.
‡For OLE correlation over a small (constant size) ring.
**For generating authenticated Beaver triples over a 128-bit prime field.

Additional Applications. From our silent OT extension protocol, we obtain the following additional results:

- *Oblivious Pseudorandom Functions (OPRFs).* An OPRF [36] is a two-party protocol for securely evaluating a pseudorandom function, whose key is known by one party, on a secret input known by the second party. OPRFs serve as the main building blocks in recent protocols for private set intersection [56]. Our silent OT construction can be used to obtain a form of batch OPRF with cost as little as 1 bit of communication per OPRF evaluation on a random input, leading to around a factor two reduction in communication for these protocols.

- *Reusable-Preprocessing NIZK.* Consider the following setting for non-interactive zero knowledge (NIZK) with reusable interactive setup: In an offline setup phase, before the statements to be proved are known, the prover and the verifier interact to securely generate correlated random seeds. The seeds can then be used to prove any polynomial number of statements by having the prover send a single message to the verifier for each statement. Such a notion was recently constructed in [14], building on [24], using their PCG for VOLE. Our silent OT extension can be used to obtain an improved reusable-preprocessing NIZK system for NP, under the standard LPN assumption over $\mathbb{F}_2$. As compared to the reusable NIZK of [14], our NIZK relies on a more standard assumption (LPN over $\mathbb{F}_2$ versus large $\mathbb{F}$), and the setup cost is independent of both the number of statements and their size (whereas in [14], the setup cost was independent of the number of statements, but grows linearly with a bound on their size). On the down side, our OT-based NIZK protocols do not have the computational complexity advantages of the VOLE-based constructions from [14].

- *Efficient Secure Matrix Multiplication.* As a stepping stone towards silent OT extension, we construct a PCG for a generalization of VOLE called *subfield VOLE*. This can be seen as a form of batch VOLE where the u value is reused across several instances, and can be applied to compute secret-shared tensor products and matrix multiplication more efficiently. Compared with naively using a PCG for standard VOLE, we reduce the seed size by at least a $O(\log n)$ factor.

Finally, our PCG for OTTT yields the following application.

- *Improved 2-PC with Sublinear Online Communication.* Standard approaches to secure computation with preprocessing (e.g., SPDZ) still require online communication that is linear in the circuit size. Recently, Couteau [25] demonstrated asymptotic feasibility of information-theoretic secure 2-party computation (2-PC) in the preprocessing model for a natural class of circuits (namely, "layered" circuits), with sublinear online communication, $O(s/\log\log s)$ for circuit size s. However, this comes at the cost of generating and storing $O(s^2)$ bits of correlated randomness.
  Our compressed one-time truth-table (OTTT) construction allows one to match the asymptotic complexity of [25], while reducing the amount of correlated randomness from quadratic to quasilinear in the circuit size, in exchange for settling for computational security and assuming the existence of one-way functions.

1.2 Paper Organization

In this extended abstract we only present our main techniques and results. For the full details of constructions and other results, we refer to the full version of this work [15]. We begin in Sect. 2 with an overview of our techniques, followed by preliminaries in Sect. 3. In Sect. 4, we present our PCG definition and foundational results. Section 5 contains our PCGs for subfield-VOLE and OT, leading to our silent OT extension construction.

2 Technical Overview of Constructions

In this section we give a high-level overview of the techniques that underlie our different PCG constructions.

2.1 Background

Our PCG constructions rely on different types of *homomorphic secret sharing* (HSS) and *function secret sharing* (FSS) schemes. Informally, HSS is a form of secret sharing that allows a secret x to be split up into shares k_0, k_1, such that a party holding k_i can *locally* obtain an additive secret share of $f(x)$, for some function f. FSS is the dual notion: starting with a function f, and splitting into shares f_0, f_1 such that each share f_i hides f, but can be used to obtain an additive sharing of $f(x)$ for some public input x.[4] FSS for a class of point functions (i.e., functions f which evaluate to 0 on all but a single input) is called a *distributed point function* [39], and can be constructed very efficiently based on a pseudorandom generator (PRG) [19]. There are HSS constructions for branching programs based on DDH [18] or lattices [22], or general circuits from strong forms of fully homomorphic encryption [31].

2.2 Overall Methodology

At a high level, our constructions can all be seen as examples of the following blueprint: construct an HSS scheme that can homomorphically evaluate the composition of a pseudorandom generator (PRG) with a function f that uses the expanded randomness to compute the desired correlation. This can be used to obtain PCGs for any *additive* correlation; i.e., that outputs random additive shares of some distribution. Of course, the main challenge lies in instantiating this *efficiently*, since plugging in even a low-degree PRG to an off-the-shelf HSS scheme is typically not practical. We instead use specialized HSS constructions that pair well with our carefully chosen PRGs.

As a stepping stone, our constructions implicitly construct a *compressible* form of HSS, which allows the sharing of inputs from some distribution $\mathcal{D}$, such that the share size is *smaller than* an uncompressed output of $\mathcal{D}$, and we can still compute some useful function f on the expanded inputs. We typically choose $\mathcal{D}$ to be a sparse distribution on vectors, or another similarly compressible distribution. We then convert these long $\mathcal{D}$-vectors to slightly shorter (but still long)

---

[4] FSS is actually equivalent to HSS for a related class of functions, but we differentiate between the two for convenience, depending on the applications.

random-looking vectors, by homomorphically multiplying by a compressive linear map. Under a suitable LPN-type assumption, this combination of expanding the compressed $\mathcal{D}$-vector followed by linear compression acts as a PRG in the above blueprint, and we can proceed to homomorphically compute the desired correlation.

For example, when $\mathcal{D}$ samples a sparse, low-weight vector e over $\mathbb{F}_2$, and the linear map is a random matrix H, then distinguishing $(H, e \cdot H)$ from random is as hard as the problem of decoding a random binary linear code, which corresponds to the standard LPN assumption [2,12]. Another example is when $\mathcal{D}$ outputs a *tensor product* of two short, uniform vectors. Recovering the short vectors given only $(x \otimes y) \cdot H$ is the problem of solving a random system of multivariate quadratic equations (MQ problem), which is believed to be hard for a suitable choice of parameters [4,11,57,63]. In particular, the decision version of MQ is polynomially reducible to its search version [11].

We remark that the resulting PRGs do not necessarily conform to standard metrics of simplicity, such as low degree or low locality, and in isolation may appear somewhat unnatural. This exemplifies an interesting observation that "HSS-friendliness" may indeed be a new type of metric that does not directly align with those previously studied.

2.3 Silent OT Extension

As a building block for silent OT extension, we start by constructing a PCG for a two-party correlation we call *subfield vector oblivious linear evaluation* (subfield VOLE). This correlation works over a field $\mathbb{F}_q$, and a subfield $\mathbb{F}_p$, where $q = p^r$. It first samples a random $x \in \mathbb{F}_q$, $u \in \mathbb{F}_p^n$, $v \in \mathbb{F}_q^n$, then outputs (u, v) to the sender and $(x, w = ux + v)$ to the receiver.[5] Our construction is a generalization of the vector-OLE construction from [14]: when $p = q$ the correlation is exactly vector-OLE, but using $q > p$ opens up additional applications. For example, viewing $x \in \mathbb{F}_q$ as a vector $x \in \mathbb{F}_p^r$, subfield VOLE can be seen as computing additive shares of the $r \times n$ tensor product $x \otimes u$, which can be useful for secure two-party matrix multiplication, and other linear algebra tasks. Compared with using r copies of VOLE [14] to achieve the same task, we reduce the seed size by a $O(\log n)$ factor and obtain more efficient computation.

To build a PCG for subfield VOLE, we consider a compressible distribution $\mathcal{D}$ that outputs random sparse vectors of weight t and length n'. First, notice that we can compress a secret-sharing of the j-th unit vector $e_j \in \{0, 1\}^{n'}$, using a distributed point function (DPF) for the point $(j, 1)$: evaluating a DPF key on input i produces a random share of 0 on all inputs except $i = j$, where it outputs a share of 1. Hence, performing all n' evaluations results in shares of the entire vector e_j. This easily extends to weight t vectors, by naively using t DPFs and summing up the shares of the t unit vectors (this step can be optimized with a multi-point DPF as described in [14]).

---

[5] We view elements of $\mathbb{F}_p$ embedded into $\mathbb{F}_q$ throughout, so that the multiplication $u \cdot x$ happens over $\mathbb{F}_q$.

Although it may appear that this only allows us to compress sparse vectors, and not perform any useful HSS computations afterwards, we observe that with a small tweak we can use this to build HSS for the family of randomized functions

$$\mathcal{F} = \{f_H : \mathbb{F}_q \to \mathbb{F}_q^n, x \mapsto x \cdot \boldsymbol{e} \cdot H \mid \boldsymbol{e} \xleftarrow{\$} \mathcal{HW}_t, H \in \mathbb{F}_p^{n' \times n}\} \qquad (1)$$

where $\mathcal{HW}_t$ is the distribution that outputs a random weight-t vector over $\mathbb{F}_p^{n'}$ (with each entry either 0 or uniform). We remark that a naive description of the class $\mathcal{F}$ gives functions with very high degree, which could *not* be evaluated using simple HSS schemes, which highlights the importance of tailoring a specific solution.

To upgrade the above sketch to get HSS for $\mathcal{F}$, we make one small modification: using t DPFs that output shares over $\mathbb{F}_q$, we specify the i-th DPF by the point $(j_i, y_i \cdot x)$ for some random index j_i and $y_i \in \mathbb{F}_p^*$, instead of $(j_i, 1)$ as before. When evaluating the DPFs, the parties now obtain additive shares of $\boldsymbol{e} \cdot x$, where $\boldsymbol{e}$ contains all t y_i's in random positions. Since additive secret sharing is linear, any linear map H can then be locally applied on the shares.

If $H \in \mathbb{F}_p^{n' \times n}$ is a compressive linear map with $n < n'$, the vector $\boldsymbol{u} = \boldsymbol{e} \cdot H$ is pseudorandom under a suitable form of the LPN (or syndrome decoding) assumption. Concretely, we require that a t-noisy random codeword in the code whose *parity check* matrix is H is pseudorandom. This immediately yields a subfield VOLE generator, where each party's seed contains a set of DPF seeds, and the sender additionally gets the points (j_i, y_i), and the receiver gets x, since additive shares of $x \cdot \boldsymbol{u}$ can be locally converted to the $(\boldsymbol{v}, \boldsymbol{w})$ components of a VOLE correlation.

Our next observation, inspired by the OT extension protocol of Ishai et al. [46], is that subfield VOLE already gives as a restricted form of oblivious transfer, known as correlated OT or Δ-OT. If we run subfield VOLE over $\mathbb{F}_2$, embedded in $\mathbb{F}_{2^r}$, then the VOLE sender obtains a set of pairs $u_i \xleftarrow{\$} \mathbb{F}_2, v_i \xleftarrow{\$} \mathbb{F}_{2^r}$, while the VOLE receiver gets $x \xleftarrow{\$} \mathbb{F}_{2^r}$ and $w_i = x \cdot u_i + v_i$, for $i = 1, \ldots, n$. Now switch the roles of sender and receiver, so the VOLE sender becomes an OT receiver with choice bit u_i and string v_i. If $u_i = 0$ then $v_i = w_i$, whilst if $u_i = 1$ then $v_i = w_i - x$, hence, this is exactly a 1-out-of-2 OT where the OT sender's (formerly VOLE receiver's) messages are all of the form $(w_i, w_i - x)$.

On its own, this type of Δ-OT is already useful for many applications such as garbled circuits and secure computation with information-theoretic MACs [59, 61]. However, most importantly, following [46], the parties can locally convert such a correlated OT into an OT on random strings, using a hash function that is pseudorandom under correlated inputs. This gives us a PCG for random oblivious transfer, where the seed size is essentially that of t distributed point functions, or $O(t\lambda \log n)$ bits. Combining this with an efficient secure protocol for setting up a pair of DPF keys [32], we obtain our silent OT extension protocol, which produces n pseudorandom string-OTs with $o(n)$ bits of communication.

2.4 One-Time Truth Tables

We next show how to adapt the above approach to produce authenticated, one-time truth table correlations, which can be used to efficiently perform table lookups in MPC [28, 30, 47]. This construction is straightforward given the above description of our subfield-VOLE generator, so we informally explain it here and defer the complete description to the full version.

The correlation we want to produce, for a lookup table $T : [n] \rightarrow \{0,1\}^m$, is an additive secret-sharing of

$$\left(\alpha, \{y_i, \gamma_i\}_{i \in [n]}\right) \quad \text{where} \quad y_i = T(s + i \bmod n), \gamma_i = y_i \cdot \alpha \in \mathbb{F}_{2^\lambda} \quad (2)$$

for $\alpha \xleftarrow{\$} \mathbb{F}_{2^\lambda}, s \xleftarrow{\$} [n]$. Here, the y_i's are equal to T shifted by a random offset s, while the γ_i's are information-theoretic MACs on y_i under the key α, used to obtain active security in the MPC protocol.

Our starting point is the observation from [52] that the y_i's can be generated locally, given secret-shares of a random unit vector. This is because, if $\boldsymbol{e}_s \in \{0,1\}^n$ is the s-th unit vector, then we have

$$T(s + i \bmod n) = \sum_{j=1}^{n} \boldsymbol{e}_s[j] \cdot T(i + j \bmod n)$$

which is linear in $\boldsymbol{e}_s$. We can further obtain the γ_i's (namely, the authenticated $\gamma_i = y_i \cdot \alpha$) if we additionally have secret-shares of the corresponding scaled vector $\alpha \cdot \boldsymbol{e}_s$.

The core observation is that a DPF gives precisely a *compressed* secret sharing of such a secret vector $(1\|\alpha) \cdot \boldsymbol{e}_s \in (\{0,1\}^{1+\lambda})^n$: requiring only $O(\lambda \log n)$ bits in the place of $O(\lambda n)$.

More concretely, this leads to the following, simple approach for a PCG to generate shares of (2): use the previous DPF-based construction of HSS for the family in (1) over $\mathbb{F}_2$, with $t = 1$, $x = (1\|\alpha)$ for $\alpha \xleftarrow{\$} \mathbb{F}_{2^\lambda}$, and H the linear map induced by T in the equation above. The resulting PCG has seed size essentially the same as one DPF, which is $O(\lambda \log n)$ bits. This gives a large compression over the previous, practical approach from [28], which required $O(\lambda n)$ bits per table. Expanding the PCG is relatively cheap in practice, since in 2-PC applications only a single entry of each table is ever used, and this can be computed on-the-fly with $O(n)$ PRG evaluations.

A downside of this construction is that it seems difficult to produce the necessary PCG seeds with good concrete efficiency in the malicious setting, since the only known approach in this setting requires evaluating a PRG inside 2-PC [32]. However, our result is still interesting for a preprocessing phase with semi-honest security, or when a trusted dealer is present. Alternatively, if one can afford the cost of distributing Gen with malicious security via general-purpose 2-PC, the resulting correlated seeds only require a small amount of storage, and their local expansion is (automatically) secure against malicious parties.

2.5   PCGs for Constant-Degree Polynomials from LPN

We construct PCGs for constant-degree polynomials, using again function secret sharing for multi-point functions together with LPN. At a high level, the construction builds upon the fact that given two sparse vectors $\boldsymbol{a}, \boldsymbol{b}$, their tensor product $\boldsymbol{a} \otimes \boldsymbol{b}$ is sparse as well, hence shares of $\boldsymbol{a} \otimes \boldsymbol{b}$ can be compressed using an FSS, as for vector-OLE generators and silent OT extension. Then, a compressive mapping can be applied to obtain $\boldsymbol{x} \otimes \boldsymbol{y}$ from $\boldsymbol{a} \otimes \boldsymbol{b}$, where $\boldsymbol{x} = (\boldsymbol{a} \cdot H)$ and $\boldsymbol{y} = (\boldsymbol{b} \cdot H)$ are *pseudorandom* under the LPN assumption, thanks to the bilinearity of the tensor product (and linearity of H). This immediately leads to a PCG for bilinear functions, which can be easily generalized to a PCG for constant-degree polynomials. However, the share size grows as $O(t^d)$, where t is the number of noisy coordinates in the LPN instance, and d is the degree of the polynomial. The computation cost grows as $O(n^{2d})$, where n is the input size.

2.6   PCGs from Ring-LWE and BGN-based HSS

We construct PCGs for more general two-party correlations, building upon the specific structure of homomorphic encryption-based HSS schemes [22,31] and group-based HSS schemes [16,18,20]. Our key observation is that in both HSS schemes encodings of large pseudorandom strings can be compressed efficiently using an "HSS-friendly PRG" as described in Sect. 2.2. For the ring-LWE based construction, we obtain compression with a PRG based on the multivariate quadratic equations problem, and present several ways of optimizing this with batching techniques for homomorphic encryption, which lead to different trade-offs for seed size and computational cost.

The group-based approach requires more involved techniques: The underlying HSS scheme uses two types of encodings, where so-called level-1 encodings are ElGamal ciphertexts, and level-2 encodings are shares of $\mathsf{sk} \cdot \boldsymbol{x}$ for a vector $\boldsymbol{x}$, where sk is the secret key of the homomorphic encryption scheme. Then, a special HSS operation allows to compute level-2 encodings of bilinear functions applied to a level-1 encoding and a level-2 encoding. Using two parallel instances of the PCG for vector-OLE of [14] allows us to efficiently compress shares of $\boldsymbol{y}$ and $\mathsf{sk} \cdot \boldsymbol{y}$, where $\boldsymbol{y}$ is a pseudorandom vector and sk is a shared value, to only $O(\lambda t \log n)$ bits, under the LPN assumption with t noisy coordinates. Furthermore, encrypting short random sparse vectors suffices for homomorphically evaluating a specific LPN-based PRG directly on the level-1 encodings, as long as they support evaluation of degree-2 functions. This can be ensured by using BGN-style pairing-based encryption for the group-based HSS. Since the HSS comes with an inverse-polynomial error probability, we further develop a new method to efficiently remove the faulty outputs, building upon our silent OT extension protocol.

For both schemes, we discuss various optimizations and provide detailed efficiency estimations.

2.7 Multi-party PCGs

As our final contribution, we construct *multi-party* PCGs for a useful class of bilinear correlations. Concretely, for a given bilinear map $e : \mathbb{G}_1 \times \mathbb{G}_2 \to \mathbb{G}_T$, we consider M-party correlations of the form $\{(a_i, b_i, c_i)\}_{i \in [M]}$, consisting of additive secret shares of random elements $a \in \mathbb{G}_1$, $b \in \mathbb{G}_2$, and their image $c = e(a, b) \in \mathbb{G}_T$. For appropriate choice of groups and bilinear operation, this captures M-party OT, M-party vector OLE, M-party Beaver triples, and more.

Our construction approach provides a semi-generic transformation from any PCG for a corresponding *2-party* correlation $\{(a, c_1), (b, c_2)\}$ for random a, b, and $c_1 + c_2 = e(a, b)$, if the PCG satisfies an additional programmability property. Roughly, this property requires a way of "reusing" the inputs a and b across instances without compromising security.

The M-party construction leverages this structure by executing $M(M - 1)$ pairwise instances of the underlying 2-party PCG, for all the "cross-terms." Namely, we think of each a_i and b_i from the final M-party correlation as playing the role of a or b in the 2-party correlation, with all possible partners. The desired M-party additive shares c_i can then be derived by combining $c_{ii} = a_i b_i$ (computable locally) together with $\{c_{ij}, c_{ji}\}_{j \in [M] \setminus \{i\}}$ resulting from the 2-party correlations for pairs (a_i, b_j) and (a_j, b_i). The resulting M-party PCG keys consist of $M(M - 1)$ keys from the 2-party PCG, together with short expandable shares of 0 for rerandomization.

We observe that the necessary programmability property is satisfied by our subfield VOLE construction and the 2-party VOLE PCG from [14], as well as the 2-party bilinear PCGs constructed in this work (including OT and Beaver triples) from group-based and lattice-based HSS and from LPN (in the full version [15]). As a corollary, we obtain M-party variants of these correlations with quadratic blowup in computation and share size. Interestingly, our silent OT extension construction does *not* seem to support the necessary programmability, since the resulting sender message pairs are implicitly defined as a function of the receiver's bit selections.

3 Preliminaries

We say that a function $\mathsf{negl} \colon \mathbb{N} \to \mathbb{R}^+$ is *negligible* if it vanishes faster than every inverse polynomial. For two families of distributions $X = \{X_\lambda\}$ and $Y = \{Y_\lambda\}$ indexed by a security parameter $\lambda \in \mathbb{N}$, we write $X \overset{c}{\approx} Y$ if X and Y are *computationally indistinguishable* (namely, any family of circuits of size $\mathsf{poly}(\lambda)$ has a negligible distinguishing advantage), $X \overset{s}{\approx} Y$ if they are *statistically indistinguishable* (namely, the above holds for arbitrary distinguishers), and $X \equiv Y$ if the two families are identically distributed.

Notation. We usually denote matrices with capital letters (A, B, C) and vectors with bold lowercase $(\boldsymbol{x}, \boldsymbol{y})$. By default, vectors are assumed to be row vectors. We write $A|_{i,j}$ to denote the entry (i, j) of a matrix A. Given a vector $\boldsymbol{x}$ of length $|\boldsymbol{x}| = n$, the notation $\mathsf{HW}(x)$ denotes the Hamming weight $\boldsymbol{x}$, *i.e.*, the number of its nonzero entries. Given a distribution $\mathcal{D}$, we denote by $\mathsf{Im}(\mathcal{D})$ the image of $\mathcal{D}$ (i.e., its support set).

3.1   Function Secret Sharing

Informally, an FSS scheme for a class of functions $\mathcal{C}$ is a pair of algorithms $\mathsf{FSS} = (\mathsf{FSS.Gen}, \mathsf{FSS.Eval})$ such that:

– $\mathsf{FSS.Gen}$ given a function $f \in \mathcal{C}$ outputs a pair of keys (K_0, K_1);
– $\mathsf{FSS.Eval}$, given K_b and input x, outputs y_b such that y_0 and y_1 form additive shares of $f(x)$.

The security requirement is that each key K_b computationally hide f, except for revealing the input and output domains of f. For a formal definition, see e.g. [19].

Some applications of FSS require applying the evaluation algorithm on *all inputs*. Following [14,19], given an FSS scheme $(\mathsf{FSS.Gen}, \mathsf{FSS.Eval})$, we denote by $\mathsf{FSS.FullEval}$ an algorithm which, on input a bit b, and an evaluation key K_b (which defines the input domain I), outputs a list of $|I|$ elements of $\mathbb{G}$ corresponding to the evaluation of $\mathsf{FSS.Eval}(b, K_b, \cdot)$ on every input $x \in I$ (in some predetermined order). While $\mathsf{FSS.FullEval}$ can always be realized with $|I|$ invocations of $\mathsf{FSS.Eval}$, it is typically possible to obtain a more efficient construction. Below, we recall some results from [19] on FSS schemes for useful classes of functions.

Distributed Point Functions. A distributed point function (DPF) [39] is an FSS scheme for the class of point functions $f_{\alpha,\beta} : \{0,1\}^\ell \to \mathbb{G}$ which satisfy $f_{\alpha,\beta}(\alpha) = \beta$, and $f_{\alpha,\beta}(x) = 0$ for any $x \neq \alpha$. A sequence of works [17,19,39] has led to highly efficient constructions of DPF schemes from any pseudorandom generator (PRG), which can be implemented in practice using block ciphers such as AES.

Theorem 1 (PRG-based DPF [19], Theorems 3.3 and 3.4). *Given a PRG* $G : \{0,1\}^\lambda \to \{0,1\}^{2\lambda+2}$, *there exists a DPF for point functions* $f_{\alpha,\beta} : \{0,1\}^\ell \to \mathbb{G}$ *with key size* $\ell \cdot (\lambda+2) + \lambda + \lceil \log_2 |\mathbb{G}| \rceil$ *bits. For* $m = \lceil \frac{\log |\mathbb{G}|}{\lambda+2} \rceil$, *the key generation algorithm* Gen *invokes* G *at most* $2(\ell + m)$ *times, the evaluation algorithm* Eval *invokes* G *at most* $\ell + m$ *times, and the full evaluation algorithm* $\mathsf{FullEval}$ *invokes* G *at most* $2^\ell(1 + m)$ *times.*

Note that a naive construction of $\mathsf{FullEval}$ from Eval would require $2^\ell(\ell + m)$ invocations of G.

FSS for Multi-point Functions. Similarly to [14], we use FSS for *multi-point functions*. A k-point function evaluates to 0 everywhere, except on k specified points. When specifying multi-point functions we often view the domain of the function as $[n]$ for $n = 2^\ell$ instead of $\{0,1\}^\ell$.

Definition 2 (Multi-point Function [14]). *An (n, t)-multi-point function over an abelian group $(\mathbb{G}, +)$ is a function $f_{S,y} : [n] \to \mathbb{G}$, where $S = (s_1, \cdots, s_t)$ is an ordered subset of $[n]$ of size t and $y = (y_1, \cdots, y_t) \in \mathbb{G}^t$, defined by $f_{S,y}(s_i) = y_i$ for any $i \in [t]$, and $f_{S,y}(x) = 0$ for any $x \in [n] \setminus S$.*

We assume that the description of S includes the input domain $[n]$ so that $f_{S,y}$ is fully specified.

A *Multi-Point Function Secret Sharing* (MPFSS) is an FSS scheme for the class of multi-point functions, where a point function $f_{S,y}$ is represented in a natural way. We assume that an MPFSS scheme leaks not only the input and output domains but also the number of points t that the multi-point function specifies. An MPFSS can be easily obtained by adding t instances of DPF; optimized constructions of MPFSS, using batch codes [48] to speed up the full domain evaluation algorithm, were presented in [14].

3.2 Learning Parity with Noise

Our constructions rely on variants of the Learning Parity with Noise (LPN) assumption [12] over either $\mathbb{F}_2$ or a large finite field $\mathbb{F}$. Unlike the LWE assumption, in LPN over $\mathbb{F}$ the noise is assumed to have a small Hamming weight. Concretely, the noise is a random field element in a small fraction of the coordinates and 0 elsewhere. Similar assumptions have been previously used in the context of secure arithmetic computation [3, 33, 37, 50, 58]. Unlike most of these works, the flavors of LPN on which we rely do not require the underlying code to have an algebraic structure and are thus not susceptible to algebraic (list-) decoding attacks.

Definition 3 (LPN). *Let $\mathcal{D}(\mathcal{R}) = \{\mathcal{D}_{k,q}(\mathcal{R})\}_{k,q \in \mathbb{N}}$ denote a family of distributions over a ring $\mathcal{R}$, such that for any $k, q \in \mathbb{N}$, $\mathsf{Im}(\mathcal{D}_{k,q}(\mathcal{R})) \subseteq \mathcal{R}^q$. Let $\mathbf{C}$ be a probabilistic code generation algorithm such that $\mathbf{C}(k, q, \mathcal{R})$ outputs a matrix $A \in \mathcal{R}^{k \times q}$. For dimension $k = k(\lambda)$, number of samples (or block length) $q = q(\lambda)$, and ring $\mathcal{R} = \mathcal{R}(\lambda)$, the $(\mathcal{D}, \mathbf{C}, \mathcal{R})$-LPN$(k, q)$ assumption states that*

$$\{(A, b) \mid A \xleftarrow{\$} \mathbf{C}(k, q, \mathcal{R}), e \xleftarrow{\$} \mathcal{D}_{k,q}(\mathcal{R}), s \xleftarrow{\$} \mathbb{F}^k, b \leftarrow s \cdot A + e\}$$
$$\overset{c}{\approx} \{(A, b) \mid A \xleftarrow{\$} \mathbf{C}(k, q, \mathcal{R}), b \xleftarrow{\$} \mathcal{R}^q\}$$

Here and in the following, all parameters are functions of the security parameter λ and computational indistinguishability is defined with respect to λ.

When $\mathcal{R} = \mathbb{F}_2$ and $\mathcal{D}$ is the Bernoulli distribution over $\mathbb{F}_2^q$, where each coordinate is 1 with probability r and 0 otherwise, this corresponds to the standard binary LPN assumption.

Note that the search LPN problem, of finding the vector can be reduced to the decisional LPN assumption as defined above when the code generator $\mathbf{C}$ outputs a uniform matrix A [5, 12]. However, this is less relevant for us as we are mainly interested in efficient variants with more structured codes. See [34] for further discussion of search-to-decision reductions in the general case.

Example: LPN with Fixed Weight Noise. For a finite field $\mathbb{F}$, we denote by $\mathcal{HW}_r(\mathbb{F})$ the distribution of uniform, weight r vectors over $\mathbb{F}$; that is, a sample from $\mathcal{HW}_r(\mathbb{F})$ is a uniformly random nonzero field element in r random positions, and zero elsewhere. The $(\mathsf{Ber}_r(\mathbb{F})^q, \mathbf{C}, \mathbb{F}) - \mathsf{LPN}(k, q)$ assumption corresponds to the standard (non-binary, fixed-weight) LPN assumption over a field $\mathbb{F}$ with code generator $\mathbf{C}$, dimension k, number of samples (or block length) q, and noise rate r.

When the block length q and noise rate r are such that k random coordinates will be all noiseless with non-negligible probability (e.g., when r is constant and $q = \Omega(k^2)$), LPN can be broken via Gaussian elimination (cf. [6]). This attack does not apply to our constructions, which typically have $q = O(k)$.

Definition 4 (dual LPN). *Let $\mathcal{D}(\mathcal{R})$ and $\mathbf{C}$ be as in Definition 3, $n, n' \in \mathbb{N}$ with $n' > n$, and define $\mathbf{C}^{\perp}(n', n, \mathcal{R}) = \{B \in \mathcal{R}^{n' \times n} : A \cdot B = 0, A \in \mathbf{C}(n' - n, n', \mathcal{R}), \mathsf{rank}(B) = n\}$.*

For $n = n(\lambda), n' = n'(\lambda)$ and $\mathcal{R} = \mathcal{R}(\lambda)$, the $(\mathcal{D}, \mathbf{C}, \mathcal{R})$-dual-LPN$(n', n)$ assumption states that

$$\{(H, \boldsymbol{b}) \mid H \xleftarrow{\$} \mathbf{C}^{\perp}(n', n, \mathcal{R}), e \xleftarrow{\$} \mathcal{D}(\mathcal{R}), \boldsymbol{b} \leftarrow e \cdot H\}$$
$$\stackrel{c}{\approx} \{(H, \boldsymbol{b}) \mid H \xleftarrow{\$} \mathbf{C}^{\perp}(n', n, \mathcal{R}), \boldsymbol{b} \xleftarrow{\$} \mathcal{R}^n\}$$

The search version of the dual LPN problem is also known as syndrome decoding. The decision version defined above is equivalent to primal variant of LPN from Definition 3 with dimension $k = n' - n$ and number of samples $q = n'$. This follows from the simple fact that $(\boldsymbol{s} \cdot A + \boldsymbol{e}) \cdot H = \boldsymbol{s} \cdot A \cdot H + \boldsymbol{e} \cdot H = \boldsymbol{e} \cdot H$, when H is the parity-check matrix of A.

Remark 5. For any code generation algorithm $\mathbf{C}$ where dual-LPN is hard, it must hold that for $H \xleftarrow{\$} \mathbf{C}^{\perp}(n', n', \mathcal{R})$, H is full rank with overwhelming probability. If that was not the case, then we could easily distinguish $\boldsymbol{e} \cdot H$ from uniform due to a linear relation between some of its outputs.

Remark 6. As a concrete example of the actual flavor of the dual-LPN assumption we will use, our construction of silent OT from Sect. 5 relies on the dual-LPN assumption of Definition 3 with respect to a random linear code over the field $\mathbb{F}_2$. For deriving our concrete parameters, we choose a *regular* error distribution of weight t, where a length-n' error vector has t non-zero coordinates spread across weight-1 blocks of length n'/t. This is known as the regular-LPN or *regular syndrome decoding* problem. When $n \geq 2^{16}$ and $n' = 4n$, a fixed-weight noise of $t \approx 32$ suffices to achieve 80-bit security against the best known attacks on this flavor of LPN, which all take time exponential in $(n'/n) \cdot t$. We will also consider alternative choices of linear codes (such as LDPC codes or quasi-cyclic codes) to improve the concrete computational efficiency in our estimates; such codes still lead to plausible variants of LPN and do not significantly improve known attacks compared with random codes.

4   Pseudorandom Correlation Generators

In this section we put forward a general notion of pseudorandom correlation generator (PCG) and study some of its limitations, capabilities, and relation with other primitives. We start with our formal definition of PCG in Sect. 4.1. We then discuss in Sect. 4.2 a simpler and more natural simulation-based definition of PCG, that would suffice for *all* applications, but is not realizable. As a second-best alternative, we show in Sect. 4.3 that PCGs can be used as a drop-in replacement for correlated randomness in every protocol that meets a slightly stronger security requirement, which is indeed met by natural MPC protocols in the correlated randomness model. In the full version [15], we also show a two-way relation between PCGs for a useful class of "low-degree correlations" and homomorphic secret sharing for low-degree polynomials.

4.1   Defining Pseudorandom Correlation Generators

At a high level, a pseudorandom correlation generator (PCG) for some relation takes as input a pair of short, correlated seeds and outputs long correlated pseudorandom strings, where the expansion procedure is deterministic and can be applied locally.

For correctness we require that the expanded output of a PCG is indistinguishable from truly random correlated strings.

For security it would be natural and straightforward to require that we can securely replace long correlated strings by short correlated seeds in any secure protocol execution. Unfortunately, as shown in the following section, this security requirement would be impossible to meet. Therefore, we will introduce (and subsequently prove useful) an indistinguishability based security notion. Namely, we require that an adversary given access to one of the short seeds k_σ, cannot distinguish the pseudorandom string $R_{1-\sigma}$ from a pseudorandom string that is chosen at random conditioned on (R_0, R_1) being correlated (where $R_\sigma = \mathsf{PCG}(k_\sigma)$). In other words, an adversary given access to a short seed cannot learn more about the other party's pseudorandom string than what is obvious given access to its own pseudorandom string.

In order to formally define pseudorandom correlations, we first introduce the concept of a *correlation generator* as a PPT algorithm outputting correlated elements.

Definition 7 (Correlation Generator). *A PPT algorithm $\mathcal{C}$ is called a* correlation generator, *if $\mathcal{C}$ on input 1^λ outputs a pair of elements in $\{0,1\}^n \times \{0,1\}^n$ for $n \in \mathsf{poly}(\lambda)$.*

In order to define security, we require the notion of a reverse-sampleable correlation generator introduced in the following.

Definition 8 (Reverse-sampleable Correlation Generator). *Let $\mathcal{C}$ be a correlation generator. We say CC is* reverse sampleable *if there exists a PPT algorithm $\mathsf{RSample}$ such that for $\sigma \in \{0,1\}$ the correlation obtained via:*

$$\{(R'_0, R'_1) \,|\, (R_0, R_1) \xleftarrow{\$} \mathcal{C}(1^\lambda), R'_\sigma := R_\sigma, R'_{1-\sigma} \xleftarrow{\$} \mathsf{RSample}(\sigma, R_\sigma)\}$$

is computationally indistinguishable from $\mathcal{C}(1^\lambda)$.

The following definition of pseudorandom correlation generators can be viewed as a generalization of the definition of the pseudorandom VOLE generator in [14]. Note though that we do not enforce perfect correctness.

Definition 9 (Pseudorandom Correlation Generator (PCG)). *Let $\mathcal{C}$ be a reverse-sampleable correlation generator. A pseudorandom correlation generator (PCG) for CC is a pair of algorithms (PCG.Gen, PCG.Expand) with the following syntax:*

- *PCG.Gen(1^λ) is a PPT algorithm that given a security parameter λ, outputs a pair of seeds $(\mathsf{k}_0, \mathsf{k}_1)$;*
- *PCG.Expand$(\sigma, \mathsf{k}_\sigma)$ is a polynomial-time algorithm that given party index $\sigma \in \{0, 1\}$ and a seed k_σ, outputs a bit string $R_\sigma \in \{0, 1\}^n$.*

The algorithms (PCG.Gen, PCG.Expand) should satisfy the following:

- **Correctness.** *The correlation obtained via:*

$$\{(R_0, R_1) \,|\, (\mathsf{k}_0, \mathsf{k}_1) \xleftarrow{\$} \mathsf{PCG.Gen}(1^\lambda), R_\sigma \leftarrow \mathsf{PCG.Expand}(\sigma, \mathsf{k}_\sigma) \text{ for } \sigma \in \{0, 1\}\}$$

is computationally indistinguishable from $\mathcal{C}(1^\lambda)$.
- **Security.** *For any $\sigma \in \{0, 1\}$, the following two distributions are computationally indistinguishable:*

$$\{(\mathsf{k}_{1-\sigma}, R_\sigma) \,|\, (\mathsf{k}_0, \mathsf{k}_1) \xleftarrow{\$} \mathsf{PCG.Gen}(1^\lambda), R_\sigma \leftarrow \mathsf{PCG.Expand}(\sigma, \mathsf{k}_\sigma)\} \text{ and}$$
$$\{(\mathsf{k}_{1-\sigma}, R_\sigma) \,|\, (\mathsf{k}_0, \mathsf{k}_1) \xleftarrow{\$} \mathsf{PCG.Gen}(1^\lambda), R_{1-\sigma} \leftarrow \mathsf{PCG.Expand}(\sigma, \mathsf{k}_{1-\sigma}),$$
$$R_\sigma \xleftarrow{\$} \mathsf{RSample}(\sigma, R_{1-\sigma})\}$$

where RSample is the reverse sampling algorithm for correlation $\mathcal{C}$.

Note that the above definition is trivial to achieve in general: We can let PCG.Gen on input 1^λ return $(R_0, R_1) \leftarrow \mathcal{C}(1^\lambda)$, and simply define Expand to be the identity. Typically, we will be interested in non-trivial constructions of PCGs, in which the seed size is significantly shorter than the output size. A pseudorandom generator with image in $\{0, 1\}^n$ is a simple example for an expanding PCG for the equality correlation $\{(R, R) \,|\, R \in \{0, 1\}^n\}$. In the following we will be interested in constructing PCGs for a much broader class of correlations, like OT correlations, OLE correlations and (authenticated) Beaver triples.

4.2   Impossibility of a Simulation-Based Definition

A natural and useful alternative to the security definition we gave in Sect. 4, is the following: In any secure protocol (say against semi-honest adversaries), one can replace sampling a pair of strings from the correlation $\mathcal{C}$ by generating a pair of seeds (which are later expanded) using a PCG for $\mathcal{C}$ without compromising security. Unfortunately, as sketched in [38], a non-trivial PCG construction cannot satisfy such a simulation-based definition. Consider the simple protocol, where P_0 samples a pair $(R_0, R_1) \leftarrow \mathcal{C}(1^\lambda)$ and sends R_1 to P_1, who simply outputs R_1. This protocol obviously realizes the protocol dictated by $\mathcal{C}$, with one-sided security against P_1. But, if P_0 instead generates $(\mathsf{k}_0, \mathsf{k}_1)$ according to the seed generation algorithm of the PCG and sends k_1 to P_1, a possible simulator runs into the following problem. Simulating the above protocol given only the output R_1 corresponds to finding a short seed k_1 that can be (deterministically) expanded to R_1. If the entropy in the second output of $\mathcal{C}$ exceeds the seed-length $|\mathsf{k}_1|$, such a compression violates correctness, as it could be used to distinguish R_1 from a string that is indeed chosen via $\mathcal{C}$.

In the full version, we present a formal and more general version of the above argument for ruling out a simulation-based definition for non-trivial correlations, based on a lower bound of Hubáček and Wichs [45].

4.3   Applying PCGs in Protocols with Correlated Randomness

In this section we show that one *can* use PCGs in a "plug-and-play" fashion in protocols consuming correlated randomness sampled by a given functionality. More precisely, we show that PCGs can be directly applied to any protocol using a weaker form of correlated randomness, where corrupted parties can influence their outputs.

A simple example is random OT, where the weaker functionality we can realize allows a corrupt sender/receiver to choose its outputs, then the other party's outputs are sampled at random correspondingly. When using OT in an MPC protocol, the OT is typically implemented from random OT by masking the actual OT inputs with fresh random OT outputs. Allowing a corrupt party to choose its own OT outputs does not affect the security of these protocols, since (intuitively) this can only weaken security for the corrupt party and not for honest parties. More generally, it turns out that many practical MPC protocols, including those based on preprocessed multiplication triples for arithmetic circuits [10,29] and binary circuits [59,61,62], use this kind of corruptible, correlated randomness, since it is often easier to design a protocol that realizes this.

More formally, the randomness is modelled by the functionality $\mathcal{F}^{\mathcal{C}}_{\mathsf{corr}*}$ (Fig. 1), where a corrupted party may first *choose* its own output, and then the honest party's output is computed with the reverse sampling algorithm for $\mathcal{C}$. As we show in the following, PCGs can be used to securely realize $\mathcal{F}^{\mathcal{C}}_{\mathsf{corr}*}$, opening up many important applications at no extra cost.

To realize $\mathcal{F}^{\mathcal{C}}_{\mathsf{corr}*}$, we use a simple protocol, $\Pi^{\mathcal{C}}_{\mathsf{corr}*}$, that calls $\mathcal{F}^{\mathsf{PCG.Gen}}_{\mathsf{corr}}$ so that each party obtains a seed k_σ, which is then expanded to get the output $\mathsf{PCG.Expand}(\sigma, \mathsf{k}_\sigma)$.

Theorem 10. *Let* $\mathsf{PCG} = (\mathsf{PCG.Gen}, \mathsf{PCG.Expand})$ *be a secure PCG for a reverse-sampleable correlation generator, $\mathcal{C}$. Then the protocol $\Pi_{\mathsf{corr}*}$ securely realizes the $\mathcal{F}^{\mathcal{C}}_{\mathsf{corr}*}$ functionality against a static, malicious adversary.*

Functionality $\mathcal{F}_{\mathsf{corr}*}^{\mathcal{C}}$

On input 1^λ, the functionality does as follows:

- If no parties are corrupt, sample $(R_0, R_1) \overset{\$}{\leftarrow} \mathcal{C}(1^\lambda)$.
- Otherwise, if P_σ is corrupt, wait to receive $R_\sigma \in \{0,1\}^{n_\sigma}$ from $\mathcal{A}$, then sample $R_{1-\sigma} \overset{\$}{\leftarrow} \mathsf{RSample}(\sigma, R_\sigma)$.

The functionality outputs R_0 to P_0 and R_1 to P_1, and then halts.

Fig. 1. Corruptible correlated randomness functionality for a reverse-sampleable correlation generator, $\mathcal{C}$

5   Silent Oblivious Transfer Extension from LPN

In this section we present a protocol for silent OT extension, which allows to generate n instances of random OT with sublinear communication complexity. To this end, we first show how to tweak the construction of Boyle et al. [14] to give correlated OT. Combining this observation with the OT extension technique of Ishai et al. [46] we obtain a PCG for random OT. Finally, we show how to use the protocol of Doerner and Shelat [32] for secure computation of the seed, giving sublinear OT extension.

5.1   Subfield Vector-OLE

Here, we introduce the notion of subfield vector oblivious linear evaluation (sVOLE), and show that sVOLE for $\mathbb{F}_q$ over subfield $\mathbb{F}_p \subset \mathbb{F}_q$ gives 1-out-of-p correlated OT. More precisely, a single big instance of sVOLE will give many 1-out-of-p OTs at once. Our construction of sVOLE comes with two additional advantages: It enjoys lower computational costs, because matrix multiplications are performed with a matrix over $\mathbb{F}_p$, and for $p = 2$ we can reduce security to the better-studied binary LPN problem, instead of its arithmetic variant over larger fields.

Subfield VOLE is a form of vector oblivious linear evaluation (VOLE) over $\mathbb{F}_q$, which computes $\boldsymbol{w} = \boldsymbol{u}x + \boldsymbol{v}$, where the vector $\boldsymbol{u}$ is restricted to lie over a subfield $\mathbb{F}_p \subset \mathbb{F}_q$, for $q = p^r$ (and we multiply $\boldsymbol{u}$ with $x \in \mathbb{F}_q$ component-wise, by viewing x as a vector over $\mathbb{F}_p$). It outputs $(\boldsymbol{u}, \boldsymbol{v})$ to the sender and $(x, \boldsymbol{w})$ to the receiver.

The construction in Fig. 2 uses the function $\mathsf{spread}_n(S, \boldsymbol{y})$, which expands a set $S = (s_1, \ldots, s_{|S|}) \subset [n]$ and a vector $\boldsymbol{y} \in \mathbb{F}_p^{|S|}$ into the vector $\boldsymbol{\mu} \in \mathbb{F}_p^n$, where $\mu_{s_i} = y_i$ for $i = 1, \ldots, |S|$, and $\mu_j = 0$ for $j \in [n] \setminus S$. It is a generalization of the VOLE generator from [14], which follows from the case $p = q$.

Theorem 11. *Suppose the $(\mathcal{HW}_t, \mathbf{C}, \mathbb{F}_p)\text{-dual-LPN}(n', n)$ assumption holds, and that MPFSS is a secure multi-point FSS scheme. Then the construction G_{sVOLE} (Fig. 2) is a secure PCG for the subfield vector-OLE correlation.*

Construction G_{sVOLE}

PARAMETERS:

- Security parameter 1^λ, integers $n' > n$, $q = p^r$, and noise weight t.
- A code generation algorithm $\mathbf{C}$ and $H_{n',n} \xleftarrow{\$} \mathbf{C}(n', n, \mathbb{F}_p)$.
- A multi-point FSS scheme (MPFSS.Gen, MPFSS.FullEval).

CORRELATION: Output $(\boldsymbol{u}, \boldsymbol{v})$ and $(x, \boldsymbol{w})$, where $x \leftarrow \mathbb{F}_q$, $\boldsymbol{u} \xleftarrow{\$} \mathbb{F}_p^n$, $\boldsymbol{v} \xleftarrow{\$} \mathbb{F}_q^n$ and $\boldsymbol{w} = \boldsymbol{u}x + \boldsymbol{v}$.

GEN: On input 1^λ:

1. Pick a random size-t subset S of $[n']$, sorted in increasing order.
2. Pick a random vector $\boldsymbol{y} \in (\mathbb{F}_p^*)^t$ and $x \xleftarrow{\$} \mathbb{F}_q$.
3. Compute $(K_0^{\text{fss}}, K_1^{\text{fss}}) \xleftarrow{\$} \text{MPFSS.Gen}(1^\lambda, f_{S, x \cdot \boldsymbol{y}})$.
4. Let $\mathsf{k}_0 \leftarrow (m, n, K_0^{\text{fss}}, S, \boldsymbol{y})$ and $\mathsf{k}_1 \leftarrow (m, n, K_1^{\text{fss}}, x)$.
5. Output $(\mathsf{k}_0, \mathsf{k}_1)$.

EXPAND: On input $(\sigma, \mathsf{k}_\sigma)$:

1. If $\sigma = 0$: parse k_0 as $(m, n, K_0^{\text{fss}}, S, \boldsymbol{y})$. Set $\boldsymbol{\mu} \leftarrow \text{spread}_{n'}(S, \boldsymbol{y})$ in $\mathbb{F}_p^{n'}$. Compute $\boldsymbol{v}_0 \leftarrow \text{MPFSS.FullEval}(0, K_0^{\text{fss}})$ in $\mathbb{F}_q^{n'}$. Output $(\boldsymbol{u}, \boldsymbol{v}) \leftarrow (\boldsymbol{\mu} \cdot H_{n',n}, -\boldsymbol{v}_0 \cdot H_{n',n})$.
2. If $\sigma = 1$: parse k_1 as $(m, n, K_1^{\text{fss}}, x)$. Compute $\boldsymbol{v}_1 \leftarrow \text{MPFSS.FullEval}(1, K_1^{\text{fss}})$ in $\mathbb{F}_q^{n'}$, and output $(x, \boldsymbol{w} \leftarrow \boldsymbol{v}_1 \cdot H_{n',n})$.

Fig. 2. PCG for subfield vector-OLE

Application to Correlated OT. Subfield VOLE immediately gives a PCG for *correlated OT* (or Δ-OT). This is a batch of 1-out-of-2 OTs where the sender's strings are of the form $(w_i, w_i \oplus \Delta)$ for some fixed string Δ, and is the main building block in practical MPC protocols such as TinyOT [59] and authenticated garbling [61,62].

To obtain correlated OT, we run subfield VOLE with $p = 2$ and $q = 2^r$, so the VOLE sender obtains $u_i \in \mathbb{F}_2, v_i \in \mathbb{F}_{2^r}$, while the VOLE receiver gets $x \in \mathbb{F}_{2^r}$ and $w_i = x \cdot u_i + v_i$, for $i = 1, \ldots, n$. Now switching the roles of sender and receiver, the VOLE sender can be seen as an OT receiver with choice bit u_i and string v_i. This gives us a correlated OT, since the OT sender (formerly VOLE receiver) can compute the strings $(w_i, w_i + x)$, and we have $v_i = w_i$ if $u_i = 0$ and $v_i = w_i + x$ if $u_i = 1$.

Application to Matrix Multiplication. Our construction for subfield VOLE can alternatively be seen as a PCG for *tensor product*: writing $x \in \mathbb{F}_q$ as $\boldsymbol{x} = (x_1, \ldots, x_r) \in \mathbb{F}_p^r$, and $\boldsymbol{u} = (u_1, \ldots, u_n) \in \mathbb{F}_p^n$, sVOLE computes secret shares of $\boldsymbol{x} \otimes \boldsymbol{u}$, that is, $x_i \cdot u_j$ for every $(i, j) \in [r] \times [n]$. This allows evaluation of secret-shared tensor products in 2-PC, which can in turn be used for matrix multiplication.

The seed size scales linearly in r, but this still improves upon the naive way of using r PCGs for VOLE over $\mathbb{F}_p$; the latter approach (with the VOLE from [14]) has seed size $O(rt \cdot (\lambda \log n + \log p))$ bits, whereas we reduce this to $O(t \cdot (\lambda \log n + r \log p))$ bits, saving at least a $\log n$ factor when $\log p = O(\lambda)$.

5.2   PCG for Random Oblivious Transfer

In the full version [15], we give the formal construction of a PCG for the random oblivious transfer correlation, based on G_{sVOLE}. Given the above observation that subfield VOLE implies correlated OT, this is straightforward, as we can apply the OT extension technique of Ishai et al. [46], which converts correlated OTs into random OTs using a suitable hash function. We extend this in a natural way to generate 1-out-of-p random OTs using subfield VOLE over $\mathbb{F}_p$. Note that for security when applying the hash function, we now need $q = \lambda^{\omega(1)}$.

We use a generalization of a correlation robust function, called $\mathbb{F}_p$-*correlation robustness* (defined in the full version). As recently shown in [41], this can be instantiated with fixed-key AES modeled as a random permutation when $p = 2$.

Theorem 12. *Suppose that* H *is an* $\mathbb{F}_p$-*correlation robust hash function and* G_{sVOLE} *is a secure PCG. Then the silent OT construction (in the full version) is a secure PCG for the random 1-out-of-p OT correlation.*

5.3   From a PCG to Silent OT Extension

To construct an OT extension protocol, we can use 2-PC to securely compute the Gen algorithm of G_{OT}, and then have each party locally expand its output using G_{OT}.Expand. Applying Theorem 10 from Sect. 4.3, this realizes a *corruptible* form of the ideal functionality for random oblivious transfer, where corrupt parties may influence their random outputs.

To do this efficiently with semi-honest security, we use the black-box protocol of Doerner and Shelat [32] (also used in [14]) for setting up distributed point function keys. For a single point function of domain size n, this requires $O(\log n)$ OTs on $O(\lambda)$-bit strings, giving $O(t \log n)$ OTs for a multi-bit point function. Implementing each OT with (non-silent) OT extension [46] costs $O(\lambda)$ bits of communication, plus a setup phase of λ base OTs. Putting this together, we obtain the following.

Theorem 13. *Suppose the* $(\mathcal{HW}_t, \mathbf{C}, \mathbb{F}_p)$-*dual-LPN*$(n', n)$ *assumption holds, and an* $\mathbb{F}_p$-*correlation robust hash function exists. Then there is a protocol that uses* $O(\lambda)$ *1-out-of-2 OTs to realize* n *instances of random 1-out-of-p OT with semi-honest security, using* $O(t\lambda \log n) + \mathsf{poly}(\lambda)$ *bits of communication.*

We remark that this gives OT with *sublinear communication* when $t = o(n/(\lambda \log n))$, which translates to an instance of LPN with noise rate

$1/\omega(\lambda \log n)$. If the matrix $H_{n',n}$ in G_{sVOLE} is uniformly random, the computational complexity is dominated by $O(n' \cdot n)$ arithmetic operations; using more structured matrices based on LDPC codes or quasi-cyclic codes, we get respective costs of $O(n')$ or $\tilde{O}(n')$ arithmetic and PRG operations.

Concrete Efficiency. In the full version, we analyze these costs more concretely and give a breakdown of the communication complexity, as well as some approximate runtime estimates based on the cost of the main operations. For example, for $n \leq 2^{22}$ OTs, the PCG seed size is under $10\,\mathrm{kB}$ and requires less than $30\,\mathrm{kB}$ of communication to create with the distributed setup procedure. After setup, we estimate that these seeds can be expanded into $16\,\mathrm{MB}$ of OTs on 128-bit strings at a rate of around 1 million per second, or 2 million per second when expanding to $1\,\mathrm{MB}$, using a single core of a CPU on a modern laptop. When including the distributed setup procedure, in these two cases we get an amortized communication complexity of just 0.2 and 2.6 bits per OT, respectively.

Acknowledgements. We would like to thank Peter Rindal and Melissa Rossi for helpful discussions and pointers, and the anonymous Crypto 2019 reviewers for their comments.

E. Boyle, N. Gilboa, and Y. Ishai supported by ERC Project NTSC (742754). E. Boyle additionally supported by ISF grant 1861/16 and AFOSR Award FA9550-17-1-0069. G. Couteau supported by ERC Project PREP-CRYPTO (724307). N. Gilboa additionally supported by ISF grant 1638/15 and a grant by the BGU Cyber Center. Y. Ishai additionally supported by ISF grant 1709/14, NSF-BSF grant 2015782, and a grant from the Ministry of Science and Technology, Israel and Department of Science and Technology, Government of India. L. Kohl supported by ERC Project PREP-CRYPTO (724307), by DFG grant HO 4534/2-2 and by a DAAD scholarship. This work was done in part while visiting the FACT Center at IDC Herzliya, Israel. P. Scholl supported by the European Union's Horizon 2020 research and innovation programme under grant agreement No 731583 (SODA), and the Danish Independent Research Council under Grant-ID DFF-6108-00169 (FoCC).

References

1. Aguilar, C., Blazy, O., Deneuville, J.C., Gaborit, P., Zémor, G.: Efficient encryption from random quasi-cyclic codes. Cryptology ePrint Archive, Report 2016/1194 (2016). http://eprint.iacr.org/2016/1194
2. Alekhnovich, M.: More on average case vs approximation complexity. In: 44th FOCS. IEEE Computer Society Press, October 2003
3. Applebaum, B., Damgård, I., Ishai, Y., Nielsen, M., Zichron, L.: Secure arithmetic computation with constant computational overhead. In: Katz, J., Shacham, H. (eds.) CRYPTO 2017, Part I. LNCS, vol. 10401, pp. 223–254. Springer, Cham (2017). https://doi.org/10.1007/978-3-319-63688-7_8
4. Applebaum, B., Haramaty, N., Ishai, Y., Kushilevitz, E., Vaikuntanathan, V.: Low-complexity cryptographic hash functions. In: ITCS 2017. LIPIcs, January 2017

5. Applebaum, B., Ishai, Y., Kushilevitz, E.: Cryptography with constant input locality. J. Cryptol. **22**(4), 429–469 (2009)
6. Arora, S., Ge, R.: New algorithms for learning in presence of errors. In: Aceto, L., Henzinger, M., Sgall, J. (eds.) ICALP 2011, Part I. LNCS, vol. 6755, pp. 403–415. Springer, Heidelberg (2011). https://doi.org/10.1007/978-3-642-22006-7_34
7. Asharov, G., Lindell, Y., Schneider, T., Zohner, M.: More efficient oblivious transfer and extensions for faster secure computation. In: ACM CCS 2013. ACM Press, November 2013
8. Beaver, D.: Efficient multiparty protocols using circuit randomization. In: Feigenbaum, J. (ed.) CRYPTO 1991. LNCS, vol. 576, pp. 420–432. Springer, Heidelberg (1992). https://doi.org/10.1007/3-540-46766-1_34
9. Beaver, D.: Correlated pseudorandomness and the complexity of private computations. In: Proceedings of the Twenty-Eighth Annual ACM Symposium on the Theory of Computing, Philadelphia, Pennsylvania, USA, 22–24 May 1996, pp. 479–488 (1996). https://doi.org/10.1145/237814.237996
10. Bendlin, R., Damgård, I., Orlandi, C., Zakarias, S.: Semi-homomorphic encryption and multiparty computation. In: Paterson, K.G. (ed.) EUROCRYPT 2011. LNCS, vol. 6632, pp. 169–188. Springer, Heidelberg (2011). https://doi.org/10.1007/978-3-642-20465-4_11
11. Berbain, C., Gilbert, H., Patarin, J.: QUAD: a practical stream cipher with provable security. In: Vaudenay, S. (ed.) EUROCRYPT 2006. LNCS, vol. 4004, pp. 109–128. Springer, Heidelberg (2006). https://doi.org/10.1007/11761679_8
12. Blum, A., Furst, M.L., Kearns, M.J., Lipton, R.J.: Cryptographic primitives based on hard learning problems. In: Stinson, D.R. (ed.) CRYPTO 1993. LNCS, vol. 773, pp. 278–291. Springer, Heidelberg (1994). https://doi.org/10.1007/3-540-48329-2_24
13. Boneh, D., Goh, E.-J., Nissim, K.: Evaluating 2-DNF formulas on ciphertexts. In: Kilian, J. (ed.) TCC 2005. LNCS, vol. 3378, pp. 325–341. Springer, Heidelberg (2005). https://doi.org/10.1007/978-3-540-30576-7_18
14. Boyle, E., Couteau, G., Gilboa, N., Ishai, Y.: Compressing vector OLE. In: ACM CCS 2018. ACM Press, October 2018
15. Boyle, E., Couteau, G., Gilboa, N., Ishai, Y., Kohl, L., Scholl, P.: Efficient pseudorandom correlation generators: Silent ot extension and more. Cryptology ePrint Archive, Report 2019/448 (2019). https://eprint.iacr.org/2019/448
16. Boyle, E., Couteau, G., Gilboa, N., Ishai, Y., Orrú, M.: Homomorphic secret sharing: optimizations and applications. In: ACM CCS 2017. ACM Press, October/November 2017
17. Boyle, E., Gilboa, N., Ishai, Y.: Function secret sharing. In: Oswald, E., Fischlin, M. (eds.) EUROCRYPT 2015, Part II. LNCS, vol. 9057, pp. 337–367. Springer, Heidelberg (2015). https://doi.org/10.1007/978-3-662-46803-6_12
18. Boyle, E., Gilboa, N., Ishai, Y.: Breaking the circuit size barrier for secure computation under DDH. In: Robshaw, M., Katz, J. (eds.) CRYPTO 2016, Part I. LNCS, vol. 9814, pp. 509–539. Springer, Heidelberg (2016). https://doi.org/10.1007/978-3-662-53018-4_19
19. Boyle, E., Gilboa, N., Ishai, Y.: Function secret sharing: improvements and extensions. In: ACM CCS 2016. ACM Press, October 2016
20. Boyle, E., Gilboa, N., Ishai, Y.: Group-based secure computation: optimizing rounds, communication, and computation. In: Coron, J.-S., Nielsen, J.B. (eds.) EUROCRYPT 2017, Part II. LNCS, vol. 10211, pp. 163–193. Springer, Cham (2017). https://doi.org/10.1007/978-3-319-56614-6_6

21. Boyle, E., Gilboa, N., Ishai, Y., Lin, H., Tessaro, S.: Foundations of homomorphic secret sharing. In: 9th Innovations in Theoretical Computer Science Conference, ITCS 2018, Cambridge, MA, USA, 11–14 January 2018, pp. 21:1–21:21 (2018). https://doi.org/10.4230/LIPIcs.ITCS.2018.21

22. Boyle, E., Kohl, L., Scholl, P.: Homomorphic secret sharing from lattices without FHE. In: Ishai, Y., Rijmen, V. (eds.) EUROCRYPT 2019, Part II. LNCS, vol. 11477, pp. 3–33. Springer, Cham (2019). https://doi.org/10.1007/978-3-030-17656-3_1

23. Brakerski, Z., Gentry, C., Vaikuntanathan, V.: (Leveled) fully homomorphic encryption without bootstrapping. In: ITCS 2012. ACM, January 2012

24. Chase, M., et al.: Reusable non-interactive secure computation. IACR Cryptology ePrint Archive 2018, 940 (2018). https://eprint.iacr.org/2018/940

25. Couteau, G.: A note on the communication complexity of multiparty computation in the correlated randomness model. In: Ishai, Y., Rijmen, V. (eds.) EUROCRYPT 2019. LNCS, vol. 11477, pp. 473–503. Springer, Cham (2019). https://doi.org/10.1007/978-3-030-17656-3_17

26. Cramer, R., Damgård, I., Ishai, Y.: Share conversion, pseudorandom secret-sharing and applications to secure computation. In: Kilian, J. (ed.) TCC 2005. LNCS, vol. 3378, pp. 342–362. Springer, Heidelberg (2005). https://doi.org/10.1007/978-3-540-30576-7_19

27. Cramer, R., Damgård, I., Nielsen, J.B.: Multiparty computation from threshold homomorphic encryption. In: Pfitzmann, B. (ed.) EUROCRYPT 2001. LNCS, vol. 2045, pp. 280–300. Springer, Heidelberg (2001). https://doi.org/10.1007/3-540-44987-6_18

28. Damgård, I., Nielsen, J.B., Nielsen, M., Ranellucci, S.: The tinytable protocol for 2-party secure computation, or: gate-scrambling revisited. In: Katz, J., Shacham, H. (eds.) CRYPTO 2017, Part I. LNCS, vol. 10401, pp. 167–187. Springer, Cham (2017). https://doi.org/10.1007/978-3-319-63688-7_6

29. Damgård, I., Pastro, V., Smart, N., Zakarias, S.: Multiparty computation from somewhat homomorphic encryption. In: Safavi-Naini, R., Canetti, R. (eds.) CRYPTO 2012. LNCS, vol. 7417, pp. 643–662. Springer, Heidelberg (2012). https://doi.org/10.1007/978-3-642-32009-5_38

30. Dessouky, G., Koushanfar, F., Sadeghi, A.R., Schneider, T., Zeitouni, S., Zohner, M.: Pushing the communication barrier in secure computation using lookup tables. In: NDSS 2017. The Internet Society, February/March 2017

31. Dodis, Y., Halevi, S., Rothblum, R.D., Wichs, D.: Spooky encryption and its applications. In: Robshaw, M., Katz, J. (eds.) CRYPTO 2016, Part III. LNCS, vol. 9816, pp. 93–122. Springer, Heidelberg (2016). https://doi.org/10.1007/978-3-662-53015-3_4

32. Doerner, J., Shelat, A.: Scaling ORAM for secure computation. In: ACM CCS 2017. ACM Press, October/November 2017

33. Döttling, N., Ghosh, S., Nielsen, J.B., Nilges, T., Trifiletti, R.: TinyOLE: efficient actively secure two-party computation from oblivious linear function evaluation. In: ACM CCS 2017. ACM Press, October/November 2017

34. Druk, E., Ishai, Y.: Linear-time encodable codes meeting the Gilbert-Varshamov bound and their cryptographic applications. In: ITCS 2014. ACM, January 2014

35. Franklin, M.K., Haber, S.: Joint encryption and message-efficient secure computation. J. Cryptol. 9(4), 217–232 (1996). https://doi.org/10.1007/BF00189261

36. Freedman, M.J., Ishai, Y., Pinkas, B., Reingold, O.: Keyword search and oblivious pseudorandom functions. In: Kilian, J. (ed.) TCC 2005. LNCS, vol. 3378, pp. 303–324. Springer, Heidelberg (2005). https://doi.org/10.1007/978-3-540-30576-7_17

37. Ghosh, S., Nielsen, J.B., Nilges, T.: Maliciously secure oblivious linear function evaluation with constant overhead. In: Takagi, T., Peyrin, T. (eds.) ASIACRYPT 2017, Part I. LNCS, vol. 10624, pp. 629–659. Springer, Cham (2017). https://doi.org/10.1007/978-3-319-70694-8_22
38. Gilboa, N., Ishai, Y.: Compressing cryptographic resources. In: Wiener, M. (ed.) CRYPTO 1999. LNCS, vol. 1666, pp. 591–608. Springer, Heidelberg (1999). https://doi.org/10.1007/3-540-48405-1_37
39. Gilboa, N., Ishai, Y.: Distributed point functions and their applications. In: Nguyen, P.Q., Oswald, E. (eds.) EUROCRYPT 2014. LNCS, vol. 8441, pp. 640–658. Springer, Heidelberg (2014). https://doi.org/10.1007/978-3-642-55220-5_35
40. Goldreich, O., Micali, S., Wigderson, A.: How to play ANY mental game or a completeness theorem for protocols with honest majority. In: 19th ACM STOC. ACM Press, May 1987
41. Guo, C., Katz, J., Wang, X., Yu, Y.: Efficient and secure multiparty computation from fixed-key block ciphers. Cryptology ePrint Archive, Report 2019/074 (2019). https://eprint.iacr.org/2019/074
42. Halevi, S., Ishai, Y., Jain, A., Kushilevitz, E., Rabin, T.: Secure multiparty computation with general interaction patterns. In: ITCS 2016. ACM, January 2016
43. Hazay, C., Orsini, E., Scholl, P., Soria-Vazquez, E.: TinyKeys: a new approach to efficient multi-party computation. In: Shacham, H., Boldyreva, A. (eds.) CRYPTO 2018, Part III. LNCS, vol. 10993, pp. 3–33. Springer, Cham (2018). https://doi.org/10.1007/978-3-319-96878-0_1
44. Heyse, S., Kiltz, E., Lyubashevsky, V., Paar, C., Pietrzak, K.: Lapin: an efficient authentication protocol based on ring-LPN. In: Canteaut, A. (ed.) FSE 2012. LNCS, vol. 7549, pp. 346–365. Springer, Heidelberg (2012). https://doi.org/10.1007/978-3-642-34047-5_20
45. Hubacek, P., Wichs, D.: On the communication complexity of secure function evaluation with long output. In: ITCS 2015. ACM, January 2015
46. Ishai, Y., Kilian, J., Nissim, K., Petrank, E.: Extending oblivious transfers efficiently. In: Boneh, D. (ed.) CRYPTO 2003. LNCS, vol. 2729, pp. 145–161. Springer, Heidelberg (2003). https://doi.org/10.1007/978-3-540-45146-4_9
47. Ishai, Y., Kushilevitz, E., Meldgaard, S., Orlandi, C., Paskin-Cherniavsky, A.: On the power of correlated randomness in secure computation. In: Sahai, A. (ed.) TCC 2013. LNCS, vol. 7785, pp. 600–620. Springer, Heidelberg (2013). https://doi.org/10.1007/978-3-642-36594-2_34
48. Ishai, Y., Kushilevitz, E., Ostrovsky, R., Sahai, A.: Batch codes and their applications. In: 36th ACM STOC. ACM Press, June 2004
49. Ishai, Y., Prabhakaran, M., Sahai, A.: Founding cryptography on oblivious transfer – efficiently. In: Wagner, D. (ed.) CRYPTO 2008. LNCS, vol. 5157, pp. 572–591. Springer, Heidelberg (2008). https://doi.org/10.1007/978-3-540-85174-5_32
50. Ishai, Y., Prabhakaran, M., Sahai, A.: Secure arithmetic computation with no honest majority. In: Reingold, O. (ed.) TCC 2009. LNCS, vol. 5444, pp. 294–314. Springer, Heidelberg (2009). https://doi.org/10.1007/978-3-642-00457-5_18
51. Katz, J., Ranellucci, S., Rosulek, M., Wang, X.: Optimizing authenticated garbling for faster secure two-party computation. In: Shacham, H., Boldyreva, A. (eds.) CRYPTO 2018, Part III. LNCS, vol. 10993, pp. 365–391. Springer, Cham (2018). https://doi.org/10.1007/978-3-319-96878-0_13
52. Keller, M., Orsini, E., Rotaru, D., Scholl, P., Soria-Vazquez, E., Vivek, S.: Faster secure multi-party computation of AES and DES using lookup tables. In: Gollmann, D., Miyaji, A., Kikuchi, H. (eds.) ACNS 2017. LNCS, vol. 10355, pp. 229–249. Springer, Cham (2017). https://doi.org/10.1007/978-3-319-61204-1_12

53. Keller, M., Pastro, V., Rotaru, D.: Overdrive: making SPDZ great again. In: Nielsen, J.B., Rijmen, V. (eds.) EUROCRYPT 2018, Part III. LNCS, vol. 10822, pp. 158–189. Springer, Cham (2018). https://doi.org/10.1007/978-3-319-78372-7_6

54. Kilian, J.: Founding cryptography on oblivious transfer. In: Proceedings of the 20th Annual ACM Symposium on Theory of Computing, Chicago, Illinois, USA, 2–4 May 1988, pp. 20–31 (1988). https://doi.org/10.1145/62212.62215

55. Kolesnikov, V., Kumaresan, R.: Improved OT extension for transferring short secrets. In: Canetti, R., Garay, J.A. (eds.) CRYPTO 2013, Part II. LNCS, vol. 8043, pp. 54–70. Springer, Heidelberg (2013). https://doi.org/10.1007/978-3-642-40084-1_4

56. Kolesnikov, V., Kumaresan, R., Rosulek, M., Trieu, N.: Efficient batched oblivious PRF with applications to private set intersection. In: ACM CCS 2016. ACM Press, October 2016

57. Matsumoto, T., Imai, H.: Public quadratic polynomial-tuples for efficient signature-verification and message-encryption. In: Barstow, D., Brauer, W., Brinch Hansen, P., Gries, D., Luckham, D., Moler, C., Pnueli, A., Seegmüller, G., Stoer, J., Wirth, N., Günther, C.G. (eds.) EUROCRYPT 1988. LNCS, vol. 330, pp. 419–453. Springer, Heidelberg (1988). https://doi.org/10.1007/3-540-45961-8_39

58. Naor, M., Pinkas, B.: Oblivious polynomial evaluation. SIAM J. Comput. **35**(5), 1254–1281 (2006)

59. Nielsen, J.B., Nordholt, P.S., Orlandi, C., Burra, S.S.: A new approach to practical active-secure two-party computation. In: Safavi-Naini, R., Canetti, R. (eds.) CRYPTO 2012. LNCS, vol. 7417, pp. 681–700. Springer, Heidelberg (2012). https://doi.org/10.1007/978-3-642-32009-5_40

60. Scholl, P.: Extending oblivious transfer with low communication via key-homomorphic PRFs. In: Abdalla, M., Dahab, R. (eds.) PKC 2018, Part I. LNCS, vol. 10769, pp. 554–583. Springer, Cham (2018). https://doi.org/10.1007/978-3-319-76578-5_19

61. Wang, X., Ranellucci, S., Katz, J.: Authenticated garbling and efficient maliciously secure two-party computation. In: ACM CCS 2017. ACM Press, October/November 2017

62. Wang, X., Ranellucci, S., Katz, J.: Global-scale secure multiparty computation. In: ACM CCS 2017. ACM Press, October/November 2017

63. Wolf, C.: Multivariate quadratic polynomials in public key cryptography. Cryptology ePrint Archive, Report 2005/393 (2005). http://eprint.iacr.org/2005/393

Various Topics

Adaptively Secure and Succinct Functional Encryption: Improving Security and Efficiency, Simultaneously

Fuyuki Kitagawa[1(✉)], Ryo Nishimaki[1(✉)], Keisuke Tanaka[2], and Takashi Yamakawa[1]

[1] NTT Secure Platform Laboratories, Tokyo, Japan
{fuyuki.kitagawa.yh,ryo.nishimaki.zk,takashi.yamakawa.ga}@hco.ntt.co.jp
[2] Tokyo Institute of Technology, Tokyo, Japan
keisuke@is.titech.ac.jp

Abstract. Functional encryption (FE) is advanced encryption that enables us to issue functional decryption keys where functions are hardwired. When we decrypt a ciphertext of a message m by a functional decryption key where a function f is hardwired, we can obtain $f(m)$ and nothing else. We say FE is selectively or adaptively secure when target messages are chosen at the beginning or after function queries are sent, respectively. In the weakly-selective setting, function queries are also chosen at the beginning. We say FE is single-key/collusion-resistant when it is secure against adversaries that are given only-one/polynomially-many functional decryption keys, respectively. We say FE is sublinearly-succinct/succinct when the running time of an encryption algorithm is sublinear/poly-logarithmic in the function description size, respectively.

In this study, we propose a generic transformation from weakly-selectively secure, single-key, and sublinearly-succinct (we call "building block") PKFE for circuits into adaptively secure, collusion-resistant, and succinct (we call "fully-equipped") one for circuits. Our transformation relies on *neither* concrete assumptions such as learning with errors *nor* indistinguishability obfuscation (IO). This is the first generic construction of fully-equipped PKFE that does not rely on IO.

As side-benefits of our results, we obtain the following primitives from the building block PKFE for circuits: (1) laconic oblivious transfer (2) succinct garbling scheme for Turing machines (3) selectively secure, collusion-resistant, and succinct PKFE for Turing machines (4) low-overhead adaptively secure traitor tracing (5) key-dependent message secure and leakage-resilient public-key encryption. We also obtain a generic transformation from simulation-based adaptively secure garbling schemes that satisfy a natural decomposability property into adaptively indistinguishable garbling schemes whose online complexity does not depend on the output length.

1 Introduction

1.1 Background

Achieving stronger cryptographic primitives by using weaker ones is one of the central and fundamental tasks in cryptography. We would like to minimize

A. Boldyreva and D. Micciancio (Eds.): CRYPTO 2019, LNCS 11694, pp. 521–551, 2019.
https://doi.org/10.1007/978-3-030-26954-8_17

assumptions to achieve more secure and advanced cryptography. A typical example is how to achieve IND-CCA secure public-key encryption from IND-CPA secure one [21,48,50]. The objective of this study is showing how to achieve more secure and efficient *functional encryption* (FE) from less secure and efficient one in a generic way.

FE [15] is an encryption scheme that enables us to issue functional decryption keys sk_f where a function f is hardwired. We can decrypt a ciphertext $\mathsf{ct_m}$ of a message m by using sk_f. A notable feature of FE is that we obtain $f(\mathsf{m})$ and nothing else when we decrypt $\mathsf{ct_m}$ by sk_f. If we can encrypt messages by a public-key (resp. a master secret key), then we call public-key (resp. secret-key) FE (PKFE and SKFE for short). FE can control what information of messages can be given to owners of functional decryption keys by using various functions. Moreover, FE is a versatile tool to achieve useful cryptographic primitives such as trapdoor permutations, universal samplers, non-interactive multi-party key-exchange [28]. The most prominent application of FE is achieving indistinguishability obfuscation (IO) [10,24] from FE [3,13,14,41,43].

There are three main performance measures of FE. One is the number of issuable functional decryption keys. Another is the level of security. The other is the size of an encryption circuit. If an FE scheme can securely release one/polynomially-many functional decryption key/s, we call it a single-key/collusion-resistant scheme. Roughly speaking, an FE scheme is secure if adversaries cannot distinguish whether a target ciphertext is an encryption of $\mathsf{m_0}$ or $\mathsf{m_1}$ chosen by them. In the security game, adversaries can send functional decryption key queries and receives sk_f for queried f as long as $f(\mathsf{m_0}) = f(\mathsf{m_1})$. If adversaries are required to commit target messages $(\mathsf{m_0}, \mathsf{m_1})$ (resp. and queries $f_1, \ldots, f_q$) at the beginning of the game, we call it *selective* (resp. *weakly selective*) security. If adversaries can decide target messages after they send functional decryption key queries[1], then we call it *adaptive* security. The size of an encryption circuit must depend on the length of messages to be encrypted. Moreover, the size might depend on the size of functions supported by the scheme as several known FE schemes do [33,51]. The dependence on the size of functions should be as low as possible to achieve better efficiency. FE is called *succinct/sublinearly-succinct* if the dependence is logarithmic/sublinear.

It is desirable to achieve the best properties of all performance measures simultaneously. Therefore, the following question is natural.

Can we achieve adaptively secure, collusion-resistant, and succinct PKFE for circuits by using only weakly-selectively secure, single-key, and sublinearly-succinct one?

This question has been extensively studied [1,4,14,29,30,35,37,44], but all previous studies gave only partial answers. The work of Garg and Srinivasan [30] is the most close to an answer to the above problem, but that is not sufficient since they need an additional algebraic assumption and the ciphertext size of the resulting scheme depends on output-length of circuits supported by the scheme.

---

[1] Of course, adversaries can send queries after they decided a pair of target messages.

In this study, we give an affirmative answer to the open question above, which was clearly stated by Garg and Srinivasan [29]. We sometimes call the building-block and goal-primitive in the question above *obf-minimum*[2] and *fully-equipped* PKFE, respectively in this paper.

One might wonder why we do not start with weakly-selectively secure, single-key, and *non-succinct* FE. This is because there is a huge gap between non-succinct FE and sublinearly-succinct one. We know that sub-exponentially-secure sublinearly-succinct FE implies IO for circuits [3,14,29,39–42]. We also know that non-succinct PKFE (resp. SKFE) is achieved by *plain public-key encryption (resp. one-way function)* [33,51]. It is unlikely that we can achieve IO from plain public-key encryption. Thus, we start with sublinearly-succinct FE. We also emphasize that we focus on transformations with *polynomial security loss* in this study. If sub-exponential security loss is allowed, we can achieve IO from obf-minimum SKFE/PKFE. We rely on neither sub-exponential security nor IO in this study. We stress that one of the big issues in cryptography is to avoid sub-exponential security loss. Sub-exponential security loss significantly degrades security and efficiency of cryptographic schemes in general. In particular, in the area of obfuscation-based (or FE-based) cryptography, avoiding sub-exponential security loss has been actively studied [2,5,6,27–29,31,46].

Hereafter, we use the following notations. Relationships between different notions of PKFE and SKFE are parameterized by $(\#\mathsf{key}, \#\mathsf{ct}, \mathsf{sec}, \mathsf{eff})$. Here, $\#\mathsf{key} \in \{1_{\mathsf{key}}, \mathsf{unb}_{\mathsf{key}}\}$ and $\#\mathsf{ct} \in \{1_{\mathsf{ct}}, \mathsf{unb}_{\mathsf{ct}}\}$ denote the number of functional-decryption-keys/ciphertexts: unb means unbounded polynomially many, $\mathsf{sec} \in \{\mathsf{w\text{-}sel}, \mathsf{sel}, \mathsf{ada}\}$ denotes weakly-selective, selective or adaptive security, and $\mathsf{eff} \in \{\mathsf{ns}, \mathsf{sls}, \mathsf{fs}\}$ denotes the efficiency: ns, sls, and fs denote non-succinct, sublinearly-succinct, and succinct, respectively. In the case of PKFE, we omit $\#\mathsf{ct}$[3].

Known Transformations for Better Security and Efficiency. There are several techniques to strengthen security and/or improve the efficiency of FE. Ananth, Brakerski, Segev, and Vaikuntanathan [1] presented a transformation from selectively secure FE to adaptively secure FE. Unfortunately, this transformation does not preserve (sublinear-)succinctness. This is because the transformation uses a $(\mathsf{unb}_{\mathsf{key}}, 1_{\mathsf{ct}}, \mathsf{ada}, \underline{\mathsf{ns}})$-SKFE scheme[4] [33] as a key building block. Garg and Srinivasan [29], and Li and Micciancio [44] presented transformations from single-key and sublinearly-succinct PKFE to collusion-resistant one. More specifically, the transformation by Garg and Srinivasan [29] is from $(1_{\mathsf{key}}, \mathsf{w\text{-}sel}, \mathsf{sls})$-PKFE to $(\mathsf{unb}_{\mathsf{key}}, \mathsf{sel}, \mathsf{fs})$-PKFE. However, these transformations do not preserve adaptive security. Ananth, Jain, and Sahai [4] and Bitansky and Vaikuntanathan [14] presented a transformation from $(\mathsf{unb}_{\mathsf{key}}, \mathsf{sel}, \mathsf{ns})$-PKFE to

---

[2] See the subsequent paragraph for the reason of naming "obf-minimum".

[3] In the case of PKFE, $\#\mathsf{ct}$ is trivially unb.

[4] In the setting of SKFE, only an entity that has a master secret-key can generate ciphertexts. Thus, adversaries is allowed to send messages as queries and receives ciphertexts in its security game. When adversaries can send one/polynomially-many message(s), we say one/many-ciphertext SKFE.

(unb$_{key}$, sel, fs)-PKFE. This transformation also does not preserve adaptive security. Ananth and Sahai [7] presented a transformation (denoted by AS16 transformation) from (unb$_{key}$, sel, fs)-PKFE for circuits to (unb$_{key}$, ada, fs)-PKFE for Turing machines (TMs) by using (1$_{key}$, 1$_{ct}$, ada, fs)-SKFE for TMs. If the building block (1$_{key}$, 1$_{ct}$, ada, fs)-SKFE is for *circuits*, then the transformation also works and we obtain the resulting PKFE for *circuits*. The difference from the transformation by Ananth et al. [1] is that we can start with (1$_{key}$, 1$_{ct}$, ada, f$\underline{s}$)-SKFE. AS16 transformation is the closest to what we want, but not satisfactory since it uses IO (that is, *sub-exponentially secure* FE). All these transformations sacrifice either adaptive security or succinctness or rely on IO. Thus, the transformation in the question above has been remaining open in the area of FE.

Crucial Ingredient: Adaptive Garbling. As we saw above, if we can obtain (1$_{key}$, 1$_{ct}$, ada, fs)-SKFE for circuits from (1$_{key}$, w-sel, sls)-PKFE, then we resolve the open question above by using the transformations of Garg and Srinivasan [29] and Ananth and Sahai [7]. In fact, (1$_{key}$, 1$_{ct}$, ada, fs)-SKFE for circuits is essentially the same as *adaptively indistinguishable garbling schemes (indistinguishability-based definition [37])* whose online computational complexity is poly(log $|C|, n, \lambda$) where C is a circuit to be garbled, n is the input length of C, and λ is the security parameter[5]. Here, the online computational complexity means the computational complexity to encode an input. We call garbling schemes whose online computational complexity is poly(log $|C|, n, \lambda$) *circuit-succinct* garbling schemes.[6] Thus, we focus on adaptive and circuit-succinct garbling schemes.

Several previous works [11,30,35–38] have proposed adaptively secure garbling schemes. The garbling scheme of Bellare, Hoang, and Rogaway is not circuit-succinct, that is, the online computational complexity is poly($|C|, \lambda$). The garbling scheme of Hemenway, Jafargholi, Ostrovsky, Scafuro, and Wichs [35] achieves online computational complexity $(n + m + w)$poly(λ) where n, m, and w are the input length, output length, and width of a circuit to be garbled, respectively (they also presented a garbling scheme for NC^1 circuits whose complexity is $(n + m)$poly(λ)). Jafargholi, Scafuro, and Wichs [37] presented an adaptively indistinguishable garbling scheme whose online computational complexity is $(n + w)$poly(λ). The garbling scheme of Garg and Srinivasan [30] (we call GS18 scheme in this paper) achieved online computational complexity $O(n+m) + $poly(log $|C|, \lambda$). Others [36,38] are garbling scheme for NC^1 circuits. None of these is satisfactory for our goal since the complexity depends on a polynomial of $|C|$, w, d, or m.

GS18 scheme is closest to our goal. However, there are two issues as follows.

1. GS18 scheme is based on a concrete assumption (the CDH, LWE, or factoring assumptions). More specifically, the scheme is based on updatable laconic

---

[5] In fact, there are subtle issues to transform a garbling scheme into a single-key and single-ciphertext SKFE (the opposite is easy). See the full version for more details.

[6] Note that this is different from succinct garbling schemes [5,12] since ours is for circuits while succinct garbling schemes are for TMs.

oblivious transfer (LOT) [19], which is achieved by the CDH, LWE, or factoring assumptions [16,19,23].
2. GS18 scheme is simulation-based secure. Therefore, the online computational complexity must be at least linear in m since Applebaum, Ishai, Kushilevitz, and Waters [8] showed the lower bound of online complexity for simulation-based secure garbled circuits.

Getting Rid of the Dependence on Output Length. If we can generically transform a simulation-based adaptively secure garbling scheme whose online computational complexity is $\text{poly}(n, m, g(|C|), \lambda)$ where $g(\cdot)$ is some function (such as $\log(\cdot)$) into an adaptively *indistinguishable* garbling scheme whose online computational complexity is $\text{poly}'(n, g(|C|), \lambda)$, then we can solve the second issue explained above by using GS18 scheme [30] as a building block. In fact, Jafargholi et al. left such a transformation as an open problem [37]. We quote their sentence in a footnote.[7] This open question is related to our main question since $(1_{\text{key}}, 1_{\text{ct}}, \text{ada}, \text{fs})$-SKFE is the crucial ingredient as explained above.

1.2   Our Contributions

We solved the open problem explained in the previous section. In particular, we prove the following theorem.

Theorem 1.1 (Main theorem). *Assume that there exists weakly-selectively secure, single-key, and sublinearly-succinct PKFE for circuits, then there exists adaptively secure, collusion-resistant, and succinct PKFE for circuits.*

All our constructions and transformations in this study incur only polynomial security loss. To obtain our crucial ingredient, $(1_{\text{key}}, 1_{\text{ct}}, \text{ada}, \text{fs})$-SKFE, we will prove the (informal) theorems below, which are of independent interests, and construct an adaptively secure garbling scheme whose online computational complexity is $\text{poly}(\log |C|, n, \lambda)$ by combining (a variant of) GS18 scheme.

Theorem 1.2 (Informal, see Theorem 4.5). *Assume that there exists $(1_{\text{key}}, \text{w-sel}, \text{sls})$-PKFE for circuits, then there exists updatable laconic oblivious transfer.*

That is, we can generically construct updatable LOT from obf-minimum FE. This solves the first issue of GS18 scheme. This itself is interesting since this is the first construction of LOT that relies on *neither* specific number theoretic assumptions *nor* IO.[8] Therefore, we obtain an adaptively secure garbling scheme whose online computational complexity is $O(n + m) + \text{poly}(\log |C|, \lambda)$ from obf-minimum PKFE via GS18 scheme. Note that, to achieve this, we need some

---

[7] Jafargholi et al. wrote *"It remains an open problem whether it is possible to show a more general transformation from garbled circuits with adaptive security (and maybe other natural properties) to garbled circuits with indistinguishability based adaptive security and online complexity independent of the output size."* [37].

[8] Ananth and Lombardi present an LOT protocol based on IO [5].

tweaks for the garbling scheme since the security level of our updatable LOT is slightly weaker than that used in GS18 scheme. In fact, we prove that such a weaker LOT is sufficient to achieve an adaptively secure garbling scheme that we need. However, for simplicity, we give only informal theorems here. See Sect. 2 for more details.

We propose two solutions for the second issue of GS18 scheme. One is proposing an extension of AS16 transformation [7] in the following theorem.

Theorem 1.3 (Informal, see Theorem 6.1). *If there exists* $(\mathsf{unb_{key}}, \mathsf{sec}, \mathsf{eff})$-*PKFE for single-bit output circuits, then there exists* $(\mathsf{unb_{key}}, \mathsf{sec}, \mathsf{eff})$-*PKFE for multi-bit output circuits where* $\mathsf{sec} \in \{\mathsf{w\text{-}sel}, \mathsf{sel}, \mathsf{ada}\}$ *and* $\mathsf{eff} \in \{\mathsf{ns}, \mathsf{sls}, \mathsf{fs}\}$. *This transformation preserves adaptive security and succinctness.*

If we set $m = 1$ (that is, single-bit output) in adaptively secure garbling scheme whose online computational complexity is $O(n, m, \log|C|, \lambda)$, then we obtain adaptively secure circuit-succinct garbling scheme for *single-bit output* circuits. We plug this into AS16 transformation, and then we obtain $(\mathsf{unb_{key}}, \mathsf{ada}, \mathsf{fs})$-PKFE for *single-bit output* circuits. Lastly, by applying the informal theorem above, we can obtain fully-equipped PKFE. See the next section for more details. Note that it is easy to transform our variant of GS18 scheme into $(1_{\mathsf{key}}, 1_{\mathsf{ct}}, \mathsf{ada}, \mathsf{fs})$-SKFE for single-bit output circuits. See the full version for details.

The other is using the transformation in the following theorem.

Theorem 1.4 (Informal). *Assume that there exists a simulation-based adaptively secure garbling scheme whose online computational complexity depends on the output length of circuits and that satisfies a natural decomposability property, then there exists an indistinguishability-based adaptively secure garbling scheme whose online computational complexity does not depend on the output length of circuits. The overhead of the transformation is not large, that is, the online complexity affected by other parameters ($|C|$, n, and λ) do not change in an asymptotic sense.*

Known adaptive garbling schemes satisfy the natural decomposability property. That is, we solve the open question by Jafargholi et al. [37]. Note that the first solution is much simpler than the second one. However, the technique used in the transformation in Theorem 1.4 is related to other our techniques in this study, and adaptively secure circuit-succinct garbling schemes are closely related to our goal as we explained so far. Moreover, Theorem 1.4 solves the open problem presented by Jafargholi et al. [37] (We think this is of an independent interest). Therefore, we also include the second solution in this paper.

More Implications of Our Results. Ananth and Lombardi [5] proved that if there exists single-key and succinct PKFE for circuits and one of CDH/LWE/factoring assumptions holds, then there exists succinct garbling scheme for TMs. The concrete assumptions come from that they use LOT. We can replace their LOT with our LOT based on FE[9]. Thus, we obtain the following corollary.

---

[9] The security level of our LOT is sufficient for their purpose.

Corollary 1.1. *If there exists* $(1_{\mathsf{key}}, \mathsf{w\text{-}sel}, \mathsf{sls})$-*PKFE for circuits, then there exists a succinct garbling scheme for TMs.*

We also obtain the following corollary by combining with the known results [7,29].

Corollary 1.2. *If there exists* $(1_{\mathsf{key}}, \mathsf{w\text{-}sel}, \mathsf{sls})$-*PKFE for circuits, then there exists* $(\mathsf{unb}_{\mathsf{key}}, \mathsf{sel}, \mathsf{fs})$-*PKFE for TMs.*

That is, we remove the concrete assumptions from the theorems of Ananth and Lombardi.[10] Agrawal and Maitra [6] also proved that if there exists succinct PKFE for circuits, then there exists PKFE for TMs. However, their PKFE for TMs supports only single/constant-bit output TMs. That is, our corollary above improves their result since ours supports multi-bit output TMs.[11]

Nishimaki, Wichs, and Zhandry [49] presented a traitor tracing scheme that supports an exponentially large identity space and whose ciphertext overhead is $O(\log n)$ where n is the length of identities. Their scheme is based on fully-equipped PKFE that was instantiated by IO previously. Thus, we obtain the following corollary.

Corollary 1.3. *If there exists* $(1_{\mathsf{key}}, \mathsf{w\text{-}sel}, \mathsf{sls})$-*PKFE for circuits, there exists an adaptively secure traitor tracing scheme whose master key size is* $\mathrm{poly}(\log n)$, *secret key size is* $\mathrm{poly}(n)$, *and ciphertext size is* $|\mathsf{m}| + \mathrm{poly}(\log n)$ *where* $|\mathsf{m}|$ *is the message length.*

Brakerski, Lombardi, Segev, and Vaikuntanathan [16] showed key-dependent message (KDM) secure and leakage-resilient PKE can be based on batch encryption, which is essentially the same as LOT. Thus, we obtain the following corollary (See the reference [16] for the details of parameters in the statement).

Corollary 1.4. *If there exists* $(1_{\mathsf{key}}, \mathsf{w\text{-}sel}, \mathsf{sls})$-*PKFE for circuits, then there exists a PKE scheme that satisfies (1) KDM security with respect to affine functions of the secret key and (2) leakage-resilience with leakage rate* $1 - o(1)$.

To the best of our knowledge, except constructions based on IO [20,47], all existing generic constructions of PKE satisfying KDM security or leakage resilience of $1 - o(1)$ rate assume some algebraic property such as homomorphism to the underlying primitive. Our construction is a generic construction of PKE satisfying the above security notions based on a polynomially secure primitive without such algebraic properties.

2 Technical Overview

In this section, we give high level overviews of our techniques. We briefly summarize how to arrive at fully-equipped PKFE from obf-minimum PKFE in Fig. 1.

---

[10] Note that we cannot obtain an adaptively secure scheme in Corollary 1.2 since the succinct garbling for TMs by Ananth and Lombardi is not adaptively secure.

[11] Note that their FE for TMs satisfies a stronger security notion called distributional indistinguishability than standard indistinguishability.

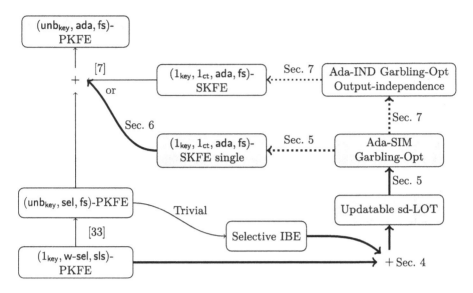

Fig. 1. Illustration of the path from our starting point to the goal: In this figure, "SKFE single" denotes SKFE for single-bit output circuits. "Updatable sd-LOT" denotes selective-database updatable laconic OT. Regarding garbling scheme, "Garbling-Opt" denotes garbling schemes with nearly optimal online complexity and "Output-independence" denotes the online complexity does not depends on output-length (See Sects. 5 and 7 for more details). Ada-SIM/Ada-IND denote simulation-/indistinguishability-based adaptively secure garbling schemes, respectively. Solid thin arrows denote known or trivial implications. Thick solid and dotted arrows denote implications that we prove in this study. Here, in the case of dotted lines, we assume specific properties of underlying tools. See each section for details.

2.1 Laconic OT from Succinct PKFE

We first show an overview of our LOT protocol based on sublinearly succinct PKFE. More precisely, we construct updatable LOT with arbitrary compression factor based on $(1, \mathsf{w\text{-}sel}, \mathsf{sls})$-PKFE.

By the transformation of Cho et al. [19] and an observation by Ananth and Lombardi [5][12], we can transform non-updatable LOT with compression factor 2 into updatable one with arbitrary compression factor using Merkle tree. Thus, to achieve our goal, we can focus on constructing non-updatable LOT with compression factor 2. Our first observation is that we might construct such LOT

---

[12] Cho et al.'s bootstrapping method is not sufficient for LOT whose security holds only when an adversary declares the challenge database before seeing CRS. Therefore, we cannot use the bootstrapping method of Cho et al. directly to make our selective-database (explained later) LOT updatable. However, we can use a *minor variant* of the bootstrapping method observed by Ananth and Lombardi [5] to bootstrap selective-database LOT into updatable one.

based on IBE. In this overview, let the length of a database D be s, that is $D \in \{0,1\}^s$, and $D[i]$ denotes the i-th bit of D.

Laconic OT Based on IBE and Its Problem. We first review the definition of LOT. An LOT consists of four algorithms Gen, Hash, Send, and Receive. We generate a CRS crs using Gen. Hash, given crs and a database D, outputs a short digest d and private state $\widehat{D}$. The algorithm Send, given d, a database location L, and two messages m_0 and m_1, outputs LOT's ciphertext e. By using Receive, a receiver who has the secret state $\widehat{D}$ can decrypt e and obtain $m_{D[L]}$. For security, we require that an honest receiver cannot obtain the other message $m_{1-D[L]}$ even if he has $\widehat{D}$.

Our basic idea for constructing LOT is as follows. When hashing a database D, we first generate a master public-key and master secret-key (MPK, MSK) of IBE and $\mathsf{sk}_{i,D[i]} \leftarrow \mathsf{KG}(\mathsf{MSK}, i\|D[i])$ for every $i \in [s]$. Then, we set MPK as a digest of D and $\{\mathsf{sk}_{i,D[i]}\}_{i\in[s]}$ as a secret state $\widehat{D}$. When generating LOT's ciphertext e for location $L \in [s]$ and two messages m_0 and m_1, we generate $e = (\mathsf{Enc}(\mathsf{MPK}, L\|0, m_0), \mathsf{Enc}(\mathsf{MPK}, L\|1, m_1))$. We see that a receiver who has $\widehat{D} = \{\mathsf{sk}_{i,D[i]}\}_{i\in[s]}$ can obtain $m_{D[L]}$. If the receiver honestly generates $\widehat{D}$ and deletes MSK, he cannot obtain $m_{\overline{D[L]}}$ based on the security of IBE. Moreover, if the size of a master public-key of IBE is independent of the identity length, the size of a digest is also independent of the database size. This construction resembles the one-time signature with encryption from IBE by Döttling and Garg [22].

The above construction seems to satisfy the syntactic and security requirement of LOT. However, the construction has a problem that the hash procedure is randomized. Though the definition of LOT by Cho et al. does not explicitly require that the hash algorithm be deterministic, we observe that the hash algorithm needs to be deterministic for the security notion defined by Cho et al. [19] to be meaningful. In fact, the above basic construction has a crucial problem that if a receiver computes a hash value by himself, he obtains a master secret-key of IBE and can decrypt any ciphertext.

Moreover, it is not clear whether we can apply the bootstrap method proposed by Cho et al. [19] if the hash function of the underlying LOT is randomized. Their bootstrapping method implicitly assumes the hash algorithm of the underlying LOT is deterministic.

Derandomization Using IO. For the above reasons, we need to derandomize the hash algorithm of the above construction. We can make the hash procedure of the above construction deterministic by using IO and puncturable pseudorandom function (PRF) as follows.

In a modified construction, we generate a CRS by obfuscating a circuit that, given a database D, first generates a random coin by using D and a puncturable PRF key and then perform the hash procedure of the basic construction using the random coin. This circuit outputs a digest that is a master public-key of IBE and secret state that is secret-keys of IBE corresponding to D, but not master secret-key.

We can prove the security of the modified construction based on the punctured programming technique proposed by Sahai and Waters [52]. However, to complete the proof, we need to require an adversary to declare the challenge database before seeing a CRS. This is because, in the security proof, we need to generate a CRS as an obfuscated circuit that has the challenge database hardwired. This security notion for LOT is weaker than that used by Garg and Srinivasan [30] to construct adaptive garbling scheme.

Selective-Database Security. In this work, we show that we can construct an adaptive garbling scheme based on LOT whose security holds only when the challenge database is selectively determined. We call an LOT scheme satisfying such a security notion *selective-database* LOT. Note that we allow an adversary for LOT to adaptively choose the challenge location and messages. In fact, in our construction of adaptive garbling scheme, we need LOT whose security holds even if the challenge messages are adaptively chosen. In contrast, the security notion defined by Cho et al. [19] that requires an adversary to declare all challenge instances before seeing CRS is not sufficient for our adaptive garbling scheme. In Sect. 2.2, we explain this issue in more detail.

By weakening the required security notion to selective-database security, LOT no longer imply collision-resistant hash function while the LOT satisfying an adaptive security notion used by Garg and Srinivasan does. This weakening seems to be necessary to achieve LOT from IO due to the substantial barrier that was shown by Asharov and Segev [9].

Replacing IO with Sublinearly Succinct PKFE. We can replace IO in the above construction with sublinearly succinct PKFE by relying on the result shown by Liu and Zhandry [46].

Liu and Zhandry generalized previous works [27–29], and showed we can replace IO with *decomposable obfuscation (dO)* that can be based on polynomially secure $(1, \mathsf{w\text{-}sel}, \mathsf{sls})$-PKFE if the circuit pair to be obfuscated satisfies some condition. Roughly speaking, they showed that if there is a polynomial size "witness" for the functional equivalence of a circuit pair to be obfuscated, IO can be replaced with dO. One particular situation where this condition is satisfied is that in the security proof we modify a circuit to be obfuscated so that it outputs a hardwired value for *a single input* and otherwise it runs in the same way as the original one.

Using the terminology by Liu and Zhandry, hardwiring a single output for an input into a circuit corresponds to *decompose* the circuit to the input. We explain this in more detail. Let C be a circuit of 3-bit input. For a bit string x of length less than 3, let C_x be a circuit $C(x\|\cdot)$, that is, C in which x is hardwired as the first $|x|$ bit of the input. We call such a circuit partial evaluation of C. When decomposing C to the input say 100, we represent C as the tuple of partial evaluations $(C_0, C_{11}, C_{100}, C_{101})$. When considering C as a complete binary tree, $(C_0, C_{11}, C_{100}, C_{101})$ corresponds to the cover of minimum size that contains 100. We see that computation of C on any input can be done using $(C_0, C_{11}, C_{100}, C_{101})$. This is essentially the same as hardwiring a single output $C(100)$ on input 100 into C.

Liu and Zhandry showed if C is obfuscated by dO, we can replace it with an obfuscated circuit that is constructed from partial evaluations $(C_0, C_{11}, C_{100}, C_{101})$ without affecting the behavior of an adversary. At a high level, this change can be done by removing C and embedding $(C_0, C_{11}, C_{100}, C_{101})$ into functional keys of the underlying PKFE. Then, we can perform security proofs in a similar way as the punctured programming.

Consider a circuit of the form $C(x) = C'(x; F_K(x))$, where C' is a circuit, F is a PRF, and K is a PRF key. For simplicity, let C be a circuit of 3 bit input as above. We show how to change the distribution of $C(100)$. By obfuscating C with dO, we can decompose C to 100, that is, we can replace obfuscated C with obfuscated circuit constructed from $(C_0, C_{11}, C_{100}, C_{101})$. Next, we change $F_K(100)$ with a truly random string. To accomplish this step, we require that $F_K(100)$ is pseudorandom even if partial evaluations of $F_K(\cdot)$ for $0, 11$, and 101 are given. Liu and Zhandry call such PRF *decomposing compatible PRF* and the construction of PRF by Goldreich, Goldwasser, and Micali [32] satisfies such a property. Once we can replace $F_K(100)$ with a truly random string, we can change the distribution of $C(100)$. Thus, we can complete the security proof.

Instantiating Our Construction with Sublinearly Succinct PKFE. The circuit to be obfuscated in our construction is of the form $C(x) = C'(x; F_K(x))$, where C' is a circuit executes a setup and key generation algorithm of IBE. In a similar manner as above, we can change the security game so that the master public-key and secret-keys related to the challenge database are generated using a truly random string. Then, we can prove the selective-database security of our LOT based on the selective security of IBE. Note that in the reduction, the challenge identity in the security game of IBE is $L^* \| 1 - D^*[L^*]$, where D^* and L^* are challenge database and position in the security game of LOT. The identity $L^* \| 1 - D^*[L^*]$ depends on the choice of L^* by an adversary for LOT. However, the reduction algorithm can guess the location with the probability at least $\frac{1}{s+1}$, which is inverse polynomial. Thus, a selectively secure IBE is sufficient for this construction.

Therefore, we can replace IO in our construction with dO, which can be based on $(1_{key}, w\text{-sel}, sls)$-PKFE. Moreover, selectively secure IBE can be constructed from $(1_{key}, w\text{-sel}, sls)$-PKFE based on the result by Garg and Srinivasan [29]. Their collusion-resistant PKFE based on $(1_{key}, w\text{-sel}, sls)$-PKFE can be used as an identity-based key encapsulation mechanism the size of whose master public-key is independent of the length of identities.[13] Thus, we can construct selective-database LOT based only on $(1_{key}, w\text{-sel}, sls)$-PKFE.

Comparison with the Construction by Ananth and Lombardi [5]. Ananth and Lombardi showed a construction of LOT based on IO. As they noted, it seems difficult to replace IO in their construction with polynomially secure PKFE.

---

[13] To achieve $\frac{1}{2}$ compression in our construction, it is sufficient that the size of a master public-key is logarithmic in the length of identities. This requirement is more natural for IBE, and thus we assume only this mild condition in the actual construction.

The reason why they need IO is that they constructed LOT based on *witness encryption* [25] by modifying the construction proposed by Cho et al. [19].

Witness encryption based on IO is outside of the framework by Liu and Zhandry. Thus, we cannot construct witness encryption from sublinearly succinct PKFE using the result by Liu and Zhandry. In fact, it is believed to be hard to construct witness encryption based on some polynomially secure primitive including PKFE [25].

2.2 Adaptive Garbling from Selective-Database Updatable Laconic OT

The adaptive garbling scheme by Garg and Srinivasan (we write GS18 scheme for short) is based on adaptively secure updatable LOT [30], where adversaries can select a database after they see a CRS. However, our LOT achieves only selective-database updatable LOT, where adversaries must commit a database before a CRS is given. In fact, we prove that we can achieve an adaptive garbling scheme by using a *selective-database* updatable LOT.

Where is the Adaptive Property of LOT Used in GS18 Scheme? In GS18 scheme, a database of an updatable LOT is determined by an input x. More specifically, the current database is determined by x, each intermediate wire values determined by x and each gate, and output values. A CRS crs of updatable LOT is generated at the offline phase (i.e., when we generate a garbled circuit $\widetilde{C}$) and crs is hardwired in circuits to be garbled by selectively secure garbling. At this point, x might not be determined yet since we consider the *adaptive* setting. Thus, a simulator must have crs before x (and a database) is fixed. This is why Garg and Srinivasan used the adaptive security of LOT.

Overcoming the Issue. The issues is that we need crs at the offline phase. Our idea is deferring using crs until we generate a garbled input (i.e., online phase). To look closer at our idea, we need to explain more on GS18 scheme. In GS18 scheme, "step circuits" are garbled by selectively secure garbling. Each step circuit has the description of each gate of the circuit C to be garbled by the adaptive garbling scheme. Roughly speaking, a step circuit takes as input a digest d of updatable LOT and does the following two procedures.

- Updating the database according to the output wire value of the gate computed from input x.
- Outputting encrypted labels of selectively secure garbling for the next gate via updatable LOT.

The important point is that crs of updatable LOT is hardwired in each step circuit to run Send and SendWrite algorithms, which was explained in Sect. 2.1. This is the problem since we do not fix crs at the offline phase. Here our idea comes in.

Instead of hardwiring crs in each step circuit, we define modified step circuits that take as input not only digest d *but also* crs. Now crs is an input for step circuits. By this change, to generate (simulated) garbled modified step circuits, we do not need crs. As a result, crs need not be determined at the offline phase. In the construction, we put crs in the state information though we generate crs at the offline phase in the construction. In the proof, a simulator can adaptively set the state information when the simulator needs it since the state information is not revealed.

The CRS crs must be fixed when a garbled input $\tilde{x}$ is generated. However, at this point, input x and a database were already determined. Therefore, we can use the selective-database security of updatable LOT because, in the simulation, an adversary of updatable LOT can simulate garbled step circuits without crs, and when x is fixed, the adversary fixes a database based on x and can receive crs in the reduction. This is the main idea behind our adaptive garbling scheme based on selective-database updatable LOT.

Although we can generate crs at the online phase, we select that we put crs in the state information for better online complexity and compatibility with the transformation given in Sect. 7.

Note that, to make our proof work, reduction algorithms attacking updatable LOT need to set the challenge messages as values computed by using CRS. That is, we allow the challenge messages to depend on the CRS. This is why we introduce a new security notion selective-database security for LOT. Our LOT satisfies this security.

From Adaptive Garbling to Adaptively Secure 1-Key 1-Ciphertext SKFE. By combining two transformations explained in this section and the previous section, we obtain an adaptive garbling scheme whose online complexity is $O(n + m) + \mathrm{poly}(\log|C|, \lambda)$ based on $(1_{\mathsf{key}}, \mathsf{w\text{-}sel}, \mathsf{sls})$-PKFE. Especially, by restricting circuits supported by garbling schemes to single-bit output circuits, we obtain an adaptive garbling scheme whose online complexity is $O(n) + \mathrm{poly}(\log|C|, \lambda)$ based on the same assumption.

In the next step, we use the transformation proposed by Ananth and Sahai [7]. In order to use their transformation, we have to transform the constructed adaptive garbling scheme into $(1_{\mathsf{key}}, 1_{\mathsf{ct}}, \mathsf{ada}, \mathsf{fs})$-SKFE. Although adaptive garbling scheme with succinct online encoding and $(1_{\mathsf{key}}, 1_{\mathsf{ct}}, \mathsf{ada}, \mathsf{fs})$-SKFE are essentially the same primitives, there is a difference between them. The security game for $(1_{\mathsf{key}}, 1_{\mathsf{ct}}, \mathsf{ada}, \mathsf{fs})$-SKFE allows an adversary to make an encryption query and key query in arbitrary order while that for adaptive garbling scheme requires an adversary to always make circuit query first. We can solve this issue with a simple transformation using a one-time pad. See the full version for details.

2.3   From Single-bit to Multi-bit Succinct FE by Leveraging Collusion-Resistance

As explained in the previous section, we obtained $(1_{\mathsf{key}}, 1_{\mathsf{ct}}, \mathsf{ada}, \mathsf{fs})$-SKFE for single-bit output functions from $(1_{\mathsf{key}}, \mathsf{w\text{-}sel}, \mathsf{sls})$-PKFE. By using $(1_{\mathsf{key}}, 1_{\mathsf{ct}}, \mathsf{ada}, \mathsf{fs})$-SKFE for single-bit output functions in the transformation by Ananth and Sahai [7], we obtain $(\mathsf{unb}_{\mathsf{key}}, \mathsf{ada}, \mathsf{fs})$-PKFE for single-bit output functions.

Here, we show that we can transform $(\mathsf{unb}_\mathsf{key}, \mathsf{ada}, \mathsf{fs})$-PKFE for single-bit output functions to one for multi-bit output functions.

The transformation is very simple. We construct a PKFE scheme MultiPKFE for multi-bit output functions from a PKFE scheme OnePKFE for single-bit output functions as follows. The encryption algorithm of MultiPKFE works completely in the same manner as that of OnePKFE. The key generation algorithm of MultiPKFE, given a function f with m-bit output, first decomposes the function to $\{f_i\}_{i \in [m]}$ where f_i is a function that computes the i-th bit of $f(\mathsf{m})$ on input m. Then it generates decryption keys sk_{f_i} for the function f_i for $i \in [m]$ by the key generation algorithm of OnePKFE, and outputs $\mathsf{sk}_f := \{\mathsf{sk}_{f_i}\}_{i \in [m]}$. The decryption algorithm of MultiPKFE, given a ciphertext CT of a message m and a decryption key $\mathsf{sk}_f = \{\mathsf{sk}_{f_i}\}_{i \in [m]}$, computes $f_i(\mathsf{m})$ for $i \in [m]$ by using the decryption algorithm of OnePKFE, and outputs $f(\mathsf{m}) = f_1(\mathsf{m}) \| \cdots \| f_m(\mathsf{m})$.

In the above construction, if OnePKFE is adaptively collusion-resistant, then so is MultiPKFE since a decryption key of MultiPKFE consists of a polynomial number of decryption keys of OnePKFE. Moreover, the transformation also preserves the succinctness of a ciphertext since a ciphertext of MultiPKFE consists of a ciphertext of OnePKFE.

We note that this transformation has not been explicitly pointed out before despite its simplicity. Although researchers in this filed might already observe this transformation, we explicitly write it since to the best of our knowledge, nobody explicitly claims.

By combining the transformation with the results of previous sections, we obtain fully-equipped PKFE for all polynomial-size functions from $(1, \mathsf{w\text{-}sel}, \mathsf{sls})$-PKFE.

2.4 Adaptively Indistinguishable Garbling with Near-Optimal Online Complexity

We explained how to construct fully-equipped PKFE for all polynomial-size functions from $(1_\mathsf{key}, \mathsf{w\text{-}sel}, \mathsf{sls})$-PKFE through Sects. 2.1, 2.2, and 2.3. As mentioned in Sect. 1, we have another option to achieve it.

In the option, after constructing adaptive garbling scheme as explained in Sect. 2.2, we transform it into adaptively *indistinguishable* garbling with near-optimal online complexity. More specifically, we construct an adaptively indistinguishable garbling scheme whose online complexity only logarithmically depends on the size of a circuit being garbled, and does not depend on the output length of the circuit. Similarly to adaptive garbling scheme, adaptively indistinguishable garbling with such online complexity can be easily transformed into $(1_\mathsf{key}, 1_\mathsf{ct}, \mathsf{ada}, \mathsf{fs})$-SKFE for (multi-bit output) circuits using one-time pad. Thus, by using the transformation by Ananth and Sahai [7] with the resulting $(1_\mathsf{key}, 1_\mathsf{ct}, \mathsf{ada}, \mathsf{fs})$-SKFE, we obtain fully equipped PKFE for circuits.

We can generalize the transformation from adaptive garbling scheme into adaptively indistinguishable garbling that removes the dependence on the output-length of online encoding so that it captures not only our (and GS18) adaptive garbling scheme but also those proposed by Hemenway et al. [35] and

Jafargholi and Wichs [38]. Thus, this transformation solves the open question posed by Jafargholi et al. [37]. Here, we give an overview of the transformation.

Basic Idea. Our starting point is the simulation-based adaptive garbling given in Sect. 5 (or in [30]), which we denote by $\mathsf{adGC}'_{\mathsf{gs}}$. Recall that the online communication complexity of $\mathsf{adGC}'_{\mathsf{gs}}$ is $n + m + \mathrm{poly}(\lambda, \log |C|)$ where C is the circuit being garbled with n-bit input and m-bit output. Especially, we remark that if we only consider circuits of single-bit output, then the online communication complexity is $n + \mathrm{poly}(\lambda, \log |C|)$. Our first attempt is to decompose a circuit of m-bit output to circuits of single-bit output, and garble each of them by using $\mathsf{adGC}'_{\mathsf{gs}}$. Namely, for garbling a circuit C of m-bit output, we garble C_i, which is a circuit that outputs the i-th bit of an output of C, for each $i \in [m]$. For an input x, the input garbling algorithm generates a single garbled input $\widetilde{x}$ by $\mathsf{adGC}'_{\mathsf{gs}}$.

At first glance, this idea would lead to a garbling scheme with online communication complexity $n + \mathrm{poly}(\lambda, \log |C|)$ since we only garble circuits of single-bit output. However, this idea does not work since a garbling scheme is defined so that 1 garbled input is associated with 1 garbled circuit whereas we need a variant of garbling scheme where 1 garbled input is associated with multiple garbled circuits. Here, we notice that such a variant of garbling scheme can be seen as a single-key SKFE (with function privacy[14]) by interpreting garbled circuits and garbled inputs as ciphertexts and decryption keys of SKFE, respectively. By this interpretation, the online communication and computational complexity as garbling are translated into the secret key length and running time of key generation, and the size of a circuit being garbled is translated into the message length. Based on this observation, we can see that what we need to construct an adaptively indistinguishable garbling with succinct online complexity is an adaptively secure single-key SKFE scheme with succinct decryption key and key generation in the sense that they only logarithmically depend on the message-length.

Single-Key SKFE with Succinct Decryption Key and Key Generation. Our idea to construct such an SKFE scheme is to plug $\mathsf{adGC}'_{\mathsf{gs}}$ into the construction of adaptively secure single-key SKFE by Gorbunov, Vaikuntanathan and Wee [33].[15] We first briefly review their construction. In their construction, for a message m, the encryption algorithm garbles the universal circuit $U(\mathsf{m}, \cdot)$, which is given a description of a function f as input and outputs $f(\mathsf{m})$, by Yao's garbling scheme to generate a garbled circuit $\widetilde{U}$ along with labels that are needed to evaluate the garbled circuit. Then it encrypts $\widetilde{U}$ and labels by a secret-key non-committing encryption for receiver (SK-NCER) to generate a ciphertext of

---

[14] We say that an SKFE scheme is function private if a decryption key does not reveal the associated function. As shown by Brakerski and Segev [17], we can generically add the function privacy to any SKFE scheme. Thus we do not care about function privacy in this overview.

[15] Though Gorbunov et al. [33] presented their construction in the public key setting, the same construction works in the secret key setting.

the SKFE scheme.[16] Here, SK-NCER is a special type of SKE in which we can generate a "fake" ciphertext that can be opened to any message that is later chosen along with a corresponding "fake" decryption key. We note that we can construct an SK-NCER scheme whose decryption-key-length is proportional to the message-length from any SKE scheme by "double-encryption" construction similarly to some previous works [18,34]. Namely, we encrypt each bit of the message under two different keys either of which is given to the decryptor. A decryption key of the SKFE scheme for a function f consists of secret keys of SK-NCER that enable one to recover labels corresponding to f. By using the decryption key, one first recovers labels corresponding to f and then evaluates the garbled circuit $\widetilde{U}$ with these labels to obtain $U(\mathsf{m}, f) = f(\mathsf{m})$. Intuitively, the security of the SKFE scheme holds since an adversary who has a decryption key for f cannot obtain labels that do not correspond to f, and thus $\widetilde{U}$ does not reveal information of m beyond the value of $U(\mathsf{m}, f) = f(\mathsf{m})$ by the security of Yao's garbling. We note that it is essential to encrypt $\widetilde{U}$ by SK-NCER for achieving the adaptive security since Yao's garbling only has the selective security and thus we cannot simulate $\widetilde{U}$ before an input is determined.[17] Since the size of $\widetilde{U}$ is proportional to the message-length of the SKFE scheme and the decryption-key-length of SK-NCER depends on its message-length, the decryption-key-length of their SKFE scheme is proportional to the message-length of the SKFE scheme.

Here, we observe that if we use an adaptive garbling scheme instead of Yao's garbling, then we need not encrypt $\widetilde{U}$ since we can simulate $\widetilde{U}$ before an input is determined by the adaptive security, and we only need to encrypt labels by SK-NCER. Since the number of labels corresponds to the online communication complexity of the underlying garbling scheme, we expect that we could obtain an SKFE scheme with succinct decryption key by plugging $\mathsf{adGC}'_{\mathsf{gs}}$ into this construction. However, there is a problem that $\mathsf{adGC}'_{\mathsf{gs}}$ does not have the *decomposability*, which means that a garbled input is obtained by choosing labels according to each bit of the input whereas the above construction requires the garbling scheme to have the decomposability. Nonetheless, we observe that $\mathsf{adGC}'_{\mathsf{gs}}$ has a similar property to the decomposability called the *quasi-decomposability*, which we introduce in this paper. The quasi-decomposability roughly means that there exists a hash function H such that a garbled input for an input x is generated by choosing labels according to each bit of $\mathsf{H}(x)$ instead of x. We prove that the quasi-decomposability is sufficient to realize the above idea.

---

[16] Though Gorbunov et al. [33] does not use an abstraction as NCER, we observe that their construction can be seen like this.

[17] Though Jafargholi and Wichs [38] showed that Yao's garbling scheme is adaptively secure for certain class of circuits like NC^1, we do not know how to prove its adaptive security for all circuits.

Now, we obtained adaptively secure single-key SKFE with succinct decryption key.[18] We can also see that the key generation algorithm of the scheme is also succinct. As discussed in the previous paragraph, such an SKFE scheme yields an adaptively indistinguishable garbling scheme with succinct online communication/computational complexity.

Other Instantiations. The above construction gives a generic construction of an adaptively indistinguishable garbling scheme whose online complexity does not depend on the output length of the circuit being garbled based on any (quasi-)decomposable adaptive garbling scheme. For example, we can also instantiate the construction with adaptive garbling schemes proposed by Hemenway et al. [35] and Jafargholi and Wichs [38] (the latter is Yao's garbling itself) since they are decomposable. As a result, we obtain adaptively indistinguishable garbling schemes for corresponding circuit classes whose online complexity do not depend on output-length. Previously, such garbling schemes are constructed in an ad hoc manner by Jafargholi et al. [37]. On the other hand, our construction is generic, and thus resolves the open question posed by Jafargholi et al. [37].

Alternative Ad-hoc Way. Knowledgeable readers might think that we can achieve an adaptively indistinguishable garbling scheme that we need by replacing selectively secure garbling schemes in the somewhere adaptive garbling scheme by Garg, Miao, and Srinivasan [26] with GS18 scheme. This idea might work. However, the idea is an ad-hoc solution. Moreover, to formally prove its security, we must use the specific property (and internal structure) of Yao's garbling scheme [45,53] and GS18 scheme at least. We cannot use those schemes in a black-box way.[19] To avoid this issue, prove security in a modular way, and achieve a general transformation, we selected the design explained above.

3 Preliminaries

Definitions of standard notations and primitives are omitted here. Omitted definitions can be found in the full version.

3.1 Known Results on Functional Encryption

Ananth and Sahai [7] proved the following theorem.

---

[18] Strictly speaking, the SKFE scheme achieves a security notion called key-adaptive security slightly weaker than the adaptive security, in which an adversary cannot make any encryption queries after making the key query. We note that this is sufficient for constructing an adaptively indistinguishable garbling scheme since the adaptive security of a garbling scheme only considers the case where a garbled input is generated after a garbled circuit is generated.

[19] We can formally prove adaptive security of the somewhere adaptive garbling scheme by Garg et al. [26] by using specific properties of Yao's selectively secure garbling scheme instead of using selective security in a black-box way.

Theorem 3.1 ([7]). *If there exist* $(\mathsf{unb}_{\mathsf{key}}, \mathsf{sel}, \mathsf{fs})$*-PKFE for circuits and* $(1_{\mathsf{key}}, 1_{\mathsf{ct}}, \mathsf{ada}, \mathsf{fs})$*-SKFE for multi-bit output (resp. single-bit output) circuits, then there exists* $(\mathsf{unb}_{\mathsf{key}}, \mathsf{ada}, \mathsf{fs})$*-PKFE for multi-bit output (resp. single-bit output) circuits.*

Garg and Srinivasan [29] proved the following theorem.

Theorem 3.2 ([29]). *If there exists* $(1_{\mathsf{key}}, \mathsf{w\text{-}sel}, \mathsf{sls})$*-PKFE for circuits, then there exists* $(\mathsf{unb}_{\mathsf{key}}, \mathsf{sel}, \mathsf{fs})$*-PKFE for circuits.*

By combining these theorems, we obtain the following theorem.

Theorem 3.3 ([7,29]). *If there exist* $(1_{\mathsf{key}}, \mathsf{w\text{-}sel}, \mathsf{sls})$*-PKFE for circuits and* $(1_{\mathsf{key}}, 1_{\mathsf{ct}}, \mathsf{ada}, \mathsf{fs})$*-SKFE for multi-bit output (resp. single-bit output) circuits, then there exists* $(\mathsf{unb}_{\mathsf{key}}, \mathsf{ada}, \mathsf{fs}) - PKFE$ *for multi-bit output (resp. single-bit output) circuits.*

4   Selective-Database Laconic OT from PKFE

In this section, we show how to construct (updatable) laconic OT satisfying a security notion we call selective-database security from sublinearly succinct PKFE. We first show that by using IO, we can construct selective-database laconic OT with the compression factor 2. Then, we show that we can replace IO in our construction with sublinearly succinct PKFE by relying on the result of Liu and Zhandry [46]. Finally, we transform our selective-database laconic OT with compression factor 2 into updatable one based on the transformation using Merkle tree proposed by Cho et al. [19].

4.1   Definition of Selective-Database Laconic OT

We use (updatable) laconic OT proposed by Cho et al. [19]. However, the security level that we need in this work is slightly different from those by Cho et al., Garg and Srinivasan [30], and Ananth and Lombardi [5].

Definition 4.1 (Selective-Database Laconic OT). *A laconic OT (LOT) A laconic OT protocol consists of four algorithms.*

$\mathsf{Gen}(1^\lambda) \to \mathsf{crs}$*: This algorithm takes as input the security parameter and outputs a common reference string* crs*.*

$\mathsf{Hash}(\mathsf{crs}, D) =: (d, \widehat{D})$*: This deterministic algorithm takes as input* crs *and a database* $D \in \{0,1\}^*$ *and outputs a digest* d *of* D *and a state* $\widehat{D}$*.*

$\mathsf{Send}(\mathsf{crs}, d, L, m_0, m_1) \to e$*: This algorithm takes as input* crs*,* d*, a database location* $L \in \mathbb{N}$*, and two messages* m_0 *and* m_1 *of length* $p(\lambda)$*, and outputs a ciphertext* e*.*

$\mathsf{Receive}^{\widehat{D}}(\mathsf{crs}, e, L) \to m$*: This is a RAM algorithm with random read access to* $\widehat{D}$*. It takes as input* crs*,* e*, and* $L \in \mathbb{N}$*, and outputs a message* m*.*

These algorithms satisfy the following three properties.

Correctness. For any database D of size at most $M = \text{poly}(\lambda)$, any memory location $L \in [M]$, any pair of messages $(m_0, m_1) \in \{0,1\}^{p(\lambda)}$, it holds that $m_{D[L]} = \text{Receive}^{\widehat{D}}(\text{crs}, \text{Send}(\text{crs}, d, L, m_0, m_1), L)$, where $\text{crs} \leftarrow \text{Gen}(1^\lambda)$ and $(d, \widehat{D}) := \text{Hash}(\text{crs}, D)$.

Selective-Database Adaptive-Message Sender Privacy Against Semi-honest Receivers. There exists a PPT simulator Sim that satisfies $|\Pr[\text{Real}_{\ell\text{OT}}^{\text{sel-db}}(\lambda) = 1] - \Pr[\text{Sim}_{\ell\text{OT}}^{\text{sel-db}}(\lambda) = 1]| \leq \text{negl}(\lambda)$, where the experiments $\text{Real}_{\ell\text{OT}}^{\text{sel-db}}(\lambda)$ and $\text{Sim}_{\ell\text{OT}}^{\text{sel-db}}(\lambda)$ are defined as follows.

$\text{Real}_{\ell\text{OT}}^{\text{sel-db}}(\lambda)$	$\text{Sim}_{\ell\text{OT}}^{\text{sel-db}}(\lambda)$
1. $(D, \text{st}) \leftarrow \mathcal{A}(1^\lambda)$	1. $(D, \text{st}) \leftarrow \mathcal{A}(1^\lambda)$,
2. $\text{crs} \leftarrow \text{Gen}(1^\lambda)$,	2. $\text{crs} \leftarrow \text{Gen}(1^\lambda)$,
3. $d := \text{Hash}(\text{crs}, D)$,	3. $d := \text{Hash}(\text{crs}, D)$,
4. $(L, m_0, m_1, \text{st}') \leftarrow \mathcal{A}(\text{st}, \text{crs})$,	4. $(L, m_0, m_1, \text{st}') \leftarrow \mathcal{A}(\text{st}, \text{crs})$,
5. $e \leftarrow \text{Send}(\text{crs}, d, L, m_0, m_1)$,	5. $e \leftarrow \text{Sim}(\text{crs}, D, L, m_{D[L]})$,
6. $b' \leftarrow \mathcal{A}(\text{crs}, e, \text{st}')$	6. $b' \leftarrow \mathcal{A}(\text{crs}, e, \text{st}')$

where $|D| = M = \text{poly}(\lambda)$, $L \in [M]$, and $m_0, m_1 \in \{0,1\}^{p(\lambda)}$.

We call this security selective-database sender privacy *for short in this paper.*

Efficiency. We require that $|d|$ is bounded by a fixed polynomial in λ independent of $|D|$, the running time of Hash is $|D| \cdot \text{poly}(\log|D|, \lambda)$, and the running time of Send and Receive are $\text{poly}(\log|D|, \lambda)$.

Selective-database adaptive-message sender privacy for updatable laconic OT [19] is defined similarly. A formal definition can be found in the full version.

4.2 Selective-Database Laconic OT with Compression Factor 2 from IO

We show how to construct laconic OT from IO in this subsection. Let $\text{IBE} = (\text{IBE.Setup}, \text{IBE.KG}, \text{IBE.Enc}, \text{IBE.Dec})$ be an IBE scheme. For simplicity, we assume that the randomness space of IBE.Setup is $\{0,1\}^\lambda$ and IBE.KG is deterministic.[20] We let the length of a master public-key of IBE be bounded by some fixed polynomial $\text{poly}_{\text{MPK}}(\lambda, n)$, where n is the length of identities. Then, there exists a polynomial $s = \text{poly}(\lambda)$ such that $s \geq \text{poly}_{\text{MPK}}(\lambda, \log s + 2)$. Let $\text{PPRF} = (\text{F}, \text{Punc})$ be a puncturable PRF whose domain and range are $\{0,1\}^{2s}$ and $\{0,1\}^\lambda$, respectively. Let $i\mathcal{O}$ be an IO.

We construct an LOT protocol $\ell\text{OT} = (\text{Gen}, \text{Hash}, \text{Send}, \text{Receive})$ whose hash algorithm Hash hashes a $2s$ bit database to a digest of $\text{poly}_{\text{MPK}}(\lambda, \log s + 2) \leq s$ bits. Thus, our construction achieves compression factor 2. In the construction, for an integer $i \in [2s]$, $\text{str}(i)$ denotes the bit representation of i.

---

[20] We can always modify any IBE scheme so that it satisfies these two conditions by using PRF.

Setup and key generation circuit SetupKG[K]

Hardwired: puncturable PRF key K.

Input: $D \in \{0,1\}^{2s}$.

Padding: circuit is padded to size pad $:= \max(|\mathsf{SetupKG}|, |\mathsf{SetupKG}^*|)$, where $\mathsf{SetupKG}^*$ is defined in the security proof.

1. Computes $r \leftarrow \mathsf{F}_K(D)$.
2. Computes $(\mathsf{MPK}, \mathsf{MSK}) \leftarrow \mathsf{IBE.Setup}(1^\lambda, 1^{\log s + 2}; r)$.
3. For every $i \in [2s]$, computes $\mathsf{sk}_i \leftarrow \mathsf{IBE.KG}(\mathsf{MSK}, \mathsf{str}(i) \| D[i])$.
4. Outputs $d := \mathsf{MPK}$ and $\widehat{D} := (D, \{\mathsf{sk}_i\}_{i \in [2s]})$.

Fig. 2. The description of SetupKG.

$\mathsf{Gen}(1^\lambda)$:
1. Generates $K \xleftarrow{r} \{0,1\}^\lambda$.
2. Computes $\mathsf{crs} \leftarrow i\mathcal{O}(1^\lambda, \mathsf{SetupKG}[K])$. The circuit SetupKG is defined in Fig. 2.
3. Outputs crs.

$\mathsf{Hash}(\mathsf{crs}, D)$:
1. Outputs $(d, \widehat{D}) \leftarrow \mathsf{crs}(D)$.

$\mathsf{Send}(\mathsf{crs}, d, L, \mathsf{m}_0, \mathsf{m}_1)$:
1. Parses $\mathsf{MPK} \leftarrow d$.
2. For $\alpha \in \{0,1\}$, computes $\mathsf{CT}_\alpha \leftarrow \mathsf{IBE.Enc}(\mathsf{MPK}, \mathsf{str}(L) \| \alpha, \mathsf{m}_\alpha)$.
3. Outputs $e := (\mathsf{CT}_0, \mathsf{CT}_1)$.

$\mathsf{Receive}^{\widehat{D}}(\mathsf{crs}, e, L)$:
1. Sets $\widehat{D} := (D, \{\mathsf{sk}_i\}_{i \in [2s]})$.
2. Parses $e \leftarrow (\mathsf{CT}_0, \mathsf{CT}_1)$.
3. Outputs $m \leftarrow \mathsf{IBE.Dec}(\mathsf{sk}_L, \mathsf{CT}_{D[L]})$.

Theorem 4.1. *Let* IBE *be a selectively secure IBE scheme and* PPRF *be a puncturable PRF. Let* $i\mathcal{O}$ *be IO. Then,* $\ell\mathsf{OT}$ *be a selective-database laconic OT.*

The proof can be found in the full version.

4.3   Replacing IO with Sublinearly Succinct PKFE

IO in our construction can be replaced with sublinearly succinct PKFE by relying on the result of Liu and Zhandry [46]. Liu and Zhandry showed we can replace IO with *decomposable obfuscation (dO)* that can be based on sublinearly succinct PKFE if the circuit pair to be obfuscated satisfies some condition by generalizing previous works [27–29]. Roughly speaking, they showed that if there is a polynomial size "witness" for the functional equivalence of a circuit pair to be obfuscated, IO can be replaced with dO. One particular situation where this condition is satisfied is that in the security proof we modify a circuit to be obfuscated so that it outputs a hard-wired value for a single input and otherwise it runs in the same way as the original one. More formally, we obtain the following theorem as a special case of the result by Liu and Zhandry.

Theorem 4.2 ([46]). *Let $C'(x, r)$ be a circuit. Let $\mathsf{PPRF} = (\mathsf{F}, \mathsf{Punc})$ be a punctured PRF and $K \in \{0, 1\}^\lambda$. Let Punc be deterministic. We define a circuit C_K as $C_K(x) = C'(x, \mathsf{F}_K(x))$. Moreover, we define a circuit C^* as*

$$
C^*_{x^*, K^*, y^*}(x) = \begin{cases} y^* & (x = x^*) \\ C'(x, \mathsf{F}_{K^*}(x)) & (otherwise) \end{cases},
$$

where x^*, $K^* \leftarrow \mathsf{Punc}(K, x^*)$, and $y^* = C(x^*)$ are hardwired into C^*. C_K and $C^*_{x^*, K^*, y^*}$ are parameterized by K and x^*, and they are functionally equivalent for all K and x^*.

Assuming $(1_{\mathsf{key}}, \mathsf{w\text{-}sel}, \mathsf{sls})$-PKFE, there exists a special type of punctured PRF and decomposable obfuscation whose indistinguishability property holds for each pair of circuits $\{(C_K, C^*_{x^*, K^*, y^*})\}_{K, x^*}$ by implementing them using the PRF.

In the above theorem, "a special type of punctured PRF" is a primitive called decomposing compatible PRF by Liu and Zhandry. Decomposing compatible PRF can be constructed from one-way functions via the construction proposed by Goldreich et al. [32], and thus its existence is implied by that of PKFE. See Sect. 2.1 or the paper by Liu and Zhandry [46] for details.

In the construction of selective-database laconic OT based on IO in Sect. 4.2, we apply IO for a pair of circuits SetupKG and SetupKG*. We see that when we apply IO to these circuits, they have exactly the same functional relationship as C and C^* in Theorem 4.2. That is, we obtain the following.

Lemma 4.1. *Circuits $\mathsf{SetupKG}[K]$ and $\mathsf{SetupKG}^*[D^*, K\{D^*\}, \mathsf{MPK}^*, \{\mathsf{sk}_i^*\}_{i \in [2s]}]$ in Sect. 4.2 fall into the circuit class C_K and $C^*_{x^*, K^*, y^*}$ defined in Theorem 4.2.*

Therefore, from Theorem 4.2 and Lemma 4.1, IO that is needed in our construction of selective-database laconic OT in Sect. 4.2 can be instantiated based on sublinearly succinct PKFE.

Moreover, selectively secure IBE can be constructed from sublinearly succinct PKFE [29], and puncturable PRF can be based on one-way functions. Thus, we obtain the following theorem.

Theorem 4.3. *Assume that there exists $(1_{\mathsf{key}}, \mathsf{w\text{-}sel}, \mathsf{sls})$-PKFE for circuits. Then, there exists selective-database laconic OT with compression factor 2.*

4.4   From Non-updatable to Updatable

Cho et al. [19] showed we could bootstrap a laconic OT with the compression factor 2 into an updatable laconic OT with arbitrary compression factor using a garbling scheme and Merkle hash tree. Their bootstrapping method considers laconic OT that satisfies a weak security notion where in addition to the challenge database, the challenge location and messages are also fixed at the beginning of the security game. As Ananth and Lombardi [5] pointed out, if we use selective-database laconic OT as a building block for the bootstrapping method, then we have to use a minor variant of the method to obtain selective-database updatable laconic OT (the original bootstrapping method is not sufficient for us). More specifically, we have to sample fresh crs_j for each depth j of the Merkle hash tree in the bootstrapping method. We use this variant since our laconic OT is selective-database secure. That is, we have the following theorem.

Theorem 4.4 ([5,19]). *Assume that there exists selective-database laconic OT with the compression factor 2. Then, there exists selective-database updatable laconic OT with arbitrary compression factor.*

By combining Theorems 4.3 and 4.4, we obtain the following theorem.

Theorem 4.5. *Assume that there exists* $(1_{key}, w\text{-}sel, sls)$-*PKFE. Then, there exists selective-database updatable laconic OT with arbitrary compression factor.*

5   Adaptive Garbling from Selective-Database Laconic OT

In this section, we present an adaptive garbling scheme with nearly optimal online communication/computational complexity based on selective-database updatable LOT. Garg and Srinivasan presented such an adaptive garbling scheme based on *adaptively secure* updatable LOT [30], which is instantiated by concrete assumptions such as CDH [16,19,23]. However, we cannot directly use their adaptive garbling scheme due to the following two reasons.

1. Our goal in this section is achieving adaptive garbling scheme from succinct PKFE (i.e., we do not rely on any specific assumption such as the CDH assumption).
2. The updatable LOT protocol presented in Sect. 4 is *selective-database* updatable LOT.

We will show that we can achieve an adaptive garbling scheme with nearly optimal online communication/computational complexity from *selective-database* updatable LOT in the rest of this section.

5.1   Description of Our Adaptive Garbling Scheme

In this section, we present our adaptive garbling scheme and properties that it satisfies.

Theorem 5.1. *If there exist selective-database updatable LOT, somewhere equivocal encryption, and selectively secure garbled circuits, then there exists an adaptively secure garbling scheme for circuits with online communication complexity* $n + m + poly(\lambda, \log |C|)$ *and online computational complexity* $O(n+m) + poly(\lambda, \log |C|)$.

From this theorem, Theorem 4.5, and the fact that selectively secure garbled circuits and somewhere equivocal encryption can be constructed from one-way functions [35], we obtain the following theorem.

Theorem 5.2. *If there exists* $(1_{\text{key}}, \text{w-sel}, \text{sls})$-*PKFE, then there exists an adaptively secure garbling scheme for circuits with online communication complexity* $n + m + \text{poly}(\lambda, \log |C|)$ *and online computational complexity* $O(n + m) + \text{poly}(\lambda, \log |C|)$.

Conventions. Without loss of generality, we assume that circuits consist of only NAND gates. Let n, m, and $N - n$ be the input length, output length, and number of NAND gates of the circuit. An index is assigned to each input and gate. That is, from 1 to n are input wires, from $n + 1$ to $N - m$ are intermediate NAND gates, and $N - m + 1$ to N are output gates of the circuit. Note that a gate whose inputs come from gate i and j has an index greater than i and j. Each gate $g \in [n + 1, N]$ is represented by a pair $(i, j) \in [g - 1] \times [g - 1]$. That is, the inputs of g are outputs of gates i and j. In this section, we use r_i, x_i, and y_i instead of $r[i]$, $x[i]$, and $y[i]$ to mean the i-th bit of r, x, and y, respectively for notational simplicity.

A Variant of GS18 Garbling Scheme. We prove Theorem 5.1 in the rest of this section. First, we describe our adaptive garbling scheme. We put red underlines at different points from the adaptive garbling scheme by Garg and Srinivasan [30]. Let $\Sigma := (\text{KeyGen}, \text{Enc}, \text{Dec}, \text{SimEnc}, \text{SimKey})$, $\text{GC} := (\text{GC.Grbl}, \text{GC.Eval})$, and $\Pi := (\text{Gen}, \text{Hash}, \text{Send}, \text{Receive}, \text{SendWrite}, \text{ReceiveWrite})$ be a somewhere equivocal encryption scheme, a (selectively secure) garbling scheme with a corresponding simulator GC.Sim, and an updatable LOT protocol, respectively. Our adaptive garbling scheme $\text{adGC}'_{\text{gs}} := (\text{GbCkt}, \text{Gblnp}, \text{GbEval})$ is as follows.

$\text{GbCkt}(1^\lambda, C)$: This algorithm garbles a circuit $C : \{0, 1\}^n \to \{0, 1\}^m$ as follows.
1. Generates $\text{sek} \leftarrow \text{KeyGen}(1^\lambda)$, and chooses $r \leftarrow \{0, 1\}^N$.
2. Generates $\text{crs} \leftarrow \text{Gen}(1^\lambda)$.
3. Chooses $\text{label}_{k,b}^g \leftarrow \{0, 1\}^\lambda$ and $\text{label}_{k,b}^{g,\text{crs}} \leftarrow \{0, 1\}^\lambda$ for $g \in [n + 1, N + 1]$, $k \in [\lambda]$, and $b \in \{0, 1\}$.
4. From $g = N$ to $g = n + 1$ (decrement g), does the following.
   (a) Interprets gate g as (i, j).
   (b) Computes

$$\widetilde{SC}_g \leftarrow \text{GC.Grbl}(1^\lambda, SC[(r_i, r_j, r_g), (i, j),$$

$$\{(\text{label}_{k,b}^{g+1}, \text{label}_{k,b}^{g+1,\text{crs}})\}_{k \in [\lambda], b \in \{0,1\}}, 0],$$

$$(\{\text{label}_{k,b}^g\}_{k \in [\lambda], b \in \{0,1\}}, \{\text{label}_{k,b}^{g,\text{crs}}\}_{k \in [\lambda], b \in \{0,1\}})).$$

5. Generates $c \leftarrow \text{Enc}(\text{sek}, \{\widetilde{SC}_g\}_{g \in [n+1,N]})$.
6. Outputs $\widetilde{C} := c$ and $\text{st} := (r, \text{sek}, \{(\text{label}_{k,b}^{n+1}, \text{label}_{k,b}^{n+1,\text{crs}})\}_{k \in [\lambda], b \in \{0,1\}}, \text{crs})$.

Gblnp(st, x): This algorithm garbles an input $x \in \{0,1\}^n$ as follows.

1. Parses $st := (r, sek, \{(label_{k,b}^{n+1}, label_{k,b}^{n+1,crs})\}_{k \in [\lambda], b \in \{0,1\}}, crs)$.
2. Sets $D := r_1 \oplus x_1 \| \cdots \| r_n \oplus x_n \| 0^{N-n}$.
3. Computes $(d, \widehat{D}) := \mathsf{Hash}(crs, D)$.
4. Outputs $\widetilde{x} := (\{(label_{k,d[k]}^{n+1}, label_{k,crs[k]}^{n+1,crs})\}_{k \in [\lambda]}, crs, r_1 \oplus x_1, \ldots, r_n \oplus x_n, sek, r_{N-m+1}, \ldots, r_N)$.

GbEval($\widetilde{C}, \widetilde{x}$): This evaluation algorithm does the following.

1. Parses $\widetilde{C} = c$ and $\widetilde{x} := (\{(label_{k,d[k]}, label_{k,crs[k]}^{crs})\}_{k \in [\lambda]}, crs, r_1 \oplus x_1, \ldots, r_n \oplus x_n, sek, r_{N-m+1}, \ldots, r_N)$.
2. Sets $D := r_1 \oplus x_1 \| \cdots \| r_n \oplus x_n \| 0^{N-n}$.
3. Computes $(d, \widehat{D}) := \mathsf{Hash}(crs, D)$.
4. Computes $\{\widetilde{SC}_g\}_{g \in [n+1, N]} \leftarrow \mathsf{Dec}(sek, c)$.
5. Set $\overline{label} := \{label_{k,d[k]}\}_{k \in [\lambda]}$ and $\overline{label}^{crs} := \{label_{k,crs[k]}^{crs}\}_{k \in [\lambda]}$.
6. For $g = n+1, \ldots, N$
   (a) Interprets g as (i, j).
   (b) Computes $(gout_1, gout_2) := \mathsf{GC.Eval}(\widetilde{SC}_g, (\overline{label}, \overline{label}^{crs}))$.
   (c) Computes $(\gamma, e) := \mathsf{Receive}^{\widehat{D}}(crs, \mathsf{Receive}^{\widehat{D}}(crs, gout_1, i), j)$.
   (d) Sets $\overline{label} := \mathsf{ReceiveWrite}^{\widehat{D}}(crs, g, \gamma, e)$ and $\overline{label}^{crs} := gout_2$.
7. Reads D from $\widehat{D}$.
8. Outputs $D_{N-m+1} \oplus r_{N-m+1} \| \cdots \| D_N \oplus r_N$.

Remark 5.1. We assume that the length of crs is λ for ease of notation instead of writing $\{label_{k',b}^{g,crs}\}_{k' \in [\mathrm{poly}(\lambda)], b \in \{0,1\}}$. We often omit the region where indices (k,b) run if it is clear from the context. That is, we often write $\{label_{k,b}^g\}$ and $\{label_{k,b}^{g,crs}\}$ to denote $\{label_{k,b}^g\}_{k \in [\lambda], b \in \{0,1\}}$ and $\{label_{k,b}^{g,crs}\}_{k \in [\lambda], b \in \{0,1\}}$.

Proofs of correctness and security can be found in the full version.

Online Complexity of Gblnp. We confirm that our garbling scheme satisfies the complexity described in Theorem 5.2.

Online Communication Complexity: We see that $|\widetilde{x}| = \lambda^2 + \lambda + |crs| + n + m + |sek|$. By the efficiency of updatable LOT, $|crs| = \lambda$ holds[21]. Recall that $|sek| = t \cdot s \cdot \mathrm{poly}(\lambda)$ where s is the block-length and t is the equivocation parameter. In our setting, we set $s := |\widetilde{SC}|$ and $t := \log N$. Moreover, by the efficiency of updatable LOT, $|\widetilde{SC}| = \mathrm{poly}(\log N, \lambda)$. Therefore, $|sek| = \mathrm{poly}(\log N, \lambda)$. Thus, $|\widetilde{x}| = n + m + \mathrm{poly}(\log |C|, \lambda)$ (note that $|C| = N$).

Online Computational Complexity: The running time of our Gblnp depends on N since it computes $\mathsf{Hash}(crs, D)$. However, we can reduce the computational complexity using a specific structure of the updatable LOT by Cho et al. [19] (recall that our updatable LOT in Sect. 4 also uses this structure)

---

[21] In fact, in our LOT protocol in Sect. 4, $|crs| = \mathrm{poly}(\lambda)$. However, it does not matter here since it is absorbed in $\mathrm{poly}(\log |C|, \lambda)$ part.

Modified Step Circuit SC

Input: A digest d and the CRS crs.
Hardwired value: (r_i, r_j, r_g), (i, j), $\{\mathsf{label}_{k,b}\}$, $\{\mathsf{label}_{k,b}^{\mathsf{crs}}\}$, and flag $\in \{0, 1\}$.

1. Generates $e_b \leftarrow \mathsf{SendWrite}(\mathsf{crs}, d, g, b, \{\mathsf{label}_{k,0}, \mathsf{label}_{k,1}\}_{k \in [\lambda]})$ for $b \in \{0, 1\}$.
2. If flag $= 0$, then $\gamma(\alpha, \beta) := \mathsf{NAND}(\alpha \oplus r_i, \beta \oplus r_j) \oplus r_g$ for all $\alpha, \beta \in \{0, 1\}$.
3. If flag $= 1$, then $\gamma(\alpha, \beta) := r_g$ for all $\alpha, \beta \in \{0, 1\}$.
4. Generates

$$f_0 \leftarrow \mathsf{Send}(\mathsf{crs}, d, j, (\gamma(0,0), e_{\gamma(0,0)}), (\gamma(0,1), e_{\gamma(0,1)}))$$
$$f_1 \leftarrow \mathsf{Send}(\mathsf{crs}, d, j, (\gamma(1,0), e_{\gamma(1,0)}), (\gamma(1,1), e_{\gamma(1,1)}))$$

5. Outputs $\mathsf{Send}(\mathsf{crs}, d, i, f_0, f_1)$ and $\{\mathsf{label}_{k,\mathsf{crs}[k]}^{\mathsf{crs}}\}$.

Fig. 3. The description of modified step circuit

by using the same technique as GS18 scheme. We briefly review it. The construction uses Merkle hash tree technique. Therefore, we can efficiently *update* a hash value. Let y and y' consist of ℓ blocks of λ-bits strings. Assume that y is different from y' only in the first k blocks. Given the Merkle hash on y and a set of $\log |y|$ hash values, there exists an efficient algorithm that computes the Merkle hash on y' and whose running time is $O(\lambda(k + \log |y|))$. By using this efficient update algorithm, we can reduce the computational complexity as follows. At offline phase, we compute a hash value on 0^N. We set each block length to be 1. That is, when $x \in \{0, 1\}^n$ is given, we update the first $\lceil n \rceil$ blocks. For updating the hash value on 0^N to the hash value on $(r \oplus x \| 0^{N-n})$, it takes $O(1 \cdot (n + \log N))$ time. That is, the running time of Gblnp is $O(n + m) + \mathsf{poly}(\log |C|, \lambda)$ since Gblnp computes the hash value and outputs $\mathsf{poly}(\lambda) + n + m$ values. Note that Gblnp need not output $(r_{n+1}, \dots, r_{N-m})$.

5.2   Secret-Key FE from Our Adaptive Garbling

We observe that $\mathsf{adGC}_{\mathsf{gs}}'$ can be seen as a single-key and single-ciphertext adaptive SKFE by considering a garbled circuit and a garbled input to be a decryption key and a ciphertext, respectively, where a master secret key is set as $\mathsf{MSK} := (r, \mathsf{sek}, \{\mathsf{label}_{k,b}^{n+1}\}, \{\mathsf{label}_{k,b}^{n+1,\mathsf{crs}}\}, \mathsf{crs}).^{22}$ Moreover, if we only consider single-bit output circuits as a function class, the scheme is fully succinct due to the succinct online complexity of $\mathsf{adGC}_{\mathsf{gs}}'$. See the full version for details.

---

[22] Actually, the direct adaptation only achieves ciphertext-adaptive security where a decryption key must be queried before the challenge ciphertext is given to an adversary. This can be easily overcome by using one-time pad without sacrificing succinctness.

By combining Theorem 5.2 with the above observation, we obtain the following theorem.

Theorem 5.3. *If there exists* $(1_{\mathsf{key}}, \mathsf{w\text{-}sel}, \mathsf{sls})$-*PKFE for circuits, then there exists* $(1_{\mathsf{key}}, 1_{\mathsf{ct}}, \mathsf{ada}, \mathsf{fs})$-*SKFE for single-bit output circuits.*

By combining Theorems 3.3 and 5.3, we obtain the following theorem.

Theorem 5.4. *If there exists* $(1_{\mathsf{key}}, \mathsf{w\text{-}sel}, \mathsf{sls})$-*PKFE for circuits, then there exists* $(\mathsf{unb}_{\mathsf{key}}, \mathsf{ada}, \mathsf{fs})$-*PKFE for single-bit output circuits.*

6   Adaptively Secure, Collusion-Resistant, and Succinct FE

In this section, we show a conversion from collusion-resistant PKFE for single-bit output circuits to one for multi-bit output circuits without sacrificing succinctness. Combined with Theorem 5.4, this gives our main theorem, Theorem 1.1.

6.1   From Single-Bit to Multi-bit Succinct FE by Leveraging Collusion-Resistance

Let $\mathsf{OnePKFE} = (\mathsf{OnePKFE.Setup}, \mathsf{OnePKFE.KG}, \mathsf{OnePKFE.Enc}, \mathsf{OnePKFE.Dec})$ be an PKFE scheme for $\mathcal{M}$, $\mathcal{Y}' := \{0,1\}$, and single-bit output circuits. Then, we construct an PKFE scheme $\mathsf{MultiPKFE} = (\mathsf{MultiPKFE.Setup}, \mathsf{MultiPKFE.KG}, \mathsf{MultiPKFE.Enc}, \mathsf{MultiPKFE.Dec})$ for $\mathcal{M}$, $\mathcal{Y} := \{0,1\}^{\ell}$, and circuits as follows.

$\mathsf{MultiPKFE.Setup}(1^{\lambda})$:
  1. Computes $(\mathsf{MPK}, \mathsf{MSK}) \leftarrow \mathsf{OnePKFE.Setup}(1^{\lambda})$.
  2. Outputs $(\mathsf{MPK}, \mathsf{MSK})$.
$\mathsf{MultiPKFE.KG}(\mathsf{MSK}, f)$:
  1. Computes $\mathsf{sk}_i \leftarrow \mathsf{OnePKFE.KG}(\mathsf{MSK}, f_i)$ for every $i \in [\ell]$ where $f_i(\mathsf{m})$ outputs the i-th bit of $f(\mathsf{m})$.
  2. Outputs $\mathsf{sk}_f := \{\mathsf{sk}_{f_i}\}_{i \in [\ell]}$.
$\mathsf{MultiPKFE.Enc}(\mathsf{MPK}, \mathsf{m})$:
  1. Computes $\mathsf{CT_m} \leftarrow \mathsf{OnePKFE.Enc}(\mathsf{MPK}, \mathsf{m})$.
  2. Outputs $\mathsf{CT} := \mathsf{CT_m}$.
$\mathsf{MultiPKFE.Dec}(\mathsf{sk}_f, \mathsf{CT_m})$:
  1. Parses $\{\mathsf{sk}_{f_i}\}_{i \in [\ell]} \leftarrow \mathsf{sk}_f$.
  2. Computes $y_i \leftarrow \mathsf{OnePKFE.Dec}(\mathsf{sk}_{f_i}, \mathsf{CT_m})$ for every $i \in [\ell]$.
  3. Outputs $y := y_1 \| \dots \| y_{\ell}$.

Correctness. Correctness of $\mathsf{MultiPKFE}$ easily follows from correctness of $\mathsf{OnePKFE}$.

Security. The security of MultiPKFE can be stated as follows.

Theorem 6.1. *If* OnePKFE *is* $(\mathsf{unb}_{\mathsf{key}}, \mathsf{sec}, \mathsf{eff})$*-PKFE for single-bit output circuits, then* MultiPKFE *is* $(\mathsf{unb}_{\mathsf{key}}, \mathsf{sec}, \mathsf{eff})$*-PKFE for multi-bit output circuits where* $\mathsf{sec} \in \{\mathsf{w\text{-}sel}, \mathsf{sel}, \mathsf{ada}\}$ *and* $\mathsf{eff} \in \{\mathsf{ns}, \mathsf{sls}, \mathsf{fs}\}$.

This can be proven by a standard hybrid argument.

The Running Time of Encryption Algorithm. Since the encryption algorithm of MultiPKFE only runs the encryption algorithm of OnePKFE, the running time of MultiPKFE.Enc is the same as that of OnePKFE.Enc. OnePKFE.Enc is succinct, so MultiPKFE.Enc is.

6.2 Fully-Equipped PKFE

By combining Theorems 5.4 and 6.1, we obtain the main theorem in this study, that is, Theorem 1.1. We obtain adaptively secure, collusion-resistant, and succinct public-key FE for circuits from weakly-selectively secure, single-key, and sublinearly-succinct public-key FE for circuits.

7   Adaptively Indistinguishable Garbling with Near-Optimal Online Complexity

In this section, we give a construction of an adaptively indistinguishable garbling scheme for all circuits whose online complexity does not depend on output-length of the circuit to garble. Namely, the length of online part in our construction is $2n + \mathrm{poly}(\log |C|, \lambda)$ where n and $|C|$ denote the input-length and circuit size, respectively. This is done by transforming our adaptive garbling scheme given in Sect. 4 (or the one by Garg and Srinivasan [30]). Our result can be stated as follows.

Theorem 7.1. *If one of the* $\{CDH, Factoring, LWE\}$ *assumptions holds or* $(1_{\mathsf{key}}, \mathsf{w\text{-}sel}, \mathsf{sls})$*-PKFE for circuits exists, then there exists an adaptively indistinguishable garbling scheme whose online communication complexity is* $2n + \mathrm{poly}(\log |C|, \lambda)$ *and online computational complexity is* $O(n) + \mathrm{poly}(\log |C|, \lambda)$ *where* C *is the circuit being garbled of* n-*bit input.*

We note the adaptively indistinguishable garbling scheme obtained by the above theorem can be seen as $(1_{\mathsf{key}}, 1_{\mathsf{ct}}, \mathsf{ada}, \mathsf{fs})$-SKFE for all circuits. This gives an alternative way to construct fully-equipped PKFE by Theorem 3.1.

Moreover, our construction gives a generic way to convert simulation-secure adaptive garbling (with a particular structure which we call *quasi-decomposability*) whose online complexity depends on output-length into adaptively indistinguishable garbling whose online complexity does not depend on output-length. By instantiating the conversion with known adaptive garbling schemes from one-way functions [35,38], we obtain the following corollary.

Corollary 7.1 (Also proven in [37]). *If one-way function exists, the following garbling schemes exist:*

1. *Adaptively indistinguishable garbling scheme for* NC^1 *whose online communication/computational complexity are* $n \cdot \operatorname{poly}(\lambda)$.
2. *Adaptively indistinguishable garbling scheme for all circuits whose online communication/computational complexity are* $(n + w) \cdot \operatorname{poly}(\lambda)$.

where n *is the input-length and* w *is the width of the circuit being garbled.*

Though Jafargholi et al. [37] already proved the same statement, their construction is obtained by modifying (simulation-based) adaptive garbling scheme by Hemenway et al. [35] in an ad hoc and complicated manner. On the other hand, our construction is generic, and gives a modular construction. See the full version for the details of these results.

Acknowledgments. The third author was supported by NTT Secure Platform Laboratories, JST OPERA JPMJOP1612, JST CREST JPMJCR14D6, JSPS KAKENHI JP16H01705, JP17H01695.

References

1. Ananth, P., Brakerski, Z., Segev, G., Vaikuntanathan, V.: From selective to adaptive security in functional encryption. In: Gennaro, R., Robshaw, M. (eds.) CRYPTO 2015, Part II. LNCS, vol. 9216, pp. 657–677. Springer, Heidelberg (2015). https://doi.org/10.1007/978-3-662-48000-7_32
2. Agrikola, T., Couteau, G., Hofheinz, D.: The usefulness of sparsifiable inputs: how to avoid subexponential iO. Cryptology ePrint Archive, Report 2018/470 (2018)
3. Ananth, P., Jain, A.: Indistinguishability obfuscation from compact functional encryption. In: Gennaro, R., Robshaw, M. (eds.) CRYPTO 2015, Part I. LNCS, vol. 9215, pp. 308–326. Springer, Heidelberg (2015). https://doi.org/10.1007/978-3-662-47989-6_15
4. Ananth, P., Jain, A., Sahai, A.: Indistinguishability obfuscation from functional encryption for simple functions. Cryptology ePrint Archive, Report 2015/730 (2015)
5. Ananth, P., Lombardi, A.: Succinct garbling schemes from functional encryption through a local simulation paradigm. In: Beimel, A., Dziembowski, S. (eds.) TCC 2018, Part II. LNCS, vol. 11240, pp. 455–472. Springer, Cham (2018). https://doi.org/10.1007/978-3-030-03810-6_17
6. Agrawal, S., Maitra, M.: FE and iO for turing machines from minimal assumptions. In: Beimel, A., Dziembowski, S. (eds.) TCC 2018, Part II. LNCS, vol. 11240, pp. 473–512. Springer, Cham (2018). https://doi.org/10.1007/978-3-030-03810-6_18
7. Ananth, P.V., Sahai, A.: Functional encryption for Turing machines. In: Kushilevitz, E., Malkin, T. (eds.) TCC 2016-A, Part I. LNCS, vol. 9562, pp. 125–153. Springer, Heidelberg (2016). https://doi.org/10.1007/978-3-662-49096-9_6
8. Applebaum, B., Ishai, Y., Kushilevitz, E., Waters, B.: Encoding functions with constant online rate, or how to compress garbled circuit keys. SIAM J. Comput. **44**(2), 433–466 (2015)

9. Asharov, G., Segev, G.: Limits on the power of indistinguishability obfuscation and functional encryption. In: 56th FOCS, pp. 191–209 (2015)
10. Barak, B., et al.: On the (im)possibility of obfuscating programs. J. ACM **59**(2), 6:1–6:48 (2012)
11. Bellare, M., Hoang, V.T., Rogaway, P.: Adaptively secure garbling with applications to one-time programs and secure outsourcing. In: Wang, X., Sako, K. (eds.) ASIACRYPT 2012. LNCS, vol. 7658, pp. 134–153. Springer, Heidelberg (2012). https://doi.org/10.1007/978-3-642-34961-4_10
12. Bitansky, N., et al.: Indistinguishability obfuscation for RAM programs and succinct randomized encodings. SIAM J. Comput. **47**(3), 1123–1210 (2018)
13. Bitansky, N., Nishimaki, R., Passelègue, A., Wichs, D.: From cryptomania to obfustopia through secret-key functional encryption. In: Hirt, M., Smith, A. (eds.) TCC 2016-B, Part II. LNCS, vol. 9986, pp. 391–418. Springer, Heidelberg (2016). https://doi.org/10.1007/978-3-662-53644-5_15
14. Bitansky, N., Vaikuntanathan, V.: Indistinguishability obfuscation from functional encryption. In: 56th FOCS, pp. 171–190 (2015)
15. Boneh, D., Sahai, A., Waters, B.: Functional encryption: definitions and challenges. In: Ishai, Y. (ed.) TCC 2011. LNCS, vol. 6597, pp. 253–273. Springer, Heidelberg (2011). https://doi.org/10.1007/978-3-642-19571-6_16
16. Brakerski, Z., Lombardi, A., Segev, G., Vaikuntanathan, V.: Anonymous IBE, leakage resilience and circular security from new assumptions. In: Nielsen, J.B., Rijmen, V. (eds.) EUROCRYPT 2018, Part I. LNCS, vol. 10820, pp. 535–564. Springer, Cham (2018). https://doi.org/10.1007/978-3-319-78381-9_20
17. Brakerski, Z., Segev, G.: Function-private functional encryption in the private-key setting. In: Dodis, Y., Nielsen, J.B. (eds.) TCC 2015, Part II. LNCS, vol. 9015, pp. 306–324. Springer, Heidelberg (2015). https://doi.org/10.1007/978-3-662-46497-7_12
18. Canetti, R., Halevi, S., Katz, J.: Adaptively-secure, non-interactive public-key encryption. In: Kilian, J. (ed.) TCC 2005. LNCS, vol. 3378, pp. 150–168. Springer, Heidelberg (2005). https://doi.org/10.1007/978-3-540-30576-7_9
19. Cho, C., Döttling, N., Garg, S., Gupta, D., Miao, P., Polychroniadou, A.: Laconic oblivious transfer and its applications. In: Katz, J., Shacham, H. (eds.) CRYPTO 2017, Part II. LNCS, vol. 10402, pp. 33–65. Springer, Cham (2017). https://doi.org/10.1007/978-3-319-63715-0_2
20. Dachman-Soled, D., Dov Gordon, S., Liu, F.-H., O'Neill, A., Zhou, H.-S.: Leakage-resilient public-key encryption from obfuscation. In: Cheng, C.-M., Chung, K.-M., Persiano, G., Yang, B.-Y. (eds.) PKC 2016, Part II. LNCS, vol. 9615, pp. 101–128. Springer, Heidelberg (2016). https://doi.org/10.1007/978-3-662-49387-8_5
21. Dolev, D., Dwork, C., Naor, M.: Nonmalleable cryptography. SIAM J. Comput. **30**(2), 391–437 (2000)
22. Döttling, N., Garg, S.: From selective IBE to Full IBE and selective HIBE. In: Kalai, Y., Reyzin, L. (eds.) TCC 2017, Part I. LNCS, vol. 10677, pp. 372–408. Springer, Cham (2017). https://doi.org/10.1007/978-3-319-70500-2_13
23. Döttling, N., Garg, S., Hajiabadi, M., Masny, D.: New constructions of identity-based and key-dependent message secure encryption schemes. In: Abdalla, M., Dahab, R. (eds.) PKC 2018, Part I. LNCS, vol. 10769, pp. 3–31. Springer, Cham (2018). https://doi.org/10.1007/978-3-319-76578-5_1
24. Garg, S., Gentry, C., Halevi, S., Raykova, M., Sahai, A., Waters, B.: Candidate indistinguishability obfuscation and functional encryption for all circuits. SIAM J. Comput. **45**(3), 882–929 (2016)

25. Garg, S., Gentry, C., Sahai, A., Waters, B.: Witness encryption and its applications. In: 45th ACM STOC, pp. 467–476 (2013)
26. Garg, S., Miao, P., Srinivasan, A.: Two-round multiparty secure computation minimizing public key operations. In: Shacham, H., Boldyreva, A. (eds.) CRYPTO 2018, Part III. LNCS, vol. 10993, pp. 273–301. Springer, Cham (2018). https://doi.org/10.1007/978-3-319-96878-0_10
27. Garg, S., Pandey, O., Srinivasan, A.: Revisiting the cryptographic hardness of finding a Nash equilibrium. In: Robshaw, M., Katz, J. (eds.) CRYPTO 2016, Part II. LNCS, vol. 9815, pp. 579–604. Springer, Heidelberg (2016). https://doi.org/10.1007/978-3-662-53008-5_20
28. Garg, S., Pandey, O., Srinivasan, A., Zhandry, M.: Breaking the sub-exponential barrier in obfustopia. In: Coron, J.-S., Nielsen, J.B. (eds.) EUROCRYPT 2017, Part III. LNCS, vol. 10212, pp. 156–181. Springer, Cham (2017). https://doi.org/10.1007/978-3-319-56617-7_6
29. Garg, S., Srinivasan, A.: Single-key to multi-key functional encryption with polynomial loss. In: Hirt, M., Smith, A. (eds.) TCC 2016-B, Part II. LNCS, vol. 9986, pp. 419–442. Springer, Heidelberg (2016). https://doi.org/10.1007/978-3-662-53644-5_16
30. Garg, S., Srinivasan, A.: Adaptively secure garbling with near optimal online complexity. In: Nielsen, J.B., Rijmen, V. (eds.) EUROCRYPT 2018, Part II. LNCS, vol. 10821, pp. 535–565. Springer, Cham (2018). https://doi.org/10.1007/978-3-319-78375-8_18
31. Garg, S., Srinivasan, A.: A simple construction of iO for Turing machines. In: Beimel, A., Dziembowski, S. (eds.) TCC 2018, Part II. LNCS, vol. 11240, pp. 425–454. Springer, Cham (2018). https://doi.org/10.1007/978-3-030-03810-6_16
32. Goldreich, O., Goldwasser, S., Micali, S.: How to construct random functions. J. ACM **33**(4), 792–807 (1986)
33. Gorbunov, S., Vaikuntanathan, V., Wee, H.: Functional encryption with bounded collusions via multi-party computation. In: Safavi-Naini, R., Canetti, R. (eds.) CRYPTO 2012. LNCS, vol. 7417, pp. 162–179. Springer, Heidelberg (2012). https://doi.org/10.1007/978-3-642-32009-5_11
34. Hazay, C., Patra, A., Warinschi, B.: Selective opening security for receivers. In: Iwata, T., Cheon, J.H. (eds.) ASIACRYPT 2015, Part I. LNCS, vol. 9452, pp. 443–469. Springer, Heidelberg (2015). https://doi.org/10.1007/978-3-662-48797-6_19
35. Hemenway, B., Jafargholi, Z., Ostrovsky, R., Scafuro, A., Wichs, D.: Adaptively secure garbled circuits from one-way functions. In: Robshaw, M., Katz, J. (eds.) CRYPTO 2016, Part III. LNCS, vol. 9816, pp. 149–178. Springer, Heidelberg (2016). https://doi.org/10.1007/978-3-662-53015-3_6
36. Jafargholi, Z., Kamath, C., Klein, K., Komargodski, I., Pietrzak, K., Wichs, D.: Be adaptive, avoid overcommitting. In: Katz, J., Shacham, H. (eds.) CRYPTO 2017, Part I. LNCS, vol. 10401, pp. 133–163. Springer, Cham (2017). https://doi.org/10.1007/978-3-319-63688-7_5
37. Jafargholi, Z., Scafuro, A., Wichs, D.: Adaptively indistinguishable garbled circuits. In: Kalai, Y., Reyzin, L. (eds.) TCC 2017, Part II. LNCS, vol. 10678, pp. 40–71. Springer, Cham (2017). https://doi.org/10.1007/978-3-319-70503-3_2
38. Jafargholi, Z., Wichs, D.: Adaptive security of Yao's garbled circuits. In: Hirt, M., Smith, A. (eds.) TCC 2016-B, Part I. LNCS, vol. 9985, pp. 433–458. Springer, Heidelberg (2016). https://doi.org/10.1007/978-3-662-53641-4_17

39. Kitagawa, F., Nishimaki, R., Tanaka, K.: From single-key to collusion-resistant secret-key functional encryption by leveraging succinctness. Cryptology ePrint Archive, Report 2017/638 (2017)

40. Kitagawa, F., Nishimaki, R., Tanaka, K.: Indistinguishability obfuscation for all circuits from secret-key functional encryption. Cryptology ePrint Archive, Report 2017/361 (2017)

41. Kitagawa, F., Nishimaki, R., Tanaka, K.: Obfustopia built on secret-key functional encryption. In: Nielsen, J.B., Rijmen, V. (eds.) EUROCRYPT 2018, Part II. LNCS, vol. 10821, pp. 603–648. Springer, Cham (2018). https://doi.org/10.1007/978-3-319-78375-8_20

42. Kitagawa, F., Nishimaki, R., Tanaka, K.: Simple and generic constructions of succinct functional encryption. In: Abdalla, M., Dahab, R. (eds.) PKC 2018, Part II. LNCS, vol. 10770, pp. 187–217. Springer, Cham (2018). https://doi.org/10.1007/978-3-319-76581-5_7

43. Komargodski, I., Segev, G.: From minicrypt to obfustopia via private-key functional encryption. In: Coron, J.-S., Nielsen, J.B. (eds.) EUROCRYPT 2017, Part I. LNCS, vol. 10210, pp. 122–151. Springer, Cham (2017). https://doi.org/10.1007/978-3-319-56620-7_5

44. Li, B., Micciancio, D.: Compactness vs collusion resistance in functional encryption. In: Hirt, M., Smith, A. (eds.) TCC 2016-B, Part II. LNCS, vol. 9986, pp. 443–468. Springer, Heidelberg (2016). https://doi.org/10.1007/978-3-662-53644-5_17

45. Lindell, Y., Pinkas, B.: A proof of security of Yao's protocol for two-party computation. J. Cryptol. **22**(2), 161–188 (2009)

46. Liu, Q., Zhandry, M.: Decomposable obfuscation: a framework for building applications of obfuscation from polynomial hardness. In: Kalai, Y., Reyzin, L. (eds.) TCC 2017, Part I. LNCS, vol. 10677, pp. 138–169. Springer, Cham (2017). https://doi.org/10.1007/978-3-319-70500-2_6

47. Marcedone, A., Pass, R., Shelat, A.: Bounded KDM security from iO and OWF. In: Zikas, V., De Prisco, R. (eds.) SCN 2016. LNCS, vol. 9841, pp. 571–586. Springer, Cham (2016). https://doi.org/10.1007/978-3-319-44618-9_30

48. Naor, M., Yung, M.: Public-key cryptosystems provably secure against chosen ciphertext attacks. In: 22nd ACM STOC, pp. 427–437 (1990)

49. Nishimaki, R., Wichs, D., Zhandry, M.: Anonymous traitor tracing: how to embed arbitrary information in a key. In: Fischlin, M., Coron, J.-S. (eds.) EUROCRYPT 2016, Part II. LNCS, vol. 9666, pp. 388–419. Springer, Heidelberg (2016). https://doi.org/10.1007/978-3-662-49896-5_14

50. Sahai, A.: Non-malleable non-interactive zero knowledge and adaptive chosen-ciphertext security. In: 40th FOCS, pp. 543–553 (1999)

51. Sahai, A., Seyalioglu, H.: Worry-free encryption: functional encryption with public keys. In: ACM CCS 2010, pp. 463–472 (2010)

52. Sahai, A., Waters, B.: How to use indistinguishability obfuscation: deniable encryption, and more. In: 46th ACM STOC, pp. 475–484 (2014)

53. Yao, A.C.-C.: How to generate and exchange secrets (extended abstract). In: 27th FOCS, pp. 162–167 (1986)

Non-interactive Non-malleability
from Quantum Supremacy

Yael Tauman Kalai[1(✉)] and Dakshita Khurana[2,3(✉)]

[1] Microsoft Research and MIT, Cambridge, USA
yael@microsoft.com
[2] Microsoft Research, Cambridge, USA
dakshita@illinois.edu
[3] UIUC, Urbana-Champaign, USA

Abstract. We construct non-interactive non-malleable commitments without setup in the plain model, under well-studied assumptions.

First, we construct non-interactive non-malleable commitments w.r.t. commitment for $\epsilon \log \log n$ tags for a small constant $\epsilon > 0$, under the following assumptions:
1. Sub-exponential hardness of factoring or discrete log.
2. Quantum sub-exponential hardness of learning with errors (LWE).
Second, as our key technical contribution, we introduce a new tag amplification technique. We show how to convert any non-interactive non-malleable commitment w.r.t. commitment for $\epsilon \log \log n$ tags (for any constant $\epsilon > 0$) into a non-interactive non-malleable commitment w.r.t. replacement for 2^n tags. This part only assumes the existence of sub-exponentially secure non-interactive witness indistinguishable (NIWI) proofs, which can be based on sub-exponential security of the decisional linear assumption.

Interestingly, for the tag amplification technique, we crucially rely on the leakage lemma due to Gentry and Wichs (STOC 2011). For the construction of non-malleable commitments for $\epsilon \log \log n$ tags, we rely on quantum supremacy. This use of quantum supremacy in classical cryptography is novel, and we believe it will have future applications. We provide one such application to two-message witness indistinguishable (WI) arguments from (quantum) polynomial hardness assumptions.

1 Introduction

Non-malleability, first introduced by Dolev, Dwork and Naor [11] aims to counter the ubiquitous problem of man-in-the-middle (MIM) attacks on cryptographic protocols. A MIM adversary participates in two or more instantiations of a protocol, trying to use information obtained in one execution to breach security in the other protocol execution. A non-malleable protocol should ensure that such an adversary gains no advantage. A long-standing problem in this area has been to build non-malleable protocols, without any additional setup or rounds of interaction. In this paper, we develop techniques to address this question based on well-studied assumptions. We focus on a core non-malleable primitive – a commitment scheme.

© International Association for Cryptologic Research 2019
A. Boldyreva and D. Micciancio (Eds.): CRYPTO 2019, LNCS 11694, pp. 552–582, 2019.
https://doi.org/10.1007/978-3-030-26954-8_18

Non-interactive Commitments. A non-interactive commitment scheme consists of a commitment algorithm, that on input a message m and randomness r, outputs a commitment to m, which is denoted by $\mathsf{com}(m; r)$[1]. A commitment scheme is required to be both binding and hiding. The (statistical) binding requirement asserts that a commitment cannot be opened to two different messages $m \neq m'$, namely, there do not exist $m \neq m'$ and randomness r, r' such that $\mathsf{com}(m; r) = \mathsf{com}(m'; r')$. The (computational) hiding property asserts that for any two messages, m and m' (of the same length), the distributions $\mathsf{com}(m)$ and $\mathsf{com}(m')$ are computationally indistinguishable. We note that one could also consider computational binding and statistical hiding, however such commitment schemes are known to require at least two rounds of interaction when dealing with non-uniform adversaries. The focus of this work is on the non-interactive setting.

Non-interactive Non-malleable Commitments. Loosely speaking, a commitment scheme is said to be non-malleable if no MIM adversary, given a commitment $\mathsf{com}(m)$, can efficiently generate a commitment $\mathsf{com}(m')$, such that the message m' is related to the original message m.

Non-malleable commitments are among the core building blocks of various cryptographic protocols such as coin-flipping, secure auctions, electronic voting, general multi-party computation (MPC) protocols, and non-malleable proof systems. Therefore, they have a direct impact on the round complexity of such protocols. For example, many constructions of concurrent MPC against Byzantine adversaries are bottlenecked by the round complexity of non-malleable commitments.

As such, there has been a long line of work on obtaining constructions of non-malleable commitments in the plain model in as few rounds as possible (e.g [2,9–11,15,17–19,23,24,26,27,29–32,34–36]). So far, the only known constructions of non-interactive non-malleable commitments (without setup) are the ones by Pandey, Pass and Vaikuntanathan [31], based on a strong non-falsifiable assumption, and Bitansky and Lin [5], based on a relatively new assumption about sub-exponential incompressible functions. We elaborate on these related works in Sect. 1.3.

Indeed, constructing non-interactive non-malleable commitment schemes (without setup) from standard assumptions, has been a long standing open problem and is the focus of this work. Three primary flavours of non-malleability have been considered in the literature:

- **Non-malleability w.r.t. commitment.** Intuitively, non-malleability w.r.t. commitment, which is the strongest of the three definitions, requires that for any two messages $m_0, m_1 \in \{0,1\}^p$, the distributions $(\mathsf{Com}(m_0), \widetilde{m}_0)$ and $(\mathsf{Com}(m_1), \widetilde{m}_1)$ are computationally indistinguishable. Here $\widetilde{m}_b$ is the message committed to by the MIM given $\mathsf{Com}(m_b)$, and is set to $\bot$ if the adversary given $\mathsf{Com}(m_b)$ outputs $\widetilde{c}$ for which there do not exist any $(\widetilde{m}, \widetilde{r})$ such that $\widetilde{c} = \mathsf{com}(\widetilde{m}; \widetilde{r})$. Another definition that is considered in the literature is that of

---

[1] We will sometimes omit explicitly writing the randomness r.

CCA-security for commitment schemes. It is known [7] that in the case of non-interactive commitments, non-malleability w.r.t. commitment is equivalent to (one-to-one) CCA-security.

– **Non-malleability w.r.t. replacement.** A weaker, yet natural, notion of malleability is non-malleability w.r.t. replacement [15]. This requires that for any two messages $m_0, m_1 \in \{0,1\}^p$, the distributions $(\mathsf{Com}(m_0), \widetilde{m}_0)$ and $(\mathsf{Com}(m_1), \widetilde{m}_1)$ are indistinguishable *whenever* $\widetilde{m}_0, \widetilde{m}_1 \neq \bot$.[2] This is exactly like non-malleability w.r.t. commitment, except that the adversary is allowed to perform "selective abort" attacks, where the event that the adversary committed to an invalid message, is allowed to be correlated with the honest message. This guarantees that a man-in-the-middle adversary cannot commit to *valid* messages that are related to the message committed in an honest protocol. We observe that the proofs in [7] demonstrate that non-interactive non-malleability w.r.t. replacement is equivalent to a weaker form of CCA-security. We further elaborate upon this in Sect. 1.2.

– **Non-malleability w.r.t. opening.** This is an even weaker[3], yet natural notion, which requires that for any two messages m_0, m_1, the joint distribution of $(\mathsf{Com}(m_0), \widetilde{m}_0)$ and $(\mathsf{Com}(m_1), \widetilde{m}_1)$ are indistinguishable *whenever* $\widetilde{m}_0, \widetilde{m}_1 \neq \bot$, where $\widetilde{m}_b$ is the message *opened* by the MIM given $\mathsf{Com}(m_b)$. The crucial difference from both the previous definitions is that $\widetilde{m}_0, \widetilde{m}_1$ represent the messages opened by the adversary, as opposed to the messages committed. Informally, this allows an adversary to commit to a message that is related to an honest message, as long the adversary is unable to convincingly open these commitments.

This work focuses on the first two definitions. We also note that all non-malleable commitment schemes assume that parties have "tags" (or id's), and require non-malleability to hold whenever the adversary is trying to commit w.r.t. $\widetilde{\mathsf{tag}}$ that is different from an honest tag. We differentiate between the following two settings:

– One-to-one setting, where the man-in-the-middle (MIM) gets a single committed message and generates a single commitment.
– Many-to-many (concurrent) setting, where the MIM receives many commitments and is allowed to generate many commitments. Here, the guarantee is that for any two sets of committed messages sent to the MIM, the joint distribution of these committed messages and the messages that the MIM commits to, are indistinguishable.

In this work, we focus on the one-to-one definition. But as a stepping stone, we define and construct many-to-many *same-tag* non-malleable commitments. This is similar to the many-to-many notion, except that it restricts the MIM to use the same tag in all commitments that he outputs.

---

[2] As earlier, $\widetilde{m}_b$ denotes the message committed to by the MIM given $\mathsf{Com}(m_b)$.

[3] Non-malleability w.r.t. replacement implies non-malleability w.r.t. opening, as defined by Goyal et al. [16].

1.1   Our Results

In this paper, we first construct non-malleable commitments w.r.t. commitment for $\epsilon \log \log n$ tags (for some small constant $\epsilon > 0$) in the many-to-many same-tag setting, based on well-studied hardness assumptions, which we elaborate on below. Then we present a general "tag amplification" compiler that converts any non-malleable commitment w.r.t. replacement with $\epsilon \log \log n$ tags in the many-to-many same tag setting, into a non-malleable commitment w.r.t. replacement with 2^n tags in the one-to-one setting, assuming sub-exponential NIWI (which can in turn be based on sub-exponential decisional linear (DLIN)).

For the first result, our contribution is primarily conceptual, and relies on using *quantum supremacy*. Our second result contains the bulk of the technical difficulty. In this part, we make a novel use of the leakage lemma due to Gentry and Wichs [13]. The use of the leakage lemma in this context is surprising, since a-priori the problem of non-malleability seems quite unrelated to leakage. In what follows, we state our results in more detail.

Non-interactive Non-malleable Commitments for $O(\log \log n)$ Tags.
We construct non-interactive non-malleable commitments w.r.t. commitment for $\epsilon \log \log n$ tags (for a small constant $\epsilon > 0$) assuming:

- Sub-exponential hardness of factoring or discrete log.
- Sub-exponential hardness of learning with errors (LWE) or learning parity with noise (LPN) against quantum circuits.

More generally, we construct non-malleable commitments w.r.t. commitment for $\epsilon \log \log n$ tags from any sub-exponentially secure bit commitment for 2 tags (denoted by com_0 and com_1), for which the hiding property of com_0 holds even given an oracle that breaks com_1, and similarly the hiding property of com_1 holds even given an oracle that breaks com_0. Such commitments are known as *adaptive* or CCA-secure commitments [28,31], and imply many-to-many non-interactive non-malleable commitments w.r.t. commitment.

Informal Theorem 1. *Assuming the existence of sub-exponentially CCA-secure many-to-many non-interactive bit commitments for 2 tags, there exist many-to-many same-tag non-interactive non-malleable string commitments w.r.t. commitment for $\epsilon \log \log n$ tags (for a small constant $\epsilon > 0$).*

To achieve this, we start with the leveraging technique of Pass and Wee [35] that allows us to construct, from any sub-exponentially secure non-interactive commitment, a series of $\epsilon \log \log n$ commitments, each harder than the previous one. But this only provides hardness in one direction, and in particular does not even yield commitments for 2 tags that are non-malleable w.r.t. each other.

Our main conceptual novelty in this part, which we describe next, is the idea of constructing a CCA secure commitment scheme for 2 tags using *quantum supremacy*. Later, we describe how we can carefully combine this insight with the technique of [35] to obtain non-malleable commitments for $\epsilon \log \log n$ tags.

Using Quantum Supremacy. Loosely speaking, in order to construct a CCA-secure commitment for 2 tags, we need two axes of hardness: One axis in which com_0 is harder than com_1, and the other in which com_1 is harder than com_0.

We build such an axis by relying on quantum supremacy, which is the ability of quantum computers to solve problems (such as factoring) that are believed to be hard for classical computers. Namely, we construct two commitment algorithms com_0 and com_1 such that for quantum algorithms, breaking com_1 is harder than breaking com_0, and yet for classical algorithms, breaking com_0 is harder than breaking com_1.

This is achieved by instantiating com_1 as a post-quantum secure commitment (such as one based on LWE or LPN [14]); and instantiating com_0 as a post-quantum *insecure* commitment (such as one based on factoring or discrete log), albeit with a much larger security parameter. Now, given a BQP oracle, com_1 is secure but com_0 is not; at the same time, classical machines can break com_1 faster than they can break com_0. We prove the following claim:

Informal Claim 1. *Assuming sub-exponential hardness of factoring/discrete log and sub-exponential quantum hardness of LWE/LPN, there exist sub-exponentially CCA secure many-to-many non-interactive commitments for 2 tags.*

Combining this with Informal Theorem 1, we have:

Informal Theorem 2. *Assuming sub-exponential hardness of factoring/discrete log, and sub-exponential quantum hardness of LWE/LPN, many-to-many same-tag non-interactive non-malleable commitments w.r.t. commitment exist for $\epsilon \log \log n$ tags, for a small constant $\epsilon > 0$.*

Prior to this work, obtaining non-interactive non-malleable commitments w.r.t. commitment, even for just two tags, required the non-standard assumption that there exist sub-exponential incompressible one-way functions, and either sub-exponentially secure time-lock puzzles or sub-exponentially secure one-way functions admitting hardness amplification [5]. The work of [29] constructed non-interactive non-malleable commitments *w.r.t. extraction* (which is similar to w.r.t. replacement) for $O(\log \log n)$ tags assuming sub-exponentially secure time-lock puzzles or sub-exponentially secure one-way functions that admit hardness amplification [5]. We show that non-interactive non-malleable commitments w.r.t. commitment for $\epsilon \log \log n$ tags (in fact, even parallel CCA commitments for 2 tags) can be constructed based on much more well-studied assumptions than previously known.

We also remark that one can substitute the assumption on sub-exponential quantum hardness of LWE with sub-exponentially secure time-lock puzzles [29], or sub-exponentially secure one-way functions [5] admitting hardness amplification, to obtain (many-to-many) non-malleable commitments w.r.t. replacement for $\epsilon \log \log n$ tags.

We believe that this idea of using quantum supremacy may have other applications in classical cryptography. In particular, the technique of complexity leveraging, which breaks hardness of one primitive while retaining hardness of another, is extensively used in cryptography. Typically, when this technique is used, the resulting scheme relies on super-polynomial (and often subexponential) hardness. We believe that in several such applications, the complexity leveraging technique can be replaced with quantum supremacy, thus converting such super-polynomial hardness assumptions to quantum polynomial hardness. For example, using our ideas, one can appropriately instantiate the protocols in [21] to obtain two-message witness indistinguishable protocols based on quantum-polynomial hardness of LWE, and polynomially hard one-way functions (such as those based on factoring or discrete log) that are invertible in BQP.

Non-interactive Tag Amplification from NIWIs. Our more involved technical contribution is a non-interactive tag amplification technique that relies only on sub-exponentially secure non-interactive witness indistinguishable (NIWI) proofs for NP.

Informal Theorem 3 (Tag Amplification from NIWIs). *Assuming many-to-many same-tag non-malleable commitments w.r.t. replacement for $\epsilon \log \log n$ tags (for an arbitrarily small constant $\epsilon > 0$) and sub-exponentially secure NIWIs for NP, there exist non-interactive non-malleable commitments w.r.t. replacement for 2^n tags.*

We note that sub-exponentially secure NIWIs can be constructed assuming the sub-exponential hardness of the decisional linear problem [20], or from derandomization assumptions [3], or assuming indistinguishability obfuscation [6]. Interestingly, to prove this theorem, we crucially rely on the Gentry-Wichs leakage lemma [13]. We provide a high-level overview of this amplification technique, as well as its proof, in Sect. 2.2. To summarize, assuming sub-exponential hardness of factoring or discrete log, as well as sub-exponential quantum hardness of LWE or LPN, there exist:

- Non-interactive non-malleable commitments w.r.t. commitment for $\epsilon \log \log n$ tags.
- Non-interactive non-malleable commitments w.r.t. replacement for 2^n tags, additionally assuming sub-exponentially secure NIWIs for NP.

1.2   Applications and Directions for Future Work

As mentioned above, our final result (for 2^n tags) satisfies non-malleability w.r.t. replacement. In what follows, we give applications of this notion. Prior to our work, these were only known under strong non-standard assumptions [5].

Applications to Other Notions of Commitment

- **Non-malleability w.r.t. Opening.** As previously mentioned, non-malleable commitments w.r.t. replacement imply non-malleable commitments w.r.t. opening, as defined in [8,16]. Therefore, we obtain the first non-interactive non-malleable commitments w.r.t. opening from well-studied assumptions.

Informal Theorem 4. *Assuming sub-exponential hardness of discrete log or factoring, sub-exponential quantum hardness of LWE or LPN, and sub-exponentially secure NIWIs, there exist non-interactive non-malleable commitments w.r.t. opening (for 2^n tags).*

- **CCA Secure Commitments.** It was observed by [7] that the definitions of (one-to-one) non-malleability w.r.t. commitment and (one-to-one) CCA-security are equivalent in the non-interactive setting. We observe that in a similar way, non-malleability w.r.t. replacement implies a weaker notion of one-to-one CCA-security, where if the adversary queries the CCA oracle with a commitment to an invalid value, the oracle self-destructs.
- **Restricted Adversaries.** When restricted to adversaries that only output valid commitments, the notions of non-malleability w.r.t. replacement and non-malleability w.r.t. commitment are equivalent. Therefore, non-malleable commitments w.r.t. replacement can be combined with an appropriate ZK proof of validity of the commitment (as is implicit in [9,19]) to obtain non-malleable commitments w.r.t. commitment. For instance, (sub-exponential) NIWI and (sub-exponential) keyless collision resistant hash functions against *uniform adversaries* are known to imply one-message zero-knowledge with soundness against uniform (sub-exponential time) adversaries [4,29], and admitting a non-uniform simulator. Combining these with our non-malleable commitments w.r.t. replacement, we have the following theorem.

Informal Theorem 5. *Assuming sub-exponential hardness of discrete log or factoring against non-uniform adversaries, sub-exponential quantum hardness of LWE or LPN against non-uniform adversaries, sub-exponentially secure keyless collision-resistant hash functions against uniform adversaries, and sub-exponentially secure NIWIs against uniform adversaries, there exist non-interactive non-malleable commitments w.r.t. commitment against uniform adversaries.*

In a similar way, our commitment with can be appended with one-message ZK arguments of validity of the commitments, against any restricted class of adversaries, to yield non-malleable commitments w.r.t. commitment, against the same restricted classes of adversaries.

Other Applications

- **Upgrading NIZKs.** Non-interactive non-malleable commitments can also be used to upgrade NIZKs to satisfy a form of simulation soundness, without modifying the CRS. Informally, to give a simulation sound NIZK for statement x with witness w, the prover can generate a non-malleable commitment to w with tag x, and provide a (standard) NIZK proof that the commitment is a valid commitment to a witness for x. Note that non-malleability with respect to replacement suffices for this application because the NIZK can be used to provide a proof of validity of the commitment.
- **Block-wise Non-Malleable Codes.** Non-interactive non-malleable commitments w.r.t. opening are known to be equivalent to block-wise non-malleable codes [8] with two blocks. Block-wise non-malleable codes are a strengthening of the notion of split-state non-malleable codes. Using our result, we obtain the first block-wise non-malleable codes that only require two blocks (or states), based on well-studied assumptions.

Informal Theorem 6. *Assuming sub-exponential hardness of discrete log or factoring, sub-exponential quantum hardness of LWE or LPN, and sub-exponentially secure NIWIs, there exist 2-block blockwise non-malleable codes.*

Directions for Future Work

- **MPC.** Non-malleable commitments w.r.t. replacement are known to be sufficient for MPC [15]. We believe that our constructions of non-malleable commitments w.r.t. replacement will help obtain constructions of two-message concurrent secure computation against malicious adversaries (with superpolynomial simulation) from well-studied assumptions. A detailed exploration is beyond the scope of this work.
- **Non-Malleable Cryptographic Primitives.** The recent works of [12,25] give constructions of non-malleable point obfuscation and non-malleable digital lockers from strong variants of the DDH assumption. We believe that our commitments will find applications to achieving non-malleability in context of witness encryption, obfuscation and many other inherently non-interactive primitives, based on well-studied assumptions.

1.3   Prior Work

The work of [29] constructed non-interactive non-malleable commitments w.r.t. commitment against a restricted class of *uniform* adversaries, assuming sub-exponentially secure time-lock puzzles, sub-exponential NIWI and sub-exponential collision-resistant hash functions against uniform adversaries. A very recent independent work [1] constructs an object called non-interactive quasi-non-malleable commitment (w.r.t. commitment), based on well-studied assumptions. This guarantees security against adversaries running in a-priori bounded polynomial time $O(n^c)$, but allows honest parties to run in longer (polynomial) time.

In this paper, our focus is on the non-interactive setting in the plain model against non-uniform adversaries with arbitrary polynomial running time. In this setting, constructions of non-malleable commitments have remained elusive, except based on non-standard assumptions. In particular, prior to our work, there were only two known constructions, described below.

Pandey et al. [31] constructed non-interactive concurrent non-malleable commitments w.r.t. commitment, starting from a non-falsifiable assumption, that already incorporates a strong form of non-malleability called *adaptive* injective one-way functions. Very recently, Bitansky and Lin [5] constructed concurrent non-interactive non-malleable commitments w.r.t. commitment, based on the (relatively new, non-standard) assumption that there exist sub-exponential incompressible functions, sub-exponentially secure NIWI proofs, and either sub-exponential injective one-way functions that admit hardness amplification or sub-exponential time-lock puzzles.

Non-interactive Tag Amplification. Tag amplification has been extensively studied in the non-malleability literature (e.g. [5,11,27,29,36]). Of these, only the recent work of [5] considers tag amplification in the non-interactive setting against general adversaries. They make a relatively non-standard assumption about the existence of sub-exponential incompressible one-way functions, in addition to assuming the existence of a sub-exponentially secure NIWI proofs. Using this incompressibility assumption, they construct a variant of one-message ZK proofs with weak soundness guarantees, and they use this variant of ZK to emulate techniques used in prior work for tag amplification.

On the other hand, our tag amplification technique only assumes the existence of a sub-exponentially secure NIWI proof, and is therefore substantially different from prior techniques for tag amplification (all of which crucially required ZK). However, while our tag amplification technique yields commitments that are non-malleable w.r.t. replacement, the one in [5] yields commitments that are (concurrent) non-malleable w.r.t. commitment.

2   Overview of Our Techniques

We now provide an informal overview of our techniques.

2.1   Non-malleable Commitments w.r.t. Commitment for $\epsilon \log \log n$ Tags

As discussed earlier, we realize sub-exponential adaptive commitments for two tags based on sub-exponential quantum hardness of LWE/LPN and sub-exponential hardness of factoring/discrete log. We now describe how we use these to obtain non-malleable commitments for a small number of tags ($\epsilon \log \log n$ tags where $\epsilon > 0$ is a small constant), which satisfy many-to-many same-tag non-malleability w.r.t. commitment. We give a formal construction of non-malleable commitments for $\epsilon \log \log n$ tags, and its proof in Sect. 4.

Assume the existence of adaptive commitments $\mathsf{com}_0, \mathsf{com}_1$, and oracles $\mathcal{O}_0, \mathcal{O}_1$ such that com_0 is *sub-exponentially* hard to invert given oracle $\mathcal{O}_1$, but com_1 is invertible in the presence of $\mathcal{O}_1$. Similarly, com_1 is *sub-exponentially* hard to invert given oracle $\mathcal{O}_0$, but com_0 is invertible in the presence of $\mathcal{O}_0$.

We show that from any such adaptive commitments, one can use complexity leveraging to derive a sequence of (bit) commitments $\{\mathsf{com}_{d,i}\}_{d \in \{0,1\}, i \in [\zeta]}$, where $\zeta = \epsilon \log \log n$ for a small constant $0 < \epsilon < 1$, and where

$$\mathsf{com}_{d,i} : \{0,1\} \times \{0,1\}^{\ell_{d,i}(n)} \to \{0,1\}^*$$

such that for each $d \in \{0,1\}$,

$$\ell_{d,1} = \omega(\log n) < \ell_{d,2} < \ldots < \ell_{d,\zeta-1} < \ell_{d,\zeta} \triangleq n$$

and for every $i, j, k \in [\zeta]$ for which $k > i$, inverting $\mathsf{com}_{d,k}$ relative to the oracle $\mathcal{O}_{1-d}$ requires more time than jointly inverting $\mathsf{com}_{d,i}$ and $\mathsf{com}_{1-d,j}$, relative to the oracle $\mathcal{O}_{1-d}$. A variant of this technique was used by Pass and Wee [35].

Construction. In order to commit to a bit b with $\mathsf{tag} \in [\zeta]$, the committer first XOR secret shares the bit b to obtain two shares b_1 and b_2. The commitment to b simply consists of $\left(\mathsf{com}_{0,\mathsf{tag}}(b_1), \mathsf{com}_{1,\zeta-\mathsf{tag}}(b_2) \right)$.

Analysis. Suppose there exists a MIM (adversary) that on input a commitment to a bit b w.r.t. tag tag, commits to a related bit b' w.r.t. $\widetilde{\mathsf{tag}} \neq \mathsf{tag}$. We have the following possibilities:

- If $\mathsf{tag} > \widetilde{\mathsf{tag}}$, then breaking $\mathsf{com}_{0,\mathsf{tag}}$ relative to oracle $\mathcal{O}_1$ is harder than jointly breaking $\mathsf{com}_{0,\widetilde{\mathsf{tag}}}$ and $\mathsf{com}_{1,\zeta-\widetilde{\mathsf{tag}}}$ relative to $\mathcal{O}_1$.
- If $\mathsf{tag} < \widetilde{\mathsf{tag}}$, then breaking $\mathsf{com}_{1,\zeta-\mathsf{tag}}$ relative to $\mathcal{O}_0$ is harder than jointly breaking $\mathsf{com}_{0,\widetilde{\mathsf{tag}}}$ and $\mathsf{com}_{1,\zeta-\widetilde{\mathsf{tag}}}$ relative to $\mathcal{O}_0$.

In the first case, we extract the bit b' committed by the MIM by jointly breaking $\mathsf{com}_{0,\widetilde{\mathsf{tag}}}$ and $\mathsf{com}_{1,\zeta-\widetilde{\mathsf{tag}}}$ relative to $\mathcal{O}_1$, and if b' is related to b, we get a contradiction to the hardness of breaking $\mathsf{com}_{0,\mathsf{tag}}$ relative to $\mathcal{O}_1$. We can use a similar argument in the second case.

We also observe that we can allow the MIM to generate an arbitrary number of commitments on the right with the same $\widetilde{\mathsf{tag}}$, and rely on the same assumptions to argue that the joint distribution of bits committed by the MIM (in many right commitments) remains independent of the honest bit. This gives us many-to-many same tag non-malleable commitments w.r.t. commitment for $\epsilon \log \log n$ tags. For simplicity, we only focused on bit commitments in this overview. However it is easy to extend this construction to obtain string commitments for $\epsilon \log \log n$ tags, based on sub-exponential adaptive bit commitments for two tags.

2.2   Non-interactive Tag Amplification

Our starting point is the following basic idea. Start with a non-malleable commitment scheme com for tags in $[\alpha]$ where $\alpha \leq \mathsf{poly}(n)$, and obtain a scheme

Com for tags in $\left[2^{\alpha/2}\right]$, as follows: To commit to a message m w.r.t. a tag T, first compute $\{t_1, t_2, \ldots t_{\alpha/2}\}$, such that each $t_i = (i\|T_i)$ where T_i denotes the ith bit of T^4. Let

$$\mathsf{Com}_T(m) \triangleq \{\mathsf{com}_{t_i}(m)\}_{i \in [\alpha/2]}.$$

Note that for any two tags $T = \{t_1, t_2, \ldots, t_{\alpha/2}\}$ and $\widetilde{T} = \{\widetilde{t}_1, \widetilde{t}_2, \ldots, \widetilde{t}_{\alpha/2}\}$ such that $\widetilde{T} \neq T$, there exists at least one index i such that $\widetilde{t}_i \notin \{t_1, t_2, \ldots t_{\alpha/2}\}$. Therefore, if the underlying com is $\alpha/2$-to-1 non-malleable, then given $\mathsf{Com}_T(m) = \{\mathsf{com}_{t_i}(m)\}_{i \in [\alpha/2]}$, it should be hard to generate $\mathsf{com}_{\widetilde{t}_i}(m')$ for a related message m'. Therefore, an adversary cannot generate a *valid* commitment $\mathsf{com}_{\widetilde{T}}(\widetilde{m})$ to a related message $\widetilde{m}$, i.e., that the resulting scheme is non-malleable w.r.t. replacement.

However, the security of this scheme completely breaks down even if the adversary receives *two commitments*. Specifically, an adversary that receives two commitments $\mathsf{Com}_T(m)$ and $\mathsf{Com}_{T'}(m)$ with different tags $T = \{t_1, t_2, \ldots, t_{\alpha/2}\}$ and $T' = \{t'_1, t'_2, \ldots, t'_{\alpha/2}\}$, can easily output $\mathsf{Com}_{\widetilde{T}}(m)$, where $\widetilde{T} = \{t_1, \ldots t_{\alpha/4}, t'_{\alpha/4+1}, \ldots t'_{\alpha_2}\}$. In other words, the resulting scheme *does not satisfy* many-to-1 non-malleability (or even 2-to-1 non-malleability), and is only non-malleable in the 1-to-1 setting.

Thus, using this idea we can go from $\eta \log\log n$ tags to $2^{\frac{\eta}{2}\log\log n} = \log^{\frac{\eta}{2}} n$ tags, but cannot continue further, since this compiler uses an underlying commitment which is many-to-one non-malleable (or more specifically, $\alpha/2$-to-1 non-malleable).

The blueprint in Khurana and Sahai [24] describes how this problem can be solved using a NIZK argument, which requires the existence of a common random string (which we want to avoid). Namely, they show that if we append to the commitment $C = \{\mathsf{com}_{t_i}(m)\}_{i \in [\alpha/2]}$ a NIZK proof that all these $\alpha/2$ commitments com_{t_i} are to the same message m, then one can indeed prove that this resulting scheme is many-to-one non-malleable[5]. Instead, in this work, we rely on non-interactive proofs satisfying a weaker hiding property, i.e., witness indistinguishability[6]. This introduces several problems that do not come up when using NIZKs. In particular, techniques in [24] rely on the reduction's ability to generate "simulated" proofs, a notion that is not applicable when using NIWIs. We discuss these barriers in further detail below.

Tag Amplification Using NIWIs: First Stab. While NIWI proofs have been extremely useful in a wide variety of cryptographic settings, they often become meaningless when trying to prove NP statements that have a single witness, such

---

[4] Our actual encoding of T to $\{t_1, t_2, \ldots t_{\alpha/2}\}$ is slightly more sophisticated, but achieves the same effect.

[5] To be precise, they need to rely on the fact that the NIZK is "more secure" than the underlying commitment scheme.

[6] As with NIZKs used in [24], we also require our NIWI to be more secure than the underlying commitment, which results in a sub-exponential assumption on the NIWI.

as the one described above. Typically, NIWI proofs are only useful for statements that have at least two independent witnesses.

One can create a statement with two independent witnesses by repeating the blueprint twice in parallel. Namely, commit to a message m by computing $C_1 = \{\mathsf{com}_{t_i}(m; r_{i,1})\}_{i \in [\alpha/2]}, C_2 = \{\mathsf{com}_{t_i}(m; r_{i,2})\}_{i \in [\alpha/2]}$ where $\{r_{i,b}\}_{i \in [\alpha/2], b \in \{0,1\}} \xleftarrow{\$} \{0,1\}^*$, and add a NIWI proving that all the commitments, in either C_1 or C_2, are to the same message.

Indeed, one can easily prove that if the underlying scheme for α tags is $(\alpha/2)$-to-1 non-malleable, then the resulting scheme is one-to-one non-malleable w.r.t. replacement (which was the case even before we started using NIWIs)[7]. Unfortunately, it is not clear if the resulting scheme satisfies even 2-to-1 non-malleability (w.r.t. replacement). Roughly speaking, the problem is as follows. For simplicity, consider a MIM that obtains commitments which are both commitments to m_1 or both to m_2, and tries to copy m_1 (or m_2). A natural approach to rule out such a MIM would be to rely on an intermediate hybrid, in which the MIM obtains a commitment to (m_1, m_2).[8] Unfortunately, we have no way to use a hybrid argument to rule out a MIM that does the following:

- In the first hybrid, on input commitments to (m_1, m_1), outputs a (valid) commitment to m_1.
- In the intermediate hybrid, on input commitments to (m_1, m_2), outputs an invalid commitment where the first repetition in the MIM's commitment consists of all commitments to m_1, and the second repetition consists of all commitments to m_2, and these commitments are accompanied with an accepting NIWI proof.
- In the final hybrid, on input commitments to (m_2, m_2), outputs a (valid) commitment to m_2.

The problem is that neither of the two pairs of adjacent hybrids can be used to get a contradiction to the one-to-one non-malleability, because neither are violating the non-malleability criterium w.r.t. replacement[9].

However, as we already noted above, many-to-one non-malleability is essential if we want to use the compiler again. In fact, it may seem like the NIWIs were not useful at all, since we could get one-to-one non-malleability even for the basic scheme described at the beginning of this overview, which did not require any NIWI (or NIZK). While at first, this approach seems to be inherently problematic, we will now describe how we can nevertheless rely on NIWIs to obtain our desired compiler, as follows.

---

[7] On the other hand, if we used a NIZK, the resulting scheme would be many-to-1 non-malleable w.r.t. commitment.

[8] This is the standard approach used in all previous work on this topic.

[9] This problem can be avoided by relying on NIZKs which would prevent the MIM from behaving as in the intermediate hybrid. However, we cannot rely on NIZKs because they require a CRS.

Overview of Our Compiler. Our idea is to have each commitment consist of $(\ell + 1)$ repetitions (as opposed to only 2), where ℓ is the number of commitments that the adversary can receive (on the left).

Namely, our new (outer) commitment scheme will consist of a matrix of (inner) commitments corresponding to the underlying small tag commitment scheme. This matrix contains $(\ell + 1)$ rows, corresponding to each of the repetitions, and $(\alpha/2)$ columns, corresponding to the small tags of the underlying scheme. The honest committer generates all $(\alpha/2) \cdot (\ell+1)$ inner commitments to the same message (with independent randomness). Additionally, the committer is required to provide a NIWI proof that ℓ out of the $(\ell + 1)$ rows satisfy the following property: The message committed using the inner commitment scheme across all $\alpha/2$ tags is identical for this row (but this message is not required to be identical across different rows).

Now, let us perform the same hybrid argument as above, where in the jth hybrid, we change the jth left outer commitment from a commitment to m_1 to a commitment to m_2. Then, for the outer commitment output by the MIM, which is an $(\ell + 1) \times (\alpha/2)$ matrix of inner commitments, the following must be true.

1. Recall that at least one small tag of the MIM differs from *every* small tag used in the jth left outer commitment. Therefore, by the non-malleability of the underlying commitment, the value committed by the MIM *in all inner commitments accross at least one column* (corresponding to this differing small tag) does not change.
2. Moreover, by the soundness of the NIWI provided by the MIM, at least ℓ of the rows satisfy the following property: the values committed across all $\alpha/2$ tags is identical for this row.

Combining (1) and (2) implies that the values committed by the MIM across at least ℓ rows do not change. In other words, the MIM may change the values committed in *at most one row in every hybrid*.

But since there are $(\ell + 1)$ rows and only ℓ hybrids, we deduce that there exists at least one row for which the messages remained unchanged at the end of *all ℓ hybrids*[10]. Therefore, no adversary can commit to a *valid* message that is related to the messages committed to in the left executions.

We show that this compiler works even if the underlying scheme is non-malleable w.r.t. replacement (as opposed to being non-malleable w.r.t. commitment). However, there is a loss in parameters when applying this compiler, i.e., the compiler converts any ℓ-to-z non-malleable commitment w.r.t. replacement into an ℓ'-to-z' non-malleable commitment w.r.t. replacement, where ℓ' and z' are smaller than ℓ and z. We do not discuss exact parameter constraints here, but refer the reader to Theorem 3 for details. We will give a more detailed explanation in Sect. 2.2.

Technical Bottlenecks. The intuition above seems to imply that the adversary cannot convert a commitment to m into a commitment to a related message m'.

---

[10] To simplify our proof, we rely on 10ℓ repetitions (instead of $\ell + 1$) repetitions, to ensure that the messages in *most* repetitions remain unchanged.

Proving this formally requires overcoming many technical difficulties. Specifically, the definition of non-malleability w.r.t. replacement[11], requires that there exist an (inefficient) extractor $\mathcal{V}_{\mathsf{Real}}$ that extracts the message committed by the adversary from a transcript of a "real" experiment with honest messages $(m_1, \ldots m_\ell)$, and an (inefficient) extractor $\mathcal{V}_{\mathsf{Ideal}}$ that extracts the message committed by the adversary from a transcript of an "ideal" experiment with honest messages $(0, 0, \ldots, 0)$, such that the joint distribution of the view of the MIM in the real experiment and the values output by $\mathcal{V}_{\mathsf{Real}}$, is indistinguishable from the joint distribution of the view of the MIM in the ideal experiment and the values output by $\mathcal{V}_{\mathsf{Ideal}}$. Furthermore, whenever the MIM generates a "valid" commitment $\tilde{c}$ to a message $\tilde{m}$ in either the real or ideal experiment, $\mathcal{V}_{\mathsf{Real}}$ and $\mathcal{V}_{\mathsf{Ideal}}$ are required to output $\tilde{m}$. Whenever the message committed by the MIM is invalid, we impose no restrictions on the output of $\mathcal{V}_{\mathsf{Real}}$ and $\mathcal{V}_{\mathsf{Ideal}}$. To formally prove security, we will need to define these extractors $\mathcal{V}_{\mathsf{Real}}$ and $\mathcal{V}_{\mathsf{Ideal}}$, and ensure that their output distributions remain indistinguishable.

It is tempting to define $\mathcal{V}_{\mathsf{Real}}$ and $\mathcal{V}_{\mathsf{Ideal}}$ to output $\widetilde{M}$ corresponding to the MIM's commitment string $\tilde{c}$, if there exists $\tilde{r}$ such that $\tilde{c} = \mathsf{com}(\widetilde{M}, \tilde{r})$, and otherwise output $\perp$. However, as observed by the intuition above, these distributions will not necessarily be indistinguishable.[12] Namely, the adversary may generate valid commitments when given commitments to m and commit to $\perp$ when given commitments to 0.

Intuitively, to make these distributions indistinguishable, we will introduce some "slack", and sometimes output a valid message even though the adversary did not commit to a "perfectly valid" message. The question is the following: Suppose that the adversary outputs a commitment that is "close to" being a valid commitment to a message $\tilde{m}$. Should the extractors $\mathcal{V}_{\mathsf{Real}}$ or $\mathcal{V}_{\mathsf{Ideal}}$ output $\tilde{m}$ or output $\perp$? This is precisely where the leakage lemma of Gentry and Wichs [13] plays a crucial role. More specifically, we define a function π that outputs the decision bit of whether to output $\perp$, or to output one of the extracted messages (and also specifies which of the extracted messages should be output). This function is inefficient.

Now informally, the leakage lemma states that for every two indistinguishable distributions (X, Y) and every unbounded leakage function π, there exists a relatively efficient simulator that outputs a leakage π' such that $(X, \pi(X))$ is indistinguishable from $(Y, \pi'(Y))$.

In our context, the decision of whether to output $\tilde{m}$ or output $\perp$ in any particular hybrid will be dictated by the leakage lemma. Specifically, we will rely on the lemma where X and Y correspond to the view of the MIM in two consecutive hybrids, and where π is the leakage function described above. The leakage lemma will help us "carry over" this leakage across indistinguishable

---

[11] We refer the reader to Definition 3 for a one-to-one definition, and Definition 2 for a many-to-many definition.

[12] We note that these distributions are indeed indistinguishable if the adversary always generates valid commitments.

hybrids in a relatively efficient manner. The proof of non-malleability of this amplification step is the primary technical contribution of our paper.

There are many additional technical subtleties that were not discussed. For instance, in order to argue that the compiler can be applied several times, we work with a strong variant of non-malleability w.r.t. replacement (which only strengthens our final result). We give a more detailed protocol description towards the end of this section, and also refer the reader to Sect. 5 for details of the construction.

Putting Things Together. We now describe how we use this compiler to obtain our final result, i.e. non-malleable commitments for 2^n tags. Our starting point is our scheme for $\eta \log \log n$ tags which is many-to-many same-tag non-malleable w.r.t. commitment, and in particular is many-to-many same-tag non-malleable w.r.t. replacement (we give an overview of this scheme in Sect. 2.1). We will use the compiler above *three times*: First we convert the scheme for $\eta \log \log n$ tags into a scheme for $\log^{\eta/2}(n)$ tags, then we convert the resulting scheme for $\log^{\eta/2}(n)$ tags into a scheme for $2^{\log^\epsilon n}$ tags (for a small constant $\epsilon > 0$). We apply the compiler one final time to the scheme for $2^{\log^\epsilon n}$ tags to get a scheme for $\omega(n^{\log n})$ tags.

We note that it is not clear that we can run the compiler on itself many times, since every time we run the compiler, there is a loss in parameters. However, we set parameters carefully so that this nevertheless goes through.

To go from $n^{\log n}$ tags to 2^n tags, we use the (standard) idea of relying on sub-exponentially secure signatures. Specifically, to commit to a message m with tag $T \in [2^n]$, we generate a random pair sk, vk of signing and verification keys for the underlying scheme, where the verification key is of length $\log^2 n$ bits. We use vk as our "small" tag for the non-malleable commitment, and sign the larger tag $T \in [2^n]$ with sk. The security of this construction follows by the (sub-exponential) unforgeability of the underlying signature scheme. We refer the reader to Sect. 6 for more details.

More Detailed Protocol Description. Finally, to help the reader navigate our tag amplification protocol, we now give a slightly more detailed description of our protocol, and the intuition for non-malleability. As mentioned above, to commit to a message m with tag $T = \{t_1, t_2, \ldots t_{\alpha/2}\}$, the committer commits to the message $k = 10\ell$ times in parallel with tags $\{t_1, t_2, \ldots t_{\alpha/2}\}$, using fresh randomness each time.

Our protocol is described informally in Fig. 1. Note that the resulting commitment is not many-to-many, because as explained above, even for ℓ-to-1 non-malleability, the size of the resulting commitment grows linearly with ℓ.

Roughly, we prove that if our underlying commitment scheme com is many-to-z non-malleable w.r.t. replacement, and is secure against 2^y-sized adversaries, then the resulting scheme is ℓ-to-y same-tag non-malleable w.r.t. replacement, for any y and ℓ such that $\ell \cdot y < \frac{z}{10}$. We require the NIWI to be WI against poly(T)-time adversaries, where T is the time required to brute-force break com.

Intuition for Non-malleability. For simplicity, let us consider a MIM that on input ℓ commitments, with corresponding tags $T_1, T_2, \ldots T_\ell$, outputs a single commitment $\tilde{c}$ with tag $\tilde{T}$ (in our actual proof, the MIM is allowed to output multiple commitments, albeit using the same tag).

We need to argue that the MIM on input ℓ commitments to messages $m_1, \ldots, m_\ell$ cannot output a *valid* commitment to a related message $\tilde{m}$. As eluded to earlier, this is done via hybrids. Let us suppose for contradiction that on input commitments to $m_1, \ldots, m_\ell$, the adversary outputs a valid commitment to $\tilde{m}$.

Parameters: Set $k = 10\ell$.

Committer Input: Message $M \in \{0,1\}^{p(n)}$, and tag $\{t_1, t_2, \ldots t_{\alpha/2}\}$.

Commit Stage:

1. **Committer Message.**
   - For every $\lambda \in [\alpha/2]$ and every $j \in [k]$, sample randomness $r_{\lambda,j} \xleftarrow{\$} \{0,1\}^{\mathsf{poly}(n)}$ and compute $C_{\lambda,j} = \mathsf{com}_{t_\lambda}(M; r_{\lambda,j})$.
   - Use witness $J = [k-1], \{M, r_{\lambda,j}\}_{\lambda \in [t/2], j \in J}$ to compute a NIWI proof Π that there exists $J \subseteq [k]$ of size at least $(k-1)$, such that: For every $j \in J$, $\exists M_j$, $\{r_{\lambda,j}\}_{\lambda \in [\alpha/2]}$ so that $\{C_{\lambda,j} = \mathsf{com}_{t_\lambda}(M_j; r_{\lambda,j})\}_{\lambda \in [\alpha/2]}$.
   - Send to the receiver the message $(\mathsf{tag}, \{(C_{\lambda,j}, t_\lambda)\}_{\lambda \in [t/2], j \in [k]}, \Pi)$.
   - **Receiver Acceptance.** Accept the comitment if and only if Π verifies.

Reveal Stage: The committer sends M and $\{r_{\lambda,j}\}_{\lambda \in [t/2], \lambda \in [k]}$ to the receiver.

Receiver Output: The receiver accepts the decommitment if all $k \cdot \alpha/2$ are valid commitments to M.

Fig. 1. Round-preserving tag amplification

We consider a hybrid where the first honest commitment (on the left) is generated as a commitment to 0 (but the rest are commitments to $m_2, \ldots m_\ell$). Letting $T_1 := \{t_{1,1}, t_{1,2}, \ldots t_{1,\alpha/2}\}$, one can argue that the distribution of the message $\tilde{m}$ committed by the MIM in the column corresponding small tag $\tilde{t}_1 \notin \{t_{1,1}, t_{1,2}, \ldots t_{1,\alpha/2}\}$ cannot change in all k rows. This follows from the many-to-z non-malleability w.r.t. commitment of com for $z \geq k$ (and relying on the fact that NIWI is hard against $\mathsf{poly}(T)$-time adversaries).

Furthermore, by the soundness of the MIM's NIWI, this implies that the MIM continues to commit to $\tilde{m}$ in at least $(k-1)$ of the rows. This implies that the MIM continues to commit to $\tilde{m}$ in least $(k-1)$ of the rows, *for every tag*. The MIM continues to commit to $\tilde{m}$ in at least $(k-2)$ of the rows, for every tag.

Continuing this way, we observe that the MIM continues to commit to $\tilde{m}$ in at least $(k-\ell)$ of the rows, w.r.t. every tag, on input ℓ commitments to messages $(0, 0, \ldots, 0)$. Therefore on input $(0, 0, \ldots 0)$, the MIM either continues to commit to $\tilde{m}$ or commits to an invalid value, and therefore, $\tilde{m}$ must be unrelated to m. This is the key intuition for the security of our scheme.

As explained above, the actual analysis of indistinguishability of the *joint distribution* of the protocol transcript and messages committed by the MIM is quite involved, and requires multiple careful applications of the leakage lemma [13]. We refer the reader to Sect. 5 for details.

3   Definitions

Let n denote the security parameter. In all our definitions, the input message to the commitment scheme will be sampled from $\{0,1\}^p$ for a polynomially bounded function $p = p$.

For any $T = T(n)$, we use $\mathcal{X} \approx_{\mathsf{poly}(T(n))} \mathcal{Y}$ to denote two distributions such that for every $(T(n))^{O(1)}$-size distinguisher $\mathcal{D}$,

$$\Pr[\mathcal{D}(x) = 1 | x \xleftarrow{\$} \mathcal{X}] - \Pr[\mathcal{D}(x) = 1 | x \xleftarrow{\$} \mathcal{Y}] = \mathsf{negl}(n).$$

We denote by $\mathcal{X} \approx \mathcal{Y}$, the event that $\mathcal{X} \approx_{\mathsf{poly}(n)} \mathcal{Y}$.

3.1   Non-malleable Commitments w.r.t. Replacement

In this section, we present the main definition of non-malleability that we achieve, which is known as *non-malleability w.r.t. replacement* ([15]). This definition is weaker than the original definition of non-malleability, which is known as *non-malleability with respect to commitment* (and is formally defined in Sect. 3.2).

Non-malleability considers a man-in-the-middle that receives a commitment to a message $m \in \{0,1\}^p$ and generates a new commitment $\widetilde{c}$. We say that the man-in-the-middle commits to $\bot$ if there does not exist any $(\widetilde{m}, \widetilde{r})$ such that $\widetilde{c} = \mathsf{com}(\widetilde{m}; \widetilde{r})$. Intuitively, the definition of non-malleability with respect to commitment requires that for any two messages $m_0, m_1 \in \{0,1\}^p$, the joint distributions of $(\mathsf{Com}(m_0), \widetilde{m}_0)$ and $(\mathsf{Com}(m_1), \widetilde{m}_1)$ are indistinguishable, where $\widetilde{m}_b$ is the message committed to by the MIM given $\mathsf{Com}(m_b)$. The definition of non-malleability w.r.t. replacement (that we achieve) intuitively requires this to hold only conditioned on $\widetilde{m}_0, \widetilde{m}_1 \neq \bot$.

We emphasize that we consider the case where the MIM gets a single committed message and generates a single commitment. This is known as the "one-to-one" definition. A stronger definition is the "many-to-many" definition (also known as concurrent non-malleability), where the MIM receives many commitments and is allowed to generate many commitments, and the guarantee is that for any two sets of messages committed to and sent to the MIM, the joint distribution of these commitments and the messages committed to by the MIM, are indistinguishable.

Definition 1 (Non-malleable Commitments w.r.t. Replacement). *A non-interactive non-malleable (one-to-one) string commitment scheme with N tags consists of a probabilistic poly-time algorithm $\mathcal{C}$, that takes as input a message $m \in \{0,1\}^p$, randomness $r \in \{0,1\}^{\mathsf{poly}(n)}$, and a tag $\in [N]$, and outputs a commitment $\mathsf{com}_{\mathsf{tag}}(m; r)$. It is said to be non-malleable w.r.t. replacement if the following two properties hold:*

1. **Statistical binding.** *There do not exist* $m_0, m_1 \in \{0,1\}^p$, $r_0, r_1 \in \{0,1\}^{\mathsf{poly}(n)}$ *and* $\mathsf{tag}_0, \mathsf{tag}_1 \in [N]$ *such that* $m_0 \neq m_1$ *and* $\mathsf{com}_{\mathsf{tag}_0}(m_0; r_0) = \mathsf{com}_{\mathsf{tag}_1}(m_1; r_1)$.

2. **One-to-One Non-malleability.** *For any poly-size adversary* $\mathcal{A}$, *any* $m \in \{0,1\}^p$ *and any* $\mathsf{tag} \in [N]$, *there exist (possibly inefficient) functions* $\mathcal{V}_{\mathsf{Real}}$ *and* $\mathcal{V}_{\mathsf{Ideal}}$ *such that the following holds:*

   (a) *Sample* $r \xleftarrow{\$} \{0,1\}^{\mathsf{poly}(n)}$ *and set* $c = \mathsf{com}_{\mathsf{tag}}(m; r)$. *Let* $(\widetilde{c}, z) = \mathcal{A}(c)$. *If there exists* $\widetilde{\mathsf{tag}} \in [N] \setminus \{\mathsf{tag}\}$, $\widetilde{M} \in \{0,1\}^{p(n)}$ *and* $\widetilde{r} \in \{0,1\}^{\mathsf{poly}(n)}$ *such that* $\widetilde{c} = \mathsf{com}_{\widetilde{\mathsf{tag}}}(\widetilde{M}; \widetilde{r})$ *then* $\widetilde{m} = \widetilde{M}$, *otherwise no restrictions are placed on* $\widetilde{m}$. *We require that*

   $$\Pr[\mathcal{V}_{\mathsf{Real}}(c, \widetilde{c}) = \widetilde{m}] = 1 - \mathsf{negl}(n).$$

   (b) *Sample* $r_{\mathsf{Ideal}} \xleftarrow{\$} \{0,1\}^{\mathsf{poly}(n)}$ *and set* $c_{\mathsf{Ideal}} = \mathsf{com}_{\mathsf{tag}}(0^p; r_{\mathsf{Ideal}})$. *Let* $(\widetilde{c}_{\mathsf{Ideal}}, z_{\mathsf{Ideal}}) = \mathcal{A}(c_{\mathsf{Ideal}})$. *If there exists* $\widetilde{\mathsf{tag}} \in [N] \setminus \{\mathsf{tag}\}$, $\widetilde{M}_{\mathsf{Ideal}} \in \{0,1\}^{p(n)}$ *and* $\widetilde{r}_{\mathsf{Ideal}} \in \{0,1\}^{\mathsf{poly}(n)}$ *such that* $\widetilde{c}_{\mathsf{Ideal}} = \mathsf{com}_{\widetilde{\mathsf{tag}}}(\widetilde{M}_{\mathsf{Ideal}}; \widetilde{r}_{\mathsf{Ideal}})$ *then* $\widetilde{m}_{\mathsf{Ideal}} = \widetilde{M}_{\mathsf{Ideal}}$, *otherwise no restrictions are placed on* $\widetilde{m}_{\mathsf{Ideal}}$. *We require that*

   $$\Pr[\mathcal{V}_{\mathsf{Ideal}}(c_{\mathsf{Ideal}}, \widetilde{c}_{\mathsf{Ideal}}) = \widetilde{m}_{\mathsf{Ideal}}] = 1 - \mathsf{negl}(n).$$

   (c) *We require:*

   $$\left(c, \widetilde{c}, z, \mathcal{V}_{\mathsf{Real}}(c, \widetilde{c})\right) \approx_c \left(c_{\mathsf{Ideal}}, \widetilde{c}_{\mathsf{Ideal}}, z_{\mathsf{Ideal}}, \mathcal{V}_{\mathsf{Ideal}}(c_{\mathsf{Ideal}}, \widetilde{c}_{\mathsf{Ideal}})\right).$$

   over the randomness of sampling r, r_{Ideal}[13].

We next present an (intermediate) security definition that we use as a stepping stone to achieve our main result. This is a many-to-many version of Definition 1, that restricts the adversary to use the same tag in all commitments that he outputs.

Definition 2 (ℓ-to-y Same-tag Non-malleable Commitments w.r.t. Replacement). *A non-interactive non-malleable commitment scheme with N tags consists of a probabilistic poly-time algorithm $\mathcal{C}$, that takes as input a message $m \in \{0,1\}^p$, randomness $r \in \{0,1\}^{\mathsf{poly}(n)}$, and a tag $\in [N]$, and outputs a commitment $\mathsf{com}_{\mathsf{tag}}(m; r)$. It is said to be ℓ-to-y same-tag non-malleable w.r.t. replacement for polynomials $\ell(\cdot)$ and $y(\cdot)$, if the following two properties hold:*

1. **Statistical binding.** *There do not exist* $m_0, m_1 \in \{0,1\}^p$, $r_0, r_1 \in \{0,1\}^{\mathsf{poly}(n)}$ *and* $\mathsf{tag}_0, \mathsf{tag}_1 \in [N]$ *such that* $m_0 \neq m_1$ *and* $\mathsf{com}_{\mathsf{tag}_0}(m_0; r_0) = \mathsf{com}_{\mathsf{tag}_1}(m_1; r_1)$.

2. **ℓ-to-y Non-malleability.** *For any poly-size adversary* $\mathcal{A}$, *any* $m_1, \ldots, m_\ell \in \{0,1\}^p$, *and any* $\mathsf{tag}_1, \ldots, \mathsf{tag}_\ell \in [N]$, *there exist (possibly inefficient) functions* $\mathcal{V}_{\mathsf{Real}}$ *and* $\mathcal{V}_{\mathsf{Ideal}}$ *such that the following holds:*

---

[13] Note that this definition explicitly considers auxiliary information z, but is equivalent to one that does not consider z. We explicitly consider z for convenience.

(a) *Sample* $r_1, \ldots, r_\ell \xleftarrow{\$} \{0,1\}^{\mathsf{poly}(n)}$, *set* $c_i = \mathsf{com}_{\mathsf{tag}_i}(m_i; r_i)$ *for every* $i \in [\ell]$, *and let* $(\widetilde{c}_1, \ldots, \widetilde{c}_y, z) = \mathcal{A}(c_1, \ldots, c_\ell)$.

If there exists $\widetilde{\mathsf{tag}} \in [N] \setminus \{\mathsf{tag}_i\}_{i \in [\ell]}$ *such that* $\widetilde{c}_1, \ldots \widetilde{c}_y$ *all use* $\widetilde{\mathsf{tag}}$, *then continue. Otherwise set* $(\widetilde{m}_1, \ldots \widetilde{m}_n) = \mathsf{abort}$.

For each $i \in [y]$, *if there exists* $\widetilde{M}_i \in \{0,1\}^p$ *and* $\widetilde{r}_i \in \{0,1\}^{\mathsf{poly}(n)}$ *for which* $\widetilde{c}_i = \mathsf{com}_{\widetilde{\mathsf{tag}}}(\widetilde{M}_i; \widetilde{r}_i)$, *set* $\widetilde{m}_i = \widetilde{M}_i$, *and otherwise no restrictions are placed on* $\widetilde{m}_i$. *We require that*

$$\Pr[\mathcal{V}_{\mathsf{Real}}(c_1, \ldots, c_\ell, \widetilde{c}_1, \ldots \widetilde{c}_y) = (\widetilde{m}_1, \ldots, \widetilde{m}_y)] = 1 - \mathsf{negl}(n)$$

(b) *Sample* $r_{\mathsf{Ideal},1}, \ldots, r_{\mathsf{Ideal},\ell} \xleftarrow{\$} \{0,1\}^{\mathsf{poly}(n)}$, *set* $c_{\mathsf{Ideal},i} = \mathsf{com}_{\mathsf{tag}_i}(0^p; r_{\mathsf{Ideal},i})$ *for every* $i \in [\ell]$, *and let* $(\widetilde{c}_{\mathsf{Ideal},1}, \ldots, \widetilde{c}_{\mathsf{Ideal},y}, z_{\mathsf{Ideal}}) = \mathcal{A}(c_{\mathsf{Ideal},1}, \ldots, c_{\mathsf{Ideal},\ell})$.

If there exists $\widetilde{\mathsf{tag}} \in [N] \setminus \{\mathsf{tag}_i\}_{i \in [\ell]}$ *such that* $\widetilde{c}_{\mathsf{Ideal},1}, \ldots \widetilde{c}_{\mathsf{Ideal},y}$ *all use* $\widetilde{\mathsf{tag}}$, *then continue. Otherwise set* $(\widetilde{m}_{\mathsf{Ideal},1}, \ldots \widetilde{m}_{\mathsf{Ideal},n}) = \mathsf{abort}$.

For each $i \in [y]$, *if there exists* $\widetilde{M}_{\mathsf{Ideal},i} \in \{0,1\}^p$ *and* $\widetilde{r}_{\mathsf{Ideal},i} \in \{0,1\}^{\mathsf{poly}(n)}$ *for which* $\widetilde{c}_{\mathsf{Ideal},i} = \mathsf{com}_{\widetilde{\mathsf{tag}}}(\widetilde{M}_{\mathsf{Ideal},i}; \widetilde{r}_{\mathsf{Ideal},i})$, *set* $\widetilde{m}_{\mathsf{Ideal},i} = \widetilde{M}_{\mathsf{Ideal},i}$, *and otherwise no restrictions are placed on* $\widetilde{m}_{\mathsf{Ideal},i}$. *We require that*

$$\Pr[\mathcal{V}_{\mathsf{Ideal}}(c_{\mathsf{Ideal},1}, \ldots, c_{\mathsf{Ideal},\ell}, \widetilde{c}_{\mathsf{Ideal},1}, \ldots, \widetilde{c}_{\mathsf{Ideal},y}) = (\widetilde{m}_{\mathsf{Ideal},1}, \ldots, \widetilde{m}_{\mathsf{Ideal},y})]$$
$$= 1 - \mathsf{negl}(n)$$

(c) *We require:*

$$\left((c_1, \ldots c_\ell), (\widetilde{c}_1, \ldots \widetilde{c}_y), z, \mathcal{V}_{\mathsf{Real}}(c_1, \ldots, c_\ell.\widetilde{c}_1, \ldots \widetilde{c}_y)\right) \approx_c$$

$$\left((c_{\mathsf{Ideal},1}, \ldots c_{\mathsf{Ideal},\ell}), (\widetilde{c}_{\mathsf{Ideal},1}, \ldots \widetilde{c}_{\mathsf{Ideal},y}), z_{\mathsf{Ideal}},\right.$$

$$\left.\mathcal{V}_{\mathsf{Ideal}}(c_{\mathsf{Ideal},1}, \ldots, c_{\mathsf{Ideal},\ell}, \widetilde{c}_{\mathsf{Ideal},1}, \ldots \widetilde{c}_{\mathsf{Ideal},y})\right)$$

over the randomness of sampling $r_1, \ldots, r_\ell$ *and* $r_{\mathsf{Ideal},1}, \ldots, r_{\mathsf{Ideal},\ell}$.

In what follows, we define a slight strengthening of ℓ-to-y same-tag non-malleability w.r.t. replacement. Namely, in the definition below we allow the MIM to *obtain as input* some restricted auxiliary information on the honest messages and randomness.

Definition 3 (ℓ-to-y Same-tag Auxiliary-Input Non-malleable Commitments w.r.t. Replacement). *A non-interactive non-malleable commitment scheme with N tags consists of a probabilistic poly-time algorithm $\mathcal{C}$, that takes as input a message $m \in \{0,1\}^p$, randomness $r \in \{0,1\}^{\mathsf{poly}(n)}$, and a* $\mathsf{tag} \in [N]$, *and outputs a commitment* $\mathsf{com}_{\mathsf{tag}}(m; r)$. *It is said to be ℓ-to-y same-tag auxiliary-input non-malleable w.r.t. replacement for polynomials $\ell(\cdot)$ and $y(\cdot)$, if the following two properties hold:*

1. **Statistical binding.** *There do not exist* $m_0, m_1 \in \{0,1\}^p$, $r_0, r_1 \in \{0,1\}^{\mathsf{poly}(n)}$ *and* $\mathsf{tag}_0, \mathsf{tag}_1 \in [N]$ *such that* $m_0 \neq m_1$ *and* $\mathsf{com}_{\mathsf{tag}_0}(m_0; r_0) = \mathsf{com}_{\mathsf{tag}_1}(m_1; r_1)$.
2. ℓ-*to*-y **Non-malleability.** *There exists a function* $t_V : \mathbb{N} \to \mathbb{N}$ *such that the following holds.*

Fix any messages $m_1, \ldots m_\ell \in \{0,1\}^p$, *any* $\mathsf{tag}_1, \ldots \mathsf{tag}_\ell$, *and any efficient auxiliary input functions* $\mathsf{aux}_1, \mathsf{aux}_2, \ldots, \mathsf{aux}_\ell$, *where for every* $i \in [\ell]$, aux_i *takes as input the commitments* $(c_1, \ldots c_\ell)$ *together with the messages and randomness used to compute* $(c_1, \ldots c_{i-1}, c_{i+1}, \ldots, c_\ell)$. *Set* $T_V(n) = 2^{t_V(n)}$.

For every $\beta \in [\ell]$ *define* ℓ *commitments* $c_{\beta,1}, \ldots, c_{\beta,\ell}$, *where* $c_{\beta,i} = \mathsf{com}_{\mathsf{tag}_i}(0^p; r_i)$ *for every* $i \in [\beta]$, *and* $c_{\beta,i} = \mathsf{com}_{\mathsf{tag}_i}(m_i; r_i)$ *for every* $i \in [\beta+1, \ell]$, *where* $r_1, \ldots, r_\ell \xleftarrow{s} \{0,1\}^{\mathsf{poly}(n)}$.

Suppose that for every $\beta \in [0, \ell-1]$,

$$
\begin{aligned}
\big(c_{\beta,1}, \ldots, c_{\beta,\ell}, \mathsf{aux}_\beta(c_{\beta,1}, \ldots, c_{\beta,\ell}, (0^p)_{\times(\beta-1)}, m_{\beta+1}, \ldots, m_\ell, \quad &(1)\\
r_1, \ldots, r_{\beta-1}, r_{\beta+1}, \ldots, r_\ell)\big) \approx_{T_V(n)} &\\
(c_{\beta,1}, \ldots, c_{\beta,\ell}, \mathsf{aux}_{\beta+1}(c_{\beta,1}, \ldots, c_{\beta,\ell}, (0^p)_{\times(\beta)}, m_{\beta+2}, \ldots, m_\ell, &\\
r_1, \ldots, r_\beta, r_{\beta+2}, \ldots, r_\ell))&
\end{aligned}
$$

where $\mathsf{aux}_0 \triangleq \mathsf{aux}_\ell$.

Fix any polynomial-size adversary $\mathcal{A}$, *and for every* $\beta \in [0, \ell]$ *let*

$$
(\widetilde{c}_{\beta,1}, \ldots, \widetilde{c}_{\beta,y}, z_\beta) =
$$

$$
\mathcal{A}(c_{\beta,1}, \ldots, c_{\beta,\ell}, \mathsf{aux}_\beta(c_{\beta,1}, \ldots c_{\beta,\ell}, (0^p)_{\times(\beta-1)}, m_{\beta+1}, \ldots, m_\ell,
$$

$$
r_1, \ldots, r_{\beta-1}, r_{\beta+1}, \ldots, r_\ell)).
$$

We require that there exist (possibly inefficient) functions $\mathcal{V}_{\mathsf{Real}}$ *and* $\mathcal{V}_{\mathsf{Ideal}}$, *each computable in time* $T_V(n)$, *such that:*
(a) *If there exists* $\widetilde{\mathsf{tag}} \in [N] \setminus \{\mathsf{tag}_i\}_{i \in [\ell]}$ *such that* $\widetilde{c}_{0,1}, \ldots \widetilde{c}_{0,y}$ *all use tag* $\widetilde{\mathsf{tag}}$, *then continue. Otherwise set* $(\widetilde{m}_1, \ldots \widetilde{m}_n) = \mathsf{abort}$.

For each $i \in [y]$, *if there exists* $\widetilde{M}_i \in \{0,1\}^p$ *and* $\widetilde{r}_i \in \{0,1\}^{\mathsf{poly}(n)}$ *for which* $\widetilde{c}_{0,i} = \mathsf{com}_{\widetilde{\mathsf{tag}}}(\widetilde{M}_i; \widetilde{r}_i)$, *set* $\widetilde{m}_i = \widetilde{M}_i$, *and otherwise no restrictions are placed on* $\widetilde{m}_i$. *We require that*

$$
\Pr[\mathcal{V}_{\mathsf{Real}}(c_{0,1}, \ldots, c_{0,\ell}, \mathsf{a}_0, \widetilde{c}_{0,1}, \ldots \widetilde{c}_{0,y}) = (\widetilde{m}_1, \ldots, \widetilde{m}_y)] = 1 - \mathsf{negl}(n)
$$

where $\mathsf{a}_0 = \mathsf{aux}_0(c_{0,1}, \ldots, c_{0,\ell}, m_1, \ldots, m_{\ell-1}, r_1, \ldots r_{\ell-1})$.
(b) *If there exists* $\widetilde{\mathsf{tag}} \in [N] \setminus \{\mathsf{tag}_i\}_{i \in [\ell]}$ *such that* $\widetilde{c}_{\ell,1}, \ldots \widetilde{c}_{\ell,y}$ *all use tag* $\widetilde{\mathsf{tag}}$, *then continue. Otherwise set* $(\widetilde{m}_1, \ldots \widetilde{m}_n) = \mathsf{abort}$.

For each $i \in [y]$, if there exists $\widetilde{M}_i \in \{0,1\}^p$ and $\widetilde{r}_i \in \{0,1\}^{\mathsf{poly}(n)}$ for which $\widetilde{c}_{\ell,i} = \mathsf{com}_{\widetilde{\mathsf{tag}}}(\widetilde{M}_i; \widetilde{r}_i)$, set $\widetilde{m}_i = \widetilde{M}_i$, and otherwise no restrictions are placed on $\widetilde{m}_i$. We require that

$$\Pr[\mathcal{V}_{\mathsf{Ideal}}(c_{\ell,1}, \ldots, c_{\ell,\ell}, \mathsf{a}_\ell, \widetilde{c}_{\ell,1}, \ldots, \widetilde{c}_{\ell,y}) = (\widetilde{m}_1, \ldots, \widetilde{m}_y)] = 1 - \mathsf{negl}(n)$$

where $\mathsf{a}_\ell = \mathsf{aux}_\ell(c_{\ell,1}, \ldots, c_{\ell,\ell}, (0^p)_{\times(\ell-1)}, r_1, \ldots r_{\ell-1})$.
   (c) We require:

$$\big((c_{0,1}, \ldots c_{0,\ell}), \mathsf{a}_0, (\widetilde{c}_{0,1}, \ldots \widetilde{c}_{0,y}), z_0, \mathcal{V}_{\mathsf{Real}}(c_{0,1}, \ldots, c_{0,\ell}, \mathsf{a}_0, \widetilde{c}_{0,1}, \ldots \widetilde{c}_{0,y})\big) \approx_c$$

$$\big((c_{\ell,1}, \ldots c_{\ell,\ell}), \mathsf{a}_\ell, (\widetilde{c}_{\ell,1}, \ldots \widetilde{c}_{\ell,y}), z_\ell, \mathcal{V}_{\mathsf{Ideal}}(c_{\ell,1}, \ldots, c_{\ell,\ell}, \mathsf{a}_\ell, \widetilde{c}_{\ell,1}, \ldots \widetilde{c}_{\ell,y})\big)$$

over the randomness of sampling $c_{0,1}, \ldots, c_{0,\ell}$ and $c_{\ell,1}, \ldots, c_{\ell,\ell}$.

Remark 1. One can strengthen these definitions, to require non-malleability to hold for *any two sets of messages* $(m_1^1, \ldots m_\ell^1)$ and $(m_1^2, \ldots, m_\ell^2)$, such that $\mathcal{V}_{\mathsf{Real}}$ (as before) considers an experiment where the honest committer generates commitments to $(m_1^1, \ldots m_\ell^1)$, whereas $\mathcal{V}_{\mathsf{Ideal}}$ considers an experiment where the honest committer generates commitments to $(m_1^2, \ldots, m_\ell^2)$ (instead of generating commitments to 0s). The proofs of Theorems 2 and 3 show that our constructions also satisfy this stronger definition.

3.2   Non-malleable Commitments w.r.t. Commitment

We also consider the stronger definition of non-malleability with respect to commitment [33]. This definition is standard in the literature; it is sometimes considered in the many-to-many setting (known as concurrent non-malleability), where the adversary (man-in-the-middle) receives many commitments "on the left" and generates many commitments "on the right". It is also sometimes considered in the one-to-one setting, where the man-in-the-middle receives a single commitment "on the left" and generates a single commitment "on the right". In this paper, we use a variant where we require the MIM to use the same tag in all "right" commitments, and we refer to this as the many-to-k same-tag variant. This definition is used as a stepping stone to achieve our main result, and is omitted from this version due to space constraints.

4   Non-malleable Commitments for Small Tags

In this section, we construct a many-to-many same-tag non-malleable commitment scheme w.r.t. commitment for $\zeta = \eta \cdot \log\log n$ tags, for a small enough constant $\eta > 0$, based on the following assumption.

Assumption 1. *There exist non-interactive bit commitments* $\mathsf{com}_0 : \{0,1\} \times \{0,1\}^n \to \{0,1\}^{L(n)}$ *and* $\mathsf{com}_1 : \{0,1\} \times \{0,1\}^n \to \{0,1\}^{L(n)}$ *with the following properties.*

1. **There exists an oracle relative to which** com_0 **is** *sub-exponentially* **hiding, but** com_1 **is extractable.** *There exists an (inefficient, possibly randomized) oracle* $\mathcal{O}_1$ *and a poly-size algorithm* $\mathcal{A}_1$ *such that for every* $n \in \mathbb{N}$ *and every* $(m,r) \in \{0,1\} \times \{0,1\}^n$,

$$\Pr[\mathcal{A}_1^{\mathcal{O}_1}(\mathsf{com}_1(m;r)) = (m,r)] = 1 - \mathsf{negl}(n).$$

where the probability is over the randomness of $\mathcal{O}_1$. *Moreover, on input any string* c *for which* $\not\exists(m,r)$ *such that* $c = \mathsf{com}_1(m;r)$, *we require that* $\mathcal{A}_1^{\mathcal{O}_1}$ *output* $\bot$.

Yet, there exists a constant $\delta > 0$ *such that for every* $n \in \mathbb{N}$, *every* $\mathsf{poly}\left(2^{n^\delta}\right)$- *size adversary* $\mathcal{A}$, *and every pair of messages* m_1 *and* m_2 *in* $\{0,1\}$,

$$\left| \Pr[\mathcal{A}^{\mathcal{O}_1}(\mathsf{com}_0(m_1;r)) = 1] - \Pr[\mathcal{A}^{\mathcal{O}_1}(\mathsf{com}_0(m_2;r)) = 1] \right| = \mathsf{negl}(n),$$

where the probability is over $r \xleftarrow{\$} \{0,1\}^n$ *and over the randomness of* $\mathcal{O}_1$.
2. **There exists an oracle relative to which** com_1 **is** *sub-exponentially* **hard to invert but** com_0 **is invertible.** *There exists an (inefficient, possibly randomized) oracle* $\mathcal{O}_0$ *and a poly-size algorithm* $\mathcal{A}_0$ *such that for every* $n \in \mathbb{N}$ *and every* $(m,r) \in \{0,1\} \times \{0,1\}^n$,

$$\Pr[\mathcal{A}_0^{\mathcal{O}_0}(\mathsf{com}_0(m;r)) = (m,r)] = 1 - \mathsf{negl}(n)$$

where the probability is over the randomness of $\mathcal{O}_0$. *Moreover, on input any string* c *for which* $\not\exists(m,r)$ *such that* $c = \mathsf{com}_0(m;r)$, *we require that* $\mathcal{A}_0^{\mathcal{O}_0}$ *output* $\bot$.

Yet, there exists a constant $\delta > 0$ *such that for every* $n \in \mathbb{N}$, *every* $\mathsf{poly}\left(2^{n^\delta}\right)$- *size adversary* $\mathcal{A}$, *and every pair of messages* m_1 *and* m_2 *in* $\{0,1\}$,

$$\left| \Pr[\mathcal{A}^{\mathcal{O}_0}(\mathsf{com}_1(m_1;r)) = 1] - \Pr[\mathcal{A}^{\mathcal{O}_0}(\mathsf{com}_1(m_2;r)) = 1] \right| = \mathsf{negl}(n),$$

where the probability is over $r \xleftarrow{\$} \{0,1\}^n$ *and over the randomness of* $\mathcal{O}_0$.

In the full version, we formally show that it suffices to instantiate com_0 as any commitment whose hiding is based on the sub-exponential hardness of factoring/discrete log or any other problem that is invertible given a BQP oracle, and it suffices to instantiate com_1 as any commitment whose hiding holds against sub-exponential quantum adversaries.

We note that Assumption 1 can be used to derive a sequence of commitments, described below [35].

There exist inefficient (possibly randomized) oracles $\mathcal{O}_0, \mathcal{O}_1$, a small constant $\eta > 0$, and a sequence $\{\mathsf{com}_{b,i}\}_{b \in \{0,1\}, i \in [\zeta]}$ of commitment functions, where $\zeta = \eta \cdot \log\log(n)$ and

$$\mathsf{com}_{b,i} : \{0,1\} \times \{0,1\}^{\ell_{b,i}(n)} \rightarrow \{0,1\}^{L(\ell_{b,i}(n))}$$

such that for each $b \in \{0, 1\}$,

$$\ell_{b,1} = \omega(\log n^{\log \log n}) < \ell_{b,2} < \ldots < \ell_{b,\zeta-1} < \ell_{b,\zeta} \triangleq n$$

and for every $i, j, k \in [\zeta]$ such that $k > i$, inverting $\mathsf{com}_{b,k}$ relative to the oracle $\mathcal{O}_{1-b}$ requires more time than jointly inverting $\mathsf{com}_{b,i}$ and $\mathsf{com}_{1-b,j}$ relative to the oracle $\mathcal{O}_{1-b}$.

Formally, for every $b \in \{0, 1\}$ and every $i \in [\zeta - 1]$ there exists a $T_{b,i} \cdot \mathsf{poly}(n)$-size algorithm $\mathcal{A}_{b,i}$ such that for every $j \in [\zeta]$, every messages $m_1, m_2 \in \{0, 1\}$, every $r \in \{0, 1\}^{\ell_{b,i}}$ and $r' \in \{0, 1\}^{\ell_{1-b,j}}$,

$$\Pr\left[\left(\mathcal{A}_{b,i}^{\mathcal{O}_{1-b}}(\mathsf{com}_{b,i}(m_1; r)) = (m_1, r)\right) \wedge \left(\mathcal{A}_{b,i}^{\mathcal{O}_{1-b}}(\mathsf{com}_{1-b,j}(m_2; r')) = (m_2, r')\right)\right]$$
$$= 1 - \mathsf{negl}(n),$$

where the probability is over the randomness of $\mathcal{O}_{1-b}$. Moreover, on input any element outside the range of $\mathsf{com}_{b,i}$ or $\mathsf{com}_{1-b,j}$, $\mathcal{A}_{b,i}^{\mathcal{O}_{1-b}}$ outputs $\perp$.

Yet, for every $\mathsf{poly}(T_{b,i})$-size adversary $\mathcal{A}$ and every $k > i$,

$$\left| \Pr[\mathcal{A}^{\mathcal{O}_{1-b}}(\mathsf{com}_{b,k}(m_1; r)) = 1] - \Pr[\mathcal{A}^{\mathcal{O}_{1-b}}(\mathsf{com}_{b,k}(m_2; r)) = 1] \right| = \mathsf{negl}(n),$$

where the probability is over $r \leftarrow \{0, 1\}^{\ell_{b,k}(n)}$ and over the randomness of $\mathcal{O}_{1-b}$. An overview of the construction of this sequence of commitments, following the technique of [35], can be found in the full version of the paper.

Our Construction of Non-malleable Commitments for $\zeta(n)$ Tags. To commit to a message $m = (m_1, \ldots, m_p) \in \{0, 1\}$ with respect to tag, using randomness $(r_i, s_i, a_i)_{i \in [p]}$, where for every $i \in [p]$, $r_i, s_i \xleftarrow{\$} \{0, 1\}^{\ell_{0,\mathsf{tag}}} \times \{0, 1\}^{\ell_{1,\zeta-\mathsf{tag}}}$ and $a_i \xleftarrow{\$} \{0, 1\}$, our commitment algorithm is defined by:

$$\mathsf{Com}_{\mathsf{tag}}\left(m; (r_i, s_i, a_i)_{i \in [p]}\right)$$
$$= \left(\mathsf{tag}, \left(\mathsf{com}_{0,\mathsf{tag}}(a_i; r_i)\right)_{i \in [p]}, \left(\mathsf{com}_{1,\zeta-\mathsf{tag}}(m_i \oplus a_i; s_i)\right)_{i \in [p]}\right).$$

Theorem 2. *If Assumption 1 holds, then there exists a constant $\eta > 0$ such that $\mathsf{Com}_{\mathsf{tag}}$ is a non-interactive many-to-many same-tag non-malleable commitment scheme w.r.t. commitment for $\zeta = \eta \cdot \log \log(n)$ tags, against all $2^{\mathsf{poly}(\log n)}$-size adversaries.*

Proof. The fact that Com is statistically binding follows from the fact that $\mathsf{com}_{b,i}$ are all statistically binding, which in turn follows from the fact that com_0 and com_1 are statistically binding. We next argue that Com is many-to-many same-tag non-malleable w.r.t. commitment against all $2^{\mathsf{poly}(\log n)}$-size adversaries. To this end, it suffices to prove that it is 1-to-many same-tag non-malleable w.r.t. commitment against all $2^{\mathsf{poly}(\log n)}$-size adversaries. This follows by a hybrid argument of [30], which proves that any commitment scheme that satisfies the one-to-many definition also satisfies the many-to-many definition.

To prove non-malleability, fix a $2^{\mathsf{poly}(\log n)}$-size adversary $\mathcal{A}$, and fix any $k \leq \mathsf{poly}(n)$. Given a message $m = (m_1, \ldots, m_p) \in \{0,1\}^p$,[14] we consider the following distribution:

Choose at random $b \xleftarrow{\$} \{0,1\}$ and $R \xleftarrow{\$} \{0,1\}^{\mathsf{poly}(n)}$. If $b = 0$ then let $c = \mathsf{Com}_{\mathsf{tag}}(0^p; R)$. If $b = 1$ then let $c = \mathsf{Com}_{\mathsf{tag}}(m; R)$. Let

$$(\widetilde{\mathsf{tag}}, \widetilde{c}_1, \ldots, \widetilde{c}_k) = \mathcal{A}(c).$$

Consider the joint distribution

$$(c, \widetilde{c}_1, \ldots \widetilde{c}_k, \widetilde{m}_1, \ldots \widetilde{m}_k),$$

where for every $i \in [k]$, if there exists $\widetilde{M}_i \in \{0,1\}^p$ and randomness $R_i \in \{0,1\}^{\mathsf{poly}(n)}$ such that $\widetilde{c}_i = \mathsf{com}_{\widetilde{\mathsf{tag}}}(\widetilde{M}_i, R_i)$, then $\widetilde{m}_i = \widetilde{M}_i$; else $\widetilde{m}_i = \bot$.

To prove that this construction is secure, it suffices to prove that for every $2^{\mathsf{poly}(\log n)}$-size adversary $\mathcal{D}$ and every message m,

$$\Pr[\mathcal{D}(c, \widetilde{c}_1, \ldots, \widetilde{c}_k, \widetilde{m}_1, \ldots, \widetilde{m}_k) = b] = \frac{1}{2} + \mathsf{negl}(n).$$

To prove this, it suffices to show that for every $2^{\mathsf{poly}(\log n)}$-size adversary $\mathcal{D}$ and every message m, if $\Pr[\widetilde{\mathsf{tag}} > \mathsf{tag}] \geq \frac{1}{\mathsf{poly}(n)}$ for some polynomial $\mathsf{poly}(\cdot)$, then

$$\Pr[\mathcal{D}(c, \widetilde{c}_1, \ldots, \widetilde{c}_k, \widetilde{m}_1, \ldots, \widetilde{m}_k) = b | \widetilde{\mathsf{tag}} > \mathsf{tag}] = \frac{1}{2} + \mathsf{negl}(n),$$

and if $\Pr[\widetilde{\mathsf{tag}} < \mathsf{tag}] \geq \frac{1}{\mathsf{poly}(n)}$ for some polynomial $\mathsf{poly}(\cdot)$, then

$$\Pr[\mathcal{D}(c, \widetilde{c}_1, \ldots, \widetilde{c}_k, \widetilde{m}_1, \ldots, \widetilde{m}_k) = b | \widetilde{\mathsf{tag}} < \mathsf{tag}] = \frac{1}{2} + \mathsf{negl}(n).$$

Suppose that $\Pr[\widetilde{\mathsf{tag}} > \mathsf{tag}] = \widehat{p} = \frac{1}{\mathsf{poly}(n)}$. Note that $\widetilde{\mathsf{tag}} > \mathsf{tag}$ implies, $\zeta - \widetilde{\mathsf{tag}} < \zeta - \mathsf{tag}$. Suppose for the sake of contradiction that there exists a $2^{\mathsf{poly}(\log n)}$-size distinguisher $\mathcal{D}$ and a non-negligible function Δ such that

$$\Pr[\mathcal{D}(c, \widetilde{c}_1, \ldots, \widetilde{c}_k, \widetilde{m}_1, \ldots, \widetilde{m}_k) = b | \widetilde{\mathsf{tag}} > \mathsf{tag}] \geq \frac{1}{2} + \Delta. \tag{2}$$

Consider the following hybrid distributions $H_0, \ldots, H_p$, where H_α is defined by choosing $m' = (m_1, \ldots, m_\alpha, 0, \ldots 0) \in \{0,1\}^p$ and setting $c = \mathsf{Com}_{\mathsf{tag}}(m'; r)$ for a randomly chosen $r \xleftarrow{\$} \{0,1\}^{\mathsf{poly}(n)}$.

By a standard hybrid argument, we conclude that there exists $\alpha \in \{0, 1 \ldots, p\}$ and a $2^{\mathsf{poly}(\log n)}$-size distinguisher $\mathcal{D}'$ such that

$$\Pr[\mathcal{D}'(c, \widetilde{c}_1, \ldots \widetilde{c}_k, \widetilde{m}_1, \ldots \widetilde{m}_k | \widetilde{\mathsf{tag}} > \mathsf{tag}, H_\alpha) = 0] -$$

$$\Pr[\mathcal{D}'(c, \widetilde{c}_1, \ldots \widetilde{c}_k, \widetilde{m}_1, \ldots \widetilde{m}_k | \widetilde{\mathsf{tag}} > \mathsf{tag}, H_{\alpha+1}) = 0] \geq \frac{\Delta}{p+1}. \tag{3}$$

---

[14] We overload notation, here m_i denotes the ith bit of m, and below each $\widetilde{m}_i$ consists of p bits.

Note that this implies that $\widetilde{m}_{\alpha+1} = 1$, since otherwise H_α and $H_{\alpha+1}$ are identical.

We use $\mathcal{D}$ to construct a $\mathsf{poly}(T_{1,\xi-\widetilde{\mathsf{tag}}})$-size adversary $\mathcal{B}^{\mathcal{O}_0}$ that breaks the hiding property of $\mathsf{com}_{1,\zeta-\mathsf{tag}}$. Recall that

$$\mathsf{Com}_{\mathsf{tag}}\left(m; (r_i, s_i, a_i)_{i\in[p]}\right)$$

$$= \left(\mathsf{tag}, \left(\mathsf{com}_{0,\mathsf{tag}}(a_i; r_i)\right)_{i\in[p]}, \left(\mathsf{com}_{1,\zeta-\mathsf{tag}}(m_i \oplus a_i; s_i)\right)_{i\in[p]}\right).$$

Fix any $\mathsf{tag} \in [\zeta]$. The algorithm $\mathcal{B}^{\mathcal{O}_0}$, given input a string C in the range of $\mathsf{com}_{1,\zeta-\mathsf{tag}}$, and oracle access to $\mathcal{D}$ does the following:

1. For each $j \in [p]$ sample $r_j \xleftarrow{\$} \{0,1\}^{\ell_{0,\mathsf{tag}}}$ and compute $y_j = \mathsf{com}_{0,\mathsf{tag}}(a_j; r_j)$.
2. For each $j \in [\alpha] \cup [\alpha+2, p]$, sample $s_j \xleftarrow{\$} \{0,1\}^{\ell_{1,\zeta-\mathsf{tag}}}$ and compute $w_j = \mathsf{com}_{1,\zeta-\mathsf{tag}}(m_j \oplus a_j; s_j)$.
3. Let $w_{\alpha+1} = C$, $c = (\mathsf{tag}, \{y_j\}_{j\in[p]}, \{w_j\}_{j\in[p]})$. Set $(\widetilde{\mathsf{tag}}, \widetilde{c}_1, \ldots, \widetilde{c}_k) = \mathcal{A}(c)$.
4. If $\widetilde{\mathsf{tag}} < \mathsf{tag}$, then output a randomly chosen $b \xleftarrow{\$} \{0,1\}$.
5. For each $\kappa \in [k]$, do the following:
   - Parse $\widetilde{c}_\kappa = (\widetilde{\mathsf{tag}}, \{\widetilde{y}_j^\kappa\}_{j\in[p]}, \{\widetilde{w}_j^\kappa\}_{j\in[p]})$.
   - For each $j \in [p]$, compute $(\widetilde{a}_j^\kappa, \widetilde{r}_j^\kappa) = \mathcal{A}_{1,\zeta-\widetilde{\mathsf{tag}}}^{\mathcal{O}_0}(\widetilde{y}_j^\kappa)$ and $(\widetilde{a}'_j^\kappa, \widetilde{s}_j^\kappa) = \mathcal{A}_{1,\zeta-\widetilde{\mathsf{tag}}}^{\mathcal{O}_0}(\widetilde{w}_j^\kappa)$.
   - If there exists $j \in [p]$ such that $a_j^\kappa = \bot$ or $a'^\kappa_j = \bot$, then set $m_\kappa = \bot$.
   - Else, set $m_\kappa = (m_1^\kappa, m_2^\kappa, \ldots m_p^\kappa)$, where $m_j^\kappa = a_j^\kappa \oplus a'^\kappa_j$.

   Recall that for every $\widetilde{\mathsf{tag}} \in [\zeta]$, $\mathcal{A}_{1,\zeta-\widetilde{\mathsf{tag}}}^{\mathcal{O}_0}$ is a $T_{1,\zeta-\widetilde{\mathsf{tag}}} \cdot \mathsf{poly}(n)$-size oracle-aided algorithm that:
   - Inverts $\mathsf{com}_{0,\widetilde{\mathsf{tag}}}$ on any element in the image of $\mathsf{com}_{0,\widetilde{\mathsf{tag}}}$ with overwhelming probability (over the randomness of $\mathcal{O}_0$), and outputs $\bot$ on input any element outside the image of $\mathsf{com}_{0,\widetilde{\mathsf{tag}}}$.
   - Inverts $\mathsf{com}_{1,\zeta-\widetilde{\mathsf{tag}}}$ on any element in the image of $\mathsf{com}_{1,\zeta-\widetilde{\mathsf{tag}}}$ with overwhelming probability (over the randomness of $\mathcal{O}_0$), and outputs $\bot$ on input any element outside the image of $\mathsf{com}_{1,\zeta-\widetilde{\mathsf{tag}}}$.

   Therefore, $(\widetilde{m}_1, \ldots \widetilde{m}_k)$ are extracted correctly w.h.p.
6. Compute $e = \mathcal{D}'(c, \widetilde{c}_1, \ldots, \widetilde{c}_k, \widetilde{m}_1, \ldots, \widetilde{m}_k)$.
7. If $e = 0$, output $b' = a_{\alpha+1}$. If $e = 1$, output uniformly random b'.

By Eq. (3), together with the fact that $\widetilde{m}_1, \ldots, \widetilde{m}_k$ were computed correctly with overwhelming probability,

$$\Pr[e = 0 | (\widetilde{\mathsf{tag}} > \mathsf{tag}) \wedge (a_{\alpha+1} \oplus b = 0)] -$$

$$\Pr[e = 0 | (\widetilde{\mathsf{tag}} > \mathsf{tag}) \wedge (a_{\alpha+1} \oplus b = 1)] \geq \frac{\Delta}{p+1}.$$

Since $a_{\alpha+1} \xleftarrow{\$} \{0,1\}$ (independently of b), this implies that

$$\Pr[(b' = b) \ \wedge \ (e = 0)|\widetilde{\text{tag}} > \text{tag}] = \frac{1}{2}\Pr[(e = 0)|\widetilde{\text{tag}} > \text{tag}] + \frac{\Delta}{4(p+1)}$$

Also note that we sample b' uniformly at random if $e = 1$. Therefore,

$$\Pr[(b' = b) \ \wedge \ (e = 1)|\widetilde{\text{tag}} > \text{tag}]-$$
$$\Pr[(b' \neq b) \ \wedge \ (e = 1)|\widetilde{\text{tag}} > \text{tag}] = 0$$

which implies

$$\Pr[(b' = b) \ \wedge \ (e = 1)|\widetilde{\text{tag}} > \text{tag}] = \frac{1}{2}\Pr[(e = 1)|\widetilde{\text{tag}} > \text{tag}]$$

This implies that

$$\Pr[\mathcal{B}^{\mathcal{O}_0}(\text{com}_{1,\zeta-\widetilde{\text{tag}}}(b)) = b|\widetilde{\text{tag}} > \text{tag}] \geq \frac{1}{2} + \frac{\Delta}{4(p+1)} - \text{negl}(n),$$

contradicting Assumption 1. The case where $\Pr[\widetilde{\text{tag}} < \text{tag}] = \frac{1}{\text{poly}(n)}$, is identical to the previous case, with the roles of com_0 and com_1 reversed, thus we omit the proof. This completes the proof of non-malleability.

5 Non-malleability Amplification

In this section, we present a non-interactive amplification technique to bootstrap non-malleable commitments for small tags into non-malleable commitments for large tags. We present a compiler that converts any $5\ell t$-to-z same-tag *auxiliary-input* non-malleable commitment scheme *w.r.t. replacement* (Definition 3) for tags in $[t]$ into an ℓ-to-y same-tag *auxiliary-input* non-malleable commitment scheme *w.r.t. replacement* (Definition 3) for tags in $\left[\binom{t}{t/2}\right]$, for any y and any ℓ such that $\ell y \leq \frac{z}{10}$. We describe our compiler in Fig. 2. We emphasize that the size of the resulting commitment scheme grows linearly with ℓ.

We denote the commitment scheme for tags in $[t]$ by Com. We require the scheme Com to be secure against $\mathcal{T}$-size adversaries, for $\mathcal{T} = \text{poly}(n \cdot 2^y)$.

Let $T_V : \mathbb{N} \to \mathbb{N}$ denote the time bound associated with Com (i.e., the time required to compute $\mathcal{V}_{\text{Real}}$ and $\mathcal{V}_{\text{Ideal}}$). Our compiler assumes the existence of a NIWI (non-interactive witness indistinguishable) proof system, where witness indistinguishability holds against $\text{poly}(T_V, \mathcal{T})$-size adversaries. From now, we assume for simplicity (and without loss of generality) that $T_V \geq \mathcal{T}$.

Parameters: Set $k = 10\ell$ and let $\mathbb{T}$ denote the unordered set of all possible subsets of $[t]$ of size $t/2$.

Language L: We define language $L = \{\{C_{\lambda,j}, s_\lambda\}_{\lambda \in [t/2], j \in [k]} : \exists J \subset [k], |J| = k - 1, \exists \{M_j, r_{\lambda,j}\}_{j \in J, \lambda \in [t/2]} \text{ s.t. } C_{\lambda,j} = \mathsf{Com}_{s_\lambda}(M_j; r_{\lambda,j}) \, \forall j \in J, \lambda \in [t/2]\}$.

Committer Input: Message $M \in \{0,1\}^{p(n)}$, and $\mathsf{tag} \in [N]$, where $N = \binom{t}{t/2}$.

Commit Stage: To commit to a message M w.r.t. tag tag, do the following:

1. Pick the ith element in $\mathbb{T}$, for $i = \mathsf{tag}$. Denote this element by $\{s_1, \ldots, s_{t/2}\}$.
2. **Committer Message.** For every $\lambda \in [t/2]$ and every $j \in [k]$, sample randomness $r_{\lambda,j} \xleftarrow{\$} \{0,1\}^{\mathsf{poly}(n)}$ and compute $C_{\lambda,j} = \mathsf{Com}_{s_\lambda}(M; r_{\lambda,j})$. Use witness $J = [k] \setminus \{1\}, \{M, r_{\lambda,j}\}_{\lambda \in [t/2], j \in J}$ to compute a NIWI proof Π for:

$$\{(C_{\lambda,j}, s_\lambda)\}_{\lambda \in [t/2], j \in [k]} \in L.$$

Send to the receiver the message

$$(\mathsf{tag}, \{(C_{\lambda,j}, s_\lambda)\}_{\lambda \in [t/2], j \in [k]}, \Pi)$$

3. **Receiver Acceptance.** The receiver accepts $(\mathsf{tag}, \{(C_{\lambda,j}, s_\lambda)\}, \Pi)$ if and only if the proof Π is accepted by the verifier of the NIWI system and $\{s_\lambda\}_{\lambda \in [t/2]}$ is the ith element in $\mathbb{T}$ for $i = \mathsf{tag}$.

Reveal Stage: The committer sends the message M and the randomness $\{r_{\lambda,j}\}_{\lambda \in [t/2], \lambda \in [k]}$ to the receiver.

Receiver Output: The receiver verifies that all the commitments were correctly decommitted, and accepts the decommitment $(M, \{r_{\lambda,j}\}_{\lambda \in [t/2], j \in [k]})$ if and only if $\forall \lambda, j \in [t/2] \times [k] : C_{\lambda,j} = \mathsf{Com}_{s_\lambda}(M; r_{\lambda,j})$.

Fig. 2. Round-preserving tag amplification

Theorem 3. *For any polynomials y, z, ℓ and t, where $\ell y \leq \frac{z}{10}$, assuming Com is $5\ell t$-to-z same-tag auxiliary-input non-malleable w.r.t. replacement (Definition 3) for tags in $[t]$ against $\mathsf{poly}(n \cdot 2^y)$-size adversaries, and assuming sub-exponentially secure NIWI, the scheme in Fig. 2 is ℓ-to-y same-tag auxiliary-input non-malleable w.r.t. replacement (Definition 3) for tags in $\left[\binom{t}{t/2}\right]$ against polynomial size adversaries.*

An overview of the intuition for this construction was provided in Sect. 2.2. In the formal proof (please refer to the full version of the paper [22]), for every $\beta \in [\ell]$, we define τ_β as the transcript generated by the MIM when the first β left commitments are to 0, and the remaining are to $m_{\beta+1}, \ldots m_\ell$. We then build a sequence of extractors $\mathcal{V}_{\beta,\mathsf{real}}$ and $\mathcal{V}_{\beta,\mathsf{ideal}}$ for $\beta \in [\ell]$, where V_{real} roughly corresponds to $\mathcal{V}_{1,\mathsf{real}}$ and V_{ideal} to $\mathcal{V}_{\ell,\mathsf{ideal}}$. These are such that the joint distribution $(\tau_\beta, \mathcal{V}_{\beta,\mathsf{ideal}}(\tau_\beta)) \approx_c (\tau_{\beta-1}, \mathcal{V}_{\beta,\mathsf{real}}(\tau_{\beta-1}))$. Roughly, we also define a $2y$-bit inefficient leakage function π_β and an efficient function f such that for every τ,

$\mathcal{V}_{\beta,\text{real}}(\tau) = f(\mathcal{V}_{\beta-1,\text{ideal}}(\tau), \pi_\beta - 1(\tau))$. Combining these equations implies that for every $\beta \in [2, \ell]$:

$$(\tau_\beta, \mathcal{V}_{\beta,\text{ideal}}(\tau_\beta)) \approx_c \tau_{\beta-1}, f(\mathcal{V}_{\beta-1,\text{ideal}}(\tau_{\beta-1}), \pi_\beta - 1(\tau_{\beta-1}))$$

We then use the leakage lemma to simulate leakage $\widehat{\pi}_{\beta-1}$ such that

$$(\tau_\beta, \mathcal{V}_{\beta,\text{ideal}}(\tau_\beta)) \approx_c \tau_{\beta-1}, f(\mathcal{V}_{\beta-1,\text{ideal}}(\tau_{\beta-1}), \pi_{\beta-1}(\tau_{\beta-1}))$$

$$\approx_c \tau_{\beta-2}, f(\mathcal{V}_{\beta-2,\text{ideal}}(\tau_{\beta-2}), \pi_{\beta-2}(\tau_{\beta-2})), \widehat{\pi}_{\beta-1}(\tau_{\beta-2}) \approx_c \tau_{\beta-3} \cdots$$

Continuing this way, we obtain efficiently simulatable leakage η and an efficiently computable function F such that $\tau_\ell, \mathcal{V}_{\ell,\text{ideal}}(\tau_\ell) \approx_c \tau_0, F(\mathcal{V}_{1,\text{real}}(\tau_0), \eta(\tau_0))$. This allows us to set $\mathcal{V}_{\text{real}}$ as $F(\mathcal{V}_{1,\text{real}}(\tau_0), \eta(\tau_0))$ while preserving indistinguishability. We refer the reader to the full version for a detailed proof.

6   Putting Things Together: Non-malleable Commitments for All Tags

In this section, we describe how one can combine results from Sects. 4 and 5 to obtain our main result.

Theorem 4. *There exists a non-interactive non-malleable commitment w.r.t. replacement satisfying Definition 1, assuming the following:*

- Sub-exponential hardness of factoring or discrete log.
- Sub-exponential quantum hardness of LWE.
- Sub-exponential non-interactive witness indistinguishable (NIWI) proofs.

Proof. To obtain this theorem, we apply the following sequence of steps:

- Let $\mathcal{C}_{[\eta \log \log n]}$ denote a many-to-many same-tag non-malleable commitment w.r.t. commitment for $\eta \log \log n$ tags where $0 < \eta < 1$, secure against $2^{\text{poly} \log n}$-size adversaries. Such a scheme is constructed in Theorem 2, assuming sub-exponential hardness of factoring or discrete log, and sub-exponential quantum hardness of LWE.
- Apply the compiler in Sect. 5 to $\mathcal{C}_{[\eta \log \log n]}$.
  Specifically, setting $y = \log^3 n, \ell = \log^3 n, z = \log^7 n, t = \eta \log \log n$ in Theorem 3, we note that $z \geq 10\ell y$ and $\mathcal{C}_{[\eta \log \log n]}$ is $5\ell t$-to-z same-tag auxiliary-input non-malleable w.r.t. replacement against $\text{poly}(n \cdot 2^y)$-size adversaries. Therefore, Theorem 3 gives a $(\log^3 n)$-to-$(\log^3 n)$ same-tag auxiliary-input non-malleable commitment w.r.t. replacement satisfying Definition 3, for $\log^\epsilon n$ tags, (for a small constant $\epsilon > 0$), against polynomial-size adversaries. Denote this resulting scheme by $\mathcal{C}_{[\log^\epsilon n]}$.

- Apply the compiler in Sect. 5 once again, this time to $\mathcal{C}_{[\log^\epsilon n]}$.
  Specifically, setting $y = 10, \ell = 10\log^2 n, z = 1000\log^2 n, t = \log^\epsilon n$ in Theorem 3, we note that $z = 10\ell y$ and that $\mathcal{C}_{[\log^\epsilon n]}$ is $5\ell t$-to-z same-tag auxiliary-input non-malleable w.r.t. replacement against $\mathsf{poly}(n \cdot 2^y)$-size adversaries.
  Therefore, Theorem 3 gives a $10\log^2 n$-to-10 same-tag auxiliary-input non-malleable commitment w.r.t. replacement satisfying Definition 3, for $2\log^2 n$ tags, against polynomial-size adversaries. Denote this resulting scheme by $\mathcal{C}_{[2\log^2 n]}$.
- Apply the compiler in Sect. 5 one final time, this time to To $\mathcal{C}_{[2\log^2 n]}$.
  Specifically, setting $\ell = y = 1, z = 10, t = 2\log^2 n$ in Theorem 3, we note that $z = 10\ell y$ and that $\mathcal{C}_{[\log^2 n]}$ is $5\ell t$-to-z same-tag auxiliary-input non-malleable w.r.t. replacement against $\mathsf{poly}(n \cdot 2^y)$-size adversaries.
  Therefore, Theorem 3 gives a 1-to-1 auxiliary-input non-malleable commitment w.r.t. replacement satisfying Definition 3, for $n^{\log n}$ tags, against polynomial-size adversaries. Denote this resulting scheme by $\mathcal{C}_{[n^{\log n}]}$.
- Next, assume the existence of a sub-exponentially secure digital signature scheme. More specifically, assume the existence of a signature scheme such that poly-size adversary cannot forge signatures w.r.t. verification keys of size $\log^2 n$ (except with negligible probability). Such a scheme is implied by sub-exponential one-way functions. Denote the keys for such a scheme by (vk, sk), the setup algorithm by $\mathsf{Setup}(1^\lambda)$ and the signing algorithm by $\mathsf{Sign}(sk, \cdot)$.
  Then starting with a non-malleable commitment scheme (w.r.t. replacement) according to Definition 1 for tags in $[n^{\log n}]$ (denoted by $\mathcal{C}_{[n^{\log n}]}$), we build non-malleable commitments for tags in $[2^n]$, satisfying Definition 1 as follows:
  To commit to message m with tag $T \in [2^n]$, sample $(vk, sk) \xleftarrow{\$} \mathsf{Setup}(1^{\log^2 n})$, compute a commitment $c \leftarrow \mathsf{Com}_{vk}(m)$, and a signature $\sigma \leftarrow \mathsf{Sign}(sk, T)$. Output (vk, c, σ). Here $\mathsf{Com}_{vk}(\cdot)$ denotes the commitment algorithm of $\mathcal{C}_{[n^{\log n}]}$ corresponding to tag vk, and we note that $|vk| = \log^2 n$ bits.
  For every PPT man-in-the-middle $\mathcal{A}$ that outputs $(\widetilde{vk}, \widetilde{c}, \widetilde{\sigma})$, one of the following holds.
  - Either $\widetilde{vk} = vk$, in which case by unforgeability of the signature scheme, if $\widetilde{T} \neq T$ then $\widetilde{\sigma}$ does not verify.
  - Or $\widetilde{vk} \neq vk$, in which case the message committed to in $\widetilde{c}$ is "unrelated" to the message committed to in c, i.e., it satisfies the non-malleability condition of Definition 1, since we assume Com_{vk} satisfies Definition 1.

References

1. Ball, M., Dachman-Soled, D., Kulkarni, M., Lin, H., Malkin, T.: Non-malleable codes against bounded polynomial time tampering. IACR Cryptology ePrint Archive 2018, 1015 (2018). https://eprint.iacr.org/2018/1015
2. Barak, B.: Constant-round coin-tossing with a man in the middle or realizing the shared random string model. In: FOCS 2002, pp. 345–355 (2002)
3. Barak, B., Ong, S.J., Vadhan, S.P.: Derandomization in cryptography. SIAM J. Comput. **37**(2), 380–400 (2007). https://doi.org/10.1137/050641958

4. Bellare, M., Palacio, A.: The knowledge-of-exponent assumptions and 3-round zero-knowledge protocols. In: Franklin, M. (ed.) CRYPTO 2004. LNCS, vol. 3152, pp. 273–289. Springer, Heidelberg (2004). https://doi.org/10.1007/978-3-540-28628-8_17

5. Bitansky, N., Lin, H.: One-message zero knowledge and non-malleable commitments. IACR Cryptology ePrint Archive 2018, 613 (2018). https://eprint.iacr.org/2018/613

6. Bitansky, N., Paneth, O.: ZAPs and non-interactive witness indistinguishability from indistinguishability obfuscation. In: Dodis, Y., Nielsen, J.B. (eds.) TCC 2015. LNCS, vol. 9015, pp. 401–427. Springer, Heidelberg (2015). https://doi.org/10.1007/978-3-662-46497-7_16

7. Broadnax, B., Fetzer, V., Müller-Quade, J., Rupp, A.: Non-malleability vs. CCA-security: the case of commitments. In: Abdalla, M., Dahab, R. (eds.) PKC 2018, Part II. LNCS, vol. 10770, pp. 312–337. Springer, Cham (2018). https://doi.org/10.1007/978-3-319-76581-5_11

8. Chandran, N., Goyal, V., Mukherjee, P., Pandey, O., Upadhyay, J.: Block-wise non-malleable codes. In: 43rd International Colloquium on Automata, Languages, and Programming, ICALP 2016, Rome, Italy, 11–15 July 2016, pp. 31:1–31:14 (2016). https://doi.org/10.4230/LIPIcs.ICALP.2016.31

9. Ciampi, M., Ostrovsky, R., Siniscalchi, L., Visconti, I.: Concurrent non-malleable commitments (and more) in 3 rounds. In: Robshaw, M., Katz, J. (eds.) CRYPTO 2016. LNCS, vol. 9816, pp. 270–299. Springer, Heidelberg (2016). https://doi.org/10.1007/978-3-662-53015-3_10

10. Ciampi, M., Ostrovsky, R., Siniscalchi, L., Visconti, I.: Four-round concurrent non-malleable commitments from one-way functions. In: Katz, J., Shacham, H. (eds.) CRYPTO 2017. LNCS, vol. 10402, pp. 127–157. Springer, Cham (2017). https://doi.org/10.1007/978-3-319-63715-0_5

11. Dolev, D., Dwork, C., Naor, M.: Non-malleable cryptography (extended abstract). In: STOC 1991 (1991)

12. Fenteany, P., Fuller, B.: Non-malleable digital lockers. Cryptology ePrint Archive, Report 2018/957 (2018). https://eprint.iacr.org/2018/957

13. Gentry, C., Wichs, D.: Separating succinct non-interactive arguments from all falsifiable assumptions. In: Fortnow, L., Vadhan, S.P. (eds.) Proceedings of the 43rd ACM Symposium on Theory of Computing, STOC 2011, San Jose, CA, USA, 6–8 June 2011, pp. 99–108. ACM (2011). http://doi.acm.org/10.1145/1993636.1993651

14. Goyal, R., Hohenberger, S., Koppula, V., Waters, B.: A generic approach to constructing and proving verifiable random functions. In: Kalai, Y., Reyzin, L. (eds.) TCC 2017. LNCS, vol. 10678, pp. 537–566. Springer, Cham (2017). https://doi.org/10.1007/978-3-319-70503-3_18

15. Goyal, V.: Constant round non-malleable protocols using one-way functions. In: STOC 2011, pp. 695–704. ACM (2011)

16. Goyal, V., Khurana, D., Sahai, A.: Breaking the three round barrier for non-malleable commitments. In: FOCS (2016)

17. Goyal, V., Lee, C.K., Ostrovsky, R., Visconti, I.: Constructing non-malleable commitments: a black-box approach. In: FOCS (2012)

18. Goyal, V., Pandey, O., Richelson, S.: Textbook non-malleable commitments. In: STOC, pp. 1128–1141. ACM, New York (2016). http://doi.acm.org/10.1145/2897518.2897657

19. Goyal, V., Richelson, S., Rosen, A., Vald, M.: An algebraic approach to non-malleability. In: FOCS 2014, pp. 41–50 (2014)

20. Groth, J., Ostrovsky, R., Sahai, A.: New techniques for noninteractive zero-knowledge. J. ACM **59**(3), 11:1–11:35 (2012). http://doi.acm.org/10.1145/2220357.2220358
21. Jain, A., Kalai, Y.T., Khurana, D., Rothblum, R.: Distinguisher-dependent simulation in two rounds and its applications. In: Katz, J., Shacham, H. (eds.) CRYPTO 2017. LNCS, vol. 10402, pp. 158–189. Springer, Cham (2017). https://doi.org/10.1007/978-3-319-63715-0_6
22. Kalai, Y., Khurana, D.: Non-interactive non-malleability from quantum supremacy. In: Electronic Colloquium on Computational Complexity (ECCC), vol. 25, p. 203 (2018). https://eccc.weizmann.ac.il/report/2018/203
23. Khurana, D.: Round optimal concurrent non-malleability from polynomial hardness. In: Kalai, Y., Reyzin, L. (eds.) TCC 2017, Part II. LNCS, vol. 10678, pp. 139–171. Springer, Cham (2017). https://doi.org/10.1007/978-3-319-70503-3_5
24. Khurana, D., Sahai, A.: How to achieve non-malleability in one or two rounds. In: 58th IEEE Annual Symposium on Foundations of Computer Science, FOCS 2017, Berkeley, CA, USA, 15–17 October 2017, pp. 564–575 (2017). https://doi.org/10.1109/FOCS.2017.58
25. Komargodski, I., Yogev, E.: Another step towards realizing random oracles: nonmalleable point obfuscation. In: Nielsen, J.B., Rijmen, V. (eds.) EUROCRYPT 2018. LNCS, vol. 10820, pp. 259–279. Springer, Cham (2018). https://doi.org/10.1007/978-3-319-78381-9_10
26. Lin, H., Pass, R.: Constant-round non-malleable commitments from any one-way function. In: STOC 2011, pp. 705–714 (2011)
27. Lin, H., Pass, R.: Non-malleability amplification. In: Proceedings of the 41st Annual ACM Symposium on Theory of Computing, STOC 2009, pp. 189–198 (2009)
28. Lin, H., Pass, R.: Black-box constructions of composable protocols without set-up. In: Safavi-Naini, R., Canetti, R. (eds.) CRYPTO 2012. LNCS, vol. 7417, pp. 461–478. Springer, Heidelberg (2012). https://doi.org/10.1007/978-3-642-32009-5_27
29. Lin, H., Pass, R., Soni, P.: Two-round and non-interactive concurrent nonmalleable commitments from time-lock puzzles. Cryptology ePrint Archive, Report 2017/273 (2017). http://eprint.iacr.org/2017/273
30. Lin, H., Pass, R., Venkitasubramaniam, M.: Concurrent non-malleable commitments from any one-way function. In: Canetti, R. (ed.) TCC 2008. LNCS, vol. 4948, pp. 571–588. Springer, Heidelberg (2008). https://doi.org/10.1007/978-3-540-78524-8_31
31. Pandey, O., Pass, R., Vaikuntanathan, V.: Adaptive one-way functions and applications. In: Wagner, D. (ed.) CRYPTO 2008. LNCS, vol. 5157, pp. 57–74. Springer, Heidelberg (2008). https://doi.org/10.1007/978-3-540-85174-5_4
32. Pass, R., Rosen, A.: Concurrent non-malleable commitments. In: Proceedings of the 46th Annual IEEE Symposium on Foundations of Computer Science, FOCS 2005, pp. 563–572 (2005)
33. Pass, R., Rosen, A.: New and improved constructions of non-malleable cryptographic protocols. In: STOC 2005, pp. 533–542 (2005)
34. Pass, R., Rosen, A.: New and improved constructions of nonmalleable cryptographic protocols. SIAM J. Comput. **38**(2), 702–752 (2008)
35. Pass, R., Wee, H.: Constant-round non-malleable commitments from subexponential one-way functions. In: Gilbert, H. (ed.) EUROCRYPT 2010. LNCS, vol. 6110, pp. 638–655. Springer, Heidelberg (2010). https://doi.org/10.1007/978-3-642-13190-5_32
36. Wee, H.: Black-box, round-efficient secure computation via non-malleability amplification. In: FOCS 2010, pp. 531–540 (2010)

Cryptographic Sensing

Yuval Ishai[1][✉], Eyal Kushilevitz[1], Rafail Ostrovsky[2], and Amit Sahai[2]

[1] Technion, Haifa, Israel
{yuvali,eyalk}@cs.technion.ac.il
[2] University of California, Los Angeles, USA
{rafail,sahai}@cs.ucla.edu

Abstract. Is it possible to measure a physical object in a way that makes the measurement signals unintelligible to an external observer? Alternatively, can one learn a natural concept by using a contrived training set that makes the labeled examples useless without the line of thought that has led to their choice? We initiate a study of "cryptographic sensing" problems of this type, presenting definitions, positive and negative results, and directions for further research.

1 Introduction

The traditional goal of cryptography is to *design* cryptographic algorithms for well-defined tasks, such as public-key encryption. In this work we study the following question: when can we *embed* a cryptographic function in a function that was not designed for this purpose, say a function created by nature?

To make the question more concrete and illustrate a potential application scenario, consider the goal of observing a physical object in total darkness. Is it possible to design a flashlight, and a matching pair of glasses, such that the flashlight will only make the object visible to the owner of the glasses? Note that we are not attempting to hide the existence of the object and the flashlight. Our goal is to embed in the physical implementation of the flashlight a hidden secret (which is only explicitly found in the glasses), such that without knowing this secret it is *computationally infeasible* to make sense of the signals directed at and reflected from the object. The latter requirement should hold *even if the flashlight can be captured and analyzed completely* by an adversary, and even if the adversary can design its own pair of glasses based on this analysis.

A bit more rigorously and abstractly, we model the object being observed as a vector $x \in \mathcal{X}$, where $\mathcal{X} = \{0,1\}^n$ by default. The flashlight is modeled as a randomized measurement algorithm Sen that can carefully choose a sequence of measurement functions $f_1, f_2, \ldots$, where each f_i is taken from some fixed and publicly known class $\mathcal{F}$. For each function f_i, the algorithm Sen learns the value $a_i = f_i(x)$. The choice of the measurement sequence f_i may either be adaptive, in the sense that each f_i can depend on $a_1, \ldots, a_{i-1}$, or non-adaptive, in the sense that all f_i are chosen together. We would like the following two requirements to hold. First, given the randomness that was used to choose the measurement

A. Boldyreva and D. Micciancio (Eds.): CRYPTO 2019, LNCS 11694, pp. 583–604, 2019.
https://doi.org/10.1007/978-3-030-26954-8_19

functions f_i, it is possible to efficiently decode the object x from the sequence (f_i, a_i). In the flashlight example, this decoding algorithm is performed by the glasses. Second, we would like the object x to remain "hidden" (in a sense that should be defined) from any polynomial-time (passive) external observer Adv who can only view the measurements (f_i, a_i) without the randomness that was used to generate them. We refer to such an algorithm Sen as a *cryptographic sensing algorithm* for the measurement class $\mathcal{F}$.

For the purpose of obtaining better efficiency or stronger security, it will sometimes be useful to relax the above goal by settling for Sen learning only partial information $g(x)$ about x (e.g., a lower resolution version of an image x or some targeted portion of x), or by allowing Adv to learn partial information $\ell(x)$ about x (e.g., the brightness level of an image). As long as Sen has a meaningful advantage over Adv, we realize a non-trivial notion of cryptographic sensing. A different type of relaxation is to consider a *distributed* setting, where two or more instances of Sen can be executed. Here Adv only has access to a bounded number of these instances (say, one out of two) but the decoder has access to all of them. This is analogous to the type of security provided by secret sharing schemes or protocols for secure multiparty computation.

One can also consider a dual formulation of the problem in the language of computational learning theory. Here the object is a secret *concept*, namely a function $f \in \mathcal{F}$, and the goal of the (active, randomized) learning algorithm Sen is to come up with a training set $x_1, x_2, \ldots$ such that given the labeled examples $(x_i, f(x_i))$ it can efficiently learn some representation of f. The unusual requirement we make here is that without the "line of thought" that has led to the choice of the training set, it should be impossible for an efficient, passive Adv to learn f from the labeled examples. There are instances of the cryptographic sensing problem that are better motivated or are more naturally cast in this dual form; however, most instances considered in this work are more naturally cast in the original "sensing" framework.

If we could choose the class $\mathcal{F}$ at will, we could simply make it rich enough to directly implement an encryption of x via a standard public-key encryption scheme, say the RSA scheme. This is akin to allowing the flashlight to shoot a miniature robot at the object, where the robot physically senses the object and sends back an encrypted image using the flashlight's public encryption key. However, our goal here is to study the possibility of coping with *natural* classes $\mathcal{F}$, such as ones that can potentially be realized by a simple physical measurement process (in the sensing formulation) or that capture simple and/or realistic classes of concepts (in the learning formulation).

Other than the type of "sensing" applications illustrated by the cryptographic flashlight metaphor, it is not hard to imagine additional potential application scenarios. For instance, consider a drug company A that must outsource expensive experiments to a company B for the purpose of determining the chemical structure of some virus. Company A would like to deter employees of B who conduct the actual experiments from selling the results to a competing drug company C. Here too, our goal is not to hide the fact that a virus is being analyzed, but rather to render the "questions and answers" that must inevitably be obtained by B in the process of analysis useless to anyone but the company A that designed (and paid for) the experiments. A similar goal can apply to other measurement and learning scenarios such as conducting polls, training deep neural nets, and many more.

1.1 Our Contribution

In this work we initiate a study of cryptographic sensing by presenting definitions, some positive and negative results, and directions for further research.

Formalizing Security. We start by putting forward different notions of security for cryptographic sensing. The weakest notion is that of *one-way security*, which ensures that Adv has a negligible success of guessing x *exactly*, when x is picked at random. Using standard cryptographic terminology, a *non-adaptive* cryptographic sensing algorithm for $\mathcal{F}$ with one-way security is equivalent to an $\mathcal{F}$-computable injective trapdoor function, namely one that can be computed by concatenating functions from $\mathcal{F}$. One-way security is typically not very useful, since it only applies to a specific object distribution and even in this case it does not rule out revealing a big amount of partial information about the object.

A stronger and more useful notion is that of *entropic security*, requiring that any two object distributions that have high min-entropy cannot be distinguished by Adv. This intuitively means that the interaction does not help Adv distinguish between objects that were sufficiently unpredictable to start with. Using standard cryptographic terminology, a non-adaptive cryptographic sensing algorithm with entropic security for $\mathcal{F}$ can be viewed as an $\mathcal{F}$-computable one-time-secure *deterministic* public-key encryption scheme [13,24,46].

As in the case of non-cryptographic sensing (e.g., compressed sensing), it is often useful to settle for *lossy decoding*, where Sen outputs some useful partial information about x such as a projection of x to a subset of the coordinates or a compressive linear sketch of x from which an approximate version (e.g., a lower resolution image) can be recovered. Note that with lossy decoding, one-way security may become meaningless. However, entropic security is still as meaningful. Lossy decoding is motivated by the possibility of obtaining better efficiency (e.g., fewer measurements) and better security (e.g., entropic security with a lower entropy bound).

Finally, we consider a useful combination of entropic security and lossy decoding we refer to as *security with background noise*. Here we aim to completely hide the object x by masking it with "background noise" r, where measurements apply jointly to (x, r). (In the case of physical measurements, r can be taken from parts of the object that are considered irrelevant, or from nearby objects.) This is analogous to the role of randomness in semantically secure probabilistic encryption [27]. We distinguish between different types of security with background noise, depending on whether r is assumed to be random and whether it is independent of x.

Constructions and Negative Results. At a first glance, obtaining cryptographic sensing algorithms for *natural* classes $\mathcal{F}$ may seem hopeless. Indeed, such classes are expected to be either hard to learn (even without any security requirements) or alternatively admit *simple* learning algorithms in which case there is no hope to embed any cryptographic hardness, let alone the intricate structure of public-key cryptography.

However, a second thought reveals that this view may be too pessimistic. First, there is a rich line of work on *low complexity cryptography* (see Sect. 1.2), showing that sophisticated cryptographic primitives can be implemented in low complexity classes under well studied intractability assumptions. Second, an even richer line of work shows how to construct code-based [2,39] or lattice-based [1,25,44] public-key encryption schemes in which encryption can be implemented by computing a *linear function* of the message and secret randomness over some finite ring $\mathbb{Z}_q$. In our language, these cryptosystems imply cryptographic sensing algorithms with $\mathbb{Z}_q$-linear measurements that achieve semantic security using random background noise. In fact, lattice-based *deterministic* public-key encryption schemes imply a similar result with entropic security [15,19,42] and without the need for background noise.

Let us pause to explain how linear functions, that are trivially "learnable" by using Gaussian elimination, can be a source for cryptographic hardness. The key feature that makes this possible is that the object x is restricted to be in $\{0,1\}^n$ (or, more generally, a vector of a small norm) whereas the linear combinations are taken over the larger domain $\mathbb{Z}_q^n$. This means that even though Adv can obtain an explicit description of affine space of objects in $\mathbb{Z}_q^n$ that are consistent with the labeled examples, it has no obvious way of making sense of this information. Indeed, the affine space is of exponential size, which makes it possible to hide inside it a low-norm object x that has sufficient entropy.

The simplicity of linear functions makes lattice-based cryptography an attractive venue for cryptographic sensing algorithms. However, even when restricting attention to linear measurements, there are several reasons why these off-the-shelf solutions from the literature are not completely satisfying.

First, they all inherently require *modular* linear measurements, modulo some finite integer $q \geq 2$. While the class of such measurements is very natural from a theory perspective, we are not aware of any realistic way of obtaining a direct physical implementation of such measurements. Note that it is crucial that no additional information except the output of the measurement is leaked. In contrast, linear combinations with small integer coefficients (or alternatively bounded-precision reals) can conceivably be realized without significant additional leakage. As a toy example, consider an implementation of a "flashlight" that shoots small balls or a spray of water at a metal board with holes. The amount of noise made by the impact (alternatively the amount of substance that bounces back) reveals a linear combination *over the integers* of the characteristic vector of the board (0 for hole, 1 for no hole) and the density vector of objects shot at it. One can easily imagine more sophisticated and scalable physical measurement processes of this type. Other disadvantages of off-the-shelf solutions is that their entropically secure variants have a poor quality of entropic security and require a large number of measurements.

We start by addressing the latter disadvantages. We show a simple cryptographic sensing algorithm that achieves a good quality of entropic security (i.e., with weak entropy requirements) and only uses a small number of linear measurements over $\mathbb{Z}_q$. The price we pay is that we settle for lossy decoding, revealing a sublinear number of linear combinations of the object x. In the context of natural objects (such as images), such compressive linear mappings are often almost as good as full recovery (see, e.g., [29] for a survey). Our algorithm is simple and intuitive, and builds on the same technique that underlies lattice-based encryption schemes such as Regev's cryptosystem [44]. The high level idea is to hide the "useful" linear combinations in a low-dimensional linear space by adding noise. Using a combination of the Learning With Errors assumption and the Leftover Hash Lemma, it is ensured that the linear space spanned by the measurements together with the measurement outcomes looks completely random to a computationally bounded Adv, assuming that the object has sufficient entropy.

Then, we use a simple generic transformation from cryptographic sensing algorithms that use linear measurements over $\mathbb{Z}_q$ to ones that use linear measurements over the integers. This transformation relies on background noise, effectively implementing mod-q reduction by adding secret random multiples of q that are harvested from the background noise. This transformation has two disadvantages: first, if the coefficients of the linear combinations are polynomially bounded, Adv gets an inverse polynomial distinguishing advantage (compared to the negligible advantage in the $\mathbb{Z}_q$ solutions). Second, the resulting algorithm relies on background noise and does not achieve entropic security. While we show that both disadvantages are in some sense inherent, there is still a lot of room for improving both the qualitative security guarantee and the quantitative parameters.

We conclude by presenting positive and negative results for other classes $\mathcal{F}$, beyond linear measurements. These results build heavily on previous results in the literature on computational learning theory or low-complexity cryptography. See Sect. 5 for details.

Can Public-Key Encryption *Really* Be Implemented by Nature? As discussed above, cryptographic sensing for naturally occurring functions essentially requires public-key encryption (PKE) to be implemented by nature. This may seem inconceivable in light of the complexity and relative scarcity of known PKE candidates. However, as our results suggest, this view may be overly pessimistic for several reasons.

First, it ignores the extra degree of freedom one has by *encoding* the output of a standard PKE scheme. Indeed, even complex functions can be encoded by randomized functions (such as NC^0 functions [9]) for which *every individual output* is a very simple function of the input. The space of possible constructions of such randomized encoding schemes for functions is far from being well understood or even systematically explored.

A second degree of freedom that our constructions exploit is the ability of the sensing algorithm to pick an arbitrary, possibly contrived, distribution over the class of measurement functions. We heavily exploit this in our sensing algorithm that uses linear measurement functions with small integer coefficients. (As argued above, this class of measurements admits simple physical realizations.) In the dual learning formulation, this amounts to using a contrived training set or input distribution. The combination of a "contrived" input distribution with a "natural" function class might be just as powerful as the usual combination of "contrived" function class with a "natural" input distribution, which is commonly used in cryptography. For instance, for all we know, even DNF formulas can compute weak pseudo-random functions or public-key encryption schemes for contrived input distributions.

Finally, as we demonstrate in Sect. 5, relaxing the basic model to a distributed setting, which allows two or more separate interactions, breaks the PKE implication and opens the space to a much larger class of cryptographic sensing and learning schemes.

1.2 Related Work

A central theme of this work is that of using *simple* forms of cryptography, that one can actually implement via physical measurements. The study of simple forms of cryptography is not new and has already lead to rich and often surprising results. This study of low-complexity cryptography includes works on local one-way functions and other cryptographic primitives [9,26] that led to the notion of randomized encoding (RE), works on low-degree polynomials [8,30], linear-time functions [31], as well as similar results for arithmetic functions [6,32].

By necessity, we will generally focus on less traditional notions of cryptographic security and correctness. For instance, we will largely eschew the traditional notion of probabilistic encryption with semantic security [27] in favor of entropic security [13,24,46] notions that have arisen primarily in the context of deterministic encryption. Moreover, we will consider relaxations of correctness, as well, inspired by compressed sensing (see, e.g., [29,33]) where not the entire message is recovered.

Finally, the interaction between cryptography and learning has rich history. Valiant [48] already pointed out that if $\mathcal{F}$ contains a cryptographic pseudorandom function (PRF) then this makes the class $\mathcal{F}$ hard to learn, even given membership queries. Other cryptographic primitives like PKE, were used to base some more advanced hardness results in learning theory, e.g., [4,35,36] (beyond hardness results for so-called "proper" learning [43]). See [23] for a more recent work in this direction. Concretely, the work of [4] may seem as an obstacle for cryptographic-sensing of sufficiently rich classes $\mathcal{F}$ (such as CNF formulae) that allow embedding of signature verification. For such classes, they prove that if $\mathcal{F}$ can be leaned from random examples and membership queries (MQs) then $\mathcal{F}$ can also be leaned from random examples and *without* membership queries, which seems to indicate that whatever the sensing algorithm can learn the adversary will be able to learn as well. This however is not the case as, in the construction of [4], for learning $f \in \mathcal{F}$ wrt distribution D and without MQs, the learner invokes a learning algorithm with MQs that learns a *different* (but related) function $f' \in \mathcal{F}$ wrt a related distribution D'. This is not possible in the physical setting of cryptographic sensing where f, D are chosen by nature and the sensing algorithm and the adversary both have access to them.

In the reverse direction, hard learning problems were proposed as a source for cryptographic assumptions [16] where the LPN and LWE assumptions (proposed by [16,44] respectively) serve, due to their convenient structure and simplicity, as some of the most useful assumptions for cryptographic constructions. There is currently a large body of work on adversarial machine learning (e.g, [22,38] and references therein); these works are mainly concerned with the correctness of the learning process in the presence of adversaries that harm the samples (e.g., by changing examples and/or their labels). In a very different direction, [34] initiated the study of private learning, whose goal is to protect the privacy of individuals whose sensitive inputs are used for learning.

1.3   Future Directions

Our work leaves many directions for future research. Which natural classes admit cryptographic sensing algorithms? We note that not much attention has been spent on finding explicit "hard distributions" for classes that are learnable with membership queries, but for which PAC learning algorithms are unknown. This includes even very simple classes such as DNF formulas. Hard input distributions for these classes can serve as a starting point for designing a cryptographic sensing algorithm. Another direction that we haven't explored at all is potential applications in the context of practical machine learning algorithms.

On the physical side: which simple functions of an object can be measured (say, using radar technologies or particle physics) without significant additional leakage? We described specific toy experiments for realizing linear measurements with small non-negative integer coefficients. Is there a direct way to measure mod-q linear combinations using quantum measurements or classical wave interference? Is there a good algorithmic way to cope with the type of additional leakage that can be expected from physical measurements?

To conclude, while the feasibility of implementing a cryptographic flashlight "in the wild" is left open, we do not see any fundamental barriers to making this idea applicable for real-world sensing and learning problems. Our results leave much room for further quantitative and qualitative improvements that can help make this happen. Alternatively, the question of cryptographic sensing can help motivate a rich line of theoretical questions that explore new kinds of interaction between cryptography and computational learning theory.

2   Preliminaries

In this section we recall some standard definitions and facts that will be useful for formalizing our security notions and analyzing the constructions.

Definition 1 (Statistical distance). *The statistical distance between distributions X and Y, denoted $\mathrm{SD}(X, Y)$, is defined as the maximum, over all functions A, of the distinguishing advantage $|\Pr[A(X) = 1] - \Pr[A(Y) = 1]|$.*

Definition 2 (Min-Entropy). *We say that a random variable X over a set S has min-entropy k, and denote $H_\infty(X) = k$, if $\max_{s \in S} \Pr[X = s] = 2^{-k}$.*

We will use the following standard Leftover Hash Lemma (LHL).

Lemma 3 (Leftover Hash Lemma [28]). Let $H = \{h\}$ be a family of pairwise-independent hash functions $h : \mathcal{D} \to \mathcal{R}$. Let X be a distribution over $\mathcal{D}$ with $H_\infty(X) \geq k$, where $k \geq \log|\mathcal{R}| + 2\log(1/\epsilon)$. Then, the distribution $(h, h(x))$ with $h \in_R H$ and x selected according to X is ϵ-close to (h, r), with $h \in_R H$ and $r \in_R \mathcal{R}$.

2.1 The LWE Assumption

We rely on well studied decisional variants of the Learning with Errors (LWE) assumption [44]. This assumption says that a random noisy codeword in a publicly known random linear code is pseudo-random. More precisely, the distribution $(M, Ms + e)$, for a random matrix $M \in_R \mathbb{Z}_q^{n \times m}$, secret vector $s \in_R \mathbb{Z}_q^m$ and appropriately chosen noise distribution $e \in \mathbb{Z}_q^n$ is computationally indistinguishable from the distribution (M, u), where u is uniformly distributed over $\mathbb{Z}_q^n$ independently of M. The noise distribution for LWE is χ^n for some distribution χ over $\mathbb{Z}_q$, which is typically a discrete Gaussian. For simplicity, it is convenient to replace the Gaussian distribution with a uniform distribution over an interval $[0, b]$, where $b = q^{\Omega(1)}$. When q is super-polynomial in λ, security with such an "interval noise" reduces to security with Gaussian noise of standard deviation $\approx b$. While no such reduction is known in the regime of polynomially large q (which is more relevant to our work), this alternative form of the LWE assumption resists known attacks.

Definition 4 (Learning With Errors). *Let λ be a security parameter. For $m = m(\lambda)$, $n = n(\lambda)$, $q = q(\lambda)$, $b = b(\lambda)$, $t = t(\lambda)$, and $\epsilon = \epsilon(\lambda)$, we say that the decisional learning with errors problem (with interval noise) $\mathsf{LWE}_{m,n,q,b}$ is (t, ϵ)-hard if for all sufficiently large λ, every circuit of size $t = t(\lambda)$ has at most an $\epsilon = \epsilon(\lambda)$ advantage in distinguishing between the distributions $(M, Ms + e)$ and (M, u), where $M \xleftarrow{R} \mathbb{Z}_q^{n \times m}$, $s \xleftarrow{R} \mathbb{Z}_q^m$, e is uniformly distributed in $[0, b]^n$, and $u \xleftarrow{R} \mathbb{Z}_q^n$. We say that LWE holds with parameters m, n, q, b, if $\mathsf{LWE}_{m,n,q,b}$ is $(t = p(\lambda), \epsilon = 1/p(\lambda))$-hard for every polynomial $p(\lambda)$.*

Our typical choice of parameters is $m = \lambda$, $n \leq \mathrm{poly}(m)$, $q \approx n^2$, and $b \approx \sqrt{m}$; however, smaller values of q and b can be used for better efficiency. See [40] and references therein for choices of LWE parameters that resist known attacks, including ones that are provably secure under worst-case hardness assumptions for integer lattices. We note that one could alternatively settle for sampling the secret s from the the same distribution as the noise instead of the uniform distribution [7]. This optimization can improve the concrete efficiency of our LWE-based constructions.

3 Defining Cryptographic Sensing

In this section we formalize our notion of cryptographic sensing. We start with the default "sensing" formulation and then describe how to modify it to get the dual "learning" formulation.

Function Classes. A *function class* $\mathcal{F}$ is defined by a polynomial-time algorithm that given a description $\hat{f}$ of a finite function f and an input x for f outputs $f(x)$. (We will often abuse notation and identify functions and other objects with their representations.) We assume that $\hat{f}$ includes a description of the input domain $\mathcal{X}_f$ and that $\mathcal{F}$ outputs $\perp$ when the input $(\hat{f}, x)$ is not of the expected form, namely when $\hat{f}$ is not a valid function description or when $x \notin \mathcal{X}_f$. We let $\mathcal{X}(\mathcal{F})$ denote the set of (descriptions of) valid input domains for $\mathcal{F}$ and $\mathcal{F}_{\mathcal{X}}$ denote the set of function descriptions $\hat{f}$ with input domain $\mathcal{X}$. The set $\mathcal{F}_{\mathcal{X}}$ defines the allowable *measurement functions* that can apply to a hidden object $x \in \mathcal{X}$. The function class $\mathcal{F}$ also assigns a *cost* measure to every function description $\hat{f}$. For instance, if $\mathcal{F}$ is the class of DNF formulas then a natural cost of $\hat{f}$ is the number of clauses and if $\mathcal{F}$ is the class of linear functions with non-negative integer coefficients then a natural cost is the sum of all coefficients.

Cryptographic Sensing: Syntax. A *cryptographic sensing algorithm for* $\mathcal{F}$ is a PPT algorithm Sen with oracle access to $\mathcal{F}$ that, given a security parameter 1^{λ} and description of an input domain $\mathcal{X} \in \mathcal{X}(\mathcal{F})$, proceeds as follows. It starts by randomly generating a secret decoding key sk. (If concrete efficiency is not a concern, one can let sk include all random coins of Sen.) It then interacts with $\mathcal{F}$, feeding it with measurement functions $\hat{f}_i \in \mathcal{F}_{\mathcal{X}}$, and receiving the outcomes $a_i = f_i(x)$ on some fixed object $x \in \mathcal{X}$ unknown to Sen. We will mostly consider *non-adaptive* sensing algorithms Sen in which all measurements $\hat{f}_i$ are chosen simultaneously before querying $\mathcal{F}$. In this case, we will sometimes consider the concatenation of all f_i as a single function f taken from the multi-output extension of $\mathcal{F}$. Once it is done querying, Sen uses sk and the interaction transcript $\mathcal{I} = ((\hat{f}_1, a_1), \ldots, (\hat{f}_m, a_m))$ to produce a guess for x.

Correctness. The default correctness requirement, which will later be relaxed, is that for every efficient non-uniform adversary that on input 1^{λ} picks an input domain $\mathcal{X} \in \mathcal{X}(\mathcal{F})$ and an object $x \in \mathcal{X}$, the interaction of $\mathsf{Sen}(1^{\lambda}, \mathcal{X})$ with $\mathcal{F}_{\mathcal{X}}$ on object x results in Sen outputting the correct value of x except with $\mathrm{neg}(\lambda)$ probability.

One-Way Security. The minimal security requirement we consider is *one-wayness*. Since it is not always natural to consider a uniform distribution over objects (let alone over *functions* in the learning formulation), we allow an arbitrary efficiently samplable distribution. Concretely, we say that Sen is one-way secure with respect to $\mathcal{F}$ if there is a PPT object sampling algorithm S such that every efficient non-uniform adversary Adv succeeds in the following game with neg(λ) probability. First, $S(1^\lambda)$ outputs a challenge input domain $\mathcal{X} \in \mathcal{X}(\mathcal{F})$ and an object $x \in \mathcal{X}$. Then, $\mathsf{Sen}(1^\lambda, \mathcal{X})$ interacts with $\mathcal{F}_\mathcal{X}$ on object x, resulting in an interaction transcript $\mathcal{I} = ((\hat{f}_1, a_1), \dots, (\hat{f}_m, a_m))$. Finally, $\mathsf{Adv}(\mathcal{X}, \mathcal{I})$ outputs a guess for x. We say that Adv succeeds if its guess is correct.

Using standard cryptographic terminology, a *non-adaptive* cryptographic sensing algorithm with one-way security for $\mathcal{F}$ is equivalent (up to the choice of input distribution) to an $\mathcal{F}$-computable injective trapdoor function, namely one that can be computed by concatenating functions from $\mathcal{F}$. One-way security is typically not very useful, since it only applies to a specific object distribution and even in this case it does not rule out revealing a big amount of partial information about the object. Below we define several stronger notions, analogously to different notions of security for (one-time) encryption in the cryptographic literature.

Entropic Security. Entropic security is in a sense the best possible notion of security for deterministic encryption. It requires that any two object distributions that have high min-entropy cannot be distinguished by Adv. This intuitively means that the interaction does not help Adv distinguish between objects that were sufficiently unpredictable to start with. Formally, let $k : \mathbb{N} \times \mathcal{X}(\mathcal{F}) \to \mathbb{R}$ be an entropy bound function, specifying a lower bound on object entropy as a function of the security parameter λ and object domain $\mathcal{X}$. For $\epsilon = \epsilon(\lambda)$ we say that Sen is (k, ϵ)-*entropically secure* if every efficient non-uniform adversary Adv succeeds in the following game with at most $1/2 + \epsilon(\lambda)$ probability for all sufficiently large λ. First, $\mathsf{Adv}(1^\lambda)$ outputs an input domain $\mathcal{X} \in \mathcal{X}(\mathcal{F})$ and a pair of circuits describing input distributions X_0, X_1 over $\mathcal{X}$ with $H_\infty(X_\sigma) \geq k$ for $\sigma = 0, 1$. Then, a challenger picks a random bit $\sigma \in \{0, 1\}$ and lets $\mathsf{Sen}(1^\lambda, \mathcal{X})$ interact with $\mathcal{F}_\mathcal{X}$ on an object x sampled from X_σ. This results in an interaction transcript $\mathcal{I} = ((\hat{f}_1, a_1), \dots, (\hat{f}_m, a_m))$. Finally, $\mathsf{Adv}(\mathcal{I})$ outputs a guess for σ. We say that Adv succeeds if its guess is correct. When ϵ is omitted we assume it is negligible; however, some of our results inherently require ϵ to be non-negligible.

To gain more flexibility, it can be convenient to give an entropy bound k as an additional input for Sen and modify the above definition accordingly (allowing Sen to declare failure in case k is too low; for instance, when $k = O(\log(\lambda))$ a brute-force search attack is possible). Using standard cryptographic terminology, a non-adaptive cryptographic sensing algorithm with entropic security for $\mathcal{F}$ can be viewed as an $\mathcal{F}$-computable one-time-secure *deterministic* public-key encryption scheme [13, 24, 46].

Lossy Decoding. A useful relaxation of the above correctness requirement settles for *lossy decoding*, where Sen outputs some useful partial information about x such as a projection of x to a subset of the coordinates or a compressive linear sketch of x from which an approximate version (e.g., a lower resolution image) can be recovered. We formalize this by introducing a *target function class* $\mathcal{G}$ with the same input domains as $\mathcal{F}$ (i.e., $\mathcal{X}(\mathcal{G}) = \mathcal{X}(\mathcal{F})$) and adding to the inputs of

Sen a description $\hat{g}$ of a target function $g : \mathcal{X} \to \mathcal{Z}$. The correctness requirement is changed in a natural way, requiring that $\mathsf{Sen}(1^\lambda, \mathcal{X}, \hat{g})$ correctly output $g(x)$. In the definition of entropic security, the entropy bound k is allowed to also depend on g (where typically k needs to grow with the output size of g). Note that with lossy decoding, one-way security may become meaningless. However, entropic security is still as meaningful.

Allowing Background Noise. A useful special case of lossy decoding is a projection to a *fixed* set of coordinates, where the other coordinates are viewed as background noise whose entropy can be exploited to protect the target output. In this case we will view the measurements of Sen as applying to (x, r), where x is the target object and r is the background noise, and require Sen to only output x. One can consider three notions of security with background noise. The strongest, referred to as security with *correlated background noise* does not assume independence between x and r and only requires entropic security when the *joint entropy* is at least k. The second, referred to as security with *independent background noise*, requires that x remain completely hidden if the background noise is independent and has high min-entropy. This is formalized as in the definition of entropic security, except that the distributions X_0 and X_1 are of the form (x_0, R) and (x_1, R) for $x_0, x_1 \in \mathcal{X}$ and an adversarially chosen R such that $H_\infty(R) \geq k$. Finally, the third and weakest notion, referred to as security with *random background noise*, is similar to the above except that the noise is picked from some specified noise distribution (uniform by default).

The weakest variant of security with background noise corresponds to the usual notion of semantically secure probabilistic encryption [27]. The strongest is equivalent to (one-time) indistinguishability under a *chosen distribution attack*, as defined in [14].

A Dual Learning Formulation. In the above, we assumed that Sen tries to recover a secret object $x \in \mathcal{X}$ using a sequence of measurement functions f_i. In the setting of computational learning theory [48], one considers the dual goal of learning a secret *concept* $\hat{f} \in \mathcal{F}$ by evaluating it on a sequence of inputs x_i. The above definitions can be adapted in a natural way to this dual formulation. However, some changes should be made. First, the role of the object domain $\mathcal{X}$, which is given as input to Sen, is replaced by a sub-class of concepts in $\mathcal{F}$ from which the target concept is picked. For instance, if $\mathcal{F}$ is the class of DNF formulas, this subclass can include all formulas with a fixed number of inputs n, or alternatively formulas with n inputs and ℓ clauses. Second, since $\mathcal{F}$ may define many equivalent representations $\hat{f}$ for the same concept f, we define the entropic security requirements semantically, namely with respect to the functions rather than their representations. Finally, our correctness requirements can accommodate relaxed notions of correctness from the machine learning literature. For instance, we can allow approximate correctness as in the PAC model (except that we need to additionally allow membership queries), and we can consider improper learning, namely allow Sen to output a general circuit representation of the target concept or its approximation.

The Distributed Setting. Finally, we will consider a distributed relaxation of the above notions, where Sen may be involved in $d \geq 2$ separate interactions, producing transcripts $\mathcal{I}_1, \ldots, \mathcal{I}_d$. The output can be decoded by Sen given all transcripts, but only a bounded number t of these transcripts is available to Adv. In the context of the drug company example from the Introduction, this corresponds to distributing the experiments among d companies $B_1, \ldots, B_d$, where security of A is only guaranteed as long as no more than t companies B_i reveal their information to C.

4 Cryptographic Sensing with Linear Measurements

In this section we describe simple cryptographic sensing algorithms that use different types of linear measurement functions: linear functions over $\mathbb{Z}_q$ and linear functions over the integers.

4.1 Linear Measurements over $\mathbb{Z}_q$

Code-based public-key encryption schemes presented by McEliece [39] and by Alekhnovich [2] imply cryptographic sensing algorithms with linear measurements over $\mathbb{Z}_2$ that require uniformly random background noise and a large number of measurements. These constructions can in fact be generalized to apply over any finite field. Lattice-based encryption schemes such as Ajtai-Dwork [1], Regev [44] and GPV [25] imply similar algorithms with linear measurements over $\mathbb{Z}_q$, where q grows with the object length n. These lattice-based constructions have the additional benefit of provable security under well-studied worst-case hardness assumptions; however they still require a random background noise and a large number of measurements.

Targeting the stronger security notion of entropic security, one could obtain lattice-based cryptographic sensing algorithms with $\mathbb{Z}_q$-linear measurements by using known lattice-based constructions of deterministic encryption schemes [19], which in turn are based on constructions of lossy injective trapdoor functions [15,42]. However, these constructions require a large number of measurements, and only tolerate a constant entropy rate.

In the following we present an LWE-based *lossy* cryptographic sensing algorithm that uses $\mathbb{Z}_q$-linear measurements and achieves entropic security, where both the entropy bound and the number of measurements are comparable to the length of the lossy output $g(x)$, independently of the length of the measured object x.

We first assume for simplicity that the object is $x \in \mathcal{X}_n = \{0,1\}^n$ and the target function class $\mathcal{G}$ is the class of mod-2 linear mappings with output length $t < n$. This is already useful for obtaining many natural approximations of x [33]. We then generalize the algorithm to the case where x is a vector of bounded-size integers and $\mathcal{G}$ includes compressive linear mappings with bounded integer coefficients. This generalization allows for a wider range of useful approximations, via compressed sensing and other linear sketching techniques (cf. [29]).

The algorithm uses the standard approach of lattice-based cryptosystems, in particular Regev's cryptosystem [44]. The high level idea is as follows. If the object x has min-entropy k, then (by Lemma 3) revealing up to $\approx k/\log q$ publicly known *random* $\mathbb{Z}_q$-linear combinations of the entries of x gives essentially no information about x. However, if we could choose special linear combinations, say ones in which each coefficient is either close to 0 or to $q/2$ (where $q \gg n$), then we could learn parities of subsets of the bits of x. Assuming LWE, we can hide such special linear combinations in the span of a small number of random-looking linear combinations. We formalize this idea below. Note that below we assume LWE for uniform noise. However, this is strictly for simplicity of exposition; all our results also hold assuming LWE with discrete Gaussian noise.

Decoding a Single Parity. We start by considering the case $t = 1$, namely the target function g computes $\langle y, x \rangle \bmod 2$ for $y \in \{0,1\}^n$, and then generalize to $t > 1$. The class of measurement functions $\mathcal{F}$ includes all linear functions mod q. That is, each measurement f_i is represented by $\ell \in \mathbb{Z}_q^n$ and returns $\langle \ell, x \rangle \bmod q$. We will also have a dimension parameter m and noise parameter b where the choice of n, m, q, b (all as functions of a security parameter λ) satisfies the LWE assumption with interval noise. Furthermore, we require that q be at most polynomial in n and that $q > 4nb$. See Sect. 2.1 for possible choices of parameters.

Algorithm. $\mathsf{Sen}(1^\lambda, 1^n, y \in \{0,1\}^n)$:

1. Pick $A \in_R \mathbb{Z}_q^{m \times n}$ and set $z = s^T A + e + \lfloor q/2 \rfloor \cdot y$ for "LWE secret" $s \in_R \mathbb{Z}_q^m$ (which serves as the secret key sk) and "noise" vector $e \in_R [0, b]^n$, as in the LWE assumption. (Note that since $s^T A + e$ is pseudorandom given A, then so is z.)
2. Make the $m+1$ measurements corresponding to the m rows of A, as well as z. Get in response $m+1$ values that are viewed as $v_1 = Ax \in \mathbb{Z}_q^m$ and $v_2 = z \cdot x$ (where all arithmetic is over $\mathbb{Z}_q$).
3. Use the secret key s to compute $w = v_2 - s^T v_1 = z \cdot x - s^T A x = (s^T A + e + \lfloor q/2 \rfloor \cdot y) \cdot x - s^T A x = e \cdot x + \lfloor q/2 \rfloor \cdot y \cdot x$ from which $g(x) = \langle y, x \rangle \bmod 2$ is decoded: 0 if w is closer to 0 than to $\lfloor q/2 \rfloor$, and 1 otherwise.

The correctness of Sen follows from its description and from the choice of parameters: we have $0 \leq e \cdot x \leq nb$, and the parity of $y \cdot x$ determines whether we add $\lfloor q/2 \rfloor$ an even number of times, implying that $w \approx 0 \bmod q$ or an odd number of times, implying that $w \approx \lfloor q/2 \rfloor \bmod q$. Hence, $\langle y, x \rangle \bmod 2$ is correctly decoded with probability 1.

Let us argue that Sen is entropically secure for entropy bound $k \approx m \log q$. Note that the view of the adversary Adv consists of the queries of Algorithm Sen, as well as the answers, namely A, z, v_1, v_2. Our goal is to argue that if the entropy condition is met, this view is indistinguishable from a random tuple in $\mathbb{Z}_q^{m \times n} \times \mathbb{Z}_q^n \times \mathbb{Z}_q^m \times \mathbb{Z}_q$. The proof will be based on the LWE assumption and the leftover hash lemma (see Lemma 3). Note that if we take the collection of matrices $A \in \mathbb{Z}_q^{m \times n}$ and consider the functions $h_A(x) = Ax$ (from $\mathbb{Z}_q^n$ to $\mathbb{Z}_q^m$), then the family $H = \{h_A\}$ is indeed known to be pairwise-independent hash family.

Security Analysis: Let X be a distribution of objects with $H_\infty(X) = k$, for $k \geq (m+1)\log q + 2\log(1/\epsilon)$. Let $\mathcal{I} = (A, z, v_1, v_2)$ be the distribution of interactions, as generated by Sen, when interacting with an object x drawn from X. Let $\mathcal{I}' = (A, z, v_1, v_2)$ be the same distribution, except that now z is selected by $z \in_R \mathbb{Z}_q^n$. By the LWE assumption, $\mathcal{I} \approx_c \mathcal{I}'$. Let B be the $(m+1) \times n$ matrix obtained by placing A on top of z and let v be the $(m+1)$-vector obtained by concatenating v_2 to v_1. Observe that $v = Bx$. By the leftover hash lemma (with $\log|\mathcal{R}| = (m+1)\log q$), since X has sufficient min-entropy then the pair $(B, v = Bx)$, for a random B, is ϵ-close to a random pair (B, v) (of the corresponding lengths). This means that $\mathcal{I}'$ is indistinguishable from a distribution $\mathcal{I}'' = (A, z, v_1, v_2)$ consisting of randomly selected elements from $\mathbb{Z}_q$ of the corresponding length. This analysis yields the following theorem.

Theorem 5. *Suppose n, m, q, b are chosen such that $\mathsf{LWE}_{m,n,q,b}$ holds, $q > 4nb$, and $k \geq m\log q + \lambda$. Then Sen is a k-entropically secure cryptographic sensing algorithm for decoding a single parity of $x \in \{0,1\}^n$ using $m+1$ linear measurements over $\mathbb{Z}_q$.*

Extensions. We now extend the previous algorithm in a few simple ways. First, we observe that, for any "small" c, we can modify Sen to learn $\langle y, x \rangle \bmod c$ (rather than only for $c = 2$, as above). This is simply done by computing $z = s^T A + e + \lfloor q/c \rfloor \cdot y$. Again, each coordinate j where $x_j y_j = 1$ will contribute $\approx \lfloor q/c \rfloor$ to the value $v_2 - s^T v_1$. As long as q is sufficiently large (say, $q > 4cnb$) the noise does not prevent the algorithm from recovering $\langle y, x \rangle \bmod c$. In fact, in this case we can let y be any vector in $[0, c-1]^n$ and the algorithm still works, as is. Moreover, it also works when x is not a binary vector but is rather an integer-valued vector from $[0, d]^n$, provided that $q > 4cdnb$.

Next, we consider the case where the sensing algorithm wishes to learn not only a single linear combination $\langle y, x \rangle \bmod 2$, but rather a few of those; namely, for $y^1, \ldots, y^t$, where each y^j is in $\{0,1\}^n$, the algorithm needs to learn all of $\langle y^1, x \rangle \bmod 2, \ldots, \langle y^t, x \rangle \bmod 2$ (this can also naturally be combined with the previous extensions, to allow learning linear combinations mod c of $x \in [0, d]^n$). The first approach that comes to mind is to independently pick queries $(A^1, z^1), \ldots, (A^t, z^t)$, as in the basic algorithm Sen. While this in principle works, it rapidly "consumes" the entropy of x (as Adv gets to see $m+1$ linear combinations per each y^j). Instead, we will pick a single matrix $A \in_R \mathbb{Z}_q^{m \times n}$ and t vectors $z^1, \ldots, z^t$, as above (namely, for each $j \in [t]$, we set $z^j = s^j A + e^j + \lfloor q/2 \rfloor \cdot y^j$, for "secret" $s^j \in_R [b]^m$). The correctness remains unchanged. As for security, as long as X has entropy $k \geq (m+t)\log q + 2\log(1/\epsilon)$, then a similar argument holds. Namely, $A, z^1, \ldots, z^t$ is still pseudorandom, by repeated application of the LWE assumption, and then the leftover hash lemma is applied where our hash function has output of length $m + t$.

Applying the above extensions to Sen, we get a general algorithm Sen′ for decoding compressive linear mappings of x over the integers using $\mathbb{Z}_q$-linear measurements.

Theorem 6. *Suppose n, m, q, b, t, c are chosen such that* $\mathsf{LWE}_{m,n,q,b}$ *holds, $q > 4c^3nb$, and $k \geq (m+t)\log q + \lambda$. Then* Sen′ *is a k-entropically secure cryptographic sensing algorithm for decoding Gx, where $x \in [0, c]^n$ and G is a $t \times n$ integer matrix with entries in $[0, c]$, using $m + t$ linear measurements over $\mathbb{Z}_q$.*

Note that unlike solutions based on deterministic encryption, Theorem 6 cannot be used to obtain full decoding of x even when x is uniformly random. Indeed, this would require choosing t so that the entropy requirement becomes impossible to meet. However, for the case of lossy decoding Theorem 6 gives near-optimal complexity.

4.2   Linear Measurements over the Integers

The LWE-based solution inherently makes use of linear measurements over $\mathbb{Z}_q$. From a physical realization perspective, it is much more desirable to use linear measurements over the *integers* (or reals), since it is not clear how to design a simple physical measurement process that reveals *only* a mod-q linear combination. However, applying the previous construction directly over the integers would render it insecure, since modular reduction is crucial for ruling out efficient real-valued approximation and decoding techniques [20].

We start by proving some inherent limitations on the type of security that can be achieved using linear measurements over the integers, and then present a positive result.

Can't Make ϵ Negligible. Our first negative result says that even if x is a single bit and we settle for semantic security with random background noise, we cannot obtain a negligible distinguishing advantage with polynomial-size linear measurement coefficients. This negative result is based on the following lemma, which says that for a random variable Z over integers in a small range, the statistical distance between Z and $Z + 1$ is noticeable.

Lemma 7. Let Z be distributed over $[0, c - 1]$. Then $\mathrm{SD}(Z, Z + 1) \geq 1/c$.

Proof: Let $Z_i = Z + i$. Since Z and $Z + c$ have disjoint supports, we have $\mathrm{SD}(Z_0, Z_c) = \mathrm{SD}(Z, Z + c) = 1$. By the triangle inequality, there must exist $0 \leq j < c$ such $\mathrm{SD}(Z_j, Z_{j+1}) \geq 1/c$. The lemma follows by observing that $\mathrm{SD}(Z, Z + 1) = \mathrm{SD}(Z_j, Z_{j+1})$.   □

It follows from the above lemma that for any vector of linear measurement coefficients $\ell \in \mathbb{N}^{m+1}$ with $\ell_1 > 0$ and $\ell_i \in [0, c-1]$, and for a random background noise $r \in_R \{0, 1\}^n$ we have $\mathrm{SD}(\langle \ell, (0, r) \rangle, \langle \ell, (1, r) \rangle) \geq 1/(cm)$. Moreover, since the distributions have polynomial-size support, a statistical distinguisher implies (non-uniform) efficient distinguisher. This rules out security with negligible distinguishing advantage $\epsilon = \mathrm{neg}(\lambda)$, polynomial background noise $m = \mathrm{poly}(\lambda)$, and $\mathrm{poly}(\lambda)$-bounded coefficients.

We note that this negative result does *not* apply to our minimal notion of one-way security. Indeed, one-way security can be achieved with polynomial-size coefficients by dividing x into λ disjoint blocks and applying the positive result presented below for each block. This exploits the fact that one-way security can be amplified via independent repetition.

Can't Get Entropic 1/Poly-Security. Next, we show that our positive result for entropic security with mod-q linear measurements (cf. Theorem 6) cannot be achieved over the integers, even if one settles for $1/\mathrm{poly}$ distinguishing advantage, and even if there is no bound on the size of the integers. The intuition is that when there is no background noise to mask the object x, there is a noticeable difference between a "bright" object and a "dark" object. Concretely, consider the case of entropy bound $k = n/3$, and let X_0 be a distribution over $\{0,1\}^n$ in which a random set of $n/3$ bits are picked at random and the rest are set to 0 (a bright object), and X_1 is a similar except that the other bits are set to 1 (a dark object). Then, for any nonzero $\ell \in \mathbb{N}^n$, a distinguisher that tests whether its input is bigger than $\sum_{i=1}^n \ell_i/2$ distinguishes between $\langle \ell, X_0 \rangle$ and $\langle \ell, X_1 \rangle$ with constant advantage. We leave open the question of obtaining security up to leakage of brightness, namely obtaining an entropic secure solution (say, with poly-bounded integer coefficients and constant fractional entropy bound) in which the view of Adv can be simulated given $\sum x_i$ with simulation error that vanishes with n.

A Positive Result. Our positive result complements the first negative result above by showing that semantic security with random background noise is indeed achievable with $\epsilon \geq 1/\mathrm{poly}(\lambda)$ by only using polynomial-size non-negative integer coefficients. More generally, we give a simple method for compiling any solution that uses linear measurements over $\mathbb{Z}_q$ into one that uses linear measurements over the integers, at the price of relying on random background noise and settling for an inverse polynomial error. More precisely, the cost of the linear measurements (namely, the magnitude of the coefficients) grows polynomially with n/ϵ.

The high level idea is to perform the $\mathbb{Z}_q$ measurements over the integers, and effectively achieve modular reduction by adding (over the integers) a large random multiple of q. (The previous negative result suggests that this is in some sense inherent.) The randomness used by this reduction is taken from the background noise. Concretely, given a bound $\mu = 2^c$ on the coefficients, we add to each original measurement a weighted sum of the form $\sum_{i=1}^c (2^i q) \cdot r_i$ where each measurement uses a disjoint set of c background points. Note that this effectively means that we add a random multiple $\beta \cdot q$ for $\beta \in_R [0, \mu - 1]$.

We turn to analyze the correctness and security of the above transformation. Decoding in the integer case can proceed as in the mod-q case, reducing the integer measurement values modulo q. This is not affected by adding multiples of q, hence correctness is maintained. The security analysis relies on the following standard lemma (cf. [12]), showing that if we add βq to a value from a bounded range $[0, B]$ and β is uniform in $[0, \mu - 1]$ (for μ sufficiently large, depending on B and q), then little is revealed beyond mod q.

Lemma 8. Let $\alpha_1, \alpha_2 \in [0, B]$ be two integers such that $\alpha_1 \equiv \alpha_2 \mod q$. Consider the two distributions Y_1, Y_2 where Y_i is obtained by $\alpha_i + \beta q$, for $\beta \in_R [0, \mu - 1]$. Then, $\mathrm{SD}(Y_1, Y_2) \leq \frac{B}{q\mu}$.

Note that when allowing a random background noise, the entropic security with lossy decoding of Theorem 6 implies semantic security with full decoding by applying the algorithm of Theorem 6 to the concatenation (x, r) and decoding only the x portion. Applying the above transformation, we get the following integer analogue.

Theorem 9. *Suppose* $\mathsf{LWE}_{m,n,q,b}$ *holds for* $m = \lambda$, $n = m^d$ *(for some constant $d > 2$), $b = \sqrt{q}$ and $q = \Theta(c^3 n^2)$ (for some positive integer $c = c(\lambda)$). Then there is a semantically ϵ-secure cryptographic sensing algorithm with random background noise for decoding Gx, where $x \in [0, c]^n$ and G is a $t \times n$ integer matrix with entries in $[0, c]$, using $m + t$ linear measurements with non-negative integer coefficients, where the cost of each measurement is* $\mathrm{poly}(n, c, 1/\epsilon)$.

Studying the extent to which the random background noise assumption can be relaxed, as well as a more refined study of the achievable tradeoffs between the parameters, are left for future work.

5   Beyond Linear Measurements

In this section, we briefly discuss other classes of measurements, beyond linear functions. Here we will typically use the learning formulation of cryptographic sensing (see Introduction and Sect. 3). We give examples for positive and negative results that follow quite easily from the literature, as well as some directions for further research.

5.1   Negative Results for Simple Classes via Occam's Razor

Our first observation in this section is that classes of functions $\mathcal{F}$ that are "learnable" in a strong sense (to be made precise below) cannot be used for cryptographic sensing. The intuition being that the adversary Adv who observes the interaction transcript $\mathcal{I}$ can simply apply the learning algorithm to the examples it sees throughout the observed interaction and learn the concept by itself. To make this a bit more formal, we first recall the notion of *OCCAM learning.*

An OCCAM Learning algorithm for a class of functions $\mathcal{F}$, using a class of hypotheses $\mathcal{H}$ and constants $a \geq 0$ and $0 \leq b < 1$, is an algorithm $\mathcal{A}$ that, given any set (sample) S of m examples in $\{0,1\}^n$, labeled by any $f \in \mathcal{F}$, outputs an hypothesis $h \in \mathcal{H}$ such that: (1) h is consistent with S (i.e., it agrees with the hidden f on the labels of all examples); and (2) h is "succinct", i.e.

size(h) is bounded by[1] $(n \cdot \text{size}(f))^a \cdot m^b$. Algorithm $\mathcal{A}$ is efficient if it runs in time polynomial in n, m and size(f).

Occam's Razor is a well-known philosophical principle. Its connection to machine learning was made by [17], who showed that it is essentially equivalent to Valiant's notion of PAC-learnability [48]. Concretely, they showed that an OCCAM learner $\mathcal{A}$ can be turned into a PAC learner $\mathcal{A}'$ (essentially showing that if $\mathcal{A}'$ feeds $\mathcal{A}$ with enough random examples, as a function of the parameters a, b of $\mathcal{A}$, the hypotheses h that $\mathcal{A}$ outputs is good enough) thus providing a natural approach for designing PAC-learning algorithms. The converse direction, namely that PAC learnability implies OCCAM learnability also holds [47].[2]

We now conclude that, for classes $\mathcal{F}$ that admit OCCAM learnability, the adversary Adv can apply the corresponding OCCAM algorithm $\mathcal{A}$ to get a hypothesis h that is consistent with f on all examples. If there is a sensing algorithm Sen that is able to identify the concept f based on these examples, then so can Adv. This rules out even our weakest notion of one-way security.

Such efficient OCCAM (alternatively PAC) learning algorithms are known for classes such as disjunctions, conjunctions and k-DNFs for constant k [48], decision lists [45], and more. Thus, all these classes are not candidates for cryptographic sensing. For a richer class such as (poly-size) DNFs, the question of its efficient learnability is wide open. Designing (even a one-way secure) cryptographic sensing algorithm for such a class would therefore imply that it cannot be PAC-learned efficiently without membership queries. While proving hardness under standard intractability assumptions may be a difficult challenge, coming up with explicit plausible candidates for hard distributions is a problem that apparently did not receive much attention.

On the optimistic side, PAC-learning algorithms are known only for limited classes of functions (hence, the above negative result is limited as well). For other classes, sensing may or may not be possible. Note that, intuitively, cryptographic sensing is closer in spirit to the stronger setting of PAC with membership queries (MQ). In such a model, one can learn more expressive classes such as Decision Trees [21] and DFAs [3].

There are several non-trivial sub-exponential algorithms for DNF. The best such algorithm is by Klivans and Servedio [37] and has complexity of roughly $2^{O(n^{1/3} \log n \log s)}$ for learning s-term DNF with n variables. Transforming this algorithm to an OCCAM learning algorithm, as above, gives a limit on the security of cryptographic sensing algorithms for DNF that one may hope to achieve. We also remark that known results on PAC-learnability of DNF under uniform distribution (this is known to be possible in quasi-polynomial time [49]) do not imply a negative result for cryptographic sensing.

---

[1] The requirement that $b < 1$ is what rules out the trivial solution where h is just the list of labels for the m points in S and forces actual "learning".

[2] In the case of *proper* PAC-learning (i.e., when $\mathcal{H} = \mathcal{F}$), [18] present a condition (called "closure under exception lists") on $\mathcal{F}$ under which PAC still implies OCCAM learning.

5.2   Local Measurements

We now go back temporarily to the sensing formulation, focusing on a simple class of measurements that corresponds to work on low-complexity cryptography. Consider d-local measurement functions, namely the class $\mathcal{F}$ of "finite" functions f that depend on at most d bits of x. We note that, despite the simplicity of such functions, we are not aware of any natural physical realization that does not involve additional leakage. Still, it is natural to study the power of this class.

Entropic security cannot be realized in NC^0, as it is easy to construct, for any d-local function f, a pair of high-entropy distributions X_0, X_1 where for every $x \in X_0$ we have $f(x) = 0$ and for every $x \in X_1$ we have $f(x) = 1$ (the entropy can be as large as, say, $n - d$). The same impossibility holds for security with independent background noise (as defined in Sect. 3). However, in the setting of *random* background noise, where noise is a uniformly random bit-string, we can get positive results for $d = 4$. Indeed, under standard cryptographic assumptions, there is 4-local PKE [9], which implies a cryptographic sensing algorithm with random background noise. The above is still not satisfactory because it does not respect physical locality. Under a less standard but still plausible security assumption, namely the security of a variant of the McEliece cryptosystem, it is possible to get an analogous result with constant physical locality [11].

The amount of background noise in the above solutions is very large, $|x| \cdot \mathrm{poly}(\lambda)$. If we do not insist on physical locality, we can trade background noise for locality by using polynomial-stretch local PRGs [5, 10, 26, 31]. This can reduce the amount of background noise to $|x|^\epsilon \cdot \mathrm{poly}(\lambda)$, for any constant ϵ, while still maintaining constant locality d.

5.3   Distributed Solution for Learning Juntas

Finally, we demonstrate the potential usefulness of the distributed variant of cryptographic sensing by showing a positive result for the class of juntas. Learning juntas on $k = O(\log n)$ inputs from random examples is conjectured to be a hard learning problem (this conjecture is attributed to Avrim Blum). However, we argue that such f can be learned in the distributed setting (see Sect. 3) via two sets of labeled examples: S_1 that contains $\mathrm{poly}(n)$ random examples (the exact polynomial depends on k), and S_2 that contains a random Hamming-neighbor for each example in S_1, namely each example in S_2 is obtained by flipping a random bit in the corresponding example in S_1. Note that each of the two interactions $\mathcal{I}_1, \mathcal{I}_2$ separately is a collection of labeled random examples from which learning f, as mentioned, is conjectured to be hard. On the other hand, putting together the two interactions allow Sen to identify each of the k sensitive variables x_i, with high probability (by selecting, with probability $\geq 2^{-k}$, an assignment to S_1 that is sensitive at x_i and selecting to S_2 its i-th neighbor). Then the function itself can recovered in polynomial time from the answers to questions from, say, S_1 that cover all 2^k assignments to the k sensitive variables. Note that here quasi-polynomial security is the best that one can hope for, since the original problem can be solved in, roughly, $n^{k+O(1)}$ time (via a naive algorithm that checks all subsets of k variables) or even slightly better via a sophisticated algorithm of [41] that runs in time $n^{ck+O(1)}$, for some $c < 1$.

Acknowledgements. We thank Brent Waters for helpful discussions.

Research supported by NSF-BSF grant 2015782. Y. Ishai and E. Kushilevitz were additionally supported by ISF grant 1709/14 and a grant from the Ministry of Science and Technology, Israel and Department of Science and Technology, Government of India. Y. Ishai was additionally supported by ERC Project NTSC (742754). R. Ostrovsky was additionally supported by NSF grant 1619348, DARPA SafeWare subcontract to Galois Inc., DARPA SPAWAR contract N66001-15-C-4065, JP Morgan Faculty Research Award, OKAWA Foundation Research Award, IBM Faculty Research Award, Xerox Faculty Research Award, B. John Garrick Foundation Award, Teradata Research Award, and Lockheed-Martin Corporation Research Award. A. Sahai was additionally supported by a DARPA/ARL SAFEWARE award, NSF Frontier Award 1413955, and NSF grant 1619348, a Xerox Faculty Research Award, a Google Faculty Research Award, an equipment grant from Intel, and an Okawa Foundation Research Grant. This material is based upon work supported by the Defense Advanced Research Projects Agency through the ARL under Contract W911NF-15-C-0205. The views expressed are those of the authors and do not reflect the official policy or position of the Department of Defense, the National Science Foundation or the U.S. Government.

References

1. Ajtai, M., Dwork, C.: A public-key cryptosystem with worst-case/average-case equivalence. In: Proceedings of the Twenty-Ninth Annual ACM Symposium on the Theory of Computing, El Paso, Texas, USA, 4–6 May 1997 (1997)
2. Alekhnovich, M.: More on average case vs approximation complexity. In: Proceedings of the 44th Symposium on Foundations of Computer Science (FOCS 2003), Cambridge, MA, USA, 11–14 October 2003 (2003)
3. Angluin, D.: Learning regular sets from queries and counterexamples. Inf. Comput. **75**(2), 87–106 (1987)
4. Angluin, D., Kharitonov, M.: When won't membership queries help? (Extended abstract). In: STOC (1991)
5. Applebaum, B.: Exponentially-hard gap-CSP and local PRG via local hardcore functions. In: FOCS (2017)
6. Applebaum, B., Avron, J., Brzuska, C.: Arithmetic cryptography. J. ACM **64**(2), 10:1–10:74 (2017)
7. Applebaum, B., Cash, D., Peikert, C., Sahai, A.: Fast cryptographic primitives and circular-secure encryption based on hard learning problems. In: Halevi, S. (ed.) CRYPTO 2009. LNCS, vol. 5677, pp. 595–618. Springer, Heidelberg (2009). https://doi.org/10.1007/978-3-642-03356-8_35
8. Applebaum, B., Haramaty, N., Ishai, Y., Kushilevitz, E., Vaikuntanathan, V.: Low-complexity cryptographic hash functions. In: ITCS (2017)
9. Applebaum, B., Ishai, Y., Kushilevitz, E.: Cryptography in NC⁰. In: FOCS (2004)
10. Applebaum, B., Ishai, Y., Kushilevitz, E.: On pseudorandom generators with linear stretch in NC⁰. In: Díaz, J., Jansen, K., Rolim, J.D.P., Zwick, U. (eds.) APPROX/RANDOM -2006. LNCS, vol. 4110, pp. 260–271. Springer, Heidelberg (2006). https://doi.org/10.1007/11830924_25

11. Applebaum, B., Ishai, Y., Kushilevitz, E.: Cryptography by cellular automata or how fast can complexity emerge in nature? In: ICS (2010)
12. Applebaum, B., Ishai, Y., Kushilevitz, E.: How to garble arithmetic circuits. In: IEEE 52nd Annual Symposium on Foundations of Computer Science, FOCS 2011, Palm Springs, CA, USA, 22–25 October 2011 (2011)
13. Bellare, M., Boldyreva, A., O'Neill, A.: Deterministic and efficiently searchable encryption. IACR Cryptology ePrint Archive 2006/186 (2006)
14. Bellare, M., et al.: Hedged public-key encryption: how to protect against bad randomness. In: Matsui, M. (ed.) ASIACRYPT 2009. LNCS, vol. 5912, pp. 232–249. Springer, Heidelberg (2009). https://doi.org/10.1007/978-3-642-10366-7_14
15. Bellare, M., Kiltz, E., Peikert, C., Waters, B.: Identity-based (lossy) trapdoor functions and applications. In: Pointcheval, D., Johansson, T. (eds.) EUROCRYPT 2012. LNCS, vol. 7237, pp. 228–245. Springer, Heidelberg (2012). https://doi.org/10.1007/978-3-642-29011-4_15
16. Blum, A., Furst, M.L., Kearns, M.J., Lipton, R.J.: Cryptographic primitives based on hard learning problems. In: Stinson, D.R. (ed.) CRYPTO 1993. LNCS, vol. 773, pp. 278–291. Springer, Heidelberg (1994). https://doi.org/10.1007/3-540-48329-2_24
17. Blumer, A., Ehrenfeucht, A., Haussler, D., Warmuth, M.K.: Occam's razor. Inf. Process. Lett. **24**(6), 377–380 (1987)
18. Board, R.A., Pitt, L.: On the necessity of Occam algorithms. In: STOC (1990)
19. Boldyreva, A., Fehr, S., O'Neill, A.: On notions of security for deterministic encryption, and efficient constructions without random oracles. In: Wagner, D. (ed.) CRYPTO 2008. LNCS, vol. 5157, pp. 335–359. Springer, Heidelberg (2008). https://doi.org/10.1007/978-3-540-85174-5_19
20. Bootle, J., Delaplace, C., Espitau, T., Fouque, P., Tibouchi, M.: LWE without modular reduction and improved side-channel attacks against BLISS. IACR Cryptology ePrint Archive 2018/22 (2018, to appear in Asiacrypt 2018)
21. Bshouty, N.H.: Exact learning via the monotone theory (extended abstract). In: FOCS (1993)
22. Bshouty, N.H., Eiron, N., Kushilevitz, E.: PAC learning with nasty noise. In: Watanabe, O., Yokomori, T. (eds.) ALT 1999. LNCS (LNAI), vol. 1720, pp. 206–218. Springer, Heidelberg (1999). https://doi.org/10.1007/3-540-46769-6_17
23. Cohen, A., Goldwasser, S., Vaikuntanathan, V.: Aggregate pseudorandom functions and connections to learning. In: Dodis, Y., Nielsen, J.B. (eds.) TCC 2015. LNCS, vol. 9015, pp. 61–89. Springer, Heidelberg (2015). https://doi.org/10.1007/978-3-662-46497-7_3
24. Dodis, Y., Smith, A.: Entropic security and the encryption of high entropy messages. In: Kilian, J. (ed.) TCC 2005. LNCS, vol. 3378, pp. 556–577. Springer, Heidelberg (2005). https://doi.org/10.1007/978-3-540-30576-7_30
25. Gentry, C., Peikert, C., Vaikuntanathan, V.: Trapdoors for hard lattices and new cryptographic constructions. In: Proceedings of the 40th Annual ACM Symposium on Theory of Computing, Victoria, British Columbia, Canada, 17–20 May 2008 (2008)
26. Goldreich, O.: Candidate one-way functions based on expander graphs. In: Goldreich, O. (ed.) Studies in Complexity and Cryptography. Miscellanea on the Interplay between Randomness and Computation. LNCS, vol. 6650, pp. 76–87. Springer, Heidelberg (2011). https://doi.org/10.1007/978-3-642-22670-0_10
27. Goldwasser, S., Micali, S.: Probabilistic encryption. J. Comput. Syst. Sci. **28**(2), 270–299 (1984)

28. Impagliazzo, R., Levin, L.A., Luby, M.: Pseudo-random generation from one-way functions. In: Proceedings of the Twenty-First Annual ACM Symposium on Theory of Computing, STOC 1989 (1989)
29. Indyk, P.: Sketching via hashing: from heavy hitters to compressed sensing to sparse Fourier transform. In: Proceedings of the 32nd ACM SIGMOD-SIGACT-SIGART Symposium on Principles of Database Systems, PODS 2013, New York, NY, USA, 22–27 June 2013 (2013)
30. Ishai, Y., Kushilevitz, E.: Randomizing polynomials: a new representation with applications to round-efficient secure computation. In: FOCS (2000)
31. Ishai, Y., Kushilevitz, E., Ostrovsky, R., Sahai, A.: Cryptography with constant computational overhead. In: STOC (2008)
32. Ishai, Y., Prabhakaran, M., Sahai, A.: Secure arithmetic computation with no honest majority. In: Reingold, O. (ed.) TCC 2009. LNCS, vol. 5444, pp. 294–314. Springer, Heidelberg (2009). https://doi.org/10.1007/978-3-642-00457-5_18
33. Kannan, S., Mossel, E., Sanyal, S., Yaroslavtsev, G.: Linear sketching over f_2. In: 33rd Computational Complexity Conference, CCC 2018, San Diego, CA, USA, 22–24 June 2018 (2018)
34. Kasiviswanathan, S.P., Lee, H.K., Nissim, K., Raskhodnikova, S., Smith, A.D.: What can we learn privately? In: FOCS (2008)
35. Kearns, M.J., Valiant, L.G.: Cryptographic limitations on learning Boolean formulae and finite automata. In: STOC (1989)
36. Kharitonov, M.: Cryptographic hardness of distribution-specific learning. In: STOC (1993)
37. Klivans, A.R., Servedio, R.A.: Learning DNF in time $2^{\tilde{o}(n^{1/3})}$. In: STOC (2001)
38. Mahloujifar, S., Diochnos, D.I., Mahmoody, M.: Learning under p-tampering attacks. In: ALT (2018)
39. McEliece, R.J.: A public-key cryptosystem based on algebraic coding theory. Deep Space Network Progress Report 44, 114–116 (1978)
40. Micciancio, D., Peikert, C.: Hardness of SIS and LWE with small parameters. In: Canetti, R., Garay, J.A. (eds.) CRYPTO 2013. LNCS, vol. 8042, pp. 21–39. Springer, Heidelberg (2013). https://doi.org/10.1007/978-3-642-40041-4_2
41. Mossel, E., O'Donnell, R., Servedio, R.A.: Learning juntas. In: STOC (2003)
42. Peikert, C., Waters, B.: Lossy trapdoor functions and their applications. In: Proceedings of the 40th Annual ACM Symposium on Theory of Computing, Victoria, British Columbia, Canada, 17–20 May 2008 (2008)
43. Pitt, L., Valiant, L.G.: Computational limitations on learning from examples. J. ACM 35(4), 965–984 (1988)
44. Regev, O.: On lattices, learning with errors, random linear codes, and cryptography. In: STOC (2005)
45. Rivest, R.L.: Learning decision lists. Mach. Learn. 2(3), 229–246 (1987)
46. Russell, A., Wang, H.: How to fool an unbounded adversary with a short key. In: Knudsen, L.R. (ed.) EUROCRYPT 2002. LNCS, vol. 2332, pp. 133–148. Springer, Heidelberg (2002). https://doi.org/10.1007/3-540-46035-7_9
47. Schapire, R.E.: The strength of weak learnability (extended abstract). In: FOCS (1989)
48. Valiant, L.G.: A theory of the learnable. In: STOC (1984)
49. Verbeurgt, K.A.: Learning DNF under the uniform distribution in quasi-polynomial time. In: COLT (1990)

Public-Key Cryptography
in the Fine-Grained Setting

Rio LaVigne[⊠], Andrea Lincoln[⊠], and Virginia Vassilevska Williams

MIT CSAIL and EECS, Cambridge, USA
{rio,andreali,virgi}@mit.edu

Abstract. Cryptography is largely based on unproven assumptions, which, while believable, might fail. Notably if $P = NP$, or if we live in Pessiland, then all current cryptographic assumptions will be broken. A compelling question is if any interesting cryptography might exist in Pessiland.

A natural approach to tackle this question is to base cryptography on an assumption from fine-grained complexity. Ball, Rosen, Sabin, and Vasudevan [BRSV'17] attempted this, starting from popular hardness assumptions, such as the Orthogonal Vectors (OV) Conjecture. They obtained problems that are hard on average, assuming that OV and other problems are hard in the worst case. They obtained proofs of work, and hoped to use their average-case hard problems to build a fine-grained one-way function. Unfortunately, they proved that constructing one using their approach would violate a popular hardness hypothesis. This motivates the search for other fine-grained average-case hard problems.

The main goal of this paper is to identify sufficient properties for a fine-grained average-case assumption that imply cryptographic primitives such as fine-grained public key cryptography (PKC). Our main contribution is a novel construction of a cryptographic key exchange, together with the definition of a small number of relatively weak structural properties, such that if a computational problem satisfies them, our key exchange has provable fine-grained security guarantees, based on the hardness of this problem. We then show that a natural and plausible average-case assumption for the key problem Zero-k-Clique from fine-grained complexity satisfies our properties. We also develop fine-grained one-way functions and hardcore bits even under these weaker assumptions.

R. LaVigne—This material is based upon work supported by the National Science Foundation Graduate Research Fellowship under Grant No. 1122374. Any opinion, findings, and conclusions or recommendations expressed in this material are those of the authors(s) and do not necessarily reflect the views of the National Science Foundation. Research also supported in part by NSF Grants CNS-1350619 and CNS-1414119, and by the Defense Advanced Research Projects Agency (DARPA) and the U.S. Army Research Office under contracts W911NF-15-C-0226 and W911NF-15-C-0236.

A. Lincoln—This work supported in part by NSF Grants CCF-1417238, CCF-1528078 and CCF-1514339, and BSF Grant BSF:2012338.

V. Williams—Partially supported by an NSF Career Award, a Sloan Fellowship, NSF Grants CCF-1417238, CCF-1528078 and CCF-1514339, and BSF Grant BSF:2012338.

A. Boldyreva and D. Micciancio (Eds.): CRYPTO 2019, LNCS 11694, pp. 605–635, 2019.
https://doi.org/10.1007/978-3-030-26954-8_20

Where previous works had to assume random oracles or the existence of strong one-way functions to get a key-exchange computable in $O(n)$ time secure against $O(n^2)$ adversaries (see [Merkle'78] and [BGI'08]), our assumptions seem much weaker. Our key exchange has a similar gap between the computation of the honest party and the adversary as prior work, while being non-interactive, implying fine-grained PKC.

1   Introduction

Modern cryptography has developed a variety of important cryptographic primitives, from One-Way Functions (OWFs) to Public-Key Cryptography to Obfuscation. Except for a few more limited information theoretic results [20,50,51], cryptography has so far required making a computational assumption, $P \neq NP$ being a baseline requirement. Barring unprecedented progress in computational complexity, such hardness hypotheses seem necessary in order to obtain most useful primitives. To alleviate this reliance on unproven assumptions, it is good to build cryptography from a variety of extremely different, believable assumptions: if a technique disproves one hypothesis, the unrelated ones might still hold. Due to this, there are many different cryptographic assumptions: on factoring, discrete logarithm, shortest vector in lattices and many more.

Unfortunately, almost all hardness assumptions used so far have the same quite stringent requirements: not only that NP is not in BPP, but that we must be able to efficiently sample polynomially-hard instances whose solution we know. Impagliazzo [31,47] defined five worlds, which capture the state of cryptography, depending on which assumptions happen to fail. The three worlds worst for cryptography are Algorithmica (NP in BPP), Heuristica (NP is not in BPP but NP problems are easy on average) and Pessiland (there are NP problems that are hard on average but solved hard instances are hard to sample, and OWFs do not exist). This brings us to our main question.

Can we have a meaningful notion of cryptography even if we live in Pessiland (or Algorithmica or Heuristica)?

This question motivates a weaker notion of cryptography: cryptography that is secure against n^k-time bounded adversaries, for a constant k. Let us see why such cryptography might exist even if $P = NP$. In complexity, for most interesting computational models, we have time hierarchy theorems that say that there are problems solvable in $O(n^2)$ time (say) that cannot be solved in $O(n^{2-\epsilon})$ time for any $\epsilon > 0$ [28,30,53]. In fact, such theorems exist also for the average case time complexity of problems [39]. Thus, even if $P = NP$, there are problems that are hard on average for specific runtimes, i.e. *fine-grained* hard on average. *Can we use such hard problems to build useful cryptographic primitives?*

Unfortunately, the problems from the time hierarchy theorems are difficult to work with, a common problem in the search for unconditional results. Thus, let us relax our requirements and consider hardness assumptions, but this time on the exact running time of our problems of interest. One simple approach is to consider all known constructions of Public Key Cryptography (PKC) to date and see what they imply if the hardness of the underlying problem is relaxed to be $n^{k-o(1)}$ for a fixed k (as it would be in Pessiland). Some of the known schemes are extremely efficient. For instance, the RSA and Diffie-Hellman cryptosystems immediately imply weak PKC if one changes their assumptions to be about polynomial hardness [23,49]. However, these cryptosystems have other weaknesses – for instance, they are completely broken in a postquantum world as Shor's algorithm breaks their assumptions in essentially quadratic time [52]. Thus, it makes sense to look at the cryptosystems based on other assumptions. Unfortunately, largely because cryptography has mostly focused on the gap between polynomial and superpolynomial time, most reductions building PKC have a significant (though polynomial) overhead; many require, for example, multiple rounds of Gaussian elimination. As a simple example, the Goldreich-Levin construction for hard-core bits uses n^ω (where $\omega \in [2, 2.373)$ is the exponent of square matrix multiplication [26,55]) time and n calls to the hard-core-bit distinguisher [27]. The polynomial overhead of such reductions means that if the relevant problem is only $n^{2-o(1)}$ hard, instead of super-polynomially hard, the reduction will not work anymore and won't produce a meaningful cryptographic primitive. Moreover, reductions with fixed polynomial overheads are no longer composable in the same way when we consider weaker, polynomial gap cryptography. Thus, new, more careful cryptographic reductions are needed.

Ball et al. [6,7] began to address this issue through the lens of the recently blossoming field of *fine-grained complexity*. Fine-grained complexity is built upon "fine-grained" hypotheses on the (worst-case) hardness of a small number of key problems. Each of these key problems K, has a simple algorithm using a combination of textbook techniques, running in time $T(n)$ on instances of size n, in, say, the RAM model of computation. However, despite decades of research, no $\tilde{O}(T(n)^{1-\epsilon})$ algorithm is known for any $\epsilon > 0$ (note that the tilde $\sim$ suppresses sub-polynomial factors). The fine-grained hypothesis for K is then that K requires $T(n)^{1-o(1)}$ time in the RAM model of computation. Some of the main hypotheses in fine-grained complexity (see [54]) set K to be CNF-SAT (with $T(n) = 2^n$, where n is the number of variables), or the k-Sum problem (with $T(n) = n^{\lceil k/2 \rceil}$), or the All-Pairs Shortest Paths problem (with $T(n) = n^3$ where n is the number of vertices), or one of several versions of the k-Clique problem in weighted graphs. Fine-grained complexity uses fine-grained reductions between problems in a very tight way (see [54]): if problem A has requires running time $a(n)^{1-o(1)}$, and one obtains an $(a(n), b(n))$-fine-grained reduction from A to B, then problem B needs runtime $b(n)^{1-o(1)}$. Using such reductions, one can obtain strong lower bounds for many problems, conditioned on one of the few key hypotheses.

The main question that Ball et al. set out to answer is: *Can one use fine-grained reductions from the hard problems from fine-grained complexity to build useful cryptographic primitives?* Their work produced worst-case to average-case fine-grained reductions from key problems to new algebraic average case problems. From these new problems, Ball et al. were able to construct fine-grained proofs of work, but they were not able to obtain stronger cryptographic primitives such as fine-grained one-way-functions or public key encryption. In fact, they gave a barrier for their approach: extending their approach would falsify the Nondeterministic Strong Exponential Time Hypothesis (NSETH) of Carmosino et al. [18]. Because of this barrier, one would either need to develop brand new techniques, or use a different hardness assumption.

What kind of hardness assumptions can be used to obtain public-key cryptography (PKC) even in Pessiland?

A great type of theorem to address this would be: for every problem P that requires $n^{k-o(1)}$ time on average, one can construct a public-key exchange (say), for which Alice and Bob can exchange a $\lg(n)$ bit key in time $O(n^{ak})$, whereas Eve must take $n^{(a+g)k-o(1)}$ time to learn Alice and Bob's key, where g is large, and a is small. As a byproduct of such a theorem, one can obtain not just OWFs, but even PKC in Pessiland under fine-grained assumptions via the results of Ball et al. Of course, due to the limitations given by Ball et al. such an ideal theorem would have to refute NSETH, and hence would be at the very least difficult to prove. Thus, let us relax our goal, and ask

What properties are sufficient for a fine-grained average-case assumption so that it implies fine-grained PKC?

If we could at least resolve this question, then we could focus our search for worst-case to average-case reductions in a useful way.

1.1 Our Contributions

Our main result is a fine-grained key-exchange that can be formed from any problem that meets three structural conditions in the word-RAM model of computation. This addresses the question of what properties are sufficient to produce fine-grained Public Key Encryption schemes (PKEs).

For our key exchange, we describe a set of properties, and any problem that has those properties implies a polynomial gap PKE. An informal statement of our main theorem is as follows.

Theorem [Fine-Grained Key-Exchange (informal)]. Let P be a computational problem for which a random instance can be generated in $O(n^g)$ time for some g, and that requires $n^{k-o(1)}$ time to be solved on average for some fixed $k > g$. Additionally, let P have three key structural properties of interest: (1) "plantable": we can generate a random-looking instance, choosing either to have or not to have a solution in the instance, and if there is a solution, we know what/where it is; (2) "average-case list-hard": given a list of n random instances of the problem, returning which one of the instances has a solution requires essentially solving all instances; (3) "splittable": when given an instance with a solution, we can split it in $O(n^g)$ time into two slightly smaller instances that both have solutions.

Then a public key-exchange can be built such that Alice and Bob exchange a $\lg(n)$ bit key in time n^{2k-g}, where as Eve must take $\tilde{\Omega}(n^{3k-2g})$ time to learn Alice and Bob's key.

Notice that as long as there is a gap between the time to generate a random instance and the time to solve an instance on average, there is a gap between $N = n^{2k-g}$ and $n^{3k-2g} = N^{3/2-1/(4(k/g)-2)}$ and the latter goes to $N^{3/2}$, as k/g grows. The key exchange requires no interaction, and we get a *fine-grained* public key cryptosystem. While our key exchange construction provides a relatively small gap between the adversary and the honest parties ($O(N^{1.5})$ vs $O(N)$), the techniques required to prove security of this scheme are novel and the result is generic as long as the three assumptions are satisfied. In fact, we will show an alternate method to achieve a gap approaching $O(N^2)$ in the full version of this paper.

Our main result above is stated formally and in more generality in Theorem 5. We will explain the formal meaning of our structural properties *plantable, average-case list-hard,* and *splittable* later.

We also investigate what plausible average-case assumptions one might be able to make about the key problems from fine-grained complexity so that the three properties from our theorem would be satisfied. We consider the Zero-k-Clique problem as it is one of the hardest worst-case problems in fine-grained complexity. For instance, it is known that if Zero-3-Clique is in $O(n^{3-\varepsilon})$ time for some $\varepsilon > 0$, then both the 3-Sum and the APSP hypotheses are violated [54,57]. It is important to note that while fine-grained problems like Zero-k-Clique and k-Sum are suspected to take a certain amount of time in the worst case, when making these assumptions for any constant k does not seem to imply $P \neq NP$ since all of these problems are still solvable in polynomial time.[1]

An instance of Zero-k-Clique is a complete k-partite graph G, where each edge is given a weight in the range $[0, R-1]$ for some integer R. The problem asks whether there is a k-clique in G whose edge weights sum to 0, modulo R. A standard fine-grained assumption (see e.g. [54]) is that in the worst case, for large enough R, say $R \geq 10n^{4k}$, Zero-k-Clique requires $n^{k-o(1)}$ time to solve. Zero-k-Clique has no non-trivial average-case algorithms for natural distributions (uniform for a range of parameters, similar to k-Sum and Subset Sum). Thus, Zero-k-Clique is a natural candidate for an average-case fine-grained hard problem.

Our other contribution addresses an open question from Ball et al.: can a fine-grained one-way function be constructed from worst case assumptions? While we do not fully achieve this, we generate new plausible average-case assumptions from fine-grained problems that imply fine-grained one-way functions.

1.2   Previous Works

There has been much prior work leading up to our results. First, there are a few results using assumptions from fine-grained complexity and applying them to cryptography. Second, there has been work with the kind of assumptions that we will be using.

---

[1] Assuming the hardness of these problems for more general k will imply $P \neq NP$, but that is not the focus of our work.

Fine-Grained Cryptography. Ball et al. [6,7] produce fine-grained wost-case to average-case reductions. Ball et al. leave an open problem of producing a one-way-function from a worst case assumption. They prove that from some fine-grained assumptions building a one-way-function would falsify NSETH [6,18]. We avoid their barrier in this paper by producing a construction of both fine-grained OWFs and fine-grained PKE from an *average-case* assumption.

Fine-Grained Key Exchanges. Fine-grained cryptography is a relatively unexplored area, even though it had its start in the 1970's with Merkle puzzles: the gap between honestly participating in the protocol versus breaking the security guarantee was only quadratic [43]. Merkle originally did not describe a plausible hardness assumption under which the security of the key exchange can be based. 30 years later, Biham, Goren, and Ishai showed how to implement Merkle puzzles by making an assumption of the existence of either a random oracle or an exponential gap one way function [16]. That is, Merkle puzzles were built under the assumption that a one-way function exists which takes time $2^{n(1/2+\delta)}$ to invert for some $\delta > 0$. So while prior work indeed succeeded in building a fine-grained key-exchange, it needed a very strong variant of OWFs to exist. It is thus very interesting to obtain fine-grained public key encryption schemes based on a fine-grained assumption (that might even work in Pessiland and below).

Another Notion of Fine-Grained Cryptography. In 2016, work by Degwekar, Vaikuntanathan, and Vasudevan [22] discussed fine-grained complexity with respect to both honest parties and adversaries restricted to certain circuit classes. They obtained constructions for some cryptographic primitives (including PKE) when restricting an adversary to a certain circuit class. From the assumption $\mathsf{NC1} \neq \oplus L/\text{poly}$ they show Alice and Bob can be in $AC^0[2]$ while being secure against $\mathsf{NC1}$ adversaries. While [22] obtains some unconditional constructions, their security relies on the circuit complexity of the adversary, and does not apply to arbitrary time-bounded adversaries as is usually the case in cryptography. That is, this restricts the types of algorithms an adversary is allowed to use beyond just how much runtime these algorithms can have. It would be interesting to get similar results in the low-polynomial time regime, without restricting an adversary to a certain circuit class. Our results achieve this, though not unconditionally.

Tight Security Reductions and Fine-Grained Crypto. Another area the world of fine-grained cryptography collides with is that of tight security reductions in cryptography. Bellare et.al. coined the term "concrete" security reductions in [12,14]. Concrete security reductions are parametrized by time (t), queries (q), size (s), and success probability (ε). This line of work tracks how a reduction from a problem to a construction of some cryptographic primitive effects the four parameters of interest. This started a rich field of study connecting theory to practical cryptographic primitives (such as PRFs, different instantiations of symmetric encryption, and even IBE for example [10,11,15,36]). In fine-grained reductions we also need to track exactly how our adversary's advantage changes throughout our reductions, however, we also track the running time of the honest parties. So, unlike in the concrete security literature, when the hard problems are polynomially hard (perhaps because $P = NP$), we can track the gap in running times between the honest and dishonest parties. This allows us to build one way functions and public key cryptosystems when the hard problems we are given are only polynomially hard (Fig. 1).

Paper	Assumptions	Crypto	Runtime	Power of Adversary
[43]	Random Oracles*	Key Exchange	$O(N)$	$O(N^2)$
[16]	Exponentially-Strong OWFs	Key Exchange	$O(N)$	$O(N^2)$
[7]	WC 3-Sum, OV, APSP, or SETH	Proof of Work	$O(N^2)$	N/A
[This work]	Zero-k-Clique or k-Sum	OWFs,	$O(N)$	$O(N^{1+\delta})$
		Key Exch. & PKE	$O(N)$	$O(N^{1.5-\delta})$
[22]	$NC1 \neq \oplus L/\text{poly}$	OWFs, and PRGs with sublinear stretch, CRHFs, and PKE	NC1	NC1
	$NC1 \neq \oplus L/\text{poly}$	PKE and CRHFs	$AC^0[2]$	NC1
	Unconditional	PRGs with poly stretch, Symmetric encryption, and CRHFs	AC^0	AC^0

Fig. 1. A table of previous works' results in this area. There have been several results characterizing different aspects of fine-grained cryptography. *It was [16] who showed that Merkle's construction could be realized with a random oracle. However, Merkle presented the construction.

Similar Assumptions. This paper uses hypotheses on the running times of problems that, while solvable in polynomial time, are variants of natural NP-hard problems, in which the size of the solution is a fixed constant. For instance, k-Sum is the variant of Subset Sum, where we are given n numbers and we need to find exactly k elements that sum to a given target, and Zero-k-Clique is the variant of Zero-Clique, in which we are given a graph and we need to find exactly k nodes that form a clique whose edge weights sum to zero.

With respect to Subset Sum, Impagliazzo and Naor showed how to directly obtain OWFs and PRGs assuming that Subset Sum is hard on average [32]. The OWF is $f(\mathbf{a}, \mathbf{s}) = (\mathbf{a}, \mathbf{a} \cdot \mathbf{s})$, where $\mathbf{a}$ is the list of elements (chosen uniformly at random from the range R) and $s \in \{0, 1\}^n$ represents the set of elements we add together. In addition to Subset Sum, OWFs have also been constructed from planted Clique, SAT, and Learning-Parity with Noise [34, 41]. The constructions from the book of Lindell and the chapter written by Barak [41] come from a definition of a "plantable" NP-hard problem that is assumed to be hard on average.

Although our OWFs are equivalent to scaled-down, polynomial-time solvable characterizations of these problems, we also formalize the property that allows us to get these fine-grained OWFs (plantability). We combine these NP constructions and formalizations to lay the groundwork for fine-grained cryptography.

In the public-key setting, there has been relatively recent work taking NP-hard problems and directly constructing public-key cryptosystems [4]. They take a problem that is NP-hard in its worst case and come up with an average-case assumption that works well for their constructions. Our approach is similar, and we also provide evidence for why our assumptions are correct.

In recent work, Subset Sum was also shown to directly imply public-key cryptography [42]. The construction takes ideas from Regev's LWE construction [48], turning a vector of subset sum elements into a matrix by writing each element out base q in a column. The subset is still represented by a 0–1 matrix, and error is handled by the lack of carrying digits. It is not clear how to directly translate this construction into the fine-grained world. First, directly converting from Subset Sum to k-Sum just significantly weakens the security without added benefit. More importantly, the security reduction has significant polynomial overhead, and would not apply in a very pessimistic Pessiland where random planted Subset Sum instances can be solved in quadratic time, say.

While it would be interesting to reanalyze the time-complexity of this construction (and others) in a fine-grained way, this is not the focus of our work. Our goal is to obtain novel cryptographic approaches exploiting the fine-grained nature of the problems, going beyond just recasting normal cryptography in the fine-grained world, and obtaining somewhat generic constructions.

1.3   Technical Overview

Here we will go into a bit more technical detail in describing our results. First, we need to describe our hardness assumptions. Then, we will show how to use them for our fine-grained key exchange, and finally, we will talk briefly about fine-grained OWFs and hardcore bits.

Our Hardness Assumption. We generate a series of properties where if a problem has these properties then a fine-grained public key-exchange can be built.

One property we require is that the problem is hard on average, in a fine-grained sense. Intuitively, a problem is average case indistinguishably hard if given an instance that is drawn with probability $1/2$ from instances with no solutions and with probability $1/2$ from instances with one solution, it is computationally hard on average to distinguish whether the instance has 0 or 1 solutions. The rest of the properties are structural; we need a problem that is *plantable*, *average-case list-hard*, and *splittable*. Informally,

- The plantable property roughly says that one can efficiently choose to generate either an instance without a solution or one with a solution, knowing where the solution is;
- The average case list-hard property says that if one is given a list of instances where all but one of them are drawn uniformly over instances with no solutions, and a random one of them is actually drawn uniformly from instances with one solution, then it is computationally hard to find the instance with a solution;
- Finally, the splittable property says that one can generate from one average case instance, two new average case instances that have the same number of solutions as the original one.

These are natural properties for problems and hypotheses to have. We will demonstrate in the full version Zero-k-Clique has all of these properties. We need our problem to have all three of these qualities for the key exchange. For our one-way function constructions we only need the problem to be plantable.

The structural properties are quite generic, and in principle, there could be many problems that satisfy them. We exhibit one: the Zero-k-Clique problem.

Because no known algorithmic techniques seem to solve Zero-k-Clique even when the weights are selected independently uniformly at random from $[0, cn^k]$ for a constant c, folklore intuition dictates that the problem might be hard on average for this distribution: here, the expected number of k-Cliques is $\Theta(1)$, and solving the decision problem correctly on a large enough fraction of the random instances seems difficult. This intuition was formally proposed by Pettie [46] for the very related k-Sum problem which we also consider.

We show that the Zero-k-Clique problem, together with the assumption that it is fine-grained hard to solve on average, satisfies all of our structural properties, and thus, using our main theorem, one can obtain a fine-grained key exchange based on Zero-k-Clique.

Key Exchange Assumption. We assume that when given a complete k-partite graph with kn nodes and random weights $[0, R - 1]$, $R = \Omega(n^k)$, any adversary running in time $n^{k-\Omega(1)}$ time cannot distinguish an instance with a zero-k-clique solution from one without with more than $2/3$ chance of success. In more detail, consider a distribution where with probability $1/2$ one generates a random instance of size n with no solutions, and with probability $1/2$ one generates a random instance of size n with exactly one solution. (We later tie in this distribution to our original uniform distribution.) Then, consider an algorithm that can determine with probability $2/3$ (over the distribution of instances) whether the problem has a solution or not. We make the conjecture that such a $2/3$-probability distinguishing algorithm for Zero-k-Clique, which can also exhibit the unique zero clique whenever a solution exists, requires time $n^{k-o(1)}$.

Public Key Exchange. So, what does the existence of a problem with our three properties, *plantable*, *average-case list-hard*, and *splittable*, imply?

The intuitive statement of our main theorem is that, if a problem has the three properties, and is n^k hard to solve on average and can be generated in n^g time (for Zero-k-Clique $g = 2$), then a key exchange exists that takes $O(N)$ time for Alice and Bob to execute, and requires an eavesdropper Eve $\tilde{\Omega}(N^{(3k-2g)/(2k-g)})$ time to break. When $k > g$ Eve takes super linear time in terms of N. When $k = 3$ and $g = 2$, an important case for the Zero-k-Clique problem, Eve requires $\tilde{\Omega}(N^{5/4})$ time.

For the rest of this overview we will describe our construction with the problem Zero-k-Clique.

To describe how we get our key exchange, it is first helpful to consider Merkle Puzzles [8,16,43]. The idea is simple: let f be a one way permutation over n bits (so a range of 2^n values) requires $2^{n(\frac{1}{2}+\epsilon)}$ time to invert for some constant $\epsilon > 0$. Then, Alice and Bob could exchange a key by each computing $f(v)$ on $10 \cdot 2^{n/2}$ random element $v \in [2^n]$ and sending those values $f(v)$ to each other. With .9 probability, Alice and Bob would agree on at least one pre-image, v. It would take an eavesdropper Eve $\Omega(2^{n(\frac{1}{2}+\epsilon)})$ time before she would be able to find the v agreed upon by Alice and Bob. So, while Alice and Bob must take $O(2^{n/2})$ time, Eve must take $O(2^{n(\frac{1}{2}+\epsilon)})$ time to break it.

Our construction will take on a similar form: Alice and Bob will send several problems to each other, and some of them will have planted solutions. By matching up where they both put solutions, they get a key exchange.

Concretely, Alice and Bob will exchange m instances of the Zero-k-Clique problem and in $\sqrt{m}$ of them (chosen at random), plant solutions. The other $m - \sqrt{m}$ will not have solutions (except with some small probability). These m problems will be indexed, and we expect Alice and Bob to have both planted a solution in the same index. Alice can check her $\sqrt{m}$ indices against Bob's, while Bob checks his, and by the end, with constant probability, they will agree on a single index as a key. In the end, Alice and Bob require $O(mn^g + \sqrt{m}n^k)$ time to exchange this index. Eve must take time $\tilde{\Omega}(n^k m)$. When $m = n^{2k-2g}$, Alice and Bob take $O(n^{2k-g})$ time and Eve takes $\tilde{\Omega}(n^{3k-2g})$. We therefore get some gap between the running time of Alice and Bob as compared to Eve for any value of $k \geq g$. Furthermore, for all $\delta > 0$ there exists some large enough k such that the difference in running time is at least $O(T(n))$ time for Alice and Bob and $\tilde{\Omega}(T(n)^{1.5-\delta})$ time for Eve. Theorem 5 is the formal theorem statement.

To show hardness for this construction we combine techniques from both fine-grained complexity and cryptography (see Fig. 2). We take a single instance and use a self-reduction to produce a list of ℓ instances where one has a solution whp if the original instance has a solution. In our reductions ℓ will be polynomial in the input size. Then, we take this list and produce two lists that have a solution in the same location with high probability if the original instance has a solution. Finally, we plant $\sqrt{\ell}$ solutions into the list, to simulate Alice and Bob's random solution planting.

One Way Functions. First, and informally, a fine-grained OWF is a function on n bits that requires $\tilde{O}(T(n)^{1-\delta})$ time to evaluate for some constant $\delta > 0$, and if any adversary attempts to invert f in time $\tilde{O}(T(n)^{1-\delta'})$ for *any* constant

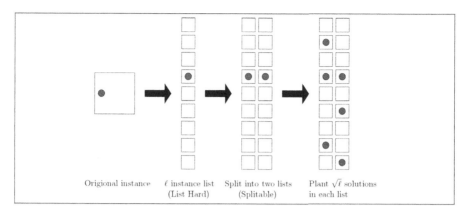

Original instance ℓ instance list   Split into two lists   Plant $\sqrt{\ell}$ solutions
(List Hard)   (Splitable)   in each list

Fig. 2. A depiction of our reduction showing hardness for our fine-grained key exchange.

$\delta' > 0$, she only succeeds with probability at most $\epsilon(n)$, where ϵ is considered "insignificant."

Ball et al. [6] defined fine-grained OWFs, keeping track of the time required to invert and the probability of inversion in two separate parameters. We streamline this definition by fixing the probability an adversary inverts to an insignificant function of input size, which we define in Sect. 2.

For this overview, we will focus on the intuition of using specific problems k-Sum-R (k-Sum modulo R) or Zero-k-Clique-R (Zero-k-Clique modulo R) to get fine-grained OWFs, though in the full version, we construct fine-grained OWFs from a general class of problems. Let N be the size of the input to these problems. Note that if R is too small (e.g. constant), then these problems are solvable quickly and the assumptions we are using are false. So, we will assume $R = \Omega(n^k)$.

OWF Assumptions. Much like for our key exchange, our assumptions are about the difficulty of distinguishing an instance of k-Sum or Zero-k-Clique with probability more than $2/3$ in time faster than $n^{k/2}$ or n^k respectively. Formally, randomly generating a k-Sum-R instance is creating a k lists of size n with values randomly chosen from $[0, R-1]$. Recall that a random Zero-k-Clique instance is a complete k-partite graph where weights are randomly chosen from $[0, R-1]$. Our 'weak' k-Sum-R and Zero-k-Clique-R assumptions state that for any algorithm running in $O(n)$ time, it cannot distinguish between a randomly generated instance with a planted solution and one without with probability greater than $2/3$.

Note that these assumptions are much weaker than the previously described key-exchange assumption, where we allowed the adversary $O(n^{k-\Omega(1)})$ time instead of sub-linear.

Theorem 1 (Fine-Grained OWFs (informal)). *If for some constant $\delta > 0$ and range $R = \Omega(n^k)$ either k-Sum-R requires $\Omega(N^{1+\delta})$ time to solve with* *probability* $>2/3$ *or Zero-k-Clique-R requires* $\Omega(N^{(1+\delta)})$ *time to solve with probability* $>2/3$ *then a fine-grained OWF exists.*

The formal theorem is proved in the full version.

Intuitively our construction of a fine-grained OWF runs a planting procedure on a random instance in time $O(N)$. By our assumptions finding this solution takes time $\Omega(N^{1+\delta})$ for some constant $\delta > 0$, and thus inverting this OWF takes $\Omega(N^{1+\delta})$.

We also get a notion of hardcore bits from this. Unlike in traditional crypto, we can't immediately use Goldreich-Levin's hardcore bit construction [27]. Given a function on N bits, the construction requires at least $\Omega(N)$ calls to the adversary who claims to invert the hardcore bit. When one is seeking super-polynomial gaps between computation and inversion of a function, factors of N can be ignored. However, in the fine-grained setting, factors of N can completely eliminate the gap between computation and inversion, and so having a notion of fine-grained hardcore bits is interesting.

We show that for our concrete constructions of fine-grained OWFs, there is a subset of the input of size $O(\lg(N))$ (or any sub-polynomial function) which itself requires $\Omega(N^{1+\delta})$ time to invert. From this subset of bits we can use Goldreich-Levin's hardcore bit construction, only losing a factor of $N^{o(1)}$ which is acceptable in the fine-grained setting.

Theorem 2 (Hardcore Bits (informal)). *If for some constant* $\delta > 0$ *and range* $R = \Omega(n^k)$ *either k-Sum-R requires* $\Omega(N^{1+\delta})$ *time to solve with probability* $>2/3$ *or Zero-k-Clique-R requires* $\Omega(N^{1+\delta})$ *time to solve with probability* $>2/3$ *then a fine-grained OWF exists with a hardcore bit that can not be guessed with probability greater than* $\frac{1}{2} + 1/q(n)$ *for any* $q(n) = n^{o(1)}$.

The formal theorem is also proved in the full version.

Intuitively, solutions for k-Sum-R and Zero-k-Clique-R can be described in $O(\log(n))$ bits—we just list the locations of the solution. Given a solution for the problem, we can just change one of the weights and use the solution location to produce a correct preimage. So, now using Goldreich-Levin, we only need to make $O(\log(n))$ queries during the security reduction.

1.4   Organization of Paper

In Sect. 2 we define our notions of fine-grained crypto primitives, including fine-grained OWFs, fine-grained hardcore bits, and fine-grained key exchanges. In Sect. 3, we describe a few classes of general assumptions (plantable, splittable, and average-case list hard), and then describe the concrete fine-grained assumptions we use (k-Sum and Zero-k-Clique). Next, in Sect. 4 we show that the concrete assumptions we made imply certain subsets of the general assumptions. In Sect. 5, we show that using an assumption that is plantable, splittable, and average-case list hard, we can construct a fine-grained key exchange.

2 Preliminaries: Model of Computation and Definitions

The running times of all algorithms are analyzed in the word-RAM model of computation, where simple operations such as $+, -, \cdot$, bit-shifting, and memory access all require a single time-step.

Just as in normal exponential-gap cryptography we have a notion of probabilistic polynomial-time (PPT) adversaries, we can similarly define an adversary that runs in time less than expected for our fine-grained polynomial-time solvable problems. This notion is something we call probabilistic fine-grained time (or PFT). Using this notion makes it easier to define things like OWFs and doesn't require carrying around time parameters through every reduction.

Definition 1. *An algorithm $\mathcal{A}$ is a $T(n)$ probabilistic fine-grained time, $\mathsf{PFT}_{T(n)}$, algorithm if there exists a constant $\delta > 0$ such that $\mathcal{A}$ runs in time $O(T(n)^{1-\delta})$.*

Note that in this definition, assuming $T(n) = \Omega(n)$, any sub-polynomial factors can be absorbed into δ.

Additionally, we will want a notion of *negligibility* that cryptography has. Recall that a function $\mathrm{negl}(n)$ is negligible if for all polynomials $Q(n)$ and sufficiently large n, $\mathrm{negl}(n) < 1/Q(n)$. We will have a similar notion here, but we will use the words *significant* and *insignificant* corresponding to non-negligible and negligible respectively.

Definition 2. *A function $\mathsf{sig}(n)$ is* significant *if*

$$\mathsf{sig}(n) = \frac{1}{n^{o(1)}}.$$

A function $\mathsf{insig}(n)$ is insignificant *if for all significant functions $\mathsf{sig}(n)$ and sufficiently large n,*

$$\mathsf{insig}(n) < \mathsf{sig}(n).$$

Note that for every polynomial f, $1/f(n)$ is insignificant. Also notice that if a probability is significant for an event to occur after some process, then we only need to run that process a sub-polynomial number of times before the event will happen almost certainly. This means our run-time doesn't increase even in a fine-grained sense; i.e. we can boost the probability of success of a randomized algorithm running in $\tilde{O}(T(n))$ from $1/\log(n)$ to $O(1)$ just by repeating it $O(\log(n))$ times, and still run in $\tilde{O}(T(n))$ time (note that '~' suppresses all sub-polynomial factors in this work).

2.1 Fine-Grained Symmetric Crypto Primitives

Ball et al. defined fine-grained one-way functions (OWFs) in their work from 2017 [6]. They parameterize their OWFs with two functions: an inversion-time function $T(n)$ (how long it takes to *invert* the function on n bits), and an probability-of-inversion function ϵ; given $T(n)^{1-\delta'}$ time, the probability any adversary can invert is $\epsilon(T(n)^{1-\delta'})$. The computation time is implicitly defined to be anything noticeably less than the time to invert: there exists a $\delta > 0$ and algorithm running in time $T(n)^{1-\delta}$ such that the algorithm can evaluate f.

Definition 3 ((δ, ϵ)-one-way functions [6]). *A function $f : \{0,1\}^* \to \{0,1\}^*$ is (δ, ϵ) -one-way if, for some $\delta > 0$, it can be evaluated on n bits in $O(T(n)^{1-\delta})$ time, but for any $\delta' > 0$ and for any adversary $\mathcal{A}$ running in $O(T(n)^{1-\delta'})$ time and all sufficiently large n,*

$$\Pr_{x \leftarrow \{0,1\}^n} \left[\mathcal{A}(f(x)) \in f^{-1}(f(x)) \right] \leq \epsilon(n, \delta).$$

Using our notation of $\mathsf{PFT}_{T(n)}$, we will similarly define OWFs, but with one fewer parameter. We will only be caring about $T(n)$, the time to invert, and assume that the probability an adversary running in time less than $T(n)$ inverts with less time is insignificant. We will show in the full version that we can compile fine-grained one-way functions with probability of inversion $\epsilon \leq 1 - \frac{1}{n^{o(1)}}$ into ones with insignificant probability of inversion. So, it makes sense to drop this parameter in most cases.

Definition 4. *A function $f : \{0,1\}^* \to \{0,1\}^*$ is $T(n)$ fine-grained one-way (is an $T(n)$-FGOWF) if there exists a constant $\delta > 0$ such that it takes time $T(n)^{1-\delta}$ to evaluate f on any input, and there exists a function $\varepsilon(n) \in \mathsf{insig}(n)$, and for all $\mathsf{PFT}_{T(n)}$ adversaries $\mathcal{A}$,*

$$\Pr_{x \leftarrow \{0,1\}^n} \left[\mathcal{A}(f(x)) \in f^{-1}(f(x)) \right] \leq \varepsilon(n).$$

With traditional notions of cryptography there was always an exponential or at least super-polynomial gap between the amount of time required to evaluate and invert one-way functions. In the fine-grained setting we have a polynomial *gap* to consider.

Definition 5. *The (relative) gap of an $T(n)$ fine-grained one-way function f is the constant $\delta > 0$ such that it takes $T(n)^{1-\delta}$ to compute f but for all $\mathsf{PFT}_{T(n)}$ adversaries $\mathcal{A}$,*

$$\Pr_{x \leftarrow \{0,1\}^n} \left[\mathcal{A}(f(x)) \in f^{-1}(f(x)) \right] \leq \mathsf{insig}(n).$$

2.2   Fine-Grained Asymmetric Crypto Primitives

In this paper, we will propose a fine-grained key exchange. First, we will show how to do it in an interactive manner, and then remove the interaction. Removing this interaction means that it implies fine-grained public key encryption! Here we will define both of these notions: a fine-grained non-interactive key exchange, and a fine-grained, CPA-secure public-key cryptosystem.

First, consider the definition of a key exchange, with interaction. This definition is modified from [16] to match our notation. We will be referring to a transcript generated by Alice and Bob and the randomness they used to generate it as a "random transcript".

Definition 6 (Fine-Grained Key Exchange). *A* $(T(n), \alpha, \gamma)$*-FG-Key Exchange is a protocol,* Π*, between two parties* A *and* B *such that the following properties hold*

- *Correctness. At the end of the protocol,* A *and* B *output the same bit (* $b_A = b_B$*) except with probability* γ*;*

$$\Pr_{\Pi, A, B}[b_A = b_B] \geq 1 - \gamma$$

  This probability is taken over the randomness of the protocol, A*, and* B*.*
- *Efficiency. There exists a constant* $\delta > 0$ *such that the protocol for both parties takes time* $\tilde{O}(T(n)^{1-\delta})$*.*
- *Security. Over the randomness of* Π*,* A*, and* B*, we have that for all* $\mathsf{PFT}_{T(n)}$ *eavesdroppers* E *has advantage* α *of guessing the shared key after seeing a random transcript. Where a transcript of the protocol* Π *is denoted* $\Pi(A, B)$*.*

$$\Pr_{A, B}[E(\Pi(A, B)) = b_B] \leq \frac{1}{2} + \alpha$$

A Strong $(T(n))$*-FG-KeyExchange is a* $(T(n), \alpha, \gamma)$*-FG-KeyExchange where* α *and* γ *are insignificant. The key exchange is considered* weak *if it is not strong.*

This particular security guarantee protects against chosen plaintext attacks. But first, we need to define what we mean by a fine-grained public key cryptosystem.

Definition 7. *An* $T(n)$*-*fine-grained public-key cryptosystem *has the following three algorithms.*

$\mathsf{KeyGen}(1^\lambda)$ *Outputs a public-secret key pair* (pk, sk)*.*
$\mathsf{Enc}(pk, m)$ *Outputs an encryption of* m*,* c*.*
$\mathsf{Dec}(sk, c)$ *Outputs a decryption of* c*,* m*.*

These algorithms must have the following properties:

- *They are efficient. There exists a constant* $\delta > 0$ *such that all three algorithms run in time* $O\left(T(n)^{1-\delta}\right)$*.*
- *They are correct. For all messages* m*,*

$$\Pr_{\mathsf{KeyGen}, \mathsf{Enc}, \mathsf{Dec}}[\mathsf{Dec}(sk, \mathsf{Enc}(pk, m)) = m | (pk, sk) \leftarrow \mathsf{KeyGen}(1^\lambda)] \geq 1 - \mathsf{insig}(n).$$

The cryptosystem is CPA-secure *if any* $\mathsf{PFT}_{T(n)}$ *adversary* $\mathcal{A}$ *has an insignificant advantage in winning the following game:*

1. *Setup. A challenger* $\mathcal{C}$ *runs* $\mathsf{KeyGen}(1^n)$ *to get a pair of keys,* (pk, sk)*, and sends* pk *to* $\mathcal{A}$*.*
2. *Challenge.* $\mathcal{A}$ *gives two messages* m_0 *and* m_1 *to the challenger. The challenger chooses a random bit* $b \xleftarrow{\$} \{0, 1\}$ *and returns* $c \leftarrow \mathsf{Enc}(pk, m_b)$ *to* $\mathcal{A}$*.*
3. *Guess.* $\mathcal{A}$ *outputs a guess* b' *and wins if* $b' = b$*.*

3 Average Case Assumptions

Below we will describe four general properties so that any assumed-to-be-hard problem that satisfies them can be used in our later constructions of one-way functions and cryptographic key exchanges. We will also propose two concrete problems with believable fine-grained hardness assumptions on it, and we will prove that these problems satisfy some, if not all, of our general properties.

Let us consider a search or decision problem P. Any instance of P could potentially have multiple witnesses/solutions. We will restrict our attention only to those instances with no solutions or with exactly one solution. We define the natural uniform distributions over these instances below.

Definition 8 (General Distributions). *Fix a size n and a search problem P. Define $D_0(P, n)$ as the uniform distribution over the set S_0, the set of all P-instances of size n that have no solutions/witnesses. Similarly, let $D_1(P, n)$ denote the uniform distribution over the set S_1, the set of all P-instances of size n that have exactly one unique solution/witness. When P and n are clear from the context, we simply use D_0 and D_1.*

3.1 General Useful Properties

We now turn our attention to defining the four properties that a fine-grained hard problem needs to have, in order for our constructions to work with it.

To be maximally general, we present definitions often with more than one parameter. The four properties are: *average case indistinguishably hard, plantable, average case list-hard* and *splittable*.

We state the formal definitions. In these definitions you will see constants for probabilities. Notably $2/3$ and $1/100$. These are arbitrary in that the properties we need are simply that $1/2 < 2/3$ and $2/3$ is much less than $1 - 1/100$. We later boost these probabilities and thus only care that there are constant gaps.

Definition 9 (Average Case Indistinguishably Hard). *For a decision or search problem P and instance size n, let D be the distribution drawing with probability $1/2$ from $D_0(P, n)$ and $1/2$ from $D_1(P, n)$.*

Let $val(I) = 0$ if I is from the support of D_0 and let $val(I) = 1$ if I is from the support of D_1.

P is Average Case Indistinguishably Hard in time $T(n)$ (T(n)-ACIH) if $T(n) = \Omega(n)$ and for any $\mathsf{PFT}_{T(n)}$ algorithm A

$$\Pr_{I \sim D}[A(I) = val(I)] \leq 2/3.$$

We also define a similar notion for search problems. Intuitively, it is hard to find a 'witness' for a problem with a solution, but we need to define what a witness is and how to verify a witness in the fine-grained world.

Definition 10 (Average Case Search Hard). *For a search problem P and instance size n, let $D_1 = D_1(P, n)$.*

Let $wit(I)$ denote an arbitrary witness of an instance I with at least one solution.

P is Average Case Search Hard in time $T(n)$ if $T(n) = \Omega(n)$ and

- *there exists a $\mathsf{PFT}_{T(n)}$ algorithm V (a fine-grained verifier) such that $V(I, wit(I)) = 1$ if I has a solution and $wit(I)$ is a witness for it and 0 otherwise*
- *and for any $\mathsf{PFT}_{T(n)}$ algorithm A*

$$\Pr_{I \sim D_1}[A(I) = wit(I)] \leq 1/100.$$

Note that ACIH implies ACSH, but not the other way around. In fact, given difficulties in dealing with problems in the average case, getting search-to-decision reductions seems very difficult.

Our next definition describes a fine-grained version of a problem (or relation) being 'plantable' [41]. The definition of a plantable problem from Lindell's book states that a plantable NP-hard problem is hard if there exists a PPT sampling algorithm G. G produces both a problem instance and a corresponding witness (x, y), and over the randomness of G, any other PPT algorithm has a negligible chance of finding a witness for x.

There are a couple of differences between our definition and the plantable definition from Lindell's book the [41]. First, we will of course have to put a fine-grained spin on it: our problem is solvable in time $T(n)$ and so we will need to be secure against $\mathsf{PFT}_{T(n)}$ adversaries. Second, we will be focusing on a decision-version of our problems, as indicated by Definition 9. Intuitively, our sampler (Generate) will also take in a bit b to determine whether or not it produces an instance of the problem that has a solution or does not.

Definition 11 (Plantable $((G(n), \epsilon)$-Plantable)). *A $T(n)$-ACIH or $T(n)$-ACSH problem P is* plantable *in time $G(n)$ with error ϵ if there exists a randomized algorithm* Generate *that runs in time $G(n)$ such that on input n and $b \in \{0, 1\}$,* Generate(n, b) *produces an instance of P of size n drawn from a distribution of total variation distance at most ϵ from $D_b(P, n)$.*

If it is a $T(n) - ACSH$ problem, then Generate$(n, 1)$ *also needs to output a witness $wit(I)$, in addition to an instance I.*

We now introduce the List-Hard property. Intuitively, this property states that when given a list of length $\ell(n)$ of instances of P, it is almost as hard to determine if there exists one instance with a solution as it is to solve an instance of size $\ell(n) \cdot n$.

Definition 12 (Average Case List-hard $((T(n), \ell(n), \delta_{LH})$-ACLH)). *A $T(n)$- ACIH or $T(n)$-ACSH problem P is* Average Case List Hard *in time $T(n)$ with list length $\ell(n)$ if $\ell(n) = n^{\Omega(1)}$, and for every $\mathsf{PFT}_{\ell(n) \cdot T(n)}$ algorithm A,* given a list of $\ell(n)$ instances, $\mathbf{I} = I_1, I_2, \ldots, I_{\ell(n)}$, each of size n distributed as follows: $i \xleftarrow{\$} [\ell(n)]$ and $I_i \sim D_1(P, n)$ and for all $j \neq i$, $I_j \sim D_0(P, n)$;

$$\Pr_{\mathbf{I}}[A(\mathbf{I}) = i] \leq \delta_{LH}.$$

It's worth noting that this definition is nontrivial only if $\ell(n) = n^{\Omega(1)}$. Otherwise $\ell(n)T(n) = \tilde{O}(T(n))$, since $\ell(n)$ would be sub-polynomial.

We now introduce the splittable property. Intuitively a splittable problem has a process in the average case to go from one instance I into a pair of average looking problems with the same number of solutions. We use the splittable property to enforce that a solution is shared between Alice and Bob, which becomes the basis of Alice and Bob's shared key (see Fig. 2).

Definition 13 ((Generalized) Splittable). *A $T(n)$-ACIH problem P is generalized splittable with error ϵ, to the problem P' if there exists a $\mathsf{PFT}_{T(n)}$ algorithm Split and a constant m such that*

- *when given a P-instance $I \sim D_0(P, n)$, $\mathsf{Split}(I)$ produces a list of length m of pairs of instances $\{(I_1^1, I_2^1), \ldots, (I_1^m, I_2^m)\}$ where $\forall i \in [1, m]$ I_1^i, I_2^i are drawn from a distribution with total variation distance at most ϵ from $D_0(P', n) \times D_0(P', n)$.*
- *when given an instance of a problem $I \sim D_1(P, n)$, $\mathsf{Split}(I)$ produces a list of length m of pairs of instances $\{(I_1^1, I_2^1), \ldots, (I_1^m, I_2^m)\}$ where $\exists i \in [1, m]$ such that I_1^i, I_2^i are drawn from a distribution with total variation distance at most ϵ from $D_1(P', n) \times D_1(P', n)$.*

3.2 Concrete Hypothesis

Problem Descriptions. Two key problems within fine-grained complexity are the k-Sum problem and the Zero-k-Clique problem.

Given k lists of n numbers $L_1, \ldots, L_k$, the k-Sum problem asks, are there $a_1 \in L_1, \ldots, a_k \in L_k$ so that $\sum_{j=1}^{k} a_j = 0$. The fastest known algorithms for k-Sum run in $n^{\lceil k/2 \rceil - o(1)}$ time, and this running time is conjectured to be optimal, in the worst case (see e.g. [2,44,54]).

The Zero-k-Clique problem is, given a graph G on n vertices and integer edge weights, determine whether G contains k vertices that form a k-clique so that the sum of all the weights of the clique edges is 0. The fastest known algorithms for this problem run in $n^{k-o(1)}$ time, and this is conjectured to be optimal in the worst case (see e.g. [1,5,17,40]). As we will discuss later, Zero-k-Clique and k-Sum are related. In particular, it is known [56] that if 3-Sum requires $n^{2-o(1)}$ time, then Zero-3-Clique requires $n^{3-o(1)}$ time. Zero-3-Clique is potentially even harder than 3-Sum, as other problems such as All-Pairs Shortest Paths are known to be reducible to it, but not to 3-Sum.

A folklore conjecture states that when the 3-Sum instance is formed by drawing n integers uniformly at random from $\{-n^3, \ldots, n^3\}$ no PFT_{n^2} algorithm can solve 3-Sum on a constant fraction of the instances. This, and more related conjectures were explicitly formulated by Pettie [46].

We propose a new hypothesis capturing the folklore intuition, while drawing some motivation from other average case hypotheses such as Planted Clique. For convenience, we consider the k-Sum and Zero-k-Clique problems modulo a number; this variant is at least as hard to solve as the original problems over the integers: we can reduce these original problems to their modular versions where the modulus is only k (for k-Sum) or $\binom{k}{2}$ (for Zero-k-Clique) times as large as the original range of the numbers.

We will discuss and motivate our hypotheses further in Sect. 4.

Definition 14. *An instance of the k-Sum problem over range R, k-Sum-R, consists of kn numbers in k lists $L_1, \ldots, L_k$. The numbers are chosen from the range $[0, R-1]$. A solution of a k-Sum-R instance is a set of k numbers $a_1 \in L_1, \ldots, a_k \in L_k$ such that their sum is zero mod R, $\sum_{i=1}^{k} a_i \equiv 0 \mod R$.*

We will also define the uniform distributions over k-Sum instances that have a certain number of solutions. We define two natural distributions over k-Sum-R instances.

Definition 15. *Define $D_{uniform}^{ksum}[R, n]$ be the distribution of instances obtained by picking each integer in the instance uniformly at random from the range $[0, R-1]$.*

Define $D_0^{ksum}[R, n] = D_0(k$-Sum-$R, n)$ to be the uniform distribution over k-Sum-R instances with no solutions. Similarly, let $D_1^{ksum}[R, n] = D_1(k$-Sum-$R, n)$ to be the uniform distribution over k-Sum-R instances with 1 solution.

The distribution $D_{ksum}[R, i, n]$ is the uniform distribution over k-Sum instances with n values chosen modulo R and where there are exactly i distinct solutions.

Let $D_0^{ksum}[R, n] = D_{ksum}[R, 0, n]$, and $D_1^{ksum}[R, n] = D_{ksum}[R, 1, n]$.

We now proceed to define the version of Zero-k-Clique that we will be using. In addition to working modulo an integer, we restrict our attention to k-partite graphs. In the worst case, the Zero-k-Clique on a general graph reduces to Zero-k-Clique on a complete k-partite graph[2][3].

Definition 16. *An instance of Zero-k-Clique-R consists of a k-partite graph with kn nodes and partitions $P_1, \ldots, P_k$. The k-partite graph is complete: there is an edge between a node $v \in P_i$ and a node $u \in P_j$ if and only if $i \neq j$. Thus, every instance has $\binom{k}{2}n^2$ edges. The weights of the edges come from the range $[0, R-1]$.*

A solution in a Zero-k-Clique-R instance is a set of k nodes $v_1 \in P_1, \ldots, v_k \in P_k$ such that the sum of all the weights on the $\binom{k}{2}$ edges in the k-clique formed by $v_1, \ldots, v_k$ is congruent to zero mod R: $\sum_{i \in [1,k]} \sum_{j \in [1,k] \text{ and } j \neq i} w(v_i, v_j) \equiv 0 \mod R$. A solution is also called a zero k-clique.

---

[2] This reduction is done using color-coding [3], an example of this lemma exists in the paper "Tight Hardness for Shortest Cycles and Paths in Sparse Graphs" [40].

We now define natural distributions over Zero-k-Clique-R instances.

Definition 17. *Define $D_{uniform}^{zkc}[R,n]$ to be the distribution of instances obtained by picking each integer edge weight in the instance uniformly at random from the range $[0, R-1]$.*

Define $D_0^{zkc}[R,n] = D_0(\text{Zero-}k\text{-Clique-}R, n)$ to be the uniform distribution over Zero-k-Clique-R instances with no solutions. Similarly, let $D_1^{zkc}[R,n] = D_1(\text{Zero-}k\text{-Clique-}R, n)$ to be the uniform distribution over Zero-k-Clique-R instances with 1 solution.

The distribution is $D_{zkc}[R,i,n]$ the uniform distribution over zero k-clique instances on kn nodes with weights chosen modulo R and where there are exactly i distinct zero k-cliques in the graph. Let $D_0^{zkc}[R,n] = D_{zkc}[R,0,k]$ and $D_1^{zkc}[R,n] = D_{zkc}[R,1,k]$.

Weak and Strong Hypotheses. The strongest hypothesis that one can make is that the average case version of a problem takes essentially the same time to solve as the worst case variant is hypothesized to take. The weakest but still useful hypothesis that one could make is that the average case version of a problem requires *super-linear* time. We formulate both such hypotheses and derive meaningful consequences from them.

We state the weak versions in terms of decision problems and the strong version in terms of search problems. Our fine-grained one-way functions and fine-grained key exchanges can both be built using the search variants. We make these choices for clarity of presentation later on.

Definition 18 (Weak k-Sum-R Hypothesis). *There exists some large enough constant c such that for all constants $c' > c$, distinguishing $D_0^{ksum}[c'R,n]$ and $D_1^{ksum}[c'R,n]$ is $n^{1+\delta}$-ACIH for some $\delta > 0$.*

Definition 19 (Weak Zero-k-Clique-R Hypothesis). *There exists some large enough constant c such that for all constants $c' > c$, distinguishing $D_0^{zkc}[c'R,n]$ and $D_1^{zkc}[c'R,n]$ is $n^{2+\delta}$-ACIH for some $\delta > 0$.*
Notice that the Zero-k-Clique-R problem is of size $O(n^2)$.

Definition 20 (Strong Zero-k-Clique-R Hypothesis for range n^{ck}). *For all $c > 1$, given an instance I drawn from the distribution $D_1^{zkc}[n^{ck},n]$ where the witness (solution) is the single zero k-clique is formed by nodes $\{v_1, \ldots, v_k\}$, finding $\{v_1, \ldots, v_k\}$ is n^k-ACSH.*

Some may find the assumption with range n^k to be the most believable assumption. This is where the probability of a Zero-k-Clique existing at all is a constant.

Definition 21 (Random Edge Zero-k-Clique Hypothesis). *Let $sol(I)$ be a function over instances of Zero-k-Clique problems where $sol(I) = 0$ if there are no zero k-cliques and $sol(I) = 1$ if there is exactly one of zero k-clique. Let $wit(I)$ be a zero k-clique in I, if one exists. Given an instance I drawn from* *the distribution* $D^{zkc}_{uniform}[n^k, n]$ *there is some large enough* n *such that for any* PFT$_{n^k}$ *algorithm* A

$$\Pr_{I \sim D}[A(I) = wit(I)|sol(I) = 1] \leq 1/200.$$

Theorem 3. *Strong Zero-k-Clique-R Hypothesis for range* $R = n^{ck}$ *is implied by the Random Edge Random Edge Zero-k-Clique Hypothesis if* $c > 1$ *is a constant.*

The proof of this Theorem is in the full version.[3]

4   Our Assumptions - Background and Justification

In this section, we justify making average-case hardness assumptions for k-SUM and Zero k-Clique—and why we do not for other fine-grained problems. We start with some background on these problems, and then justify why our hypotheses are believable.

4.1   Background for Fine-Grained Problems

Among the most popular hypotheses in fine-grained complexity is the one concerning the 3-Sum problem defined as follows: given three lists A, B and C of n numbers each from $\{-n^t, \ldots, n^t\}$ for large enough t, determine whether there are $a \in A, b \in B, c \in C$ with $a + b + c = 0$. There are multiple equivalent variants of the problem (see e.g. [25]).

The fastest 3-Sum algorithms run in $n^2(\log \log n)^{O(1)}/\log^2 n$ time (Baran, Demaine and Patrascu for integer inputs [9], and more recently Chan'18 for real inputs [19]). Since the 1990s, 3-Sum has been an important problem in computational geometry. Gajentaan and Overmars [25] formulated the hypothesis that 3-Sum requires quadratic time (nowadays this means $n^{2-o(1)}$ time on a word-RAM with $O(\log n)$ bit words), and showed via reductions that many geometry problems also require quadratic time under this hypothesis. In recent years, many more consequences of this hypothesis have been derived, for a variety of non-geometric problems, such as sequence local alignment [1], triangle enumeration [37,44], and others.

As shown by Vassilevska Williams and Williams [56], 3-Sum can be reduced to a graph problem, 0-Weight Triangle, so that if 3-Sum requires $n^{2-o(1)}$ time on inputs of size n, then 0-Weight Triangle requires $N^{3-o(1)}$ time in N-node graphs. In fact, Zero-Weight Triangle is potentially harder than 3-Sum, as one can also reduce to it the All-Pairs Shortest Paths (APSP) problem, which is widely believed to require essentially cubic time in the number of vertices. There is no known relationship (via reductions) between APSP and 3-Sum.

The Zero-Weight Triangle problem is as follows: given an n-node graph with edge weights in the range $\{-n^c, \ldots, n^c\}$ for large enough c, denoted by the

---

[3] Thank you to Russell Impagliazzo for discussions related to the sizes of ranges R.

function $w(\cdot, \cdot)$, are there three nodes p, q, r so that $w(p, q) + w(q, r) + w(r, p) =$ 0? Zero-Weight Triangle is just Zero-3-Clique where the numbers are from a polynomial range. An equivalent formulation assumes that the input graph is tripartite and complete (between partitions).

Both 3-Sum and Zero-Weight Triangle have generalizations for $k \geq 3$: k-Sum and Zero-Weight k-Clique, defined in the natural way. We give their definitions in Definitions 14 and 16 respectively.

4.2   Justifying the Hardness of Some Average-Case Fine-Grained Problems

The k-Sum problem is conjectured to require $n^{\lceil k/2 \rceil - o(1)}$ time (for large enough weights), and the Zero-Weight k-Clique problem is conjectured to require $n^{k - o(1)}$ time (for large enough weights), matching the best known algorithms for both problems (see [54]). Both of these conjectures have been used in fine-grained complexity to derive conditional lower bounds for other problems (e.g. [1,5,17, 40]).

It is tempting to conjecture average-case hardness for the key hard problems within fine-grained complexity: Orthogonal Vectors (OV), APSP, 3-Sum. However, it is known that APSP is not hard on average, for many natural distributions (see e.g. [21,45]), and OV is likely not (quadratically) hard on average (see e.g. [35]).

On the other hand, it is a folklore belief that 3-Sum is actually hard on average. In particular, if one samples n integers uniformly at random from $\{-cn^3, \ldots, cn^3\}$ for constant c, the expected number of 3-Sums in the instance is $\Theta(1)$, and there is no known truly subquadratic time algorithm that can solve 3-Sum reliably on such instances. The conjecture that this is a hard distribution for 3-Sum was formulated for instance by Pettie [46].

The same folklore belief extends to k-Sum. Here a hard distribution seems to be to generate k lists uniformly from a large enough range $\{-cn^k, \ldots, cn^k\}$, so that the expected number of solutions is constant.

Due to the tight relationship between 3-Sum and Zero-Weight Triangle, one might also conjecture that uniformly generated instances of the latter problem are hard to solve on average. In fact, if one goes through the reductions from the worst-case 3-Sum problem to the worst-case Zero-Weight Triangle, via the 3-Sum Convolution problem [44,57] starting from an instance of 3-Sum with numbers taken uniformly at random from a range, then one obtains a list of Zero-Weight Triangle instances that are essentially average-case. This is easier to see in the simpler but less efficient reduction in [57] which from a 3-Sum instance creates $n^{1/3}$ instances of (complete tripartite) Zero-Weight Triangle on $O(n^{2/3})$ nodes each and whose edge weights are exactly the numbers from the 3-Sum instance. Thus, at least for $k = 3$, average-case hardness for 3-Sum is strong evidence for the average-case hardness for Zero-Weight Triangle.

In the full version we give a reduction between uniform instances of uniform Zero-Weight k-Clique with range $\Theta(n^k)$ and instances of planted Zero-Weight k-Clique with large range. Working with instances of planted Zero-Weight k-Clique with large range is easier for our hardness constructions, so we use those in most of this paper.

Justifying the Hardness of Distinguishing. Now, our main assumptions consider distinguishing between the distributions D_0 and D_1 for 3-Sum and Zero-Weight Triangle. Here we take inspiration from the Planted Clique assumption from Complexity [29, 33, 38]. In Planted Clique, one first generates an Erdös-Renyi graph that is expected to not contain large cliques, and then with probability $1/2$, one plants a clique in a random location. Then the assertion is that no polynomial time algorithm can distinguish whether a clique was planted or not.

We consider the same sort of process for Zero-k-Clique. Imagine that we first generate a uniformly random instance that is expected to have no zero k-Cliques, by taking the edge weights uniformly at random from a large enough range, and then we plant a zero k-Clique with probability $1/2$ in a random location. Similarly to the Planted Clique assumption, but now in a fine-grained way, we can assume that distinguishing between the planted and the not-planted case is computationally difficult.

Our actual hypothesis is that when one picks an instance that has no zero k-Cliques at random with probability $1/2$ and picks one that has a zero k-Clique with probability $1/2$, then distinguishing these two cases is hard. As we show later, this hypothesis is essentially equivalent to the planted version (up to some slight difference between the underlying distributions).

Similarly to Planted Clique, no known approach for Zero-k-Clique seems to work in this average-case scenario, faster than essentially n^k, so it is natural to hypothesize that the problem is hard. We leave it as a tantalizing open problem to determine whether the problem is actually hard, either by reducing a popular worst-case hypothesis to it, or by providing a new algorithmic technique.

5   Fine-Grained Key Exchange

Now we will explain a construction for a *key exchange* using general distributions. We will then specify the properties we need for problems to generate a secure key exchange. We will finally generate a key exchange using the strong Zero-k-Clique hypothesis. Sketches for most of proofs of these theorems are provided here, while full proofs can be found in the full version.

Before doing this, we will define a class of problems as being Key Exchange Ready (KER).

Definition 22 (Key Exchange Ready (KER)). *A problem P is $\ell(n)$-KER with generate time $G(n)$, solve time $S(n)$ and lower bound solving time $T(n)$ if*

- *there is an algorithm which runs in $\tilde{\Theta}(S(n)))$ time that determines if an instance of P of size n has a solution or not,*
- *the problem is $(\ell(n), \delta_{LH})$-ACLH where $\delta_{LH} \leq \frac{1}{34}$,*

- *is Generalized Splittable with error $\leq 1/(128\ell(n))$ to the problem P' and,*
- *P' is plantable in time $G(n)$ with error $\leq 1/(128\ell(n))$.*
- *$\ell(n)T(n) \in \tilde{\omega}\left(\ell(n)G(n) + \sqrt{\ell(n)}S(n)\right)$, and*
- *there exists an n' such that for all $n \geq n'$, $\ell(n) \geq 2^{14}$.*

5.1 Description of a Weak Fine-Grained Interactive Key Exchange

The high level description of the key exchange is as follows. Alice and Bob each produce $\ell(n) - \sqrt{\ell(n)}$ instances using $\mathsf{Generate}(n, 0)$ and $\sqrt{\ell(n)}$ generate instances with $\mathsf{Generate}(n, 1)$. Alice then shuffles the list of $\ell(n)$ instances so that those with solutions are randomly distributed. Bob does the same thing (with his own private randomness). Call the set of indices that Alice chooses to plant solutions S_A and the set Bob picks S_B. The likely size of $S_A \cap S_B$ is 1. The index $S_A \cap S_B$ is the basis for the key.

Alice determines the index $S_A \cap S_B$ by brute forcing all problems at indices S_A that Bob published. Bob can brute force all problems at indices S_B that Alice published and learn the set $S_A \cap S_B$.

If after brute forcing for instances either Alice or Bob find a number of solutions not equal to 1 then they communicate this and repeat the procedure (using interaction). They only need to repeat a constant number of times.

More formally our key exchange does the following:

Construction 4 (Weak Fine-Grained Interactive Key Exchange). *A fine-grained key exchange for exchanging a single bit key.*

- $\mathsf{Setup}(1^n)$: *output* $\mathrm{MPK} = (n, \ell(n))$ *and* $\ell(n) > 2^{14}$.
- $\mathsf{KeyGen}(\mathrm{MPK})$: *Alice and Bob both get parameters* (n, ℓ).
  - *Alice generates a random* $S_A \subset [\ell]$, $|S_A| = \sqrt{\ell}$. *She generates a list of instances* $\mathbf{I}_A = (I_A^1, \ldots, I_A^\ell)$ *where for all* $i \in S_A$, $I_i = \mathsf{Generate}(n, 1)$ *and for all* $i \notin S_A$, $I_A^i = \mathsf{Generate}(n, 0)$ *(using Alice's private randomness). Alice publishes* $\mathbf{I}_A$ *and a random vector* $\mathbf{v} \xleftarrow{\$} \{0, 1\}^{\log \ell}$.
  - *Bob computes* $\mathbf{I}_B = (I_B^1, \ldots, I_B^\ell)$ *similarly: generating a random* $S_B \subset [\ell]$ *of size* $\sqrt{\ell}$ *and for every instance* $I_j \in \mathbf{I}_B$, *if* $j \in S_B$, $I_j = \mathsf{Generate}(n, 1)$ *and if* $j \notin S_B$, $I_j = \mathsf{Generate}(n, 0)$. *Bob publishes* $\mathbf{I}_B$.
- *Compute shared key: Alice receives* $\mathbf{I}_B$ *and Bob receives* $\mathbf{I}_A$.
  - *Alice computes what she believes is* $S_A \cap S_B$: *for every* $i \in S_A$, *she brute force checks if* I_B^i *has a solution or not. For each* i *that does, she records in list* L_A.
  - *Bob computes what he thinks to be* $S_B \cap S_A$: *for every* $j \in S_B$, *he checks if* I_A^j *has a solution. For each that does, he records it in* L_B.
- *Check: Alice takes her private list* L_A: *if* $|L_A| \neq 1$, *Alice publishes that the exchange failed. Bob does the same thing with his list* L_B: *if* $|L_B| \neq 1$, *Bob publishes that the exchange failed. If either Alice or Bob gave or received a failure, they both know, and go back to the* KeyGen *step.*
  If no failure occurred, then $|L_A| = |L_B| = 1$. *Alice interprets the index* $i \in L_A$ *as a vector and computes* $i \cdot \mathbf{v}$ *as her key. Bob uses the index in* $j \in L_B$ *and also computes* $j \cdot \mathbf{v}$. *With high probability,* $i = j$ *and so the keys are the same.*

5.2   Correctness and Soundness of the Key Exchange

We want to show that with high probability, once the key exchange succeeds, both Alice and Bob get the same shared index. The full proofs for Lemmas 1, 2, and 3 can be found in the full version of this paper.

Lemma 1. *After running Construction 4, Alice and Bob agree on a key k with probability at least $1 - \frac{1}{10,000\ell e}$.*

Sketch of Proof. We notice that the only way Alice and Bob fail to exchange a key is if they *both* generate a solution accidentally in each other's sets (that is Alice generates exactly one accidental solution in S_B and Bob in S_A), and $S_A \cap S_B = \emptyset$. All other 'failures' are detectable in this interactive case and simply require Alice and Bob to run the protocol again. So, we just bound the probability this happens, and since $\epsilon_{plant} \leq \frac{1}{100\sqrt{\ell}}$, we get the bound $1 - \frac{1}{10,000\ell e}$. $\qquad\square$

We next show that the key-exchange results in gaps in running time and success probability between Alice and Bob and Eve. Then, we will show that this scheme can be boosted in a fine-grained way to get larger probability gaps (a higher chance that Bob and Alice exchange a key and lower chance Eve gets it) while preserving the running time gaps.

First, we need to show that the time Alice and Bob take to compute a shared key is less (in a fine-grained sense) than the time it takes Eve, given the public transcript, to figure out the shared key. This includes the number of times we expect Alice and Bob to need to repeat the process before getting a usable key.

Time for Alice and Bob.

Lemma 2. *If a problem P is $\ell(n)$-KER with plant time $G(n)$, solve time $S(n)$ and lower bound $T(n)$ when $\ell(n) > 100$, then Alice and Bob take expected time $O(\ell G(n) + \sqrt{\ell}S(n))$ to run the key exchange.*

Time for Eve.

Lemma 3. *If a problem P is $\ell(n)$-KER with plant time $G(n)$, solve time $S(n)$ and lower bound $T(n)$ when $\ell(n) \geq 2^{14}$, then an eavesdropper Eve, when given the transcript $\mathbf{I}_T$, requires $\tilde{\Omega}(\ell(n)T(n))$ time to solve for the shared key with probability $\frac{1}{2} + \mathsf{sig}(n)$.*

Sketch of Proof. This is proved in two steps. First, if Eve can determine the shared key in time $\mathsf{PFT}_{\ell(n)T(n)}$ with advantage δ_{Eve}, then she can also figure out the index in $\mathsf{PFT}_{\ell(n)T(n)}$ time with probability $\delta_{Eve}/4$. Second, if Eve can compute the index with advantage $\delta_{Eve}/4$, we can use Eve to solve the list-version of P in $\mathsf{PFT}_{\ell(n)T(n)}$ with probability $\delta_{Eve}/16$, which is a contradiction to the list-hardness of our problem. This first part follows from a fine-grained Goldreich-Levin hardcore-bit theorem, proved in the full version.

The second part, proving that once Eve has the index, then she can solve an instance of P, uses the fact that P is list-hard, generalized splittable, and plantable. Intuitively, since P is already list hard, we will start with a list of average problem instances $(I_1, \ldots, I_\ell)$, and our goal will be to have Eve tell us which instance (index) has a solution. We apply the splittable property to this list to get lists of pairs of problems. For one of these lists of pairs, there will exist an index where both instances have solutions. These lists of pairs will *almost* look like the transcript between Alice and Bob during the key exchange: if I had a solution then there should be one index such that both instances in a pair have a solution. Now, we just need to plant $\sqrt{\ell} - 1$ solutions in the left instances and $\sqrt{\ell} - 1$ on the right, and this will be indistinguishable from a transcript between Alice and Bob. If Eve can find the index of the pair with solutions, we can quickly check that she is right (because the instances inside the list are relatively small), and simply return that index.   □

Now, we can put all of these together to get a weak fine-grained key exchange. We will then boost it to be a strong fine-grained key exchange (see the Definition 6 for weak versus strong in this setting).

Theorem 5. *If a problem P is $\ell(n)$-KER with plant time $G(n)$, solve time $S(n)$ and lower bound $T(n)$ when $\ell(n) \geq 2^{14}$, then Construction 4 is a $((\ell(n)T(n), \alpha, \gamma)$-FG-KeyExchange, with $\gamma \leq \frac{1}{10,000\ell(n)e}$ and $\alpha \leq \frac{1}{4}$.*

Proof. This is a simple combination of the correctness of the protocol, and the fact that an eavesdropper must take more time than the honest parties. We have that the $\Pr[b_A = b_B] \geq 1 - \frac{1}{10,000\ell e}$, implying $\gamma \leq \frac{1}{10,000\ell e}$ from Lemma 1. We have that Alice and Bob take time $O(\ell(n)G(n) + \sqrt{\ell(n)}S(n))$ and Eve must take time $\tilde{\Omega}(\ell(n)T(n))$ to get an advantage larger than $\frac{1}{4}$ by Lemmas 2 and 3. Because P is KER, $\ell(n)T(n) \in \tilde{\omega}\left(\ell(n)G(n) + \sqrt{\ell(n)}S(n)\right)$, implying there exists $\delta > 0$ so that $\ell(n)G(n) + \sqrt{\ell(n)}S(n) \in \tilde{O}(\ell(n)T(n)^{1-\delta})$. So, we have correctness, efficiency and security.   □

Next, we are going to amplify the security of this key exchange using parallel repetition, drawing off of strategies from [24] and [13].

Theorem 6. *If a weak $(\ell(n)T(n), \alpha, \gamma)$-FG-KeyExchange exists where $\gamma = O\left(\frac{1}{n^c}\right)$ for some constant $c > 0$, but $\alpha = O(1)$, then a Strong $(\ell(n)T(n))$-FG-KeyExchange also exists.*

The proof of Theorem 6 is in the full version of this paper.

Remark 1. It is not obvious how to amplify correctness *and* security of a fine-grained key exchange at the same time. If we have a weak $(\ell(n)T(n), \alpha, \gamma)$-FG-KeyExchange, where $\alpha = \text{insig}(n)$ but $\gamma = O(1)$, then we can use a standard repetition error-correcting code to amplify γ. That is, we can run the key exchange $\log^2(n)$ times to get $\log^2(n)$ keys (most of which will agree between Alice and Bob), and to send a message with these keys, send that message $\log^2(n)$ times. With all but negligible probability, the decrypted message will agree with the sent message a majority of the time. Since with very high probability the adversary cannot recover any of the keys in $\mathsf{PFT}_{\ell(n)T(n)}$ time, this repetition scheme is still secure.

As discussed in Theorem 6, we can also amplify a key exchange that has constant correctness and polynomial soundness to one with $1 - \mathsf{insig}(n)$ correctness and polynomial soundness. However, it is unclear how to amplify both at the same time in a fine-grained manner.

Corollary 1. *If a problem P is $\ell(n)$-KER, then a **Strong** $(\ell(n)T(n))$-**FG-KeyExchange** exists.*

The proof of Corollary 1 is included in the full version of this paper.

Finally, using the fact that Alice and Bob do not use each other's messages to produce their own in Construction 4, we prove that we can remove all interaction through repetition to get a $T(n)$-fine-grained public key cryptosystem. The key insight is that if there are no false positives Then L_A and L_B are the same, they will either both fail or both succeed. The proof Theorem 7 below is included in the full version of the paper.

Theorem 7. *If a problem P is $\ell(n)$-KER, then a $\ell(n) \cdot T(n)$-fine-grained public key cryptosystem exists.*

Note that this encryption scheme can be used to send any sub-polynomial number of bits, just by running it in sequence sub-polynomially many times. We also want to note that the adversary's advantage cannot be any less than $\frac{1}{\mathsf{poly}(n)}$ since, due to the fine-grained nature of the scheme, the adversary can always solve the hard problem via guessing.

Corollary 2. *Given the strong Zero-k-Clique-R Hypothesis over range $R = n^k$, there exists a $(\ell(n)T(n), 1/4, \mathsf{insig}(n))$-**FG-KeyExchange**, where Alice and Bob can exchange a sub-polynomial-sized key in time $\tilde{O}\left(n^{2k-2}\right)$ when $\ell(n) = n^{2k-4}$.*

There also exists a $\ell(n)T(n)$-fine-grained public-key cryptosystem, where we can encrypt a sub-polynomial sized message in time $\tilde{O}\left(n^{2k-2}\right)$.

The Zero-3-Clique hypothesis (the Zero Triangle hypothesis) is the most believable version of the Zero-k-Clique hypothesis. Note that even with the strong Zero-3-Clique hypothesis we get a key exchange with a gap in the running times of Alice and Bob vs Eve. In this case, the gap is $t = 5/4 = 1.2$.

References

1. Abboud, A., Williams, V.V., Weimann, O.: Consequences of faster alignment of sequences. In: Esparza, J., Fraigniaud, P., Husfeldt, T., Koutsoupias, E. (eds.) ICALP 2014. LNCS, vol. 8572, pp. 39–51. Springer, Heidelberg (2014). https://doi.org/10.1007/978-3-662-43948-7_4
2. Abboud, A., Williams, V.V.: Popular conjectures imply strong lower bounds for dynamic problems. In: 55th IEEE Annual Symposium on Foundations of Computer Science, FOCS 2014, Philadelphia, PA, USA, 18–21 October 2014, pp. 434–443 (2014)

3. Alon, N., Yuster, R., Zwick, U.: Color coding. Encyclopedia of Algorithms, pp. 335–338. Springer, New York (2016). https://doi.org/10.1007/978-1-4939-2864-4_76

4. Applebaum, B., Barak, B., Wigderson, A.: Public-key cryptography from different assumptions. In: Proceedings of the Forty-Second ACM Symposium on Theory of Computing, STOC 2010, pp. 171–180. ACM, New York (2010)

5. Backurs, A., Tzamos, C.: Improving viterbi is hard: better runtimes imply faster clique algorithms. CoRR, abs/1607.04229 (2016)

6. Ball, M., Rosen, A., Sabin, M., Vasudevan, P.N.: Average-case fine-grained hardness. In: Proceedings of the 49th Annual ACM SIGACT Symposium on Theory of Computing, STOC 2017, Montreal, QC, Canada, 19–23 June 2017, pp. 483–496 (2017)

7. Ball, M., Rosen, A., Sabin, M., Vasudevan, P.N.: Proofs of work from worst-case assumptions. In: Shacham, H., Boldyreva, A. (eds.) CRYPTO 2018. LNCS, vol. 10991, pp. 789–819. Springer, Cham (2018). https://doi.org/10.1007/978-3-319-96884-1_26

8. Barak, B., Mahmoody-Ghidary, M.: Merkle puzzles are optimal—an $O(n^2)$-query attack on any key exchange from a random oracle. In: Halevi, S. (ed.) CRYPTO 2009. LNCS, vol. 5677, pp. 374–390. Springer, Heidelberg (2009). https://doi.org/10.1007/978-3-642-03356-8_22

9. Baran, I., Demaine, E.D., Patrascu, M.: Subquadratic algorithms for 3SUM. Algorithmica **50**(4), 584–596 (2008)

10. Bellare, M., Canetti, R., Krawczyk, H.: Pseudorandom functions revisited: the cascade construction and its concrete security. In: 37th Annual Symposium on Foundations of Computer Science, FOCS 1996, Burlington, Vermont, USA, 14–16 October 1996, pp. 514–523 (1996)

11. Bellare, M., Desai, A., Jokipii, E., Rogaway, P.: A concrete security treatment of symmetric encryption. In: 38th Annual Symposium on Foundations of Computer Science, FOCS 1997, Miami Beach, Florida, USA, 19–22 October 1997, pp. 394–403 (1997)

12. Bellare, M., Guérin, R., Rogaway, P.: XOR MACs: new methods for message authentication using finite pseudorandom functions. In: Coppersmith, D. (ed.) CRYPTO 1995. LNCS, vol. 963, pp. 15–28. Springer, Heidelberg (1995). https://doi.org/10.1007/3-540-44750-4_2

13. Bellare, M., Impagliazzo, R., Naor, M.: Does parallel repetition lower the error in computationally sound protocols? In: Proceedings of the 38th Annual Symposium on Foundations of Computer Science, FOCS 1997, p. 374. IEEE Computer Society, Washington, DC (1997)

14. Bellare, M., Kilian, J., Rogaway, P.: The security of cipher block chaining. In: Desmedt, Y.G. (ed.) CRYPTO 1994. LNCS, vol. 839, pp. 341–358. Springer, Heidelberg (1994). https://doi.org/10.1007/3-540-48658-5_32

15. Bellare, M., Ristenpart, T.: Simulation without the artificial abort: simplified proof and improved concrete security for waters' IBE scheme. In: Joux, A. (ed.) EUROCRYPT 2009. LNCS, vol. 5479, pp. 407–424. Springer, Heidelberg (2009). https://doi.org/10.1007/978-3-642-01001-9_24

16. Biham, E., Goren, Y.J., Ishai, Y.: Basing weak public-key cryptography on strong one-way functions. In: Canetti, R. (ed.) TCC 2008. LNCS, vol. 4948, pp. 55–72. Springer, Heidelberg (2008). https://doi.org/10.1007/978-3-540-78524-8_4

17. Bringmann, K., Gawrychowski, P., Mozes, S., Weimann, O.: Tree edit distance cannot be computed in strongly subcubic time (unless APSP can). In: Proceedings of the Twenty-Ninth Annual ACM-SIAM Symposium on Discrete Algorithms, SODA 2018, New Orleans, LA, USA, 7–10 January 2018, pp. 1190–1206 (2018)

18. Carmosino, M.L., Gao, J., Impagliazzo, R., Mihajlin, I., Paturi, R., Schneider, S.: Nondeterministic extensions of the strong exponential time hypothesis and consequences for non-reducibility. In: Proceedings of the 2016 ACM Conference on Innovations in Theoretical Computer Science, Cambridge, MA, USA, 14–16 January 2016, pp. 261–270 (2016)
19. Chan, T.M.: More logarithmic-factor speedups for 3SUM, (median, +)-convolution, and some geometric 3SUM-hard problems. In: Proceedings of the Twenty-Ninth Annual ACM-SIAM Symposium on Discrete Algorithms, SODA 2018, New Orleans, LA, USA, 7–10 January 2018, pp. 881–897 (2018)
20. Chor, B., Kushilevitz, E., Goldreich, O., Sudan, M.: Private information retrieval. J. ACM **45**(6), 965–981 (1998)
21. Cooper, C., Frieze, A.M., Mehlhorn, K., Priebe, V.: Average-case complexity of shortest-paths problems in the vertex-potential model. Random Struct. Algorithms **16**(1), 33–46 (2000)
22. Degwekar, A., Vaikuntanathan, V., Vasudevan, P.N.: Fine-grained cryptography. In: Robshaw, M., Katz, J. (eds.) CRYPTO 2016. LNCS, vol. 9816, pp. 533–562. Springer, Heidelberg (2016). https://doi.org/10.1007/978-3-662-53015-3_19
23. Diffie, W., Hellman, M.: New directions in cryptography. IEEE Trans. Inf. Theor. **22**(6), 644–654 (2006)
24. Dwork, C., Naor, M., Reingold, O.: Immunizing encryption schemes from decryption errors. In: Cachin, C., Camenisch, J.L. (eds.) EUROCRYPT 2004. LNCS, vol. 3027, pp. 342–360. Springer, Heidelberg (2004). https://doi.org/10.1007/978-3-540-24676-3_21
25. Gajentaan, A., Overmars, M.H.: On a class of $O(n^2)$ problems in computational geometry. Comput. Geom. **45**(4), 140–152 (2012)
26. Gall, F.L.: Powers of tensors and fast matrix multiplication. In: International Symposium on Symbolic and Algebraic Computation, ISSAC 2014, Kobe, Japan, 23–25 July 2014, pp. 296–303 (2014)
27. Goldreich, O., Levin, L.A.: A hard-core predicate for all one-way functions. In: Proceedings of the Twenty-First Annual ACM Symposium on Theory of Computing, STOC 1989, pp. 25–32. ACM, New York (1989)
28. Hartmanis, J., Stearns, R.E.: On the computational complexity of algorithms. Trans. Am. Math. Soc. **117**, 285–306 (1965)
29. Hazan, E., Krauthgamer, R.: How hard is it to approximate the best nash equilibrium? SIAM J. Comput. **40**(1), 79–91 (2011)
30. Hennie, F.C., Stearns, R.E.: Two-tape simulation of multitape turing machines. J. ACM **13**(4), 533–546 (1966)
31. Impagliazzo, R.: A personal view of average-case complexity. In: Proceedings of the Tenth Annual Structure in Complexity Theory Conference, Minneapolis, Minnesota, USA, 19–22 June 1995, pp. 134–147 (1995)
32. Impagliazzo, R., Naor, M.: Efficient cryptographic schemes provably as secure as subset sum, vol. 9, no. 02 (2002)
33. Jerrum, M.: Large cliques elude the metropolis process. Random Struct. Algorithms **3**(4), 347–360 (1992)
34. Juels, A., Peinado, M.: Hiding cliques for cryptographic security. Des. Codes Crypt. **20**(3), 269–280 (2000)
35. Kane, D.M., Williams, R.R.: The orthogonal vectors conjecture for branching programs and formulas. CoRR, abs/1709.05294 (2017)

36. Katz, J., Wang, N.: Efficiency improvements for signature schemes with tight security reductions. In: Proceedings of the 10th ACM Conference on Computer and Communications Security, CCS 2003, Washington, DC, USA, 27–30 October 2003, pp. 155–164 (2003)

37. Kopelowitz, T., Pettie, S., Porat, E.: Higher lower bounds from the 3SUM conjecture. In: Proceedings of the Twenty-Seventh Annual ACM-SIAM Symposium on Discrete Algorithms, SODA 2016, Arlington, VA, USA, 10–12 January 2016, pp. 1272–1287 (2016)

38. Kucera, L.: Expected complexity of graph partitioning problems. Discrete Appl. Math. **57**(2–3), 193–212 (1995)

39. Levin, L.A.: On storage capacity of algorithms. Soviet Math. Dokl. **14**(5), 1464–1466 (1973)

40. Lincoln, A., Williams, V.V., Williams, R.R.: Tight hardness for shortest cycles and paths in sparse graphs. In: Proceedings of the Twenty-Ninth Annual ACM-SIAM Symposium on Discrete Algorithms, SODA 2018, New Orleans, LA, USA, 7–10 January 2018, pp. 1236–1252 (2018)

41. Lindell, Y.: Tutorials on the Foundations of Cryptography: Dedicated to Oded Goldreich, 1st edn. Springer, Cham (2017). https://doi.org/10.1007/978-3-319-57048-8

42. Lyubashevsky, V., Palacio, A., Segev, G.: Public-key cryptographic primitives provably as secure as subset sum. In: Micciancio, D. (ed.) TCC 2010. LNCS, vol. 5978, pp. 382–400. Springer, Heidelberg (2010). https://doi.org/10.1007/978-3-642-11799-2_23

43. Merkle, R.C.: Secure communications over insecure channels. Commun. ACM **21**(4), 294–299 (1978)

44. Patrascu, M.: Towards polynomial lower bounds for dynamic problems. In: Proceedings of the 42nd ACM Symposium on Theory of Computing, STOC 2010, Cambridge, Massachusetts, USA, 5–8 June 2010, pp. 603–610 (2010)

45. Peres, Y., Sotnikov, D., Sudakov, B., Zwick, U.: All-pairs shortest paths in $O(n^2)$ time with high probability. J. ACM **60**(4), 26:1–26:25 (2013)

46. Pettie, S.: Higher lower bounds from the 3SUM conjecture. In: Fine-Grained Complexity and Algorithm Design Workshop at the Simons Institute (2015)

47. Razborov, A.A., Rudich, S.: Natural proofs. In: Proceedings of the Twenty-Sixth Annual ACM Symposium on Theory of Computing, Montréal, Québec, Canada, 23–25 May 1994, pp. 204–213 (1994)

48. Regev, O.: On lattices, learning with errors, random linear codes, and cryptography. In: Proceedings of the Thirty-Seventh Annual ACM Symposium on Theory of Computing, STOC 2005, pp. 84–93. ACM, New York (2005)

49. Rivest, R.L., Shamir, A., Adleman, L.: A method for obtaining digital signatures and public-key cryptosystems. Commun. ACM **21**(2), 120–126 (1978)

50. Russell, A., Wang, H.: How to fool an unbounded adversary with a short key. In: Knudsen, L.R. (ed.) EUROCRYPT 2002. LNCS, vol. 2332, pp. 133–148. Springer, Heidelberg (2002). https://doi.org/10.1007/3-540-46035-7_9

51. Shamir, A.: How to share a secret. Commun. ACM **22**(11), 612–613 (1979)

52. Shor, P.W.: Algorithms for quantum computation: discrete logarithms and factoring. In: Proceedings of the 35th Annual Symposium on Foundations of Computer Science, SFCS 1994, pp. 124–134. IEEE Computer Society, Washington, DC (1994)

53. Tseitin, G.S.: Seminar on math, logic (1956)

54. Williams, V.V.: On some fine-grained questions in algorithms and complexity. In: Proceedings of the International Congress of Mathematicians (2018, to appear)

55. Williams, V.V.: Multiplying matrices faster than coppersmith-winograd. In: Proceedings of the 44th Symposium on Theory of Computing Conference, STOC 2012, New York, NY, USA, 19–22 May 2012, pp. 887–898 (2012)
56. Williams, V.V., Williams, R.: Subcubic equivalences between path, matrix and triangle problems. In: 51th Annual IEEE Symposium on Foundations of Computer Science, FOCS 2010, Las Vegas, Nevada, USA, 23–26 October 2010, pp. 645–654 (2010)
57. Williams, V.V., Williams, R.: Finding, minimizing, and counting weighted subgraphs. SIAM J. Comput. **42**(3), 831–854 (2013)

Zero Knowledge II

Exploring Constructions of Compact NIZKs from Various Assumptions

Shuichi Katsumata[1,2]($\boxtimes$), Ryo Nishimaki[3], Shota Yamada[1],
and Takashi Yamakawa[3]

[1] AIST, Tokyo, Japan
{shuichi.katsumata,yamada-shota}@aist.go.jp
[2] The University of Tokyo, Tokyo, Japan
[3] NTT Secure Platform Laboratories, Tokyo, Japan
{ryo.nishimaki.zk,takashi.yamakawa.ga}@hco.ntt.co.jp

Abstract. A non-interactive zero-knowledge (NIZK) protocol allows a prover to non-interactively convince a verifier of the truth of the statement without leaking any other information. In this study, we explore shorter NIZK proofs for all **NP** languages. Our primary interest is NIZK proofs from falsifiable pairing/pairing-free group-based assumptions. Thus far, NIZKs in the common reference string model (CRS-NIZKs) for **NP** based on falsifiable pairing-based assumptions all require a proof size at least as large as $O(|C|\kappa)$, where C is a circuit computing the **NP** relation and κ is the security parameter. This holds true even for the weaker designated-verifier NIZKs (DV-NIZKs). Notably, constructing a (CRS, DV)-NIZK with proof size achieving an *additive*-overhead $O(|C|)+\mathsf{poly}(\kappa)$, rather than a multiplicative-overhead $|C|\cdot\mathsf{poly}(\kappa)$, based on any falsifiable pairing-based assumptions is an open problem.

In this work, we present various techniques for constructing NIZKs with *compact* proofs, i.e., proofs smaller than $O(|C|)+\mathsf{poly}(\kappa)$, and make progress regarding the above situation. Our result is summarized below.
- We construct CRS-NIZK for all **NP** with proof size $|C| + \mathsf{poly}(\kappa)$ from a (non-static) falsifiable Diffie-Hellman (DH) type assumption over pairing groups. This is the first CRS-NIZK to achieve a compact proof without relying on either lattice-based assumptions or non-falsifiable assumptions. Moreover, a variant of our CRS-NIZK satisfies universal composability (UC) in the erasure-free adaptive setting. Although it is limited to **NP** relations in **NC**[1], the proof size is $|w| \cdot \mathsf{poly}(\kappa)$ where w is the witness, and in particular, it matches the state-of-the-art UC-NIZK proposed by Cohen, shelat, and Wichs (CRYPTO'19) based on lattices.
- We construct (multi-theorem) DV-NIZKs for **NP** with proof size $|C| + \mathsf{poly}(\kappa)$ from the computational DH assumption over *pairing-free* groups. This is the first DV-NIZK that achieves a compact proof from a standard DH type assumption. Moreover, if we further assume the **NP** relation to be computable in **NC**[1] and assume hardness of a (non-static) falsifiable DH type assumption over *pairing-free* groups, the proof size can be made as small as $|w| + \mathsf{poly}(\kappa)$.

© International Association for Cryptologic Research 2019
A. Boldyreva and D. Micciancio (Eds.): CRYPTO 2019, LNCS 11694, pp. 639–669, 2019.
https://doi.org/10.1007/978-3-030-26954-8_21

Another related but independent issue is that all (CRS, DV)-NIZKs require the running time of the prover to be at least $|C| \cdot \mathsf{poly}(\kappa)$. Considering that there exists NIZKs with efficient verifiers whose running time is strictly smaller than $|C|$, it is an interesting problem whether we can construct *prover-efficient* NIZKs. To this end, we construct prover-efficient CRS-NIZKs for **NP** with compact proof through a generic construction using laconic functional evaluation schemes (Quach, Wee, and Wichs (FOCS'18)). This is the first NIZK in any model where the running time of the prover is strictly smaller than the time it takes to compute the circuit C computing the **NP** relation.

Finally, perhaps of an independent interest, we formalize the notion of *homomorphic equivocal commitments*, which we use as building blocks to obtain the first result, and show how to construct them from pairing-based assumptions.

1 Introduction

1.1 Background

Zero-knowledge (ZK) protocols, introduced by Goldwasser, Micali, and Rackoff [37], allow a prover to convince a verifier of the truth of a statement without leaking any knowledge other than the fact that the statement is indeed true. A practically useful and theoretically alluring feature for a ZK protocol to have is *non-interactiveness*, where a prover simply outputs a single message (called a proof) and convinces the verifier of the truth of the statement. Unfortunately, it is known that non-interactive ZK (NIZK) for non-trivial languages do not exist in the plain model where there is no trusted setup [36]. However, Blum, Feldman, and Micali [10] showed how to construct a NIZK in a setting where the prover and verifier have access to a shared *common reference string* (as known as CRS-NIZK). Since then, NIZKs have been used as a ubiquitous building block for cryptography ranging from the early chosen-ciphertext secure public key encryption schemes [27,59,66], advanced signature schemes [5,19,65], and multi-party computation [35].

Compact NIZK. One of the important research topics for NIZK is making the proof size as small as possible. So far, CRS-NIZK for all of **NP** in the standard model is known to exist from (doubly-enhanced) trapdoor permutation [6,28,34], pairing [30,40,41,43,44,53], indistinguishability obfuscation (iO) [8,9,15,67], or correlation intractable hash function [12,13,46]. Among these, CRS-NIZKs that have proof size independent of the size of the circuit C computing the **NP** relation are limited to those based on either a knowledge assumption [30,41,53] or iO [67]. There also exist generic conversions from standard CRS-NIZKs to CRS-NIZKs with proof size independent of $|C|$. However, they rely on fully homomorphic encryption (FHE) [31,32] or homomorphic trapdoor functions (HTDF) [20] whose existence is only implied from lattice-based assumptions. Put differently, the classical CRS-NIZKs based on trapdoor permutations or (falsifiable [33,58]) pairing-based assumptions all require a large proof size that is polynomially related to the circuit size $|C|$. Notably, even the most well-known Groth-Ostrovsky-Sahai NIZK (GOS-NIZK) [43] based on the decisional linear or subgroup decision assumptions over pairing groups requires the proof size to be as large as $O(|C|\kappa)$, where κ is the security parameter. In fact, the CRS-NIZK with the shortest proof that does not rely on any of the above strong tools is the NIZK of Groth [40] based on the security of Naccache-Stern public key encryption scheme [57] which achieves proof size $|C| \cdot \mathsf{polylog}(\kappa)$. Therefore, it remains an interesting open problem to construct CRS-NIZKs with proof size smaller than the current state-of-the-art while avoiding to rely on strong tools such as knowledge assumptions, iO, FHE, and HTDF. Specifically, in this paper, one of the primary interest is to obtain a CRS-NIZK with proof size achieving an *additive*-overhead $O(|C|) + \mathsf{poly}(\kappa)$, rather than a multiplicative-overhead $|C| \cdot \mathsf{poly}(\kappa)$ (or $|C| \cdot \mathsf{polylog}(\kappa)$), based on any falsifiable pairing-based assumptions. Hereafter, we call such NIZKs with proof size $O(|C|) + \mathsf{poly}(\kappa)$ as NIZKs with *compact* proofs for simplicity.

Designated Verifier NIZKs and Compact Proofs. A relaxation of CRS-NIZKs called the *designated verifier* NIZKs (DV-NIZKs) [24,61] retain most of the useful properties of CRS-NIZKs and in some applications can be used as a substitute for CRS-NIZKs. The main difference between CRS and DV-NIZKs is that the latter limits the proof to only be verifiable by a designated party in possession of a verification key; the proof can still be generated by anybody as in CRS-NIZKs. Due to this extra secret information possessed by the verifier, DV-NIZKs suffer from the so-called verifier rejection attack. Specifically, a prover may learn partial information of the secret verification key and break soundness if the verifier uses the same verification key for verifying multiple statements. In this paper, our primary interest is *multi-theorem* DV-NIZKs (also known as *reusable* or *unbounded-soundness* DV-NIZKs) where the verification key can be reused for multiple statements without compromising soundness. Surprisingly, most DV-NIZKs [17,18,24,55,61,69] (that are not a simple downgrade of CRS-NIZKs) are known to either suffer from the verifier rejection attack or to be limited to specific **NP** languages. It was not until recently that the first multi-theorem DV-NIZK for all **NP** languages was (concurrently and independently) shown by Couteau and Hofheinz [21], Katsumata et al. [47], and Quach et al. [63]. They proposed a tweak to the classical Feige-Lapidot-Shamir (FLS) NIZK protocol [28] and showed for the first time how to construct DV-NIZKs from the computational Diffie-Hellman (CDH) assumption over *pairing-free* groups; an assumption which is not yet known to imply CRS-NIZKs. However, one drawback of their DV-NIZK is that the CRS size and proof size are huge, i.e., $\mathsf{poly}(\kappa, |C|)$. This is due to the fact that the FLS NIZK, which they base their construction on, is highly specific to the **NP**-complete Hamiltonicity problem. It is unclear if we can make their scheme compact since all other (CRS-)NIZKs following the footsteps of FLS NIZK such as [40, 48, 50] suffer from the same problem of having large CRS and proof size. Therefore, it is unclear whether such a weak assumption as CDH over pairing-free groups can be used to construct a DV-NIZK with compact proofs. In fact, constructing DV-NIZKs with compact proof from any *pairing/pairing-free* group assumptions remains open.

Prover-Efficient NIZKs. Continuing the line of NIZKs with compact proofs, it is very natural and appealing to consider NIZKs that enjoy *efficient provers*, i.e., the running time of the prover is small. We say the prover is efficient if its running time is strictly smaller than the time it takes to compute $C(x, w)$ for statement x and witness w, where recall C was the circuit computing the **NP** relation. As an example, we can imagine a case where a user (acting as a prover) is given some sort of credential w as a witness by a trusted authority and is required to prove in zero-knowledge the fact that it possesses a valid credential to make some action. More concretely, in group signatures [5] a trusted authority will provide users with a credential which allows them to sign anonymously on behalf of the group. In such a case, it would be appealing if the user could generate a proof without requiring to invest computational time-dependent of $|C|$, since if zero-knowledge was not required, the prover could have simply output the credential w in the clear and completely outsourced the computation of $C(x, w)$ to the verifier. Since the authority is providing a valid credential w to the user, in principle, the user should never need to compute $C(x, w)$ to check whether w is valid.

As far as our knowledge goes, all NIZKs, regardless of CRS or DV, have a prover with running time at least $|C| \cdot \mathsf{poly}(\kappa)$ which is much larger than the time it takes to simply compute the circuit C. We emphasize that solutions to the counterpart notion of *efficient verifiers* are well known and studied. Specifically, NIZKs with compact proofs with the additional property of having efficient verifiers are known as ZK-succinct non-interactive arguments (ZK-SNARGs) or ZK-succinct non-interactive arguments of knowledge (ZK-SNARKs).[1] They have been the subject of extensive research, e.g., [7,25,30,40,42,53,54,60], where constructions are known to exist either in the random oracle model or based on non-falsifiable assumptions. We also note that it would be impossible to construct a NIZK where both the prover *and* the verifier are efficient since the circuit C representing the **NP** relation must be computed by at least one of the parties to check the validity of the witness w. Therefore, it is an interesting question of whether there exists an opposite flavor of the current NIZKs where we have an efficient prover instead of an efficient verifier.

1.2 Our Contribution

In this paper, we provide new constructions of CRS-NIZK and DV-NIZK with compact proofs. The former is instantiated on a pairing group and the latter on a paring-free group. The tools and techniques which we use for our CRS-NIZK can be slightly modified to construct universally composable NIZK (UC-NIZK) [43] with compact proofs over pairing groups. Finally, we provide a generic construction of a CRS-NIZK with an efficient prover using as a building block

---

[1] We note that in ZK-SNARG/SNARK, it is conventional to require an efficient verifier to have running time that is only poly-logarithmic dependent of $|C|$, rather than being just strictly smaller than $|C|$.

the recently proposed laconic functional evaluation (LFE) scheme of Quach, Wee, and Wichs [64]. We summarize our results below and refer to Tables 1, 2, and 3 for a comparison between prior works. We note that we only include multi-theorem NIZKs supporting all of **NP** based on falsifiable assumptions in the table.

1. We construct CRS-NIZKs for **NP** with compact proof from a (non-static) assumption over pairing groups, namely, the (n, m)-computational Diffie-Hellman exponent and ratio (CDHER) assumption introduced by [47]. This is the first CRS-NIZK to achieve a compact proof without relying on either lattice-based assumptions, knowledge assumptions, or indistinguishability obfuscation. The proof size has an additive-overhead $|C| + \mathsf{poly}(\kappa)$, rather than a multiplicative-overhead $|C| \cdot \mathsf{poly}(\kappa)$, where C is the circuit that computes the **NP** relation (See Table 1). Moreover, if we assume the **NP** relation to be computable in $\mathbf{NC}^1$, we can make the proof size as small as $|w| + \mathsf{poly}(\kappa)$, where w is the witness. This matches the proof size of the CRS-NIZK of Gentry et al. [32] based on fully-homomorphic encryption.

2. We construct UC-NIZKs for **NP** relations in $\mathbf{NC}^1$ with compact proof from the (n, m)-CDHER assumption. Although it is limited to **NP** relations in $\mathbf{NC}^1$, it matches the smallest proof size among all the UC-NIZKs secure against adaptive corruptions in the erasure-free setting (See Table 2). The proof size is small as $|w| \cdot \mathsf{poly}(\kappa)$, and in particular, matches the recent UC-NIZK of Cohen, shelat, and Wichs [20] based on lattice-assumptions. Here, note that for $\mathbf{NC}^1$ circuits, the dependence on the depth d they have can be ignored, since asymptotically d is smaller than κ.

3. We construct (multi-theorem) DV-NIZKs for **NP** with compact proof from the CDH assumption over *pairing-free* groups. This is the first DV-NIZK that achieves a compact proof from a weak and static Diffie-Hellman type assumption such as CDH. Specifically, similarly to the above CRS-NIZK, the proof size of our DV-NIZK is $|C| + \mathsf{poly}(\kappa)$, whereas all previous DV-NIZKs had proof size $\mathsf{poly}(|C|, \kappa)$ (See Table 3). Moreover, if we further assume the **NP** relation to be computable in $\mathbf{NC}^1$ and assume the hardness of the parameterized ℓ-computational Diffie-Hellman inversion (CDHI) assumption over *pairing-free* groups [16,56], we can make the proof size as small as $|w| + \mathsf{poly}(\kappa)$.

4. Finally, we construct prover-efficient CRS-NIZKs for **NP** through a generic construction using LFE schemes [64]. This is the first NIZK in any model (e.g., CRS, DV) where the running time of the prover is strictly smaller than the time it takes to compute the circuit C computing the **NP** relation. Using any non-prover-efficient CRS-NIZK, we generically construct a CRS-NIZK where the running time of the prover (and the proof size) is $\mathsf{poly}(\kappa, |x|, |w|, d)$, independent of the circuit size $|C|$, by instantiating the LFE scheme by the sub-exponential security of the learning with errors (LWE) assumption with sub-exponential modulus-to-noise ratio, where x is the statement and d is the depth of C. Moreover, if we use as building block a CRS-NIZK whose prover running time is smaller than $|C| \cdot \mathsf{poly}(\kappa)$ (e.g., [43]), the running time and

proof size can be made as small as $\tilde{O}(|x| + |w|) \cdot \mathsf{poly}(\kappa, d)$ by instantiating the LFE scheme by the *adaptive* LWE assumption with sub-exponential modulus-to-noise ratio introduced in [64].

Along the way of obtaining our first and second results, we formalize a new tool called *homomorphic equivocal commitments* (HEC)[2], which may be of independent interest. An HEC is a commitment with two additional properties called *equivocality* and *homomorphism*. The equivocality enables one to generate a commitment that can be opened to any message by using a master secret key. The homomorphism for a circuit family $\mathcal{C} = \{C : \mathcal{X} \rightarrow \mathcal{Z}\}$ informally requires that one can commit to a message $\mathbf{x} \in \mathcal{X}$, where its commitment com can be further publicly modified to a commitment com_C on the message $C(\mathbf{x}) \in \mathcal{Z}$ for any circuit $C \in \mathcal{C}$. Here, a decommitment for com_C can be computed by the knowledge of the message $\mathbf{x}$, decommitment of com, and the circuit C. To the knowledgeable readers, we note that HEC is a strictly weaker primitive compared to homomorphic trapdoor functions [39]. Previously, an HEC supporting the family of all polynomial-sized circuits were only (implicitly) known from lattice-based assumptions [39]. Apart from their construction, known (implicit) constructions of HEC only support linear functions [62] or group operations on a pairing group [2]. In this paper, we provide the first instantiation of HEC supporting $\mathbf{NC}^1$ based on any pairing-based assumptions, namely, the (n, m)-CDHER assumption introduced in [47]. The construction is inspired by the recent construction of compact homomorphic signatures of Katsumata et al. [47]. The proposed HEC enjoys a particular form of compactness which is especially useful for generically converting CRS-NIZKs with non-compact proofs to CRS-NIZKs with compact proofs. Concretely, for any polynomially-sized circuit C, the evaluated commitment com_C and its decommitment of our HEC are of size $\mathsf{poly}(\kappa)$ independent of $|C|$, and one can verify the validity of the decommitment in time $\mathsf{poly}(\kappa)$ independent of $|C|$. Somewhat surprisingly, we also construct another instantiation of HEC supporting $\mathbf{NC}^1$ based on the CDH assumption over pairing groups. Although this HEC does not enjoy compactness, and hence cannot be used for our compact CRS-NIZK conversion, we believe it to be an interesting primitive on its own since we achieve homomorphic computations in $\mathbf{NC}^1$ from such a weak assumption as CDH.

1.3   Technical Overview

Our results can be broken up into three parts. The first two results concerning CRS and UC-NIZKs with short proof are obtained through a generic conversion from NIZKs with non-compact proofs to NIZKs with compact proofs using homomorphic equivocal commitments (HEC); a primitive which we formalize and provide instantiations in this work. The third result concerning DV-NIZKs

---

[2] This primitive was already informally mentioned in [39] and we do not take credit for proposing the concept of HEC. We note that Abe et al. [2] also introduced a similar primitive with the name *homomorphic trapdoor commitments*.

Table 1. Comparison of CRS-NIZKs for **NP**.

Reference	CRS size	Proof size	Assumption (Misc.)
FLS [28]	$\mathsf{poly}(\kappa, \lvert C \rvert)$	$\mathsf{poly}(\kappa, \lvert C \rvert)$	Trapdoor permutation[†]
Groth [40]	$\lvert C \rvert \cdot k_{\mathsf{tpm}} \cdot \mathsf{polylog}(\kappa)$ $+\mathsf{poly}(\kappa)$	$\lvert C \rvert \cdot k_{\mathsf{tpm}} \cdot \mathsf{polylog}(\kappa)$ $+\mathsf{poly}(\kappa)$	Trapdoor permutation[†]
Groth [40]	$\lvert C \rvert \cdot \mathsf{polylog}(\kappa)+\mathsf{poly}(\kappa)$	$\lvert C \rvert \cdot \mathsf{polylog}(\kappa) +$ $\mathsf{poly}(\kappa)$	Naccache-Stern PKE
GOS [43]	$\mathsf{poly}(\kappa)$	$O(\lvert C \rvert \kappa)$	DLIN/SD
CHK, Abusalah [3,14]	$\mathsf{poly}(\kappa, \lvert C \rvert)$	$\mathsf{poly}(\kappa, \lvert C \rvert)$	CDH (pairing group)
GGIPSS [32]	$\mathsf{poly}(\kappa)$	$\lvert w \rvert + \mathsf{poly}(\kappa)$	FHE and CRS-NIZK circular security
Sect. 3	$\mathsf{poly}(\kappa, \lvert C \rvert)$	$\lvert C \rvert + \mathsf{poly}(\kappa)$	(n, m)-CDHER
Sect. 3	$\mathsf{poly}(\kappa, \lvert C \rvert, 2^d)$	$\lvert w \rvert + \mathsf{poly}(\kappa)$	(n, m)-CDHER (limited to **NC**^{1} relation)
Sect. 5	$\mathsf{poly}(\kappa, \lvert x \rvert, \lvert w \rvert, d)$	$\mathsf{poly}(\kappa, \lvert x \rvert, \lvert w \rvert, d)$	LFE and CRS-NIZK (prover-efficient, implied by sub-exp. LWE)
Sect. 5	$(\lvert x \rvert + \lvert w \rvert) \cdot \mathsf{poly}(\kappa, d)$	$\tilde{O}(\lvert x \rvert + \lvert w \rvert) \cdot$ $\mathsf{poly}(\kappa, d)$	LFE and CRS-NIZK[‡] (prover-efficient, implied by adaptive LWE)

In column "CRS size" and "Proof size", κ is the security parameter, $\lvert x \rvert$, $\lvert w \rvert$ is the statement and witness size, $\lvert C \rvert$ and d are the size and depth of the circuit computing the **NP** relation, and k_{tpm} is the length of the domain of the trapdoor permutation. In column "Assumption", DLIN stands for the decisional linear assumption, SD stands for the subgroup decision assumption, (n, m)-CDHER stands for the (parameterized) computational DH exponent and ratio assumption, LFE stands for laconic functional evaluation, and sub-exp. LWE stands for sub-exponentially secure learning with errors (LWE).
[†]If the domain of the permutation is not $\{0, 1\}^n$, we further assume they are doubly enhanced [34].
[‡]We additionally require a mild assumption that the prover run time is linear in the size of the circuit computing the **NP** relation.

with short proof size based on pairing-free groups, that is, CDH and ℓ-CDHI, are obtained by extending the recent result of Katsumata et al. [47] which constructs the first NIZKs in the preprocessing model (PP-NIZKs) with short proof size from pairing-free groups. As explained later, PP-NIZK is a strictly weaker primitive compared to DV-NIZK. Finally, the fourth result concerning prover-efficient NIZK is obtained by a generic construction based on the recently developed laconic function evaluation scheme of Quach et al. [64]. In the following, we explain these approaches in more detail.

Generic Construction of Compact (CRS, UC)-NIZK from HEC. Here, we explain our construction of compact CRS-NIZK. Our starting point is the

Table 2. Comparison of UC-NIZKs for **NP**.

Reference	Security (erasure-free)	CRS size	Proof size	Assumption (Misc.)
GOS [43]	Adaptive ($\checkmark$)	$\mathsf{poly}(\kappa)$	$O(\lvert C\rvert\kappa)$	DLIN/SD
GGIPSS [32]	Adaptive ($\times$)	$\mathsf{poly}(\kappa)$	$\lvert w\rvert + \mathsf{poly}(\kappa)$	FHE and UC-NIZK (circular security)
CsW [20]	Adaptive ($\checkmark$)	$\mathsf{poly}(\kappa, d)$	$\lvert w\rvert \cdot \mathsf{poly}(\kappa, d)$	HTDF and UC-NIZK
Sect. 3	Adaptive ($\checkmark$)	$\mathsf{poly}(\kappa, \lvert C\rvert, 2^d)$	$\lvert w\rvert \cdot \mathsf{poly}(\kappa)$	(n, m)-CDHER (limited to **NC**^{1} relation)

In column "CRS size" and "Proof size", κ is the security parameter, $\lvert w\rvert$ is the witness size, $\lvert C\rvert$ and d are the size and depth of circuit computing the **NP** relation. In column "Assumption", DLIN stands for the decisional linear assumption, SD stands for the subgroup decision assumption, HTDF stands for homomorphic trapdoor functions, and (n, m)-CDHER stands for the (parameterized) computational DH exponent and ratio assumption.

Table 3. Comparison of DV-NIZKs for **NP**.

Reference	CRS size	Proof size	Verification key size	Assumption (Misc.)
CH, KNYY, QRW [21, 47, 63]	$\mathsf{poly}(\kappa, \lvert C\rvert)$	$\mathsf{poly}(\kappa, \lvert C\rvert)$	$\mathsf{poly}(\kappa, \lvert C\rvert)$	CDH (pairing-free group)
Sect. 4	$\mathsf{poly}(\kappa)$	$\lvert C\rvert + \mathsf{poly}(\kappa)$	$\mathsf{poly}(\kappa)$	CDH (pairing-free group)
Sect. 4	$2^d \cdot \mathsf{poly}(\kappa)$	$\lvert w\rvert + \mathsf{poly}(\kappa)$	$\mathsf{poly}(\kappa)$	ℓ-CDHI (pairing-free group, limited to **NC**^{1} relation)

In the columns concerning sizes, κ is the security parameter, $\lvert w\rvert$ is the witness-size, $\lvert C\rvert$ and d are the size and depth of the circuit computing the **NP** relation. In column "Assumption", ℓ-CDHI stands for the ℓ-computational Diffie-Hellman inversion assumption.

recent result by Katsumata et al. [47], who constructed a *designated prover* NIZK (DP-NIZK) with compact proof, where DP-NIZK is an analogue of DV-NIZK where the prover requires secret information to generate proofs and anybody can publicly verify the proofs. Since the construction of Katsumata et al. is an instantiation of the generic conversion from homomorphic signature to DP-NIZK proposed by Kim and Wu [51], we first briefly review Kim and Wu's conversion. Recall that in homomorphic signature, a signature σ on a message $\mathbf{m} \in \{0, 1\}^{\ell}$ generated by a secret key sk, can be homomorphically evaluated to a signature

σ on $C(\mathbf{m})$ for a circuit $C : \{0,1\}^\ell \to \{0,1\}$. Anybody can verify the validity of the signature by using a public verification key vk and the circuit C. As for the security requirements, we need that given a verification key vk and a signature σ on $\mathbf{m}$, it is computationally hard to forge a signature σ^* on z such that $z \neq C(\mathbf{m})$ (unforgeability) and an honestly evaluated signature σ on z does not reveal information about $\mathbf{m}$ beyond the fact that it was derived from a signature on $\mathbf{m}$ such that $C(\mathbf{m}) = z$ (context-hiding). Furthermore, as an efficiency requirement, we need that the size of σ is independent of the size of the circuit C. In Kim and Wu's construction of DP-NIZK, the prover is given a signature σ on a secret key $\mathbf{k}$ of a secret key encryption (SKE) scheme as the secret proving key. When the designated prover proves that x is in some language $\mathcal{L}$ that is specified by a relation $\mathcal{R}$, it generates an encryption ct of the witness w such that $(x, w) \in \mathcal{R}$ and homomorphically evaluates the signature σ with respect to a circuit that computes $f_{x,\mathsf{ct}}$, where $f_{x,\mathsf{ct}}$ is a function that takes as input $\mathbf{k}'$ and outputs whether $(x, \mathsf{SKE}.\mathsf{Dec}(\mathbf{k}', \mathsf{ct})) \in \mathcal{R}$. The proof for DP-NIZK is then set as ct and the homomorphically evaluated signature σ. The verifier prepares the function $f_{x,\mathsf{ct}}$ from ct and x, and simply checks σ is a correct signature on 1 with respect to the evaluated function $f_{x,\mathsf{ct}}$. The soundness of the protocol follows from the unforgeability of the homomorphic signature since $f_{x,\mathsf{ct}}(\mathbf{k}') = 0$ for any $\mathbf{k}'$ when $\mathbf{x}$ is not in the language induced by the relation $\mathcal{R}$. Furthermore, the zero-knowledge property of the protocol follows from the security of SKE and the context-hiding property of the homomorphic signature. Katsumata et al. [47] gave a new homomorphic signature scheme with short evaluated signature σ that supports the function class of $\mathbf{NC}^1$ circuits based on a newly introduced (non-static) pairing-based assumption called the (n, m)-computational Diffie-Hellman exponent and ratio (CDHER) assumption. Plugging this homomorphic signature into the Kim-Wu conversion, they obtained the first compact DP-NIZK for all $\mathbf{NP}$ based on any pairing-based assumptions.[3]

The aim of our work is to modify the Kim-Wu conversion and remove the necessity of the prover keeping secret information to generate a proof so that we can convert the compact DP-NIZK of Katsumata et al. into a compact CRS-NIZK. The main reason why their construction cannot be used as a CRS-NIZK is because the prover cannot generate the signature σ on the fly without knowing the signing key sk of the homomorphic signature. To this end, our first idea is to let the prover choose vk, sk, and $\mathbf{k}$ on its own. This would allow the prover to generate a proof as in the designated prover setting since it can generate the signature σ on $\mathbf{k}$ on its own by using the signing key sk. The proof for the CRS-NIZK will then consist of the verification key vk and a proof of the DP-NIZK. Unfortunately, there are multiple of problems with this naive approach. The first problem is that the size of the verification key vk used in Katsumata et al. [47] is polynomially dependent on the size of the circuit that computes the relation to be

---

[3] Note that any $\mathbf{NP}$ relation can be converted to an $\mathbf{NP}$ relation in $\mathbf{NC}^1$ by expanding the witness size as large as the circuit computing the original $\mathbf{NP}$ relation. Notably, a homomorphic signature scheme supporting the function class of $\mathbf{NC}^1$ circuits is sufficient for constructing DP-NIZK for all of $\mathbf{NP}$.

proven, and thus, this ruins the compactness property of the original DP-NIZK proof. The second problem is that we can no longer invoke the unforgeability of the homomorphic signature to prove soundness since unforgeability holds against adversaries who only has access to a verification key vk and a signature σ. Indeed, in the specific case of Katsumata et al.'s homomorphic signature scheme, an adversary will be able to completely break the soundness of the resulting scheme if it is further given the signing key sk. Therefore, to resolve these problems, we make use of the special structure that the homomorphic signature scheme of Katsumata et al. has and abstract it to a primitive which we call homomorphic equivocal commitments (HEC).

Our key observation is that in the Katsumata et al.'s homomorphic signature scheme, the reverse direction of the signing procedure is possible *without* the knowledge of the secret signing key sk if we are allowed to program part of the verification key vk. Namely, the verification key vk can be divided into two parts vk_0 and vk_1 where the size of vk_1 is compact (i.e., independent of the size of the circuit), and for a fixed vk_0 and $\mathbf{k}$, one can sample a signature σ and efficiently compute the remaining part of the verification key vk_1 without knowledge of the secret signing key sk so that σ is a valid signature on $\mathbf{k}$ with respect to the entire verification key $vk = (vk_0, vk_1)$. We then modify our above idea using this reverse direction of computation. Namely, we put the non-compact part of the verification key vk_0 in the common reference string. The prover first choose $\mathbf{k}, \sigma$ on its own and then computes the remaining compact part of the verification key vk_1 from them so that σ is a valid signature on $\mathbf{k}$ with respect to the verification key vk. Notably, the prover no longer requires knowledge of the secret signing key sk, and thus, the prover can generate a proof publicly. The resulting proof is the same as in the case for the above naive construction except that we now only append vk_1 to the underlying DP-NIZK proof, rather than vk_0 *and* vk_1. The first problem of having a large proof size we encountered in our above attempt is now resolved since we moved the non-compact part of the verification key vk_0 to the common reference string and the proof now only contains the compact vk_1 and the compact proof of the underlying DP-NIZK. At first glance, the second problem of losing soundness seems to be resolved as well, as the prover is choosing the signature σ without knowledge of the underlying secret signing key sk. However, we encounter a new problem. Namely, once again, we cannot directly use the unforgeability of the homomorphic signature to prove soundness, since this time the part of the verification key vk_1 that the adversary appends to the underlying DP-NIZK proof may be maliciously chosen in a way that deviates from the security setting of the homomorphic signature. However, luckily, the proof for unforgeability provided by Katsumata et al. can be adapted without much change to the setting where vk_1 follows an arbitrary distribution since their proof does not depend on the specific distribution which vk_1 is chosen from. In this work, to capture this special security requirement as well as the syntactic structure that we require for the homomorphic signature, we introduce a new primitive that we call *homomorphic equivocal commitment* (HEC) and instantiate it by mimicking the homomorphic signature scheme of Katsumata et al. [47]. Roughly speaking, in our formulation, we regard vk_1 as a commitment of a message $\mathbf{k}$ with respect to a randomness σ.

While the above explanation conveys our main idea, we need some more modification to obtain our final construction. In the above construction, an honest prover outputs a "commitment" vk_1 of a secret key $\mathbf{k}$. However, a malicious prover may choose the commitment that does not correspond to any secret key. In this case, we can no longer argue soundness. To avoid the problem, we rely on a non-compact NIZK to prove the well-formedness of the commitment. Since the size of the circuit for checking the well-formedness is independent of the size of the circuit for computing the relation to be proven, this does not harm the compactness of the proof. We finally remark that the construction we explained so far is still slightly different from the one we give in Sect. 3.2. There, we change the scheme so that the prover provides the proof of knowledge of σ instead of sending σ as part of the proof in the clear. While our scheme is secure without this change, this makes it easier to extend our construction to the UC-secure setting.

The proof size of the resulting CRS-NIZK is $|C| + \mathsf{poly}(\kappa)$ since our HEC only supports $\mathbf{NC}^1$ and thus we have to expand the witness to the concatenation of all values corresponding to each wire of the circuit verifying the relation to make the verification of the relation be done in $\mathbf{NC}^1$. On the other hand, if the relation can be verified in $\mathbf{NC}^1$ from the beginning, then the expansion is not needed and the proof size is as small as $|w| + \mathsf{poly}(\kappa)$.

Interestingly, our CRS-NIZK can also be seen as a variant of the UC-NIZK recently proposed by Cohen, shelat, and Wichs [20]. The differences from their scheme are (1) an HTDF is replaced with an HEC, (2) a witness is encrypted by SKE of which key is committed by a HEC instead of the witness itself, and (3) one-time signatures are omitted. If we are to construct a UC-NIZK in the adaptive non-erasure setting as is done in [20], the modifications (2) and (3) are no longer applicable, but (1) is still applicable. Based on this observation, we obtain a UC-NIZK for $\mathbf{NC}^1$ in the adaptive non-erasure setting with a similar proof size to that of [20] based on a HEC instead of a HTDF. A caveat of our construction is that the scheme only supports NP languages verifiable in $\mathbf{NC}^1$ whereas their scheme supports all of NP (verifiable by a polynomial-size circuit). On the other hand, our abstraction as HEC instead of HTDF enables us to instantiate the scheme based on a pairing assumption instead of lattices. In particular, it seems difficult to construct HTDF based on a pairing assumption.

Compact DV-NIZKs Based on Pairing-Free Groups. Here, we explain our constructions of compact DV-NIZKs. Actually, we give a generic compiler to convert any non-compact DV-NIZK to a compact one additionally assuming the existence of PKE and $\mathbf{NC}^1$-decryptable SKE with additive ciphertext overhead. In this overview, we discuss a specific instantiation based on the CDH assumption in pairing-free groups.

The starting point of our constructions is the recent construction of compact NIZKs in the preprocessing model (PP-NIZKs) by Katsumata et al. [47] based on inner-product functional encryptions (IPFE) [1].[4] PP-NIZK is a relaxation

---

[4] Actually, their construction is based on a variant of IPFE called IPFE on exponent (expIPFE). We note that their construction works with standard IPFE. They used

of (CRS, DV, DP)-NIZK where both the prover and the verifier are given proving and verification keys, respectively, which should be hidden from each other. Katsumata et al. first constructed a context-hiding homomorphic MAC for arithmetic circuits by adding the context-hiding property to the non-context-hiding homomorphic MAC of Catalano and Fiore [16] by using an IPFE. They then plugged the context-hiding homomorphic MAC into the generic conversion by Kim and Wu [51] to obtain PP-NIZKs.[5] Recall that in the PP-NIZK construction of Kim and Wu, a prover key consists of an SKE key $\mathbf{k}$ and a signature σ on $\mathbf{k}$, and a verification key consists of a verification key vk of a homomorphic MAC scheme. The reason why their scheme is PP-NIZK and not DV-NIZK is that a prover has to obtain a signature σ on $\mathbf{k}$ which should be generated by a trusted third party who has the corresponding signing key sk.[6] Similarly to the case of our CRS-NIZK explained in the previous section, we observe the following fact. If one can choose σ and vk in the reverse order, that is, if one can first choose the signature σ, and then define vk so that σ is a valid signature on $\mathbf{k}$, then we could modify the scheme to be a DV-NIZK by letting the prover choose $\mathbf{k}$ and σ on its own. Below, we observe that the homomorphic MAC of Katsumata et al. [47] indeed has this property. To explain this, we first recall the structure of their homomorphic MAC.

In their homomorphic MAC scheme, a verification key vk (which is also a signing key) consists of $s \xleftarrow{\$} \mathbb{Z}_p^*$, $\mathbf{r} \xleftarrow{\$} \mathbb{Z}_p^\ell$ and a decryption key of an IPFE corresponding to the vector $(s, \ldots, s^D) \in \mathbb{Z}_p^D$ where p is a sufficiently large prime, ℓ is the message length, and D is the degree of the arithmetic circuits supported by the homomorphic MAC scheme.[7] A signature on $\mathbf{k}$ is defined to be $\sigma := (\mathbf{r} - \mathbf{k}) \cdot s^{-1} \mod p$. From the form of σ, we can see that for any fixed $\mathbf{k}$ and s, one can set σ and $\mathbf{r}$ in the reverse order, that is, one can first pick σ and then set $\mathbf{r} := \mathbf{k} + \sigma \cdot s \mod p$.

Going back to the construction of NIZK, this structure enables us to get close to DV-NIZK. Namely, a prover can now choose $\mathbf{k}$ and σ by itself, and it no longer needs any proving key generated by a trusted third party. However, there is an important problem still remaining on how the verifier gets to know $\mathbf{r} = \mathbf{k} + \sigma \cdot s \mod p$, which is required for verification. Recall that $\mathbf{r}$ was part of the private verification key of the PP-NIZK of Kim and Wu. If s is given to a prover, then we cannot rely on unforgeability of the homomorphic MAC to prove soundness, and if the prover sends $\mathbf{k}$ and σ in the clear, then we cannot rely on the security of SKE to prove zero-knowledge. Therefore the prover has to transmit $\mathbf{r} = \mathbf{k} + \sigma \cdot s \mod p$ to the verifier without knowing s nor revealing

---

the notion of expIPFE instead of IPFE for making it possible to instantiate the scheme based on the DDH-based scheme by Agrawal, Libert, and Stehlé [4].

[5] Kim and Wu [51] showed that if one uses their generic conversion on homomorphic MACs instead of homomorphic signatures, it would result in PP-NIZKs instead of DP-NIZKs.

[6] In a homomorphic MAC, we can let sk := vk since both are kept private.

[7] We remark that we cannot include the master secret key of IPFE in vk since the context-hiding property should hold even against the verifier who sees vk.

$\mathbf{k}$ and $\boldsymbol{\sigma}$ to the verifier. We observe that this task can be done by using IPFE. Namely, we give a secret key corresponding to the vector $(1, s)$ of IPFE to the verifier as a part of his verification key, and a prover encrypts vectors (k_i, σ_i) for each $i \in [\ell]$ where k_i and σ_i are the i-th entry of $\mathbf{k}$ and $\boldsymbol{\sigma}$, respectively, and sends the ciphertexts as a part of the proof. Then a verifier can obtain $\mathbf{r} = \mathbf{k} + \boldsymbol{\sigma} \cdot s$ mod p by simply decrypting the IPFE ciphertexts with his decryption key.

Though the above idea seems to work at first glance, there is a problem that was also addressed in [47]. Namely, since a standard security notion of IPFE does not consider a malicious encryptor, an adversary may generate a malformed ciphertext whose decryption result is perfectly under his control, which breaks soundness. To prevent such an attack, Katsumata et al. [47] required a property called an *extractability* for an IPFE, which means that one can extract a corresponding message from any possibly malformed ciphertext if it does not decrypt to $\perp$. They then showed that the DDH-based IPFE scheme of Agrawal, Libert, and Stehlé [4] can be used as an extractable IPFE. However, unfortunately, we will not be able to simply plug in the extractable IPFE of Agrawal et al. into our DV-NIZK. This is because the IPFE of Agrawal et al. embeds the message into the exponent of a group element, and forces one to compute the discrete logarithm to decrypt. Therefore, unless we can be sure that the exponent will be small, the IPFE of Agrawal et al. is difficult to use. Here, the reason why the PP-NIZK of Katsumata et al. [47] did not face any issue with this somewhat awkward decryption algorithm was because the verification algorithm only consisted of checking whether the decryption result is equal to a certain value, which could be tested in the exponent, using the verification key $(s, \mathbf{r})$. However, in our case, the verifier must first decrypt $\mathbf{r}$ using the IPFE secret key corresponding to the vector $(1, s)$ to recover $\mathbf{r}$, and only then it can run the internal verification algorithm of [47] using the pair $(s, \mathbf{r})$. Notably, the verifier would have to solve the discrete logarithm for a random value in $\mathbb{Z}_p$ to recover the piece $\mathbf{r}$ of the verification key used in the PP-NIZK of Katsumata et al. However, obviously, there is no way to compute this efficiently. Therefore, in this work, we must take a different approach. Concretely, instead of relying on the extractability of IPFE, we require a prover to provide a proof that he has honestly generated ciphertexts by using another (non-compact) DV-NIZK. Here, since the validity check of IPFE ciphertexts can be done with computational complexity independent of the size of the language the prover really wants to prove, we can use a non-compact DV-NIZK for this part while keeping the whole proof size compact. In summary, we can convert the PP-NIZK of [47] to a DV-NIZK by adding ℓ IPFE ciphertexts along with their validity proof whose sizes are $\mathsf{poly}(\kappa)$. Since the proof size of the PP-NIZK of [47] is $|C| + \mathsf{poly}(\kappa)$, the proof size of the resulting DV-NIZK is also $|C| + \mathsf{poly}(\kappa)$. Moreover, we note that single-key secure IPFE suffices for the above construction of DV-NIZK. Since single-key secure functional encryption for all polynomial-sized functions exist under the existence of PKE [38] and DV-NIZK for all of **NP** exists under the CDH assumption on a pairing-free group [21,47,63], we can instantiate the above DV-NIZK based on the CDH assumption on a pairing-free group.[8] Finally, we note that by using the idea of the compact homomorphic MAC based on the ℓ-CDHI assumption by Catalano and Fiore [16], we can further reduce the proof size to be $|w| + \mathsf{poly}(\kappa)$ in the case when the language to be proven is computable in $\mathbf{NC}^1$.

Generic Construction of Prover-Efficient NIZK from LFE. To achieve prover-efficient NIZKs, we use laconic function evaluation (LFE) recently introduced by Quach, Wee, and Wichs [64]. LFE schemes are defined for a class of circuits $\mathcal{C}$. We can generate a short digest of circuit $C \in \mathcal{C}$ from a CRS and the circuit C. Anybody can then generate a ciphertext ct of a message m from the CRS, the digest, and m. Finally, anybody can decrypt the ciphertext to $C(m)$ using the ciphertext ct and the circuit C. Here, the security of LFE imposes that the ciphertext ct leaks no additional information other than the value $C(m)$. The attractive feature of LFE is that the size of the CRS, digest, ciphertext ct, and the running time of the encryption algorithm are all strictly smaller than the size of the circuits in $\mathcal{C}$.

Our design idea is to impose the computation of the circuit C computing the NP-relation on the verifier by using LFE. Specifically, we put a digest of C (and a CRS of LFE) in the CRS of our NIZK. The prover then computes an LFE ciphertext of message (x, w) where x is a statement and w is its witness using the digest of C. A verifier can check the validity of the statement by decrypting the ciphertext with C. By the security of LFE, the verifier obtains nothing beyond $C(x, w)$, hence, zero-knowledge of our NIZK follows naturally. Furthermore, by the efficiency property of LFE, the running time of the prover is smaller than the size of C. However, this basic idea is not yet sufficient. This is because a cheating prover may not honestly compute an LFE ciphertext of the message (x, w) and may possibly break soundness of our NIZK. To overcome this issue, a prover must generate not only an LFE ciphertext of (x, w) but also a NIZK proof to prove that the prover honestly generated the LFE ciphertext of (x, w) with the CRS of LFE and the digest of C. We point out that this additional NIZK proof does not harm prover efficiency since the additional statement which the prover must prove is independent of the size of the circuit C owing to the feature of LFE. In particular, we can check the validity of the ciphertext by computing the encryption circuit of LFE whose size is independent of the size of C.

Using any non-prover-efficient NIZK for $\mathbf{NP}$ as building block and instantiating the LFE scheme by the sub-exponential security of LWE assumption with sub-exponential modulus-to-noise ratio, we obtain a prover-efficient CRS-NIZK for $\mathbf{NP}$ whose prover running time is $\mathsf{poly}(\kappa, |x|, |w|, d)$, where d is the depth of the circuit C computing the $\mathbf{NP}$ relation. In particular, the prover running time is independent of $|C|$. In fact, we can further reduce the prover running time to be as small as $\tilde{O}(|x| + |w|) \cdot \mathsf{poly}(\kappa, d)$ where the dependence of the statement x and witness w size is only quasi-linear if we further use the following

---

[8] One may wonder why we only need CDH though [47] assumed DDH. Recall that the DDH in their construction comes from the necessity of an extractable expIPFE. We show that this can be replaced with any IPFE and DV-NIZK both of which exist under the CDH assumption based on the same idea as explained above.

two assumptions (1) the prover running time of the underlying NIZK is linear in the size of the circuit that computes the **NP** relation, that is, $|C| \cdot \mathsf{poly}(\kappa)$ (2) a natural variant of the above LWE assumption introduced by Quach et al. [64], called the *adaptive* LWE assumption. Note that the assumption we make on the underlying NIZK is not that strong, and in particular, we can use the NIZK of Groth, Ostrovsky, and Sahai [43].

1.4 Related Works

Other than CRS and DV-NIZKs, which have been the main interest of this paper, there are other variants of NIZKs. One is PP-NIZK and the other is DP-NIZK as we briefly mentioned in Sect. 1.3. Similarly to DV-NIZKs, due to the extra secret information shared by the prover and/or verifier, the soundness (resp. zero-knowledge) property of (PP, DP)-NIZKs may be compromised after verifying (resp. proving) multiple statements. In fact most of the PP or DP-NIZKs [22, 23, 26, 45, 49, 52] are known only to be secure for bounded statements. The first multi-theorem PP and DP-NIZKs (that are not a trivial downgrade of CRS-NIZKs) where given by Kim and Wu [51] who proposed a generic construction of them via homomorphic MACs and homomorphic signatures, respectively. Since homomorphic signatures were implied by lattice-based assumptions [39], this implied the first DP-NIZKs based on lattices. Subsequently, Katsumata et al. [47] constructed a homomorphic signature based on the CDHER assumption and a homomorphic MAC based on the DDH assumption over pairing-free groups, and thus constructed DP and PP-NIZKs relative to those assumptions. One attractive feature of the NIZKs of Kim and Wu [51] and Katsumata et al. [47] is that the proof size are compact: the DP-NIZK of [51] has proof size $|w| + \mathsf{poly}(\kappa, d)$ and the (PP, DP)-NIZK of [47] have proof size $|C| + \mathsf{poly}(\kappa)$, where d is the depth of the circuit C computing the **NP** relation.

2 Homomorphic Equivocal Commitment

2.1 Definition

We introduce a new primitive which we call homomorphic equivocal commitment (HEC), which can be seen as a relaxed variant of HTDF defined by Gorbunov et al. [39]. A HEC scheme with message space $\mathcal{X}$, randomness space $\mathcal{R}$, and a randomness distribution $\mathcal{D}_\mathcal{R}$ over $\mathcal{R}$ for a circuit class $\mathcal{C} = \{C : \mathcal{X} \to \mathcal{Z}\}$ consists of PPT algorithms (HEC.Setup, HEC.Commit, HEC.Open, HEC.Eval^{in}, HEC.Eval^{out}, HEC.Verify).

HEC.Setup(1^κ): The setup algorithm takes as input the security parameter 1^κ and outputs a public parameter pp, an evaluation key ek, and a master secret key msk.

HEC.Commit(pp, $\mathbf{x}$; R): The commit algorithm takes as input a public parameter pp and a message $\mathbf{x} \in \mathcal{X}$ along with a randomness $R \in \mathcal{R}$, and outputs a commitment com. When we omit R to denote HEC.Commit(pp, $\mathbf{x}$), we mean that R is chosen according to the distribution $\mathcal{D}_\mathcal{R}$.

HEC.Open(msk, $(\mathbf{x}, R), \mathbf{x}'$): The open algorithm takes as input a master secret key msk, a message $\mathbf{x} \in \mathcal{X}$, a randomness $R \in \mathcal{R}$, and a fake message $\mathbf{x}' \in \mathcal{X}$, and outputs a fake randomness $R' \in \mathcal{R}$.

HEC.Eval^{in}(ek, $C, \mathbf{x}, R$): The inner evaluation algorithm takes as input an evaluation key ek, a circuit $C \in \mathcal{C}$, a message $\mathbf{x} \in \mathcal{X}$, and a randomness $R \in \mathcal{R}$, and outputs a proof π.

HEC.Eval^{out}(ek, C, com): The outer evaluation algorithm is a deterministic algorithm that takes as input an evaluation key ek, a circuit $C \in \mathcal{C}$, and a commitment com, and outputs an evaluated commitment com_{eval}.

HEC.Verify(pp, $\text{com}_{\text{eval}}, z, \pi$): The verification algorithm takes as input a public parameter pp, an evaluated commitment com_{eval}, a message $z \in \mathcal{Z}$, and a proof π, and outputs $\top$ if the proof is valid and $\bot$ otherwise.

Evaluation Correctness. For all $\kappa \in \mathbb{Z}$, (pp, ek, msk) $\xleftarrow{\$}$ HEC.Setup(1^κ), $\mathbf{x} \in \mathcal{X}$, $R \in \mathcal{R}$, com := HEC.Commit(pp, $\mathbf{x}; R$), $C \in \mathcal{C}$, $\pi \xleftarrow{\$}$ HEC.Eval^{in}(msk, $C, \mathbf{x}, R$), and com_{eval} := HEC.Eval^{out}(ek, C, com), we have

$$\Pr[\text{HEC.Verify}(\text{pp}, \text{com}_{\text{eval}}, C(\mathbf{x}), \pi) = \top] = 1.$$

Distributional Equivalence of Open. We have

$$\{(\text{pp}, \text{ek}, \text{msk}, \mathbf{x}, R, \text{com})\} \overset{\text{stat}}{\approx} \{(\text{pp}, \text{ek}, \text{msk}, \mathbf{x}, R', \text{com}')\}$$

where (pp, ek, msk) $\xleftarrow{\$}$ HEC.Setup(1^κ), $(\mathbf{x}, \overline{\mathbf{x}}) \in \mathcal{X}^2$ are arbitrary random variables that may depend on (pp, ek, msk), $R \xleftarrow{\$} \mathcal{D}_\mathcal{R}$, com := HEC.Commit(pp, $\mathbf{x}; R$), $\overline{R} \xleftarrow{\$} \mathcal{D}_\mathcal{R}$, com' := HEC.Commit(pp, $\overline{\mathbf{x}}; \overline{R}$), and $R' \xleftarrow{\$}$ HEC.Open(msk, $(\overline{\mathbf{x}}, \overline{R}), \mathbf{x}$).

Computational Binding for Evaluated Commitment. For all PPT adversary $\mathcal{A}$,

$$\Pr\left[\begin{array}{l} \text{HEC.Verify}(\text{pp}, \text{com}_{\text{eval}}, z^*, \pi^*) = \top \\ z^* \neq C(\mathbf{x}) \end{array} \middle| \begin{array}{l} (\text{pp}, \text{ek}, \text{msk}) \xleftarrow{\$} \text{HEC.Setup}(1^\kappa), \\ (\mathbf{x}, R, C, z^*, \pi^*) \xleftarrow{\$} \mathcal{A}(\text{pp}, \text{ek}), \\ \text{com} := \text{HEC.Commit}(\text{pp}, \mathbf{x}; R) \\ \text{com}_{\text{eval}} := \text{HEC.Eval}^{out}(\text{ek}, C, \text{com}) \end{array} \right] \leq \text{negl}(\kappa).$$

Efficient Committing. There exists a polynomial poly such that for all (pp, ek, msk) $\xleftarrow{\$}$ HEC.Setup(1^κ), $\mathbf{x} \in \mathcal{X}$, $R \in \mathcal{R}$, the running time of com := HEC.Commit(pp, $\mathbf{x}; R$) is bounded by $|\mathbf{x}| \cdot \text{poly}(\kappa)$.

Efficient Verification (optional). There exists a polynomial poly such that for all (pp, ek, msk) $\xleftarrow{\$}$ HEC.Setup(1^κ), $\mathbf{x} \in \mathcal{X}$, $R \in \mathcal{R}$, com := HEC.Commit(pp, $\mathbf{x}; R$), $C \in \mathcal{C}$, $\pi \xleftarrow{\$}$ HEC.Eval^{in}(ek, $C, \mathbf{x}, R$), com_{eval} := HEC.Eval^{out}(ek, C, com), and $z \in \mathcal{Z}$, we have $|\pi| \leq \text{poly}(\kappa)$ and $|\text{com}_{\text{eval}}| \leq \text{poly}(\kappa)$ and the running time of HEC.Verify(pp, $\text{com}_{\text{eval}}, z, \pi$) is at most $\text{poly}(\kappa)$. We remark that poly does not depend on C.

Context-Hiding (optional). There exists a PPT simulator HEC.ProofSim such that for all $\kappa \in \mathbb{N}$, $(\mathsf{pp}, \mathsf{ek}, \mathsf{msk}) \xleftarrow{\$} \mathsf{HEC.Setup}(1^\kappa)$, $\mathbf{x} \in \mathcal{X}$, $C \in \mathcal{C}$, $R \in \mathcal{R}$, and $\mathsf{com} := \mathsf{HEC.Commit}(\mathsf{pp}, \mathbf{x}; R)$, we have

$$\{\pi \xleftarrow{\$} \mathsf{HEC.Eval}^{in}(\mathsf{ek}, C, \mathbf{x}, R))\} \stackrel{\mathrm{stat}}{\approx} \{\pi' \xleftarrow{\$} \mathsf{HEC.ProofSim}(\mathsf{msk}, \mathsf{com}, C, C(\mathbf{x})))\}$$

where the probability is only over the randomness used by the algorithms $\mathsf{HEC.Eval}^{in}$ and $\mathsf{HEC.ProofSim}$.

Remark 2.1. We can generically convert any HEC scheme to a context-hiding one by using any statistical CRS-NIZK scheme. Namely, instead of directly using π as an output of the inner evaluation algorithm, it outputs a NIZK proof for the statement that there exists π that passes the verification.

Remark 2.2. The following properties immediately follow from the distributional equivalence of open.

Equivocality. We have

$$\Pr[\mathsf{HEC.Commit}(\mathsf{pp}, \overline{\mathbf{x}}; \overline{R}) \neq \mathsf{HEC.Commit}(\mathsf{pp}, \mathbf{x}; R)] = \mathsf{negl}(\kappa)$$

where $(\mathsf{pp}, \mathsf{ek}, \mathsf{msk}) \xleftarrow{\$} \mathsf{HEC.Setup}(1^\kappa)$, $(\mathbf{x}, \overline{\mathbf{x}}) \in \mathcal{X}^2$ are arbitrary random variables that may depend on $(\mathsf{pp}, \mathsf{ek}, \mathsf{msk})$, $\overline{R} \xleftarrow{\$} \mathcal{D}_\mathcal{R}$, and $R \xleftarrow{\$} \mathsf{HEC.Open}(\mathsf{msk}, (\overline{\mathbf{x}}, \overline{R}), \mathbf{x})$.

Hiding. We have

$$\{\mathsf{pp}, \mathsf{ek}, \mathsf{com} \xleftarrow{\$} \mathsf{HEC.Commit}(\mathsf{pp}, \mathbf{x})\} \stackrel{\mathrm{stat}}{\approx} \{\mathsf{pp}, \mathsf{ek}, \mathsf{com}' \xleftarrow{\$} \mathsf{HEC.Commit}(\mathsf{pp}, \mathbf{x}')\},$$

where $(\mathsf{pp}, \mathsf{ek}, \mathsf{msk}) \xleftarrow{\$} \mathsf{HEC.Setup}(1^\kappa)$ and $(\mathbf{x}, \mathbf{x}') \in \mathcal{X}^2$ are arbitrary random variables that may depend on $(\mathsf{pp}, \mathsf{ek}, \mathsf{msk})$. We say that a scheme is computationally hiding if the above two distributions are computationally indistinguishable.

Remark 2.3. If we require neither efficient verification nor context-hiding, then there is a trivial construction of HEC based on any equivocal commitment. Namely, we can just set $\mathsf{com}_{\mathsf{eval}} := C\|\mathsf{com}$ and $\pi := (\mathbf{x}, R)$. The verification algorithm can verify them by checking if com is a commitment of $\mathbf{x}$ with randomness R and $z = C(\mathbf{x})$ holds. On the other hand, if we require either of efficient verification or context hiding, then there does not seem to be such a trivial solution.[9] This is reminiscent of the similar situation for fully homomorphic encryption where a scheme without compactness nor function privacy is trivial to construct but a scheme with either of them is non-trivial [31].

---

[9] As remarked in Remark 2.1, we can convert the trivial construction to a context-hiding one additionally assuming a statistical CRS-NIZK for all of **NP**. Though this is less interesting than schemes with efficient verification, we do not consider it a "trivial solution" since the existence of a statistical CRS-NIZK is an additional assumption to an equivocal commitment.

2.2 Constructions of HEC

Here, we show that we can construct an HEC scheme based on a non-static falsifiable pairing assumption called the (n, m)-computational Diffie-Hellman exponent ratio (CDHER) assumption [47].

(n, m)-**Computational Diffie-Hellman Exponent and Ratio Assumption.** Let BGGen be a PPT algorithm that on input 1^κ returns a description $\mathcal{G} = (\mathbb{G}, \mathbb{G}_T, p, g, e(\cdot, \cdot))$ of symmetric pairing groups where $\mathbb{G}$ and $\mathbb{G}_T$ are cyclic groups of prime order p, g is the generator of $\mathbb{G}$, and $e : \mathbb{G} \times \mathbb{G} \to \mathbb{G}_T$ is an efficiently computable (non-degenerate) bilinear map.

Definition 2.1 ((n, m)-Computational Diffie-Hellman Exponent and Ratio Assumption) [47]. *Let* BGGen *be a group generator and* $n := n(\kappa) = \mathsf{poly}(\kappa)$, $m := m(\kappa) = \mathsf{poly}(\kappa)$. *We say that the* (n, m)-*decisional Diffie-Hellman exponent and ratio (CDHER) assumption holds with respect to* BGGen, *if for all PPT adversaries* $\mathcal{A}$, *we have*

$$\Pr\left[\mathcal{A}(\mathcal{G}, \Psi) \to e(g, g)^{sa^{m+1}}\right] = \mathsf{negl}(\kappa)$$

where $\mathcal{G} = (\mathbb{G}, \mathbb{G}_T, p, g, e(\cdot, \cdot)) \xleftarrow{\$} \mathsf{BGGen}(1^\lambda)$, $s, a, b_1, \ldots, b_n, c_1, \ldots c_n \xleftarrow{\$} \mathbb{Z}_p^*$, *and*

$$\Phi := \begin{pmatrix} \left\{g^{a^j}\right\}_{j \in [m]}, & \left\{g^{c_i}\right\}_{i \in [n]}, & \left\{g^{a^j/b_i}\right\}_{\substack{i \in [n], j \in [2m] \\ j \neq m+1}}, & \left\{g^{a^{m+1}c_{i'}/b_i c_i}\right\}_{i, i' \in [n], i \neq i'}, \\ & \left\{g^{ac_i}\right\}_{i \in [n]}, & \left\{g^{a^j/b_i c_i}\right\}_{i \in [n], j \in [2m+1]}, & \left\{g^{a^j c_{i'}/b_i}\right\}_{i, i' \in [n], j \in [m]}, \\ g^s, & \left\{g^{sb_i}\right\}_{i \in [n]}, & \left\{g^{sa^{m+1}b_i/b_{i'}c_{i'}}\right\}_{i, i' \in [n], i \neq i'}, & \left\{g^{sa^j b_i/b_{i'}}\right\}_{\substack{i, i' \in [n], j \in [m] \\ i \neq i'}} \end{pmatrix}.$$

Katsumata et al. showed that the CDHER assumption holds on the generic group model introduced by Shoup [68].

Construction of HEC Based on CDHER Assumption. We show the following theorem.

Theorem 2.1. *If the* (n, m)-*CDHER assumption holds on a pairing group for all* $n = \mathsf{poly}(\kappa)$ *and* $m = \mathsf{poly}(\kappa)$, *then there exists an HEC scheme that supports* $\mathbf{NC^1}$ *that satisfies evaluation correctness, distributional equivalence of open, computational binding for evaluated commitments, efficient committing, efficient verification, and context-hiding.*

The construction is obtained by a tweak to the homomorphic signature scheme by Katsumata et al. [47] as explained in Sect. 1.3. The full description of the construction and its security proof can be found in the full version.

In the full version, we also show that we can construct a context-hiding HEC scheme *without efficient verification* based on the weaker CDH assumption on a pairing group. Though this is not useful for constructing compact NIZKs as is done in Sect. 3, this can be used for constructing (non-compact) context-hiding homomorphic signature scheme as shown in the full version.

3   Compact CRS-NIZK from HEC

Here, we give a construction of a compact CRS-NIZK scheme based on any non-compact CRS-NIZK scheme and HEC with efficient verification. If we instantiate the construction with the HEC given in Sect. 2.2, then the proof size of the resulting CRS-NIZK scheme is $|C| + \mathsf{poly}(\kappa)$. Moreover, if the relation supported by the scheme is verifiable in $\mathbf{NC}^1$, then the proof size is $|w| + \mathsf{poly}(\kappa)$.

3.1   Extractable CRS-NIZK

First, we define extractability for CRS-NIZK, which is needed for our construction of compact CRS-NIZK scheme. We note that the extractability defined here is a mild property, and we can convert any CRS-NIZK scheme to the one with extractability if we additionally assume the existence of PKE as shown in Lemma 3.1.

An extractable CRS-NIZK is a CRS-NIZK with an additional deterministic algorithm Extract which takes as input a randomness r_{Setup} used in Setup and a proof π, and outputs a witness w that satisfies the following.

Extractability. For all PPT adversary $\mathcal{A}$, we have

$$\Pr\left[\begin{array}{c} \mathsf{Verify}(\mathsf{crs}, x, \pi) = \top \\ (x, w) \notin \mathcal{R} \end{array} \middle| \begin{array}{c} \mathsf{crs} \xleftarrow{\$} \mathsf{Setup}(1^\kappa) \\ (x, \pi) \xleftarrow{\$} \mathcal{A}(\mathsf{crs}) \\ w \xleftarrow{\$} \mathsf{Extract}(r_{\mathsf{Setup}}, \pi) \end{array}\right] \leq \mathsf{negl}(\kappa).$$

where r_{Setup} is the randomness used in Setup to generate crs.

The following lemma is easy to prove. The proof can be found in the full version.

Lemma 3.1. *If there exist CRS-NIZK for all of **NP** and a CPA-secure PKE scheme, then there exists CRS-NIZK for all of **NP** with extractability.*

3.2   Construction of Compact CRS-NIZK

Before describing the construction, we prepare some building blocks and notations.

- Let $\mathcal{L}$ be an **NP** language defined by a relation $\mathcal{R} \subseteq \{0,1\}^* \times \{0,1\}^*$. Let $n(\kappa)$ and $m(\kappa)$ be any fixed polynomials. Let C be a circuit that computes the relation $\mathcal{R}$ on $\{0,1\}^n \times \{0,1\}^m$, i.e., for $(x, w) \in \{0,1\}^n \times \{0,1\}^m$, we have $C(x, w) = 1$ if and only if $(x, w) \in \mathcal{R}$.
- Let $\Pi_{\mathsf{SKE}} = (\mathsf{SKE.KeyGen}, \mathsf{SKE.Enc}, \mathsf{SKE.Dec})$ be a symmetric key encryption (SKE) scheme with ciphertext space $\mathcal{CT}$ and key space $\{0,1\}^\ell$.

In the following, for $x \in \{0,1\}^n$ and $\mathsf{ct} \in \mathcal{CT}$, we define the function

$$f_{x,\mathsf{ct}}(K) := C(x, \mathsf{SKE.Dec}(K, \mathsf{ct})).$$

- Let Π_{HEC} = (HEC.Setup, HEC.Commit, HEC.Open, HEC.Eval^{in}, HEC.Eval^{out}, HEC.Verify) be a HEC scheme with the message space that contains $\{0,1\}^{\ell}$ and randomness space $\mathcal{R}$ on which a distribution $\mathcal{D}_{\mathcal{R}}$ is defined. We need the HEC scheme to support a function class containing $\{f_{x,\mathsf{ct}}\}_{x \in \{0,1\}^n, \mathsf{ct} \in \mathcal{CT}}$.
- Let Π_{CRSNIZK} = (Setup, Prove, Verify) be an extractable CRS-NIZK for the language corresponding to the relation $\widetilde{\mathcal{R}}$ defined below:
  $((\mathsf{pp}, \mathsf{com}, \mathsf{com}_{\mathsf{eval}}), (K, R, \pi_{\mathsf{HEC}})) \in \widetilde{\mathcal{R}}$ if and only if the followings are satisfied:
  1. $K \in \{0,1\}^{\ell}$,
  2. HEC.Commit$(\mathsf{pp}, K; R) = \mathsf{com}$,
  3. HEC.Verify$(\mathsf{pp}, \mathsf{com}_{\mathsf{eval}}, 1, \pi_{\mathsf{HEC}}) = \top$.

  We note that extractable CRS-NIZK for all of **NP** exists assuming (non-extractable) CRS-NIZK for all of **NP** and CPA secure PKE as shown in Lemma 3.1.

The CRS-NIZK Π'_{CRSNIZK} = (Setup', Prove', Verify') for $\mathcal{L}$ is described as follows.

Setup'(1^{κ}): This algorithm generates crs $\xleftarrow{\$}$ Setup(1^{κ}) and $(\mathsf{pp}, \mathsf{ek}, \mathsf{msk}), \xleftarrow{\$}$ HEC.Setup(1^{κ}). It outputs a common reference string crs' $= (\mathsf{crs}, \mathsf{pp}, \mathsf{ek})$.

Prove'(crs', x, w): This algorithm aborts if $\mathcal{R}(x, w) = 0$. Otherwise it parses $(\mathsf{crs}, \mathsf{pp}, \mathsf{ek}) \leftarrow \mathsf{crs}'$, picks $K \xleftarrow{\$}$ SKE.KeyGen(1^{κ}) and $R \xleftarrow{\$} \mathcal{D}_{\mathcal{R}}$, computes ct $\xleftarrow{\$}$ SKE.Enc(K, w), generates com := HEC.Commit$(\mathsf{pp}, K; R)$, $\pi_{\mathsf{HEC}} \xleftarrow{\$}$ HEC.Eval$^{in}(\mathsf{ek}, f_{x,\mathsf{ct}}, K, R)$, $\mathsf{com}_{\mathsf{eval}}$:= HEC.Eval$^{out}(\mathsf{ek}, f_{x,\mathsf{ct}}, \mathsf{com})$, and $\pi_{\mathsf{NIZK}} \xleftarrow{\$}$ Prove$(\mathsf{crs}, (\mathsf{pp}, \mathsf{com}, \mathsf{com}_{\mathsf{eval}}), (K, R, \pi_{\mathsf{HEC}}))$, and outputs a proof $\pi' := (\mathsf{ct}, \mathsf{com}, \pi_{\mathsf{NIZK}})$.

Verify'(crs', x, π'): This algorithm parses $(\mathsf{crs}, \mathsf{pp}, \mathsf{ek}) \leftarrow \mathsf{crs}'$ and $(\mathsf{ct}, \mathsf{com}, \pi_{\mathsf{NIZK}}) \leftarrow \pi'$, computes $\mathsf{com}_{\mathsf{eval}}$:= HEC.Eval$^{out}(\mathsf{ek}, f_{x,\mathsf{ct}}, \mathsf{com})$, and outputs $\top$ if Verify$(\mathsf{crs}, (\mathsf{pp}, \mathsf{com}, \mathsf{com}_{\mathsf{eval}}), \pi_{\mathsf{NIZK}}) = \top$, and outputs $\bot$ otherwise.

Correctness. Suppose that $(\mathsf{ct}, \mathsf{com}, \pi_{\mathsf{NIZK}})$ is an honestly generated proof on $(x, w) \in \mathcal{R}$. Then we have ct $\xleftarrow{\$}$ SKE.Enc(K, w) and com = HEC.Commit$(\mathsf{pp}, K; R)$ with some K and R. By the correctness of Π_{SKE}, we have $f_{x,\mathsf{ct}}(K) = 1$, and by the correctness of Π_{HEC}, we have HEC.Verify$(\mathsf{pp}, \mathsf{com}_{\mathsf{eval}}, 1, \pi_{\mathsf{HEC}}) = \top$ where we generate $\mathsf{com}_{\mathsf{eval}}$:= HEC.Eval$^{out}(\mathsf{ek}, f_{x,\mathsf{ct}}, \mathsf{com})$ and $\pi_{\mathsf{HEC}} \xleftarrow{\$}$ HEC.Eval$^{in}(\mathsf{ek}, f_{x,\mathsf{ct}}, K, R)$. Since we have $((\mathsf{pp}, \mathsf{com}, \mathsf{com}_{\mathsf{eval}}), (K, R, \pi_{\mathsf{HEC}})) \in \widetilde{\mathcal{R}}$, if we generate $\pi_{\mathsf{NIZK}} \xleftarrow{\$}$ Prove$(\mathsf{crs}, (\mathsf{pp}, \mathsf{com}, \mathsf{com}_{\mathsf{eval}}), (K, R, \pi_{\mathsf{HEC}}))$, then we have Verify$(\mathsf{crs}, (\mathsf{pp}, \mathsf{com}, \mathsf{com}_{\mathsf{eval}}), \pi_{\mathsf{NIZK}}) = \top$ by the correctness of Π_{CRSNIZK}.

Security. The security of NIZK' is stated as follows. The proofs can be found in the full version.

Theorem 3.1 (Soundness). *If Π_{CRSNIZK} satisfies extractability and HEC satisfies computational binding for evaluated commitment, then Π'_{CRSNIZK} satisfies computational soundness.*

Theorem 3.2 (Zero-knowledge). *If Π_{CRSNIZK} satisfies zero-knowledge, HEC is computationally hiding,[10] and SKE is CPA secure, then Π'_{CRSNIZK} satisfies zero-knowledge.*

3.3 Instantiations

Here, we discuss that by appropriately instantiating Π_{CRSNIZK}, we can achieve compact proof size. In particular, we consider instantiating the HEC scheme with our construction in Sect. 2.2. Since our HEC scheme only supports $\mathbf{NC}^1$ circuits, we have to ensure that $f_{x,\mathsf{ct}}$ is computable in $\mathbf{NC}^1$. For ensuring this, we use the fact that any efficiently verifiable relation can be verified in $\mathbf{NC}^1$ at the cost of making the witness size as large as the size of a circuit that verifies the relation (e.g., [29]). This is done by considering all values corresponding to all gates when computing the circuit on input (x, w) to be the new witness. In addition, we use an SKE scheme whose decryption circuit is in $\mathbf{NC}^1$ with additive ciphertext overhead (i.e., the ciphertext length is the message length plus $\mathsf{poly}(\kappa)$) and the key size $\ell = \kappa$, which exists under the CDH assumption [47]. Then $f_{x,\mathsf{ct}}$ is computable in $\mathbf{NC}^1$ for every x and ct. In this case, we have that $|\mathsf{ct}| \leq |C| + \mathsf{poly}(\kappa)$. In order to bound the length of the proof π', we also bound $|\mathsf{com}|$ and $|\pi_{\mathsf{NIZK}}|$. By the efficient committing property of HEC, $|\mathsf{com}|$ and the size of the circuit computing HEC.Commit is bounded by $|K| \cdot \mathsf{poly}(\kappa) \leq \mathsf{poly}(\kappa)$. Furthermore, by the efficient verification property of HEC, the size of the circuit computing HEC.Verify is bounded by $\mathsf{poly}(\kappa)$. Therefore, the size of the circuit computing $\widetilde{\mathcal{R}}$ is bounded by $\mathsf{poly}(\kappa)$, which implies that $|\pi_{\mathsf{NIZK}}|$ is bounded by $\mathsf{poly}(\kappa)$ as well (even if Π_{CRSNIZK} is non-compact). To sum up, we have that the proof size of Π_{CRSNIZK} is $|C| + \mathsf{poly}(\kappa)$. Moreover, if we only consider a relation computable in $\mathbf{NC}^1$ in the first place, then we need not expand the witness, and the proof size can be further reduced to be $|w| + \mathsf{poly}(\kappa)$. Finally, we remark that (non-compact) CRS-NIZK for all of $\mathbf{NP}$ exists under the CDH assumption on a pairing group [3,14], which in particular holds under the CDHER assumption. In summary, we obtain the following corollary.

Corollary 3.1. *If the CDHER assumption holds on a pairing group, then there exists CRS-NIZK for all of $\mathbf{NP}$ with proof size $|C| + \mathsf{poly}(\kappa)$. Moreover, if the corresponding relation is computable in $\mathbf{NC}^1$, then the proof size is $|w| + \mathsf{poly}(\kappa)$.*

Variant with Sublinear Proof Size. Katsumata et al. [47] showed that their DP-NIZK achieves sublinear proof size i.e., $|w| + |C|/\log \kappa + \mathsf{poly}(\kappa)$ if C is a leveled circuit [11] whose gates are divided into L levels, and all incoming wires to a gate of level $i + 1$ come from gates of level i. Exactly the same idea can be applied to our CRS-NIZK to achieve sublinear proof size. More detailed explanation can be found in the full version. Namely, we obtain the following corollary:

---

[10] Recall that the computational hiding (or even statistical hiding) follows from the distributional equivalence of open.

Corollary 3.2. *If the CDHER assumption holds on a pairing group, then there exists CRS-NIZK for all **NP** languages whose corresponding relation is computable by a leveled circuit with proof size* $|w| + |C|/\log \kappa + \mathsf{poly}(\kappa)$.

Variant with UC-Security. We can modify the above scheme to satisfy the UC security in the non-erasure adaptive setting. Namely, we can show the following theorem. The proof can be found in the full version.

Theorem 3.3. *If the DLIN assumption and the CDHER assumption hold in a bilinear group, then for any relation* $\mathcal{R}$ *that is computable in* $\mathbf{NC^1}$*, there exists a UC-secure NIZK scheme for* $\mathcal{R}$ *tolerating an adaptive, malicious adversary.*

4   Compact DV-NIZK

4.1   Preliminaries

Lemma 4.1 *(Implicit in [47]). Let* C *be a boolean circuit that computes a relation* $\mathcal{R}$ *on* $\{0,1\}^n \times \{0,1\}^m$*, i.e., for* $(x,w) \in \{0,1\}^n \times \{0,1\}^m$*, we have* $C(x,w) = 1$ *if and only if* $(x,w) \in \mathcal{R}$*, and* p *be an integer larger than* $|C|$*. Then there exists a deterministic algorithm* $\mathsf{Exp}_{C,x}$ *and an arithmetic circuit* $\tilde{C}$ *on* $\mathbb{Z}_p$ *with degree at most 3 such that we have*

- $|\mathsf{Exp}_{C,x}(w)| = |C(x,\cdot)|$ *for all* $w \in \{0,1\}^m$*.*
- *If* $C(x,w) = 1$*, then we have* $\tilde{C}(x, \mathsf{Exp}_{C,x}(w)) = 1 \mod p$*.*
- *For any* $x \in \{0,1\}^n$*, if there does not exist* $w \in \{0,1\}^m$ *such that* $C(x,w) = 1$*, then there does not exist* $w' \in \{0,1\}^{|C(x,\cdot)|}$ *such that* $\tilde{C}(x,w') = 1 \mod p$

Lemma 4.2 *([47]). There exists a deterministic polynomial-time algorithm* Coefficient *that satisfies the following: for any* $p \in \mathbb{N}$*, arithmetic circuit* f *over* $\mathbb{Z}_p$ *of degree* D*,* $\mathbf{x} = (x_1,\ldots,x_\ell) \in \mathbb{Z}_p^\ell$ *and* $\boldsymbol{\sigma} = (\sigma_1,\ldots,\sigma_\ell) \in \mathbb{Z}_p^\ell$*,* Coefficient$(1^D, p, f, \mathbf{x}, \boldsymbol{\sigma})$ *outputs* $(c_1,\ldots,c_D) \in \mathbb{Z}_p^D$ *such that*

$$f(\sigma_1 Z + x_1,\ldots,\sigma_\ell Z + x_\ell) = f(x_1,\ldots,x_\ell) + \sum_{j=1}^{D} c_j Z^j \mod p. \qquad (1)$$

where Z *is an indeterminate.*

4.2   Construction

Here, we give a generic construction of compact DV-NIZK. Namely, we construct DV-NIZK with the proof size $|C| + \mathsf{poly}(\kappa)$ from any (non-compact) DV-NIZK, SKE scheme whose decryption circuit is in $\mathbf{NC^1}$ with additive ciphertext overhead, and PKE scheme. First, we prepare notations and the building blocks.

- Let $\mathcal{L}$ be an **NP** language defined by a relation $\mathcal{R} \subseteq \{0,1\}^* \times \{0,1\}^*$. Let $n(\kappa)$ and $m(\kappa)$ be any fixed polynomials. Let C be a circuit that computes the relation $\mathcal{R}$ on $\{0,1\}^n \times \{0,1\}^m$, i.e., for $(x,w) \in \{0,1\}^n \times \{0,1\}^m$, we have $C(x,w) = 1$ if and only if $(x,w) \in \mathcal{R}$. Let $\mathsf{Exp}_{C,x}$ and $\tilde{C}$ be as defined in Lemma 4.1.

- Let $\Pi_{\mathsf{IPFE}} = (\mathsf{IPFE.Setup}, \mathsf{IPFE.KeyGen}, \mathsf{IPFE.Enc}, \mathsf{IPFE.Dec})$ be an adaptively single-key secure IPFE scheme with a prime modulus $p > |C|$. Such an IPFE scheme can be constructed from any PKE scheme [38].
- Let $\Pi_{\mathsf{SKE}} = (\mathsf{SKE.KeyGen}, \mathsf{SKE.Enc}, \mathsf{SKE.Dec})$ be a CPA-secure symmetric key encryption scheme over a ciphertext space $\mathcal{CT}$ and a key space $\{0,1\}^{\ell}$ with additive ciphertext overhead (i.e., the ciphertext size is the message size plus $\mathsf{poly}(\kappa)$) whose decryption algorithm is computed in $\mathbf{NC}^1$. Especially, the decryption circuit can be expressed by an arithmetic circuit over $\mathbb{Z}_p$ of degree $\mathsf{poly}(\kappa)$. We note that such an SKE scheme exists under the CDH assumption [47].
- For $x \in \{0,1\}^n$ and $\mathsf{ct} \in \mathcal{CT}$, we define the function $f_{x,\mathsf{ct}}(K) := \tilde{C}(x, \mathsf{SKE.Dec}(K, \mathsf{ct}))$. Let D be the maximal degree of $f_{x,\mathsf{ct}}$ (as a multivariate polynomial). Since $\tilde{C}$'s degree is at most 3 and $\mathsf{SKE.Dec}(\cdot, \mathsf{ct})$'s degree is $\mathsf{poly}(\kappa)$, we have $D = \mathsf{poly}(\kappa)$ (which especially does not depend on $|C|$).
- Let $\Pi_{\mathsf{DVNIZK}} = (\mathsf{Setup}, \mathsf{Prove}, \mathsf{Verify})$ be DV-NIZK for the language corresponding to the relation $\tilde{\mathcal{R}}$ defined below:

$$\left((\mathsf{pp}_{\mathsf{IPFE}}, \{\mathsf{ct}^i_{\mathsf{IPFE}}\}_{i\in[\ell]}, \mathsf{pp}'_{\mathsf{IPFE}}, \mathsf{ct}'_{\mathsf{IPFE}}), \; (\{(K_i, \sigma_i, R_i)\}_{i\in[\ell]}, (c_1, \ldots, c_D, R')) \right) \in \tilde{\mathcal{R}}$$

if and only if the following conditions are satisfied:
1. For all $i \in [\ell]$, $K_i \in \{0,1\}$,
2. For all $i \in [\ell]$, $\mathsf{IPFE.Enc}(\mathsf{pp}_{\mathsf{IPFE}}, (K_i, \sigma_i); R_i) = \mathsf{ct}^i_{\mathsf{IPFE}}$,
3. $\mathsf{IPFE.Enc}(\mathsf{pp}'_{\mathsf{IPFE}}, (c_1, \ldots, c_D); R') = \mathsf{ct}'_{\mathsf{IPFE}}$.

The DV-NIZK $\Pi'_{\mathsf{DVNIZK}} = (\mathsf{Setup}', \mathsf{Prove}', \mathsf{Verify}')$ for $\mathcal{L}$ is described as follows.

$\mathsf{Setup}'(1^\kappa)$: This algorithm picks $s \xleftarrow{\$} \mathbb{Z}_p^*$ and generates $(\mathsf{crs}, k_\mathsf{V}) \xleftarrow{\$}$ $\mathsf{Setup}(1^\kappa)$, $(\mathsf{pp}_{\mathsf{IPFE}}, \mathsf{msk}_{\mathsf{IPFE}}) \xleftarrow{\$} \mathsf{IPFE.Setup}(1^\kappa, 1^2)$, $(\mathsf{pp}'_{\mathsf{IPFE}}, \mathsf{msk}'_{\mathsf{IPFE}}) \xleftarrow{\$}$ $\mathsf{IPFE.Setup}(1^\kappa, 1^D)$, $\mathsf{sk}_{\mathsf{IPFE}} \xleftarrow{\$} \mathsf{IPFE.KeyGen}(\mathsf{msk}_{\mathsf{IPFE}}, (1, s))$, and $\mathsf{sk}'_{\mathsf{IPFE}} \xleftarrow{\$}$ $\mathsf{IPFE.KeyGen}(\mathsf{msk}'_{\mathsf{IPFE}}, (s, \ldots, s^D))$. It outputs a common reference string $\mathsf{crs}' := (\mathsf{crs}, \mathsf{pp}_{\mathsf{IPFE}}, \mathsf{pp}'_{\mathsf{IPFE}})$ and a verifier key $k'_\mathsf{V} := (k_\mathsf{V}, s, \mathsf{sk}_{\mathsf{IPFE}}, \mathsf{sk}'_{\mathsf{IPFE}})$.

$\mathsf{Prove}'(\mathsf{crs}', x, w)$: This algorithm aborts if $(x, w) \notin \mathcal{R}$. Otherwise it parses $(\mathsf{crs}, \mathsf{pp}_{\mathsf{IPFE}}, \mathsf{pp}'_{\mathsf{IPFE}}) \leftarrow \mathsf{crs}'$, picks $K \xleftarrow{\$} \mathsf{SKE.KeyGen}(1^\kappa)$ and $\sigma_i \xleftarrow{\$}$ $\mathbb{Z}_p$ for $i \in [\ell]$, and generates $\mathsf{ct}_{\mathsf{SKE}} \xleftarrow{\$} \mathsf{SKE.Enc}(K, \mathsf{Exp}_{C,x}(w))$ and $(c_1, \ldots, c_D) \leftarrow \mathsf{Coefficient}(1^D, p, f_{x, \mathsf{ct}_{\mathsf{SKE}}}, K = (K_1, \ldots, K_\ell), (\sigma_1, \ldots, \sigma_\ell))$. Then it generates $\mathsf{ct}^i_{\mathsf{IPFE}} := \mathsf{IPFE.Enc}(\mathsf{pp}_{\mathsf{IPFE}}, (K_i, \sigma_i); R_i)$ for $i \in [\ell]$ (where R_i is the randomness used by the encryption algorithm), $\mathsf{ct}'_{\mathsf{IPFE}} := \mathsf{IPFE.Enc}(\mathsf{pp}'_{\mathsf{IPFE}}, (c_1, \ldots, c_D); R')$ (where R' is the randomness used by the encryption algorithm), and $\pi \xleftarrow{\$} \mathsf{Prove}$ $(\mathsf{crs}, (\mathsf{pp}_{\mathsf{IPFE}}, \{\mathsf{ct}^i_{\mathsf{IPFE}}\}_{i\in[\ell]}, \mathsf{pp}'_{\mathsf{IPFE}}, \mathsf{ct}'_{\mathsf{IPFE}}), (\{(K_i, \sigma_i, R_i)\}_{i\in[\ell]}, (c_1, \ldots, c_D, R')))$ and outputs a proof $\pi' := (\pi, \mathsf{ct}_{\mathsf{SKE}}, \{\mathsf{ct}^i_{\mathsf{IPFE}}\}_{i\in[\ell]}, \mathsf{ct}'_{\mathsf{IPFE}})$.

$\mathsf{Verify}'(\mathsf{crs}', k'_\mathsf{V}, x, \pi')$: This algorithm parses $(\mathsf{crs}, \mathsf{pp}_{\mathsf{IPFE}}, \mathsf{pp}'_{\mathsf{IPFE}}) \leftarrow \mathsf{crs}'$, $(k_\mathsf{V}, s, \mathsf{sk}_{\mathsf{IPFE}}, \mathsf{sk}'_{\mathsf{IPFE}}) \leftarrow k'_\mathsf{V}$, and $(\pi, \mathsf{ct}_{\mathsf{SKE}}, \{\mathsf{ct}^i_{\mathsf{IPFE}}\}_{i\in[\ell]}, \mathsf{ct}'_{\mathsf{IPFE}}) \leftarrow \pi'$, computes $r_i \xleftarrow{\$} \mathsf{IPFE.Dec}(\mathsf{pp}_{\mathsf{IPFE}}, \mathsf{ct}^i_{\mathsf{IPFE}}, \mathsf{sk}_{\mathsf{IPFE}})$ for $i \in [\ell]$ and $t \xleftarrow{\$} \mathsf{IPFE.Dec}$

$(pp'_{\mathsf{IPFE}}, ct'_{\mathsf{IPFE}}, sk'_{\mathsf{IPFE}})$, and outputs $\top$ if we have $\mathsf{Verify}(crs, (pp_{\mathsf{IPFE}}, \{ct^i_{\mathsf{IPFE}}\}_{i\in[\ell]},$
$pp'_{\mathsf{IPFE}}, ct'_{\mathsf{IPFE}}), \pi) = \top$ and

$$f_{x,ct_{\mathsf{SKE}}}(r_1, \ldots, r_\ell) = 1 + t \mod p,$$

and outputs $\bot$ otherwise.

Correctness. Suppose that $(\pi, ct_{\mathsf{SKE}}, \{ct^i_{\mathsf{IPFE}}\}_{i\in[\ell]}, ct'_{\mathsf{IPFE}})$ is an honestly generated proof on $(x, w) \in \mathcal{R}$. Then it is clear that we have $\mathsf{Verify}(crs, (pp_{\mathsf{IPFE}}, \{ct^i_{\mathsf{IPFE}}\}_{i\in[\ell]}, pp'_{\mathsf{IPFE}}, ct'_{\mathsf{IPFE}}), \pi) = \top$ by the way of generating the proof and the correctness of Π_{DVNIZK}. By the way of generating $(\{ct^i_{\mathsf{IPFE}}\}_{i\in[\ell]}, ct'_{\mathsf{IPFE}})$ and correctness of Π_{IPFE}, we have $r_i = K_i + \sigma_i s \mod p$ for $i \in [\ell]$ and $t = \sum_{j\in[D]} c_j s^j$ where r_i and t are generated as in the verification. Since we have $f_{x,ct_{\mathsf{SKE}}}(K_1 + \sigma_1 Z, \ldots, K_\ell + \sigma_\ell Z) = 1 + \sum_{j\in[D]} c_j Z^j$ for an indeterminate Z by the correctness of Π_{SKE} and Lemma 4.2, we have $f_{x,ct_{\mathsf{SKE}}}(r_1, \ldots, r_\ell) = 1 + t$ by substituting s for Z.

Proof Size. First, we remark that the relation $\tilde{\mathcal{R}}$ can be verified by a circuit whose size is a fixed polynomial in $(\kappa, \ell, \log p, D)$ that does not depend on $|C|$. Moreover, we have $|\mathsf{Exp}_{C,x}(w)| = |C(x, \cdot)| \le |C|$ for all $w \in \{0,1\}^m$ by Lemma 4.1. Then we have $|\pi| = \mathsf{poly}(\kappa, \ell, \log p, D)$, $|ct_{\mathsf{SKE}}| = |C(x, \cdot)| + \mathsf{poly}(\kappa)$, $|ct^i_{\mathsf{IPFE}}| = \mathsf{poly}(\kappa, \log p)$, and $|ct'_{\mathsf{IPFE}}| = \mathsf{poly}(\kappa, \log p, D)$. By setting $\ell = \kappa$ and $p = 2^{O(\kappa)}$ and remarking that $D = \mathsf{poly}(\kappa)$, we have $|\pi'| = |C(x, \cdot)| + \mathsf{poly}(\kappa) \le |C| + \mathsf{poly}(\kappa)$.

Security. The security of our scheme Π'_{DVNIZK} is stated as follows. The proofs are similar to the security proof for PP-NIZK by Katsumata et al. [47], and thus given in the full version.

Theorem 4.1 (Soundness). *If Π_{DVNIZK} satisfies statistical (resp. computational) soundness and $p = \kappa^{\omega(1)}$, then Π'_{DVNIZK} satisfies statistical (resp. computational) soundness.*

Theorem 4.2 (Zero-knowledge). *If SKE is CPA secure, Π_{IPFE} is adaptively single-key secure, and Π_{DVNIZK} satisfies zero-knowledge, then Π'_{DVNIZK} satisfies zero-knowledge.*

Instantiation. The above construction can be instantiated based on the CDH assumption on a pairing-free group since

- An adaptively single-key secure IPFE scheme exists under any PKE scheme [38], and there exists a PKE scheme based on the CDH assumption.
- An SKE scheme whose decryption circuit is in $\mathbf{NC}^1$ with additive ciphertext overhead exists under the CDH assumption [47].
- DV-NIZK for all of $\mathbf{NP}$ exists under the CDH assumption [21,47,63]

Therefore we obtain the following corollary.

Corollary 4.1. *If the CDH assumption holds on a pairing-free group, then there exists DV-NIZK for all of* **NP** *with proof size* $|C| + \mathsf{poly}(\kappa)$.

Variant with Sublinear Proof Size. Similarly to the case of CRS-NIZK as discussed in Sect. 3.3, we can make the proof size of the above DV-NIZK sublinear in $|C|$ if C is a leveled circuit. More detailed explanation can be found in the full version. Namely, we obtain the following corollary:

Corollary 4.2. *If the CDH assumption holds on a pairing-free group, then there exists DV-NIZK for all* **NP** *languages whose corresponding relation is computable by a leveled circuit with proof size* $|w| + |C|/\log \kappa + \mathsf{poly}(\kappa)$.

Variant with Shorter Proof Size for NC^1 Relations. We can further reduce the proof size to $|w| + \mathsf{poly}(\kappa)$ if the relation to prove is computable in **NC**^{1} and we additionally assume ℓ-computational Diffie-Hellman inversion (CDHI) assumption [16,56].

Theorem 4.3. *If the ℓ-CDHI assumption holds for all $\ell = \mathsf{poly}(\kappa)$, then there exists DV-NIZK for all relations for all* **NP** *languages whose corresponding relation is computable in* **NC**^{1} *with proof size* $|w| + \mathsf{poly}(\kappa)$.

The construction and security proofs can be found in the full version.

5   CRS-NIZK with Efficient Prover from Laconic Function Evaluation

In this section, we present a NIZK proof system where a prover is efficient, that is, the running time of a prover is smaller than the size of circuit that computes the relation. We use laconic function evaluation to achieve our NIZK proof system.

Before describing the construction, we prepare some building blocks and notations.

- Let $\mathcal{L}$ be an **NP** language defined by a relation $\mathcal{R} \subseteq \{0,1\}^* \times \{0,1\}^*$. Let $n(\kappa)$ and $m(\kappa)$ be any fixed polynomials. Let C be a circuit that computes the relation $\mathcal{R}$ on $\{0,1\}^n \times \{0,1\}^m$, i.e., for $(x,w) \in \{0,1\}^n \times \{0,1\}^m$, we have $C(x,w) = 1$ if and only if $(x,w) \in \mathcal{R}$
- Let $\mathsf{LFE} = (\mathsf{LFE.crsGen}, \mathsf{LFE.Compress}, \mathsf{LFE.Enc}, \mathsf{LFE.Dec})$ be a LFE scheme whose function class $\mathcal{C}$ is the class of all circuits with $\mathsf{params} = (1^k, 1^d)$ consisting of the input size k and the depth d of the circuits and contains $\{C\}$ that computes the relation $\mathcal{R}$ for NP-complete language.
- Let $\Pi_{\mathsf{CRSNIZK}} = (\mathsf{Setup}, \mathsf{Prove}, \mathsf{Verify})$ be a CRS-NIZK for the language corresponding to the relation $\tilde{\mathcal{R}}$ defined below:

$$((x, \mathsf{lfe.crs}, \mathsf{digest}_C, \mathsf{lfe.ct}), (w, r)) \in \tilde{\mathcal{R}} \iff \mathsf{LFE.Enc}(\mathsf{lfe.crs}, \mathsf{digest}_C, (x, w); r) = \mathsf{lfe.ct}.$$

The CRS-NIZK $\Pi'_{\mathsf{CRSNIZK}} = (\mathsf{Setup}', \mathsf{Prove}', \mathsf{Verify}')$ for $\mathcal{L}$ is described as follows.

Setup$'(1^\kappa)$: This algorithm generates crs $\xleftarrow{\$}$ Setup(1^κ) and lfe.crs $\xleftarrow{\$}$ LFE.crsGen$(1^\kappa, \text{params})$. It generates digest$_C :=$ LFE.Compress(lfe.crs, C). It outputs a common reference string crs$' = (\text{crs}, \text{lfe.crs}, \text{digest}_C)$.

Prove$'(\text{crs}', x, w)$: This algorithm aborts if $\mathcal{R}(x, w) = 0$. Otherwise it parses (crs, lfe.crs, digest$_C$) $\leftarrow$ crs$'$, generates lfe.ct $:=$ LFE.Enc(lfe.crs, digest$_C$, (x, w); r) where r is the randomness for LFE.Enc and $\pi_{\text{NIZK}} \xleftarrow{\$}$ Prove(crs, $(x, \text{lfe.crs}, \text{digest}_C, \text{lfe.ct}), (w, r))$. It outputs a proof $\pi' := (\text{lfe.ct}, \pi_{\text{NIZK}})$.

Verify$'(\text{crs}', x, \pi')$: This algorithm parses (crs, lfe.crs, digest$_C$) $\leftarrow$ crs$'$, (lfe.ct, $\pi_{\text{NIZK}}) \leftarrow \pi'$, and computes $t :=$ Verify(crs, $(x, \text{lfe.crs}, \text{digest}_C, \text{lfe.ct}), \pi_{\text{NIZK}})$. If $t = \bot$ or $0 \xleftarrow{\$}$ LFE.Dec(lfe.crs, C, lfe.ct), then outputs $\bot$. Otherwise, outputs $\top$.

Completeness. By the completeness of Π_{CRSNIZK}, the proof π_{NIZK} in an honestly generated proof π' passes the verification of Π_{CRSNIZK}. That is, it holds that Verify(crs, $(x, \text{lfe.crs}, \text{digest}_C, \text{lfe.ct}), \pi_{\text{NIZK}}) = \top$. By the correctness of LFE, it holds that $1 = C(x, w) \xleftarrow{\$}$ LFE.Dec(lfe.crs, C, lfe.ct) with probability 1. Thus, the completeness follows.

Prover Efficiency. First, we remark that the relation $\tilde{\mathcal{R}}$ can be verified by a circuit whose size is $|\text{LFE.Enc}|$ since the relation is about the validity of LFE ciphertexts. The running time of Prove$'$ is the sum of those of LFE.Enc and Prove. We defer concrete efficiency analysis until Sect. 5.1 since the running time depends on instantiations of LFE.Enc and Prove.

Security. The security of the scheme is stated as follows. See the full version for the proofs.

Theorem 5.1 (Soundness). Π'_{CRSNIZK} *is computationally/statistically sound if* Π_{CRSNIZK} *is computationally/statistically sound, respectively.*

Theorem 5.2 (Zero-Knowledge). Π'_{CRSNIZK} *is computational zero-knowledge if* Π_{CRSNIZK} *is zero-knowledge and* LFE *is adaptively secure.*

5.1   Instantiations

We can consider two cases since there are two instantiations of adaptively secure LFE.

1. (Under sub-exponential security of the LWE assumption with sub-exponential modulus-to-noise ratio): By the result of [64], it holds that $|\text{lfe.crs}| = \text{poly}(\kappa, |x|, |w|, d)$, $|\text{digest}_C| = \text{poly}(\kappa)$, $|\text{lfe.ct}| = \text{poly}(\kappa, |x|, |w|, d)$, and the running time of LFE.Enc is $\text{poly}(\kappa, |x|, |w|, d)$ where d is the depth of C since the input length of C is $|x| + |w|$. In this case, we use a NIZK whose prover running time is $\text{poly}(\tilde{C}, \kappa)$ where $\tilde{C}$ is a circuit that computes the relation $\tilde{\mathcal{R}}$, which holds for any NIZK. In this case, $\tilde{C}$ just runs LFE.Enc, so it takes $|\text{LFE.Enc}| + \text{poly}(|\text{LFE.Enc}|, \kappa)$ time to generate π_{NIZK}. Thus, the running time of the prover is $\text{poly}(\kappa, |x|, |w|, d)$.

2. (Under the *adaptive* LWE assumption with sub-exponential modulus-to-noise ratio): By the result of [64], it holds that $|\mathsf{lfe.crs}| = (|x| + |w|) \cdot \mathsf{poly}(\kappa, d)$, $|\mathsf{digest}_C| = \mathsf{poly}(\kappa)$, $|\mathsf{lfe.ct}| = \tilde{O}(|x| + |w|) \cdot \mathsf{poly}(\kappa, d)$, and the running time of $\mathsf{LFE.Enc}$ is $\tilde{O}(|x| + |w|) \cdot \mathsf{poly}(\kappa, d)$ where d is the depth of C since the input length of C is $|x| + |w|$. In this case, we use a NIZK whose prover running time is $|\tilde{C}| \cdot \mathsf{poly}(\kappa)$. An example of such a NIZK is the NIZK by Groth et al. [43]. By using the efficiency of Groth et al. NIZK, it takes $|\mathsf{LFE.Enc}| + |\mathsf{LFE.Enc}| \cdot \mathsf{poly}(\kappa)$ time to generate π_{NIZK}. Thus, the running time of the prover is $\tilde{O}(|x| + |w|) \cdot \mathsf{poly}(\kappa, d) \cdot \mathsf{poly}(\kappa) = \tilde{O}(|x| + |w|) \cdot \mathsf{poly}(\kappa, d)$.

Therefore, we obtain the following two corollaries.

Corollary 5.1. *If a CRS-NIZK scheme for all of **NP** exists and the sub-exponentially secure LWE assumption with sub-exponential modulus-to-noise ratio holds, then there exists a CRS-NIZK scheme for all of **NP** whose prover running time is $\mathsf{poly}(\kappa, |x|, |w|, d)$.*

Corollary 5.2. *If the DLIN assumption in a bilinear group and the adaptive LWE assumption with sub-exponential modulus-to-noise ratio hold, then there exists a CRS-NIZK scheme for all of **NP** whose prover running time is $\tilde{O}(|x| + |w|)\mathsf{poly}(\kappa, d)$.*

Acknowledgement. We thank anonymous reviewers of Crypto 2019 for their helpful comments. The first and the third authors were supported by JST CREST Grant Number JPMJCR19F6. The third author was supported by JSPS KAKENHI Grant Number 16K16068.

References

1. Abdalla, M., Bourse, F., De Caro, A., Pointcheval, D.: Simple functional encryption schemes for inner products. In: Katz, J. (ed.) PKC 2015. LNCS, vol. 9020, pp. 733–751. Springer, Heidelberg (2015). https://doi.org/10.1007/978-3-662-46447-2_33
2. Abe, M., Fuchsbauer, G., Groth, J., Haralambiev, K., Ohkubo, M.: Structure-preserving signatures and commitments to group elements. J. Cryptol. **29**(2), 363–421 (2016)
3. Abusalah, H.: Generic instantiations of the hidden bits model for non-interactive zero-knowledge proofs for NP. Master's thesis, RWTH-Aachen University (2013)
4. Agrawal, S., Libert, B., Stehlé, D.: Fully secure functional encryption for inner products, from standard assumptions. In: Robshaw, M., Katz, J. (eds.) CRYPTO 2016. LNCS, vol. 9816, pp. 333–362. Springer, Heidelberg (2016). https://doi.org/10.1007/978-3-662-53015-3_12
5. Bellare, M., Micciancio, D., Warinschi, B.: Foundations of group signatures: formal definitions, simplified requirements, and a construction based on general assumptions. In: Biham, E. (ed.) EUROCRYPT 2003. LNCS, vol. 2656, pp. 614–629. Springer, Heidelberg (2003). https://doi.org/10.1007/3-540-39200-9_38
6. Bellare, M., Yung, M.: Certifying permutations: noninteractive zero-knowledge based on any trapdoor permutation. J. Cryptol. **9**(3), 149–166 (1996)

7. Bitansky, N., Canetti, R., Chiesa, A., Tromer, E.: From extractable collision resistance to succinct non-interactive arguments of knowledge, and back again. In: ITCS 2012, pp. 326–349 (2012)
8. Bitansky, N., Paneth, O.: ZAPs and non-interactive witness indistinguishability from indistinguishability obfuscation. In: Dodis, Y., Nielsen, J.B. (eds.) TCC 2015. LNCS, vol. 9015, pp. 401–427. Springer, Heidelberg (2015). https://doi.org/10.1007/978-3-662-46497-7_16
9. Bitansky, N., Paneth, O., Wichs, D.: Perfect structure on the edge of chaos. In: Kushilevitz, E., Malkin, T. (eds.) TCC 2016. LNCS, vol. 9562, pp. 474–502. Springer, Heidelberg (2016). https://doi.org/10.1007/978-3-662-49096-9_20
10. Blum, M., Feldman, P., Micali, S.: Non-interactive zero-knowledge and its applications (extended abstract). In: 20th ACM STOC, pp. 103–112 (1988)
11. Boyle, E., Gilboa, N., Ishai, Y.: Breaking the circuit size barrier for secure computation under DDH. In: Robshaw, M., Katz, J. (eds.) CRYPTO 2016. LNCS, vol. 9814, pp. 509–539. Springer, Heidelberg (2016). https://doi.org/10.1007/978-3-662-53018-4_19
12. Canetti, R., et al.: Fiat-Shamir: from practice to theory. In: STOC 2019 (2019, to appear)
13. Canetti, R., Chen, Y., Reyzin, L., Rothblum, R.D.: Fiat-Shamir and correlation intractability from strong KDM-secure encryption. In: Nielsen, J.B., Rijmen, V. (eds.) EUROCRYPT 2018. LNCS, vol. 10820, pp. 91–122. Springer, Cham (2018). https://doi.org/10.1007/978-3-319-78381-9_4
14. Canetti, R., Halevi, S., Katz, J.: A forward-secure public-key encryption scheme. J. Cryptol. 20(3), 265–294 (2007)
15. Canetti, R., Lichtenberg, A.: Certifying trapdoor permutations, revisited. In: Beimel, A., Dziembowski, S. (eds.) TCC 2018. LNCS, vol. 11239, pp. 476–506. Springer, Cham (2018). https://doi.org/10.1007/978-3-030-03807-6_18
16. Catalano, D., Fiore, D.: Practical homomorphic message authenticators for arithmetic circuits. J. Cryptol. 31(1), 23–59 (2018)
17. Chaidos, P., Couteau, G.: Efficient designated-verifier non-interactive zero-knowledge proofs of knowledge. In: Nielsen, J.B., Rijmen, V. (eds.) EUROCRYPT 2018, Part III. LNCS, vol. 10822, pp. 193–221. Springer, Cham (2018). https://doi.org/10.1007/978-3-319-78372-7_7
18. Chaidos, P., Groth, J.: Making sigma-protocols non-interactive without random oracles. In: Katz, J. (ed.) PKC 2015. LNCS, vol. 9020, pp. 650–670. Springer, Heidelberg (2015). https://doi.org/10.1007/978-3-662-46447-2_29
19. Chaum, D., van Heyst, E.: Group signatures. In: Davies, D.W. (ed.) EUROCRYPT 1991. LNCS, vol. 547, pp. 257–265. Springer, Heidelberg (1991). https://doi.org/10.1007/3-540-46416-6_22
20. Cohen, R., Shelat, A., Wichs, D.: Adaptively secure MPC with sublinear communication complexity. In: Boldyreva, A., Micciancio, D. (eds.) CRYPTO 2019, LNCS, vol. 11693, pp. 30–60. Springer, Cham (2019)
21. Couteau, G., Hofheinz, D.: Designated-verifier pseudorandom generators, and their applications. In: Ishai, Y., Rijmen, V. (eds.) EUROCRYPT 2019. LNCS, vol. 11477, pp. 562–592. Springer, Cham (2019). https://doi.org/10.1007/978-3-030-17656-3_20
22. Cramer, R., Damgård, I.: Secret-key zero-knowlegde and non-interactive verifiable exponentiation. In: Naor, M. (ed.) TCC 2004. LNCS, vol. 2951, pp. 223–237. Springer, Heidelberg (2004). https://doi.org/10.1007/978-3-540-24638-1_13

23. Damgård, I.: Non-interactive circuit based proofs and non-interactive perfect zero-knowledge with preprocessing. In: Rueppel, R.A. (ed.) EUROCRYPT 1992. LNCS, vol. 658, pp. 341–355. Springer, Heidelberg (1993). https://doi.org/10.1007/3-540-47555-9_28

24. Damgård, I., Fazio, N., Nicolosi, A.: Non-interactive zero-knowledge from homomorphic encryption. In: Halevi, S., Rabin, T. (eds.) TCC 2006. LNCS, vol. 3876, pp. 41–59. Springer, Heidelberg (2006). https://doi.org/10.1007/11681878_3

25. Danezis, G., Fournet, C., Groth, J., Kohlweiss, M.: Square span programs with applications to succinct NIZK arguments. In: Sarkar, P., Iwata, T. (eds.) ASIACRYPT 2014. LNCS, vol. 8873, pp. 532–550. Springer, Heidelberg (2014). https://doi.org/10.1007/978-3-662-45611-8_28

26. De Santis, A., Micali, S., Persiano, G.: Non-interactive zero-knowledge with preprocessing. In: Goldwasser, S. (ed.) CRYPTO 1988. LNCS, vol. 403, pp. 269–282. Springer, New York (1990). https://doi.org/10.1007/0-387-34799-2_21

27. Dolev, D., Dwork, C., Naor, M.: Nonmalleable cryptography. SIAM J. Comput. **30**(2), 391–437 (2000)

28. Feige, U., Lapidot, D., Shamir, A.: Multiple noninteractive zero knowledge proofs under general assumptions. SIAM J. Comput. **29**(1), 1–28 (1999)

29. Garg, S., Gentry, C., Halevi, S., Raykova, M., Sahai, A., Waters, B.: Candidate indistinguishability obfuscation and functional encryption for all circuits. SIAM J. Comput. **45**(3), 882–929 (2016)

30. Gennaro, R., Gentry, C., Parno, B., Raykova, M.: Quadratic span programs and succinct NIZKs without PCPs. In: Johansson, T., Nguyen, P.Q. (eds.) EUROCRYPT 2013. LNCS, vol. 7881, pp. 626–645. Springer, Heidelberg (2013). https://doi.org/10.1007/978-3-642-38348-9_37

31. Gentry, C.: A fully homomorphic encryption scheme. Ph.D. thesis, Stanford University (2009)

32. Gentry, C., Groth, J., Ishai, Y., Peikert, C., Sahai, A., Smith, A.D.: Using fully homomorphic hybrid encryption to minimize non-interative zero-knowledge proofs. J. Cryptol. **28**(4), 820–843 (2015)

33. Gentry, C., Wichs, D.: Separating succinct non-interactive arguments from all falsifiable assumptions. In: 43rd ACM STOC, pp. 99–108, June 2011

34. Goldreich, O.: Foundations of Cryptography: Volume 2, Basic Applications. Cambridge, New York (2004)

35. Goldreich, O., Micali, S., Wigderson, A.: How to play any mental game or a completeness theorem for protocols with honest majority. In: 19th ACM STOC, pp. 218–229 (1987)

36. Goldreich, O., Oren, Y.: Definitions and properties of zero-knowledge proof systems. J. Cryptol. **7**(1), 1–32 (1994)

37. Goldwasser, S., Micali, S., Rackoff, C.: The knowledge complexity of interactive proof systems. SIAM J. Comput. **18**(1), 186–208 (1989)

38. Gorbunov, S., Vaikuntanathan, V., Wee, H.: Functional encryption with bounded collusions via multi-party computation. In: Safavi-Naini, R., Canetti, R. (eds.) CRYPTO 2012. LNCS, vol. 7417, pp. 162–179. Springer, Heidelberg (2012). https://doi.org/10.1007/978-3-642-32009-5_11

39. Gorbunov, S., Vaikuntanathan, V., Wichs, D.: Leveled fully homomorphic signatures from standard lattices. In: STOC 2015, pp. 469–477 (2015)

40. Groth, J.: Short non-interactive zero-knowledge proofs. In: Abe, M. (ed.) ASIACRYPT 2010. LNCS, vol. 6477, pp. 341–358. Springer, Heidelberg (2010). https://doi.org/10.1007/978-3-642-17373-8_20

41. Groth, J.: Short pairing-based non-interactive zero-knowledge arguments. In: Abe, M. (ed.) ASIACRYPT 2010. LNCS, vol. 6477, pp. 321–340. Springer, Heidelberg (2010). https://doi.org/10.1007/978-3-642-17373-8_19

42. Groth, J.: On the size of pairing-based non-interactive arguments. In: Fischlin, M., Coron, J.-S. (eds.) EUROCRYPT 2016. LNCS, vol. 9666, pp. 305–326. Springer, Heidelberg (2016). https://doi.org/10.1007/978-3-662-49896-5_11

43. Groth, J., Ostrovsky, R., Sahai, A.: New techniques for noninteractive zero-knowledge. J. ACM **59**(3), 11:1–11:35 (2012)

44. Groth, J., Sahai, A.: Efficient noninteractive proof systems for bilinear groups. SIAM J. Comput. **41**(5), 1193–1232 (2012)

45. Ishai, Y., Kushilevitz, E., Ostrovsky, R., Sahai, A.: Zero-knowledge proofs from secure multiparty computation. SIAM J. Comput. **39**(3), 1121–1152 (2009)

46. Kalai, Y.T., Rothblum, G.N., Rothblum, R.D.: From obfuscation to the security of Fiat-Shamir for proofs. In: Katz, J., Shacham, H. (eds.) CRYPTO 2017, Part II. LNCS, vol. 10402, pp. 224–251. Springer, Cham (2017). https://doi.org/10.1007/978-3-319-63715-0_8

47. Katsumata, S., Nishimaki, R., Yamada, S., Yamakawa, T.: Designated verifier/prover and preprocessing NIZKs from Diffie-Hellman assumptions. In: Ishai, Y., Rijmen, V. (eds.) EUROCRYPT 2019. LNCS, vol. 11477, pp. 622–651. Springer, Cham (2019). https://doi.org/10.1007/978-3-030-17656-3_22

48. Kilian, J.: On the complexity of bounded-interaction and noninteractive zero-knowledge proofs. In: 35th FOCS, pp. 466–477 (1994)

49. Kilian, J., Micali, S., Ostrovsky, R.: Minimum resource zero-knowledge proofs (extended abstract). In: Brassard, G. (ed.) CRYPTO 1989. LNCS, vol. 435, pp. 545–546. Springer, New York (1990). https://doi.org/10.1007/0-387-34805-0_47

50. Kilian, J., Petrank, E.: An efficient noninteractive zero-knowledge proof system for NP with general assumptions. J. Cryptol. **11**(1), 1–27 (1998)

51. Kim, S., Wu, D.J.: Multi-theorem preprocessing NIZKs from lattices. In: Shacham, H., Boldyreva, A. (eds.) CRYPTO 2018. LNCS, vol. 10992, pp. 733–765. Springer, Cham (2018). https://doi.org/10.1007/978-3-319-96881-0_25

52. Lapidot, D., Shamir, A.: Publicly verifiable non-interactive zero-knowledge proofs. In: Menezes, A.J., Vanstone, S.A. (eds.) CRYPTO 1990. LNCS, vol. 537, pp. 353–365. Springer, Heidelberg (1991). https://doi.org/10.1007/3-540-38424-3_26

53. Lipmaa, H.: Progression-free sets and sublinear pairing-based non-interactive zero-knowledge arguments. In: Cramer, R. (ed.) TCC 2012. LNCS, vol. 7194, pp. 169–189. Springer, Heidelberg (2012). https://doi.org/10.1007/978-3-642-28914-9_10

54. Lipmaa, H.: Succinct non-interactive zero knowledge arguments from span programs and linear error-correcting codes. In: Sako, K., Sarkar, P. (eds.) ASIACRYPT 2013, Part I. LNCS, vol. 8269, pp. 41–60. Springer, Heidelberg (2013). https://doi.org/10.1007/978-3-642-42033-7_3

55. Lipmaa, H.: Optimally sound sigma protocols under DCRA. In: Kiayias, A. (ed.) FC 2017. LNCS, vol. 10322, pp. 182–203. Springer, Cham (2017). https://doi.org/10.1007/978-3-319-70972-7_10

56. Mitsunari, S., Saka, R., Kasahara, M.: A new traitor tracing. IEICE Trans. **E85-A**(2), 481–484 (2002)

57. Naccache, D., Stern, J.: A new public key cryptosystem based on higher residues. In: ACM CCS 1998, pp. 59–66 (1998)

58. Naor, M.: On cryptographic assumptions and challenges. In: Boneh, D. (ed.) CRYPTO 2003. LNCS, vol. 2729, pp. 96–109. Springer, Heidelberg (2003). https://doi.org/10.1007/978-3-540-45146-4_6

59. Naor, M., Yung, M.: Public-key cryptosystems provably secure against chosen ciphertext attacks. In: 22nd ACM STOC, pp. 427–437 (1990)
60. Parno, B., Howell, J., Gentry, C., Raykova, M.: Pinocchio: nearly practical verifiable computation. Commun. ACM **59**(2), 103–112 (2016)
61. Pass, R., Shelat, A., Vaikuntanathan, V.: Construction of a non-malleable encryption scheme from any semantically secure one. In: Dwork, C. (ed.) CRYPTO 2006. LNCS, vol. 4117, pp. 271–289. Springer, Heidelberg (2006). https://doi.org/10.1007/11818175_16
62. Pedersen, T.P.: Non-interactive and information-theoretic secure verifiable secret sharing. In: Feigenbaum, J. (ed.) CRYPTO 1991. LNCS, vol. 576, pp. 129–140. Springer, Heidelberg (1992). https://doi.org/10.1007/3-540-46766-1_9
63. Quach, W., Rothblum, R.D., Wichs, D.: Reusable designated-verifier NIZKs for all NP from CDH. In: Ishai, Y., Rijmen, V. (eds.) EUROCRYPT 2019. LNCS, vol. 11477, pp. 593–621. Springer, Cham (2019). https://doi.org/10.1007/978-3-030-17656-3_21
64. Quach, W., Wee, H., Wichs, D.: Laconic function evaluation and applications. In: 59th FOCS, pp. 859–870 (2018)
65. Rivest, R.L., Shamir, A., Tauman, Y.: How to leak a secret. In: Boyd, C. (ed.) ASIACRYPT 2001. LNCS, vol. 2248, pp. 552–565. Springer, Heidelberg (2001). https://doi.org/10.1007/3-540-45682-1_32
66. Sahai, A.: Non-malleable non-interactive zero knowledge and adaptive chosen-ciphertext security. In: 40th FOCS, pp. 543–553 (1999)
67. Sahai, A., Waters, B.: How to use indistinguishability obfuscation: deniable encryption, and more. In: 46th ACM STOC, pp. 475–484 (2014)
68. Shoup, V.: Lower bounds for discrete logarithms and related problems. In: Fumy, W. (ed.) EUROCRYPT 1997. LNCS, vol. 1233, pp. 256–266. Springer, Heidelberg (1997). https://doi.org/10.1007/3-540-69053-0_18
69. Ventre, C., Visconti, I.: Co-sound zero-knowledge with public keys. In: Preneel, B. (ed.) AFRICACRYPT 2009. LNCS, vol. 5580, pp. 287–304. Springer, Heidelberg (2009). https://doi.org/10.1007/978-3-642-02384-2_18

New Constructions of Reusable Designated-Verifier NIZKs

Alex Lombardi[1]([✉]), Willy Quach[2]([✉]), Ron D. Rothblum[3], Daniel Wichs[2], and David J. Wu[4]

[1] MIT, Cambridge, MA, USA
alexjl@mit.edu
[2] Northeastern University, Boston, MA, USA
quach.w@husky.neu.edu, wichs@ccs.neu.edu
[3] Technion, Haifa, Israel
rothblum@cs.technion.ac.il
[4] University of Virginia, Charlottesville, VA, USA
dwu4@virginia.edu

Abstract. Non-interactive zero-knowledge arguments (NIZKs) for NP are an important cryptographic primitive, but we currently only have instantiations under a few specific assumptions. Notably, we are missing constructions from the learning with errors (LWE) assumption, the Diffie-Hellman (CDH/DDH) assumption, and the learning parity with noise (LPN) assumption.

In this paper, we study a relaxation of NIZKs to the *designated-verifier* setting (DV-NIZK), where a trusted setup generates a common reference string together with a secret key for the verifier. We want *reusable* schemes, which allow the verifier to reuse the secret key to verify many different proofs, and soundness should hold even if the malicious prover learns whether various proofs are accepted or rejected. Such reusable DV-NIZKs were recently constructed under the CDH assumption, but it was open whether they can also be constructed under LWE or LPN.

We also consider an extension of reusable DV-NIZKs to the *malicious designated-verifier* setting (MDV-NIZK). In this setting, the only trusted setup consists of a common random string. However, there is also an additional untrusted setup in which the verifier chooses a public/secret key needed to generate/verify proofs, respectively. We require that zero-knowledge holds even if the public key is chosen maliciously by the verifier. Such reusable MDV-NIZKs were recently constructed under the

A. Lombardi—Research supported in part by an NDSEG fellowship. Research supported in part by NSF Grants CNS-1350619 and CNS-1414119, and by the Defense Advanced Research Projects Agency (DARPA) and the U.S. Army Research Office under contracts W911NF-15-C-0226 and W911NF-15-C-0236.

R. D. Rothblum—Supported in part by the Israeli Science Foundation (Grant No. 1262/18) and the Technion Hiroshi Fujiwara cyber security research center and the Israel cyber directorate.

D. Wichs—Research supported by NSF grants CNS-1314722, CNS-1413964, CNS-1750795 and the Alfred P. Sloan Research Fellowship.

D. J. Wu—Part of this work was done while visiting the Technion.

© International Association for Cryptologic Research 2019
A. Boldyreva and D. Micciancio (Eds.): CRYPTO 2019, LNCS 11694, pp. 670–700, 2019.
https://doi.org/10.1007/978-3-030-26954-8_22

"one-more CDH" assumption, but constructions under CDH/LWE/LPN remained open.

In this work, we give new constructions of (reusable) DV-NIZKs and MDV-NIZKs using generic primitives that can be instantiated under CDH, LWE, or LPN.

1 Introduction

Zero-knowledge proofs [28] allow a prover to convince a verifier that a statement is true without revealing anything beyond this fact. While standard zero-knowledge proof systems are interactive, Blum, Feldman, and Micali [4] introduced the concept of a non-interactive zero-knowledge (NIZK) proof, which consists of a single message sent by the prover to the verifier. Although such NIZKs cannot exist in the plain model, they are realizable in the *common reference string (CRS)* model, where a trusted third party generates and publishes a common reference string chosen either uniformly random or from some specified distribution. We currently have NIZKs for general NP languages under several specific assumptions, such as: (doubly-enhanced) trapdoor permutations, which can be instantiated from factoring [4,23,26,50,51], the Diffie-Hellman assumption over bilinear groups [11,32], optimal hardness of the learning with errors (LWE) assumption[1] [10], and circular-secure fully homomorphic encryption [12]. We also have such NIZKs in the random-oracle model [24]. However, we are lacking constructions from several standard assumptions, most notably the computational or decisional Diffie-Hellman assumptions (CDH, DDH), the plain learning with errors (LWE) assumption, and the learning parity with noise (LPN) assumption.

Designated-Verifier NIZK. We consider a relaxation of NIZKs to the *designated verifier* model (DV-NIZK). In this model, a trusted third party generates a CRS together with a secret key, which is given to the verifier and is used to verify proofs. Throughout this work, we focus on the problem of achieving *reusable* (i.e., multi-theorem) security. This means that soundness should hold even if the scheme is used multiple times and a malicious prover can test whether the verifier accepts or rejects various proofs.

While reusable DV-NIZKs appear to be a non-trivial relaxation of standard NIZKs,[2] we did not (until recently) have any constructions of such DV-NIZKs under assumptions not known to imply standard NIZKs. Very recently, the works of [14,35,46] constructed such DV-NIZKs under the CDH assumption. However, it was left as an open problem whether such DV-NIZKs can be constructed under LWE or LPN.

We note that the work [37] constructed an orthogonal notion of reusable "designated-prover" NIZKs (DP-NIZK) under LWE, where the trusted third

---

[1] This means that no polynomial-time attacker can break LWE with any probability better than random guessing.

[2] The public verifiability of traditional NIZKs immediately implies reusable soundness.

party generates a CRS together with a secret key that is given to the prover and needed to generate proofs. In addition, the work [8] constructed "preprocessing NIZKs" (PP-NIZK), in which the trusted third party generates both a secret proving key and a secret verification key, under variants of the LPN assumption over large fields.

Malicious-Designated-Verifier NIZK. We also consider a strengthening of DV-NIZKs to the malicious-designated-verifier model (MDV-NIZKs) introduced by [46]. In this model, a trusted party only generates a common *uniformly random* string. The verifier can then choose a public/secret key pair, which is used to generate/verify proofs, respectively. Soundness is required to hold when the verifier generates these keys honestly, while zero-knowledge is required to hold even when the verifier may generate the public key maliciously. MDV-NIZKs can equivalently be thought of as 2-round zero-knowledge protocols in the common random string model, in which the verifier's first-round message is reusable; namely, the public key chosen by the verifier can be thought of as a first-round message.

Very recently, the work of [46] showed how to construct such MDV-NIZKs under the "one-more CDH assumption." This is an interactive assumption that has received much less scrutiny than standard CDH/DDH.

1.1 Our Results

In this work, we propose a framework for constructing reusable DV-NIZKs from generic assumptions. One instantiation of this framework yields reusable DV-NIZKs generically from any public-key encryption together with a secret-key encryption scheme satisfying a weak form of key-dependent message (KDM) security Both components can be instantiated under any of the CDH/LWE/LPN assumptions, so we obtain constructions of DV-NIZKs under these assumptions. In particular, we obtain the following theorem:

Theorem 1.1 (informal). *Assuming the existence of public-key encryption and secret-key encryption that is KDM-secure with respect to projections (see Definition 2.12), there exist reusable designated-verifier NIZK arguments for NP. In particular, there exist reusable DV-NIZKs under either the CDH assumption, the LWE assumption, or the LPN assumption with noise rate $O(\frac{1}{\sqrt{n}})$.*

We then show how to construct reusable *malicious* DV-NIZKs from any (receiver-extractable) 2-round oblivious transfer (OT) in the common random string model and the same form of KDM-secure SKE. This yields instantiations of MDV-NIZKs under the CDH/LWE/LPN assumptions using the OT constructions of [21,45], as summarized by the following theorem.

Theorem 1.2 (informal). *Assuming the existence of "receiver-extractable 2-message OT" and secret-key encryption that is KDM-secure with respect to projections, there exist reusable* malicious *designated-verifier NIZK arguments for NP. In particular, there exist reusable MDV-NIZKs under the CDH assumption, the LWE assumption, or the LPN assumption with noise rate $n^{-(\frac{1}{2}+\varepsilon)}$ for any $\varepsilon > 0$.*

More generally, we give a compiler converting any Σ-protocol (or even more generally, any "zero-knowledge PCP" [34,36]) into a DV-NIZK using a form of *single-key attribute-based encryption* (ABE) satisfying a certain "function-hiding (under decryption queries)" property. Collusion-resistant ABE is only known from specific algebraic assumptions over bilinear maps [31,49] or lattices [6,30], but *single-key* ABE can be constructed from any public-key encryption scheme [29,48]. While we are unable to construct our variant of ABE (i.e., one that satisfies our function-hiding property) from an arbitrary public-key encryption (PKE) scheme, we show how to construct it by additionally relying on KDM-secure SKE, using a technique recently developed in [38,39]. However, in addition to this construction, we outline an alternate approach for building single-key ABE with our function-hiding property (using the standard lattice-based ABE [6]) in the full version of this paper [40]. As a result, we believe that our new notion may be helpful in order to construct DV-NIZKs from other assumptions in the future. Note that if one could construct DV-NIZKs from any semantically-secure PKE scheme, it would show that semantically-secure PKE generically implies CCA-secure PKE (via the Naor-Yung paradigm [42]), which would resolve a major long-standing open problem. More modestly, one could hope to construct DV-NIZKs generically from any CCA-2 secure encryption. Our techniques may offer some hope towards realizing these exciting possibilities.

Our techniques depart significantly from the prior constructions of DV-NIZKs and MDV-NIZKs in [14,35,46]. In particular, those works relied on the hidden-bits model from [23] and used a variant of the Cramer-Shoup hash-proof system under CDH [16,17] to instantiate the hidden bits for a designated verifier. Unfortunately, we do not have good hash-proof systems under LWE/LPN and so it does not appear that these techniques can be used when starting from "noisy assumptions" (among other concerns). As we describe below, we take a vastly different approach and do not rely on the hidden bits model. One disadvantage of our results is that, while [14,35,46] achieve *statistically* sound (M)DV-NIZK proofs, we only get argument systems with *computational* soundness[3].

Application to Reusable Non-interactive Secure Computation. We note that MDV-NIZKs can be used to obtain new solutions to the problem of reusable non-interactive secure computation (rNISC) [13]. In this setting, there is a public function f and a receiver (Rachel) publishes a "query" using her secret input x. Later a sender (Sam) can send a "response" using his secret input y and ensure that Rachel only learns $f(x, y)$. We further want Rachel's query to be reusable so that Sam can send many different responses with various values y_i and have Rachel learn $f(x, y_i)$ without compromising security. The main difficulty is that a malicious Sam can send malformed responses and, by observing whether Rachel aborts or not, can potentially learn information about her input x. Previously, we had instantiations of rNISC (in the CRS model) using 2-round (malicious) oblivious transfer (OT) *and* NIZKs, or more recently, via a black-box use of oblivious linear-function evaluation (OLE) [13]. However, we had no constructions under

---

[3] Our construction is also computational zero-knowledge. None of the recent constructions of DV-NIZKs satisfy statistical zero knowledge.

many standard assumptions, including any of CDH/DDH, LPN or LWE. It turns out that we can easily use MDV-NIZKs instead of standard NIZKs (along with 2-round malicious OT) to solve this problem. In particular, Rachel sends OT queries corresponding to her input x as well as the public-key of an MDV-NIZK. Sam then creates a garbled circuit for $f(\cdot, y)$ with his input y hard-coded, and sends the labels via the OT responses; in addition he encrypts y (under a public key in the CRS) and proves that he computed the garbled circuit and the OT responses correctly and consistently with the encrypted y. We can simulate Sam's view (including Rachel's output) by checking the MDV-NIZK to decide if Rachel aborts or not; if the MDV-NIZK verifies then we can extract y from the encryption and be sure that Rachel correctly outputs $f(x, y)$. Using our instantiations of MDV-NIZKs along with known constructions of 2-round OT from [21,45], we get instantiations of rNISC under CDH, LPN or LWE.

1.2 Our Techniques

Our approach starts with the construction of *non-reusable* DV-NIZKs from any public-key encryption, due to Pass, shelat, and Vaikuntanathan [43]. The [43] construction relies on a Σ-protocol [15] with 1-bit challenges for an NP-complete language, such as Blum's protocol for graph Hamiltonicity [3]. Recall that a Σ-protocol is a 3-round protocol, where the prover sends a value a, the challenger chooses a bit $b \in \{0, 1\}$, and the prover replies with a response z; the verifier checks the validity of the transcript (a, b, z) at the end. The protocol should have special soundness (if there are two accepting transcripts $(a, 0, z_0), (a, 1, z_1)$ with the same a then the statement must be true) and special honest-verifier zero-knowledge (given b ahead of time, we can simulate the transcript (a, b, z) without knowing a witness). The scheme also relies on a public-key encryption scheme PKE. The non-reusable DV-NIZK of [43] is defined by invoking λ (security parameter) independent copies of the following base scheme in parallel:

- **Setup:** The common reference string consists of PKE public keys, $(\mathsf{pk}_0, \mathsf{pk}_1)$. The verifier's secret verification key (b, sk_b) consists of a random bit b along with the secret key sk_b for the corresponding public key pk_b.
- **Proof generation:** On input a statement x and a witness w, the prover P first computes the first message a of the Σ-protocol. Then, the prover computes responses (z_0, z_1) for both possible challenge bits $b \in \{0, 1\}$, respectively, and outputs $(a, \mathsf{ct}_0 = \mathsf{Encrypt}(\mathsf{pk}_0, z_0), \mathsf{ct}_1 = \mathsf{Encrypt}(\mathsf{pk}_1, z_1))$.
- **Proof verification:** Given a proof $(a, \mathsf{ct}_0, \mathsf{ct}_1)$, and verification key (b, sk_b), the verifier computes $z = \mathsf{Decrypt}(\mathsf{sk}_b, \mathsf{ct}_b)$ and accepts if and only if (a, b, z) is a valid transcript.

Zero-knowledge of the DV-NIZK holds because the simulator knows the bits b of the verifier in each invocation and can therefore simulate the Σ-protocol transcripts (a, b, z_b) without knowing a witness. It can create the ciphertext ct_b by encrypting z_b and can put an arbitrary dummy value in the "other" ciphertext ct_{1-b}; this is indistinguishable by the security of the encryption.

Non-reusable soundness of the DV-NIZK follows from the special soundness of the Σ-protocol. If the statement is false then, for each a, there is only one challenge bit b that has a valid response z, and therefore the prover would have to correctly guess the bit b in each of the λ invocations of the above base protocol. This can only happen with negligible probability.

Unfortunately, as noted in [43], the soundness of this scheme is completely broken if the prover is allowed to query a verification oracle to test whether arbitrary proofs accept or reject—by creating a proof of a true statement and putting an incorrect value in (say) the ciphertext ct_0 of the ith copy of the protocol, the adversary learns the verifier's bit b in the ith copy after learning whether the proof accepts or rejects. The adversary can eventually recover all of the verifier's bits b this way and, once it does so, it is easy to construct a valid proof of a false statement by using the Σ-protocol simulator to generate valid transcripts (a, b, z_b).

To overcome this problem, we replace the use of public-key encryption with a form of *attribute-based encryption*, so that every instance x yields a *different* sequence of challenge bits b associated to it.

Function-Hiding ABE. The main tool that we use in this work is a variant of single-key ABE satisfying a certain *function-hiding* property. Recall that an ABE scheme (Setup, KeyGen, Encrypt, Decrypt) allows for the encryption of a message m under public parameters pp with respect to an *attribute* x resulting in a ciphertext ct. The ciphertext ct can be decrypted using a secret key sk_f associated with a function f and the message m is recovered if $f(x) = 1$. On the other hand, if $f(x) = 0$, then semantic security holds and nothing about the message is revealed even given sk_f. In this work, we focus on schemes satisfying semantic security in the presence of a *single* secret key sk_f; ABE schemes satisfying single-key security can be constructed from any public-key encryption scheme [29,48].

The function-hiding property we consider in this work requires that for any function f, oracle access to the decryption oracle Decrypt($sk_f, \cdot$) does not reveal anything about the function f beyond whether sk_f was qualified to decrypt the ciphertexts in question. More formally, we consider schemes where the attribute x is given in the clear as part of the ciphertext ct, and require that an oracle call of the form Decrypt(sk_f, ct) can be simulated using the master secret key msk along with the value $f(x)$, but without any additional knowledge of f.

At first glance, this property seems closely related to the standard notion of *CCA-security*, in which access to a decryption oracle does not compromise semantic security. However, these two notions appear to be incomparable. In particular, function-hiding can hold even if access to the decryption oracle completely breaks semantic security while CCA-2 security can hold even if access to the decryption oracle completely reveals the function f. Nonetheless, we observe that some of the techniques previously developed for obtaining CCA-security are also useful for obtaining our form of function-hiding.

Given this notion, our main contributions can be broken down into two steps: (1) showing that function-hiding ABE yields DV-NIZKs, and (2) giving constructions of function-hiding ABE. With respect to (1), we note that assuming the existence of public-key encryption, our notion of function-hiding ABE is actually *equivalent* to DV-NIZKs for NP; we show the converse to (1) in the full version of this paper [40].

The Compiler. Here, we describe a simplified version of our DV-NIZK protocol using three main ingredients:

- A Σ-protocol [15] with 1-bit challenges for an NP-complete language $\mathcal{L}$, such as Blum's protocol for graph Hamiltonicity [3]. (In Sect. 4, we describe our compiler more generally in the language of zero-knowledge PCPs, which can be instantiated via Σ-protocols as a special case).
- An ABE scheme ABE = (Setup, KeyGen, Encrypt, Decrypt) satisfying single-key security and function-hiding as described above. (In Sect. 4, we describe our compiler more generally using a new primitive called attribute-based secure function evaluation (AB-SFE), for which ABE is a special case).
- A pseudorandom function PRF that can be evaluated by ABE. In this simplified scheme, it suffices for PRF to output a single bit. (In Sect. 4, we describe our compiler by reusing the same PRF and ABE parameters across invocations, while here we apply parallel repetition of completely independent schemes).

Our DV-NIZK protocol is defined by invoking λ (security parameter) independent copies of the following base scheme in parallel.

- **Setup:** The common reference string consists of the public parameters pp for ABE. The verifier's secret verification key (k, sk_f) consists of a PRF key k along with an ABE secret key sk_f for evaluating the function

$$f(x, b) = 1 \iff \mathsf{PRF}(k, x) = b.$$

- **Proof generation:** On input a statement x and a witness w, the prover P computes the first message a in the Σ-protocol. Then, the prover computes responses (z_0, z_1) for both possible challenge bits $b \in \{0, 1\}$, respectively, and computes an ABE encryption of z_b with respect to attribute (x, b). This yields ciphertexts $(\mathsf{ct}_0, \mathsf{ct}_1)$; the prover sends $(a, \mathsf{ct}_0, \mathsf{ct}_1)$ to the verifier.
- **Proof verification:** The verifier first computes $y = \mathsf{PRF}(k, x)$. Then, the verifier decrypts ct_y using its secret verification key sk_f to obtain the prover's response z_y. Finally, the verifier checks that the proof (a, y, z_y) is valid and accepts if this is the case.

We claim that the DV-NIZK is reusably sound. Consider any fixed statement[4] $x \notin \mathcal{L}$ and an adversary that makes arbitrary verification queries and eventually produces an accepting proof for x. First, without loss of generality, we claim

---

[4] This suffices for *non-adaptive* soundness. Adaptive soundness (in which the cheating prover is allowed to adaptively select a false statement $x \notin \mathcal{L}$ after seeing the common reference string) can be achieved either by complexity leveraging [5] (see Remark 2.4) or by relying on a *trapdoor Σ-protocol* [12] (see Remark 4.4).

that we can consider an adversary that never makes a verification query on x itself; if an adversary had a non-negligible probability of making such a query and getting an accepting response then it would be able to win the game without making the query! Second, we claim that the challenges $y = \mathsf{PRF}(k, x)$ for each invocation, which are used when verifying the adversary's final proof for x, are pseudorandom from the prover's perspective. This holds *even* if the prover is given oracle access to the verifier on all statements $x' \neq x$ since, by the function-hiding of ABE, these queries can be simulated given only the values $\mathsf{PRF}(k, x')$ without revealing any additional info about k. But, by the special soundness of the Σ-protocol, the only way that the adversary can produce an accepting proof would be to guess all of the values y used in each of the λ invocations, which only happens with negligible probability.

Moreover, we claim that the DV-NIZK is zero-knowledge. In an honestly-generated proof $\pi = (a, \mathsf{ct}_0, \mathsf{ct}_1)$, on instance x, the verifier can compute the response z_y for $y = \mathsf{PRF}(k, x)$, but the response z_{1-y} is computationally hidden by semantic security of ABE. This means that π can be simulated given only $(k, (a, z_y))$, which is in turn simulatable given only x by the special honest-verifier zero-knowledge of the Σ-protocol.

We provide the formal description of our compiler in Sect. 4.

Constructing Function-Hiding ABE. We now describe two ways[5] to construct a (single-key) ABE scheme that satisfies our function-hiding property. Combined with our compiler above, this suffices to construct DV-NIZKs (i.e., the results from Theorem 1.1). In the body of the paper, we will focus on the second candidate based on KDM-secure SKE for two main reasons: (1) it enables instantiations from CDH/LWE/LPN (and correspondingly, DV-NIZKs from these assumptions); and (2) it readily generalizes to notions beyond ABE, which as we discuss in greater detail below, enables constructions of *MDV-NIZKs* from CDH/LWE/LPN.

– **Lattice-based ABE:** First, we observe that a simple variant of the lattice-based ABE construction from [6] satisfies our notion of function-hiding. Namely, we can modify the construction [6] so that the decryption algorithm (with either the master secret key or a function key) can *fully recover* the encryption randomness used to construct a particular ciphertext, and in doing so, verify that a ciphertext is well-formed (i.e., could be output by the honest encryption algorithm). If the scheme supports this randomness recovery property, function-privacy essentially follows from (perfect) correctness of the underlying scheme. This high-level idea of leveraging *randomness recovery* is a common theme in our constructions. We provide additional details in the full version of this paper [40].
– **PKE and KDM-secure SKE:** Following the approach of [38,39], we show that any single-key ABE scheme can be used to construct an ABE scheme satisfying function-hiding with respect to decryption queries. The amplification procedure additionally requires the existence of a secret-key encryption

---

[5] We refer to a previous version of this work [41] for an additional approach based on lossy trapdoor functions.

scheme SKE that is KDM-secure for a simple class of functions. As shown in [2,7,9,19,20], such secret-key encryption schemes can be constructed from the CDH/LWE/LPN assumptions, and hence, give instantiations of function-hiding ABE from CDH/LWE/LPN.

In fact, the exact construction of *CCA-secure* ABE in [39] (and the modification introduced in [38]) can also be shown to satisfy function-hiding. However, as noted above, CCA-security does not generically imply our notion of function-hiding or vice versa. In this work, we describe a simplified variant of the [38] compiler that suffices to construct function-hiding ABE and then analyze its security.

We now provide a description of (our simplification of) the [38,39] construction. Take any (single-key) ABE scheme ABE, a secret-key encryption scheme SKE, a public-key encryption scheme PKE, an equivocable commitment scheme Com, and consider the following modified ABE scheme:

- **Public parameters:** ABE public parameters pp, PKE public key pk, and commitment common reference string crs.
- **Key generation:** This is unmodified from ABE: an ABE master secret key is used to generate keys sk_f associated to functions f.
- **Encryption algorithm:** On input the public parameters (pp, pk, crs), an attribute x and a message m:
  1. Sample a SKE secret key $s \leftarrow \{0,1\}^\lambda$.
  2. Sample random strings ρ_i (for $i \in [\lambda]$) and $R_{i,b}$ (for $i \in [\lambda], b \in \{0,1\}$).
  3. Output commitments $com_i = \mathsf{Com}(crs, s_i; \rho_i)$ to the bits of the secret key s, a "joint encryption matrix" $M = \{ct_{i,b}\}_{i \in [\lambda], b \in \{0,1\}}$ consisting of λ ABE ciphertexts and λ PKE ciphertexts using the strings $R_{i,b}$ as encryption randomness. Lastly, also output a symmetric encryption $ct_0 \leftarrow \mathsf{SKE.Encrypt}(s, m \| \{R_{i,s_i}\}_{i \in [\lambda]})$ of the message m concatenated with a subset of $\{R_{i,b}\}$ corresponding to the bits of s (using fresh encryption randomness).

  We now elaborate on the ciphertexts $ct_{i,b}$:
  * For every index $i \in [\lambda]$, $ct_{i,0}$ is an ABE ciphertext computed using (pp, x) and randomness $R_{i,0}$, while $ct_{i,1}$ is a PKE ciphertext computed using pk and randomness $R_{i,1}$.
  * As for the underlying messages: for every index $i \in [\lambda]$, ct_{i,s_i} is an encryption of ρ_i, while $ct_{i,1-s_i}$ is an encryption of $\perp$ (a dummy message).

Following [38,39], we provide some high-level intuition for this encryption algorithm. For a fixed pair (i,b), call a ciphertext $ct_{i,b}$ "good" with respect to commitment com_i if there exists commitment randomness ρ_i such that $com_i = \mathsf{Com}(crs, b; \rho_i)$ and $ct_{i,b}$ is a well-formed encryption of ρ_i. Then, given a qualified secret key sk_f, an honestly-generated matrix $M = \{ct_{i,b}\}$ encodes the SKE-secret key s: we have $s_i = b$ if and only if $ct_{i,b}$ is "good," so s_i can be identified by decrypting $ct_{i,0}$ (using sk_f) and checking whether the underlying message is $\perp$.[6]

---

[6] In the actual decryption procedure, a more sophisticated mechanism is employed to identify s in order to handle malformed ciphertexts.

Moreover, the binding property of the commitment scheme Com guarantees that for every $(i, \mathsf{com}_i, \mathsf{ct}_{i,0}, \mathsf{ct}_{i,1})$, there is *at most one bit* b such that $\mathsf{ct}_{i,b}$ is "good"; in other words, even malformed ciphertexts encode at most one secret key s. This introduces enough redundancy in the scheme so that CCA-like security properties can be guaranteed *without* the decryption procedure fully recovering the encryption randomness. In particular, the randomness $\{R_{i,1-s_i}\}$ can be left unrecoverable (even given a qualified key sk_f), which is what allows for a proof of semantic security.

We leave a detailed discussion of the decryption algorithm to Sect. 5, but decryption roughly proceeds by recovering some of the overall encryption randomness (using sk_f)—namely, $(s, \rho, \{R_{i,s_i}\}_{i\in[\lambda]})$—and then checking that each ciphertext of the form ct_{i,s_i} is "good" (which can be done *without* using sk_f). To argue semantic security, we proceed in three steps:

- Switch the commitment crs to an "equivocal mode" so that com $=$ $(\mathsf{com}_i)_{i\in[\lambda]}$ can be explained as a commitment to *any string* (with an appropriate choice of randomness).
- Show that (in equivocal mode) $M = \{\mathsf{ct}_{i,b}\}$ can be simulated (using ρ and $\{R_{i,b}\}$) without knowing s.
- At this point, ct_0 is guaranteed to hide m by invoking KDM-security of SKE.

To argue function-hiding, we show that the ciphertext ct can be decrypted in two equivalent ways: (1) by using the "honest" decryption algorithm with the ABE secret key sk_f; and (2) using *the* PKE *secret key associated with* pk (and outputting a message only when $f(x) = 1$). Semantic security of the scheme is guaranteed to hold in the presence of sk_f (the secret key of the honest decryptor), but an adversary with oracle access to one of these two decryption functions cannot distinguish them. Since the second procedure hides $f(x')$ for any attribute x' not queried by the adversary, function-hiding follows.

Combined with the instantiations of KDM-secure SKE from various assumptions [2,7,9,19,20] and the fact that single-key ABE follows from PKE [29,48], this approach gives a single-key function-hiding ABE scheme from any of the CDH/LWE/LPN assumptions. For our LPN instantiation, we require noise rate $1/\sqrt{n}$ to instantiate the public-key encryption scheme [1]. We describe this construction and its analysis in Sect. 5.

Obtaining Malicious Security. So far, we have shown how to construct DV-NIZKs from function-hiding single-key ABE and provided several instantiations of the latter object from concrete assumptions. However, the DV-NIZKs obtained in this fashion necessarily requires that the verifier's secret key be generated by a trusted party; indeed, if the verifier is malicious and allowed to set up this DV-NIZK, it can simply sample an ABE key-pair (pp, msk) and remember the entire master secret key. This clearly breaks zero-knowledge.

To construct a malicious DV-NIZK scheme, we intuitively have to replace the trusted setup of an ABE scheme with a form of reusable *non-interactive* two-party computation that implements a similar functionality. Specifically, we introduce a more general primitive called *attribute-based secure function evaluation* (AB-SFE, see Definition 3.1). At a high-level, an AB-SFE scheme is a two-party protocol between a sender and a receiver and parameterized by a public function $F: \mathcal{X} \times \mathcal{Y} \to \{0,1\}$. The sender holds a public attribute $x \in \mathcal{X}$ and a secret message m while the receiver holds a secret input $y \in \mathcal{Y}$. At the end of the protocol, the receiver should learn m only if $F(x, y) = 1$ (otherwise, the receiver should learn nothing). The protocol should be non-interactive in the following sense: at the beginning of the protocol, the receiver publishes a public key pk_y based on its secret input y; thereafter, the sender with its attribute-message pair (x, m) can send a single message to the receiver that allows the receiver to learn m whenever $F(x, y) = 1$. The receiver's initial message pk_y should both hide y and be *reusable* for arbitrarily many protocol executions. We say AB-SFE schemes satisfying this property are "key-hiding". In addition, we are interested in security even against malicious receivers that choose pk_y maliciously. We note that a single-key ABE scheme can be used to construct a secure AB-SFE scheme satisfying a much weaker security notion where a trusted party generates the receiver's message pk_y.

Similarly to our use of ABE in the generic compiler above, an AB-SFE scheme can be used to compile a Σ-protocol (or more generally, zero-knowledge PCPs) to obtain a reusable DV-NIZK; moreover, this compiled DV-NIZK is secure even against *malicious* verifiers and is therefore an MDV-NIZK. Specifically, in our construction, we replace the ABE scheme with an AB-SFE scheme with respect to the function F where $F((x, b), k) = 1$ if and only if $\mathsf{PRF}(k, x) = b$. If we use a maliciously-secure AB-SFE scheme, we only rely on a trusted setup to generate a *uniformly random* common reference string. We then allow the verifier to (1) sample a PRF key k and (2) compute the receiver message pk_k for the AB-SFE protocol (with private input k) itself. Malicious security of the AB-SFE protocol exactly allows us to prove malicious zero-knowledge of the compiled protocol. As in the case of ABE, *soundness* of the compiled protocol relies on a form of AB-SFE security where the receiver's input y is hidden from the sender even given access to an appropriately-defined decryption oracle.

We obtain AB-SFE schemes that can be plugged into our compiler in two steps:

- **Constructing weak key-hiding AB-SFE.** First, we combine a form of malicious-secure 2-message OT [21,45] with garbled circuits to obtain an AB-SFE scheme that satisfies *weak key-hiding*. Namely, the receiver's input y is hidden to an adversary that does *not* have access to the decryption oracle. We describe this construction in Sect. 5.2.
- **Amplifying weak key-hiding to strong key-hiding.** Then, we apply the [38,39] transformation to the weak key-hiding AB-SFE scheme from above to obtain an AB-SFE scheme that satisfies strong key-hiding where the receiver's input y is hidden even in the presence of the decryption oracle. This allows for new instantiations of MDV-NIZK from any of the CDH/LWE/LPN assumptions (Theorem 1.2). Our LPN-based instantiation requires noise rate $n^{-(\frac{1}{2}+\epsilon)}$

for some $\epsilon > 0$ in order to implement the [21] OT protocol. We describe this construction in Sect. 5.3.

We provide a formal definition of AB-SFE in Sect. 3, and the full construction and analysis in Sect. 5.

1.3 Recent Related Work

In this section, we describe several recent works that are directly related to this work. Several of these works [21,38] have yielded new instantiations of our general framework for constructing designated-verifier NIZKs (relative to a preliminary version of this work [41]).

NIZKs from LWE. In a concurrent and independent work, Peikert and Shiehian [44] construct NIZKs from the plain LWE assumption, which in particular yields reusable (M)DV-NIZKs from LWE. While the [44] NIZK has the major advantage of being publicly verifiable, we note that our usage of LWE only relies on plain Regev (public-key) encryption [47] rather than more complex lattice-based primitives.

KDM-Secure SKE and Hinting PRGs. In a concurrent work, Kitagawa, Matsuda and Tanaka [38] modify the "signaling technique" of [39] with the goal of constructing CCA-secure encryption (similarly to [39]). The [38] modification of [39] can be plugged into our construction of (M)DV-NIZKs to obtain our LPN-based instantiation of DV-NIZKs.

2-Message OT from CDH/LPN. In another concurrent work, Döttling, Garg, Hajiabadi, Masny, and Wichs [21] construct 2-round OT from the CDH/LPN assumptions. Their construction can be directly combined with our generic transformations to obtain the CDH/LPN-based instantiations of MDV-NIZKs in this paper.

2 Preliminaries

We write λ to denote a security parameter. We say that a function f is negligible in λ, denoted $\mathsf{negl}(\lambda)$, if $f(\lambda) = o(1/\lambda^c)$ for all $c \in \mathbb{N}$. We say an event happens with negligible probability if the probability of the event happening is negligible, and that it happens with overwhelming probability if its complement occurs with negligible probability. We say that an algorithm is efficient if it runs in probabilistic polynomial-time (PPT) in the length of its inputs. We write $\mathsf{poly}(\lambda)$ to denote a function bounded by a (fixed) polynomial in λ. We say that two families of distributions $\mathcal{D}_1 = \{\mathcal{D}_{1,\lambda}\}_{\lambda \in \mathbb{N}}$ and $\mathcal{D}_2 = \{\mathcal{D}_{2,\lambda}\}_{\lambda \in \mathbb{N}}$ are computationally indistinguishable if no PPT adversary can distinguish samples from $\mathcal{D}_1$ and $\mathcal{D}_2$ except with negligible probability, and we denote this by writing $\mathcal{D}_1 \overset{c}{\approx} \mathcal{D}_2$. We write $\mathcal{D}_1 \overset{s}{\approx} \mathcal{D}_2$ to denote that $\mathcal{D}_1$ and $\mathcal{D}_2$ are statistically indistinguishable (i.e., the statistical distance between $\mathcal{D}_1$ and $\mathcal{D}_2$ is bounded by a negligible function).

For an integer $n \geq 1$, we write $[n]$ to denote the set of integers $\{1, \ldots, n\}$. For a finite set S, we write $x \xleftarrow{\text{R}} S$ to denote that x is sampled uniformly at random from S. For a distribution $\mathcal{D}$, we write $x \leftarrow \mathcal{D}$ to denote that x is sampled from $\mathcal{D}$. For two finite sets $\mathcal{X}$ and $\mathcal{Y}$, we write $\mathsf{Funs}[\mathcal{X}, \mathcal{Y}]$ to denote the set of functions from $\mathcal{X}$ to $\mathcal{Y}$. In the full version of this paper [40], we also review the definitions of core cryptographic primitives such as pseudorandom functions, public-key encryption, (receiver-extractable) 2-message oblivious transfer, garbling schemes, and non-interactive equivocable commitments.

2.1 Designated-Verifier NIZKs

We now introduce the notion of a designated-verifier non-interactive zero-knowledge (DV-NIZK) argument. We use a refined notion where there are separate setup and key-generation algorithms. The setup algorithm outputs a common reference string (possibly a common *random* string) for the scheme. The CRS can be reused by different verifiers, who would generate their own public and private keys. In the traditional notion of designated-verifier NIZKs, the setup and key-generations algorithms are combined, and the public key pk is simply included as part of the CRS.

Definition 2.1 (Designated-Verifier NIZK Argument). *Let $\mathcal{L}$ be an* NP *language associated with an* NP *relation $\mathcal{R}$. A designated-verifier non-interactive zero-knowledge (DV-NIZK) argument for $\mathcal{L}$ consists of a tuple of three efficient algorithms* dvNIZK = (dvNIZK.Setup, dvNIZK.KeyGen, dvNIZK.Prove, dvNIZK.Verify) *with the following properties:*

- dvNIZK.Setup$(1^\lambda) \to$ crs*: On input the security parameter λ, the setup algorithm outputs a common reference string* crs*. If* dvNIZK.Setup *outputs a uniformly random string, then we say that the DV-NIZK scheme is in the* common random string *model.*
- dvNIZK.KeyGen(crs) $\to$ (pk, sk)*: On input a common reference string* crs*, the key-generation algorithm outputs a public key* pk *and a secret verification key* sk*.*
- dvNIZK.Prove(crs, pk, x, w) $\to \pi$*: On input the common reference string* crs*, a public key* pk*, a statement x, and a witness w, the prove algorithm outputs a proof π.*
- dvNIZK.Verify(crs, sk, x, π) $\to \{0, 1\}$*: On input the common reference string* crs*, a secret key* sk*, a statement x, and a proof π, the verification algorithm outputs a bit $b \in \{0, 1\}$.*

Moreover, dvNIZK *should satisfy the following properties:*

- **Completeness:** *For all $(x, w) \in \mathcal{R}$, and taking* crs $\leftarrow$ dvNIZK.Setup(1^λ) *and* (pk, sk) $\leftarrow$ dvNIZK.KeyGen(crs)*, we have that*

$$\Pr\left[\pi \leftarrow \mathsf{dvNIZK.Prove}(\mathsf{crs}, \mathsf{pk}, x, w) : \mathsf{dvNIZK.Verify}(\mathsf{crs}, \mathsf{sk}, x, \pi) = 1\right] = 1.$$

- **Soundness:** *We consider two variants of soundness:*

- **Non-adaptive soundness:** *For all $x \notin \mathcal{L}$, all PPT adversaries $\mathcal{A}$,*

$$\Pr\left[\pi \leftarrow \mathcal{A}^{\mathsf{dvNIZK.Verify(crs,sk,\cdot,\cdot)}}(1^\lambda, \mathsf{crs}, \mathsf{pk}, x) :\right.$$

$$\left.\mathsf{dvNIZK.Verify}(\mathsf{crs}, \mathsf{sk}, x, \pi) = 1\right] = \mathsf{negl}(\lambda),$$

where $\mathsf{crs} \leftarrow \mathsf{dvNIZK.Setup}(1^\lambda)$ *and* $(\mathsf{pk}, \mathsf{sk}) \leftarrow \mathsf{dvNIZK.KeyGen}(\mathsf{crs})$.
- **Adaptive soundness:** *For all PPT adversaries $\mathcal{A}$,*

$$\Pr\left[(x, \pi) \leftarrow \mathcal{A}^{\mathsf{dvNIZK.Verify(crs,sk,\cdot,\cdot)}}(1^\lambda, \mathsf{crs}) :\right.$$

$$\left.x \notin \mathcal{L} \wedge \mathsf{dvNIZK.Verify}(\mathsf{crs}, \mathsf{sk}, x, \pi) = 1\right] = \mathsf{negl}(\lambda),$$

for $(\mathsf{crs}, \mathsf{pk}, \mathsf{sk}) \leftarrow \mathsf{dvNIZK.Setup}(1^\lambda)$ *and* $(\mathsf{pk}, \mathsf{sk}) \leftarrow \mathsf{dvNIZK.KeyGen}(\mathsf{crs})$.
- **Zero-knowledge:** *For all PPT adversaries $\mathcal{A}$, there exists a PPT simulator $\mathcal{S} = (\mathcal{S}_1, \mathcal{S}_2)$ such that*

$$\left|\Pr[\mathcal{A}^{\mathcal{O}_0(\mathsf{crs,pk},\cdot,\cdot)}(\mathsf{crs}, \mathsf{pk}, \mathsf{sk}) = 1] - \Pr[\mathcal{A}^{\mathcal{O}_1(\mathsf{st}_\mathcal{S},\cdot,\cdot)}(\overline{\mathsf{crs}}, \overline{\mathsf{pk}}, \overline{\mathsf{sk}}) = 1]\right| = \mathsf{negl}(\lambda),$$

where $\mathsf{crs} \leftarrow \mathsf{dvNIZK.Setup}(1^\lambda)$, $(\mathsf{pk}, \mathsf{sk}) \leftarrow \mathsf{dvNIZK.KeyGen}(\mathsf{crs})$, *and* $(\mathsf{st}_\mathcal{S}, \overline{\mathsf{crs}}, \overline{\mathsf{pk}}, \overline{\mathsf{sk}}) \leftarrow \mathcal{S}_1(1^\lambda)$, *the oracle* $\mathcal{O}_0(\mathsf{crs}, \mathsf{pk}, x, w)$ *outputs* $\mathsf{dvNIZK.Prove}(\mathsf{crs}, \mathsf{pk}, x, w)$ *if* $\mathcal{R}(x, w) = 1$ *and* $\perp$ *otherwise, and the oracle* $\mathcal{O}_1(\mathsf{st}_\mathcal{S}, x, w)$ *outputs* $\mathcal{S}_2(\mathsf{st}_\mathcal{S}, x)$ *if* $\mathcal{R}(x, w) = 1$ *and* $\perp$ *otherwise.*

Definition 2.2 (Malicious Designated-Verifier NIZKs [46]). *Let* dvNIZK *be a DV-NIZK for a language $\mathcal{L}$ (with associated NP relation $\mathcal{R}$). For an adversary $\mathcal{A}$, and a simulator $\mathcal{S} = (\mathcal{S}_1, \mathcal{S}_2)$, we define two experiments $\mathsf{ExptReal}_\mathcal{A}(\lambda)$ and $\mathsf{ExptSim}_{\mathcal{A},\mathcal{S}}(\lambda)$ as follows:*

- **Setup:** *In* $\mathsf{ExptReal}_\mathcal{A}(\lambda)$, *the challenger samples* $\mathsf{crs} \leftarrow \mathsf{dvNIZK.Setup}(1^\lambda)$ *and in* $\mathsf{ExptSim}_{\mathcal{A},\mathcal{S}}(\lambda)$, *the challenger samples* $(\mathsf{st}_\mathcal{S}, \overline{\mathsf{crs}}) \leftarrow \mathcal{S}_1(1^\lambda)$. *In* $\mathsf{ExptReal}_\mathcal{A}(\lambda)$, *the challenger gives* crs *to $\mathcal{A}$, while in* $\mathsf{ExptSim}_{\mathcal{A},\mathcal{S}}(\lambda)$, *the challenger gives* $\overline{\mathsf{crs}}$ *to $\mathcal{A}$. Then, $\mathcal{A}$ outputs a public key* pk.
- **Verification queries:** *Algorithm $\mathcal{A}$ is then given access to a verification oracle. In both experiments, if* $\mathcal{R}(x, w) \neq 1$, *then the challenger replies with $\perp$. Otherwise, in* $\mathsf{ExptReal}_\mathcal{A}(\lambda)$, *the challenger replies with* $\pi \leftarrow \mathsf{dvNIZK.Prove}(\mathsf{crs}, \mathsf{pk}, x, w)$, *and in* $\mathsf{ExptSim}_{\mathcal{A},\mathcal{S}}(\lambda)$, *the challenger replies with* $\overline{\pi} \leftarrow \mathcal{S}_2(\mathsf{st}_\mathcal{S}, \mathsf{pk}, x)$.
- **Output:** *At the end of the experiment, the adversary outputs a bit* $b' \in \{0, 1\}$, *which is the output of the experiment.*

We say that dvNIZK *provides* zero-knowledge against malicious verifiers *if for all PPT adversaries $\mathcal{A}$, there exists an efficient simulator $\mathcal{S}$ such that* $\mathsf{ExptReal}_\mathcal{A}(\lambda) \overset{c}{\approx} \mathsf{ExptSim}_{\mathcal{A},\mathcal{S}}(\lambda)$. *If* dvNIZK *satisfies this property (in addition to completeness and soundness), then we say that* dvNIZK *is a* malicious-designated-verifier NIZK *(MDV-NIZK).*

Remark 2.3 (Reusability of the CRS with Many Public Keys). The zero-knowledge property of Definition 2.2 only provides (multi-theorem) zero-knowledge with respect to a *single* maliciously-generated public key pk. Using the "OR trick" transformation from [23], any MDV-NIZK can be generically compiled into one where a single CRS can be reused with an arbitrary polynomial number of (potentially maliciously-generated) public keys, while preserving zero-knowledge. Note that the original transformation compiled any NIZK in the CRS model with single-theorem zero-knowledge into a multi-theorem version; we note that it also directly applies to the (malicious) designated-verifier setting (essentially because proofs can still be generated publicly). Additionally, if the original MDV-NIZK is in the common random string model, then the resulting protocol is also in the common random string model.

Remark 2.4 (Adaptive Soundness via Complexity Leveraging). Using the standard technique of complexity leveraging [5], a DV-NIZK satisfying non-adaptive soundness also satisfies adaptive soundness at the expense of a super-polynomial loss in the security reduction.

2.2   Zero-Knowledge PCPs

Definition 2.5 (Zero-Knowledge PCP [34,36]**).** *Let* $\mathcal{R} \colon \{0,1\}^n \times \{0,1\}^h \to \{0,1\}$ *be an* NP *relation and* $\mathcal{L} \subseteq \{0,1\}^n$ *be the associated language. A non-adaptive, ℓ-query zero-knowledge PCP (with alphabet Σ) for $\mathcal{L}$ is a tuple of algorithms* zkPCP $=$ (zkPCP.Prove, zkPCP.Query, zkPCP.Verify) *with the following properties:*

- zkPCP.Prove$(x, w) \to \pi$: *On input a statement* $x \in \{0,1\}^n$ *and a witness* $w \in \{0,1\}^h$*, the prove algorithm outputs a proof* $\pi \in \Sigma^m$*.*
- zkPCP.Query$(x) \to (\mathsf{st}_x, q_1, \ldots, q_\ell)$: *On input a statement* $x \in \{0,1\}^n$*, the query-generation algorithm outputs a verification state* st_x *and ℓ query indices* $q_1, \ldots, q_\ell \in [m]$*.*
- zkPCP.Verify$(\mathsf{st}_x, s_1, \ldots, s_\ell) \to \{0,1\}$: *On input the verification state* st *and a set of responses* $s_1, \ldots, s_\ell \in \Sigma$*, the verify algorithm outputs a bit* $b \in \{0,1\}$*.*

Moreover, zkPCP *should satisfy the following properties:*

- **Efficiency:** *The running time of* zkPCP.Prove, zkPCP.Query, *and* zkPCP.Verify *should be bounded by* poly(n)*. In particular, this means that* $m = $ poly(n)*.*
- **Completeness:** *For all* $x \in \{0,1\}^n$ *and* $w \in \{0,1\}^h$ *where* $\mathcal{R}(x, w) = 1$*,*

$$\Pr[\mathsf{zkPCP.Verify}(\mathsf{st}_x, \pi_{q_1}, \ldots, \pi_{q_\ell}) = 1] = 1,$$

where $\pi \leftarrow$ zkPCP.Prove(x, w) *and* $(\mathsf{st}_x, q_1, \ldots, q_\ell) \leftarrow$ zkPCP.Query(x)*.*
- **Soundness:** *For all* $x \notin \mathcal{L}$*, all proof strings* $\pi \in \Sigma^m$*,*

$$\Pr[\mathsf{zkPCP.Verify}(\mathsf{st}_x, \pi_{q_1}, \ldots, \pi_{q_\ell}) = 1] = \mathsf{negl}(n),$$

where $(\mathsf{st}_x, q_1, \ldots, q_\ell) \leftarrow$ zkPCP.Query(x)*.*

– **Zero-knowledge:** *For all PPT adversaries* $\mathcal{A} = (\mathcal{A}_1, \mathcal{A}_2)$, *there exists an efficient simulator* $\mathcal{S}$ *such that*

$$\left| \Pr[b = 1 \mid \mathcal{R}(x, w) = 1] - \Pr[\tilde{b} = 1 \mid \mathcal{R}(x, w) = 1] \right| = \mathsf{negl}(n),$$

where $(\mathsf{st}_\mathcal{A}, x, w, q_1, \ldots, q_\ell) \leftarrow \mathcal{A}_1(1^n)$, $\pi \leftarrow \mathsf{zkPCP.Prove}(x, w)$, $(\tilde{\pi}_1, \ldots, \tilde{\pi}_\ell)$ $\leftarrow \mathcal{S}(x, q_1, \ldots, q_\ell)$, $b \leftarrow \mathcal{A}_2(\mathsf{st}_\mathcal{A}, \pi_{q_1}, \ldots, \pi_{q_\ell})$, *and* $\tilde{b} \leftarrow \mathcal{A}_2(\mathsf{st}_\mathcal{A}, \tilde{\pi}_1, \ldots, \tilde{\pi}_\ell)$,

Semi-malicious Zero-Knowledge. The zero-knowledge requirement in Definition 2.5 requires that there exists a PPT simulator for an adversary that reads any set of ℓ bits of the PCP, including subsets that would never be output by zkPCP.Query. In our constructions, we can rely on the relaxed notion of *semi-malicious* zero-knowledge which only requires simulation for subsets of bits that are output by an invocation of zkPCP.Query (for some setting of the randomness). Specifically, we define the following:

Definition 2.6 (Semi-Malicious Zero-Knowledge). *A zero-knowledge PCP* zkPCP *for a language* $\mathcal{L}$ *with associated* NP *relation* $\mathcal{R}$ *satisfies semi-malicious zero-knowledge if for all PPT adversaries* $\mathcal{A} = (\mathcal{A}_1, \mathcal{A}_2)$, *there exists a PPT simulator* $\mathcal{S}$ *such that*

$$\left| \Pr[\mathcal{A}_2(\mathsf{st}_\mathcal{A}, \pi_{q_1}, \ldots, \pi_{q_\ell}) = 1 \mid \mathcal{R}(x, w) = 1] - \right.$$

$$\left. \Pr[\mathcal{A}_2(\mathsf{st}_\mathcal{A}, \tilde{\pi}_1, \ldots, \tilde{\pi}_\ell) = 1 \mid \mathcal{R}(x, w) = 1] \right| = \mathsf{negl}(n),$$

for $(\mathsf{st}_\mathcal{A}, x, w, r) \leftarrow \mathcal{A}_1(1^n)$, $(q_1, \ldots, q_\ell) \leftarrow \mathsf{zkPCP.Query}(x; r)$, $\pi \leftarrow$ zkPCP.Prove(x, w), *and* $(\tilde{\pi}_1, \ldots, \tilde{\pi}_\ell) \leftarrow \mathcal{S}(x, q_1, \ldots, q_\ell)$.

Instantiating Zero-Knowledge PCPs. As noted by Ishai et al. [34], the original zero-knowledge protocol by Goldreich et al. [27] makes implicit use of an honest-verifier zero-knowledge PCP for graph 3-coloring. To briefly recall, the prover takes a 3-coloring of the graph, randomly permutes the colors, and writes down the colors for each vertex as the PCP. To check the PCP, the (honest) verifier samples a random edge in the graph and reads the colors for the two nodes associated with the edge. It is straightforward to see that if zkPCP.Query always outputs a pair of nodes corresponding to some edge in the graph, then this PCP satisfies semi-malicious zero-knowledge. To achieve negligible soundness, we rely on parallel amplification (e.g., by concatenating many independent copies of the PCP) and note that semi-malicious zero-knowledge is indeed preserved under parallel repetition. We state this instantiation below:

Theorem 2.7 (Semi-Malicious Zero-Knowledge PCP [27]). *Let* $\mathcal{L} \subseteq \{0, 1\}^n$ *be an* NP *language. Then, there exists an* ℓ-query zero-knowledge PCP for $\mathcal{L}$ *with alphabet* $\Sigma = \{0, 1, 2\}$ *and* $\ell = \mathsf{poly}(n)$.

We note that there are many other ways to instantiate the zero-knowledge PCP with the desired properties. For instance, Blum's protocol for graph Hamiltonicity [3] also implicitly uses a (semi-malicious) zero-knowledge PCP. We can also construct zero-knowledge PCPs (with fully malicious zero knowledge) using multiparty computation (MPC) protocols by using the MPC-in-the-head technique of Ishai et al. [33]. More broadly, Σ-protocols with a polynomial-size challenge space can generally be viewed as implicitly implementing a (semi-malicious) zero-knowledge PCP.

2.3   Attribute-Based Encryption

Definition 2.8 (Attribute-Based Encryption). *An attribute-based encryption (ABE) scheme over a message space $\mathcal{M}$, an attribute space $\mathcal{X}$, and a function family $\mathcal{F} = \{f \colon \mathcal{X} \to \{0,1\}\}$ is a tuple of algorithms* ABE = (ABE.Setup, ABE.KeyGen, ABE.Encrypt, ABE.Decrypt) *with the following properties:*

- ABE.Setup$(1^\lambda) \to$ (pp, msk): *On input the security parameter λ, the setup algorithm outputs the public parameters* pp *and the master secret key* msk.
- ABE.KeyGen$($pp, msk, $f) \to$ sk$_f$: *On input the public parameters* pp, *the master secret key* msk *and a function $f \in \mathcal{F}$, the key-generation algorithm outputs a decryption key* sk$_f$.
- ABE.Encrypt$($pp, $x, m) \to$ ct$_{x,m}$: *On input the public parameters* pp, *an attribute $x \in \mathcal{X}$, and a message $m \in \mathcal{M}$, the encryption algorithm outputs a ciphertext* ct$_{x,m}$.
- ABE.Decrypt$($pp, sk, ct$) \to (x, m)$: *On input the public parameters* pp, *a secret key* sk *(which could be the master secret key), and a ciphertext* ct, *the decryption algorithm either outputs an attribute-message pair $(x, m) \in \mathcal{X} \times \mathcal{M}$ or a special symbol $\bot$.*

Definition 2.9 (Correctness). *An ABE scheme* ABE *is (perfectly) correct if for all messages $m \in \mathcal{M}$, all attributes $x \in \mathcal{X}$, and all predicates $f \in \mathcal{F}$, and setting* (pp, msk) $\leftarrow$ ABE.Setup(1^λ),

- $\Pr\left[\text{ABE.Decrypt}\big(\text{pp}, \text{msk}, \text{ABE.Encrypt}(\text{pp}, x, m)\big) = (x, m)\right] = 1.$
- *If $f(x) = 1$, then*

ABE.Decrypt$\big($pp, ABE.KeyGen(pp, msk, f), ABE.Encrypt(pp, x, m)$\big) = (x, m)$

with probability 1.

Definition 2.10 (Security). *Let* ABE *be an ABE scheme over an attribute space $\mathcal{X}$, message space $\mathcal{M}$, and function family $\mathcal{F}$. For a security parameter λ and an adversary $\mathcal{A}$, we define the ABE security experiment* $\mathsf{Expt}_{\mathcal{A}}^{\mathsf{ABE}}(\lambda, b)$ *as follows. The challenger begins by sampling* (pp, msk) $\leftarrow$ ABE.Setup(1^λ) *and gives* pp *to the adversary $\mathcal{A}$. Then $\mathcal{A}$ is given access to the following oracles:*

- **Key-generation oracle:** *On input a function $f \in \mathcal{F}$, the challenger responds with a key* sk$_f$ $\leftarrow$ ABE.KeyGen(pp, msk, f).

– **Challenge oracle:** *On input an attribute* $x \in \mathcal{X}$ *and a pair of messages* $m_0, m_1 \in \mathcal{M}$, *the challenger responds with a ciphertext* ct $\leftarrow$ ABE.Encrypt(pp, x, m_b).

At the end of the game, the adversary outputs a bit $b' \in \{0, 1\}$, *which is also the output of the experiment. An adversary* $\mathcal{A}$ *is admissible for the attribute-based encryption security game if it makes one challenge query* (x, m_0, m_1), *and for all key-generation queries* f *the adversary makes,* $f(x) = 0$. *We say that* ABE *is secure if for all efficient and admissible adversaries* $\mathcal{A}$,

$$\left| \Pr[\mathsf{Expt}_{\mathcal{A}}^{\mathsf{ABE}}(\lambda, 0) = 1] - \Pr[\mathsf{Expt}_{\mathcal{A}}^{\mathsf{ABE}}(\lambda, 1) = 1] \right| = \mathsf{negl}(\lambda).$$

Moreover, we say that ABE *is* single-key secure *if the above property holds for all efficient and admissible adversaries* $\mathcal{A}$ *that make at most one key-generation query.*

Function Hiding. Our generic constructions of designated-verifier NIZKs from ABE (and generalizations thereof) relies on an additional (weak) notion of function hiding. While the traditional notion of function hiding asks that the secret decryption key hides the function, our construction relies on a *weaker* notion where we require that *oracle access* to the decryption function does not reveal information about the underlying function (other than what can be directly inferred by the input-output behavior of the function). We give the formal definition below:

Definition 2.11 (Weak Function Hiding). *Let* ABE *be an ABE scheme, and let* $t = t(\lambda)$ *be a bound on the length of ciphertext in* ABE. *We say that* ABE *satisfies* weak function hiding *if there exists an efficient simulator* $\mathcal{S}$ *such that for all functions* $f \in \mathcal{F}$, (pp, msk) $\leftarrow$ ABE.Setup(1^λ), *and* sk$_f \leftarrow$ ABE.KeyGen(pp, msk, f)

$$\left| \Pr[\mathcal{A}^{\mathcal{O}_1(\mathsf{pp},\mathsf{sk}_f,\cdot)}(1^\lambda, \mathsf{pp}) = 1] - \Pr[\mathcal{A}^{\mathcal{O}_2(\mathsf{pp},\mathsf{msk},\cdot)}(1^\lambda, \mathsf{pp}) = 1] \right| = \mathsf{negl}(\lambda),$$

where the oracles $\mathcal{O}_1, \mathcal{O}_2$ *are defined as follows:*

– **Real decryption oracle:** *On input* pp, sk$_f$, ct $\in \{0, 1\}^t$, *the real decryption oracle* $\mathcal{O}_1$(pp, sk$_f$, ct) *outputs* ABE.Decrypt(pp, sk$_f$, ct).
– **Ideal decryption oracle:** *On input* pp, msk, *and a string* ct $\in \{0, 1\}^t$, *the ideal decryption oracle* $\mathcal{O}_2$(pp, msk, ct) *outputs* $\mathcal{S}^{f(\cdot)}$(pp, msk, ct). *Moreover, we restrict the simulator* $\mathcal{S}$ *to make at most one oracle query to* f *per invocation.*

2.4   KDM-Secure Secret-Key Encyryption

Definition 2.12 (One-Time KDM-Secure SKE). *A secret-key encryption (SKE) scheme* SKE $=$ (SKE.Encrypt, SKE.Decrypt) *is said to be* one-time KDM secure *for a function class* $\mathcal{F}$ *(with many-bit outputs) if for every function* $f \in \mathcal{F}$, *the following two distributions are computationally indistinguishable:*

$$\{s \xleftarrow{\text{R}} \{0,1\}^\lambda : \mathsf{SKE.Encrypt}(s, f(s))\} \overset{c}{\approx} \{s \xleftarrow{\text{R}} \{0,1\}^\lambda : \mathsf{SKE.Encrypt}(s, 0^{|f(s)|})\}$$

Remark 2.13 (KDM-Secure SKE Constructions for Projection Functions). We say a function $f \colon \{0,1\}^\lambda \to \{0,1\}^m$ is a *projection function* if each bit of $f(s)$ depends on at most one bit of s. As in [38], we consider the class $\mathcal{F} = \mathcal{F}_{\text{proj}}$ of projection functions. Secret-key encryption schemes that are KDM-secure for the class of projection functions can be constructed from the CDH [7,9], LWE (with polynomial modulus) [2,9], and constant-noise LPN [2] assumptions.

3   Attribute-Based Secure Function Evaluation

In this section, we formally introduce our notion of an attribute-based secure function evaluation scheme (AB-SFE), which can be viewed as a generalization of a single-key ABE scheme. We then define two main security requirements on AB-SFE schemes: message-hiding and key-hiding. For each notion, we introduce a "weak" variant and a "strong" variant of the notion.

Definition 3.1 (Attribute-Based Secure Function Evaluation). *An attribute-based secure function evaluation (AB-SFE) scheme for a function* $F \colon \mathcal{X} \times \mathcal{Y} \to \{0,1\}$ *with message space* $\mathcal{M}$ *consists of a tuple of PPT algorithms* $\mathsf{ABSFE} = (\mathsf{ABSFE.Setup}, \mathsf{ABSFE.KeyGen}, \mathsf{ABSFE.Encrypt}, \mathsf{ABSFE.Decrypt})$ *with the following properties:*

- $\mathsf{ABSFE.Setup}(1^\lambda) \to \mathsf{crs}$: *On input the security parameter* λ, *the setup algorithm outputs a* common reference string crs. *We say that the AB-SFE scheme is in the* common random string model *if* Setup *simply outputs a uniformly random string.*
- $\mathsf{ABSFE.KeyGen}(\mathsf{crs}, y) \to (\mathsf{pk}, \mathsf{sk})$: *On input the common reference string* crs *and a value* $y \in \mathcal{Y}$, *the key-generation algorithm outputs a public key* pk *and a secret key* sk.
- $\mathsf{ABSFE.Encrypt}(\mathsf{crs}, \mathsf{pk}, x, m) \to \mathsf{ct}$: *On input the common reference string* crs, *a public key* pk, *a value* $x \in \mathcal{X}$, *and a message* $m \in \mathcal{M}$, *the encryption algorithm outputs a ciphertext* ct.
- $\mathsf{ABSFE.Decrypt}(\mathsf{crs}, \mathsf{sk}, x, \mathsf{ct}) \to m$: *On input the common reference string* crs, *a secret key* sk, *an attribute* $x \in \mathcal{X}$, *and a ciphertext* ct, *the decryption algorithm outputs a message* $m \in \mathcal{M} \cup \{\bot\}$.

Definition 3.2 (Correctness). *An AB-SFE scheme* ABSFE *is (perfectly) correct if for all messages* $m \in \mathcal{M}$, *all* $x \in \mathcal{X}, y \in \mathcal{Y}$ *where* $F(x,y) = 1$,

$$\Pr\left[\mathsf{ABSFE.Decrypt}(\mathsf{crs}, \mathsf{sk}, x, \mathsf{ABSFE.Encrypt}(\mathsf{crs}, \mathsf{pk}, x, m)) = m\right] = 1,$$

where $\mathsf{crs} \leftarrow \mathsf{ABSFE.Setup}(1^\lambda)$ *and* $(\mathsf{pk}, \mathsf{sk}) \leftarrow \mathsf{ABSFE.KeyGen}(\mathsf{crs}, y)$.

Message-Hiding. The first security requirement on an AB-SFE scheme is message-hiding. The basic notion (or "weak" notion) is essentially semantic security: namely, a ciphertext with attribute $x \in \mathcal{X}$ encrypted under a public key for $y \in \mathcal{Y}$ where $F(x, y) = 0$ should hide the underlying message. Next, we define a "strong" notion of message-hiding, which says semantic security holds even in the setting where the public-key is *maliciously* chosen. In this case, we require that there exists an efficient algorithm that can extract an attribute y from any (possibly malformed) public key pk, and ciphertexts encrypted to any attribute x where $F(x, y) = 0$ still hide the underlying message.

Definition 3.3 (Weak Message-Hiding). *Let* ABSFE *be an AB-SFE scheme. For a bit* $b \in \{0, 1\}$, *we define the following game between an adversary* $\mathcal{A}$ *and a challenger:*

- **Setup:** *The adversary* $\mathcal{A}$ *begins by sending an input* $y \in \mathcal{Y}$ *to the challenger. The challenger samples* crs $\leftarrow$ ABSFE.Setup(1^λ), (pk, sk) $\leftarrow$ ABSFE.KeyGen (crs, y) *and gives* crs, pk, sk *to* $\mathcal{A}$.
- **Challenge query:** *The adversary* $\mathcal{A}$ *then makes a challenge query* (x, m_0, m_1) *to the challenger where* $x \in \mathcal{X}$, $m_0, m_1 \in \mathcal{M}$, *and* $F(x, y) = 0$. *The challenger replies with* ct $\leftarrow$ ABSFE.Encrypt(crs, pk, x, m_b) *and gives* ct *to* $\mathcal{A}$.
- **Output:** *The adversary* $\mathcal{A}$ *outputs a bit* $b' \in \{0, 1\}$.

We say that ABSFE *provides* weak message-hiding *if for all PPT adversaries* $\mathcal{A}$,

$$|\Pr[b' = 1 | b = 0] - \Pr[b' = 1 | b = 1]| = \mathsf{negl}(\lambda).$$

Definition 3.4 (Strong Message-Hiding). *An AB-SFE scheme* ABSFE *provides* strong message-hiding *if there exists a PPT "extractable-setup" algorithm* (crs, td) $\leftarrow$ ABSFE.SetupExt(1^λ) *and a PPT extractor* $y \leftarrow$ ABSFE.Ext(td, pk) *with the following properties:*

- **CRS indistinguishability:** *The CRS distributions output by* ABSFE.Setup *and* ABSFE.SetupExt *are computationally indistinguishable:*

$$\{\mathsf{crs} \leftarrow \mathsf{ABSFE.Setup}(1^\lambda) : \mathsf{crs}\} \overset{c}{\approx} \{(\mathsf{crs}, \mathsf{td}) \leftarrow \mathsf{ABSFE.SetupExt}(1^\lambda) : \mathsf{crs}\}.$$

- **Ciphertext indistinguishability in extraction mode:** *For a bit* $b \in \{0, 1\}$, *we define the following game between an adversary* $\mathcal{A}$ *and a challenger:*
  - **Setup:** *The challenger samples* (crs, td) $\leftarrow$ ABSFE.SetupExt(1^λ) *and gives* crs *to* $\mathcal{A}$.
  - **Public key selection:** *The adversary chooses a public key* pk. *The challenger computes* $y \leftarrow$ ABSFE.Ext(td, pk) *and gives* $y \in \mathcal{Y}$ *to* $\mathcal{A}$.
  - **Challenge query:** *The adversary* $\mathcal{A}$ *makes a challenge query* (x, m_0, m_1) *where* $x \in \mathcal{X}$, $m_0, m_1 \in \mathcal{M}$, *and* $F(x, y) = 0$. *The challenger computes* ct $\leftarrow$ ABSFE.Encrypt(crs, pk, x, m_b) *and gives* ct *to* $\mathcal{A}$.
  - **Output:** *The adversary* $\mathcal{A}$ *outputs a bit* $b' \in \{0, 1\}$.

We require that for all PPT adversaries $\mathcal{A}$, $\left| \Pr[b' = 1|b = 0] - \Pr[b' = 1|b = 1] \right| = \mathsf{negl}(\lambda)$.

Remark 3.5 (Multiple Challenge Queries). By a standard hybrid argument, any AB-SFE scheme that satisfies weak message-hiding (resp., strong message-hiding) against an adversary that makes a single challenge query (x, m_0, m_1) is also secure against an adversary that makes polynomially-many challenge queries. Note that in the strong message-hiding setting, the challenger encrypts each challenge message with respect to the *same* public key chosen by the adversary (and correspondingly, the *same* value of y is used to check admissibility of each of the adversary's challenge queries). It is essential for the hybrid argument to use the same public key together with the same extracted attribute y, which is known to the adversary (otherwise, the reduction algorithm is unable to simulate the other ciphertexts in the hybrid argument, and correspondingly, single-challenge security does not necessarily imply multiple-challenge security).

Key-Hiding. The second security requirement on an AB-SFE scheme is key-hiding. Similar to the case of message-hiding security, we consider a "weak" notion and a "strong" notion. The weak notion requires that a public key pk associated with an attribute y hides y, while the strong notion requires that y remains hidden even if the adversary has access to a decryption oracle (with the associated secret key sk). Strong key-hiding is reminiscent of the weak function-hiding property we defined for ABE (Definition 2.11), and indeed, we show in Sect. 5.1 that ABE schemes satisfying weak function-hiding imply AB-SFE schemes that satisfy strong key-hiding.

Definition 3.6 (Weak Key-Hiding). *An AB-SFE scheme* ABSFE *satisfies weak key-hiding if there exists a PPT simulator $\mathcal{S}$ such that for all $y \in \mathcal{Y}$ and all PPT adversaries $\mathcal{A}$,*

$$\left| \Pr[\mathcal{A}(1^\lambda, \mathsf{crs}, \mathsf{pk}) = 1] - \Pr[\mathcal{A}(1^\lambda, \overline{\mathsf{crs}}, \overline{\mathsf{pk}}) = 1] \right| = \mathsf{negl}(\lambda),$$

where $\mathsf{crs} \leftarrow \mathsf{ABSFE.Setup}(1^\lambda)$, $(\mathsf{pk}, \mathsf{sk}) \leftarrow \mathsf{ABSFE.KeyGen}(\mathsf{crs}, y)$, *and* $(\overline{\mathsf{crs}}, \overline{\mathsf{pk}}) \leftarrow \mathcal{S}(1^\lambda)$.

Definition 3.7 (Strong Key-Hiding). *An AB-SFE scheme* ABSFE *satisfies strong key-hiding if there exists a PPT simulator $\mathcal{S} = (\mathcal{S}_1, \mathcal{S}_2)$ such that for all $y \in \mathcal{Y}$ and all PPT adversaries $\mathcal{A}$ we have:*

$$\left| \Pr[\mathcal{A}^{\mathcal{O}_1(\mathsf{crs},\mathsf{sk},\cdot,\cdot)}(1^\lambda, \mathsf{crs}, \mathsf{pk}) = 1] - \Pr[\mathcal{A}^{\mathcal{O}_2(\mathsf{st},\cdot,\cdot)}(1^\lambda, \overline{\mathsf{crs}}, \overline{\mathsf{pk}}) = 1] \right| = \mathsf{negl}(\lambda),$$

where $\mathsf{crs} \leftarrow \mathsf{ABSFE.Setup}(1^\lambda)$, $(\mathsf{pk}, \mathsf{sk}) \leftarrow \mathsf{ABSFE.KeyGen}(\mathsf{crs}, y)$, $(\mathsf{st}_\mathcal{S}, \overline{\mathsf{crs}}, \overline{\mathsf{pk}}) \leftarrow \mathcal{S}_1(1^\lambda)$ *and the oracles $\mathcal{O}_1, \mathcal{O}_2$ are defined as follows:*

- *Real decryption oracle $\mathcal{O}_1$: On input a string crs, a secret key sk, a value $x \in \mathcal{X}$, and a ciphertext ct, output $\mathsf{ABSFE.Decrypt}(\mathsf{crs}, \mathsf{sk}, x, \mathsf{ct})$.*
- *Ideal decryption oracle $\mathcal{O}_2$: On input a state $\mathsf{st}_\mathcal{S}$, $x \in \mathcal{X}$ and a ciphertext ct, output $\mathcal{S}_2(\mathsf{st}_\mathcal{S}, x, \mathsf{ct}, F(x, y))$.*

4   Designated-Verifier NIZKs from AB-SFE

In this section, we show how to construct a DV-NIZK from any AB-SFE scheme that provides weak message-hiding and strong key-hiding. In the full version of this paper [40], we show that a converse of this statement also holds: given any public-key encryption scheme and a DV-NIZK, we can obtain an AB-SFE scheme that provides weak message-hiding and strong key-hiding. This means that assuming public-key encryption exists, our notion of AB-SFE is *equivalent* to DV-NIZK. Next, we strengthen our construction and show that if the underlying AB-SFE scheme satisfies strong message-hiding (and strong key-hiding), then we obtain a DV-NIZK with security against malicious verifiers. We give our main construction below:

Construction 4.1 (Designated-Verifier NIZKs from AB-SFE). *Let λ be a security parameter. Let $\mathcal{L} \subseteq \{0,1\}^n$ be an NP language associated with an NP relation $\mathcal{R} \subseteq \{0,1\}^n \times \{0,1\}^h$, where $n = n(\lambda), h = h(\lambda)$. Our construction relies on the following building blocks:*

- *Let* zkPCP $=$ (zkPCP.Prove, zkPCP.Query, zkPCP.Verify) *be an efficient ℓ-query, non-adaptive, zero-knowledge PCP (with alphabet Σ) for $\mathcal{L}$ (Definition 2.5). Let $m = m(\lambda)$ be the length of the PCP and $\rho = \rho(\lambda)$ be a bound on the number of random bits needed for* zkPCP.Query.
- *Let* PRF: $\mathcal{K} \times \{0,1\}^n \to \{0,1\}^\rho$ *be a pseudorandom function.*
- *Let F: $(\{0,1\}^n \times [m]) \times \mathcal{K} \to \{0,1\}$ be the function*

$$F((x,i),k) := \begin{cases} 1 & \exists j \in [\ell] \text{ where } i = q_j \\ 0 & \text{otherwise,} \end{cases} \qquad (4.1)$$

where $(\mathsf{st}_x, q_1, \ldots, q_\ell) \leftarrow$ zkPCP.Query$(x; \mathsf{PRF}(k,x))$.
- *Let* ABSFE $=$ (ABSFE.Setup, ABSFE.KeyGen, ABSFE.Encrypt, ABSFE.Decrypt) *be an AB-SFE scheme (Definition 3.1) for F with message space $\mathcal{M} = \Sigma$ and attribute spaces $\mathcal{X} = \{0,1\}^n \times [m]$ and $\mathcal{Y} = \mathcal{K}$.*

We construct a designated-verifier NIZK dvNIZK $=$ (dvNIZK.Setup, dvNIZK.KeyGen, dvNIZK.Prove, dvNIZK.Verify) *for $\mathcal{L}$ as follows:*

- dvNIZK.Setup(1^λ): *Output* crs $\leftarrow$ ABSFE.Setup(1^λ).
- dvNIZK.KeyGen(crs): *Sample $k \xleftarrow{\text{R}} \mathcal{K}$, and $(\mathsf{pk}', \mathsf{sk}') \leftarrow$ ABSFE.KeyGen(crs, k). Output the public key* pk $=$ pk′, *and the secret verification key* sk $=$ (k, sk').
- dvNIZK.Prove$(\mathsf{crs}, \mathsf{pk}, x, w)$: *Construct a PCP $\pi^{(\mathsf{PCP})} \leftarrow$ zkPCP.Prove(x, w). Then, for each $i \in [m]$, compute ciphertexts $\mathsf{ct}_i \leftarrow$ ABSFE.Encrypt$(\mathsf{crs}, \mathsf{pk}, (x,i), \pi_i^{(\mathsf{PCP})})$, and finally, output the proof $\pi = (\mathsf{ct}_1, \ldots, \mathsf{ct}_m)$.*
- dvNIZK.Verify$(\mathsf{crs}, \mathsf{sk}, x, \pi)$: *On input the verification key* sk $=$ (k, sk'), *a statement $x \in \{0,1\}^n$ and a proof $\pi = (\mathsf{ct}_1, \ldots, \mathsf{ct}_m)$, compute $(\mathsf{st}_x, q_1, \ldots, q_\ell) \leftarrow$ zkPCP.Query$(x; \mathsf{PRF}(k,x))$. For each $j \in [\ell]$, compute $s_j \leftarrow$ ABSFE.Decrypt $(\mathsf{crs}, \mathsf{sk}, (x, q_j), \mathsf{ct}_{q_j})$, and finally, output zkPCP.Verify$(\mathsf{st}_x, s_1, \ldots, s_\ell)$.*

Security Analysis. We now state the completeness, soundness, and zero-knowledge theorems for Construction 4.1, but defer the proofs to the full version of this paper [40].

Theorem 4.2 (Completeness). *If* zkPCP *is complete and* ABSFE *is correct, then* dvNIZK *from Construction 4.1 is complete.*

Theorem 4.3 (Soundness). *If* PRF *is a secure PRF,* ABSFE *satisfies strong key-hiding, and* zkPCP *is sound, then* dvNIZK *from Construction 4.1 satisfies non-adaptive computational soundness.*

Remark 4.4 (Adaptive Soundness without Complexity Leveraging). Theorem 4.3 shows that Construction 4.1 gives a non-adaptively sound DV-NIZK. As noted in Remark 2.4, we can always use complexity leveraging to obtain adaptive soundness. Here, we note that we can avoid complexity leveraging and sub-exponential hardness assumptions if we instead apply our general compiler to zero-knowledge PCPs based on "trapdoor Σ-protocols" [12]. We refer the reader to the full version of this paper [40] (Remark 4.4 and Appendix A) for more details.

Theorem 4.5 (Zero-Knowledge). *If* ABSFE *satisfies weak message-hiding (resp., strong message-hiding) and* zkPCP *satisfies semi-malicious zero-knowledge, then the designated-verifier NIZK* dvNIZK *from Construction 4.1 satisfies computational zero-knowledge (resp., computational zero-knowledge against malicious verifiers).*

Remark 4.6 (DV-NIZKs in the Common Random String Model). If the public parameters of ABSFE (i.e., the output of ABSFE.Setup) in Construction 4.1 are uniformly random strings, then the resulting DV-NIZK is also in the common random string model. More generally, because we are working with computational notions of soundness *and* zero-knowledge, this is true even if the public parameters are only *pseudorandom*. In this case, computational soundness and zero-knowledge would still follow by a standard hybrid argument, but completeness may be downgraded from perfect to statistical.

5   Constructing AB-SFE Schemes

In this section, we describe several approaches to construct AB-SFE schemes satisfying different flavors of message-hiding and key-hiding. First, in Sect. 5.1, we show how to build weak message-hiding AB-SFE from any single-key ABE scheme. In Sect. 5.2, we show how to construct AB-SFE schemes with strong message-hiding (and weak key-hiding) from receiver-extractable OT. Then, in Sect. 5.3, we show how to generically boost an AB-SFE scheme satisfying weak key-hiding into one that satisfies strong key-hiding (Definition 3.7) via a KDM-secure secret-key encryption scheme (while preserving weak/strong message-hiding). Combining the constructions in Sects. 5.2 and 5.3, we obtain AB-SFE schemes that provide both strong message-hiding and strong key-hiding (which suffice to realize our strongest notion of MDV-NIZK via Construction 4.1). Finally, in Sect. 5.4, we describe how to instantiate the different building blocks from the CDH, DDH, or LWE assumptions.

5.1 Weak Message-Hiding AB-SFE from Single-Key ABE

As noted in Sect. 1.2, an AB-SFE scheme can be viewed as a generalization of a single-key ABE scheme. In the full version of this paper [40], we describe two simple constructions of AB-SFE schemes from single-key ABE schemes (which are in turn implied by public-key encryption [29,48]). Both of these schemes provide *weak message-hiding*.

5.2 Strong Message-Hiding AB-SFE from Receiver-Extractable OT

Towards our goal of obtaining a malicious-designated-verifier NIZK, we show in this section how to construct an AB-SFE scheme that provides *strong message-hiding* from any receiver-extractable 2-message OT scheme. The resulting scheme satisfies weak key-hiding, and we show how to amplify key-hiding security in Sect. 5.3.

Construction 5.1 (Strong Message-Hiding AB-SFE from OT). *Take a function* $F\colon \mathcal{X} \times \mathcal{Y} \to \{0,1\}$ *and a message space* $\mathcal{M}$. *Our construction relies on the following ingredients:*

- *For an attribute* $x \in \mathcal{X}$ *and a message* $m \in \mathcal{M}$, *let* $C_{x,m}\colon \mathcal{Y} \to \mathcal{M} \cup \{\bot\}$ *be a circuit that on input* y' *outputs* m *if* $F(x,y') = 1$ *and* $\bot$ *otherwise. Let* $\ell = \mathsf{poly}(\lambda)$ *be a bound on the bit-length of elements in* $\mathcal{Y}$.
- *Let* $\mathsf{Yao} = (\mathsf{Yao.Garble}, \mathsf{Yao.Eval})$ *be a garbling scheme that supports the circuit class* $\mathcal{C} = \{x \in \mathcal{X}, m \in \mathcal{M} : C_{x,m}\}$.
- *Let* $\mathsf{OT} = (\mathsf{OT.Setup}, \mathsf{OT}_1, \mathsf{OT}_2, \mathsf{OT.Receive})$ *be a 2-message batch OT scheme that is receiver-extractable with* k-*bit messages with batch size* ℓ *(see the full version of this paper [40] for the formal definitions), where* $k = \mathsf{poly}(\lambda)$ *is a bound on the length of the labels output by* Yao. *Let* $\{0,1\}^\tau$ *be the randomness space for the first OT message.*

We construct an AB-SFE scheme as follows:

- $\mathsf{ABSFE.Setup}(1^\lambda)$: *Output* $\mathsf{crs} \leftarrow \mathsf{OT.Setup}(1^\lambda)$.
- $\mathsf{ABSFE.KeyGen}(\mathsf{crs}, y)$: *Sample* $\mathsf{sk} = r \xleftarrow{\mathrm{R}} \{0,1\}^\tau$, *and set* $\mathsf{pk} \leftarrow \mathsf{OT}_1(\mathsf{crs}, y; r)$. *Output* $(\mathsf{pk}, \mathsf{sk})$.
- $\mathsf{ABSFE.Encrypt}(\mathsf{crs}, \mathsf{pk}, x, m)$: *Compute* $(\widetilde{C}_{x,m}, \overline{\mathsf{lab}}) \leftarrow \mathsf{Yao.Garble}(1^\lambda, C_{x,m})$, *where* $\overline{\mathsf{lab}} = \{\mathsf{lab}_{i,b}\}_{i \in [\ell], b \in \{0,1\}}$ *and* $\mathsf{lab}_{i,b} \in \{0,1\}^t$ *for all* $i \in [\ell]$ *and* $b \in \{0,1\}$. *Output the ciphertext* $\mathsf{ct} = (\widetilde{C}_{x,m}, \mathsf{OT}_2(\mathsf{crs}, \mathsf{pk}, \overline{\mathsf{lab}}))$.
- $\mathsf{ABSFE.Decrypt}(\mathsf{crs}, \mathsf{sk}, x, \mathsf{ct})$: *On input the common reference string* crs, *a secret key* $\mathsf{sk} = r$, *an attribute* $x \in \mathcal{X}$, *and a ciphertext* $\mathsf{ct} = (\widetilde{C}, \mathsf{ct}')$, *the decryption algorithm computes* $\overrightarrow{\mathsf{lab}} \leftarrow \mathsf{OT.Receive}(\mathsf{crs}, r, \mathsf{ct}')$ *and outputs* $\mathsf{Yao.Eval}(\widetilde{C}, \overrightarrow{\mathsf{lab}})$.

We state the properties of Construction 5.1 in the following theorem, but defer the proof to the full version of this paper [40].

Theorem 5.2 (Strong Message-Hiding AB-SFE from OT). *If Yao is a secure garbling scheme and* OT *is a receiver-extractable 2-message batch OT scheme on k-bit messages, then the AB-SFE scheme* ABSFE *from Construction 5.1 satisfies strong message-hiding and weak key-hiding.*

5.3   Amplifying Weak Key-Hiding AB-SFE to Strong Key-Hiding AB-SFE

In the full version of this paper [40], we show how to generically upgrade weak key-hiding to strong key-hiding via KDM-secure secret-key encryption (Definition 2.12) and an equivocable non-interactive commitment scheme [18]. Before presenting our main construction, we first define a useful property on PKE and AB-SFE schemes that we will use in our construction.

Definition 5.3 (Recovery from Randomness [39]). *A public-key encryption scheme* PKE = (PKE.KeyGen, PKE.Encrypt, PKE.Decrypt) *with message space* $\mathcal{M}$ *satisfies the* recover from randomness *property if there exists an efficient algorithm* PKE.Recover *with the following property:*

- PKE.Recover$(\mathsf{pk}, \mathsf{ct}, r) \to m/\perp$: *On input a public key* pk, *a ciphertext* ct, *and a string* r, *output a message* $m \in \mathcal{M}$ *or* $\perp$.

Then, for all messages $m \in \mathcal{M}$, *if* $(\mathsf{pk}, \mathsf{sk}) \leftarrow \mathsf{PKE.KeyGen}(1^\lambda)$, ct $\leftarrow$ PKE.Encrypt $(\mathsf{pk}, m; r)$, *then* Recover$(\mathsf{pk}, \mathsf{ct}, r) = m$. *Alternatively, if there is no pair* (m, r) *where* ct = PKE.Encrypt$(\mathsf{pk}, m; r)$, *then* Recover$(\mathsf{pk}, \mathsf{ct}, r) = \perp$. *We extend this definition to the AB-SFE setting accordingly: in this case,* ABSFE.Recover$(\mathsf{crs}, \mathsf{pk}, \mathsf{ct}, r)$ *either outputs* (x, m) *if* ct = ABSFE.Encrypt$(\mathsf{crs}, \mathsf{pk}, x, m; r)$ *and* $\perp$ *if there does not exist any* (x, m) *such that* ct = ABSFE.Encrypt$(\mathsf{crs}, \mathsf{pk}, x, m; r)$.

Remark 5.4 (Recovery from Randomness [39]). It is straightforward to upgrade any PKE (resp., AB-SFE) scheme to have the recovery from randomness property. As noted in [39], we simply modify the encryption algorithm to use part of the encryption randomness to construct a symmetric encryption of the underlying message (resp., underlying attribute-message pair).

Construction 5.5 (Weak Key-Hiding to Strong Key-Hiding). *Let* ABSFE *be an AB-SFE scheme for* $F: \mathcal{X} \times \mathcal{Y} \to \{0, 1\}$ *with message space* $\mathcal{M}$ *that satisfies weak key-hiding and the recovery from randomness property (Definition 5.3, Remark 5.4). To construct an AB-SFE scheme satisfying strong key-hiding, we additionally rely on the following building blocks:*

- *Let* PKE *be a public-key encryption scheme with message space* $\{0, 1\}^\lambda$ *and which supports the recovery from randomness property (Remark 5.4).*
- *Let* $\ell = \ell(\lambda)$ *be a bound on the number of bits of randomness* PKE.Encrypt *and* ABSFE.Encrypt *use.*
- *Let* SKE *denote a secret-key encryption scheme with message-space* $\mathcal{M} \times \{0, 1\}^{\ell \lambda}$ *that is one-time KDM-secure for the class of projection functions (Definition 2.12, Remark 2.13).*

– Let Com *be a non-interactive equivocable commitment scheme with message space* $\{0, 1\}$.

We construct an augmented AB-SFE scheme Aug *as follows:*

– Aug.Setup(1^λ): *Sample* ABSFE.crs $\leftarrow$ ABSFE.Setup(1^λ), (PKE.pk, PKE.sk) $\leftarrow$ PKE.Gen(1^λ), *and for each* $i \in [\lambda]$, Com.crs$_i$ $\leftarrow$ Com.Setup(1^λ). *It outputs the common reference string* crs = (ABSFE.crs, PKE.pk, $\{$Com.crs$_i\}_{i \in [\lambda]}$).
– Aug.KeyGen(crs, y): *On input* crs = (ABSFE.crs, PKE.pk, $\{$Com.crs$_i\}_{i \in [\lambda]}$), *sample a key-pair* (ABSFE.pk, ABSFE.sk) $\leftarrow$ ABSFE.KeyGen(ABSFE.crs, y) *and output the public key* pk = ABSFE.pk *and the secret key* sk = (y, ABSFE.pk, ABSFE.sk).
– Aug.Encrypt(crs, pk, x, m): *Parse* crs = (ABSFE.crs, PKE.pk, $\{$Com.crs$_i\}_{i \in [\lambda]}$) *and* pk = ABSFE.pk, *and proceed as follows:*
  • *Sample a secret key* $s \xleftarrow{\text{R}} \{0, 1\}^\lambda$ *for* SKE.
  • *For every* $i \in [\lambda]$, *sample* $\rho_i \xleftarrow{\text{R}} \{0, 1\}^\lambda$ *and compute* $c_i \leftarrow$ Com.Commit(Com.crs$_i$, s_i; ρ_i).
  • *For every* $i \in [\lambda]$, *define* $M_{i,s_i} = \rho_i$ *and* $M_{i,1-s_i} = \bot$. *Then, sample* $R_{i,0}, R_{i,1} \xleftarrow{\text{R}} \{0, 1\}^\ell$ *and construct the ciphertexts*

$$\text{ct}_{i,0} \leftarrow \text{ABSFE.Encrypt(ABSFE.crs, ABSFE.pk, } x, M_{i,0}; R_{i,0})$$
$$\text{ct}_{i,1} \leftarrow \text{PKE.Encrypt(PKE.pk, } M_{i,1}; R_{i,1}).$$

  • *Let* ct$_0$ $\leftarrow$ SKE.Encrypt(s, (m, $(R_{i,s_i})_{i \in [\lambda]}$)).
  • *Output* ct = $\big($ct$_0$, $(c_i, \text{ct}_{i,0}, \text{ct}_{i,1})_{i \in [\lambda]}\big)$.
– Aug.Decrypt(crs, sk, x, ct): *On input* crs = (ABSFE.crs, PKE.pk, $\{$Com.crs$_i\}_{i \in [\lambda]}$), *a secret key* sk = (y, ABSFE.pk, ABSFE.sk), *and a ciphertext* ct = $\big($ct$_0$, $(c_i, \text{ct}_{i,0}, \text{ct}_{i,1})_{i \in [\lambda]}\big)$, *proceed as follows:*
  1. *If* $F(x, y) = 0$, *output* $\bot$.
  2. *For every* $i \in [\lambda]$, *compute* $\rho'_i \leftarrow$ ABSFE.Decrypt(ABSFE.crs, ABSFE.sk, x, ct$_{i,0}$). *If* $\rho'_i \neq \bot$ *and* Com.Commit(Com.crs$_i$, 0; ρ'_i) = c_i, *set* $s'_i = 0$; *otherwise, set* $s'_i = 1$.
  3. *Compute* $(m', (r'_i)_{i \in [\lambda]}) \leftarrow$ SKE.Decrypt(s', ct$_0$).
  4. *For every* $i \in [\lambda]$, *perform the following checks:*
     • *If* $s'_i = 0$, *then check if* Recover(ABSFE.crs, ABSFE.pk, ct$_{i,0}$, r'_i) = (x, $\tilde{\rho}_i$) *for some* $\tilde{\rho}_i$, *and output* $\bot$ *if the check fails.*
     • *If* $s'_i = 1$, *then compute* $\tilde{\rho}_i \leftarrow$ PKE.Recover(PKE.pk, ct$_{i,1}$, r'_i) *and output* $\bot$ *if the recovery procedure fails.*
     • *Finally, check if* $c_i =$ Com.Commit(Com.crs$_i$, s'_i; $\tilde{\rho}_i$). *Output* $\bot$ *if this check fails.*
  5. *If all checks pass, output* m'.

5.4   Instantiations

In this section, we describe how to instantiate each of the building blocks needed to obtain an AB-SFE scheme satisfying strong key-hiding and strong (respectively, weak) message-hiding from either the CDH assumption, the LWE assumption, or the LPN assumption with noise rate $n^{-(\frac{1}{2}+\varepsilon)}$ (respectively, the CDH assumption, the LWE assumption, or the LPN assumption with noise rate $O(1/\sqrt{n})$). All of our LWE-based instantiations can use a polynomial modulus-to-noise ratio.

The resulting weak message-hiding AB-SFE instantiations correspondingly yield DV-NIZKs. Moreover, the resulting strong message-hiding AB-SFE schemes have *uniformly random* public parameters, thus yielding designated-verifier NIZKs with security against malicious verifiers in the common *random* string model. We instantiate each building block as follows (with more details in the full version of this paper [40]):

- There exists a receiver-extractable 2-message batch OT scheme in the common random string model under the CDH/LWE/LPN assumptions (with the parameters specified above). There exists a garbling scheme from one-way functions. Thus, by Theorem 5.2, we obtain an AB-SFE scheme with strong message-hiding and weak key-hiding under the CDH/LWE/LPN assumptions in the common random string model.
- There exist public-key encryption schemes with pseudorandom (or uniformly random) public keys from the CDH assumption [25], the LWE assumption [47], or the LPN assumption [1] with the parameters specified above. Because we only use the associated secret key in the proof of security, we can replace the public key PKE.pk from Construction 5.5 with a uniformly random string, while maintaining security (by a standard hybrid argument) and perfect correctness.
- From Sect. 5.1, there exists an AB-SFE scheme with weak message-hiding and weak key-hiding under any assumption implying PKE.
- By Remark 2.13, there exists a KDM-secure secret-key encryption scheme for projection functions under the CDH assumption, the LWE assumption, or the LPN assumption with constant noise rate.
- There exists a non-interactive equivocable commitment scheme from one-way functions in the common random string model.

Remark 5.6 (Almost-All-Keys Perfect Decryption Correctness). Some of the PKE/OT schemes above (such as the PKE scheme of [1]) do not actually satisfy perfect decryption correctness. However, the transformation of [22] shows that these encryption schemes can be modified to satisfy the following "almost-all-keys perfect correctness" property: with probability $1 - \mathsf{negl}(\lambda)$ over the randomness of PKE.KeyGen($\cdot$), decryption is perfectly correct with probability 1 over the choice of encryption randomness. Encryption schemes satisfying this notion of almost-all-keys perfect correctness suffice for all of the constructions in this paper.

Instantiations. Combining the above primitives in Construction 5.5, we now obtain the following corollaries. In all cases, we only rely on polynomial hardness of the underlying assumption.

Corollary 5.7 (Weak Message-Hiding, Strong Key-Hiding AB-SFE from LPN). *Assuming polynomial hardness of the LPN assumption with noise rate $O(\frac{1}{\sqrt{n}})$, there exists an AB-SFE scheme with that satisfies strong key-hiding and weak message-hiding.*

Corollary 5.8 (Strong Message-Hiding, Strong Key-Hiding AB-SFE from CDH/LWE/LPN). *Assuming polynomial hardness of either CDH, LWE, or LPN with noise rate $n^{-(\frac{1}{2}+\varepsilon)}$ for any $\varepsilon > 0$, there exists an AB-SFE scheme with uniformly random public parameters that satisfies strong key-hiding and strong message-hiding security.*

Combining Theorem 2.5 now with Construction 4.1 (and Remarks 4.4 and 4.6), we obtain the following instantiations of designated-verifier NIZKs:

Corollary 5.9 (Designated-Verifier NIZKs from LPN). *Assuming polynomial hardness of the LPN assumption with noise rate $O(\frac{1}{\sqrt{n}})$, there exists a designated-verifier NIZK argument for NP that is adaptively sound and provides computational zero-knowledge in the common reference string model.*

Corollary 5.10 (Malicious-Designated-Verifier NIZKs from CDH/LWE/LPN). *Assuming polynomial hardness of either CDH, LWE, or LPN with noise rate $n^{-(\frac{1}{2}+\varepsilon)}$ for any $\varepsilon > 0$, there exists a designated-verifier NIZK argument for NP that is adaptively sound and provides computational zero-knowledge against malicious verifiers in the common random string model.*

Acknowledgments. We thank Yuval Ishai and Brent Waters for many helpful discussions and comments on this work.

References

1. Alekhnovich, M.: More on average case vs approximation complexity. In: FOCS, pp. 298–307 (2003)
2. Applebaum, B., Cash, D., Peikert, C., Sahai, A.: Fast cryptographic primitives and circular-secure encryption based on hard learning problems. In: Halevi, S. (ed.) CRYPTO 2009. LNCS, vol. 5677, pp. 595–618. Springer, Heidelberg (2009). https://doi.org/10.1007/978-3-642-03356-8_35
3. Blum, M.: How to prove a theorem so no one else can claim it. In: Proceedings of the International Congress of Mathematicians, vol. 1, p. 2 (1986)
4. Blum, M., Feldman, P., Micali, S.: Non-interactive zero-knowledge and its applications (extended abstract). In: STOC, pp. 103–112 (1988)
5. Boneh, D., Boyen, X.: Efficient selective-ID secure identity-based encryption without random oracles. In: Cachin, C., Camenisch, J.L. (eds.) EUROCRYPT 2004. LNCS, vol. 3027, pp. 223–238. Springer, Heidelberg (2004). https://doi.org/10.1007/978-3-540-24676-3_14
6. Boneh, D., et al.: Fully key-homomorphic encryption, arithmetic circuit ABE and compact garbled circuits. In: Nguyen, P.Q., Oswald, E. (eds.) EUROCRYPT 2014. LNCS, vol. 8441, pp. 533–556. Springer, Heidelberg (2014). https://doi.org/10.1007/978-3-642-55220-5_30

7. Boneh, D., Halevi, S., Hamburg, M., Ostrovsky, R.: Circular-secure encryption from decision Diffie-Hellman. In: Wagner, D. (ed.) CRYPTO 2008. LNCS, vol. 5157, pp. 108–125. Springer, Heidelberg (2008). https://doi.org/10.1007/978-3-540-85174-5_7
8. Boyle, E., Couteau, G., Gilboa, N., Ishai, Y.: Compressing vector OLE. In: ACM CCS, pp. 896–912 (2018)
9. Brakerski, Z., Lombardi, A., Segev, G., Vaikuntanathan, V.: Anonymous IBE, leakage resilience and circular security from new assumptions. In: Nielsen, J.B., Rijmen, V. (eds.) EUROCRYPT 2018. LNCS, vol. 10820, pp. 535–564. Springer, Cham (2018). https://doi.org/10.1007/978-3-319-78381-9_20
10. Canetti, R., Chen, Y., Holmgren, J., Lombardi, A., Rothblum, G.N., Rothblum, R.D.: Fiat-Shamir from simpler assumptions. IACR Cryptology ePrint Archive 2018:1004 (2018)
11. Canetti, R., Halevi, S., Katz, J.: A forward-secure public-key encryption scheme. IACR Cryptology ePrint Archive 2003:83 (2003)
12. Canetti, R., Lombardi, A., Wichs, D.: Fiat-Shamir: from practice to theory, part ii (NIZK and correlation intractability from circular-secure FHE). IACR Cryptology ePrint Archive 2018:1248 (2018)
13. Chase, M., et al.: Reusable non-interactive secure computation. In: Boldyreva, A., Micciancio, D. (eds.) CRYPTO 2019. LNCS, vol. 11694, pp. 462–488. Springer, Cham (2019)
14. Couteau, G., Hofheinz, D.: Designated-verifier pseudorandom generators, and their applications. In: Ishai, Y., Rijmen, V. (eds.) EUROCRYPT 2019. LNCS, vol. 11477, pp. 562–592. Springer, Cham (2019). https://doi.org/10.1007/978-3-030-17656-3_20
15. Cramer, R., Damgård, I., Schoenmakers, B.: Proofs of partial knowledge and simplified design of witness hiding protocols. In: Desmedt, Y.G. (ed.) CRYPTO 1994. LNCS, vol. 839, pp. 174–187. Springer, Heidelberg (1994). https://doi.org/10.1007/3-540-48658-5_19
16. Cramer, R., Shoup, V.: A practical public key cryptosystem provably secure against adaptive chosen ciphertext attack. In: Krawczyk, H. (ed.) CRYPTO 1998. LNCS, vol. 1462, pp. 13–25. Springer, Heidelberg (1998). https://doi.org/10.1007/BFb0055717
17. Cramer, R., Shoup, V.: Universal hash proofs and a paradigm for adaptive chosen ciphertext secure public-key encryption. In: Knudsen, L.R. (ed.) EUROCRYPT 2002. LNCS, vol. 2332, pp. 45–64. Springer, Heidelberg (2002). https://doi.org/10.1007/3-540-46035-7_4
18. Crescenzo, G.D., Ishai, Y., Ostrovsky, R.: Non-interactive and non-malleable commitment. In: STOC, pp. 141–150 (1998)
19. Döttling, N., Garg, S.: Identity-based encryption from the Diffie-Hellman assumption. In: Katz, J., Shacham, H. (eds.) CRYPTO 2017. LNCS, vol. 10401, pp. 537–569. Springer, Cham (2017). https://doi.org/10.1007/978-3-319-63688-7_18
20. Döttling, N., Garg, S., Hajiabadi, M., Masny, D.: New constructions of identity-based and key-dependent message secure encryption schemes. In: Abdalla, M., Dahab, R. (eds.) PKC 2018. LNCS, vol. 10769, pp. 3–31. Springer, Cham (2018). https://doi.org/10.1007/978-3-319-76578-5_1
21. Döttling, N., Garg, S., Hajiabadi, M., Masny, D., Wichs, D.: Two-round oblivious transfer from CDH or LPN. IACR Cryptology ePrint Archive 2019 (2019)
22. Dwork, C., Naor, M., Reingold, O.: Immunizing encryption schemes from decryption errors. In: Cachin, C., Camenisch, J.L. (eds.) EUROCRYPT 2004. LNCS, vol. 3027, pp. 342–360. Springer, Heidelberg (2004). https://doi.org/10.1007/978-3-540-24676-3_21

23. Feige, U., Lapidot, D., Shamir, A.: Multiple non-interactive zero knowledge proofs under general assumptions. SIAM J. Comput. **29**(1), 1–28 (1999)

24. Fiat, A., Shamir, A.: How to prove yourself: practical solutions to identification and signature problems. In: Odlyzko, A.M. (ed.) CRYPTO 1986. LNCS, vol. 263, pp. 186–194. Springer, Heidelberg (1987). https://doi.org/10.1007/3-540-47721-7_12

25. ElGamal, T.: A public key cryptosystem and a signature scheme based on discrete logarithms. In: Blakley, G.R., Chaum, D. (eds.) CRYPTO 1984. LNCS, vol. 196, pp. 10–18. Springer, Heidelberg (1985). https://doi.org/10.1007/3-540-39568-7_2

26. Goldreich, O.: Basing non-interactive zero-knowledge on (enhanced) trapdoor permutations: the state of the art. In: Goldreich, O. (ed.) Studies in Complexity and Cryptography. Miscellanea on the Interplay between Randomness and Computation. LNCS, vol. 6650, pp. 406–421. Springer, Heidelberg (2011). https://doi.org/10.1007/978-3-642-22670-0_28

27. Goldreich, O., Micali, S., Wigderson, A.: Proofs that yield nothing but their validity and a methodology of cryptographic protocol design (extended abstract). In: FOCS, pp. 174–187 (1986)

28. Goldwasser, S., Micali, S., Rackoff, C.: The knowledge complexity of interactive proof systems. SIAM J. Comput. **18**(1), 186–208 (1989)

29. Gorbunov, S., Vaikuntanathan, V., Wee, H.: Functional encryption with bounded collusions via multi-party computation. In: Safavi-Naini, R., Canetti, R. (eds.) CRYPTO 2012. LNCS, vol. 7417, pp. 162–179. Springer, Heidelberg (2012). https://doi.org/10.1007/978-3-642-32009-5_11

30. Gorbunov, S., Vaikuntanathan, V., Wee, H.: Attribute-based encryption for circuits. In: STOC, pp. 545–554 (2013)

31. Goyal, V., Pandey, O., Sahai, A., Waters, B.: Attribute-based encryption for fine-grained access control of encrypted data. In: ACM CCS, pp. 89–98 (2006)

32. Groth, J., Ostrovsky, R., Sahai, A.: Non-interactive zaps and new techniques for NIZK. In: Dwork, C. (ed.) CRYPTO 2006. LNCS, vol. 4117, pp. 97–111. Springer, Heidelberg (2006). https://doi.org/10.1007/11818175_6

33. Ishai, Y., Kushilevitz, E., Ostrovsky, R., Sahai, A.: Zero-knowledge from secure multiparty computation. In: STOC, pp. 21–30 (2007)

34. Ishai, Y., Mahmoody, M., Sahai, A.: On efficient zero-knowledge PCPs. In: Cramer, R. (ed.) TCC 2012. LNCS, vol. 7194, pp. 151–168. Springer, Heidelberg (2012). https://doi.org/10.1007/978-3-642-28914-9_9

35. Katsumata, S., Nishimaki, R., Yamada, S., Yamakawa, T.: Designated verifier/prover and preprocessing NIZKs from Diffie-Hellman assumptions. In: Ishai, Y., Rijmen, V. (eds.) EUROCRYPT 2019. LNCS, vol. 11477, pp. 622–651. Springer, Cham (2019). https://doi.org/10.1007/978-3-030-17656-3_22

36. Kilian, J., Petrank, E., Tardos, G.: Probabilistically checkable proofs with zero knowledge. In: STOC, pp. 496–505 (1997)

37. Kim, S., Wu, D.J.: Multi-theorem preprocessing NIZKs from lattices. In: Shacham, H., Boldyreva, A. (eds.) CRYPTO 2018. LNCS, vol. 10992, pp. 733–765. Springer, Cham (2018). https://doi.org/10.1007/978-3-319-96881-0_25

38. Kitagawa, F., Matsuda, T., Tanaka, K.: CCA security and trapdoor functions via key-dependent-message security. IACR Cryptology ePrint Archive 2019:291 (2019)

39. Koppula, V., Waters, B.: Realizing chosen ciphertext security generically in attribute-based encryption and predicate encryption. IACR Cryptology ePrint Archive 2018:847 (2018)

40. Lombardi, A., Quach, W., Rothblum, R.D., Wichs, D., Wu, D.J.: New constructions of reusable designated-verifier NIZKs. IACR Cryptology ePrint Archive 2019:242 (2019)

41. Lombardi, A., Quach, W., Rothblum, R.D., Wichs, D., Wu, D.J.: New constructions of reusable designated-verifier NIZKs. IACR Cryptology ePrint Archive, 2019 (2019). Preliminary Version

42. Naor, M., Yung, M.: Public-key cryptosystems provably secure against chosen ciphertext attacks. In: STOC, pp. 427–437 (1990)

43. Pass, R., Shelat, A., Vaikuntanathan, V.: Construction of a non-malleable encryption scheme from any semantically secure one. In: Dwork, C. (ed.) CRYPTO 2006. LNCS, vol. 4117, pp. 271–289. Springer, Heidelberg (2006). https://doi.org/10.1007/11818175_16

44. Peikert, C., Shiehian, S.: Noninteractive zero knowledge for NP from (plain) learning with errors. In: Boldyreva, A., Micciancio, D. (eds.) CRYPTO 2019. LNCS, vol. 11692, pp. 89–114. Springer, Cham (2019)

45. Peikert, C., Vaikuntanathan, V., Waters, B.: A framework for efficient and composable oblivious transfer. In: Wagner, D. (ed.) CRYPTO 2008. LNCS, vol. 5157, pp. 554–571. Springer, Heidelberg (2008). https://doi.org/10.1007/978-3-540-85174-5_31

46. Quach, W., Rothblum, R.D., Wichs, D.: Reusable designated-verifier NIZKs for all NP from CDH. In: Ishai, Y., Rijmen, V. (eds.) EUROCRYPT 2019. LNCS, vol. 11477, pp. 593–621. Springer, Cham (2019). https://doi.org/10.1007/978-3-030-17656-3_21

47. Regev, O.: On lattices, learning with errors, random linear codes, and cryptography. In: STOC, pp. 84–93 (2005)

48. Sahai, A., Seyalioglu, H.: Worry-free encryption: functional encryption with public keys. In: ACM CCS, pp. 463–472 (2010)

49. Sahai, A., Waters, B.: Fuzzy identity-based encryption. In: Cramer, R. (ed.) EUROCRYPT 2005. LNCS, vol. 3494, pp. 457–473. Springer, Heidelberg (2005). https://doi.org/10.1007/11426639_27

50. De Santis, A., Di Crescenzo, G., Ostrovsky, R., Persiano, G., Sahai, A.: Robust noninteractive zero knowledge. In: Kilian, J. (ed.) CRYPTO 2001. LNCS, vol. 2139, pp. 566–598. Springer, Heidelberg (2001). https://doi.org/10.1007/3-540-44647-8_33

51. De Santis, A., Micali, S., Persiano, G.: Non-interactive zero-knowledge proof systems. In: Pomerance, C. (ed.) CRYPTO 1987. LNCS, vol. 293, pp. 52–72. Springer, Heidelberg (1988). https://doi.org/10.1007/3-540-48184-2_5

Scalable Zero Knowledge with No Trusted Setup

Eli Ben-Sasson[1,2(✉)], Iddo Bentov[3], Yinon Horesh[1], and Michael Riabzev[1,2]

[1] Technion, Haifa, Israel
[2] StarkWare Industries Ltd., Netanya, Israel
eli@starkware.co
[3] Cornell Tech, New York, NY, USA

Abstract. One of the approaches to constructing zero knowledge (ZK) arguments relies on "PCP techniques" that date back to influential works from the early 1990's [Babai et al., Arora et al. 1991-2]. These techniques require only minimal cryptographic assumptions, namely, the existence of a family of collision-resistant hash functions [Kilian, STOC 1992], and achieve two remarkable properties: (i) all messages generated by the verifier are public random coins, and (ii) total verification time is merely poly-logarithmic in the time needed to naïvely execute the computation being verified [Babai et al., STOC 1991].

Those early constructions were never realized in code, mostly because proving time was too large. To address this, the model of interactive oracle proofs (IOPs), which generalizes the PCP model, was recently suggested. Proving time for ZK-IOPs was reduced to *quasi-linear*, even for problems that require nondeterministic exponential time to decide [Ben-Sasson et al., TCC 2016, ICALP 2017].

Despite these recent advances it was still not clear whether ZK-IOP systems can lead to concretely efficient succinct argument systems. Our main claim is that this is indeed the case. We present a new construction of an IOP of knowledge (which we call a zk-STIK) that improves, asymptotically, on the state of art: for log-space computations of length T it is the first to $O(T \log T)$ arithmetic prover complexity and $O(\log T)$ verifier arithmetic complexity. Prior IOPs had additional $\text{poly} \log T$ factors in both prover and verifier. Additionally, we report a C++ realization of this system (which we call libSTARK). Compared to prevailing ZK realizations, it has the fastest proving and (total) verification time for sufficiently large *sequential* computations.

1 Introduction

By the early 1990s, a combination of works [5–7,39,44,54] showed the existence of proof systems that satisfy the following conditions, simultaneously:

1. **universality:** such systems can be constructed for any language $L \in \mathsf{NEXP}$;
2. **zero knowledge (ZK):** the proof for the membership of $x \in L$ reveals no meaningful information about the nondeterministic witness w provided to show $x \in L$;

© International Association for Cryptologic Research 2019
A. Boldyreva and D. Micciancio (Eds.): CRYPTO 2019, LNCS 11694, pp. 701–732, 2019.
https://doi.org/10.1007/978-3-030-26954-8_23

3. **argument of knowledge (ARK):** the witness w can be "extracted" from a prover that succeeds in showing $x \in L$;
4. **scalable (succinct) verification:** for instances of size n, verifying membership in L requires time at most $\mathsf{poly}(\log \mathsf{T}(n), n)$, where $\mathsf{T}(n)$ is the running time of the nondeterministic machine[1] deciding membership in L on instances of size n;
5. **public coins:** all messages and queries sent by the verifier are public random coins ("Arthur-Merlin" protocols); we choose to refer to such protocols as *transparent* and this allows us to compress terminology (one word instead of two) while emphasizing the benefits of such systems.
6. **"simple" cryptographic assumptions:** the soundness of these constructions assumes only the existence of a family of collision resistant hash functions[2].

The early theoretical constructions that achieved the six properties above were based on the celebrated PCP Theorem [2,3,5,6] and ZK variants of PCPs (ZK-PCPs) [39,52,55]. But these theoretical constructions were never *realized*[3] in code, mostly due to prover (in)efficiency problems. Recent advances in the study of quasilinear PCPs [17,25,27,38,62] and ZK Interactive Oracle Proofs (IOPs) [13,15,22,67] have shown the existence of ZK-IOP systems that achieve all six properties along with the following property, simultaneously:

7. **scalable (quasilinear) proving:** the running time of the prover is $\tilde{O}(\mathsf{T}(n)) := \mathsf{T}(n) \cdot \log^{O(1)} \mathsf{T}(n)$.

Nevertheless, the constructions that achieve all seven properties were inefficient in terms of both prover and verifier running times. Indeed, a proof-of-concept IOP-based system without ZK but with the remaining six properties, called SCI [9], was reported recently but was relatively inefficient, and the cost of adding ZK to it would further deteriorate its performance. The recent Aurora system [21] describes a ZK-IOP (along with an accompanying implementation) that is designed for arithmetic circuits and provides succinct proofs (poly-logarithmic in the size of the arithmetic circuit). However, verifier running time scales linearly with the input size, meaning the system is not (doubly) scalable according to our definition of the term. Therefore, a valid question to ask is whether IOPs are a viable approach to obtaining ZK systems for any concretely realizable computational setting? The main point of this paper is to provide a positive answer to this question.

Contributions. We make four:

---

[1] The machine could either be a Turing machine or a RAM machine.
[2] In the "random oracle" model where all parties have access to the same random function, these systems can be made non-interactive [22,60].
[3] Henceforth, a proof system *realization* refers to an implementation in code, along with reported measurements, of it.

1. The first *strictly scalable* ZK-IOP for log-space computations, in arithmetic complexity (see Definition 3 and Theorem 1). In words, this is the first ZK-IOP for computations requiring $T(n)$ time and $O(\log T(n))$ space (on instances of size n) in which the arithmetic complexity of the prover is $O(T(n) \cdot \log T(n))$ and that of the verifier is $O(\log T(n))$. All prior ZK-IOP constructions had poly-log factors in the verifier and/or prover with an exponent (in the poly-log) that is strictly greater than 1.

2. A scalable ZK-IOP for general sequential computations (with no restrictions on memory access) in NEXP, which is more efficient in terms of asymptotic prover and verifier complexity than the prior state of the art (Theorem 2). It is the first scalable ZK-IOP system with *strictly* quasi-linear ($O(T(n) \log T(n))$) proof length (measured in field elements) and *strictly* logarithmic ($O(\log T(n))$) query complexity.

3. A code realization (in C++) of an argument system that implements this pair of IOP systems. The code base, called libSTARK, is published under the permissive MIT license [10]. Furthermore, the ZK-STARK prover is $\geq 10\times$ faster than prior ZKprovers for general sequential computations (see Sect. 3). This reduction is significant because prover complexity is the main bottleneck encountered when scaling ZKproof systems to deal with large computations. Compared to SCI [9], the prior state-of-the-art scalable IOP system, our ZK-STARK reduces proving time by $7\times$–$40\times$ and communication complexity by $3\times$–$20\times$; the improved verifier complexity (but not prover complexity) relies on a new set of algebraic conjectures—different than those relied upon by SCI (and other ZK constructions). These conjectures, which are of independent interest, are discussed in Sect. 4.3.

4. For the benefit of future and alternative constructions, we formally define the notions of a scalable and transparent IOP of knowledge (STIK) and a scalable and transparent argument of knowledge (STARK), which is a system that achieves, simultaneously, all seven properties listed earlier.

1.1   The Virtues of Transparent Scalability

No prior ZK system realized in code has achieved both transparency *and* full (or double) scalability for general programs, meaning the simultaneous combination of quasilinear proving time *and* polylogarithmic (succinct) verification time. We briefly discuss the importance of the combined effect of scalability and transparency in ZK systems.

Transparency. Non-transparent protocols require an elaborate *setup phase* that is hard to perform securely [20]. This phase constitutes a single point of failure that might be exploited by powerful parties to compromise the system (especially when that system carries significant value, as is the case with Zcash [64]). The complexity of performing the setup leads to another security threat: to minimize the number of times the setup is invoked, projects using non-transparent systems will batch together many system improvements within a single roll-out, adding to operational security risks; this is already the case with Zcash's recent "Sapling" upgrade.

A different benefit of transparency relates to decentralized open source code. It is far easier to build transparent systems in this manner, because they do not require an extra setup procedure, one that requires additional trust assumptions and governance structures (who will be trusted to perform and manage the setup phase?). For the reasons above, leading crypto-currencies that care about financial privacy (including Ethereum, Monero and Zcash) agree that a move to *transparent* ZK ARKs is inevitable.

Scalability. An aspect of proof systems (with or without ZK) that was first noted by [5,6] is their potential for truly scaling computation in a sound and trustless manner. As articulated by Babai et al.: *"a single reliable PC can monitor the operation of a herd of supercomputers working with possibly extremely powerful but unreliable software and untested hardware"* [5].

A STARK (even without ZKcapabilities) can deliver on this promise in an extreme way, facilitating *exponential* savings in verification time and space (like compressing Bitcoin's blockchain to a logarithmic size proof that would attest to the validity of its latest UTXO set); notably, a *transparent* proof system achieves this exponential compression without any auxiliary key management issues and their associated trust assumptions and governance problems.

Organization of the Paper. In Sect. 2 we define the notions STIK and STARK and state the theorems backing our construction (proofs appear in the full online version [12]). Section 3 compares our work to other ZKsolutions, theoretically and practically. Section 4 explains the main novel components in our IOP and STARK constructions, showing how the asymptotic efficiency of Theorems 1 and 2 is translated to concrete efficiency of the realized system. In Appendix A we provide a self-contained overview of the ZK-STARK protocol from start to end, along with an example "toy problem" to assist readers unfamiliar with ZK-IOP constructions. Full details appear in the online version [12].

2   Theory—Definitions and Main Results

This section describes our theoretical contributions. After recalling the interactive oracle proof model, we define a particularly efficient class of IOP protocols called scalable and transparent IOPs of knowledge (STIK), present our main theorems for this model (proofs omitted due to space limitations) and define the notion of a STARK.

2.1   Interactive Oracle Proofs (IOP)

The IOP[4] model suggested in [22,67] is a generalization of the IP [44], PCP [2], and interactive PCP (IPCP) [53] models. It is an information theoretic model

---

[4] Reingold et al. [67] use the name "Probabilistically Checkable Interactive Proofs" (PCIP).

in which soundness can be proven unconditionally, as in the PCP, IP and MIP models. But, like those earlier models, the IOP model is unrealistic. To realize it, additional cryptographic assumptions are needed, and those are discussed later.

Remark 1 (The computational integrity language). Our statements and constructions apply to large classes of languages (like NP and NEXP). But we advise the reader to focus on the specific *computational integrity* (CI) language L (also called the *universal language* and the *bounded-halting language*), comprised of quadruples (C, x, y, T) such that the computation specified by a program C, on public input x and auxiliary (private) witness w, reaches output y within T cycles. In fact, to achieve scalable verification it is *necessary* to use succinctly represented instances, such as sequential programs that are short and require execution time that is greater than the program description.

Informally, during an IOP protocol for a nondeterministic language L the prover and verifier receive public input x and then interact over a number of rounds; the prover's goal is to establish in zero knowledge that it knows a nondeterministic witness w for the fact that x belongs to L. During each round the verifier sends a message (in the case of transparent IOPs, like ours, all messages are public random coins), and the prover replies with an oracle, a long message which the verifier may query at random locations and need not read in entirety (jumping ahead, these oracles will be implemented in our ZK-STARK using Merkle-tree commitments). The verifier may query these oracles at any time during the interaction but for transparent systems (like ours) all queries can be postponed to the very last stage, after all prover-side oracles have been sent. Once the interaction has terminated and the verifier has made the required queries, it posts a decision—whether to accept x as a member of L or to reject it. Completeness means that an honest prover knowing w will succeed in making the verifier accept with probability 1, soundness means that for $x \notin L$ the prover has only negligible probability ϵ of convincing the verifier to accept, and knowledge soundness means that a prover succeeding with probability $\gg \epsilon$ in convincing the verifier to accept x has provided oracles that, if opened, will be found to encode a witness w that shows $x \in L$ directly. We now present the formal definitions.

A nondeterministic machine (see footnote 1) M that decides a language $L \in \mathsf{NTIME}(T(n))$ in time $T(n)$ (n denotes instance size) *induces* a binary relation R_M consisting of all pairs (x, w) where $x \in L$ and w is a sequence of nondeterministic choices of $M(x)$ that lead to an accepting state. In this case we say $R = R_M$ is *induced* by L and implicitly assume M is fixed and known. We recall the IOP definition from [22].

Definition 1 (Interactive Oracle Proof (IOP)). *Let R be a binary relation induced by a nondeterministic language L and let $\epsilon \in [0, 1]$ denote soundness error. An Interactive Oracle Proof (IOP) system S for R with soundness ϵ is a pair of interactive randomized algorithms $S = (P, V)$ that satisfy the properties below; P is the prover and V is the verifier.*

- **operation:** *The input of the verifier is* x, *and the input of the prover is* (x, w) *for some string* w. *The number of interactive rounds, denoted* r(x), *is called the* round complexity *of the system. During a single round the prover sends a message (which may depend on* w *and prior messages) to which the verifier is given oracle access, and the verifier responds with a message to the prover. We denote by* ⟨P(x, w) ↔ V(x)⟩ *the output of* V *after interacting with* P; *this output is either* accept *or* reject.
- **completeness** *If* (x, w) ∈ R *then*

$$\Pr\left[\langle P(x, w) \leftrightarrow V(x)\rangle = \mathsf{accept}\right] = 1$$

- **soundness** *If* x ∉ L *then for any* P*,

$$\Pr\left[\langle P^* \leftrightarrow V(x)\rangle = \mathsf{accept}\right] \leq \epsilon$$

The proof length, *denoted* ℓ(x), *is the sum of lengths of all messages sent by the prover. The* query complexity *of the protocol, denoted* q(x), *is the number of entries read by* V *from the various prover messages. Given witness* w *such that* (x, w) ∈ R, prover complexity, *denoted* tp(x, w), *is the complexity required to generate all prover messages, and* verifier complexity, *similarly defined, is denoted* tv(x).

2.2   ZK-STIK

Next, we introduce the definition of a scalable and transparent IOP of knowledge (STIK). Most of the work described in later sections is related to constructing a new, concretely efficient, ZK-STIK; soundness is proved *information-theoretically*, with no cryptographic assumptions.

Definition 2 (Scalable Transparent IOP of Knowledge (STIK)). *Let* R *be a binary relation induced by a nondeterministic language* L ∈ NTIME($T(n)$) *for* $T(n) \geq n$ *and let* S = (P, V) *be an IOP for* L *with soundness error* $\epsilon(n) < 1$. *We say* S *is*

- **transparent** *if all verifier messages and queries are public random coins.*
- **(doubly) scalable** *if for every instance* x *of length* n, *both of the following hold:*
  1. **scalable verifier:** tv(n) = poly(n, log $T(n)$, log $1/\epsilon(n)$)
  2. **scalable prover:** tp(n) = $T(n)$ · poly(n, log $T(n)$, log $1/\epsilon(n)$)
- **a proof of knowledge** *if there exists a* knowledge error function $\epsilon'(n) \in [0, 1]$ *and a randomized extractor* E *that, given oracle access to any prover* P* *that causes the verifier to accept* x *with probability* $p(n) > \epsilon'(n)$, *outputs in expected time* poly $\left(\frac{T(n)}{p(n)-\epsilon'(n)}\right)$ *a witness* w *such that* (x, w) ∈ R.

- **witness indistinguishable (privacy preserving)** *if there exists a randomized simulator* Sim *that samples (perfectly) the distribution on transcripts of interactions between* V *and* P, *and runs in time* $\mathsf{poly}(T(n))$.

A (doubly) scalable and transparent IOP of knowledge will be denoted by STIK. *A witness indistinguishable* STIK *is denoted by wi-*STIK, *and when* $T(n) = \mathsf{poly}(n)$ *it will be called a* zero knowledge STIK, *denoted* ZK-STIK.

Remark 2 (Zero knowledge vs. witness indistinguishability). In this work we construct (ZK) simulators that run in time that is polynomial in the *prover's* running time. For languages in NP, prover and verifier running times are both polynomial in the input size, so our simulator gives perfect zero knowledge. However, for languages in super-polynomial time, as stated in Theorem 2, our simulator only shows that the system is witness indistinguishable. The question of presenting a *succinct* simulator is left as an interesting open question; cf. [14] where a similar ZK simulator of NEXP is presented for a different IOP construction.

Remark 3 (History). PCP systems are, by definition, transparent (1-round) IOP systems. The first such system with a scalable verifier was given in the works[5] of Babai et al. [5,6] and the first doubly scalable PCP, i.e., the first STIK construction, appears in the works[6] of Ben-Sasson et al. [17,25]. The first ZK-STIK for NP appears in the work of Ben-Sasson et al. [16], later extended to a ZK-STIK for NEXP [13].

For languages with logarithmic space our construction in Theorem 1 has prover and verifier complexity that are asymptotically better than previous constructions, and lead to a *strictly scalable* construction in arithmetic complexity, as defined next.

Definition 3 (Strictly scalable IOPs). *Using the notation of Definition 2, we say that* S *is a* strictly scalable transparent IOP of Knowledge (strict STIK) *if for every instance* x *of length* n, *both of the following hold:*

1. **strictly scalable verifier:** $\mathsf{tv}(n) = O(\log T(n)) + \mathsf{poly}(n, \log 1/\epsilon(n))$
2. **strictly scalable prover:** $\mathsf{tp}(n) = O(T(n) \log T(n)) + \mathsf{poly}(n, \log 1/\epsilon(n))$

When the complexity of prover and verifier is measured as the number of arithmetic operations over a finite field of size $O(T(n))$, *we say that* S *is a* strict arithmetic STIK.

---

[5] The first work [6] shows this for NEXP and the second [5] scales it down to NP.
[6] The first work [25] presents a PCP with scalable verification and quasi-linear *proof length*, the second work [17] bounds the prover running time and also proves the proof of knowledge property.

2.3   Main Theorems

We now state the two main theorems regarding IOP systems that underlie our construction. IOP constructions use finite fields, so prover and verifier complexity are most naturally stated using arithmetic complexity over the ambient field, the size of which is derived from the size of the instance x; we use $\mathsf{tv}^{\mathbb{F}}$ and $\mathsf{tp}^{\mathbb{F}}$ to denote arithmetic complexity, assuming the field $\mathbb{F}$ is understood from context. In contrast to other ZKapproaches, the size of the field does not need to grow with the security parameter. In particular, our libSTARK implementation [10] uses the finite field of size 2^{64}, and could use even smaller fields, yet achieves soundness error $2^{-128} \ll 1/|\mathbb{F}|$. This unlinking of the security parameter from the ambient field size is one reason (out of several) our libSTARK prover is fast.

Let $\mathsf{NTimeSpace}(T(n), S(n))$ denote the class of nondeterministic languages that are decidable in simultaneous time $T(n)$ and space $S(n)$. Our first theorem applies to space bounded sequential computations.

Theorem 1 (ZK-STIK for space bounded computations). *Let* L *be a language in* $\mathsf{NTimeSpace}(T(n), S(n)), T(n) \geq n$ *and let* R *be induced by* L. *Then* R *has a transparent witness indistinguishable IOP of knowledge with the following parameters, stated for soundness error* $\mathsf{err} = 2^{-\lambda}$ *(that may depend on* n*)*

- *perfect completeness and soundness error at most* $\mathsf{err}(n)$ *for instances of size* n
- *knowledge error bound* $\mathsf{err}'(n) = O(\mathsf{err}(n))$
- *round complexity* $\mathsf{r}(n) = \frac{\log T(n)}{2} + O(1)$
- *query complexity* $\mathsf{q}(n) = 36(\lambda + 2) \cdot (\log T(n) + \frac{S(n)}{\log T(n)} + O(1))$
- *alphabet size: each query answer belongs to a binary field* $\mathbb{F}, |\mathbb{F}| = 2^{\mathsf{n}}$ *for* $\mathsf{n} = \lambda + \log T(n) + O(1)$
- *verifier arithmetic complexity* $\mathsf{tv}^{\mathbb{F}}(n) = \tilde{O}(n) + O(\lambda \cdot (\frac{S(n)}{\log T(n)} + \log T(n)))$
- *prover arithmetic complexity* $\mathsf{tp}^{\mathbb{F}}(n) = O(S(n) \cdot T(n))$
- *proof length* $O(S(n) \cdot T(n)/\log T(n))$, *measured in field elements.*

In particular, for $S(n) = \mathsf{poly}\log T(n)$, this IOP is doubly scalable, i.e., the system is a wi-STIK (see Remark 2). Moreover, for $S(n) = O(\log T(n))$ the IOP is a strict arithmetic STIK (see Definition 3), meaning the prover arithmetic complexity is $O(T(n) \log T(n))$ and verifier arithmetic complexity is $O(\log T(n)) + \mathsf{poly}(n)$. Finally, when $T(n) = \mathsf{poly}(n)$, the system has perfect ZK, i.e., it is a ZK-STIK.

For computations with super-poly-logarithmic space the theorem above is not scalable, neither for prover nor for verifier. The following theorem is doubly scalable for any nondeterministic language, i.e., it can be said to be a *universal* wi-STIK (see Remark 1). Comparing Theorem 2 to the previous Theorem 1, the following result is more general, as it makes no assumptions regarding space. For computations requiring space $S(n) = o(\log^2 T(n))$ Theorem 1 has lower asymptotic prover complexity, but for $S(n) = \omega(\log^2 T(n))$ the more general Theorem 2 has more efficient prover complexity.

Theorem 2 (wi-STIK for NEXP). *Let* L *be a language in* NTIME($T(n)$), $T(n) \geq n$ *and* R *be induced by* L. *Then* R *has a doubly scalable, transparent, and witness indistinguishable (see Remark 2) IOP of knowledge (wi-STIK) with the following parameters, stated for soundness error* err $= 2^{-\lambda}$ *(that may depend on n)*

- *perfect completeness and soundness error* err(n) *for instances of size* n
- *knowledge extraction bound* err$'(n) = O($err$(n))$
- *round complexity* r(n) $= \frac{\log T(n)}{2} + O(1)$
- *query complexity* $O(\lambda \cdot \log T(n))$
- *alphabet size: each query answer belongs to a binary field* $\mathbb{F}, |\mathbb{F}| = 2^{\mathsf{n}}$ *for* $\mathsf{n} = \lambda + \log T(n) + \log \log T(n) + O(1)$
- *verifier arithmetic complexity* tv$^{\mathbb{F}}(n) = \tilde{O}(n) + O(\lambda \cdot \log T(n))$,
- *prover arithmetic complexity* tp$^{\mathbb{F}}(n) = O(T(n) \log^2 T(n))$,
- *proof length* $O(T(n) \log T(n))$, *measured in field elements.*

For $T(n) = $ poly(n) *the system has perfect ZK, i.e., it is a ZK-STIK.*

We point out that this is the first construction of a scalable ZK-IOP system with strictly quasi-linear ($O(T(n) \log T(n))$) proof length and strictly logarithmic ($O(\log T(n))$) query complexity. Prior IOP systems, even without ZK, required query complexity $\log^c T(n)$ for exponent $c > 1$ for any quasi-linear length proofs [9,13,17].

2.4   STARK as a Realization of STIK

Definition 2 refers to the IOP model, in which results can be proved with no cryptographic assumptions. A number of fundamental transformations have been suggested in the past to realize PCP systems using various cryptographic assumptions, and these transformations were adapted to the IOP model [22]. In all such realizations the prover must be computationally bounded, and such systems are commonly called *argument systems*, and, consequently, the realization of a STIK results in a *Scalable Transparent ARgument of Knowledge* (STARK).

The two main transformations of proof systems into realizable argument systems are:

- **Interactive STARK (iSTARK)** As shown by Kilian [54] for the PCP model, a family of collision-resistant hash functions can be used to convert a STIK into an interactive argument of knowledge system; if the STIK has perfect ZK, then the argument system has computational ZK. Any realization of a STIK using this technique will be called an *interactive* STARK (iSTARK); when one wants to emphasize that the STIK is zero knowledge, the term ZK-iSTARK will be used.

- **Non-interactive** STARK (nSTARK) As shown by Micali [61] and Valiant [77] for the PCP model, and by Ben-Sasson et al. [22] for the IOP model, any STIK can be compiled into a non-interactive argument of knowledge in the random oracle model (called a *non-interactive random-oracle proof (NIROP)* there); if the STIK had perfect zero knowledge then the resulting construction has computational zero knowledge. Any realization of a STIK using this technique will be called an *non-interactive* STARK (nSTARK); when one wants to emphasize that the STIK is zero knowledge, the term ZK-nSTARK will be used.

While non-interactive STARKs have the advantage of being comprised of a single message from the prover, they also rely on stronger assumptions. Thus, we leave the choice of which particular realization mode to use for a (ZK)-STIK—(ZK)-iSTARK vs. (ZK)-nSTARK—to be made by system designers based on particular use cases, and refer to both realization modes of a STIK as a STARK; to emphasize the ZKaspect of the STIK we may refer to the realization as a ZK-STARK.

3   Evaluation and Comparison

In this section we compare our ZK-STARK to other implemented systems. We start in Sect. 3.1 by comparing our approach to other implemented ZKapproaches from a purely *asymptotic* and *theoretical* point of view, and show that the combination of full scalability, transparency and lean cryptographic assumptions for *universal* computations is *unique* to our system. We continue in Sect. 3.2, where we measure implemented systems for similar circuit size and topology as that which our system deals with. In Sect. 3.3 we compare our system to the previous state-of-the-art IOP system, called SCI [9], and show our system is faster while also adding ZK, which SCI did not obtain (see Remark 4 for a discussion of performance compared to the recent Aurora system [21]).

3.1   Comparison to Prior Works—Theory

The literature on ZKrealizations is vast, and rapidly expanding, so we limit the discussion to approaches that are *ZK and universal*, i.e., apply to any language in NP (thus, we sadly omit reference to many *verifiable computation* approaches that do not achieve ZK, like the recent [81]). For the purposes of this discussion, we consider four properties: asymptotic (i) prover scalability (quasilinear running time), (ii) asymptotic verifier scalability (poly-logarithmic verification time, including setup/parameter generation time), (iii) transparency (public randomness), and (iv) cryptographic assumptions.

Figure 1 summarizes our discussion, and we provide details next. Later, when we evaluate the performance of our system against other methods (Sect. 3) we will use the classification below.

	prover scalability (quasilinear time)	verifier scalability (polylogarithmic time)	transparency (public randomness)	cryptographic assumptions
A. hPKC	Yes	Only repeated computation	No	KoE, DL, FS
B. DLP	Yes	No	Yes	DL, FS
C. IP	Yes	No	Yes	none (interactive) / FS (noninteractive)
D. MPC	Yes	No	Yes	CRH (interactive) / FS (noninteractive)
E. IVC+hPKC	Yes	Yes	No	KoE, DL, FS
F. Aurora	Yes	No	Yes	CRH (interactive) / FS (noninteractive)
G. This work	Yes	Yes	Yes	CRH (interactive) / FS (noninteractive)

Fig. 1. Theoretical comparison of universal (NP complete) realized ZKsystems. KoE stands for "knowledge of exponent" assumptions, DL for "hardness of discrete log", CRH for "collision resistant hash" and FS for Fiat-Shamir heuristic.

A. Homomorphic Public-Key Cryptography (hPKC): This approach, initiated by Ishai et al. [50] (for the "designated verifier" case) and Groth [45] (for the "publicly verifiable" case), uses an efficient information-theoretic model called a "linear PCP" that is then "compiled" into a cryptographic system using hPKC. An extremely efficient instantiation, based on Quadratic Span Programs, was introduced by Gennaro et al. [41] (see [29,40,47–49,58] for related work and further improvements). It serves, e.g., as the proof system behind Zerocash and Zcash™. The first implementation of a QSP based system is called Pinocchio [63], with subsequent implementations including libSNARK [19,68] which is used in the Zerocash and Zcash™ implementations; additional implementations appear in [24,37,70–73,79,82].

The theoretical differences between hPKC and ZK-STARK are the lack of transparency and the reliance on number-theoretic knowledge of exponent assumptions (which are vulnerable to attacks by quantum computers). Verification time in hPKC is scalable only for computations that are repeated many times, because the hPKC "setup phase" requires time $\geq \mathsf{T}$, where T denotes running time of the nondeterministic computation (see Footnote 1) being verified.

B. Discrete Logarithm Problem (DLP): An approach initiated by Groth [46] (cf. [69]) and implemented in [30], relies on the hardness of the DLP to construct a system that is transparent. Shor's quantum factoring algorithm solves the DLP efficiently, rendering this approach quantum-susceptible. Additionally, verifier complexity in the DLP approach requires time $\geq \mathsf{T}_C$ hence it is non-scalable (according to our definition of the term), although communication complexity in the DLP approach is logarithmic. We refer to the initial implementation of this system as BCCGP [30], and a recent improved version is called BulletProofs [31].

C. Interactive Proofs (IP) Based: IP protocols can be performed with zero knowledge [8] but only recently have IP protocols been efficiently "scaled down" to small depth (non-sequential) computations via so-called "proofs for muggles" of Goldwasser et al. [43,67]. This led to a line of realizations in code, early works lacked ZK [35,36,76,78], but the state-of-the-art ones, like [82] and Hyrax [80], do have it.

Like ZK-STARK, most of these IP-based proofs (but for [82]) are transparent and have a scalable prover, but their verifier is not scalable, as its running time grows linearly with computation time for "standard" (i.e., sequential) computations. In terms of cryptographic assumptions, some are plausibly post-quantum secure while others rely on number theoretic assumptions that are susceptible to quantum attacks.

D. Secure Multi-Party Computation (MPC): This approach, suggested by Ishai et al. [51] and implemented first in the ZKBoo [42] system, and more recently, in Ligero [1], "compiles" secure MPC protocols into ZK-PCP systems, by requiring the prover to commit to the transcript of a secure MPC protocol, and then reveal the view of one of the parties.

Like ZK-STARK, the MPC-based proofs are transparent and have scalable (quasilinear) proving time. However, MPC based systems have a non-scalable verifier, one that runs in time $\geq T$. Additionally, their communication complexity is non-scalable, it is $\sqrt{T}$ in the state of the art system [1]; nevertheless, for concrete circuits and amortized computations verification time and communication complexity are extremely efficient.

E. Incrementally Verifiable Computation (IVC): This approach, suggested by Valiant [77] (cf. [28,34]) reduces prover space consumption by relying on knowledge extraction assumptions; this approach can be applied on top of other proof systems with succinct (sub-linear) verifiers, including ZK-STARK, but thus far has been realized only for a single hPKC system [23].

Compared with ZK-STARK, systems built this way inherit most properties from the underlying proof system. In particular, the hPKC-based IVC is non-transparent and quantum-susceptible; however the verifier is scalable even for a computation executed only once, because the setup phase runs in poly-logarithmic time.

F. Aurora: The Aurora system is a recently posted ZK-IOP by Ben-Sasson et al., that is optimized for arithmetic circuits [21]. For a circuit with N gates, prover running time is scalable—$O(N \log N)$ arithmetic operations over the ambient field—and proof length scales succinctly, poly-logarithmically in N. However, verification time scales *linearly* in N. Aurora shares many similarities with our ZK-STARK: both are IOP-based, plausibly post-quantum secure and require only symmetric cryptographic assumptions (for the interactive setting; the non-interactive one relies on the Fiat-Shamir heuristic). Furthermore, both use the FRI protocol for asserting proximity to RS codes. The main difference between Aurora and our system regards verifier time: Aurora's verifier scales linearly with the computation size whereas our system has poly-logarithmic verification time.

Summary

ZK-IOPs have a combination of beneficial attributes not achieved by any other code-realized approach; these are *full* scalability (prover- and verifier-side) and transparency. Additionally, the cryptographic assumptions needed by the ZK-IOP approach are rather minimal, although obtained by other approaches—MPC and IP. As we shall see later, the theoretical attributes are complemented by practical benefits, like the *fastest* proving time for ZK proofs of sequential computations.

3.2 Comparison to Prior Works—Concrete Performance

In this section we compare measurements of different ZKsystems on the same hardware, a server with 32 AMD cores at clock speed of 3.2 GHz, and 512 GB of DDR3 RAM. Each pair of cores shares memory; this roughly corresponds to a machine with 16 cores and hyper-threading.

Comparison Method. All *prior* realized ZKsystems we are aware of use arithmetic circuits over prime fields, and their complexity is mostly affected by arithmetic circuit (i) depth and (ii) size—the number of addition and multiplication gates; typically multiplication complexity dominates addition complexity. (See Remark 4 for a discussion of our system compared to the recent Aurora system [21].) Since these systems are affected mostly by the circuit topology—size and depth—the exact nature of the computation (beyond these parameters) does not significantly affect their complexity measures.

To generate circuits for other systems, we started with a program written in TinyRAM assembly [18]—the exhaustive subset-sum program reported for SCI in [9]. This computation does not access RAM memory, which is a requirement when comparing to other ZKsystems that deal with circuits, not RAM machines (in the next section we shall also discuss RAM computations, when comparing ZK-STARK to SCI). This program was compiled into a ZK-STARK system, and also into a set of quadratic arithmetic program (QAP) constraints by libSNARK. This offers a rather direct comparison between the following three systems—SCI (an IOP system with no ZK), libSNARK (an hPKC system, with ZK) and our ZK-STARK. All three apply to the same computation, running on the same machine, and use multi-threading (see Remark 5 for a more thorough discussion of the comparison method).

We extracted depth and multiplication complexity numbers from the libSNARK compiler and requested the authors of the following systems to measure them on our server for arbitrary circuits with similar depth and multiplication complexity. Figure 1 shows the resulting proving time, verifying time and communication complexity. Since several of the systems operate only in single-threaded

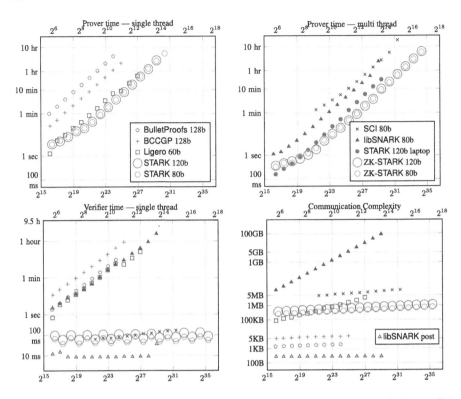

Fig. 2. A comparison of different realized proof systems as a function of the number of machine cycles (top axis) and multiplication gates (bottom axis); each cycle of the TinyRAM program corresponds to $\approx 2000 \approx 2^{11}$ multiplication gates. The estimated level of security of each system is denoted on the legend above (e.g., "STARK 80b" means estimated soundness error of $\leq 2^{-80}$). All systems were tested on the same server (specs below) and executed a computation of size and structure corresponding to the "exhaustive subset-sum" program from [9, Section 3]; our ZK-STARK was *also* executed on the same program on a weaker laptop (quad core i7-8550U CPU @ 1.80 GHz clock with 32 GB of DDR4 RAM), see right top plot. Notice that even on this weaker machine the ZK-STARK prover is faster, and reaches larger circuit size, than all other systems.

proving mode (all systems use single-thread for verification), we have a separate comparison of single-threaded ZK-STARK vs. the other single-treaded systems. Recall the classification of ZKapproaches from Sect. 3.1. The systems that have performed the above testing procedure on our machine are:

- hPKC-based: libSNARK with 80 bits (80b) of security (commit dc78fd, September 7, 2017);
- DLP-based: The system of BCCGP with logarithmic communication complexity [30], and the BulletProofs system of [31]; both systems are single-threaded and have 128b security.

- MPC-based: Ligero strong with 60b security, single-threaded [1] (this system has sublinear communication complexity, compared with linear complexity of ZKBoo, hence we include only it in our measurements).

Regarding ZK-STARK, we evaluated it in single- and multi-theard mode, for 80 and 120 bits of security, using Blake2s (with 128-bits of security) as our CRH for constructing the Merkle tree commitments to oracles. To address concerns about the ability to execute ZK-STARK on weaker machines, we also plot the measured proving time on a Lenovo T440 laptop with 32 GB of DDR4 RAM and a quad-core Intel i7-8550U CPU 1.80 GHz clock speed.

Let us discuss prover time, verifier time, and communication complexity, addressing the systems above. We hope to add measurements for IP based systems like Hyrax in the future [80].

Prover Complexity. All systems surveyed here have prover complexity that scales either linearly or nearly-linearly in computation size. However, as shown in Fig. 2, our ZK-STARK prover is the fastest among the single-threaded systems (though not by a large margin) and is at least $10\times$ faster than the second fastest prover (that of libSNARK) when multi-threading is allowed; all systems were tested up to maximal proving time of 12 h. Notice that even when executed not on a large server but on a weaker laptop with 32 GB of RAM, our ZK-STARK prover is noticeably faster, and reaches larger circuit size, than all other systems (which were measured only on the stronger and bigger server). This shows that ZK-STARK proving efficiency is not an artifact of using a strong machine, but rather follows from the efficiency of the underlying protocol (the interested reader is welcome to test libSTARK on her laptop, using the runSubsetsumTests.sh procedure there [10].)

The speedup of multi-threaded over single-threaded execution of libSTARK on the server is plotted in Fig. 3. For very small instances multi-threading gives moderate improvements, possibly due to short running time and cost of opening many threads, and for very large instances it drops somewhat, perhaps because memory swapping contributes more significantly to running time.

Verifier Complexity. The *total* verifier running time (including setup/parameter generation and post-processing) of all prior works grows at least like $\sqrt{T}$, and, often, like T; in contrast, our ZK-STARK scales like $a + \log T$ (see Theorems 1 and 2). Consequently, for medium- and large-scale *sequential* computations our ZK-STARK total verification time is better than all prior solutions, as shown by Fig. 2. The efficiency of ZK-IOP systems tailored specifically for small depth, parallel computations (the setting which Hyrax is tailored to) is left to future work.

hPKC-based systems like Pinocchio and libSNARK, and IVC+hPKC systems like that of [23] are different in this respect. They have a setup that is performed only once per circuit. For Pinocchio and libSNARK pre-processing time grows *linearly* with circuit size. E.g., the libSNARK system requires ≈ 16 s for a computation with 2^{20} gates. In Fig. 1 we plot both post-processing verification time

multi-threading speedup over single-thread

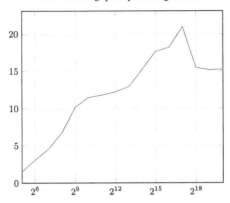

Fig. 3. The ratio of multi-threaded to single-threaded proving time of ZK-STARK for the exhaustive subset-sum computation, as a function of the number of cycles. Recall that the server used for testing has 32 AMD cores, which correspond to 16 cores with hyperthreading.

(and CC) using open blue triangles and total time/CC (including setup) using filled blue triangles. For the IVC+hPKC system, pre-processing time is *constant* and does not depend on circuit size; this constant ($\approx$10 s) is quite large compared to our verifier time, but on the other hand is needed only once, so amortized over many computations it approaches 0.

Communication Complexity (CC). The use of a pre-processing phase in the hPKC and IVC+hPKC systems leads to extremely small post-processing CC; the BCCGP and BulletProofs systems also enjoy extremely short CC and, because pre-processing is transparent, can be effectively replaced with a short seed to a pseudo-random generator. Concretely, for all computations measured in practice, post-processing CC of Pinocchio, libSNARK and the IVC+hPKC system are less than 300 bytes, that of BCCGP is less than 7 KB, and BulletProofs is roughly 3× smaller, less than 2.5 KB [30,31] (see also Fig. 2). However, pre-processing key length scales linearly with circuit size for hPKC; the IVC+hPKC system is different in this respect, it has succinct pre-processing length even for large computation size, but once again, this length is concretely large—more than 40 MB for our computation. For Ligero, communication complexity scales like $70\sqrt{\text{mult}_n}$ field elements [1, Section 5.3].

Discussion

Among all ZKsystems compared above, our ZK-STARK has the fastest prover in single- and multi-thread modes; in particular, it is $\approx$10× faster than the second fastest measured system—libSNARK. Other systems perform better (shorter communication, faster verification) on small circuits (ZKBoo, Ligero), small-depth circuits (Hyrax), and on computations repeated many times with the same fixed circuit (BulletProofs, Pinocchio, libSNARK). However, for general large scale sequential computations our ZK-STARK has verification time and communication complexity that outperforms all other *transparent* systems published thus far for this range of parameters. In other words, our particular ZK-STARK realization shows that the asymptotic benefits of full scalability and transparency are manifested already for concrete computations, and suggest that ZK-IOP systems are of interest not merely as a theoretical construct but also as a viable approach to building future ZK-systems.

Remark 4 (Runtime comparison to Aurora). For computations that are specified simply as arithmetic circuits, Aurora out-performs our ZK-STARK (and Ligero) (see [21, Figures 10–12]). However, for sequential computations specified by succinct programs, verification time in our ZK-STARK out-performs that of Aurora. Concretely, Aurora verification time for a circuit with a million gates requires ~ 1 s (see Fig. 12 there) and scales linearly with N, whereas our ZK-STARK verifier scales quite slowly and requires less than 0.1 s even for a circuit with 34 billion gates (see Fig. 2).

Summarizing, we view Aurora and our ZK-STARK as complementary: both are IOP-based, transparent, plausibly post-quantum secure and have concretely efficient provers. Arora is better when dealing with computations specified as generic arithmetic circuits but does not offer full scalability, while our ZK-STARK is better when dealing with sequential programs because its verification time scales poly-logarithmically with computation time.

Remark 5 (On validity of the comparison method). The reader might ask whether the method outlined above—compiling the particular exhaustive subset-sum program into (i) arithmetic circuits over prime fields and (ii) AIRs over binary fields, is fair and valid. Wouldn't it better to "hand optimize" the circuit/AIR for a particular computation, and perhaps do it over the same ambient field?

The choice of program—the exhaustive subset-sum—was dictated by the constraint of including a comparison to SCI, the prior IOP state of the art; this limited us to choosing one of the programs provided there. Hand-optimizing AIRs and arithmetic circuits for the same computation for all the various proof systems surveyed here is beyond the scope of this work, as these systems are provided by different teams and some of the code-bases (SCI, for instance) are not updateable.

The compilation process that converts a program (in our case, written in TinyRAM assembly) to an arithmetic circuit, and to an AIR, leads to a construction that is less efficient than a "hand-written" circuit/AIR of the very same computation. It is hard to estimate which approach (AIR vs. circuits) suffers more from compilation inefficiency but the fundamental complexity measures for circuits and STARKs—number of gates per cycle (for arithmetic circuit), and "total degree" per cycle (= state width × constraint degree/code rate)—are roughly similar for this particular choice of program and compilation: roughly 2,000 multiplication gates per cycle (for arithmetic circuits), and total degree roughly 9,000 per cycle (because our program leads to 94 state width, the constraint degree is 12 and the code rate is $1/8$).

3.3 SCI vs. ZK-STARK

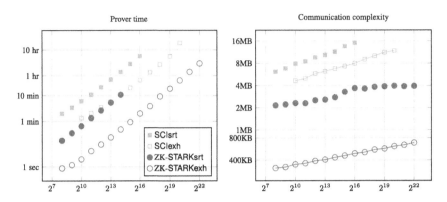

Fig. 4. SCI vs. ZK-STARK comparison of prover time and communication complexity. Both systems measured at 80 bits of security on the same machine.

To compare SCI and ZK-STARK we use the exact same pair of TinyRAM programs used by SCI and reported in [9], namely:

- exh: the exhaustive-search subset-sum program which does not require RAM access (no use of LOAD/STORE TinyRAM opcodes); this corresponds to Theorem 1
- srt: the sorted subset-sum program which does require RAM access (with LOAD/STORE opcodes), corresponding to Theorem 2

Both systems were executed with an 80-bit security level and measured on the machine specified at the beginning of Sect. 3.2. Figure 4 shows that ZK-STARK prover time is 7×–40× faster than that of SCI and has communication complexity that is 3×–20× smaller than that of SCI. Notably, ZK-STARK has ZK, which SCI does not (the cost of adding ZK increases computational complexity across the board).

As pointed out earlier (Sect. 4), this improvement is due to the better arithmetization which uses many RS codewords (one per register), tighter soundness analysis, the use of the more efficient FRI protocol and the efficient additive FFTs of [57].

The improvement of ZK-STARK over SCI is more noticeable for the program that does not use RAM. The reason for this is verifying correct RAM requires certain tools that incur large blow-ups in communication complexity and prover time. These blowups are due to the need to verify that an arbitrary RAM access pattern was executed correctly. This is solved in both SCI and ZK-STARK using switching networks to "route" accesses to memory, following the method of [17]. We refer the reader to Appendices C.3 and G in the online version of this paper [12] for full details.

4   Novel Ingredients in the Construction

Our new ZK-STARK builds significantly on recent ZK-IOP research [11,13,15, 22], and its main advantage is *improved efficiency*, leading to it being the first strictly scalable IOP for space bounded computation (Theorem 1). Our main improvements are four, listed below. We briefly recount the prior state of the art as background and then explain how ZK-STARK improves on it.

Background—SCI *and* FRI. The SCI system [9] is an IOP without zero knowledge. It uses an arithmetization process that reduces a witness of membership in a language to a *pair* of univariate polynomial, and reduces the transition function of the computation to a *single* low-degree multivariate polynomial. Then, it employs an IOP version of the quasilinear PCP of Proximity (PCPP) of [27] to solve the low-degree testing problem. This PCPP, and the IOP emerging from it, require quasi-linear proving time and poly-logarithmic verification time, but both algorithms are not *strictly* quasi-linear (cf. Definition 3). Due to the reliance on bivariate polynomials in that IOP, when converting it to an argument system via Merkle trees, different queries to the proof oracles led to different authentication paths, resulting in increased communication complexity.

Another component that is used in ZK-STARK (and in Aurora [21]) is the recent strictly quasi-linear IOP of proximity (IOPP) for univariate polynomials called FRI and discussed further below [11].

Improvements. In addition to the qualitative improvement over SCI of adding ZK, our system is asymptotically and concretely more efficient in terms of verifier complexity and communication complexity than SCI, and has a prover that is more efficient, for sequential computations, than all other existing systems. The main novel components in ZK-STARK that facilitate this are:

1. ZK-STARK uses the FRI protocol of [11], which is vastly more efficient, both asymptotically and concretely, than the Ben-Sasson–Sudan PCPP used by SCI. Asymptotically, FRI has prover arithmetic complexity that is strictly linear in blocklength (prior IOPPs required quasi-linear proving time) and strictly logarithmic verifier arithmetic complexity (prior verifiers required poly-logarithmic complexity, with an exponent greater than 1).
2. The FRI oracle structure is used by our ZK-STARK to significantly reduce Merkle-tree authentication path complexity; this aspect is explained in Sect. 4.1;
3. Our ZK-STARK uses an arithmetization with one RS codeword per register, as opposed to one RS codeword for *all* registers; we then use a round of interaction to solve the RPT problem only once over all different RS codewords; see Sect. 4.2.
4. in similar fashion to the step above, our new *algebraic linking IOP* (ALI) protocol "compresses" all of the constraints that enforce the computational integrity of the transition function, into a *single* random combination of them all. This dramatically reduces the memory and computational complexity of the prover. The specification of the ALI protocol and its analysis appear in the full version of the paper [12, Sections B.5, D].

Below we elaborate on the second and last items of the list above.

4.1 Reduced Authentication Path Complexity

The largest contributor to communication complexity, and to verifier time and space complexity in our ZK-STARK (and prior related works [9,17,27,33]) is the cost of checking authentication paths. We now discuss the way our ZK-STARK reduces this cost. Let λ denote the number of output bits of the cryptographic hash function used to construct a Merkle tree in our system; let AP_{total} denote the total number of authentication path nodes in all subtrees of Merkle trees whose leaves are query answers, and let q_{total} denote the total number of queries, made to all proof oracles. The total communication complexity (CC) of the proof system is

$$\mathsf{CC} = \mathsf{q}_{total} \cdot \log |\mathbb{F}| + \mathsf{AP}_{total} \cdot \lambda \tag{1}$$

Compared to prior works, most notably SCI, our ZK-STARK reduces the second summand in two separate ways:

1. The ZK-STARK verifier queries *rows* of the (low degree extension of the) execution trace, each row comprises a field elements that represent the state at some point in the computation (or its low degree extension). To reduce communication complexity, the ZK-STARK prover places each such row in a *single* sub-tree of the Merkle tree, and therefore only *one* authentication path is required per row (as opposed to a many paths in prior solutions).
2. The verifier of the FRI protocol queries functions on cosets of a fixed subspace; i.e., the entries of each oracle accessed by the verifier can be *partitioned*, so that a single authentication path covers all entries required by the verifier in a single test. Accordingly, the ZK-STARK prover places each member of the partition in a *single* sub-tree of the Merkle tree, thereby reducing the number of authentication paths to one-per-coset (as opposed to one per field element).

4.2 Algebraic Linking Interactive Oracle Proof (ALI)

The main bottleneck for prover time and space complexity is the cost of performing *polynomial interpolation* and its inverse operation—multi-point *polynomial evaluation*. The complexity measure that dominates this bottleneck is the *maximal degree* of a polynomial which the prover must interpolate and/or evaluate; for a computation involving a $\mathsf{T} \times \mathsf{a}$ execution trace specified by s constraints of degree at most d, we denote this degree by $\mathsf{d}^{\max} = \mathsf{d}^{\max}(\mathsf{T}, \mathsf{a}, \mathsf{s}, \mathsf{d})$. Prior state-of-the-art [9,17,27,33] gave

$$\mathsf{d}^{\max}_{\mathsf{old}}(\mathsf{T}, \mathsf{a}, \mathsf{s}, \mathsf{d}) = \mathsf{T} \cdot \mathsf{a} \cdot \mathsf{d} + \mathsf{T} \cdot \mathsf{s}. \tag{2}$$

which leads to concretely large values. Our ZK-STARK reduces $\mathsf{d}^{\max}$ to

$$\mathsf{d}^{\max}_{\mathsf{ZK\text{-}STARK}}(\mathsf{T}, \mathsf{a}, \mathsf{s}, \mathsf{d}) = \mathsf{T} \cdot \mathsf{d} \tag{3}$$

The improved efficiency of our ZK-STARK is due to two reasons, explained next. The first one completely removes the second summand of (2) and the second one removes a from its first summand.

Algebraic linking IOP (ALI). The second summand of (2) arises because our prover needs to apply a "local map" induced by the AIR constraint system. Prior state-of-the-art systems, like [9], used a local map that checks each constraint of the AIR separately, leading to this second summand. Instead, our ZK-STARK uses a single round of interaction to reduce all s constraints to a *single constraint* that is a *random linear combination* of all AIR constraints, thereby completely removing the second summand of (2). See [12, Sections B.5, D] for a specification of the protocol.

Register-Based Encoding. Prior systems, like [9], encoded the *full* execution trace by a *single* Reed-Solomon codeword, leading to degree T · a; this degree is then multiplied by d to account for application of the AIR constraints to this codeword, resulting in the first summand of (2). Our ZK-STARK uses a *separate* Reed-Solomon codeword for each register[7], leading to a many codewords, each of lower degree T. At first glance this tradeoff may seem wasteful, because we now have to solve an RPT problem for each of these a codewords. However, the interaction and use of randomness allowed by the IOP model once again come to our aid: it suffices to solve a *single* RPT problem, applied to a *random* linear combination of all a codewords. The use of a single codeword per register also helps with reducing communication complexity, as explained in Sect. 4.1.

4.3 Algebraic Security Assumptions

In our measurements (Sect. 3.2) we rely on two conjectures. Informally, the first, which appears in the full version [12, Conjecture B.17] due to space limitations, says that any efficient attacker will be presenting proof oracles $f^{(0)}, g^{(0)}$ that are maximally far from the respective RS codes, and the second, stated below, says that δ-far words are rejected by the FRI protocol with probability $\approx \delta$. Both conjectures match our current understanding of the best possible attacks against the ZK-STIK system; it is reasonable to use such an approach when running comparisons to other implemented systems, because all other systems use a similar "security-based" approach when setting parameters (group size in an elliptic curve, field size in a discrete-log based approach, bit-length in a cryptographic hash function, etc.). To be fair, these other assumptions have received more scrutiny than ours but by stating this conjecture we hope it, too, will be further inspected by the research community.

Conjecture 1 (FRI soundness—informal). For *any* rate parameter ρ and constant δ, if $f : S \to \mathbb{F}$ is δ-far from $\mathsf{RS}[\mathbb{F}, S, \rho]$, then the FRI protocol rejects f with probability at least $\delta - \frac{O(1)}{|\mathbb{F}|}$.

---

[7] For simplicity, the current description discusses the case of space bounded computations; the case of computations with large space also uses multiple codewords but the reduction is more complicated, and discussed in the online version of the paper.

For a code of rate $\rho = 2^{-\mathcal{R}}$, the conjecture implies that to reach a security level of λ bits (or error probability $< 2^{-\lambda}$), the QUERY phase of the FRI protocol should be invoked $\lambda/\mathcal{R}$ times. See [11, 26] for a discussion of the conjecture.

Without Conjecture 1 and [12, Conjecture B.17], the number of FRI-verifier tests would increase at most *three-fold*, to $3 \cdot \lambda/\mathcal{R}$ (to achieve λ bits of security). This would entail a ×3 increase in communication complexity and verifier running time (both scale linearly with the number of FRI-verifier tests), however, there would be no other change to the system parameters, such as field size, the schedule of reductions, etc. Regarding prover time—the main bottleneck in proof systems—the impact would be negligible ($< 1\%$ for all reasonable sized computations) because producing query answers requires only poly-logarithmic running time (whereas producing the proof requires quasi-linear running time and vastly dominates overall proving time).

We stress that in terms of security, our ZK-STARK is *qualitatively better* than most prior ZKapproaches (but for Ligero and Aurora that are similar in this respect). Consider the effect of refuting, in the strongest possible way, either of the Knowledge of Exponent (KoE) or Discrete Log Problem (DLP) hardness assumptions discussed in Sect. 3.1, say, by an efficient algorithm that breaks them (or by a large scale quantum computer). In such a case, the systems relying on KoE/DLP would be rendered completely broken and useless. In stark contrast (pun intended), if Conjecture 1 and [12, Conjecture B.17] were to be refuted in the strongest possible way, the effect on ZK-STARK would only be to increase communication complexity and verifier complexity by a factor of $\leq$ ×3. This is thanks to *proven, information-theoretic* bounds that show that for any $\delta \leq 1 - \sqrt[3]{\rho} = 1 - 2^{-\mathcal{R}/3}$ the conjecture above is in fact a theorem (see [26] for more details)[8].

Acknowledgements. We thank Arie Tal, Yechiel Kimchi and Gala Yadgar for help optimizing code performance. We thank the Andrea Cerulli, Venkitasubramaniam Muthuramakrishnan, Madars Virza, and the other authors of [1, 30] for assistance in obtaining the data reported in Fig. 2. We thank Alessandro Chiesa, Yuval Ishai and the anonymous referees for commenting on earlier drafts of this paper.

A   Standalone Construction

In this section we give an overview of the process leading to the main theorems specified above (Sect. 2.3). For didactic reasons we accompany our description with a simple and concrete "toy" computation as an example, marked in boxed texts, and gloss over some of the (numerous) technicalities (a few examples are discussed in the last part in this section); nevertheless, the same steps apply to more complex computations. Further details and formal definitions appear in the full version of this paper [12].

---

[8] Our ZK-STARK still requires a collision resistant hash function, and in the interactive setting even the Fiat-Shamir heuristic, and, obviously, we make no information-theoretic claims on those.

Many ZKsystems (including ours) use *arithmetization*, a technique introduced to prove circuit lower bounds [66,75] and adapted later to interactive proof systems [4,59]. Arithmetization is the reduction of *computational* problems to *algebraic* problems, that involve "low degree" polynomials over a finite field $\mathbb{F}$; in this context, "low degree" means degree is significantly smaller than field size.

The start point for arithmetization in all proof systems is a computational integrity statement which the prover wishes to prove, like the following instance of the CI language (see Remark 1):

$$\text{"I know private input } y, \text{ such that executing } \mathsf{C} \text{ for } \mathsf{T} \text{ steps on public input } x$$
$$\text{and private input } y \text{ leads to result } z. \text{"} \tag{*}$$

For our ZK-STIK and for related prior systems [9,25,27], the end point of arithmetization is a pair of *Reed-Solomon (RS) proximity testing (RPT)* problems[9], and the scalability of our ZK-STIK relies on a new solution to it—the FRI protocol discussed below [11]. For $S \subset \mathbb{F}$ and rate parameter $\rho \in (0,1)$, the RS code with evaluation domain S and *rate* ρ is the space of evaluations of low-degree functions over S,

$$\mathsf{RS}[\mathbb{F}, S, \rho] = \{f : S \to \mathbb{F} \mid \deg(f) < \rho|S|\}.$$

The RPT problem for $\mathsf{RS}[\mathbb{F}, S, \rho]$ is one of deciding, with a small number of queries, whether a function $f : S \to \mathbb{F}$ is a member of $\mathsf{RS}[\mathbb{F}, S, \rho]$ or far from all members of the code in relative Hamming distance.

> **Toy problem** For concreteness, consider the following special case of (*), which computes the T entry in a "multiplicative modular Fibonacci sequence":
>
> $\quad$ *"I know initial values $y_0, y_1 \in \mathbb{F}$, such that $z \in \mathbb{F}^*$ is the Tth element in the*
> $\quad$ *sequence defined inductively by $y_i = y_{i-2} \cdot y_{i-1}$ for $i > 1$ (i.e., $z = y_\mathsf{T}$)"* $\quad$ (**)
>
> We call this a multiplicative modular Fibonacci sequence because, fixing g to be a generator of $\mathbb{F}^*$, and setting $y_i = g^{j_i}$ one sees that the correct output z is $z = g^{F_\mathsf{T}}$ where F_T is the Tth element in the Fibonacci sequence that starts with j_0, j_1, and is computed modulo $|\mathbb{F}^*| = |\mathbb{F}| - 1$. We choose this simple computation as our toy problem because it is non-trivial to compute over all fields (the standard modular Fibonacci sequence is trivial over binary fields).

Our process has 4 parts (see Fig. 5). When reading the description below, the main thing to notice is that from start to end, verification costs are logarithmic in T (and polynomial in the description of the computation C). To see this it is useful to think informally of $\mathsf{T} \gg |\mathsf{C}|$, like $\mathsf{T} = 2^{|\mathsf{C}|}$. In each of the reductions, the verifier receives only an instance (denoted x) as its input, whereas the prover additionally receives a witness (denoted w) for membership of x in the relevant language.

---

[9] The other solutions described in Sect. 3.1 like those based on Homomorphic public-key cryptography (hPKC) have different end points.

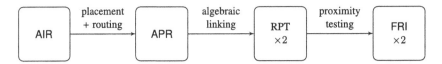

Fig. 5. The reduction from an AIR instance to a pair of RPT problems, solved using the FRI protocol, explained later in this section. Briefly, the Algebraic Intermediate Representation (AIR) is converted via the Algebraic Placement and Routing (APR) reduction to an APR instance. This is reduced via the Algebraic Linking IOPP (ALI) protocol to a pair of RPT problems, which are solved using two applications of the FRI protocol.

Part I. The starting point is a natural *algebraic intermediate representation*[10] (AIR) of x and w, denoted x_{AIR}, w_{AIR}. The verifier receives x_{AIR} and the prover also receives w_{AIR}. Informally, x_{AIR} corresponds to the statement (*) and w_{AIR} corresponds to an execution trace witnessing correctness of (*), i.e., w_{AIR} is a $T \times a$ array in which the ith row describes the state of the computation at time i and the jth column tracks the contents of the jth register over time (this column will later give rise to f_j). Each entry of this array is an element in the field $\mathbb{F}$. The transition relation of the computation is specified by a set of multivariate polynomials over variables $X_1, \ldots, X_a, Y_1, \ldots, Y_a$ that correspond to the current state registers (X variables) and next state registers (Y variables). These constraints enforce the validity of the transition from one state to the next.

> In our toy problem (**), we shall use an execution trace of dimensions $T \times 2$, where an honest prover is expected to fill the ith row with entries y_{i-1}, y_i. Using X_0, X_1 and Y_0, Y_1 to denote the registers in two consecutive sets, our toy transition relation is captured by the pair of polynomial constraints
>
> $$C_0(Y_0, X_1) := Y_0 - X_1; \quad C_1(X_0, X_1, Y_1) := Y_1 - X_0 \cdot X_1.$$
>
> Satisfying a constraint means assigning values to its variables as to make it vanish (evaluate to 0). The first constraint above ensures we move the latest element in the sequence to the first register and the second constraint ensures we compute the next element correctly. x_{AIR} contains these two constraints, along with the boundary constraint that "forces" the $[T, 2]$-entry of w_{AIR} to equal z (the public input of the statement (**)).

Notice that $|x_{AIR}|$ can be much smaller than $|w_{AIR}|$; this is crucial for (full) scalability because tv must be bounded by a polynomial in $|x_{AIR}|$ and $\log T$. Another point to bear in mind is that constructing an AIR for simple computations is straightforward (as shown in our toy example); additional examples appear in Vitalik Buterin's blog posts I and III on STARKs [32], in the examples in libSTARK [10], and in previous works like [9, Appendix B] and [65].

---

[10] AIRs are called algebraic constraint satisfaction problems (ACSPs) in prior works like [9,27]; we prefer the mono-syllable term AIRs which also relates to the notion of an intermediate representation used in other areas of computer science.

Part II. We reduce the AIR representation into a different one, in which states of the execution trace are "placed" on nodes of an *affine graph*, so that consecutive states are connected by an edge in that graph. Informally, an affine graph is a "circuit" that has "algebraic" topology. The process of "placing" machine states on nodes of a circuit is roughly analogous to the process of *placement and routing* which is commonly used in computer and circuit design, although our design space is constrained by *algebra* rather than by physical reality. We refer to this particular transformation as the *algebraic placement and routing* (APR) reduction, and the resulting representation is an APR instance/witness pair $(\mathsf{x}_{\mathsf{APR}}, \mathsf{w}_{\mathsf{APR}})$. The affine graph will necessarily be quite large, larger than $|\mathsf{w}_{\mathsf{APR}}| \geq \mathsf{T}$, but the verifier requires only a *succinct* representation of this graph, via a constant size set of (edge) generators. This succinct representation is crucial for obtaining verifier scalability and avoiding the "computation unrolling" costs incurred by other ZKapproaches. We first explain how a prover computes this transformation, and then address the verifier's transformation.

The (honest) prover interprets the jth column of the algebraic execution trace as a partial function $\hat{f}_j$ from a domain that is a subset of $\mathbb{F}$ and which maps into the field $\mathbb{F}$. Thus, the prover now interpolates this function $\hat{f}_j$ to obtain a polynomial $P_j(X)$, and then evaluates this polynomial on a different domain $S \subset \mathbb{F}$ of size $|S| = \beta \cdot \mathsf{T}$, to obtain a function f_j. The final step of this stage on the prover-side is providing the verifier with oracle access to the sequence $\boldsymbol{f} = (f_1, \ldots, f_{\mathsf{a}})$ where $f_i : S \to \mathbb{F}$, noticing this sequence is an encoding of columns (registers) of the execution trace via RS codewords. (in the ZK-STARK, this oracle access will be realized via Merkle-tree commitments to $\boldsymbol{f}$).

The verifier, on receiving $\mathsf{x}_{\mathsf{AIR}}$, computes the size $\beta \cdot \mathsf{T}$ and picks the same domain $S \subset \mathbb{F}$ as the prover (notice S does not depend on $\mathsf{w}_{\mathsf{AIR}}$). Then, the verifier computes the succinct set of affine transformations that correspond to edges in the affine graph, and obtains an APR instance, denoted $\mathsf{x}_{\mathsf{APR}}$.

In the toy problem (**) the APR reduction involves picking a multiplicative subgroup G of $\mathbb{F}^*$ of size $|G| = \mathsf{T}$ (for simplicity we assume such G exists; in libSTARK we use additive subgroups instead of multiplicative ones and pad the execution trace to size $|G|$). Let g denote a generator of G. The affine graph in this case has vertex set G and directed edges $(h, \mathsf{g} \cdot h)$. Using this, we now view the execution trace as a pair of mappings $\hat{f}_0, \hat{f}_1 : G \to \mathbb{F}$, one mapping per register/column of the execution trace. The prover interpolates each function to obtain a pair of polynomials $P_0(X), P_1(X)$ and evaluates them over a set S that is a union of cosets of G, creating the first proof oracle $\boldsymbol{f} = (f_0, f_1)$ (when constructing the ZK-STARK, this means the prover computes the Merkle root of $\boldsymbol{f}$ and sends it to the verifier).

The reduction in this step is deterministic on the verifier side, i.e., involves no verifier-side randomness and no interaction; as such, it also has perfect completeness and perfect soundness. On the prover side, randomness is used to create a zero knowledge version of the execution trace, by allowing the prover to use polynomials of degree slightly greater than T, as to allow for Shamir-style secret sharing techniques to hide individual entries of the execution trace.

Part III. The APR representation is used to produce, via a 1-round IOP, a pair of instances of the Reed-Solomon proximity testing (RPT) problem. In our case, the two codes resulting from the reduction are over the same field $\mathbb{F}$ but may have different evaluation domains and different code rates. To maintain verifier scalability, we point out that specifying the code parameters—S and ρ, will be done in a succinct manner, one that requires space $\log|T|$; thus, this part of our construction also supports verifier-side scalability.

The witness in this case is a pair of purported codewords $(f^{(0)}, g^{(0)})$. The first function $f^{(0)}$ is simply a random linear combination of f to which the prover committed in the previous step. The second function $g^{(0)}$ is obtained after the various constraints that enforce execution trace validity are randomly "linked" into a single (random) constraint. We thus refer to this step as the *algebraic linking IOP* (ALI) protocol.

For the toy problem (**) the ALI protocol works thus. After receiving oracle access to f (or its Merkle commitment), the verifier samples $r_0, r_1, r'_0, r'_1 \in \mathbb{F}$ and sends them to the prover. The prover is expected to compute $f^{(0)} = r_0 \cdot f_0 + r_1 \cdot f_1$. To construct $g^{(0)}$, the prover first constructs the single random constraint

$$C(X_0, X_1, Y_0, Y_1) := r'_0 \cdot C_0(Y_0, X_1) + r'_1 \cdot C_1(X_0, X_1, Y_1)$$

where C_0, C_1 are as defined in step 1. Then, the prover recalls the interpolating polynomials P_0, P_1 from step 2 and computes

$$Q(X) := C(P_0(X), P_1(X), P_0(\mathbf{g} \cdot X), P_1(\mathbf{g} \cdot X)).$$

Let $\mathsf{Zero}_G(X) := \prod_{\xi \in G}(X - \xi)$. The prover computes $g^{(0)} : S \to \mathbb{F}$ as the evaluation of $Q(X)/\mathsf{Zero}_G(X)$ on S. Notice that $g^{(0)}$ is well-defined because $G \cap S = \emptyset$. Recalling the verifier has oracle access to f, notice that each entry of $f^{(0)}$ can be computed by querying a single row of the execution trace f (one query from f_0 and one from f_1; similarly, each entry of $g^{(0)}$ can be computed by reading two consecutive rows (4 entries) of f. Thus, even though the next step will assume oracle access to $f^{(0)}, g^{(0)}$, the protocol does not require the prover to send another set of oracles during this step, the oracles can be "locally computed" from f.

Finally, notice that if the prover is honest, then it holds that $f^{(0)}$ is a codeword of the RS code of rate $|G|/|S|$ over evaluation domain S. Similarly, since $Q(X)$ vanishes on all $\xi \in G$, we deduce that $Q(X)/\mathsf{Zero}_G(X)$ is a polynomial of degree at most $\deg(C) \cdot |S| - \deg(\mathsf{Zero}_G) = |S|$, so $g^{(0)}$ is also a codeword of $\mathsf{RS}[\mathbb{F}, S, |G|/|S|]$.

Part IV. In the last step of our reduction, for each of the two functions (oracles) $f^{(0)}, g^{(0)}$, the prover and verifier interact according to the *fast RS IOP of proximity* (FRI) protocol from [11] (cf. [12, Appendix B.6]). That protocol has a scalable verifier and query complexity that is logarithmic in the size of the evaluation domain of the code, further establishing verifier scalability. And thus, from start to end, verifier side complexity remains scalable—logarithmic in T (and polynomial in $|C|$).

> In this last step our toy problem (**) behaves no differently than the general case. We apply the FRI protocol to each of $f^{(0)}, g^{(0)}$ described in the prior step, and compute the entries of each function by making oracle access to f.

Regarding prover scalability, inspection reveals that the main bottleneck in the process is the low-degree extension part, in which each function $\hat{f}_j$ that encodes a register gets interpolated and then evaluated on a domain of size $\beta \cdot T$. For this part we use so-called *additive FFTs*; in particular, libSTARK uses the recent innovative algorithm of [56] that performs this computation with $O(\beta T \log(\beta T))$ arithmetic operations. All other steps of the prover's computation are merely *linear* in $|T|$; in particular, the FRI computation is such.

In closing we briefly mention some of the subtle issues that were glossed over in our toy example and are discussed at length in our formal proofs, and implemented in the code:

1. The toy construction is not zero knowledge, because each entry of f does reveal some information about y_0, y_1. To achieve zero knowledge we slacken the degree constraint on f_0, f_1, allowing the prover to sample a random polynomial that agrees with $\hat{f}_0, \hat{f}_1$ on G, and thus hide information regarding y_0, y_1 for query-limited verifiers (in a manner resembling Shamir secret sharing [74]).

2. We did not enforce the boundary condition stating that the last entry is z. To enforce this, the verifier interpolates a polynomial corresponding to all boundary constraints (in our toy example there is only one such constraint) and "incorporates it" in the proof oracle f.

3. Verifier scalability requires that Zero_G be computed efficiently. This is indeed the case (because G is a subgroup of $\mathbb{F}$), and holds also for additive subgroups (as implemented by libSTARK [10]).

4. The toy computation does not make use of random memory access (RAM); maintaining scalability for programs that make significant use of RAM complicates the construction, requiring more elaborate affine graphs that embed DeBruijn switching networks; these issues are addressed by Theorem 2 and its proof.

References

1. Ames, S., Hazay, C., Ishai, Y., Venkitasubramaniam, M.: Ligero: lightweight sublinear arguments without a trusted setup. In: Proceedings of the 24th ACM Conference on Computer and Communications Security (2017)

2. Arora, S., Lund, C., Motwani, R., Sudan, M., Szegedy, M.: Proof verification and the hardness of approximation problems. J. ACM **45**(3), 501–555 (1998). Preliminary version in FOCS 1992

3. Arora, S., Safra, S.: Probabilistic checking of proofs: a new characterization of NP. J. ACM **45**(1), 70–122 (1998). Preliminary version in FOCS 1992

4. Babai, L., Fortnow, L.: Arithmetization: a new method in structural complexity theory. Comput. Complex. **1**(1), 41–66 (1991). https://doi.org/10.1007/BF01200057. ISSN 1420–8954

5. Babai, L., Fortnow, L., Levin, L.A., Szegedy, M.: Checking computations in poly-logarithmic time. In: Proceedings of the 23rd Annual ACM Symposium on Theory of Computing, STOC 1991, pp. 21–32 (1991)
6. Babai, L., Fortnow, L., Lund, C.: Nondeterministic exponential time has two-prover interactive protocols. In: Proceedings of the 31st Annual Symposium on Foundations of Computer Science, FOCS 1990, pp. 16–25 (1990)
7. Bellare, M., Goldreich, O.: On defining proofs of knowledge. In: Brickell, E.F. (ed.) CRYPTO 1992. LNCS, vol. 740, pp. 390–420. Springer, Heidelberg (1993). https://doi.org/10.1007/3-540-48071-4_28
8. Ben-Or, M., et al.: Everything provable is provable in zero-knowledge. In: Goldwasser, S. (ed.) CRYPTO 1988. LNCS, vol. 403, pp. 37–56. Springer, New York (1990). https://doi.org/10.1007/0-387-34799-2_4
9. Ben-Sasson, E., et al.: Computational integrity with a public random string from quasi-linear PCPs. In: IACR Cryptology ePrint Archive 2016, p. 646 (2016). http://eprint.iacr.org/2016/646
10. Ben-Sasson, E., Bentov, I., Horesh, Y., Riabzev, M.: libSTARK: a library for zero knowledge (ZK) scalable transparent argument of knowledge (STARK). https://github.com/elibensasson/libSTARK
11. Ben-Sasson, E., Bentov, I., Horesh, Y., Riabzev, M.: Fast reed-solomon interactive oracle proofs of proximity. In: 45th International Colloquium on Automata, Languages, and Programming, ICALP 2018, Prague, Czech Republic, 9–13 July 2018, pp. 14:1–14:17 (2018). https://doi.org/10.4230/LIPIcs.ICALP.2018.14
12. Ben-Sasson, E., Bentov, I., Horesh, Y., Riabzev, M.: Scalable, transparent, and post-quantum secure computational integrity. Cryptology ePrint Archive, Report 2018/046 (2018). https://eprint.iacr.org/2018/046
13. Ben-Sasson, E., Chiesa, A., Forbes, M.A., Gabizon, A., Riabzev, M., Spooner, N.: On probabilistic checking in perfect zero knowledge. In: Electron. Colloq. Comput. Complex. (ECCC) **23**, 156 (2016). http://eccc.hpi-web.de/report/2016/156
14. Ben-Sasson, E., Chiesa, A., Forbes, M.A., Gabizon, A., Riabzev, M., Spooner, N.: Zero knowledge protocols from succinct constraint detection. In: Kalai, Y., Reyzin, L. (eds.) TCC 2017, Part II. LNCS, vol. 10678, pp. 172–206. Springer, Cham (2017). https://doi.org/10.1007/978-3-319-70503-3_6
15. Ben-Sasson, E., Chiesa, A., Gabizon, A., Riabzev, M., Spooner, N.: Short interactive oracle proofs with constant query complexity, via composition and sumcheck. Electron. Colloq. Comput. Complex. (ECCC) **23**, 46 (2016)
16. Ben-Sasson, E., Chiesa, A., Gabizon, A., Virza, M.: Quasi-linear size zero knowledge from linear-algebraic PCPs. In: Kushilevitz, E., Malkin, T. (eds.) TCC 2016. LNCS, vol. 9563, pp. 33–64. Springer, Heidelberg (2016). https://doi.org/10.1007/978-3-662-49099-0_2
17. Ben-Sasson, E., Chiesa, A., Genkin, D., Tromer, E.: On the concrete efficiency of probabilistically-checkable proofs. In: Proceedings of the 45th ACM Symposium on the Theory of Computing, STOC 2013, pp. 585–594 (2013)
18. Ben-Sasson, E., Chiesa, A., Genkin, D., Tromer, E., Virza, M.: TinyRAM architecture specification v2. 00 (2013). http://scipr-lab.org/tinyram
19. Ben-Sasson, E., Chiesa, A., Genkin, D., Tromer, E., Virza, M.: SNARKs for C: verifying program executions succinctly and in zero knowledge. In: Canetti, R., Garay, J.A. (eds.) CRYPTO 2013. LNCS, vol. 8043, pp. 90–108. Springer, Heidelberg (2013). https://doi.org/10.1007/978-3-642-40084-1_6

20. Ben-Sasson, E., Chiesa, A., Green, M., Tromer, E., Virza, M.: Secure sampling of public parameters for succinct zero knowledge proofs. In: 2015 IEEE Symposium on Security and Privacy, SP 2015, San Jose, CA, USA, 17–21 May 2015, pp. 287–304 (2015). https://doi.org/10.1109/SP.2015.25

21. Ben-Sasson, E., Chiesa, A., Riabzev, M., Spooner, N., Virza, M., Ward, N.P.: Aurora: transparent succinct arguments for R1CS. Cryptology ePrint Archive, Report 2018/828 (2018). https://eprint.iacr.org/2018/828. To appear in Eurocrypt 2019

22. Ben-Sasson, E., Chiesa, A., Spooner, N.: Interactive oracle proofs. In: Hirt, M., Smith, A. (eds.) TCC 2016, Part II. LNCS, vol. 9986, pp. 31–60. Springer, Heidelberg (2016). https://doi.org/10.1007/978-3-662-53644-5_2. ISBN 978-3-662-53644-5

23. Ben-Sasson, E., Chiesa, A., Tromer, E., Virza, M.: Scalable zero knowledge via cycles of elliptic curves. In: Garay, J.A., Gennaro, R. (eds.) CRYPTO 2014. LNCS, vol. 8617, pp. 276–294. Springer, Heidelberg (2014). https://doi.org/10.1007/978-3-662-44381-1_16. Extended version at http://eprint.iacr.org/2014/595

24. Ben-Sasson, E., Chiesa, A., Tromer, E., Virza, M.: Succinct non-interactive zero knowledge for a von Neumann architecture. In: Proceedings of the 23rd USENIX Security Symposium, Security 2014, pp. 781-796 (2014). Extended version at http://eprint.iacr.org/2013/879

25. Ben-Sasson, E., Goldreich, O., Harsha, P., Sudan, M., Vadhan, S.: Short PCPs verifiable in polylogarithmic time. In: Proceedings of the 20th Annual IEEE Conference on Computational Complexity, CCC 2005, pp. 120–134 (2005)

26. Ben-Sasson, E., Kopparty, S., Saraf, S.: Worst-case to average case reductions for the distance to a code. In: 33rd Computational Complexity Conference, CCC 2018, San Diego, CA, USA, 22–24 June 2018, pp. 24:1–24:23 (2018). https://doi.org/10.4230/LIPIcs.CCC.2018.24

27. Ben-Sasson, E., Sudan, M.: Short PCPs with polylog query complexity. SIAM J. Comput. $38(2)$, 551–607 (2008). Preliminary version appeared in STOC 2005

28. Bitansky, N., Canetti, R., Chiesa, A., Tromer, E.: Recursive composition and bootstrapping for SNARKs and proof-carrying data. In: Proceedings of the 45th ACM Symposium on the Theory of Computing, STOC 2013, pp. 111–120 (2013)

29. Bitansky, N., Chiesa, A., Ishai, Y., Paneth, O., Ostrovsky, R.: Succinct non-interactive arguments via linear interactive proofs. In: Sahai, A. (ed.) TCC 2013. LNCS, vol. 7785, pp. 315–333. Springer, Heidelberg (2013). https://doi.org/10.1007/978-3-642-36594-2_18

30. Bootle, J., Cerulli, A., Chaidos, P., Groth, J., Petit, C.: Efficient zero-knowledge arguments for arithmetic circuits in the discrete log setting. In: Fischlin, M., Coron, J.-S. (eds.) EUROCRYPT 2016, Part II. LNCS, vol. 9666, pp. 327–357. Springer, Heidelberg (2016). https://doi.org/10.1007/978-3-662-49896-5_12

31. Bünz, B., Bootle, J., Boneh, D., Poelstra, A., Wuille, P., Maxwell, G.: Bulletproofs: efficient range proofs for confidential transactions. Cryptology ePrint Archive, Report 2017/1066 (2017). https://eprint.iacr.org/2017/1066

32. Buterin, V.: (2017). https://vitalik.ca/

33. Chiesa, A., Zhu, Z.A.: Shorter arithmetization of nondeterministic computations. Theor. Comput. Sci. **600**, 107–131 (2015)

34. Chiesa, A., Tromer, E.: Proof-carrying data and hearsay arguments from signature cards. In: Proceedings of the 1st Symposium on Innovations in Computer Science, ICS 2010, pp. 310–331 (2010)

35. Cormode, G., Mitzenmacher, M., Thaler, J.: Practical verified computation with streaming interactive proofs. In: Proceedings of the 4th Symposium on Innovations in Theoretical Computer Science. ITCS 2012, pp. 90–112 (2012)

36. Cormode, G., Thaler, J., Yi, K.: Verifying computations with streaming interactive proofs. Proc. VLDB Endow. **5**(1), 25–36 (2011)

37. Danezis, G., Fournet, C., Groth, J., Kohlweiss, M.: Square span programs with applications to succinct NIZK arguments. In: Sarkar, P., Iwata, T. (eds.) ASIACRYPT 2014, Part I. LNCS, vol. 8873, pp. 532–550. Springer, Heidelberg (2014). https://doi.org/10.1007/978-3-662-45611-8_28. ISBN 978-3-662-45611-8

38. Dinur, I.: The PCP theorem by gap amplification. J. ACM **54**(3), 12 (2007)

39. Dwork, C., Feige, U., Kilian, J., Naor, M., Safra, M.: Low communication 2-prover zero-knowledge proofs for NP. In: Brickell, E.F. (ed.) CRYPTO 1992. LNCS, vol. 740, pp. 215–227. Springer, Heidelberg (1993). https://doi.org/10.1007/3-540-48071-4_15

40. Gennaro, R., Gentry, C., Parno, B.: Non-interactive verifiable computing: outsourcing computation to untrusted workers. In: Rabin, T. (ed.) CRYPTO 2010. LNCS, vol. 6223, pp. 465–482. Springer, Heidelberg (2010). https://doi.org/10.1007/978-3-642-14623-7_25. http://dl.acm.org/citation.cfm?id=1881412.1881445. ISBN 3-642-14622-8, 978-3-642-14622-0

41. Gennaro, R., Gentry, C., Parno, B., Raykova, M.: Quadratic span programs and succinct NIZKs without PCPs. In: Johansson, T., Nguyen, P.Q. (eds.) EUROCRYPT 2013. LNCS, vol. 7881, pp. 626–645. Springer, Heidelberg (2013). https://doi.org/10.1007/978-3-642-38348-9_37

42. Giacomelli, I., Madsen, J., Orlandi, C.: ZKBoo: faster zero-knowledge for boolean circuits. In: 25th USENIX Security Symposium (USENIX Security 16), pp. 1069–1083. USENIX Association, Austin (2016). https://www.usenix.org/conference/usenixsecurity16/technical-sessions/presentation/giacomelli. ISBN 978-1-931971-32-4

43. Goldwasser, S., Kalai, Y.T., Rothblum, G.N.: Delegating computation: interactive proofs for Muggles. In: Proceedings of the 40th Annual ACM Symposium on Theory of Computing, STOC 2008, pp. 113–122 (2008)

44. Goldwasser, S., Micali, S., Rackoff, C.: The knowledge complexity of interactive proof systems. SIAM J. Comput. **18**(1), 186–208 (1989). Preliminary version appeared in STOC 1985

45. Groth, J.: Short pairing-based non-interactive zero-knowledge arguments. In: Abe, M. (ed.) ASIACRYPT 2010. LNCS, vol. 6477, pp. 321–340. Springer, Heidelberg (2010). https://doi.org/10.1007/978-3-642-17373-8_19

46. Groth, J.: Efficient zero-knowledge arguments from two-tiered homomorphic commitments. In: Lee, D.H., Wang, X. (eds.) ASIACRYPT 2011. LNCS, vol. 7073, pp. 431–448. Springer, Heidelberg (2011). https://doi.org/10.1007/978-3-642-25385-0_23

47. Groth, J.: On the size of pairing-based non-interactive arguments. In: Fischlin, M., Coron, J.-S. (eds.) EUROCRYPT 2016, Part II. LNCS, vol. 9666, pp. 305–326. Springer, Heidelberg (2016). https://doi.org/10.1007/978-3-662-49896-5_11

48. Groth, J., Maller, M.: Snarky signatures: minimal signatures of knowledge from simulation-extractable SNARKs. In: Katz, J., Shacham, H. (eds.) CRYPTO 2017, Part II. LNCS, vol. 10402, pp. 581–612. Springer, Cham (2017). https://doi.org/10.1007/978-3-319-63715-0_20

49. Groth, J., Sahai, A.: Efficient non-interactive proof systems for bilinear groups. In: Smart, N. (ed.) EUROCRYPT 2008. LNCS, vol. 4965, pp. 415–432. Springer, Heidelberg (2008). https://doi.org/10.1007/978-3-540-78967-3_24

50. Ishai, Y., Kushilevitz, E., Ostrovsky, R.: Efficient arguments without short PCPs. In: Proceedings of the Twenty-Second Annual IEEE Conference on Computational Complexity, CCC 2007, pp. 278–291 (2007)
51. Ishai, Y., Kushilevitz, E., Ostrovsky, R., Sahai, A.: Zero-knowledge from secure multiparty computation. In: Proceedings of the Thirty-Ninth Annual ACM Symposium on Theory of Computing, pp. 21–30. ACM (2007)
52. Ishai, Y., Mahmoody, M., Sahai, A., Xiao, D.: On Zero-Knowledge PCPs: Limitations, Simplifications, and Applications (2015). http://www.cs.virginia.edu/~mohammad/files/papers/ZKPCPs-Full.pdf
53. Kalai, Y.T., Raz, R.: Interactive PCP. In: Aceto, L., Damgård, I., Goldberg, L.A., Halldórsson, M.M., Ingólfsdóttir, A., Walukiewicz, I. (eds.) ICALP 2008. LNCS, vol. 5126, pp. 536–547. Springer, Heidelberg (2008). https://doi.org/10.1007/978-3-540-70583-3_44
54. Kilian, J.: A note on efficient zero-knowledge proofs and arguments. In: Proceedings of the 24th Annual ACM Symposium on Theory of Computing, STOC 1992, pp. 723–732 (1992)
55. Kilian, J., Petrank, E., Tardos, G.: Probabilistically checkable proofs with zero knowledge. In: Proceedings of the 29th Annual ACM Symposium on Theory of Computing, STOC 1997, pp. 496–505 (1997)
56. Lin, S.-J., Al-Naffouri, T.Y., Han, Y.S., Chung, W.-H.: Novel polynomial basiswith fast fourier transform and its application to Reed-Solomon erasure codes. IEEE Trans. Inf. Theory **62**(11), 6284–6299 (2016)
57. Lin, S.-J., Chung, W.-H., Han, Y.S.: Novel polynomial basis and its application to Reed-Solomon erasure codes. In: Proceedings of the 2014 IEEE 55th Annual Symposium on Foundations of Computer Science, FOCS 2014, pp. 316–325. IEEE Computer Society, Washington, DC (2014). https://doi.org/10.1109/FOCS.2014.41. ISBN 978-1-4799-6517-5
58. Lipmaa, H.: Progression-free sets and sublinear pairing-based non-interactive zero-knowledge arguments. In: Cramer, R. (ed.) TCC 2012. LNCS, vol. 7194, pp. 169–189. Springer, Heidelberg (2012). https://doi.org/10.1007/978-3-642-28914-9_10
59. Lund, C., Fortnow, L., Karloff, H.J., Nisan, N.: Algebraic methods for interactive proof systems. J. ACM **39**(4), 859–868 (1992)
60. Micali, S.: Computationally sound proofs. SIAM J. Comput. **30**(4), 1253–1298 (2000). Preliminary version appeared in FOCS 1994
61. Micali, S.: Computationally sound proofs. SIAM J. Comput. **30**(4), 1253–1298 (2000). https://doi.org/10.1137/S0097539795284959
62. Mie, T.: Polylogarithmic two-round argument systems. J. Math. Cryptol. **2**(4), 343–363 (2008)
63. Parno, B., Gentry, C., Howell, J., Raykova, M.: Pinocchio: nearly practical verifiable computation. In: Proceedings of the 34th IEEE Symposium on Security and Privacy, Oakland 2013, pp. 238–252 (2013)
64. Peck, M.: A blockchain currency that beat s bitcoin on privacy [News]. IEEE Spectr. **53**(12), 11–13 (2016). https://doi.org/10.1109/MSPEC.2016.7761864. ISSN 0018-9235
65. Pergament, E.: Algebraic RAM. MA thesis. Technion—Israel Institute of Technology (2017)
66. Razborov, A.A.: Lower bounds on the size of bounded depth circuits over a complete basis with logical addition. Math. Notes Acad. Sci. USSR **41**(4), 333–338 (1987)

67. Reingold, O., Rothblum, G.N., Rothblum, R.D.: Constant-round interactive proofs for delegating computation. In: Proceedings of the 48th Annual ACM SIGACT Symposium on Theory of Computing, STOC 2016, Cambridge, MA, USA, 18–21 June 2016, pp. 49–62 (2016). https://doi.org/10.1145/2897518.2897652
68. SCIPR Lab. libsnark: a C++ library for zkSNARK proofs. https://github.com/scipr-lab/libsnark
69. Seo, J.H.: Round-efficient sub-linear zero-knowledge arguments for linear algebra. In: Catalano, D., Fazio, N., Gennaro, R., Nicolosi, A. (eds.) PKC 2011. LNCS, vol. 6571, pp. 387–402. Springer, Heidelberg (2011). https://doi.org/10.1007/978-3-642-19379-8_24
70. Setty, S., Blumberg, A.J., Walfish, M.: Toward practical and unconditional verification of remote computations. In: Proceedings of the 13th USENIX Conference on Hot Topics in Operating Systems, HotOS 2011, p. 29 (2011)
71. Setty, S., Braun, B., Vu, V., Blumberg, A.J., Parno, B., Walfish, M.: Resolving the conflict between generality and plausibility in verified computation. In: Proceedings of the 8th EuoroSys Conference, EuroSys 2013, pp. 71–84 (2013)
72. Setty, S., McPherson, M., Blumberg, A.J., Walfish, M.: Making argument systems for outsourced computation practical (sometimes). In: Proceedings of the 2012 Network and Distributed System Security Symposium, NDSS 2012 (2012)
73. Setty, S., Vu, V., Panpalia, N., Braun, B., Blumberg, A.J., Walfish, M.: Taking proof-based verified computation a few steps closer to practicality. In: Proceedings of the 21st USENIX Security Symposium, Security 2012, pp. 253–268 (2012)
74. Shamir, A.: IP = PSPACE. J. ACM 39(4), 869–877 (1992)
75. Smolensky, R.: Algebraic methods in the theory of lower bounds for Boolean circuit complexity. In: Proceedings of the Nineteenth Annual ACM Symposium on Theory of Computing, pp. 77–82. ACM (1987)
76. Thaler, J.: Time-optimal interactive proofs for circuit evaluation. In: Canetti, R., Garay, J.A. (eds.) CRYPTO 2013. LNCS, vol. 8043, pp. 71–89. Springer, Heidelberg (2013). https://doi.org/10.1007/978-3-642-40084-1_5
77. Valiant, P.: Incrementally verifiable computation or proofs of knowledge imply time/space efficiency. In: Canetti, R. (ed.) TCC 2008. LNCS, vol. 4948, pp. 1–18. Springer, Heidelberg (2008). https://doi.org/10.1007/978-3-540-78524-8_1. http://dl.acm.org/citation.cfm?id=1802614.1802616. ISBN 3-540-78523-X, 978-3-540-78523-1
78. Vu, V., Setty, S., Blumberg, A.J., Walfish, M.: A hybrid architecture for interactive verifiable computation. In: Proceedings of the 34th IEEE Symposium on Security and Privacy, Oakland 2013, pp. 223–237 (2013)
79. Wahby, R.S., Setty, S.T.V., Ren, Z., Blumberg, A.J., Walfish, M.: Efficient RAM and control flow in verifiable outsourced computation. In: 22nd Annual Network and Distributed System Security Symposium, NDSS 2015, San Diego, California, USA, 8–11 February 2014 (2015)
80. Wahby, R.S., Tzialla, I., Shelat, A., Thaler, J., Walfish, M.: Doubly-efficient zkSNARKs without trusted setup. Cryptology ePrint Archive, Report 2017/1132 (2017). https://eprint.iacr.org/2017/1132
81. Zhang, Y., Genkin, D., Katz, J., Papadopoulos, D., Papamanthou, C.: vRAM: faster verifiable RAM with program-independent preprocessing. In: 2018 IEEE Symposium on Security and Privacy (SP), pp. 203–220 (2018). https://doi.org/10.1109/SP.2018.00013
82. Zhang, Y., Genkin, D., Katz, J., Papadopoulos, D., Papamanthou, C.: A zero-knowledge version of vSQL. Cryptology ePrint Archive, Report 2017/1146 (2017). https://eprint.iacr.org/2017/1146

Libra: Succinct Zero-Knowledge Proofs with Optimal Prover Computation

Tiacheng Xie[1][✉], Jiaheng Zhang[1][✉], Yupeng Zhang[1,2],
Charalampos Papamanthou[3], and Dawn Song[1]

[1] University of California, Berkeley, USA
{tianc.x,jiaheng_zhang,dawnsong}@berkeley.edu
[2] Texas A&M University, College Station, USA
zhangyp@tamu.edu
[3] University of Maryland, College Park, USA
cpap@umd.edu

Abstract. We present Libra, the first zero-knowledge proof system that has both optimal prover time and succinct proof size/verification time. In particular, if C is the size of the circuit being proved (i) the prover time is $O(C)$ irrespective of the circuit type; (ii) the proof size and verification time are both $O(d \log C)$ for d-depth log-space uniform circuits (such as RAM programs). In addition Libra features an one-time trusted setup that depends only on the size of the input to the circuit and not on the circuit logic. Underlying Libra is a new linear-time algorithm for the prover of the interactive proof protocol by Goldwasser, Kalai and Rothblum (also known as GKR protocol), as well as an efficient approach to turn the GKR protocol to zero-knowledge using small masking polynomials. Not only does Libra have excellent asymptotics, but it is also efficient in practice. For example, our implementation shows that it takes 200 s to generate a proof for constructing a SHA2-based Merkle tree root on 256 leaves, outperforming all existing zero-knowledge proof systems. Proof size and verification time of Libra are also competitive.

1 Introduction

Zero-knowledge proofs (ZKP) are cryptographic protocols between two parties, a *prover* and a *verifier*, in which the prover can convince the verifier about the validity of a statement without leaking any extra information beyond the fact that the statement is true. Since they were first introduced by Goldwasser et al. [31], ZKP protocols have evolved from pure theoretical constructs to practical implementations, achieving proof sizes of just hundreds of bytes and verification times of several milliseconds, regardless of the size of the statement being proved. Due to this successful transition to practice, ZKP protocols have found numerous applications not only in the traditional computation delegation setting but most importantly in providing privacy of transactions in deployed cryptocurrencies (e.g., Zcash [9]) as well as in other blockchain research projects (e.g., Hawk [37]).

Despite such progress in practical implementations, ZKP protocols are still notoriously hard to scale for large statements, due to a particularly high overhead on generating the proof. For most systems, this is primarily because the

© International Association for Cryptologic Research 2019
A. Boldyreva and D. Micciancio (Eds.): CRYPTO 2019, LNCS 11694, pp. 733–764, 2019.
https://doi.org/10.1007/978-3-030-26954-8_24

prover has to perform a large number of cryptographic operations, such as exponentiation in an elliptic curve group. And to make things worse the asymptotic complexity of computing the proof is typically more than linear, e.g., $O(C \log C)$ or even $O(C \log^2 C)$, where C is the size of the statement.

Unfortunately, as of today we are yet to construct a ZKP system whose prover time is *optimal*, i.e., linear in the size of the statement C (this is irrespective of whether the ZKP system has per-statement trusted setup, one-time trusted setup or no trusted setup at all). The only notable exception is the recent work by Bünz et al. [16] that however suffers from linear verification time—for a detailed comparison see Table 1. Therefore designing ZKP systems that enjoy linear prover time as well as succinct[1] proof size and verification time is an open problem, whose resolution can have significant practical implications.

Our Contributions. In this paper we propose Libra, the first ZKP protocol with *linear prover time* and *succinct proof size and verification time* in the size of the arithmetic circuit representing the statement C, when the circuit is *log-space uniform*. Libra is based on the doubly efficient interactive proof protocol proposed by Goldwasser et al. in [30] (referred as GKR protocol in this paper), and the verifiable polynomial delegation scheme proposed by Zhang et al. in [50]. As such it comes with *one-time trusted* setup (and not per-statement trusted setup) that depends only on the size of the input (witness) to the statement that is being proved. Not only does Libra have excellent asymptotic performance but also its prover outperforms in practice all other ZKP systems while verification time and proof size are also very competitive—see Table 1. Our concrete contributions are:

- **GKR with linear prover time.** Libra features a new linear-time algorithm to generate a GKR proof. Our new algorithm does not require any pattern in the circuit and our result subsumes all existing improvements on the GKR prover assuming special circuit structures, such as regular circuits in [43], data-parallel circuits in [43,46], circuits with different sub-copies in [51]. See related work for more details.
- **Adding zero-knowledge.** We propose an approach to turn Libra into zero-knowledge efficiently. In particular, we show a way to mask the responses of our linear-time prover with small random polynomials such that the zero-knowledge variant of the protocol introduces minimal overhead on the verification time compared to the original (unmasked) construction.
- **Implementation and evaluation.** We implement Libra. Our implementation takes an arithmetic circuit with various types of gates (fan-in 2 and degree ≤ 2, such as $+, -, \times$, AND, XOR, etc.) and compiles it into a ZKP protocol. We conduct thorough comparisons to all existing ZKP systems (see Sect. 1.1). We plan to release our system as an open-source implementation.

1.1 Comparing to Other ZKP Systems

Table 1 shows a detailed comparison between Libra and existing ZKP systems. First of all, Libra is the best among all existing systems in terms of practical

---

[1] In ZKP literature, "succinct" is poly-logarithmic in the size of the statement C.

Table 1. Comparison of Libra to existing ZKP systems, where $(\mathcal{G}, \mathcal{P}, \mathcal{V}, |\pi|)$ denote the trusted setup algorithm, the prover algorithm, the verification algorithm and the proof size respectively. Also, C is the size of the log-space uniform circuit with depth d, and n is the size of its input. The numbers are for a circuit computing the root of a Merkle tree with 256 leaves (511 instances of SHA256).

	libSNARK [13]	Ligero [6]	Bulletproofs [16]	Hyrax [48]	libSTARK [8]	Aurora [11]	Libra
$\mathcal{G}$	$O(C)$ per-statement trusted setup	no trusted setup					$O(n)$ one-time trusted setup
$\mathcal{P}$	$O(C \log C)$	$O(C \log C)$	$O(C)$	$O(C \log C)$	$O(C \log^2 C)$	$O(C \log C)$	$O(C)$
$\mathcal{V}$	$O(1)$	$O(C)$	$O(C)$	$O(\sqrt{n} + d \log C)$	$O(\log^2 C)$	$O(C)$	$O(d \log C)$
$|\pi|$	$O(1)$	$O(\sqrt{C})$	$O(\log C)$	$O(\sqrt{n} + d \log C)$	$O(\log^2 C)$	$O(\log^2 C)$	$O(d \log C)$
$\mathcal{G}$	1027 s	NA					210 s
$\mathcal{P}$	360 s	400 s	13,000 s	1,041 s	2,022 s	3199 s	201 s
$\mathcal{V}$	0.002 s	4 s	900 s	9.9 s	0.044 s	15.2 s	0.71 s
$|\pi|$	0.13 KB	1,500 KB	5.5 KB	185 KB	395 KB	174.3 KB	51 KB

prover time. In terms of asymptotics, Libra is the only system with linear prover time and succinct verification and proof size for log-space uniform circuits. The only other system with linear prover time is Bulletproofs [16] whose verification time is linear, *even for log-space uniform circuits*. In the practical front, Bulletproofs prover time and verification time are high, due to the large number of cryptographic operations required for every gate of the circuit.

The proof and verification of Libra are also competitive to other systems. In asymptotic terms, our proof size is only larger than libSNARK [13] and Bulletproofs [16], and our verification is slower than libSNARK [13] and libSTARK [8]. Compared to Hyrax [48], which is also based on similar techniques with our work, Libra improves the performance in all aspects (yet Hyrax does not have any trusted setup). One can refer to Sect. 5 for a detailed description of our experimental setting as well as a more detailed comparison.

Finally, among all systems, libSNARK [13] requires a trusted setup for every statement, and Libra requires an one-time trusted setup that depends on the input size.

Log-Space Uniform Circuits. Though the prover time in Libra is optimal for all circuits, the verification time is succinct only when the circuit is structured (log-space uniform with logarithmic depth). This is the best that can be achieved for all ZKP protocols without per-circuit setup, as the verifier must read the entire circuit, which takes linear time in the worst case. We always refer to log-space uniform circuits when we say our scheme is succinct in this paper, to differentiate from schemes with linear verification time on all circuits (irrespective of whether the circuits are log-space uniform or not). Schemes such as libSTARK [8], zkVSQL [49] and Hyrax [48] also have such property.

In practice, with the help of auxiliary input and circuit squashing, most computations can be expressed as log-space uniform circuits with low depth, such as matrix multiplication, image scaling and Merkle hash tree in Sect. 5. Asymptotically, as shown in [8,13,51], all random memory access (RAM) programs can be validated by circuits that are log-space uniform with log-depth in the running time of the programs (but linear in the size of the programs) by RAM-to-circuit reduction, which justifies the expressiveness of such circuits.

1.2 Our Techniques

Our main technical contributions are a GKR protocol with linear prover time and an efficient approach to turn the GKR protocol into zero-knowledge. We summarize the key ideas behind these two contributions. The detailed protocols are presented in Sects. 3 and 4 respectively.

GKR with Linear Prover. Goldwasser et al. [30] showed an approach to model the evaluation of a layered circuit as a sequence of summations on polynomials defined by values in consecutive layers of the circuit. Using the famous sumcheck protocol (see Sect. 2.3), they developed a protocol (the GKR protocol) allowing the verifier to validate the circuit evaluation in logarithmic time with a logarithmic size proof. However, the polynomials in the protocol are multivariate with $2s$ variables, where S is the number of gates in one layer of the circuit and $s = \log S$. Naively running the sumcheck protocol on these polynomials incurs S^2 prover time, as there are at least $2^{2s} = S^2$ monomials in a $2s$-variate polynomial. Later, Cormode et al. [23] observed that these polynomials are sparse, containing only S nonzero monomials and improved the prover time to $S \log S$.

In our new approach, we divide the protocol into two separate sumchecks. In each sumcheck, the polynomial only contains s variables, and can be expressed as the product of two multilinear polynomials. Utilizing the sparsity of the circuit, we develop new algorithms to scan through each gate of the circuit and compute the closed-form of all these multilinear polynomials explicitly, which takes $O(S)$ time. With this new way of representation, the prover can deploy a dynamic programming technique to generate the proofs in each sumcheck in $O(S)$ time, resulting in a total prover time of $O(S)$.

Efficient Zero-Knowledge GKR. The original GKR protocol is not zero-knowledge, since the messages in the proof can be viewed as weighed sums of the values in the circuit and leak information. In [48,49], the authors proposed to turn the GKR protocol into zero-knowledge by hiding the messages in homomorphic commitments, which incurs a big overhead in the verification time. In [22], Chiesa et al. proposed an alternative approach by masking the protocol with random polynomials. However, the masking polynomials are as big as the original ones and the prover time becomes exponential, making the approach mainly of theoretical interest.

In our scheme, we first show that in order to make the sumcheck protocol zero-knowledge, the prover can mask it with a "small" polynomial. In particular, the masking polynomial only contains logarithmically many random coefficients. The intuition is that though the original polynomial has $O(2^{\ell})$ or more terms (ℓ is the number of variables in the polynomial), the prover only sends $O(\ell)$ messages in the sumcheck protocol. Therefore, it suffices to mask the original polynomial with a random one with $O(\ell)$ coefficients to achieve zero-knowledge.

In particular, we set the masking polynomial as the sum of ℓ univariate random polynomials with the same variable-degree. In Sect. 4.1, we show that the entropy of this mask exactly counters the leakage of the sumcheck, proving that it is sufficient and optimal.

Besides the sumcheck, the GKR protocol additionally leaks two evaluations of the polynomial defined by values in each layer of the circuit. To make these evaluations zero-knowledge, we mask the polynomial by a special low-degree random polynomial. In particular, we show that after the mask, the verifier in total learns 4 messages related to the evaluations of the masking polynomial and we can prove zero-knowledge by making these messages linearly independent. Therefore, the masking polynomial is of constant size: it consists of 2 variables with variable degree 2.

1.3 Related Work

In recent years there has been significant progress in efficient ZKP protocols and systems. In this section, we discuss related work in this area, with the focus on those with sublinear proofs.

QAP-Based. Following earlier work of Ishai [34], Groth [33] and Lipmaa [38], Gennaro et al. [28] introduced quadratic arithmetic programs (QAPs), which forms the basis of most recent implementations [10,14,19,24,27,42,47] including libSNARK [13]. The proof size in these systems is constant, and the verification time depends only on the input size. Both these properties are particularly appealing and have led to real-world deployments, e.g., ZCash [9]. One of the main bottlenecks, however, of QAP-based systems is the high overhead in the prover running time and memory consumption, making it hard to scale to large statements. In addition, a separate trusted setup for every statement is required.

IOPs. Based on "(MPC)-in-the-head" introduced in [21,29,35], Ames et al. [6] proposed a ZKP scheme called Ligero. It only uses symmetric key operations and the prover time is fast in practice. However, it generates proofs of size $O(\sqrt{C})$, which is several megabytes in practice for moderate-size circuits. In addition, the verification time is quasi-linear to the size of the circuit. It is categorized as interactive PCP, which is a special case of interactive oracle proofs (IOPs). IOP generalizes the probabilistically checkable proofs (PCPs) where earlier works of Kilian [36] and Micali [41] are built on. In the IOP model, Ben-Sasson et al. built libstark [8], a zero-knowledge transparent argument of knowledge (zkSTARK).libstark does not rely on trusted setup and executes in the RAM model of computation. Their verification time is only linear to the description of the RAM program, and succinct (logarithmic) in the time required for program execution. Recently, Ben-Sasson et al. [11] proposed Aurora, a new ZKP system in the IOP model with the proof size of $O(\log^2 C)$.

Discrete Log. Before Bulletproof [16], earlier discrete-log based ZKP schemes include the work of Groth [32], Bayer and Groth [7] and Bootle et al. [17].

Hash-Based. Bootle et al. [18] proposed a ZKP scheme with linear prover time and verification time. The verification only requires $O(C)$ field additions. However, the proof size is $O(\sqrt{C})$ and the constants are large.

Interactive Proofs. The line of work that relates to our paper the most is based on interactive proofs [31]. In the seminal work of [30], Goldwasser et al. proposed an efficient interactive proof for layered arithmetic circuits. Later, Cormode et al. [23] improved the prover complexity of the interactive proof in [30] to $O(C \log C)$ using multilinear extensions instead of low degree extensions. Several follow-up works further reduce the prover time assuming special structures of the circuit. For regular circuits where the wiring pattern can be described in constant space and time, Thaler [43] introduced a protocol with $O(C)$ prover time; for data parallel circuits with many copies of small circuits with size C', a $O(C \log C')$ protocol is presented in the same work, later improved to $O(C + C' \log C)$ by Wahby et al. in [46]; for circuits with many non-connected but different copies, Zhang et al. showed a protocol with $O(C \log C')$ prover time.

In [50], Zhang et al. extended the GKR protocol to an argument system using a protocol for verifiable polynomial delegation. Zhang et al. [51] and Wahby et al. [48] make the argument system zero-knowledge by putting all the messages in the proof into homomorphic commitments, as proposed by Cramer and Damgard in [25]. This approach introduces a high overhead on the verification time compared to the plain argument system without zero-knowledge, as each addition becomes a multiplication and each multiplication becomes an exponentiation in the homomorphic commitments. The multiplicative overhead is around two orders of magnitude in practice. Additionally, the scheme of [48], Hyrax, removes the trusted setup of the argument system by introducing a new polynomial delegation, increasing the proof size and verification time to $O(\sqrt{n})$.

2   Preliminaries

2.1   Notation

In this paper, we use λ to denote the security parameter, and $\mathsf{negl}(\lambda)$ to denote the negligible function in λ. "PPT" stands for probabilistic polynomial time. We use $f(), h()$ for polynomials, x, y, z for vectors of variables and g, u, v for vectors of values. x_i denotes the i-th variable in x. We use bold letters such as $\mathbf{A}$ to represent arrays. For a multivariate polynomial f, its "variable-degree" is the maximum degree of f in any of its variables.

Assumptions. Our scheme uses bilinear pairing and relies on the q-Strong Bilinear Diffie-Hellman (q-SBDH) assumption and an extended version of the Power Knowledge of Exponent (PKE) assumption [49,50]. We present bilinear pairing and the assumptions formally in the full version of the paper.

2.2   Interactive Proofs and Zero-Knowledge Arguments

Interactive Proofs. An interactive proof allows a prover $\mathcal{P}$ to convince a verifier $\mathcal{V}$ the validity of some statement. The interactive proof runs in several rounds, allowing $\mathcal{V}$ to ask questions in each round based on $\mathcal{P}$'s answers of previous rounds. We phrase this in terms of $\mathcal{P}$ trying to convince $\mathcal{V}$ that $f(x) = 1$. The proof system is interesting only when the running time of $\mathcal{V}$ is less than the time of directly computing the function f. We give the formal definition of interactive proofs in the full version.

Zero-Knowledge Arguments. An argument system for an NP relationship R is a protocol between a computationally-bounded prover $\mathcal{P}$ and a verifier $\mathcal{V}$. At the end of the protocol, $\mathcal{V}$ is convinced by $\mathcal{P}$ that there exists a witness w such that $(x; w) \in R$ for some input x. We focus on arguments of knowledge which have the stronger property that if the prover convinces the verifier of the statement validity, then the prover must know w. We use $\mathcal{G}$ to represent the generation phase of the public key pk and the verification key vk. Formally, consider the definition below, where we assume R is known to $\mathcal{P}$ and $\mathcal{V}$.

Definition 1. *Let R be an NP relation. A tuple of algorithm $(\mathcal{G}, \mathcal{P}, \mathcal{V})$ is a zero-knowledge argument of knowledge for R if the following holds.*

- **Correctness.** *For every* (pk, vk) *output by* $\mathcal{G}(1^\lambda)$ *and* $(x, w) \in R$,

$$\langle \mathcal{P}(\mathsf{pk}, w), \mathcal{V}(\mathsf{vk}) \rangle (x) = \mathsf{accept}$$

- **Soundness.** *For any PPT prover $\mathcal{P}$, there exists a PPT extractor ε such that for every* (pk, vk) *output by* $\mathcal{G}(1^\lambda)$ *and any x, it holds that*

$$\Pr[\langle \mathcal{P}(\mathsf{pk}), \mathcal{V}(\mathsf{vk}) \rangle (x) = \mathsf{accept} \wedge (x, w) \notin R | w \leftarrow \varepsilon(\mathsf{pk}, x)] \leq \mathsf{negl}(\lambda)$$

- **Zero knowledge.** *There exists a PPT simulator $\mathcal{S}$ such that for any PPT adversary $\mathcal{A}$, auxiliary input $z \in \{0,1\}^{\mathsf{poly}(\lambda)}$, $(x; w) \in R$, it holds that*
$$\Pr\left[\langle \mathcal{P}(\mathsf{pk}, w), \mathcal{A} \rangle = \mathsf{accept} : (\mathsf{pk}, \mathsf{vk}) \leftarrow \mathcal{G}(1^\lambda); (x, w) \leftarrow \mathcal{A}(z, \mathsf{pk}, \mathsf{vk}) \right] =$$
$$\Pr\left[\langle \mathcal{S}(\mathsf{trap}, z, \mathsf{pk}), \mathcal{A} \rangle = \mathsf{accept} : (\mathsf{pk}, \mathsf{vk}, \mathsf{trap}) \leftarrow \mathcal{S}(1^\lambda); (x, w) \leftarrow \mathcal{A}(z, \mathsf{pk}, \mathsf{vk}) \right]$$

*We say that $(\mathcal{G}, \mathcal{P}, \mathcal{V})$ is a **succinct** argument system if the running time of $\mathcal{V}$ and the total communication between $\mathcal{P}$ and $\mathcal{V}$ (proof size) are* $\mathsf{poly}(\lambda, |x|, \log |w|)$.

2.3 GKR Protocol

In [30], Goldwasser et al. proposed an efficient interactive proof protocol for layered arithmetic circuits, which we use as a building block for our new zero-knowledge argument and is referred as the *GKR* protocol. We present the detailed protocol here.

Sumcheck Protocol. The sumcheck problem is a fundamental problem that has various applications. The problem is to sum a polynomial $f : \mathbb{F}^\ell \to \mathbb{F}$ on the binary hypercube $\sum_{b_1, b_2, \dots, b_\ell \in \{0,1\}} f(b_1, b_2, \dots, b_\ell)$. Directly computing the sum requires exponential time in ℓ, as there are 2^ℓ combinations of $b_1, \dots, b_\ell$. Lund et al. [39] proposed a *sumcheck* protocol that allows a verifier $\mathcal{V}$ to delegate the computation to a computationally unbounded prover $\mathcal{P}$, who can convince $\mathcal{V}$ that H is the correct sum. We provide a description of the sumcheck protocol in Protocol 1. The proof size of the sumcheck protocol is $O(d\ell)$, where d is the variable-degree of f, as in each round, $\mathcal{P}$ sends a univariate polynomial of one variable in f, which can be uniquely defined by $d+1$ points. The verifier time of the protocol is $O(d\ell)$. The prover time depends on the degree and the sparsity of f, and we will give the complexity later in our scheme. The sumcheck protocol is complete and sound with $\epsilon = \frac{d\ell}{|\mathbb{F}|}$.

Protocol 1 (Sumcheck) *The protocol proceeds in ℓ rounds.*

- *In the first round, $\mathcal{P}$ sends a univariate polynomial*

$$f_1(x_1) \overset{def}{=} \sum\nolimits_{b_2,\ldots,b_\ell \in \{0,1\}} f(x_1, b_2, \ldots, b_\ell),$$

  $\mathcal{V}$ checks $H = f_1(0) + f_1(1)$. Then $\mathcal{V}$ sends a random challenge $r_1 \in \mathbb{F}$ to $\mathcal{P}$.
- *In the i-th round, where $2 \le i \le l-1$, $\mathcal{P}$ sends a univariate polynomial*

$$f_i(x_i) \overset{def}{=} \sum\nolimits_{b_{i+1},\ldots,b_\ell \in \{0,1\}} f(r_1, \ldots, r_{i-1}, x_i, b_{i+1}, \ldots, b_\ell),$$

  $\mathcal{V}$ checks $f_{i-1}(r_{i-1}) = f_i(0) + f_i(1)$, and sends a random challenge $r_i \in \mathbb{F}$ to $\mathcal{P}$.
- *In the ℓ-th round, $\mathcal{P}$ sends a univariate polynomial*

$$f_\ell(x_\ell) \overset{def}{=} f(r_1, r_2, \ldots, r_{l-1}, x_\ell),$$

  $\mathcal{V}$ checks $f_{\ell-1}(r_{\ell-1}) = f_\ell(0) + f_\ell(1)$. The verifier generates a random challenge $r_\ell \in \mathbb{F}$. Given oracle access to an evaluation $f(r_1, r_2, \ldots, r_\ell)$ of f, $\mathcal{V}$ will accept if and only if $f_\ell(r_\ell) = f(r_1, r_2, \ldots, r_\ell)$. The instantiation of the oracle access depends on the application of the sumcheck protocol.

Definition 2 (Multi-linear Extension). *Let $V : \{0,1\}^\ell \to \mathbb{F}$ be a function. The multilinear extension of V is the unique polynomial $\tilde{V} : \mathbb{F}^l \to \mathbb{F}$ such that $\tilde{V}(x_1, x_2, ..., x_l) = V(x_1, x_2, ..., x_l)$ for all $x_1, x_2, \ldots, x_l \in \{0,1\}^l$. $\tilde{V}$ can be expressed as:*

$$\tilde{V}(x_1, x_2, ..., x_l) = \sum\nolimits_{b \in \{0,1\}^\ell} \prod\nolimits_{i=1}^{l} [((1-x_i)(1-b_i) + x_i b_i) \cdot V(b)]$$

where b_i is i-th bit of b.

Multilinear Extensions of Arrays. Inspired by the close form equation of the multilinear extension given above, we can view an array $\mathbf{A} = (a_0, a_1, \ldots, a_{n-1})$ as a function $A : \{0,1\}^{\log n} \to \mathbb{F}$ such that $\forall i \in [0, n-1], A(i) = a_i$. Therefore, in this paper, we abuse the use of multilinear extension on an array as the multilinear extension $\tilde{A}$ of A.

High Level Ideas of GKR. Let C be a layered arithmetic circuit with depth d over a finite field $\mathbb{F}$. Each gate in the i-th layer takes inputs from two gates in the $(i+1)$-th layer; layer 0 is the output layer and layer d is the input layer. The protocol proceeds layer by layer. Upon receiving the claimed output from $\mathcal{P}$, in the first round, $\mathcal{V}$ and $\mathcal{P}$ run the sumcheck protocol to reduce the claim about the output to a claim about the values in the layer above. In the i-th round, both parties reduce a claim about layer $i-1$ to a claim about layer i through the sumcheck protocol. Finally, the protocol terminates with a claim about the input layer d, which can be checked directly by $\mathcal{V}$, or is given as an oracle access. If the check passes, $\mathcal{V}$ accepts the claimed output.

Notation. Before describing the GKR protocol, we introduce some additional notations. We denote the number of gates in the i-th layer as S_i and let $s_i = \lceil \log S_i \rceil$. (For simplicity, we assume S_i is a power of 2, and we can pad the layer with dummy gates otherwise.) We then define a function $V_i : \{0,1\}^{s_i} \to \mathbb{F}$ that takes a binary string $b \in \{0,1\}^{s_i}$ and returns the output of gate b in layer i, where b is called the gate label. With this definition, V_0 corresponds to the output of the circuit, and V_d corresponds to the input layer. Finally, we define two additional functions $add_i, mult_i : \{0,1\}^{s_{i-1}+2s_i} \to \{0,1\}$, referred as *wiring predicates* in the literature. add_i $(mult_i)$ takes one gate label $z \in \{0,1\}^{s_{i-1}}$ in layer $i-1$ and two gate labels $x, y \in \{0,1\}^{s_i}$ in layer i, and outputs 1 if and only if gate z is an addition (multiplication) gate that takes the output of gate x, y as input. With these definitions, V_i can be written as follows:

$$V_i(z) = \sum_{x,y \in \{0,1\}^{s_{i+1}}} (add_{i+1}(z,x,y)(V_{i+1}(x) + V_{i+1}(y)) \\ + mult_{i+1}(z,x,y)(V_{i+1}(x)V_{i+1}(y))) \tag{1}$$

for any $z \in \{0,1\}^{s_i}$.

In the equation above, V_i is expressed as a summation, so $\mathcal{V}$ can use the sumcheck protocol to check that it is computed correctly. As the sumcheck protocol operates on polynomials defined on $\mathbb{F}$, we rewrite the equation with their multilinear extensions:

$$\tilde{V}_i(g) = \sum_{x,y \in \{0,1\}^{s_{i+1}}} f_i(x,y) \\ = \sum_{x,y \in \{0,1\}^{s_{i+1}}} (\tilde{add}_{i+1}(g,x,y)(\tilde{V}_{i+1}(x) + \tilde{V}_{i+1}(y)) \\ + \tilde{mult}_{i+1}(g,x,y)(\tilde{V}_{i+1}(x)\tilde{V}_{i+1}(y))), \tag{2}$$

where $g \in \mathbb{F}^{s_i}$ is a random vector.

Protocol. With Eq. 2, the GKR protocol proceeds as follows. The prover $\mathcal{P}$ first sends the claimed output of the circuit to $\mathcal{V}$. From the claimed output, $\mathcal{V}$ defines polynomial $\tilde{V}_0$ and computes $\tilde{V}_0(g)$ for a random $g \in \mathbb{F}^{s_0}$. $\mathcal{V}$ and $\mathcal{P}$ then invoke a sumcheck protocol on Eq. 2 with $i = 0$. As described in Sect. 2.3, at the end of the sumcheck, $\mathcal{V}$ needs an oracle access to $f_i(u,v)$, where u,v are randomly selected in $\mathbb{F}^{s_{i+1}}$. To compute $f_i(u,v)$, $\mathcal{V}$ computes $\tilde{add}_{i+1}(u,v)$ and $\tilde{mult}_{i+1}(u,v)$ locally (they only depend on the wiring pattern of the circuit, but not on the values), asks $\mathcal{P}$ to send $\tilde{V}_1(u)$ and $\tilde{V}_1(v)$ and computes $f_i(u,v)$ to complete the sumcheck protocol. In this way, $\mathcal{V}$ and $\mathcal{P}$ reduces a claim about the output to two claims about values in layer 1.

Combining Two Claims: Condensing to One Claim. In [30], Goldwasser et al. presented a protocol to reduce two claims $\tilde{V}_i(u)$ and $\tilde{V}_i(v)$ to one as following. $\mathcal{V}$ defines a line $\gamma : \mathbb{F} \to \mathbb{F}^{s_i}$ such that $\gamma(0) = u, \gamma(1) = v$. $\mathcal{V}$ sends $\gamma(x)$ to $\mathcal{P}$. Then $\mathcal{P}$ sends $\mathcal{V}$ a degree s_i univariate polynomial $h(x) = \tilde{V}_i(\gamma(x))$. $\mathcal{V}$ checks that $h(0) = \tilde{V}_i(u), h(1) = \tilde{V}_i(v)$. Then $\mathcal{V}$ randomly chooses $r \in \mathbb{F}$ and computes a new claim $h(r) = \tilde{V}_i(\gamma(r)) = \tilde{V}_i(w)$ on $w = \gamma(r) \in \mathbb{F}^{s_i}$. $\mathcal{V}$ sends r, w to $\mathcal{P}$. In this way, the two claims are reduced to one claim $\tilde{V}_i(w)$. Combining this protocol with the sumcheck protocol on Eq. 2, $\mathcal{V}$ and $\mathcal{P}$ can reduce a claim on layer i to one claim on layer $i+1$, and eventually to a claim on the input.

Combining Two Claims: Random Linear Combination. In [22], Chiesa et al. proposed an alternative approach using random linear combinations. Upon receiving the two claims $\tilde{V}_i(u)$ and $\tilde{V}_i(v)$, $\mathcal{V}$ selects $\alpha_i, \beta_i \in \mathbb{F}$ randomly and computes $\alpha_i \tilde{V}_i(u) + \beta_i \tilde{V}_i(v)$. Based on Eq. 2, this can be written as

$$
\begin{aligned}
&\alpha_i \tilde{V}_i(u) + \beta_i \tilde{V}_i(v) \\
={}&\alpha_i \sum_{x,y\in\{0,1\}^{s_{i+1}}} (\widetilde{add}_{i+1}(u,x,y)(\tilde{V}_{i+1}(x) + \tilde{V}_{i+1}(y)) + \widetilde{mult}_{i+1}(u,x,y)(\tilde{V}_{i+1}(x)\tilde{V}_{i+1}(y))) \\
+{}&\beta_i \sum_{x,y\in\{0,1\}^{s_{i+1}}} (\widetilde{add}_{i+1}(v,x,y)(\tilde{V}_{i+1}(x) + \tilde{V}_{i+1}(y)) + \widetilde{mult}_{i+1}(v,x,y)(\tilde{V}_{i+1}(x)\tilde{V}_{i+1}(y))) \\
={}&\sum_{x,y\in\{0,1\}^{s_{i+1}}} ((\alpha_i \widetilde{add}_{i+1}(u,x,y) + \beta_i \widetilde{add}_{i+1}(v,x,y))(\tilde{V}_{i+1}(x) + \tilde{V}_{i+1}(y)) \\
&+ (\alpha_i \widetilde{mult}_{i+1}(u,x,y) + \beta_i \widetilde{mult}_{i+1}(v,x,y))(\tilde{V}_{i+1}(x)\tilde{V}_{i+1}(y)))
\end{aligned}
\tag{3}
$$

$\mathcal{V}$ and $\mathcal{P}$ then execute the sumcheck protocol on Eq. 3 instead of Eq. 2. At the end of the sumcheck protocol, $\mathcal{V}$ still receives two claims about $\tilde{V}_{i+1}$, computes their random linear combination and proceeds to an layer above recursively. In our new ZKP scheme, we will mainly use the second approach.

Theorem 1. [23,30,43,45]. *Let $C : \mathbb{F}^n \to \mathbb{F}^k$ be a depth-d layered arithmetic circuit. The GKR protocol is an interactive proof for the function computed by C with soundness $O(d\log|C|/|\mathbb{F}|)$. It uses $O(d\log|C|)$ rounds of interaction and running time of the prover $\mathcal{P}$ is $O(|C|\log|C|)$. Let the optimal computation time for all $\widetilde{add}_i$ and $\widetilde{mult}_i$ be T, the running time of $\mathcal{V}$ is $O(n + k + d\log|C| + T)$. For log-space uniform circuits it is $T = \mathsf{polylog}\,|C|$.*

2.4 Zero-Knowledge Verifiable Polynomial Delegation Scheme

Let $\mathbb{F}$ be a finite field, $\mathcal{F}$ be a family of ℓ-variate polynomial over $\mathbb{F}$, and d be a variable-degree parameter. A zero-knowledge verifiable polynomial delegation scheme (zkVPD) for $f \in \mathcal{F}$ and $t \in \mathbb{F}^\ell$ consists of the following algorithms:

- $(\mathsf{pp}, \mathsf{vp}) \leftarrow \mathsf{KeyGen}(1^\lambda, \ell, d)$,

---

Algorithm 1. $\mathcal{F} \leftarrow$ FunctionEvaluations$(f, \mathbf{A}, r_1, \ldots, r_\ell)$

Input: Multilinear f on ℓ variables, initial bookkeeping table $\mathbf{A}$, random $r_1, \ldots, r_\ell$;
Output: All function evaluations $f(r_1, \ldots, r_{i-1}, t, b_{i+1}, \ldots, b_\ell)$;
1: **for** $i = 1, \ldots, \ell$ **do**
2:     **for** $b \in \{0,1\}^{\ell-i}$ **do**   // b is both a number and its binary representation.
3:         **for** $t = 0, 1, 2$ **do**
4:             Let $f(r_1, \ldots, r_{i-1}, t, b) = \mathbf{A}[b] \cdot (1-t) + \mathbf{A}[b + 2^{\ell-i}] \cdot t$
5:         $\mathbf{A}[b] = \mathbf{A}[b] \cdot (1 - r_i) + \mathbf{A}[b + 2^{\ell-i}] \cdot r_i$
6: Let $\mathcal{F}$ contain all function evaluations $f(.)$ computed at Step 4
7: **return** $\mathcal{F}$

- com $\leftarrow$ Commit(f, r_f, pp),
- $\{\mathsf{accept}, \mathsf{reject}\} \leftarrow$ CheckComm$(\mathsf{com}, \mathsf{vp})$,
- $(y, \pi) \leftarrow$ Open(f, t, r_f, pp),
- $\{\mathsf{accept}, \mathsf{reject}\} \leftarrow$ Verify$(\mathsf{com}, t, y, \pi, \mathsf{vp})$.

A zkVPD scheme satisfies correctness, soundness and zero knowledge. We give the formal definitions in the full version.

3   GKR Protocol with Linear Prover Time

In this section we present a new algorithm for the prover of the GKR protocol [30] that runs in linear time for *arbitrary layered circuits*. Before that, we present some necessary building blocks.

3.1   Linear-Time Sumcheck for a Multilinear Function [43]

In [43], Thaler proposed a linear-time algorithm for the prover of the sumcheck protocol on a multilinear function f on ℓ variables (the algorithm runs in $O(2^\ell)$ time). We review this algorithm here. Recall that in the i-th round of the sumcheck protocol the prover sends the verifier the univariate polynomial on x_i

$$\sum\nolimits_{b_{i+1}, \ldots, b_\ell \in \{0,1\}} f(r_1, \ldots, r_{i-1}, x_i, b_{i+1}, \ldots, b_\ell),$$

where $r_1, \ldots, r_{i-1}$ are random values chosen by the verifier in previous rounds. Since f is multilinear, it suffices for the prover to send two evaluations of the polynomial at points $t = 0$ and $t = 1$, namely the evaluations

$$\sum\nolimits_{b_{i+1}, \ldots, b_\ell \in \{0,1\}} f(r_1, \ldots, r_{i-1}, 0, b_{i+1}, \ldots, b_\ell) \tag{4}$$

and

$$\sum\nolimits_{b_{i+1}, \ldots, b_\ell \in \{0,1\}} f(r_1, \ldots, r_{i-1}, 1, b_{i+1}, \ldots, b_\ell). \tag{5}$$

To compute the above sums the prover maintains a *bookkeeping table* $\mathbf{A}$ for f. This table, at round i, has $2^{\ell-i+1}$ entries storing the values

---

Algorithm 2. $\{a_1, \ldots, a_\ell\} \leftarrow \mathsf{SumCheck}(f, \mathbf{A}, r_1, \ldots, r_\ell)$

Input: Multilinear f on ℓ variables, initial bookkeeping table $\mathbf{A}$, random $r_1, \ldots, r_\ell$;
Output: ℓ sumcheck messages for $\sum_{x \in \{0,1\}^\ell} f(x)$. Each message a_i consists of 3 elements (a_{i0}, a_{i1}, a_{i2});
1: $\mathcal{F} \leftarrow \mathsf{FunctionEvaluations}(f, \mathbf{A}, r_1, \ldots, r_\ell)$
2: **for** $i = 1, \ldots, \ell$ **do**
3:     **for** $t \in \{0, 1, 2\}$ **do**
4:         $a_{it} = \sum_{b \in \{0,1\}^{\ell-i}} f(r_1, \ldots, r_{i-1}, t, b)$ *// All evaluations needed are in $\mathcal{F}$.*
5: **return** $\{a_1, \ldots, a_\ell\}$;

$f(r_1, \ldots, r_{i-1}, b_i, b_{i+1}, \ldots, b_\ell)$ for all $b_i, \ldots, b_\ell \in \{0, 1\}$ and is initialized with evaluations of f on the hypercube. For every entry of $\mathbf{A}$, the prover subsequently computes, as in Step 4 of Algorithm 1 FunctionEvaluations[2] two values $f(r_1, \ldots, r_{i-1}, 0, b_{i+1}, \ldots, b_\ell)$ and $f(r_1, \ldots, r_{i-1}, 1, b_{i+1}, \ldots, b_\ell)$. Once these function evaluations are in place, the prover can easily sum over them and compute the required sumcheck messages as required by Relations 4 and 5. This is done in Algorithm 2.

Complexity Analysis. Both Algorithms 1 and 2 run in $O(2^\ell)$ time: The first iteration takes $O(2^\ell)$, the second $O(2^{\ell-1})$ and so on. Therefore the bound holds.

3.2 Linear-Time Sumcheck for Products of Multilinear Functions [43]

The linear-time sumcheck in the previous section can be generalized to a product of two multilinear functions. Let now f and g be two multilinear functions on ℓ variables each, we describe a linear-time algorithm to compute the messages of the prover for the sumcheck on the product $f \cdot g$, as proposed in [43]. Note that we cannot use Algorithm 2 here since $f \cdot g$ is not multilinear. However, similarly with the single-function case, the prover must now send, at round i, the following evaluations at points $t = 0$, $t = 1$ and $t = 2$

$$\sum\nolimits_{b_{i+1}, \ldots, b_{\ell}, \in \{0,1\}} f(r_1, \ldots, r_{i-1}, t, b_{i+1}, \ldots, b_\ell) \cdot g(r_1, \ldots, r_{i-1}, t, b_{i+1}, \ldots, b_\ell)$$

The above can be easily computed by computing evaluations for functions f and g *separately* using Algorithm 1 and the combining the results using our new Algorithm 3 SumCheckProduct. We now have the following lemma:

Lemma 1. *Algorithm* SumCheckProduct *runs in time* $O(2^\ell)$

---

[2] To be compatible with other protocols later, we use three values $t = 0, 1, 2$ in our evaluations instead of just two.

3.3   Linear-Time Sumcheck for GKR Functions

Let us now consider the sumcheck problem on a particular class of functions that are relevant for the GKR protocol (that is why we call them GKR functions). In particular we want to compute the sumcheck

$$\sum_{x,y\in\{0,1\}^\ell} f_1(g,x,y)f_2(x)f_3(y), \tag{6}$$

for a fixed point $g \in \mathbb{F}^\ell$, where $f_2(x), f_3(x) : \mathbb{F}^\ell \to \mathbb{F}$ are multilinear extensions of arrays $\mathbf{A}_{f_2}, \mathbf{A}_{f_3}$ of size 2^ℓ, and function $f_1 : \mathbb{F}^{3\ell} \to \mathbb{F}$ is the multilinear extension of a sparse array with $O(2^\ell)$ (out of $2^{3\ell}$ possible) nonzero elements. It is not hard to see that the sumcheck polynomials in GKR given by Eqs. 2 and 3 satisfy these properties.

Algorithm 3. $\{a_1, \ldots, a_\ell\} \leftarrow \mathsf{SumCheckProduct}(f, \mathbf{A}_f, g, \mathbf{A}_g, r_1, \ldots, r_\ell)$

Input: Multilinear f and g, initial bookkeeping tables $\mathbf{A}_f$ and $\mathbf{A}_g$, random $r_1, \ldots, r_\ell$;
Output: ℓ sumcheck messages for $\sum_{x\in\{0,1\}^\ell} f(x)g(x)$. Each message a_i consists of 3 elements (a_{i0}, a_{i1}, a_{i2});

1: $\mathcal{F} \leftarrow \mathsf{FunctionEvaluations}(f, \mathbf{A}_f, r_1, \ldots, r_\ell)$
2: $\mathcal{G} \leftarrow \mathsf{FunctionEvaluations}(g, \mathbf{A}_g, r_1, \ldots, r_\ell)$
3: **for** $i = 1, \ldots, \ell$ **do**
4:     **for** $t \in \{0, 1, 2\}$ **do**
5:         $a_{it} = \sum_{b\in\{0,1\}^{\ell-i}} f(r_1, \ldots, r_{i-1}, t, b) \cdot g(r_1, \ldots, r_{i-1}, t, b)$ // *All*
    evaluations needed are in $\mathcal{F}$ and $\mathcal{G}$.
6: **return** $\{a_1, \ldots, a_\ell\}$;

We note here that applying Algorithm 1 FunctionEvaluations for this particular class of polynomials would lead to quadratic prover time. This is because f_1 has $2^{2\ell}$ variables to sum on yielding $O(2^{2\ell})$ complexity. However, one could take advantage of the sparsity of f_1: the prover can store only the $O(2^\ell)$ non-zero values of the bookkeeping table $\mathbf{A}$. This is exactly the approach used in many prior work [23,46,51]. However, with this approach, the number of nonzero values that must be considered in Step 2 is always at most 2^ℓ, since it is not guaranteed that this number will reduce to half (i.e., to $2^{\ell-i}$) after every update in Step 5 because it is sparse. Therefore, the overall complexity becomes $O(\ell \cdot 2^\ell)$.

In this section we effectively reduce this bound to $O(2^\ell)$. Our protocol divides the sumcheck into two phases: the first ℓ rounds bounding the variables of x to a random point u, and the last ℓ rounds bounding the variables of y to a random point v. The central idea lies in rewriting Eq. 6 as follows

$$\sum_{x,y\in\{0,1\}^\ell} f_1(g,x,y)f_2(x)f_3(y) = \sum_{x\in\{0,1\}^\ell} f_2(x) \sum_{y\in\{0,1\}^\ell} f_1(g,x,y)f_3(y)$$

$$= \sum_{x\in\{0,1\}^\ell} f_2(x)h_g(x),$$

where $h_g(x) = \sum_{y\in\{0,1\}^\ell} f_1(g,x,y)f_3(y)$.

Algorithm 4. $\mathbf{A}_{h_g} \leftarrow$ Initialize_PhaseOne$(f_1, f_3, \mathbf{A}_{f_3}, g)$

Input: Multilinear f_1 and f_3, initial bookkeeping tables $\mathbf{A}_{f_3}$, random $g = g_1, \ldots, g_\ell$;
Output: Bookkeeping table $\mathbf{A}_{h_g}$;

1: **procedure** $\mathbf{G} \leftarrow$ Precompute(g) // $\mathbf{G}$ *is an array of size* 2^ℓ.
2:     Set $\mathbf{G}[0] = 1$
3:     **for** $i = 0, \ldots, \ell - 1$ **do**
4:        **for** $b \in \{0,1\}^i$ **do**
5:           $\mathbf{G}[b, 0] = \mathbf{G}[b] \cdot (1 - g_{i+1})$
6:           $\mathbf{G}[b, 1] = \mathbf{G}[b] \cdot g_{i+1}$
7: $\forall x \in \{0,1\}^\ell$, set $\mathbf{A}_{h_g}[x] = 0$
8: **for** every (z, x, y) such that $f_1(z, x, y)$ is non-zero **do**
9:     $\mathbf{A}_{h_g}[x] = \mathbf{A}_{h_g}[x] + \mathbf{G}[z] \cdot f_1(z, x, y) \cdot \mathbf{A}_{f_3}[y]$
10: **return** $\mathbf{A}_{h_g}$;

Phase One. With the formula above, in the first ℓ rounds, the prover and the verifier are running exactly a sumcheck on a product of two multilinear functions $f_2 \cdot h_g$, since functions f_2 and h_g can be viewed as functions only in x—y can be considered constant (it is always summed on the hypercube). To compute the sumcheck messages for the first ℓ rounds, given their bookkeeping tables, we can call

$$\mathsf{SumCheckProduct}(h_g(x), \mathbf{A}_{h_g}, f_2(x), \mathbf{A}_{f_2}, u_1, \ldots, u_\ell)$$

in Algorithm 3. By Lemma 1 this will take $O(2^\ell)$ time. We now show how to initialize the bookkeeping tables in linear time.

Initializing the Bookkeeping Tables:

Initializing the bookkeeping table for f_2 in $O(2^\ell)$ time is trivial, since f_2 is a multilinear extension of an array and therefore the evaluations on the hypercube are known. Initializing the bookkeeping table for h_g in $O(2^\ell)$ time is more challenging but we can leverage the sparsity of f_1. Consider the following lemma.

Lemma 2. *Let $\mathcal{N}_x$ be the set of $(z, y) \in \{0,1\}^{2\ell}$ such that $f_1(z, x, y)$ is non-zero. Then for all $x \in \{0,1\}^\ell$, it is $h_g(x) = \sum_{(z,y) \in \mathcal{N}_x} I(g, z) \cdot f_1(z, x, y) \cdot f_3(y)$, where $I(g, z) = \prod_{i=1}^\ell ((1 - g_i)(1 - z_i) + g_i z_i)$.*

Proof. As f_1 is a multilinear extension, as shown in [43], we have $f_1(g, x, y) = \sum_{z \in \{0,1\}^\ell} I(g, z) f_1(z, x, y)$, where I is the multilinear extension of the identity polynomial, i.e., $I(w, z) = 1$ iff $w = z$ for all $w, z \in \{0,1\}^\ell$. Therefore, we have

$$h_g(x) = \sum_{y \in \{0,1\}^\ell} f_1(g, x, y) f_3(y) = \sum_{z,y \in \{0,1\}^\ell} I(g, z) f_1(z, x, y) f_3(y)$$
$$= \sum_{(z,y) \in \mathcal{N}_x} I(g, z) \cdot f_1(z, x, y) \cdot f_3(y)$$

Moreover, $I(w, z) = \prod_{i=1}^\ell ((1 - w_i)(1 - z_i) + w_i z_i))$ is the unique polynomial that evaluates to 1 iff $w = z$ for all $w, z \in \{0,1\}^\ell$. As the multilinear extension is unique, we have $I(g, z) = \prod_{i=1}^\ell ((1 - g_i)(1 - z_i) + g_i z_i))$. $\qquad \square$

Algorithm 5. $\mathbf{A}_{f_1} \leftarrow$ Initialize_PhaseTwo(f_1, g, u)

Input: Multilinear f_1, random $g = g_1, \ldots, g_\ell$ and $u = u_1, \ldots, u_\ell$;
Output: Bookkeeping table $\mathbf{A}_{f_1}$;

1: $\mathbf{G} \leftarrow$ Precompute(g)
2: $\mathbf{U} \leftarrow$ Precompute(u)
3: $\forall y \in \{0, 1\}^\ell$, set $\mathbf{A}_{f_1}[y] = 0$
4: **for** every (z, x, y) such that $f_1(z, x, y)$ is non-zero **do**
5:     $\mathbf{A}_{f_1}[y] = \mathbf{A}_{f_1}[y] + \mathbf{G}[z] \cdot \mathbf{U}[x] \cdot f_1(z, x, y)$
6: **return** $\mathbf{A}_{f_1}$;

Lemma 3. *The bookkeeping table $\mathbf{A}_{h_g}$ can be initialized in time $O(2^\ell)$.*

Proof. As f_1 is sparse, $\sum_{x \in \{0,1\}^\ell} |\mathcal{N}_x| = O(2^\ell)$. From Lemma 2, given the evaluations of $I(g, z)$ for all $z \in \{0, 1\}^\ell$, the prover can iterate all $(z, y) \in \mathcal{N}_x$ for all x to compute $\mathbf{A}_{h_g}$. The full algorithm is presented in Algorithm 4.

Procedure Precompute(g) is to evaluate $\mathbf{G}[z] = I(g, z) = \prod_{i=1}^\ell ((1 - g_i)(1 - z_i) + g_i z_i))$ for $z \in \{0, 1\}^\ell$. By the closed-form of $I(g, z)$, the procedure iterates each bit of z, and multiples $1 - g_i$ for $z_i = 0$ and multiples g_i for $z_i = 1$. In this way, the size of $\mathbf{G}$ doubles in each iteration, and the total complexity is $O(2^\ell)$.

Step 8–9 computes $h_g(x)$ using Lemma 2. When f_1 is represented as a map of (z, x, y), $f_1(z, x, y)$ for non-zero values, the complexity of these steps is $O(2^\ell)$. In the GKR protocol, this is exactly the representation of a gate, where z, x, y are labels of the gate, its left input and its right input, and $f_1(z, x, y) = 1$. $\square$

With the bookkeeping tables, the prover runs SumCheckProduct$(h_g(x), \mathbf{A}_{h_g}, f_2(x), \mathbf{A}_{f_2}, u_1, \ldots, u_\ell)$ in Algorithm 3 and the complexity for phase one is $O(2^\ell)$.

Phase Two. At this point, all variables in x have been bounded to random numbers u. In the second phase, the equation to sum on becomes

$$\sum_{y \in \{0,1\}^\ell} f_1(g, u, y) f_2(u) f_3(y)$$

Note here that $f_2(u)$ is merely a single value which we already computed in phase one. Both $f_1(g, u, y)$ and $f_3(y)$ are polynomials on y with ℓ variables. Similar to phase one, to compute the messages for the last ℓ rounds we can call

SumCheckProduct$(f_1(g, u, y), \mathbf{A}_{f_1}, f_3(y) \cdot f_2(u), \mathbf{A}_{f_3} \cdot f_2(u), , v_1, \ldots, v_\ell)$.

Note here that $\mathbf{A}_{f_1}$ is the bookkeeping table for $f_1(g, u, y)$, not the original sparse function $f_1(g, x, y)$.

Initializing the Bookkeeping Table for f_1:
It now remains to initialize the bookkeeping table for $f_1(g, u, y)$ efficiently. Similar to phase one, we have the following lemma:

Lemma 4. *Let $\mathcal{N}_y$ be the set of $(z, x) \in \{0, 1\}^{2\ell}$ such that $f_1(z, x, y)$ is non-zero. Then for all $y \in \{0, 1\}^\ell$, it is $f_1(g, u, y) = \sum_{(z,x) \in \mathcal{N}_y} I(g, z) \cdot I(u, x) \cdot f_1(z, x, y)$.*

Proof. This immediately follows from the fact that f_1 is a multilinear extension. We have $f_1(g, u, y) = \sum_{z,y \in \{0,1\}^\ell} I(g, z) \cdot I(u, x) \cdot f_1(z, x, y)$, where the closed from of I is given in Lemma 2.   □

Lemma 5. *The bookkeeping table $\mathbf{A}_{f_1}$ can be initialized in time $O(2^\ell)$.*

Proof. Similar to Algorithm 4, he prover again iterates all non-zero indices of f_1 to compute it using Lemma 4. The full algorithm is presented in Algorithm 5.   □

3.4 Putting Everything Together

The sumcheck protocol in GKR given by Eq. 2 can be decomposed into several instances that have the form of Eq. 6 presented in the previous section. The term

$$\sum_{x,y \in \{0,1\}^{s_{i+1}}} \tilde{mult}_{i+1}(g, x, y)(\tilde{V}_{i+1}(x)\tilde{V}_{i+1}(y))$$

is exactly the same as Eq. 6. The term $\sum_{x,y \in \{0,1\}^{s_{i+1}}} \tilde{add}_{i+1}(g, x, y)(\tilde{V}_{i+1}(x) + \tilde{V}_{i+1}(y))$ can be viewed as:

$$\sum_{x,y \in \{0,1\}^{s_{i+1}}} \tilde{add}_{i+1}(g, x, y)\tilde{V}_{i+1}(x) + \sum_{x,y \in \{0,1\}^{s_{i+1}}} \tilde{add}_{i+1}(g, x, y)\tilde{V}_{i+1}(y)$$

The first sum can be computed using the same protocol in Sect. 3.3 without $f_3(y)$, and the second sum can be computed without $f_2(x)$. The complexity for both cases remains linear. Due to linearity of the sumcheck protocol, the prover can execute these 3 instances simultaneously in every round, and sum up the individual messages and send them to the verifier.

Combining Two Claims. After the sumcheck in the GKR protocol is completed, as described in Sect. 2.3, the prover and the verifier need to combine the two claims about $\tilde{V}_{i+1}$ received at the end of the sumcheck protocol to one to avoid the exponential blow-up. There are two ways to combine the two claims and we show how to do each of them in linear time.

The second approach using random linear combinations is rather straight forward. After the output layers, $\mathcal{P}$ and $\mathcal{V}$ execute sumcheck protocol on Eq. 3 instead of Eq. 2, which still satisfies the properties of Eq. 6. One could view it as 6 instances of Eq. 6 and the prover time is still linear. Moreover, there is a better way to further improve the efficiency. Taking $\sum_{x,y \in \{0,1\}^{s_{i+1}}} (\alpha_i \tilde{mult}_{i+1}(u, x, y) + \beta_i \tilde{mult}_{i+1}(v, x, y))\tilde{V}_{i+1}(x)\tilde{V}_{i+1}(y)$ as an example, in Algorithm 4, the prover runs Precompute twice on u and v to generate two arrays ($\mathbf{G}_1$ and $\mathbf{G}_2$), and sets $\mathbf{G}[b] = \alpha_i \mathbf{G}_1[b] + \beta_i \mathbf{G}_2[b]$ for all b. The rest of the algorithms remains the same. This only incurs a small overhead in practice in our implementation, compared to the original algorithm on Eq. 6.

Though with the approach above we already have a linear prover GKR protocol, the technique to condense two points to one proposed in the original GKR protocol [30] may still be interesting in some scenarios (e.g., in our implementation, we use this approach in the last layer and only make one query to the multi-linear extension of the input, which is more efficient practice). We present an algorithm to reduce the prover time of this approach to linear in the full version of the paper.

4   Zero Knowledge Argument Protocols

In this section, we present the construction of our new zero-knowledge argument system. In [50], Zhang et al. proposed to combine the GKR protocol with a verifiable polynomial delegation protocol, resulting in an argument system. Later, in [48,49], the construction was extended to zero-knowledge, by sending all the messages in the GKR protocol in homomorphic commitments and performing all the checks by zero-knowledge equality and product testing. This incurs a high overhead for the verifier compared to the plain version without zero-knowledge, as each multiplication becomes an exponentiation and each equality check becomes a Σ-protocol, which is around $100\times$ slower in practice.

In this paper, we follow the same blueprint of combining GKR and VPD to obtain an argument system, but instead show how to extend it to be zero-knowledge efficiently. In particular, the prover masks the GKR protocol with special random polynomials so that the verifier runs a "randomized" GKR that leaks no extra information and her overhead is small. A similar approach was used by Chiesa et al. in [22]. In the following, we present the zero-knowledge version of each building block, followed by the whole zero-knowledge argument.

4.1   Zero Knowledge Sumcheck

As a core step of the GKR protocol, $\mathcal{P}$ and $\mathcal{V}$ execute a sumcheck protocol on Eq. 2, during which $\mathcal{P}$ sends $\mathcal{V}$ evaluations of the polynomial at several random points chosen by $\mathcal{V}$. These evaluations leak information about the values in the circuit, as they can be viewed as weighted sums of these values.

To make the sumcheck protocol zero-knowledge, we take the approach proposed by Chiesa et al. in [22], which is masking the polynomial in the sumcheck protocol by a random polynomial. In this approach, to prove

$$H = \sum\nolimits_{x_1,x_2,\ldots,x_\ell \in \{0,1\}} f(x_1, x_2, \ldots, x_\ell),$$

the prover generates a random polynomial g with the same variables and individual degrees of f. She commits to the polynomial g, and sends the verifier a claim $G = \sum\nolimits_{x_1,x_2,\ldots,x_\ell \in \{0,1\}} g(x_1, x_2, \ldots, x_\ell)$. The verifier picks a random number ρ, and execute a sumcheck protocol with the prover on

$$H + \rho G = \sum\nolimits_{x_1,x_2,\ldots,x_\ell \in \{0,1\}} (f(x_1, x_2, \ldots, x_\ell) + \rho g(x_1, x_2, \ldots, x_\ell)).$$

At the last round of this sumcheck, the prover opens the commitment of g at $g(r_1, \ldots, r_\ell)$, and the verifier computes $f(r_1, \ldots, r_l)$ by subtracting $\rho g(r_1, \ldots, r_\ell)$ from the last message, and compares it with the oracle access of f. It is shown that as long as the commitment and opening of g are zero-knowledge, the protocol is zero-knowledge. Intuitively, this is because all the coefficients of f are masked by those of g. The soundness still holds because of the random linear combination of f and g.

Unfortunately, the masking polynomial g is as big as f, and opening it to a random point later is expensive. In [22], the prover sends a PCP oracle of g, and executes a zero-knowledge sumcheck to open it to a random point, which incurs an exponential complexity for the prover. Even replacing it with the zkVPD protocol in [49], the prover time is slow in practice.

In this paper, we show that it suffices to mask f with a small polynomial to achieve zero-knowledge. In particular, we set $g(x_1, \ldots, x_\ell) = a_0 + g_1(x_1) + g_2(x_2) + \ldots + g_\ell(x_\ell)$, where $g_i(x_i) = a_{i,1}x_i + a_{i,2}x_i^2 + \ldots + a_{i,d}x_i^d$ is a random univariate polynomial of degree d (d is the variable degree of f). Note here that the size of g is only $O(d\ell)$, while the size of f is exponential in ℓ.

The intuition of our improvement is that the prover sends $O(d\ell)$ messages in total to the verifier during the sumcheck protocol, thus a polynomial g with $O(d\ell)$ random coefficients is sufficient to mask all the messages and achieve zero-knowledge. We present the full protocol in Construction 1.

The completeness of the protocol holds obviously. The soundness follows the soundness of the sumcheck protocol and the random linear combination in step 2 and 3, as proven in [22]. We give a proof of zero knowledge in the full version.

Theorem 2 (Zero knowledge). *For every verifier $\mathcal{V}^*$ and every ℓ-variate polynomial $f : \mathbb{F}^\ell \to \mathbb{F}$ with variable degree d, there exists a simulator $\mathcal{S}$ such that given access to $H = \sum_{x_1, x_2, \ldots, x_\ell \in \{0,1\}} f(x_1, x_2, \ldots, x_\ell)$, $\mathcal{S}$ is able to simulate the partial view of $\mathcal{V}^*$ in step 1–4 of Construction 1.*

Construction 1. *We assume the existence of a zkVPD protocol defined in Sect. 2.4. For simplicity, we omit the randomness r_f and public parameters pp, vp without any ambiguity. To prove the claim $H = \sum\limits_{x_1, x_2, \ldots, x_\ell \in \{0,1\}} f(x_1, x_2, \ldots, x_\ell)$:*

1. *$\mathcal{P}$ selects a polynomial $g(x_1, \ldots, x_\ell) = a_0 + g_1(x_1) + g_2(x_2) + \ldots + g_l(x_\ell)$, where $g_i(x_i) = a_{i,1}x_i + a_{i,2}x_i^2 + \ldots + a_{i,d}x_i^d$ and all $a_{i,j}s$ are uniformly random. $\mathcal{P}$ sends $H = \sum\limits_{x_1, x_2, \ldots, x_\ell \in \{0,1\}} f(x_1, x_2, \ldots, x_\ell)$, $G = \sum\limits_{x_1, x_2, \ldots, x_\ell \in \{0,1\}} g(x_1, x_2, \ldots, x_\ell)$ and $\mathsf{com}_g = \mathsf{Commit}(g)$ to $\mathcal{V}$.*

2. *$\mathcal{V}$ uniformly selects $\rho \in \mathbb{F}^*$, computes $H + \rho G$ and sends ρ to $\mathcal{P}$.*

3. *$\mathcal{P}$ and $\mathcal{V}$ run the sumcheck protocol on*

$$H + \rho G = \sum_{x_1, x_2, \ldots, x_\ell \in \{0,1\}} (f(x_1, x_2, \ldots, x_\ell) + \rho g(x_1, x_2, \ldots, x_\ell))$$

4. *At the last round of the sumcheck protocol, $\mathcal{V}$ obtains a claim $h_\ell(r_\ell) = f(r_1, r_2, \ldots, r_\ell) + \rho g(r_1, r_2, \ldots, r_\ell)$. $\mathcal{P}$ and $\mathcal{V}$ opens the commitment of g at $r = (r_1, \ldots, r_\ell)$ by $(g(r), \pi) \leftarrow \mathsf{Open}(g, r), \mathsf{Verify}(\mathsf{com}_g, g(r), r, \pi)$. If Verify outputs reject, $\mathcal{V}$ aborts.*

5. *$\mathcal{V}$ computes $h_\ell(r_\ell) - \rho g(r_1, \ldots, r_\ell)$ and compares it with the oracle access of $f(r_1, \ldots, r_\ell)$.*

4.2   Zero Knowledge GKR

To achieve zero-knowledge, we replace the sumcheck protocol in GKR with the zero-knowledge version described in the previous section. However, the protocol still leaks additional information. In particular, at the end of the zero-knowledge sumcheck, $\mathcal{V}$ queries the oracle to evaluate the polynomial on a random point. When executed on Eq. 2, this reveals two evaluations of the polynomial $\tilde{V}_i$ defined by the values in the i-th layer of the circuit: $\tilde{V}_i(u)$ and $\tilde{V}_i(v)$.

To prevent this leakage, Chiesa et al. [22] proposed to replace the multi-linear extension $\tilde{V}_i$ with a low degree extension, such that learning $\tilde{V}_i(u)$ and $\tilde{V}_i(v)$ does not leak any information about V_i. Define a low degree extension of V_i as

$$\dot{V}_i(z) \stackrel{def}{=} \tilde{V}_i(z) + Z_i(z) \sum\nolimits_{w \in \{0,1\}^\lambda} R_i(z, w), \tag{7}$$

where $Z(z) = \prod_{i=1}^{s_i} z_i(1 - z_i)$, i.e., $Z(z) = 0$ for all $z \in \{0,1\}^{s_i}$. $R_i(z, w)$ is a random low-degree polynomial and λ is the security parameter. With this low degree extension, Eq. 2 becomes

$$\dot{V}_i(g) = \sum\nolimits_{x,y \in \{0,1\}^{s_{i+1}}} \widetilde{mult}_{i+1}(g, x, y)(\dot{V}_{i+1}(x)\dot{V}_{i+1}(y))$$
$$+ \widetilde{add}_{i+1}(g, x, y)(\dot{V}_{i+1}(x) + \dot{V}_{i+1}(y)) + Z_i(g) \sum\nolimits_{w \in \{0,1\}^\lambda} R_i(g, w) \tag{8}$$

$$= \sum\nolimits_{x,y \in \{0,1\}^{s_{i+1}}, w \in \{0,1\}^\lambda} (I(\mathbf{0}, w) \cdot \widetilde{mult}_{i+1}(g, x, y)(\dot{V}_{i+1}(x)\dot{V}_{i+1}(y))$$
$$+ \widetilde{add}_{i+1}(g, x, y)(\dot{V}_{i+1}(x) + \dot{V}_{i+1}(y)) + I((x, y), \mathbf{0})Z_i(g)R_i(g, w)) \tag{9}$$

where $I(\boldsymbol{a}, \boldsymbol{b})$ is an identity polynomial $I(\boldsymbol{a}, \boldsymbol{b}) = 0$ iff $\boldsymbol{a} = \boldsymbol{b}$. The first equation holds because $\dot{V}_i$ agrees with $\tilde{V}_i$ on the Boolean hyper-cube $\{0,1\}^{s_i}$, as $Z_i(z) = 0$ for binary inputs. The second equation holds because the mask in $\dot{V}_i$ is in the form of a "sum" and can be moved into the sumcheck equation.

When executing the zero-knowledge sumcheck protocol on Eq. 8, at the end of the protocol, $\mathcal{V}$ receives $\dot{V}_{i+1}(u)$ and $\dot{V}_{i+1}(v)$ for random points $u, v \in \mathbb{F}^{s_{i+1}}$ chosen by $\mathcal{V}$. They no longer leak information about V_{i+1}, as they are masked by $Z_{i+1}(z) \sum_{w \in \{0,1\}^\lambda} R_{i+1}(z, w)$ for $z = u$ and $z = v$. $\mathcal{V}$ computes $\widetilde{mult}_{i+1}(g, u, v)$ and $\widetilde{add}_{i+1}(g, u, v)$ as before, computes $Z_i(g), I(\mathbf{0}, c), I((u, v), \mathbf{0})$ where $c \in \mathbb{F}^\lambda$ is a random point chosen by $\mathcal{V}$ for variable w, opens $R_i(g, w)$ at c with $\mathcal{P}$ through a polynomial commitment, and checks that together with $\dot{V}_{i+1}(u), \dot{V}_{i+1}(v)$ received from $\mathcal{P}$ they are consistent with the last message of the sumcheck. $\mathcal{V}$ then uses $\dot{V}_{i+1}(u), \dot{V}_{i+1}(v)$ to proceed to the next round.

Unfortunately, similar to the zero-knowledge sumcheck, the masking polynomial R_i is very large in [22]. Opening R_i at a random point takes exponential time for $\mathcal{P}$ either using a PCP oracle as in [22] or potentially using a zkVPD, as R has $s_i + 2s_{i+1} + \lambda$ variables.

In this section, we show that we can set R_i to be a small polynomial to achieve zero-knowledge. In particular, R_i has only two variables with variable degree 2. This is because in the $(i - 1)$-th round, $\mathcal{V}$ receives two evaluations of V_i, $\dot{V}_i(u)$ and $\dot{V}_i(v)$, which are masked by $\sum_w R_i(u, w)$ and $\sum_w R_i(v, w)$; in the

i-th sumcheck, $\mathcal{V}$ opens R_i at $R_i(u,c)$ and $R_i(v,c)$. It suffices to make these four evaluations linearly independent, assuming the commitment and opening of R_i are using a zkVPD. Therefore, we set the low-degree term in Eq. 7 as $Z_i(z)\sum_{w\in\{0,1\}}R_i(z_1,w)$, i.e. R_i only takes two variables, the first variable z_1 of z and an extra variable $w\in\{0,1\}$ instead of $\{0,1\}^\lambda$, with variable degree 2.

The full protocol is presented in Construction 2. Here we use superscriptions (e.g., $u^{(i)}$) to denote random numbers or vectors for the i-th layer of the circuit.

Construction 2. 1. *On a layered arithmetic circuit C with d layers and input* in, *the prover $\mathcal{P}$ sends the output of the circuit* out *to the verifier $\mathcal{V}$.*

2. *$\mathcal{P}$ randomly selects polynomials $R_1(z_1,w),\ldots,R_d(z_1,w):\mathbb{F}^2\to\mathbb{F}$ with variable degree 2. $\mathcal{P}$ commits to these polynomials by sending $\mathsf{com}_i\leftarrow\mathsf{Commit}(R_i)$ to $\mathcal{V}$ for $i\in[1,d]$.*

3. *$\mathcal{V}$ defines $\dot{V}_0(z)=\tilde{V}_0(z)$, where $\tilde{V}_0(z)$ is the multilinear extension of* out. *$\dot{V}_0(z)$ can be viewed as a special case with $R_0(z_1,w)$ being the 0 polynomial. $\mathcal{V}$ evaluates it at a random point $\dot{V}_0(g^{(0)})$ and sends $g^{(0)}$ to $\mathcal{P}$.*

4. *$\mathcal{P}$ and $\mathcal{V}$ execute the zero knowledge sumcheck protocol presented in Construction 1 on*

$$\dot{V}_0(g^{(0)})=\sum_{x,y\in\{0,1\}^{s_1}}\tilde{\mathrm{mult}}_1(g^{(0)},x,y)(\dot{V}_1(x)\dot{V}_1(y))$$
$$+\tilde{\mathrm{add}}_1(g^{(0)},x,y)(\dot{V}_1(x)+\dot{V}_1(y))$$

If $u_1^{(1)}=v_1^{(1)}$, $\mathcal{P}$ aborts. At the end of the protocol, $\mathcal{V}$ receives $\dot{V}_1(u^{(1)})$ and $\dot{V}_1(v^{(1)})$. $\mathcal{V}$ computes $\tilde{\mathrm{mult}}_1(g^{(0)},u^{(1)},v^{(1)})$, $\tilde{\mathrm{add}}_1(g^{(0)},u^{(1)},v^{(1)})$ and checks that

$$\tilde{\mathrm{mult}}_1(g^{(0)},u^{(1)},v^{(1)})\dot{V}_1(u^{(1)})\dot{V}_1(v^{(1)})+\tilde{\mathrm{add}}_1(g^{(0)},u^{(1)},v^{(1)})(\dot{V}_1(u^{(1)})+\dot{V}_1(v^{(1)}))$$

equals to the last message of the sumcheck (evaluation oracle).

1. *For layer $i=1,\ldots,d-1$:*
   (a) *$\mathcal{V}$ randomly selects $\alpha^{(i)},\beta^{(i)}\in\mathbb{F}$ and sends them to $\mathcal{P}$.*
   (b) *Let $Mult_{i+1}(x,y)=\alpha^{(i)}\tilde{\mathrm{mult}}_{i+1}(u^{(i)},x,y)+\beta^{(i)}\tilde{\mathrm{mult}}_{i+1}(v^{(i)},x,y)$ and $Add_{i+1}(x,y)=\alpha^{(i)}\tilde{\mathrm{add}}_{i+1}(u^{(i)},x,y)+\beta^{(i)}\tilde{\mathrm{add}}_{i+1}(v^{(i)},x,y)$. $\mathcal{P}$ and $\mathcal{V}$ run the zero knowledge sumcheck on the equation*
   $\alpha^{(i)}\dot{V}_i(u^{(i)})+\beta^{(i)}\dot{V}_i(v^{(i)})=$

$$\sum_{\substack{x,y\in\{0,1\}^{s_{i+1}}\\w\in\{0,1\}}}(I(\mathbf{0},w)\cdot Mult_{i+1}(x,y)(\dot{V}_{i+1}(x)\dot{V}_{i+1}(y))$$

$$+Add_{i+1}(x,y)(\dot{V}_{i+1}(x)+\dot{V}_{i+1}(y))$$

$$+I((x,y),\mathbf{0})(\alpha^{(i)}Z_i(u^{(i)})R_i(u_1^{(i)},w)+\beta^{(i)}Z_i(v^{(i)})R_i(v_1^{(i)},w)))$$

If $u_1^{(i+1)} = v_1^{(i+1)}$, $\mathcal{P}$ aborts.

(c) *At the end of the zero-knowledge sumcheck protocol, $\mathcal{P}$ sends $\mathcal{V}$*
$\dot{V}_{i+1}(u^{(i+1)})$ *and* $\dot{V}_{i+1}(v^{(i+1)})$.

(d) *$\mathcal{V}$ computes*

$$a_{i+1} = \alpha^{(i)}\widetilde{mult}_{i+1}(u^{(i)}, u^{(i+1)}, v^{(i+1)}) + \beta^{(i)}\widetilde{mult}_{i+1}(v^{(i)}, u^{(i+1)}, v^{(i+1)})$$

and

$$b_{i+1} = \alpha^{(i)}\widetilde{add}_{i+1}(u^{(i)}, u^{(i+1)}, v^{(i+1)}) + \beta^{(i)}\widetilde{add}_{i+1}(v^{(i)}, u^{(i+1)}, v^{(i+1)})$$

locally. $\mathcal{V}$ computes $Z_i(u^{(i)}), Z_i(v^{(i)}), I(\mathbf{0}, c^{(i)}), I((u^{(i+1)}, v^{(i+1)}), \mathbf{0})$ locally.

(e) *$\mathcal{P}$ and $\mathcal{V}$ open R_i at two points $R_i(u_1^{(i)}, c^{(i)})$ and $R_i(v_1^{(i)}, c^{(i)})$ using* Open *and* Verify.

(f) *$\mathcal{V}$ computes the following as the evaluation oracle and uses it to complete the last step of the zero-knowledge sumcheck.*

$$I(\mathbf{0}, c^{(i)})(a_{i+1}(\dot{V}_{i+1}(u^{(i+1)})\dot{V}_{i+1}(v^{(i+1)}))+$$
$$b_{i+1}(\dot{V}_{i+1}(u^{(i+1)}) + \dot{V}_{i+1}(v^{(i+1)})))+$$
$$I((u^{(i+1)}, v^{(i+1)}), \mathbf{0})(\alpha^{(i)}Z_i(u^{(i)})R_i(u_1^{(i)}, c^{(i)}) + \beta^{(i)}Z_i(v^{(i)})R_i(v_1^{(i)}, c^{(i)}))$$

If all checks in the zero knowledge sumcheck and Verify *passes, $\mathcal{V}$ uses $\dot{V}_{i+1}(u^{(i+1)})$ and $\dot{V}_{i+1}(v^{(i+1)})$ to proceed to the $(i+1)$-th layer. Otherwise, $\mathcal{V}$ outputs* reject *and aborts.*

6. *At the input layer d, $\mathcal{V}$ has two claims $\dot{V}_d(u^{(d)})$ and $\dot{V}_d(v^{(d)})$. $\mathcal{V}$ opens R_d at 4 points $R_d(u_1^{(d)}, 0), R_d(u_1^{(d)}, 1), R_d(v_1^{(d)}, 0), R_d(v_1^{(d)}, 1)$ and checks that $\dot{V}_d(u^{(d)}) = \tilde{V}_d(u^{(d)}) + Z_d(u^{(d)}) \sum_{w \in \{0,1\}} R_d(u_1^{(d)}, w)$ and $\dot{V}_d(v^{(d)}) = \tilde{V}_d(v^{(d)}) + Z_d(v^{(d)}) \sum_{w \in \{0,1\}} R_d(v_1^{(d)}, w)$, given oracle access to two evaluates of $\tilde{V}_d$ at $u^{(d)}$ and $v^{(d)}$. If the check passes, output* accept; *otherwise, output* reject.

Theorem 3. *Construction 2 is an interactive proof protocol, for a function f defined by a layered arithmetic circuit C such that $f(\mathsf{in}, \mathsf{out}) = 1$ iff $C(\mathsf{in}) = \mathsf{out}$. In addition, for every verifier $\mathcal{V}^*$ and every layered circuit C, there exists a simulator $\mathcal{S}$ such that given oracle access to out, $\mathcal{S}$ is able to simulate the partial view of $\mathcal{V}^*$ in step 1–5 of Construction 2.*

The completeness follows from the construction explained above and the completeness of the zero knowledge sumcheck. The soundness follows the soundness of the GKR protocol with low degree extensions, as proven in [30] and [22]. We defer the proof of zero knowledge to the full version.

4.3   Zero Knowledge VPD

In this section, we present the instantiations of the zkVPD protocol, as described in Sect. 2.4. For every intermediate layer i, we use the same zkVPD protocol as proposed by Zhang et al. in [49] to commit and open the masking polynomials $g_i(x), R_i(z_1, w)$. In fact, as we show in the previous sections, these polynomials are very small (g_i is the sum of univariate polynomials and R_i has 2 variables with variable degree 2), the zkVPD protocols become very simple. The complexity of KeyGen, Commit, Open, Verify and proof size are all $O(s_i)$ for g_i and are all $O(1)$ for R_i. We omit the full protocols due to space limit.

For the zkVPD used for the input layer, we design a customized protocol based on the zkVPD protocol in [49]. Recall that at the end of the GKR protocol, $\mathcal{P}$ sends two evaluations of $\dot{V}_d(z) = \tilde{V}_d(z) + Z_d(z) \sum_{w \in \{0,1\}} R_d(z_1, w)$ at $z = u^{(d)}$ and $z = v^{(d)}$. In our zero knowledge proof protocol, which will be presented in Sect. 4.4, $\mathcal{P}$ commits to $\dot{V}_d(z)$ using the zkVPD at the beginning, and opens it to the two points selected by $\mathcal{V}$.

The protocol in [49] works for any polynomial with ℓ variables and any variable degree, and is particularly efficient for multilinear polynomials. We modify the protocol for our zero-knowledge proof scheme and preserve the efficiency. Note that though $\dot{V}_d(z)$ is a low degree extension of the input, it can be decomposed to the sum of $\tilde{V}_d(z)$, a multilinear polynomial, and $Z_d(z) \sum_{w \in \{0,1\}} R_d(z_1, w)$. Moreover, $Z_d(u^{(d)})$ and $Z_d(v^{(d)})$ can be computed directly by $\mathcal{V}$. Therefore, in our construction, $\mathcal{P}$ commits to $\tilde{V}_d(z)$ and $\sum_{w \in \{0,1\}} R_d(z_1, w)$ separately, and later opens the sum together given $Z_d(u^{(d)})$ and $Z_d(v^{(d)})$, which is naturally supported because of the homomorphic property of the commitment. Another optimization is that unlike other layers of the circuit, $R_d(z_1, w)$ itself is not opened at two points ($\mathcal{V}$ does not receive $R_d(u^{(d)}, c^{(d)})$ and $R_d(v^{(d)}, c^{(d)})$ in Construction 2). Therefore, it suffices to set $\dot{V}_d(z) = \tilde{V}_d(z) + Z_d(z) R_d(z_1)$, where R_d is a univariate linear polynomial. We will give the full protocol in the full version.

4.4   Putting Everything Together

In this section, we present our zero knowledge argument scheme. At a high level, similar to [48–50], $\mathcal{V}$ can use the GKR protocol to verify the correct evaluation of a circuit C on input x and a witness w, given an oracle access to the evaluation of a polynomial defined by x, w on a random point. We instantiate the oracle using the zkVPD protocol. Formally, we present the construction in Construction 3, which combines our zero knowledge GKR and zkVPD protocols. Similar to the protocols in [48,49], Step 6 and 7 are to check that $\mathcal{P}$ indeed uses x as the input to the circuit.

Construction 3. *Let λ be the security parameter, $\mathbb{F}$ be a prime field, n be an upper bound on input size, and S be an upper bound on circuit size. We use $\mathsf{VPD}_1, \mathsf{VPD}_2, \mathsf{VPD}_3$ to denote the zkVPD protocols for input layer, masking polynomials g_i and R_i described in Construction 2.*

- $\mathcal{G}(1^\lambda, n, S)$: *run* $(\mathsf{pp}_1, \mathsf{vp}_1) \leftarrow \mathsf{VPD}_1.\mathsf{KeyGen}(1^\lambda, \log n)$, $(\mathsf{pp}_2, \mathsf{vp}_2) \leftarrow \mathsf{VPD}_2.\mathsf{KeyGen}(1^\lambda, \log S)$, $(\mathsf{pp}_3, \mathsf{vp}_3) \leftarrow \mathsf{VPD}_3.\mathsf{KeyGen}(1^\lambda)$. *Output* $\mathsf{pk} = (\mathsf{pp}_1, \mathsf{pp}_2, \mathsf{pp}_3)$ *and* $\mathsf{vk} = (\mathsf{vp}_1, \mathsf{vp}_2, \mathsf{vp}_3)$.
- $\langle \mathcal{P}(\mathsf{pk}, w), \mathcal{V}(\mathsf{vk})\rangle(x)$: *Let C be a layered arithmetic circuit over $\mathbb{F}$ with d layers, input x and witness w such that $|x| + |w| \le n$, $|C| \le S$ and $C(x; w) = 1$. Without loss of generality, assume $|w|/|x| = 2^m - 1$ for some $m \in \mathbb{N}$.*
    1. $\mathcal{P}$ *selects a random bivariate polynomial R_d with variable degree 2 and commits to the input of C by sending $\mathsf{com}_d \leftarrow \mathsf{VPD}_1.\mathsf{Commit}(\dot{V}_d, r_V, r_R, \mathsf{pp}_1)$ to $\mathcal{V}$, where $\tilde{V}_d$ is the multilinear extension of array $(x; w)$ and $\dot{V}_d = \tilde{V}_d + R_d$*
    2. $\mathcal{V}$ *runs $\mathsf{VPD}_1.\mathsf{CheckComm}(\mathsf{com}_d, \mathsf{vp}_1)$. If it outputs reject, $\mathcal{V}$ aborts and outputs reject.*
    3. $\mathcal{P}$ *and $\mathcal{V}$ execute Step 1–5 of the zero knowledge GKR protocol in Construction 2, with the zkVPDs instantiated with VPD_2 and VPD_3. If Construction 2 rejects, $\mathcal{V}$ outputs reject and aborts. Otherwise, by the end of this step, $\mathcal{V}$ receives two claims of $\dot{V}_d$ at $u^{(d)}$ and $v^{(d)}$.*
    4. $\mathcal{P}$ *runs* $(y_1, \pi_1) \leftarrow \mathsf{VPD}_1.\mathsf{Open}(\dot{V}, r_V, r_R, u^{(d)}, \mathsf{pp}_1)$, $(y_2, \pi_2) \leftarrow \mathsf{VPD}_1.\mathsf{Open}(\dot{V}, r_V, r_R, v^{(d)}, \mathsf{pp}_1)$ *and sends y_1, π_1, y_2, π_2 to $\mathcal{V}$.*
    5. $\mathcal{V}$ *runs* $\mathsf{Verify}(\mathsf{com}_d, u^{(d)}, y_1, \pi_1, \mathsf{vp}_1)$ *and* $\mathsf{Verify}(\mathsf{com}_d, v^{(d)}, y_2, \pi_2, \mathsf{vp}_1)$ *and output reject if either check fails. Otherwise, $\mathcal{V}$ checks $\dot{V}_d(u^{(d)}) = y_1$ and $\dot{V}_d(v^{(d)}) = y_2$, and rejects if either fails.*
    6. $\mathcal{V}$ *computes the multilinear extension of input x at a random point $r_x \in \mathbb{F}^{\log |x|}$ and sends r_x to $\mathcal{P}$.*
    7. $\mathcal{P}$ *pads r_x to $r_x' \in \mathbb{F}^{\log |x|} \times 0^{\log |w|}$ with $\log |w|$ 0s and sends $\mathcal{V}$ $(y_x, \pi_x) \leftarrow \mathsf{VPD}_1.\mathsf{Open}(\tilde{V}_d, r_V, r_R, r_x', \mathsf{pp}_1)$. $\mathcal{V}$ checks $\mathsf{Verify}(\mathsf{com}_d, r_x', y_x, \pi_x, \mathsf{vp}_1)$ and y_x equals the evaluation of the multilinear extension on x. $\mathcal{V}$ outputs reject if the checks fail. Otherwise, $\mathcal{V}$ outputs accept.*

Theorem 4. *For an input size n and a finite field $\mathbb{F}$, Construction 3 is a zero knowledge argument for the relation*

$$\mathcal{R} = \{(C, x; w) : C \in \mathcal{C}_\mathbb{F} \wedge |x| + |w| \le n \wedge C(x; w) = 1\},$$

as defined in Definition 1, under the q-SBDH and the extended PKE assumptions. Moreover, for every $(C, x; w) \in \mathcal{R}$, the running time of $\mathcal{P}$ is $O(|C|)$ field operations and $O(n)$ multiplications in the base group of the bilinear map. The running time of $\mathcal{V}$ is $O(|x| + d \cdot \log |C|)$ if C is log-space uniform with d layers. $\mathcal{P}$ and $\mathcal{V}$ interact $O(d \log |C|)$ rounds and the total communication (proof size) is $O(d \log |C|)$. In case d is $\mathsf{polylog}(|C|)$, the protocol is a succinct argument.

Proof Sketch. The correctness and the soundness follow from those of the two building blocks, zero knowledge GKR and zkVPD.

To prove zero knowledge, consider a simulator $\mathcal{S}$ that calls the simulator $\mathcal{S}_{GKR}$ of zero knowledge GKR given in Sect. 4.2 as a subroutine, which simulates the partial view up to the input layer. At the input layer, the major challenge is that $\mathcal{S}$ committed to (a randomly chosen) $\dot{V}_d^*$ at the beginning of the protocol, before knowing the points $u^{(d)}, v^{(d)}$ to evaluate on. If $\mathcal{S}$ opens the commitment honestly, with high probability the evaluations are not consistent with the last message of the GKR (sumcheck in layer $d-1$) and a malicious $\mathcal{V}^*$ can distinguish the ideal world from the real world. In our proof, we resolve this issue by using the simulator $\mathcal{S}_{VPD}$ of our zkVPD protocol. Given the trapdoor trap used in KeyGen, $\mathcal{S}_{VPD}$ is able to open the commitment to any value in zero knowledge, and in particular it opens to those messages that are consistent with the GKR protocol in our scheme, which completes the construction of $\mathcal{S}$.

The complexity of our zero knowledge argument scheme follows from our new GKR protocol with linear prover time, and the complexity of the zkVPD protocol for the input layer analyzed in Sect. 4.3. The masking polynomials g_i, R_i and their commitments and openings introduce no asymptotic overhead and are efficient in practice.

Removing Interactions. Our construction can be made non-interactive in the random oracle model using Fiat—Shamir heuristic [26]. Though GKR protocol is not constant round, recent results [12,20] show that applying Fiat-Shamir only incurs a polynomial soundness loss in the number of rounds in GKR. In our implementation, the GKR protocol is on a 254-bit prime field matching the bilinear group used in the zkVPD. The non-interactive version of our system provides a security level of 100+ bits.

5   Implementation and Evaluation

Software. We fully implement Libra, our new zero knowledge proof system in C++. There are around 3000 lines of code for the zkGKR protocol, 1000 lines for the zkVPD protocol and 700 lines for circuit generators. Our system provides an interface to take a generic layered arithmetic circuit and turn it into a zero knowledge proof. We implement a new class for large integers named u512, and use it together with the GMP [2] library for large numbers and field arithmetic. We use the ate-pairing [1] library on a 254-bit elliptic curve for the bilinear map used in zkVPD. We plan to open-source our system.

Hardware. We run all of the experiments on Amazon EC2 c5.9xlarge instances with 70 GB of RAM and Intel Xeon platinum 8124 m CPU with 3 GHz virtual core. Our current implementation is not parallelized and we only use a single CPU core in the experiments. We report the average running time of 10 executions.

In the implementation, we developed a concrete optimization to support various types of gates with no extra overhead, instead of only addition and multiplication. It may be of independent interest and is presented in the full version.

Table 2. Prover time of our linear GKR and previous GKR variants.

Matrix multiplication	Matrix size	4×4	16×16	64×64	256×256
	[43]	0.0003 s	0.006 s	0.390 s	29.0 s
	Ours	0.0004 s	0.014 s	0.788 s	50.0 s
Image scaling	#pixels	112×112	176×176	560×560	1072×1072
	[46]	0.445 s	0.779 s	7.54 s	29.2 s
	Ours	0.337 s	1.25 s	19.8 s	79.2 s
Image scaling with different parameters	#pixels	112×112	176×176	560×560	1072×1072
	[50]	5.45 s	21.8 s	348 s	1441 s
	Ours	0.329 s	1.22 s	19.3 s	77.2 s
Random circuit	#gates per layer	2^8	2^{12}	2^{16}	2^{20}
	[23]	0.008 s	0.179 s	3.79 s	83.1 s
	Ours	0.002 s	0.039 s	0.635 s	10.8 s

5.1   Improvements on GKR Protocols

In this section, we compare the performance of our new GKR protocol with linear prover time with all variants of GKR in the literature on different circuits.

Methodology and Benchmarks. For fair comparisons, we re-implement all of these variants in C++ with the same libraries. The variants include: (1) $O(C)$ for regular circuits, proposed in [43], where the two inputs of a gate can be described by two mapping functions with constant size in constant time. See [43] for the formal definition of regular circuits. (2) $O(C+C' \log C')$ for data-parallel circuits with a small copy of size C', proposed in [46]. (3) $O(C \log C')$ for circuits with non-connected different copies of size C', proposed in [51]. (4) $O(C \log C)$ for arbitrary circuits, proposed in [23].

We compare our GKR protocol to these variants on the benchmarks below:

- **Matrix multiplication:** $\mathcal{P}$ proves to $\mathcal{V}$ that it knows two matrices whose product equals a public matrix. The representation of this function with an arithmetic circuit is highly regular[3]. We evaluate on different dimensions from 4×4 to 256×256 and the elements in the matrices are 32-bit integers.
- **Image scaling:** It computes a low-resolution image by scaling from a high-resolution image. We use the classic Lanczos re-sampling [44] method. It computes each pixel of the output as the convolution of the input with a sliding window and a kernel function defined as: $k(x) = \mathrm{sinc}(x)/\mathrm{sinc}(ax)$, if $-a < x < a$; $k(x) = 0$, otherwise, where a is the scaling parameter and $\mathrm{sinc}(x) = \sin(x)/x$. This function is data parallel, where each sub-circuit computes the same function to generate one pixel of the output image. We evaluate by

---

[3] We use the circuit representation of matrix multiplication with $O(n^3)$ gates for fair comparisons, not the special protocol proposed in [43].

fixing the window size as 16×16 and increase the image size from 112×112 to 1072×1072. The pixels are 8-bit integers for greyscale images.

- **Image scaling of different parameters:** It is the same computation as above with different scaling parameters in the kernel function for different pixels. The circuit of this function consists of different sub-copies. We evaluate it with the same image sizes as above.
- **Random circuit:** It is randomly generated layered circuit. We randomly sample the type of each gate, input value and the wiring patterns. We fix the depth as 3 and increase the number of gates per layer from 2^8 to 2^{20}.

To be consistent with the next section, all the protocols are executed on a 254-bit prime field. This does not affect the comparison at all, as all the protocols are in the same field. In Table 2, we report the prover time of the protocols. The proof size and the verification time of all the variants are similar.

Results. As shown in Table 2, the performance of our GKR protocol is comparable to those special protocols for structured circuits, and much better than the state-of-the-art on generic circuits. For example, for matrix multiplication, our protocol is slower by 1.3–$2.4\times$, because the protocol in [43] writes the wiring of matrix multiplication explicitly and does not need to compute $\tilde{add}$ and $\tilde{mult}$. For image scaling, our protocol is slower by 2.5–$4\times$. This gap would become even smaller when the size of each sub-copy is larger. Here we use a small 16×16 block, while the number of copies is 49–4489.

For image scaling with different parameters and generic random circuits, our protocol has a speedup of 4–$8\times$, and the speedup will increase with the scale of the circuits, as indicated by the complexity.

Besides the speedup on complicated circuits, a significant advantage of our new GKR protocol is on the prover interface of the system. In prior work such as [46,51], as the protocols are particularly efficient for structured circuits, the circuits must be represented as small copies and the numbers of each copy. Even worse, the structure is explored per layer of the circuit, making the numbers of each copy potentially different in different layers. (E.g., 6 gates may be considered 3 copies with 2 gates and 2 copies with 3 gates in two different layers for efficiency purposes.) This constraint makes the interface of these systems hard to use and generalize. Our result gives a unified solution for arbitrary circuits, and it is the main reason that our prover can take the description of any layered arithmetic circuit potentially generated by other tools like Verilog.

5.2   Comparing to Other ZKP Schemes

In this section, we show the performance of Libra as a whole and compare it with several state-of-the-art zero knowledge proof systems.

Methodology. We compare with the following systems: libSNARK [13], Ligero [6], libSTARK [8], Hyrax [48], Bulletproofs [16] and Aurora [11]. See Sect. 1 for more explanations of these systems and their asymptotic.

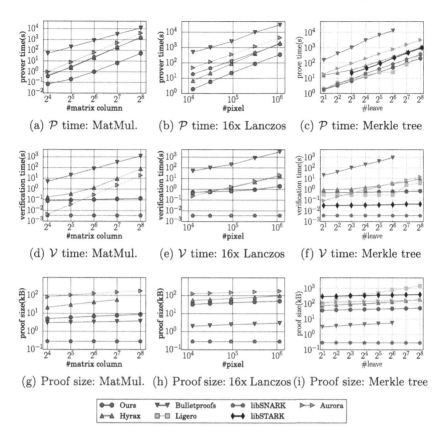

(a) $\mathcal{P}$ time: MatMul.   (b) $\mathcal{P}$ time: 16x Lanczos   (c) $\mathcal{P}$ time: Merkle tree

(d) $\mathcal{V}$ time: MatMul.   (e) $\mathcal{V}$ time: 16x Lanczos   (f) $\mathcal{V}$ time: Merkle tree

(g) Proof size: MatMul.   (h) Proof size: 16x Lanczos (i) Proof size: Merkle tree

Fig. 1. Comparisons of prover time, proof size and verification time between Libra and existing zero knowledge proof systems.

- libSNARK: We use jsnark [4] to write the circuits (rank one constraint system (R1CS)), which compiles them to ZKP using the libSNARK backend [5].
- Ligero: As the system is not open-source, we use the same number reported in [6] on computing hashes.
- libSTARK: After communications with the authors of [8], we obtain numbers for proving the same number of hashes in the 3rd benchmark below from the authors. The experiments are executed on a server with 512GB of DDR3 RAM (1.6GHz) and 16 cores (2 threads per core) at speed of 3.2GHz.
- Hyrax: We use the open-source implementation of the system at [3].
- Bulletproofs: We use the system re-implemented by [48] at [3].
- Aurora: As a recently accepted paper, the system is not available and we extrapolate its performance using the numbers reported in the paper [11] for circuits with $2^{10} - 2^{20}$ R1CS constrains.

Benchmarks. We evaluate the systems on three benchmarks: matrix multiplication, image scaling and Merkle Tree [40], which are used in [48]. Matrix multiplication and image scaling are the same as explained in Sect. 5.1. In the third benchmark, $\mathcal{P}$ proves to $\mathcal{V}$ that it knows the value of the leaves of a Merkle tree [40] that computes to a public root value [15]. We use SHA-256 for the hash function. We implement it with a flat circuit where each sub-computation is one instance of the hash function. The consistency of the input and output of corresponding hashes are then checked by the circuit. There are $2M - 1$ SHA256 invocations for a Merkle tree with M leaves. We increase the number of leaves from 16 to 256. We use the SHA-256 implemented by jsnark [4] in R1CS format to run libSNARK and estimate Aurora, and we use the SHA-256 arithmetic circuit implemented by Hyrax to run Hyrax, Bulletproofs and Libra. We only show the performance of Ligero and libSTARK on the third benchmark.

We report the prover time, proof size and verification time in Fig. 1.

Prover Time. As shown in Fig. 1(a), (b) and (c), the prover in Libra is the fastest among all systems in all three benchmarks we tested. Ligero is one of the best existing ZKP systems on prover time as it is purely based on symmetric key operations. Comparing to Ligero, the prover time of Libra is 1.15× faster on a Merkle tree with 2 leaves and 2× faster with 256 leaves. Comparing to other systems, Libra improves the prover time by 3.4–8.9× vs. Hyrax, 7.1–16.1× vs. Aurora, 10.1–12.4× vs. libSTARK and 65–166× vs. Bulletproof.

Libra is also faster than libSNARK on general circuits by 5–10×, as shown in Fig. 1(a) and (b). The performance of Libra is comparable to libSNARK on Merkle trees in Fig. 1(c). This is because (1) most values in the circuit of SHA256 are binary, which is friendly to the prover of libSNARK as the time of exponentiation is proportional to the bit-length of the values; (2) The R1CS of SHA256 is highly optimized by jsnark [4] and real world products like Zcash [9]. There are only 26,000 constrains in one hash. In the arithmetic circuit used by Libra, there are 60,000 gates with 38,000 of them being multiplication gates. Even so, Libra is still as fast as libSNARK on a Merkle tree with 2 leaves and 2× faster with 256 leaves. We plan to further optimize the implementation of SHA256 as an arithmetic circuit in the future.

The gap between Libra and other systems will become bigger as the size of the circuit grows, as the prover time in these systems (other than Bulletproof) scales quasi-linearly with the circuit size. The evaluations justify that the prover time in Libra is both optimal asymptotically, and efficient in practice.

Verification Time. Figure 1(d), (e) and (f) show the verification time. Our verifier is much slower than libSNARK and libSTARK, which runs in 1.8 ms and 28–44 ms respectively in all the benchmarks.

Other than these two systems, the verification time of Libra is faster, as it grows sub-linearly with the circuit size. In particular, our verification time ranges from 0.08–1.15 s in the benchmarks we consider. In Fig. 1(f), the verification time of Libra is 8× slower than Aurora when $M = 2$, and 15× faster when $M = 256$. Libra is 2.5× slower than Ligero with $M = 2$ and 4× faster with $M = 256$. Comparing to Hyrax and Bulletproof, our verification is 1.2–9× and 27–900× faster respectively. Again, the gap increases with the scale of the circuits as our verification is succinct.

Proof Size. We report the proof size in Fig. 1(g), (h) and (i). Our proof size is much bigger than libSNARK, which is 128 bytes for all circuits, and Bulletproof, which ranges in 2–5.5 KBs. The proof size in Libra is in the range of 30–60 KBs, except for the matrix multiplications where it reduces to 5–9 KBs. This is better than Aurora, Hyrax and libSTARK, which also have poly-logarithmic proof size to the circuit. Finally, the proof size in Ligero is $O(\sqrt{C})$ and grows to several MBs.

Setup Time. Among all the systems, only Libra and libSNARK require trusted setup. Thanks to the optimization described in the beginning of this section, it only takes 202 s to generate the public parameters in our largest instance with $n = 2^{24}$. Libra only needs to perform this setup once and it can be used for all benchmarks and all circuits with no more inputs. libSNARK requires a per-circuit setup. For example, it takes 1027 s for the Merkle tree with 256 leaves, and takes 210 s for 64×64 matrix multiplications.

Acknowledgments. This material is in part based upon work supported by DARPA under Grant No. N66001-15-C-4066 and Center for Long-Term Cybersecurity (CLTC). Any opinions, findings, and conclusions or recommendations expressed in this material are those of the author(s) and do not necessarily reflect the views of DARPA or CLTC. Charalampos Papamanthou's work was supported by NSF grants #1652259 and #1514261 and by a NIST grant.

References

1. Ate-pairing. https://github.com/herumi/ate-pairing
2. The GNU multiple precision arithmetic library. https://gmplib.org/
3. Hyrax reference implementation. https://github.com/hyraxZK/hyraxZK
4. jsnark. https://github.com/akosba/jsnark
5. libsnark. https://github.com/scipr-lab/libsnark
6. Ames, S., Hazay, C., Ishai, Y., Venkitasubramaniam, M.: Ligero: lightweight sublinear arguments without a trusted setup. In: Proceedings of the ACM SIGSAC Conference on Computer and Communications Security (2017)
7. Bayer, S., Groth, J.: Efficient zero-knowledge argument for correctness of a shuffle. In: Pointcheval, D., Johansson, T. (eds.) EUROCRYPT 2012. LNCS, vol. 7237, pp. 263–280. Springer, Heidelberg (2012). https://doi.org/10.1007/978-3-642-29011-4_17
8. Ben-Sasson, E., Bentov, I., Horesh, Y., Riabzev, M.: Scalable, transparent, and post-quantum secure computational integrity. Cryptology ePrint (2018)
9. Ben-Sasson, E., et al.: Zerocash: decentralized anonymous payments from bitcoin. In: Proceedings of the Symposium on Security and Privacy SP (2014)
10. Ben-Sasson, E., Chiesa, A., Genkin, D., Tromer, E., Virza, M.: SNARKs for C: verifying program executions succinctly and in zero knowledge. In: Canetti, R., Garay, J.A. (eds.) CRYPTO 2013. LNCS, vol. 8043, pp. 90–108. Springer, Heidelberg (2013). https://doi.org/10.1007/978-3-642-40084-1_6
11. Ben-Sasson, E., Chiesa, A., Riabzev, M., Spooner, N., Virza, M., Ward, N.P.: Aurora: transparent succinct arguments for R1CS. Cryptology ePrint (2018)

12. Ben-Sasson, E., Chiesa, A., Spooner, N.: Interactive oracle proofs. In: Hirt, M., Smith, A. (eds.) TCC 2016. LNCS, vol. 9986, pp. 31–60. Springer, Heidelberg (2016). https://doi.org/10.1007/978-3-662-53644-5_2

13. Ben-Sasson, E., Chiesa, A., Tromer, E., Virza, M.: Succinct non-interactive zero knowledge for a von Neumann architecture. In: Proceedings of the USENIX Security Symposium (2014)

14. Ben-Sasson, E., Chiesa, A., Tromer, E., Virza, M.: Scalable zero knowledge via cycles of elliptic curves. In: Garay, J.A., Gennaro, R. (eds.) CRYPTO 2014. LNCS, vol. 8617, pp. 276–294. Springer, Heidelberg (2014). https://doi.org/10.1007/978-3-662-44381-1_16

15. Blum, M., Evans, W., Gemmell, P., Kannan, S., Naor, M.: Checking the correctness of memories. Algorithmica **12**(2–3), 225–244 (1994)

16. Bünz, B., Bootle, J., Boneh, D., Poelstra, A., Wuille, P., Maxwell, G.: Bulletproofs: short proofs for confidential transactions and more. In: Proceedings of the Symposium on Security and Privacy (SP), pp. 319–338 (2018)

17. Bootle, J., Cerulli, A., Chaidos, P., Groth, J., Petit, C.: Efficient zero-knowledge arguments for arithmetic circuits in the discrete log setting. In: Fischlin, M., Coron, J.-S. (eds.) EUROCRYPT 2016. LNCS, vol. 9666, pp. 327–357. Springer, Heidelberg (2016). https://doi.org/10.1007/978-3-662-49896-5_12

18. Bootle, J., Cerulli, A., Ghadafi, E., Groth, J., Hajiabadi, M., Jakobsen, S.K.: Linear-time zero-knowledge proofs for arithmetic circuit satisfiability. In: Takagi, T., Peyrin, T. (eds.) ASIACRYPT 2017. LNCS, vol. 10626, pp. 336–365. Springer, Cham (2017). https://doi.org/10.1007/978-3-319-70700-6_12

19. Braun, B., Feldman, A.J., Ren, Z., Setty, S.T.V., Blumberg, A.J., Walfish, M.: Verifying computations with state. In: ACM SIGOPS 24th Symposium on Operating Systems Principles, SOSP (2013)

20. Canetti, R., Chen, Y., Holmgren, J., Lombardi, A., Rothblum, G.N., Rothblum, R.D.: Fiat-Shamir from simpler assumptions. IACR Cryptology ePrint Archive 2018:1004 (2018)

21. Chase, M., et al.: Post-quantum zero-knowledge and signatures from symmetric-key primitives. In: Proceedings of the 2017 ACM SIGSAC Conference on Computer and Communications Security, pp. 1825–1842. ACM (2017)

22. Chiesa, A., Forbes, M.A., Spooner, N.: A zero knowledge sumcheck and its applications. CoRR abs/1704.02086 (2017). http://arxiv.org/abs/1704.02086

23. Cormode, G., Mitzenmacher, M., Thaler, J.: Practical verified computation with streaming interactive proofs. In: Proceedings of the 3rd Innovations in Theoretical Computer Science Conference, ITCS 2012 (2012)

24. Costello, C., et al.: Geppetto: Versatile verifiable computation. In: S&P (2015)

25. Cramer, R., Damgård, I.: Zero-knowledge proofs for finite field arithmetic, or: can zero-knowledge be for free? In: Krawczyk, H. (ed.) CRYPTO 1998. LNCS, vol. 1462, pp. 424–441. Springer, Heidelberg (1998). https://doi.org/10.1007/BFb0055745

26. Fiat, A., Shamir, A.: How to prove yourself: practical solutions to identification and signature problems. In: Odlyzko, A.M. (ed.) CRYPTO 1986. LNCS, vol. 263, pp. 186–194. Springer, Heidelberg (1987). https://doi.org/10.1007/3-540-47721-7_12

27. Fiore, D., Fournet, C., Ghosh, E., Kohlweiss, M., Ohrimenko, O., Parno, B.: Hash first, argue later: adaptive verifiable computations on outsourced data. In: ACM SIGSAC Conference on Computer and Communications Security (2016)

28. Gennaro, R., Gentry, C., Parno, B., Raykova, M.: Quadratic span programs and succinct NIZKs without PCPs. In: Johansson, T., Nguyen, P.Q. (eds.) EURO-CRYPT 2013. LNCS, vol. 7881, pp. 626–645. Springer, Heidelberg (2013). https://doi.org/10.1007/978-3-642-38348-9_37

29. Giacomelli, I., Madsen, J., Orlandi, C.: ZKBoo: faster zero-knowledge for boolean circuits. In: USENIX Security Symposium, pp. 1069–1083 (2016)

30. Goldwasser, S., Kalai, Y.T., Rothblum, G.N.: Delegating computation: interactive proofs for Muggles. J. ACM **62**(4), 27:1–27:64 (2015)

31. Goldwasser, S., Micali, S., Rackoff, C.: The knowledge complexity of interactive proof systems. SIAM J. Comput. **18**(1), 186–208 (1989)

32. Groth, J.: Linear algebra with sub-linear zero-knowledge arguments. In: Halevi, S. (ed.) CRYPTO 2009. LNCS, vol. 5677, pp. 192–208. Springer, Heidelberg (2009). https://doi.org/10.1007/978-3-642-03356-8_12

33. Groth, J.: Short pairing-based non-interactive zero-knowledge arguments. In: Abe, M. (ed.) ASIACRYPT 2010. LNCS, vol. 6477, pp. 321–340. Springer, Heidelberg (2010). https://doi.org/10.1007/978-3-642-17373-8_19

34. Ishai, Y., Kushilevitz, E., Ostrovsky, R.: Efficient arguments without short PCPs. In: 22nd Annual IEEE Conference on Computational Complexity (CCC 2007) (2007)

35. Ishai, Y., Kushilevitz, E., Ostrovsky, R., Sahai, A.: Zero-knowledge from secure multiparty computation. In: Proceedings of the Annual ACM Symposium on Theory of Computing, pp. 21–30. ACM (2007)

36. Kilian, J.: A note on efficient zero-knowledge proofs and arguments (extended abstract). In: Proceedings of the ACM Symposium on Theory of Computing (1992)

37. Kosba, A., Miller, A., Shi, E., Wen, Z., Papamanthou, C.: Hawk: the blockchain model of cryptography and privacy-preserving smart contracts. In: Proceedings of Symposium on Security and Privacy (SP) (2016)

38. Lipmaa, H.: Progression-free sets and sublinear pairing-based non-interactive zero-knowledge arguments. In: Cramer, R. (ed.) TCC 2012. LNCS, vol. 7194, pp. 169–189. Springer, Heidelberg (2012). https://doi.org/10.1007/978-3-642-28914-9_10

39. Lund, C., Fortnow, L., Karloff, H., Nisan, N.: Algebraic methods for interactive proof systems. J. ACM **39**(4), 859–868 (1992)

40. Merkle, R.C.: A digital signature based on a conventional encryption function. In: Pomerance, C. (ed.) CRYPTO 1987. LNCS, vol. 293, pp. 369–378. Springer, Heidelberg (1988). https://doi.org/10.1007/3-540-48184-2_32

41. Micali, S.: Computationally sound proofs. SIAM J. Comput. (2000)

42. Parno, B., Howell, J., Gentry, C., Raykova, M.: Pinocchio: nearly practical verifiable computation. In: S&P 2013, pp. 238–252 (2013)

43. Thaler, J.: Time-optimal interactive proofs for circuit evaluation. In: Canetti, R., Garay, J.A. (eds.) CRYPTO 2013. LNCS, vol. 8043, pp. 71–89. Springer, Heidelberg (2013). https://doi.org/10.1007/978-3-642-40084-1_5

44. Turkowski, K.: Filters for common resampling tasks. In: Graphics Gems, pp. 147–165. Academic Press Professional, Inc. (1990)

45. Vu, V., Setty, S., Blumberg, A.J., Walfish, M.: A hybrid architecture for interactive verifiable computation. In: Proceedings of the 2013 IEEE Symposium on Security and Privacy, SP 2013 (2013)

46. Wahby, R.S., et al.: Full accounting for verifiable outsourcing. In: Proceedings of the 2017 ACM SIGSAC Conference on Computer and Communications Security. ACM (2017)

47. Wahby, R.S., Setty, S.T., Ren, Z., Blumberg, A.J., Walfish, M.: Efficient RAM and control flow in verifiable outsourced computation. In: NDSS (2015)

48. Wahby, R.S., Tzialla, I., Shelat, A., Thaler, J., Walfish, M.: Doubly-efficient zkSNARKs without trusted setup. In: 2018 IEEE Symposium on Security and Privacy (SP), pp. 926–943. IEEE (2018)
49. Zhang, Y., Genkin, D., Katz, J., Papadopoulos, D., Papamanthou, C.: A zero-knowledge version of vSQL. Cryptology ePrint (2017)
50. Zhang, Y., Genkin, D., Katz, J., Papadopoulos, D., Papamanthou, C.: vSQL: verifying arbitrary SQL queries over dynamic outsourced databases. In: 2017 IEEE Symposium on Security and Privacy (SP), pp. 863–880. IEEE (2017)
51. Zhang, Y., Genkin, D., Katz, J., Papadopoulos, D., Papamanthou, C.: vRAM: faster verifiable RAM with program-independent preprocessing. In: Proceeding of IEEE Symposium on Security and Privacy (S&P) (2018)

Key Exchange and Broadcast Encryption

Highly Efficient Key Exchange
Protocols with Optimal Tightness

Katriel Cohn-Gordon[1], Cas Cremers[2(✉)], Kristian Gjøsteen[3],
Håkon Jacobsen[4], and Tibor Jager[5(✉)]

[1] Oxford, UK
me@katriel.co.uk
[2] CISPA Helmholtz Center for Information Security, Saarbrücken, Germany
cremers@cispa.saarland
[3] NTNU - Norwegian University of Science and Technology, Trondheim, Norway
kristian.gjosteen@ntnu.no
[4] McMaster University, Hamilton, Canada
jacobseh@mcmaster.ca
[5] Paderborn University, Paderborn, Germany
tibor.jager@upb.de

Abstract. In this paper we give nearly-tight reductions for modern implicitly authenticated Diffie-Hellman protocols in the style of the Signal and Noise protocols, which are extremely simple and efficient. Unlike previous approaches, the combination of nearly-tight proofs and efficient protocols enables the first real-world instantiations for which the parameters can be chosen in a theoretically sound manner.

Our reductions have only a linear loss in the number of users, implying that our protocols are more efficient than the state of the art when instantiated with theoretically sound parameters. We also prove that our security proofs are optimal: a linear loss in the number of users is unavoidable for our protocols for a large and natural class of reductions.

1 Introduction

Key exchange protocols serve as a building block for almost all secure communication today. However, deploying a key exchange protocol requires implementors to carefully choose concrete values for several parameters, such as group and key sizes, which we here abstract into a single security parameter n. But how should n be selected? An answer is to select it based on formal reductionist arguments in the style of concrete security [7]. These arguments relate the security parameter n of a protocol to the security parameter $f(n)$ of an assumed-hard problem, such that breaking the protocol with parameter n would lead to an attack on

Supported by the European Research Council (ERC) under the European Union's Horizon 2020 research and innovation programme, grant agreement 802823, and the Deutsche Forschungsgemeinschaft (DFG), project number 265919409.

K. Cohn-Gordon—Independent Scholar.

A. Boldyreva and D. Micciancio (Eds.): CRYPTO 2019, LNCS 11694, pp. 767–797, 2019.
https://doi.org/10.1007/978-3-030-26954-8_25

the hard problem with parameter $f(n)$. We say a protocol is deployed in a *theoretically sound* way if n is chosen such that the underlying problem is "hard enough" with parameter $f(n)$.

Unfortunately, for most deployed protocols the parameters are actually *not* chosen in a theoretically sound way. This means that the formal security arguments are in reality vacuous since $f(n)$ is too small for the underlying problem to be hard. For example, existing security proofs for TLS [11,22,27] have a security loss which is quadratic in the total number of sessions, but the parameters chosen in practice does not account for this. If one aims for "128-bit security", and assumes 2^{30} users and up to 2^{30} sessions per user (very plausible for TLS), then a theoretically sound choice of parameters would have to provide at least "248-bit security". In the particular case of the algebraic groups used for Diffie-Hellman (DH) in TLS, this would require a group of order $|\mathbb{G}| \approx 2^{496}$ instead of the common 128-bit-secure choice of $|\mathbb{G}| \approx 2^{256}$. But larger parameters typically leads to worse performance so this is not done in practice. Thus, for TLS as actually used, the proofs do not provide any meaningful security guarantees since they relate the hardness of breaking TLS to a DH instance which is too easy to solve.

It would be desirable if protocols could be instantiated in a theoretically sound way without sacrificing efficiency. This has led to the study of so-called *tight security*, in which one aims to construct proofs such that the gap between n and $f(n)$ is as small as possible. While there have been several recent advances in this field [3,19], typically they trade tighter proofs for the use of more complex primitives and constructions—which themselves require more or larger keys. This leads to the perhaps counter-intuitive observation that the resulting protocols have a tighter security proof, but are substantially less efficient in practice. For example, the recent protocol of Gjøsteen and Jager [19] has a constant security loss, meaning that an attack on their protocol leads to an attack on decisional DH with essentially the same parameter. However, it is a signed DH protocol, and thus must be instantiated with a tightly-secure signature scheme. The solution used by Gjøsteen and Jager [19] requires a total of 17 exponentiations which can negate the efficiency savings from using a smaller group. In some sense they overshoot their target: they achieve tightness without reaching the actual goal of *efficient* theoretically sound deployment in practice.

In this work we will instead aim between the two extremes of real-world protocols on the one end having very non-tight proofs, and the more theoretical protocols on the other having fully tight proofs, focusing instead on the actual end-goal of achieving efficient theoretically sound deployments in practice. Our constructions fall into the class of implicitly authenticated DH protocols, which often are more efficient than signed DH variants, and can additionally offer various forms of deniability. Implicitly authenticated key exchange protocols have been studied extensively in the literature, and in the past few years have also started to see deployments in the real world. Perhaps the most well-known example is the Signal protocol [38], which encrypts messages for WhatsApp's 1.5 billion users. Another example is the Noise protocol framework [36], whose so-called IK pattern powers the new Linux kernel VPN Wireguard [16]. Similar protocols in the literature include KEA+ [30] and UM [24].

We will give a security proof for a simple instance of this class, very close to Signal's basic design. In and of itself this isn't particularly noteworthy. What *is* noteworthy, however, is the *tightness* of the proof. Unlike any other proof for a protocol as simple and efficient as ours, our proof only incurs a security loss which is *linear* in the number of users μ and *constant* in the number of sessions per user ℓ. This is in stark contrast to most other key exchange proofs that are typically *quadratic* in at least one of these parameters, and most of the time quadratic even in their product $\mu\ell$.

Our Contributions. Our contributions revolve around three protocols which all aim for high practical efficiency when instantiated with theoretically sound parameters. The first protocol, which we call Π, is a simple and clean implicitly authenticated DH protocol very close to Signal, Noise-KK, KEA+ and UM, and provides weak forward secrecy. In protocol Π users exchange a single group element and perform four group exponentiations to establish a session key. Protocol Π—specified precisely in Sect. 4—aims for maximal efficiency under the strong DH assumption.

The other two protocols, which can be seen as variants of protocol Π, are designed to avoid the strong DH assumption of Π. The first protocol, which we call Π_{Twin}, adapts the "twinning" technique of Cash et al. [13] to protocol Π, and needs four more exponentiations. The second, which we call Π_{Com}, additionally adapts the "commitment" technique of Gjøsteen and Jager [19], and only needs two more exponentiations than protocol Π. On the other hand, it requires one more round of communication. Both Π_{Twin} and Π_{Com} are slightly more costly than protocol Π, but in return require only the standard CDH and DDH assumptions.

Common to all our protocols is that they are simple and conventional, with no heavyweight cryptographic machinery. They exchange ephemeral keys and derive a session key from the combination of static-ephemeral, ephemeral-static and ephemeral-ephemeral DH values via a hash function H. In our proofs H will be a random oracle.

Our first core contribution is thus to give new reductions for all these protocols with a linear loss $L = O(\mu)$ in the random oracle model. This is better than almost all known AKE protocols. As we will see, even though the loss is not constant, our protocols are so efficient that they perform better than both fully-tight protocols as well as the most efficient non-tight AKEs[1]. In contrast to previous works, our proofs enable theoretically sound deployment of conventional protocols while maintaining high efficiency.

Our second core contribution is to show that the $O(\mu)$ tightness loss is essentially optimal for the protocols considered in this paper, at least for "simple" reductions. A "simple" reduction runs a *single* copy of the adversary only *once*. To the best of our knowledge, all known security reductions for AKE protocols

---

[1] When instantiated with theoretically sound parameters under reasonable assumptions on μ and ℓ in modern deployment settings.

are either of this type or use the forking lemma (which of necessity leads to a non-tight proof). Hence, to give a tighter security proof, one would have to develop a completely new approach to prove security.

The lower-bound proof will be based on the *meta-reduction* techniques described by Bader et al. [4]. However, these techniques are only able to handle tight reductions from *non-interactive* assumptions, while our first protocol is based on the *interactive* strong DH assumption. Therefore we develop a new variant of the approach, which makes it possible to also handle the strong DH assumption.

Finally, we prove that our protocols can be enhanced to also provide explicit entity authentication by adding key-confirmation messages, while still providing tight security guarantees. To do so, we generalise a theorem of Yang [41] in two ways: we apply it to n-message protocols for $n > 2$, and we give a tight reduction to the multi-user versions of the underlying primitives.

To summarise:

1. We give three protocols with linear-loss security reductions, making them faster than both fully-tight protocols and the most efficient non-tight ones when instantiated in a theoretically sound manner for reasonable numbers of users and sessions.
2. We prove optimality of linear loss for our protocols under "simple" reductions.
3. We tightly extend our protocols with key confirmation messages to provide explicit entity authentication.

Related Work. We briefly touch upon some other protocols with non-quadratic security loss. KEA+ [30] achieves $L = O(\mu\ell)$ under the Gap-DH assumption, and where the reduction for pairing-friendly curves takes $O(t \log t)$ time. However, for non-pairing-friendly curves the reduction takes $O(t^2)$ time. Moreover, KEA+ also does not achieve weak forward secrecy in a modern model: only one side's long term key can be corrupted.

The first AKE protocols with L *independent* of μ and ℓ were described by Bader et al. [3] at TCC 2015. They describe two protocols, one with constant security loss $L = O(1)$ and another with loss $L = O(\kappa)$ linear in the security parameter. Both protocols make use of rather heavy cryptographic building blocks, such as tree-based signature schemes, Groth-Sahai proofs [20], and cryptographic pairings, and are therefore not very efficient.

As already mentioned, Gjøsteen and Jager [19] recently described a more practical protocol, which essentially is a three-message variant of "signed Diffie-Hellman". Even though their protocol uses a rather complex signature scheme to achieve tightness (a single key exchange requires 17 exponentiations and the exchange of in total 16 group elements/exponents), when instantiated with theoretically sound parameters it turns out to be more efficient than even plain signed DH with ECDSA, at least for large-scale deployments. Unlike [3], the security analysis in [19] is in the random oracle model [8] since the paper aims at maximal practical efficiency.

2   Background

In this section we recap some background and standard definitions. Let $\mathbb{G}$ be a cyclic group of prime order p with generator g.

Diffie-Hellman Problems. The computational and decisional Diffie-Hellman problems are natural problems related to breaking the Diffie-Hellman protocol.

Definition 1. *Consider the following experiment involving an adversary $\mathcal{A}$. The experiment samples $x, y \xleftarrow{\$} \mathbb{Z}_p$ and starts $\mathcal{A}(g^x, g^y)$. The advantage of $\mathcal{A}$ in solving the* computational Diffie-Hellman *problem is defined as*

$$\mathrm{Adv}_{\mathbb{G},g}^{\mathsf{CDH}}(\mathcal{A}) := \Pr\left[\mathcal{A}(g^x, g^y) = g^{xy}\right]$$

Definition 2. *Consider the following experiment involving an adversary $\mathcal{A}$. The experiment samples $x, y, z \xleftarrow{\$} \mathbb{Z}_p$ and tosses a coin $\hat{b} \xleftarrow{\$} \{0, 1\}$. If $\hat{b} = 1$ then it sets $Z := g^{xy}$, while if $\hat{b} = 0$ then it sets $Z = g^z$. We define the advantage of $\mathcal{A}$ in solving the* decisional Diffie-Hellman *problem as*

$$\mathrm{Adv}_{\mathbb{G},g}^{\mathsf{DDH}}(\mathcal{A}) := \left|\Pr\left[\mathcal{A}(g^x, g^y, Z) = \hat{b}\right] - 1/2\right|$$

Let $\mathsf{DDH}(g^x, g^y, g^z)$ be an oracle that returns 1 if and only if $xy = z$. The *gap* Diffie-Hellman problem asks to solve the computational Diffie-Hellman problem, given access to the oracle $\mathsf{DDH}(\cdot, \cdot, \cdot)$. The *strong* Diffie-Hellman problem is related to the gap Diffie-Hellman problem, except that the adversary now gets a less capable oracle where the first input is fixed, i.e., $\mathsf{stDH}_x(\cdot, \cdot) = \mathsf{DDH}(g^x, \cdot, \cdot)$.

Definition 3. *Consider the following experiment involving an adversary $\mathcal{A}$. The experiment samples $x, y \xleftarrow{\$} \mathbb{Z}_p$ and starts $\mathcal{A}^{\mathsf{stDH}_x(\cdot, \cdot)}(g^x, g^y)$. The advantage of $\mathcal{A}$ in solving the* strong Diffie-Hellman *problem is defined as*

$$\mathrm{Adv}_{\mathbb{G},g}^{\mathsf{stDH}}(\mathcal{A}) := \Pr\left[\mathcal{A}^{\mathsf{stDH}_x(\cdot, \cdot)}(g^x, g^y) = g^{xy}\right].$$

One may wonder to which extent the number of oracle queries to the strong DH oracle affects the concrete security of this assumption. That is, how does the security of strong DH degrade with the number of queries to the stDH oracle? We are not aware of any concrete attacks that exploit the oracle to solve the CDH problem more efficiently than other algorithms for CDH. In particular, in many elliptic curves with practical bilinear pairings it is reasonable to assume hardness of CDH, even though the bilinear pairing is a much stronger tool than a strong DH oracle.

   A crucial technique in any tight proof using Diffie-Hellman problems is rerandomisation [6], where a single Diffie-Hellman problem instance can be turned into many, in such a way that an answer to any one of them can be turned into an answer to the original instance. We will use this technique in our proofs.

The Strong Twin Diffie-Hellman Problem. The strong twin Diffie-Hellman problem was introduced by Cash, Kiltz, and Shoup [13] at EUROCRYPT 2008. It is closely related to the standard computational Diffie-Hellman (CDH) problem, except that it "twins" certain group elements, in order to enable an efficient "trapdoor-DDH" test that makes it possible to simulate a strong-CDH oracle. This makes it possible to show that the twin-DH problem is *equivalent* to the standard CDH problem. Let $\mathsf{twinDH}_{x_0,x_1}(Y, Z_0, Z_1)$ be an oracle which returns 1 if and only if $\mathsf{DDH}(g^{x_0}, Y, Z_0) = 1$ *and* $\mathsf{DDH}(g^{x_1}, Y, Z_1) = 1$.

Definition 4. *Consider the following experiment involving an adversary $\mathcal{A}$. The experiment samples $x_0, x_1, y \xleftarrow{\$} \mathbb{Z}_p$ and starts $\mathcal{A}^{\mathsf{twinDH}_{x_0,x_1}(\cdot,\cdot,\cdot)}(g^{x_0}, g^{x_1}, g^y)$. The advantage of $\mathcal{A}$ in solving the* strong twin Diffie-Hellman *problem is defined as*

$$\mathrm{Adv}_{\mathbb{G},g}^{\text{2-CDH}}(\mathcal{A}) := \Pr\left[\mathcal{A}^{\mathsf{twinDH}_{x_0,x_1}(\cdot,\cdot,\cdot)}(g^{x_0}, g^{x_1}, g^y) = (g^{x_0 y}, g^{x_1 y})\right]$$

The following theorem was proven by Cash, Kiltz, and Shoup [[13], Theorem 3].

Theorem 1. *Let $\mathcal{A}$ be a strong twin DH adversary that makes at most Q queries to oracle $\mathcal{O}$ and runs in time $t_{\mathcal{A}}$. Then one can construct a DH adversary $\mathcal{B}$ that runs in time $t_{\mathcal{A}} \approx t_{\mathcal{B}}$ such that*

$$\mathrm{Adv}_{\mathbb{G},g}^{\text{2-CDH}}(\mathcal{A}) \leq \mathrm{Adv}_{\mathbb{G},g}^{\mathsf{CDH}}(\mathcal{B}) + Q/p.$$

3   AKE Security Model

In this section we define our game-based key exchange security model. It is based on the real-or-random ("RoR") security definition of Abdalla, Fouque, and Pointcheval [2], and incorporates the extension of Abdalla, Benhamouda, and MacKenzie [1] to capture forward secrecy. The central feature of the RoR-model is that the adversary can make *many* Test-queries, and that all queries are answered with a "real" or "random" key based on the *same* random bit $\hat{b}$.

We prefer to work in a RoR-model because it automatically lends itself to tight composition with protocols that use the session keys of the key exchange protocol. For security models where there is only a single Test-query, or where each Test-query is answered based on an individual random bit [3,19], such a composition is not automatically tight.

Although we mainly consider key exchange protocols with *implicit* authentication in this paper, we show in Sect. 8 how they can easily be upgraded to also have *explicit* authentication by adding key-confirmation messages to the protocol. The advantage of working in the RoR-model is that it allows us to do this transformation tightly.

Execution Environment. We consider μ parties $1, \ldots, \mu$. Each party i is represented by a set of ℓ oracles, $\{\pi_i^1, \ldots, \pi_i^\ell\}$, where each oracle corresponds to a session, i.e., a single execution of a protocol role, and where $\ell \in \mathbb{N}$ is the maximum number of protocol sessions per party. Each oracle is equipped with a randomness tape containing random bits, but is otherwise deterministic. Each oracle π_i^s has access to the long-term key pair (sk_i, pk_i) of party i and to the public keys of all other parties, and maintains a list of internal state variables that are described in the following:

- Pid$_i^s$ ("peer id") stores the identity of the intended communication partner.
- $\Psi_i^s \in \{\emptyset, \texttt{accept}, \texttt{reject}\}$ indicates whether oracle π_i^s has successfully completed the protocol execution and "accepted" the resulting key.
- k_i^s stores the session key computed by π_i^s.
- sent$_i^s$ contains the list of messages sent by π_i^s in chronological order.
- recv$_i^s$ contains the list of messages received by π_i^s in chronological order.
- role$_i^s \in \{\emptyset, \texttt{init}, \texttt{resp}\}$ indicates π_i^s's role during the protocol execution.

For each oracle π_i^s these variables are all initialized to the empty string $\emptyset$. The computed session key is assigned to the variable k_i^s if and only if π_i^s reaches the accept state, that is, we have $k_i^s \neq \emptyset \iff \Psi_i^s = \texttt{accept}$.

Partnering. To define when two oracles are supposed to derive the same session key we use a variant of matching conversations. In addition to agreement on their message transcripts, they should also agree upon each other's identities and have compatible roles (one being the initiator the other the responder). We remark that our protocol messages consist only of group elements and deterministic functions of them. This means that they are not vulnerable to the "no-match" attacks of Li and Schäge [32].

Definition 5 (Origin-oracle). *An oracle π_j^t is an* origin-oracle *for an oracle π_i^s if $\Psi_j^t \neq \emptyset$, $\Psi_i^s = \texttt{accept}$, and the messages sent by π_j^t equal the messages received by π_i^s, i.e., if* sent$_j^t$ = recv$_i^s$.

Definition 6 (Partner oracles). *We say that two oracles π_i^s and π_j^t are partners if (1) each is an origin-oracle for the other; (2) each one's identity is the other one's peer identity, i.e.,* Pid$_i^s = j$ *and* Pid$_j^t = i$; *and (3) they do not have the same role, i.e.,* role$_i^s \neq$ role$_j^t$.

Attacker Model. The adversary $\mathcal{A}$ interacts with the oracles through queries. It is assumed to have full control over the communication network, modeled by a Send query which allows it to send arbitrary messages to any oracle. The adversary is also granted a number of additional queries that model the fact that various secrets might get lost or leaked. The queries are described in detail below.

- Send(i, s, j, m): This query allows $\mathcal{A}$ to send any message m of its choice to oracle π_i^s on behalf of party P_j. The oracle will respond according to the protocol specification and depending on its internal state. For starting a role there are additional actions:
  [Initiator] If (Pid$_i^s, \Psi_i^s) = (\emptyset, \emptyset)$ and $m = \emptyset$, then this means that $\mathcal{A}$ requests π_i^s to start the initiator role with peer P_j. In this case, π_i^s will set Pid$_i^s := j$ and role$_i^s := \texttt{init}$.
  [Responder] If (Pid$_i^s, \Psi_i^s) = (\emptyset, \emptyset)$ and $m \neq \emptyset$, then this means that $\mathcal{A}$ requests π_i^s to start the responder role with peer P_j with first message m. In this case, π_i^s will set Pid$_i^s := j$ and role$_i^s := \texttt{resp}$.
- RevLTK(i): For $i \leq \mu$, this query allows the adversary to learn the long-term private key sk_i of user i. After the query i is said to be *corrupted*, and all oracles $\pi_i^1, \ldots, \pi_i^\ell$ now respond with $\bot$ to all queries.

- RegisterLTK(i, pk_i): For $i > \mu$, this query allows the adversary to register a new party i with public key pk_i. We do not require that the adversary knows the corresponding private key. After the query the pair (i, pk_i) is distributed to all other parties. Parties registered by RegisterLTK are corrupted by definition.
- RevSessKey(i, s): This query allows the adversary to learn the session key derived by an oracle. That is, query RevSessKey(i, s) returns the contents of k_i^s. Recall that we have $k_i^s \neq \emptyset$ if and only if $\Psi_i^s = \mathsf{accept}$. After this query π_i^s is said to be *revealed*.

Note that unlike, e.g., [10,12], we do not allow the adversary to learn the sessions' ephemeral randomness.

Security Experiment. To define the security of a key exchange protocol we want to evaluate the attacker's knowledge of the session keys. Formally, we have an AKE security game, played between an adversary $\mathcal{A}$ and a challenger $\mathcal{C}$, where the adversary can issue the queries defined above. Additionally, it is given access to a special Test query, which, depending on a secret bit $\hat{b}$ chosen by the challenger, either returns real or random keys. The goal of the adversary is to guess $\hat{b}$.

- Test(i, s): If $\Psi_i^s \neq \mathsf{accept}$, return $\bot$. Else, return $k_{\hat{b}}$, where $k_0 = k_s^i$ and $k_1 \overset{\$}{\leftarrow} \mathcal{K}$ is a random key. If a Test query is repeated in the case $b = 1$, the same random key is returned. After the query, oracle π_i^s is said to be *tested*.

The adversary can issue many Test queries, to different oracles, but all are answered using the *same* bit $\hat{b}$.

The AKE security game, denoted $G_\Pi(\mu, \ell)$, is parameterized by the protocol Π and two numbers μ (the number of honest parties) and ℓ (the maximum number of protocol executions per party), and is run as follows.

1. $\mathcal{C}$ begins by drawing a random bit $\hat{b} \overset{\$}{\leftarrow} \{0, 1\}$, then generates μ long-term key pairs $\{(sk_i, pk_i) \mid i \in [1, \ldots, \mu]\}$, and initializes the collection of oracles $\{\pi_i^s \mid i \in [1, \ldots, \mu], s \in [1, \ldots, \ell]\}$.
2. $\mathcal{C}$ now runs $\mathcal{A}$, providing all the public keys $pk_1, \ldots, pk_\mu$ as input. During its execution, $\mathcal{A}$ may adaptively issue Send, RevLTK, RevSessKey, RegisterLTK and Test queries any number of times and in arbitrary order. The only requirement is that all tested oracles remain *fresh* throughout the game (see Definition 7 below). Otherwise, the game aborts and outputs a random bit.
3. The game ends when $\mathcal{A}$ terminates with output b', representing its guess of $\hat{b}$. If not all test oracles are fresh, the security game outputs a random bit. If all test oracles are fresh and $b' = \hat{b}$, it outputs 1. Otherwise, it outputs 0.

Definition 7 (Freshness). *An oracle π_i^s is fresh, written* fresh(i, s), *if:*

(i) RevSessKey(i, s) *has not been issued,*
(ii) *no query* Test(j, t) *or* RevSessKey(j, t) *has been issued, where π_j^t is a partner of π_i^s, and*
(iii) Pid$_i^s$ *was:*
   (a) not corrupted before π_i^s accepted if π_i^s has an origin-oracle, and

(b) *not corrupted at all if π_i^s has no origin-oracle.*

Definition 8 (Winning Events). *We define the following three winning events on game $G_\Pi(\mu, \ell)$.*

(i) *Event* break$_{\text{Sound}}$ *occurs if there exist two partner oracles π_i^s and π_j^t with $k_i^s \neq k_j^t$. In other words, there are two partner oracles which compute different session keys.*

(ii) *Event* break$_{\text{Unique}}$ *occurs if for some oracle π_i^s there exist distinct oracles π_j^t and $\pi_{j'}^{t'}$ such that π_i^s is a partner oracle to both π_j^t and $\pi_{j'}^{t'}$. In other words, there exists an oracle with more than one partner oracle.*

(iii) *Let* guess$_{\text{KE}}$ *be the output of game $G_\Pi(\mu, \ell)$. We define* break$_{\text{KE}}$ *to be the event* guess$_{\text{KE}} = 1$.

Definition 9 (AKE Security). *An attacker $\mathcal{A}$ breaks the security of protocol Π, if at least one of* break$_{\text{Sound}}$, break$_{\text{Unique}}$, *or* break$_{\text{KE}}$ *occurs in $G_\Pi(\mu, \ell)$. The advantage of the adversary $\mathcal{A}$ against AKE security of Π is*

$$\text{Adv}_\Pi^{\text{AKE}}(\mathcal{A}) = \max\left\{\Pr\left[\text{break}_{\text{Sound}}\right], \Pr\left[\text{break}_{\text{Unique}}\right], |\Pr\left[\text{break}_{\text{KE}}\right] - 1/2|\right\}.$$

We say that $\mathcal{A}$ $(\epsilon_{\mathcal{A}}, t, \mu, \ell)$-breaks Π if its running time is t and $\text{Adv}_\Pi^{\text{AKE}}(\mathcal{A}) \geq \epsilon_{\mathcal{A}}$. The running time of $\mathcal{A}$ includes the running time of the security experiment (see [19, Remark 1]).

Security Properties. The core aspects of the security properties in our model are captured by the break$_{\text{KE}}$ event, combined with the adversary's capabilities and the restrictions imposed on them through the freshness predicate.

The freshness clauses (i) and (ii) imply that we only exclude the reveal of session keys for tested oracles as well as their partners. This encodes both (a) key independence if the revealed key is different from the session key: knowing some keys must not enable computing other keys, as well as (b) implicitly ensuring agreement on the involved parties, since sessions that compute the same session key but disagree on the parties would not be partnered, and reveal the Test session's key.

Our freshness clause (iii) encodes *weak forward secrecy*: the adversary can learn the peer's long-term key after the tested oracle accepted, but only if it has been passive in the run of the oracle [26]. Another property captured by our model is resistance to *key-compromise impersonation* attacks. Recall that KCI attacks are those where the adversary uses a party A's own private long-term key to impersonate other users towards A. This is (implicitly) encoded by the absence of any adversary restrictions on learning the private long-term key of a test-oracle itself. Additionally, the break$_{\text{Unique}}$ event captures the resistance to replay attacks. The break$_{\text{Sound}}$ event ensures that two parties that execute the protocol together in the absence of an attacker (or at least a passive one), compute the same session key.

Some recent protocols also offer *post-compromise security*, in which the communication partner π_j^t may be corrupted before π_i^s has accepted. However, in this work we consider only stateless protocols, which cannot achieve this goal [14].

4   Protocol Π

Protocol Π, defined in Fig. 1, uses a mix of static-ephemeral and ephemeral-ephemeral Diffie-Hellman key exchanges to get a protocol that is extremely efficient in terms of communications as well as computational effort required. Specifically, the two protocol participants exchange ephemeral Diffie-Hellman shares g^r and g^s for random r, s, and then compute a session key from three Diffie-Hellman shared secrets (static-ephemeral, ephemeral-static, ephemeral-ephemeral) as well as identities and a transcript. Note that this is very close to the Noise-KK pattern [36].

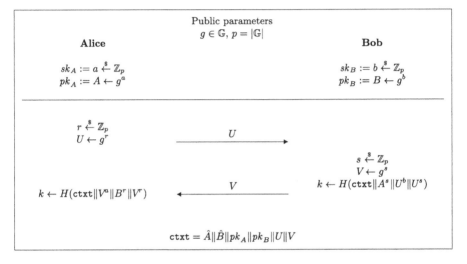

Fig. 1. Protocol Π. The session key is derived from the combination of the parties' static-ephemeral, ephemeral-static, and ephemeral-ephemeral DH values.

Theorem 2. *Consider the protocol* Π *defined in Fig. 1 where H is modeled as a random oracle. Let $\mathcal{A}$ be an adversary against the AKE security of* Π. *Then there exist adversaries $\mathcal{B}_1$, $\mathcal{B}_2$ and $\mathcal{B}_3$ against strong Diffie-Hellman such that*

$$\mathrm{Adv}_{\Pi}^{\mathsf{AKE}}(\mathcal{A}) \leq \mu \cdot \mathrm{Adv}_{\mathbb{G},g}^{\mathsf{stDH}}(\mathcal{B}_1) + \mathrm{Adv}_{\mathbb{G},g}^{\mathsf{stDH}}(\mathcal{B}_2) + \mu \cdot \mathrm{Adv}_{\mathbb{G},g}^{\mathsf{stDH}}(\mathcal{B}_3) + \frac{\mu\ell^2}{p}.$$

The strong Diffie-Hellman adversaries all run in essentially the same time as $\mathcal{A}$, and make at most as many queries to their strong DH-oracle as $\mathcal{A}$ makes to its hash oracle H.

The proof of the theorem is structured as a sequence of games running variations on the security experiment, with the first game identical to the experiment. We bound the difference in the probability of the event that the experiment outputs 1 in each game. As a side effect, along the way we also get a bound on

$\mathsf{break_{Unique}}$. Then we argue that the probability that the experiment outputs 1 is $1/2$ in the final game, which gives us a bound on $\mathsf{break_{KE}}$. Since the scheme has perfect correctness, the theorem follows.

To achieve this result in the final game, we shall have our oracles choose session keys at random, without reference to secret keys or messages. Obviously, we have to ensure consistency with what the adversary can learn. This means that we have to make sure that partnered oracles both choose the same key (Game 2); that keys the adversary should be able to compute on his own are the same as chosen by the oracle (Game 2), and that corruptions of long-term keys that enable the adversary to compute session keys on his own return results consistent with previous RevSessKey-queries (Game 3 and 5).

The general technique we use is to have our oracles refrain from computing the input to the key derivation hash oracle, but instead check to see if the adversary somehow computes it. The idea is that computing the hash input is hard to simulate in the strong Diffie-Hellman game, but checking if someone else has computed the hash input is easy using the strong DH oracle provided.

We call an oracle *honest* (at some point) if the user it belongs to has not yet been corrupted (at that point). There are five types of oracles that we will have to deal with in separate ways, and the first four are essentially fresh oracles:

- (I) initiator oracles whose response message comes from a responder oracle, which has the same `ctxt` (i.e., they agree on the message transcript and participant identities and public keys) and which is honest when the response is received;
- (II) other initiator oracles whose intended peer is honest until the oracle accepts;
- (III) responder oracles whose initial message comes from an initiator, which has the same `ctxt` up to the responder message (thus agreeing on the first message and participant identities and public keys) and which is honest when the response is received;
- (IV) other responder oracles whose intended peer is honest until the oracle accepts; and
- (V) oracles whose intended peer is corrupted.

Note that at the time an initiator oracle starts, we cannot know if it will be of type I or II. However, we will know what type it is when it is time to compute the oracle's session key. We also remark that types I and III correspond to case (iii)a in the definition of freshness. Types II and IV correspond to case (iii)b.

In the following, let S_j denote the event that the experiment in Game j outputs 1.

Game 0. Our starting point Game 0 is the security experiment defining AKE security. We have that

$$\Pr\left[\mathsf{break_{KE}}\right] = \Pr[S_0]. \tag{1}$$

We begin with an administrative step to avoid pathologies where honest players choose the same random nonces.

Game 1. In this game, we abort if two initiator oracles or two responder oracles ever arrive at the same `ctxt`. The probability of this happening can be upper-bounded by the probability of two oracles for the same peer choosing the same random exponents, and we get that

$$|\Pr[S_1] - \Pr[S_0]| \leq \frac{\mu\ell^2}{p}. \tag{2}$$

We also note that the event in this game that corresponds to $\text{break}_{\text{Unique}}$ cannot happen in this game. It follows that

$$\Pr[\text{break}_{\text{Unique}}] \leq \frac{\mu\ell^2}{p}. \tag{3}$$

4.1 Preparing Oracles

Our goal in this game is to change every oracle so that it no longer computes the input to the key derivation hash H, but instead checks if the adversary computes this input and adapts accordingly. This is essential for later games, since it allows us to replace every use of the secret key with queries to a strong DH oracle.

Game 2. In this game, we modify how our oracles determine their session keys. Note that at the point in time where an initiator oracle determines its session key, we know its type exactly.

A type III, IV or V responder oracle with $\text{ctxt} = \hat{i}\|\hat{j}\|pk_i\|pk_j\|U\|V$, secret key b and random exponent s does the following to determine its session key k: First, it checks to see if any oracle queries $\hat{i}\|\hat{j}\|pk_i\|pk_j\|U\|V\|W_1\|W_2\|W_3$ have been made satisfying

$$W_1 = pk_i^s \qquad\qquad W_2 = U^b \qquad\qquad W_3 = U^s. \tag{4}$$

If any such query is found k is set to the corresponding hash value. Otherwise, the session key is chosen at random. And if such a hash query happens later, the hash value is set to the chosen session key.

A type I initiator oracle will simply use the key from the corresponding responder oracle.

A type II or V initiator oracle with $\text{ctxt} = \hat{i}\|\hat{j}\|pk_i\|pk_j\|U\|V$, secret key a and random exponent r does the following to determine its session key k: First, it checks to see if any oracle queries $\hat{i}\|\hat{j}\|pk_i\|pk_j\|U\|V\|W_1\|W_2\|W_3$ have been made satisfying

$$W_1 = V^a \qquad\qquad W_2 = pk_j^r \qquad\qquad W_3 = V^r. \tag{5}$$

If any such query is found, k is set to the corresponding hash value. Otherwise, the session key is chosen at random. And if such a hash query happens later, the hash value is set to the chosen session key.

The only potential change in this game is at which point in time the key derivation hash oracle value is first defined, which is unobservable. It follows that

$$\Pr[S_2] = \Pr[S_1]. \tag{6}$$

4.2   Type IV Responder Oracles

Game 3. In this game type IV oracles choose their session key at random, but do not modify the hash oracle unless the intended peer is corrupted. If the adversary corrupts the intended peer i of a type IV oracle running as user j with secret key b, random exponent s and chosen key k, then from that point in time, any query of the form

$$\hat{i}\|\hat{j}\|pk_i\|pk_j\|U\|V\|pk_i^s\|U^b\|U^s$$

to the key derivation hash oracle H will result in the hash value k.

Unless one of these queries happen before user i is corrupted, the only change is at which point in time the key derivation hash oracle value is first defined, which is unobservable. Let F be the event that a query as above happens before the corresponding long-term key is corrupted. Then

$$|\Pr[S_3] - \Pr[S_2]| \le \Pr[F].$$

Let F_i be the same event as F, but with the intended peer being user i. We then have that $\Pr[F] = \sum_i \Pr[F_i]$.

Next, consider the event E_i which is that for some type IV oracle as above, any query of the form

$$\hat{i}\|\hat{j}\|pk_i\|pk_j\|U\|V\|W_1\|W_2\|W_3 \qquad\qquad W_1 = pk_i^s = V^a \qquad (7)$$

to the key derivation hash oracle H happens before user i is corrupted. Then $\Pr[F_i] \le \Pr[E_i]$.

We shall now bound the probability of the event E_i by constructing an adversary against strong Diffie-Hellman. This adversary will embed its DH challenge in some user i's public key and type IV oracle responses for oracles whose intended peer is user i, and recover the solution to its DH challenge from the hash query in event E_i.

Strong Diffie-Hellman Adversary $\mathcal{B}_1$. The algorithm $\mathcal{B}_1$ takes as input a DH challenge $(X, Y) = (g^x, g^y)$ and outputs a group element Z. It has access to a strong Diffie-Hellman oracle $\mathsf{stDH}_x(\cdot, \cdot)$.

Reduction $\mathcal{B}_1$ runs Game 2 with the following changes: it chooses i uniformly at random and sets user i's public key to $pk_i = X$ (and thus implicitly sets i's private key to the unknown value x). For type IV oracles whose intended peer is user i, $\mathcal{B}_1$ sets $V = Y \cdot g^{\rho_0}$, with ρ_0 random. If the adversary corrupts user i, the reduction $\mathcal{B}_1$ aborts. (For other users, the reduction simply returns the secret key, as in Game 2.)

We need to recognise hash queries of the form (4) and (5) that involve user i, as well as queries of the form (7). For (4), where user i acts in the responder role, we know the oracle's random exponent s, so we only need to recognise if W_2 is U raised to user i's secret key, which can be done by checking if $\mathsf{stDH}_x(U, W_2) = 1$.

For (5), where user i is the initiator, we know the oracle's random exponent r, so we only need to recognise if W_1 is V raised to user i's secret key, which can be done by checking if $\mathsf{stDH}_x(V, W_1) = 1$.

Finally, for (7), we need to recognise if a group element W_1 is V raised to user i's secret key, which can be done by checking if $\mathsf{stDH}_x(V, W_1) = 1$. When we recognise a query of the form (7), since we know that $V = Y \cdot g^{\rho_0}$, we output

$$Z = W_1 X^{-\rho_0} = V^x X^{-\rho_0} = Y^x g^{\rho_0 x} g^{-x\rho_0} = Y^x.$$

In other words, our adversary $\mathcal{B}_1$ succeeds whenever E_i would happen in Game 2. Furthermore, E_i in Game 2 can only happen before user i is corrupted, so whenever E_i would happen in Game 2, $\mathcal{B}_1$ would not have aborted.

We get that

$$\mathsf{Adv}^{\mathsf{stDH}}_{\mathbb{G},g}(\mathcal{B}_1) \geq \frac{1}{\mu} \sum_i \Pr[E_i] \geq \frac{1}{\mu} \sum_i \Pr[F_i] = \frac{1}{\mu} \Pr[F],$$

from which it follows that

$$|\Pr[S_3] - \Pr[S_2]| \leq \Pr[F] \leq \mu \cdot \mathsf{Adv}^{\mathsf{stDH}}_{\mathbb{G},g}(\mathcal{B}_1). \tag{8}$$

4.3   Type III Responder Oracles

Game 4. In this game type III responder oracles choose their session key at random, and do not modify the key derivation hash oracle.

Consider a type III responder oracle for user j with secret key b, random exponent s and intended peer i, who has secret key a. Unless the adversary ever makes a hash query of the form

$$\hat{i}\|\hat{j}\|pk_i\|pk_j\|U\|V\|W_1\|W_2\|W_3 \qquad\qquad W_3 = U^s, \tag{9}$$

this change is unobservable. Call this event F. We thus have

$$|\Pr[S_4] - \Pr[S_3]| \leq \Pr[F]. \tag{10}$$

We shall bound the probability of F by constructing an adversary against strong Diffie-Hellman. This adversary will embed its challenge in type I or II initiator oracles' message, as well as in type III responder oracles' message. It will recover the solution to its DH challenge from the hash query in event F.

Strong Diffie-Hellman Adversary $\mathcal{B}_2$. The algorithm $\mathcal{B}_2$ takes as input a DH challenge $(X, Y) = (g^x, g^y)$ and outputs a group element Z. It has access to a strong DH-oracle $\mathsf{stDH}_x(\cdot, \cdot)$.

Our reduction $\mathcal{B}_2$ runs Game 3 with the following changes: for type I and II initiator oracles (we cannot distinguish these at this point in time), it computes $U = X \cdot g^{\rho_0}$, with ρ_0 random. For type III responder oracles, it computes $V = Y \cdot g^{\rho_1}$, with ρ_1 random. Note that in this game, the reduction knows all static secret keys, so user corruption is handled exactly as in Game 3.

We need to recognise hash queries of the form (5) for type II initiator oracles, as well as queries of the form (9) for type III oracles. Although we do not know the oracle's random exponents, we do know their secret keys. This means that we only need to recognise if W_3 is V raised to $\log_g U = x + \rho_0$. Of course, if $W_3 = V^{x+\rho_0}$, then $W_3 V^{-\rho_0} = V^x$, which we can detect by checking if $\mathsf{stDH}_x(V, W_3 V^{-\rho_0}) = 1$. If this is the case for a query of the form (9), then we output

$$Z = W_3 \cdot V^{-\rho_0} \cdot X^{-\rho_1} = V^x \cdot X^{-\rho_1} = g^{yx+\rho_1 x} g^{-x\rho_1} = Y^x$$

as the solution to the DH challenge. In other words, $\mathcal{B}_2$ succeeds whenever F would happen in Game 3, hence

$$|\Pr[S_4] - \Pr[S_3]| \leq \Pr[F] \leq \mathsf{Adv}_{\mathbb{G},g}^{\mathsf{stDH}}(\mathcal{B}_2). \tag{11}$$

Note that we do not stop the simulation in the case we detect a hash query of the form (5) for a type II initiator oracle, because in this case the responder message V does not contain the embedded DH challenge.

4.4   Type II Initiator Oracles

Game 5. In this game type II initiator oracles choose their session key at random, but do not modify the hash oracle unless the intended peer is corrupted. If the adversary corrupts the intended peer j of a type II oracle running as user i with secret key a, random exponent r and chosen key k, then from that point in time, any query of the form

$$\hat{i}\|\hat{j}\|pk_i\|pk_j\|U\|V\|V^a\|pk_j^r\|V^r$$

to the key derivation hash oracle H will result in the hash value k.

Unless one of these queries happen before the user j is corrupted, the only change is at which point in time the key derivation hash oracle value is first defined, which is unobservable. Let F be the event that a query as above happens before the corresponding long-term key is corrupted. Then

$$|\Pr[S_5] - \Pr[S_4]| \leq \Pr[F].$$

Let F_j be the same event as F, but with the intended peer being user j. We then have that $\Pr[F] = \sum_j \Pr[F_j]$.

Next, consider the event E_j which is that for some type II oracle as above, any query of the form

$$\hat{i}\|\hat{j}\|pk_i\|pk_j\|U\|V\|W_1\|W_2\|W_3 \qquad\qquad W_2 = pk_j^r = U^b \tag{12}$$

to the key derivation hash oracle H happens before user j is corrupted. Then $\Pr[F_j] \leq \Pr[E_j]$.

We shall now bound the probability of the event E_j by constructing an adversary against strong Diffie-Hellman. This adversary will embed its DH challenge in some user j's public key and type II oracle messages for oracles whose intended peer is user j, and recover the solution to its DH challenge from the hash query in event E_j.

Strong Diffie-Hellman Adversary $\mathcal{B}_3$. The algorithm $\mathcal{B}_3$ takes as input a DH challenge $(X, Y) = (g^x, g^y)$ and outputs a group element Z. It has access to a strong DH-oracle $\mathsf{stDH}_x(\cdot, \cdot)$.

Our reduction $\mathcal{B}_3$ runs Game 4 with the following changes: It chooses j uniformly at random and sets user j's public key to $pk_j = X$ (and thus implicitly sets j's private key to the unknown value $b = x$). For type I and II initiator oracles whose intended peer is user j, $\mathcal{B}_3$ sets $U = Y \cdot g^{\rho_0}$, with ρ_0 random. If the adversary corrupts user j, the reduction $\mathcal{B}_3$ aborts. (For other users, the reduction simply returns the secret key, as in Game 4.)

We need to recognise hash queries of the form (4) and (5) that involve user j, as well as queries of the form (12). For (4), where user j is the responder, we know the oracle's random exponent s, so we only need to recognise if W_2 is U raised to user j's secret key, which can be done by checking if $\mathsf{stDH}_x(U, W_2) = 1$. For (5), where user j is the initiator, we know the oracle's random exponent r, so we only need to recognise if W_1 is V raised to user j's secret key, which can be done by checking if $\mathsf{stDH}_x(V, W_1) = 1$. Finally, for (12), we need to recognise if a group element W_2 is U raised to user j's secret key, which can be done by checking if $\mathsf{stDH}_x(U, W_2) = 1$.

When we recognise a query of the form (12), meaning that $W_2 = U^x$ where know that $U = Y \cdot g^{\rho_0}$, then we output

$$Z = W_2 X^{-\rho_0} = U^x X^{-\rho_0} = Y^x g^{\rho_0 x} g^{-x \rho_0} = Y^x.$$

In other words, our adversary $\mathcal{B}_3$ succeeds whenever E_j would happen in Game 4. Furthermore, E_j in Game 4 can only happen before user j is corrupted, so whenever E_j would happen in Game 4, $\mathcal{B}_3$ would not have aborted. We get that

$$\mathrm{Adv}_{\mathbb{G},g}^{\mathsf{stDH}}(\mathcal{B}_3) \geq \frac{1}{\mu} \sum_j \Pr[E_j] \geq \frac{1}{\mu} \sum_j \Pr[F_j] = \frac{1}{\mu} \Pr[F],$$

from which it follows that

$$|\Pr[S_5] - \Pr[S_4]| \leq \Pr[F] \leq \mu \cdot \mathrm{Adv}_{\mathbb{G},g}^{\mathsf{stDH}}(\mathcal{B}_3). \tag{13}$$

4.5   Summary

Note that in Game 5, every session key is chosen at random independent of every key and sent message.

For type V oracles, the key derivation oracle is immediately programmed so that the session key is available to the adversary. But type V oracles are never fresh and therefore never subject to a Test query.

For type II and IV oracles, the key derivation hash oracle is programmed to make the session key available to the adversary only after the intended peer is corrupted. But if the intended peer is corrupted, a type II or IV oracle will become non-fresh, hence no Test query can be made to it.

For type I and III oracles, the key derivation hash oracle will never make the session key available to the adversary.

This means that for any oracle subject to a Test query, the session key is and will remain independent of every key and sent message. Which means that the adversary cannot distinguish the session key from a random key. It follows that

$$\Pr[S_5] = \frac{1}{2}. \tag{14}$$

Furthermore, (3) from Game 1 gives us $\Pr[\mathsf{break_{Unique}}] \leq \mu \ell^2 / p$. Because of perfect correctness $\Pr[\mathsf{break_{Sound}}] = 0$. It is now easy to see that Theorem 2 follows from the construction of $\mathcal{B}_1$, $\mathcal{B}_2$ and $\mathcal{B}_3$ as well as Eqs. (1), (2), (6), (8), (11), (13) and (14).

5 Avoiding the Strong Diffie-Hellman Assumption

The proof of Π relies on the strong Diffie-Hellman assumption, which is an interactive assumption. A natural goal is to look for a protocol whose proof relies on standard non-interactive assumptions. In this section we present two protocols that solve this problem. Both can be seen as different modifications of Π.

5.1 Protocol Π_{Twin}

The first protocol, which we call Π_{Twin}, applies the twinning technique of [13] to the different DH values in Π. This requires some additional exponentiations over protocol Π, as well as the need to transmit one extra group element. The details are given in Fig. 2: instead of sending a single Diffie-Hellman share, the protocol initiator samples and sends two ephemeral shares, and both shares are used in the key derivation. This duplication allows us to reduce to twin Diffie-Hellman.

Theorem 3. *Consider the protocol Π_{Twin} defined in Fig. 2 where H is modeled as a random oracle. Let $\mathcal{A}$ be an adversary against the AKE security of Π_{Twin}. Then there exists adversaries $\mathcal{B}_1$, $\mathcal{B}_2$ and $\mathcal{B}_3$ against twin Diffie-Hellman such that*

$$\mathrm{Adv}^{\mathsf{AKE}}_{\Pi_{\mathrm{Twin}}}(\mathcal{A}) \leq \mu \cdot \mathrm{Adv}^{\mathsf{2\text{-}CDH}}_{\mathbb{G},g}(\mathcal{B}_1) + \mathrm{Adv}^{\mathsf{2\text{-}CDH}}_{\mathbb{G},g}(\mathcal{B}_2) + \mu \cdot \mathrm{Adv}^{\mathsf{2\text{-}CDH}}_{\mathbb{G},g}(\mathcal{B}_3) + \frac{\mu \ell^2}{p}.$$

The adversaries all run in essentially the same time as $\mathcal{A}$ and make at most as many queries to their twin DH oracle as $\mathcal{A}$ makes to its hash oracle H.

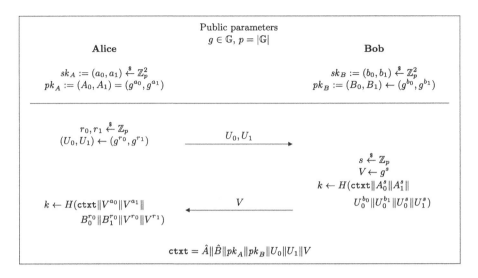

Fig. 2. Protocol Π_{Twin}. It is obtained from protocol Π by applying the twinning trick of [13] to the DH values

The proof is given in the full version. Note that by Theorem 1, we can tightly replace the twin Diffie-Hellman terms in the theorem statement by ordinary computational Diffie-Hellman terms.

5.2 Protocol Π_{Com}

The second protocol, which we call Π_{Com}, again uses the twinning technique of [13], but this time only applied to the static DH values in Π. This provides tight implicit authentication. However, instead of also twinning the ephemeral DH values we use a variant of the commitment trick of [19]. This reduces the number of exponentiations compared to Π_{Twin}, but adds another round of communication. Also, we need to rely on the Decision Diffie-Hellman assumption instead of computational Diffie-Hellman. The details are given in Fig. 3. The proof of the following theorem is given in the full version.

Theorem 4. *Consider the protocol* Π_{Com} *defined in Fig. 3 where H and G are modeled as random oracles. Let $\mathcal{A}$ be an adversary against the AKE security of* Π_{Com}*. Then there exists adversaries $\mathcal{B}_1$ and $\mathcal{B}_3$ against computational Diffie-Hellman and an adversary $\mathcal{B}_2$ against Decision Diffie-Hellman such that*

$$\text{Adv}^{\text{AKE}}_{\Pi_{\text{Twin}}}(\mathcal{A}) \leq \mu \cdot \text{Adv}^{\text{CDH}}_{\mathbb{G},g}(\mathcal{B}_1) + \text{Adv}^{\text{DDH}}_{\mathbb{G},g}(\mathcal{B}_2) + \mu \cdot \text{Adv}^{\text{CDH}}_{\mathbb{G},g}(\mathcal{B}_3) + \frac{\mu \ell^2 (1 + 2t)}{p}.$$

The adversaries all run in essentially the same time t as $\mathcal{A}$ and make at most as many queries to their twin DH oracle as $\mathcal{A}$ makes to its hash oracle H.

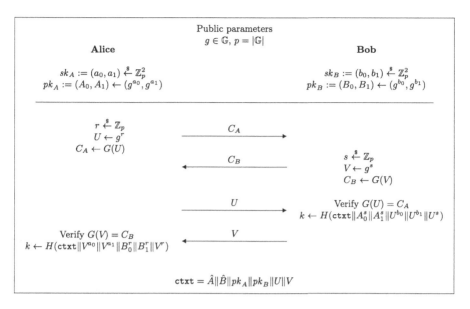

Fig. 3. Protocol Π_{Com}. It is obtained from protocol Π by applying the twinning trick of [13] to the static DH values and the commitment trick of [19] to the ephemeral DH values.

6   Efficiency Analysis

In this section we argue that our protocols are more efficient than other comparable[2] protocols in the literature when instantiated with theoretically sound parameter choices. There are two reasons for this. First, the most efficient key protocols do not have tight proofs. Hence, for theoretically sound deployment they must use larger parameters to compensate for the proof's security loss, which directly translates into more expensive operations. The result is that although some protocols require fewer operations than ours (typically group exponentiations), the increase in computational cost *per operation* dominates whatever advantage they might have over our protocols in terms of *number of operations*.

Second, the few known key exchange protocols which *do* have tight proofs, require a large number of operations or heavy cryptographic machinery. Thus, even though they can use small parameters, such as the P-256 elliptic curve, here the sheer number of operations dominates their advantage over our protocols.

To illustrate the first point in more detail, here are some examples of very efficient key exchange protocols having non-tight security proofs: UM [33], KEA+ [30], HMQV [26], CMQV [39], $\mathcal{TS}1/2/3$ [24], Kudla-Paterson [28], and NAXOS [29]. Typically, these proofs have a tightness loss between $L = O(\mu\ell)$ and $L = O(\mu^2\ell^2)$ as illustrated for a few of the protocols in Table 1.

---

[2] Comparing protocols is complex, and we return to this at the end of this section.

Table 1. The number of group exponentiations in our protocols compared to other protocols in the literature. All protocols are one-round except Π_{Com}, which has two rounds of communication. All security proofs are in the random oracle model. The security loss is in terms of the number of users (μ), the number of protocol instances per user (ℓ), and reduction's running time (t).

Protocol	#Exponentiations	Assumption	Security loss $O(\cdot)$
HMQV [26]	2.5	CDH	$\mu^2\ell^2$
NAXOS [29]	3	Gap-DH	$\mu^2\ell^2$
UM [33]	3	Gap-DH	$\mu^2\ell^2$
Kudla-Paterson [28]	3	Gap-DH	$\mu^2\ell$
KEA+ [30]	3	Gap-DH	$\mu\ell^\dagger$
Π (Fig. 1)	4	Strong-DH	μ
Π_{Twin} (Fig. 2)	8/7	CDH	μ
Π_{Com} (Fig. 3)	6	DDH	μ
GJ [19]	17	DDH	1

$\dagger$ Only when using pairing-friendly curves; otherwise $L = O(\mu\ell t)$.

Suppose we now want to compare the efficiency of the protocols Π, Π_{Twin}, Π_{Com} and HMQV, aiming for around 110-bits of security. Following Gjøsteen and Jager [19], let us imagine two different scenarios: a small-to-medium-scale setting with $\mu = 2^{16}$ users and $\ell = 2^{16}$ sessions per user, and a large-scale setting with $\mu = 2^{32}$ users and $\ell = 2^{32}$ sessions per user. To instantiate the protocols in a theoretically sound manner we need to select a group large enough so that the underlying DH-assumptions are still hard even when accounting for the security loss. For simplicity, we only consider selecting among elliptic curve groups based on the NIST curves P-256, P-384, and P-521, and assume that the CDH, DDH, and Gap-DH problems are equally hard in each group.

HMQV. Supposing HMQV has a tightness loss of $L \approx \mu^2\ell^2$, this translates into a loss of 2^{64} in the small-to-medium-scale setting, and a loss of 2^{128} in the large-scale setting. To compensate we have to increase the group size by a factor of $L^2 \approx 2^{128}$ and $L^2 \approx 2^{256}$, respectively. With a target of 110-bit security, this means that we have to instantiate HMQV with curve P-384 and P-521, respectively.

Π, Π_{Twin}, Π_{Com}. Our protocols' security proofs have a tightness loss of $L \approx \mu$, which translates into 2^{16} in the small-to-medium-scale setting and 2^{32} in the large-scale setting. In the first setting P-256 is still sufficient for 110-bit security, but in the later setting P-384 must be used instead.

We can now compare these instantiations by multiplying the number of exponentiations required with the cost of an exponentiation in the relevant group. For the latter values we use the OpenSSL benchmark numbers from Gjøsteen and Jager [19] (reproduced in Table 2). Calculating the numbers we get:

	HMQV	Π	Π_{Twin}	Π_{Com}
S-M	$2.5 \times 5.6 = 14$	$4 \times 2.1 = 8.4$	$8 \times 2.1 = 16.8$	$6 \times 2.1 = 12.6$
L	$2.5 \times 16.1 = 40.3$	$4 \times 5.6 = 22.4$	$8 \times 5.6 = 44.8$	$6 \times 5.6 = 33.6$

Table 2. OpenSSL benchmark results for NIST curves [19, Table 1].

Curve	Exp./Sec.	Time/Exp.
NIST P-256	476.9	2.1 ms
NIST P-384	179.7	5.6 ms
NIST P-521	62.0	16.1 ms

Observe that Π is more efficient than HMQV in both the small-to-medium-scale setting as well as in the large-scale setting despite needing more exponentiations. This is because it can soundly use smaller curves than HMQV due to the relative tightness of its reduction. Protocol Π_{Twin} is about as efficient as HMQV in both settings, while Π_{Com} lies somewhere in between Π and Π_{Twin}, but since it requires one extra round of communication a direct comparison is more difficult. Of course, the main reason to prefer Π_{Twin} and Π_{Com} over Π is the reliance on the weaker CDH and DDH assumptions rather than strong DH. A complicating factor in comparing with HMQV is the difference in security properties and security models (see the end of this section).

To illustrate the second point mentioned above—that our protocols are also more efficient than protocols with fully tight proofs—we also compute the numbers for the recent protocol of Gjøsteen and Jager (GJ) which is currently the most efficient key exchange protocol with a fully tight proof. Since GJ can use P-256 independent of the number of users and sessions its cost is $17 \times 2.1 = 35.7$ in both the small-to-medium scale setting as well as the large-scale setting. Nevertheless, we observe that the large number of exponentiations in GJ dominates its tightness advantage in realistic settings.

Thus, absent a fully tight proof, our protocols hit a proverbial "sweet spot" between security loss and computational complexity: they can be instantiated soundly on relatively small curves using only a few exponentiations.

Communication Complexity. For completeness we also briefly mention communication complexity. Since in most implicitly-authenticated DH-based protocols each user only sends one or two group elements, there is in practice little difference between Π, Π_{Twin}, and Π_{Com}, and protocols like HMQV when it comes to communication cost. Especially if elliptic curve groups are used.

This is in contrast to the fully tight signature-based GJ protocol, which in total needs to exchange two group elements for the Diffie-Hellman key exchange, two signatures (each consisting of a random 256-bit exponent, two group elements, and four 256-bit exponents), and one hash value. Altogether, this gives a total of ≈ 545 bytes communicated when instantiated for a security level of, say, 128 bits [19, Sect. 5]. In comparison, Π, Π_{Twin}, and Π_{Com} would only need to exchange around 160 to 224 bytes for the same security level. This assumes curve P-384 and includes the addition of two 256-bit key-confirmation messages to provide explicit entity authentication in order to make the comparison with the GJ protocol fair.

On the (Im)possibility of Fairly Comparing Protocols. Our protocols are the first implicitly authenticated key exchange protocols that were designed to provide efficient deployment in a theoretically sound manner. This implies that we must compare their efficiency with other protocols with slightly different goals. In Table 1 we included protocols with closely related goals and similar structure, but not aiming for exactly the same target.

One example of such a different goal is that NAXOS was designed to be proven in the eCK model, which also allows the reveal of the randomness of the tested session, similar to HMQV. Our protocols, like TLS 1.3, currently do not offer this property. We conjecture that the NAXOS transformation could be directly applied to our protocols to obtain eCK-secure protocols without adding exponentiations, but it is currently unclear if this could be done with a *tight* proof, and hence we leave this to future work.

7   Optimality of Our Security Proofs

In this section we will show that the tightness loss of $L = O(\mu)$ in Theorems 2, 3 and 4 is essentially optimal—at least for "simple" reductions. Basically, a "simple" reduction runs a *single* copy of the adversary only *once*. To the best of our knowledge, all known security reductions for AKE protocols are either of this type or use the forking lemma. For example, the original reduction for HMQV uses the forking lemma and thus is very non-tight, but does not fall under our lower bound. In contrast, the HMQV reduction by Barthe et al. [5] is simple and thus our lower bound applies. Hence, in order to give a tighter security proof, one would have to develop a completely new approach to prove security for such protocols.

Tightness bounds for different cryptographic primitives were given in [4,15, 17,18,21,23,25,31,35,37,40], for instance. Bader et al. [4] describe a generic framework that makes it possible to derive tightness lower bounds for many different primitives. However, these techniques are only able to consider tight reductions from *non-interactive* assumptions, while our first protocol is based on the *interactive* strong Diffie-Hellman assumption. Morgan and Pass [34] showed how to additionally capture *bounded-round* interactive assumptions, but the strong Diffie-Hellman assumption does not bound the number of possible oracle queries, so we cannot use their approach directly.

Therefore we develop a new variant of the approach of Bader et al. [4], which makes it possible to capture interactive assumptions with an unbounded number of oracle queries, such as strong Diffie-Hellman assumption. For clarity and simplicity, we formulate this specifically for the class of assumptions and protocols that we consider, but we discuss possible extensions below.

Considered Class of Protocols. In the following we consider protocols where public keys are group elements of the form $pk = g^x$ and the corresponding secret key is $sk = x$. We denote the class of all protocols with this property with Π_{DH}. Note that this class contains, in particular, NAXOS [29], KEA+ [30], and HMQV [26].

Remark 1. One can generalize our results to *unique and verifiable* secret keys, which essentially requires that for each value pk there exists only one unique matching secret key sk, and that there exists an efficiently computable relation R such that $R(pk, sk) = 1$ if and only if (pk, sk) is a valid key pair. Following Bader et al. [4], one can generalize this further to so-called *efficiently re-randomizable* keys. We are not aware of concrete examples of protocols that would require this generality, and thus omit it here. All protocols considered in the present paper and the vast majority of high-efficiency protocols in the literature have keys of the form $(pk, sk) = (g^x, x)$, so we leave such extensions for future work.

Why Does GJ18 Not Contradict Our Lower Bound? As mentioned in Remark 1, our bound applies to protocols with *unique and verifiable* secret keys. In contrast, the protocol of Gjøsteen and Jager [19] constructs a tightly-secure digital signature scheme based on OR-proofs, where secret keys are *not* unique. As explained in [19, Section 1.1], these non-unique secret keys seem inherently necessary to achieve fully-tight security.

Simple Reductions from (Strong) Diffie-Hellman. Intuitively, a *simple* reduction $\mathcal{R} = \mathcal{R}^{\mathcal{O}}$ from (strong) CDH takes as input a CDH instance (g^x, g^y) and may query an oracle $\mathcal{O}$ that, on input Y, Z, returns 1 if and only if $Y^x = Z$ (cf. Definition 3). More formally:

Definition 10. *A simple* reduction $\mathcal{R}$ *interacts with an adversary* $\mathcal{A}$ *as follows.*

1. $\mathcal{R}$ *receives as input a CDH instance* (g^x, g^y).
2. *It generates* μ *public keys and starts* $\mathcal{A}(pk_1, \dots, pk_\mu)$. $\mathcal{R}$ *provides* $\mathcal{A}$ *with access to all queries provided in the security model described in Sect. 3.*
3. $\mathcal{R}$ *outputs a value* h.

We say that $\mathcal{R}$ *is a* $(t_\mathcal{R}, \epsilon_\mathcal{R}, \epsilon_\mathcal{A})$-reduction, *if it runs in time at most* $t_\mathcal{R}$ *and for any adversary* $\mathcal{A}$ *with* $\epsilon_\mathcal{A} = \mathrm{Adv}_\Pi^{\mathsf{AKE}}(\mathcal{A})$ *holds that*

$$\Pr[h = g^{xy}] \geq \epsilon_\mathcal{R}.$$

We say that $\mathcal{R} = \mathcal{R}^{\mathcal{O}}$ *is a reduction from the* strong *CDH problem if it makes at least one query to its oracle* $\mathcal{O}$, *and a reduction from the CDH problem if not.*

Remark 2. The formalization in this section very specifically considers the computational problems CDH and sCDH, as concrete examples of reasonable hardness assumptions that a typical security proof for the protocols considered in this work may be based on. We will later discuss how our results can be extended to other interactive and non-interactive problems.

Theorem 5. *Let* Π *be an AKE protocol such that* $\Pi \in \Pi_{\mathsf{DH}}$. *Let* $|\mathcal{K}|$ *denote the size of the key space of* Π. *For any simple* $(t_{\mathcal{R}}, \epsilon_{\mathcal{R}}, 1 - 1/|\mathcal{K}|)$-*reduction* $\mathcal{R}^{\mathcal{O}}$ *from (strong) CDH to breaking* Π *in the sense of Definition 9 there exists an algorithm* $\mathcal{M}^{\mathcal{O}}$, *the meta-reduction, that solves the (strong) CDH problem in time* $t_{\mathcal{M}}$ *and with success probability* $\epsilon_{\mathcal{M}}$ *such that* $t_{\mathcal{M}} \approx \mu \cdot t_{\mathcal{R}}$ *and*

$$\epsilon_{\mathcal{M}} \geq \epsilon_{\mathcal{R}} - \frac{1}{\mu}.$$

Remark 3. Note that the lower bound $\epsilon_{\mathcal{M}} \geq \epsilon_{\mathcal{R}} - 1/\mu$ implies that the success probability $\epsilon_{\mathcal{R}}$ cannot significantly exceed $1/\mu$, as otherwise there exists an efficient algorithm $\mathcal{M}$ for a computationally hard problem. Note also that this implies that the reduction cannot be tight, as it "loses" a factor of at least $1/\mu$, even if the running time of $\mathcal{R}$ is not significantly larger than that of the adversary.

In the sequel we write $[\mu \setminus i]$ as a shorthand for $[1 \ldots i - 1, i + 1 \ldots \mu]$.

Proof. We describe a *meta-reduction* $\mathcal{M}$ that uses $\mathcal{R}$ as a subroutine to solve the (strong) CDH problem. Following Hofheinz et al. [21] and Bader et al. [4], we will first describe a *hypothetical* inefficient adversary $\mathcal{A}$. Then we explain how this adversary is efficiently simulated by $\mathcal{M}$. Finally, we bound the success probability of $\mathcal{M}$, which yields the claim.

Hypothetical Adversary. The hypothetical adversary $\mathcal{A}$ proceeds as follows.

1. Given μ public keys $pk_1 = g^{x_1}, \ldots, pk_\mu = g^{x_\mu}$, $\mathcal{A}$ samples a uniformly random index $j^* \xleftarrow{\$} [\mu]$. Then it queries $\mathsf{RevLTK}(i)$ for all $i \in [\mu \setminus j^*]$ to obtain all secret keys except for sk_{j^*}.
2. Next, $\mathcal{A}$ computes $sk_{j^*} = x_{j^*}$ from $pk_{j^*} = g^{x_{j^*}}$, e.g., by exhaustive search.[3]
3. Then $\mathcal{A}$ picks an arbitrary oracle, say π_s^1 for $s = (j^* + 1) \bmod \mu$, and executes the protocol with π_s^1, impersonating user j^*. That is, $\mathcal{A}$ proceeds exactly as in the protocol specification, but on behalf of user j^*. Note that $\mathcal{A}$ it is able to compute all messages and the resulting session key on behalf of user j^*, because it "knows" sk_{j^*}.
4. Finally, $\mathcal{A}$ asks $\mathsf{Test}(s, 1)$. Note that this is a valid Test-query, as $\mathcal{A}$ has never asked any $\mathsf{RevSessKey}$-query or $\mathsf{RevLTK}(j^*)$ to the peer j^* of oracle π_s^1. If the experiment returns the "real" key, then $\mathcal{A}$ outputs "1". Otherwise it outputs "0".

Note that $\mathcal{A}$ wins the security experiment with optimal success probability $1 - 1/|\mathcal{K}|$, where $|\mathcal{K}|$ is the size of the key space. The loss of $1/|\mathcal{K}|$ is due to the fact that the random key chosen by the Test-query may be equal to the actual session key.

Description of the Meta-reduction. Meta-reduction $\mathcal{M}$ interacts with reduction $\mathcal{R}$ by simulating the hypothetical adversary $\mathcal{A}$ as follows.

---

[3] Note that we are considering an inefficient adversary here. As usual for meta-reductions, we will later describe how $\mathcal{A}$ can be simulated *efficiently*.

1. $\mathcal{M}$ receives as input a CDH instance (g^x, g^y). It starts $\mathcal{R}$ on input (g^x, g^y).
2. Whenever $\mathcal{R}$ issues a query to oracle $\mathcal{O}$, $\mathcal{M}$ forwards it to its own oracle. Note that both oracles are equivalent, because $\mathcal{M}$ has simply forwarded the CDH instance.
3. When $\mathcal{R}$ outputs public keys $pk_1 = g^{x_1}, \ldots, pk_\mu = g^{x_\mu}$ to $\mathcal{A}$, $\mathcal{M}$ makes a snapshot of the current state $st_\mathcal{R}$ of $\mathcal{R}$.
4. For $j \in [1 \ldots \mu]$, $\mathcal{M}$ now proceeds as follows.
    (a) It lets $\mathcal{A}$ query $\mathsf{RevLTK}(i)$ for all $i \in [\mu \setminus j]$, in order to obtain all secret keys except for sk_j. Note that the reduction may or may not respond to all $\mathsf{RevLTK}(i)$ queries. For instance, $\mathcal{R}$ may abort for certain queries.
    (b) Then it resets $\mathcal{R}$ to state $st_\mathcal{R}$.
5. Now $\mathcal{M}$ proceeds to simulate the hypothetical adversary. That is:
    (a) It picks a uniformly random index $j^* \overset{\$}{\leftarrow} [1 \ldots \mu]$ and queries $\mathsf{RevLTK}(i)$ for all $i \in [\mu \setminus j^*]$.
    (b) Then it executes the protocol with π_s^1, impersonating user j^*. Note that this works only if $\mathcal{M}$ was able to obtain sk_{j^*} in Step (4).
    (c) Finally, $\mathcal{M}$ lets $\mathcal{A}$ ask $\mathsf{Test}(s, 1)$. If the experiment returns the "real" key, then $\mathcal{A}$ outputs "1". Otherwise it outputs "0".
6. If $\mathcal{R}$ outputs some value h throughout the experiment, then $\mathcal{M}$ outputs the same value.

Note that $\mathcal{M}$ provides a perfect simulation of the hypothetical adversary, provided that it "learns" sk_{j^*} in the loop in Step (4).

Analysis of the Meta-reduction. $\mathcal{M}$ essentially runs reduction $\mathcal{R}$ at most μ times. Apart from that, it performs only minor additional operations, such that we have $t_\mathcal{M} \approx \mu \cdot t_\mathcal{R}$.

In order to analyse the success probability of $\mathcal{M}$, let us say that bad occurs, if j^* is the *only* index for which $\mathcal{R}$ did not abort in Step (4) of the meta-reduction. Note that in this case $\mathcal{M}$ learns all secret keys, *except* for sk_{j^*}, in which is the only case where the simulation of $\mathcal{A}$ in Step (5.b) fails. Since we may assume without loss of generality that the reduction $\mathcal{R}$ works for at least one index $j \in [\mu]$ and we chose $j^* \overset{\$}{\leftarrow} [\mu]$ uniformly random, we have

$$\Pr[\mathsf{bad}] \leq \frac{1}{\mu}.$$

Let $\mathsf{win}(\mathcal{R}, \mathcal{A})$ denote the event that $\mathcal{R}$ outputs $h = g^{xy}$ when interacting with $\mathcal{A}$, and $\mathsf{win}(\mathcal{R}, \mathcal{M})$ the corresponding event with $\mathcal{M}$. Since $\mathcal{M}$ simulates $\mathcal{A}$ perfectly unless bad occurs, we have

$$|\Pr[\mathsf{win}(\mathcal{R}, \mathcal{A})] - \Pr[\mathsf{win}(\mathcal{R}, \mathcal{M})]| \leq \Pr[\mathsf{bad}].$$

Furthermore, note that by definition we have $\epsilon_\mathcal{R} = \Pr[\mathsf{win}(\mathcal{R}, \mathcal{A})]$ and $\epsilon_\mathcal{M} = \Pr[\mathsf{win}(\mathcal{R}, \mathcal{M})]$. Hence we get $|\epsilon_\mathcal{R} - \epsilon_\mathcal{M}| \leq 1/\mu$, which in turn yields the lower bound $\epsilon_\mathcal{M} \geq \epsilon_\mathcal{R} - 1/\mu$.

Generalizations. The tightness lower bound proven above makes several very specific assumptions about the considered protocols, hardness assumptions, and security models. The main purpose of this is to keep the formalization and proof focused on the type of protocols that we are considering in this paper. However, a natural question is to which extent the results also apply to more general protocols, models, and assumptions, and whether and how the tightness bound can be evaded by tweaking the considered setting.

First of all, we consider only protocols where long-term secrets are of the form $(pk, sk) = (g^x, x)$. As already briefly discussed above, one can generalize this to other protocols, as long as the simulation of the hypothetical adversary by the meta-reduction is able to recover properly distributed secret keys. In particular, one can generalize to arbitrary *efficiently re-randomizable* long-term keys, as defined by Bader et al. [4]. Note that current AKE protocols with tight security proofs [3,19] do *not* have efficiently rerandomizable keys, and therefore do not contradict our result.

In order to obtain a tighter security proof one may try to make different complexity assumptions. These can be either *non-interactive* (i.e., the reduction does not have access to an oracle $\mathcal{O}$, such as e.g. DDH), or stronger *interactive* assumptions. Let us first consider non-interactive assumptions. A very general class of such assumptions was defined abstractly in Bader et al. [4], and it is easy to verify that our proof works exactly the same way with such an abstract non-interactive assumption instead of CDH.

Some stronger assumptions may yield tight security proofs, but not all of them do. Consider for instance the *gap Diffie-Hellman* assumption, which is identical to strong Diffie-Hellman, except that the first input to the provided DDH-oracle is not fixed, but can be arbitrary. It is easy to verify that our proof also works for this assumption, in exactly the same way. More generally, our proof works immediately for any assumption for which the "winning condition" of the reduction is independent of the sequence of oracle queries issued by the reduction. An example of an interactive assumptions where this does *not* hold is the trivial interactive assumption that the protocol is secure (which, of course, immediately yields a tight security proof).

Finally, we note that our impossibility result holds also for many weaker or stronger AKE security models. We only require that the model allows for active attacks and provides a RevLTK query. Thus, the result immediately applies also to weaker models that, e.g., do not provide a RevSessKey-query or only a single Test-query, and trivially also for stronger models, such as eCK-style *ephemeral key reveals* [10,12]. It remains an interesting open question whether stronger impossibility results (e.g., with quadratic lower bound) can be proven for such eCK-style definitions.

8   Adding Explicit Entity Authentication

In this section we describe how explicit entity authentication (EA) [9] can be added to our protocols by doing an additional key-confirmation step. Recall that

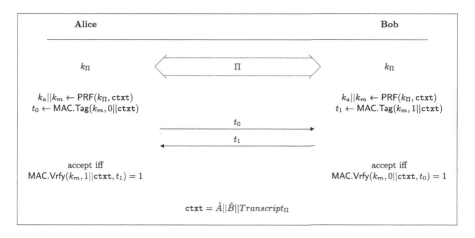

Fig. 4. Generic compiler from an AKE protocol Π with implicit authentication to a protocol Π^+ with explicit entity authentication.

EA is the aliveness property that fresh oracles are guaranteed to have a partner once they accept. Our construction is a generic compiler which transforms an arbitrary AKE protocol Π, secure according to Definition 9, into one that also provides EA. The details of the compiler are given in Fig. 4.

Specifically, protocol Π^+ begins by running protocol Π to obtain a session key k_Π. This key, which we henceforth call the *intermediate key* for protocol Π^+, is then used to derive two additional keys: k_a and k_m. The first key becomes the final session key of protocol Π^+, while k_m is used to compute a key-confirmation message, i.e., a MAC, for each party. The EA property of Π^+ reduces to the AKE security of the initial protocol Π, the *multi-user* PRF security of the function used to derive k_a and k_m, as well as the *multi-user strong UF-CMA* (mu-SUF-CMA) security of the MAC scheme (see the full version for the formal definitions).

Theorem 6. *Let Π be an AKE protocol, let Π^+ be the protocol derived from Π as defined in Fig. 4, and let $\mathcal{A}$ be an adversary against the EA security of protocol Π^+. Then there exists adversaries $\mathcal{B}_1$, $\mathcal{B}_2$, $\mathcal{D}$, and $\mathcal{F}$, such that*

$$\mathrm{Adv}_{\Pi^+}^{\mathsf{EA}}(\mathcal{A}) \leq \mathrm{Adv}_{\Pi}^{\mathsf{AKE}}(\mathcal{B}_1) + 2 \cdot \mathrm{Adv}_{\Pi}^{\mathsf{AKE}}(\mathcal{B}_2) + \mathrm{Adv}_{\mathsf{PRF},\mu\ell}^{\mathsf{mu\text{-}PRF}}(\mathcal{D}) + \mathrm{Adv}_{\mathsf{MAC},\mu\ell}^{\mathsf{mu\text{-}SUF\text{-}CMA}}(\mathcal{F}),$$

where $\mu\ell$ is the number of sessions created by $\mathcal{A}$. The adversaries $\mathcal{B}_1$, $\mathcal{B}_2$, $\mathcal{D}$, and $\mathcal{F}$ all run in essentially the same time as $\mathcal{A}$.

Our result is basically a restatement of the theorem proved by Yang [41], but with two minor differences: (1) our result is stated for arbitrary protocols and not only two-message protocols, and (2) since we use the AKE-RoR model the proof is tighter and slightly simpler.

9 Conclusion

We showed that it is possible to achieve highly efficient AKE protocols that can be instantiated with theoretically sound parameters. Specifically, we gave protocol constructions that have only a linear tightness loss in the number of users, while using only a handful of exponentiations. Our constructions are at least as efficient as the best known AKE protocols in this setting. Perhaps surprisingly, our constructions only use standard building blocks as used by widely deployed protocols and are very similar to protocols like Noise-KK, and offer similar security guarantees.

While our proofs have a linear loss we have showed that this is actually unavoidable: any reduction from a protocol in our class to a wide class of hardness assumptions must lose a factor of at least μ. Thus, our reductions are optimal in this regard. Additionally, we proved that adding a key confirmation step tightly provides explicit authentication.

Taken together, these results demonstrate for the first time that AKE protocols can be instantiated in a theoretically sound way in real-world deployments without sacrificing performance.

References

1. Abdalla, M., Benhamouda, F., MacKenzie, P.: Security of the J-PAKE password-authenticated key exchange protocol. In: 2015 IEEE Symposium on Security and Privacy, pp. 571–587. IEEE Computer Society Press, May 2015
2. Abdalla, M., Fouque, P.-A., Pointcheval, D.: Password-based authenticated key exchange in the three-party setting. In: Vaudenay, S. (ed.) PKC 2005. LNCS, vol. 3386, pp. 65–84. Springer, Heidelberg (2005). https://doi.org/10.1007/978-3-540-30580-4_6
3. Bader, C., Hofheinz, D., Jager, T., Kiltz, E., Li, Y.: Tightly-secure authenticated key exchange. In: Dodis, Y., Nielsen, J.B. (eds.) TCC 2015. LNCS, vol. 9014, pp. 629–658. Springer, Heidelberg (2015). https://doi.org/10.1007/978-3-662-46494-6_26
4. Bader, C., Jager, T., Li, Y., Schäge, S.: On the impossibility of tight cryptographic reductions. In: Fischlin, M., Coron, J.-S. (eds.) EUROCRYPT 2016. LNCS, vol. 9666, pp. 273–304. Springer, Heidelberg (2016). https://doi.org/10.1007/978-3-662-49896-5_10
5. Barthe, G., Crespo, J.M., Lakhnech, Y., Schmidt, B.: Mind the gap: modular machine-checked proofs of one-round key exchange protocols. In: Oswald, E., Fischlin, M. (eds.) EUROCRYPT 2015. LNCS, vol. 9057, pp. 689–718. Springer, Heidelberg (2015). https://doi.org/10.1007/978-3-662-46803-6_23
6. Bellare, M., Boldyreva, A., Micali, S.: Public-key encryption in a multi-user setting: security proofs and improvements. In: Preneel, B. (ed.) EUROCRYPT 2000. LNCS, vol. 1807, pp. 259–274. Springer, Heidelberg (2000). https://doi.org/10.1007/3-540-45539-6_18
7. Bellare, M., Desai, A., Jokipii, E., Rogaway, P.: A concrete security treatment of symmetric encryption. In: 38th FOCS, pp. 394–403. IEEE Computer Society Press, October 1997

8. Bellare, M., Rogaway, P.: Random oracles are practical: a paradigm for designing efficient protocols. In: Denning, D.E., Pyle, R., Ganesan, R., Sandhu, R.S., Ashby, V. (eds.) ACM CCS 1993, pp. 62–73. ACM Press, November 1993

9. Bellare, M., Rogaway, P.: Entity authentication and key distribution. In: Stinson, D.R. (ed.) CRYPTO 1993. LNCS, vol. 773, pp. 232–249. Springer, Heidelberg (1994). https://doi.org/10.1007/3-540-48329-2_21

10. Bergsma, F., Jager, T., Schwenk, J.: One-round key exchange with strong security: an efficient and generic construction in the standard model. In: Katz, J. (ed.) PKC 2015. LNCS, vol. 9020, pp. 477–494. Springer, Heidelberg (2015). https://doi.org/10.1007/978-3-662-46447-2_21

11. Bhargavan, K., Fournet, C., Kohlweiss, M., Pironti, A., Strub, P.-Y., Zanella-Béguelin, S.: Proving the TLS handshake secure (as it is). In: Garay, J.A., Gennaro, R. (eds.) CRYPTO 2014. LNCS, vol. 8617, pp. 235–255. Springer, Heidelberg (2014). https://doi.org/10.1007/978-3-662-44381-1_14

12. Canetti, R., Krawczyk, H.: Analysis of key-exchange protocols and their use for building secure channels. In: Pfitzmann, B. (ed.) EUROCRYPT 2001. LNCS, vol. 2045, pp. 453–474. Springer, Heidelberg (2001). https://doi.org/10.1007/3-540-44987-6_28

13. Cash, D., Kiltz, E., Shoup, V.: The twin Diffie-Hellman problem and applications. In: Smart, N. (ed.) EUROCRYPT 2008. LNCS, vol. 4965, pp. 127–145. Springer, Heidelberg (2008). https://doi.org/10.1007/978-3-540-78967-3_8

14. Cohn-Gordon, K., Cremers, C.J.F., Garratt, L.: On post-compromise security. In: IEEE 29th Computer Security Foundations Symposium, CSF 2016, Lisbon, Portugal, 27 June–1 July 2016, pp. 164–178. IEEE Computer Society (2016). https://doi.org/10.1109/CSF.2016.19

15. Coron, J.-S.: Optimal security proofs for PSS and other signature schemes. In: Knudsen, L.R. (ed.) EUROCRYPT 2002. LNCS, vol. 2332, pp. 272–287. Springer, Heidelberg (2002). https://doi.org/10.1007/3-540-46035-7_18

16. Donenfeld, J.A.: WireGuard: next generation Kernel network tunnel. In: NDSS 2017. The Internet Society, February/March 2017

17. Fleischhacker, N., Jager, T., Schröder, D.: On tight security proofs for Schnorr signatures. In: Sarkar, P., Iwata, T. (eds.) ASIACRYPT 2014. LNCS, vol. 8873, pp. 512–531. Springer, Heidelberg (2014). https://doi.org/10.1007/978-3-662-45611-8_27

18. Garg, S., Bhaskar, R., Lokam, S.V.: Improved bounds on security reductions for discrete log based signatures. In: Wagner, D. (ed.) CRYPTO 2008. LNCS, vol. 5157, pp. 93–107. Springer, Heidelberg (2008). https://doi.org/10.1007/978-3-540-85174-5_6

19. Gjøsteen, K., Jager, T.: Practical and tightly-secure digital signatures and authenticated key exchange. In: Shacham, H., Boldyreva, A. (eds.) CRYPTO 2018. LNCS, vol. 10992, pp. 95–125. Springer, Cham (2018). https://doi.org/10.1007/978-3-319-96881-0_4

20. Groth, J., Sahai, A.: Efficient non-interactive proof systems for bilinear groups. In: Smart, N. (ed.) EUROCRYPT 2008. LNCS, vol. 4965, pp. 415–432. Springer, Heidelberg (2008). https://doi.org/10.1007/978-3-540-78967-3_24

21. Hofheinz, D., Jager, T., Knapp, E.: Waters signatures with optimal security reduction. In: Fischlin, M., Buchmann, J., Manulis, M. (eds.) PKC 2012. LNCS, vol. 7293, pp. 66–83. Springer, Heidelberg (2012). https://doi.org/10.1007/978-3-642-30057-8_5

22. Jager, T., Kohlar, F., Schäge, S., Schwenk, J.: On the security of TLS-DHE in the standard model. In: Safavi-Naini, R., Canetti, R. (eds.) CRYPTO 2012. LNCS, vol. 7417, pp. 273–293. Springer, Heidelberg (2012). https://doi.org/10.1007/978-3-642-32009-5_17

23. Jager, T., Stam, M., Stanley-Oakes, R., Warinschi, B.: Multi-key authenticated encryption with corruptions: reductions are lossy. In: Kalai, Y., Reyzin, L. (eds.) TCC 2017. LNCS, vol. 10677, pp. 409–441. Springer, Cham (2017). https://doi.org/10.1007/978-3-319-70500-2_14

24. Jeong, I.R., Katz, J., Lee, D.H.: One-round protocols for two-party authenticated key exchange. In: Jakobsson, M., Yung, M., Zhou, J. (eds.) ACNS 2004. LNCS, vol. 3089, pp. 220–232. Springer, Heidelberg (2004). https://doi.org/10.1007/978-3-540-24852-1_16

25. Kakvi, S.A., Kiltz, E.: Optimal security proofs for full domain hash, revisited. In: Pointcheval, D., Johansson, T. (eds.) EUROCRYPT 2012. LNCS, vol. 7237, pp. 537–553. Springer, Heidelberg (2012). https://doi.org/10.1007/978-3-642-29011-4_32

26. Krawczyk, H.: HMQV: a high-performance secure Diffie-Hellman protocol. In: Shoup, V. (ed.) CRYPTO 2005. LNCS, vol. 3621, pp. 546–566. Springer, Heidelberg (2005). https://doi.org/10.1007/11535218_33

27. Krawczyk, H., Paterson, K.G., Wee, H.: On the security of the TLS protocol: a systematic analysis. In: Canetti, R., Garay, J.A. (eds.) CRYPTO 2013. LNCS, vol. 8042, pp. 429–448. Springer, Heidelberg (2013). https://doi.org/10.1007/978-3-642-40041-4_24

28. Kudla, C., Paterson, K.G.: Modular security proofs for key agreement protocols. In: Roy, B. (ed.) ASIACRYPT 2005. LNCS, vol. 3788, pp. 549–565. Springer, Heidelberg (2005). https://doi.org/10.1007/11593447_30

29. LaMacchia, B., Lauter, K., Mityagin, A.: Stronger security of authenticated key exchange. In: Susilo, W., Liu, J.K., Mu, Y. (eds.) ProvSec 2007. LNCS, vol. 4784, pp. 1–16. Springer, Heidelberg (2007). https://doi.org/10.1007/978-3-540-75670-5_1

30. Lauter, K., Mityagin, A.: Security analysis of KEA authenticated key exchange protocol. In: Yung, M., Dodis, Y., Kiayias, A., Malkin, T. (eds.) PKC 2006. LNCS, vol. 3958, pp. 378–394. Springer, Heidelberg (2006). https://doi.org/10.1007/11745853_25

31. Lewko, A., Waters, B.: Why proving HIBE systems secure is difficult. In: Nguyen, P.Q., Oswald, E. (eds.) EUROCRYPT 2014. LNCS, vol. 8441, pp. 58–76. Springer, Heidelberg (2014). https://doi.org/10.1007/978-3-642-55220-5_4

32. Li, Y., Schäge, S.: No-match attacks and robust partnering definitions: defining trivial attacks for security protocols is not trivial. In: Thuraisingham, B.M., Evans, D., Malkin, T., Xu, D. (eds.) ACM CCS 2017, pp. 1343–1360. ACM Press, October/November 2017

33. Menezes, A., Ustaoglu, B.: Security arguments for the UM key agreement protocol in the NIST SP 800-56A standard. In: Abe, M., Gligor, V. (eds.) ASIACCS 2008, pp. 261–270. ACM Press, March 2008

34. Morgan, A., Pass, R.: On the security loss of unique signatures. In: Beimel, A., Dziembowski, S. (eds.) TCC 2018. LNCS, vol. 11239, pp. 507–536. Springer, Cham (2018). https://doi.org/10.1007/978-3-030-03807-6_19

35. Paillier, P., Vergnaud, D.: Discrete-log-based signatures may not be equivalent to discrete log. In: Roy, B.K. (ed.) ASIACRYPT 2005. LNCS, vol. 3788, pp. 1–20. Springer, Heidelberg (2005)

36. Perrin, T.: Noise protocol framework (2018). http://noiseprotocol.org
37. Seurin, Y.: On the exact security of Schnorr-type signatures in the random oracle model. In: Pointcheval, D., Johansson, T. (eds.) EUROCRYPT 2012. LNCS, vol. 7237, pp. 554–571. Springer, Heidelberg (2012). https://doi.org/10.1007/978-3-642-29011-4_33
38. Signal Messenger: Technical information (2018). https://signal.org/docs
39. Ustaoglu, B.: Obtaining a secure and efficient key agreement protocol from (H)MQV and NAXOS. Des. Codes Crypt. **46**(3), 329–342 (2008)
40. Wang, Y., Matsuda, T., Hanaoka, G., Tanaka, K.: Memory lower bounds of reductions revisited. In: Nielsen, J.B., Rijmen, V. (eds.) EUROCRYPT 2018. LNCS, vol. 10820, pp. 61–90. Springer, Cham (2018). https://doi.org/10.1007/978-3-319-78381-9_3
41. Yang, Z.: Modelling simultaneous mutual authentication for authenticated key exchange. In: Danger, J.-L., Debbabi, M., Marion, J.-Y., Garcia-Alfaro, J., Zincir Heywood, N. (eds.) FPS -2013. LNCS, vol. 8352, pp. 46–62. Springer, Cham (2014). https://doi.org/10.1007/978-3-319-05302-8_4

Strong Asymmetric PAKE
Based on Trapdoor CKEM

Tatiana Bradley$^{(\boxtimes)}$, Stanislaw Jarecki$^{(\boxtimes)}$, and Jiayu Xu$^{(\boxtimes)}$

University of California, Irvine, USA
{tebradle,sjarecki,jiayux}@uci.edu

Abstract. Password-Authenticated Key Exchange (PAKE) protocols allow two parties that share a password to establish a shared key in a way that is immune to offline attacks. Asymmetric PAKE (aPAKE) [20] adapts this notion to the common client-server setting, where the server stores a one-way hash of the password instead of the password itself, and server compromise allows the adversary to recover the password only via the (inevitable) offline dictionary attack. Most aPAKE protocols, however, allow an attacker to *pre*-compute a dictionary of hashed passwords, thus instantly learning the password on server compromise. Recently, Jarecki, Krawczyk, and Xu formalized a Universally Composable *strong* aPAKE (saPAKE) [23], which requires the password hash to be salted so that the dictionary attack can only start after the server compromise leaks the salt and the salted hash. The UC saPAKE protocol shown in [23], called OPAQUE, uses 3 protocol flows, 3–4 exponentiations per party, and relies on the One-More Diffie-Hellman assumption in ROM.

We propose an alternative UC saPAKE construction based on a novel use of the encryption+SPHF paradigm for UC PAKE design [19,26]. Compared to OPAQUE, our protocol uses only 2 flows, has comparable costs, avoids hashing onto a group, and relies on different assumptions, namely Decisional Diffie-Hellman (DDH), Strong Diffie-Hellman (SDH), and an assumption that the Boneh-Boyen function $f_s(x) = g^{1/(s+x)}$ [9] is a *Salted Tight One-Way Function* (STOWF). We formalize a UC model for STOWF and analyze the Boneh-Boyen function as UC STOWF in the generic group model and ROM.

Our saPAKE protocol employs a new form of Conditional Key Encapsulation Mechanism (CKEM), a generalization of SPHF, which we call an *implicit-statement* CKEM. This strengthening of SPHF allows for a UC (sa)PAKE design where only the client commits to its password, and only the server performs an SPHF, compared to the standard UC PAKE design paradigm where the encrypt+SPHF subroutine is used symmetrically by both parties.

1 Introduction

Passwords are the most common form of authentication on the Internet, and the almost-universal password authentication method is password-over-TLS. In this method, the user (client) sends their encrypted password over TLS to a

© International Association for Cryptologic Research 2019
A. Boldyreva and D. Micciancio (Eds.): CRYPTO 2019, LNCS 11694, pp. 798–825, 2019.
https://doi.org/10.1007/978-3-030-26954-8_26

server, who then decrypts the password and verifies it against a locally stored password file. The password file does not contain the correct password pw in cleartext, but rather a random salt s and a salted password hash $F_s(pw)$, which is a randomized one-way function of the password. Function F must be a (salted) *tight* one-way function [7] in the sense that an attacker who compromises the server and learns its password file $(s, F_s(pw))$, can find pw only by running an exhaustive offline dictionary attack, at cost which is linear in the number of tested password guesses.

However, there are at least two major disadvantages of password-over-TLS: (1) the cleartext password is handled by the server during login, which could leak the password without an offline dictionary attack if the server is compromised; and (2) a Public Key Infrastructure (PKI) is needed to authenticate the server to the client, and the client loses all security if the TLS channel uses a compromised public key, e.g., due to a phishing attack (see also multiple other PKI attacks listed in [23]). Both problems of password-over-TLS are well known and have been partly addressed by the literature on Password Authentication Key Exchange (PAKE). Only one existing PAKE proposal, however, maintains password-over-TLS's advantage of forcing a full offline dictionary attack after server compromise, while mitigating its disadvantages of potential cleartext password leakage and reliance on PKI. We propose another, and to motivate our contribution we first discuss past work on PAKE.

Cryptographic PAKE and aPAKE Protocols. Standard PAKE, introduced by Bellovin and Merritt in [4], formalized in a game-based indistinguishability approach by Bellare et al. [3], and in the Universally Composable (UC) framework by Canetti et al. [14], considers secure key exchange between two parties who share the same password. Because passwords have low entropy, PAKE protocols cannot prevent the active attacker from performing an *online* impersonation attack by guessing the password, but they do guarantee security against *offline* attacks, i.e., active attacks must be the only way to verify a guessed password. Crucially, PAKE requires only passwords as inputs, and does not rely on authentic distribution of public keys via PKI, thus solving problem (2) of the password-over-TLS method. However, the shared-password PAKE model of [3,14] makes problem (1) even worse: to participate in the protocol, the server needs to *store*, not just briefly handle, the cleartext password.

To solve problem (1) and (2) together, Bellovin and Merritt [5] introduced the notion of *asymmetric* PAKE (aPAKE), a.k.a. *augmented* or *verifier-based*, which allows the server party to execute the protocol on a one-way function of the password instead of the password itself. This notion was formalized in the simulation-based approach by Boyko et al. [11], and in the UC framework by Gentry et al. [20]. There are several aPAKE's proposed in the literature, both in the simulation-based model [7,11,28,29] and in the UC model [20,21,25]. Several aPAKE protocols have also been proposed with only ad-hoc security arguments – see [23] for their discussion.

In all the above aPAKE protocols, however, passwords are hashed via some *deterministic* one-way function, making password files vulnerable to pre-computation attacks: An attacker who pre-computes a list of hashes for all passwords in an assumed dictionary can *instantly* find a user's password on server compromise. This attack is allowed by aPAKE models because, despite guaranteeing that the offline attack takes work linear in the dictionary size, they do not require that this work be done before server compromise [11, 20].

All aPAKE protocols using a deterministic one-way function allow for the password hash to be randomized if the random salt assigned to a given user account is "public" i.e., if it is revealed in the authentication protocol. This makes the pre-computation attack harder, because the adversary must engage in the online protocol to gather the (public) salt values assigned to user accounts, and pre-compute separate $(pw, F_s(pw))$ tables for each user-specific salt value s. Yet the core of the problem remains: the adversary can pre-compute hash values for a dictionary of the most probable passwords, thus learning the real password immediately on server compromise.

Strong aPAKE. To prevent pre-computation attacks, Jarecki, Krawczyk, and Xu have recently proposed a UC *strong* aPAKE (saPAKE) notion [23], which enforces that the offline dictionary attack takes $O(|D|)$ work *after* server compromise. Strong aPAKE thus bridges the security gap between password-over-TLS and PAKE, with no cleartext passwords on the server, no reliance on PKI, and no instant password retrieval on server compromise.

In the same paper [23] presented an efficient UC saPAKE protocol, called OPAQUE: It relies on standard prime-order groups, the client C and server S make respectively only 4 and 3 (multi-)exponentiations, and the protocol has 3 message flows.[1] The security of OPAQUE relies on ROM and an interactive hardness assumption of One-More Diffie-Hellman (OMDH), which states that an adversary who is allowed n queries to the Diffie-Hellman oracle $(\cdot)^k$ can compute the $(\cdot)^k$ function on at most n out of $n + 1$ random challenge group elements.

Our saPAKE Contribution. We propose a new UC saPAKE construction family based on a novel application of the encryption+SPHF paradigm. Our saPAKE construction requires ROM, as OPAQUE [23] does[2], it has only 2 message flows, and it has comparable computational costs to OPAQUE, with 1 variable-base multi-exponentiation and (at most) 11 fixed-base exponentiations for the client and 2 variable-base multi-exponentiations and 2 fixed-base exponentiations for the server. Unlike OPAQUE, it does not require hashing

---

[1] The conference paper [23] reported it as 2 message flows but the full version [24] explain why 3 flows seem necessary.

[2] ROM appears to be a minimal model necessary to achieve UC aPAKE [20], and thus UC saPAKE. To satisfy the UC (s)aPAKE notion, we need some idealized computation model (e.g., RO or a generic group) that allows us to "count" the number of times $F(x)$ is called in the adversary's *local computation*, and also to extract the effective inputs x on which the adversary computes F values.

onto a curve, which simplifes its implementation over some curves. Our protocol is also based on different hardness assumptions, namely DDH and Strong
DH, and any assumptions necessary for the (hashed) Boneh-Boyen function
$F_s(x) = g^{1/(s+\mathsf{H}(x))}$ [9] to realize what we call a *Salted Tight One-Way* (STOWF)
function. The protocol family we show can also be used with different STOWF
function candidates, possibly leading to further efficiency improvements and
weaker security assumptions for saPAKE's.

Our Approach: Using Implicit-Statement and CCA-Secure CKEM.
Our approach is inspired by the encryption+SPHF paradigm in UC PAKE
design, which began with the work of [19,26]. In this paradigm, both the client
C and the server S commit to their passwords, respectively pw_C and pw_S, using
an encryption scheme Enc whose public key pk is in the CRS. Party C uses
the ciphertext c_S sent by S to derive a secret key k_C via a Smooth Projective
Hash Function (SPHF) on input statement $x_C = (pw_C, c_S, pk)$, where the SPHF
operates on language $\mathcal{L}$ of statements (pw, c, pk) such that $c = \mathsf{Enc}_{pk}(pw)$.
Recall that an SPHF allows the hashing party C to compute a *projection key*
hp_C such that S can derive the secret key k_C given only the projection key hp_C
and a witness for $x_C \in \mathcal{L}$. The witness is the randomness r that S used to
encrypt $c_S = \mathsf{Enc}_{pk}(pw_S; r)$, and r is a valid witness for the client's statement
$(pw_C, c_S, pk) \in \mathcal{L}$ only if c_S also encrypts pw_C, i.e., if $pw_C = pw_S$. The protocol
is symmetrical, i.e. server S follows the same process with C's ciphertext to form
k_S, and the final key is a combination of the two keys, e.g. $k_C \oplus k_S$.

It is not immediately clear how to apply this paradigm to the setting of
saPAKE, because S cannot use the same SPHF as C, as it does not hold pw, but
only the password file (s, z) for $z = F_s(pw)$. Benhamouda and Pointcheval [7]
showed how to solve this problem in the context of a game-based aPAKE (but
not *strong* aPAKE) by using SPHF's for two different languages, one to verify
the client's encryption of pw using a (randomized but with public salt) one-way
function $F(pw)$ held by the server, and another to verify the server's encryption
of $z = F(pw)$. (Jutla and Roy [25] also applied this approach in the context of
a UC aPAKE.) In saPAKE, however, the client cannot compute $z = F_s(pw)$, as
the random salt s must be private on the server, so it is not clear how to adopt
this approach to the saPAKE setting.

Instead, we condense the encryption+SPHF paradigm so that a single SPHF
authenticates both the client and the server. To do this, we start from a generalized SPHF protocol called a *Conditional Key Encapsulation Mechanism*
(CKEM), introduced by Benhamouda, Couteau, Pointcheval, and Wee [6] as
an *Implicit Zero-Knowledge* protocol, and we strengthen its security properties
so that the CKEM public message m, which corresponds to the SPHF projection
key, can be used as a one-time secret authenticator: If S uses our CKEM to verify
that C's ciphertext c_C encrypts pre-image pw of S's password file $z = F_s(pw)$,
then S's CKEM message commits to its statement $x_S = (pk, c_C, F_s(pw))$, and
hence it can also act as S's authentication to C. This commitment cannot be
publicly verifiable, since x_S reveals $F_s(pw)$, but the statement-committing and

statement-privacy properties of our CKEM require that the commitment is verifiable only by a party (in our case, the client C) that holds a witness for $x_S \in \mathcal{L}$. Furthermore, for the message m to work as an authenticator for S in the UC model we need to make the sender's statement extractable by the ideal-world simulator. Moreover, standard CKEMs assume that both parties have the full language statements as inputs, but in our case the server's statement involves a password file (s, z) which cannot be made public. For that reason we develop a CKEM variant we call an *Implicit Statement* CKEM, where the sender effectively encrypts the statement it assumes in the CKEM message, and the receiver decrypts it and verifies that it agrees with its witness.

Perhaps surprisingly, we can meet all these requirements by adding just one (multi-)exponentiation for the receiver to the cost of the standard SPHF for the same language $\mathcal{L}$, with the slight caveat that SPHF-to-strong-CKEM compiler assumes ROM. However, recall that realizing the UC (s)aPAKE functionality already seems to require an idealized model like ROM, hence it is natural to use ROM to reduce the cost of all the tools used in an saPAKE protocol.

Another cost-reducing feature of our saPAKE construction is that the encryption scheme used by C to commit to a password does not need to be non-malleable, but only indistinguishable. This weaker requirement lets us use ElGamal encryption, which has half the cost of Cramer-Shoup encryption, and the SPHF for the language $\mathcal{L}$ of "encryptions of password file pre-image" is also correspondingly cheaper. This cost-saving is enabled by CCA-like security of our implicit-statement CKEM, i.e., the CKEM for statement $x = (pk, c, z)$ is secure even to the adversary who has access to a trapdoor-receiver oracle (which corresponds to a decryption oracle in CCA encryption) as long as the "trapdoor-decrypted" CKEM messages are different from the challenge CKEM message.[3] Indeed, the techniques we use to compile our (non-malleable) CKEM from (malleable) SPHF resemble the Fujisaki-Okamoto transform [17] from indistinguishable encryption to CCA-secure encryption.

On the Use of Idealized Models. Our saPAKE scheme makes use of both the (non-programmable) Random Oracle Model (ROM) and the (programmable) Generic Group Model (GGM). However, GGM is isolated so that it is used only in the offline parts of the protocol, i.e., we use it to show that the adversary may only make offline queries after it steals a password file, and cannot perform any meaningful pre-computation. By contrast, we use ROM in both the offline and online parts of the protocol. As we have mentioned, it appears that *some* programmable idealized computational model like the Random Oracle Model, the Ideal Cipher Model, or the Generic Group Model, is necessary in any UC (s)aPAKE, because of the strong constraints which the UC (s)aPAKE model imposes on the local computation of the real-world adversary. Essentially, the simulator must provide the adversary with a password file before it knows the

---

[3] These CCA-like properties were achieved already by the CKEM of [6] in the standard model, i.e. without ROM. Here we show the same properties for *implicit-statement* (and statement-private) CKEM's, and we assume ROM to minimize the costs.

actual password, then detect offline password guesses, and, if a guess is correct, program the ideal model so that the password file turns out to correspond to the correct password. That said, it may be possible to construct a UC (s)aPAKE which uses ROM/IC/GGM only in the offline part. A similar argument was used by VPAKE [7] in the context of a game-base aPAKE, to justify using both GGM and ROM only in the security analysis of the offline dictionary attacks on the password file. We analyze the security of our saPAKE protocol candidate assuming GGM only in the offline part, and ROM in both the offline and the online parts, where the latter choice is made to optimize the concrete efficiency of the resulting protocol.

Summary of Contributions. In summary, our contributions are as follows:

- We construct the first two round protocol that realizes the UC saPAKE functionality of [23]. Our protocol is based on two primitives which we introduce: implicit-statement trapdoor CKEM and salted tight one-way functions (STOWF).
- We introduce and realize a strong notion of an implicit-statement conditional key encapsulation mechanism (CKEM). Implicit-statement CKEM differs from standard CKEM in that the sender's statement is private to anyone who does not a witness for it, and the receiver runs the protocol using only a witness, and might not the same statement which the sender uses.
- We formalize the notion of a salted tight one way function (STOWF) as a UC functionality $\mathcal{F}_{\mathsf{STOWF}}$, and we show that the (hashed) Boneh-Boyen function $F_s(x) = g^{1/(s+\mathsf{H}(x))}$ realizes $\mathcal{F}_{\mathsf{STOWF}}$ in the programmable generic group model and ROM.

In Table 1 we summarize a comparison between our saPAKE protocol with several previous work on asymmetric PAKE's, in terms of efficiency, security model, and security assumptions. We stress that there are other aPAKE protocol proposals which were shown with only ad-hoc security arguments, and we refer to [23] for references.

Paper Roadmap. In Sect. 2 we define the strong (simulation-sound and statement-private) notion of implicit-statement CKEM described above, and show a generic construction of such CKEM from an SPHF for the same language in ROM. In Sect. 3 we propose the UC model for Salted Tight One-Way Functions (STOWF), and we show that the (hashed) Boneh-Boyen function $F_s(x) = g^{1/(s+\mathsf{H}(x))}$ realizes this UC functionality in GGM and ROM. In Sect. 4 we show an saPAKE protocol based on these STOWF and CKEM tools, and we show that it realizes the UC saPAKE functionality of [23] in ROM assuming that function f is a UC STOWF. Finally, in Sect. 5 we show a highly efficient instantiation of this UC saPAKE using the Boneh-Boyen function as the STOWF and the generic CKEM construction of Sect. 2 applied to the specific language implied by this STOWF instantiation.

Table 1. We compare several asymmetric PAKE protocol proposals regarding security claims, number of rounds, security assumptions, and client and server efficiency, where v and f are resp. variable-base (multi-)exponentiations and fixed-based exponentiations. All protocols rely on ROM, except [7,25] only in the offline part. GB and SIM indicate resp. game-based and simulatability-based aPAKE security notions. (1) GGM used only in the offline part; (2) OPAQUE costs reflect "multiplicative blinding" OPRF optimization reported in [24]; (3) [25] also uses a significant number of exponentiations; (4) GMR and HJKLSX are compilers from UC PAKE to UC aPAKE, here instantiated with the two-round UC PAKE of [12] secure under DDH in ROM, with resp. $1v+4f$ and $1v+2f$ costs for client and server; In the Ideal Cipher (IC) the UC PAKE of [12] reduces these costs by resp. $3f$ and $1f$ for client and server; (5) The 1-flow version of aPAKE of [7] uses a few more mostly fixed-base exponentiations.

	Security	Client	Server	Rounds	Assumptions
This work	UC saPAKE	$1v+11f$	$2v+2f$	2	DDH, 2-SDH, GGM[1]
OPAQUE[2] [24]	UC saPAKE	$2v+2f$	$2v+1f$	3	OMDH
Jutla-Roy [25]	UC aPAKE	$O(1)$ pairings[3]		1	SXDH, MDDH
HJKLSX[4] [21]	UC aPAKE	$2v+4f$	$1v+4f$	3	DDH
GMR[4] [20]	UC aPAKE	$1v+5f$	$2v+2f$	3	DDH
VPAKE [7]	GB aPAKE	$3v+8f$	$3v+4f$	2 or 1[5]	DDH, GGM[1]
PAK-X [11]	SIM aPAKE	$3v+1f$	$2v+1f$	3	DDH

2   Conditional Key Encapsulation Mechanisms

Notation. Throughout the paper, κ denotes the security parameter; "$\leftarrow$" denotes either a deterministic or a randomized assignment; and "$\leftarrow_R$" denotes uniform sampling from a given set.

Basic CKEM. A *Conditional Key Encapsulation Mechanism (CKEM)* scheme [1,6,8,16,27] implements a transfer of a random key between two parties, the sender and the receiver, under the condition that a given statement, known by both parties, belongs to some language. A CKEM can be implemented with a Smooth Projective Hash Function (SPHF), but it generalizes SPHF to interactive and only computationally secure protocols.

Let $\mathcal{L}$ be an NP language, a subset of implicit universe $\mathcal{U}$, and let $\mathcal{R}[\mathcal{L}]$ be an efficiently verifiable relation associated with $\mathcal{L}$. A CKEM for language $\mathcal{L}$ is a triple $(\mathsf{PG}, \mathsf{Snd}, \mathsf{Rec})$ where PG is a parameter generation algorithm that on input a security parameter κ outputs public parameters π, while Snd and Rec are interactive algorithms executed resp. by Sender and Receiver, where Snd runs on input parameters π, label ℓ identifying the protocol instance, and statement x, and Rec runs on inputs π, ℓ, x and a witness w, and both algorithms locally output a key ck. (To reduce visual clutter we will denote inputs π, ℓ as indices, e.g. $\mathsf{Snd}_{\pi,\ell}(x)$ will denote $\mathsf{Snd}(\pi, \ell, x)$, etc.) CKEM correctness requires that if the sender and the receiver hold the same statement in $\mathcal{L}$, and the receiver holds a witness for it, then they output the same key, i.e. for all κ, ℓ, all $\pi \leftarrow \mathsf{PG}(1^\kappa)$ and all $(x, w) \in \mathcal{R}[\mathcal{L}]$, if $(ck_\mathsf{S}, ck_\mathsf{R}) \leftarrow [\mathsf{Snd}_{\pi,\ell}(x), \mathsf{Rec}_{\pi,\ell}(x, w)]$ then $ck_\mathsf{S} = ck_\mathsf{R}$. The basic security property of CKEM is *soundness*, which states that if $x \notin \mathcal{L}$ then an efficient adversary interacting with $\mathsf{Snd}_{\pi,\ell}(x)$ cannot distinguish Snd's output key from a random string. In other words, if the sender generates its key on a false statement then this key is pseudorandom to the receiver.

Trapdoor CKEM. Benhamouda et al. [6] defined a *trapdoor* CKEM, called an *Implicit Zero-Knowledge* therein, which allows a simulator holding a global trapdoor to compute the sender's key even on false statements. This simulatability property makes CKEM a stronger protocol building block because it allows the simulator to perform any subsequent actions an honest party would do using a key received via a CKEM on a statement proving honest behavior. (Recall that the simulator typically does not have a witness for such statement because it needs to simulate an honest party without knowing its private data.) A trapdoor CKEM scheme includes two additional algorithms, the trapdoor parameter generation procedure TPG, which outputs parameters π together with a *simulation trapdoor* td, and a trapdoor receiver algorithm TRec which satisfies the *zero-knowledge* property [6], which states that for any $(x, w) \in \mathcal{R}[\mathcal{L}]$, an interaction with $\mathsf{TRec}_{\pi,\ell}(x, td)$ (including its local output) is indistinguishable from an interaction with $\mathsf{Rec}_{\pi,\ell}(x, w)$. Moreover, in parallel to zero-knowledge proofs, a trapdoor CKEM should satisfy *simulation-soundness* [6], which states that for any $x \notin \mathcal{L}$ an adversary interacting with $\mathsf{Snd}_{\pi,\ell}(x)$ cannot distinguish Snd's output key from a random string, even given access to oracle $\mathsf{TRec}_{\pi,\ell'}(x', td)$ for any $(\ell', x') \neq (\ell, x)$.

Implicit-Statement CKEM. We introduce a new CKEM variant we call an *implicit-statement* CKEM, in which the receiver might not know the statement used by the sender, and has only a witness as its input. This makes a difference for languages where the same value can be a witness for many statements. Note that in the context of saPAKE application a language of pre-images of a salted hash function in an example of such language because password pw is a witness to correctness of password file $(s, f_s(pw))$ for every salt value s (see Sect. 3). Recall also that an saPAKE server must hide the salt value, to prevent precomputation in a dictionary attack that can be staged after server compromise, so the statement assumed by the saPAKE server cannot be sent to the client in the clear. An implicit-statement CKEM allows the sender to embed its statement into the CKEM message so that the receiver reconstructs it together with the sender's key *only if* this statement is matched by the receiver's witness.

Since our implicit-statement CKEM construction is non-interactive we state all definitions below in this context, but they can be easily adapted to the interactive setting. Thus we define CKEM scheme as a tuple of non-interactive algorithms $(\mathsf{PG}, \mathsf{TPG}, \mathsf{Snd}, \mathsf{Rec}, \mathsf{TRec})$ where $\mathsf{PG}, \mathsf{TPG}$ are as above, $\mathsf{Snd}_{\pi,\ell}$ on input x outputs key ck and a message m, and $\mathsf{Rec}_{\pi,\ell}$ and $\mathsf{TRec}_{\pi,\ell}$, output (ck, x) on inputs resp. (w, m) and (td, m). The implicit-statement CKEM *correctness* requires that for all κ, ℓ and $(x, w) \in \mathcal{R}[\mathcal{L}]$ if $\pi \leftarrow \mathsf{PG}(1^\kappa)$, $(ck, m) \leftarrow \mathsf{Snd}_{\pi,\ell}(x)$, and $(ck', x') \leftarrow \mathsf{Rec}_{\pi,\ell}(w, m)$ then $(ck', x') = (ck, x)$. We require two additional syntactic properties of CKEM: *statement verification* for the receiver, which states that for all w, m, ℓ if $\pi \leftarrow \mathsf{PG}(1^\kappa)$ and $(ck, x) \leftarrow \mathsf{Rec}_{\pi,\ell}(w, m)$ then (a) if $x \neq \perp$ then $(x, w) \in \mathcal{R}[\mathcal{L}]$ and (b) if $x = \perp$ then ck is a fresh uniform random string, and *statement recovery* for the trapdoor receiver, which states that for all ℓ and $x \in \mathcal{U}$, if $(\pi, td) \leftarrow \mathsf{PG}(1^\kappa)$, $(ck, m) \leftarrow \mathsf{Snd}_{\pi,\ell}(x)$, and $(ck', x') \leftarrow \mathsf{TRec}_{\pi,\ell}(td, m)$, then $\Pr[x' \neq x] \leq \mathsf{negl}(\kappa)$.

An implicit-statement CKEM scheme must satisfy the *parameter indistinguishability*, *zero-knowledge*, and *simulation soundness* properties [6], which we adjust to implicit-statement CKEM's as follows:

(I) parameter indistinguishability: Distributions $\{\pi\}_{\pi \leftarrow \mathsf{PG}(1^\kappa)}$ and $\{\pi\}_{(\pi, td) \leftarrow \mathsf{TPG}(1^\kappa)}$ are computationally indistinguishable.

(II) zero-knowledge: The zero-knowledge defined in [6] required that the real-world receiver output $\mathsf{Rec}_{\pi,\ell}(x, w, m)$ is indistinguishable from the simulator output $\mathsf{TRec}_{\pi,\ell}(x, td, m)$. By contrast, in implicit-statement CKEM, Rec runs only on w, so it is not obvious what the corresponding ideal-world interaction should be, because w might correspond to many statements. However, since we require that Rec outputs statement x extracted from m along with key ck, and that Rec outputs $x \neq \perp$ only if $(x, w) \in \mathcal{R}[\mathcal{L}]$, the ZK property for implicit-statement CKEM will compare Rec's output with TRec's output modified by a wrapper that overwrites TRec's output (ck, x) with $(\$, \perp)$ if w is not a witness for x.[4] Formally, implicit-statement CKEM is *zero-knowledge* if for every efficient algorithm $\mathcal{A} = (\mathcal{A}_1, \mathcal{A}_2)$ we have:

$$\{\mathcal{A}_2(st, ck, x)\}_{(ck,x) \leftarrow \mathsf{Rec}_{\pi,\ell}(w,m)} \approx \{\mathcal{A}_2(st, ck, x)\}_{(ck,x) \leftarrow \mathsf{Wrap}_w(\mathsf{TRec}_{\pi,\ell}(td,m))}$$

where $(\pi, td) \leftarrow \mathsf{TPG}(1^\kappa)$ and $(st, \ell, w, m) \leftarrow \mathcal{A}_1(\pi, td)$ in both distributions, and Wrap_w is an algorithm which outputs (ck, x) on input (ck, x) if $(x, w) \in \mathcal{R}[\mathcal{L}]$ and otherwise outputs $(ck', \perp)$ for $ck' \leftarrow_\mathrm{R} \{0, 1\}^\kappa$.

(III) simulation soundness: If $x \notin \mathcal{L}$ then $(ck, m) \leftarrow \mathsf{Snd}_{\pi,\ell}(x)$ is indistinguishable from $(\$, m)$ even if the adversary interacts with a trapdoor receiver on any $(\ell', m') \neq (\ell, m)$. Formally, for every efficient algorithm $\mathcal{A} = (\mathcal{A}_1, \mathcal{A}_2)$:

$$\{\mathcal{A}_2^{\mathsf{TRec}_{\mathsf{Block}(\ell, m)}(\pi, \cdot, td, \cdot)}(st, ck, m)\} \approx \{\mathcal{A}_2^{\mathsf{TRec}_{\mathsf{Block}(\ell, m)}(\pi, \cdot, td, \cdot)}(st, ck', m)\}$$

where $(\pi, td) \leftarrow \mathsf{TPG}(1^\kappa)$, $(st, \ell, x) \leftarrow \mathcal{A}_1^{\mathsf{TRec}(\pi, \cdot, td, \cdot)}(\pi)$ s.t. $x \notin \mathcal{L}$, $(ck, m) \leftarrow \mathsf{Snd}_{\pi,\ell}(x)$, $ck' \leftarrow_\mathrm{R} \{0, 1\}^\kappa$, and oracle $\mathsf{TRec}_{\mathsf{Block}(\ell, m)}(\pi, \cdot, td, \cdot)$ returns $\mathsf{TRec}_{\pi,\ell'}(td, m')$ on any query $(\ell', m') \neq (\ell, m)$.

Statement Privacy. As said above, an implicit-statement CKEM can support applications in which the statement assumed by the sender is hidden from everyone except the receiver who holds the matching witness. This is captured

---

[4] To see that this wrapper is necessary, observe that TRec should output $(\cdot, x)$ on input m output by $\mathsf{Snd}(x)$, whereas $\mathsf{Rec}(w)$ outputs $(\cdot, \perp)$ if $(x, w) \notin \mathcal{R}[\mathcal{L}]$.

by the *statement privacy* property of CKEM, that for any statements x_0, x_1, both *not* in language $\mathcal{L}$, an adversary cannot tell whether the sender's message is produced on x_0 or x_1. Formally, we call CKEM *statement private* if for every efficient algorithm $\mathcal{A} = (\mathcal{A}_1, \mathcal{A}_2)$:

$$\{\mathcal{A}_2^{\mathsf{TRec}_{\mathsf{Block}(\ell, m_0)}(\pi, \cdot, td, \cdot)}(st, ck_0, m_0)\} \approx \{\mathcal{A}_2^{\mathsf{TRec}_{\mathsf{Block}(\ell, m_1)}(\pi, \cdot, td, \cdot)}(st, ck_1, m_1)\}$$

for $(\pi, td) \leftarrow \mathsf{TPG}(1^\kappa)$, and $(st, \ell, x_0, x_1) \leftarrow \mathcal{A}_1^{\mathsf{TRec}(\pi, \cdot, td, \cdot)}(\pi)$ s.t. $x_0, x_1 \notin \mathcal{L}$, $(ck_b, m_b) \leftarrow \mathsf{Snd}(\pi, \ell, x_b)$ for $b \in \{0, 1\}$, and oracle $\mathsf{TRec}_{\mathsf{Block}(\ell, m)}(\pi, \cdot, td, \cdot)$ acts as in the definition of simulation soundness above.

Note on Statement Privacy: It may be surprising that we define statement privacy only for incorrect statements, $x_0, x_1 \notin \mathcal{L}$. Indeed, there are many ways to express the intuitive notion of statement privacy. We chose to state it only for statements $x_0, x_1 \notin \mathcal{L}$ but to allow the adversary to see both the sender's message m and the sender's local output ck, for $(ck, m) \leftarrow \mathsf{Snd}_{\pi, \ell}(x_b)$ for $b = 0, 1$. We could have instead allowed *any* adversarially chosen statements, including those in $\mathcal{L}$, but let the adversary see only the message m, and not the sender's local output ck. We cannot allow both because if the adversary chooses $(x_b, w_b) \in \mathcal{R}[\mathcal{L}]$ and then learns $(ck, m) \leftarrow \mathsf{Snd}_{\pi, \ell}(x_b)$, it can then run the receiver algorithm on (w_b, m) to test if it returns the same value ck. Our choice to restrict statements works better in the context of the higher-level saPAKE protocol of Sect. 4: Even though statement x used by the real-world sender party might be true (which is the case if the two parties have matching passwords), in the protocol simulation the statement is guaranteed to be false (the saPAKE simulator does not know any party's password when the protocol starts), and therefore the above statement privacy property suffices.

CKEM Security and Privacy Combined. The notion of simulation soundness and statement privacy can be combined into a single notion we call *simulatability*. Let $\mathsf{Snd}_{\pi, \ell}^{\mathsf{sim}}$ be the following simulator algorithm: $\mathsf{Snd}_{\pi, \ell}^{\mathsf{sim}}$ picks an arbitrary false statement $x' \notin \mathcal{L}$, computes $(ck, m) \leftarrow \mathsf{Snd}_{\pi, \ell}(x')$, picks $ck' \leftarrow_{\mathsf{R}} \{0, 1\}^\kappa$, and outputs (ck', m). We say that an implicit-statement CKEM is *simulatable* if for any efficient algorithm $\mathcal{A} = (\mathcal{A}_1, \mathcal{A}_2)$:

$$\{\mathcal{A}_2^{\mathsf{TRec}_{\mathsf{Block}(\ell, m)}(\pi, \cdot, td, \cdot)}(st, ck_0, m_0)\} \approx \{\mathcal{A}_2^{\mathsf{TRec}_{\mathsf{Block}(\ell, m')}(\pi, \cdot, td, \cdot)}(st, ck', m_1)\}$$

for $(\pi, td) \leftarrow \mathsf{TPG}(1^\kappa)$, and $(st, \ell, x) \leftarrow \mathcal{A}_1^{\mathsf{TRec}(\pi, \cdot, td, \cdot)}(\pi)$ s.t. $x \notin \mathcal{L}$, $(ck_0, m_0) \leftarrow \mathsf{Snd}_{\pi, \ell}(x)$ and $(ck', m_1) \leftarrow \mathsf{Snd}_{\pi, \ell}^{\mathsf{sim}}$.

Lemma 1. *An Implicit-statement CKEM is simulatable if and only if it is simulation sound and statement private.*

Proof Sketch: Simulatability implies simulation soundness because $\mathcal{A}_1$ can output $x_0 = x_1$. Simulatability also implies statement privacy, because if $(ck_0, m_0) \approx (\$, m_1)$, i.e., a distribution where the ck_1 part of (ck_1, m_1) is overwritten by a random string, and by simulation soundness $(\$, m_1) \approx (ck_1, m_1)$, then $(ck_0, m_0) \approx (ck_1, m_1)$. For the opposite direction, since statement privacy implies $(ck_0, m_0) \approx (ck_1, m_1)$, and simulation soundness implies $(ck_1, m_1) \approx (\$, m_1)$, together they imply that $(ck_0, m_0) \approx (\$, m_1)$.

Relation to CCA Security and Privacy. We note that simulation soundness and statement privacy for CKEM are analogous to CCA-security and CCA-anonymity for public key KEM. If we view a statement as an encryption public key, and its witness as a private key, then the Snd procedure is analogous to public key KEM encryption and the Rec procedure is analogous to decryption. Moreover, the TRec procedure can be used by the simulator to implement access to the decryption oracle in the CCA security experiment: Recall that in the CCA security notion of KEM the adversary receives a challenge KEM ciphertext and must distinguish from random the KEM key encrypted in this ciphertext, given access to a decryption oracle which blocks the challenge ciphertext. The simulation soundness game follows the same structure, with the TRec$_{Block}$ oracle acting as the decryption oracle and the KEM message m playing the role of the ciphertext. The CCA anonymity KEM game is similar to the CCA security game, but with (key,ciphertext) challenge being generated on two randomly generated public keys. If the public keys are implemented as language statement, and if the language is a hard promise problem, i.e., if a random correct statement (=public key) cannot be distinguished from a random incorrect statement, then statement privacy implies CCA anonymity. Our notion of CKEM can be thus thought of as a generalization of CCA secure and anonymous PKE to CCA secure and anonymous *witness encryption* [18]. Indeed, the construction of simulation-sound CKEM from an SPHF in Sect. 2.1 below can be seen as a generalization of the Fujisaki-Okamoto transform [17] from IND PKE to CCA PKE.

2.1   Implicit-Statement CKEM Construction in ROM from SPHF's

We construct a non-interactive implicit-statement CKEM which is zero-knowledge, simulation sound, and statement private, for any language $\mathcal{L}$ which has a statement private Smooth Projective Hash Function (SPHF) [15]. Our construction, which is secure in the Random Oracle Model (ROM), is efficient: Its costs are as in the underlying SPHF plus, for the receiver, the cost of verifying that a projection key and a hash were computed correctly given the hash key. This verification can be done with a single multi-exponentiation using known batch signature verification techniques. We first describe the SPHF notion, and then show how to create a CKEM assuming an SPHF with the desired properties. We exemplify this generic construction in Sect. 5.1 for the case of language $\mathcal{L}$ used in our saPAKE construction.

Statement Private SPHF. We say that an algorithm tuple (Hash, PHash) is an SPHF for language $\mathcal{L} \subseteq \mathcal{U}$ (for $\mathcal{U}$ an implicit universe) if Hash on input a statement x outputs a *projection key* hp and a *hash value* v,[5] and PHash on input a witness w and hp outputs another hash value v'. Procedure Hash must be randomized and we will refer to its randomness as a *hash key* hk. Note that we assume that procedure PHash does not take a statement x as input, which is important for languages where one witness can correspond to many statements. Correctness requires that for all $(x, w) \in \mathcal{R}[\mathcal{L}]$, if $(v, hp) \leftarrow$ Hash(x) then $v \leftarrow$ PHash(w, hp). We will consider SPHF schemes that satisfy the statistical smoothness and statement privacy properties, defined as follows:

(I) Smoothness: For all $x \notin \mathcal{L}$

$$\{v, hp\}_{(v,hp) \leftarrow \mathsf{Hash}(x)} \stackrel{(s)}{\approx} \{v', hp\}_{(v,hp) \leftarrow \mathsf{Hash}(x), v' \leftarrow_{\mathrm{R}} \{0,1\}^\kappa}$$

(II) Statement Privacy: For all $x_0, x_1 \in \mathcal{U}$ close:

$$\{hp\}_{(v,hp) \leftarrow \mathsf{Hash}(x_0)} \stackrel{(s)}{\approx} \{hp\}_{(v,hp) \leftarrow \mathsf{Hash}(x_1)}$$

CKEM Construction. Let SPHF $=$ (Hash, PHash) be a statement private SPHF for $\mathcal{L}$, let $\mathsf{H}_0 : \{0,1\}^* \rightarrow (\{0,1\}^\kappa)^2$ and $\mathsf{H}_1 : \{0,1\}^* \rightarrow \{0,1\}^\kappa$ be hash functions, and let (E, D) be an indistinguishable symmetric encryption with κ-bit keys. Consider CKEM $=$ (PG, TPG, Snd, Rec, TRec) defined as follows:

- PG(1^κ) and TPG(1^κ) output descriptions of H_0 and H_1 as π. The trapdoor td output by TPG is access to the adversary's queries to random oracles $\mathsf{H}_0, \mathsf{H}_1$.
- Snd$_{\pi,\ell}(x)$:
  1. Generate $(v, hp) \leftarrow$ SPHF.Hash$(x; hk)$ for random hk;
  2. Compute $(ek, ck) \leftarrow \mathsf{H}_0(v)$, $e \leftarrow \mathsf{E}_{ek}(hk, x)$, and $\tau \leftarrow \mathsf{H}_1(v, hp, e, \ell)$;
  3. Output (ck, m) for $m = (hp, e, \tau)$.
- Rec$_{\pi,\ell}(w, m)$ for $m = (hp, e, \tau)$:
  1. Compute $v \leftarrow$ SPHF.PHash(w, hp);
  2. Compute $(ek, ck) \leftarrow \mathsf{H}_0(v)$, $(hk, x) \leftarrow \mathsf{D}_{ek}(e)$, and $\tau' \leftarrow \mathsf{H}_1(v, hp, e, \ell)$;
  3. Output (ck, x) if $\tau' = \tau$, $(v, hp) =$ SPHF.Hash$(x; hk)$, and $(x, w) \in \mathcal{R}[\mathcal{L}]$; Otherwise output $(ck, \perp)$ for $ck \leftarrow_{\mathrm{R}} \{0,1\}^\kappa$.
- TRec$_{\pi,\ell}(td, m)$ for $m = (hp, e, \tau)$:
  1. Among adversary's H_1 queries find $\tilde{v}$ s.t. $\tau = \mathsf{H}_1(\tilde{v}, hp, e, \ell)$; If none or more than one $\tilde{v}$ found, output $(ck, \perp)$ for $ck \leftarrow_{\mathrm{R}} \{0,1\}^\kappa$;
  2. If unique $\tilde{v}$ found, set $(ek, ck) \leftarrow \mathsf{H}_0(\tilde{v})$ and $(hk, x) \leftarrow \mathsf{D}_{ek}(e)$;
  3. Output (ck, x) if $(\tilde{v}, hp) =$ SPHF.Hash$(x; hk)$; Otherwise output $(ck, \perp)$ for $ck \leftarrow_{\mathrm{R}} \{0,1\}^\kappa$.

Theorem 1. *If* SPHF *is a smooth and statement private SPHF for $\mathcal{L}$ and* E *is an indistinguishable encryption, then the above is a zero-knowledge, simulation sound, and statement private implicit-statement CKEM for $\mathcal{L}$ in ROM.*

---

[5] Standard SPHF syntax uses two separate algorithms, KG $\rightarrow$ (hp, hk) and Hash$(x, hk) \rightarrow v$, which we combine for notational convenience in our context.

Due to limited space, we defer the full proof of Theorem 1 to the full version, and give a short sketch of the main arguments below.

Proof of Theorem 1 (Sketch). Correctness, statement verification, and parameter indistinguishability can be easily verified by inspection of the protocol. In particular, correctness follows directly from correctness of the SPHF and correctness of the encryption scheme E. Property (a) of statement verification holds because Rec checks if $(x, w) \in \mathcal{L}$, and property (b) holds because Rec picks a random ck when $x = \bot$. Finally, parameter indistinguishability holds trivially because PG and TPG generate public parameters in an identical way.

Statement recovery holds because a sender message commits to values (hp, e, τ) via the random oracle, and TRec, given access to the RO table, can then deterministically compute the statement x. In particular, the sender sets $\tau = H_1(v, hp, e, \ell)$, where v is the SPHF value, so TRec will find v in the RO table except with the negligible probability of a collision in H_1. If v is found, then TRec will get the same statement x from $D_{ek}(e)$ by correctness of the symmetric encryption, as the key ek is deterministically computed by $H_0(v)$.

Zero-knowledge follows from the correctness of the underlying SPHF scheme. Recall that zero-knowledge requires, essentially, that no efficient adversary can distinguish between the outputs of Rec and TRec for valid (statement,witness) pairs. We give an intuitive argument as to why this is the case. In our construction, as long as Rec and TRec find the same SPHF hash key v that was used to generate the message m, they will end up with the same statement x, which will lead to identical outputs (if the message is invalid, i.e., not computed by Snd, this also will be detected). A challenge is then in showing that Rec and TRec do indeed find the same SPHF hash value v. Intuitively, this is the case because the adversary commits to message elements hp and e along with hash value v via the random oracle hash H_1. Because of this commitment, TRec will find the hash value v in the random oracle table, and can check its validity through the call to SPHF.Hash. By SPHF correctness, if $(w, x) \in \mathcal{R}[\mathcal{L}]$, and hp is valid, then Rec's call to SPHF.PHash(w, hp) will produce the same hash value v. Rec checks both that $\mathcal{A}$ indeed committed to the hash value by checking if $\tau = H_1(v, hp, e, \ell)$, and checks the validity of the hash value through the call to SPHF.Hash. Rec also checks directly if $(x, w) \in \mathcal{R}[\mathcal{L}]$, which is not performed by TRec (since TRec has no witness w), but it is performed in the ZK experiment by the wrapper Wrap$_w$ over the (ck, x) output of TRec. The full proof captures the above in a sequence of game changes showing that adversary's interactions with the Rec and the (wrapped) TRec procedures are indistinguishable.

By Lemma 1, simulation soundness and statement privacy follow from the *simulatability* property that captures them both. Simulatability of our CKEM construction follows from the smoothness and statement privacy of the underlying SPHF scheme, and the indistinguishability of the symmetric encryption scheme. Simulatability requires that no efficient adversary can distinguish between the real output (key, message) from Snd on input x_0, and a pair (random key, message) where the message is from Snd on input x_1, even in the presence of a trapdoor receiver oracle. Because the CKEM key is computed as the hash of the SPHF hash value v, we know that the CKEM key will appear random as long as the hash value is not known. SPHF smoothness gives us that hash values v computed from SPHF.Hash$(x; hk)$ on $x \notin \mathcal{L}$ appear random and independent of projection keys hp as long as key hk used in this hash remains secret. However, an encryption of the randomness hk used to generate v is provided to the adversary, and the encryption key is in turn created from $H_0(v)$. This is a circular encryption, but in the random oracle model we avoid this circularity by first assuming that the adversary does not query either H_1 on v, which means that the encryption key appears random, which in turn means, by indistinguishability of E, that the ciphertext e does not reveal anything about hk. Further, if the adversary also does not query H_1 on v, then the tag τ appears random as well. At this point, we can safely invoke the SPHF smoothness property to say that v appears random and independent of hp, and the probability of querying either random oracle on v is then negligible. Finally, we use SPHF statement privacy, which gives us that projection keys hp_0, hp_1 are indistinguishable if created via Hash on two different statements not in the language $\mathcal{L}$, to show that we may always create the projection key with x_1 without being detected.   □

3 Security of a Password File Against Dictionary Attacks

In a strong asymmetric PAKE protocol, the salted function F used to hash a password must be a *one-way* function. However, not all one-way functions will work: To use the Encryption+SPHF approach to UC PAKE construction F needs to have an arithmetic structure that admits an efficient SPHF for the authentication protocol. Unfortunately, an arithmetic structure makes it harder to characterize F's resistance to brute-force attacks, i.e., to lower-bound the computational complexity of finding pw given $(s, F_s(pw))$ where s is a random salt and pw is sampled from a polynomial-size "password dictionary" set D.

To quantify post-compromise resistance of a password file to brute-force attacks, Benhamouda and Pointcheval introduced the notion of *tight one-wayness* [7], which we will adapt to the case where the one-way function is *salted*, i.e., randomized, as is necessary in an saPAKE, and we propose to model the resulting *Strong* Tight One-Way Function (STOWF) notion with a UC functionality. We explain why some STOWF candidates do not work for our purposes, we propose a new STOWF candidate, an SPHF-friendly function that uses the Boneh-Boyen signature [9] with the hashed password as a key and the salt as a signed message, and we show that this function realizes the $\mathcal{F}_{\mathsf{STOWF}}$ functionality in the *programmable* Generic Group Model (GGM) and the Random Oracle Model.

While it seems unavoidable to use GGM to analyze the fine-grained hardness of an algebraic salted one-way function F_s, we do not rely on GGM in the security analysis of the saPAKE protocol that uses $(s, F_s(pw))$ as the password file. Abstracting the one-wayness property as a UC functionality $\mathcal{F}_{\mathsf{STOWF}}$ helps keep this argument modular, and in Sect. 4 we show an saPAKE protocol that realizes the ideal saPAKE functionality given *any* realization of $\mathcal{F}_{\mathsf{STOWF}}$ which satisfies some additional properties which we explain below.

Modeling the Password File with *Salted* Tight One-Way Function.
Since we assume that passwords come from a polynomial-sized dictionary, the
adversary can learn the correct password by computing $F(pw)$ for all passwords
pw in the dictionary. More precisely, if the argument pw is known to come from
some domain subset D then given $z = f(pw)$ an algorithm that evaluates F on
any fraction ϵ of D will find pw with probability ϵ. This sets an upper bound
on the hardness for the problem of inverting F on a subdomain, and we call F
a *tight one-way function* (TOWF) [7] if this is also the lower bound, i.e., if for
any polynomial-size subset D of the domain of F any algorithm which runs in
time $\epsilon \cdot |D|$ has at most ϵ probability of inverting $F(x)$ for $x \leftarrow_{\mathrm{R}} D$. For example,
this holds if function F is a random oracle. On the other hand, any additional
structure in the one-way function might make it not tight. For example, if F
is additively homomorphic, e.g. $F(x) = g^x$ where g generates a multiplicative
group, and D is an integer interval, then the Baby-Step Giant-Step algorithm
finds x given $F(x)$ in time $O(\sqrt{|D|})$ with probability 1.

The goal of a *strong* asymmetric PAKE is to further constrain the adversary
so that an ϵ-advantage attacker must perform $\epsilon \cdot |D|$ computation *after* server
compromise. This means that the password file must be created by a random-
ized, a.k.a. *salted*, one-way function. Let $\{F_s\}_{s \in R}$ be a family of functions that
share the same domain and range and are indexed by values s we call *salt*.
Informally, we call $\{F_s\}$ a family of *salted tight one-way functions* (STOWF)
if for any domain subset $D \subseteq X$ it holds that any efficient algorithm $\mathcal{A}$ that
has ϵ probability of computing $F_s^{-1}(z)$ given $(s, z) = (s, F_s(x))$ for $s \leftarrow_{\mathrm{R}} R$ and
$x \leftarrow_{\mathrm{R}} D$, must perform at least $\epsilon \cdot |D|$ computation *after* receiving (s, z) as an
input. In other words, no efficient pre-computation can help the adversary to
avoid the *post-compromise* cost $\Omega(|D|)$ to recover pw given the compromised
server password file $(s, F_s(pw))$ if $(s, pw) \leftarrow_{\mathrm{R}} R \times D$.

Formally, STOWF is defined by a pair of efficient algorithms $(\mathsf{PG}, \mathsf{Eval})$ where
(1) $\mathsf{PG}(1^\kappa)$ outputs a description of a function family F, with domain X, salt
domain R, and range Y, such that $F_s : X \rightarrow Y$ for every $s \in R$, and (2)
algorithm Eval evaluates $F_s(x)$ given $(s, x) \in R \times X$ and the description of F.

Examples of Salted Tight One-Way Functions. In the Password-over-TLS
authentication used on the web today the server-held password file is (s, z) for
$z = F_s(pw) = \mathsf{H}(s, pw)$, and to authenticate the client sends password pw'
over the server-to-client PKI-authenticated TLS session and the server accepts
if $\mathsf{H}(s, pw') = z$. This method enforces the STOWF lower bound if H is a random
oracle: If $|s| = \Omega(\kappa)$ then regardless of any (efficient) pre-computation the adver-
sary can recover the client's password only by computing $\mathsf{H}(s, x)$ for $x \in D$ after
server compromise. However, a plain random oracle has no arithmetic structure,
so it is not clear how to use it as a STOWF in an saPAKE protocol.

The recently proposed PKI-free saPAKE scheme OPAQUE [23] gives a different example of a tight STOWF. The syntax differs slightly, as the password
file is $(s, F_{s,r}(pw))$ where r is an additional randomness needed to evaluate F,
but the crux of the scheme is that s is implemented as a key k of an Obliv-

ious PRF (OPRF) function F^*, and $F_{s,r}(pw)$ includes public keys pk_C and pk_S for the client and the server, the private key sk_S for the server, and a ciphertext $c \leftarrow \mathsf{E}_{rw}(sk_C)$ which encrypts the client private key sk_C under key $rw = F_k^*(pw)$ (see [23] for details). To authenticate, the client computes rw via an OPRF instance with the server on resp. inputs pw and k, decrypts sk_C from c, and the two parties run a standard AKE using resp. keys sk_C and sk_S. The STOWF bound is enforced because from a server compromise the attacker learns (k, c) and needs to compute $sk_C = \mathsf{D}_{rw}(c)$ for $rw = F_k^*(pw)$. The strong UC OPRF properties [22], realizable efficiently in ROM, imply that F^* is pseudorandom even if one holds key k, hence the only strategy for finding pw (and sk_C) given (k, c) is to evaluate F_k^* on guesses pw' and verify if $sk_C' = \mathsf{D}_{rw'}(c)$ for $rw' = F_k^*(pw')$ corresponds to pk_C.

A natural SPHF-friendly STOWF candidate is $F_s(pw) = s^{\mathsf{H}(pw)}$ where $s \leftarrow_\mathrm{R} \mathbb{G}$, where $\mathbb{G}$ is a cyclic group in which the discrete logarithm problem is hard, and H is an RO hash onto $\mathbb{Z}_p$. Using this function, we could create an authentication protocol based on an efficient SPHF scheme for the language that server-held value $z = s^{\mathsf{H}(pw)}$ and client's extractable password commitment $c = (g^r, y^r g^{\mathsf{H}(pw')})$ for $g, y \in \mathbb{G}$ are of the correct form, and indeed [7] construct their aPAKE based on this STOWF candidate along these lines. This function realizes the UC STOWF functionality we define below in GGM, and the proof is a straightforward adaptation of the proof that it satisfies a game-based TOWF property given in [7]. However, this function is *malleable* in the following sense: Given (s, z) for $z = F_s(pw)$, it is easy to create (s', z') for $z' = F_{s'}(pw)$ and $s' \neq s$, by computing $s' = s^r$ and $z' = z^r$ for any r. This creates a problem for UC security of saPAKE: An adversary who learns (s, z) via server compromise can impersonate the server using a randomized file (s', z') without learning pw via an offline attack, but the UC simulator cannot detect that such impersonation attacks because if (s, z) is an STOWF challenge and an adversary does not stage an offline attack then the simulator does not know the trapdoor $\mathsf{H}(pw) = \mathsf{DL}(s, z)$ needed to recognize (s, z, s', z') as DDH tuples. One can prove UC security of a protocol based on this STOWF function but the proof would use GGM in the online part, whereas we hope to use GGM only to analyze the tightness of F against offline computation, and not involve it in the analysis of the online protocol.[6]

Boneh-Boyen Function: SPHF-Friendly and *Unforgeable* STOWF. Fortunately, we can avoid GGM in the security proof of saPAKE based on UC secure STOWF by using the *hashed* Boneh-Boyen (BB) function $F_s(x) = g^{1/(s+\mathsf{H}(x))}$ [9] as the STOWF candidate, where $s \leftarrow_\mathrm{R} \mathbb{Z}_p$ and H hashes onto $\mathbb{Z}_p$. We also define another STOWF candidate we call *unhashed* BB function, $f_s(x) = g^{1/(s+x)}$, which can be used to define F as $F_s(x) = f_s(\mathsf{H}(x))$. The reason for introducing the unhashed BB function f is that the saPAKE security proof will rely on the STOWF candidate f satisfying some additional properties

---

[6] Similar approach was taken by [7] who contain both GGM and ROM to the offline part of analysis, while we contain GGM to the offline part but use ROM throughout.

we define below, but it will implement the password file as $(s, f_s(\mathsf{H}(pw))$. If f is instantiated as the *unhashed* BB then the saPAKE protocol effectively uses the *hashed* BB function for its password file. This will in particular imply that we can rely on the offline-hardness of STOWF F while also benefitting of the algebraic properties of f.

UC Model for Salted Tight One-Way Function. We propose a UC functionality $\mathcal{F}_{\mathsf{STOWF}}$, shown in Fig. 1, to model the offline security of the password file in an ideal saPAKE scheme, i.e., the potential leakage of the password file via server compromise and the offline dictionary attack possible after this leakage. If a function realizes this UC functionality then for every efficient real-world adversary $\mathcal{A}$ there exists an efficient ideal-world adversary (simulator) SIM, such that $\mathcal{A}$'s offline computation can be simulated by SIM on access to $\mathcal{F}_{\mathsf{STOWF}}$, which essentially implements an ideal black-box point function, namely a function which outputs 1 for $x = pw$ and 0 for all $x \neq pw$.

Leak Function Value

- On (FVal, sid, x) from S: Store (sid, x) and send $(\mathsf{FVal}, sid, \mathsf{S})$ to $\mathcal{A}$.

Offline Test Evaluation

- On $(\mathsf{OfflineEval}, sid, x')$ from $\mathcal{A}$: If there is a record (sid, x) return "correct guess" if $x = x'$ and "wrong guess" otherwise.

Fig. 1. UC functionality $\mathcal{F}_{\mathsf{STOWF}}$ for Tight One-Way Function (STOWF)

Modification of the UC Framework. The standard UC framework applied to functionality $\mathcal{F}_{\mathsf{STOWF}}$ does not express all required properties of the STOWF function, because it does not impose a tight relation between the time complexity of $\mathcal{A}$ and SIM. For example, the unhashed Boneh-Boyen function F realizes $\mathcal{F}_{\mathsf{STOWF}}$ in (programmable) GGM, but if $\mathcal{A}$ makes T generic group model operations then SIM must be allowed to make $O(T^2)$ queries to $\mathcal{F}_{\mathsf{STOWF}}$, which means that $\mathcal{A}$ can test $|D|$ passwords using only $O(\sqrt{|D|})$ group operations, as is indeed possible if D is an integer interval. Using a hashed Boneh-Boyen function heals this problem by effectively changing D into a *random* subset of $\mathbb{Z}_p$, but we need to make an adjustment to the UC model so that it imposes a tight relation between the work of the real-world adversary $\mathcal{A}$ and the simulator SIM.

As pointed out in [20], in order for the UC (s)aPAKE model to enforce that the real-world adversary performs some minimal local computation to offline test each password, we need to change the UC framework slightly, so that both the local computation of the real-world adversary and the OfflineTestPwd messages of the simulator are accounted for by the environment. For example, when the real-world adversary performs some local computation which corresponds to an offline password verification, e.g. a random oracle query or a generic group model query, this idealized computational element would send a special "flag" signal to the environment. In the ideal world, the same flag would be sent to the environment whenever $\mathcal{F}_{\mathsf{STOWF}}$ receives an OfflineTestPwd query from the simulator. (In the context of $\mathcal{F}_{\mathsf{STOWF}}$ such flag will be sent on every OfflineEval message from the ideal-world adversary.) If the environment's view of the ideal-world and the real-world executions are indistinguishable in such regime this would prevent the simulator from sending OfflineTestPwd messages to the functionality without an offline attack taking place in the real world.[7]

The necessity of such modification to the UC framework was also observed by [23] in the context of saPAKE, because otherwise $\mathcal{F}_{\mathsf{aPAKE}}$ and $\mathcal{F}_{\mathsf{saPAKE}}$ would be equivalent. The only difference between aPAKE and saPAKE is that OfflineTestPwd queries are allowed in saPAKE only *after* the adversary compromises the server. However, if the timing of the local computation of the real-world adversary and the simulator's OfflineTestPwd queries is not observed by the environment, then the simulator may accumulate all the offline password tests made by the real-world adversary before server compromise, and then send all the OfflineTestPwd queries these password tests represented right after server compromise, effectively bypassing the intended enforcement of no pre-computation of offline dictionary queries in the real-world.

Additional STOWF Properties. For the saPAKE application we need to extend the STOWF notion with a secondary "leakage function" $\hat{F}$, because in the saPAKE protocol of Sect. 4 the client will commit not to the (hashed) password itself but to another algebraic function of it, which enables both straight-line extraction of the committed password and an efficient SPHF that the committed password is the pre-image of the STOWF function value stored by the server. Formally, we extend the STOWF syntax to a triple of algorithms (PG, Eval, Leak), where PG and Eval are as before except PG also outputs a description of a leakage function $\hat{F}$ with domain X and range $\hat{Y}$ such that $\hat{F} : X \to \hat{Y}$, and (2) algorithm Leak evaluates $\hat{F}(x)$ given $x \in X$ and the description of $\hat{F}$. When it is unambiguous, we will use the shorthand (PG, F, $\hat{F}$) to refer to a specific STOWF scheme.

We define the following three properties of an STOWF candidate. Since we will claim them only about the *unhashed* BB function f we will use notation (PG, f, $\hat{f}$) to specify the properties below:

(I) One-time unforgeability. An efficient adversary who gets the server's password file $(s, f_s(x))$ for *random* $x \leftarrow_{\mathrm{R}} X$ and $s \leftarrow_{\mathrm{R}} R$, must be unable to generate an alternate file (s', z') for $z' = f_{s'}(x)$ and $s' \neq s$, except with negligible probability.

(II) Leakage-function hiding. An efficient adversary who gets the server's password file $(s, f_s(x))$ for *random* $x \leftarrow_{\mathrm{R}} X$ and $s \leftarrow_{\mathrm{R}} R$, must be unable to output $\hat{f}(x)$, except with negligible probability.

(III) Collision resistance. For all $s \in R$, if $x_1 \neq x_2$ then $f_s(x_1) \neq f_s(x_2)$.

---

[7] In [20] the environment sends permissions to the real-or-ideal adversary rather than receiving signals about the computation performed, but the effect seems the same.

Security of Boneh-Boyen Function as STOWF. We consider both the unhashed and hashed Boneh-Boyen functions. The parameter generator $\mathsf{PG}(1^\kappa)$ for both functions fixes a prime-order cyclic group $(\mathbb{G}, p)$ two random group elements $g, g' \leftarrow_{\mathrm{R}} \mathbb{G}$, and the randomness domain is $R = \mathbb{Z}_p$. The unhashed BB function pair $(f, \hat{f})$ is defined on domain $X = \mathbb{Z}_p$ as $f_s(x) = g^{1/(s+x)}$ and $\hat{f}(x) = (g')^x$, while the hashed BB function pair $(F, \hat{F})$ is defined as $F_s(x) = f_s(\mathsf{H}(x))$ and $\hat{F}(x) = \hat{f}(\mathsf{H}(x))$ where $\mathsf{H} : \{0, 1\}^* \to \mathbb{Z}_p$.

We make the following claims about the unhashed and hashed Boneh-Boyen functions. Recall that the q-DDH assumption [10] says that given $(g, g^x, ..., g^{x^q})$ for $x \leftarrow_{\mathrm{R}} \mathbb{Z}_p$ no efficient algorithm can find $(c, g^{1/(x+c)})$ for any $c \in \mathbb{Z}_p$.

Theorem 2. *The unhashed Boneh-Boyen function f satisfies the properties of one-time unforgeability, leakage-function hiding, and collision resistance under the q-SDH assumption for $q = 2$.*

Proof (Sketch). Boneh-Boyen [10] show that a signature/MAC scheme $S_x(m) = g^{1/(x+m)}$ for key $x \leftarrow_{\mathrm{R}} \mathbb{Z}_p$ is unforgeable against chosen-message attack with q queries under the q-SDH assumption. Our one-time unforgeability notion is strictly weaker than this, because the adversary sees a signature $z = S_x(m)$ on only one randomly chosen message $m = s$. By a simple modification of Lemma 9 of [10] adapted to the setting where the challenger does not generate the public verification key, the BB function is one-time unforgeable under the q-SDH assumption for $q = 1$. Similarly, the leakage-function hiding property reduces to the 2-SDH assumption by a simple modification of the same reduction from one-time unforgeability of f to q-SDH. Finally, collision resistance holds for f because g is an element of group $\mathbb{G}$ of prime order p and division modulo p is a one-to-one function. (Formally, the domain of f_s must be restricted to exclude message value $x = -s \bmod p$.) □

Theorem 3. *The unhashed Boneh-Boyen STOWF function realizes UC functionality $\mathcal{F}_{\mathsf{STOWF}}$ in the (programmable) Generic Group Model (GGM) for $\mathbb{G}$, assuming that the i-th generic group operation made by the real-world adversary triggers i "offline password test computation" flags to the environment, which allows the simulator to issue a batch of i OfflineTestPwd queries to $\mathcal{F}_{\mathsf{STOWF}}$.*

Proof (Sketch). The proof of the above theorem, included in [13], is a straightforward generalization of the $O(T^2)$ bound on the number of discrete logarithm candidates which can be tested in GGM in T steps. Such lower-bound holds because the i-th generic group operation can test at most i new discrete logarithm candidates, limiting the total number of values tested in T steps to $\sum_{i=1}^{T}(i) = O(T^2)$. Moreover, in the programmable GGM the simulator can embed the result of OfflineTestPwd queries in the result of the generic group operation: The "correct guess" response implies that the new group element should collide with a specific previously computed element, while for the "wrong guess" the new group element representation is a fresh random string. □

Theorem 4. *The hashed Boneh-Boyen STOWF function realizes UC function-ality $\mathcal{F}_{STOWF}$ in the (programmable) Generic Group Model (GGM) for $\mathbb{G}$ and (non-programmable) ROM, assuming that each generic group operation made by the real-world adversary triggers $O(1)$ "offline password test computation" flags to the environment, which allows the simulator to issue a batch of (amortized) $O(1)$ OfflineTestPwd queries to $\mathcal{F}_{STOWF}$.*

Proof (Sketch). The proof is a modification of the proof of Theorem 3 utilizing a theorem shown by Schnorr [30], which shows that for a polynomial-sized subset D of *random* points in $\mathbb{Z}_p$, which we define as H outputs on values hashed by the real-world adversary, the generic group model algorithm must make $\Omega(|D|)$ operations to test if a discrete logarithm challenge is solved by the candidates in set D.[8]   □

4   Strong aPAKE from Implicit-Statement CKEM

We show the saPAKE protocol we propose in Fig. 2. The construction relies on several building blocks: (1) hash function $H : \{0,1\}^* \rightarrow \mathbb{Z}_p$ modeled as a random oracle; (2) zero-knowledge, simulation sound, and statement private implicit-statement CKEM scheme (PG, Snd, Rec) for language $\mathcal{L}$ described below; (3) one-time unforgeable, leakage-function hiding, and collision-resistant UC STOWF scheme (PG, f, $\hat{f}$); and (4) CPA-secure public key encryption scheme (KG, Enc, Dec) on message space $\hat{Y}$, the range of the leakage function $\hat{f}$. The common reference string (CRS) consists of a public key $pk \leftarrow KG(1^\kappa)$, CKEM parameters $\pi \leftarrow CKEM.PG(1^\kappa)$, and functions $(f, \hat{f})$ generated by STOWF generator $PG(1^\kappa)$.

The high-level idea of this construction is as follows. The server S's password file contains a random salt and salted hash (s, z) for $z = f_s(hw_S)$, where $hw_S = H(pw_S)$. To authenticate, client C encrypts its hashed password $hw_C = H(pw_C)$ under the public key pk from the CRS, and sends the resulting ciphertext c to S. Server S uses the CKEM scheme to form a key k_S and message m conditioned on the statement $x_S = (s, z, c)$ that c encrypts the same value hw as was used to form $z = f_s(hw)$. Client C uses hw_C and the randomness in c as its witness in the CKEM receiver procedure, which computes the key k_C. (The receiver algorithm also outputs the value x_C implicit in m, but this value is not used by the client.) The properties of CKEM guarantee that if x_C does not match C's witness then the client's key k_C will be random independent of the server's view, so S fails to authenticate to C. Likewise, if C doesn't have a witness for S's statement x_S for which S created this CKEM message, then the server's key k_S will be independent of the client's view, so C fails to authenticate to S.

---

[8] A variant of the theorem of Schnorr was also shown by Benhamouda-Pointcheval [7], but customized to n-bit passwords for $n < |p|/4$.

CKEM Language. The CKEM used in the saPAKE protocol saPAKE of Fig. 2 is defined as follows:

$$\mathcal{L}_{pk} = \{(s, z, c) \mid \exists\ (h, r) \text{ s.t. } z = f_s(h) \text{ and } c = \mathsf{Enc}_{pk}(\hat{f}(h); r)\} \quad (1)$$

Since key pk is part of a CRS, we will leave it as implicit and refer to $\mathcal{L}_{pk}$ as simply $\mathcal{L}$. Note that if function $\hat{f}$ is hard to invert then $\mathsf{Enc}_{pk}(\hat{f}(m))$ is not a standard encryption scheme, as there is no efficient decryption procedure. However, since it is used to encrypt a hashed password, i.e. $m = \mathsf{H}(pw)$, it still implements a commitment with straight-line extractor in ROM, which the simulator uses to extract the client's password in the proof of Theorem 5 below.

Public parameters:	**Password Registration (offline):**
Parameters $(pk, \pi, f, \hat{f})$ for	On $(\mathsf{StorePwdFile}, sid, \mathsf{C}, pw_\mathsf{S})$
$(pk, \cdot) \leftarrow \mathsf{KG}(1^\kappa)$,	$\mathtt{file}[sid] \leftarrow (s, z \leftarrow f_s(hw_\mathsf{S}))$
$\pi \leftarrow \mathsf{CKEM.PG}(1^\kappa)$,	for $hw_\mathsf{S} \leftarrow \mathsf{H}(pw_\mathsf{S})$
and $(f, \hat{f}) \leftarrow \mathsf{STOWF.PG}(1^\kappa)$	

Party C, on input		Party S, on input
$(\mathsf{CltSession}, sid, ssid, \mathsf{S}, pw_\mathsf{C})$:		$(\mathsf{SvrSession}, sid, ssid)$:
$\ell \leftarrow (sid, ssid)$		$\ell \leftarrow (sid, ssid)$
$hw_\mathsf{C} \leftarrow \mathsf{H}(pw_\mathsf{C})$		retrieve $\mathtt{file}[sid] = (s, z)$
$r \leftarrow_\mathsf{R} \{0,1\}^\kappa$		
$c \leftarrow \mathsf{Enc}_{pk}(\hat{f}(hw_\mathsf{C}); r)$	$\xrightarrow{(\mathsf{flow1}, sid, ssid, c)}$	
		$x_\mathsf{S} \leftarrow (s, z, c)$
	$\xleftarrow{(\mathsf{flow2}, sid, ssid, m)}$	$(k_\mathsf{S}, m) \leftarrow \mathsf{Snd}_{\pi, \ell}(x_\mathsf{S})$
$w \leftarrow (hw_\mathsf{C}, r)$		output k_S
$(k_\mathsf{C}, x_\mathsf{C}) \leftarrow \mathsf{Rec}_{\pi, \ell}(w, m)$		
output k_C		

Steal password file: On $\mathcal{A}$'s message $(\mathsf{StealPwdFile}, sid)$ send $\mathtt{file}[sid]$ to $\mathcal{A}$

Fig. 2. Strong aPAKE scheme saPAKE based on an implicit-statement CKEM

4.1 Security Analysis

We now show that saPAKE is a secure realization of functionality $\mathcal{F}_{\mathsf{saPAKE}}$, originally proposed by [23]. The formal security claim about protocol saPAKE is as follows:

Theorem 5. *The saPAKE protocol shown in Fig. 2 securely realizes functionality $\mathcal{F}_{\mathsf{saPAKE}}$ in ROM, provided that function f securely realizes functionality $\mathcal{F}_{\mathsf{STOWF}}$ and is (one-time) unforgeable, leakage-function hiding and collision-resistant, PKE is a CPA-secure public-key encryption, and CKEM is a zero-knowledge, simulatable CKEM for language $\mathcal{L}$.*

Public parameters: Parameters $(pk, \pi, f, \hat{f})$ and secret trapdoors (sk, td)
for $(pk, sk) \leftarrow \mathsf{KG}(1^\kappa)$, $(\pi, td) \leftarrow \mathsf{CKEM.TPG}(1^\kappa)$, and $(f, \hat{f}) \leftarrow \mathsf{STOWF.PG}(1^\kappa)$.
Assume that $\mathcal{Z}$ fixes $(sid, ssid)$ and $\ell = (sid, ssid)$, and that all flows contain $(sid, ssid)$.

$$\xleftarrow{\quad pw_{\mathsf{C}} \quad} \mathcal{Z} \xrightarrow{\quad pw_{\mathsf{S}} \quad}$$

$c \leftarrow \mathsf{Enc}_{pk}(\hat{y})$ for $\hat{y} \leftarrow_{\mathsf{R}} \hat{Y}$ $\quad\xrightarrow{\quad c \quad} \mathcal{A} \xrightarrow{\quad c' \quad}\quad$ if $c = c'$: **connect**
$\qquad\qquad\qquad\qquad\qquad\qquad\qquad\qquad\qquad\qquad d \leftarrow \mathsf{Dec}_{sk}(c')$
$\qquad\qquad\qquad\qquad\qquad\qquad\qquad\qquad\qquad\qquad$ find $(pw, h) \in \mathsf{T_H}$ s.t. $\hat{f}(h) = d$
$\qquad\qquad\qquad\qquad\qquad\qquad\qquad\qquad\qquad\qquad$ if none: $pw \leftarrow \bot$
$\qquad\qquad\qquad\qquad\qquad\qquad\qquad\qquad\qquad\qquad$ if more than one pw: abort
$\qquad\qquad\qquad\qquad\qquad\qquad\qquad\qquad\qquad\qquad$ send (TestPwd, S, pw) to $\mathcal{F}$
$\qquad\qquad\qquad\qquad\qquad\qquad\qquad\qquad\qquad\qquad$ if "correct": **compromise**
$\qquad\qquad\qquad\qquad\qquad\qquad\qquad\qquad\qquad\qquad$ if "wrong": **interrupt**
$\qquad\qquad\qquad\qquad\qquad\qquad\qquad\qquad\qquad\qquad$ **compromise** :
$\qquad\qquad\qquad\qquad\qquad\qquad\qquad\qquad\qquad\qquad\quad$ if no record (s, z):
$\qquad\qquad\qquad\qquad\qquad\qquad\qquad\qquad\qquad\qquad\qquad s \leftarrow_{\mathsf{R}} \mathbb{G};\ z \leftarrow f_s(h)$
$\qquad\qquad\qquad\qquad\qquad\qquad\qquad\qquad\qquad\qquad\qquad$ record (s, z)
$\qquad\qquad\qquad\qquad\qquad\qquad\qquad\qquad\qquad\qquad\quad (k_{\mathsf{S}}, m) \leftarrow \mathsf{Snd}_{\pi, \ell}(s, z, c')$
$\qquad\qquad\qquad\qquad\qquad\qquad\qquad\qquad\qquad\qquad$ **connect OR interrupt** :
$\qquad\qquad\qquad\qquad\qquad\qquad\qquad\qquad\qquad\qquad\quad (k_{\mathsf{S}}, m) \leftarrow \mathsf{Snd}^{\mathsf{sim}}_{\pi, \ell}$

if $(c', m') = (c, m)$: **connect** $\quad\xleftarrow{\ m'\ } \mathcal{A} \xleftarrow{\ m\ }\quad$ send (NewKey, S, k_{S}) to $\mathcal{F}$
$(\tilde{k}_{\mathsf{C}}, (\tilde{s}, \tilde{z}, \tilde{c})) \leftarrow \mathsf{TRec}_{\pi, \ell}(td, m')$
if S compromised $\wedge\ (\tilde{s}, \tilde{z}, \tilde{c}) = (s, z, c)$:
$\quad$ send Impersonate to $\mathcal{F}$,
$\quad$ if "correct": **compromise**; if "wrong": **interrupt**
find $(pw, h) \in \mathsf{T_H}$ s.t. $\tilde{z} = f_{\tilde{s}}(h)$
if none: $pw \leftarrow \bot$
if more than one pw: abort
send (TestPwd, C, pw) to $\mathcal{F}$;
if "correct": **compromise**; if "wrong": **interrupt**
compromise :
$\quad k_{\mathsf{C}} \leftarrow \tilde{k}_{\mathsf{C}}$
connect OR interrupt :
$\quad k_{\mathsf{C}} \leftarrow_{\mathsf{R}} \{0,1\}^\kappa$
send (NewKey, C, k_{C}) to $\mathcal{F}$

On $\mathcal{A}$'s message (StealPwdFile, sid), find record (s, z), if no such record found send pair
(s, z) outut by $\mathsf{SIM_{STOWF}}$ on (FVal, sid, C, S);
On query (OfflineEval, sid, h) from $\mathsf{SIM_{STOWF}}$, find $(pw', h) \in \mathsf{T_H}$. If none found, reply
"wrong guess", else send (OfflineTestPwd, sid, pw') to $\mathcal{F}$ and forward reply to $\mathsf{SIM_{STOWF}}$.

Fig. 3. Simulator alg. SIM for saPAKE interacting with $\mathcal{A}$, $\mathcal{F}$ and $\mathsf{SIM_{STOWF}}$

Due to space limits, we include here only the simulator for the protocol and the quick overview of the proof ideas, deferring the full proof of the theorem to the full version of this paper [13]. To prove Theorem 5, we construct a simulator SIM, shown in Fig. 3, s.t. that for any efficient environment $\mathcal{Z}$ and adversary $\mathcal{A}$, the environment's view of the real-world execution, where adversary $\mathcal{A}$ interacts with the honest parties that execute protocol saPAKE, is indistinguishable from its view of the ideal-world execution, where simulator SIM (which uses $\mathcal{A}$ as an oracle) interacts with the ideal-world honest parties via the ideal functionality $\mathcal{F}_{\mathsf{saPAKE}}$. Without loss of generality, we assume that $\mathcal{A}$ is a "dummy" adversary who merely passes all messages between $\mathcal{Z}$ and SIM. In the description of the simulator in Fig. 3 we shorten $\mathcal{F}_{\mathsf{saPAKE}}$ as $\mathcal{F}$. Note that because by assumption function f securely realizes functionality $\mathcal{F}_{\mathsf{STOWF}}$, there exists a simulator $\mathsf{SIM}_{\mathsf{STOWF}}$ such that no efficient environment can distinguish between interacting with the real STOWF protocol and with $\mathsf{SIM}_{\mathsf{STOWF}}$ and $\mathcal{F}_{\mathsf{STOWF}}$. The saPAKE protocol simulator SIM shown in Fig. 3 uses this $\mathsf{SIM}_{\mathsf{STOWF}}$ as a black box. It also uses the CKEM sender simulator algorithm $\mathsf{Snd}^{\mathsf{sim}}$ defined for Lemma 1 in Sect. 2.

Proof Overview. The proof uses a sequence of games, starting from the real world and ending at the ideal world. The first step is to let the game abort if there is a collision in H, or H outputs 0. Then consider the case that $\mathcal{A}$ merely passes all messages between C and S: if C and S use the same password then they output the same key, otherwise C outputs an independent random key. The resultant game is indistinguishable to the previous one due to CKEM correctness and statement verification. Then according to the zero-knowledge property of CKEM, we modify the client-side code so that it computes k_C with the trapdoor receiver TRec and trapdoor td instead of the standard receiver Rec and witness w, and then performs a check that the client's statement is in the language. Now the witness $w = (hw_C, r)$ and the secret key sk are not used in the game, so we change client's ciphertext to a "dummy" one $c \leftarrow \mathsf{Enc}_{pk}(\hat{y})$ for $\hat{y} \leftarrow_{\mathrm{R}} \hat{Y}$. After that, in the case that (1) the ciphertext sent to S, c', is new and invalid, or (2) $c' = c$, we let S output a random key k_S and send a "dummy" message m on a fixed false statement x'; this move can be made due to CKEM simulatability. Then we let C detect server impersonation and extract password guess, i.e., (1) if S is compromised, and $(\tilde{s}, \tilde{z}, \tilde{c}) = (s, z, c)$, or (2) if there is a pw s.t. $\tilde{z} = f_{\tilde{s}}(\mathsf{H}(pw))$, k_C is decided according to whether $pw_C = pw_S$. Then we remove the query $\mathsf{H}(pw_C)$ from the client-side code, and postpone the $\mathsf{H}(pw_S)$ query until server compromise. Finally, when $\mathcal{A}$ compromises S, invoke $\mathsf{SIM}_{\mathsf{STOWF}}$ to simulate $\mathcal{A}$'s view in offline password tests.

5   Efficient Instantiation of Strong aPAKE

The efficiency of the generic saPAKE construction in Fig. 2 depends on the choices of the salted tight one-way function (STOWF), the encryption scheme, and a CKEM. A particularly efficient instantiation of this framework, protocol saPAKE-BB shown in Fig. 4, results from implementing the STOWF scheme $(\mathsf{PG}, f, \hat{f})$ as the unhashed Boneh-Boyen function $f_s(x) = g^{1/(s+x)}$ for $s \leftarrow_{\mathrm{R}} \mathbb{Z}_p$ and $\hat{f}(x) = (g')^x$ for $g, g' \leftarrow_{\mathrm{R}} \mathbb{G}$ (see Sect. 3). Since in the generic protocol in Fig. 2 function f is evaluated on hashed password $hw \leftarrow \mathsf{H}(pw)$, the server's password file (s, z) in protocol saPAKE-BB is effectively computed using the *hashed* Boneh-Boyen function, i.e. $z = f_s(\mathsf{H}(pw)) = g^{1/(s+\mathsf{H}(pw))}$. PKE Enc is instantiated as ElGamal, i.e. $\mathsf{Enc}_{pk}(m; r) = (c, d) = (g^r, y^r \cdot m)$ where $pk = y$ for $y \leftarrow_{\mathrm{R}} \mathbb{G}$, and CKEM is implemented using the SPHF-based CKEM construction of Sect. 2.1 instantiated for a language defined in Eq. (2) below.

Public parameters: Prime-order cyclic group $(\mathbb{G}, p)$, random group elements $g, g', y \leftarrow_R \mathbb{G}$; hash functions H, H_0, H_1 onto resp. $\mathbb{Z}_p$, $(\{0,1\}^\kappa)^2$, and $\{0,1\}^\kappa$.	**Password Registration (offline):** On $(\text{StorePwdFile}, sid, C, pw_S)$ $\text{file}[sid] \leftarrow (s, z \leftarrow g^{1/(s+hw_S)})$ for $s \leftarrow_R \mathbb{Z}_p$ and $hw_S \leftarrow H(pw_S)$.

Party C, on input
$(\text{CltSession}, sid, ssid, S, pw_C)$:

$\ell \leftarrow (sid, ssid)$
$hw_C \leftarrow H(pw_C)$
$r \leftarrow_R \mathbb{Z}_p$
$(c, d) \leftarrow (g^r, y^r (g')^{hw_C})$

$\xrightarrow{\quad (c,d) \quad}$

Party S, on input
$(\text{SvrSession}, sid, ssid)$:

$\ell \leftarrow (sid, ssid)$
retrieve $(s, z) \leftarrow \text{file}[sid]$

$hk \leftarrow (\alpha, \beta, \gamma) \leftarrow_R \mathbb{Z}_p^3$
$(v, hp_1, hp_2) \leftarrow ((gz^{-s})^\alpha c^\beta d^\gamma, z^\alpha (g')^\gamma, g^\beta y^\gamma)$
$hp \leftarrow (hp_1, hp_2); \ x_S \leftarrow (s, z, c, d)$
$(ek, k_S) \leftarrow H_0(v); \ e \leftarrow E_{ek}(hk, x_S)$
$\tau \leftarrow H_1(v, hp, e, \ell)$
output k_S

$\xleftarrow{\quad (hp, e, \tau) \quad}$

$v \leftarrow hp_1^{hw_C} \cdot hp_2^r$ where
$(hp_1, hp_2) \leftarrow hp$
$(ek, k_C) \leftarrow H_0(v)$
$((\alpha, \beta, \gamma), (s, z, c', d')) \leftarrow D_{ek}(e)$
$\tau' \leftarrow H_1(v, hp, e, \ell)$
output k_C if $\tau' = \tau$, $(c', d') = (c, d)$, $z = g^{\frac{1}{s+hw_C}}$,
    and $(v, hp_1, hp_2) = ((gz^{-s})^\alpha c^\beta d^\gamma, z^\alpha (g')^\gamma, g^\beta y^\gamma)$
otherwise output $k_C \leftarrow_R \{0,1\}^\kappa$

Steal password file: On $\mathcal{A}$'s message $(\text{StealPwdFile}, sid)$, send $\text{file}[sid]$ to $\mathcal{A}$

Fig. 4. saPAKE-BB: Instantiation of protocol saPAKE with Boneh-Boyen STOWF, ElGamal PKE, and SPHF-based CKEM

In the following two subsections we explain how the generic CKEM scheme of Sect. 2.1 is instantiated for a language implied by the above Enc and f_s choices, and then we discuss the implications of these choices to the efficiency of protocol saPAKE-BB.

5.1   Efficient CKEM for Commitment to STOWF Preimage

Since the CKEM construction of Sect. 2.1 is based on SPHF, it is efficient for language $\mathcal{L}_{pk}$ of "encryptions of a leakage function applied to the pre-image of a tight one-way function," defined in Eq. (1), if PKE Enc and STOWF $(f, \hat{f})$ are instantiated so that $\mathcal{L}_{pk}$ has an efficient SPHF. Recall that there are efficient SPHF's for "linear function" languages, i.e., languages whose relation can be expressed as

$$\mathcal{R}[\mathcal{L}] = \{(x, w) \text{ s.t. } x = (C, M) \text{ and } C = w \cdot M\}$$

where C, M are resp. vector and matrix of elements of $\mathbb{G}$, w is a vector of integers, and product $w \cdot M$ denotes an exponentiation, e.g. if $w = [\alpha_1, \ldots, \alpha_n]$ and $M = [g_1, \ldots, g_n]^T$ then $w \cdot M = \prod_{i=1}^{n} g_i^{\alpha_i}$. If C and M are resp. $1 \times m$ and $n \times m$ matrices in $\mathbb{G}$ then the following algorithms form an SPHF for $\mathcal{L}$:

Hash$(x; hk)$ for $x = (C, M)$ and $hk \leftarrow_{\text{R}} (\mathbb{Z}_p)^m$ outputs $(v, hp) = (C \cdot hk, M \cdot hk)$.
PHash(w, hp) outputs $v = w \cdot hp$.

Correctness follows because if $C = w \cdot M$ then $w \cdot hp = w \cdot (M \cdot hk) = (w \cdot M) \cdot hk = C \cdot hk$, smoothness because $(C, M) \notin \mathcal{L}$ if and only if C is not in the row span of M, in which case $v = C \cdot hk$ is independent of $hp = M \cdot hk$, and statement privacy holds if for every (C, M) in universe $\mathcal{U}$ matrix M has full row rank.

CKEM for ElGamal Encryption and Boneh-Boyen Function. If f_s, $\hat{f}$, and Enc are defined as $f_s(h) = g^{1/(s+h)}$, $\hat{f}(h) = (g')^h$, and $\text{Enc}_y(m; r) = (g^r, y^r m)$ then language $\mathcal{L}_{pk}$ in Eq. (1) is an example of a linear function language which admits an SPHF defined above. Note that if $z = g^{1/(s+h)}$ then $z^h = gz^{-s}$, and therefore in this instantiation language $\mathcal{L}_{pk}$ becomes:

$$\mathcal{L}_{pk} = \{(s, z, c, d) \mid \exists\, w = (h, r) \text{ s.t. } (gz^{-s}, c, d) = w \cdot \begin{bmatrix} z & 1 & g' \\ 1 & g & y \end{bmatrix} \} \tag{2}$$

Note on Shared Group Setting. Note that the Boneh-Boyen function parameters are $\pi = (\mathbb{G}, p, g, g')$ and the ElGamal public key is $pk = (\mathbb{G}, p, g, y)$. The two schemes share group setting $(\mathbb{G}, p)$, but note that prime-order groups are typically standardized and re-used across many cryptosystems. All group elements g, g', y in the CRS are chosen at random, because the unforgeability of the Boneh-Boyen function assumes that base g is a random group element and the leakage-function hiding property of STOWF assumes that base g' is another random group element. Note that while typically ElGamal encryption is defined for a fixed group generator g, under the DDH assumption on $\mathbb{G}$ it can also be instantiated with a random generator g.

Efficient CKEM for $\mathcal{L}_{pk}$. The generic CKEM construction of Sect. 2.1 instantiated with the linear-language SPHF for $\mathcal{L}_{pk}$ results in the following CKEM procedures (Snd, Rec) for $\pi = (\mathbb{G}, p, g, g', y)$, hash functions $\text{H}_0 : \{0,1\}^* \to (\{0,1\}^\kappa)^2$ and $\text{H}_1 : \{0,1\}^* \to \{0,1\}^\kappa$, and IND-SKE encryption scheme (E, D):

$\text{Snd}_\pi(\ell, x)$ for $x = (s, z, c, d)$:
  1. Set $(v, hp_1, hp_2) \leftarrow ((gz^{-s})^\alpha c^\beta d^\gamma, z^\alpha (g')^\gamma, g^\beta y^\gamma)$ for $(\alpha, \beta, \gamma) \leftarrow_{\text{R}} \mathbb{Z}_p^3$;
  2. Set $hp \leftarrow (hp_1, hp_2)$ and $hk \leftarrow (\alpha, \beta, \gamma)$;
  3. Compute $(ek, ck) \leftarrow \text{H}_0(v)$, $e \leftarrow \text{E}_{ek}(hk, x)$, and $\tau \leftarrow \text{H}_1(v, hp, e, \ell)$;
  4. Output (ck, m) for $m = (hp, e, \tau)$.

$\text{Rec}_\pi(\ell, w, m)$ for $w = (h, r)$ and $m = (hp, e, \tau)$:
  1. Compute $v \leftarrow hp_1^h \cdot hp_2^r$ where $hp = (hp_1, hp_2)$;
  2. Set $(ek, ck) \leftarrow \text{H}_0(v)$, $(hk, x) \leftarrow \text{D}_{ek}(e)$;
  3. Parse $(\alpha, \beta, \gamma) \leftarrow hk$ and $(s, z, c, d) \leftarrow x$, and set $\tau' \leftarrow \text{H}_1(v, hp, e, \ell)$;

4. Output (ck, x) if $\tau' = \tau$, $(v, hp_1, hp_2) = ((gz^{-s})^\alpha c^\beta d^\gamma, z^\alpha (g')^\gamma, g^\beta y^\gamma)$ and $(gz^{-s}, c, d) = (z^h, g^r, (g')^h y^r)$; Otherwise output $(ck, \perp)$ for $ck \leftarrow_R \{0, 1\}^\kappa$.

Note that Step 4 of Rec, which validates that $(v, hp) = \mathsf{Hash}_{pk}(x; hk)$ and $(x, w) \in \mathcal{R}[\mathcal{L}]$, involves a *verification* of six multiexponentiation equations, rather than their recomputation. Batch verification techniques, e.g. [2], allow this to be done with a single multi-exponentiation. However, using fixed-base exponentiations instead is likely to be more efficient, because when this CKEM is used in the context of the saPAKE-BB protocol shown in Fig. 4 the client who runs CKEM Rec algorithm already knows that elements (c, d) are formed correctly, and it will know the representation of (c, d) in bases (g, g', y). Likewise after verifying that $z = g^{(1/(s+h))}$ for $h = hw_C$, base z can be replaced by base g in the verification equations for (v, hp_1, hp_2), hence all these values can be verified by the client using at most 8 fixed-base exponentiations. (We note that these costs can be reduced further if some of the base elements g, g', y are combined, i.e. if g' is equated with either g or y, but we leave the verification of security of such variants to future work.)

5.2   Communication and Computation Costs of Protocol saPAKE-BB

Protocol saPAKE-BB uses only 2 message flows whose total bandwidth is 7 group elements and 2κ additional bits: c, d in flow1 and hp_1, hp_2 in flow2, as well as z, c, d encrypted in e and κ bits each in salt s and hash τ. It is easy to see, however, that (c, d) do not need to be included in the server's ciphertext e, and that they can intead be added to the inputs of hash τ. This optimized protocol would thus take 5 group elements plus 2κ bits, which e.g., on EC-224 comes to about $1120 + 320 = 1440$ bits.

The client's verification in the last step that $(v, hp_1, hp_2) = \mathsf{Hash}_{pk}(x; hk)$ and that statement (s, z, c', d') extracted from the CKEM message m corresponds to the client's witness (hw_C, r), can be implemented with a single multi-exponentiation, but as explained in the previous subsection, it can also be implemented with seven fixed-base exponentiation. The total computational cost will therefore be dominated by **1** variable-base multi-exps and **11** fixed-base exps for the client, and **2** variable base multi-exps and **2** fixed-base exps for the server.

References

1. Aiello, B., Ishai, Y., Reingold, O.: Priced oblivious transfer: how to sell digital goods. In: Pfitzmann, B. (ed.) EUROCRYPT 2001. LNCS, vol. 2045, pp. 119–135. Springer, Heidelberg (2001). https://doi.org/10.1007/3-540-44987-6_8
2. Bellare, M., Garay, J.A., Rabin, T.: Fast batch verification for modular exponentiation and digital signatures. In: Nyberg, K. (ed.) EUROCRYPT 1998. LNCS, vol. 1403, pp. 236–250. Springer, Heidelberg (1998). https://doi.org/10.1007/BFb0054130

3. Bellare, M., Pointcheval, D., Rogaway, P.: Authenticated key exchange secure against dictionary attacks. In: Preneel, B. (ed.) EUROCRYPT 2000. LNCS, vol. 1807, pp. 139–155. Springer, Heidelberg (2000). https://doi.org/10.1007/3-540-45539-6_11

4. Bellovin, S.M., Merritt, M.: Encrypted key exchange: password-based protocols secure against dictionary attacks. In: IEEE Symposium on Security and Privacy – S&P 1992, pp. 72–84. IEEE (1992)

5. Bellovin, S.M., Merritt, M.: Augmented encrypted key exchange: a password-based protocol secure against dictionary attacks and password file compromise. In: ACM Conference on Computer and Communications Security – CCS 1993, pp. 244–250. ACM (1993)

6. Benhamouda, F., Couteau, G., Pointcheval, D., Wee, H.: Implicit zero-knowledge arguments and applications to the malicious setting. In: Gennaro, R., Robshaw, M. (eds.) CRYPTO 2015. LNCS, vol. 9216, pp. 107–129. Springer, Heidelberg (2015). https://doi.org/10.1007/978-3-662-48000-7_6

7. Benhamouda, F., Pointcheval, D.: Verifier-based password-authenticated key exchange: new models and constructions. IACR Cryptology ePrint Archive 2013, 833 (2013)

8. Blake, I.F., Kolesnikov, V.: Strong conditional oblivious transfer and computing on intervals. In: Lee, P.J. (ed.) ASIACRYPT 2004. LNCS, vol. 3329, pp. 515–529. Springer, Heidelberg (2004). https://doi.org/10.1007/978-3-540-30539-2_36

9. Boneh, D., Boyen, X.: Efficient selective-ID secure identity-based encryption without random oracles. In: Cachin, C., Camenisch, J.L. (eds.) EUROCRYPT 2004. LNCS, vol. 3027, pp. 223–238. Springer, Heidelberg (2004). https://doi.org/10.1007/978-3-540-24676-3_14

10. Boneh, D., Boyen, X.: Short signatures without random oracles and the SDH assumption in bilinear groups. J. Cryptol. **21**(2), 149–177 (2008). https://doi.org/10.1007/s00145-007-9005-7

11. Boyko, V., MacKenzie, P., Patel, S.: Provably secure password-authenticated key exchange using Diffie-Hellman. In: Preneel, B. (ed.) EUROCRYPT 2000. LNCS, vol. 1807, pp. 156–171. Springer, Heidelberg (2000). https://doi.org/10.1007/3-540-45539-6_12

12. Bradley, T., Camenisch, J., Jarecki, S., Lehmann, A., Neven, G., Xu, J.: Password-authenticated public-key encryption. In: Deng, R.H., Gauthier-Umaña, V., Ochoa, M., Yung, M. (eds.) ACNS 2019. LNCS, vol. 11464, pp. 442–462. Springer, Cham (2019). https://doi.org/10.1007/978-3-030-21568-2_22

13. Bradley, T., Jarecki, S., Xu, J.: Strong asymmetric PAKE based on trapdoor CKEM. IACR Cryptology ePrint Archive (2019). https://eprint.iacr.org/2019/

14. Canetti, R., Halevi, S., Katz, J., Lindell, Y., MacKenzie, P.: Universally composable password-based key exchange. In: Cramer, R. (ed.) EUROCRYPT 2005. LNCS, vol. 3494, pp. 404–421. Springer, Heidelberg (2005). https://doi.org/10.1007/11426639_24

15. Cramer, R., Shoup, V.: Universal hash proofs and a paradigm for adaptive chosen ciphertext secure public-key encryption. In: Knudsen, L.R. (ed.) EUROCRYPT 2002. LNCS, vol. 2332, pp. 45–64. Springer, Heidelberg (2002). https://doi.org/10.1007/3-540-46035-7_4

16. Di Crescenzo, G., Ostrovsky, R., Rajagopalan, S.: Conditional oblivious transfer and timed-release encryption. In: Stern, J. (ed.) EUROCRYPT 1999. LNCS, vol. 1592, pp. 74–89. Springer, Heidelberg (1999). https://doi.org/10.1007/3-540-48910-X_6

17. Fujisaki, E., Okamoto, T.: Secure integration of asymmetric and symmetric encryption schemes. In: Wiener, M. (ed.) CRYPTO 1999. LNCS, vol. 1666, pp. 537–554. Springer, Heidelberg (1999). https://doi.org/10.1007/3-540-48405-1_34

18. Garg, S., Gentry, C., Sahai, A., Waters, B.: Witness encryption and its applications. In: ACM Conference on Computer and Communications Security – CCS 2013, pp. 467–476. ACM (2013)

19. Gennaro, R., Lindell, Y.: A framework for password-based authenticated key exchange. In: Biham, E. (ed.) EUROCRYPT 2003. LNCS, vol. 2656, pp. 524–543. Springer, Heidelberg (2003). https://doi.org/10.1007/3-540-39200-9_33

20. Gentry, C., MacKenzie, P., Ramzan, Z.: A method for making password-based key exchange resilient to server compromise. In: Dwork, C. (ed.) CRYPTO 2006. LNCS, vol. 4117, pp. 142–159. Springer, Heidelberg (2006). https://doi.org/10.1007/11818175_9

21. Hwang, J.Y., Jarecki, S., Kwon, T., Lee, J., Shin, J.S., Xu, J.: Round-reduced modular construction of asymmetric password-authenticated key exchange. In: Catalano, D., De Prisco, R. (eds.) SCN 2018. LNCS, vol. 11035, pp. 485–504. Springer, Cham (2018). https://doi.org/10.1007/978-3-319-98113-0_26

22. Jarecki, S., Kiayias, A., Krawczyk, H., Xu, J.: Highly-efficient and composable password-protected secret sharing (or: how to protect your bitcoin wallet online). In: IEEE European Symposium on Security and Privacy - EuroS&P 2016, pp. 276–291. IEEE (2016)

23. Jarecki, S., Krawczyk, H., Xu, J.: OPAQUE: an asymmetric PAKE protocol secure against pre-computation attacks. In: Nielsen, J.B., Rijmen, V. (eds.) EUROCRYPT 2018. LNCS, vol. 10822, pp. 456–486. Springer, Cham (2018). https://doi.org/10.1007/978-3-319-78372-7_15

24. Jarecki, S., Krawczyk, H., Xu, J.: OPAQUE: An asymmetric PAKE protocol secure against pre-computation attacks. IACR Cryptology ePrint Archive 2018, 163 (2018)

25. Jutla, C.S., Roy, A.: Smooth NIZK arguments. In: Beimel, A., Dziembowski, S. (eds.) TCC 2018. LNCS, vol. 11239, pp. 235–262. Springer, Cham (2018). https://doi.org/10.1007/978-3-030-03807-6_9

26. Katz, J., Ostrovsky, R., Yung, M.: Efficient password-authenticated key exchange using human-memorable passwords. In: Pfitzmann, B. (ed.) EUROCRYPT 2001. LNCS, vol. 2045, pp. 475–494. Springer, Heidelberg (2001). https://doi.org/10.1007/3-540-44987-6_29

27. Laur, S., Lipmaa, H.: A new protocol for conditional disclosure of secrets and its applications. In: Katz, J., Yung, M. (eds.) ACNS 2007. LNCS, vol. 4521, pp. 207–225. Springer, Heidelberg (2007). https://doi.org/10.1007/978-3-540-72738-5_14

28. MacKenzie, P.: More efficient password-authenticated key exchange. In: Naccache, D. (ed.) CT-RSA 2001. LNCS, vol. 2020, pp. 361–377. Springer, Heidelberg (2001). https://doi.org/10.1007/3-540-45353-9_27

29. MacKenzie, P., Patel, S., Swaminathan, R.: Password-authenticated key exchange based on RSA. In: Okamoto, T. (ed.) ASIACRYPT 2000. LNCS, vol. 1976, pp. 599–613. Springer, Heidelberg (2000). https://doi.org/10.1007/3-540-44448-3_46

30. Schnorr, C.P.: Small generic hardcore subsets for the discrete logarithm: short secret DL-keys. Inf. Process. Lett. **79**(2), 93–98 (2001)

Broadcast and Trace with N^ε Ciphertext Size from Standard Assumptions

Rishab Goyal[1($\boxtimes$)], Willy Quach[2($\boxtimes$)], Brent Waters[1,3], and Daniel Wichs[2]

[1] University of Texas at Austin, Austin, USA
goyal@utexas.edu, bwaters@cs.utexas.edu
[2] Northeastern University, Boston, USA
quach.w@husky.neu.edu, wichs@ccs.neu.edu
[3] NTT Research, Tokyo, Japan

Abstract. We construct a *broadcast and trace* scheme (also known as *trace and revoke* or *broadcast, trace and revoke*) with N users, where the ciphertext size can be made as low as $O(N^\varepsilon)$, for any arbitrarily small constant $\varepsilon > 0$. This improves on the prior best construction of broadcast and trace under standard assumptions by Boneh and Waters (CCS '06), which had ciphertext size $O(N^{1/2})$. While that construction relied on bilinear maps, ours uses a combination of the learning with errors (LWE) assumption and bilinear maps.

Recall that, in both *broadcast encryption* and *traitor-tracing* schemes, there is a collection of N users, each of which gets a different secret key sk_i. In broadcast encryption, it is possible to create ciphertexts targeted to a subset $S \subseteq [N]$ of the users such that only those users can decrypt it correctly. In a traitor tracing scheme, if a subset of users gets together and creates a decoder box D that is capable of decrypting ciphertexts, then it is possible to trace at least one of the users responsible for creating D. A broadcast and trace scheme intertwines the two properties, in a way that results in more than just their union. In particular, it ensures that if a decoder D is able to decrypt ciphertexts targeted toward a set S of users, then it should be possible to trace one of the users in the set S responsible for creating D, even if other users outside of S also participated. As of recently, we have essentially optimal broadcast encryption (Boneh, Gentry, Waters CRYPTO '05) under bilinear maps and traitor tracing (Goyal, Koppula, Waters STOC '18) under LWE, where the ciphertext size is at most poly-logarithmic in N. The main contribution of our paper is to carefully combine LWE and bilinear-map based components, and get them to interact with each other, to achieve broadcast and trace.

R. Goyal—Supported by IBM PhD Fellowship.
B. Waters—Supported by NSF CNS-1908611, CNS-1414082, DARPA SafeWare and Packard Foundation Fellowship.
D. Wichs—Research supported by NSF grants CNS-1314722, CNS-1413964, CNS-1750795 and the Alfred P. Sloan Research Fellowship.

A. Boldyreva and D. Micciancio (Eds.): CRYPTO 2019, LNCS 11694, pp. 826–855, 2019.
https://doi.org/10.1007/978-3-030-26954-8_27

1   Introduction

Broadcast Encryption. In *broadcast encryption*, as introduced by Fiat and Naor [FN94], a broadcaster can encrypt a message m to an arbitrary subset $S \subseteq [N]$ of indexed users, which results in a ciphertext ct. The i-th user is given a secret key sk_i and can decrypt the ciphertext ct iff $i \in S$. When designing broadcast encryption systems, a primary goal is to achieve short ciphertexts, ideally independent of the number of users N. (In order to decrypt, one must also know the description of S, but we count this separately from the ciphertext size.) Almost all of the earliest proposed solutions were not collusion resistant [FN94, Sti97, SVT98, GSW00, HS02, DF02, GST04], but in 2005 Boneh, Gentry and Waters [BGW05] gave a collusion-resistant system from bilinear maps with ciphertext size that is independent of N; in particular, ciphertexts consist of just three group elements.[1]

Traitor Tracing. A closely related primitive called *traitor tracing* was introduced by Chor, Fiat and Naor [CFN94]. Here, a broadcaster encrypts messages to the entire set of N users, where the i-th user is given a secret key sk_i that always decrypts the broadcaster's ciphertexts. If some subset $T \subseteq [N]$ of users ("traitors") gets together and pools their secret keys to produce a decoder algorithm D that can decrypt the broadcaster's ciphertexts, then there is a tracing procedure that can identify at least one of the users in the set T.[2] While earlier tracing systems [CFN94, SW98, CFNP00, SSW01, PST06] were not collusion resistant, Boneh, Sahai and Waters [BSW06] showed how to leverage bilinear maps to provide collusion resistant systems with $N^{\frac{1}{2}}$ sized ciphertexts. Very recently, Goyal, Koppula and Waters [GKW18] constructed a traitor tracing scheme with essentially optimal ciphertext size, which only scales poly-logarithmically in the number of users N, under the Learning with Errors (LWE) assumption.

Broadcast and Trace. The concepts of broadcast encryption and traitor tracing are naturally intertwined to form a *broadcast and trace* system [NP00, NNL01] (also known as a "trace and revoke" or "broadcast,trace and revoke" system). Here we want the ability to broadcast to an arbitrary set of users *and* the ability to trace any rogue decoding algorithm or box. However, the combination of broadcast and tracing security is more than just the sum of the parts – the two requirements interact with each other in a non-trivial way. In particular, the tracing property now also incorporates the broadcast set S as follows. If some subset T of users get together and construct a decoder algorithm D that can decrypt ciphertexts targeted to a certain set S, then there is a tracing procedure that can identify at least one of the users in $T \cap S$ that contributed to constructing D, even if some other users outside of S also participated. At that point one

---

[1] In a collusion-resistant system, there is no a-priori bound on the number of secret keys the adversary can see. Our discussion and comparisons will be in the collusion resistant setting.

[2] For both broadcast and traitor tracing, we require that the encryption procedure is public key. In traitor tracing, while some prior works also require that the tracing procedure is public key, here we consider secret-key tracing.

might take certain punitive actions against such a user and most likely remove them from the broadcast set S used in future encryptions.

The requirement that the tracing procedure identifies a user in the set $T \cap S$ rather than just any user in T is important here. For example, consider a scenario where a broadcast encryption scheme is used to encrypt messages to various subgroups within a company, and one of the board members colludes with an intern to publish a decoder that decrypts ciphertexts targeted to the set S of all board members. In this case, we want to trace the responsible board member and *not* just the intern. Alternately, even in setting involving a flat hierarchy where with no distinctions between different types of users (e.g., broadcasting cable TV), this requirement is important. Assume some user i publishes an illegal decoder D online, and then gets identified and revoked from the broadcast set S, causing D to stop working. But then a new traitor j colludes with i to publish a new decoder D' that is able to decrypt newly created ciphertexts for the new broadcast set S. In this case, we need to identify the *new* traitor j (and not just the old traitor i who is already known) so that we can also revoke j them from the broadcast set, and eventually revoke all misbehaving users through this process.

The requirement that the tracing procedure identifies a user in $T \cap S$ and not just T is also what makes the problem of achieving broadcast and trace more technically challenging than just tackling the problems of broadcast encryption and traitor tracing separately. Otherwise, one could trivially construct a broadcast and trace cryptosystem with a basic combination of a broadcast encryption and a traitor tracing, by secret sharing the message across the two systems.

Historically, progress on broadcast and trace has followed progress on the two problems separately. For example, soon after the construction of the first broadcast with optimally succinct ciphertexts [BGW05] and the first traitor tracing scheme with $N^{\frac{1}{2}}$ sized ciphertexts [BSW06], the work of Boneh and Waters [BW06] built upon these works to give a broadcast and trace system with $N^{\frac{1}{2}}$ sized ciphertexts by carefully combining techniques from the two bilinear map-based schemes. We also have essentially optimal constructions of broadcast and trace using (positional) witness encryption [GVW19], but we don't currently have any construction that beats the $N^{\frac{1}{2}}$ barrier under any standard assumptions. Very recently, we finally reached the point where we have essentially optimal ciphertext size in both broadcast and traitor tracing separately, and therefore the time is ripe to revisit the problem of constructing an optimal broadcast and trace system under standard assumptions. However, the optimal broadcast scheme [BGW05] is based on bilinear maps and the optimal traitor tracing scheme [GKW18] is based on LWE.[3] Can we still come up with a way to combine these different techniques to get an optimal broadcast and trace scheme? In particular, can we meaningfully combine bilinear-map and LWE based components and get them to interact with each other to get something beyond just the sum of the parts?

Our Results. In this work, we show how to combine bilinear-map and LWE based techniques to construct broadcast and trace.

---

[3] There are actually no known collusion resistant broadcast encryption schemes from LWE other than the trivial one with N-sized ciphertexts.

Theorem 1.1 (informal). *Under the Decisional Bilinear Diffie-Hellman Exponent (DBDHE) assumption and the Learning with Errors (LWE) assumptions, for any constant $\varepsilon > 0$, there exists a broadcast and trace scheme with ciphertext size $\widetilde{O}(N^\varepsilon)\mathsf{poly}(\lambda)$, where N is the number of users and λ is the security parameter.*

As a tool in our construction, we rely on a black-box use of *attribute-based encryption (ABE)* with *succinct ciphertexts*, whose size is essentially independent of the attribute size (the attribute is assumed to be known by the decryption procedure but is not counted in the ciphertext size). This can be seen as a generalization of broadcast encryption, which is a special case of succinct ABE where the attribute is S and keys sk_i are associated with policies that allow decryption iff $i \in S$. Currently, we can instantiate such succinct ABE schemes for $\mathbf{NC}^1$ circuits using bilinear maps [HLR10, ALDP11, AHL+12, YAHK14]. However we note that: (1) while the best current construction of succinct ABE relies on the DBDHE assumption, it is very conceivable that this could be improved to milder bilinear assumptions in future work, and (2) while current constructions only work for $\mathbf{NC}^1$ circuits, if we had a succinct ABE for even the slightly larger class of $\mathbf{TC}^1$ circuits, we could leverage it to get essentially optimal broadcast and trace with only a poly-logarithmic dependence on N. Therefore, we state the following more general result of our work, which shows that future advances in succinct ABE will also lead to advances in broadcast and trace:

Theorem 1.2 (informal). *Assuming the existence of ABE with succinct ciphertexts for $\mathbf{NC}^1$ and the LWE assumption, for any constant $\varepsilon > 0$, there exists a broadcast and trace scheme with ciphertext size $\widetilde{O}(N^\varepsilon)\mathsf{poly}(\lambda)$. Assuming the existence of ABE with succinct ciphertexts for $\mathbf{TC}^1$ and the LWE assumption, there exists a broadcast and trace scheme with ciphertext size $\mathsf{poly}(\log N, \lambda)$.*

Overall, picking a smaller constant ε yields shorter ciphertexts, at the cost of making both the secret keys bigger and the decryption time longer, with the exact tradeoff depending on the parameters of the underlying ABE.

Our main technique is to use a bilinear-based succinct ABE scheme for $\mathbf{NC}^1$ and use it to evaluate an LWE-based scheme, which we carefully engineer to be in $\mathbf{NC}^1$. This allows us to meaningfully combine the cryptographic properties of both schemes and achieve more than just their union. We provide a detailed technical overview below.

1.1   Technical Overview

We now give a technical overview of our result. We start by giving a high-level description of the state of the art construction of traitor tracing based on the works of [BSW06, GKW18, CVW+18a]. Then we discuss our approach to incorporate broadcast and get a broadcast and trace system. Concretely, we describe a 3-step construction of traitor tracing and then show how to augment each of the steps to also accommodate broadcast. Finally, we discuss the complications that arise in realizing the augmented steps and our solutions.

Traitor Tracing in Three Steps. The following is a high-level description of a 3-step approach to construct traitor-tracing based on the works of [BSW06, GKW18,CVW+18a].

Step 1: Traitor Tracing from PLBE. The first step is to construct traitor tracing from a conceptually simpler primitive called *private linear broadcast encryption* (PLBE) [BSW06]. A PLBE scheme is initialized with a master public key pk, a master secret key msk, and N user secret keys $sk_1, \ldots, sk_N$. There is a "public encryption" procedure which encrypts a message m under pk and guarantees that every user secret key sk_i will decrypt it correctly. There is also a "secret encryption" procedure which encrypts a message m under msk with respect to some index ind $\in [N+1]$ and guarantees that a user secret key sk_i will decrypt m correctly iff $i \geq$ ind. Moreover, one cannot distinguish a public encryption from a secret encryption or a secret encryption with one index ind versus another index ind$'$ unless one has a secret key sk_i that correctly decrypts in one case but not the other. Lastly, a secret encryption with the index ind $= N + 1$ should hide the message m even given all the secret keys. An important subtlety, discovered by [GKW18], is that these indistinguishability properties must hold even if the adversary is given a single arbitrary query to the secret encryption oracle, in addition to getting the challenge ciphertext.

A PLBE scheme can directly be used as a traitor tracing scheme, where the "secret encryption" procedure is used to implement the tracing algorithm. Assume some subset of users get together and create a decoder D that can correctly decrypt ciphertexts produced by the public encryption procedure. Then D should also correctly decrypt ciphertexts produced by the secret encryption procedure with index ind $= 1$ (since these are indistinguishable even given all the user secret keys). On the other hand the decoder cannot correctly decrypt ciphertexts produced by the secret encryption procedure with index ind $= N+1$ (since these are undecryptable even given all the user secret keys). Therefore there must be at least one index ind* where the decoder's probability of successful decryption drops significantly between being given secret encryptions with index ind* and ind$^* + 1$. But this can only be the case if the decoder was created with knowledge of sk_{ind^*} (since otherwise the two cases are indistinguishable). Therefore, this allows the tracing algorithm to finger user ind* as a traitor.[4]

Step 2: PLBE from ABE and mixed FE. The work of [GKW18] showed how to construct PLBE from two simpler primitives. The first primitive is a *(key-policy) attribute-based encryption (ABE)* [SW05] for circuits, which is already

---

[4] The above argument implicitly assumes that, if an adversary can create a decoder D that can distinguish between certain types of ciphertexts, then the adversary himself can also distinguish. As observed by [GKW18], this is more subtle than it appears and not true in general. The issue arises from a discrepancy between the decoder's advantage, which is calculated only over the choice of the encryption randomness after the keys have been fixed, and the advantage of the adversary, which is calculated also over the choice of the keys and randomness simultaneously. To make this step work, [GKW18] showed that one needs to start with a stronger form of PLBE security, where the adversary also gets one query to the secret encryption oracle.

known from LWE [GVW13]. The second primitive is a restricted form of functional encryption for the comparison function, called *mixed functional encryption (Mixed FE)*.

In Mixed FE, private keys sk_i are associated with values i and the adversary can collect an unrestricted number of such keys. There is a "secret encryption" algorithm which requires the master secret key and is used to encrypt an index ind. If a user with a secret key for input i decrypts a ciphertext encrypting an index ind, the output is 1 if $i \geq$ ind and 0 otherwise. Security says that, given an encryption of ind and many secret keys $\{\mathsf{sk}_i\}_{i \in T}$, the adversary does not learn anything about ind beyond the decryptions. Security must hold even if the attacker is also allowed to make 1 query to the secret encryption oracle, in addition to getting the challenge ciphertext. So far, the above can be thought of as a secret-key FE scheme for the comparison functions with security for unbounded number of keys and two ciphertexts, which can actually be constructed based only on one-way functions via garbled circuits [GVW12, KMUW18]. The additional property that makes mixed FE different, is that it also requires a public encryption algorithm, which only uses a public key and generates ciphertexts ct that always decrypt to 1 under all private keys. Such an algorithm is a bit unusual in that there is no further choice in the index. The security of the system requires that an attacker who makes a single query to the "secret encryption" oracle cannot distinguish a public encryption versus a secret encryption or a secret encryption with one index ind versus another index ind' unless he has a secret key sk_i that decrypts to 0 in one case and 1 in the other. The name "Mixed FE" is derived from the fact that the scheme has both a public and secret encryption procedure.

The semantics of mixed FE scheme are already very close a PLBE; in both cases there is a "public encryption" and "secret encryption" algorithm and one should not be able to distinguish different types of ciphertexts without having a secret key that decrypts differently in one case versus the other. The one important difference is that, in PLBE, the ciphertext also incorporates a message m, while in mixed FE there is no message. The work of [GKW18] showed how to use ABE on top of a mixed FE to incorporate a message into the ciphertext and get PLBE. Essentially, the PLBE scheme uses a mixed FE ciphertext as an attribute and then encrypts the message m under this attribute via an ABE scheme. In more detail, to implement public PLBE encryption (resp. secret PLBE encryption for index ind), first create public mixed-FE ciphertext (resp. secret mixed-FE ciphertext for the index ind) denoted $\mathsf{ct}_{\mathrm{mfe}}$ and then use the ABE scheme to encrypt the message m under the attribute $\mathsf{ct}_{\mathrm{mfe}}$. To create a PLBE secret key sk_i for index i, first create a mixed-FE secret key $\mathsf{sk}_{\mathrm{mfe},i}$ for the index i and then set sk_i to be an ABE secret key for the function $f_{\mathsf{sk}_{\mathrm{mfe},i}}$ which takes as input $\mathsf{ct}_{\mathrm{mfe}}$ and decrypts it with $\mathsf{sk}_{\mathrm{mfe},i}$. This incorporates the message m into the PLBE scheme, while having the mixed FE dictate whether or not the message is decryptable and preserving the mixed FE security properties.

Step 3: Constructing mixed FE. The work of [GKW18] gave a self-contained albeit somewhat complex construction of mixed FE from the LWE assumption.

Later, the work of [CVW+18a] gave two simple and modular constructions of mixed FE from previously studied primitives: one from lockable (AKA, compute-and-compare) obfuscation [WZ17, GKW17] and one from (key-homomorphic) private constrained PRFs (PCPRFs) [CC17, BTVW17, CVW18b]. Since either of these can be instantiated under LWE, so can the final mixed FE and traitor-tracing schemes.

We recall the PCPRF-based construction of mixed FE from [CVW+18a], which we will later rely on for our results. A PCPRF consists of a pseudorandom function (PRF) family $F_K(\cdot)$ with a key K. The constrained property states that given K, there is a way to generate a constrained key K_P for some program P such that $F_K(x) = F_{K_P}(x)$ if $P(x) = 0$. In addition, the constraints are private in that, one cannot distinguish between seeing the constrained key K_P, along the evaluations of $y_i = F_K(x_i)$ on various inputs x_i for which $P(x_i) = 1$, versus being given a "dummy key" that does not depend on P along with uniformly random values y_i.

Given a PCPRF for the comparison functions $P_{\mathsf{ind}}(i) = 1$ iff $i \geq \mathsf{ind}$, one can construct a simple mixed FE scheme as follows. The master secret key is a PRF key K and the secret key for an input i is the value $y = F_K(i)$. An encryption is a PRF key K^* and the decryption algorithm outputs 1 iff $y \neq F_{K^*}(x)$. A public encryption consists of a "dummy key" K^*. A secret encryption of some index ind consists of the constrained key $K^* = K_{P_{\mathsf{ind}}}$. It's relatively easy to see that the above gives a mixed FE scheme that is secure with $q = 0$ queries to the secret encryption oracle. In particular, the only way to distinguish different types of PRF keys is to have an evaluation on some i for which one is constrained and the other is not.

To get a mixed FE scheme with security for $q = 1$ queries to the secret encryption oracle, which is needed for traitor tracing, we rely on a PCPRF with an additional key homomorphic property saying that $F_K(x) + F_{K'}(x) = F_{K+K'}(x)$. The construction is only slightly more complex. Now the master secret key consists of 2λ PRF keys $\{K_{j,b}\}_{j \in \lambda, b \in \{0,1\}}$ and the secret key for an input i consists of the values $\{y_{j,b} = F_{K_{j,b}}(i)\}_{j \in \lambda, b \in \{0,1\}}$. An encryption is a PRF key K^* and some "tag" value $z \in \{0,1\}^\lambda$ and the decryption algorithm outputs 1 iff $\sum_{j=1}^\lambda y_{j,z_j} \neq F_{K^*}(i)$. A public encryption consists of a random z and a "dummy key" K^*. A secret encryption for some index ind consists of a random z along with the constrained key $K'_{P_{\mathsf{ind}}}$ where $K' = \sum_{j=1}^\lambda K_{j,z_j}$. The above gives a mixed FE scheme which is secure with $q = 1$ queries to the secret encryption oracle. With overwhelming probability, the z value used in the challenge ciphertext differs from the one used by the oracle in answering the encryption query in some position j, and therefore we can rely on the security of the PRF $F_{K_{j,z_j}}$ in essentially the same way as was done in the $q = 0$ query case.

Adding Broadcast to Traitor Tracing. We now discuss how to "upgrade" the above ideas to construct a broadcast and trace scheme.

Perhaps the first approach one would try is to combine broadcast and traitor-tracing directly; e.g., secret-share the message and encrypt one share via a broadcast scheme and the other share via a traitor-tracing scheme. Indeed, we can use the broadcast scheme to restrict the set S of users that can recover the first share and therefore the encrypted message. Also, any decoder D that decrypts the full ciphertext correctly must also necessarily decrypt the second share, and therefore we can use the traitor-tracing scheme to trace at least one user $i \in [N]$ that participated in constructing D. However, even if the decoder D can decrypt ciphertexts targeted toward some restricted set S of users, the traitor tracing procedure might find a user $i \notin S$, which is not good enough for a broadcast and trace scheme, as explained earlier. To fix this, we need to incorporate the broadcast set S into the tracing procedure itself. We revisit the 3-step approach outlined above and show how to upgrade it to get a broadcast and trace scheme.

Updated Step 1: Broadcast and Trace from AugBE. We previously saw how traitor-tracing can be constructed from "private linear broadcast encryption" (PLBE). The work of [BW06] showed that broadcast and trace can analogously be constructed from an augmented version of PLBE, called "augmented broadcast encryption" (AugBE), which can be thought of as combining PLBE and broadcast encryption. In particular, an AugBE scheme has a master public key pk, a master secret key msk, and N user secret keys $\mathsf{sk}_1, \ldots, \mathsf{sk}_N$. There is a "public encryption" procedure using pk, which encrypts a message m to a target set S, and guarantees that a secret key sk_i will decrypt correctly iff $i \in S$. There is also a "secret encryption" procedure using msk, which encrypts a message m to a target set S with respect to some index $\mathsf{ind} \in [N + 1]$, and guarantees that a secret key sk_i will decrypt correctly iff $i \in S \land i \geq \mathsf{ind}$. Moreover, one cannot distinguish a public encryption from a secret encryption or a secret encryption with one index ind versus another index ind' (all with the same set S) unless one has a secret key sk_i that correctly decrypts in one case but not the other. A secret encryption with the index $\mathsf{ind} = N + 1$ should hide the message even given all the secret keys. As before, these indistinguishability properties must hold even if the adversary is given a single query to the secret encryption oracle. We want the ciphertext size to be small, much smaller than N. As in broadcast encryption, the decryption algorithm is also given the set S separately, but we do not count it as part of the ciphertext size.

The notion of AugBE already incorporates the broadcast encryption requirements directly in the definition. To see that it also allows us to trace a traitor in the set S, one can adapt the previous argument that PLBE implies tracing. The tracing algorithm tests the decoder's success probability on secret encryptions with the fixed broadcast set S and all possible values of $\mathsf{ind} \in [N + 1]$. As before, the decoder must be successful when $\mathsf{ind} = 1$ (since it is successful with public encryptions and the two are indistinguishable) but cannot be successful when $\mathsf{ind} = N + 1$ (since such encryptions hide the message by definition) and so there must be some value ind^* such that success probability drops significantly between ind^* and $\mathsf{ind}^* + 1$. But this means that the decoder can distinguish between these two types of ciphertexts and, in order for that to happen, the decoder must have been created using knowledge of $\mathsf{sk}_{\mathsf{ind}^*}$ with $\mathsf{ind}^* \in S$. Thus the tracing algorithm can finger the user $\mathsf{ind}^* \in S$ as a traitor.

Updated Step 2: AugBE from Succinct ABE and BMFE. Recall that the work of [GKW18] constructed of PLBE from ABE and mixed FE. As our first contribution, we given an analogous result showing how to construct AugBE (the augmented form of PLBE) from two simpler primitives: a (succinct) ABE scheme and an augmented variant of mixed FE that we call "broadcast mixed FE" (BMFE). At a high level, we incorporate the set S into the ABE to ensure that only users $i \in S$ can decrypt correctly. But we also incorporate the set S into the mixed FE to ensure that the keys of users $i \notin S$ cannot help to distinguish between ciphertexts with different values of the index ind. We now go into more detail on how this is done.

A BMFE scheme can be thought of as an augmented form of mixed FE that includes the set S. In particular, a BMFE has master public key pk, a master secret key msk and allows us to create user secret keys sk_i for values $i \in [N]$. There is a "public encryption" procedure using pk, which takes as input a set $S \subseteq [N]$ and outputs a ciphertext ct that decrypts to 1 under *all* secret keys sk_i. There is also a "secret encryption" procedure using msk, which takes as input a set S and an index ind and outputs a ciphertext ct that decrypts to 1 under sk_i if $i \notin S \vee i \geq \mathsf{ind}$ and decrypts to 0 otherwise. The security of the system requires that an attacker with $q = 1$ queries to the "secret encryption" oracle cannot distinguish a public encryption versus a secret encryption or a secret encryption with one index ind versus another index ind' (all with the same set S) unless he has a secret key sk_i that decrypts to 0 in one case and 1 in the other.

Note that the decryptability conditions of AugBE ($i \in S \wedge i \geq \mathsf{ind}$) and of BMFE ($i \notin S \vee i \geq \mathsf{ind}$) differ from each other. However, these decryptability conditions match up to ensure that the only way to distinguish between ciphertexts with some index ind versus ones with index $\mathsf{ind}' > \mathsf{ind}$ is to have a key sk_i for some $i \in S \cap [\mathsf{ind}, \mathsf{ind}')$.

We can construct AugBE by combining together ABE with BMFE. In particular, the ABE scheme allows us to simultaneously add a message m to the BMFE and also to ensure that only the users in S can decrypt correctly. In more detail, the AugBE encryption consists of creating a BMFE ciphertext $\mathsf{ct}_{\mathsf{bmfe}}$ with some set S and index ind and then using the ABE to encrypt the message m under attribute $a = (S, \mathsf{ct}_{\mathsf{bmfe}})$. The AugBE secret key sk_i is an ABE secret key for a function $f_{i,\mathsf{sk}_{\mathsf{bmfe},i}}$ which has the BMFE secret key $\mathsf{sk}_{\mathsf{bmfe},i}$ inside it and checks that $i \in S$ and that $\mathsf{ct}_{\mathsf{bmfe}}$ decrypts to 1 under $\mathsf{sk}_{\mathsf{bmfe},i}$. It is easy to see that the above construction ensures that the set S and the index ind correctly determine whether an AugBE ciphertext is decryptable while preserving the BMFE indistinguishability properties.

Up until now we have completely ignored efficiency and, in particular, the requirement that ciphertexts are small. To ensure this we need the following:

– Firstly, we need a succinct ABE where the ciphertext size is essentially independent of the attribute size, since the attribute includes the set S (the decryption algorithm gets the attribute, but we don't count it as part of the ciphertext). Succinct ABE can be thought of as generalizing broadcast encryption, where the latter is a special case of succinct ABE in which attributes are sets S, and keys are associated with policies of the form $f_i(S) = 1$ iff $i \in S$. Unfortunately, the current ABE systems from the LWE assumption [GVW13, BGG+14] do not satisfy this form of succinctness, and we do not know how to achieve even broadcast encryption from LWE. On the positive side, we do have constructions of succinct ABE from bilinear maps [HLR10, ALDP11, AHL+12, YAHK14]; however, these constructions can only support policies for circuits in $\mathbf{NC}^1$, unlike the LWE-based ones that can support circuits of arbitrary depth. Recall that, in our case, the ABE policy checks that $i \in S$ and that a BMFE ciphertext decrypts to 1. The first part is in $\mathbf{NC}^1$ and therefore we need to ensure that the BMFE decryption is in $\mathbf{NC}^1$.

– Secondly, we need a succinct BMFE scheme, where decryption is in $\mathbf{NC}^1$ and the ciphertext size is much smaller than N (the decryption procedure gets S but we do not count it in the ciphertext size). We next show how to construct this primitive under LWE.

Note that we are using a bilinear-based succinct ABE to evaluate the decryption of an LWE-based BMFE scheme, which will be in $\mathbf{NC}^1$. This allows us to meaningfully combine the security properties of a bilinear-based scheme and an LWE-based scheme to achieve more than just the union of their capabilities.

Updated Step 3: Constructing BMFE in $\mathbf{NC}^1$. Our goal now is to construct a succinct BMFE with decryption in $\mathbf{NC}^1$. Recall that BMFE is an augmented form of mixed FE for which we have constructions from LWE [GKW18, CVW+18a]. We face two challenges:

– We need to incorporate the set S into mixed FE to get BMFE.
– We need to ensure that BMFE decryption is in $\mathbf{NC}^1$.

Let's start by showing how to augment mixed FE to get BMFE. Recall that we previously outlined the [CVW+18a] construction of mixed FE from (key-homomorphic) private constrained PRFs (PCPRFs) for comparison constraints: $P_{\mathsf{ind}}(i) = 1$ iff $i \geq \mathsf{ind}$. We now outline how to upgrade this construction to get a BMFE scheme. For simplicity, we describe how to get BMFE with security against $q = 0$ queries to the secret encryption oracle; to get security for $q = 1$ queries, as is needed for broadcast and trace, we then employ the same trick as in the mixed FE case. The master secret key of the BMFE scheme now consists of N PCPRF keys $\{K_j\}_{j \in N}$. The secret key of user i consists of the values $\{y_{i,j} = F_{K_j}(i)\}_{j \neq i}$ for $i, j \in [N]$. To create a "secret encryption" to a set S with respect to an index ind, the encryptor computes a key $K^+ = \sum_{j \notin S} K_j$ and then constrains it on the program P_{ind} to get $K^* = K^+_{P_{\mathsf{ind}}}$. To create a "public encryption" to a set S, the encryptor chooses a dummy constrained key K^*. The decryption procedure takes a ciphertext K^* and outputs 1 iff $F_{K^*}(i) \neq \sum_{j \notin S} y_{i,j}$. We rely on the fact that, the only way to distinguish different types of BMFE ciphertexts (i.e., PRF keys), is to have a complete set of values $\{F_{K_j}(i)\}_{j \notin S}$ for some

i which is constrained in one case but not the other, which requires having the BMFE key of some user i such that $i \in S$ (as no secret key contain the value $F_{K_i}(i)$), and where i is constrained in one case but not the other.

In our BMFE scheme, the decryption procedure is in $\mathbf{NC}^1$ if the underlying PCPRF evaluation $F_{K^*}(i)$ with a constrained key K^* is in $\mathbf{NC}^1$. If we go under the hood, and look at the PCPRF construction of [CVW18b], the constrained keys consist of $\log N$ tuples of square matrices $\{\mathbf{D}_{j,0}, \mathbf{D}_{j,1}\}_{j \in [\log N]}$ of dimension $\mathsf{poly}(\lambda)$, and the evaluation on some input $i = (b_1, \ldots, b_{\log N})$ computes a subset-product $\prod_{j=1}^{\log N} \mathbf{D}_{j,b_j}$ followed by rounding. While the product of a constant number of matrices and the rounding are in $\mathbf{NC}^1$, multiplying $\log N$ matrices is only known to be in $\mathbf{TC}^1$, which is not good enough for us.

We solve this problem by "pre-processing" the key which makes it longer but allows us to evaluate in $\mathbf{NC}^1$. In particular, we first group the $\log N$ matrix tuples into c groups of $(\log N)/c$ tuples each. Next, we pre-compute all possible $2^{(\log N)/c} = N^{1/c}$ subset-products within each group. This increases the key size from $2 \log N$ original matrices to $c \cdot N^{1/c}$ pre-processed matrices, but now the evaluation only needs to multiply together c of the pre-processed matrices; as long as c is a constant (which can be arbitrarily large), this can be done in $\mathbf{NC}^1$. In other words, for any constant $\varepsilon > 0$ there is a PCPRF with key size $O(N^\varepsilon)$ (ignoring factors $\mathsf{poly}(\lambda)$ independent of ε) and evaluation in $\mathbf{NC}^1$. This translates into a BMFE with ciphertext size $O(N^\varepsilon)$ and decryption in $\mathbf{NC}^1$. Combining with succinct ABE for $\mathbf{NC}^1$, this in turn leads to an a AugBE scheme and eventually a Broadcast and Trace scheme with ciphertext size $O(N^\varepsilon)$. Note that if we instead had a succinct ABE for $\mathbf{TC}^1$ then we could avoid the pre-processing step and that would lead to the ciphertext size only $\mathsf{poly} \log N$.

2   Preliminaries

Notations. Let PPT denote probabilistic polynomial-time. We denote the set of all positive integers upto n as $[n] := \{1, 2, \ldots, n\}$. Throughout this paper, unless specified, all polynomials we consider are positive polynomials. For any finite set S, $x \leftarrow S$ denotes a uniformly random element x from the set S. Similarly, for any distribution $\mathcal{D}$, $x \leftarrow \mathcal{D}$ denotes an element x drawn from distribution $\mathcal{D}$. The distribution $\mathcal{D}^n$ is used to represent a distribution over vectors of n components, where each component is drawn independently from the distribution $\mathcal{D}$.

2.1   Broadcast and Trace Systems

Here we recall the framework of broadcast and trace systems[5] and describe its security properties. In this work, we study broadcast and trace systems with secret key tracing. A broadcast and trace scheme BT, for message spaces $\mathcal{M} = \{\mathcal{M}_\lambda\}_{\lambda \in \mathbb{N}}$, consists of four polytime algorithms (Setup, Enc, Dec, Trace) with the following syntax:

---

[5] Prior works [NP00,NNL01,BW06] referred to such systems as Trace and Revoke.

Setup$(1^\lambda, 1^N) \rightarrow (\mathsf{pk}, \mathsf{tk}, \{\mathsf{sk}_1, \mathsf{sk}_2, \ldots, \mathsf{sk}_N\})$. The setup algorithm takes as input a security parameter λ and number of users N. It outputs a public key pk, tracing key tk, and secret keys for N users $\{\mathsf{sk}_1, \mathsf{sk}_2, \ldots, \mathsf{sk}_N\}$ respectively.

Enc$(\mathsf{pk}, S, m) \rightarrow \mathsf{ct}$. The encryption algorithm takes as input public key pk, a set $S \subseteq [N]$ of users, a message m and outputs a ciphertext ct.

Dec$(\mathsf{sk}_i, S, \mathsf{ct}) \rightarrow m$ or $\bot$. The decryption algorithm takes as input a user secret key, a set of users $S \subseteq [N]$, a ciphertext ct, and outputs either a message m or special reject symbol $\bot$.

Trace$^D(\mathsf{tk}, S_D, m_0, m_1, 1^{1/\epsilon}) \rightarrow S^*$. The tracing algorithm takes as input a tracing key tk, a set of users S_D, two messages m_0, m_1 and parameter $\epsilon < 1$. The algorithm has a black-box access to the decoder D and outputs a set of indices $S^* \subseteq [N]$.

Intuitively, the goal of the tracing algorithm is that when the decoder D can distinguish between encryptions of messages m_0 and m_1 encrypted to the set S_D with probability more than ϵ, the tracing algorithm should output a set S^* which is a subset of traitors (i.e., keys used to build decoder D). Here we consider the notion of secret key tracing, that is the algorithm takes as input a *private* tracing key to carry out the tracing procedure.

Correctness. A broadcast and trace system is said to be correct if there exists a negligible function $\mathsf{negl}(\cdot)$ such that for every $\lambda \in \mathbb{N}$, any number of users $N \in \mathbb{N}$, every subset of users $S \subseteq [N]$, every message $m \in \mathcal{M}_\lambda$, every user $i \in S$, the following holds

$$\Pr\left[\mathsf{Dec}(\mathsf{sk}_i, S, \mathsf{ct}) = m : \begin{array}{c} (\mathsf{pk}, \mathsf{tk}, \{\mathsf{sk}_i\}_{i \in [N]}) \leftarrow \mathsf{Setup}(1^\lambda, 1^N); \\ \mathsf{ct} \leftarrow \mathsf{Enc}(\mathsf{pk}, S, m) \end{array}\right] \geq 1 - \mathsf{negl}(\lambda).$$

where the probability is taken over the random coins used during setup and encryption.

Security. Intuitively, the system is said to be secure if it is IND-CPA secure as well as if no poly-time adversary can produce a decoder that can fool the tracing algorithm. We formally define both of these properties below.

Definition 2.1 (Selective IND-CPA security). *We say that a broadcast and trace scheme is selective IND-CPA secure if for every stateful PPT adversary $\mathcal{A}$, there exists a negligible function $\mathsf{negl}(\cdot)$ such that for all $\lambda \in \mathbb{N}$, the following holds*

$$\Pr\left[\mathcal{A}(\mathsf{ct}) = b : \begin{array}{c} (1^N, S^*) \leftarrow \mathcal{A}(1^\lambda); \\ (\mathsf{pk}, \mathsf{tk}, \{\mathsf{sk}_i\}_{i \in [N]}) \leftarrow \mathsf{Setup}(1^\lambda, 1^N); \\ (m_0, m_1) \leftarrow \mathcal{A}(\mathsf{pk}, \{\mathsf{sk}_i\}_{i \in [N] \setminus S^*}); \\ b \leftarrow \{0, 1\}; \mathsf{ct} \leftarrow \mathsf{Enc}(\mathsf{pk}, S^*, m_b) \end{array}\right] \leq \frac{1}{2} + \mathsf{negl}(\lambda).$$

Next, we describe the secure tracing definition and experiment. Intuitively, it states that if an adversary $\mathcal{A}$ outputs a decoding box D such that D can distinguish between encryptions of messages m_0 and m_1 encrypted to the set $S_D \subseteq [N]$ with some non-negligible probability ϵ, then the tracing algorithm

Trace, given oracle access to D, outputs (with all but negligible probability) a non-empty set of user indices such that all of them were corrupted by $\mathcal{A}$. Formally, it is described below (Fig. 1).

Definition 2.2 (Selective Secure Tracing). *Let* BT $=$ (Setup, Enc, Dec, Trace) *be a broadcast and trace scheme. For any non-negligible function* $\epsilon(\cdot)$ *and stateful PPT adversary* $\mathcal{A}$, *consider the experiment* Expt-BT$_{\mathcal{A},\epsilon}(\lambda)$ *defined as follows.*

Experiment Expt-BT$_{\mathcal{A},\epsilon}(\lambda)$

- $(1^N, S_D) \leftarrow \mathcal{A}(1^\lambda)$.
- $(\mathsf{pk}, \mathsf{tk}, (\mathsf{sk}_1, \ldots, \mathsf{sk}_N)) \leftarrow \mathsf{Setup}(1^\lambda, 1^N)$.
- $(D, m_0, m_1) \leftarrow \mathcal{A}^{O(\cdot)}(\mathsf{pk})$.
- $S^* \leftarrow \mathsf{Trace}^D(\mathsf{tk}, S_D, m_0, m_1, 1^{1/\epsilon(\lambda)})$.

Here, $O(\cdot)$ is an oracle that has keys $\{\mathsf{sk}_i\}_{i \in [N]}$ hardwired, takes as input an index $i \in [N]$ and outputs i^{th} key sk_i. Let S be the set of indices queried by $\mathcal{A}$.

Fig. 1. Experiment Expt-BT

Based on the above experiment, we now define the following (probabilistic) events and the corresponding probabilities (which are a functions of λ, parameterized by $\mathcal{A}, \epsilon$):

- Good-Decoder : $\Pr[D(\mathsf{ct}) = b : b \leftarrow \{0,1\}, \mathsf{ct} \leftarrow \mathsf{Enc}(\mathsf{pk}, S_D, m_b)] \geq 1/2 + \epsilon(\lambda)$
  $\mathrm{Pr}\text{-}\mathsf{G}\text{-}\mathsf{D}_{\mathcal{A},\epsilon}(\lambda) = \Pr[\text{Good-Decoder}]$
- Cor-Tr : $|S^*| > 0, S^* \subseteq S \cap S_D$
  $\mathrm{Pr}\text{-}\mathsf{Cor}\text{-}\mathsf{Tr}_{\mathcal{A},\epsilon}(\lambda) = \Pr[\text{Cor-Tr}]$
- Fal-Tr : $S^* \nsubseteq S \cap S_D$
  $\mathrm{Pr}\text{-}\mathsf{Fal}\text{-}\mathsf{Tr}_{\mathcal{A},\epsilon}(\lambda) = \Pr[\text{Fal-Tr}]$

A broadcast and trace scheme BT *is said to satisfy selective secure tracing property if for every PPT adversary* $\mathcal{A}$, *polynomial* $q(\cdot)$ *and non-negligible function* $\epsilon(\cdot)$, *there exists negligible functions* $\mathsf{negl}_1(\cdot)$, $\mathsf{negl}_2(\cdot)$ *such that for all* $\lambda \in \mathbb{N}$ *satisfying* $\epsilon(\lambda) > 1/q(\lambda)$, *the following holds*

$$\mathrm{Pr}\text{-}\mathsf{Fal}\text{-}\mathsf{Tr}_{\mathcal{A},\epsilon}(\lambda) \leq \mathsf{negl}_1(\lambda), \quad \mathrm{Pr}\text{-}\mathsf{Cor}\text{-}\mathsf{Tr}_{\mathcal{A},\epsilon}(\lambda) \geq \mathrm{Pr}\text{-}\mathsf{G}\text{-}\mathsf{D}_{\mathcal{A},\epsilon}(\lambda) - \mathsf{negl}_2(\lambda).$$

2.2 Augmented Broadcast Encryption

In this section, we define Augmented Broadcast Encryption (AugBE) and its security properties. The notion of AugBE was introduced by Boneh and Waters [BW06] as a building block towards realizing broadcast and trace systems. The original definition was described such that it could be used to build broadcast and trace scheme with public traceability. Here we relax the original definition since we only target secret key traceability. Specifically, the index encryption algorithm will now be a secret key algorithm, instead of being a public key algorithm. Below we describe the syntax.

Setup$(1^\lambda, 1^N) \rightarrow (\mathsf{pk}, \mathsf{msk}, \{\mathsf{sk}_1, \ldots, \mathsf{sk}_N\})$. The setup algorithm takes as input security parameter λ and number of users N. It outputs a public key pk, a master secret key msk and user secret keys $\{\mathsf{sk}_1, \ldots, \mathsf{sk}_N\}$, where sk_i is the secret key for user i.

Enc$(\mathsf{pk}, S, m) \rightarrow \mathsf{ct}$. The encryption algorithm takes as input public key pk, a set of users $S \subseteq [N]$, and a message m. It outputs a ciphertext ct.

Enc-index$(\mathsf{msk}, S, m, \mathsf{ind}) \rightarrow \mathsf{ct}$. The index encryption algorithm takes as input master secret key msk, a set of users $S \subseteq [N]$, a message m, and an index $\mathsf{ind} \in [N+1]$. It outputs a ciphertext ct.

Dec$(\mathsf{sk}_i, S, \mathsf{ct}) \rightarrow m$ or $\perp$. The decryption algorithm takes as input a secret key for i^{th} user sk_i, a set of users $S \subseteq [N]$, a ciphertext ct, and outputs a message m or $\perp$.

Correctness. An AugBE system is said to be correct if there exists a negligible function $\mathsf{negl}_1(\cdot), \mathsf{negl}_2(\cdot)$ such that for every $\lambda \in \mathbb{N}$, any number of users $N \in \mathbb{N}$, every subset of users $S \subseteq [N]$, any index $\mathsf{ind} \in [N+1]$, every message $m \in \mathcal{M}_\lambda$, every user $i \in S$, the following holds

$$\Pr\left[\mathsf{Dec}(\mathsf{sk}_i, S, \mathsf{ct}) = m : \begin{array}{l} (\mathsf{pk}, \mathsf{msk}, \{\mathsf{sk}_i\}_{i \in [N]}) \leftarrow \mathsf{Setup}(1^\lambda, 1^N); \\ \mathsf{ct} \leftarrow \mathsf{Enc}(\mathsf{pk}, S, m) \end{array}\right] \geq 1 - \mathsf{negl}_1(\lambda),$$

$$i \geq \mathsf{ind} \Rightarrow \Pr\left[\mathsf{Dec}(\mathsf{sk}_i, S, \mathsf{ct}) = m : \right.$$
$$\left. \begin{array}{l} (\mathsf{pk}, \mathsf{msk}, \{\mathsf{sk}_i\}_{i \in [N]}) \leftarrow \mathsf{Setup}(1^\lambda, 1^N); \\ \mathsf{ct} \leftarrow \mathsf{Enc\text{-}index}(\mathsf{msk}, S, m, \mathsf{ind}) \end{array}\right] \geq 1 - \mathsf{negl}_2(\lambda).$$

where the probabilities are taken over the random coins used during setup and encryption.

Security. Below we describe the security properties required from an AugBE scheme. The definitions are modelled after the bounded-ciphertext-query PLBE definitions [GKW18].

Definition 2.3 (q-query Selective Normal Hiding Security). *Let $q(\cdot)$ be any fixed polynomial. An AugBE scheme is said to satisfy q-query selective normal hiding security if for every stateful PPT adversary $\mathcal{A}$, there exists a negligible function $\mathsf{negl}(\cdot)$ such that for every $\lambda \in \mathbb{N}$, the following holds:*

$$\Pr\left[\mathcal{A}^{\mathsf{Enc\text{-}index}(\mathsf{msk},\cdot,\cdot,1)}(\mathsf{ct}_b) = b \; : \; \begin{array}{c} (1^N, S^*) \leftarrow \mathcal{A}(1^\lambda); \\ (\mathsf{pk}, \mathsf{msk}, \{\mathsf{sk}_i\}_{i \in [N]}) \leftarrow \mathsf{Setup}(1^\lambda, 1^N) \\ m \leftarrow \mathcal{A}^{\mathsf{Enc\text{-}index}(\mathsf{msk},\cdot,\cdot,1)}(\mathsf{pk}, \{\mathsf{sk}_i\}_{i \in [N]}) \\ b \leftarrow \{0,1\}; \; \mathsf{ct}_0 \leftarrow \mathsf{Enc}(\mathsf{pk}, S^*, m) \\ \mathsf{ct}_1 \leftarrow \mathsf{Enc\text{-}index}(\mathsf{msk}, S^*, m, 1) \end{array}\right] \leq \frac{1}{2} + \mathsf{negl}(\lambda)$$

where $\mathcal{A}$ can make at most $q(\lambda)$ queries to $\mathsf{Enc\text{-}index}(\mathsf{msk}, \cdot, \cdot, 1)$ oracle. Note that here $\mathcal{A}$ is only allowed to query for ciphertexts corresponding to index 1.

Definition 2.4 (q-query Selective Index Hiding Security). *Let $q(\cdot)$ be any fixed polynomial. An AugBE scheme is said to satisfy q-query selective index hiding security if for every (admissible) stateful PPT adversary $\mathcal{A}$, there exists a negligible function $\mathsf{negl}(\cdot)$ such that for every $\lambda \in \mathbb{N}$, the following holds:*

$$\Pr\left[\mathcal{A}^{O(\cdot),\mathsf{Enc\text{-}index}(\mathsf{msk},\cdot,\cdot,\cdot)}(\mathsf{ct}) = b \; : \; \begin{array}{c} (1^N, \mathsf{ind} \in [N], S^*) \leftarrow \mathcal{A}(1^\lambda) \\ (\mathsf{pk}, \mathsf{msk}, \{\mathsf{sk}_i\}_{i \in [N]}) \leftarrow \mathsf{Setup}(1^\lambda, 1^N) \\ m \leftarrow \mathcal{A}^{O(\cdot),\mathsf{Enc\text{-}index}(\mathsf{msk},\cdot,\cdot,\cdot)}(\mathsf{pk}) \\ b \leftarrow \{0,1\}; \; \mathsf{ct} \leftarrow \mathsf{Enc\text{-}index}(\mathsf{msk}, S^*, m, \mathsf{ind} + b) \end{array}\right] \leq \frac{1}{2} + \mathsf{negl}(\lambda)$$

where $\mathcal{A}$ can make at most $q(\lambda)$ queries to $\mathsf{Enc\text{-}index}(\mathsf{msk}, \cdot, \cdot, \cdot)$ oracle. Here $O(\cdot)$ is an oracle that has keys $\{\mathsf{sk}_i\}_{i \in [N]}$ hardwired, takes as input an index $i \in [N]$ and outputs sk_i. Let the set of keys queried by the adversary be S. The adversary is admissible *if and only if the challenge index ind it chooses satisfies $\mathsf{ind} \notin (S^* \cap S)$.*

Definition 2.5 (q-bounded Selective Message Hiding Security). *Let $q(\cdot)$ be any fixed polynomial. An AugBE scheme is said to satisfy q-query selective message hiding security if for every stateful PPT adversary $\mathcal{A}$, there exists a negligible function $\mathsf{negl}(\cdot)$ such that for every $\lambda \in \mathbb{N}$, the following holds:*

$$\Pr\left[\mathcal{A}^{\mathsf{Enc\text{-}index}(\mathsf{msk},\cdot,\cdot,\cdot)}(\mathsf{ct}) = b \; : \; \begin{array}{c} (1^N, S^*) \leftarrow \mathcal{A}(1^\lambda); (\mathsf{pk}, \mathsf{msk}, \{\mathsf{sk}_i\}_{i \in [N]}) \leftarrow \mathsf{Setup}(1^\lambda, 1^N) \\ (m_0, m_1) \leftarrow \mathcal{A}^{\mathsf{Enc\text{-}index}(\mathsf{msk},\cdot,\cdot,\cdot)}(\mathsf{pk}, \{\mathsf{sk}_i\}_{i \in [N]}) \\ b \leftarrow \{0,1\}; \; \mathsf{ct} \leftarrow \mathsf{Enc\text{-}index}(\mathsf{msk}, S^*, m_b, N + 1) \end{array}\right] \leq \frac{1}{2} + \mathsf{negl}(\lambda)$$

where $\mathcal{A}$ can make at most $q(\lambda)$ queries to $\mathsf{Enc\text{-}index}(\mathsf{msk}, \cdot, \cdot, \cdot)$ oracle.

We refer for the full version of the paper for a construction of a broadcast and trace system from an AugBE scheme. The formal theorem is provided later.

2.3   Key-Policy Attribute Based Encryption with Short Ciphertexts

In this work we require a key-policy attribute based encryption (KP-ABE) scheme with short ciphertexts for obtaining our final result. Here we recall the definition of KP-ABE with short ciphertexts, and state the prior results with explicit succinctness guarantees.

A KP-ABE scheme ABE, for set of attribute spaces $\mathcal{X} = \{\mathcal{X}_\kappa\}_\kappa$, predicate classes $\mathcal{C} = \{\mathcal{C}_\kappa\}_\kappa$ and message spaces $\mathcal{M} = \{\mathcal{M}_\kappa\}_\kappa$, consists of four polytime algorithms (Setup, Enc, KeyGen, Dec) with the following syntax:

Setup($1^\lambda, 1^\kappa$) $\rightarrow$ (pp, msk). The setup algorithm takes as input the security parameter λ and a functionality index κ, and outputs the public parameters pp and master secret key msk.

Enc(pp, x, m) $\rightarrow$ ct. The encryption algorithm takes as input public parameters pp, an attribute $x \in \mathcal{X}_\kappa$ and a message $m \in \mathcal{M}_\kappa$. It outputs a ciphertext ct.

KeyGen(msk, C) $\rightarrow$ sk$_C$. The key generation algorithm takes as input master secret key msk and a predicate $C \in \mathcal{C}_\kappa$. It outputs a secret key sk$_C$.

Dec(sk$_C$, ct, x) $\rightarrow m$ or $\bot$. The decryption algorithm takes as input a secret key sk$_C$, a ciphertext ct and an attribute x. It outputs either a message $m \in \mathcal{M}_\kappa$ or a special symbol $\bot$.

We point out that in our syntax the decryption algorithm takes the attribute x as explicit input. This is done so to simplify stating the succinctness requirement. Below we describe the correctness and security requirements, and later state the results achieving the requisite notion.

Correctness. A key-policy attribute based encryption scheme is said to be correct if there exists negligible functions negl($\cdot$) such that for all $\lambda, \kappa \in \mathbb{N}$, for all $x \in \mathcal{X}_\kappa$, $C \in \mathcal{C}_\kappa$, $m \in \mathcal{M}_\kappa$, such that $C(x) = 1$ the following holds

$$\Pr\left[\text{Dec(sk}_C, \text{ct}, x) = m : \begin{array}{l} (\text{pp}, \text{msk}) \leftarrow \text{Setup}(1^\lambda, 1^\kappa); \\ \text{sk}_C \leftarrow \text{KeyGen}(\text{msk}, C); \\ \text{ct} \leftarrow \text{Enc}(\text{pp}, x, m) \end{array} \right] \geq 1 - \text{negl}(\lambda)$$

where negl($\cdot$) is a negligible function, and the probabilities are taken over the random coins used during setup, key generation, and encryption procedures.

Security. The standard notion of security for a KP-ABE scheme is that of IND-CPA security. It is formally defined as follows.

Definition 2.6. *A key-policy attribute based encryption scheme* ABE $=$ (Setup, Enc, KeyGen, Dec) *is said to be selectively secure if for every stateful PPT adversary $\mathcal{A}$, there exists a negligible function negl($\cdot$), such that for every $\lambda \in \mathbb{N}$ the following holds:*

$$\left| \Pr\left[\mathcal{A}^{\text{KeyGen}(\text{msk}, \cdot)}(\text{ct}) = b : \begin{array}{l} (1^\kappa, x) \leftarrow \mathcal{A}(1^\lambda); \\ (\text{pp}, \text{msk}) \leftarrow \text{Setup}(1^\lambda, 1^\kappa) \\ (m_0, m_1) \leftarrow \mathcal{A}^{\text{KeyGen}(\text{msk}, \cdot)}(\text{pp}) \\ b \leftarrow \{0, 1\}; \text{ct} \leftarrow \text{Enc}(\text{pp}, x, m_b) \end{array} \right] - \frac{1}{2} \right| \leq \text{negl}(\lambda)$$

where every predicate query C, made by adversary $\mathcal{A}$ to the KeyGen(msk, ·) *oracle, must satisfy the condition that $C(x) = 0$.*

Below we state the result proved in [AHL+12] about a KP-ABE scheme with short ciphertexts from assumptions over bilinear maps. Concretely, they relied on the n-DBDHE assumption studied in [BGW05, BBG05]. Below we state the formal theorem.

Theorem 2.7 ([AHL+12, **Theorem 4, Paraphrased**]). *Assuming κ-DBDHE assumption holds, there exists a selectively-secure (Definition 2.6) KP-ABE scheme for non-monotonic access structures with length κ attributes (/number of parties). Additionally, the size of public parameters, secret keys, ciphertexts grow with λ and κ as follows—$|\mathsf{pp}| = O(\kappa \cdot \lambda)$, $|\mathsf{sk}_C| = O(\kappa \cdot \lambda \cdot |C|)$, and $|\mathsf{ct}| = O(\lambda)$.*

We point out that the size of the ciphertext does not depend on the length of the attributes, that is the KP-ABE scheme has short ciphertexts.

2.4   Key-Homomorphic Private Constrained PRFs

In this section, we recall the notion of almost-key-homomorphic private constrained PRFs (PCPRFs) from [CVW+18a]. As in [CVW+18a], we also work with PCPRFs that satisfy simulation-based security given one constrained key and many input queries. The existence of a simulator will be useful for the purpose of this paper. Below we describe the syntax and definition of PCPRFs.

A constrained PRF consists of five PPT algorithms (PPGen, SKGen, Constrain, Eval, Constrain.Eval) along with a domain family $\{D_\lambda\}_{\lambda \in \mathbb{N}}$, a range family $\{R_\lambda\}_{\lambda \in \mathbb{N}}$, and a constraint family $\mathcal{C} = \{\mathcal{C}_\lambda = \{C : D_\lambda \to \{0, 1\}\}\}_{\lambda \in \mathbb{N}}$.

PPGen(1^λ) → PP. The public parameter generation algorithm takes the security parameter λ and generates the public parameters PP.

SKGen(1^λ, PP) → SK. The secret key generation algorithm takes the security parameter λ, and the public parameters PP, and generates a secret key SK.

Eval(SK, x) → y. The evaluation algorithm takes SK, an input $x \in D_\lambda$, and deterministically outputs $y \in R_\lambda$. We will also use the alternative notation $y = F_{\mathsf{SK}}(x)$.

Constrain(1^λ, PP, SK, C) → CK_C. The constraining algorithm takes SK, a constraint $C \in \mathcal{C}_\lambda$, outputs the constrained key CK_C.

Constrain.Eval(CK_C, x) → y. The constrained evaluation algorithm takes a constrained key CK_C, an input x, outputs $y = F_{\mathsf{CK}_C}(x)$.

Definition 2.8 (Key-homomorphic private constrained PRF). *A constrained PRF (PPGen, SKGen, Constrain, Eval, Constrain.Eval) is a family of almost-key-homomorphic private constrained PRF for $\mathcal{C}$ if it satisfies the following properties:*

Functionality preservation for $C(x) = 0$. *For any constraint $C \in \mathcal{C}_\lambda$, any input $x \in D_\lambda$ s.t. $C(x) = 0$,*

$$\Pr[\mathsf{Eval}(\mathsf{SK}, x) = \mathsf{Constrain.Eval}(\mathsf{CK}_C, x)] \geq 1 - \mathsf{negl}(\lambda),$$

where the probability is taken over the randomness used in algorithms PPGen, SKGen *and* Constrain.

Pseudorandomness and constraint-hiding. *There exists a polynomial time algorithm* Sim *such that for every stateful PPT adversary* $\mathcal{A}$, *there exists a negligible function* negl$(\cdot)$ *such that for all* $\lambda \in \mathbb{N}$, *the following holds:*

$$\Pr\left[\mathcal{A}^{\mathsf{Eval}(\mathsf{SK},\cdot)}(\mathsf{PP},\mathsf{CK}_C) = 1 \ : \ \begin{array}{c} C \leftarrow \mathcal{A}(1^\lambda); \mathsf{PP} \leftarrow \mathsf{PPGen}(1^\lambda) \\ \mathsf{SK} \leftarrow \mathsf{SKGen}(1^\lambda, \mathsf{PP}) \\ \mathsf{CK}_C \leftarrow \mathsf{Constrain}(1^\lambda, \mathsf{PP}, \mathsf{SK}, C) \end{array}\right]$$

$$- \Pr\left[\mathcal{A}^{O(\cdot)}(\mathsf{PP},\mathsf{CK}_C) = 1 \ : \ \begin{array}{c} C \leftarrow \mathcal{A}(1^\lambda); \\ (\mathsf{PP},\mathsf{CK}_C) \leftarrow \mathsf{Sim}(1^\lambda, 1^{|C|}) \end{array}\right] \leq \frac{1}{2} + \mathsf{negl}(\lambda).$$

where the oracle $O(\cdot)$ *is defined as follows. On each query* x *made by the adversary, if* $C(x) = 0$ *then it responds with* $y = $ Constrain.Eval(CK_C, x), *otherwise it responds with* $y \leftarrow R_\lambda$.

Distribution requirement on the secret keys. *The space of keys* K_λ *is a group for all* $\lambda \in \mathbb{N}$. *Let* $+$ *denote the group operation over* K_λ. *We additionally require that for* PP $\leftarrow$ PPGen(1^λ), *for* $\mathsf{SK}_1, \mathsf{SK}_2, \mathsf{SK}'$ *sampled from* SKGen$(1^\lambda, \mathsf{PP})$ *with uniform and independent randomness,* $\mathsf{SK}_1 + \mathsf{SK}_2$, $\mathsf{SK}_1 + (-\mathsf{SK}_2)$, *and* SK' *are identically distributed.*

Almost-key-homomorphism. *Let* $B \in \mathbb{N}$, *and suppose* R_λ *is endowed with a norm* $\|\cdot\|$ *and a group operation* $+$ *(by abuse of notation; whether we are considering addition over* R_λ *or over* K_λ *will be clear from the context) for all* $\lambda \in \mathbb{N}$. *A constrained PRF (*PPGen, SKGen, Constrain, Eval, Constrain.Eval*) with domain* D_λ *and range* R_λ *is called B-almost-key-homomorphic if for* PP $\leftarrow$ PPGen(1^λ), $\mathsf{SK}_1, \mathsf{SK}_2 \leftarrow$ SKGen$(1^\lambda, \mathsf{PP})$, *and any input* $x \in D_\lambda$:

$$\|\mathsf{Eval}(\mathsf{SK}_1, x) + \mathsf{Eval}(\mathsf{SK}_2, x) - \mathsf{Eval}(\mathsf{SK}_1 + \mathsf{SK}_2, x)\| \leq B.$$

To instantiate the definition above, we will use PCPRFs from LWE [CC17, CVW18b], which happen to satisfy 1-almost-key homomorphism. We defer a more detailed exposition of the parameters and the efficiency of those PCPRFs to Sect. 6.1.

3 Broadcast Mixed FE for Comparison

The notion of mixed functional encryption was introduced in [GKW18] towards building efficient collusion-resistant Traitor Tracing systems. In this work, we adapt the notion of Mixed FE to additionally provide broadcast capability. We call this new primitive to Broadcast Mixed FE. This new notion is a central component of our approach to building Broadcast and Trace schemes. Let us first recall the notion of Mixed FE scheme for comparisons. In such a scheme, both the secrets keys as well as ciphertexts are associated with a message string (say all natural numbers for instance) with the comparison predicate being implemented. In a Mixed FE system, there are two modes of encryption—secret-key and public-key. In the public-key (or normal) encryption mode, the algorithm takes as input only the public parameters and outputs a encryption of 'one' (i.e., inherently it encrypts a "canonical" *always-accepting* function '≥ 1'). Whereas in the secret-key mode, it takes as input the master secret key and a string x, and encrypts x. Now the functional secret keys are associated with a unique string as well. The decryption algorithm in a Mixed FE system works similar to that in standard FE, that is decrypting an encryption of message x using secret key for string i outputs 1 iff '$i \geq x$' (i.e., decryption evaluates the comparison function).

Here we extend this to provide a broadcast functionality as well. This means that now in both the public-key and secret-key modes, the encryption algorithms also take as input a set $S \subseteq [N]$. And, now the decryption functionality is altered as follows—decrypting an encryption of message x for set S using secret key for string i outputs 1 iff '$i \notin S \lor i \geq x$'. In other words, the decryption algorithm evaluates the comparison function *only if* $i \in S$, so that users outside of the broadcast set S cannot infer any information about x from their secret key. Next, we formally describe it.

A broadcast mixed functional encryption scheme BMFE consists of four poly-time algorithms (Setup, Enc, SK-Enc, Dec) with the following syntax:

Setup$(1^\lambda, 1^N) \rightarrow (\text{pp}, \text{msk}, \{\text{sk}_1, \ldots, \text{sk}_N\})$. The setup algorithm takes as input the security parameter λ and number of users N, and outputs the public parameters pp, the master secret key msk and N user keys $\{\text{sk}_i\}_{i \in [N]}$.

Enc$(\text{pp}, S) \rightarrow \text{ct}$. The normal encryption algorithm takes as input public parameters pp and a set $S \subseteq [N]$, and outputs a ciphertext ct.

SK-Enc$(\text{msk}, S, j) \rightarrow \text{ct}$. The secret key encryption algorithm takes as input master secret key msk, set $S \subseteq [N]$, and an index $j \in [N+1]$. It outputs a ciphertext ct.

Dec$(\text{sk}_i, S, \text{ct}) \rightarrow \{0, 1\}$. The decryption algorithm takes as input a secret key sk_i, set $S \subseteq [N]$ and a ciphertext ct, and it outputs a single bit.

Correctness. A broadcast mixed functional encryption scheme is said to be correct if there exists negligible functions $\text{negl}_1(\cdot), \text{negl}_2(\cdot), \text{negl}_3(\cdot)$ such that for all $\lambda, N \in \mathbb{N}$, for every set $S \subseteq [N]$, and for all user indices $i \in [N]$ and $j \in [N+1]$, the following holds

$$\Pr\left[\text{Dec}(\text{sk}_i, S, \text{ct}) = 1 : \begin{array}{l} (\text{pp}, \text{msk}, \{\text{sk}_i\}_{i \in [N]}) \leftarrow \text{Setup}(1^\lambda, 1^N); \\ \text{ct} \leftarrow \text{Enc}(\text{pp}, S) \end{array}\right] \geq 1 - \text{negl}_1(\lambda),$$

$$(i \in S \land i < j) \Rightarrow \Pr\left[\text{Dec}(\text{sk}_i, S, \text{ct}) = 0 : \right.$$

$$\left. \begin{array}{l} (\text{pp}, \text{msk}, \{\text{sk}_i\}_{i \in [N]}) \leftarrow \text{Setup}(1^\lambda, 1^N); \\ \text{ct} \leftarrow \text{SK-Enc}(\text{msk}, S, j) \end{array}\right] \geq 1 - \text{negl}_2(\lambda).$$

where the probabilities are taken over the random coins used during setup and encryption.

Security. The security notions are derived from the mixed FE security notions of function indistinguishability and accept indistinguishability as follows. Informally, the idea is that no PPT adversary should be able to distinguish between a normal ciphertext and a secret-key ciphertext encrypting index 1. Additionally, it should be hard to distinguish between two secret-key ciphertexts unless the adversary can trivially distinguish between using the keys given to it. As in prior works, we are only interested in broadcast mixed FE schemes that guarantee security against adversaries which make a bounded number of secret key encryption queries. Below we formally define it.

Definition 3.1 (q-query Selective Index Indistinguishability). *Let $q(\cdot)$ be any fixed polynomial. A broadcast mixed functional encryption scheme* BMFE = (Setup, Enc, SK-Enc, Dec) *is said to satisfy q-query selective index indistinguishability security if for every stateful PPT adversary $\mathcal{A}$, there exists a negligible function* negl$(\cdot)$, *such that for every $\lambda \in \mathbb{N}$ the following holds:*

$$\Pr\left[\mathcal{A}^{\mathsf{SK\text{-}Enc}(\mathsf{msk},\cdot,\cdot)}(\mathsf{pp}, \mathsf{ct}, \mathsf{Keys}) = b : \begin{array}{c} (1^N, \mathsf{ind} \in [N], S^*) \leftarrow \mathcal{A}(1^\lambda) \\ (\mathsf{pp}, \mathsf{msk}, \{\mathsf{sk}_i\}_{i \in [N]}) \leftarrow \mathsf{Setup}(1^\lambda, 1^N) \\ b \leftarrow \{0,1\}; \ \mathsf{ct} \leftarrow \mathsf{SK\text{-}Enc}(\mathsf{msk}, S^*, \mathsf{ind} + b) \end{array}\right] \leq \frac{1}{2} + \mathsf{negl}(\lambda)$$

where $\mathcal{A}$ can make at most $q(\lambda)$ queries to SK-Enc$(\mathsf{msk}, \cdot, \cdot)$ *oracle. And,* Keys *is the following set of secret keys—*Keys = $\{\mathsf{sk}_i\}_{i \in [N] \setminus \{\mathsf{ind}\}}$ *if* ind $\in S^*$, *otherwise* Keys = $\{\mathsf{sk}_i\}_{i \in [N]}$.

Definition 3.2 (q-query Selective Mode Indistinguishability). *Let $q(\cdot)$ be any fixed polynomial. A broadcast mixed functional encryption scheme* BMFE = (Setup, Enc, SK-Enc, Dec) *is said to satisfy q-query selective mode indistinguishability security if for every stateful PPT adversary $\mathcal{A}$, there exists a negligible function* negl$(\cdot)$, *such that for every $\lambda \in \mathbb{N}$ the following holds:*

$$\Pr\left[\mathcal{A}^{\mathsf{SK\text{-}Enc}(\mathsf{msk},\cdot,1)}(\mathsf{pp}, \mathsf{ct}_b, \{\mathsf{sk}_i\}_{i \in [N]}) = b : \begin{array}{c} (1^N, S^*) \leftarrow \mathcal{A}(1^\lambda); \\ (\mathsf{pp}, \mathsf{msk}, \{\mathsf{sk}_i\}_{i \in [N]}) \leftarrow \mathsf{Setup}(1^\lambda, 1^N) \\ b \leftarrow \{0,1\}; \ \mathsf{ct}_0 \leftarrow \mathsf{Enc}(\mathsf{pp}, S^*) \\ \mathsf{ct}_1 \leftarrow \mathsf{SK\text{-}Enc}(\mathsf{msk}, S^*, 1) \end{array}\right] \leq \frac{1}{2} + \mathsf{negl}(\lambda)$$

where $\mathcal{A}$ can make at most $q(\lambda)$ queries to SK-Enc$(\mathsf{msk}, \cdot, 1)$ *oracle.*

4 Building Augmented BE from Broadcast Mixed FE and Key-Policy ABE with Short Ciphertexts

In this section we provide our construction for augmented BE from broadcast mixed FE and KP-ABE with short ciphertexts.

Let ABE $=$ (ABE.Setup, ABE.Enc, ABE.KeyGen, ABE.Dec) be a key-policy attribute based encryption scheme for set of attribute spaces $\{\mathcal{X}_\kappa\}_\kappa$, predicate classes $\{\mathcal{C}_\kappa\}_\kappa$ and message spaces $\{\mathcal{M}_\kappa\}_\kappa$, and BMFE $=$ (BMFE.Setup, BMFE.Enc, BMFE.SK-Enc, BMFE.Dec) be a broadcast mixed functional encryption scheme for comparison with ciphertexts of length $\ell = \ell(\lambda, N)$. Also, let $\kappa = \kappa(\lambda, N)$ be the lexicographically smallest functionality index such that every string of length ℓ can be uniquely represented in attribute class $\mathcal{X}_\kappa$ (i.e., $\{0, 1\}^\ell \subseteq \mathcal{X}_\kappa$). We will suppose that for all $i \in [N]$ and bmfe.sk generated by BMFE.Setup, $\mathcal{C}_\kappa$ contains the circuit $C_{i,\mathsf{bmfe.sk}}$ defined as:

$$C_{i,\mathsf{bmfe.sk}}(\mathsf{bmfe.ct}, S) := (i \in S) \wedge (\mathsf{BMFE.Dec}(\mathsf{bmfe.sk}, S, \mathsf{bmfe.ct}) = 1),$$

which composes a BMFE decryption with testing membership in $S \subseteq [N]$.

Below we describe our construction.

Setup$(1^\lambda, 1^N) \rightarrow \Big(\mathsf{pk}, \mathsf{msk}, \{\mathsf{sk}_i\}_{i\in[N]}\Big)$. The setup algorithm runs ABE.Setup and BMFE.Setup to generate ABE and broadcast mixed FE public parameters and master secret key as $(\mathsf{abe.pp}, \mathsf{abe.msk}) \leftarrow \mathsf{ABE.Setup}(1^\lambda, 1^\kappa)$ and $(\mathsf{bmfe.pp}, \mathsf{bmfe.msk}, \{\mathsf{bmfe.sk}_i\}_{i\in[N]}) \leftarrow \mathsf{BMFE.Setup}(1^\lambda, 1^N)$. Now let $C_{i,\mathsf{bmfe.sk}_i} : \{0, 1\}^\ell \times [N] \rightarrow \{0, 1\}$ denote the following circuit:

$$C_{i,\mathsf{bmfe.sk}_i}(\mathsf{bmfe.ct}, S) := (i \in S) \wedge (\mathsf{BMFE.Dec}(\mathsf{bmfe.sk}_i, S, \mathsf{bmfe.ct}) = 1).$$

That is, it corresponds to BMFE decryption circuit with key $\mathsf{bmfe.sk}_i$ hardwired along with a set membership check for index i. Next, it computes N ABE secret keys $\mathsf{abe.sk}_i$ as

$$\forall\, i \in [N], \quad \mathsf{abe.sk}_i \leftarrow \mathsf{ABE.KeyGen}(\mathsf{abe.msk}, C_{i,\mathsf{bmfe.sk}_i})$$

Finally, it sets $\mathsf{pk} = (\mathsf{abe.pp}, \mathsf{bmfe.pp})$, $\mathsf{msk} = (\mathsf{abe.msk}, \mathsf{bmfe.msk})$ and $\mathsf{sk}_i = \mathsf{abe.sk}_i$ for $i \in [N]$.

Enc$(\mathsf{pk}, S, m) \rightarrow \mathsf{ct}$. Let $\mathsf{pp} = (\mathsf{abe.pp}, \mathsf{bmfe.pp})$. The encryption algorithm first computes $\mathsf{ct}_{\mathsf{attr}} \leftarrow \mathsf{BMFE.Enc}(\mathsf{bmfe.pp}, S)$. Next, it encrypts message m as $\mathsf{ct} \leftarrow \mathsf{ABE.Enc}(\mathsf{abe.pp}, \mathsf{attr} = (\mathsf{ct}_{\mathsf{attr}}, S), m)$, and outputs ciphertext $(\mathsf{ct}, \mathsf{ct}_{\mathsf{attr}})$.

Enc-index$(\mathsf{msk}, S, m, \mathsf{ind}) \rightarrow \mathsf{ct}$. Let $\mathsf{msk} = (\mathsf{abe.msk}, \mathsf{bmfe.msk})$. The index-encryption algorithm first computes $\mathsf{ct}_{\mathsf{attr}} \leftarrow \mathsf{BMFE.SK\text{-}Enc}(\mathsf{bmfe.msk}, S, \mathsf{ind})$. Next, it encrypts message m as $\mathsf{ct} \leftarrow \mathsf{ABE.Enc}(\mathsf{abe.pp}, \mathsf{attr} = (\mathsf{ct}_{\mathsf{attr}}, S), m)$, and outputs ciphertext $(\mathsf{ct}, \mathsf{ct}_{\mathsf{attr}})$.

Dec$(\mathsf{sk}, S, (\mathsf{ct}, \mathsf{ct}_{\mathsf{attr}})) \rightarrow m$ or $\perp$. The decryption algorithm runs ABE.Dec on ct using key sk as $y = \mathsf{ABE.Dec}(\mathsf{sk}, \mathsf{ct}, (\mathsf{ct}_{\mathsf{attr}}, S))$, and sets y as the output of decryption.

We now state the correctness and security of the above construction. Their proofs are included in the full version of the paper.

Theorem 4.1. *Suppose* ABE $=$ (ABE.Setup, ABE.Enc, ABE.KeyGen, ABE.Dec) *is a correct attribute based encryption for set of attribute spaces* $\{\mathcal{X}_\kappa\}_\kappa$, *predicate classes* $\{\mathcal{C}_\kappa\}_\kappa$ *and message spaces* $\{\mathcal{M}_\kappa\}_\kappa$, *and* BMFE $=$

(BMFE.Setup, BMFE.Enc, BMFE.SK-Enc, BMFE.Dec) *is a correct broadcast mixed functional encryption scheme for comparison, then the above construction satisfies correctness.*

Theorem 4.2. *If* ABE $=$ (ABE.Setup, ABE.Enc, ABE.KeyGen, ABE.Dec) *is a selectively-secure attribute based encryption for set of attribute spaces* $\{\mathcal{X}_\kappa\}_\kappa$, *predicate classes* $\{\mathcal{C}_\kappa\}_\kappa$ *and message spaces* $\{\mathcal{M}_\kappa\}_\kappa$ *satisfying Definition 2.6, and* BMFE $=$ (BMFE.Setup, BMFE.Enc, BMFE.SK-Enc, BMFE.Dec) *is a broadcast mixed functional encryption scheme satisfying 1-query selective mode indistinguishability (Definition 3.2) and 1-query selective index indistinguishability (Definition 3.1) properties, then the above construction is a secure augmented broadcast encryption scheme, for messages spaces* $\{\mathcal{M}_\kappa\}_\kappa$, *satisfying 1-query selective normal, index and message hiding security properties as per Definitions 2.3 to 2.5. Additionally, the size of ciphertexts in the AugBE system is* $\ell + \widetilde{\ell}$, *where* $\ell = \ell(\lambda, N)$ *and* $\widetilde{\ell} = \widetilde{\ell}(\lambda, \kappa)$ *are the sizes of broadcast mixed FE and ABE ciphertexts, respectively.*

5   Building Broadcast Mixed FE for Comparison from PCPRFs

In this section we present our construction of a broadcast mixed FE for comparison with 1-query security based on almost-key-homomorphic private constrained PRFs.

In the following, if we let $N \in \mathbb{N}$ (which is the number of users), we will consider $N+1$ tuples of PCPRF keys indexed by $\{0, \ldots, N\}$. This can be viewed as adding a dummy user "0" who is never authorized to decrypt, so that no sums are empty (and in particular our scheme makes sense even if the set $S \subseteq [N]$ is $[N]$). As a result, in this whole section, whenever we consider a sum, unless specified otherwise, the set of indices live in $\{0, \ldots, N\}$; for instance, for $S \subseteq [N]$, $j \notin S$ will stand for $j \in \{0, \ldots, N\} \setminus S$.

Let PCPRF $=$ (PPGen, SKGen, Constrain, Eval, Constrain.Eval) along with a family of constraints $\mathcal{C}$ be a PCPRF (Definition 2.8) satisfying B-almost-key homomorphism. For all $j \in D_\lambda$, let $C_j : i \mapsto [i \geq j]$ be a circuit that outputs 1 if $i \geq j$ and 0 otherwise. We will suppose that for all $j \in D_\lambda$, $C_j \in \mathcal{C}_\lambda$, that is C_j are valid constraints for the PCPRF. Let $|C_\lambda| = \mathsf{poly}(\lambda)$ be a common size for such circuits.

We define our broadcast mixed FE scheme as follows:

Setup($1^\lambda, 1^N$) $\rightarrow$ (pp, msk, $\{\mathsf{sk}_1, \ldots, \mathsf{sk}_N\}$): The setup algorithm first samples PP $\leftarrow$ PPGen($1^\lambda, \mathcal{F}_\lambda$). It then generates for all $0 \leq i \leq N$, $t \in [\lambda]$ and $b \in \{0,1\}$: $\mathsf{SK}_{i,t,b} \leftarrow$ SKGen(1^λ, PP).
　　It then sets pp $=$ PP, msk $= \{\mathsf{SK}_{i,t,b}\}_{0 \leq i \leq N, t \in [\lambda], b \in \{0,1\}}$, and for all $i \in [N]$: $\mathsf{sk}_i = \{i, \mathsf{Eval}(\mathsf{SK}_{j,t,b}, i)\}_{j \neq i, t \in [\lambda], b \in \{0,1\}}$.
Enc(pp, S) $\rightarrow$ ct. The normal encryption algorithm first picks a random tag $\mathbf{z} \leftarrow \{0,1\}^\lambda$. It then runs the PCPRF simulator: CK $\leftarrow$ Sim($1^\lambda, 1^{|C_\lambda|}$), and sets ct $= (\mathbf{z}, \mathsf{CK})$.

SK-Enc$(\mathsf{msk}, S, j) \to \mathsf{ct}$. The secret key encryption algorithm first samples $\mathbf{z} \leftarrow \{0,1\}^\lambda$. It computes:

$$\mathsf{SK}_{S,\mathbf{z}} = \sum_{i \notin S, t \in [\lambda]} \mathsf{SK}_{i,t,\mathbf{z}_t},$$

(where the sum denotes the group operation over PCPRF keys). Note that this sum is never empty (as $i \notin S$ stands here for $i \in \{0, \ldots, N\} \setminus S$, so that it always contains the secret keys $\mathsf{SK}_{0,t,b}$ for all $t \in [\lambda], b \in \{0,1\}$). The algorithm computes the constrained key

$$\mathsf{CK}_{S,\mathbf{z},j} \leftarrow \mathsf{Constrain}(1^\lambda, \mathsf{PP}, \mathsf{SK}_{S,\mathbf{z}}, C_j),$$

where C_j is defined above. It finally sets $\mathsf{ct} = (\mathbf{z}, \mathsf{CK}_{S,\mathbf{z},j})$.

Dec$(\mathsf{sk}_i, S, \mathsf{ct}) \to \{0,1\}$. The decryption algorithm parses ct as $(\mathbf{z}, \mathsf{CK})$. If $i \notin S$ where i is the secret key index, the decryption algorithm outputs 1. Otherwise, it computes $\mathsf{Constrain.Eval}(\mathsf{CK}, i)$, and outputs:

$$\begin{cases} 0 & \text{if } \|\mathsf{Constrain.Eval}(\mathsf{CK}, i) - \sum_{j \notin S, t \in [\lambda]} \mathsf{Eval}(\mathsf{SK}_{j,t,\mathbf{z}_t}, i)\| \le (N+1) \cdot \lambda \cdot B \\ 1 & \text{otherwise.} \end{cases}$$

We now state the correctness and security of the above construction. The proofs are included in the full version of the paper.

Theorem 5.1. *Suppose* PCPRF $=$ (PPGen, SKGen, Constrain, Eval, Constrain. Eval) *along with a constraint family $\mathcal{C}$ and range R_λ is a PCPRF (Definition 2.8) satisfying B-almost-key homomorphism for a norm $\|\cdot\|$. Suppose furthermore that $\Pr_{x \leftarrow R_\lambda}[\|x\| \le (N+1)\lambda B] \le \mathsf{negl}(\lambda)$, that is, random elements in the range of the PCPRF have large norm. Then the above construction satisfies correctness.*

Theorem 5.2. *If* PCPRF $=$ (PPGen, SKGen, Constrain, Eval, Constrain.Eval) *along with a constraint family $\mathcal{C}$ is a PCPRF (Definition 2.8) satisfying B-almost-key homomorphism, then the above construction is a secure BMFE for comparison satisfying 1-query selective index indistinguishability and 1-query selective mode indistinguishability, as per Definitions 3.1 and 3.2.*

6   Efficiency

In this section we analyze the efficiency of our different constructions, in order to evaluate the efficiency of our broadcast and trace scheme.

6.1   Efficient PCPRF for Comparison Constraints

We first focus on the PCPRF used in Sect. 5. Looking ahead, it will be crucial that the resulting BMFE has *short ciphertext* and *efficient decryption*. More precisely, we will require to have the BMFE to have decryption in $\mathbf{NC}^1$ while having as short ciphertexts as possible.

Looking at our construction in Sect. 5, we first need to analyze the complexity of evaluating a PCPRF constrained evaluation for comparison constraints (which is performed during BMFE decryption, and therefore required be in $\mathbf{NC}^1$), as well as the size of the constrained keys (which are the BMFE ciphertexts). We do so by analyzing and tailoring the PCPRFs from the literature ([CC17, CVW18b]) for our needs.

Almost-Key-Homomorphic PCPRFs from LWE. For our constructions, we will focus on constructions of PCPRFs from LWE supporting (polynomial length) branching program constraints [CC17, CVW18b], where the range is $R_\lambda = \mathbb{Z}_p^{m \times m}$ where p is the output modulus of the PRF, and $m = \mathsf{poly}(n)$ where n is the lattice dimension in the underlying learning with errors assumption. They additionally satisfy 1-almost-key-homomorphism with the infinity norm $\| \cdot \|_\infty$ [CVW+18a]. For more details on the parameters, we refer the reader tà the relevant sections of [CC17, CVW18b].

Again, we will be most interested in both the *size of the constrained keys* and the complexity of computing a *constrained evaluation*. In the constructions of [CC17, CVW18b], if we consider branching programs of constant width and length $h \in \mathbb{N}$, then constrained keys consist of a set of $2h$ matrices in $\mathbb{Z}_q^{m \times m}$ and a single matrix in $\mathbb{Z}_q^{n \times m}$, where $m = \mathsf{poly}(n)$ and n and q are respectively the lattice dimension and modulus of the underlying learning with errors assumption. In other words, the constrained keys are of the form:

$$\mathsf{CK} = (\mathbf{A}, \{\mathbf{D}_{i,b}\}_{i \in [h], b \in \{0,1\}}),$$

where $\mathbf{A} \in \mathbb{Z}_q^{n \times m}$ and $\mathbf{D}_{i,b} \in \mathbb{Z}_q^{m \times m}$ for all $i \in [h], b \in \{0,1\}$, and where $m = \mathsf{poly}(n)$, and q is exponential in h (for correctness). Constrained evaluation is performed by multiplying elements in the constrained key, namely the matrix $\mathbf{A}$, and a subset of h matrices determined by the input to the evaluation. For an input $x \in \{0,1\}^\ell$, we have:[6]

$$\mathsf{Constrain.Eval}(\mathsf{CK}, x) = \left\lfloor \mathbf{A} \cdot \prod_{i \in [h]} \mathbf{D}_{i, x_{(i \bmod \ell)}} \right\rceil_p,$$

where, for $q > p \geq 2$, $\lfloor \cdot \rceil_p : \mathbb{Z}_q \mapsto \mathbb{Z}_p$ rounds element in $\mathbb{Z}_q$ to $\mathbb{Z}_p$, that is, $\lfloor x \rceil_p = \lfloor x \cdot p/q \rceil$ where $\lfloor \cdot \rceil$ denotes the usual rounding to the nearest integer; and $\lfloor \cdot \rceil_p$ extends over matrices by applying the rounding pointwise. In particular, for $m = \mathsf{poly}(n)$ and $q \leq 2^{\mathsf{poly}(n)}$, such a computation can be implemented by a circuit of depth $O(\log h \cdot \log n)$ (by computing the h matrix products using a binary tree). Actually, as both matrix multiplication and rounding (which is computable using

---

[6] Later, we will need the index-to-input map ι of the branching program to be independent of the program; we consider here $\iota : i \mapsto (i \bmod \ell)$ for simplicity. This is without loss of generality up to a blow-up in the branching program length by a factor ℓ.

integer multiplication, division and rounding) can be performed in $\mathbf{TC}^0$ in this regime (e.g. [RT92]), constrained evaluation can be performed in $\mathbf{TC}^1$.

Theorem 6.1 (PCPRFs from LWE [CC17, CVW18b]**).** *Assuming the hardness of LWE (with appropriate parameters), there exists PCPRFs satisfying 1-almost-key-homomorphism supporting branching program constraints. Additionally for any class of branching program constraints of width $O(1)$ and length $h \leq \mathsf{poly}(n)$, the constrained keys have size $O(h \cdot \mathsf{poly}(n) \cdot \log q)$, and constrained evaluation can be computed in $\mathbf{TC}^1$, where n and q are respectively the lattice dimension and modulus of the underlying LWE assumption.*

Pre-processing the Constrained Evaluation. As noted earlier, we will crucially need to be able to compute constrained evaluations in $\mathbf{NC}^1$. We note here that in the constructions of [CC17, CVW18b] of PCPRFs for branching program constraints (with index-to-input map independent of the program), we can improve the complexity of computing a constrained evaluation by pre-process the constrained keys. Recall that constrained keys contains matrices $\{\mathbf{D}_i^b\}_{i \in [h], b \in \{0,1\}}$, where $h \in \mathbb{N}$ is the length of the branching program. Let $0 < \varepsilon < 1$ be a fixed constant, such that $1/\varepsilon \in \mathbb{N}$, and that $\varepsilon h \in \mathbb{N}$ (this is without loss of generality up to padding the branching program with a constant number $\leq 1/\varepsilon$ of dummy levels). To pre-process the constrained keys, we pre-compute all the products of blocks of εh matrices.[7] In other words, for all $y \in \{0,1\}^{\varepsilon h}$ and all $j \in \{0, \ldots, 1/\varepsilon - 1\}$, the pre-processing phase computes:

$$\mathbf{M}_{j,y} = \prod_{i=1}^{\varepsilon h} \mathbf{D}_{j\varepsilon h + i, \, y_i \bmod \ell}.$$

For $x \in \{0,1\}^\ell$, $j \in \{0, \ldots, 1/\varepsilon - 1\}$, let $y^{(j)} = (x_{j\varepsilon h + 1 \bmod \ell}, \ldots, x_{(j+1)\varepsilon h \bmod \ell})$ be the j-th block of εh consecutive coordinates of x, ranging from $j\varepsilon h + 1 \bmod \ell$ to $(j+1)\varepsilon h \bmod \ell$. Then, given those $2^{\varepsilon h} \cdot 1/\varepsilon$ matrices $\{\mathbf{M}_{j,y}\}_{0 \leq j < 1/\varepsilon, \, y \in \{0,1\}^{\varepsilon h}}$, and the original matrix $\mathbf{A}$, one can compute for all $x \in \{0,1\}^\ell$:

$$\mathsf{Constrain.Eval}(\mathsf{CK}, x) = \left\lfloor \mathbf{A} \cdot \prod_{j=0}^{1/\varepsilon - 1} \mathbf{M}_{j, y^{(j)}} \right\rceil_p.$$

In other words, given the pre-processed constrained key, constrained evaluation can be performed by multiplying the appropriate $(1/\varepsilon)$ pre-computed block products together with $\mathbf{A}$ (and rounding). In particular, this only requires a *constant* number of matrix multiplications (as opposed to h originally). This is at the cost of using a pre-processed constrained key consisting of $2^{\varepsilon h} \times 1/\varepsilon$ matrices (which can seen as pre-processed constrained keys).

Efficient Construction for Comparison Constraints. We note now that the BMFE of Sect. 5 does not need to support general constraints, but only *comparison*

---

[7] We rely here on the fact that the index-to-input ι is independent of the branching program.

functions. Recall that for a parameter $N \in \mathbb{N}$ and for $\mathsf{ind} \in [N]$, the function P_{ind}, on input $i \in [N]$, outputs 1 if $i \geq \mathsf{ind}$ and 0 otherwise.

However, naively invoking Barrington theorem [Bar86] to obtain a generic branching program computing P_{ind}, only yields a branching program of length $\log^2(N)$, which makes the pre-processing described above output *super-polynomially* many matrices. Instead, we directly build a branching program for comparison constraints, with constant width and length $O(\log N)$, which will be good enough for our purposes.

Lemma 6.2. *Let $N \in \mathbb{N}$ be an integer. Then for all $\mathsf{ind} \in [N]$, there exists a (non-permutation) branching program of width 3 and length $\log N + 2$ computing P_{ind} (defined as $P_{\mathsf{ind}}(i) = 1$ if $i \geq \mathsf{ind}$ and 0 otherwise), with index-to-input map ι is independent of ind.*

We exhibit such a branching program in the full version of the paper. Note that this particular branching program is *not* a permutation branching program, which excludes the PCPRF of [CC17]. Fortunately [CVW18b] does support general (non-permutation) branching program constraints. Now, for $0 < \varepsilon < 1$ being a fixed constant, pre-processing the constrained keys results in N^ε matrices of size $\mathsf{poly}(n) \log q$ (where n and q are respectively the lattice dimension and the modulus of the underlying LWE assumption), while now multiplying $1/\varepsilon$ matrices can be performed using a circuit of depth $O(\log(1/\varepsilon) \log(n))$. The following Lemma follows by the fact that rounding can be computed in $\mathbf{TC}^0$ ([RT92]).

Lemma 6.3. *Let $N \in \mathbb{N}$ be an integer and $0 < \varepsilon < 1$ be a constant. Assuming the hardness of LWE (with appropriate parameters), there exists a PCPRF for comparison constraints (as defined above) satisfying 1-almost-key homomorphism. Furthermore, for $\mathcal{C}_\lambda = \{P_{\mathsf{ind}}\}_{\mathsf{ind} \in [N]}$ (defined above), that is if the constraints compare integers in $[N]$, then the constrained keys have size $N^\varepsilon \cdot \mathsf{poly}(n)$ (where n is the lattice dimension in the underlying LWE assumption) and constrained evaluation is in $\mathbf{NC}^1$.*

6.2 Wrapping-Up

Efficiency and Parameters of the BMFE. We are here most interested in the *size* of a BMFE ciphertext and its *decryption complexity*. First, adding polynomially many $\mathsf{poly}(n)$-bit numbers, and comparing $\mathsf{poly}(n)$-bit numbers can be done in $\mathbf{TC}^0$, and therefore in $\mathbf{NC}^1$. Therefore, combined with Lemma 6.3, we obtain that BMFE decryption from Sect. 5 can be evaluated in $\mathbf{NC}^1$, as summing PCPRF evaluations, taking their infinity norm and comparing them to the threshold are in $\mathbf{NC}^1$ as well.

Alternatively, we can directly use the PCPRFs of [CVW18b] (without pre-processing the constrained keys). Combined our branching program for comparison (Lemma 6.2), this gives a BMFE with ciphertext size $\log N \cdot \mathsf{poly}(\lambda)$ with decryption in $\mathbf{TC}^1$.

Lemma 6.4. *Suppose* $N = \mathsf{poly}(\lambda)$*, and let* ε *be a constant such that* $0 < \varepsilon < 1$*. Assuming the hardness of LWE with (sufficiently large) quasi-polynomial modulus-to-noise ratio, there exists:*

- *a BMFE for comparison with ciphertext size* $N^\varepsilon \cdot \mathsf{poly}(\lambda)$ *and decryption in* $\mathbf{NC^1}$*;*
- *a BMFE for comparison with ciphertext size* $\log(N) \cdot \mathsf{poly}(\lambda)$ *and decryption in* $\mathbf{TC^1}$*.*

For the parameters of the LWE assumption, we can take those of [CVW18b, Remark 7.2] for branching programs of width $w = 3$ and length $h = \log N + 2$, with the additional requirement that $p \geq C \cdot N\lambda$ for some fixed constant $C > 1$ (e.g. $C = 1.1$), which we use to argue correctness of the BMFE. In particular, for $N = \mathsf{poly}(\lambda)$, this corresponds to assuming the hardness of LWE with a quasi-polynomial modulus to noise ratio. Looking ahead, this will be parameters of the LWE assumption of our final broadcast and trace scheme.

Efficiency of the Broadcast and Trace. The final broadcast and trace system directly inherits the ciphertext size from the augmented BE. Using the construction from Sect. 4, the resulting augmented BE scheme inherits its ciphertext size from its underlying ABE, assuming the ABE support the class of predicates $C_{i,\mathsf{bmfe.sk}_i}(\mathsf{bmfe.ct}, S) := (i \in S) \wedge (\mathsf{BMFE.Dec}(\mathsf{bmfe.sk}_i, S, \mathsf{bmfe.ct}) = 1)$ defined by the BMFE decryption procedure.

In conclusion, assuming the ABE has *succinct* ciphertexts of size independent of their attribute, then our broadcast and trace system has ciphertext size dominated by the size of the BMFE ciphertexts. Overall, Combining Lemma 6.4, and Theorem 2.7, we get the desired result:

Theorem 6.5. *Let* $N = \mathsf{poly}(\lambda)$*, and let* ε *be a constant such that* $0 < \varepsilon < 1$*. Assuming the hardness of LWE with (sufficiently large) quasi-polynomial modulus-to-noise ratio, and:*

- *assuming that the N-DBDHE assumption holds, there exists a broadcast and trace scheme with ciphertext size* $N^\varepsilon \cdot \mathsf{poly}(\lambda)$*.*
- *assuming the existence of an ABE for* $\mathbf{TC^1}$ *predicates with ciphertext size polylogarithmic in its attribute length, there exists a broadcast and trace scheme with ciphertext size* $\mathsf{poly}(\log N, \lambda)$*.*

References

[AHL+12] Attrapadung, N., Herranz, J., Laguillaumie, F., Libert, B., De Panafieu, E., Ràfols, C.: Attribute-based encryption schemes with constant-size ciphertexts. Theor. Comput. Sci. **422**, 15–38 (2012)

[ALDP11] Attrapadung, N., Libert, B., de Panafieu, E.: Expressive key-policy attribute-based encryption with constant-size ciphertexts. In: Catalano, D., Fazio, N., Gennaro, R., Nicolosi, A. (eds.) PKC 2011. LNCS, vol. 6571, pp. 90–108. Springer, Heidelberg (2011). https://doi.org/10.1007/978-3-642-19379-8_6

[Bar86]   Barrington, D.A.: Bounded-width polynomial-size branching programs recognize exactly those languages in NC^1. In: Proceedings of the Eighteenth Annual ACM Symposium on Theory of Computing, STOC 1986 (1986)

[BBG05]   Boneh, D., Boyen, X., Goh, E.-J.: Hierarchical identity based encryption with constant size ciphertext. In: Cramer, R. (ed.) EUROCRYPT 2005. LNCS, vol. 3494, pp. 440–456. Springer, Heidelberg (2005). https://doi.org/10.1007/11426639_26

[BGG+14] Boneh, D., et al.: Fully key-homomorphic encryption, arithmetic circuit ABE and compact garbled circuits. In: Nguyen, P.Q., Oswald, E. (eds.) EUROCRYPT 2014. LNCS, vol. 8441, pp. 533–556. Springer, Heidelberg (2014). https://doi.org/10.1007/978-3-642-55220-5_30

[BGW05]   Boneh, D., Gentry, C., Waters, B.: Collusion resistant broadcast encryption with short ciphertexts and private keys. In: Shoup, V. (ed.) CRYPTO 2005. LNCS, vol. 3621, pp. 258–275. Springer, Heidelberg (2005). https://doi.org/10.1007/11535218_16

[BSW06]   Boneh, D., Sahai, A., Waters, B.: Fully collusion resistant traitor tracing with short ciphertexts and private keys. In: Vaudenay, S. (ed.) EUROCRYPT 2006. LNCS, vol. 4004, pp. 573–592. Springer, Heidelberg (2006). https://doi.org/10.1007/11761679_34

[BTVW17] Brakerski, Z., Tsabary, R., Vaikuntanathan, V., Wee, H.: Private constrained PRFs (and more) from LWE. In: Kalai, Y., Reyzin, L. (eds.) TCC 2017, Part I. LNCS, vol. 10677, pp. 264–302. Springer, Cham (2017). https://doi.org/10.1007/978-3-319-70500-2_10

[BW06]   Boneh, D., Waters, B.: A fully collusion resistant broadcast, trace, and revoke system. In: Proceedings of the 13th ACM Conference on Computer and Communications Security, CCS 2006, Alexandria, VA, USA, 30 October–3 November 2006, pp. 211–220 (2006)

[CC17]   Canetti, R., Chen, Y.: Constraint-hiding constrained PRFs for NC^1 from LWE. In: Coron, J.-S., Nielsen, J.B. (eds.) EUROCRYPT 2017. LNCS, vol. 10210, pp. 446–476. Springer, Cham (2017). https://doi.org/10.1007/978-3-319-56620-7_16

[CFN94]   Chor, B., Fiat, A., Naor, M.: Tracing traitors. In: Desmedt, Y.G. (ed.) CRYPTO 1994. LNCS, vol. 839, pp. 257–270. Springer, Heidelberg (1994). https://doi.org/10.1007/3-540-48658-5_25

[CFNP00] Chor, B., Fiat, A., Naor, M., Pinkas, B.: Tracing traitors. IEEE Trans. Inf. Theory **46**(3), 893–910 (2000)

[CVW+18a] Chen, Y., Vaikuntanathan, V., Waters, B., Wee, H., Wichs, D.: Traitor-tracing from LWE made simple and attribute-based. In: Beimel, A., Dziembowski, S. (eds.) TCC 2018. LNCS, vol. 11240, pp. 341–369. Springer, Cham (2018). https://doi.org/10.1007/978-3-030-03810-6_13

[CVW18b] Chen, Y., Vaikuntanathan, V., Wee, H.: GGH15 beyond permutation branching programs: proofs, attacks, and candidates. In: Shacham, H., Boldyreva, A. (eds.) CRYPTO 2018, Part II. LNCS, vol. 10992, pp. 577–607. Springer, Cham (2018). https://doi.org/10.1007/978-3-319-96881-0_20

[DF02]   Dodis, Y., Fazio, N.: Public key broadcast encryption for stateless receivers. In: Feigenbaum, J. (ed.) DRM 2002. LNCS, vol. 2696, pp. 61–80. Springer, Heidelberg (2003). https://doi.org/10.1007/978-3-540-44993-5_5

[FN94] Fiat, A., Naor, M.: Broadcast encryption. In: Stinson, D.R. (ed.) CRYPTO 1993. LNCS, vol. 773, pp. 480–491. Springer, Heidelberg (1994). https://doi.org/10.1007/3-540-48329-2_40

[GKW17] Goyal, R., Koppula, V., Waters, B.: Lockable obfuscation. In: 58th IEEE Annual Symposium on Foundations of Computer Science, FOCS 2017, pp. 612–621 (2017)

[GKW18] Goyal, R., Koppula, V., Waters, B.: Collusion resistant traitor tracing from learning with errors. In: STOC (2018)

[GST04] Goodrich, M.T., Sun, J.Z., Tamassia, R.: Efficient tree-based revocation in groups of low-state devices. In: Franklin, M. (ed.) CRYPTO 2004. LNCS, vol. 3152, pp. 511–527. Springer, Heidelberg (2004). https://doi.org/10.1007/978-3-540-28628-8_31

[GSW00] Garay, J.A., Staddon, J., Wool, A.: Long-lived broadcast encryption. In: Bellare, M. (ed.) CRYPTO 2000. LNCS, vol. 1880, pp. 333–352. Springer, Heidelberg (2000). https://doi.org/10.1007/3-540-44598-6_21

[GVW12] Gorbunov, S., Vaikuntanathan, V., Wee, H.: Functional encryption with bounded collusions via multi-party computation. In: Safavi-Naini, R., Canetti, R. (eds.) CRYPTO 2012. LNCS, vol. 7417, pp. 162–179. Springer, Heidelberg (2012). https://doi.org/10.1007/978-3-642-32009-5_11

[GVW13] Gorbunov, S., Vaikuntanathan, V., Wee, H.: Attribute-based encryption for circuits. In: STOC (2013)

[GVW19] Goyal, R., Vusirikala, S., Waters, B.: Collusion resistant broadcast and trace from positional witness encryption. In: Lin, D., Sako, K. (eds.) PKC 2019. LNCS, vol. 11443, pp. 3–33. Springer, Cham (2019). https://doi.org/10.1007/978-3-030-17259-6_1

[HLR10] Herranz, J., Laguillaumie, F., Ràfols, C.: Constant size ciphertexts in threshold attribute-based encryption. In: Nguyen, P.Q., Pointcheval, D. (eds.) PKC 2010. LNCS, vol. 6056, pp. 19–34. Springer, Heidelberg (2010). https://doi.org/10.1007/978-3-642-13013-7_2

[HS02] Halevy, D., Shamir, A.: The LSD broadcast encryption scheme. In: Yung, M. (ed.) CRYPTO 2002. LNCS, vol. 2442, pp. 47–60. Springer, Heidelberg (2002). https://doi.org/10.1007/3-540-45708-9_4

[KMUW18] Kowalczyk, L., Malkin, T., Ullman, J., Wichs, D.: Hardness of non-interactive differential privacy from one-way functions. In: Shacham, H., Boldyreva, A. (eds.) CRYPTO 2018. LNCS, vol. 10991, pp. 437–466. Springer, Cham (2018). https://doi.org/10.1007/978-3-319-96884-1_15

[NNL01] Naor, D., Naor, M., Lotspiech, J.: Revocation and tracing schemes for stateless receivers. In: Kilian, J. (ed.) CRYPTO 2001. LNCS, vol. 2139, pp. 41–62. Springer, Heidelberg (2001). https://doi.org/10.1007/3-540-44647-8_3

[NP00] Frankel, Y. (ed.): FC 2000. LNCS, vol. 1962. Springer, Heidelberg (2001). https://doi.org/10.1007/3-540-45472-1

[PST06] Phan, D.H., Safavi-Naini, R., Tonien, D.: Generic construction of hybrid public key traitor tracing with full-public-traceability. In: Bugliesi, M., Preneel, B., Sassone, V., Wegener, I. (eds.) ICALP 2006, Part II. LNCS, vol. 4052, pp. 264–275. Springer, Heidelberg (2006). https://doi.org/10.1007/11787006_23

[RT92] Reif, J., Tate, S.: On threshold circuits and polynomial computation. SIAM J. Comput. 21(5), 896–908 (1992)

[SSW01] Staddon, J., Stinson, D.R., Wei, R.: Combinatorial properties of frameproof and traceability codes. IEEE Trans. Inf. Theory **47**(3), 1042–1049 (2001)

[Sti97] Stinson, D.R.: On some methods for unconditionally secure key distribution and broadcast encryption. In: Kranakis, E., Van Oorschot, P. (eds.) Selected Areas in Cryptography, pp. 3–31. Springer, Boston (1997). https://doi.org/10.1007/978-1-4615-5489-9_2

[SVT98] Stinson, D.R., Trung, T.V.: Some new results on key distribution patterns and broadcast encryption. Des. Codes Crypt. **14**(3), 261–279 (1998)

[SW98] Stinson, D.R., Wei, R.: Combinatorial properties and constructions of traceability schemes and frameproof codes. SIAM J. Discrete Math. **11**(1), 41–53 (1998)

[SW05] Sahai, A., Waters, B.: Fuzzy identity-based encryption. In: Cramer, R. (ed.) EUROCRYPT 2005. LNCS, vol. 3494, pp. 457–473. Springer, Heidelberg (2005). https://doi.org/10.1007/11426639_27

[WZ17] Wichs, D., Zirdelis, G.: Obfuscating compute-and-compare programs under LWE. In: 58th IEEE Annual Symposium on Foundations of Computer Science, FOCS 2017, pp. 600–611 (2017)

[YAHK14] Yamada, S., Attrapadung, N., Hanaoka, G., Kunihiro, N.: A framework and compact constructions for non-monotonic attribute-based encryption. In: Krawczyk, H. (ed.) PKC 2014. LNCS, vol. 8383, pp. 275–292. Springer, Heidelberg (2014). https://doi.org/10.1007/978-3-642-54631-0_16

Author Index

Printed in the United States
By Bookmasters